# Ethical Obligations and Decision Making in Accounting

**Text and Cases**

Third Edition

# Ethical Obligations and Decision Making in Accounting

**Text and Cases**

**Third Edition**

**Steven M. Mintz, DBA, CPA**

*Professor of Accounting*
*California Polytechnic State University,*
*San Luis Obispo*

**Roselyn E. Morris, Ph.D., CPA**

*Professor of Accounting*
*Texas State University–San Marcos*

McGraw Hill Education

ETHICAL OBLIGATIONS AND DECISION MAKING IN ACCOUNTING: TEXT AND CASES,
THIRD EDITION
International Edition 2014

10 09 08 07 06 05 04 03 02 01
20 15 14 13
CTP    SLP

**When ordering this title, use ISBN 978-981-4581-29-5 or MHID 981-4581-29-1**

Printed in Singapore

www.mhhe.com

# Dedication

"Whatever we learn to do, we learn by doing it."
—Aristotle

We hope this book inspires students to engage in the learning process, to make ethical choices in their lives, and always strive for excellence in whatever they do.

# About the Authors

**STEVEN M. MINTZ, DBA, CPA,** is a professor of accounting in the Orfalea College of Business at the California Polytechnic State University–San Luis Obsipo. Dr. Mintz received his DBA from George Washington University. His first book, titled *Cases in Accounting Ethics and Professionalism,* was also published by McGraw-Hill. Dr. Mintz develops individual courses in professional accounting ethics for Bisk Education that meet each state's board of accountancy mandatory requirements for continuing education in ethics. He also writes two popular ethics blogs under the names "ethicssage" and "work-placeethicsadvice." Dr. Mintz has received the Faculty Excellence Award of the California Society of CPAs and Service Award from the California Board of Accountancy for his work on the Advisory Committee on Accounting Ethics Curriculum.

**ROSELYN E. MORRIS, PH.D., CPA,** is a professor of accounting in the Accounting Department at the McCoy College of Business, Texas State University–San Marcos. Dr. Morris received her Ph.D. in business administration from the University of Houston. She is a past president of the Accounting Education Foundation and a member of the Qualifications Committee of the Texas Board of Public Accountancy. Dr. Morris has received the Outstanding Educator Award from the Texas Society of CPAs.

Both Professors Mintz and Morris have developed and teach an accounting ethics course at their respective universities.

# Preface

## Why Did We Write This Book?

The first edition of *Ethical Obligations and Decision Making in Accounting: Text and Cases* was written in the wake of the dot.com bubble and accounting scandals at companies such as Enron and WorldCom. The second edition was written in the wake of the financial meltdown of 2007–2008 that was due to high-risk lending and borrowing practices. The result of these scandals has been an increased call by professional and regulatory bodies for ethics education of accounting students in values, ethics, and attitudes to support professional and ethical judgments and act in the public interest. We dedicate ourselves to this goal through our book.

Several states now require their accounting students to complete an ethics course prior to certification. Texas was first state to do so, and it requires accounting students in Texas and those moving into the state to complete an ethics course at a Texas university or in their home institution. California and Colorado require separate accounting ethics courses; states such as Maryland, New York, and West Virginia also have separate ethics course requirements. This book is written to enable instructors to address the content material that state boards typically expect to be covered in qualifying courses.

*Ethical Obligations and Decision Making in Accounting* was written to guide students through the minefields of ethical conflict in meeting their responsibilities under the professions' codes of conduct. Our book is devoted to helping students cultivate the ethical commitment needed to ensure that their work meets the highest standards of integrity, independence, and objectivity. We hope that this book and classroom instruction will work together to provide the tools to help you make ethical judgments and carry through with ethical actions.

Our book blends ethical reasoning, components of behavioral ethics, reflection, and the principles of ethical conduct that embody the values of the accounting profession. We incorporate these elements into a framework to consider the ethical obligations of accountants and auditors and how to make ethical decisions that address the following material:

- The role of moral and cognitive development in ethical reasoning, ethical judgment, and ethical orientation
- Professional codes of conduct in accounting
- Ethical corporate governance systems
- Fraud detection and prevention
- Legal and regulatory obligations of auditors
- Whistleblowing obligations of accountants and auditors
- Earnings management issues and the quality of financial reporting
- Ethical systems, global ethics standards, and corporate governance considerations in doing business worldwide

### Attributes of This Textbook

*Ethical Obligations and Decision Making in Accounting* is designed to provide the instructor with comprehensive coverage of ethical and professional issues encountered by accounting professionals. Our material provides the best flexibility and pedagogical effectiveness of any book on the market. To that end, it includes numerous features designed to make both learning and teaching easier, such as:

- Ethical reflections that set the tone for each chapter
- 160 discussion questions
- 76 cases (10 per Chapters 1–7 and 6 in Chapter 8), about one-third of which are from the SEC enforcement files
- 6 additional major cases that can be used for comprehensive testing, a group project, a research assignment, or a capstone to the book
- Dozens of additional cases and instructional resources, which are available to enrich student learning
- Links to videos for instructors

Pedagogical approach:

- The book is comprehensive enough to serve as a stand-alone text, yet flexible enough to act as a co-text or supplementary text across the accounting curricula or within an auditing or financial accounting course.
- There is sufficient case and supplementary material to allow the instructor to vary the course over at least two to three terms.
- The writing style is pitched specifically to students, making the material easy to follow and absorb.
- Group discussions and role-play opportunities using case studies
- Video links to bring case material to life

The **Instructor Edition of the Online Learning Center,** www.mhhe.com/mintz3e, offers materials to support the efforts of first-time and seasoned instructors of accounting ethics. A comprehensive **Instructor's Manual** provides teaching notes, grading suggestions and rubrics, sample syllabi, extra cases and projects, and guidelines for incorporating writing into the accounting ethics course; a **Test Bank** that provides a variety of multiple-choice, short answer, and essay questions for building quizzes and tests; additional cases that can be assigned, including some that were not carried over from the first and second editions; links to videos to enhance the learning experience and bring case discussions to life; and **PowerPoint** presentations for every chapter make a convenient and powerful lecture tool.

## Changes in This Edition

The behavioral approach to ethics leads to understanding and explaining moral behavior in a systematic way. We have expanded our discussion of ethics beyond the traditional philosophical moral reasoning methods that teach students how they should behave when facing ethical dilemmas and now also engage them to understand their own behavior better and compare it to how they would ideally like to behave. We incorporate those discussions in addressing ethical obligations of accountants and auditors under professional codes of conduct and in areas such as whistleblowing considerations under Sarbanes-Oxley (SOX) and the Dodd-Frank Financial Reform Act.

This revision also includes:

- Emphasis on values, ethics, and behaviors in a professional setting
- Expanded coverage of professional codes of conduct and failure to maintain independence, integrity, objectivity, and professional skepticism
- New audit requirements and clarified Statements on Auditing Standards effective in 2014 that collectively better address financial statement fraud and the risk of material misstatements

- Broadened perspective on earnings management, including the role of earnings expectations, the use of accruals, income smoothing, risk assessment and materiality, and financial restatements
- Public interest and ethical considerations in developing international financial reporting standards, cultural considerations when operating overseas, corporate governance systems, and global bribery
- Restoring public trust and confidence in the accounting profession

This edition of *Ethical Obligations and Decision Making in Accounting* has dozens of new discussion questions. The material that was replaced to keep the book fresh is available to instructors in the Instructor's Manual for testing purposes. For the first time, we provide video links to many of the cases in the book in the IM.

In a project of this kind, errors are bound to occur. As authors, we accept full responsibility for all errors and omissions. We welcome feedback on the book and suggestions for improvements. The authors have collectively had more than 30 years of experience teaching accounting ethics and welcome the opportunity to share our insights with you on how best to use the book and teach ethics to accounting students.

## Acknowledgments

The authors want to express their sincere gratitude to these reviewers for their comments and guidance. Their insights were invaluable in developing this edition of the book.

**Russell Calk**
*New Mexico State University*

**Jeffrey Cohen**
*Boston College*

**Dan Hubbard**
*University of Mary Washington*

**Lorraine Lee**
*University of North Carolina–Wilimington*

**Stephen A. McNett**
*Texas A&M University–Central Texas*

**Barbara Porco**
*Fordham University*

We also appreciate the assistance and guidance given us on this project by the staff of Mc-Graw-Hill Education, including Tim Vertovec, Managing Director; James Heine, Executive Brand Manager; Michelle Nolte, Marketing Manager; Lori Bradshaw, development editor; Judi David, project manager; Jennifer Pickel, buyer; Studio Montage, design coordinator; and Prashanthi Nadipalli, media project manager. We greatly appreciate the role of Shyam Ramasubramony, project manager, and Susan McClung, copyeditor of the book.

Finally, we would like to acknowledge the contributions of our students, who have provided invaluable comments and suggestions on the content and use of these cases.

If you have any questions, comments, or suggestions concerning *Ethical Obligations and Decision Making in Accounting,* please send them to us at smintz@calpoly.edu and rmorris@txstate.edu.

*Steve Mintz*

*Rosie Morris*

# Case Descriptions

| Case #     | Case Name/Description |
| ---------- | --------------------- |

| Case # | Case Name/Description |
| --- | --- |

| Case # | Case Name/Description |
| --- | --- |

| Case # | Case Name/Description |
|---|---|
| **7-1** | **Nortel Networks** <br> *Use of reserves and revenue recognition techniques to manage earnings.* |
| **7-2** | **Solutions Network, Inc.** <br> *Use of the Fraud Triangle to evaluate management's actions.* |
| **7-3** | **Cubbies Cable** <br> *Differences of opinion with management over whether to capitalize or expense cable construction costs.* |
| **7-4** | **Solway, Inc.** <br> *Use of year-end accruals to manage earnings and whistleblowing considerations.* |
| **7-5** | **Dell Computer** <br> *Use of "cookie-jar" reserves to smooth net income and meet financial analysts' earnings projections.* |
| **7-6** | **Sweat Construction Company** <br> *Pressure on the controller to ignore higher estimated costs on a construction contract to improve earnings and secure needed financing.* |
| **7-7** | **Sunbeam Corporation** <br> *Use of cookie-jar reserves and "channel stuffing" by a turnaround artist to manage earnings.* |
| **7-8** | **Diamond Foods** <br> *Link between projecting financial results and earnings management.* |
| **7-9** | **The North Face, Inc.** <br> *Questions about financial structuring and revenue recognition on barter transactions to achieve desired results.* |
| **7-10** | **Vivendi Universal** <br> *Improper adjustments to EBITDA and operating free cash flow by a French multinational company to meet ambitious earnings targets and conceal liquidity problems.* |

| Case # | Case Name/Description |
|---|---|
| **8-1** | ***SEC v. Siemens Aktiengesellschaft*** <br> *Bribery committed by a German company, using slush funds, off-book accounts, and business consultants and intermediaries to facilitate illegal payments.* |
| **8-2** | **Parmalat: Europe's Enron** <br> *Fictitious accounts at Bank of America and the use of nominee entities to transfer debt off the books by an Italian company led to one of Europe's largest fraud cases.* |
| **8-3** | **Satyam: India's Enron** <br> *CEO's falsification of financial information and misuse of corporate funds for personal purposes.* |
| **8-4** | **Royal Dutch Shell plc** <br> *Overstatement of estimated recoverable proved oil and gas reserves by Dutch-U.K. company in violation of SEC regulations.* |

8-5       **Autonomy**
          *Investigations by U.S. SEC and UK Serious Fraud Office into accounting for an acquisition of a British software maker by Hewlett-Packard (HP).*

8-6       **Olympus**
          *Major corporate scandal in Japan where Olympus committed a $1.7 billion fraud involving concealment of investment losses through fraudulent accounting.*

## Major Cases

| Chapter Coverage | Case Name/Description |
| --- | --- |
| 1 | **Adelphia Communications Corporation**<br>*SEC action against Deloitte & Touche for failing to exercise the proper degree of professional skepticism in examining complex related-party transactions and contingencies that were not accounted for in accordance with GAAP.* |
| 2 | **Royal Ahold N.V. (Ahold)**<br>*Court finding that Deloitte & Touche should not be held liable for the efforts of the client to deprive the auditors of accurate information needed for the audit and masking the true nature of other evidence.* |
| 3 | **MicroStrategy, Inc.**<br>*SEC action against MicroStrategy for improper revenue recognition of accounting for multiple deliverables contracts and questions about independence of PwC.* |
| 4 | **Cendant Corporation**<br>*SEC action against Cendant for managing earnings through merger reserve manipulations and improper accounting for membership sales, and questions about the audit of Ernst & Young.* |
| 5 | **Navistar International**<br>*Confidentiality issues that arise when Navistar management questions the competency of Deloitte & Touche auditors by referring to PCAOB inspection reports and fraud at the company.* |
| 6 | **Waste Management**<br>*Failure of Andersen auditors to enforce agreement with the board of directors to adopt proposed adjusting journal entries that were required in restated financial statements.* |

# Brief Contents

# Table of Contents

# Chapter 4
# AICPA Code of Professional Conduct    175

# Chapter 5
# Fraud in Financial Statements and Auditor Responsibilities   246

## Chapter 7
## Earnings Management and the Quality of Financial Reporting    410

## Chapter 8
## International Financial Reporting: Ethics and Corporate Governance Considerations    475

# Ethical Reasoning: Implications for Accounting

## PENN STATE CHILD ABUSE SCANDAL: A CULTURE OF INDIFFERENCE

What motivates an otherwise ethical person to do the wrong thing when faced with an ethical dilemma? Why did Joe Paterno and administrators at Penn State University look the other way and fail to act on irrefutable evidence that former assistant football coach Jerry Sandusky had raped and molested young boys, an offense for which Sandusky currently is serving a 30- to 60-year sentence? According to the independent report by Louis Freeh that investigated the sexual abuse, four of the most powerful people at Penn State, including president Graham Spanier, athletic director Timothy Curley, senior vice president Gary Schultz, and head football coach Joe Paterno, sheltered a child predator harming children for over a decade by concealing Sandusky's activities from the board of trustees, the university community, and authorities. The Freeh report characterizes the inactions as lacking empathy for the victims by failing to inquire as to their safety and well-being. Not only that, but they exposed the first abused child to additional harm by alerting Sandusky, who was the only one who knew the child's identity, of what assistant coach Mike McQueary saw in the shower on the night of February 9, 2001.[1] McQueary testified at the June 2012 trial of Sandusky that when he was a graduate assistant, he walked into the locker room and heard sounds of slapping

and observed Sandusky up against a boy, whose hands were up against the wall.[2] He reported the suspected child abuse to Paterno who reported the incident to his superiors but did not confront Sandusky or report the incident to the board of trustees or the police.[3]

## REASONS FOR UNETHICAL ACTIONS

The report gives the following explanations for the failure of university leaders to take action to identify this child victim and for not reporting Sandusky to the authorities:

- The desire to avoid the bad publicity that reporting the incident would bring
- The failure of the university's board of trustees to have reporting mechanisms in place to ensure disclosure of major risks to the university
- A president who discouraged discussion and dissent
- A lack of awareness of child abuse issues and the Clery Act, which requires all colleges and universities participating in federal financial aid programs to keep and disclose information about crimes committed on and near their campuses
- A lack of whistleblower policies and protections
- A culture of reverence for the football program that was ingrained at all levels of the campus community

*(Continued)*

## EXPLANATIONS FOR UNETHICAL ACTIONS

Former Penn State president Spanier who was fired by the board of trustees in November 2011, is quoted as saying in an interview with Jeffrey Toobin of the *New Yorker* online after the trial of Sandusky that ended on June 22, 2012, about how the university worked that "honesty, integrity, and always doing what was in the *best interests of the university* [italics added] was how everyone agreed to operate and . . . we've always operated as a family. Our personal and social and professional lives were all very intertwined."[4]

At Penn State, a culture existed that placed the interests of the university, as perceived by its leadership, ahead of the interests of the abused children and the public trust. The tone that was set by Paterno and Spanier was to cover up any potentially damaging information about the institution and its football program. This happens in other organizations as well, such as Enron and WorldCom, where acting ethically took a back seat to self-interest, including maximizing earnings and share price. The culture of an organization should be built on ethical values such as honesty, integrity, responsibility, and accountability. While Penn State may have claimed to follow such principles, the reality was that its actions did not match these behavioral norms.

## ETHICAL BLIND SPOTS

Leaders of organizations who may be successful at what they do and see themselves as ethical and moral still cultivate a collection of what Max Bazerman and Ann Trebrunsel call *blind spots*.[5] Blind spots are the gaps between who you want to be and the person you actually are. In other words,

most of us want to do the right thing—to act ethically—but internal and external pressures get in the way. These authors attribute blind spots to the concept of *bounded ethicality;* that is, psychological processes that lead even good people to engage in ethically questionable behavior that contradicts their own preferred ethics. At Penn State, bounded ethicality came into play because individuals such as Paterno decided to keep the scandal quiet, thereby enabling the abuse and harm to the affected children to continue even though that harm was inconsistent with their purported beliefs and preferences.

Our workday lives can create ethical challenges where there is a difference between knowing the right thing to do and doing it. One reason is organizational goals (such as what is in the best interests of Penn State), rewards, compliance systems, and informal pressures, all of which can contribute to *ethical fading,* a process by which the ethical dimensions are eliminated from a decision and replaced by "avoiding bad publicity" or making the deal at any costs. Enron had a code of conduct in place, but that didn't stop it from rewarding officers involved in conflicts of interest such as the former chief financial officer (CFO), Andy Fastow, who managed special-purpose-entities that dealt directly with Enron at the same time he served as Enron's CFO.

As you read this chapter, think about the following questions: (1) What would you have done if you had been in Joe Paterno's position, and why? (2) What factors might have enabled you to act in accordance with your own values and beliefs? (3) What factors might have served as disablers and made it more difficult to act on your values and beliefs?

---

Have the courage to say no. Have the courage to face the truth. Do the right thing because it is right. These are the magic keys to living your life with integrity.

*W. Clement Stone (1902–2002)*

---

This quote by William Clement Stone, a businessman, philanthropist, and self-help book author, underscores the importance of integrity in decision making. Notice that the quote addresses integrity in one's personal life. That is because one has to act with integrity when making personal decisions in order to be best equipped to act with integrity on a professional level. Integrity, indeed all of ethics, is not a spigot that can be turned on or off depending on one's whims or whether the matter at hand is personal or professional. As the ancient Greeks knew, we learn how to be ethical by practicing and exercising those virtues that enable us to lead a life of excellence.

Joe Paterno and other university leaders did not act with integrity. They let external considerations of reputation and image dictate their internal actions. Ironically, the very factor—reputation—that they guarded so closely was the first to be brought down by the disclosure of a cover-up in the sex scandal case.

In accounting, internal accountants and auditors may be pressured by superiors to manipulate financial results. The external auditors may have to deal with pressures imposed on them by clients to put the best face on the financial statements regardless of whether they conform to generally accepted accounting principles (GAAP). It is the ethical value of integrity that provides the moral courage to resist the temptation to stand by silently while a company misstates its financial statement amounts.

## Integrity: The Basis of Accounting

According to Mintz (1995), "Integrity is a fundamental trait of character that enables a CPA to withstand client and competitive pressures that might otherwise lead to the subordination of judgment."[6] A person of integrity will act out of moral principle and not expediency. That person will do what is right, even if it means the loss of a job or client. In accounting, the public interest (i.e., investors and creditors) always must be placed ahead of one's own self-interest or the interests of others, including a supervisor or client.

Integrity means that a person acts on principle—a conviction that there is a right way to act when faced with an ethical dilemma. For example, assume that your tax client fails to inform you about an amount of earned income for the year, and you confront the client on this issue. The client tells you not to record it and reminds you that there is no W-2 or 1099 form to document the earnings. The client adds that you will not get to audit the company's financial statements anymore if you do not adhere to the client's wishes. Would you decide to "go along to get along"? If you are a person of integrity, you should not allow the client to dictate how the tax rules will be applied in the client's situation. You are the professional and know the tax regulations best, and you have an ethical obligation to report taxes in accordance with the law. If you go along with the client and the Internal Revenue Service (IRS) investigates and sanctions you for failing to follow the IRS Tax Code, then you may suffer irreparable harm to your reputation. An important point is that a professional must never let loyalty to a client cloud good judgment and ethical decision making.

### WorldCom: Cynthia Cooper: Hero and Role Model

Cynthia Cooper's experience at WorldCom illustrates how the internal audit function should work and how a person of integrity can put a stop to financial fraud. It all unraveled in April and May 2002 when Gene Morse, an auditor at WorldCom, couldn't find any documentation to support a claim of $500 million in computer expenses. Morse approached Cooper, the company's director of internal auditing and Morse's boss, who instructed Morse to "keep going." A series of obscure tips led Morse and Cooper to suspect that WorldCom was cooking the books. Cooper formed an investigation team to determine whether their hunch was right.

In its initial investigation, the team discovered $3.8 billion of misallocated expenses and phony accounting entries.[7] Cooper approached the CFO, Scott Sullivan, but was dissatisfied with his explanations. The chief executive officer (CEO) of the company, Bernie Ebbers, had already resigned under pressure from WorldCom's board of directors, so Cooper went to the audit committee. The committee interviewed Sullivan about the accounting issues and did not get a satisfactory answer. Still, the committee was reluctant to take any action. Cooper persisted anyway. Eventually, one member of the audit committee told her to approach the outside auditors to get their take on the matter. Cooper gathered additional evidence of fraud, and ultimately KPMG, the firm that had replaced Arthur Andersen LLP—the auditors during the fraud—supported Cooper. Sullivan was asked to resign, refused to do so, and was fired.[8]

One tragic result of the fraud and cover-up at WorldCom is the case of Betty Vinson. It is not unusual for someone who is genuinely a good person to get caught up in fraud. Vinson, a former WorldCom mid-level accounting manager, went along with the fraud because her superiors told her to do so. She was convinced that it would be a one-time action. It rarely works that way, however, because once a company starts to engage in accounting fraud, it feels compelled to continue the charade into the future to keep up the appearance that each period's results are as good as or better than prior periods. The key to maintaining one's integrity and ethical perspective is not to take the first step down the proverbial *ethical slippery slope*.

Vinson pleaded guilty in October 2002 to participating in the financial fraud at the company. She was sentenced to five months in prison and five months of house arrest. Vinson represents the typical "pawn" in a financial fraud: an accountant who had no interest or desire to commit fraud but got caught up in it when Sullivan, her boss, instructed her to make improper accounting entries. The rationalization by Sullivan that the company had to "make the numbers appear better than they really were" did nothing to ease her guilty conscience. Judge Barbara Jones, who sentenced Vinson, commented that "Ms. Vinson was among the least culpable members of the conspiracy at WorldCom. . . . Still, had Vinson refused to do what she was asked, it's possible this conspiracy might have been nipped in the bud."[9]

Accounting students should reflect on what they would do if they faced a situation similar to the one that led Vinson to do something that was out of character. Once she agreed to go along with making improper entries, it was difficult to turn back. The company could have threatened to disclose her role in the original fraud and cover-up if Vinson then acted on her beliefs. From an ethical (and practical) perspective it is much better to just do the right thing from the very beginning, so that you can't be blackmailed or intimidated later.

Vinson became involved in the fraud because she had feared losing her job, her benefits, and the means to provide for her family. She must live with the consequences of her actions for the rest of her life. On the other hand, Cynthia Cooper, on her own initiative, ordered the internal investigation that led to the discovery of the $11 billion fraud at WorldCom. Cooper did all the right things to bring the fraud out in the open. Cooper received the Accounting Exemplar Award in 2004 given by the American Accounting Association and was inducted into the American Institute of Certified Public Accountants (AICPA) Hall of Fame in 2005.

Cooper truly is a positive role model. She discusses the foundation of her ethics that she developed as a youngster because of her mother's influence in her book *Extraordinary Circumstances: The Journey of a Corporate Whistleblower*. Cooper says: "Fight the good fight. Don't ever allow yourself to be intimidated. . . . Think about the consequences of your actions. I've seen too many people ruin their lives."[10]

## Religious and Philosophical Foundations of Ethics

Virtually all the world's great religions contain in their religious texts some version of the Golden Rule: "Do unto others as you would wish them to do unto you." In other words, we should treat others the way we would want to be treated. This is the basic ethic that guides all religions. If we believe honesty is important, then we should be honest with others and expect the same in return. One result of this ethic is the concept that every person shares certain inherent human rights, which will be discussed later in this chapter and the next. Exhibit 1.1 provides some examples of the universality of the Golden Rule in world religions provided by the character education organization Teaching Values.[11]

Integrity is the key to carrying out the Golden Rule. A person of integrity acts with truthfulness, courage, sincerity, and honesty. Integrity means to have the courage to stand by your principles even in the face of pressure to bow to the demands of others. As previously mentioned, integrity has particular importance for certified public accountants (CPAs), who often are pressured by their employers and clients to give in to their demands. The ethical responsibility of a CPA in these instances is to adhere to the ethics of the accounting profession and not to subordinate professional judgment to others. Integrity encompasses the whole of the person, and it is the foundational virtue of the ancient Greek philosophy of virtue.

**EXHIBIT 1.1**
**The Universality of the Golden Rule in the World Religions**

| Religion | Expression of the Golden Rule | Citation |
|---|---|---|
| Christianity | All things whatsoever ye would that men should do to you, Do ye so to them; for this is the law and the prophets. | Matthew 7:1 |
| Confucianism | Do not do to others what you would not like yourself. Then there will be no resentment against you, either in the family or in the state. | Analects 12:2 |
| Buddhism | Hurt not others in ways that you yourself would find hurtful. | Udānavarga 5,1 |
| Hinduism | This is the sum of duty, do naught onto others what you would not have them do unto you. | Mahabharata 5, 1517 |
| Islam | No one of you is a believer until he desires for his brother that which he desires for himself. | Sunnah |
| Judaism | What is hateful to you, do not do to your fellowman. This is the entire Law; all the rest is commentary. | Talmud, Shabbat 3id |
| Taoism | Regard your neighbor's gain as your gain, and your neighbor's loss as your own loss. | Tai Shang Kan Yin P'ien |
| Zoroastrianism | That nature alone is good which refrains from doing another whatsoever is not good for itself. | Dadisten-I-dinik, 94, 5 |

The origins of Western philosophy trace back to the ancient Greeks, including Socrates, Plato, and Aristotle. The ancient Greek philosophy of virtue deals with questions such as: What is the best sort of life for human beings to live? Greek thinkers saw the attainment of a good life as the *telos,* the end or goal of human existence. For most Greek philosophers, the end is *eudaimonia,* which is usually translated as "happiness." However, the Greeks thought that the end goal of happiness meant much more than just experiencing pleasure or satisfaction. The ultimate goal of happiness was to attain some objectively good status, the life of excellence. The Greek word for excellence is *arete,* the customary translation of which is "virtue." Thus for the Greeks, "excellences" or "virtues" were the qualities that made a life admirable or excellent. They did not restrict their thinking to characteristics we regard as moral virtues, such as courage, justice, and temperance, but included others we think of as nonmoral, such as wisdom.[12]

Modern philosophies have been posited as ways to living an ethical life. Unlike virtue theory that relies on both the characteristics of a decision and the person making that decision, these philosophies rely more on methods of ethical reasoning, and they, too, can be used to facilitate ethical decision making. We review these philosophies later in the chapter.

# What Is Ethics?

The term *ethics* is derived from the Greek word *ethikos,* which itself is derived from the Greek word *ethos,* meaning "custom" or "character." Morals are from the Latin word *moralis,* meaning "customs," with the Latin word *mores* being defined as "manners, morals, character." Therefore, ethics and morals are essentially the same.

In philosophy, ethical behavior is that which is "good." The Western tradition of ethics is sometimes called "moral philosophy." The field of ethics or moral philosophy involves developing, defending, and recommending concepts of right and wrong behavior. These concepts do not change as one's desires and motivations change. They are not relative to the situation. They are immutable.

In a general sense, ethics (or moral philosophy) addresses fundamental questions such as: How should I live my life? That question leads to others, such as: What sort of person should I strive to be? What values are important? What standards or principles should I live by?[13] There are various ways to define the concept of ethics. The simplest may be to say that ethics deals with "right" and "wrong." However, it is difficult to judge what may be right or wrong in a particular situation without some frame of reference.

Ethics must be based on accepted standards of behavior. For example, in virtually all societies and cultures, it is wrong to kill someone or steal property from someone else. These standards have developed over time and come from a variety of sources, including:

- The influence of religious writing and interpretations
- The influence of philosophical thought
- The influence of community (societal) values

In addition, the ethical standards for a profession, such as accounting, are heavily influenced by the practices of those in the profession, state laws and board of accountancy rules, and the expectations of society. Gaa and Thorne define ethics as "the field of inquiry that concerns the actions of people in situations where these actions have effects on the welfare of both oneself and others."[14] We adopt that definition and emphasize that it relies on ethical reasoning to evaluate the effects of actions on others—*the stakeholders*.

## Norms, Values, and the Law

Ethics deals with well-based standards of how people *ought* to act, does *not* describe the way people *actually* act, and is prescriptive, not descriptive. Ethical people always strive to make the right decision in all circumstances. They do not rationalize their actions based on their own perceived self-interests. Ethical decision making entails following certain well-established norms of behavior. The best way to understand ethics may be to differentiate it from other concepts.

### Values and Ethics

*Values* are basic and fundamental beliefs that guide or motivate attitudes or actions. In accounting, the values of the profession are embedded in its codes of ethics that guide the actions of accountants and auditors in meeting their professional responsibilities.

Values are concerned with how a person behaves in certain situations and is predicated on personal beliefs that may or may not be ethical, whereas ethics is concerned with how a moral person should behave to act in an ethical manner. A person who values prestige, power, and wealth is likely to act out of self-interest, whereas a person who values honesty, integrity, and trust will typically act in the best interests of others. It does not follow, however, that acting in the best interests of others always precludes acting in one's own self-interest. Indeed, the Golden Rule prescribes that we should treat others the way we want to be treated.

The Golden Rule requires that we try to understand how our actions affect others; thus, we need to put ourselves in the place of the person on the receiving end of the action. The Golden Rule is best seen as a consistency principle, in that we should not act one way toward others but have a desire to be treated differently in a similar situation. In other words, it would be wrong to think that separate standards of behavior exist to guide our personal lives but that a different standard (a lower one) exists in business.

### Laws versus Ethics

Being ethical is not the same as following the law. Although ethical people always try to be law-abiding, there may be instances where their sense of ethics tells them it is best not to follow the law. These situations are rare and should be based on sound ethical reasons.

Assume that you are driving at a speed of 45 miles per hour (mph) on a two-lane divided roadway (double yellow line) going east. All of a sudden, you see a young boy jump into the road to retrieve a ball. The boy is close enough to your vehicle so that you know you cannot continue straight down the roadway and stop in time to avoid hitting him. You quickly look to your right and notice about 10 other children off the road. You cannot avoid hitting 1 or more of them if you swerve to the right to avoid hitting the boy in the middle of the road. You glance to the left on the opposite side of the road and notice no traffic going west or any children off the road. What should you do?

### Ethical Perspective

If you cross the double yellow line that divides the roadway, you have violated the motor vehicle laws. We are told never to cross a double yellow line and travel into oncoming traffic. But the ethical action would be to do just that, given that you have determined it appears to be safe. It is better to risk getting a ticket than hit the boy in the middle of your side of the road or those children off to the side of the road.

## Laws and Ethical Obligations

Benjamin Disraeli (1804–1881), the noted English novelist, debater, and former prime minister, said, "When men are pure, laws are useless; when men are corrupt, laws are broken." A person of goodwill honors and respects the rules and laws and is willing to go beyond them when circumstances warrant. As indicated by the previous quote, such people do not need rules and laws to guide their actions. They always try to do the right thing. On the other hand, the existence of specific laws prohibiting certain behaviors will not stop a person who is unethical (e.g., does not care about others) from violating those laws. Just think about a Ponzi scheme such as the one engaged in by Bernie Madoff, whereby he duped others to invest with him by promising huge returns that, unbeknownst to each individual investor, would come from additional investments of scammed investors and not true returns. Madoff's story will be discussed in more detail in Chapter 3.

Laws create a minimum set of standards. Ethical people often go beyond what the law requires because the law cannot cover every situation a person might encounter. When the facts are unclear and the legal issues uncertain, an ethical person should decide what to do on the basis of well-established standards of ethical behavior. This is where moral philosophies come in and, for accountants and auditors, the ethical standards of the profession.

Ethical people often do less than is permitted by the law and more than is required. A useful perspective is to ask these questions:

- What does the law require of me?
- What do ethical standards of behavior demand of me?
- How should I act to conform to both?

## The Gray Area

When the rules are unclear, an ethical person looks beyond his / her own self-interest and evaluates the interests of the stakeholders potentially affected by the action or decision. Ethical decision making requires that a decision maker be willing, at least sometimes, to take an action that may not be in his / her best interest. This is known as the "moral point of view."

Sometimes people believe that the ends justify the means. In ethics it all depends on one's motives for acting. If one's goals are good and noble, and the means we use to achieve them are also good and noble, then the ends do justify the means. However, if one views the concept as an excuse to achieve one's goals through any means necessary, no matter how immoral, illegal, or offensive to others the means may be, then that person is attempting to justify the wrongdoing by pointing to a good outcome regardless of ethical considerations such as how one's actions affect others. Nothing could be further from the truth. The process you follow to decide on a course of action is more important than achieving the end goal. If this were not true from a moral point of view, then we could rationalize all kinds of actions in the name of achieving a desired goal, even if that goal does harm to others while satisfying our personal needs and desires.

Imagine that you work for a CPA firm and are asked to evaluate three software packages for a client. Your boss tells you that the managing partners are pushing for one of these packages, which just happens to be the firm's internal software. Your initial numerical analysis of the packages based on functionality, availability of upgrades, and customer service indicates that a competitor's package is better than the firm's software. Your boss tells you, in no uncertain terms, to redo the analysis. You know what she wants. Even though you feel uncomfortable with the situation, you decide to "tweak" the numbers to show a preference for the firm's package. The end result desired in this case is to choose the firm's package. The means to that end was to alter the analysis, an unethical act because it is dishonest and unfair to the other competitors (not to mention the client) to change the objectively determined results. In this instance, ethical decision making requires that we place the client's interests (to get the best software package for his needs) above those of the firm (to get the new business and not upset the boss).

## Ethical Relativism

*Ethical relativism* is the philosophical view that what is right or wrong and good or bad is not absolute but variable and relative, depending on the person, circumstances, or social situation. Ethical relativism holds that morality is relative to the norms of one's culture. That is, whether an action is right or wrong depends on the moral norms of the society in which it is practiced. The same action may be morally right in one society but be morally wrong in another. For the ethical relativist, there are no universal moral standards—standards that can be universally applied to all peoples at all times. The only moral standards against which a society's practices can be judged are its own. If ethical relativism is correct, then there can be no common framework for resolving moral disputes or for reaching agreement on ethical matters among members of different societies.

Most ethicists reject the theory of ethical relativism. Some claim that while the moral practices of societies may differ, the fundamental moral principles underlying these practices do not. For example, there was a situation in Singapore in the 1990s where a young American spray-painted graffiti on several cars. The Singaporean government's penalty was to "cane" the youngster by striking him on the buttocks four times. In the United States, some said it was cruel and unusual punishment for such a minor offense. In Singapore, the issue is that to protect the interests of society, the government treats harshly those who commit relatively minor offenses. After all, it does send a message that in Singapore, this and similar types of behavior will not be tolerated. While such a practice might be condemned in the United States, most people would agree with the underlying moral principle—the duty to protect the safety and security of the public (life and liberty concerns). Societies, then, may differ in their application of fundamental moral principles but agree on the principles.

## Situation Ethics

*Situation ethics*, a term first coined in 1966 by an Episcopalian priest, Joseph Fletcher, is a body of ethical thought that takes normative principles—like the virtues, natural law, and Kant's categorical imperative that relies on the universality of actions—and generalizes them so that an agent can "make sense" out of one's experience when confronting ethical dilemmas. Unlike ethical relativism that denies universal moral principles, claiming the moral codes are strictly subjective, situational ethicists recognize the existence of normative principles but question whether they should be applied as strict directives (i.e., imperatives) or, instead, as guidelines that agents should use when determining a course of ethical conduct. In other words, situationists ask: Should these norms, as generalizations about what is desired, be regarded as intrinsically valid and universally obliging of all human beings? For situationists, the circumstances surrounding an ethical dilemma can and should influence an agent's decision-making process and may alter an agent's decision when warranted. Thus, situation ethics holds that "what in some times and in some places is ethical can be in other times and in other places unethical."[15] A problem with a situation ethics perspective is that it can be used to rationalize actions such as those in the Penn State scandal.

### Student Cheating

Another danger of situational ethics is it can be used to rationalize cheating. Cheating in general is at epidemic proportions in society. The *2012 Report Card on the Ethics of American Youth,* conducted by the Josephson Institute of Ethics, found that of 43,000 high school students surveyed, 51 percent admitted to having cheated on a test during 2012, 55 percent admitted to lying and 20 percent admitted to stealing.[16]

Cheating in college is prevalent as well. The estimates of number of students engaging in some form of academic dishonesty at least once ranges from 50 to 70 percent.[17] In 1997, McCabe and Treviño surveyed 6,000 students in 31 academic institutions and found contextual factors, such as peer influence, had the most effect on student cheating behavior.[18] Contextual appropriateness, rather than what is good or right, suggests that situations alter cases, thus changing the rules and principles that guide behavior.[19]

A comprehensive study of 4,950 students at a small southwestern university identified neutralizing techniques to justify violations of accepted behavior. In the study, students rationalized their cheating behavior without challenging the norm of honesty. The most common rationale was denial of responsibility (i.e., circumstances beyond their control, such as excessive hours worked on a job, made cheating okay in that instance). Then, they blamed the faculty and testing procedures (i.e., exams that try to trick students rather than test knowledge). Finally, the students appealed to a higher loyalty by arguing that it is more important to help a friend than to avoid cheating. One student blamed the larger society for his cheating: "In America, we're taught that results aren't achieved through beneficial means, but through the easiest means." The authors concluded that the use of these techniques of neutralization conveys the message that students recognize and accept cheating as an undesirable behavior but one that can be excused under certain circumstances, reflecting a situational ethic.[20]

### Student Cheating and Workplace Behavior

Some educators feel that a student's level of academic integrity goes hand in hand with a student's ethical values on other real-world events that present ethical challenges.[21] In other words, developing a sound set of ethical standards in one area of decision making, such as personal matters, will carry over and affect other areas such as workplace ethics.

Some educators believe that ethics scandals in the business world can be attributed to the type of education that graduates of MBA programs obtained in business schools.[22] In 2006, McCabe, Butterfield, and Treviño reported on their findings regarding the extent of cheating among MBA students compared to non-business graduate students at 32 universities in the United States and Canada. The authors found that 56 percent of business students admitted to cheating, versus 47 percent of non-business students.[23]

Several researchers have examined student cheating in college and the tendency of those students to cheat in the workplace. Lawson surveyed undergraduate and graduate students enrolled in business schools and found a strong relationship between "students' propensity to cheat in an academic setting and their attitude toward unethical behavior in the business world."[24] Another study looked at the issue of graduate students cheating versus workplace dishonesty. Sims surveyed MBA students and found that students who engaged in behaviors considered severely dishonest in college also engaged in behaviors considered severely dishonest at work.[25]

If students who cheat in the university setting subsequently cheat in the workplace, then ethics education is all the more important. Once a student rationalizes cheating by blaming others or circumstances, it is only a small step to blaming others in the workplace for one's inability to get things done or unethical behavior.

## Cultural Values

Between 1967 and 1973, Dutch researcher Geert Hofstede conducted one of the most comprehensive studies of how values in the workplace are influenced by culture. Using responses to an attitude study of approximately 116,000 IBM employees in 39 countries, Hofstede identified four cultural dimensions that can be used to describe general similarities and differences in cultures around the world: (1) individualism, (2) power distance, (3) uncertainty avoidance, and (4) masculinity.[26] In 2001, a fifth dimension, long-term orientation—initially called Confucian dynamism—was identified.[27] More recently, a sixth variable was added—indulgence versus restraint—as a result of Michael Minkov's analysis of data from the World Values Survey.[28] We briefly discuss Hofstede's cultural variables in this chapter, and in Chapter 8, we extend it to Gray's model, which overlies accounting values and systems and their linkage to societal values and institutional norms. Exhibit 1.2 summarizes the five dimensions from Hofstede's work for Japan, the United Kingdom, and the United States, representing leading industrialized nations; and the so-called BRIC countries (Brazil, Russia, India, and China), which represent four major emerging economies.[29]

Individualism (IDV) focuses on the degree that the society reinforces individual or collective achievement and interpersonal relationships. In individualist societies (high IDV), people are supposed to look after themselves and their direct family, while in collectivist societies (low IDV), people belong to "in-groups" that take care of them in exchange for loyalty. Imagine, for example, you are the manager of workers from different cultures and cheating/unethical behavior occurs in the workplace. A workgroup with collectivist values such as China and Japan (low IDV) might be more prone to covering up the behavior of one member of the group, whereas in the United Kingdom and United States (high IDV), there is a greater likelihood of an individual blowing the whistle.

Uncertainty Avoidance (UAI) is another cultural value that has important implications for workplace behavior, as it describes the tolerance for uncertainty and ambiguity within society. A high UAI ranking indicates that a country has a low tolerance of uncertainty

**EXHIBIT 1.2**
**Hofstede's Cultural Dimensions***

| Cultural Variables | Countries/Scores | | | | | | |
|---|---|---|---|---|---|---|---|
| | Brazil | Russia | India | China | Japan | U.K. | U.S. |
| Power Distance (PDI) | 69 | 93 | 77 | 80 | 54 | 35 | 40 |
| Individualism (IDV) | 38 | 39 | 48 | 20 | 46 | 89 | 91 |
| Masculinity (MAS) | 49 | 36 | 56 | 66 | 95 | 66 | 62 |
| Uncertainty Avoidance (UAI) | 76 | 95 | 40 | 30 | 92 | 35 | 46 |
| Long-Term Orientation (LTO) | 65 | N/A | 61 | 118 | 80 | 25 | 29 |

*High scores indicate a propensity towards the cultural variable; low scores indicate the opposite.

and ambiguity. Such a society is likely to institute laws, rules, regulations, and controls to reduce the amount of uncertainty. A country such as Russia has a high UAI, while the United States and United Kingdom have lower scores (low UAI), indicating more tolerance for a variety of opinions. One implication is the difficulty of doing business in a country like Russia, which has strict rules and regulations about what can and cannot be done by multinational enterprises.

Other variables have important implications for workplace behavior as well, such as the Power Distance index (PDI), which focuses on the degree of equality between people in the country's society. A high PDI indicates inequalities of wealth and power have been allowed to grow within society, as has occurred in China and Russia as they develop economically. Long-term orientation (LTO) versus short-term orientation has been used to illustrate one of the differences between Asian cultures, such as China and Japan, and the United States and United Kingdom. In societies like China and Japan, high LTO scores reflect the values of long-term commitment and respect for tradition, as opposed to low-LTO countries, such as the United Kingdom and United States, where change can occur more rapidly. Time can often be a stumbling block for Western-cultured organizations entering the China market. The length of time it takes to get business deals done in China can be two or three times that in the West. One final point is to note that Brazil and India show less variability in their scores than other countries, perhaps reflecting fewer extremes in cultural dimensions.

Our discussion of cultural dimensions is meant to explain how workers from different cultures *might* interact in the workplace. The key point is that cultural sensitivity is an essential ingredient in establishing workplace values and may affect ethical behavioral patterns.

# The Six Pillars of Character

It has been said that ethics is all about how we act when no one is looking. In other words, ethical people do not do the right thing because someone observing their actions might judge them otherwise, or because they may be punished as a result of their actions. Instead, ethical people act as they do because their "inner voice" or conscience tells them that it is the right thing to do. Assume that you are leaving a shopping mall, get into your car to drive away, and hit a parked car in the lot on the way out. Let's also assume that no one saw you hit the car. What are your options? You could simply drive away and forget about it, or you can leave a note for the owner of the parked car with your telephone number. What would you do and why? Your actions will reflect the character of your inner being.

According to "virtue ethics," there are certain ideals, such as excellence or dedication to the common good, toward which we should strive and which allow the full development of our humanity. These ideals are discovered through thoughtful reflection on what we as human beings have the potential to become.

*Virtues* are attitudes, dispositions, or character traits that enable us to be and to act in ways that develop this potential. They enable us to pursue the ideals we have adopted. Honesty, courage, compassion, generosity, fidelity, integrity, fairness, self-control, and prudence are all examples of virtues in Aristotelian ethics. A quote attributed to Aristotle is, "We are what we repeatedly do. Therefore, excellence is not an act. It is a habit."[30]

The Josephson Institute of Ethics identifies Six Pillars of Character that provide a foundation to guide ethical decision making. These ethical values include trustworthiness, respect, responsibility, fairness, caring, and citizenship. Josephson believes that the Six Pillars act as a multilevel filter through which to process decisions. So, being trustworthy is not enough—we must also be caring. Adhering to the letter of the law is not enough; we must accept responsibility for our actions or inactions.[31]

## Trustworthiness

The dimensions of trustworthiness include being honest, acting with integrity, being reliable, and exercising loyalty in dealing with others.

### Honesty

Honesty is the most basic ethical value. It means that we should express the truth as we know it and without deception. In accounting, the full disclosure principle supports transparency and requires that the accounting professional disclose all the information that owners, investors, creditors, and the government need to know to make informed decisions. To withhold relevant information is dishonest. Transparent information is that which helps one understand the process followed to reach a decision. In other words it supports an ethical ends versus means belief.

Let's assume that you are a member of a discussion group in your Intermediate Accounting II class, and in an initial meeting with all members, the leader asks whether there is anyone who has not completed Intermediate I. You failed the course last term and are retaking it concurrently with Intermediate II. However, you feel embarrassed and say nothing. Now, perhaps the leader thinks that this point is important because a case study assigned to your group uses knowledge gained from Intermediate I. You internally justify the silence by thinking: Well, I did complete the course, albeit with a grade of F. This is an unethical position. You are rationalizing silence by interpreting the question in your own self-interest rather than in the interests of the entire group. The other members need to know whether you have completed Intermediate I because the leader may choose not to assign a specific project to you that requires the Intermediate I prerequisite knowledge.

### Integrity

The integrity of a person is an essential element in trusting that person. MacIntyre, in his account of Aristotelian virtue, states, "There is at least one virtue recognized by tradition which cannot be specified except with reference to the wholeness of a human life—the virtue of integrity or constancy."[32] A person of integrity takes time for self-reflection, so that the events, crises, and challenges of everyday living do not determine the course of that person's moral life. Such a person is trusted by others because that person is true to her word.

Going back to the previous example, if you encounter a conflict with another group member who pressures you to plagiarize a report available on the Internet that the two of you are working on, you will be acting with integrity if you refuse to go along. Integrity requires that you have the courage of your convictions. You know it's wrong to plagiarize another writer's material. Someone worked hard to get this report published. You would not want another person to take material you had published without permission and proper citation. Why do it to that person, then? If you do it simply because it might benefit you, then you act out of self-interest, or egoism, and that is wrong.

### Reliability

The promises that we make to others are relied on by them, and we have a moral duty to follow through with action. Our ethical obligation for promise keeping includes avoiding bad-faith excuses and unwise commitments. Imagine that you are asked to attend a group meeting on Saturday and you agree to do so. That night, though, your best friend calls and says he has two tickets to the basketball game between the Dallas Mavericks and San Antonio Spurs. The Spurs are one of the best teams in basketball and you don't get this kind of opportunity very often, so you decide to go to the game instead of the meeting. You've broken your promise, and you did it out of self-interest. You figured, who wouldn't want to see the Spurs play? What's worse, you call the group leader and say that you can't attend the meeting because you are sick. Now you've also lied. You've started the slide down the ethical slippery slope, and it will be difficult to climb back to the top.

### Loyalty

We all should value loyalty in friendship. After all, you wouldn't want the friend who invited you to the basketball game to telephone the group leader later and say that you went to the game on the day of the group meeting.

Loyalty requires that friends not violate the confidence we place in them. In accounting, loyalty requires that we keep financial and other information confidential when it deals with our employer and client. For example, if you are the in-charge accountant on an audit of a client for your CPA firm-employer and you discover that the client is "cooking the books," you shouldn't telephone the local newspaper and tell the story to a reporter. Instead, you should go to the partner in charge of the engagement and tell her. Your ethical obligation is to report what you have observed to your supervisor and let her take the appropriate action.

### A Word about Whistleblowing

There are limits to the confidentiality obligation. For example, let's assume that you are the accounting manager at a publicly owned company and your supervisor (the controller) pressures you to keep silent about the manipulation of financial information. You then go to the CFO, who tells you that both the CEO and board of directors support the controller. Out of a misplaced duty of loyalty in this situation, you might rationalize your silence as did Betty Vinson. Ethical values sometimes conflict, and loyalty is the one value that should never take precedence over other values such as honesty and integrity. Otherwise, we can imagine all kinds of cover-ups of information in the interest of loyalty or friendship.

Internal whistleblowing typically is appropriate to clarify the positions of your superiors and bring matters of concern to the highest levels within an organization, including the audit committee of the board of directors. In fact, the ethics of the accounting profession [Interpretation 102-4 of the AICPA Code of Professional Conduct][33]obligates the CPA to do just that. The prior example may represent a situation where you may be tempted to take the matter outside your employer or circumvent the firm-employer relationship to air your concerns. You should be careful if you choose to do this; get legal advice before acting. Informing parties outside an entity violates confidentiality. While acting out of conscience and a sense that the right thing to do is the highest ethical choice one can make, it is important to be aware of the consequences of one's actions before taking the ultimate step of external whistleblowing. Exhibit 1.3 describes the ethical standards for CPAs under Interpretation 102-4. More will be said about whistleblowing in Chapter 3.

Notice that the process is clearly defined and requires bringing any concerns to higher-ups in the organization, including the audit committee, and preparing an informative memorandum that would summarize the various positions, including that of members of top management. The memo should help provide a defense of due care and compliance with ethical standards in case it becomes a regulatory or legal matter.

While attending a Josephson Institute of Ethics training program for educators, one of the authors of this book heard Michael Josephson make an analogy about loyal behavior that sticks with him to this day. Josephson said: "Dogs are loyal to their master, while cats are loyal to the house." How true it is that dogs see their ultimate allegiance to their owner while cats get attached to the place they call home—their own personal space. Now, in a business context, this means that a manager should try to encourage "cat" behavior in the organization (sorry, dog lovers). In that way, if a cover-up of a financial wrongdoing exists, the "cat loyalty" mentality incorporated into the business environment dictates that the information be disclosed because it is not in the best interests of the organization to hide or ignore it. If we act with "dog loyalty," we will cover up for our supervisor, who has a say about what happens to us in the organization. Recall our discussion of cultural

**EXHIBIT 1.3**
**Ethical Responsibilities of Industry CPAs to Avoid Subordinating Judgment***

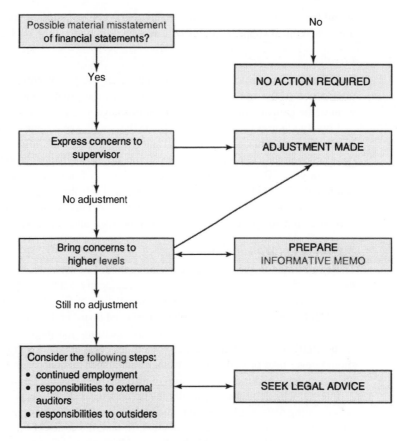

*A depiction of the requirements of Interpretation 102-4 developed by Steven Mintz.

values, and that someone from a country or group with a low score on individualism (a collectivist society) is more likely to hide a damaging fact out of loyalty to the controller and her superiors, while someone from a more individualistic society is more likely to come forward with information about the wrongdoing. A cover-up may be an understandable position because of internal pressures that work against voicing one's concerns, but it is unethical all the same. Moreover, once we go along with the cover-up, we have started the slide down the ethical slippery slope, and there may be no turning back. In fact, our supervisor may come to us during the next period and expect us to go along with the same cover-up in a similar situation. If we refuse at that point, the first instance may be brought up and used as a threat against us because we've already violated ethical standards once and don't want to get caught. It is important to emphasize that we should not act ethically out of fear of the consequences of hiding information. Instead, we should act ethically out of a positive sense that it is the right way to behave.

Often when we cover up information in the present, it becomes public knowledge later. The consequences at that time are more serious because trust has been destroyed. We have already discussed the Penn State scandal and forfeiture of trust by Joe Paterno for failing to take steps to stop child abuse. Another example is Lance Armstrong, who for years denied taking performance-enhancing drugs while winning seven Tour de France titles. In 2012, he finally admitted to doing just that, and as a result, all those titles were stripped away by the U.S. Anti-Doping Agency. Or consider former president Richard Nixon, who went along with the cover-up in the Watergate break-in only to be forced to resign the presidency once the cover-up became public knowledge.

## Respect

All people should be treated with dignity. We do not have an ethical duty to hold all people in high esteem, but we should treat everyone with respect, regardless of their circumstances in life. In today's slang, we might say that respect means giving a person "props." The Golden Rule encompasses respect for others through notions such as civility, courtesy, decency, dignity, autonomy, tolerance, and acceptance.[34]

By age 16, George Washington had copied by hand 110 *Rules of Civility & Decent Behavior in Company and Conversation.* They are based on a set of rules composed by French Jesuits in 1595. While many of the rules seem out of place in today's society, Washington's first rule is noteworthy: "Every Action done in Company, ought to be with Some Sign of Respect, to those that are Present."[35]

Washington's vernacular was consistent with the times as indicated by the last of his rules: "Labour to keep alive in your Breast that Little Spark of Celestial fire Called Conscience."[36] We have found many definitions of conscience, but the one we like best is the universal lexical English wordnet used for research and developed by the Cognitive Sciences Laboratory at Princeton University. The definition is: "Motivation deriving logically from ethical or moral principles that govern a person's thoughts and actions."[37]

As a member of the case discussion group in the previous example, it would be wrong to treat another member with discourtesy or prejudice because you have drawn conclusions about that person on the basis of national origin or some other factor rather than her abilities and conduct. You would not want to be treated unfairly because of how you dress or walk or talk, so others should not be judged based on similar considerations. We should judge people based on their character.

The Nobel Peace Prize–winning activist Dr. Martin Luther King said it best in his "I Have a Dream" speech, delivered on the steps at the Lincoln Memorial in Washington, D.C., on August 28, 1963. Dr. King said the following in reference to the true meaning of the nation's creed: "'We hold these truths to be self-evident; that all men are created equal.' … I have a dream that my four little children will one day live in a nation where they will not be judged by the color of their skin but by the content of their character."[38]

## Responsibility

Josephson points out that our capacity to reason and our freedom to choose make us morally responsible for our actions and decisions. We are accountable for what we do and who we are.[39]

A responsible person carefully reflects on alternative courses of action using ethical principles. A responsible person acts diligently and perseveres in carrying out moral action. Imagine if you were given the task by your group to interview five CPAs in public practice about their most difficult ethical dilemma, and you decided to ask one person, who was a friend of the family, about five dilemmas that person faced in the practice of public accounting. Now, even if you made an "honest" mistake in interpreting the requirement, it is clear that you did not exercise the level of care that should be expected in this instance in carrying out the instructions to interview five different CPAs. The due care test is whether a "reasonable person" would conclude that you had acted with the level of care, or diligence, expected in the circumstance. The courts have used this test for many years to evaluate the actions of professionals.

## Fairness

A person of fairness treats others equally, impartially, and openly. In business, we might say that the fair allocation of scarce resources requires that those who have earned the right to a greater share of corporate resources as judged objectively by performance measures should receive a larger share than those whose performance has not met the standard.

Let's assume that your instructor told the case study groups at the beginning of the course that the group with the highest overall numerical average would receive an A, the group with second highest a B, and so on. At the end of the term, the teacher gave the group with the second-highest average—90.5—an A and the group with the highest average—91.2—a B. Perhaps the instructor took subjective factors into account in deciding on the final grading. You might view the instructor's action as unfair to the group with the highest average. It certainly contradicts his original stated policy, is capricious and unfair, especially if the instructor does not explain his reason for doing this. As Josephson points out, "Fairness implies adherence to a balanced standard of justice without relevance to one's own feelings or inclinations."[40]

## Caring

The late Edmund L. Pincoffs, a philosopher who formerly taught at the University of Texas at Austin, believed that virtues such as caring, kindness, sensitivity, altruism, and benevolence enable a person who possesses these qualities to consider the interests of others.[41] Josephson believes that caring is the "heart of ethics and ethical decision making."[42]

The essence of caring is empathy. *Empathy* is the ability to understand, be sensitive to, and care about the feelings of others. Caring and empathy support each other and enable a person to put herself in the position of another. This is essential to ethical decision making.

Let's assume that on the morning of an important group meeting, your child comes down with a temperature of 103 degrees. You call the group leader and say that you can't make it to the meeting. Instead, you suggest that the meeting be taped and you will listen to the discussions later that day and telephone the leader with any questions. The leader reacts angrily, stating that you are not living up to your responsibilities. Assuming that your behavior is not part of a pattern and you have been honest with the leader up to now, you would have a right to be upset with the leader, who seems uncaring. In the real world, emergencies do occur, and placing your child's health and welfare above all else should make sense in this situation to a person of rational thought. You also acted diligently by offering to listen to the discussions and, if necessary, follow up with the leader.

Putting yourself in the place of another is sometimes difficult to do because the circumstances are unique to the situation. For example, what would you do if a member of your team walked into a meeting all bleary-eyed? You might ignore it, or you might ask that person if everything is all right. If you do and are informed that the person was up all night with a crying baby, then you might say something like, "If there's anything I can do to lighten the load for you today, just say the word."

A person who can empathize seems to know just what to say to make the other person feel better about circumstances. On the other hand, if you have never been married and have not had children, you might not be able to understand the feelings of a mother who has just spent the night trying to comfort a screaming child.

## Citizenship

Josephson points out that "citizenship includes civic virtues and duties that prescribe how we ought to behave as part of a community."[43] An important part of good citizenship is to obey the laws, be informed about the issues, volunteer in your community, and vote in elections. President Barack Obama has called for citizens to engage in some kind of public service to benefit society as a whole.

## Reputation

It might be said that judgments made about one's character contribute toward how another party views that person's reputation. In other words, what is the estimation in which a person is commonly held, whether favorable or not? The reputation of a CPA is critical to a client's trusting that CPA to perform services competently and maintain the confidentiality of client information (except for whistleblowing instances). One builds "reputational capital" through favorable actions informed by ethical behavior.

All too often in politics and government, a well-respected leader becomes involved in behavior that, once disclosed, tears down a reputation earned over many years of service. The example of former senator and presidential candidate John Edwards shows how quickly one's reputation can be destroyed—in this case because of the disclosure of an extramarital affair that Edwards had with a 42-year-old campaign employee, Rielle Hunter, that Edwards covered up.

In 2006, Edwards's political action committee (PAC) paid Hunter's video production firm $100,000 for work. Then the committee paid another $14,086 on April 1, 2007. The Edwards camp said the latter payment from the PAC was in exchange for 100 hours of unused videotape Hunter shot. The same day, the Edwards presidential campaign had injected $14,034.61 into the PAC for a "furniture purchase," according to federal election records.

Edwards, a U.S. senator representing North Carolina from 1998 until his vice presidential bid in 2004, acknowledged in May 2009 that federal investigators were looking into how he used campaign funds. Edwards was accused of soliciting nearly $1 million from wealthy backers to finance a cover-up of his illicit affair during his 2008 bid for the White House.

Edwards admitted to ABC News[44] in an interview with Bob Woodruff in August 2009 that he repeatedly lied about having an affair with Hunter. Edwards strenuously denied being involved in paying the woman hush money or fathering her newborn child, admitted the affair was a mistake in the interview, and said: "Two years ago, I made a very serious mistake, a mistake that I am responsible for and no one else. In 2006, I told Elizabeth [his wife] about the mistake, asked her for her forgiveness, asked God for His forgiveness. And we have kept this within our family since that time." Edwards said he told his entire family about the affair after it ended in 2006, and that his wife Elizabeth was "furious" but that their marriage would survive. On January 21, 2010, he also finally admitted to fathering Hunter's child, Quinn (and since the girl was born in 2008, that indicates pretty clearly that Edwards's statement that the affair ended in 2006 was less than truthful).

On May 31, 2012, a jury found him not guilty on one of six counts in the campaign-finance trial and deadlocked on the remaining charges; the Department of Justice decided not to retry him on those charges. On the courthouse steps, Edwards acknowledged his moral shortcomings.

Edwards violated virtually every tenet of ethical behavior and destroyed his reputation. He lied about the affair and attempted to cover it up, including allegations that he fathered Hunter's baby. He violated the trust of the public and lied after telling his family about the affair in 2006. He even had the audacity to run for the Democratic nomination for president in 2008. One has to wonder what it says about Edwards's ethics that he was willing to run for president of the United States while hiding the knowledge of his affair, without considering what might happen if he had won the Democratic nomination in 2008, and then the affair became public knowledge during the general election campaign. His behavior is the ultimate example of ethical blindness and the pursuit of one's own self-interests to the detriment of all others. Perhaps the noted Canadian-American chemist and author Orlando Aloysius Battista (1917–1995), said it best: "An error doesn't become a mistake until you refuse to correct it." In other words, when you do something wrong, admit it, take responsibility for your actions, accept the consequences, and move on. Unfortunately, most adulterers like Edwards go to great lengths to cover up their moral failings and don't admit to them until they have been caught.

# The Public Interest in Accounting

Following the disclosure of numerous accounting scandals in the early 2000s at companies such as Enron and WorldCom, the accounting profession and professional bodies turned their attention to examining how to rebuild the public trust and confidence in financial reporting. Stuebs and Wilkinson point out that restoring the accounting profession's public interest focus is a crucial first step in recapturing the public trust and securing the profession's future.[45] Copeland believes that in order to regain the trust and respect the profession enjoyed prior to the scandals, the profession must rebuild its reputation on its historical foundation of ethics and integrity.[46]

In response to widespread financial statement fraud and the failure of accountants and auditors to meet their professional responsibilities, regulatory bodies have turned their attention to developing ethics education requirements for university accounting students. In the United States, the state boards of accountancy are charged with protecting the public interest in licensing candidates to become CPAs. The National Association of State Boards of Accountancy (NASBA) provides a forum for discussion of the different state board requirements to develop an ideal set of regulations in the Uniform Accountancy Act. In 2009, NASBA revised its Rule 5.2 on education and set an either/or approach that recommends either the integration of the course material throughout the undergraduate and/or graduate curriculum or a three-hour stand-alone course in ethics.[47]

Even before NASBA's involvement, in 2003 the Texas legislature reacted to the implosion of Enron and its subsequent bankruptcy that shocked the Houston business community by questioning the Texas State Board of Public Accountancy (TSBPA) about how the CPAs at Andersen failed to see the ethical problems at Enron that led to its financial statement fraud. The board called for a mandated three-unit course in ethics for applicants initially taking the CPA exam, effective July 1, 2005. Rule 511.58 details that the required course "should provide students with a framework of ethical reasoning, professional values and attitudes for exercising professional skepticism, and other behavior that is in the best interest of the public and profession and include the core values of integrity, objectivity, and independence."[48]

Other states requiring a stand-alone ethics course at the time of this writing included California, Colorado, Maryland, New York, and West Virginia. The Colorado Board of Accountancy requires a separate course in accounting ethics beginning July 1, 2015,[49] while the California Board is phasing in that requirement during the 2014–2017 period.[50]

The California and Texas requirements provide a broad framework to identify the foundation of accounting ethics education. According to the California requirements, "Ethics Study Guidelines" means a program of learning that provides students with a framework of ethical reasoning, professional values and attitudes for exercising professional skepticism, and other behavior that is in the best interest of the investing and consuming public and the profession, and the core values of integrity, objectivity, and independence consistent with International Education Standard 4 (IES 4) of the International Accounting Education Standards Board (IAESB), the International Federation of Accountants Code of Ethics (IFAC Code) and the AICPA Code.[51] These international organizations will be discussed more fully in Chapter 8.

## Professional Accounting Associations

The accounting profession is a community with values and standards of behavior. These are embodied in the various codes of conduct in the profession. The AICPA is a voluntary association of CPAs with nearly 370,000 members in 128 countries, including CPAs in business and industry, public accounting, government, education, student affiliates, and international associates. Other professional associations exist in the United States. The Institute of Management Accountants (IMA), with a membership of more than 60,000, is the worldwide association for accountants and financial professionals working in business. We discuss ethics standards of the IMA later in this chapter. The Institute of Internal Auditors (IIA) is an international professional association representing the internal audit profession with 175,000 members. We look at the IIA's standards in Chapter 3. On an international level, the largest professional accounting association is the Institute of Chartered Accountants [equivalent to CPAs] in England and Wales (ICAEW) that has over 138,000 members worldwide. A truly global professional association is the International Federation of Accountants (IFAC). IFAC is a global professional body dedicated to serve the public interest with 173 members and associate members in 129 countries representing approximately 2.5 million accountants. Standards related to IFAC will be discussed in Chapter 8.

## AICPA Code of Conduct

Given the broader scope of membership in the AICPA and the fact that state boards of accountancy generally recognize its ethical standards in state board rules of conduct, we emphasize the AICPA Code of Professional Conduct in most of this book. Moreover, the previously discussed ethics education requirement pertains to those students who sit for the CPA exam, so it seems only natural to focus on AICPA rules. The Principles section of the AICPA Code, which mirrors virtues-based principles, are discussed next. We discuss the Rules of Conduct that are the enforceable provisions of the AICPA Code in Chapter 4. Later in this chapter, we explain the IMA Statement of Ethical Professional Practice.

The Principles of the AICPA Code are aspirational statements that form the foundation for the Code's enforceable rules. The Principles guide members in the performance of their professional responsibilities and call for an unyielding commitment to honor the public trust, even at the sacrifice of personal benefits. While CPAs cannot be legally held to the Principles, they do represent the expectations for CPAs on the part of the public in the performance of professional services. In this regard, the Principles are based on values of the profession and traits of character (virtues) that enable CPAs to meet their obligations to the public.

The Principles include (1) Responsibilities, (2) The Public Interest, (3) Integrity, (4) Objectivity and Independence, (5) Due Care, and (6) Scope and Nature of Services.[52]

The umbrella statement in the Code is that the overriding responsibility of CPAs is to exercise sensitive professional and moral judgments in all activities. By linking professional conduct to moral judgment, the AICPA Code recognizes the importance of moral reasoning in meeting professional obligations. That is one reason why we discuss the classic moral philosophies later in the chapter.

The second principle defines the public interest to include "clients, credit grantors, governments, employers, investors, the business and financial community, and others who rely on the objectivity and integrity of CPAs to maintain the orderly functioning of commerce." This principle calls for resolving conflicts between these stakeholder groups by recognizing the primacy of a CPA's responsibility to the public as the way to best serve clients' and employers' interests.

Integrity has been discussed already in this chapter. As a principle of CPA conduct, integrity recognizes that the public trust is served by (1) being honest and candid within the constraints of client confidentiality, (2) not subordinating the public trust to personal gain and advantage, (3) observing both the form and spirit of technical and ethical standards, and (4) observing the principles of objectivity and independence and of due care.

Objectivity requires that all CPAs maintain a mental attitude of impartiality and intellectual honesty and be free of conflicts of interest in meeting professional responsibilities. Independence applies only to CPAs who provide attestation services (i.e., auditing), not tax and advisory services. The reason lies in the scope and purpose of an audit. When conducting an audit of a client's financial statements, the CPA gathers evidence to support an opinion on whether the financial statements present fairly, in all material respects, the client's financial position and the results of operations and cash flows in accordance with GAAP. The audit opinion is relied on by the public (external users), thereby triggering the need to be independent of the client entity to enhance assurances. In tax and advisory engagements, the service is provided primarily for the client (internal user) so that the CPA might become involved in some relationships with the client that might otherwise impair audit independence but do not come into play when providing nonattest services; nonattest services do require objectivity in decision making to protect the public interest.

Independence is required both in fact and in appearance. Because it is difficult to determine independence in fact because it involves identifying a mindset, CPAs should avoid relationships with a client entity that may be seen as impairing objective judgment by a "reasonable" observer. The foundational standard of independence is discussed in the context of the audit function in Chapter 4.

The due care standard (diligence) calls for continued improvement in the level of competency and quality of services by (1) performing professional services to the best of one's abilities, (2) carrying out professional responsibilities with concern for the best interests of those for whom the services are performed, (3) carrying out those responsibilities in accordance with the public interest, (4) following relevant technical and ethical standards, and (5) properly planning and supervising engagements. A CPA who undertakes to perform professional services without having the necessarily skills violates the due care standard. The requirement for continuing education to maintain one's CPA certificate helps meet the due care standard. Most states now require CPAs to complete a specified number of continuing education hours in ethics to maintain their license to practice.

What follows is an example of the importance of the due care standard. Imagine if a CPA were asked to perform an audit of a school district and the CPA never engaged in governmental auditing before and never completed a course of study in governmental auditing. While the CPA or CPA firm may still obtain the necessary skills to perform the audit—for example, by hiring someone with the required skills—the CPA/firm would have a hard time supervising such work without the proper background and knowledge.

The due care standard also relates to the scope and nature of services performed by a CPA. The latter requires that CPAs practice in firms that have in place internal quality control procedures to ensure that services are competently delivered and adequately supervised and that such services are consistent with one's role as a professional. Also, CPAs should determine, in their individual judgments, whether the scope and nature of other services provided to an audit client would create a conflict of interest in performing an audit for that client.

A high-quality audit features the exercise of professional judgment by the auditor and, importantly, a mindset that includes professional skepticism throughout the planning and performance of the audit. Professional skepticism is an essential attitude that enhances the auditor's ability to identify and respond to conditions that may indicate possible misstatement of the financial statements. It includes a questioning mind and critical assessment of audit evidence. Professional judgment is a critical component of ethical behavior in accounting. The qualities of behavior that enable professional judgment come not only from the profession's codes of conduct, but also the virtues and ability to reason through ethical conflicts using ethical reasoning methods.

## Virtue, Character, and CPA Obligations

Traits of character such as honesty, integrity, and trustworthiness enable a person to act with virtue and apply the moral point of view. Kurt Baier, a well-known moral philosopher, discusses the moral point of view as being one that emphasizes practical reason and

**EXHIBIT 1.4**
**Virtues and Ethical**
**Obligations of CPAs**

| Aristotle's Virtues | Ethical Standards for CPAs |
| --- | --- |
| Trustworthiness, benevolence, altruism | **Integrity** |
| Honesty, integrity | Truthfulness, non-deception |
| Impartiality, open-mindedness | Objectivity, independence |
| Reliability, dependability, faithfulness | Loyalty (confidentiality) |
| Trustworthiness | Due care (competence and prudence) |

rational choice.[53] To act ethically means to incorporate ethical values into decision making and to reflect on the rightness or wrongness of alternative courses of action. The ethical values in accounting flow from its professional codes of conduct and include those identified by state boards of accountancy: the core values of integrity, objectivity, and independence; attitudes for exercising professional skepticism; and a framework for ethical reasoning.

Aristotle believed that deliberation (reason and thought) precedes the choice of action and we deliberate about things that are in our power (voluntary) and can be realized by action. The deliberation that leads to the action always concerns choices, not the ends. We take the end for granted—a life of excellence or virtue—and then consider in what manner and by what means it can be realized. In accounting, we might say that the end is to gain the public trust and serve the public interest, and the means to achieve that end is by acting in accordance with the profession's ethical standards.

Aristotle's conception of virtue incorporates positive traits of character that enable reasoned judgments to be made, and in accounting, they support integrity—the inner strength of character to withstand pressures that might otherwise overwhelm and negatively influence their professional judgment. A summary of the virtues is listed in Exhibit 1.4.[54]

## Modern Moral Philosophies

The ancient Greeks believed that reason and thought precede the choice of action and that we deliberate about things we can influence with our decisions. In making decisions, most people want to follow laws and rules. However, rules are not always clear, and laws may not cover every situation. Therefore, it is the ethical foundation that we develop and nurture that will determine how we react to unstructured situations that challenge our sense of right and wrong. In the end, we need to rely on moral principles to guide our decision making. However, the ability to reason out ethical conflicts may not be enough to assure ethical decision making occurs in accounting as discussed in Chapters 2 through 5. This is because while we believe that we should behave in accordance with core values, we may wind up deviating from these values that trigger ethical reasoning in accounting because of internal pressures from supervisors and others in top management. In the end, a self-interest motive may prevail over making a decision from an ethical perspective, and unethical behavior may result. This is the moral of the story of Betty Vinson's role in the WorldCom fraud.

Moral philosophies provide specific principles and rules that we can use to decide what is right or wrong in specific instances. They can help a business decision maker formulate strategies to deal with ethical dilemmas and resolve them in a morally appropriate way. There are many such philosophies, but we limit the discussion to those that are most applicable to the study of accounting ethics, including teleology, deontology, justice, and virtue ethics. Our approach focuses on the most basic concepts needed to help you understand the ethical decision making process in business and accounting that we outline in Chapter 2. We do not favor any one of these philosophies because there is no one correct way to resolve ethical issues in business. Instead, we present them to aid in resolving ethical dilemmas in accounting. Exhibit 1.5 summarizes the basis for making ethical judgments for each of the major moral philosophies. The discussion that follows elaborates on these principles and applies them to a common situation in accounting.

## Teleology

Recall that *telos* is the Greek word for "end" or "purpose." In *teleology,* an act is considered morally right or acceptable if it produces some desired result such as pleasure, the realization of self-interest, fame, utility, wealth, and so on. Teleologists assess the moral worth of behavior by looking at its consequences, and thus moral philosophers often refer to these theories as *consequentialism.* Two important teleological philosophies that typically guide decision making in individual business decisions are egoism and utilitarianism.

### Egoism and Enlightened Egoism

*Egoism* defines right or acceptable behavior in terms of its consequences for the individual. *Egoists* believe that they should make decisions that maximize their own self-interest, which is defined differently by each individual. In other words, the individual should "[d]o the act that promotes the greatest good for oneself."[55] Many believe that egoistic people and companies are inherently unethical, are short-term-oriented, and will take advantage of others to achieve their goals. Our laissez-faire economic system enables the selfish pursuit of individual profit, so a regulated marketplace is essential to protect the interests of those affected by individual (and corporate) decision making.

There is one form of egoism that emphasizes more of a direct action to bring about the best interests of society. *Enlightened egoists* take a long-range perspective and allow for the well-being of others because they help achieve some ultimate goal for the decision maker, although their own self-interest remains paramount. For example, enlightened egoists may abide by professional codes of ethics, avoid cheating on taxes, and create safe working conditions. They do so not because their actions benefit others, but because they help achieve some ultimate goal for the egoist, such as advancement within the firm.[56]

Let's examine the following example from the perspectives of egoism and enlightened egoism. The date is Friday, January 17, 2014, and the time is 5:00 p.m. It is the last day of fieldwork on an audit, and you are the staff auditor in charge of receivables. You are wrapping up the test of subsequent collections of accounts receivable to determine whether certain receivables that were outstanding on December 31, 2013, and that were not confirmed by the customer as being outstanding have now been collected. If these receivables have been collected and in amounts equal to the year-end outstanding balances, then you will be confident that the December 31 balance is correct and this aspect of the receivables audit can be relied on. One account receivable for $1 million has not been collected, even though it is 90 days past due. You go to your supervisor and discuss whether to establish an allowance for uncollectibles for part of or for the entire amount. Your supervisor contacts the manager in charge of the audit, who goes to the CFO to discuss the matter. The CFO says in no uncertain terms that you should not record an allowance of any amount. The CFO does not want to reduce earnings below the current level because that will cause the company to fail to meet financial analysts' estimates of earnings for the year. Your supervisor informs you that the firm will go along with the client on this matter, even though the $1 million amount is material. In fact, it is 10 percent of the overall accounts receivable balance on December 31, 2013.

The junior auditor faces a challenge to integrity in this instance. The client is attempting to circumvent GAAP. The ethical obligation of the staff auditor is not to subordinate judgment to others, including top management of the firm.

**EXHIBIT 1.5  Ethical Reasoning Method Bases for Making Ethical Judgments**

| | Teleology | | | Deontology | Justice | Virtue Ethics |
|---|---|---|---|---|---|---|
| | **Egoism** | **Enlightened Egoism** | **Utilitarianism** | **Rights Theory** | | |
| **Ethical Judgments** | Defines "right" behavior by consequences for the decision maker | Considers well-being of others within the scope of deciding on a course of action based on self-interest. | Evaluates consequences of actions (harms and benefits) on stakeholders<br><br>*Act*<br>Evaluate whether the intended *action* provides the greatest net benefits.<br><br>*Rule*<br>Select the action that conforms to the correct *moral rule* that produces the greatest net benefits | Considers "rights" of stakeholders and related duties to them.<br><br>Treats people as an end and not merely as a means to an end.<br><br>*Universality*<br>*Perspective:* Would I want others to act in a similar manner for similar reasons in this situation? | Emphasizes rights, fairness, and equality.<br><br>Those with equal claims to justice should be treated equally; those with unequal claims should be treated unequally. | Only method where ethical reasoning methods—"virtues" (internal traits of character)—apply both to the *decision maker* and the *decision*<br><br>Judgments are made not by applying rules, but by possessing those traits that enable the decision maker to act for the good of others.<br><br>Similar to Principles of AICPA Code and IMA Standards. |
| ***Problems with Implementation*** | Fails to consider interests of those affected by the decision | Interests of others are subservient to self-interest. | Can be difficult to assign values to harms and benefits. | Relies on moral absolutes—no exceptions; need to resolve conflicting rights | Can be difficult to determine the criteria to distinguish equal from unequal claims. | Virtues may conflict, requiring choices to be made. |

23

If you are an egoist, you might conclude that it is in your best interests to go along with the firm's position to support the client's presumed interests. After all, you do not want to lose your job. An enlightened egoist would consider the interests of others, including the investors and creditors, but still might reason that it is in her long-run interests to go along with the firm's position to support the client because she may not advance within the firm unless she is perceived to be a "team player."

### Utilitarianism

*Utilitarians* follow a relatively straightforward method for deciding the morally correct course of action for any particular situation. First, they identify the various courses of action that they could perform. Second, they determine the utility of the consequences of all possible alternatives and then select the one that results in the greatest net benefit. In other words, they identify all the foreseeable benefits and harms (consequences) that could result from each course of action for those affected by the action would result from each course of action for those affected by the action of the decision maker,, and then choose the course of action that provides the greatest benefits after the costs have been taken into account.[57] Given its emphasis on evaluating the benefits and harms of alternatives on stakeholders, utilitarianism requires that people look beyond self-interest to consider impartially the interest of all persons affected by their actions.

The utilitarian theory was first formulated in the eighteenth century by the English writer Jeremy Bentham (1748–1832) and later refined by John Stuart Mill (1806–1873). Bentham sought an objective basis that would provide a publicly acceptable norm for determining what kinds of laws England should enact. He believed that the most promising way to reach an agreement was to choose the policy that would bring about the greatest net benefits to society once the harms had been taken into account. His motto became "the greatest good for the greatest number." Over the years, the principle of utilitarianism has been expanded and refined so that today, there are many different variations of the principle. Modern utilitarians often describe benefits and harms in terms of satisfaction of personal preferences or in purely economic terms of monetary benefits over monetary costs.[58]

Utilitarians differ in their views about the kind of question we ought to ask ourselves when making an ethical decision. Some believe the proper question is: What effect will my doing this action in this situation have on the general balance of good over evil? If lying would produce the best consequences in a particular situation, we ought to lie.[59] These *act-utilitarians* examine the specific action itself, rather than the general rules governing the action, to assess whether it will result in the greatest utility. For example, a rule such as "don't subordinate judgment" would serve only as a general guide for an act-utilitarian. If the overall effect of giving in to the client's demands brings net utility to all the stakeholders, then the rule is set aside.

*Rule-utilitarians,* on the other hand, claim that we must choose the action that conforms to the general rule that would have the best consequences. For the rule-utilitarian, actions are justified by appealing to rules such as "don't subordinate judgment." According to the rule-utilitarian, an action is selected because it is required by the correct moral rules that everyone should follow. The correct moral rules are those that maximize intrinsic value and minimize intrinsic disvalue. For example, a rule such as "don't deceive" (an element of truthfulness) might be interpreted as requiring the full disclosure of the possibility that the client will not collect on a material, $1 million receivable. A rule-utilitarian might reason that the long-term effects of deceiving the users of financial statements are a breakdown of the trust that exists between the users and preparers and auditors of financial information.

In other words, we must ask ourselves: What effect would everyone's doing this kind of action (subordination of judgment) have on the general balance of good over evil? So, for

example, the rule "to always tell the truth" in general promotes the good of everyone and therefore should always be followed, even if lying would produce the best consequences in certain situations. Notwithstanding differences between act- and rule-utilitarians, most hold to the general principle that morality must depend on balancing the beneficial and harmful consequences of conduct.[60]

While utilitarianism is a very popular ethical theory, there are some difficulties in relying on it as a sole method for moral decision making because the utilitarian calculation requires that we assign values to the benefits and harms resulting from our actions. But it is often difficult, if not impossible, to measure and compare the values of certain benefits and costs. Let's go back to our receivables example. It would be difficult to quantify the possible effects of going along with the client. How can a utilitarian measure the costs to the company of possibly having to write off a potential bad debt after the fact, including possible higher interest rates to borrow money in the future because of a decline in liquidity? What is the cost to one's reputation for failing to disclose an event at a point in time that might have affected the analysis of financial results? On the other hand, how can we measure the benefits to the company of *not* recording the allowance? Does it mean the stock price will rise and, if so, by how much?

## Deontology

The term *deontology* is derived from the Greek word *deon,* meaning "duty." *Deontology* refers to moral philosophies that focus on the rights of individuals and on the intentions associated with a particular behavior, rather than on its consequences. *Deontologists* believe that moral norms establish the basis for action. Deontology differs from rule-utilitarianism in that the moral norms (or rules) are based on reason, not outcomes. Fundamental to deontological theory is the idea that equal respect must be given to all persons.[61] In other words, individuals have certain inherent rights and I, as the decision maker, have a duty (obligation, commitment, or responsibility) to respect those rights.

Philosophers claim that rights and duties are correlative. That is, my rights establish your duties and my duties correspond to the rights of others. The deontological tradition focuses on duties, which can be thought of as establishing the ethical limits of my behavior. From my perspective, duties are what I owe to others. Other people have certain claims on my behavior; in other words, they have certain rights against me.[62]

As with utilitarians, deontologists may be divided into those who focus on moral rules and those who focus on the nature of the acts themselves. In act deontology, principles are or should be applied by individuals to each unique circumstance allowing for some space in deciding the right thing to do. Rule deontologists believe that general moral principles determine the relationship between the basic rights of the individual and a set of rules governing conduct. It is particularly appropriate to the accounting profession, where the Principles of the AICPA Code support the rights of investors and creditors for accurate and reliable financial information and the duty of CPAs to act in accordance with the profession's rules of conduct. In this book, we adopt the rule deontological perspective when evaluating rights theories as a method of moral reasoning. Rule deontologists believe that conformity to general moral principles based on logic determines ethicalness. Examples include Kant's categorical imperative, discussed next, and the Golden Rule of the Judeo-Christian tradition: "Do unto others as you would have them do unto you." Unlike act deontologists, who hold that actions are the proper basis on which to judge morality or ethicalness and treat rules only as guidelines in the decision-making process, rule deontologists argue there are some things we should never do.[63] Similarly, unlike act-utilitarians, rule deontologists argue that some actions would be wrong regardless of utilitarian benefits. For example, rule deontologists would consider it wrong for someone who has no money to steal bread, because it violates the right of the storeowner to gain from his hard work baking and selling the bread. This is the dilemma in the classic novel *Les Misérables* by Victor Hugo. The main character, Jean Valjean, serves a 19-year sentence at hard labor for stealing a loaf of bread to feed his starving family.

### Rights Principles

A *right* is a justified claim on others. For example, if I have a right to freedom, then I have a justified claim to be left alone by others. Turned around, I can say that others have a duty or responsibility to leave me alone.[64] In accounting, because investors and creditors have a right to accurate and complete financial information, I have the duty to ensure that the financial statements "present fairly" the financial position, results of operations, and changes in cash flows.

Formulations of *rights theories* first appeared in the seventeenth century in writings of Thomas Hobbes and John Locke. One of the most important and influential interpretations of moral rights is based on the work of Immanuel Kant (1724–1804), an eighteenth-century philosopher. Kant maintained that each of us has a worth or dignity that must be respected. This dignity makes it wrong for others to abuse us or to use us against our will. Kant expressed this idea as a moral principle: Humanity must always be treated as an end, not merely as a means. To treat a person as a mere means is to use her to advance one's own interest. But to treat a person as an end is to respect that person's dignity by allowing each the freedom to choose for himself.[65]

An important contribution of Kantian philosophy is the so-called categorical imperative: "Act only according to that maxim by which you can at the same time will that it should become universal law."[66] The "maxim" of our acts can be thought of as the intention behind our acts. The maxim answers the question: What am I doing, and why? In other words, moral intention is a prerequisite to ethical action, as we discuss more fully in the next chapter.

Kant tells us that we should act only according to those maxims that could be universally accepted and acted on. For example, Kant believed that truth telling could be made a universal law, but lying could not. If we all lied whenever it suited us, rational communication would be impossible. Thus, lying is unethical. Imagine if every company falsified its financial statements. It would be impossible to evaluate the financial results of one company accurately over time and in comparison to other companies. The financial markets might ultimately collapse because reported results were meaningless, or even misleading. This condition of universality, not unlike the Golden Rule, prohibits us from giving our own personal point of view special status over the point of view of others. It is a strong requirement of impartiality and equality for ethics.[67]

One problem with deontological theory is that it relies on moral absolutes—absolute principles and absolute conclusions. Kant believed that a moral rule must function without exception. The notions of rights and duties are completely separate from the consequences of one's actions. This could lead to making decisions that might adhere to one's moral rights and another's attendant duties to those rights, but which also produce disastrous consequences for other people. For example, imagine if you were the person hiding Anne Frank and her family in the attic of your home and the Nazis came banging at the door and demanded, "Do you know where the Franks are?" Now, a strict application of rights theory requires that you tell the truth to the Nazi soldiers. However, isn't this situation one in which an exception to the rule should come into play for humanitarian reasons?

Whenever we are confronted with a moral dilemma, we need to consider whether the action would respect the basic rights of each of the individuals involved. How would the action affect the well-being of those individuals? Would it involve manipulation or deception—either of which would undermine the right to truth that is a crucial personal right? Actions are wrong to the extent that they violate the rights of individuals.[68]

Sometimes the rights of individuals will come into conflict, and one has to decide which right has priority. There is no clear way to resolve conflicts between rights and the corresponding moral duties to respect those rights. One of the most widely discussed cases of this kind is taken from William Styron's *Sophie's Choice*. Sophie and her two children are at a Nazi concentration camp. A guard confronts Sophie and tells her that one of her children will be allowed to live and one will be killed. Sophie must decide which child will be killed. She can prevent the death of either of her children, but only by condemning the other to be killed. The guard makes the situation even more painful for Sophie by telling her that if she chooses neither, then both will be killed. With this added factor, Sophie has a morally compelling reason to choose one of her children. But for each child, Sophie has an equally strong reason to save him or her. Thus, the same moral precept gives rise to conflicting obligations.[69]

Now, we do not face such morally excruciating decisions in accounting (thank goodness). The ultimate obligation of accountants and auditors is to honor the public trust. The public interest obligation that is embedded in the profession's codes of ethics requires that if a conflict exists between the obligations of a decision maker to others, the decision maker should always decide based on protecting the public's right (i.e., investors and creditors), such as in the receivables example, to receive accurate and reliable financial information about uncollectibles.

## Justice

Justice is usually associated with issues of rights, fairness, and equality. A just act respects your rights and treats you fairly. Justice means giving each person what she or he deserves. *Justice* and *fairness* are closely related terms that are often used interchangeably, although differences do exist. While *justice* usually has been used with reference to a standard of rightness, *fairness* often has been used with regard to an ability to judge without reference to one's feelings or interests. This is the basis of the objectivity principle in the AICPA Code. When people differ over what they believe should be given, or when decisions have to be made how benefits and burdens should be distributed among a group of people, questions of justice or fairness inevitably arise. These are questions of *distributive justice.*[70]

The most fundamental principle of justice, defined by Aristotle more than 2,000 years ago, is that "equals should be treated equally and unequals unequally." In other words, individuals should be treated the same unless they differ in ways that are relevant to the situation in which they are involved. The problem with this interpretation is in determining which criteria are morally relevant to distinguish between those who are equal and those who are not. It can be a difficult theory to apply in business if, for example, a CEO of a company decides to allocate a larger share of the resources than is warranted (justified) based on the results of operations, to one product line over another to promote that operation because it is judged to have more long-term expansion and income potential. If I am the manager in charge of the operation getting fewer resources but producing equal or better results, then I may believe that my operation has been (I have been) treated unfairly. On the other hand, it could be said that the other manager deserves to receive a larger share of the resources because of the long-term potential of that other product line. That is, the product lines are not equal; the former deserves more resources because of its greater upside potential.

In our discussion of ethical behavior in this and the following chapters, questions of fairness will be tied to making objective judgments. Auditors should render objective judgments about the fair presentation of financial results. In this regard, auditors should act as impartial arbiters of the truth, just as judges who make decisions in court cases should. The ethical principle of objectivity requires that such judgments be made impartially, unaffected by pressures that may exist to do otherwise. An objective auditor with knowledge about the failure to allow for the uncollectible receivables would not stand idly by and allow the financial statements to be materially misleading.

For purposes of future discussions about ethical decision making, we elaborate on the concept of *procedural justice.* Procedural justice considers the processes and activities that produce a particular outcome. For example, an ethical organization environment should positively influence employees' attitudes and behaviors toward work-group cohesion. When there is strong employee support for decisions, decision makers, organizations, and outcomes, procedural justice is less important to the individual. In contrast, when employees' support for decisions, decision makers, and organizations, or outcomes is not very strong, then procedural justice becomes more important.[71] Consider, for example, a potential whistleblower who feels confident about bringing her concerns to top management because specific procedures are in place to support that person. Unlike the Betty Vinson situation, an environment built on procedural justice supports the whistleblower, who perceives the fairness of procedures used to make decisions.

## Virtue Ethics

Virtue considerations apply both to the decision maker and to the act under consideration by that party. This is one of the differences between virtue theory and the other moral philosophies that focus on the act. To make an ethical decision, I must internalize the traits of character that make me an ethical (virtuous) person. This philosophy is called *virtue ethics,* and it posits that what is moral in a given situation is not only what conventional morality or moral rules require but also what a well-intentioned person with a "good" moral character would deem appropriate.

Virtue theorists place less emphasis on learning rules and instead stress the importance of developing *good habits of character,* such as benevolence. Plato emphasized four virtues in particular, which were later called *cardinal virtues:* wisdom, courage, temperance, and justice. Other important virtues are fortitude, generosity, self-respect, good temper, and sincerity. In addition to advocating good habits of character, virtue theorists hold that we should avoid acquiring bad character traits, or vices, such as cowardice, insensibility, injustice, and vanity. Virtue theory emphasizes moral education because virtuous character traits are developed in one's youth. Adults, therefore, are responsible for instilling virtues in the young. Virtue characteristics are particularly relevant to the cognitive moral development models discussed in Chapter 2.

The philosopher Alasdair MacIntyre states that the exercise of virtue requires "a capacity to judge and to do the right thing in the right place at the right time in the right way." Judgment is exercised not through a routinizable application of the rules, but as a function of possessing those dispositions (tendencies) that enables choices to be made about what is good for people and by holding in check desires for something other than what will help achieve this goal.[72]

At the heart of the virtue approach to ethics is the idea of "community." A person's character traits are not developed in isolation, but within and by the communities to which he belongs, such as the Principles in the AICPA Code that pertain to standards of acceptable behavior in the accounting profession (its community).

MacIntyre relates virtues to the internal rewards of a practice (i.e., the accounting profession). He differentiates between the external rewards of a practice (such as money, fame, and power) and the internal rewards, which relate to the intrinsic value of a particular practice. MacIntyre points out that every practice requires a certain kind of relationship between those who participate in it. The virtues are the standards of excellence (i.e., principles of conduct) that characterize relationships within the practice. To enter into a practice is to accept the authority of those standards, obedience to the rules, and commitment to achieve the internal rewards. Some of the virtues that MacIntyre identifies are truthfulness, trust, justice, courage, and honesty.[73]

Mintz points out that the accounting profession is a practice with inherent virtues that enable accountants to meet their ethical obligations to clients, employers, the government, and the public at large. For instance, for auditors to render an objective opinion of a client's financial statements, they must be committed to perform such services without bias and to avoid conflicts of interest. Impartiality is an essential virtue for judges in our judicial system. CPAs render judgments on the fairness of financial statements. Therefore, they should act impartially in carrying out their professional responsibilities.[74]

The virtues enable accounting professionals to resolve conflicting duties and loyalties in a morally appropriate way. They provide accountants with the inner strength of character to withstand pressures that might otherwise overwhelm and negatively influence their professional judgment in a relationship of trust.[75] For example, if your boss, the CFO, pressures you to overlook a material misstatement in financial statements, the virtues of honesty and trustworthiness will lead you to place your obligation to the public, including investors and creditors, ahead of any perceived loyalty obligation to your immediate supervisor or other members of top management (as occurred in the Betty Vinson case). The virtue of integrity enables you to withstand the pressure to look the other way. Now, in the real world, this is easier said than done. You may be tempted to be silent because you fear losing your job. However, the ethical standards of the accounting profession, as depicted in part in Exhibit 1.3, obligate accountants and auditors to bring these issues to the attention of those in the highest positions in an organization, including the audit committee of the board of directors, as did Cynthia Cooper in the WorldCom fraud.

We realize that for students, it may be difficult to internalize the concept that, when forced into a corner by one's supervisor to go along with financial wrongdoing, you should stand up for what you know to be right, even if it means losing your job. However, ask yourself the following questions: Do I even want to work for an organization that does not value my professional opinion? If I go along with it this time, might the same demand be made at a later date? Will I begin to slide down that ethical slippery slope where there is no turning back? How much is my reputation for honesty and integrity worth? Would I be proud if others found out what I did (or didn't do)? To quote the noted Swiss psychologist and psychiatrist, Carl Jung: "You are what you do, not what you say you'll do."

# Application of Ethical Reasoning in Accounting

In this section, we discuss the application of ethical reasoning in its entirety to a common dilemma faced by internal accountants and auditors. The case deals with the classic example of when pressure is imposed on accountants by top management to ignore material misstatements in financial statements.

As we have seen, accountants have ethical obligations under the AICPA Code that require them to place the public interest ahead of all other interests, including their own self-interest and that of an employer or client, and to be independent of the client; make decisions objectively; exercise due care in the performance of professional services; and act with integrity. Many internal accountants, such as controllers and CFOs, are CPAs and members of the IMA. The IMA's Statement of Ethical Professional Practice[76] is presented in Exhibit 1.6. Other than independence, which is a specific ethical requirement of an external audit, the standards of the IMA are similar to the Principles of Professional Conduct in the AICPA Code. Most important, read through the "Resolution of Ethical Conflict" section, which defines the steps to be taken by members when they are pressured to go along with financial statement improprieties. Specific steps to be taken include discussing matters of concern with the highest levels of the organization, including the audit committee. Recall that Interpretation 102-4 of the AICPA Code contains a similar provision.

**EXHIBIT 1.6** **Institute of Management Accountants Statement of Ethical Professional Practice**

Members of IMA shall behave ethically. A commitment to ethical professional practice includes overarching principles that express our values, and standards that guide our conduct.

### Principles

IMA's overarching ethical principles include: Honesty, Fairness, Objectivity, and Responsibility. Members shall act in accordance with these principles and shall encourage others within their organizations to adhere to them.

### Standards

A member's failure to comply with the following standards may result in disciplinary action.

### I. Competence

Each member has a responsibility to:

1. Maintain an appropriate level of professional expertise by continually developing knowledge and skills.
2. Perform professional duties in accordance with relevant laws, regulations, and technical standards.
3. Provide decision support information and recommendations that are accurate, clear, concise, and timely.
4. Recognize and communicate professional limitations or other constraints that would preclude responsible judgment or successful performance of an activity.

### II. Confidentiality

Each member has a responsibility to:

1. Keep information confidential except when disclosure is authorized or legally required.
2. Inform all relevant parties regarding appropriate use of confidential information. Monitor subordinates' activities to ensure compliance.
3. Refrain from using confidential information for unethical or illegal advantage.

### III. Integrity

Each member has a responsibility to:

1. Mitigate actual conflicts of interest, regularly communicate with business associates to avoid apparent conflicts of interest. Advise all parties of any potential conflicts.
2. Refrain from engaging in any conduct that would prejudice carrying out duties ethically.
3. Abstain from engaging in or supporting any activity that might discredit the profession.

### IV. Credibility

Each member has a responsibility to:

1. Communicate information fairly and objectively.
2. Disclose all relevant information that could reasonably be expected to influence an intended user's understanding of the reports, analyses, or recommendations.
3. Disclose delays or deficiencies in information, timeliness, processing, or internal controls in conformance with organization policy and/or applicable law.

### Resolution of Ethical Conduct

In applying the Standards of Ethical Professional Practice, you may encounter problems identifying unethical behavior or resolving an ethical conflict. When faced with ethical issues, you should follow your organization's established policies on the resolution of such conflict. If these policies do not resolve the ethical conflict, you should consider the following courses of action:

1. Discuss the issue with your immediate supervisor except when it appears that the supervisor is involved. In that case, present the issue to the next level. If you cannot achieve a satisfactory resolution, submit the issue to the next management level. If your immediate superior is the chief executive officer or equivalent, the acceptable reviewing authority may be a group such as the audit committee, executive committee, board of directors, board of trustees, or owners. Contact with levels above the immediate superior should be initiated only with your superior's knowledge, assuming he or she is not involved. Communication of such problems to authorities or individuals not employed or engaged by the organization is not considered appropriate, unless you believe there is a clear violation of the law.
2. Clarify relevant ethical issues by initiating a confidential discussion with an IMA Ethics Counselor or other impartial advisor to obtain a better understanding of possible courses of action.
3. Consult your own attorney as to legal obligations and rights concerning the ethical conflict.

## DigitPrint Case Study

DigitPrint was formed in March 2013 with the goal of developing an outsource business for high-speed digital printing. The company is small and does not yet have a board of directors. The comparative advantage of the company is that its founder and president, Henry Higgins, owned his own print shop for several years before starting DigitPrint. Higgins recently hired Liza Doolittle to run the start-up business. Wally Wonderful, who holds the Certified Management Accountant (CMA) certification from the IMA, was hired to help set up a computerized system to track incoming purchase orders, sales invoices, cash receipts, and cash payments for the printing business.

DigitPrint received $2 million as venture capital to start the business. The venture capitalists were given an equity share in return. From the beginning, they were concerned about the inability of the management to bring in customer orders and earn profits. In fact, only $200,000 net income had been recorded during the first year. Unfortunately, Wonderful had just discovered that $1 million of accrued expenses had not been recorded at year-end. Had that amount been recorded, the $200,000 net income of DigitPrint would have changed to an $800,000 loss.

Wonderful approached his supervisor, Doolittle, with what he had uncovered. She told him in no uncertain terms that the $1 million of expenses and liabilities could not be recorded, and warned him of the consequences of pursuing the matter any further. The reason was that the venture capitalists might pull out from financing DigitPrint because of the reduction of net income, working capital, and the higher level of liabilities. Wonderful is uncertain whether to inform Higgins. On one hand, he feels a loyalty obligation to go along with Doolittle. On the other hand, he believes he has an ethical obligation to the venture capitalists and other financiers that might help fund company operations.

We provide a brief analysis of ethical reasoning methods based on the following. First, consider the ethical standards of the IMA and evaluate potential actions for Wonderful. Then, use ethical reasoning with reference to the obligations of an accountant to analyze what you think Wonderful should do.

### IMA Standards

Wonderful is obligated by the competence standard to follow relevant laws, regulations, and technical standards, including GAAP, in reporting financial information. Of particular importance is his obligation to disclose all relevant information, including the accrued expenses, that could reasonably be expected to influence an intended user's understanding (i.e., venture capitalists) of the financial reports. Doolittle has refused to support his position and told him in no uncertain terms not to pursue the matter. At this point, Wonderful should follow the Resolution of Ethical Conduct procedures outlined in the IMA Standards and take the matter up the chain of command. Typically, in a public corporation, this would mean to go as far as the audit committee of the board of directors. However, DigitPrint is a small company without a board, so Henry Higgins, the founder and president, is the final authority. If Higgins backs Doolittle's position of nondisclosure, then Wonderful should seek outside advice from a trusted adviser, including an attorney, to help evaluate legal obligations and rights concerning the ethical conflict. The danger for Wonderful would be if he goes along with the improper accounting for the accrued expenses, the venture capitalists find out about the material misstatement in the financial statements at a later date, and then Wonderful is blamed both by the company and the venture capitalists.

### Utilitarianism

Wonderful should attempt to identify the harms and benefits of the act of recording the transactions versus not recording them. The consequences of failing to inform the venture capitalists about the accrued expenses are severe, not only for Wonderful but also for

DigitPrint. These include a possible lawsuit, investigation by regulators for failing to record the information, and, most important, a loss of reputational capital in the marketplace. The primary benefit to Wonderful is acceptance by his superiors, and he can be secure in the knowledge that he'll keep his job. Utilitarian values are difficult to assign to each potential act. Still, Wonderful should act in accordance with the moral rule that honesty requires not only truth telling, but disclosing all the information that another party has a need (or right) to know.

### Rights Theory

The venture capitalists have an ethical right to know about the higher level of payables, lower income, and the effect of the unrecorded transactions on working capital; the company has a duty to the venture capitalists to record the information. Wonderful should take the necessary steps to support such an outcome. The end goal of securing needed financing should not cloud Wonderful's judgment about the means chosen to accomplish the goal (i.e., nondisclosure). Wonderful should ask whether he believes that others in a similar situation should cover up the existence of $1 million in accrued expenses. Assuming that this is not the case, he shouldn't act in this way.

### Justice

In this case, the justice principle is linked to the fairness of the presentation of the financial statements. The omission of the $1 million of unrecorded expenses means that the statements would not "present fairly" financial position and results of operations. It violates the rights of the venture capitalists to receive accurate and reliable (fair presentation) financial information. As previously explained, a procedural justice perspective applied to the case means to assess the support for employee decisions on the part of the company. As a new employee, Wonderful needs to understand the corporate culture at DigitPrint.

### Virtue Considerations

Wonderful is expected to reason through the ethical dilemma and make a decision that is consistent with virtue considerations. The virtue of integrity requires Wonderful to have the courage to withstand the pressure imposed by Doolittle and not subordinate his judgment to hers. Integrity is the virtue that enables Wonderful to act in this way. While he has a loyalty obligation to his employer, it should not override his obligation to the venture capitalists, who expect to receive truthful financial information. A lie by omission is dishonest and inconsistent with the standards of behavior (virtues) in the accounting profession.

### What Should Wonderful Do?

Wonderful should inform Doolittle that he will take his concerns to Higgins. That may force Doolittle's hand and cause her to back off from pressuring Wonderful. As president of the company, Higgins has a right to know about the situation. After all, he hired Doolittle because of her expertise and, presumably, based on certain ethical expectations. Higgins may decide to disclose the matter immediately and cut his losses because this is the right thing to do. On the other hand, if Higgins persists in covering up the matter, then, after seeking outside/legal advice, Wonderful must decide whether to go outside the company. His conscience may move him in this direction. However, the confidentiality standard requires that he not do so unless legally required.

### A Message for Students

As you can tell from the DigitPrint case, ethical matters in accounting are not easy to resolve. On one hand, the accountant feels an ethical obligation to his employer or the client. On the other hand, the profession has strong codes of ethics that require accountants and auditors to place the public interest ahead of all other interests. Accounting professionals should analyze conflicting situations and evaluate the ethics by considering professional standards and the moral principles discussed in this chapter. A decision should be made after careful consideration of these factors and by applying logical reasoning to resolve the dilemma. Keep in mind that you may be in a position during your career where you feel pressured to remain silent about financial wrongdoing. You might rationalize that you didn't commit the unethical act, so your hands are clean. That's not good enough, though, as your ethical obligation to the public and the profession is to do whatever it takes to prevent a fraud from occurring and, if it does, take the necessary steps to correct the matter. Betty Vinson learned this lesson the hard way. We hope that you will internalize the importance of acting ethically and in accordance with the ethical values of the accounting profession, and look at the bigger picture when pressured by a superior to go along with financial wrongdoing. The road is littered with CFO/CPAs who masterminded (or at least directed) financial frauds at companies such as Enron, WorldCom, and Tyco. The result of their trials was a jail sentence for Andy Fastow of 10 years, Scott Sullivan of 5 years, and Mark Swartz of 8 1/3 to 25 years. Most important is they lost their livelihood, as well as the respect of the community. A reputation for trust takes a long time to build, but it can be destroyed in no time at all.

## Scope and Organization of the Text

The overriding philosophy of this text is that the ethical obligations of accountants and auditors are best understood in the context of professional responsibilities, including one's role in the corporate governance system, the requirements of financial reporting, the audit function, obligations to prevent and detect fraud, and legal liabilities. Given the rapid pace of globalization in the business world, we also believe that today's accounting students should gain an appreciation for ethical issues related to international financial reporting and global ethics standards.

Accounting professionals serve as internal accountants and auditors, external auditors, tax preparers and advisers, and consultants to their clients in a variety of advisory services. The ethics standards of the accounting profession, as defined by the AICPA Code of Professional Conduct and IMA's Statement of Ethical Professional Practice, provide the foundation for ethical decision making in the performance of professional responsibilities. These are discussed throughout this book. We also look at the Institute of Internal Auditors Code of Ethics (Chapter 3), and the Global Code of Ethics (Chapter 8).

Ethical decision making in accounting is predicated on moral reasoning. In this chapter, we have attempted to introduce the complex philosophical reasoning methods that help to fulfill the ethical obligations of accounting professionals. In Chapter 2, we address theories of moral development and the link to ethical reasoning and professional judgment in accounting. We also introduce a decision-making model that provides a framework for ethical decision making and can be used to help analyze cases presented at the end of each chapter. In Chapter 3, we transition to the culture of an organization and how processes and procedures can help to create and sustain an ethical organization environment, including effective corporate governance systems.

The remainder of this book focuses more directly on accounting ethics. Chapter 4 addresses the rules of professional conduct in the AICPA Code; investigations of the profession leading up to the Sarbanes-Oxley (SOX) Act, which created the Public Accounting Oversight Board; and whistleblowing obligations of accounting professionals under SOX and Dodd-Frank Financial Reform Act, which was signed into law by President Obama on July 21, 2010, in response to the financial meltdown in 2007–2008.

The accounting profession has been investigated by Congress several times over a number of years following disclosures of financial fraud. A common question has been: Where were the auditors? In Chapter 5, we review generally accepted auditing standards (GAAS), the basis for the independent audit and expectations for professional accountants and auditors. Students do not need to have completed an Auditing course to understand this discussion. We also address the important topic of financial statement fraud, including the Fraud Triangle, which describes the elements of fraud and so-called red flags that increase fraud risk.

In Chapter 6, we look at legal liability issues and regulatory requirements building on the discussion of laws that define acceptable behavior in accounting including whistleblowing requirements. The techniques used to manipulate earnings and obscure financial statement items are discussed in the context of earnings management in Chapter 7. Finally, in Chapter 8, we address global ethics considerations related to international financial reporting that have become increasingly more important for U.S. and non-U.S. companies. Recent estimates indicate that many U.S. companies earn 50 percent or more of their revenue from overseas operations, including Intel (85 percent), Dow Chemical (67 percent), IBM (64 percent), McDonald's (66 percent), General Electric (54 percent), and Ford (51 percent).[77]

There are 160 discussion questions, 76 cases, and 6 major cases in the end-of-chapter materials at the back of the book. These cases may be used by your instructor to supplement chapter material and for individual and group projects, including in-class case presentations. About one-third of the cases in this book have been taken from the files of the Securities and Exchange Commission (SEC) to give a real-life dimension to the text. Many of them deal with well-known examples of financial statement fraud, both nationally and internationally.

This book covers a variety of areas in financial reporting. Most students will have taken the Intermediate Accounting sequence before using this book, so the financial reporting areas relevant to accounting ethics such as financial statement reporting, GAAP, and informative disclosure already will have been covered.

In most of the cases, we have purposefully kept the materials as brief as possible. The reason for the brevity is we hope that students will focus on the ethical issues and not get too bogged down with numerical calculations.

## Concluding Thoughts

Our culture seems to have morphed toward exhibitionist tendencies where people do silly (stupid) things just to get their 15 minutes of fame through a YouTube video and with the promise of their own reality television show. Think about the "balloon boy" incident in October 2009, when the whole world watched a giant balloon fly through the air as a tearful family expressed fears that their six-year-old boy could be inside, all the while knowing the whole thing was staged. Perhaps the height of ridiculousness is the television show *Here Comes Honey Boo Boo*. This series, which debuted in 2012, follows the travails of a 7-year-old beauty pageant queen, Alana Thompson, aka "Honey Boo Boo," and her hillbilly family. The show is one of the most popular on cable television—in fact, during the 2012 Republican National Convention, it drew more viewers between 18 and 49 years old than Fox News's coverage, and during the Democratic Convention a month later, it tied with CNN. Some critics have characterized the show as "offensive," "outrageous," and "exploitative," while others call it "must-see TV."

When was the last time you picked up a newspaper and read a story about someone doing the right thing because it was the right thing to do? It is rare these days. We seem to read and hear more about pursuing one's own selfish interests, even to the detriment of others. It might be called the "What's in it for me?" approach to life. Nothing could be more contrary to leading a life of virtue and, as the ancient Greeks knew, benevolence is an important virtue.

In a classic essay on friendship, Ralph Waldo Emerson said: "The only reward of virtue is virtue; the only way to have a friend is to be one."[78] In other words, virtue is its own reward, just as we gain friendship in life by being a friend to someone else. In accounting, integrity is its own reward because it builds trust in client relationships and helps honor the public trust that is the foundation of the accounting profession.

We want to conclude on a positive note. Heroes in accounting do exist: brave people who have spoken out about irregularities in their organizations, such as Cynthia Cooper from WorldCom, whom we have already discussed. Another such hero is David Walker, who served as comptroller general of the United States and head of the Government Accountability Office from 1998 to 2008. Walker appeared before an appropriations committee of the U.S. Senate in 2008 and spoke out about billions of dollars in waste spent by the U.S. government, including on the Iraqi war effort. Then there was auditor Joseph St. Denis, who spoke out about improper accounting practices at his former company, AIG, which received a $150 billion bailout from the U.S. government during the financial crisis of 2008. All three received the Accounting Exemplar Award from the Public Interest Section of the American Accounting Association and serve as role models in the profession.

## Discussion Questions

1. A common ethical dilemma used to distinguish between philosophical reasoning methods is the following. Imagine that you are standing on a footbridge spanning some trolley tracks. You see that a runaway trolley is threatening to kill five people. Standing next to you, in between the oncoming trolley and the five people, is a railway worker wearing a large backpack. You quickly realize that the only way to save the people is to push the man off the bridge and onto the tracks below. The man will die, but the bulk of his body and the pack will stop the trolley from reaching the others. (You quickly understand that you can't jump yourself because you aren't large enough to stop the trolley, and there's no time to put on the man's backpack.) Legal concerns aside, would it be ethical for you to save the five people by pushing this stranger to his death? Use the deontological and teleological methods to reason out what you would do and why.

2. Another ethical dilemma deals with a runaway trolley heading for five railway workers who will be killed if it proceeds on its present course. The only way to save these people is to hit a switch that will turn the trolley onto a side track, where it will run over and kill one worker instead of five. Ignoring legal concerns, would it be ethically acceptable for you to turn the trolley by hitting the switch in order to save five people at the expense of one person? Use the deontological and teleological methods to reason out what you would do and why.

3. The following two statements about virtue were made by noted philosophers/writers:

   a. MacIntyre, in his account of Aristotelian virtue, states that integrity is the one trait of character that encompasses all the others. How does integrity relate to, as MacIntrye said, "the wholeness of a human life"?

   b. David Starr Jordan (1851–1931), an educator and writer, said, "Wisdom is knowing what to do next; virtue is doing it." Explain the meaning of this phrase as you see it.

4. a. Do you think it is the same to act in your own self-interest as it is to act in a selfish way? Why or why not?

   b. Do you think "enlightened self-interest" is a contradiction in terms, or is it a valid basis for all actions? Evaluate whether our laissez-faire, free-market economic system does (or should) operate under this philosophy.

5. In this chapter, we have discussed the Joe Paterno matter at Penn State. Another situation where a respected individual's reputation was tarnished by personal decisions is the resignation of former U.S. military general and head of the Central Intelligence Agency (CIA), David Petraeus. On November 9, 2012, Petraeus resigned from the CIA after it was announced he had an extramarital affair with a biographer, Paula Broadwell, who wrote a glowing book about his life. Petraeus acknowledged that he exercised poor judgment by engaging in the affair. When Federal Bureau of Investigation (FBI) agents investigated the matter because of concerns there may have been security leaks, they discovered a substantial number of classified documents on her computer. Broadwell told investigators that she ended up with the secret military documents after taking them from a government building. No security leaks had been found. In accepting Petraeus's resignation, President Obama praised Petraeus's leadership during the Iraq and Afghanistan wars and said: "By any measure, through his lifetime of service, David Petraeus has made our country safer and stronger." Should our evaluation of Petraeus's lifetime of hard work and Petraeus's success in his career be tainted by one act having nothing to do with job performance?

6. One explanation about rights is that "there is a difference between what we have the right to do and what is the right thing to do." Explain what you think is meant by this statement.

7. Steroid use in baseball is an important societal issue. Many members of society are concerned that their young sons and daughters may be negatively influenced by what apparently has been done at the major league level to gain an advantage and the possibility of severe health problems for young children from continued use of the body mass enhancer now and in the future. Mark McGwire, who broke Roger Maris's 60-home-run record, initially denied using steroids. He has never come close to the 75 percent positive vote to be in the Hall of Fame. Unfortunately for McGwire, his approval rating has been declining each year since he received 23.7 percent of the vote in 2010 and only 16.9 percent of the sportscasters voted in 2013 to elect him into the Hall. Some believe that Barry Bonds and Roger Clemens, who were the best at what they did, should be listed in the record books with an asterisk after their names and an explanation that their records were established at a time when baseball productivity might have been positively affected by the use of steroids. Some even believe they should be denied entrance to the baseball Hall of Fame altogether. The results for Bonds (36.2 percent) and Clemens (37.6 percent) in their initial year of eligibility (2013) were not close to meeting the 75 percent requirement and that led some to question whether these superstars would ever be voted into the Hall.[79] Evaluate whether Bonds and Clemens should be elected to the Hall of Fame from a situational ethics point of view.

8. Your best friend is from another country. One day after a particularly stimulating lecture on the meaning of ethics by your instructor, you and your friend disagree about whether culture plays a role in ethical behavior. You state that good ethics are good ethics, and it doesn't matter where you live and work. Your friend tells you that in her country, it is common to pay bribes to gain favor with important people. Comment on both positions from a relativistic ethics point of view. What do you believe and why?

9. Hofstede's Cultural Dimensions in Exhibit 1.2 indicate that China has a score of only 30 in Uncertainty Avoidance, while the U.S. score is 46. Does this seem counterintuitive to you? Why or why not? Be sure to include an explanation of why China's score is relatively low compared to the United States

10. a. What is the relationship between the ethical obligation of honesty and truth telling?

    b. Is it ever proper to not tell someone something that he or she has an expectation of knowing? If so, describe under what circumstances this might be the case. How does this square with rights theory?

11. Is there a difference between cheating on a math test, lying about your age to purchase a cheaper ticket at a movie theater, and using someone else's ID to get a drink at a bar?

12. Assume that you have been hired by the head of a tobacco industry group to do a cost–benefit analysis of whether the tobacco firms should disclose that nicotine is addictive. Assume that this is before the federal government required such disclosure on all packages of cigarettes. Explain how you would go about determining what are the potential harms and potential benefits of disclosing this information voluntarily. Is there any information that you believe cannot be included in the evaluation? What is it? Why can't you include it? If you could include it, would it affect your recommendation to the head of the industry group? Analyze the situation from a rights perspective, justice, and virtue theory. How might these considerations affect your recommendation to the head of the industry group?

13. How does virtue theory apply to both the decision maker and the act under consideration by that party? Explain.

14. Distinguish between ethical rights and obligations from the perspective of accountants and auditors.

15. Assume in the DigitPrint case that the venture capitalists do not provide additional financing to the company, even though the accrued expense adjustments have not been made. The company hires an audit firm to conduct an audit of its financial statements to take to a local bank for a loan. The auditors become aware of the unrecorded $1 million in accrued expenses. Liza Doolittle pressures them to delay recording the expenses until after the loan is secured. The auditors do not know whether Henry Higgins is aware of all the facts. Identify the stakeholders in this case. What alternatives are available to the auditors? Use the AICPA Code of Professional Conduct and Josephson's Six Pillars of Character to evaluate the ethics of the alternative courses of action.

16. IFAC, the global organization for the accountancy profession dedicated to serving the public interest, issued IFAC Policy Position Paper #4, titled *A Public Interest Framework for the Accountancy Profession,* on November 4, 2010. In that paper, IFAC identifies three criteria for the accounting profession serving the public interest:

    • Consideration of costs and benefits for society as a whole

    • Adherence to democratic principles and processes

    • Respect for cultural and ethical diversity

    Review the policy statement and any changes since it was first issued and explain how these three criteria might enable us to assess whether or not (and the degree to which) a policy, action, process, or condition is in the public interest.[80]

17. The *2011 National Business Ethics Survey, Workplace Ethics in Transition,* issued by the Ethics Resource Center (ERC), reports the following results[81]:

    • The percentage of employees who witnessed misconduct at work fell to a new low of 45 percent, compared to 49 percent in 2009 and well below the record high of 55 percent in 2007.

    • Those who reported bad behavior reached a record high of 65 percent, up from 64 percent in 2009 and the record low of 53 percent in 2005.

    • Retaliation against whistleblowers rose, with 22 percent who reported misconduct saying they experienced some form of retaliation, compared to 15 percent in 2009 and 12 percent in 2007.

    • The percentage of employees who perceived pressure to compromise standards in order to do their jobs climbed 5 points to 13 percent, just shy of the all-time high of 14 percent in 2000.

    These results show a declining rate of instances of misconduct in workplace behavior, an increase in reporting it, an increase in retaliation against whistleblowers, and an increase in pressure to compromise standards. How should we interpret these somewhat-contradictory findings with respect to corporate culture and ethics in the workplace?

18. In the discussion of loyalty in this chapter, a statement is made that "your ethical obligation is to report what you have observed to your supervisor and let her take the appropriate action." We point out that you may want to take your concerns to others. The IMA Statement of Ethical Professional Practice includes a confidentiality standard that requires members to "keep information confidential except when disclosure is authorized or legally required."

    Do you think there are any circumstances when you should go outside the company to report financial wrongdoing? If so, to what person/organization would you go? Why? If not, why would you not take the information outside the company?

19. Assume that a corporate officer or other executive asks you, as the accountant for the company, to omit or leave out certain financial figures from the balance sheet that may paint the business in a bad light to the public and investors. Because the request does not involve a direct manipulation of numbers or records, would you agree to go along with the request? What ethical considerations exist for you in deciding on a course of action?

20. Sir Walter Scott (1771–1832), the Scottish novelist and poet, wrote: "Oh what a tangled web we weave, when first we practice to deceive." Comment on what you think Scott meant by this phrase.

## Endnotes

1. Freeh, Sporkin, and Sullivan, LLP, *Report of the Special Investigative Counsel Regarding the Actions of The Pennsylvania State University Related to the Child Sexual Abuse Committed by Gerald A. Sandusky,* July 12, 2012, www.thefreehreportonpsu.com/REPORT_FINAL_071212.pdf.

2. Graham Winch, "Witness: I Saw Sandusky Raping Boy in Shower," June 12, 2012, Available at: www.hlntv.com/article/2012/06/12/witness-i-saw-sandusky-raping-child. http://www.hlntv.com/article/2012/06/12/witness-i-saw-sandusky-raping-child.

3. Eyder Peralta, "Paterno, Others Slammed In Report For Failing To Protect Sandusky's Victims," July 12, 2012, Available at: www.npr.org/blogs/thetwo-way/2012/07/12/156654260/was-there-a-coverup-report-on-penn-state-scandal-may-tell-us.

4. Jeffrey Toobin, "Former Penn State President Graham Spanier Speaks," the *New Yorker* online, August 22, 2012, Available at: www.newyorker.com/online/blogs/newsdesk/2012/08/graham-spanier-interview-on-sandusky-scandal.html#ixzz2PQ326lkq.

5. Max H. Bazerman and Ann E. Trebrunsel, *Blind Spots: Why We Fail to Do What's Right and What to Do about It* (Princeton, NJ: Princeton University Press, 2011).

6. Steven M. Mintz, "Virtue Ethics and Accounting Education," *Issues in Accounting Education* 10, no. 2 (Fall 1995), p. 257.

7. Susan Pulliam and Deborah Solomon, "Ms. Cooper Says No to Her Boss," *The Wall Street Journal,* October 30, 2002, p. A1.

8. Lynne W. Jeter, *Disconnected: Deceit and Betrayal at WorldCom* (Hoboken, NJ: Wiley, 2003).

9. Securities Litigation Watch, *Betty Vinson Gets 5 Months in Prison,* http://slw.issproxy.com/securities_litigation_blo/2005/08/betty_vinson_ge.html.

10. Cynthia Cooper, *Extraordinary Circumstances* (Hoboken, NJ: Wiley, 2008).

11. Teaching Values, *The Golden Rule in World Religions,* www.teachingvalues.com/goldenrule.html.

12. William J. Prior, *Virtue and Knowledge: An Introduction to Ancient Greek Ethics* (London: Routledge, 1991).

13. William H. Shaw and Vincent Barry, *Moral Issues in Business* (Belmont, CA: Wadsworth Cengage Learning, 2010), p. 5.

14. James C. Gaa and Linda Thorne, "An Introduction to the Special Issue on Professionalism and Ethics in Accounting Education," *Issues in Accounting Education* 1, no. 1 (February 2004), p. 1.

15. Joseph Fletcher, *Situation Ethics: The New Morality* (Louisville: KY: Westminster John Knox Press), 1966.

16. *2012 Report Card on the Ethics of American Youth's Values and Actions* (Los Angeles: Josephson Institute of Ethics), http://charactercounts.org/programs/reportcard/2012/index.html.

17. Eric G. Lambert, Nancy Lynee Hogan, and Shannon M. Barton, "Collegiate Academic Dishonesty Revisited: What Have They Done, How Often Have They Done It, Who Does It, and Why Do They Do It?" *Electronic Journal of Sociology,* 2003, www.sociology.org/content/vol7.4/lambert_etal.html.

18. Donald L. McCabe and Linda Klebe Treviño, "Individual and Contextual Influences on Academic Dishonesty: A Multicampus Investigation," *Research in Higher Education* 38, no. 3, 1997.

19. Paul Edwards, *The Encyclopedia of Philosophy,* Vol. 3, edited by Paul Edwards (New York: Macmillan Company and Free Press, 1967).

20. Emily E. LaBeff, Robert E. Clark, Valerie J. Haines, and George M. Diekhoff, "Situational Ethics and College Student Cheating," *Sociological Inquiry* 60, no. 2 (May 1990), pp. 190–197.

21. See, for example: Donald L. McCabe, Kenneth D. Butterfield, and Linda Klebe Treviño, "Academic Dishonesty in Graduate Business Programs: Prevalance, Causes, and Proposed Action," *Academy of Management Learning & Education* 5 (2006): 294–305.

22. See, for example, Kathy Lund Dean and Jeri Mullins Beggs, "University Professors and Teaching Ethics: Conceptualizations and Expectations, *Journal of Management Education,* 30, no. 1 (2006), pp. 15–44.

23. McCabe, Butterfield, and Treviño.

24. Raef A. Lawson, "Is Classroom Cheating Related to Business Students' Propensity to Cheat in the 'Real World'?" *Journal of Business Ethics,* 49, no. 2, (2004), pp. 189–199.

25. Randi L. Sims, "The Relationship between Academic Dishonesty and Unethical Business Practices," *Journal of Education for Business,* 68, no. 12, (1993), pp. 37–50.

26. Geert Hofstede, *Culture's Consequences: International Differences in Work-Related Values* (London: Sage, 1980).

27. Geert Hofstede, *Culture's Consequences: Comparing Values, Behaviours, Institutions, and Organizations* (Thousand Oaks, CA: Sage, 2001), p. 359.

28. Michael Minkov, *What Makes Us Different and Similar: A New Interpretation of the World Values Survey and Other Cross-Cultural Data* (Sofia, Bulgaria: Klasika y Stil Publishing House, 2007).

29. The results are published on a website devoted to Hofstede's work: www. http://geert-hofstede .com/countries.html.

30. Aristotle, *Nicomachean Ethics,* trans. W. D. Ross (Oxford, U.K.: Oxford University Press, 1925).

31. Michael Josephson, *Making Ethical Decisions,* rev. ed. (Los Angeles: Josephson Institute of Ethics, 2002).

32. Alasdair MacIntyre, *After Virtue,* 2d ed. (Notre Dame, IN: University of Notre Dame Press, 1984).

33. American Institute of Certified Public Accountants (AICPA), *AICPA Professional Standards. Volume 2 as of June 1, 2009,* Section 102-4 (New York: AICPA, 2009).

34. Josephson.

35. George Washington, *George Washington's Rules of Civility and Decent Behavior in Company and Conversation* (Bedford, ME: Applewood Books, 1994), p. 9.

36. Washington.

37. Cognitive Sciences Laboratory at Princeton University, *WordNet,* http.wordnet.princeton.edu.

38. Martin Luther King Jr., *The Peaceful Warrior* (New York: Pocket Books, 1968).

39. Josephson.

40. Josephson.

41. Edmund L. Pincoffs, *Quandaries and Virtues against Reductivism in Ethics* (Lawrence: University Press of Kansas, 1986).

42. Josephson.

43. Josephson.

44. Rhonda Schwartz, Brian Ross, and Chris Francescani, "Edwards Admits Sexual Affair; Lied as Presidential Candidate" (Interview with *Nightline*), August 8, 2008.

45. Martin Steubs and Brett Wilkinson, "Restoring the Profession's Public Interest Role," *The CPA Journal* 79, no. 11, (2009) pp. 62–66.

46. James E. Copeland, Jr., "Ethics as an Imperative," *Accounting Horizons* 19, no. 1 (2005), pp. 35–43.

47. National Association of State Boards of Accountancy, Uniform Accountancy Act (UAA) Model Rules Revised (2011), Nashville, TN: NASBA.

48. Texas Administrative Code (2011) Title 22, Part 22, Chapter 511, Subchapter C, §511.58 (c). www.tsbpa.state.tx.us/education/ethic-course-requirements.html.

49. Colorado Board of Accountancy (2010) Rules of the Colorado State Board of Accountancy www.dora.state.co.us/accountants/Rules103010.pdf.

50. California Board of Accountancy (2011) *SB 773.* www.legiscan.com/gaits/text/353631.

51. S B 773.

52. American Institute of Certified Public Accountants, *Code of Professional Conduct* at June 1, 2012 (New York: AICPA, 2012); www.aicpa.org/Research/Standards/CodeofConduct/Pages/ default.aspx.

53. Kurt Baier, *The Rational and Moral Order: The Social Roots of Reason and Morality* (Oxford, U.K.: Oxford University Press, 1994).

54. Steven M. Mintz, "Virtue Ethics and Accounting Education," *Issues in Accounting Education* 10, no. 2 (1995), p. 260.

55. O. C. Ferrell, John Fraedrich, and Linda Ferrell, *Business Ethics: Ethical Decision Making and Cases,* 9th ed. (Mason, OH: South-Western, Cengage Learning, 2011), p. 157.

56. Ferrell et al., p. 157.

57. Ferrell et al., p. 158.

58. Manuel Velasquez, Claire Andre, Thomas Shanks, and Michael J. Meyer, "Calculating Consequences: The Utilitarian Approach to Ethics," *Issues in Ethics* 2, no. 1 (Winter 1989), www.scu.edu/ethics.

59. Velasquez et al., 1989.

60. Velasquez et al., 1989.

61. Velasquez et al., 1989

62. Velasquez et al., 1989.

63. Ferrell et al., pp. 160–161.

64. Manuel Velasquez, Claire Andre, Thomas Shanks, and Michael J. Meyer, "Rights," *Issues in Ethics* 3, no. 1 (Winter 1990), www.scu.edu/ethics.

65. Velasquez et al., 1990.

66. Immanuel Kant, *Foundations of Metaphysics of Morals,* trans. Lewis White Beck (New York: Liberal Arts Press, 1959), p. 39.

67. Velasquez et al., 1990.

68. Velasquez, et al. 1990.

69. William Styron, *Sophie's Choice* (London: Chelsea House, 2001).

70. Manuel Velasquez, Claire Andre, Thomas Shanks, and Michael J. Meyer, "Justice and Fairness," *Issues in Ethics* 3, no. 2 (Spring 1990).

71. Ferrell et al., p. 165.

72. MacIntyre, pp. 187–190.

73. MacIntyre, pp. 190–192.

74. Mintz, 1995.

75. Mintz, 1995.

76. IMA—The Association of Accountants and Financial Professionals in Business, *IMA Statement of Ethical Professional Practice,* www.imanet.org/pdfs/statement%20of%20Ethics_web.pdf.

77. "Why U.S. Companies Aren't So American Anymore," June 30, 2011, www.money.usnews.com/money/blogs/flowchart/2011/06/30/why-us-companies-arent-so-american-anymore.

78. Ralph Waldo Emerson, *Essays: First and Second Series* (New York: Vintage Paperback, 1990).

79. See: www.espn.go.com/mlb/story/_/id/8828339/no-players-elected-baseball-hall-fame-writers.

80. International Federation of Accountants (IFAC), *A Public Interest Framework for the Accountancy Profession,* November 4, 2010, www.ifac.org/publications-resources/public-interest-framework-accountancy-profession.

81. Ethics Resource Center (ERC), *2011 National Business Ethics Survey: Workplace Ethics in Transition,* www.ethics.org/nbes/files/FinalNBES-web.pdf.

# Chapter 1 Cases

## Case 1-1

# Harvard Cheating Scandal

Yes. Cheating occurs at the prestigious Harvard University. In 2012, Harvard forced dozens of students to leave in its largest cheating scandal in memory but the institution would not address assertions that the blame rested partly with a professor and his teaching assistants. The issue is whether cheating is truly cheating when students collaborate with each other to find the right answer—in a take-home final exam.

Harvard released the results of its investigation into the controversy, in which 125 undergraduates were alleged to have cheated on an exam in May 2012.[1] The university said that more than half of the students were forced to withdraw, a penalty that typically lasts from two to four semesters. Of the remaining cases, about half were put on disciplinary probation—a strong warning that becomes part of a student's official record. The rest of the students avoided punishment.

In previous years, students thought of Government 1310 as an easy class with optional attendance and frequent collaboration. But students who took it in spring 2012 said that it had suddenly become quite difficult, with tests that were hard to comprehend, so they sought help from the graduate teaching assistants who ran the class discussion groups, graded assignments, and advised them on interpreting exam questions.

Administrators said that on final-exam questions, some students supplied identical answers (right down to typographical errors in some cases), indicating that they had written them together or plagiarized them. But some students claimed that the similarities in their answers were due to sharing notes or sitting in on sessions with the same teaching assistants. The instructions on the take-home exam explicitly prohibited collaboration, but many students said they did not think that included talking with teaching assistants.

The first page of the exam contained these instructions: "The exam is completely open book, open note, open Internet, etc. However, in all other regards, this should fall under similar guidelines that apply to in-class exams. More specifically, students may not discuss the exam with others—this includes resident tutors, writing centers, etc."

Students complained about confusing questions on the final exam. Due to "some good questions" from students, the instructor clarified three exam questions by email before the due date of the exams.

Students claim to have believed that collaboration was allowed in the course. The course's instructor and the teaching assistants sometimes encouraged collaboration, in fact. The teaching assistants who graded the exams—graduate students graded the exams and ran weekly discussion sessions—varied widely in how they prepared students for the exams, so it was common for students in different sections to share lecture notes and reading materials. During the final exam, some teaching assistants even worked with students to define unfamiliar terms and help them figure out exactly what certain test questions were asking.

Some have questioned whether it is the test's design, rather than the students' conduct, that should be criticized. Others place the blame on the teaching assistants who opened the door to collaboration outside of class by their own behavior in helping students to understand the questions better.

Answer the following questions about the Harvard cheating scandal.

1. Using Josephson's Six Pillars of Character, which of the character traits (virtues) apply to the Harvard cheating scandal and how do they apply with respect to the actions of each of the stakeholders in this case?

2. Who is at fault for the cheating scandal? Is it the students, the teaching assistants, the professor, or the institution? Use the concepts of egoism and enlightened egoism to support your answer.

3. From a deontological perspective and the point of view of achieving justice, were anyone's rights violated by the events of the scandal and outcome of the case? Explain why or why not.

[1]The facts of this case are taken from Richard Perez-Peña,"Students Disciplined in Harvard Scandal," February 1, 2013, Available at www.nytimes.com/2013/02/02/education/harvard-forced-dozens-to-leave-in-cheating-scandal.html?_r=0.

## Case 1-2

# Giles and Regas

Ed Giles and Susan Regas have never been happier than during the past four months since they have been seeing each other. Giles is a 35-year-old CPA and a partner in the medium-sized accounting firm of Saduga & Mihca. Regas is a 25-year-old senior accountant in the same firm. Although it is acceptable for peers to date, the firm does not permit two members of different ranks within the firm to do so. A partner should not date a senior in the firm any more than a senior should date a junior staff accountant. If such dating eventually leads to marriage, then one of the two must resign because of the conflicts of interest. Both Giles and Regas know the firm's policy on dating, and they have tried to be discreet about their relationship because they don't want to raise any suspicions.

While most of the staff seem to know about Giles and Regas, it is not common knowledge among the partners that the two of them are dating. Perhaps that is why Regas was assigned to work on the audit of CAA Industries for a second year, even though Giles is the supervising partner on the engagement.

As the audit progresses, it becomes clear to the junior staff members that Giles and Regas are spending personal time together during the workday. On one occasion, they were observed leaving for lunch together. Regas did not return to the client's office until three hours later. On another occasion, Regas seemed distracted from her work, and later that day, she received a dozen roses from Giles. A friend of Regas's who knew about the relationship, Ruth Revilo, became concerned when she happened to see the flowers and a card that accompanied them. The card was signed, "Love, Poochie." Regas had once told Revilo that it was the nickname that Regas gave to Giles.

Revilo pulls Regas aside at the end of the day and says, "We have to talk."

"What is it?" Regas asks.

"I know the flowers are from Giles," Revilo says. "Are you crazy?"

"It's none of your business," Regas responds.

Revilo goes on to explain that others on the audit engagement team are aware of the relationship between the two. Revilo cautions Regas about jeopardizing her future with the firm by getting involved in a serious dating relationship with someone of a higher rank. Regas does not respond to this comment. Instead, she admits to being distracted lately because of an argument that she had with Giles. It all started when Regas had suggested to Giles that it might be best if they did not go out during the workweek because she was having a hard time getting to work on time. Giles was upset at the suggestion and called her ungrateful. He said, "I've put everything on the line for you. There's no turning back for me." She points out to Revilo that the flowers are Giles's way

of saying he is sorry for some of the comments he had made about her.

Regas promises to talk to Giles and thanks Revilo for her concern. That same day, Regas telephones Giles and tells him she wants to put aside her personal relationship with him until the CAA audit is complete in two weeks. She suggests that, at the end of the two-week period, they get together and thoroughly examine the possible implications of their continued relationship. Giles reluctantly agrees, but he conditions his acceptance on having a "farewell" dinner at their favorite restaurant. Regas agrees to the dinner.

Giles and Regas have dinner that Saturday night. As luck would have it, the controller of CAA Industries, Mark Sax, is at the restaurant with his wife. Sax is startled when he sees Giles and Regas together. He wonders about the possible seriousness of their relationship, while reflecting on the recent progress billings of the accounting firm. Sax believes that the number of hours billed is out of line with work of a similar nature and the fee estimate. He had planned to discuss the matter with Herb Morris, the managing partner of the firm. He decides to call Morris on Monday morning.

"Herb, you son of a gun, it's Mark Sax."

"Mark. How goes the audit?"

"That's why I'm calling," Sax responds. "Can we meet to discuss a few items?"

"Sure," Morris replies. "Just name the time and place."

"How about first thing tomorrow morning?" asks Sax.

"I'll be in your office at 8:00 a.m.," says Morris.

"Better make it at 7:00 a.m., Herb, before your auditors arrive."

Sax and Morris meet to discuss Sax's concerns about seeing Giles and Regas at the restaurant and the possibility that their relationship is negatively affecting audit efficiency. Morris asks whether any other incidents have occurred to make him suspicious about the billings. Sax says that he is only aware of this one instance, although he sensed some apprehension on the part of Regas last week when they discussed why it was taking so long to get the audit recommendations for adjusting entries. Morris listens attentively until Sax finishes and then asks him to be patient while he sets up a meeting to discuss the situation with Giles. Morris promises to get back to Sax by the end of the week.

## Questions

1. Analyze the behavior of each party from the perspective of the Six Pillars of Character. Assess the personal responsibility of Ed Giles and Susan Regas for the relationship that developed between them. Who do you think is mostly to blame?

2. If Giles were a person of integrity but just happened to have a "weak moment" in starting a relationship with Regas, what do you think he will say when he meets with Herb Morris? Why?

3. Assume that Ed Giles is the biggest "rainmaker" in the firm. What would you do if you were in Herb Morris's position when you meet with Giles? In your response, consider how you would resolve the situation in regard to both the completion of the CAA Industries audit and the longer-term issue of the continued employment of Giles and Regas in the accounting firm.

## Case 1-3

# NYC Subway Death: Bystander Effect or Moral Blindness

On December 3, 2012, a terrible incident occurred in the New York City subway when Ki-Suck Han was pushed off a subway platform by Naeem Davis. Han was hit and killed by the train, while observers did nothing other than snap photos on their cell phones as Han was struggling to climb back onto the platform before the oncoming train struck him. Davis was arraigned on a second-degree murder charge and held without bail in the death of Han.

One of the most controversial aspects of this story is that of R. Umar Abbasi, a freelance photographer for the *New York Post*, who was waiting for a train when he said he saw a man approach Han at the Times Square station, get into an altercation with him, and push him into the train's path. He too chose to take pictures of the incident, and the next day, the *Post* published the photographer's handiwork: a photo of Han with his head turned toward the approaching train, his arms reaching up but unable to climb off the tracks in time.

Abbasi told NBC's *Today* show that he was trying to alert the motorman to what was going on by flashing his camera. He said he was shocked that people nearer to the victim didn't try to help in the 22 seconds before the train struck. "It took me a second to figure out what was happening . . . I saw the lights in the distance. My mind was to alert the train," Abbasi said. "The people who were standing close to him . . . they could have moved and grabbed him and pulled him up. No one made an effort," he added.

In a written account Abbasi gave the *Post*, he said that a crowd took videos and snapped photos on their cell phones after Han's mangled body was pulled onto the platform. He said that he shoved the onlookers back while a doctor and another man tried to resuscitate the victim, but Han died in front of them.

Some have attributed the lack of any attempt by those on the subway platform to get involved and go to Han's aid as the bystander effect. The term *bystander effect* refers to the phenomenon in which the greater the number of people present, the less likely people will be to help a person in distress. When an emergency situation occurs, observers are more likely to take action if there are few or no other witnesses. One explanation for the bystander effect is that each individual thinks that others will come to the aid of the threatened person. But when you are alone, either you will help, or no one will.

## Questions

1. Do you think the bystander effect was at work in the subway death incident? How might that effect translate to a situation where members of a work group observe financial improprieties committed by one of their group that threatens the organization? In general, do you think that someone would come forward? How might culture play into the action that would be taken?

2. Another explanation for the inaction in the subway incident is a kind of *moral blindness,* where a person fails to perceive the existence of moral issues in a particular situation. Do you believe moral blindness existed in the incident? Be sure to address the specific moral issues that give rise to your answer.

## Case 1-4

# Lone Star School District

Jose and Emily work as auditors for the state of Texas. They have been assigned to the audit of the Lone Star school district. There have been some problems with audit documentation for the travel and entertainment reimbursement claims of the manager of the school district. The manager knows about the concerns of Jose and Emily, and he approaches them about the matter. The following conversation takes place:

**Manager:** Listen, I've requested the documentation you asked for, but the hotel says it's no longer in their system.

**Jose:** Don't you have the credit card receipt or credit card statement?

**Manager:** I paid cash.

**Jose:** What about a copy of the hotel bill?

**Manager:** I threw it out.

**Emily:** That's a problem. We have to document all your travel and entertainment expenses for the city manager's office.

**Manager:** Well, I can't produce documents that the hotel can't find. What do you want me to do?

## Questions

1. Assume that Jose and Emily are CPAs and members of the AICPA. What ethical standards in the Code of Professional Conduct should guide them in dealing with the manager's inability to support travel and entertainment expenses?

2. Using Josephson's Six Pillars of Character as a guide, evaluate the statements and behavior of the manager.

3. a. Assume that Jose and Emily report to Sharon, the manager of the school district audit. Should they inform Sharon of their concerns? Why or why not?

   b. Assume that they don't inform Sharon, but she finds out from another source. What would you do if you were in Sharon's position?

## Case 1-5

# Reneging on a Promise

## Part A

Billy Tushoes recently received an offer to join the accounting firm of Tick and Check LLP. Billy would prefer to work for Foot and Balance LLP but has not received an offer from the firm the day before he must decide whether to accept the position at Tick and Check. Billy has a friend at Foot and Balance and is thinking about calling her to see if she can find out whether an offer is forthcoming.

## Question

1. Should Billy call his friend? Provide reasons why you think he should or should not. Is there any other action you suggest Billy take prior to deciding on the offer of Tick and Check? Why do you recommend that action?

## Part B

Assume that Billy calls his friend at Foot and Balance and she explains the delay is due to the recent merger of Vouch and Trace LLP with Foot and Balance. She tells Billy that the offer should be forthcoming. However, Billy gets nervous about the situation and decides to accept the offer of Tick and Check. A week later, he receives a phone call from the partner at Foot and Balance who had promised to contact him about the firm's offer. Billy is offered a position at Foot and Balance at the same salary as Tick and Check. He has one week to decide whether to accept that offer. Billy is not sure what to do. On one hand, he knows it's wrong to accept an offer and then renege on it. On the other hand, Billy hasn't signed a contract with Tick and Check, and the offer with Foot and Balance is his clear preference because he has many friends at that firm.

## Questions

1. Do you think it is ever right to back out of a promise that you gave to someone else? If so, under what circumstances? If not, why not?

2. Identify the stakeholders and their interests in this case.

3. Evaluate the alternative courses of action for Billy using ethical reasoning. What should Billy do? Why?

## Case 1-6

# Capitalization versus Expensing

Gloria Hernandez is the controller of a public company. She just completed a meeting with her superior, John Harrison, who is the CFO of the company. Harrison tried to convince Hernandez to go along with his proposal to combine 12 expenditures for repair and maintenance of a plant asset into one amount ($1 million). Each of the expenditures is less than $100,000, the cutoff point for capitalizing expenditures as an asset and depreciating it over the useful life. Hernandez asked for time to think about the matter. As the controller and chief accounting officer of the company, Hernandez knows it's her responsibility to decide how to record the expenditures. She knows that the $1 million amount is material to earnings and the rules in accounting require expensing of each individual item, not capitalization. However, she is under a great deal of pressure to go along with capitalization to meet financial analysts' earnings expectations and provide for a bonus to top management including herself. Her job may be at stake, and she doesn't want to disappoint her boss.

## Questions

1. What would motivate you to speak up and act or to stay silent?

2. Assume that you were in Gloria Hernandez's position. What would you do and why?

## Case 1-7

# Eating Time

Kevin Lowe is depressed. He has been with the CPA firm Stooges LLP for only three months. Yet the partners in charge of the firm—Bo Chambers and his brother, Moe—have asked for a "sit-down." Here's how it goes:

"Kevin, we asked to see you because your time reports indicate that it takes you 50 percent longer to complete audit work than your predecessor," Moe said.

"Well, I am new and still learning on the job," replied Lowe.

"That's true," Bo responded, "but you have to appreciate that we have fixed budgets for these audits. Every hour over the budgeted time costs us money. While we can handle it in the short run, we will have to bill the clients whose audit you work on a larger fee in the future. We don't want to lose clients as a result."

"Are you asking me to cut down on the work I do?" Lowe asked.

"We would never compromise the quality of our audit work," Moe said. "We're trying to figure out why it takes you so much longer than other staff members."

At this point, Lowe started to perspire. He wiped his forehead, took a glass of water, and asked: "Would it be better if I took some of the work home at night and on weekends, completed it, but didn't charge the firm or the client for my time?"

Bo and Moe were surprised by Kevin's openness. On one hand, they valued that trait in their employees. On the other hand, they couldn't answer with a yes. Moe looked at Bo, and then turned to Kevin and said: "It's up to you to decide how to increase your productivity on audits. As you know, this is an important element of performance evaluation."

Kevin cringed. Was the handwriting on the wall in terms of his future with the firm?

"I understand what you're saying," Kevin said. "I will do better in the future—I promise."

"Good," responded Bo and Moe. "Let's meet 30 days from now and we'll discuss your progress on the matters we've discussed today and your future with the firm."

## Questions

1. Given the facts in the case, evaluate using deontological and teleological reasoning whether Kevin should take work home and not charge it to the job.

2. What would you do if you were Kevin and why? How would you explain your position to Bo and Moe when you meet in 30 days?

## Case 1-8

# A Faulty Budget

Jackson Daniels graduated from Lynchberg State College two years ago. Since graduating from the college, he has worked in the accounting department of Lynchberg Manufacturing. Daniels was recently asked to prepare a sales budget for the year 2014. He conducted a thorough analysis and came out with projected sales of 250,000 units of product. That represents a 25 percent increase over 2013.

Daniels went to lunch with his best friend, Jonathan Walker, to celebrate the completion of his first solo job. Walker noticed Daniels seemed very distant. He asked what the matter was. Daniels stroked his chin, ran his hand through his bushy, black hair, took another drink of scotch, and looked straight into the eyes of his friend of 20 years. "Jon, I think I made a mistake with the budget."

"What do you mean?" Walker answered.

"You know how we developed a new process to manufacture soaking tanks to keep the ingredients fresh?"

"Yes," Walker answered.

"Well, I projected twice the level of sales for that product than will likely occur."

"Are you sure?" Walker asked.

"I checked my numbers. I'm sure. It was just a mistake on my part," Daniels replied.

"So, what are you going to do about it?" asked Walker.

"I think I should report it to Pete. He's the one who acted on the numbers to hire additional workers to produce the soaking tanks," Daniels said.

"Wait a second," Walker said. "How do you know there won't be extra demand for the product? You and I both know

demand is a tricky number to project, especially when a new product comes on the market. Why don't you sit back and wait to see what happens?"

"But what happens if I'm right and the sales numbers were wrong? What happens if the demand does not increase beyond what I now know to be the correct projected level?" Daniels asks.

"Well, you can tell Pete about it at that time. Why raise a red flag now when there may be no need?" Walker states.

As the lunch comes to a conclusion, Walker pulls Daniels aside and says, "Jack, this could mean your job. If I were in your position, I'd protect my own interests first."

## Questions

1. What should an employee do when he or she discovers that there is an error in a projection? Why do you suggest that action? Would your answer change if the error was not likely to affect other aspects of the operation such as employment? Why or why not?

2. Identify the stakeholders potentially affected by what Daniels decides to do. How might each stakeholder be affected by Daniels's action and decision? Use ethical reasoning to support your answer.

3. Assume that Daniels is both a CPA and holds the CMA certification granted by the IMA. Use the ethical standards of these two organizations to identify what Daniels should do in this situation.

## Case 1-9

# Cleveland Custom Cabinets

Cleveland Custom Cabinets is a specialty cabinet manufacturer for high-end homes in the Cleveland Heights and Shaker Heights areas. The company manufactures cabinets built to the specifications of homeowners and employs 125 custom cabinetmakers and installers. There are 30 administrative and sales staff members working for the company.

James Leroy owns Cleveland Custom Cabinets. His accounting manager is Marcus Sims. Sims manages 15 accountants. The staff is responsible for keeping track of manufacturing costs by job and preparing internal and external financial reports. The internal reports are used by management for decision making. The external reports are used to support bank loan applications.

The company applies overhead to jobs based on direct labor hours. For 2014, it estimated total overhead to be $9.6 million and 80,000 direct labor hours. The cost of direct materials used during the first quarter of the year is $600,000, and direct labor cost is $400,000 (based on 20,000 hours worked). The company's accounting system is old and does not provide actual overhead information until about four weeks after the close of a quarter. As a result, the applied overhead amount is used for quarterly reports.

On April 10, 2014, Leroy came into Sims's office to pick up the quarterly report. He looked at it aghast. Leroy had planned to take the statements to the bank the next day and meet with the vice president to discuss a $1 million expansion loan. He knew the bank would be reluctant to grant the loan based on the income numbers in Exhibit 1.

---

**EXHIBIT 1**
**CLEVELAND CUSTOM CABINETS**
Net Income for the Quarter Ended March 31, 2014

| | |
|---|---|
| Sales | $6,400,000 |
| Cost of goods sold | 4,800,000 |
| Gross margin | $1,600,000 |
| Selling and administrative expenses | 1,510,000 |
| Net income | $   90,000 |

---

Leroy asked Sims to explain how net income could have gone from 14.2 percent of sales for the year ended December 31, 2013, to 1.4 percent for March 31, 2014. Sims pointed out that the estimated overhead cost had doubled for 2014 compared to the actual cost for 2013. He explained to Leroy that rent had doubled and the cost of utilities skyrocketed. In addition, the custom-making machinery was wearing out more rapidly, so the company's repair and maintenance costs also doubled from 2013.

Leroy understood but wouldn't accept Sims's explanation. Instead, he told Sims that as the sole owner of the company, there was no reason not to "tweak" the numbers on a one-time basis. "I own the board of directors, so no worries there. Listen, this is a one-time deal. I won't ask you to do it again," Leroy stated. Sims started to soften and asked Leroy just how he expected the tweaking to happen. Leroy flinched, held up his hands, and said, "I'll leave the creative accounting to you."

## Questions

1. Do you agree with Leroy's statement that it doesn't matter what the numbers look like because he is the sole owner? Even if it is true that Sims "owns" the board of directors, what should be their role in this matter?

2. a. Assume that Sims is a CPA and holds the CMA. What are the ethical considerations for him in deciding whether to tweak the numbers? What should Sims do and why?

   b. Assume that Sims did a utilitarian analysis to help decide what to do. Evaluate the harms and benefits of alternative courses of action.

3. Assume that Sims decided to reduce the estimated overhead for the year by 50 percent. How would that change the net income for the quarter? What would it be as a percentage of sales? Do you think Leroy would like the result? Do you think he will be content with the tweaking occurring just this one time, or will he be tempted to do it again in the future?

## Case 1-10

# Telecommunications, Inc.

Telecommunications, Inc., is a U.S. company, a global leader in information technology, and it specializes in building data network systems. The company is a major player in the industry, although it is no match for companies like Cisco Systems. Recently, however, it has been more successful in securing contracts to build and support data network systems outside the United States. In one recent competitive bidding situation with companies from two other countries, the Latin American country of Bolumbia awarded Telecommunications a multimillion-dollar contract to develop a network for the corporate community. The job went so well that Telecommunications believes it will have a leg up on other companies in bidding for future contracts.

Telecommunications was the prime contractor on that job. It was responsible for the selection of subcontractors to perform the work that Telecommunications did not want to do, or when the company believed it was advantageous to use a local contractor. According to the company's contract with Bolumbia, only Latin American companies could be selected for subcontract work. In a recent competitive bidding selection process, Bolumbia National Communications (BNC), S.A. was chosen to assist in infrastructure connectivity. (S.A., Sociedad Anonima, is the designation for a Spanish company.) BNC wasn't as well established as other companies such as Telefonica, the Spanish multinational company that operates throughout the Spanish- and Portuguese-speaking world, but it had submitted a bid that met all the specifications of the job, including some that were unusual requests. Telefonica did not include these items in its subcontractor bid.

Ed Keller is employed as an engineer for Telecommunications, Inc. Keller recently graduated with a master's degree in engineering and joined the company six months ago. Keller had a 3.92 grade point average and could have worked for a variety of engineering firms. He chose Telecommunications because of the opportunity it afforded to travel around the world and as a result of its reputation for quality service and high moral standards.

During lunch at the office one day, Keller was talking to several of the more senior members of the engineering staff of Telecommunications, who told him about their recent trip to Bolumbia. They visited four cities and a resort in one week, and all their expenses were paid for by BNC. Keller knew that BNC had just completed its work on the contract for infrastructure connectivity. Out of curiosity, Keller questioned the engineering staff about the propriety of accepting an all-expenses-paid trip from a major subcontractor. Keller was told that it was common practice for Latin American companies to make gestures of gratitude, such as free travel and entertainment, in certain situations. Keller is told by one of the senior engineers that the culture in Bolumbia is one where the rules are not necessarily followed. Moreover, "There's nothing wrong with accepting such gratuities.

After all, the offer of free travel was made after the decision to accept the bid of BNC and the completion of the job. We were not responsible for making the selection decision. All we did was to establish the engineering specifications for the job."

Keller viewed this as an opportunity to learn more about the bidding process, so he approached Sam Jennings, the head of the internal audit department of Telecommunications. Keller grew up with Jennings's son, and Sam Jennings has been a close friend of the Keller family for many years.

Keller asked Jennings to have lunch with him one day. Jennings was curious about the request because they hadn't had lunch during the six months that Keller worked for Telecommunications. Keller said he had some questions about reporting expenses on trips that he might be assigned to in the future. Because it was a work-related request and their families go back a long time, Jennings cleared his calendar and agreed to have lunch with Keller.

During the lunch, Keller raised the issue of whether there was a conflict of interest when members of the senior engineering staff, such as those who worked on developing specifications for the BNC job, accept free travel and entertainment from a subcontractor. At first, Jennings was furious because Keller had misled him about the purpose of the lunch, but he gave Keller the benefit of the doubt and proceeded to answer the question.

Jennings informed Keller that the relationship between the engineers in question and BNC, and whether there was any inappropriate influence one way or the other, had been examined because of the company's concern about a possible violation of the Foreign Corrupt Practices Act (FCPA). Jennings went on to explain that the act prohibits U.S. multinationals or their agents from making payments that improperly influence government officials in another country, or their representatives, in the normal course of carrying out their responsibilities. Jennings told Keller that no evidence existed that the awarding of the contract was a prepayment for the promise of later free travel and entertainment, as Keller had expected. Moreover, explained Jennings, the decision to accept the BNC bid was made by Richard Kimble, the engineering division manager, and Bob Gerard, the vice president for engineering, and neither of them received any free travel or lodging. The fact was, according to Jennings, the rejected bids, while lower than BNC's, were inadequate and did not meet the specifications of the contract. Only BNC's proposal could do that.

Keller felt better about the situation after discussing it with Jennings. Still, he wondered about the values of a company that condones accepting free travel and entertainment from a subcontractor, as well as the value system of the engineers, who should be beyond reproach in carrying out their responsibilities.

# Questions

1. An important issue in conducting business overseas is whether a company should follow its home country's ethical standards or those of the host country. The ancient adage "When in Rome, do as the Romans do" is quite instructive on this matter. The argument in favor of behaving according to the host country's socially accepted morals is that it shows respect both to the citizens and the culture of the hosting country in which the business is conducting affairs. Evaluate these statements and the implications for conducting business outside's one's home country from an ethical relativistic point of view.

2. Some research into the effects of cultural variables on the application of ethical standards in a given society have shown that people in individualistic cultures tend to be more pervasive in applying their ethical standards to all, while people in collectivistic cultures tend to be more particularistic, applying differential ethical value standards to members of their in-groups and out-groups. We might conclude based on this research that people from different nations have distinct conceptions of ethical and unethical behavior. Assume that the score on Hofstede's scale for Individualism in Bolumbia is 13, while in the United States, it is 91; the scores for Uncertainty Avoidance for these countries are 80 and 46, respectively. How might these cultural differences influence your judgment whether it is acceptable for the engineers to have accepted the gratuities?

3. Assume that the engineers of Telecommunications did influence the decision-making process by establishing engineering specifications that only BNC could meet. The engineers received free travel and lodging from BNC, *but only after the job was completed*. Is there anything wrong with this picture? Consider the ethical values of objectivity and integrity in answering the question.

# 2

# Cognitive Processes and Ethical Decision Making in Accounting

## Arthur Andersen and Enron

One event more than any other that demonstrates the failure of professional judgment and ethical reasoning in the period of accounting frauds of the late 1990s and early 2000s is the relationship between Enron and its auditors, Arthur Andersen LLP. Bazerman and Tenbrunsel characterize it as *motivated blindness,* a term that describes the common failure of people to notice others' unethical behavior when seeing that behavior would harm the observer.[1] In 2000, Enron paid Andersen a total of $52 million: $25 million in audit fees and $27 million for consulting services. This amount was enough to make Enron Andersen's second largest account in 2000 and the largest client in the Houston office. Andersen's judgment was compromised by this relationship and led to moral blindness with respect to Enron's accounting for so-called special-purpose entities (SPEs)— entities set up by the firm and kept off the balance sheet. Andersen was constantly pressured by Enron to keep the debt accumulated by the SPEs off Enron's books. When Enron declared bankruptcy, there was $13.1 billion in debt on the company's books, $18.1 billion on its non-consolidated subsidiaries' books, and an estimated $20 billion more off the balance sheets.[2] Barbara Toffler points out in *Final Accounting,* her book about the rise and fall of Andersen,[3] that *The Powers Report,* named after an Enron director and the head investigator of Enron's failure, denounced Andersen for failing to fulfill its professional and ethical obligations in

connection with its auditing of Enron's financial statements, as well as to bring to the attention of Enron's board of directors concerns about Enron's internal controls over these related-party transactions.

The possibility of an accounting fraud at Enron was first discussed in an article by two *Fortune* magazine reporters, Bethany McLean and Peter Elkind. A few years later, in 2004, they wrote a book, that became the basis for a movie of the same name, titled *The Smartest Guys in the Room,*[4] in which they criticized Andersen for failing to use the professional skepticism that requires that an auditor approach the audit with a questioning mind and a critical assessment of audit evidence. David Duncan, the lead auditor, had personal relationships with some of Enron's executives that clouded his judgment, and he was influenced by the size of the fees that Andersen earned from Enron. The firm didn't seem to care about the conflict of interest because Duncan was able to generate 20 to 25 percent in additional fees each year.

Andersen's independence was called into question shortly after Enron disclosed that a large portion of the 1997 earnings restatement consisted of adjustments that the auditors had proposed at the end of the 1997 audit but had allowed to go uncorrected. Congressional investigators wanted to know why Andersen tolerated $51 million of known misstatements during a year when Enron reported only $105 million of earnings. Andersen chief executive officer (CEO) Joseph Berardino explained that Enron's 1997 earnings were artificially low due to several hundred million dollars of nonrecurring expenses and write-offs. The proposed adjustments were not material, Berardino testified, because they represented less than 8 percent of "normalized" earnings.[5]

The Enron-Andersen relationship illustrates how a certified public accounting (CPA) firm can lose sight of its professional obligations. While examining Enron's financial statements, the auditors at Andersen knew that diligent application of strict auditing standards required one decision, but that the consequences for the firm were harmful to its own business interests. From an ethical perspective, the accounting firm compromised its professional judgment and acted out of egoism, failing to see that the rights of investors and creditors for accurate and reliable information had been compromised by its actions.

Some Andersen auditors paid a steep price for their ethical failings: their licenses to practice as CPAs in Texas were revoked. David Duncan was charged with failing to exercise due care and professional skepticism in failing to conduct an audit in accordance with generally accepted auditing standards (GAAS) and acting recklessly in issuing unqualified opinions on the 1998–2000 audits, thus violating Section 10(b) of the Securities and Exchange Act.[6]

In this chapter, we explore the process of ethical decision making and how it influences professional judgment. Ethical decision making relies on the ability to make moral judgments using the reasoning methods discussed in Chapter 1. However, the ability to reason ethically does not ensure that ethical action will be taken. The decision maker must follow up ethical intent with ethical action. Think about the following questions as you read this chapter: (1) What is the role of virtue in auditors' ethical decision making? (2) What would you do if your attitudes and beliefs conflict with your intended behavior? Such conflicts create the problem of cognitive dissonance, which can affect professional judgment and ethical decision making.

Every act is to be judged by the intention of the agent.

*Unknown*

---

This quote emphasizes one's intent in making decisions. Moral intent is a critical component of ethical decision making. By internalizing the virtues discussed in the previous chapter and acting in accordance with the principles of the philosophical reasoning methods, an accountant is better equipped to make ethical, professional judgments.

## Kohlberg and the Cognitive Development Approach

Cognitive development refers to the thought process followed in one's moral development. An individual's ability to make reasoned judgments about moral matters develops in stages. The psychologist Lawrence Kohlberg concluded, on the basis of 20 years of research, that people develop from childhood to adulthood through a sequential and hierarchical series of cognitive stages that characterize the way they think about ethical dilemmas. Moral reasoning processes become more complex and sophisticated with development. Higher stages rely upon cognitive operations that are not available to individuals at lower stages, and higher stages are thought to be "morally better" because they are consistent with philosophical theories of justice and rights.[7] Kohlberg's views on ethical development are helpful in understanding how individuals may internalize moral standards and, as they become more sophisticated in their use, apply them more critically to resolve ethical conflicts.

Kohlberg developed his theory by using data from studies on how decisions are made by individuals. The example of Heinz and the Drug, given here, illustrates a moral dilemma used by Kohlberg to develop his stage-sequence model.

## Heinz and the Drug

In Europe, a woman was near death from a rare type of cancer. There was one drug that the doctors thought might save her. It was a form of radium that a druggist in the same town had recently discovered. The drug was expensive to make, but the druggist was charging 10 times what the drug cost him to make: It cost $200 for the radium and charged $2,000 for a small dose of the drug. The sick woman's husband, Heinz, went to everyone he knew to borrow the money, but he could get together only about $1,000—half the cost. He told the druggist that his wife was dying and asked him to sell it cheaper or let him pay later. But the druggist said, "No, I discovered the drug and I'm going to make money from it." Heinz got desperate and broke into the man's store to steal the drug for his wife.

Should the husband have done that? Was it right or wrong? Most people say that Heinz's theft was morally justified, but Kohlberg was less concerned about whether they approved or disapproved than with the reasons they gave for their answers. Kohlberg monitored the reasons for judgments given by a group of 75 boys ranging in age from 10 through 16 years and isolated the six stages of moral thought. The boys progressed in reasoning sequentially, with most never reaching the highest stages. He concluded that the universal principle of justice is the highest claim of morality. Kohlberg's justice orientation has been criticized by Carol Gilligan, a noted psychologist and educator.[8] Gilligan claims that because the stages were derived exclusively from interviews with boys, the stages reflect a decidedly male orientation and they ignore the care-and-response orientation that characterizes female moral judgment. For males, advanced moral thought revolves around rules, rights, and abstract principles. The ideal is formal justice, in which all parties evaluate one another's claims in an impartial manner. But this conception of morality, Gilligan argues, fails to capture the distinctly female voice on moral matters. Gilligan believes that women need more information before answering the question: Should Heinz steal the drug? Females look for ways of resolving the dilemma where no one—Heinz, his wife, or the druggist—will experience pain. Gilligan sees the hesitation to judge as a laudable quest for nonviolence, an aversion to cruel situations where someone will get hurt. However, much about her theories has been challenged in the literature. For example, Kohlberg considered it a sign of ethical relativism, a waffling that results from trying to please everyone (Stage 3). Moreover, Gilligan's beliefs seem to imply that men lack a caring response when compared to females. Rest argues that Gilligan has exaggerated the extent of the sex differences found on Kohlberg's scale.[9]

The dilemma of Heinz illustrates the challenge of evaluating the ethics of a decision. Table 2.1 displays three types of responses.[10]

Kohlberg considered how the responses were different and what problem-solving strategies underlie the three responses. Response A (Preconventional) presents a rather uncomplicated approach to moral problems. Choices are made based on the wants of the individual decision maker (egoism). Response B (Conventional) also considers the wife's needs. Here, Heinz is concerned that his actions should be motivated by good intentions (i.e., the ends justify the means). In Response C (Postconventional), a societywide

**TABLE 2.1**
**Three Sample Responses to the Heinz Dilemma**

**A:** It really depends on how much Heinz likes his wife and how much risk there is in taking the drug. If he can get the drug in no other way and if he really likes his wife, he'll have to steal it.

**B:** I think that a husband would care so much for his wife that he couldn't just sit around and let her die. He wouldn't be stealing for his own profit; he'd be doing it to help someone he loves.

**C:** Regardless of his personal feelings, Heinz has to realize that the druggist is protected by the law. Since no one is above the law, Heinz shouldn't steal it. If we allowed Heinz to steal, then all society would be in danger of anarchy.

perspective is used in decision making. Law is the key in making moral decisions[11] (for example, rule utilitarianism; justice orientation).

The examples in Table 2.2 demonstrate the application of Kohlberg's model of cognitive development to possible decision making in business.

**TABLE 2.2** Kohlberg's Stages of Moral Development

### Level 1—Preconventional

At the preconventional level, the individual is very self-centered. Rules are seen as something external imposed on the self.

#### Stage 1: Obedience to Rules; Avoidance of Punishment

At this stage, what is right is judged by one's obedience to rules and authority.

*Example:* A company forbids making payoffs to government or other officials to gain business. Susan, the company's contract negotiator, might justify refusing the request of a foreign government official to make a payment to gain a contract as being contrary to company rules, or Susan might make the payment if she believes there is little chance of being caught and punished.

#### Stage 2: Satisfying One's Own Needs

In Stage 2, rules and authority are important only if acting in accordance with them satisfies one's own needs (egoism).

*Example:* Here, Susan might make the payment even though it is against company rules if she perceives that such payments are a necessary part of doing business. She views the payment as essential to gain the contract. Susan may believe that competitors are willing to make payments, and that making such payments are part of the culture of the host country. She concludes that if she does not make the payment, it might jeopardize her ability to move up the ladder within the organization and possibly forgo personal rewards of salary increases, bonuses, or both. Because everything is *relative*, each person is free to pursue her individual interests.

### Level 2—Conventional

At the conventional level, the individual becomes aware of the interests of others and one's duty to society. Personal responsibility becomes an important consideration in decision making.

#### Stage 3: Fairness to Others

In Stage 3, an individual is not only motivated by rules but seeks to do what is in the perceived best interests of others, especially those in a family, peer group, or work organization. There is a commitment to loyalty in the relationship.

*Example:* Susan wants to be liked by others. She might be reluctant to make the payment but agrees to do so, not because it benefits her interests, but in response to the pressure imposed by her supervisor, who claims that the company will lose a major contract and employees will be fired if she refuses to go along.

#### Stage 4: Law and Order

Stage 4 behavior emphasizes the morality of law and duty to the social order. One's duty to society, respect for authority, and maintaining the social order become the focus of decision making.

*Example:* Susan might refuse to make the illegal payment, even though it leads to a loss of jobs in her company (or maybe even the closing of the company itself), because she views it as her duty to do so in the best interests of society. She does not want to violate the law.

### Level 3—Postconventional

Principled morality underlies decision making at this level. The individual recognizes that there must be a societywide basis for cooperation. There is an orientation to principles that shape whatever laws and role-systems a society may have.

#### Stage 5: Social Contract

In Stage 5, an individual is motivated by upholding the basic rights, values, and legal contracts of society. That person recognizes in some cases that legal and moral points of view may conflict. To reduce such conflict, individuals at this stage base their decisions on a rational calculation of benefits and harms to society.

*Example:* Susan might weigh the alternative courses of action by evaluating how each of the groups is affected by her decision to make the payment. For instance, the company might benefit by gaining the contract. Susan might even be rewarded for her action. The employees are more secure in their jobs. The customer in the other country gets what it wants. On the other hand, the company will be in violation of the Foreign Corrupt Practices Act (FCPA), which prohibits payments to foreign government officials. Susan then weighs the consequences of making an illegal payment, including any resulting penalties, against the ability to gain additional business. Susan might conclude that the harms of prosecution, fines, other sanctions, and the loss of one's reputational capital are greater than the benefits.

*(Continued)*

**TABLE 2.2** *(Continued)*

**Stage 6: Universal Ethical Principles**

Kohlberg was still working on Stage 6 at the time of his death in 1987. He believed that this stage rarely occurred. Still, a person at this stage believes that right and wrong are determined by universal ethical principles that everyone should follow. Stage 6 individuals believe that there are inalienable rights, which are universal in nature and consequence. These rights, laws, and social agreements are valid not because of a particular society's laws or customs, but because they rest on the premise of universality. Justice and equality are examples of principles that are deemed universal. If a law conflicts with an ethical principle, then an individual should act in accordance with the principle.

An example of such a principle is Immanuel Kant's categorical imperative, the first formulation of which can be stated as: "Act only according to that maxim [reason for acting] by which you can at the same time will that it would become a universal law."[12] Kant's categorical imperative creates an absolute, unconditional requirement that exerts its authority in all circumstances, and is both required and justified as an end in itself.

*Example:* Susan would go beyond the norms, laws, and authority of groups or individuals. She would disregard pressure from her supervisor or the perceived best interests of the company when deciding what to do. Her action would be guided only by universal ethical principles that would apply to others in a similar situation.

Let's return to the receivables example in Chapter 1 that applies ethical reasoning to the methods discussed in Exhibit 1.5 (Ethical Reasoning Method Bases for Making Ethical Judgments). In the receivables example, an auditor who reasons at Stage 3 might go along with the demands of a client out of loyalty or because she thinks the company will benefit by such inaction. At Stage 4, the auditor places the needs of society and abiding by the law above all else, so the auditor will insist on recording an allowance for uncollectibles.

An auditor who reasons at Stage 5 would not want to violate the public interest principle embedded in the profession's ethical standards, which values the public trust above all else. Investors and creditors have a right to know about the uncertainty surrounding collectibility of the receivables. At Stage 6, the auditor would ask whether she would want other auditors to insist on providing an allowance for the uncollectibles if they were involved in a similar situation. The auditor reasons that the orderly functioning of markets and a level playing field require that financial information should be accurate and reliable, so another auditor should also decide that the allowance needs to be recorded. The application of virtues such as objectivity and integrity enables her to carry out the ethical action.

Kohlberg's model suggests that people continue to change their decision priorities over time and with additional education and experience. They may experience a change in values and ethical behavior.[13] In the context of business, an individual's moral development can be influenced by corporate culture, especially ethics training.[14] Ethics training and education have been shown to improve managers' moral development. More will be said about corporate culture in Chapter 3.

## Universal Sequence

Kohlberg maintains that his stage sequence is universal; it is the same in all cultures. This seems to run contrary to Geert Hofstede's five cultural dimensions discussed in Chapter 1. For example, we might expect those in a highly collectivist-oriented society to exhibit Stage 3 features more than in an individualistic one that reflects Stage 2 behavior.

William Crain addresses whether different cultures socialize their children differently, thereby teaching them different moral beliefs.[15] He points out that Kohlberg's response has been that different cultures do teach different beliefs, but that his stages refer not to specific beliefs, but to underlying modes of reasoning. We might assume, then, that in a collectivist society, blowing the whistle on a member of a work group would be considered improper because of the "family" orientation, (Stage 3) while in a more individualistic one, it is considered acceptable because it is in the best interests of society (Stage 4). Thus, individuals in different cultures at the same stage-sequence might hold different beliefs about the appropriateness of whistleblowing but still reason the same because from a fairness perspective, it is the right way to behave.

# The Ethical Domain in Accounting and Auditing

The ethical domain for accountants and auditors usually involves four key constituent groups, including (1) the client organization that hires and pays for accounting services; (2) the accounting firm that employs the practitioner, typically represented by the collective interests of the firm's management; (3) the accounting profession, including various regulatory bodies such as the Securities and Exchange Commission (SEC) and the Public Company Accounting Oversight Board (PCAOB); and (4) the general public, who rely on the attestations and representations of the practitioner and the firm.[16] Responsibilities to each of these groups may conflict. For example, fees are paid by the client organization rather than by the general public, including investors and creditors who are the direct beneficiary of the independent auditing services so that the public interest may conflict with client interests.

The accounting profession has instituted mechanisms such as professional standards and codes of conduct (i.e., the AICPA Code and IMA Ethical Standards) to encourage the individual practitioner's ethical behavior in a way that is consistent with the stated rules and guidelines of the profession. These positive factors work in conjunction with an individual's attitudes and beliefs and ethical reasoning capacity to influence professional judgment and ethical decision making.

Kohlberg's theory of ethical development provides a framework that can be used to consider the effects of conflict areas on ethical reasoning in accounting. For example, if an individual accountant is influenced by the firm's desire to "make the client happy," then the result may be reasoning at Stage 3. The results of published studies during the 1990s by accounting researchers indicate that CPAs reason primarily at Stages 3 and 4. One possible implication of these results is that a larger percentage of CPAs may be overly influenced by their relationship with peers, superiors, and clients (Stage 3) or by rules (Stage 4). A CPA who is unable to apply the technical accounting standards and rules of conduct critically when these requirements are unclear is likely to be influenced by others in the decision-making process.[17] If an auditor reasons at the post conventional level, then that person may refuse to give in to the pressure applied by the supervisor to overlook the client's failure to follow GAAP. This is the ethical position to take, although it may go against the culture of the firm to "go along to get along."

Empirical studies have explored the underlying ethical reasoning processes of accountants and auditors in practice. Findings show that ethical reasoning may be an important determinant of professional judgment, such as the disclosure of sensitive information[18] and auditor independence.[19] Results also show that unethical and dysfunctional audit behavior, such as the underreporting of time on an audit budget, may be systematically related to the auditor's level of ethical reasoning.[20] In reviewing these and other works, Ponemon and Gabhart conclude that the results imply that ethical reasoning may be an important cognitive characteristic that may affect individual judgment and behavior under a wide array of conditions and events in extant professional practice.[21]

# Rest's Four-Component Model of Ethical Decision Making

Cognitive-developmental researchers have attempted to understand the process of ethical decision making. In particular, James Rest asserts that ethical actions are not the outcome of a single, unitary decision process, but result from a combination of various cognitive structures and psychological processes. Rest's model of ethical action is based on the presumption that an individual's behavior is related to her level of moral development. Rest built on Kohlberg's work by developing a four-component model of the ethical decision-making process. The four-component model describes the cognitive processes that individuals use in ethical decision making; that is, it depicts how an individual first identifies an ethical dilemma and then continues through to his intention and finally courage to behave ethically.[22]

## Moral Sensitivity

The first step in moral behavior requires that the individual interpret the situation as moral. Absent the ability to recognize that one's actions affect the welfare of others, it would be virtually impossible to make the most ethical decision when faced with a moral dilemma. For example, let's assume that you go into a store to order a pizza. You go to the counter and place your order. As you move down to the cashier, you notice a $50 bill in the refrigerated open area that contains cold sodas, which is just below the counter that spans the distance from the order line to the payment area. You notice that two people are ahead of you at the cashier and wonder whether either of them dropped the money. What would you do? Why?

This is an ethical situation because if you decide to keep the money, someone is $50 poorer. You, of course, are $50 richer. Should you act in your own self-interest? If so, how will you justify it? Will you say to yourself: Finders keepers, losers weepers? Or, will you say: If I had dropped the $50, then I would hope that the money would be returned to me.

Our ability to identify an ethical situation enables us to focus on how alternative courses of action might affect ourselves and others. If we simply acted without reflecting on the ethics of the situation in the store, we probably would have looked around, made sure no one was watching, and then pocketed the money. The important point to remember is that ethics is all about how we act when no one is looking.

## Moral Judgment

An individual's ethical cognition of what "ideally" ought to be done to resolve an ethical dilemma is called *prescriptive reasoning*.[23] The outcome of one's prescriptive reasoning is his ethical judgment of the ideal solution to an ethical dilemma. Generally, an individual's prescriptive reasoning reflects his cognitive understanding of an ethical situation as measured by his level of moral development.[24] Once a person is aware of possible lines of action and how people would be affected by the alternatives, a judgment must be made about which course of action is more morally justifiable (which alternative is just or right).

## Moral Motivation

Moral motivation reflects an individual's willingness to place ethical values (e.g., honesty, integrity, trustworthiness, caring, and empathy) ahead of nonethical values (e.g., wealth, power, and fame) that relate to self-interest. An individual's ethical motivation influences her intention to comply or not comply with her ethical judgment in the resolution of an ethical dilemma. In the previous example, if you decide to keep the $50, then enhancing your wealth (self-interest) overtakes the ethical values of honesty and empathy.

## Moral Character

Individuals do not always behave in accordance with their ethical intention. An individual's intention to act ethically and her ethical actions may not be aligned because of a lack of ethical character. As previously noted, individuals with strong ethical character will be more likely to carry out their ethical intentions with ethical action than individuals with a weak ethical character because they are better able to withstand any pressures (integrity) to do otherwise. Once a moral person has considered the ethics of the alternatives, she must construct an appropriate plan of action, avoid distractions, and maintain the courage to continue.

The four components of Rest's model are processes that must take place for moral behavior to occur. Rest does not offer the framework as a linear decision-making model, suggesting instead that the components interact through a complicated sequence of "feed-back" and "feed-forward" loops. An individual who demonstrates adequacy in one component may not necessarily be adequate in another and moral failure can occur when there is a deficiency in any one component.[25] For example, an individual who has good moral reasoning capacity, a skill that can be developed (Component 2), may fail to perceive an ethical problem because she does not clearly understand how others might feel or react—a lack of empathy (Component 1).

# Rest's Model and Organizational Behavior

Moral sensitivity is particularly important for a person to become aware of ethical issues. Extending moral sensitivity to a corporate setting, Schminke et al. found that a heightened moral sensitivity in a corporation created a culture that supported ethical action.[26] However, sometimes moral agents in an organization may have to overcome opposition to carrying out the course of action. Johnson points out that this helps explain why there is only a moderate correlation between moral judgment and moral behavior. Many times, deciding does not lead to doing.[27] In other words, how we think we should behave is different from how we decide to behave. This creates a problem of *cognitive dissonance*, a term first coined by Leon Festinger in 1956. The inconsistency between our thoughts, beliefs, or attitudes and behavior creates the need to resolve contradictory or conflicting beliefs, values, and perceptions.[28] Tompkins and Lawley point out that:

> This dissonance only occurs when we are "attached" to our attitudes or beliefs, i.e., they have emotional significance or consequences for our self-concept or sense of coherence about how the world works. The psychological opposition of irreconcilable ideas (cognitions) held simultaneously by one individual, create[s] a motivated force that [c]ould lead, under proper conditions, to the adjustment of one's beliefs to fit one's behavior instead of changing one's behavior to fit one's beliefs (the sequence conventionally assumed).[29]

The Betty Vinson situation at WorldCom, discussed in Chapter 1, is a case in point about cognitive dissonance. Vinson knew it was wrong to "cook the books." She felt it in her inner being, but she did not act on those beliefs. Instead, she followed the orders from superiors and later justified her behavior by rationalizing it as a one-time act and demanded by people who knew accounting better than herself

Rest's model can be applied to the situation faced by Sherron Watkins in the Enron failure. Watkins had come up through the ranks of Andersen to become an audit manager. Later, she joined Enron, one of Andersen's largest clients, and rose to the position of vice president. Watkins was savvy about accounting issues and was the first person at Enron to point out to top management that the accounting maneuvers conducted over a number of years, up until the time when the company went bankrupt in December 2001, had jeopardized its ability to remain in business. In a now-famous memo to the former chair of the board of directors of Enron, Ken Lay, Watkins commented on the sudden resignation of the company's CEO, Jeff Skilling, by stating: "Skilling's departure . . . [will] raise suspicions of accounting improprieties and valuation issues." Watkins went on to say that she is "incredibly nervous that [Enron] will implode in a wave of accounting scandals."[30]

Watkins clearly identified the ethical issues in the Enron debacle. She was motivated to do the right thing and managed to get the company to review its accounting practices, although to no avail. Still, Watkins put her professional future in jeopardy, both at Enron (somewhat of a moot point at the time) and possibly with other employers. She did not know how her actions would affect her ability to work and earn a living in the future.

It is difficult to hypothesize whether Watkins used proper moral judgment. She seemed to consider the interests of employees at Enron but may have been motivated by self-interest (enlightened egoism). One statement Watkins made in the memo to Lay appears to support this contention: "My eight years of Enron work history will be worth nothing on my resume, the business world will consider the past successes as nothing but an elaborate accounting hoax." Notice how she thinks of herself and does not mention the interests of the thousands of stockholders who lost millions of dollars from a decline in Enron stock and thousands of employees who lost their jobs and most of their retirement money if it had been invested in 401(k) plans that included Enron stock. We don't mean to be too critical of Watkins; she took an important step that no one else at Enron was willing to take. She became somewhat of an outcast at the company that had blinders on with respect to Enron's unethical actions.

Watkins's actions illustrate the difference between blowing the whistle internally and external whistleblowing. Watkins did go to the board chair so that internal whistleblowing practices were followed. However, she did not go outside the company (i.e., to the SEC) and disclose what she knew. Had Watkins gone to the SEC with her story on or around August 15, 2001, the day Skilling resigned, instead of or in addition to writing the internal memo to Lay, her actions may have saved thousands of people millions of dollars because the stock price was at $36 on that day, and ultimately, when all the dust settled on December 2, 2001, the stock sold for less than $1 a share. On the other hand, Watkins may have truly believed that Enron was still salvageable if Lay had acted on her concerns, so employees would still have their jobs and the stock price may have recovered. Moreover, the ethical obligation of confidentiality probably weighed heavily on Watkins's mind, so we can understand why she would have been reluctant to go to the SEC. Nevertheless, her actions can be differentiated from those of Cynthia Cooper at WorldCom who did enlist the aid of the outside auditors—KPMG—to put an end to the fraud.

How does a person develop the courage to withstand pressures that challenge one's commitment to act in an ethical manner? An important element is to have a supportive environment in the organization. An ethical tone must be set by top management. When an organization attempts to foster an ethical culture, the employees feel that they will be supported if they bring matters of concern out into the open. In this case, employees feel comfortable making decisions consistent with their beliefs rather than making decisions and then altering their beliefs to coincide with their behavior. The notion of creating an ethical organization environment will be explored in the next chapter.

The culture at Enron was to make the deal, regardless of which ethical standards had to be sacrificed, "for the good of the organization." An amusing story that made the rounds on the Internet was described in a book written by Watkins and Mimi Swartz, titled *Power Failure: The Inside Story of the Collapse at Enron*. It speaks volumes about what motivated behavior at Enron[31] and deals with how Enron defined capitalism with respect to its activities:

| | |
|---|---|
| **Feudalism:** | You have two cows. Your lord takes some of the milk. |
| **Fascism:** | You have two cows. The government takes both, hires you to take care of them, and sells you the milk. |
| **Communism:** | You have two cows. You must take care of them, but the government takes all the milk. |
| **Capitalism:** | You have two cows. You sell one and buy a bull. Your herd multiplies, and the economy grows. You sell them and retire on the income. |
| **Enron Capitalism:** | You have two cows. You sell three of them to your publicly listed company, using letters of credit opened by your brother-in-law at the bank, then execute a debt-equity swap with an option so that you get all four cows back, with a tax exemption for five cows. The milk rights of the six cows are transferred through an intermediary to a Cayman Island company secretly owned by the majority shareholder, who sells the rights to all seven cows to your listed company. The Enron annual report says the company owns eight cows, with an option on one more. |

# Professional Judgment in Accounting: Transitioning from Moral Intent to Moral Action

One question that arises from Rest's model is how to align ethical behavior with ethical intent. The answer is through the exercise of virtue, according to a study conducted by Libby and Thorne.[32] The authors point out that audit failures at companies such as Enron and WorldCom demonstrate that the rules in accounting cannot replace auditors' professional judgment. Transactions (i.e., special-purpose entities at Enron) can be structured around rules, and rules cannot be made to fit every situation. The rules may be unclear or nonexistent, in which case professional judgment is necessary for decisions to be made in accordance with the values of the profession as embodied in its codes of conduct such as the AICPA Code and IMA Ethical Standards discussed in Chapter 1. Professional judgment requires not only technical competence, but also depends on auditors' ethics and virtues.

Libby and Thorne surveyed members of the Canadian accounting community with the help of the Canadian Institute of Chartered Accountants (CICA), the equivalent of the AICPA in the United States, to develop a set of virtues important in the practice of auditing.[33] The authors divided the virtues into two categories: intellectual virtues, which indirectly influence an individual's intentions to exercise professional judgment; and instrumental virtues, which directly influence an individual's actions. Their results are consistent with the principles and standards of behavior discussed in Chapter 1. The most important intellectual virtues were found to be integrity, truthfulness, independence, objectivity, dependability, being principled, and healthy skepticism. The most important instrumental virtues were diligence (i.e., due care) and being alert, careful, resourceful, consultative, persistence, and courageous. The authors concluded from their study that virtue plays an integral role in both the intention to exercise professional judgment and the exercise of professional judgment, and the necessity of possessing both intellectual and instrumental virtues for auditors.[34]

Generally accepted auditing standards (GAAS) require that auditors should obtain "sufficient competent evidential matter . . . through inspection, observation, inquiries, and confirmations to afford a reasonable basis for an opinion regarding the financial statements under audit."[35] That evidence enables an auditor to make judgments that help determine whether the client's financial statements accurately record, in all material respects, the client's actual income, financial position, and cash flows. An example of when an auditor might fail to live up to this standard is if she relies extensively on information provided by the client, often in the form of oral representations of management, and fails to obtain sufficient documentary and other evidence from independent sources to verify management's representations. To carry out her professional responsibilities, the auditor should approach the engagement with a healthy dose of skepticism and objective mindset that supports the intention to do what it takes to gather the evidence necessary to support professional judgment. Such evidence is gathered by being careful and alert to circumstances that might bring into question the reliability of the evidence and persistent in cases where the client fails to cooperate. According to Gaa, the matter of due professional care concerns what the auditor does and how well she does it.[36]

Returning now to Rest's model, in her seminal paper on the role of virtue on auditors' ethical decision making, Thorne contends that the model fails to provide a theoretical description of the role of personal characteristics, except for level of moral development, in auditors' ethical decision processes. Thorne develops a model of individuals' ethical decision processes that integrates Rest's components with the basic tenets of virtue ethics theory. Her model relies on virtue-based characteristics, which tend to increase the decision maker's propensity to exercise sound ethical judgment. Thorne believes that virtue

**FIGURE 2.1**
**Thorne's Integrated Model of Ethical Decision Making**[1]

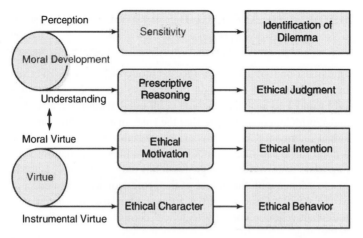

[1]Linda Thorne, "The Role of Virtue in Auditors' Ethical Decision Making: An Integration of Cognitive-Developmental and Virtue Ethics Perspectives," *Research on Accounting Ethics,* no. 4 (1998), pp. 291–308.

theory is similar to the approach advocated by the cognitive-developmental perspective in three ways. First, both perspectives suggest that ethical action is the result of a rational decision-making process. Second, both perspectives are concerned with an individual's ethical decision-making process. Third, both perspectives acknowledge the critical role of cognition in individuals' ethical decision making. Figure 2.1 presents Thorne's integrated model of the ethical decision-making process.[37]

Figure 2.1 indicates that moral development and virtue are both required for ethical behavior. In her examination of the model, Armstrong suggests that moral development comprises sensitivity to the moral content of a situation or dilemma and prescriptive reasoning, or the ability to understand the issues, think them through, and arrive at an ethical judgment. Similarly, virtue comprises ethical motivation, which describes an individual's willingness to place the interests of others ahead of her own interest; and ethical character, which leads to ethical behavior.[38]

The best way to explain how virtue-based ethical reasoning and ethical decision making should take place is through an example. The following case is a real-life example of how a government auditor acted on her beliefs in the face of strong resistance from her superiors, including retaliation for her actions.

## Diem-Thi Le and Whistleblowing at the DCCA

Diem-Thi Le is a senior auditor with the Defense Contract Audit Agency (DCCA) and CPA in the state of California. On September 10, 2008, Le testified before the U.S. Senate Committee on Homeland Security and Governmental Affairs that an audit opinion she had developed on the audit of a contractor receiving funds from the U.S. government had been changed by a branch manager at the DCCA without her knowledge or approval. So begins the story of Le, who was responsible for a ruling by the U.S. Office of the Special Counsel that the DCCA violated the Whistleblower Protection Act when it retaliated against Le for blowing the whistle on fraudulent practices. Le's experiences and how she dealt with them stand as an example of moral reasoning and ethical action under fire. She knew that she had to do everything possible to change the culture at DCCA, which sanctioned manipulated audits by supervisors without consideration of the facts (and sometimes in response to pressure from federal procurement officials and the contractors themselves), potentially costing taxpayers millions of dollars. Here is a summary of the facts of the case as Le described them to the committee.[39]

In September 2005, Le was performing an accounting system audit at the corporate office of a contractor that was a publicly traded engineering, construction, maintenance, and project management company. She found that the accounting system was inadequate in part, and as a result, the contractor was misallocating and mischarging costs to the government. Le's supervisor concurred with her audit findings; however, subsequently, the supervisor told Le that their branch manager disagreed with her. Le's requests to meet with the branch manager to explain her findings were denied. She followed the guidelines given in the agency's Contract Audit Manual and asked for her supervisor's approval to elevate the unreconciled difference of audit opinion to the regional audit manager who was the supervisor of her branch manager. She also heard from other senior auditors that her experience was not the first time an audit opinion on a contractor's inadequate system had been changed by a branch manager.

The regional audit manager told Le that because the branch manager was the one who signed the audit report, her opinion took precedence over Le's. Essentially, the person performing the audit had no say in the final audit report opinion. Moreover, the regional manager instructed Le's supervisor to put Le's working papers in the "superseded work paper folder." Her supervisor then deleted the audit findings from Le's working papers and, without performing any additional audit work, represented those changed working papers as Le's original working papers to support the change in the audit opinion from an inadequate accounting system to an adequate system. Shortly afterward, the audit report was issued, and the contractor accounting system was deemed adequate. Consequently, the contractor did not have to propose or implement any corrective actions to eliminate its accounting system deficiencies, which resulted in misallocating and mischarging costs to the government contracts. For the calendar year 2006, the contractor reported over $14 billion in revenue, including $2.9 billion in revenue from government business.

Le was skeptical, persistent, consultative, and courageous (instrumental virtues) in her actions. She recognized the importance of standing by her principles and acting with integrity (intellectual virtues). To satisfy her curiosity and give her branch manager the benefit of the doubt, she went to the office common drive that contained other audits and reviewed some system audits. She had hoped her experience was an anomaly, but as it turned out, it was not. She discovered a pattern of changing auditors' opinions by the branch manager, but Le did not know why these branch managers were doing it. She found out the reason after consulting with other supervisory auditors of other offices. By making the contractor systems and related internal controls adequate, less audit risk would be perceived and, consequently, fewer audit hours would be incurred on other audits. Because one of the DCAA's performance metrics is productivity rate, which measures the hours incurred versus the dollar examined, having fewer audit hours incurred for the same amount of dollars examined would increase the productivity rate. The productivity rate was one of the factors on which a branch manager's annual performance review was based.

Le told the committee that because of the emphasis on the increase of the productivity rate, DCAA auditors, including her, were pressured by management to perform audits within certain numbers of budgeted hours. Given the change in audit opinions by management without performing additional audit work or without discussing it with the auditors whose opinions were altered, she concluded that it was a lack of due professional care, at best, and negligent and fraudulent, at worst. She confided with other colleagues about her findings and was told she had no choice but to call the Department of Defense Inspector General (DoD IG) Hotline. She did so in November 2005.

Le said she never imagined that she would call the hotline and make an allegation against her management. She became disillusioned when she found out the complaint was sent back to her own agency for investigation. The independent process of review and determination of action by DoD IG personnel had been compromised. She followed up on her complaint several times, and in February 2006, she was told that it might take a long time for someone to work on her case due to limited staff. She then decided to contact the local office of the Defense Criminal Investigative Services (DCIS) and met with a special agent on March 4, 2006. She also found out that her complaint had been referred to DCAA headquarters, and that the referral included specific personal identifying information about her, such as her name and cell phone number, as well as details of the accounting system audit that triggered the hotline complaint. She concluded that her identity as a whistle-blower had not been adequately protected; therefore, she suffered reprisal from DCAA management.

Exhibit 2.1 summarizes Le's description to the committee of the scope and nature of the retaliation by the DCAA.

Le concluded her testimony by stating that it was her opinion that DCAA manage-ment had become so metric driven that the quality of their audits and independence had suffered. Audits were not dictated by audit risks, but rather by the established budgeted hours and due dates. The pressure to close out audits and to meet the productivity rate was so intense that it often prevented auditors from following their instincts in questioning

**EXHIBIT 2.1**
**Summary of Retaliation Against Diem-Thi Le by the DCAA**

- In September 2005, my management overruled my audit findings. In October 2005, I was transferred to another team. In the November 2005 Staff Conference, the regional audit manager stated that if we auditors did not like management's audit opinion, we should find another job.

- In early July 2006, I was transferred to another team. In late July 2006, my management was interviewed by the DCIS special agent. In October 2006, I found out that I was the only auditor with an "Outstanding" performance rating who did not get a performance award.

- In early April 2007, the Office of Special Counsel (OSC) investigator contacted DCAA Western Region management to inform them of my OSC complaint. Shortly after that hap-pened, my supervisor told me that I should seek mental health counseling because of the stress I was under. She gave me an Employee Assistance Form and asked that I sign it.

- In August 2007, I was given my annual performance evaluation for the period of July 2006 through June 2007. I was downgraded from an "Outstanding" rating to a "Fully Successful" rating (two notches down). Also, my promotion points came down from 78 (out of a maxi-mum of 120) to 58 points. Please note that prior to this job performance evaluation, I had been an outstanding auditor for several years.

- On August 31, 2007, I was given a memorandum signed by my supervisor and prepared by the DCAA headquarters legal counsel. The memo instructed me that I was not allowed to provide any documents generated by a government computer, including emails and job performance evaluations, to any investigative units, including the OSC. Failure to follow those instructions would result in disciplinary actions. Subsequently, I discovered that Section 8 of Appendix A of the DCAA Personnel Management Manual Chapter 50 considers the reprisal against an employee for providing information or disclosures to an inspector general or OSC investigator a violation of the employee's rights.

- On September 10, 2007, my supervisor advised me to read the 18 USC 641, Theft of Government Property. My supervisor stated that the unauthorized distribution of agency documents is theft, and it does not matter if the purpose is to respond to a hotline or OSC complaint.

- In August 2008, I was given my job performance evaluation for the period of July 2007 through June 2008. I remained at "Fully Successful," which is one notch above the rating that one would be put on a Performance Improvement Plan (PIP). My promotion points came down to 53.

the contractor costs, reporting internal control deficiencies, and evaluating any suspected irregular conduct. In the end, contractors were "getting away with murder" because they knew that DCAA was so metric driven. She also pointed out that DCAA management had reduced the number of audit staff and created layers of personnel who did nothing but monitor metrics. She had hoped the culture would change and enable auditors to perform high-quality audits in accordance with generally accepted government auditing standards in order to protect the government's interest and taxpayers' money.

After a great deal of agonizing and disappointment with Le's treatment by the DCAA, and vocal complaints that reached the highest levels of the agency, the Government Accountability Office (GAO) issued its report in July 2008, two years after she had complained, and with her career hanging in the balance. It is the GAO's responsibility to determine whether government entities (i.e., DCAA) are doing what they are supposed to, that funds are being spent for the intended purpose, and that applicable laws and regulations are being complied with. The GAO looked at seven of Le's cases that had been overruled by her supervisors, as well as three other cases. The GAO report supported Le's conclusions; indeed, it went even further, finding that the DCAA had a climate of cutting corners, rubber-stamping multi-billion-dollar contracts in the name of expediency, and cost-cutting.

As a result of the congressional investigation and GAO report, April Stephenson was removed as head of the DCAA in late October 2009. U.S. Army Auditor General Patrick J. Fitzgerald was chosen by President Barack Obama to take over the embattled agency. The audits were retooled to be less reliant on quantity and more focused on quality. Le got a promotion and was assigned to train auditors. She applied for whistleblower protection from the OSC, which ensured that the Department of Defense changed her employment ratings to the highest level and gave her retroactive performance awards. Correction and disciplinary actions were taken against her supervisors.

In reflecting on the incident in an interview with the *Orange County Register*,[40] Le admitted to struggling with her conscience for weeks, trying through sleepless nights to get the courage to report the bad audits. She said," I got to live with myself when I look in the mirror at the end of the day." She told the interviewer that management viewed her as the enemy, and even sympathetic coworkers were afraid of being associated with her. When [I] walked into the break room, everybody walked out."

The process of ethical decision making in an organization is sometimes fraught with danger, as was the case with Diem-Thi Le. Like Cynthia Cooper's experience at WorldCom, Le took the ultimate step even though she feared for her job. She knew early on there would be strong push-back by management against her. She was influenced in her actions by professional responsibilities as a CPA, virtue-based reasoning, and a genuine desire to improve the culture at the DCAA. Le's experience illustrates the difficulty of transitioning from knowing the right thing to do and actually doing it. It demonstrates the process that she followed to convert her moral intention into moral action.

## Behavioral Ethics

The field of behavioral ethics emphasizes the need to consider how individuals actually make decisions, rather than how they would make decisions in an ideal world. Research in behavioral ethics reveals that our minds have two distinct modes of decision making—"System 1" and "System 2" thinking.[41] Daniel Kahneman, the Nobel Prize–winning behavioral economist, points out that System 1 thinking is our intuitive system of processing information: fast, automatic, effortless, and emotional decision processes; on the other hand, "System 2" thinking is slower, conscious, effortful, explicit, and a more reasoned decision process.[42] Many times in our lives, we use System 1 thinking and that is fine. For example, we see an article of clothing in the store. We like it, so we buy it. We act rather instinctively and decide whether we like it rather than whether we should consider other options that might better complement our appearance. What follows is an example of using System 1 thinking instead of the more deliberate approach of System 2, and you draw the wrong conclusion as a result. To illustrate, answer the following question: A baseball bat and ball together cost $110. If the bat costs $100 more than the ball, how much does the ball cost? Most people say $10. They decide quickly, without doing the math or thinking through the question. However, it is the wrong answer. The ball actually cost $5, and the bat cost $105.

The broader point of this exercise is to explain how System 1 thinking can lead to snap decisions that make it more difficult to resolve an ethical dilemma in a morally appropriate way. It may occur because you lack important information regarding a decision, fail to notice available information, or face time and cost constraints. You don't have the time or inclination and fail to see the dangers of deciding too quickly.

Imagine for a moment what would have happened if Diem-Thi Le had used System 1 thinking. She may have concluded from the beginning that it would take too much time and effort to bring the audit opinion changes to top management's attention, given that in the end, she might be risking her job and entire career. But if she exhibits System 2 thinking, as she did, she considers the consequences of her action for herself and other stakeholders. She weighs the costs and benefits of alternative courses of action. She seeks advice from others who might help clarify issues before deciding. It is a reflective, mentally challenging process.

Many decisions in business and accounting have ethical challenges. This is because of the impacts of those decisions and the fact that outcomes are likely to affect stakeholders in different ways and will express different ethical values. A decision-making model built on System 2 thinking can provide a more systematic analysis that enables comprehensible judgment, clearer reasons, and a more justifiable and defensible action than otherwise would have been the case. An important part of a decision-making model is to address the professional values, behaviors, and attitudes discussed in Chapter 1 and use the ethical reasoning methods to judge the alternative courses of action. In the end, however, it is the virtues that will bridge the gap between moral judgment and ethical behavior. Virtue-based decision making is a reflective process that relies on deliberation and reason to think through conflict situations and it provides the courage (i.e., integrity) to carry through with ethical action. Diem-Thi Le is a virtuous person. She struggled with her dilemma, thought through alternative courses of action, and withstood pressures to accept management's decision to change her audit opinion.

# Ethical Decision-Making Model

A variety of ethical decision-making models exist, including the philosophical approach that combines the principles of utilitarianism, rights, and justice and states the principles in terms of questions. By answering these six questions, it should be possible to reach a decision.[43]

1. What benefits and harms will each course of action produce?
2. Which course of action will produce the greatest overall benefit for all stakeholders?
3. What are the rights of stakeholders?
4. Which course of action respects the rights of individuals?
5. Which course of action treats people fairly and equally?
6. Which course of action results in a fair distribution of benefits and burdens?

Virtue is not specifically recognized in the philosophical model, although it is implied by the considerations. It would be difficult to answer these questions in a morally appropriate way without being an honest, trustworthy person in evaluating these considerations and willing to act out of integrity in deciding on the preferred course of action.

One of the first models suggested for accounting ethics education was proposed by Langenderfer and Rockness and adopted by the American Accounting Association in 1989.[44] The model consists of seven steps that broadly identify important considerations in making ethical decisions in accounting.

1. What are the facts?
2. What are the ethical issues?
3. What are the norms, principles, and values?
4. What are the alternative courses of action?
5. What is the best course of action?
6. What are the consequences of each possible course of action?
7. What is the decision?

The appeal of the model is its simplicity. However, this is also a shortcoming, in that it leaves out important considerations such as the basis for determining "norms, principles, and values," virtue considerations, and reflection. Armstrong criticizes the model because of its reliance on consequences to drive the decision. This utilitarian approach seems to relegate rights to a secondary role.[45] We agree with her criticism.

Reflection can be seen as consciously thinking about and analyzing what one has done (or is doing). A decision-making process can help organize the various elements of ethical reasoning and professional judgment. A good model should be based on the virtues discussed in Chapter 1 that mirrors the obligations of accountants and auditors under the profession's ethics codes and standards. The model should allow for the use of ethical reasoning to evaluate stakeholder interests, analyze the relevant operational and accounting issues, and identify alternative courses of action.

We have developed a comprehensive model for students to use when analyzing ethics cases in the book. The model, presented in Exhibit 2.2, is a tool for ethical analysis. Each step of the model may not be necessary in a given case, but the steps do identify important considerations in evaluating ethical dilemmas in accounting. In order to make the process more workable and to integrate Rest's model of moral behavior, we also present an abbreviated version of the model below that is used to analyze the Diem-Thi Le conflict at DCAA.

The condensed model links to Rest's framework as follows:

**Integrated Ethical Decision-Making Process**

1. **Identify the ethical and professional issues (ethical sensitivity)**
   - *What are the ethical and professional issues in this case (i.e., GAAP and GAAS)?*
   - *Who are the stakeholders?*
   - *Which ethical standards apply (i.e., AICPA Code Principles, IMA Ethical Standards and IFAC standards)*
2. **Identify and evaluate alternative courses of action (ethical judgment)**
   - *What can and cannot be done in resolving the conflict under professional standards?*
   - *Which ethical reasoning methods apply to help reason through alternatives (i.e., rights theory, utilitarianism, justice, and virtue)?*
3. **Reflect on the core professional values, ethics, and attitudes to help carry through with ethical action (ethical intent)**
   - *Consider how virtue considerations (i.e., moral virtues: intellectual and instrumental) motivate ethical actions.*
   - *Consider how IES 4[46] standards (i.e., independence, objectivity, integrity, professional skepticism) motivate ethical actions and behaviors.*

**EXHIBIT 2.2**
Comprehensive
Ethical Decision-
Making Model

1. **Frame the ethical issue.** *What is the primary ethical issue in this case?* For example, in the uncollectibles situation discussed in Chapter 1, the ethical issue was whether the junior auditor should compromise his values and give in to the pressure of the audit manager not to report the estimated uncollectibles of $1 million that is currently unrecorded.

2. **Gather all the facts.** *Specify the relevant facts, including disagreements and other conflict situations.* Make a conscious effort to understand the situation and distinguish facts from mere opinion. An ethical judgment made after gathering the relevant facts is a more reasonable ethical judgment than one made without regard for the facts.

3. **Identify the stakeholders and obligations.** *Identify and consider all the people affected by a decision—the stakeholders.* These include all of the groups and/or individuals affected by a decision, policy, operation, or the ethics standards of a firm or the accounting profession. Determine the obligations of the decision maker to each of the stakeholder groups.

4. **Identify the accounting and auditing issues.** Assuming that the case deals with whether the financial reports are accurate and reliable, an important step is to describe the accounting (GAAP) and auditing (GAAS) issues clearly. These might include revenue and expense recognition, asset valuation, disclosures, audit independence, due care, and gathering of sufficient audit evidence to warrant the expression of an opinion. In a tax matter, the principle that helps to establish ethical behavior is to judge a proposed tax position by the "realistic possibility of success" standard, which we will discuss in Chapter 4.

5. **Identify the operational issues.** Accounting decisions are not made in a vacuum; factors such as reporting responsibilities, the culture of an organization and its own ethics standards, internal controls, and the corporate governance system must be considered to highlight operational problems that should be corrected.

6. **Identify the relevant accounting ethics standards involved in the situation.** *Identify the most important ethical values of the accounting profession that should be considered in evaluating the facts and alternative courses of action.* Emphasis must be placed on the profession's ethical standards (i.e., AICPA Principles and IMA Ethics Standards) because they provide the context within which ethical decision making takes place.

7. **List all the possible alternatives that you can or cannot do.** Most ethical issues are not black or white—there are shades of gray, and the alternatives should account for that uncertainty. Once you have examined the facts, identified the stakeholders, and described the operational and accounting issues, the next step is to consider the available alternatives. Creativity in identifying options, or "moral imagination," helps distinguish good people who make ethically responsible decisions from good people who do not.

8. **Compare and weigh the alternatives.**
   • Is it *legal;* i.e., in conformity with SEC laws and Public Company Accounting Oversight Board (PCAOB) rules?
   • Is it *consistent with professional standards* (AICPA Principles, IMA Ethics Standards and IFAC standards; GAAP and GAAS)?
   • Is it consistent with *in-house rules* (firm policies and its own code of ethics)?
   • Is it right?
   • What are the potential *harms and benefits* to the stakeholders?
   • Is it *fair* to the stakeholders?
   • Is it consistent with *virtue considerations?* This is where the decision maker should form a professional judgment after evaluating her moral intention and willingness to act in a principled manner, including having the courage to stand by what she knows is the right thing to do.

9. **Decide on a course of action.** After evaluating the ethics of the alternatives, select the one that best meets the ethical requirements of the situation.

10. **Reflect on your decision.** Before taking action, think about what you are about to do and why. Double-check the correctness of your proposed action by asking: How would I feel if my decision was made public and I had to defend it? Would I be proud if I had to explain my decision to my spouse or child?

**4. Take action (ethical behavior)**
- *Decide on a course of action consistent with one's professional obligations.*
- *How can virtue considerations support turning ethical intent into ethical action?*
- *What steps can I take to strengthen my position and argument?*

# Application of the Model

The application of the integrated model in the case of Diem-Thi Le at DCAA follows. Our purpose is not to cover every aspect of the case, but to illustrate some of the more important considerations in dealing with the ethical conflict.

**1. Ethical and Professional Issues**
- Inadequacy of accounting system at contractor that misallocated and mischarged costs to the government
- Change of audit opinion by supervisor without consultation—integrity issues
- Altered work papers—due professional care issues
- Sanctioning of contractor's inappropriate accounting by top management—objectivity and independence issues
- Use of operating metrics to dictate audit procedures and findings—responsibility issues
- Failure to act in accordance with the public interest

**2. Evaluation of Alternatives**
- **Don't take the matter to higher-ups:** Violates laws and regulations; violates accounting and auditing standards; inconsistent with professional obligations to protect the public interest; violates fiduciary obligation to the public
- **Take the matter to higher-ups:** Consistent with ethical and professional obligations; utilizes hot-line and whistleblowing procedures in place to protect the public interest; principled decision
- **Find another solution:** It's always wise to consider another alternative that might achieve the goal of reversing the altered audit opinion and improve the culture of DCAA, such as enlisting the help of coworkers to bring this matter (i.e., systemwide internal control failure at the agency) that affects other audits and auditors out in the open

**3. Reflection**
- Am I being true to myself and my personal and professional values if I take the intended action?
  - Le understood the importance of objective audit decisions and independence from contractors
  - Le struggled with her conscience and decided early on that she couldn't stand idly by and condone the fraudulent accounting and improper audit changes made by her supervisor
  - Le understood her obligations to the public that expects government agencies to use resources efficiently and closely monitor those who do business with the agency

**4. Take Action**
- What do I need to do to get my point across?
- Who should I approach?
- Can I elicit support from coworkers?
- How can I convince higher-ups to support my position?

**Concluding Thoughts**

We purposefully kept this chapter short to encourage students to think about the ethical decision-making process, how it might personally benefit them to use elements of it in daily life, and how to apply it to their professional obligations after joining the accounting profession. Ethical decision making requires both the ability to reason through alternative courses of action using moral reasoning methods and virtue in following one's decisions with ethical behavior. In accounting, ethical decision making is required by the Principles of the AICPA Code of Professional Conduct and Ethical Standards of the IMA.

Ethical dilemmas in accounting occur when the rules are unclear or nonexistent, or rules are in conflict or inconsistent. To make matters worse, pressure may be imposed on accountants and auditors by supervisors to go along with materially false and misleading financial information. The environment of ethical decision making in accounting requires that the accounting professional must overcome those pressures through integrity and do the right thing: that is, make sure that the financial statements are accurate, reliable, and transparent. A decision-making model that integrates ethical judgment with ethical action helps to focus on the critical ethical and professional issues, stakeholders affected by alternative courses of action, technical and ethical standards in the profession specific to the dilemma, virtues that enable ethical action to occur, and reflection to consider carefully how best to carry out ethical action with intended ethical behavior.

In this book, we discuss several examples of unethical behavior by accountants and auditors and members of top management from CEOs and CFOs at Enron and WorldCom to financial scam artists like Bernie Madoff and a host of other fraudsters. We purposefully focused on examples of ethical behavior in the first two chapters to demonstrate that you can stand up for what you know is the right thing to do. You can withstand the pressure to compromise your values and ethics. You can follow the lead of Cynthia Cooper at WorldCom and Diem-Thi Le at the DCAA and be respected for your actions by your peers and the accounting profession.

**Discussion Questions**

The following story applies to questions 1 and 2:

On October 15, 2009, in Fort Collins, Colorado, the parents of a six-year-old boy, Falcon Henne, claimed that he had floated away in a homemade helium balloon that was shaped to resemble a silver flying saucer. Some in the media referred to the incident as "Balloon Boy." The authorities had closed down Denver International Airport, called in the National Guard, and a police pursuit ensued. After an hour-long flight that covered more than 50 miles across three counties, the empty balloon was found near the airport. It was later determined that the boy was hiding in the house all along in an incident that was a hoax and motivated by publicity that might lead to a reality television show. The authorities blamed the father, Richard, for the incident and decided to prosecute him. Richard Heene pleaded guilty on November 13, 2009, to the felony count of falsely influencing authorities. He pled to protect his wife, Mayumi, a Japanese citizen, who he believed may have been deported if Richard was convicted of a more serious crime. Richard also agreed to pay $36,000 in restitution.

1. Identify the stakeholders and how they were affected by Heene's actions using ethical reasoning.

2. What stage of moral reasoning in Kohlberg's model is exhibited by Richard Heene's actions? Do you believe the punishment fit the crime? In other words, was justice done in this case? Why or why not?

3. How do you assess at what stage of moral development in Kohlberg's model you reason at in making decisions? Are you satisfied with that stage? Do you believe there are factors or forces preventing you from reasoning at a higher level? If so, what are they?

4. Using the child abuse scandal at Penn State discussed in Chapter 1, explain the actions that would have been taken by Joe Paterno if he had been reasoning at each stage in Kohlberg's model and why.

5. Aristotle believed that there was a definite relationship between having practical wisdom (i.e., knowledge or understanding that enables one to do the right thing) and having moral virtue, but these were not the same thing. Explain why. How do these virtues interact in Rest's Four-Component Model of Ethical Decision Making?

6. In the text, we point out that Rest's model is not linear in nature. An individual who demonstrates adequacy in one component may not necessarily be adequate in another, and moral failure

can occur when there is a deficiency in any one component. Give an example in accounting when ethical intent may not be sufficient to produce ethical behavior and explain why that is the case.

7. In teaching about moral development, instructors often point out the threefold nature of morality: It depends on emotional development (in the form of ability to feel guilt or shame), social development (manifested by the recognition of the group and the importance of moral behavior for the group's existence), and cognitive development (especially the ability to adopt another's perspective). How does this perspective of morality relate to ethical reasoning by accountants and auditors?

8. Some empirical research suggests that accountants and auditors may not achieve their higher levels of ethical reasoning. Why do you think this statement may be correct?

9. Do you agree with Carol Gilligan's criticism of Kohlberg's model that women reason differently than men and rely more on a care-and-response orientation? Why or why not? Do you believe Kohlberg's model is culturally biased? Why or why not?

10. Arthur Andersen LLP was the auditor for Enron, WorldCom, Waste Management, and other companies that committed fraud. Andersen was forced to shut its doors forever after a U.S. Department of Justice lawsuit against it concluded that it had obstructed justice and lied to the government in the Enron case. One thing Andersen had done was to shred documents related to its audit of Enron before the government could get its hands on them. Some in the profession thought that the government had gone too far given the facts and mediating circumstances (including top management's deception); others believed that the punishment was unjustified because most accounting firms got caught up in similar situations during the late 1990s and early 2000s (pre–Sarbanes-Oxley). What do you believe? Use ethical reasoning to support your answer.

11. In this chapter, we discussed the role of Sherron Watkins in the Enron fraud. Evaluate Watkins's thought process and actions from the perspective of Kohlberg's model. Do you think she went far enough in bringing her concerns out in the open? Why or why not?

12. You are in charge of the checking account for a small business. One morning, your accounting supervisor enters your office and asks you for a check for $150 for expenses that he tells you he incurred entertaining a client last night. He submits receipts from a restaurant and lounge. Later, your supervisor's girlfriend stops by to pick him up for lunch, and you overhear her telling the receptionist what a great time she had at dinner and dancing with your supervisor the night before. What would you do and why?

13. Do you believe that our beliefs trigger our actions, or do we act and then justify our actions by changing our beliefs? Explain.

14. Do you think Betty Vinson was a victim of "motivated blindness"? Why or why not?

15. In her case against the Defense Contract Audit Agency (DCAA) that resulted from actions against her for blowing the whistle on improper agency practices, Diem-Thi Le sought to provide DCAA documents to the Office of Special Counsel (OSC) to back up her claims of retaliation. DCAA provided Le with a memo that said she was "not permitted to access or copy or possess any Agency document for [her] private purposes, including preparation of complaints in any forum," according to the OSC report, which directly quoted the memo. DCAA Assistant General Counsel John Greenlee drafted the template of the August 31, 2007 memo, which bore the signature of Sharon Kawamoto, one of Le's supervising auditors.

Le wanted clarification. Kawamoto told Greenlee in a September 7, 2007, email that Le wanted to know if she could "access documents related to audits cited in her performance appraisals in order to prepare complaints to OSC and the Equal Employment Opportunity Office," states the OSC report. Le wanted copies of her performance appraisals and related emails. Greenlee responded that Le "may not distribute or disclose those documents to anyone else—period—without asking permission. That permission will not be granted her."

Do you think Le should have been provided access to her performance appraisals and related emails, given that some aspects of this information contained work-related matters and client information? Does she have an "ethical right" to such information? What ethical limitations might have existed for Le with respect to using this information, assuming that she was a member of the Institute of Management Accountants (IMA)?

16. In this chapter, we discuss the study by Libby and Thorne of the association between auditors' virtue and professional judgment by asking members of the Canadian Institute of Chartered Accountants to rate the importance of a variety of virtues. The most important virtues identified were truthful, independent, objective, and having integrity. The authors note that the inclusion of these virtues in professional codes of conduct (such as the Principles of the AICPA Code of Professional Conduct) may account for their perceived importance.[47] Explain how these virtues relate to an auditor's intention to make ethical decisions.

17. Interpretation 102-4 of the AICPA Code of Professional Conduct, which was discussed in Chapter 1, provides that a CPA should not knowingly misrepresent facts or subordinate her judgment when performing professional services. Explain how Rest's model of moral development influences the steps that a CPA should take to avoid subordinating professional judgment.

18. Explain what you think each of the following statements means in the context of moral development.

    a. How far are you willing to go to do the right thing?

    b. How much are you willing to give up to do what you believe is right?

    c. We may say that we would do the right thing, but when it requires sacrifice, how much are we willing to give up?

19. In a June 1997 paper published in the *Journal of Business Ethics,* Sharon Green and James Weber reported the results of a study of moral reasoning of accounting students prior to and after taking an auditing course. The study also compared the results between accounting and nonaccounting students prior to the auditing course. The authors found that (1) accounting students, after taking an auditing course that emphasized the AICPA Code, reasoned at higher levels than students who had not taken the course; (2) there were no differences in moral reasoning levels when accounting and nonaccounting majors were compared prior to an auditing course; and (3) there was a significant relationship between the students' levels of ethical development and the choice of an ethical versus unethical action.[48] Comment on the results of this study.

20. A major theme of this chapter is that our cognitive processes influence ethical decision making. Use the theme to comment on the following statement, which various religions claim as their own and has been attributed to Lao Tzu and some say the Dalai Lama:

    "Watch your thoughts; they become your words.

    Watch your words; they become your actions.

    Watch your actions; they become your habits.

    Watch your habits; they become your character.

    Watch your character; it becomes your destiny."

# Endnotes

1. Max H. Bazerman and Ann E. Trebrunsel, *Blind Spots: Why We Fail to Do What's Right and What to Do About It* (Princeton, NJ: Princeton University Press, 2011).

2. Wendy Zellner, "The Fall of Enron," *Business Week,* December 17, 2001, p. 30.

3. Barbara Ley Toffler with Jennifer Reingold, *Final Accounting: Ambition, Greed, and the Fall of Arthur Andersen* (New York: Broadway Books, 2003), p. 217.

4. Bethany McLean and Peter Elkind, *The Smartest Guys in the Room: The Amazing Rise and Scandalous Fall of Enron* (New York: Penguin Group, 2003).

5. Paul M. Clikeman, *Called to Account: Fourteen Financial Frauds That Shaped the American Accounting Profession* (New York: Routledge, 2009).

6. Daniel Edelman and Asgley Nicholson, "Arthur Andersen Auditors and Enron: What Happened to Their Texas CPA Licenses?" *Journal of Finance and Accountancy,* http://www.aabri.com/manuscripts/11899.pdf.

7. Lawrence Kohlberg, "Stage and Sequence: The Cognitive Developmental Approach to Socialization," in *Handbook of Socialization Theory and Research,* ed. D. A. Goslin (Chicago: Rand McNally, 1969), pp. 347–480.

8. Carol Gilligan, *In a Different Voice: Psychological Theory and Women's Development* (Cambridge, MA: Harvard University Press, 1982).

9.  James R. Rest and Darcia Narvaez, *Moral Development in the Professions: Psychology and Applied Ethics* (New York: Psychology Press, 1994), p. 4.

10. Rest and Narvaez.

11. Rest and Narvaez.

12. Muriel J. Bebeau and S. J. Thoma, "'Intermediate' Concepts and the Connection to Moral Education," *Educational Psychology Review* 11, no. 4 (1999), p. 345.

13. O. C. Ferrell, John Fraedrich, and Linda Ferrell, *Business Ethics: Ethical Decision Making and Cases* (Mason, OH: South-Western, Cengage Learning, 2009 Update), pp. 162–163.

14. Clare M. Pennino, "Is Decision Style Related to Moral Development Among Managers in the U.S.?" *Journal of Business Ethics* 41 (December 2002), pp. 337–347.

15. William Crain, *Theories of Development: Concepts and Applications,* 6th ed. (Upper Saddle River, NJ, 2010).

16. Lawrence A. Ponemon and David R. L. Gabhart, "Ethical Reasoning Research in the Accounting and Auditing Professions," in James R. Rest and Darcia Narvaez, *Moral Development in the Professions: Psychology and Applied Ethics* (New York: Psychology Press, 1994), pp. 101–120.

17. See Michael K. Shaub, "An Analysis of the Association of Traditional Demographic Variables with the Moral Reasoning of Auditing Students and Auditors," *Journal of Accounting Education* (Winter 1994), pp. 1–26; and Lawrence A. Ponemon, "Ethical Reasoning and Selection Socialization in Accounting," *Accounting, Organizations, and Society* 17 (1992), pp. 239–258.

18. David Arnold and Larry Ponemon, "Internal Auditors' Perceptions of Whistle-blowing and the Influence of Moral Reasoning: An Experiment," *Auditing: A Journal of Practice and Theory* (Fall 1991), pp. 1–15.

19. Larry Ponemon and David Gabhart, "Auditor Independence Judgments: A Cognitive Developmental Model and Experimental Evidence," *Contemporary Accounting Research* (1990), pp. 227–251.

20. Larry Ponemon, "Auditor Underreporting of Time and Moral Reasoning: An Experimental-Lab Study," *Contemporary Accounting Research* (1993), pp. 1–29.

21. Ponemon and Gabhart, 1994, p. 108.

22. James R. Rest, "Morality," in *Handbook of Child Psychology: Cognitive Development,* Vol. 3, series ed. P. H. Mussen and vol. ed. J. Flavell (New York: Wiley, 1983), pp. 556–629.

23. Lawrence Kohlberg, *The Meaning and Measurement of Moral Development* (Worcester, MA: Clark University Press, 1979).

24. Rest and Narvaez, p. 24.

25. Steven Dellaportas, Beverley Jackling, Philomena Leung, Barry J. Cooper, "Developing an Ethics Education Framework for Accounting," *Journal of Business Ethics Education* 8, no. 1 (2011), pp. 63–82.

26. Marshall Schminke, Anke Arnaud, and Maribeth Kuenzi, "The Power of Ethical Work Climates," *Organizational Dynamics* 35, no. 2 (January 2007), pp. 171–186.

27. Craig E. Johnson, *Meeting the Ethical Challenges of Leadership,* 3rd ed. (Thousand Oaks, CA: Sage Publications, Inc., 2009), p. 206.

28. Leon Festinger, *A Theory of Cognitive Dissonance* (Evanston, IL: Row & Peterson, 1957).

29. Penny Tompkins and James Lawley, "Cognitive Dissonance and Creative Tension—The Same or Different?" http://www.cleanlanguage.co.uk/articles/articles/262/0/Cognitive-Dissonance-and-Creative-Tension/Page0.html.

30. Mimi Swartz and S. Watkins, *Power Failure: The Inside Story of the Collapse of Enron* (New York: Doubleday, 2003).

31. Swartz and Watkins, pp. 350–351.

32. Theresa Libby and Linda Thorne, "While Virtue Is Back in Fashion, How Do You Define It and Measure Its Importance to an Auditor's Role?" *CA Magazine,* November 2003, www.camagazine.com/archives/print-edition/2003/nov/regulars/camagazine24374.aspx.

33. Libby and Thorne.

34. Edmund L. Pincoffs, *Quandaries and Virtues Against Reductivism in Ethics* (Lawrence: University Press of Kansas, 1986).

35. Michael Gibbins and Alister K. Mason, "Professional Judgment in Financial Reporting," *CICA Research Study* (Toronto, Ontario, Canada: Canadian Institute of Chartered Accountants, 1988).

36. James C. Gaa, "Discussion of Auditors' Ethical Decision Process," *Auditing: A Journal of Practice and Theory* (1992), pp. 60–67.

37. Linda Thorne, "The Role of Virtue in Auditors' Ethical Decision Making: An Integration of Cognitive-Developmental and Virtue Ethics Perspectives," *Research on Accounting Ethics,* no. 4 (1998), pp. 293–294.

38. Mary Beth Armstrong, J. Edward Ketz, and Dwight Owsen, "Ethics Education in Accounting: Moving Toward Ethical Motivation and Ethical Behavior," *Journal of Accounting Education* 21 (2003), pp. 1–16.

39. Statement of Diem-Thi Le, DCAA Auditor, Before the Senate Committee on Homeland Security and Governmental Affairs, September 10, 2008, www.hsgac.senate.gov/download/091008le.

40. Tony Saavedra, "The Whistleblower Saved You Money," *Orange County Register,* November 3, 2011, www.ocregister.com/articles/agency-325266-whistleblower-defense.html.

41. Richard F. West and Keith Stanovich, "Individual Differences in Reasoning: Implications for the Rationality Debate," *Behavioral & Brain Sciences* (2000), 23, pp. 645–665.

42. Daniel Kahneman, "A Perspective on Judgment and Choice: Mapping Bounded Rationality," *American Psychologist* (2003), 58, pp. 697–720.

43. Courtney Clowes, "A Critical Examination of Ethical Decision Making Models," www.aux.zicklin.baruch.cuny.edu/critical/html2/8062clowes.html.

44. Harold Q. Langenderfer and Joanee W. Rockness, "Integrating Ethics into the Accounting Curriculum: Issues, Problems, and Solutions," *Issues in Accounting Education* 4 (Spring), pp. 58–69.

45. Mary Beth Armstrong, "Professional Ethics and Accounting Education: A Critique of the 8-Step Method," *Business & Professional Ethics Journal* 9, nos. 1 & 2 (1990), pp. 181–191.

46. The phrase "IES standards" refers to International Education Standards issues by the International Federation of Accountants. IES 4 calls for ethics education to enhance and maintain professional values, ethics, and attitudes. The standards are consistent with those in the AICPA Code and IMA Ethical Standards. More will be said about IES 4 in Chapter 8.

47. Theresa Libby and Linda Thorne, "The Development of a Measure of Auditors' Virtue," *Journal of Business Ethics* 71 (2007), pp. 89–99.

48. Sharon Green and James Weber, "Influencing Ethical Development: Exposing Students to the AICPA Code of Conduct," *Journal of Business Ethics* 16, no. 8 (June 1997), pp. 777–790.

# Chapter 2 Cases

## Case 2-1

# WorldCom

The WorldCom fraud was the largest in U.S. history, surpassing even that of Enron. Beginning modestly during mid-year 1999 and continuing at an accelerated pace through May 2002, the company, under the direction of Bernie Ebbers, the CEO, Scott Sullivan, the CFO, David Myers, the controller, and Buford Yates, the director of accounting, "cooked the books" to the tune of about $11 billion of misstated earnings. Investors collectively lost $30 billion as a result of the fraud.

The fraud was accomplished primarily in two ways:

1. Booking "line costs" for interconnectivity with other telecommunications companies as capital expenditures rather than operating expenses;
2. Inflating revenues with bogus accounting entries from "corporate unallocated revenue accounts."

During 2002, Cynthia Cooper, the vice president of internal auditing, responded to a tip about improper accounting by having her team do an exhaustive hunt for the improperly recorded line costs that were also known as "prepaid capacity." That name was designed to mask the true nature of the costs and treat them as capitalizable costs rather than as operating expenses. The team worked tirelessly, often at night and secretly, to investigate and reveal $3.8 billion worth of fraud.

Soon thereafter, Cooper notified the company's audit committee and board of directors of the fraud. The initial response was not to take action, but to look for explanations from Sullivan. Over time, Cooper realized that she needed to be persistent and not give in to pressure that Sullivan was putting on her to back off. Cooper even approached KPMG, the auditors that had replaced Arthur Andersen, to support her in the matter. Ultimately, Sullivan was dismissed, Myers resigned, Andersen withdrew its audit opinion for 2001, and the Securities and Exchange Commission (SEC) began an investigation into the fraud on June 26, 2002.

In an interview with David Katz and Julia Homer for *CFO Magazine* on February 1, 2008, Cynthia Cooper was asked about her whistleblower role in the WorldCom fraud. When asked when she first suspected something was amiss, Cooper said: "It was a process. My feelings changed from curiosity to discomfort to suspicion based on some of the accounting entries my team and I had identified, and also on the odd reactions I was getting from some of the finance executives."[1]

Cooper did exactly what is expected of a good auditor. She approached the investigation of line-cost accounting with a healthy dose of skepticism and maintained her integrity throughout, even as Sullivan was trying to bully her into dropping the investigation.

When asked whether there was anything about the culture of WorldCom that contributed to the scandal, Cooper laid blame on Bernie Ebbers for his risk-taking approach that led to loading up the company with $40 billion in debt to fund one acquisition after another. He followed the same reckless strategy with his own investments, taking out loans and using his WorldCom stock as collateral. Cooper believed that Ebbers's personal decisions then affected his business decisions; he ultimately saw his net worth disappear, and he was left owing WorldCom some $400 million for loans approved by the board. Ebbers was sentenced to 25 years in jail for his offenses.

Betty Vinson, the company's former director of corporate reporting, was one of five former WorldCom executives who pleaded guilty to fraud. At the trial of Ebbers, Vinson said she was told to make improper accounting entries because Ebbers did not want to disappoint Wall Street. "I felt like if I didn't make the entries, I wouldn't be working there," Vinson testified. She said that she even drafted a resignation letter in 2000, but ultimately she stayed with the company.

Vinson said that she took her concerns to Sullivan, who told her that Ebbers did not want to lower Wall Street expectations. Asked how she chose which accounts to alter, Vinson testified: "I just really pulled some out of the air. I used some spreadsheets."[2]

Her lawyer had urged the judge to sentence Vinson to probation, citing the pressure placed on her by Ebbers and Sullivan. "She expressed her concern about what she was being directed to do to upper management, and to Sullivan and Ebbers, who assured her and lulled her into believing that all was well," he said. In the end, Vinson was sentenced to five months in prison and five months of house arrest.

## Questions

1. What is the difference between accrual earnings and cash earnings? In addition to the effect on accrual earnings of capitalizing the line costs, how might the treatment mask the true nature of operating cash flows?
2. Identify the stakeholders in the WorldCom case and how their interests were affected by the financial fraud.
3. Use ethical reasoning to compare the actions of Cynthia Cooper in the WorldCom case to those of Sherron Watkins in the Enron case, discussed earlier in this chapter.

[1]David K. Katz and Julia Homer, "WorldCom Whistle-blower Cynthia Cooper," *CFO Magazine*, February 1, 2008. Available at: www.cfo.com/article.cfm/10590507.

[2]Susan Pulliam, "Ordered to Commit Fraud, a Staffer Balked, Then Caved: Accountant Betty Vinson Helped Cook the Books at WorldCom," *The Wall Street Journal*, June 23, 2003. Available at www.people.tamu.edu/~jstrawser/acct229h/Current%20 Readings/E.%20WSJ.com%20-%20A%20Staffer%20 Ordered%20to%20Commit%20Fraud,%20Balked.pdf.

## Case 2-2

# Better Boston Beans

Better Boston Beans is a coffee shop located in the Faneuil Hall Marketplace near the waterfront and Government Center in Boston. It specializes in exotic blends of coffee, including Sumatra Dark Roast Black, India Mysore "Gold Nuggets," and Guatemala Antigua. It also serves a number of blended coffees, including Reggae Blend, Jamaican Blue Mountain Blend, and Marrakesh Blend. For those with more pedestrian tastes, the shop serves French Vanilla, Hazelnut, and Hawaiian Macadamia Nut varieties. The coffee of the day varies, but the most popular is Colombia Supremo. The coffee shop also serves a variety of cold-blended coffees.

Cindie Rosen has worked for Better Boston Beans for six months. She took the job right out of college because she wasn't sure whether she wanted to go to graduate school before beginning a career in financial services. Cindie hoped that by taking a year off before starting her career or going on to graduate school, she would experience "the real world" and find out firsthand what it is like to work a 40-hour week. (She did not have a full-time job during her college years because her parents helped pay for the tuition.)

Because Cindie is the "new kid on the block," she is often asked to work the late shift, from 4 p.m. to midnight. She works with one other person, Jeffrey Lyndell, who is the assistant shift supervisor. Lyndell has been with Boston Beans for three years but recently was demoted from shift supervisor.

For the past two weeks, Lyndell has been leaving before 11 p.m., after most of the stores in the Marketplace close, and he has asked Cindie to close up by herself. Cindie feels that this is wrong and it is starting to concern her, but she hasn't spoken to Lyndell and has not informed the store manager either. However, something happened one night that is causing Cindie to consider taking the next step.

At 11 p.m., 10 Japanese tourists came into the store for coffee. Cindie was alone and had to rush around and make five different cold-blended drinks and five different hot-blended coffees. While she was working, one of the Japanese tourists, who spoke English very well, approached her and said that he was shocked that such a famous American coffee shop would only have one worker in the store at any time during the workday. Cindie didn't want to ignore the man's comments, so she answered that her coworker had to go home early because he was sick. That seemed to satisfy the tourist.

It took Cindie almost 20 minutes to make all the drinks and also field two phone calls that came in during that time. After she closed for the night, Cindie reflected on the experience. She realized that it could get worse before it gets better because Lyndell was now making it a habit to leave work early.

At this point, she realizes that she has to either approach Lyndell about it or speak with the store manager. She feels much more comfortable talking to the store manager. In fact, in Cindie's own words, "Lyndell gives me the creeps."

## Questions

1. Consider Kohlberg's six stages of moral development. What would Cindie do and why if she reasoned at each of the six stages?

2. Assume that Cindie approached Lyndell about her concerns. Lyndell tells Cindie that he has an alcohol problem. Lately, it's gotten to him real bad. That's why he's left early—to get a drink and calm his nerves. Lyndell also said that this is the real reason he was demoted. He had been warned that if one more incident occurred, the store manager would fire him. He pleaded with Cindie to work with him through these hard times. How would you react to Lyndell's request if you were Cindie? Would you honor his request for confidentiality and support? Why or why not? What if Lyndell was a close personal friend—would that change your answer? Be sure to consider the implications of your decision on other parties potentially affected by your actions.

3. Assume that Cindie keeps quiet. The following week, another incident occurred: Cindie got into a shouting match with a customer who became tired of waiting for his coffee after 10 minutes. Cindie felt terrible about it, apologized to the customer after serving his coffee, and left work that night wondering if it was time to apply to graduate school. The customer was so irate that he contacted the store manager and expressed his displeasure about both the service and Cindie's attitude. What do you think the store manager should do? Support your answer with ethical reasoning.

## Case 2-3

# The Tax Return

Brenda Sells sent the tax return that she prepared for the president of Purple Industries, Inc., Harry Kohn, to Vincent Dim, the manager of the tax department at her accounting firm. Dim asked Sells to come to his office at 9 a.m. on Friday, April 12, 2013. Sells had no idea why Dim wanted to speak to her. The only reason she could come up with was the tax return for Kohn.

"Brenda, come in," Vincent said.

"Thank you, Vincent," Brenda responded.

"Do you know why I asked to see you?"

"I'm not sure. Does it have something to do with the tax return for Mr. Kohn?" asked Brenda.

"That's right," answered Vincent.

"Is there a problem?" Brenda asked.

"I just spoke with Kohn. I told him that you want to report his winnings from the lottery. He was incensed."

"Why?" Brenda asked. "You and I both know that the tax law is quite clear on this matter. When a taxpayer wins money by playing the lottery, then that amount must be reported as revenue. The taxpayer can offset lottery gains with lottery losses, if those are supportable. Of course, the losses cannot be higher than the amount of the gains. In the case of Mr. Kohn, the losses exceed the gains, so there is no net tax effect. I don't see the problem."

"Let me tell you the problem," Vincent stated sharply. "It's taken me years to gain Kohn's trust. Our firm now audits his company's books, prepares its annual tax return, prepares Kohn's personal tax return, and provides financial planning services for both. Kohn and Purple Industries together are the largest clients in our office. I can't afford to lose any of the business these clients provide for our firm. As you know, we are under increasing competition from larger regional firms that are looking for new clients. If we don't support Kohn, some other firm will step in and do it. Poof, there goes 20 percent of our revenues."

Brenda didn't know what to say. Vincent seemed to be telling her the lottery amounts shouldn't be reported. But that was against the law. She turned to Vincent and asked: "Are you telling me to forget about the lottery amounts on Mr. Kohn's tax return?"

"I want you to go back to your office and think carefully about the situation. Consider that this is a one-time request and we value our staff members who are willing to be flexible in such situations. Let's meet again in my office tomorrow at 9 a.m."

## Questions

1. Assume that Brenda has no reason to doubt Vincent's veracity with respect to the statement that it is "a one-time request." Should that make a difference in what Brenda decides to do? Why or why not?

2. Analyze the alternatives available to Brenda using Kohlberg's six stages of moral development. That is, what would Brenda's position be when she meets with Vincent assuming that her judgment was influenced by relevant factors at each of the six different stages of moral development?

3. Assume that Brenda decides to go along with Vincent and omits the lottery losses and gains. Next year, the same situation arises, but now it's with gambling losses and gains. If you were Brenda, and Vincent asked you to do the same thing you did last year regarding omitting the lottery losses and gains, what would you do this second year? Why?

## Case 2-4

# Shifty Industries

Shifty Industries is a small business that sells home beauty products in the San Luis Obispo, California, area. The company has experienced a cash crunch and is unable to pay its bills on a timely basis. A great deal of pressure exists to minimize cash outflows such as income tax payments to the Internal Revenue Service (IRS) by interpreting income tax regulations as liberally as possible. You are the tax accountant at the company and report to the controller. You are concerned about the fact that

the controller approved the income statement shown here for the company at December 31, 2012, for financial reporting purposes. Your concern relates to the accounting treatment of depreciation in light of the IRS Section 179 depreciation regulations displayed in Exhibit 1. The depreciation relates to the purchase of one item of office machinery in 2012 for $40,000. The asset is expected to have a five-year useful life, with no salvage value, and the company uses the straight-line method

---

**EXHIBIT 1**
**FIRST-YEAR EXPENSING (IRS SECTION 179 DEDUCTION)**

**Shifty Industries**
**Income Statement**
**For the Year Ended December 31, 2012**

| | | | |
|---|---|---|---|
| **Sales Revenue:** | | | |
| Total Sales | $137,460 | | |
| Less: Sales Returns | (2,060) | | |
| Sales Discounts | (5,190) | | |
| Net Sales Revenue | | | $130,210 |
| **Less: Cost of Goods Sold:** | | | |
| Beginning Inventory | $ 12,300 | | |
| Add: Purchases | 67,310 | | |
| Freight-In | 4,450 | $ 84,060 | |
| Less: Purchase Discounts | (3,900) | | |
| Purchase Returns | (1,000) | (4,900) | |
| Less: Ending Inventory | | (16,170) | |
| Cost of Goods Sold | | | 62,990 |
| Gross Profit | | | $67,220 |
| **Operating Expenses** | | | |
| **Selling Expenses:** | | | |
| Freight-Out | $6,150 | | |
| Advertising Expense | 5,790 | | |
| Sales Commissions Expense | 3,470 | | |
| **Administrative Expenses:** | | | |
| Office Salaries Expense | 18,510 | | |
| Office Rent Expense | 14,000 | | |
| Office Supplies Expense | 5,330 | | |
| Depreciation of Office Machinery | 40,000 | | |
| Total Operating Expenses | | | (93,250) |
| Operating Loss | | | $(26,030) |
| **Other Incomes and Expenses:** | | | |
| Gains on Sale Equipment | | $2,430 | |
| Less: Loss on Sales of Investments | (1,640) | | |
| Interest Expense | (930) | (2,570) | |
| Net Other Incomes and Expenses | | | (140) |
| Net Loss | | | ($26,170) |

of depreciation for all office machinery in its financial reports. You reviewed the income statement to help prepare the income tax return for the company that will be filed on April 30, 2013.

A special rule known as "expensing" lets small businesses write off the entire cost of certain depreciable assets in the year they are purchased.

In other words, you get to treat the cost as a business expense (hence "expensing"), such as salary paid or utilities, rather than an asset that has to be depreciated over a number of years. Property that qualifies for this tax break includes machinery, tools, furniture, fixtures, computers, software, and vehicles. (This special rule often goes by the alias "the Section 179 deduction" to give homage to the section of the tax law that allows it.)

This deduction is limited in several ways:

- **Dollar limit.** For assets placed in service in 2012, you can take a maximum expensing deduction of $500,000—a higher-than-normal level approved by Congress to help the struggling economy.

- **Investment limit.** As a way to focus this tax break on smaller businesses, firms whose investment in new property exceeds a threshold amount gradually lose the right to expensing. For 2012, the investment threshold is $2,000,000. For example, if you purchased $2,020,000 of otherwise eligible equipment in 2012, you can't expense more than $480,000 (the $500,000 expensing maximum minus the excess investment of $20,000).

- **Taxable income limit.** Your total first-year expensing deduction cannot exceed your business's taxable income. Say, for example, that you bought $40,000 of property eligible for expensing in 2012, but your firm's taxable income before taking expensing into account is just $20,000. That means your expensing deduction is limited to $20,000; you can carry over the disallowed $20,000 to 2013 and claim an expensing deduction then, assuming that you have sufficient business income.

## Questions

Consider the professional and ethical standards and ethical reasoning methods discussed in Chapters 1 and 2 in answering the following questions.

1. Has the company properly handled the depreciation of the one item of machinery reflected on its income statement for the year ended December 31, 2012? Why or why not?

2. How would you handle the depreciation deduction for income tax purposes?

3. How should the controller handle the matter, assuming that the financial reports have not been issued as yet, and that he reasons at stages 3, 4, and 5 in Kohlberg's model?

## Case 2-5

# Blues Brothers

Assume that it is December 31, the last day of the fiscal year, and you are an internal accountant for Saturday Night Accessories, a privately owned company run by the Blues Brothers, that provides personal services to consumers. On that date, a $1.2 million major contract for one year of future services is received. You are instructed by your supervisor who reports to the "Brothers" to record the full amount of the $1.2 million as revenue on December 31. You know that management will receive a bonus for the boosted revenue and you will receive recognition in an upcoming performance review.

## Questions

1. What is the proper way to account for the revenue in this case? Why?
2. How might you go about convincing your supervisor of the proper accounting? That is, what factors might enable you to get your point across, and what are disablers that might prevent you from achieving that result?
3. Under what circumstances might you consider going to the "Brothers" to discuss the matter?

## Case 2-6

# Supreme Designs, Inc.

Supreme Designs, Inc., is a small manufacturing company located in Detroit, Michigan. The company has three stockholders—Gary Hoffman, Ed Webber, and John Sullivan. Hoffman manages the business, including the responsibility for the financial statements. Webber and Sullivan do most of the sales work, and they cultivate potential customers for Supreme Designs.

Hoffman recently hired his daughter, Janet, to manage the office. Janet has successfully managed a small clothing boutique in downtown Detroit for the past eight years. She sold the shop to a regional department store that wanted to expand its operations. Gary Hoffman hopes that his daughter will take over as an owner in a few years when he reaches retirement age. Webber and Sullivan are significantly younger than Gary Hoffman.

Janet is given complete control over the payroll, and she approves disbursements, signs checks, and reconciles the general ledger cash account to the bank statement balance. Previously, the bookkeeper was the only employee with such authority. However, the bookkeeper recently left the company, and Hoffman needed someone whom he could trust to be in charge of these sensitive operations. He did ask his daughter to hire someone as soon as possible to help with these and other accounting functions. Janet hired Kevin Greenberg shortly thereafter, based on a friend's recommendation. Greenberg is a relatively inexperienced accountant, but he was willing to work for less than what the company had paid the former bookkeeper.

On April 29, 2013, about one year after hiring Greenberg, Janet discovers that she needs surgery. Even though the procedure is fairly common and the risks are minimal, she plans on spending five weeks in recovery because of related medical problems that could flare up if she returns to work too soon. She tells Greenberg to approve vouchers for payment and present them to her father during this time, and her father will write the checks during her absence. Janet had previously discussed this plan with her father, and they both agreed that Greenberg was ready to assume the additional responsibilities. They did not, however, discuss the matter with either Webber or Sullivan.

The bank statement for April arrives on May 3, 2013. Janet did not tell Greenberg to reconcile the bank statements. In fact, she specifically told him to just put those aside until her return. However, Greenberg decides to reconcile the April bank statement as a favor to Janet and to lighten her workload after she returns.

Although everything appears to be in order, Greenberg is not sure what to make of his finding that Janet approved and signed five checks payable to herself, each for the same amount, during April 2013. Each check appears in correct numerical sequence, 1 check of every 10 checks written during the month. Greenberg was surprised because if these were payroll checks (as he had suspected because they were for the same amount), it was highly unusual. This is because the payroll is processed once a month for all employees of Supreme Designs. In fact, he found only one canceled check for each of the other employees, including himself.

Curiosity gets the better of Greenberg, and he decides to trace the checks paid to Janet to the cash disbursements journal. He looked for supporting documentation but couldn't find any. He noticed that four of the five checks were coded to different accounts: one each to supplies, travel and entertainment, and books and magazines, and two to miscellaneous expenses.

After considering what his findings might mean and whether he should contact Janet, Greenberg decided to expand his search. He reviewed the bank statements for January through March 2013. In all, there were 15 additional checks made payable to Janet, each for the same amount as the 5 in April. These 20 checks totaled $30,000. Greenberg still thought it was possible that these amounts represented Janet's salary because he knows that her annual salary is $50,000. Perhaps she took out a little more this year.

Greenberg doesn't know what to do. He could contact Janet, but he knows that she would be unhappy that he opened the bank statements and went so far as to reconcile cash for April even though she specifically told him not to. Perhaps he should contact the three stockholders. Then again, it may be best to keep quiet about the entire matter.

## Questions

1. Do you think Greenberg did the "right" thing by opening the April bank statement and reconciling it to the general ledger? Why or why not? What about the previous bank statements?

2. Explain what Greenberg should do if he reasons at each of the six stages of Kohlberg's model of moral development. Be sure to consider stakeholder effects in your answer.

3. Evaluate what steps should be taken in each of the following independent situations:

   a. If you were Janet and Greenberg dropped by the hospital to tell you about his discovery, how would you react?

   b. Assume that Greenberg contacts Janet's father because he did not want to upset her after the surgery. Hoffman talks to his daughter, who informs him that she had a shortage in her personal funds and planned to repay the $30,000 after she returns. What would you do if you were Gary Hoffman? Why?

   c. Assume that Hoffman does nothing because of his daughter's explanation. Janet returns to work and fires Kevin Greenberg. What would you do if you were Greenberg? Why? How do you think his action (or inaction) might affect his opportunity for other jobs? Should that matter in terms of what he decides to do?

## Case 2-7

# Milton Manufacturing Company

Milton Manufacturing Company produces a variety of textiles for distribution to wholesale manufacturers of clothing products. The company's primary operations are located in Long Island City, New York, with branch factories and warehouses in several surrounding cities. Milton Manufacturing is a closely held company, and Irv Milton is the president. He started the business in 2002, and it grew in revenue from $500,000 to $5 million in 10 years. However, the revenues declined to $4.5 million in 2012. Net cash flows from all activities also were declining. The company was concerned because it planned to borrow $20 million from the credit markets in the fourth quarter of 2013.

Irv Milton met with Ann Plotkin, the chief accounting officer (CAO), on January 15, 2013, to discuss a proposal by Plotkin to control cash outflows. She was not overly concerned about the recent decline in net cash flows from operating activities because these amounts were expected to increase in 2013 as a result of projected higher levels of revenue and cash collections.

Plotkin knew that if overall capital expenditures continued to increase at the rate of 26 percent per year, Milton Manufacturing probably would not be able to borrow the $20 million. Therefore, she suggested establishing a new policy to be instituted on a temporary basis. Each plant's capital expenditures for 2013 would be limited to the level of capital expenditures in 2011. Irv Milton pointedly asked Plotkin about the possible negative effects of such a policy,

but in the end, he was convinced that it was necessary to initiate the policy immediately to stem the tide of increases in capital expenditures. A summary of cash flows appears in Exhibit 1.

Sammie Markowicz is the plant manager at the headquarters in Long Island City. He was informed of the new capital expenditure policy by Ira Sugofsky, the vice president for operations. Markowicz told Sugofsky that the new policy could negatively affect plant operations because certain machinery and equipment, essential to the production process, had been breaking down more frequently during the past two years. The problem was primarily with the motors. New and better models with more efficient motors had been developed by an overseas supplier. These were expected to be available by April 2013. Markowicz planned to order 1,000 of these new motors for the Long Island City operation, and he expected that other plant managers would do the same. Sugofsky told Markowicz to delay the acquisition of new motors for one year, after which time the restrictive capital expenditure policy would be lifted. Markowicz reluctantly agreed.

Milton Manufacturing operated profitably during the first six months of 2013. Net cash inflows from investing activities exceeded outflows by $250,000 during this time period. It was the first time in three years that there was a positive cash flow from investing activities. Production operations accelerated during the third quarter as a result of increased

---

**EXHIBIT 1**
**MILTON MANUFACTURING COMPANY**
Summary of Cash Flows
For the Years Ended December 31, 2012 and 2011 (000 omitted)

|  | December 31, 2012 | December 31, 2011 |
|---|---|---|
| **Cash Flows from Operating Activities** | | |
| Net income | $    372 | $    542 |
| Adjustments to reconcile net income to net cash provided by operating activities | 1,350 | 1,383 |
| Net cash provided by operating activities | $ 1,722 | $ 1,925 |
| **Cash Flows from Investing Activities** | | |
| Capital expenditures | $ (2,420) | $ (1,918) |
| Other investing inflows (outflows) | 176 | 84 |
| Net cash used in investing activities | $ (2,244) | $ (1,834) |
| **Cash Flows from Financing Activities** | | |
| Net cash provided (used in) financing activities | $    168 | $    (376) |
| **Increase (decrease) in cash and cash equivalents** | $    (354) | $    (285) |
| **Cash and cash equivalents—beginning of the year** | $    506 | $    791 |
| **Cash and cash equivalents—end of the year** | $    152 | $    506 |

demand for Milton's textiles. An aggressive advertising campaign initiated in late 2012 seemed to bear fruit for the company. Unfortunately, the increased level of production put pressure on the machines, and the degree of breakdown was increasing. A big problem was that the motors wore out prematurely.

Markowicz was concerned about the machine breakdown and increasing delays in meeting customer demands for the shipment of the textile products. He met with the other branch plant managers, who complained bitterly to him about not being able to spend the money to acquire new motors. Markowicz was very sensitive to their needs. He informed them that the company's regular supplier had recently announced a 25 percent price increase for the motors. Other suppliers followed suit, and Markowicz saw no choice but to buy the motors from the overseas supplier. That supplier's price was lower, and the quality of the motors would significantly enhance the machines' operating efficiency. However, the company's restrictions on capital expenditures stood in the way of making the purchase.

Markowicz approached Sugofsky and told him about the machine breakdowns and the concerns of other plant managers. Sugofsky seemed indifferent. He reminded Markowicz of the capital expenditure restrictions in place and that the Long Island City plant was committed to keep expenditures at the same level as it had in 2011. Markowicz argued that he was faced with an unusual situation and he had to act now. Sugofsky hurriedly left, but not before he said to Markowicz: "A policy is a policy."

Markowicz reflected on the comment and his obligations to Milton Manufacturing. He was conflicted because he viewed his primary responsibility and that of the other plant managers to ensure that the production process operated smoothly. The last thing the workers needed right now was a stoppage of production because of machine failure.

At this time, Markowicz learned of a 30-day promotional price offered by the overseas supplier to gain new customers by lowering the price for all motors by 25 percent. Coupled with the 25 percent increase in price by the company's supplier, Markowicz knew he could save the company $1,500, or 50 percent of cost, on each motor purchased from the overseas supplier.

After carefully considering the implications of his intended action, Markowicz contacted the other plant managers and informed them that while they were not obligated to follow his lead because of the capital expenditure policy, he planned to purchase 1,000 motors from the overseas supplier for the headquarters plant in Long Island City.

Markowicz made the purchase in the fourth quarter of 2013 without informing Sugofsky. He convinced the plant accountant to record the $1.5 million expenditure as an operating (not capital) expenditure because he knew that the higher level of operating cash inflows would mask the effect of his expenditure. In fact, Markowicz was proud that he had "saved" the company $1.5 million, and he did what

was necessary to ensure that the Long Island City plant continued to operate.

The acquisitions by Markowicz and the other plant managers enabled the company to keep up with the growing demand for textiles, and the company finished the year with record high levels of net cash inflows from all activities. Markowicz was lauded by his team for his leadership. The company successfully executed a loan agreement with Second Bankers Hours & Trust Co. The $20 million borrowed was received on January 3, 2014.

During the course of an internal audit on January 21, 2014, Beverly Wald, the chief internal auditor (and also a CPA), discovered that there was an unusually high number of motors in inventory. A complete check of the inventory determined that $1 million worth of motors remained on hand.

Wald reported her findings to Ann Plotkin, and together they went to see Irv Milton. After being informed of the situation, Milton called in Sugofsky. When Wald told him about her findings, Sugofsky's face turned beet red. He paced the floor, poured a glass of water, drank it quickly, and then began his explanation. Sugofsky told them about his encounter with Markowicz. Sugofsky stated in no uncertain terms that he had told Markowicz not to increase plant expenditures beyond the 2011 level. "I left the meeting believing that he understood the company's policy. I knew nothing about the purchase," he stated.

At this point, Wald joined in and explained to Sugofsky that the $1 million is accounted for as inventory, not as an operating cash outflow: "What we do in this case is transfer the motors out of inventory and into the machinery account once they are placed into operation because, according to the documentation, the motors added significant value to the asset." Sugofsky had a perplexed look on his face. Finally, Irv Milton took control of the accounting lesson by asking: "What's the difference? Isn't the main issue that Markowicz did not follow company policy?" The three officers in the room shook their head simultaneously, perhaps in gratitude for being saved the additional lecturing. Milton then said he wanted the three of them to brainstorm some alternatives on how best to deal with the Markowicz situation and present the choices to him in one week.

## Questions

Use the Integrated Ethical Decision-Making Process explained in this chapter to help you assess the following:

1. Identify the ethical and professional issues of concern to Beverly Wald in this case.

2. Identify and evaluate the alternative courses of action for Wald, Plotkin, and Sugofsky to present in their meeting with Milton.

3. How do virtue considerations influence the alternatives presented?

4. If you were in Milton's place, which of the alternatives would you choose and why?

## Case 2-8

# Juggyfroot

"I'm sorry, Lucy. That's the way it is," Ricardo Rikey said.

"I just don't know if I can go along with it, Rikey," Lucy replied.

"We have no choice. Juggyfroot is our biggest client, Lucy. They've warned us that they will put the engagement up for bid if we refuse to go along with the reclassification of marketable securities," Rikey explained.

"Have you spoken to Fred and Ethel about this?" Lucy asked.

"Are you kidding? They're the ones who made the decision to go along with Juggyfroot," Rikey responded.

The previous scene took place in the office of Deziloo LLP, a large CPA firm in Beverly Hills, California. Lucy Spheroid is the partner on the engagement of Juggyfroot, a publicly owned global manufacturer of pots and pans and other household items. Ricardo Rikey is the managing partner of the office. Fred and Ethel are the two members of the firm that make final judgments on difficult accounting issues, especially when there is a difference of opinion with the client. All four are CPAs.

Ricardo Rikey is preparing for a meeting with Norman Baitz, the CEO of Juggyfroot. Rikey knows that the company expects to borrow $5 million next quarter and it wants to put the best possible face on its financial statements to impress the banks. That would explain why the company reclassified a $2 million market loss on a trading investment to the available-for-sale category so that the "loss" would now show up in stockholder's equity, not as a charge against current income. The result was to increase earnings in 2013 by 8 percent. Rikey also knows that without the change, the earnings would have declined by 2 percent and the company's stock price would have taken a hit.

In the meeting, Rikey points out to Baitz that the investment in question was marketable, and in the past, the company had sold similar investments in less than one year. Rikey adds there is no justification under generally accepted accounting principles (GAAP) to change the classification from trading to available-for-sale.

## Questions

1. Explain the rules in accounting to determine whether an investment in a marketable security should be accounted for as trading, available-for-sale, or held-to-maturity. Include in your discussion how such classification affects the financial statements.

2. Who are the stakeholders in this case? What expectations should they have, and what are the ethical obligations of Deziloo and its CPAs to the stakeholders? Use ethical reasoning to answer this question.

3. Using the AICPA Code of Professional Conduct as a reference, what ethical issues exist for Rikey, Lucy, Fred, Ethel, and Deziloo LLP in this matter? What role does auditor virtue play in determining what to do in this case?

## Case 2-9

# Phar-Mor

## The Dilemma

The story of Phar-Mor shows how quickly a company that built its earnings on fraudulent transactions can dissolve like an Alka-Seltzer.

One day, Stan Cherelstein, the controller of Phar-Mor, discovered cabinets stuffed with held checks totaling $10 million. Phar-Mor couldn't release the checks to vendors because it did not have enough cash in the bank to cover the amount. Cherelstein wondered what he should do.

## Background

Phar-Mor was a chain of discount drugstores, based in Youngstown, Ohio, and founded in 1982 by Michael Monus and David Shapira. In less than 10 years, the company grew from 15 to 310 stores and had 25,000 employees. According to Litigation Release No. 14716 issued by the SEC,[1] Phar-Mor had cumulatively overstated income by $290 million between 1987 and 1991. In 1992, prior to disclosure of the fraud, the company overstated income by an additional $238 million.

## The Cast of Characters

Mickey Monus personifies the hard-driving entrepreneur who is bound and determined to make it big whatever the cost. He served as the president and chief operating officer (COO) of Phar-Mor from its inception until a corporate restructuring was announced on July 28, 1992.

David Shapira was the CEO of both Phar-Mor and Giant Eagle, Phar-Mor's parent company and majority stockholder. Giant Eagle also owned Tamco, which was one of Phar-Mor's major suppliers. Shapira left day-to-day operations of Phar-Mor to Monus until the fraud became too large and persistent to ignore.

Patrick Finn was the CFO of Phar-Mor from 1988 to 1992. Finn, who holds the Certified Management Accountant (CMA) certification, initially brought Monus the bad news that following a number of years of eroding profits, the company faced millions in losses in 1989.

John Anderson was the accounting manager at Phar-Mor. Hired after completing a college degree in accounting at Youngstown State University, Anderson became a part of the fraud.

[1] Securities and Exchange Commission, Litigation Release No. 14716, November 9, 1995, *SEC v. Michael Monus, Patrick Finn, John Anderson and Jeffrey Walley,* Case No. 4:95, CV 975 (N.D. OH, filed May 2, 1995), www.sec.gov/litigation/litreleases/lr14716.txt.

Coopers & Lybrand, prior to its merger with Price Waterhouse, were the auditors of Phar-Mor. The firm failed to detect the fraud as it was unfolding.

## How It Started

The facts of this case are taken from the SEC filing and a PBS *Frontline* episode called "How to Steal $500 Million." The interpretation of the facts is consistent with reports, but some literary license has been taken to add intrigue to the case.

Finn approached Monus with the bad news. Monus took out his pen, crossed off the losses, and then wrote in higher numbers to show a profit. Monus couldn't bear the thought of his hot growth company that had been sizzling for five years suddenly flaming out. In the beginning, it was to be a short-term fix to buy time while the company improved efficiency, put the heat on suppliers for lower prices, and turned a profit. Finn believed in Monus's ability to turn things around, so he went along with the fraud. Finn prepared the reports, and Monus changed the numbers for four months before turning the task over to Finn. These reports with the false numbers were faxed to Shapira and given to Phar-Mor's board. Basically, the company was lying to its owners.

The fraud occurred by dumping the losses into a "bucket account" and then reallocating the sums to one of the company's hundreds of stores in the form of increases in inventory amounts. Phar-Mor issued fake invoices for merchandise purchases and made phony journal entries to increase inventory and decrease cost of sales. The company overcounted and double-counted merchandise in inventory.

The fraud was helped by the fact that the auditors from Coopers observed inventory in only 4 out of 300 stores, and that allowed the finance department at Phar-Mor to conceal the shortages. Moreover, Coopers informed Phar-Mor in advance which stores they would visit. Phar-Mor executives fully stocked the 4 selected stores but allocated the phony inventory increases to the other 296 stores. Regardless of the accounting tricks, Phar-Mor was heading for collapse and its suppliers threatened to cut off the company for nonpayment of bills.

## Stan Cherelstein's Role

Cherelstein, a CPA, was hired to be the controller of Phar-Mor in 1991, long after the fraud had begun. One day, Anderson, Phar-Mor's accounting manager, called Cherelstein into his office and explained that the company had been keeping two sets of books—one that showed the true state of the company with the losses and the other, called the "subledger," that showed the falsified numbers that were presented to the auditors.

Cherelstein and Anderson discussed what to do about the fraud. Cherelstein was not happy about it at all and demanded to meet with Monus. Cherelstein did get Monus to agree to repay the company for the losses from Monus's (personal) investment of company funds into the World Basketball League (WBL). But Monus never kept his word. In the beginning, Cherelstein felt compelled to give Monus some time to turn things around through increased efficiencies and by using a device called "exclusivity fees," which vendors paid to get Phar-Mor to stock their products. Over time, Cherelstein became more and more uncomfortable as the suppliers called more and more frequently, demanding payment on their invoices.

## Accounting Fraud

### *Misappropriation of Assets*

The unfortunate reality of the Phar-Mor saga was that it involved not only bogus inventory but also the diversion of company funds to feed Monus's personal habits. One example was the movement of $10 million in company funds to help start the WBL.

### *False Financial Statements*

According to the ruling by the U.S. Court of Appeals that heard Monus's appeal of his conviction on all 109 counts of fraud, the company submitted false financial statements to Pittsburgh National Bank, which increased a revolving credit line for Phar-Mor from $435 million to $600 million in March 1992. It also defrauded Corporate Partners, an investment group that bought $200 million in Phar-Mor stock in June 1991. The list goes on, including the defrauding of Chemical Bank, which served as the placing agent for $155 million in 10-year senior secured notes issued to Phar-Mor; Westinghouse Credit Corporation, which had executed a $50 million loan commitment to Phar-Mor in 1987; and Westminster National Bank, which served as the placing agent for $112 million in Phar-Mor stock sold to various financial institutions in 1991.

### *Tamco Relationship*

The early financial troubles experienced by Phar-Mor in 1988 can be attributed to at least two transactions. The first was that the company provided deep discounts to retailers to stock its stores with product. There was concern early on that the margins were too thin. The second was that its supplier, Tamco, was shipping partial orders to Phar-Mor while billing for full orders. Phar-Mor had no way of knowing this because it was not logging in shipments from Tamco.

After the deficiency was discovered, Giant Eagle agreed to pay Phar-Mor $7 million in 1988 on behalf of Tamco. Phar-Mor later bought Tamco from Giant Eagle in an additional effort to solve the inventory and billing problems. However, the losses just kept on coming.

## Back to the Dilemma

Cherelstein looked out the window at the driving rain. He thought about the fact that he didn't start the fraud or engage in the cover-up. Still, he knows about it now and feels compelled to do something. Cherelstein thought about the persistent complaints by vendors that they were not being paid and their threats to cut off shipments to Phar-Mor. Cherelstein knows that without any product in Phar-Mor stores, the company could not last much longer.

## Questions

1. How do you assess blame for the fraud? That is, to what extent was it caused by Finn's willingness to go along with the actions of Monus? What about Shapira's lax oversight? Should all the blame go to Monus? What role did Coopers & Lybrand play with respect to its professional judgment?

2. Assume Cherelstein decides to use Rest's Model of Morality to reason out what the right thing to do is and how to carry out the action. Apply the logic of the model to Cherelstein's decision-making process. What do you think he should do at this point and why?

3. What is the ethical message of Phar-Mor? That is, explain what you think is the moral of this story.

## Case 2-10

# Gateway Hospital

Troy just returned from a business trip for health care administrators in Orlando. Kristen, a relatively new employee who reports to him, also attended the conference. Troy works for Gateway Hospital, a for-profit hospital in the St. Louis area. The Orlando conference included training in the newest regulations over health care, networking with other hospital administrators, and reports on upcoming legislation in health care. The conference was in early March and coincided with Troy's kids school spring break, so the entire family traveled to Orlando.

The hospital's expense reimbursement policy is very clear on the need for receipts for all reimbursements. Meals are covered for those not included in the conference, but only within a pre-set range. Troy has never had a problem following those guidelines. However, the trip to Orlando was more expensive than Troy expected. He did not attend all sessions of the conference to enjoy time with his family. Upon return to St. Louis, Troy's wife suggested that Troy submit three meals and one extra night at the hotel as business expenses, even though they were personal expenses. Her rationale was that the hospital policies would not totally cover the business costs of the trip. Troy often has to travel and misses family time that cannot be recovered or replaced. Troy also knows that his boss has a reputation of signing forms without reading or careful examination.

Kristen is approached by the head of the accounting department about Troy's expenses, which seem high and not quite right. Kirsten is asked about the extra night because she did not ask for reimbursement for that time. Kristen knows it can be easily explained by saying Troy had to stay an extra day for additional meetings, a common occurrence for administrators, although that was not the case. She also knows that the hospital has poor controls and a culture of "not rocking the boat," and that other employees have routinely inflated expense reports in the past. Assume that you are in Kristen's position. How would you respond to the inquiry of the head of the accounting department? In considering your response, address the following issues.

## Questions

1. What is at stake for the key parties? What is at stake for you [Kristen]?

2. What are the main arguments that you are trying to counter, assuming that you know Troy's position on the matter, and what are the reasons and rationalizations that you need to address?

3. What should Kristen do and what ethical considerations should influence her decision?

# 3

# Creating an Ethical Organization Environment and Effective Corporate Governance Systems

## THE *CHALLENGER* SHUTTLE DISASTER

The culture of an organization can affect the behavior of employees, as occurred at Penn State and Enron. As we learned in Chapters 1 and 2, even if your attitudes and beliefs conform to your intended actions, there may be obstacles within the organization that constrain those actions. This may be caused by *ethical fading*, a process by which the ethical dimensions are eliminated from a decision and replaced by considerations such as avoiding bad publicity or making the deal at all costs. In Chapter 2, we learned that *cognitive dissonance* occurs because how we think we should behave differs from how we decide to behave, so we adjust our beliefs to fit our behavior. Both factors were in play at the National Aeronautics and Space Administration (NASA) in the *Challenger* shuttle launch on January 28, 1986, when the solid rocket booster seals failed on takeoff, and 75 seconds after the launch, the space craft erupted into flames killing all aboard including schoolteacher Christa McAuliffe, America's first private citizen in space.

On January 27, the night before the launch, engineers and managers from NASA and from shuttle craft contractor Morton Thiokol met to discuss whether it was safe to launch the *Challenger* at a low temperature. In 7 of the shuttle program's 24 previous launches, problems with the O-rings that kept the seals intact had been detected. Now, under intense time pressure by management, Morton Thiokol engineers quickly put together a presentation that led to their recommendation not to launch because at low temperatures (it was 27°F at launch time), the likelihood of O-ring failure increased.

During a teleconference call, NASA personnel reacted to the engineers' recommendation not to launch with hostility, according to Roger Boisjoly, a Morton Thiokol engineer who participated in the meeting. NASA had already scrubbed the launching twice, and the entire public was watching to see the first "average citizen" in space. Morton Thiokol manager Joe Kilminster asked for a five-minute, offline caucus to reevaluate the data, and as soon as the mute button was pressed, according to Boisjoly,

*(Continued)*

"our general manager, Jerry Mason, said in a soft voice, 'We have to make a management decision.'" "Boisjoly concluded that it was obvious that management was going to change the decision to a launch decision to accommodate the company's major customer.

The general manager of Thiokol turned to his three senior managers and asked what they wanted to do. Two agreed to go to a launch recommendation, and one refused. "So he [the general manager] turns to him and said 'take off your engineering hat and put on your management hat'—and that's exactly what happened," said Boisjoly. "He changed his hat and changed his vote, just 30 minutes after he was the one to give the recommendation not to launch. I didn't agree with one single statement made on the recommendations given by the managers.'"

The teleconference resumed, and NASA heard that Thiokol had changed its decision and gave a recommendation to launch. NASA did not ask why.

"I went home, opened the door and didn't say a word to my wife," added Boisjoly. "She asked me what was wrong and I told her, 'Oh nothing, honey, it was a great day, we just had a meeting to go launch tomorrow and kill the astronauts, but outside of that, it was a great day.'"

How should we evaluate Boisjoly's behavior in the *Challenger* disaster? Unlike Betty Vinson in the WorldCom accounting fraud, Boisjoly did not actively do anything to bring about the failure. However, he did have the technical expertise to know the launch was fraught with danger. According to Johnson, he recognized the ethical problem of launching the shuttle in cold weather but failed to generate a "creative strategy" for preventing the launch. He stopped objecting and deferred to management. "Boisjoly made no effort to go outside the chain of command to express his concerns to the agency director or to the press."[1]

In analyzing the decision-making process in the *Challenger* disaster, Bazerman and Trebrunsel point out that an organization's ethical gap is more than just the sum of the individual gaps of its employees. Group work, the building block of organizations, creates additional ethical gaps. Groupthink—the tendency for cohesive groups to avoid a realistic appraisal of alternative courses of action in favor of unanimity—can prevent groups from challenging questionable decisions, as was the case with NASA's decision to launch the *Challenger.* Morton Thiokol's decision to treat the dilemma as a management decision led to the fading of the ethical dimensions of the problem under consideration, as if it were possible to ignore the human lives at stake.[2]

As you read this chapter, reflect on the following questions: (1) How does organization culture influence ethical decisionmaking? (2) What are the components of a strong system of corporate governance? (3) When should an employee consider blowing the whistle on wrongdoing?

"The thing I have learned at IBM is that culture is everything. Underneath all the sophisticated processes, there is always the company's sense of values and identity."

*Louis V. Gerstner, Jr. former CEO IBM*

This statement by former IBM chief executive officer (CEO) Louis Gerstner highlights one of the themes of this chapter that the culture of an organization establishes the boundaries within which ethical decisions must be made. As we learned from previous chapters, it is one thing to know that you should behave in a certain way, but it is quite another to do it (or even want to do it) given the pressures that may exist from within the organization.

## Seven Signs of Ethical Collapse

In her book *The Seven Signs of Ethical Collapse,* Marianne Jennings analyzes the indicators of possible ethical collapse in companies and provides advice how to avoid impending disaster. She starts with a description of ethical collapse, saying that it "occurs when any organization has drifted from the basic principles of right and wrong," and she uses financial reporting standards and accounting rules as one area where this might occur. She points out that "not all companies that have drifted ethically have violated any laws."[3] Enron did not necessarily violate generally accepted accounting principles (GAAP) in treating the effects of *some* of its transactions with special-purpose entities off-balance-sheet. However, the company ignored conflicts of interest of Andy Fastow who managed some of the entities while wearing a second hat as CFO of Enron during the time the two entities had mutual dealings.

According to Jennings, "When an organization collapses ethically, it means that those in the organization have drifted into rationalizations and legalisms, and all for the purpose of getting the results they want and need at almost any cost." The *Challenger* shuttle disaster is a case in point. Putting the management hat on and taking the engineer's hat off was just a way of rationalizing the launch decision. Jennings links the rationalizations and legalisms to a culture that leads to behavior based on the notion "Everybody does this" and "It's not a question of should we do it." It is a culture of "Can we do it legally?" This mentality occurs because of the combination of the seven factors working together to cloud judgment.[4]

Jennings identifies seven common ethical signs of moral meltdowns in companies that have experienced ethical collapse. The common threads she found that make good people at companies do really dumb things include (1) pressure to maintain numbers; (2) fear and silence; (3) young 'uns and a bigger-than-life CEO (i.e., loyalty to the boss); (4) weak board of directors; (5) conflicts of interest overlooked or unaddressed; (6) innovation like no other company; and (7) goodness in some areas atones for evil in others.[5] We briefly address the signs here and elaborate on some of them later on.

## Pressure to Maintain the Numbers

Jennings points out that the tension between ethics and the bottom line will always be present. The first sign of a culture at risk for ethical collapse occurs when there is not just a focus on numbers and results, but an unreasonable and unrealistic obsession with meeting quantitative goals. This "financial results at all costs" approach was a common ethical problem at both Enron and WorldCom. At WorldCom, the mantra was that financial results had to improve in every quarter, and the shifting of operating expenses to capitalized costs was used to accomplish the goal regardless of the propriety of the accounting treatment. It was an "ends justifies means" culture that sanctioned wrongdoing in the name of earnings. Accountants like Betty Vinson got caught up in the culture and did not know how to extricate themselves from the situation.

## Fear of Reprisals

Fear and silence characterizes a culture where employees are reluctant to raise issues of ethical concern because they may be ignored, treated badly, transferred, or worse. It underlies the whistleblowing process in many organizations where ethical employees want to blow the whistle but fear reprisals, so they stay silent. One aspect of such a culture is a "kill the messenger syndrome," whereby an employee brings bad news to higher-ups with the best intentions of having the organization correct the matter, but instead the messenger is treated as an outcast.

## Loyalty to the Boss

Dennis Kozlowski was the dominant, larger-then-life CEO of Tyco International, who had an appetite for a lavish style of living. He surrounded himself with young people who were taken by his stature and would not question his actions. Kozlowski, who once spent $6,000 on a shower curtain for an apartment paid for by the company, made sure these "young 'uns" received all the trappings of success so they would be reluctant to speak up when ethical and legal issues existed for fear of losing their expensive homes, boats, and cars and the prestige that comes along with financial success at a young age. They were selected by the CEO for their positions based on their inexperience, possible conflicts of interest, and unlikelihood to question the boss's decisions. Of course, not all bigger-than-life CEO's are unethical (e.g., Steve Jobs and Warren Buffet).

## Weak Board of Directors

A weak board of directors characterizes virtually all the companies with major accounting frauds in the early part of the 2000s. One example is HealthSouth, one of the largest healthcare providers in the United States specializing in patient rehabilitation services, Richard Scrushy surrounded himself with a weak board so that when he made decisions as CEO at HealthSouth that contributed to an accounting scandal where the company's earnings were falsely inflated by $1.4 billion, the board would go along, in part because of their interrelationships with Scrushy and HealthSouth that created conflicts of interest. Jennings identifies the following conflicts of interest:[6]

- One director earned $250,000 per year from a consulting contract with HealthSouth over a seven-year period.
- Another director had a joint investment venture with Scrushy on a $395,000 investment property.
- Another director's company was awarded a $5.6 million contract to install glass at a hospital being built by HealthSouth.
- MedCenter District, a hospital-supply company that was run online, did business with HealthSouth and was owned by Scrushy, six directors, and the wife of one of those directors.
- The same three directors had served on both the audit committee and the compensation committee for several years.
- Two of the directors had served on the board for 18 years.
- One director received a $425,000 donation to his favorite charity from HealthSouth just prior to his going on the board.

# A Culture of Conflicting Interests

A good example of a culture of conflicts is the dual relationship between financial analysts and investment bankers. Conflicts of interest occur in the financial services industry because of the dual tasks performed by investment banks. On the one hand, they research and conduct financial analysis on corporations issuing securities such as in an initial public offering (IPO); on the other hand, the firms hope to be chosen as the investment banker to underwrite these securities by selling them to the public on behalf of the issuing corporation. Investment banks often combine research and underwriting because the information that is produced for one task is also useful for another task. These relationships are not unlike the conflict that might exist when an audit firm also conducts a financial information systems design and installation engagement for the same client. Doing both for the same client places the firm in the position of having to examine its own work in the course of gathering data to help render an opinion on the client's financial statements.

A conflict of interest arises between research and underwriting because the investment bank attempts to serve the needs of two client groups—the firms for which it is issuing the securities and the investors to whom it sells these securities. These client groups have different information needs: Issuers benefit from optimistic research, whereas investors desire unbiased research. Due to economies of scope, however, both groups will receive the same information.

When the potential revenues from underwriting greatly exceed brokerage commissions, the investment bank has a strong incentive to alter the information provided to both types of clients so as to favor the issuing firms' needs. If the information provided is not favorable to the issuing firm, it might take its business to a competitor that is willing to put out more positive information and thereby entice more people to buy the newly issued stock. For example, an internal Morgan Stanley memo excerpted in *The Wall Street Journal* on July 14, 1992, stated: "Our objective . . . is to adopt a policy, fully understood by the entire firm, including the Research Department, that we do not make negative or controversial comments about our clients as a matter of sound business practice."[7] Because of directives like this one, analysts in investment banks might be persuaded to distort their research to please the underwriting department of their bank and the corporations issuing the securities, and indeed, this seems to have happened during the technology boom of the 1990s. Of course, such actions undermine the reliability of the information that investors use to make their financial decisions and, as a result, diminish the efficiency of securities markets.

## Innovation and Ethics

Sanjay Kumar, the former CEO of Computer Associates (CA), was sentenced to 12 years in prison on August 13, 2007, for his conviction of securities fraud, obstruction of justice, and false statements. A jury found that Kumar presided over a scheme to inflate CA's quarterly sales numbers falsely by adopting a 35-day month internally. Along with the imprisonment, Kumar was ordered to pay an $8 million fine and to make restitution for up to $800 million in losses suffered by investors who lost money as a result of his accounting fraud scheme. Jennings points out that Kumar had an attitude that the company was above the fray because it was so innovative. He is quoted as saying: "Standard accounting rules [were] not the best way to measure [Computer Associate's] results because it had changed to a new business model offering its clients more flexibility."[8]

## Community Involvement and Ethics

Should companies that act ethically in one aspect of their operations be judged less harshly when they violate ethical norms in other areas? This question came up when it was revealed that John Rigas, founder of Adelphia Communications, was convicted on July 8, 2004, of conspiracy, bank fraud, and securities fraud for looting the cable company and duping its investors. Rigas became fond of using the company's money as his personal piggy bank. Most people in the small town of Coudersport, Pennsylvania, where the company was headquartered, were shocked to learn what Rigas had done. He was known for his generosity in supporting people in financial need in the community and in financially supporting projects that enhanced the image of the town.

Jennings sums it up quite well in her book by saying that remedies for the good/evil balancing act include rethinking the popular notions of social responsibility and business and rethinking company activities, perceptions, and realities. "Be very skeptical about 'doing well by doing good.' Instead, companies need to rely on virtue ethics and simplicity: truth, honesty, fairness, and egalitarianism."[9]

## Organizational Influence on Ethical Decision Making

The previous examples illustrate how the ethics of an organization can influence decision making through the culture established by those at the very top. Those who work for an organization need to understand the culture and limitations that it creates. This includes accountants and auditors who work for the company and must meet their responsibilities given that culture. Decisions are not made in a vacuum, but in the context of organizational relationships and expectations for behavior.

Thomas Jones developed an explanatory model that merged Rest's four-step moral reasoning model with Fiske and Taylor's[10] work on social cognition to illustrate the ethical decision-making process of an individual who encounters an ethical dilemma within the context of work. Of particular importance is the role that moral intensity plays in recognizing moral issues. Recall that in Rest's model, ethical perception is the first stage in the decision-making process. Jones argues that the characteristics of the moral issue, what he collectively termed *moral intensity,* influence ethical decision making. Moral issues of high intensity will be more salient because the magnitude of consequences is greater, their effects stand out, and their effects involve significant others (greater social, cultural, psychological, or physical proximity).[11]

## Individual-Organization Interchange

While Jones's model illustrates the impact that moral intensity has on ethical choices and behavior and acknowledges that organizational factors influence the establishment of moral intent and behavior—the last two steps in Rest's model—the model fails to address what Burchard calls the cyclical, ongoing dynamic exchange between the individual and organization, which affects the development and sustaining of one's code of conduct in the organizational context.[12] It was left to Jones and Hiltebeitel to fill the gap when they conducted a study of organizational influence on moral decisions and proposed a model that demonstrated organizational influence on the moral decision-making process. As Jones had done with his previous model, Jones and Hiltebeitel based their model on Rest's moral reasoning and Kohlberg's moral development theory.[13]

The Jones-Hiltebeitel model looks at the role of one's personal code of conduct in ethical behavior within an organization. When an employee is called upon to perform routine tasks—those with no internal conflict or cognitive dissonance—the actions taken were almost automatic. However, when those tasks diverged from the routine, the employee would refer to her personal code of conduct for ethical cues.[14] The implications for ethical behavior within the organization are significant because an unethical individual might act dishonestly in one case, while a virtuous person acts in a truthful, trustworthy manner.

According to the model, when one's personal code is insufficient to make the necessary moral decision, the individual will look at the factors that influenced the formation of the code, including professional and organizational influences to resolve the conflict. The influences that are strongest are the ones that determine the reformation of the individual's code of conduct. The implications for the culture of an organization are significant because an organization that values profits above all else might elicit one kind of response, such as to go along with improper accounting, while an organization that values integrity above all else might lead to questioning improper accounting and doing what one can to reverse false and misleading financial results.

## Ethical Dissonance Model

Burchard points out that the Jones-Hiltebeitel model and others like it pay too little attention to the examination of ethical person-organization fit upon the person-organization exchange, within each of the four potential fit options. Burchard presents what he calls "the Ethical Dissonance Model" to illustrate the interaction between the individual and the organization, based on the person-organization ethical fit at various stages of the contractual relationship in each potential ethical fit scenario.[15] The model is complex, so we restrict our coverage to the basics of the person-organization interchange and its implications for ethical behavior within organizations. This is an important consideration because the ethics of an individual influences the values that one brings to the workplace and decision making, while the ethics (through its culture) of an organization influences that behavior. To keep it simple, we adopt the idea that there can be a dissonance between what is considered ethical and what may actually be "best" for the subject inviting ethical consideration.

Of the four potential fit options, two possess high person-organization fit: (1) high organizational ethics, high individual ethics (High-High), and (2) low organizational ethics, low individual ethics (Low-Low); and two possess low person-organization fit: (1) high organizational ethics, low individual ethics (High-Low) and (2) low organizational ethics, high individual ethics (Low-High).[16]

Let's pause for a moment and consider the practical implications of this model. Imagine that you are interviewing for a position with a mid-sized company in your town. You can easily find out information about the company on the Internet to prepare for the interview, such as the scope of its operations, products and services, customer base, and geographical locations. However, it is less easy to find out about its reputation for ethics, although reports in the media about specific events might be of some use. Now, let's assume that you knew (and understood) what is meant by organizational fit and in this case the fit is Low-High. Would that affect whether you interview with the company? Might you ask questions to better understand why that fit exists? Would it affect your final decision whether to work for the company? The information you might gather during the process could be invaluable when you face ethical dilemmas in the workplace.

In two of the fit options (High-High and Low-Low), no ethical dissonance exists. Person-organization fit is optimal, and the organization is highly effective, either to constructive or destructive ends. The other two (High-Low and Low-High) demonstrate a lack of person-organization fit in the realm of ethics and values.[17]

### *High Organizational Ethics, High Individual Ethics (High-High)[18]*

Assume that you know your values and beliefs are an ethical match for the company you work for. You are likely to continue to stay employed in the organization. The issue for us is how you might assess organizational ethics. Koh and Boo identified three distinct measures of organizational ethics: support for ethical behavior from top management, the ethical climate of the organization, and the connection between career success and ethical behavior.[19] These three factors relate to the culture of the organization and may have implications for actions such as whistleblowing, as will be discussed later in this chapter. Koh and Boo found that positive ethical culture and climate produces favorable organizational outcomes by setting down the ethical philosophy and rules of conduct and practices (i.e., code of ethics).

### *Low Organizational Ethics, Low Individual Ethics (Low-Low)[20]*

When both the individual and organization possess low moral and ethical development, the fit is there, but it is turns in a negative direction. A culture of corruption is difficult to change, and for the employee, it takes more conscious effort to stop the corruption than to participate in it. You might say that the employee adopts the attitude of going along to get along. Padilla et al. contend that "dysfunctional leader behaviors and susceptible followers interacting in the context of a contributing environment produce negative organizational outcomes in which 'followers must consent to, or be unable to resist, a destructive leader.'"[21] Imagine if Diem-Thi Le, whose story was discussed in Chapter 2, had low individual ethics in the low organization ethical environment at Defense Contract Audit Agency (DCAA). It is hard to imagine her taking the steps that she did to stop the misallocation and mischarging of contractor costs to the government.

### *High Organizational Ethics, Low Individual Ethics (High-Low)[22]*

According to Kelman and Hamilton, if the individual possesses lower ethics than that which is held by the organization, the discovery of an individual's lack of person-organization fit is often pointed out by socialized members within the ethical organization.[23] Those assimilated members of the organization may attempt to socialize the individual to the ways of the organization to alleviate the ethical dissonance. Once this dissonance is discovered, the likelihood that the mismatched employee will leave the company rises. The more the individual's personal decisions are seen to be in conflict with the ethical decisions that are perceived to be encouraged by the organization, the greater the discomfort of the individual. Imagine, for example, a newly hired employee thought there was nothing wrong with accepting free gifts from contractors doing business with one's employer, but the employer has a code of ethics forbidding such practices. The culture of the organization conflicts with the individual's low ethical standards in this instance, and others in the organization that identify with organizational values may attempt to resolve the dissonance and alter the employee's behavior. If the employee's behavior does not change, the employee may be let go for cause or insubordination.

### Low Organizational Ethics, High Individual Ethics (Low-High)

A reduction in job satisfaction is likely if an employee striving to be ethical perceives little top management support for ethical behavior, an unfavorable ethical climate in the organization, and/or little association between ethical behavior and job success.[24] Once this ethical dissonance is discovered, the likelihood of employee turnover rises. Sims and Keon found a significant relationship between the ethical rift between one's personal decisions and the perceived unwritten/informal policies of the organization, and the individual's level of comfort within the organization. The greater the difference between the decisions that the individual made and the decisions perceived as expected and reinforced by the organization, the greater levels of discomfort the individual would feel, and the more likely the individual would be to report these feelings of discomfort.[25] The case of Cynthia Cooper, discussed in Chapter 1, illustrates the low organizational, high individual ethics environment. Cooper reported her concerns to top management, and once she was convinced that nothing would be done to address the improper accounting for capitalized costs, she blew the whistle by going to the audit committee and external auditors.

## Business Ethics

There are many definitions of *business ethics*. The one we adopt is by Ferrell, Fraedrich, and Ferrell (referred to as just Ferrell et al. in the text) because of its simplicity. These authors define business ethics as comprising the principles, values, and standards that guide behavior in the world of business.

### Guiding Principles

The principles are specific and pervasive boundaries for behavior that are universal and absolute.[26] For example, the guiding principles of Starbucks,[27] shown in Exhibit 3.1, are part of the company's mission statement and establish a tone that defines what Starbucks stands for.

**EXHIBIT 3.1**
**Starbucks Mission Statement and Guiding Principles**

Establish Starbucks as the premier purveyor of the finest coffee in the world while maintaining our uncompromising principles while we grow.

The following six guiding principles will help us measure the appropriateness of our decisions:

1. Provide a great work environment and treat each other with respect and dignity.
2. Embrace diversity as an essential component in the way we do business.
3. Apply the highest standards of excellence to the purchasing, roasting and fresh delivery of our coffee.
4. Develop enthusiastically satisfied customers all of the time.
5. Contribute positively to our communities and our environment.
6. Recognize that profitability is essential to our future success.

Notice how profitability is at the bottom of this list, which implies that profits will occur if members of the Starbucks community live by the guiding principles. Clearly, issues of responsibility, trust, and work environment are key fundamentals that Starbucks views as critical to its success. The results speak for themselves: Starbucks has been named one of "The World's Most Ethical Companies"[28] for six years in a row by Ethisphere, a well-respected organization that promotes sound business ethics principles. No other company has been on the list longer than Starbucks.

## Values

*Values* are beliefs or convictions that guide behavior and support the overall organization vision. Values help define or describe the desired culture; further, they communicate what is important to the organization, as well as what key practices and behaviors will be recognized and rewarded. Johnson points out that if a mission statement identifies the final destination of a company, then the values that it adopts serve as a moral compass to guide the journey. Values provide a frame of reference, helping a company to set priorities and to determine right from wrong.[29] For example, if a company values diversity, then it will do what it can to hire people with a mix of abilities, experiences, knowledge, and personal attributes.

Values give the means to the end, such as the financial goals of an organization. According to Jennings, just meeting numbers does not define an organization's values. Values determine what the organization will and will not do to get to the numbers.[30] At WorldCom, the goal was to show a continuing trend of earnings increase over time to satisfy financial analysts and investors. Russ McGuire, a former WorldCom employee, who left after two months because of concerns about the environment at the company, writes about the culture that Bernie Ebbers nurtured at WorldCom as follows: "During my brief stay at WorldCom, the company's priorities were clearly communicated. Each department within the company had firm financial goals to meet. Whenever possible, individuals had specific financial goals. If you missed your goals for 1 month, you were put on warning. If you missed them for 3 months, you were gone. It was as simple as that. These requirements were always discussed within the context of creating shareholder value."[31] WorldCom valued growth above or else, and employees were expected to do whatever it took, including manipulate the numbers, to achieve that goal.

## Ethical Standards

The principles of behavior are sometimes considered the organization's ethical standards. Generally, these would be principles that when followed, promote values such as trust, good behavior, fairness, and caring. There is not one consistent set of standards that all companies follow, but each company has the right to develop the standards that are meaningful for their organization. Ethical standards are not always easily enforceable, as they are frequently vaguely defined and somewhat open to interpretation. For example, "Treat the customer with respect and kindness."

In accounting, the ethical standards for the profession are embodied in its codes of conduct. We have already discussed the codes of the American Institute of Certified Public Accountants (AICPA) and Institute of Management Accountants (IMA) in Chapter 1. Exhibit 3.2[32] presents the code of the Institute of Internal Auditors (IIA). The IIA represents about 170,000 members, many of whom hold the designation of certified internal auditor (CIA).

The IIA Code of Ethics states the principles and expectations governing the behavior of individuals and organizations in the conduct of internal auditing. It describes the minimum requirements for conduct and lists behavioral expectations rather than specific activities. The purpose of the IIA Code is to promote an ethical culture in the profession of internal auditing.

**EXHIBIT 3.2    The IIA Code of Ethics**

---

**Principles**

Internal auditors are expected to apply and uphold the following principles:

**1. Integrity**

The integrity of internal auditors establishes trust and thus provides the basis for reliance on their judgment.

**2. Objectivity**

Internal auditors exhibit the highest level of professional objectivity in gathering, evaluating, and communicating information about the activity or process being examined. Internal auditors make a balanced assessment of all the relevant circumstances and are not unduly influenced by their own interests or by others in forming judgments.

**3. Confidentiality**

Internal auditors respect the value and ownership of information they receive and do not disclose information without appropriate authority unless there is a legal or professional obligation to do so.

**4. Competency**

Internal auditors apply the knowledge, skills, and experience needed in the performance of internal audit services.

**Rules of Conduct**

**1. Integrity**

Internal auditors:

- 1.1. Shall perform their work with honesty, diligence, and responsibility.
- 1.2. Shall observe the law and make disclosures expected by the law and the profession.
- 1.3. Shall not knowingly be a party to any illegal activity, or engage in acts that are discreditable to the profession of internal auditing or to the organization.
- 1.4. Shall respect and contribute to the legitimate and ethical objectives of the organization.

**2. Objectivity**

Internal auditors:

- 2.1. Shall not participate in any activity or relationship that may impair or be presumed to impair their unbiased assessment. This participation includes those activities or relationships that may be in conflict with the interests of the organization.
- 2.2. Shall not accept anything that may impair or be presumed to impair their professional judgment.
- 2.3. Shall disclose all material facts known to them that, if not disclosed, may distort the reporting of activities under review.

**3. Confidentiality**

Internal auditors:

- 3.1. Shall be prudent in the use and protection of information acquired in the course of their duties.
- 3.2. Shall not use information for any personal gain or in any manner that would be contrary to the law or detrimental to the legitimate and ethical objectives of the organization.

**4. Competency**

Internal auditors:

- 4.1. Shall engage only in those services for which they have the necessary knowledge, skills, and experience.
- 4.2. Shall perform internal audit services in accordance with the *International Standards for the Professional Practice of Internal Auditing.*
- 4.3. Shall continually improve their proficiency and the effectiveness and quality of their services.

---

Source: Republished with permission of The Institute of Internal Auditors Research Foundation, The IIA Code of Ethics. Permission conveyed through Copyright Clearance Center, Inc.

Notice how similar the IIA standards are to those of the AICPA and IMA. In particular, integrity, objectivity, and competency (due care) appear in all three codes. We refer to elements of the IIA code in this chapter because of the role of the internal auditor in establishing an ethical organization environment, as will be discussed later.

## Business Ethics versus Personal Ethics

While many definitions and characterizations of business ethics exist, one important issue to discuss at this point is whether there is a difference between business and personal ethics.

John Maxwell contends there is no such thing as "business" ethics. Maxwell believes that a single standard of ethics applies to both our business and to our personal lives. Maxwell identifies the standard as the Golden Rule. He says in making ethical decisions, we should ask the question: How would I like to be treated in a particular situation? To Maxwell, the Golden Rule is an integrity guideline for all situations.[33] Maxwell's perspective implies that we should treat others the way that we would like to be treated. His view is consistent with Kant's notion of universality; that is, we should act in ways that we would want others to act in similar situations for similar reasons. Imagine, for example, your boss asks you to charge his personal travel expenses to the company for reimbursement because he is short of funds this month. Absent a low-low organizational fit, we can assume you would not cheat in such a way in your personal life or with your own business expenses, so you should act consistently and refuse to do so for your boss. Predictability and consistency of behavior enhances one's ethical judgments and makes them more understandable to outsiders. In business, it is an important element of trust. In this situation, ethical dissonance occurs because you know that it is wrong to "fudge" an expense report of your boss, but it is presented to you as being in the boss's best interest.

Many people seem to have a different standard of behavior in the workplace than in their personal lives. The following example illustrates how dangerous this can be. You arrive home one night and see your daughter working on an art project. She has a variety of markers on the table to help with the project. Now, you know that there are no such markers in the house, so you ask your daughter where they came from. She admits taking them from the classroom to help with the project. You lecture her on how wrong it was to do that. She says to you: "But Mommy, you take supplies from your office and use them at home all the time." Remember, ethics involves consistent behavior based on underlying ethical principles. What kind of example do you set for your daughter if you do improper things in business while touting ethical behavior at home in your personal life? Recall that the last step of the comprehensive decision-making model discussed in Chapter 2 provides for a final reflection before taking action that considers how you would feel if your child knew what you were about to do.

## Ends versus Means

While most people recognize that business must earn a profit to survive, it is the steps taken in business dealings and financial reporting to make the profit that concern ethicists. As Kant points out, the ends do not justify the means. If they did, then businesses could rationalize accelerating the recording of revenue into an earlier period to inflate profit. A company places its own self-interests (perhaps in the guise of maximizing shareholder wealth) ahead of the interests of society if it decides to inflate revenue and earnings artificially.

A good example of ends versus means can be seen in the actions of commercial and investment banks during the financial crisis of 2007–2008, to transfer risk to others by making risky home mortgage loans, group dozens of them into securitized financial instruments, and then selling the instruments to investment banks. The investment banks proceeded to sell the financial instruments to unsuspecting investors, who trusted that these investments were based on solid financial analysis. The goal of the banks was to transfer risk to others. The means to accomplish the goal was to sell off the instruments to outside investors, most of whom did not fully understand the instruments and were misled into thinking that a high level of returns would be forthcoming.

## Trust in Business

Trust in business is the cornerstone of relationships with customers, suppliers, employees, and others who have dealings with an organization. Trust means to be reliable and carry through words with deeds. Looking back at Rest's model, trust is gained when an employee follows through ethical intent with ethical action. Trust becomes pervasive only if the organization's values are followed and supported by top management. By modeling the organization's values, senior leaders provide a benchmark for all employees.

A good example of building trust in an organization is from Paul O'Neill, former CEO at Alcoa Inc., the world's third-largest producer of aluminum. O'Neill created a reputation for trust among his employees by setting strict ethical standards and carrying through with them. In an interview with *PBS Newshour* on July 9, 2002, O'Neill was asked by reporter Jim Lehrer why Alcoa was able to avoid the accounting scandals that infected so many companies in the late 1990s and early 2000s. He responded with the following statement: "When I went there [to Alcoa], I called the chief financial officer and the controller and I said to them, 'I don't want to ever be accused of or guilty of managing earnings,' that is to say making earnings that really aren't as a consequence of operations."[34] O'Neill went on to express in the interview his dismay at the number of cases where employees of a company were told that these are the company's values, and then senior management totally ignored those same values.

Alcoa stands as an example of a company that walks the talk of ethics. Alcoa's values statement, which appears in Exhibit 3.3, was recognized in the 2011 Covalence Ethical Ranking, a global ranking organization headquartered in Geneva, Switzerland, which listed Alcoa number 1 in the basic resources sector and the only basic resources company among the top-ranked companies for ethics. Alcoa also was recognized by the Dow Jones Sustainability Indexes for North America and the World, which also rank Alcoa number 1 among aluminum companies.

Trust can be lost, even if once gained in the eyes of the public, if an organization no longer follows the guiding principles that helped to create its reputation for trust. A good example is what has happened with Johnson & Johnson. The company was a model of ethical behavior during the Tylenol incident but has come under intense scrutiny lately over questions about the safety of its other products.

**EXHIBIT 3.3**  **Alcoa Values and Vision Statement**

**Our Vision**
Alcoa. Advancing each generation.

Since 1888, the people of Alcoa have partnered to create innovative and sustainable solutions that move the world forward.

**Our Values**
We live our Values every day, everywhere, collaborating for the benefit of our customers, investors, employees, communities, and partners.

**Integrity**
We are open, honest, and accountable.

**Environment, Health, & Safety**
We work safely, promote wellness, and protect the environment.

**Innovation**
We creatively transform ideas into value.

**Respect**
We treat all people with dignity and provide a diverse, inclusive work environment.

**Excellence**
We relentlessly pursue outstanding and sustainable results.

## Johnson & Johnson: A Case of Dr. Jekyll and Mr. Hyde?

In addition to a statement of values, standards of business practices, and a code of ethics, some companies use a credo to instill virtue. A credo is an aspirational statement that encourages employees to internalize the values of the company. A good example of a corporate credo is that of Johnson & Johnson, which appears in Exhibit 3.4.[35]

The Johnson & Johnson credo clearly sets a positive ethical tone. Notice how it emphasizes the company's primary obligations to those who use and rely on the safety of its products. The Johnson & Johnson credo implies that shareholders will earn a fair return if the company operates in accordance with its ethical values. Johnson & Johnson was

**EXHIBIT 3.4**
**Johnson & Johnson Credo**

We believe our first responsibility is to the doctors, nurses, and patients,
to mothers and fathers and all others who use our products and services.
In meeting their needs, everything we do must be of high quality.
We must constantly strive to reduce our costs
in order to maintain reasonable prices.
Customers' orders must be serviced promptly and accurately.
Our suppliers and distributors must have an opportunity
to make a fair profit.

We are responsible to our employees,
the men and women who work with us throughout the world.
Everyone must be considered as an individual.
We must respect their dignity and recognize their merit.
They must have a sense of security in their jobs.
Compensation must be fair and adequate,
and working conditions clean, orderly, and safe.
We must be mindful of ways to help our employees fulfill
their family responsibilities.
Employees must feel free to make suggestions and complaints.
There must be equal opportunity for employment, development,
and advancement for those qualified.
We must provide competent management,
and their actions must be just and ethical.

We are responsible to the communities in which we live and work,
and to the world community as well.
We must be good citizens—support good works and charities
and bear our fair share of taxes.
We must encourage civic improvements and better health and education.
We must maintain in good order
the property we are privileged to use,
protecting the environment and natural resources.

Our final responsibility is to our stockholders.
Business must make a sound profit.
We must experiment with new ideas.
Research must be carried on, innovative programs developed,
and mistakes paid for.
New equipment must be purchased, new facilities provided,
and new products launched.
Reserves must be created to provide for adverse times.

When we operate according to these principles,
the stockholders should realize a fair return.

credited with being an ethical organization in part because of the way it handled the Tylenol poisoning incidents in 1982. However, more recent events bring into question whether the company is suffering from a "Dr. Jekyll and Mr. Hyde" syndrome.

### Tylenol Poisoning

In the fall of 1982, seven people in the Chicago area collapsed suddenly and died after taking Tylenol capsules that had been laced with cyanide. These five women and two men became the first victims ever to die from what came to be known as "product tampering."

McNeil Consumer Products, a subsidiary of Johnson & Johnson, was confronted with a crisis when it was determined that each of the seven people had ingested an Extra-Strength Tylenol capsule laced with cyanide. The news of this incident traveled quickly and was the cause of a massive, nationwide panic.

Tamara Kaplan, a professor at Penn State University, contends that Johnson & Johnson used the Tylenol poisonings to launch a public relations program immediately to preserve the integrity of both their product and their corporation as a whole. We find this to be a vacuous position, however. By Kaplan's own admission, "Johnson & Johnson's top management put customer safety first, before they worried about their company's profit and other financial concerns."[36] This hardly sounds like a company that used a catastrophic event to boost its image in the eyes of the public.

Johnson & Johnson's stock price dropped precipitously after the initial incident was made public. In the end, the stock price recovered because the company's actions gained the support and confidence of the public. Johnson & Johnson acted swiftly to remove all the product from the shelves of supermarkets, provide free replacements of Tylenol capsules with the tablet form of the product, and make public statements of assurance that the company would not sell an unsafe product. To claim that the company was motivated by a public relations agenda (even though in the end, its actions did provide a public relations boon for the company) is to ignore a basic point that Johnson & Johnson's management may have known all along. That is, good ethics is good business. But don't be fooled by this expression. It is good for the company if it benefits as a result of an ethical action. However, the main reason to make ethical decisions, as did Johnson & Johnson, is that it is the proper way to act. Much like Alcoa, Johnson & Johnson's credo instills a sense of pride for what the company stands for.

Appendix 1 of this chapter presents an analysis of Johnson & Johnson's actions from the perspective of the comprehensive ethical decision-making model starting from the first public disclosure of the poisoning and how the company should have (and did) act in response. We provide the analysis to help students gain proficiency in using the model and identifying the ethical issues and stakeholders that provide the basis for making ethical judgments.

### Johnson & Johnson Records a $3.3 Billion Charge for Product Liability

Johnson & Johnson announced in January 2012 that it recorded pretax charges and special items totaling $3.3 billion for the fourth quarter of 2011 in order to provide a reserve for probable losses from product liability lawsuits. The pending lawsuits are attributable to misleading marketing practices and manufacturing-quality lapses.

On August 2, 2012, the company disclosed in a securities filing that it had reached an agreement in principle with the U.S. Justice Department and some states on settling investigations into marketing practices, including the illegal promotion of the antipsychotic Risperdal. One of the company's operating units paid state officials to get Risperdal on approved drug lists, marketed it for unapproved uses to children and the elderly, and lied about its safety and effectiveness. The company did not give a dollar amount of its liability, which *The Wall Street Journal* has said could be as much as $2.2 billion, depending on how many of the states suing the company join in the lawsuit.[37]

Unfortunately, the problems for Johnson & Johnson go further back. Here is a brief summary of the investigations against the company:

1. On December 21, 2011, it was announced that Johnson & Johnson must defend a lawsuit claiming that it misled investors about quality control failures at manufacturing plants that led to recalls of the popular over-the-counter drug Motrin. Allegedly, top executives made misleading statements about details of the recalls, leading to stock losses after the true reasons for the recalls became public.

2. Earlier in 2011, a lawsuit filed by a group of consumers alleging that Johnson & Johnson's baby shampoo includes potentially cancer-causing chemicals was allowed to go forward after evidence came out that the product contained a chemical ingredient called methylene chloride, which is banned by the U.S. Food and Drug Administration (FDA) for use in cosmetics.

3. In January 2011, it was announced that Johnson & Johnson might have to pay up to $1 billion for lawsuits concerning its subsidiary DePuy Orthopaedics, which sold metal-on-metal hip implants that were found to shed minute metal particles into a patient's bloodstream over time. Lawsuits over the implants have piled up across the country, accusing DePuy of manufacturing a defective product, failing to warn patients and doctors of problems with the implant, and negligence in designing, manufacturing, and selling the product.

   It is worth noting that Johnson & Johnson raised its product-liability reserves to $570 million at the end of 2010 and allotted $280 million for medical costs of patients directly affected by the recalled hip implants.

4. Women who have suffered serious injury and disfiguration filed lawsuits in 2012 against Johnson & Johnson subsidiary Ethicon, claiming that vaginal mesh manufactured by Ethicon caused them life-altering complications. Upon investigation, a number of doctors and scientists concluded that the Ethicon vaginal mesh and bladder slings did not meet reasonable safety standards. The FDA issued Public Health Notifications regarding the use of vaginal mesh products to treat pelvic organ prolapse and stress urinary incontinence in October 2008, in February 2009, and in July 2011.

Some might say that Johnson & Johnson made withdrawals from its "trust" bank in recent years. They reacted slowly to a variety of crises, at first failing to admit any culpability and disclaiming financial liability. We can't escape the logical conclusion that "where there is smoke, there is fire." The disappointing fact is that these instances occurred as a result of management and internal actions and reflect a culture that has changed dramatically from the days of the Tylenol poisoning. Perhaps Johnson & Johnson is learning the hard way that it takes a long time to build a reputation for trust, but not very long to tear it down.

### Employees Perceptions of Ethics in the Workplace

Given the organization-person fit and values that provide part of the culture for ethical decision making in the workplace, it is important to understand how employees view the ethics of the organizations they work for, in part to better understand corporate governance systems and whistleblowing, which are discussed later in this chapter. The 2011 National Business Ethics Survey (NBES) conducted by the Ethics Resource Center provides interesting data about ethics in the workplace. The report is the seventh in a series. The 2011 survey provides information on the views of 4,683 respondents that represent a broad array of employees in the for-profit sector.[38] Exhibit 3.5 summarizes some of the survey results.

The results of the NBES survey are mixed. On the one hand, the percentage of employees who witnessed misconduct at work has declined by 10 percent from 2007 to 2011, and those reporting misconduct increased by 7 percent. On the other hand, pressure to compromise

**EXHIBIT 3.5**
**Views of Employees
on Ethics in the
Workplace from
the 2011 National
Business Ethics
Survey**[39]

| Item | 2011 | 2009 | 2007 |
|---|---|---|---|
| Pressure to compromise ethical standards | 13% | 8% | 10% |
| Weak/weak-leaning ethical culture | 42% | 35% | 39% |
| Negative view of supervisors' ethics | 34% | 24% | 26% |
| Observed misconduct | 45% | 49% | 55% |
| Reported observed misconduct | 65% | 63% | 58% |
| Experienced retaliation after reporting (i.e., whistleblowing) | 22% | 15% | 12% |

ethical standards trended upwards in 2011, after a decline between 2007 and 2009. The same is true of the view of a weak ethical culture. A troubling result is retaliation against employee whistleblowers almost doubled. When employees were asked whether they could question management without fear of retaliation, 19 percent said it was not safe to do so.

The five most frequently observed types of misconduct reported in 2011 were (1) misuse of company time (33 percent); (2) abusive behavior (21 percent); (3) and (4) company resource abuse and lying to employees (20 percent each); and (5) violating company Internet use policies (16 percent). The latter is a growing problem, with more and more employees turning to social networking while on the job. Most of the active networkers who reported misconduct in the workplace say that they experienced retaliation as a result: 56 percent, compared to just 18 percent of less active social networkers and non-networkers. These results may indicate that a company turns more quickly on an employee who reports wrongdoing if that employee also uses social networking at work. The NBES survey also indicates that active social networkers show a higher tolerance for certain activities that could be considered questionable. For example, among active social networkers, half believe that it is acceptable to keep copies of confidential work documents in case they need them in their next job, compared to only 15 percent of their colleagues.[40]

We have already discussed common ways to improve the ethical culture of an organization, including values-based decision making and having a code of conduct. The NBES survey reports that ethics and compliance programs have grown since the establishment of the U.S. Federal Sentencing Guidelines for Organizations (FSGO). The U.S. Congress passed the FSGO in 1991 to create an incentive for organizations to develop and implement programs designed to foster ethical and legal compliance. These guidelines, which were developed by the U.S. Sentencing Commission, apply to all felonies and class A misdemeanors committed by employees in association with their work. As an incentive, organizations that demonstrated due diligence in developing effective compliance programs to discourage unethical and illegal conduct may be subject to reduced organizational penalties if an employee commits a crime. The essence of the law is that legal violations can be prevented through organizational values and a commitment to ethical conduct. Some have called the law the "good parenting statute."[41] In 2011, organizations subject to the law had the following ethical measures in place as part of their culture.

| | |
|---|---|
| Disciplining of employees who violate the standards of the organization or the law | 85% |
| Written standards for ethical conduct | 82% |
| Provision of a mechanism of reporting misconduct anonymously | 77% |
| Training on company standards of ethical workplace conduct | 76% |
| Provision of a mechanism for seeking ethics-related advice or information | 68% |
| Assessment of ethical conduct as a part of employee performance evaluations | 67% |

# Stakeholder Perspective

The well-known ethicist Archie Carroll points out that questions of right, wrong, fairness, and justice permeate an organization's activities as it attempts to interact successfully with major stakeholder groups, including investors and creditors, employees, customers, government, and society at large. He believes that the principal task of management is not only to deal with the various stakeholder groups in an ethical fashion, but also to reconcile the conflicts of interest that occur between the organization and the stakeholder groups.[42]

Ferrell et al. state that the degree to which an organization understands and addresses stakeholder demands can be referred to as a *stakeholder orientation*.[43] This orientation comprises three sets of activities: (1) the organization-wide generation of data about stakeholder groups and assessment of the firm's effects on these groups, (2) the distribution of this information throughout the firms, and (3) the responsiveness of the organization as a whole to this information.[44]

Generating data about stakeholders begins with identifying the stakeholders that are relevant to the firm followed by the concerns about the organization's conduct that each relevant stakeholder group shares. At this stage, the values and standards of behavior are used to evaluate stakeholder interests and concerns from an ethical perspective. The ethical reasoning methods previously discussed help to make the necessary judgments.

Stakeholder management requires that an individual consider issues from a variety of perspectives other than one's own or that of the organization. The case of the Ford Pinto illustrates how important stakeholder concerns can be left out of the decision-making process.

## The Case of the Ford Pinto

The case of the Ford Pinto illustrates a classic example of how a company can make a fatal mistake in its decision making by failing to consider the interests of the stakeholders adequately. The failure was due to total reliance on utilitarian thinking instead of the universality perspective of rights theory, to the detriment of the driving public and society in general.

The Pinto was Ford Motor Company's first domestic North American subcompact automobile, marketed beginning on September 11, 1970. It competed with the AMC Gremlin and Chevrolet Vega, along with imports from makes such as Volkswagen, Datsun, and Toyota. The Pinto was popular in sales, with 100,000 units delivered by January 1971, and was also offered as a wagon and Runabout hatchback. Its reputation suffered over time, however, especially from a controversy surrounding the safety of its gas tank.

The public was shocked to find out that if the Pinto cars experienced an impact at speeds of only 30 miles per hour or less, they might become engulfed in flames, and passengers could be burned or even die. Ford faced an ethical dilemma: what to do about the apparently unsafe gas tanks that seemed to be the cause of these incidents. At the time, the gas tanks were routinely placed behind the license plate, so a rear-end collision was more likely to cause an explosion (whereas today's gas tanks are placed on the side of the vehicle). However, the federal safety standards at the time did not address this issue, so Ford was in compliance with the law. Ford's initial response was based on ethical legalism—the company complied with all the laws and safety problems, so it was under no obligation to take any action.

Eventually, Ford did use ethical analysis to develop a response. It used a risk-benefit analysis to aid decision making. This was done because the National Highway Traffic Safety Administration (NHTSA) excused a defendant from being penalized if the monetary costs of making a production change were greater than the "societal benefit" of that change. The analysis followed the same approach modeled after Judge Learned Hand's ruling in *United States v. Carroll Towing* in 1947 that boiled the theory of negligence down to the following: If the expected harm exceeded the cost to prevent it, the defendant was obligated to take the precaution, and if he (or it, in the case of a company) did not, liability would result. But if the cost was larger than the expected harm, the defendant was not expected to take the precaution. If there was an accident, the defendant would not be found guilty.[45] A summary of the Ford analysis follows.

### Ford's Risk-Benefit Analysis[46]

#### Benefits of Fixing the Pintos

*Savings:* 180 burn deaths, 180 serious burn injuries, 2,100 burned vehicles

*Unit cost:* $200,000 per death (figure provided by the government); $67,000 per burn injury and $700 to repair a burned vehicle (company estimates)

*Total benefits:* 180 × ($200,000) + 180 × ($67,000) + 2,100 × ($700) = **$49.5 million**

#### Costs of Fixing the Pintos

*Sales:* 11 million cars, 1.5 million light trucks

*Unit cost:* $11 per car, $11 per light truck

*Total cost:* 11,000,000 × ($11) + 1,500,000 × ($11) = **$137 million**

Based on this analysis and other considerations, including not being required by law to change its product design, Ford decided not to change the placement of the fuel tank. Ford relied on ethical legalism reasoning to justify (rationalize) its actions.

In 2009, Toyota encountered a problem with some of its models when news broke that there may be a sudden unintended acceleration on certain models. Toyota was hesitant at first to do anything, but after being forced to explain its actions to the U.S. Congress, the company did take corrective action. You might say that Toyota was nudged by congressional and public opinion to see that the rights of the driving public outweighed any benefits of inaction. Toyota's fix was to first cut the length of the accelerator pedals until replacement pedal assemblies become available and to install a brake-to-idle algorithm on affected models. In December 2012, the company agreed to pay about $1.1 billion to settle a class-action lawsuit stemming from complaints about the unintended acceleration.

Returning to the Pinto problem, Ford decided to do a risk-benefit analysis relying only on act-utilitarian reasoning that focused only on costs and benefits, an approach that ignores the rights of various stakeholders. A rule-utilitarian approach might have led Ford to follow the rule "Never sacrifice public safety." A rights theory approach would have led to the same conclusion, based on the reasoning that the driving public has an ethical right to expect that their cars will not blow up if there is a crash at low speeds.

The other danger of utilitarian reasoning is that an important factor may be omitted from the analysis. Ford did not include as a potential cost the lawsuit judgments that might be awarded to the plaintiffs and against the company. For example, in May 1972, Lily Gray was traveling with 13-year-old Richard Grimshaw when their Pinto was struck by another car traveling approximately 30 miles per hour. The impact ignited a fire in the Pinto, which killed Gray and left Grimshaw with devastating injuries. A judgment was rendered against Ford, and the jury awarded the Gray family $560,000 and Matthew Grimshaw, the father of Richard Grimshaw, $2.5 million in compensatory damages. The surprise came when the jury also awarded $125 million in punitive damages. This was subsequently reduced to $3.5 million.[47]

In the aftermath of the scandal, it is interesting to consider whether any of the Ford executives who were involved in the decision-making process would have predicted in advance that they would have made such an unethical choice. Dennis Gioia, who was in charge of recalling defective automobiles at Ford, did not advocate ordering a recall. Gioia eventually came to view his decision not to recall the Pinto as a moral failure—what

De Cremer and Tenbrunsel call a failure to think outside his prevailing background narrative or script at the point of decision. "My own schematized (scripted) knowledge influenced me to perceive recall issues in terms of the prevailing decision environment and to unconsciously overlook key features of the Pinto case...mainly because they did not fit an existing script." While personal morality was very important to Gioia, he admits that the framing narrative of his workplace "did not include ethical dimension."[48] The moral mistake was that there were other, better choices that he could have made—albeit ones outside the purview of Gioai's framing narrative. The Pinto situation is much like the *Challenger* disaster discussed earlier in the chapter. The decisionmakers in each case made the same mistake of viewing the decision as a business decision rather than an ethical decision. The result, as previously noted, was ethical fading, where the ethical dimensions of the problem disappear from consideration and issues of costs and benefits and image take center stage.

# Fraud in Organizations

*Fraud* can be defined as a deliberate misrepresentation to gain an advantage over another party. Fraud comes in many different forms, including fraud in financial statements, the misappropriation of assets (theft) and subsequent cover-up, and disclosure fraud. We discuss fraud in the financial statements more fully in Chapter 5. In this chapter, we will look at the results of the *2012 Global Fraud Survey: Report to the Nations on Occupational Fraud and Abuse,* conducted by the Association of Certified Fraud Examiners (ACFE).

## Fraudulent Business Practices

Fraudulent business practices occur when an organization purposely engages in an act that harms another person, such as a customer. A good example is that of Sears. The Sears case illustrates what can happen when the culture of an organization allows for deceptive business practices. One way to prevent this from happening is to establish an ethical tone at the top that sends the message to employees that such practices will not be tolerated. Sears violated its obligations to its most important stakeholder—its customers, and the company's reputation was tarnished as a result of these events. In the end, Sears had to shut down its auto-repair operation.

In 1992, Sears paid $15 million to settle accusations in 41 states that auto-repair sales representatives were finding problems where none existed to get commissions on repair work. This was not an example of a few rogue employees acting alone to line their pockets with money they didn't rightfully earn. The company had instilled a culture of overcharging hundreds of customers at its auto-repair centers for performing four-wheel alignments, even though only the front wheels can be aligned on many vehicles. Mechanics at Sears also told customers they would conduct a "free" vehicle inspection, but then went on to charge for unauthorized repairs supposedly discovered during the inspections. Sears's actions were repeated over and over again. In New Jersey alone, there were at least 350 instances of the alleged overcharges for wheel alignments at 19 separate Sears stores. This wasn't the first time Sears has faced lawsuits because of its fraudulent business practices. In 1992, Sears agreed to pay as much as $20 million to settle 19 class action lawsuits that stemmed from charges that it bilked auto-repair customers by recommending unneeded repairs. California state authorities sent in undercover investigators for simple brake jobs that Sears had advertised. The government subsequently charged that about half of the 72 auto centers had recommended unnecessary replacement of such parts. Under the terms of the settlement, Sears offered a coupon worth $50 to some 933,000 customers nationwide who had the various (unnecessary) services performed at a Sears auto center from August 1, 1990, through January 31, 1992. There was a persistent and pervasive pattern of fraud and deception, according to the lawsuits. The unassailable conclusion is that Sears was responsible for a moral erosion of business ethics in its auto-repair business. One has to wonder whether unethical behavior fed into other business lines of Sears as well.

## Occupational Fraud

The 2012 ACFE survey is a follow-up to its *2010 Global Fraud Study* and its *2008 Report to the Nation on Occupational Fraud and Abuse.* The survey took on a distinctly international flavor in 2010 and 2012. The 2012 survey reports on 1,388 cases of occupational fraud that were reported by the Certified Fraud Examiners (CFEs) who investigated them. These offenses occurred in nearly 100 countries on six continents.[49]

As previously discussed, trust is the basis of business relationships, and it is essential for companies to entrust their employees with resources and responsibilities. The ACFE report focuses on *occupational fraud* schemes in which an employee abuses the trust placed in him by an employer for personal gain. The ACFE defines occupational fraud as "the use of one's occupation for personal enrichment through the deliberate misuse or misapplication of the employing organization's resources or assets."[50] A summary of the findings follows:

- Survey participants estimated that the typical organization loses 5 percent of its revenues to fraud each year.
- The median loss caused by the occupational fraud cases studied was $140,000.
- The frauds reported lasted a median of 18 months before being detected.
- Asset misappropriation schemes were the most common type of occupational fraud, comprising 87 percent of the reported cases.
- Financial statement fraud schemes made up just 8 percent of the cases, but caused the greatest median loss at $1 million.
- Occupational fraud is more likely to be detected by a tip than by any other method.
- Corruption and billing schemes pose the greatest risks to organizations throughout the world.
- The presence of anti-fraud controls is correlated with significant decreases in the cost and duration of occupational fraud schemes.
- Perpetrators with higher levels of authority tend to cause much larger losses.
- The longer a perpetrator has worked for an organization, the higher fraud losses tend to be.
- In 81 percent of the cases, the fraudster displayed one or more behavioral red flags that are often associated with fraudulent activities.
- Nearly half of the victim organizations do not recover any losses they suffer due to fraud.

A variety of observations from the results are discussed below given the focus in this chapter on ethics in organizations and creating an ethical culture.

### How Occupational Fraud Is Committed and Detected

Asset misappropriation schemes include when an employee steals or misuses resources, such as charging personal expenses to the company while traveling on business trips. Corruption schemes include misusing one's position or influence in an organization for personal gain, something that Dennis Kozlowski, the former CEO at Tyco, was known for doing. Kozlowski and chief financial officer (CFO) Mark Swartz were convicted on June 21, 2005, of taking bonuses worth more than $120 million without the approval of Tyco's directors, abusing an employee loan program, and misrepresenting the company's financial condition to investors to boost the stock price while selling $575 million in stock. Perhaps the most egregious offense by Kozlowski was to charge the company for half the cost of a birthday party thrown for his wife on the Italian island of Sardinia, claiming that business was conducted during the weeklong event.

**EXHIBIT 3.6**
**Initial Detection of**
**Occupational Frauds**
**from the ACFE 2012**
**Global Survey: 2012**
*Report to the Nations*
*on Occupational*
*Fraud and Abuse*

| Detection Method | Percentage Reported | Median Loss |
| --- | --- | --- |
| Tip | 43.3% | $144,000 |
| Management Review | 14.6% | $123,000 |
| Internal Audit | 14.4% | $81,000 |
| By Accident | 7.0% | $166,000 |
| Account Reconciliation | 4.8% | $124,000 |
| Document Examination | 4.1% | $105,000 |
| External Audit | 3.3% | $370,000 |
| Notified by Police | 3.0% | $1,000,000 |
| Surveillance/Monitoring | 1.9% | N/A |
| Confession | 1.5% | $225,000 |
| IT Controls | 1.1% | $110,000 |
| Other | 1.1% | $378,000 |

A surprising result is that a "tip" was the most common way of detecting fraud, at 43.3 percent in 2012. According to the ACFE report, detection by tip has been the most common method of initial detection since the first survey in 2002. It could be that tips are primarily provided by whistleblowers, but the study does not reach that conclusion. Exhibit 3.6 shows the frequency of detection methods as reported by survey respondents.

An important conclusion from these results is that controls such as management reviews and internal audits account for a significant percentage of detection methods (29 percent) and the external audit does not seem to be a reliable method to detect fraud at only 3.3 percent. These results have implications for our discussion of corporate governance later on.

### Red-Flag Warnings of Fraud

The ACFE study found that most occupational fraudsters' crimes are motivated at least in part by some kind of financial pressure. In addition, while committing a fraud, an individual will frequently display certain behavioral traits associated with stress or a fear of being caught.[51] These warning signs should alert internal auditors that trouble may lie ahead with respect to actual fraud. Exhibit 3.7 shows the fraud indicators identified in the study.

The results of the survey clearly indicate that internal auditors should have their "eyes wide open" with respect to whether senior officers have adopted a lavish living style that creates the incentive to "cook the books" in a way that provides financial results to support their lifestyle. If earnings go up, stock prices often rise as well. Top managers typically own stock in their companies, so an incentive exists to boost earnings sometimes at any cost. A good example is the former CEO of HealthSouth, Richard Scrushy. Recall that we earlier identified the company as one that showed signs of ethical collapse because of its weak board of directors. Scrushy was behind the $2.7 billion earnings overstatement at HealthSouth.

Scrushy allegedly received $226 million in compensation over seven years, while HealthSouth was losing $1.8 billion during the same period. A skeptical auditor would have asked where all that money was going and would have looked for warnings that Scrushy might have been living beyond his means. Scrushy was charged with knowingly engaging in financial transactions using criminally derived property, including the purchase of land, aircraft, boats, cars, artwork, jewelry, and other items. At his trial, it become known that he had used money from his compensation for several residences in the state of Alabama and property in Palm Beach, Florida; a 92-foot Tarrab yacht called *Chez Soiree,* a 38-foot Intrepid Walkaround watercraft and a 42-foot Lightning boat; a 1998 Cessna Caravan

| Behavioral Indicators of Fraud | Percentage Reported |
|---|---|
| Living Beyond Means | 35.6% |
| Financial Difficulties | 27.1% |
| Unusually Close Association with Vendor/Customer | 19.2% |
| Control Issues, Unwillingness to Share Duties | 18.2% |
| Divorce/Family Problems | 14.8% |
| Wheeler-Dealer Attitude | 14.8% |
| Instability, Suspiciousness or Defensiveness | 12.6% |
| Addiction Problems | 8.4% |
| Past Employment-Related Problems | 8.1% |
| Complained About Inadequate Pay | 7.9% |
| Refusal to Take Vacations | 6.5% |
| Excessive Pressure Within Organization | 6.5% |
| Past Legal Problems | 5.3% |
| Complained About Lack of Authority | 4.8% |
| Excessive Family/Peer Pressure for Success | 4.7% |
| Instability in Life Circumstance | 4.1% |

675, together with amphibious floats and other equipment, and a 2001 Cessna Citation 525 aircraft; diamond jewelry; several luxury automobiles, including a 2003 Lamborghini Murcielago, a 2000 Rolls Royce Corniche, and two 2002 Cadillac Escalades; and paintings by Pablo Picasso, Marc Chagall, Pierre-August Renoir, among others.

It is not just the internal auditors who wore blinders and the board that looked the other way. The external auditors did not detect the fraud either.

## Financial Statement Fraud

Financial statement fraud schemes occur because an employee—typically a member of top management—causes a misstatement or omission of material information in the organization's financial reports. Examples include recording fictitious revenues, understating reported expenses, artificially inflating reported assets, and failing to accrue expenses at the end of the year, such as what occurred in the DigitPrint case in Chapter 1.

A report by Ernst & Young, *Detecting Financial Statement Fraud: What Every Manager Needs to Know,*[52] provides examples of common methods to overstate revenue, understate expenses, and make improper asset valuations. Revenue overstatements include the following:

- Recording gross, rather than net, revenue
- Recording revenues of other companies when acting as a "middleman"
- Recording sales that never took place
- Recording future sales in the current period
- Recording sales of products that are out on consignment

Common methods of understating expenses include the following:

- Reporting cost of sales as a non-operating expense so that it does not negatively affect gross margin
- Capitalizing operating costs, recording them as assets on the balance sheet instead of as expenses on the income statement (i.e., WorldCom)
- Not recording some expenses at all, or not recording expenses in the proper period

Examples of improper asset valuations include the following:

- Manipulating reserves
- Changing the useful lives of assets
- Failing to take a write-down when needed
- Manipulating estimates of fair market value

One of the most bizarre examples of financial statement fraud involved Miniscribe, a manufacturer of computer hard drive disks that committed inventory fraud in the 1980s in the amount of $15 million. This was a mere pittance compared to the $11 billion fraud at WorldCom some 15 years later, but the efforts of Miniscribe's management to cover up the fraud were as audacious as any ever seen. Exhibit 3.8 summarizes this fraud. Of particular note is the unethical behavior at the highest levels of management that created a culture of blindness to what was right and wrong and led to the perpetuation of the fraud. An important point in the Miniscribe fraud is that top management committed the fraud and overrode internal controls in the process. The corporate governance system at Miniscribe failed because the company lacked independent members on its board of directors to serve as a check against excessive management behavior.

## EXHIBIT 3.8   Miniscribe Fraud[53]

Miniscribe was a Colorado-based manufacturer of computer hard disk drives whose top officers were convicted of management fraud by covering up a multimillion-dollar inventory overstatement between December 1986 and January 1989, which falsely inflated Miniscribe's profits and accelerated its descent into bankruptcy.

Patrick Schleibaum was the former CFO and vice president of Miniscribe. Quentin T. Wiles was the former chairman of the board and CEO of Miniscribe. Both Schleibaum and Wiles were convicted of making false statements to the government and securities fraud.

Miniscribe began operations in 1981 in Longmont, Colorado. Miniscribe was then a privately owned company manufacturing computer disk drives operating out of the basement of its founder, Terry Johnson. Miniscribe went public in 1983, but it soon grew beyond its capacity. In 1985, a venture capital group, Hambrecht & Quist, invested $20 million in Miniscribe and gained control of its management. By 1986, Miniscribe was a profitable, publicly owned corporation with operations in Colorado, Hong Kong, and Singapore. Miniscribe, whose common stock was traded on the NASDAQ exchange, was subject to the Securities Exchange Act of 1934, as well as the rules and regulations of the Securities and Exchange Commission (SEC).

Following its change in management, Wiles headed Miniscribe from his office in Sherman Oaks, California. Wiles had a reputation as a successful, demanding executive who expected performance. Salaries and bonuses at Miniscribe often depended upon Miniscribe "making the numbers."

Assisting Wiles was a management team consisting largely of certified public accountants (CPAs). Schleibaum initially served as Miniscribe's CFO.

Despite reported growth and profitability, Miniscribe's financial position began to deteriorate early in 1987. In January 1987, Miniscribe conducted its annual inventory count to determine the value of inventory on hand. The accuracy of the inventory count was critical to the proper preparation of Miniscribe's 1986 year-end financial statements.

Management retained the independent accounting firm of Coopers & Lybrand to audit Miniscribe and verify the accuracy of its inventory count. The standard procedure for verifying a company's inventory count is through a test count—an inventory sampling deemed representative of the entire inventory. Problems arose when, unbeknownst to the auditors, management detected an inventory hole of between $2 million and $4 million. This inventory hole appeared because the actual inventory count, and thus dollar value of the inventory, was less than the value of the inventory recorded on Miniscribe's books. The overstatement of inventory led to the understatement of cost of goods sold and inflated earnings equal to the amount of the inventory overstatement.

At this point, Wiles was unaware of the inventory hole. Schleibaum properly decided to charge a portion of the hole against an emergency fund known as "inventory reserves." The remainder of the hole also should have been charged off or expensed as a cost of goods sold, with a corresponding reduction in profits. But when the division manager, Warren Perry, suggested this approach, Schleibaum balked. Instead, Schleibaum directed his subordinates to conceal the remainder of the inventory hole through improper means so that Miniscribe could continue to "make the numbers."

*(Continued)*

**EXHIBIT 3.8**    (*Continued*)

With Schleibaum's knowledge and approval, Perry and operations controllers Kenneth A. Huff and Steven Wolfe decided to cover the inventory hole by falsely inflating the inventory count. To hide the false count from the auditors, Wolfe and Perry broke into the auditors' work trunks at Miniscribe after business hours and altered the test count to match the inflated inventory count. The inflated numbers were then entered into Miniscribe's computer system and reflected as additional inventory. Schleibaum signed a management representation letter to the auditors indicating that Miniscribe's financial statements were accurate, including its inventory valuation. Miniscribe cleared the 1986 audit.

Miniscribe reported the false profits resulting from concealment of the inventory hole on its 1986 income statement and 1987 first-quarter earnings statement. Miniscribe disseminated this information to the public through its 1986 annual report and 1987 first-quarter financial report. Schleibaum signed the 1986 10-K report (annual report to the SEC) and 1987 first-quarter 10-Q report, which contained Miniscribe's false financial statements. Miniscribe filed the 10-K and 10-Q reports with the SEC as required by law. Miniscribe's reported success allowed the company to raise funds through a $97 million issue of debentures early in 1987.

In the spring of 1987, Wiles became concerned about Miniscribe's internal controls and financial strength. He worried that if an inventory problem actually existed, Miniscribe and its officers might be liable to those investors purchasing the debentures on the basis of the company's reported financial strength. Ultimately, a $15 million hole in inventory was discovered. Wiles had decided that Miniscribe could not afford to write off the inventory hole in 1987; instead, it had to cover it up to maintain investor confidence. Wiles planned to write off the inventory hole over six quarters, beginning with the first quarter of 1988.

In December 1987, independent auditors began preparing for Miniscribe's 1987 year-end audit. Miniscribe again faced the problem of clearing the independent audit. In mid-December, Miniscribe's management, with Wiles's approval and Schleibaum's assistance, engaged in an extensive cover-up, which included recording the shipment of bricks as in-transit inventory. To implement the plan, Miniscribe employees first rented an empty warehouse in Boulder, Colorado, and procured 10 exclusive-use trailers. They then purchased 26,000 bricks from the Colorado Brick Company.

On Saturday, December 18, 1987, Schleibaum and others gathered at the warehouse. Wiles did not attend. From early morning to late afternoon, those present loaded the bricks onto pallets, shrink-wrapped the pallets, and boxed them. The weight of each brick pallet approximated the weight of a pallet of disk drives. The brick pallets then were loaded onto the trailers and taken to a farm in Larimer County, Colorado.

Miniscribe's books, however, showed the bricks as in-transit inventory worth approximately $4 million. Employees at two of Miniscribe's buyers, CompuAdd and CalAbco, agreed to refuse fictitious inventory shipments from Miniscribe totaling $4 million. Miniscribe then added the fictitious inventory shipments to the company's inventory records.

Additionally, the officers employed other means to cover the inventory hole, including (1) recording the shipment of nonexistent inventory from Colorado to the Far East, (2) packaging scrap as inventory, (3) double-counting inventory, and (4) failing to record payables upon the receipt of materials. These various means distributed the inventory hole throughout Miniscribe's three facilities, making the problem more difficult for the independent auditors to detect.

Again, Schleibaum signed a management representation letter to the auditors stating that Miniscribe's 1987 financial reports were accurate and truthful, and Miniscribe cleared the independent audit. The result of the cover-up was that Miniscribe's book inventory and reported profits for 1987 were overstated by approximately $15 million and $22 million, respectively. These figures represented 17 percent of Miniscribe's inventory and 70 percent of its profits for the year.

Eventually, Miniscribe got caught up in its own fraud, as it became more and more difficult to cover the inventory hole and questions were asked about its accounting. The sharp decline in the stock market in October 1987 hastened the day when the house of cards that was Miniscribe collapsed. The company finally declared bankruptcy in 1990.

# Foundations of Corporate Governance Systems

An essential part of creating an ethical organization environment is to put in place effective corporate governance systems that establish control mechanisms to ensure that organizational values guide decision making and that ethical standards are being followed. The characteristics of such systems include accountability, oversight, and control. *Accountability* refers to the relationship between workplace decisions, strategic direction, and compliance with legal and ethical considerations. *Oversight* provides a system of checks and balances that limit employees' and managers' opportunities to deviate from established policies and strategies aimed at preventing unethical and illegal activities. *Control* is the process of auditing and improving organizational decisions and actions, which relies on internal audit and internal control processes.[54]

## Defining Corporate Governance

There is no single, accepted definition of *corporate governance*. A fairly narrow definition given by Shleifer and Vishny emphasizes the separation of ownership and control in corporations. They define corporate governance as dealing with "the ways in which the suppliers of finance to corporations assure themselves of getting a return on their investment."[55] Parkinson defines it as a process of supervision and control intended to ensure that the company's management acts in accordance with the interests of shareholders.[56]

A corporate governance regime typically includes mechanisms to ensure that the agent (management) runs the firm for the benefit of one or more principals (shareholders, creditors, suppliers, clients, employees, and other parties with whom the firm conducts its business). The mechanisms include internal ones, such as the board of directors, its committees, executive compensation policies, and internal controls, and external measures, which include monitoring by large shareholders and creditors (in particular banks), external auditors, and the regulatory framework of a securities exchange commission, the corporate law regime, and stock exchange listing requirements and oversight.

The definition of corporate governance that we like the best is by Tricker, who says that governance is not concerned with running the business of the company per se, but with giving overall direction to the enterprise, with overseeing and controlling the executive actions of management, and with satisfying legitimate expectations of accountability and regulation by interests beyond the corporate boundaries.[57] In this regard, corporate governance can be seen as a set of rules that define the relationship between stakeholders, management, and board of directors of a company and influence how that company is operating. At its most basic level, corporate governance deals with issues that result from the separation of ownership and control. But corporate governance goes beyond simply establishing a clear relationship between shareholders and managers.

## Views of Corporate Governance

Differences exist about the role of corporate governance in business. Some organizations take the view that so long as they are maximizing shareholder wealth and profitability, they are fulfilling their core responsibilities. Other firms take a broader view based on the stakeholder perspective.

The shareholder model of corporate governance is founded on classic economic precepts, including maximizing wealth for investors and creditors. In a public corporation, firm decisions should be oriented toward serving the best interests of investors. Underlying these decisions is a classic agency problem, in which ownership (investors) and control (managers) are separate. Managers act as the agents of the investors (principals), who expect those decisions to increase the value of the stock they own.[58] However, managers may have motivations beyond stockholder value such as increasing market share, or more personal ones including maximizing executive compensation. In these instances, decisions may be based on an egoist approach to ethical decision making that ignores the interests of others.

Because shareholder owners of public companies are not normally involved in the daily operations, the board of directors oversee the companies, and CEOs and other members of top management run them. Albrecht points out that the principal-agent relationship involves a transfer of trust and duty to the agent, while also assuming that the agent is opportunistic and will pursue interests that are in conflict with those of the principal, thereby creating an "agency problem."[59] Because of these potential differences, corporate governance mechanisms are needed to align investor and management interests.

One traditional approach is for shareholders to give the CEO shares or options of stock that vest over time, thus inducing long-term behavior and deterring short-term actions that can harm future company value. When the interests of top management are brought in line with interests of shareholders, agency theory argues that management will fulfill its duty to shareholders, not so much out of any sense of moral duty to shareholders, but because doing what shareholders have provided incentives for maximizes their own utility.[60]

Jensen and Meckling demonstrate how investors in publicly traded corporations incur (agency) costs in monitoring managerial performance. In general, agency costs arise whenever there is an "information asymmetry" between the corporation and outsiders because insiders (the corporation) know more about a company and its future prospects than do outsiders (investors).[61]

Agency costs can occur if the board of directors fails to exercise due care in its oversight role of management. Enron's board of directors did not monitor the company's incentive compensation plans properly, thereby allowing top executives to "hype" the company's stock so that employees would add it to their 401(k) retirement plans. While the hyping occurred, often through positive statements about the company made by CEO Ken Lay, Lay himself sold about 2.3 million shares for $123.4 million.

The agency problem can never be perfectly solved, and shareholders may experience a loss of wealth due to divergent behavior of managers. Investigations by the SEC and U.S. Department of Justice of 20 corporate frauds during the Enron-WorldCom era indicate that $236 billion in shareholder value was lost between the time the public first learned of the first fraud and September 3, 2002, the measurement date.

An alternative to agency theory that has been proposed in recent years is stewardship theory. In this theory, managers are viewed as stewards of their companies, predominately motivated to act in the best interests of the shareholders. The theory holds that as stewards, managers will choose the interests of shareholders, perhaps psychologically identified as the best interests of "the company," over self-interests, regardless of personal motivations or incentives.[62]

Unlike agency theory, stewardship theory focuses on enabling managers rather than controlling them because they can be trusted to act in the best interests of the shareholders. The board provides feedback on intended actions of managers rather than controlling them. The steward recognizes the trust placed in him or her and is motivated to act accordingly.[63] Under this theory, the steward-CEO can best act when he or she is also the chairperson of the board; the dual roles are enablers, whereas they would be viewed as a violation of control mechanisms under agency theory. Looking back at the discussion of cultural variables in Chapter 1, the culture of agency theory reflects high individualism and high power distance, whereas collectivism and low power distance are characteristic of stewardship approaches to management.[64]

Other theories of management exist, including the "power perspective theory" and "resource dependency." However, our goal is not to address all such theories but to provide the framework within which control mechanisms exist to enhance behavior in accordance with laws and ethics.

## The Importance of Good Governance

The presence of strong governance standards provides better access to capital and aids economic growth. Various survey results in the decade of the 2000s indicate that the investment community is willing to pay more for a company with strong and effective corporate governance policies. A 2005 survey of institutional investors conducted by the Economist Intelligence Unit, which polled 136 senior executives and 65 institutional investors in

October 2004, indicates that transparency of corporate dealings is the most important element of investment decisions (68 percent) followed by high standards of corporate governance (62 percent) and ethical behavior of staff (46 percent).[65]

The survey found that corporate responsibility is a "central" or "important" consideration in business decisions: 85 percent ranked corporate responsibility as central or important, compared with 44 percent in 2000. According to the report, corporate governance has become a mainstream business concern. The increased presence of corporate responsibility in daily business operations is being driven by a variety of factors, such as the erosion of trust in large companies.[66] There is no doubt that in the United States, the Sarbanes-Oxley Act (SOX) that was passed by Congress in 2002 and follow-up SEC regulations is largely responsible for the increased emphasis on good governance.

## Executive Compensation

One of the most common approaches to the agency problem is to link managerial compensation to the financial performance of the corporation in general and the performance of the company's shares. Typically, this occurs by creating long-term compensation packages and stock option plans that tie executive wealth to an increase in the corporation's stock price. These incentives aim to encourage managers to maximize the market value of shares. One of the biggest issues that corporate boards of directors face is executive compensation. It has been found that most boards spend more time deciding how much to compensate top executives than they do ensuring the integrity of the company's financial reporting systems.[67]

### *Excessive Pay Packages*

A problem arises when top management purposefully manipulates earnings amounts to drive up the price of stock so they can cash in more lucrative stock options. During the financial crisis, Congress charged executives at some of the nation's largest companies with gaining pay packages in the millions while their companies suffered losses, and they may have even accepted funds from the government to keep them liquid. The Obama administration named a "compensation czar," Kenneth Feinberg, to set salaries and bonuses at some of the biggest firms at the heart of the economic crisis, as part of a broader government campaign to reshape pay practices across corporate America. The initiative reflected public uproar over executive compensation at companies such as American International Group (AIG) that received a $180 billion bailout from the government and decided to pay $165 million in bonuses to executives.

A study conducted by a professor at Purdue University in 2009 that used a new type of theoretical analysis found that chief executives in 35 of the top *Fortune* 500 companies were overpaid by 129 times their "ideal salaries" in 2008. The authors noted that the ratio of CEO pay to the lowest employee salary has gone up from about 40:1 in the 1970s to as high as 344:1 in recent years in the United States. At the same time, the ratio remained around 20:1 in Europe and 11:1 in Japan.[68] Other studies have found that compensation for big-company CEOs was more than 400 times the pay for average workers in past years.

We do not know whether CEOs at top American companies are overpaid. After all, they have the daunting task of running multibillion-dollar companies in an increasingly globalized, competitive environment. However, it does give us pause when we read that in 2011, the chief executives of the 500 biggest companies in the United States (as measured by a composite ranking of sales, profits, assets, and market value) got a collective pay raise of 16 percent that year, to $5.2 billion. This compares with a 3 percent pay raise for the average American worker.[69]

*Backdating Stock Options*

An executive compensation scandal erupted in 2006 when it was discovered that some companies had changed the grant dates of their options to coincide with a dip in the stock price, making the options worth more because less money would be needed to exercise them and buy stock. Although backdating was legal, it must be expensed and disclosed properly in the financial statements. Legalities aside, it is difficult to justify such a practice from an ethical perspective because it purposefully manipulates the option criteria that determine their value.

In the wake of this scandal, hundreds of companies conducted internal probes and the SEC launched investigations into more than 140 firms. The agency filed charges against 24 companies and 66 individuals for backdating-related offenses, and at least 15 people have been convicted of criminal conduct. An interesting case is that of Nancy Heinen, Apple Computer's general counsel until she left in 2006. She was investigated by the SEC for receiving backdated options and wound up agreeing to pay $2.2 million in disgorgement (return of ill-gotten gains), interest, and penalties. Steve Jobs, the former CEO of Apple, apologized on behalf of the company, stating that he did not understand the relevant accounting laws. Of course, ignorance of the law is no excuse for violating it—at least in spirit—especially by someone like Jobs, who presumably had dozens of accountants on staff to advise on these matters. Notably, SOX includes stricter reporting requirements that are supposed to cut down on such practices.

*Clawbacks*

Clawbacks have been on the regulatory radar screen in a big way since 2002, when SOX gave the SEC power to recover compensation and stock profits from CEOs and CFOs of public companies in the event of financial restatements caused by misconduct. The Dodd-Frank Act that is discussed in greater detail below requires that publicly listed companies themselves recover the compensation. Clawback policies among Fortune 100 companies were already on the rise before the financial crisis, jumping from 17.6 percent in 2006 to 42.1 percent in 2007. In 2010, the year Dodd-Frank was passed, 82.1 percent of the Fortune 100 had them. In 2012, 86.5 percent of the Fortune 100 firms had adopted publicly disclosed policies. The ethical justification for clawbacks is the breach of fiduciary duty owed by top management to shareholders and inequities when they benefit from their own wrongful acts.

*Say on Pay*

The Dodd-Frank Wall Street Reform and Consumer Protection Act (H.R. 4173)[70] was signed into federal law by President Barack Obama on July 21, 2010. Passed as a response to the late-2000s recession, it brought the most significant changes to financial regulation in the United States since the regulatory reform that followed the Great Depression. It made changes in the American financial regulatory environment that affect all federal financial regulatory agencies and almost every part of the nation's financial services industry today.

Two areas where Dodd-Frank relates to corporate governance are in executive compensation and whistleblowing procedures that will be discussed later on. The Act includes "say-on-pay" provisions (Section 951) that require SEC-registered issuers to provide shareholders at least once every three calendar years with a separate nonbinding say-on-pay vote regarding the compensation of the company's named executive officers (i.e., CEO and CFO), and the company's three other most highly compensated officers. Although the vote on compensation is nonbinding, the company must include a statement in the "Compensation Discussion and Analysis" of the proxy statement whether and, if so, how its compensation policies and decisions have taken into account the results of the shareholder-say-on-pay vote. The idea is for the vote of the shareholders to be taken seriously not only by the company, but also by other companies in the same marketplace.

In perhaps the most widely followed shareholder action, in April 2012, 55 percent of Citigroup's shareholders voted against CEO Vikram Pandit's $15 million compensation package for 2011, a year when the bank's stock tumbled. At the time of the vote, Pandit had received nearly $7 million in cash for 2011, with the remainder to be paid in restricted stock and cash over the next few years (and thus subject to possible restructuring by the board). Citigroup's shareholders expressed concerns that the compensation package lacked significant and important goals to provide incentives for improvement in the shareholder value of the institution. Soon after the vote, a shareholder filed a derivative lawsuit against the CEO, the board of directors, and other directors and executives for allegedly awarding excessive pay to its senior officers.

Questions raised by shareholders and others about the size of executive compensation packages and say-on-pay votes are designed to build equity into the compensation system. Issues with respect to whether CEOs are overpaid, as many have said, do bring up questions of fairness and justice. Over the long haul, the question is whether these nonbinding referendums are likely to have any impact on the potential civil liability of directors for approving allegedly excessive executive compensation that the shareholders reject. According to Robert Scully, who analyzes the law in the January 2011 *The Federal Lawyer,* the answer is probably not. Scully maintains that Dodd-Frank does not preempt state fiduciary law or entirely occupy the field of director liability for excessive compensation. Instead, the act focuses on the process by which public company executive compensation is set, thereby enforcing the primacy of the business judgment rule in determining executive compensation.[71]

## Corporate Governance Mechanisms

In his book *Corporate Governance and Ethics,* Zabihollah Rezaee points out that corporate governance is shaped by internal and external mechanisms, as well as policy interventions through regulations. Internal mechanisms help manage, direct, and monitor corporate governance activities to create sustainable stakeholder value. Examples include the board of directors, particularly independent directors; the audit committee; management; internal controls; and the internal audit function. External mechanisms are intended to monitor the company's activities, affairs, and performance to ensure that the interests of insiders (management, directors, and officers) are aligned with the interests of outsiders (shareholders and other stakeholders). Examples of external mechanisms include the financial markets, state and federal statutes, court decisions, and shareholder proposals.[72] Two points of note include (1) independent directors enhance governance accountability and (2) separate meetings between the audit committee and external auditors strengthen control mechanisms.

### The Role of the Board of Directors

For public corporations, boards of directors hold the ultimate responsibility for their firms' success or failure, as well as for the ethics of their own actions. The members of the board are legally responsible for the firm's resources and decisions, and they appoint its top executive officers.

The directors and officers of a corporation are responsible for managing and directing the business and affairs of the corporation. They often face difficult questions concerning whether to acquire other businesses, sell assets, expand into other areas of business, or issue stocks and dividends. They may also face potential hostile takeovers by other businesses. To help directors and officers meet these challenges without fear of liability, courts have given substantial deference to the decisions the directors and officers must make. Under the *business judgment rule,* the officers and directors of a corporation are immune from liability to the corporation for losses incurred in corporate transactions within their authority, so long as the transactions are made in good faith and with reasonable skill and prudence.

Board members have a fiduciary duty to safeguard corporate assets and make decisions that promote shareholder interests. They owe a duty of care in carrying out their responsibilities, which means to act in the best interests of the shareholders. This is typically defined as a level of care expected of a reasonable person under the same circumstances (notice the universality dimension). The board exercises diligence by performing vigilant oversight of the company's business and financial affairs, ensuring that reliable financial information is reported, and monitoring compliance with applicable laws, rules, and regulations. Failure to adhere to these obligations may constitute a breach of the fiduciary duty of care that is expected of directors. A good example is the accounting fraud at Waste Management, where Andersen auditors developed a plan called "Summary of Action Steps" to correct for the company's past misstatements in its financial reports. The idea was to correct for past adjustments by spreading out their effects over a number of years in the future, a practice that did not conform to GAAP. Rather than insist on immediate recognition of the full amount of the adjustment as required by GAAP, all members of top management agreed to the plan. The board failed in its fiduciary role by accepting the plan without questioning its appropriateness.

Despite the fact that board members have been given greater responsibilities under SOX and SEC regulations, there is scant evidence that they have been held more accountable for their own misconduct. The SEC does not usually pursue corporate directors for misconduct unless it can be proved that they acted in bad faith. One example is the civil charges brought against three directors of DHB Industries for allegedly ignoring red flags indicating misconduct in the company. According to the accusations, these directors tried to hide the fraud by hiring two separate firms to perform audits, perhaps in the hope that at least one of the firms would sign off on the financial statements. Because the SEC saw indications of corruption within the board, it filed a lawsuit against the directors. However, this type of action tends to be the exception rather than the norm.[73]

## Audit Committee

In the aftermath of accounting scandals at companies such as Enron and WorldCom, Congress passed SOX in 2002[74] to strengthen corporate governance mechanisms. One important requirement is for the audit committee of the board of directors to be completely independent of management. National stock exchanges such as the New York Stock Exchange (NYSE) adopted listing requirements that a majority of directors must be independent of management. In the accounting scandals, the audit committee either didn't know about the fraud or chose to look the other way. A conscientious and diligent committee is an essential ingredient of an effective corporate governance system—one that takes its role in financial statement oversight to heart and follows basic principles of responsibility, accountability, and transparency.

The Audit Committee Institute at the international accounting firm KPMG, issued "Ten To-Do's for Audit Committees in 2011." The most important of these are (1) focus on financial reporting and strong internal controls, (2) review the company's whistleblower processes and compliance program, (3) understand the significance of risks to the company's operations and financial reporting, (4) consider whether the company's disclosures provide investors with the information needed to understand the state of the business, (5) set clear expectations for the internal audit function and communication with the external auditors, and (6) understand the audit committee's role in information technology.[75]

Traditionally, the audit committee's primary role has been to monitor the integrity of the financial statements produced by management. Deloitte and Touche LLP elaborates on the role of audit committees in financial reporting and provides helpful advice for audit committees to discharge their expanded responsibilities under SOX, including the following:[76]

- Audit committees should be aware of the universe of corporate reporting and its various financial and nonfinancial components.
- Audit committees should review the financial statements, Management Discussion & Analysis (MD&A) and related news releases as a single package of information.
- The effectiveness of the audit committee's review of earnings news releases, financial statements, and MD&A depends not only on its understanding of accounting standards and regulations, but to a great extent on its knowledge of the company's business and the industries in which the company operates.
- In addition to approving the financial statements, MD&A and earnings news release, the audit committee must understand and agree with the process by which these documents were prepared.
- The audit committee should seek assurances from the CEO and CFO as part of the CEO/CFO financial statement certification process that they have put in place and effective disclosure controls and procedures to ensure that all reports have been prepared and filed properly with the appropriate authorities in accordance with applicable requirements.
- Audit committees should review their oversight responsibilities regularly to determine whether they should include additional financial and/or nonfinancial disclosures.

There can be no doubt that financial reports would be more reliable if audit committees adhered to these guidelines. The goal should be to establish an ethical corporate culture that supports good corporate governance. In addition to a watchful audit committee, an organization must establish effective internal controls to ferret out fraud, a strong internal audit oversight role to deal with fraud, diligent members of the board of directors to oversee management, and a management group that recognizes its primary responsibility is to conduct business operations in a responsible manner and report financial information in accordance with established accounting rules. Organizations that create such an environment are better prepared to deal with the challenges of maintaining an effective corporate governance system.

Following the passage of SOX, the audit committee was seen as the one body that was (or at least should be) capable of preventing identified fraudulent financial reporting. The audit committee has an oversight responsibility for the financial statements. The internal auditors should have direct and unrestricted access to the audit committee so that they can take any matters of concern directly to that group without having to go through top management. The external auditors rely on the support and actions of the audit committee to resolve differences with management over proper financial reporting. Section 401 of SOX amended the Securities Exchange Act of 1934 to include the requirement that each financial statement filed with the SEC should reflect all material correcting adjustments that have been identified by the audit firm in accordance with GAAP and the rules and regulations of the commission. Even though the fraud at Waste Management preceded passage of the Act, it is clear that the law would have been violated by writing off material adjustments over a period of time in the future rather than charging them against retained earnings.

An effective device to ensure audit committee independence is for the committee to meet separately with the senior executives, the internal auditors, and the external auditors. The perception of internal auditors as the "eyes and ears" of the audit committee suggests that the head of the internal audit department attend all audit committee meetings.[77] Recall the role of Cynthia Cooper at WorldCom. She informed the audit committee every step of the way as her department uncovered the fraud, and ultimately she gained the support of the external auditors.

## Internal Controls as a Monitoring Device

The internal controls that are established by management should help prevent and detect fraud, including materially false and misleading financial reports, asset misappropriations, and inadequate disclosures in the financial statements. These controls are designed to ensure that management policies are followed, laws are strictly adhered to, and ethical systems are built into corporate governance. However, even the best internal controls can be overridden by top management. For example, top executives at Tyco and Adelphia used corporate resources for their own benefit without getting proper authority from the board of directors, thereby violating their fiduciary duty and duty of care to the stockholders. The board at each company claimed to have been uninformed about the use of hundreds of millions of dollars from interest-free loans for personal purposes. We can assume that each company had a series of internal controls in place to prevent such an occurrence. Still, the CEOs circumvented their own controls to accomplish their self-interest-oriented goals. The tone at the top of these organizations apparently was that employees should do what the CEO says, not what she does. It creates a cynical attitude on the part of employees who may come to view the organization as not following its own ethical standards, while at the same time expecting its employees to adhere to those standards.

The risk that internal controls will not help prevent or detect a material misstatement in the financial statements is a critical evaluation to provide reasonable assurance that the financial statements are free from material misstatement. Auditing Standard No. 5 issued by the Public Company Accounting Oversight Board (PCAOB) establishes requirements and provides direction that applies when an auditor is engaged to perform an audit of management's assessment of the effectiveness of internal control over financial reporting that is integrated with an audit of the financial statements, a requirement of SOX. These standards are discussed in Chapter 5.

The system of internal controls and whether it operates as intended enables the auditor to either gain confidence about the internal processing of transactions or create doubt for the auditor that should be pursued. *Internal Control—Integrated Framework,* published by the Committee of Sponsoring Organizations (COSO) of the Treadway Commission in 1992, establishes a framework that defines internal control as a process, effected by an entity's board of directors, management, and other personnel, designed to provide reasonable assurance regarding the achievement of the following objectives: (a) effectiveness and efficiency of operations; (b) reliability of financial reporting; and (c) compliance with applicable laws and regulations.[78]

The COSO report states that management should enact five components related to these objectives as part of the framework including: (1) the control environment; (2) risk assessment; (3) control activities; (4) monitoring; and (5) information and communication.

1. The *control environment* sets the tone of an organization, influencing the control consciousness of its people. It is the foundation for all aspects of internal control, providing discipline and structure.
2. *Risk assessment* is the entity's identification and evaluation of how risk might affect the achievement of objectives.
3. *Control activities* are the strategic actions established by management to ensure that its directives are carried out.
4. *Monitoring* is a process that assesses the efficiency and effectiveness of internal controls over time.
5. *Information and communication* systems provide the information in a form and at a time that enables people to carry out their responsibilities.

The COSO framework emphasizes the roles and responsibilities of management, the board of directors, internal auditors, and other personnel in creating an environment that supports the objectives of internal control. One important contribution of COSO is in the area of corporate governance. COSO notes that if members of the board and audit committee do not take their responsibilities seriously, then the system will likely break down as occurred in Enron and WorldCom. The COSO *Integrated Framework* is the foundation for control assessment of internal financial reporting required by SOX under Section 404. More will be said about the framework in Chapter 5.

The results for a company can be devastating when internal controls fail or are overridden by management. A good example is what happened to Groupon after it announced a restatement in its financial statements on March 30, 2012, that resulted from a material weakness in its internal controls with respect to the inadequacy of its reserve for coupon returns. Exhibit 3.9 presents a summary of the facts surrounding the restatement. There can be no doubt that the company's fortunes changed on a dime after the announcement as its IPO share price close of $26.11 on March 30, 2012, trended downward and continued going in the wrong direction declining to $4.14 as of November 30, 2012. The stock has since rebounded somewhat to $7.69 as of June 1, 2013.

## Internal Auditors

Internal auditors interact with top management, and as such, should assist them to fulfill their role in developing accurate and reliable financial statements and compliance with

**EXHIBIT 3.9**
**Internal Control**
**Disaster at Groupon**

Groupon, Inc., offers online retail services and provides daily deals on things to do, eat, see, and buy in more than 500 markets in 44 countries. It has offices across North America, Europe, Latin America, Asia, and other parts of the world.

On November 5, 2011, Groupon took its company public in an IPO with a buy-in price set at $20 per share. Groupon shares rose from their IPO price of $20 by 40 percent in early trading on NASDAQ and ended at the 4 p.m. market close at $26.11, up 31 percent. The closing price valued Groupon at $16.6 billion, making it more valuable than companies such as Adobe Systems and nearly the size of Yahoo.

Groupon employees broke out the champagne, as did Silicon Valley and Wall Street, as financial analysts took Groupon's stock market debut as a sign that investors are still willing to make risky bets on fast-growing but unprofitable young Internet companies, even as the IPO environment had shifted downward since the financial troubles that started in 2007.

At a size of up to $805 million, Groupon ranked as the third-largest Internet IPO sold in the United States in 2011, after a $1.4 billion issue by Russian search-engine operator Yandex NV in May and a $855 million issue by China social networking platform Renren, according to Dealogic. It was the ninth-largest ever, on a list topped by the $1.9 billion sale by Google in 2004.

Less than five months later, on March 30, 2012, Groupon announced that it had revised its financial results, an unexpected restatement that deepened losses and raised questions about its accounting practices. As part of the revision, Groupon disclosed a "material weakness" in its internal controls, saying that it had failed to set aside enough money to cover customer refunds. The accounting issue increased the company's losses in the fourth quarter to $64.9 million from $42.3 million. The news that day sent shares of Groupon tumbling 6 percent, to $17.29. Shares of Groupon had fallen by 30 percent since it went public.

In its announcement of the restatement, Groupon explained that it had encountered problems related to certain assumptions and forecasts the company used to calculate its results. In particular, the company said that it underestimated customer refunds for higher-priced offers, such as laser eye surgery. Groupon collects more revenue on such deals, but it also sees a higher number of refunds. The company honors customer refunds for the life of its

*(Continued)*

**EXHIBIT 3.9**
(*Continued*)

coupons, so these payments can affect its financials at various times. Groupon deducts refunds within 60 days from receiving revenue; after that, the company has to take an additional accounting charge related to the payments.

As Groupon prepared its financial statements for 2011, its independent auditor, Ernst & Young, determined that the company did not account accurately for the possibility of higher refunds. By the firm's assessment, that constituted a "material weakness." Groupon said in its annual report, "We did not maintain effective controls to provide reasonable assurance that accounts were complete and accurate."

In an interesting twist, in response to the conclusion that the company's internal controls contained a material weakness, Groupon blamed Ernst & Young in part for not identifying the weakness. The auditors were at fault for not identifying problems with the financial controls earlier, said Herman Leung, a financial analyst at Susquehanna Financial Group in San Francisco. "This should have been highlighted by the auditors. The business is growing so fast that it sounds like they don't have the proper financial controls to deal with the growth."[79] In fact, it was management's assessment of the material weakness in internal controls over financial reporting that led to the disclosure. Ernst & Young had signed the fourth-quarter audit report included in Groupon's annual report, giving a clean (unmodified) opinion.

In a related issue, on April 3, 2012, a shareholder lawsuit was brought against Groupon, accusing the company of misleading investors about its financial prospects in its IPO and concealing weak internal controls. According to the complaint, the company overstated revenue, issued materially false and misleading financial results, and concealed how its business was not growing as fast and was not nearly as resistant to competition, such as from LivingSocial and Amazon, as it had suggested.

These claims bring up a gap in the sections of SOX that deal with companies' internal controls. There is no requirement to disclose a control weakness in a company's IPO prospectus. Groupon had no obligation to disclose the problem until it filed its first quarterly or annual report as a public company—which is what it did.

laws and regulations. Exhibit 3.10 presents the framework of financial reporting that supports a strong control environment identified in the Treadway Commission Report titled *Report of the National Commission on Fraudulent Financial Reporting.*[80] Notice how the internal auditors should have direct and unrestricted access to the audit committee. One problem for Cynthia Cooper as she struggled to get WorldCom to act on the fraudulent capitalization of line costs was periodic interference by Scott Sullivan, the CFO and mastermind of the fraud. But Cooper didn't let that stop her dogged pursuit of the truth about the causes of the fraud.

Internal auditors have a crucial role to play in risk management. PricewaterhouseCoopers (PwC) released a study, *2012 PwC State of the Internal Audit Profession,* that indicates risks are increasing because of global economic uncertainty. It topped the list as the biggest perceived risk to companies that year, according to nearly three-quarters of the chief audit executives (CAEs) and other poll respondents.[81]

The survey indicated that other significant risks have emerged, and businesses are asking internal auditing to play a bigger role in helping companies navigate the changing risk landscape. While concerns about further economic uncertainty continue to be the main ones for business leaders, issues such as fraud and ethics, mergers and acquisitions, large programs, new product introductions, and business continuity were identified among the top risks affecting businesses.

The single most requested area for increased internal audit focus was data privacy and security, with 46 percent of stakeholders asking for added capabilities in this area. With regulations escalating and evolving, the second-largest requested area for increased focus involves regulations and government policies, with 32 percent of stakeholders asking internal auditing to get more involved in supporting the business in understanding and

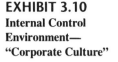

**EXHIBIT 3.10**
**Internal Control Environment— "Corporate Culture"**

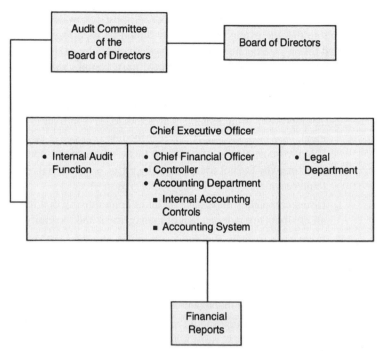

managing this risk. Survey respondents also indicated that they were concerned about areas such as fraud and ethics.

The report found that internal audit groups at leading companies provide stakeholders with advice on risks and controls rather than just reporting on gaps. A total of 78 percent of the survey respondents whose companies were better at managing risk said their CAEs played a more active role during executive meetings, compared to only 61 percent of companies that were not as well managed. In addition, the better managed companies take into consideration the organization's enterprise risk management process and adapt their approach quickly when changes are needed.

## Audited Financial Statements

The Securities and Exchange Act of 1934 established mandatory independent audits of publicly traded companies in order to give third parties confidence that the companies' books could be trusted. The financial statements prepared by management report the financial results in accordance with GAAP. The audit involves an examination of those statements in accordance with generally accepted auditing standards (GAAS) and the rendering of the opinion about whether the financials conform to GAAP. Because the purpose of an audit is to provide "reasonable assurance" to investors and creditors that the financial statements are free of material misstatement, the audit plays an important role in corporate governance. The audit function will be discussed in greater detail in Chapter 5.

## NYSE Listing Requirements

Corporate governance provisions in the United States establish benchmark standards by which publicly owned companies should measure their practices. Control procedures required by the New York Stock Exchange (NYSE) provide a blueprint of good governance practices. While there is no required formal report on corporate governance, as in many other countries outside the United States, listed companies in the United States must adopt and disclose corporate governance guidelines and CEOs must certify compliance.

Non-U.S. companies listed on the NYSE must follow U.S. corporate governance provisions so that the listing requirements should be used as part of the comparative analysis. What follows are the final corporate governance rules of the NYSE (2003) approved by the SEC. Companies listed on the exchange must comply with standards regarding corporate governance as codified in Section 303A.

1. Listed companies must have a majority of independent directors.
2. To empower non-management directors to serve as a more effective check on management, they must meet at regularly scheduled executive sessions without management. "Non-management" directors are those who are not company officers and include directors who are not independent by virtue of a material relationship, former status or family membership, or for any other reason.
3. Listed companies must have an audit committee with a minimum of three members, all of whom are independent of management and the entity.
4. From time to time, the audit committee should meet separately with management, internal auditors (or other personnel responsible for the internal audit function), and independent auditors.
5. The audit committee should review with the independent auditor any audit problems or difficulties and management's response.
6. The audit committee should report regularly to the board of directors.
7. Each listed company must have an internal audit function.
8. Each listed company CEO must certify to the NYSE each year that he or she is not aware of any violation by the company of NYSE corporate governance listing standards.
9. Listed companies must adopt and disclose corporate governance guidelines.
10. Listed foreign private issuers must disclose any significant ways in which their corporate governance practices differ from those followed by domestic companies under NYSE listing standards.

On December 14, 2009, the NYSE amended its corporate governance listing standards and they were approved by the SEC.[82] Some of the amendments relate to our discussions of corporate governance mechanisms and include the following new requirements:

- *Enhanced Notification Requirements.* A company's CEO must notify NYSE after an executive officer becomes aware of *any* noncompliance with NYSE corporate governance listing standards, regardless of its materiality.
- *Communications with Directors.* The amendments clarify that a company must disclose a method for *all* interested parties, not only shareholders, to communicate with the presiding director or the non-management or independent directors as a group.
- *Disclosure of Business Conduct and Ethics Waivers.* The amended listing standards clarify that companies must disclose any waivers of their codes of conduct and ethics granted to executive officers and directors within four business days, the same time frame required by the SEC, either through a press release, on the company's website or on a Form 8-K.
- *Executive Sessions.* A company can hold regular executive sessions of independent directors as an alternative to executive sessions of non-management directors.

These amendments should improve corporate governance disclosures of deviations from accepted governance standards because there no longer can be a materiality evaluation. In addition, it accelerates the reporting by listed companies of waivers from the code of ethics granted to executive officers and directors. Recall that this was an area creating a conflict of interest at Enron when the CFO, Andy Fastow, who also managed some of the special-purpose-entities, was given a waiver from the company's code of ethics that prohibited such related-party relationships. There was no disclosure at the time to members of the board or the outside auditors.

## Code of Ethics for CEOs and CFOs

In virtually all the frauds of the late 1990s and early 2000s, the CEOs and CFOs knew about the company's materially misstated financial statements. One important provision of SOX that helps protect the public against fraudulent financial statements is the requirement of Section 302 that the CEO and CFO must certify that to the best of their knowledge, there are no material misstatements in the financial statements. Another requirement of SOX is that public companies must have a code of ethics for its CEO and principal financial officers. This code must be separate from the company's code of ethics. An excellent example of such a code is the code for finance professionals of Microsoft which appears in Appendix 2 of this chapter. Notice how the code includes many provisions that are part of an ethical culture, reliance on virtues to instill the desired standards of behavior, and links to corporate governance. You know that a company takes its ethical obligations seriously when it establishes a series of steps for employees to follow when reporting violations of the standards of business practice (whistleblowing) and concerns about questionable accounting or auditing practices.

A valid question, now that SOX is more than 10 years old, is whether its promise of holding CEOs and CFOs criminally responsible for fraud has been a success. The law states that if top corporate executives knowingly sign off on a false financial report, they're subject to a prison term of up to 10 years and a fine of up to $1 million, with penalties escalating to 20 years and $5 million if their misconduct is willful. In practice, very few defendants have even been charged with false certification, and fewer still have been convicted.

As previously discussed, Richard Scrushy, the former HealthSouth Corporation CEO, falsely certified the financial statements of the company but was not sent to jail for that crime. On the other hand, CFO Weston L. Smith was sentenced in 2005 to 27 months in prison for his role in the company's $2.7 billion accounting fraud. Smith had pleaded guilty to one count each of conspiracy to commit wire and securities fraud, falsely certifying a financial report, and falsifying a report to the SEC.

In 2007, the former CFO of a medical equipment financing company called DVI pleaded guilty to mail fraud and false certification and was sentenced to 30 months in prison. In a more recent case, a SOX false certification charge against former Vitesse CEO Louis Tomasetta was dismissed.

What about using SOX to prosecute bank executives for their role in the mortgage crisis? Frankel points out that there has been renewed interest in SOX as a potential tool in investigations of companies involved in the financial meltdown of 2007–2008, including J.P. Morgan Chase that engaged in risky credit default swap trading.

So, the question in the end is, why have there not been more prosecutions under Section 302? Frankel believes that the answer may lie partly in how corporations have responded to SOX. Most major corporations have implemented internal compliance systems that make it very difficult to show that the CEO or CFO knowingly signed a false certification. And when prosecutors have enough evidence to show that those internal systems failed and top executives knowingly engaged in wrongdoing, they often prefer, for strategic reasons, to charge crimes other than false certification.[83]

The jury is still out on whether SOX serves as an adequate deterrent to financial fraud. We should not be surprised if the answer is "no" because laws do not necessarily lead to ethical behavior. Any law—including SOX—establishes the rules of the game and how violators will be punished. As we have learned throughout these first three chapters, ethical behavior comes from within; it comes from a desire to do the right thing, not because we may be punished if we do not. In the end, it is a post-conventional mindset that guides ethical reasoning when the chips are down, not a conventional one. Laws are needed, but they serve as only a minimum standard of ethical conduct. Codes of ethics are needed because they help to establish an ethical organization environment. But it is virtuous behavior that should guide corporate officers through the minefield of conflicts and pressures that exist in decision making.

## Compliance Function

The Ethics and Compliance Officer Association (ECOA) has recognized its increased responsibilities resulting from SOX. The mission of the ECOA is to promote "ethical business practices and [serve] as a global forum for the exchange of information and strategies among organizations and individuals responsible for ethics, compliance, and business conduct programs."[84] An important step in encouraging the reporting of wrongdoing is to appoint a trusted member of the management team to be the organization's ethics officer. This person should take the lead in ensuring that the organization is in compliance with the laws and regulations, including SEC securities laws, SOX, and Dodd-Frank. A chief compliance officer (CCO) should serve as a sounding board for management to try out new ideas to see if it passes the ethics "smell" test. The ethics officer plays a critical role in helping create a positive ethical tone in organizations.

The 2012 State of Compliance study conducted by PwC found that oversight of the compliance function has been changing. Fewer compliance officers report to the general counsel on a daily basis (35 percent in 2012, compared to 41 percent in 2011), although the number reporting on a daily basis to the CEO held steady at 32 percent. On a formal basis, 32 percent of respondents report to the audit committee, almost as many as who report to the general counsel (33 percent) and much more than those reporting to the CEO. This falls in line with the FSGO revisions from 2010, which favor an independent compliance function that preferably reports to the audit committee and board.[85]

Over the past decade, heightened regulations related to SOX and Dodd-Frank have elevated the importance and visibility of the chief compliance officer role. Now an official member of the c-suite, compliance leaders are tasked with building comprehensive and robust programs that not only address existing requirements, but also anticipate regulatory changes and their likely impact.

# Bernie Madoff's Ponzi Scheme

A *Ponzi scheme* is an investment fraud that involves the payment of purported returns to existing investors from funds contributed by new investors.[86] Ponzi scheme organizers often solicit new investors by promising to invest funds in opportunities claimed to generate high returns with little or no risk. In many Ponzi schemes, the fraudsters focus on attracting new money to make promised payments to earlier-stage investors and to use for personal expenses instead of engaging in any legitimate investment activity. With little or no legitimate earnings, the schemes require a consistent flow of money from new investors to continue. Ponzi schemes tend to collapse when it becomes difficult to recruit new investors or when a large number of investors ask to cash out.

The case of Bernie Madoff illustrates what can happen in a Ponzi scheme when regulators ignore warnings by whistleblowers.[87]

Madoff was a trusted investment adviser. He had served as chair of the board of directors and served on the board of governors of the National Association of Securities Dealers (NASDAQ), a self-regulator securities industry organization. He had personal relationships with his investors and was a pillar of the community. Madoff used his reputation to gain favor with his investors and assure them about the promised level of returns.

As the stock market tanked in the period between 2007 and 2009, many Madoff investors asked to have their funds returned. Madoff could return some of the money, typically to favored investors, but he couldn't meet most of the claims. By the time the dust had settled, Madoff had perpetrated a $65 billion fraud. Two of his sons involved in the business, Andrew and Mark, notified the federal authorities on December 11, 2008, and Madoff was arrested. He was sentenced to serve a 150-year sentence on June 16, 2009, and $170 billion of his ill-gotten gains is supposed to be restored to the victims of his crime.

The trustee assigned to handle repayments is Irving Picard, who has been bringing lawsuits against former investors who benefited disproportionately when Madoff did return money. The recovery actions are facilitated through "clawback" lawsuits to recover some of the money. In December 2010, Picard and Preet Bharara, U.S. Attorney for the Southern District of New York, cleared a major hurdle in dealing with Madoff's mess. They announced a $7.2 billion settlement with Barbara Picower, the widow of Jeffrey Picower, considered the biggest beneficiary of Madoff's scheme. According to the trustee, Picower had withdrawn $7.8 billion from Madoff's firm since the 1970s, even though he only deposited $619 million. His widow agreed to hand over the difference, $7.2 billion, to benefit Madoff's victims, many of whom were left destitute in the wake of his fraud. On March 19, 2012, a settlement was reached with the best-known Madoff investors in the clawback actions. Picard had filed suit against the owners of the New York Mets, Fred Wilpon and Saul Katz. He initially sought $1 billion, claiming that they enriched themselves over many years of profitable investing with Madoff while ignoring repeated warnings that he might have been a fraud. The owners agreed to pay $162 million, but that figure is likely to be reduced or wiped out altogether as the complex bankruptcy litigation involving Madoff's investment operation plays out.

The SEC brought an action against Madoff's auditors, Friehling & Horowitz, claiming that the firm enabled Madoff's conduct by falsely representing to investors that Bernard L. Madoff Investment Securities (BMIS) LLC was financially sound and that the firm employed independent auditors who conducted audits of BMIS each year. In documents that the firm knew were distributed or submitted to investors and the SEC, Friehling knowingly or with reckless disregard falsely stated the following:[88]

- The firm audited BMIS's financial statements pursuant to GAAS, including the requirements to maintain auditor independence, and to perform audit procedures regarding custody of securities.
- BMIS's financial statements were presented in conformity with GAAP.
- Friehling & Horowitz had reviewed the internal control environment at BMIS, including internal controls over the custody of securities, and found no material inadequacies.

According to the SEC, all of these statements were materially false because Friehling & Horowitz did not perform anything remotely resembling an audit of BMIS and, critically, did not perform procedures to confirm the securities that BMIS purportedly held on behalf of its customers even existed. Instead, the firm merely pretended to conduct minimal audit procedures of certain accounts to make it seem as though it were conducting an audit, and even then, it failed to document its purported findings and conclusions as required under GAAS. If properly stated, those financial statements, along with BMIS's related disclosures regarding reserve requirements, would have shown that BMIS owed tens of billions of dollars in additional liabilities to its customers and thus was insolvent. Similarly, Friehling & Horowitz did not conduct any procedures with respect to BMIS's internal controls, or it knew or recklessly disregarded that it had absolutely no basis to represent that BMIS had adequate internal controls. On November 3, 2009, Friehling & Horowitz agreed not to contest the SEC's findings and consented to a partial judgment without admitting or denying the allegations of the SEC's complaint.

A sad part of the Bernie Madoff story is what happened to his family in the aftermath of the public disclosure of the Ponzi scheme. No longer able to deal with the hatred against his family and his own role in the scandal, on December 11, 2010 (the two-year anniversary of his father's downfall), Mark Madoff killed himself. On June 20, 2012, another son,

Peter, pleaded guilty to one count of conspiracy to commit securities fraud and one count of falsifying records. Prosecutors said Peter Madoff will agree to forfeit $143.1 billion, a staggering amount based on the total funds that passed through the Madoff firm during his tenure. On December 20, 2012, Peter was sentenced to a ten-year jail term for crimes including conspiracy to commit securities fraud. Peter was the chief compliance officer of the firm. It is hard to feel sorry for him because he either did know about the fraud or should have known as the compliance officer. No charges had been filed against Andrew Madoff in the fraud. Bernie Madoff's wife, Ruth, disclaimed any knowledge of the fraud and denied any guilt for the fraud in a *60 Minutes* interview with Morley Safer in October 2011.

Who is to blame for the fraud at Madoff? Clearly, Madoff himself violated every standard of ethical behavior and acted strictly in his own self-interests. He even ignored the interests of his family, claiming that they knew nothing of the fraud (which is somewhat hard to believe in the light of subsequent evidence) and left them to pick up the pieces of their smashed lives. Friehling & Horowitz shares the blame with Madoff for failing to live up to its ethical obligations as a CPA firm. Perhaps most important was the benign role played by the SEC in acting on tips that it had received by an external whistleblower, Harry Markopolos, an investment adviser who was skeptical of Madoff's approach to earning the purported large returns for his investors.

Markopolos testified in February 2009, in hearings held by the U.S. House of Representatives, that the SEC ignored his repeated warnings about Madoff's dealings. Markopolos asserted that he had submitted warnings about Madoff since 2000 and he assailed the agency for ignoring his warnings or brushing them aside. "Nothing was done," he declared. "There was an abject failure by the regulatory agencies we entrust as our watchdog." Markopolos stated publicly that his experience with most SEC officials "proved to be a systemic disappointment, and lead me to conclude that the SEC securities lawyers, if only through their investigative ineptitude and financial illiteracy, colluded to maintain large frauds such as the one to which Madoff later confessed."

Markopolos said he began his investigation of Madoff after his superior at Rampart Investment Management asked him to try to match the returns of Madoff's firm. Markopolos said his analysis showed it was impossible for Madoff to outperform the markets and other managers consistently, as he was claiming. He described Madoff as "one of the most powerful men on Wall Street" and said there was "great danger" in raising questions about him. During his years of investigation, "my team and I surmised that if Madoff gained knowledge of our activities, he may have felt threatened enough to seek to stifle us." He also said, "I became fearful for the safety of my family until the SEC finally acknowledged, after Madoff had been arrested, that it had received credible evidence of Madoff's Ponzi scheme several years earlier."

In the wake of the Madoff fraud, the SEC's office of the inspector general launched an internal investigation in December 2008 to determine why the agency did not detect the scheme. The SEC initiated a variety of actions to prevent such a regulatory failure from occurring in the future. Some of the more relevant steps affecting the accounting profession include:[89]

- Require all investment advisers who control or have custody of their clients' assets to hire an independent public accountant to conduct an annual "surprise exam" to verify that those assets actually exist.

- Require all investment advisers who do not use independent firms to maintain their clients' assets to obtain a third-party written report assessing the safeguards that protect the clients' assets. The report—prepared by an accountant registered and inspected by the PCAOB—would, among other things, describe the controls that are in place to protect the assets, the tests performed on the controls, and the results of those tests.

The SEC is advocating for expanded authority from Congress to reward whistleblowers who bring forward substantial evidence to the agency about significant federal securities violations. It proposed legislation that a fund would be established to pay whistleblowers using money collected from wrongdoers that is not otherwise distributed to investors. The SEC got its way on August 12, 2011, when a rule[90] was adopted under the Dodd-Frank Act to establish a whistleblower program that requires the commission to pay an award, under regulations prescribed by the commission and subject to certain limitations, to eligible whistleblowers who voluntarily provide it with original information about a violation of the federal securities laws that leads to the successful enforcement of a covered judicial or administrative action, or a related action. Dodd-Frank also prohibits retaliation by employers against individuals who provide the commission with information about possible securities violations.

# Whistleblowing

There is no one set definition of whistleblowing, although most definitions characterize the practice as disclosing to others in an organization (internal whistleblowing) an action that violates organizational norms or the law. External whistleblowing entails going to an organization outside the employer to report wrongdoing. Near and Miceli take a broad view of whistleblowing as "the disclosure by organization members (former or current) of illegal, immoral, or illegitimate practices under the control of their employers, to persons or organizations that may be able to effect action." They identify four elements of the whistleblowing process: the whistleblower, the whistleblowing act or complaint, the party to whom the complaint is made, and the organization against which the complaint is lodged. In discussing the act itself, they label it as an act of "dissidence" somewhat analogous to civil disobedience.[91] The term *organizational dissidence* fits in with our discussion of cognitive dissonance in Chapter 2, which emphasized the difference between our thoughts, beliefs or attitudes, and behavior.

## Detection, Reporting, and Retaliation

Ferrell et al. define whistleblowing as exposing an employer's wrongdoing to outsiders such as the media or government regulatory agencies. They acknowledge that the term is sometimes used to refer to corporate internal acts but prefer to label them as form of reporting. For example, reporting of misconduct to management, especially through anonymous reporting mechanisms, often involving hotlines.[92] The ACFE study of global fraud identified hotlines as one of 16 anti-fraud controls used in organizations to report wrongdoing.

Recall the discussion about Sherron Watkins's role as an internal whistleblower in the Enron case in Chapter 2. Watkins initially wrote a letter to Ken Lay, the CEO of the company, questioning the potential effects on the company of improper accounting practices once they are discovered. She did not go any further than reporting it to Lay, and no further action was taken. She became an external whistleblower only after investigations of Enron by the federal government were underway and she testified before Congress.

The evidence shows that nearly all whistleblowers who use external channels to report wrongdoing do so after first using internal channels; they may go outside because the wrongdoing was not corrected after the internal report, because they experienced retaliation, or because the nature of the wrongdoing required it (e.g., some types of wrongdoing, such as fraud or workplace violence, must be reported to authorities).[93]

*Retaliation* refers to an undesirable action taken against a whistleblower in direct response to his or her action. This might include being viewed as an outcast by others in the organization, being written up for poor performance even though the evidence indicates otherwise, demotion, and being passed over for a deserved promotion. In Chapter 2, we discussed the case of Diem-Thi Le, who blew the whistle on illegal practices at the DCAA and experienced virtually all these forms of retaliation.

A study by the Ethics Resource Center (ERC), *Inside the Mind of a Whistleblower,* indicates that the top five reasons given by whistleblowers for coming forward are (1) the belief that corrective action would take place (79 percent); (2) support of management (75 percent); (3) support of coworkers (72 percent); (4) the fact that they could report anonymously (63 percent); and (5) their belief that no one else would (49 percent). The top reasons for not reporting include (1) the conviction that no corrective action would take place; (2) fear of retaliation; (3) fear that they wouldn't remain anonymous; and (4) the assumption that someone else would do it.[94]

The notion that an employee might not engage in whistleblowing because she believes someone else would raises the issue of "bystander apathy." In a post on the Corporate Social Responsibility Newswire, Kristy Mathewson refers to "the bystander effect" as situations where passersby don't offer assistance when other parties are present. Mathewson raises a number of questions with respect to why passersby don't act, including whether there may be an assumption that others will help or that if no one is helping, why should I? Studies have shown that the greater number of parties present, the fewer the incidents of assistance; we take our cues from the behavior of others, and it is, after all, less stress and hassle to ourselves to assume that others will intervene.[95]

There may be implications for reporting corporate fraud if the bystander effect carries over to whistleblowing. The ERC study indicates that employees may go outside their company to report wrongdoing. They may do so because they do not trust the company to handle the matter appropriately or because they are angry or frustrated after their attempts at internal reporting proved to be futile. However, while almost all whistleblowers make some effort to root out wrongdoing internally before going outside the organization, only 2 percent of employees go solely outside their companies to report misconduct. The bystander effect may account for some of that reluctance. A bystander may be concerned that if others have remained silent, then why should he go out on a limb?

Compliance officers have an important role to play in managing the risks of wrong-doing and encouraging reporting. The results of the ERC study on whistleblowing clearly indicate that an ethical organization environment enhances the likelihood the wrongdoings will be reported, while a weak environment or culture of indifference often works against reporting. Compliance officers can help to set an ethical tone that treats whistleblowers with respect rather than derision. The ERC study highlights the toll that whistleblowing can take on employees, as 11 percent of all whistleblowers said they planned to leave their company within one year and an additional 23 percent who reported misconduct and then experienced retaliation planned to leave within one year. The study also indicates that 62 percent who experienced retaliation would be willing to go to the federal government with their concerns, even if their job was at risk.[96]

### Legal Protection for Whistleblowers

Legal protection for whistleblowers exists to encourage reporting of misconduct. Whistleblower laws have provisions against retaliation and are enforced by a number of government agencies. For example, under SOX, the U.S. Department of Labor directly protects whistleblowers who report violations of the law and refuse to engage in any action made unlawful. The Corporate and Criminal Fraud Accountability Act protects employees of publicly traded companies from retaliation if they report violations of any law or regulation of the SEC, or any provision of federal law relating to fraud against shareholders.[97]

### Section 806 of SOX

Section 806 of the Sarbanes-Oxley Act of 2002, Protection for Employees of Publicly Traded Companies Who Provide Evidence in Fraud Cases, confers legal protection upon employees of public companies that report suspected violations of a range of federal offenses—including those relating to fraud against shareholders.[98] This whistleblower provision protects employees who provide information on a fraud by prohibiting the discharge, demotion, discrimination, suspension, or threatening or harassing action against an employee who provides information in a federal or regulatory investigation or to Congress or to the employee's supervisor. A person who alleges discharge or discrimination under this section can file a complaint with the Secretary of Labor. An employee who brings a successful action will be entitled to "reinstatement with the same seniority status that the employee would have had, but for the discrimination; the amount of back pay with interest; and compensation for any special damages sustained as a result of the discrimination, including litigation costs, expert witness fees, and reasonable attorney fees."

The Department of Labor delegated to the Occupational Safety and Health Administration (OSHA) enforcement authority over the whistleblower provisions of SOX. OSHA's regulations require that an employee first establish a *prima facie* case of retaliation. This is generally interpreted as meaning that the employee must be engaged in a protected activity or conduct; that the employer knew "actually or constructively" that the conduct occurred; that the employee suffered an unfavorable personnel action; and that the circumstances "were sufficient to raise the inference that the protected activity was a contributing factor to the unfavorable action."

### R. Allen Stanford Ponzi Scheme and Whistleblower Action

SOX and FSGO have institutionalized internal whistleblowing to encourage discovery of organizational misconduct. A good case study is that of R. Allen Stanford. On March 6, 2012, Stanford was convicted of a $7 billion Ponzi scheme in the style of Bernie Madoff and sentenced to 110 years in federal prison and to forfeit $5.9 billion of personal/business funds. Approximately 20,000 investors lost billions of dollars. Stanford cheated investors by selling them certificates of deposit through the bank he controlled in Antigua (in the West Indies) and telling them that the money would be invested in stocks and bonds. Instead, he diverted $2 billion into risky real-estate ventures and his own businesses. He bribed an Antiguan regulator and an outside auditor. James Davis, Stanford's CFO, pled guilty to fraud and conspiring to obstruct a federal proceeding, and he testified against Stanford.

Lost in the news reports of the scandal is the role of whistleblower Leyla Wydler. Wydler, who had worked for Stanford, alerted the SEC back in 2003. She sent a letter to the commission about her former employer, the Stanford Financial Group. A year earlier, it had fired her for refusing to sell certificates of deposit that she rightly suspected were being misleadingly advertised to investors. The company, Wydler warned in her letter, "is the subject of a lingering corporate fraud scandal perpetrated as a massive Ponzi scheme that will destroy the life savings of many, damage the reputation of all associated parties, ridicule securities and banking authorities, and shame the U.S."[99]

Wydler had resisted Stanford's pressure to get her clients to invest in his scheme. Eventually, she concluded that it was a Ponzi scheme, and she refused to sell the scheme to her clients. Stanford reacted by firing her. The SEC ignored her warnings and allowed Stanford to dupe thousands more of investors after the reporting. But she did not stop with the SEC. She also sent copies of the letter to the National Association of Securities Dealers (NASD)—now called Financial Industry Regulatory Authority (FINRA)—the trade group responsible for enforcing regulations throughout the industry, as well as various newspapers, including *The Wall Street Journal*.

Wydler was not able to sue Stanford in court because of a forced arbitration agreement. The securities arbitrator not only rejected her whistleblower retaliation claim but also ordered her to repay her $100,000 signing bonus from the company. (Under the 2010 Dodd-Frank Act, whistleblowers like Wydler are no longer bound by forced arbitration agreements.)

Why did the regulators ignore Wydler? It seemed to be a pattern of behavior at the time. Recall that Harry Markopolos reported concerns about Bernie Madoff's Ponzi scheme to the SEC, and his warnings were ignored as well. Perhaps the SEC did not have the resources to investigate all such allegations. Perhaps it just lacked the motivation to carry through with what would have been an exhaustive investigation. Or perhaps the SEC has failed in its obligations to protect the investing public.

## Incentivizing Whistleblowing under Dodd-Frank

The 2010 passage of Dodd-Frank proposed additional incentives for whistleblowers who provide information that aids in the recovery of over $1 million. The whistleblower could receive 10 to 30 percent of that amount. The belief is that monetary incentives will prompt observers of corporate misconduct to come forward, which could prevent future scandals like those leading up to the 2007–2008 financial crisis. One major concern with this new provision is that it may cause would-be whistleblowers to go external with the information rather than internal using the organization's prescribed reporting mechanisms, as previously discussed. The reason is the potential for monetary rewards may encourage whistleblowers to go straight to the SEC with their reports rather than first reporting the misconduct to the company's internal compliance officers.[100]

Under Dodd-Frank, whistleblowers who report violations of the securities laws are supposed to be protected from being fired. These protections—which can include reinstatement, double back pay, and special damages—are designed to serve as an incentive for whistleblowers to come forward despite the risk that they will be retaliated against for exposing their employer's wrongdoing.

There are many unanswered questions about Dodd-Frank, including whether specific whistleblowers are entitled to invoke the whistleblower protections under the law, even though they never reported the alleged wrongdoing to the government. A court decision in *Asadi v. G. E. Energy*[101] on June 28, 2012, indicates that whistleblowers who merely report internally are not necessarily protected; external reporting to the SEC may also be required to invoke Dodd-Frank protections. One concern we have here from an ethical perspective is that it may be better for all involved—the whistleblower, the offending company, and the public—if the whistleblower works with the company to fix the matter without getting the government (and the press) involved. Another concern is that it may force the whistleblower to take a more adverse position against the company and endure greater scrutiny and exposure when they come forward. In fact, one of the biggest concerns that surrounded the passing of Dodd-Frank whistleblower provisions was that it would undermine companies' internal compliance programs by encouraging whistleblowers to bypass them completely. Some even argued on behalf of a requirement that whistleblowers report internally first before going to the government. However, such a precondition was rejected, and the concerns about upending compliance programs have not really been borne out.

## Accountants' Obligations for Whistleblowing

Accountants are increasingly being asked to blow the whistle on corporate wrongdoing to stem the tide of recent massive financial fraud such as at Enron and WorldCom, and Ponzi schemes like those of Madoff and Stanford. The question during congressional investigations of the financial services industry role in the 2007–2008 financial meltdown was: Where were the auditors? Dodd-Frank contains provisions to encourage accountants and auditors to report corporate wrongdoing to meet their public interest responsibilities.

The whistleblower provisions of Dodd-Frank exclude two categories of accountants from award eligibility because of their preexisting legal duty to report securities violations:

1. Individuals with internal compliance or audit responsibilities at an entity, including CPAs, who receive information about potential violations, cannot receive whistleblower

awards because it is part of their job responsibilities to report suspicion of illegal acts to management. However, these individuals will not be excluded from receiving a whistleblower award where:

a. Disclosure to the SEC is needed to prevent "substantial injury" to the financial interest of an entity or its investors,

b. The whistleblower reasonably believes the entity is impeding investigation of the misconduct, or

c. The whistleblower has first reported the violation internally and at least 120 days have passed.

2. CPAs who receive information about potential violations of a client or its directors or officers through an audit or other engagement required under the federal securities laws are not eligible to receive whistleblower awards. The SEC included this exclusion so as not to undermine the legal duty that auditors have under Section 10A of the Securities and Exchange Act of 1934 to report illegal acts by officers, directors, and other client personnel up the chain of command. If the issues are not addressed adequately by management, the auditor must then resign from the engagement and file a report with the SEC.

Notably, the whistleblower exclusions do not apply to CPAs who report information about potential violations regarding their own firms' performance of audit services for a client. This is true even where the CPA's information about his or her firm leads to a successful enforcement action against one of the firm's clients.

Several members of the public accounting industry, including KPMG, Ernst & Young, PwC, and the Center for Audit Quality, have expressed concerns to the SEC that the accountant exclusion in the whistleblower provisions is too narrow. Those entities believe that permitting CPAs to obtain monetary rewards by blowing the whistle on their own firms' performance of services for clients could create several significant problems with respect to maintaining the confidentiality of client information.

The issue of confidentiality is an important one for CPAs who have an ethical obligation under the AICPA Code of Professional Conduct not to divulge client confidential information unless under a valid court order or subpoena to do so, for ethics investigations of the CPA's services, peer reviews, or if disclosure is approved by the client. The question of whether reporting to the SEC under Dodd-Frank under the conditions explained above would violate the confidentiality obligation of a CPA can be answered by referring to Rule 301 of the AICPA Code. In addition to the aforementioned exceptions, the rule specifies that the confidentiality obligation "does not prohibit a member's compliance with applicable laws and government regulations,"[102] which presumably would include SEC regulations and Dodd-Frank. More will be said about the confidentiality obligation in Chapters 4 and 5.

The confidentiality obligation of internal accountants and auditors who are members of the IMA provide that confidential employer information should be kept confidential except when disclosure is authorized or legally required. The legal requirement aspect would once again seem to protect the whistleblower given Dodd-Frank requirements.

## Has the Whistleblowing Program Been Successful?

In an August 2012 interview with *Directorship,* a publication of the National Association of Corporate Directors (NACD), Sean McKessy, chief of the Office of the Whistleblower, said that his office is receiving about eight tips a day and is preparing for an increase in tip volume. McKessy said the first payment may open the "tipster floodgates." The whistleblower set to receive the SEC's first payment has requested anonymity and will receive almost $50,000—30 percent of what the SEC has collected in the case, and the maximum that the SEC is allowed to pay out for providing evidence, which in this case is of securities fraud.

McKessy wondered about the long-term success of the program, given a study by the Ethics Resource Center stating that only 2 percent of employees went outside the company to report wrongdoing. He said that a significant majority of those who brought tips to the

Office of the Whistleblower who were reporting on their current or former company claim that they first tried to report to someone internally—a boss, a compliance hotline, or the board of directors. "I think that speaks to the fact that—notwithstanding the claims we are destroying internal compliance—most people view their own company as the first line of defense." While McKessy says that some may measure the success of the whistleblower program by the payments made, he points to another benchmark: "The program is successful if it shows people came forward who otherwise wouldn't have."

The SEC released its annual report on the Dodd-Frank Whistleblower Program for fiscal year 2012 on November 30, 2012. The commission reported that it received 3,001 tips in fiscal year 2012, with the lowest number (166) in November 2011 and the highest number (314) in May 2012. These numbers confirm the results of the "Whistleblower" study of the ERC that more employees have been reporting whistleblowing in current years compared to the past.

The value of the Whistleblower Program has been questioned in a survey by BDO International, the fifth-largest accountancy network in the world. According to the survey, 51 percent of corporate board members said the Whistleblower Program "has undermined internal anti-fraud and compliance programs." But 83 percent said that there has been no increase or decrease in the number of internal whistleblower reports at their businesses since the SEC program began. According to Lee Graul, a BDO partner who specializes in corporate governance, "I guess if somebody is going to look outside and report, that steals some of the thunder and the responsibilities those people feel they have to identify and evaluate those situations internally."[103] The BDO results seem to contradict the SEC's observation of the value of the program. Perhaps, as with so many things in business, it depends on one's perspective as to whether a controversial program is working. We believe that the jury is still out on this question.

## The Ethics of Whistleblowing

We have already discussed whistleblowing with respect to the confidentiality obligation of accountants and auditors under professional ethics codes. We also have expressed the concern that the whistleblowing provision of Dodd-Frank may lead an individual to report the matter to the SEC rather than work within internal channels to correct the wrongdoing. We believe employees who discover improprieties have an ethical obligation to do whatever is necessary to work within the system to correct the situation. A related issue is the "incentivization" of whistleblowing under Dodd-Frank. Some have called it a "bounty hunter" program. Is it ethical to provide financial incentives to motivate employees to come forward and report financial wrongdoing? This is not an easy question to answer.

Employees have a loyalty obligation to their employers that include maintaining confidentiality and not doing anything to harm their employers. However, as discussed in Chapter 1, the loyalty obligation should never be used to mask one's ethical obligation to be honest. Assuming the internal reporting process has played out and nothing has been done to correct for the wrongdoing, we believe from an ethical perspective external whistleblowing is the proper course of action especially if it is the *only* way for the public to know. An employee should not fall victim to the bystander effect and assume others will report it. Along with knowledge comes the responsibility to correct wrongdoings, which is in the best long-term interests of the organization. For CPAs, it honors the public trust to report an activity like fraud.

A valid question is whether the incentive provision itself is ethical. In other words, is Dodd-Frank replacing one unethical action (i.e., fraud) with another unethical practice (i.e., incentivizing the reporting of fraud with monetary reward)? Ideally, whistleblowing should be encouraged for the sole purpose of being the morally correct thing to do, not because of a reward that may come at the end of the process. The reward may be necessary to get someone to come forward, but it does not address the issue whether the government should pay for information about fraud or other illegal action.

## Concluding Thoughts

Fraud in business continues to persist in spite of efforts to improve the ethical climate of organizations and strengthen regulatory requirements and sanctions for wrongdoing. The post-Enron era ushered in a period of financial services fraud including firms involved in making risky mortgages and individuals like Bernie Madoff and Allen Stanford taking the traditional Ponzi scheme to a new (low) level. The greed of CEOs such as Dennis Kozlowski showed just how jaded one's actions can be when given the power and control to run a major corporation. Internal corporate governance systems have been strengthened and compliance programs enhanced. Yet, the National Business Ethics Survey indicates that pressure to compromise standards in the workplace is up. More employees believe that the ethical culture of their organization has weakened. An increasing number of employees are reporting fraud and other improper behavior, and retaliation against whistleblowers has increased. Perhaps all this will change over time with the help of whistleblower provisions in laws such as SOX and Dodd-Frank, which seem to be encouraging more external reporting after exhausting internal means of reporting. From an ethical perspective, we are concerned that employees may increasingly turn on their companies and violate the trust placed in them for personal reasons or just to receive a reward, and blow the whistle rather than to engage in that practice because it is the moral thing to do. So we end with a question that all students should ask: Notwithstanding regulatory obligations to blow the whistle, do the means of gathering and reporting information externally about an employer's wrongdoing justify the ends of whistleblowing?

## Discussion Questions

1. In her book *The Seven Signs of Ethical Collapse,* Jennings explains: "When an organization collapses ethically, it means that those in the organization have drifted into rationalizations and legalisms, and all for the purpose of getting the results they want and need at almost any cost." Discuss what you think Jennings meant by this statement.

2. Five months before the new 2002 Lexus ES hit showroom floors, the company's U.S. engineers sent a test report to Toyota City in Japan: The luxury sedan shifted gears so roughly that it was "not acceptable for production." The warning was sent to Toyota executive vice president Katsuaki Watanabe on May 16, 2001. Days later, another Japanese executive sent an email to top managers saying that despite misgivings among U.S. officials, the 2002 Lexus was "marginally acceptable for production." The new ES went on sale across the nation on October 1, 2001.

   In years to come, thousands of Lexus buyers would discover firsthand that the vehicle's transmission problems, which caused it to hesitate when motorists hit the gas, or lurch forward unintentionally, were far from fixed. The 2002–2006 ES models would become the target of lawsuits, federal safety investigations, and hundreds of consumer complaints, including claims of 49 injuries.

   In an August 15, 2005, memo explaining the company's position, a staff attorney wrote: "The objective will be to limit the number of vehicles to be serviced to those owners who complain and to limit the per-vehicle cost."

   In 2010, Toyota was fined a record $16.4 million for delays in notifying federal safety officials about defects that could lead to sudden acceleration. The reaction of a Toyota spokesperson was: "Given the concerns raised by some customers about this drivability issue, we did not meet the very high customer satisfaction standards we set for ourselves. However, we fully stand behind the engineering and production quality of the vehicle, as well as our after-sale customer service and technical support."

   Evaluate Toyota's actions from a corporate governance perspective. How would you characterize the ethical culture at Toyota, at least with respect to the Lexus incident? Can you draw any parallels between the Toyota experience and how Ford handled the matter with the Pinto?

3. The following questions deal with issues related to executive compensation:

   a. What is the business judgment rule and how does it relate to executive compensation?

   b. On August 9, 2005, Chancellor William B. Chandler III of the Delaware Chancery Court[104] ruled that the directors of the Walt Disney Company acted in good faith when Michael Ovitz was hired in 1995 to be the CEO of Disney and then allowed to walk away 15 months later with a severance package valued at $130 million after being fired by Michael Eisner, the chair of the Disney's board of directors. Is it "fair" that Ovitz was allowed to walk away with such a lucrative severance package only 15 months after being fired? Include in your discussion what constitutes fairness in this instance from an ethical perspective.

4. Explain the "say on pay rule" and whether you believe that it is likely to have an effect on large compensation packages of CEOs.

5. Distinguish between agency theory, stakeholder theory, and stewardship theory with respect to controlling the actions of managers.

6. Do you believe that a member of the audit engagement team servicing a client should also serve on the audit committee of the board of directors of the client entity? Why or why not?

7. COSO explains the importance of the control environment to internal controls by stating that it sets the tone of an organization, influencing the control consciousness of its people. It is the foundation for all aspects of internal control, providing discipline and structure. Explain what is meant by this statement.

8. According to the IIA Code of Ethics, internal auditors should make a balanced assessment of all the relevant circumstances and should not be unduly influenced by their own interests or by others in forming judgments. Which interests are being referred to in that statement, and how might they influence the ethical decisions of a member of the IIA?

9. In the accounting fraud at the cable company Adelphia, top management had established a "cash management" system that enabled the founder of Adelphia and former CEO and chair of the board of directors, John Rigas, to dip into the fund for personal expenses whenever he wanted. The final approval for such expenditures rested with Timothy Rigas, the son of John Rigas and Adelphia's CEO during the final years that fraud had occurred. What's wrong with the founder of a company, its former CEO and board chair, using corporate assets for personal reasons? Can you think of any circumstances where it would be permissible? That is, what would have to happen for this to be acceptable?

10. The 2011 National Business Ethics Survey defines "active social networkers" as people who spend more than 30 percent of the workday participating on social networking sites. Such employees are much more likely to view their current jobs as temporary; 72 percent of active social networkers polled said they plan to change employers within the next five years, compared to 39 percent of nonactive social networkers.

   That feeling of transience may lead to such workers thinking that it's no big deal to swipe a few things from the office supply cabinet: 46 percent of active social networkers said that they thought it was acceptable to take a copy of work software home and use it on their personal computers, while just 7 percent of nonactive social networkers said the same.

   Why do you think there is a difference in responses with respect to the use of company software at home on personal computers between active and nonactive social networkers? Do you believe that it is an ethics failing to take software home without asking for the company's permission? What about simply checking your Facebook page once a day at work?

11. How do the concepts of cognitive dissonance, organizational dissonance, and ethical dissonance relate to whether an accountant might choose to blow the whistle on corporate wrongdoing?

12. According to the Business Roundtable, "Effective corporate governance requires a clear understanding of the respective roles of the board and senior management and their relationships with others in the corporate structure. The relationships of the board and management with stockholders should be characterized with candor; their relationships with employees should be characterized by fairness; their relationships with communities in which they operate should be characterized by good citizenship; and their relationships with government should be characterized by a commitment to compliance." Discuss what is meant by each element of the statement with respect to creating an ethical organization environment.

13. Explain the components of Burchard's Ethical Dissonance Model and how it describes the ethical person-organization fit at various stages of the contractual relationship in each potential fit scenario. Assume a Low Organizational Ethics, High Individual Ethics (Low-High) fit. How might this relationship influence your motivation to blow the whistle on corporate wrongdoing?

14. Brief and Motowidlo define prosocial behavior within the organizational setting as "behavior which is (a) performed by a member of an organization, (b) directed toward an individual, group, or organization with whom she interacts while carrying out her organizational role, and (c) performed with the intention of promoting the welfare of the individual, group, or organization toward which it is directed."[105]

The research on whistleblowing that has used this model has generally argued that stages 5 and 6 represent cognitive moral development consistent with prosocial behavior. Discuss why stages 5 and 6 of Kohlberg's model are more likely to be associated with prosocial behavior than lower stages of moral development.

15. Compare the role of Sherron Watkins as a whistleblower in the Enron case to that of Leyla Wydler in the Allen Stanford Ponzi scheme in terms of the nature of the whistleblowing and the motivation to blow the whistle. Can you characterize each one's actions from the perspective of organization-person fit?

16. In October 2010, it was reported that Cheryl Eckard, a quality-assurance manager at the pharmaceutical company GlaxoSmithKline (GSK) who had blown the whistle on the safety of products made in its Puerto Rico plant, had been fired as a result of what the company called a "redundancy" related to the merger of Glaxo Wellcome and SmithKline Beecham a couple of years before. Of course, the suspicion was that Eckard was fired because she refused to go along in a cover-up of the quality assurance and compliance problems at the plant. She had made recommendations to her superiors that were ignored, reportedly because the company was too busy preparing for an FDA inspection that they hoped would clear the way for approval to market two new products, including the diabetes drug Avandamet. Eckard had found that the manufacturing facility had a contaminated water system, an air system that allowed products to be cross-contaminated, and pills of different strengths mixed in the same bottles, among other problems.

    Eckard filed a federal lawsuit against GSK under the U.S. False Claims Act. She won $96 million as part of a $750 million penalty against GSK. GSK agreed to pay millions in fines, penalties, and settlements to resolve claims that it knowingly made and sold adulterated drugs, including Paxil, a popular antidepressant, with the intent to defraud and mislead.

    How do you view whistleblowers that approach the government under the False Claims Act and win large awards from the settlement? Are they just out for the money? Should they profit from the wrongdoing of their employer? Or are they performing an important public service?

17. It is a distinguishing mark of actions labeled whistleblowing that the agent intends to force attention to a serious moral problem. How does this statement relate to whistleblowers who come forward under provisions of the Dodd-Frank Financial Reform Act? Respond to the question by considering the motivations to blow the whistle as discussed in this chapter.

18. Do you believe that the Dodd-Frank Whistleblower Program, which incentivizes reporting fraud and other wrongdoings in return for a monetary reward, is ethical? Use the ethical reasoning methods discussed in Chapter 1 to answer this question.

19. Because of their access and knowledge, accountants are in an ideal position to provide their clients and the SEC with early and invaluable assistance in identifying the scope, participants, victims and ill-gotten gains associated with corporate wrongdoing. Historically, when CPAs discovered attempted or actual fraud, client confidentiality rules limited their ability to publicly report their observations. With the advent of Dodd-Frank, accountants no longer need to choose between doing the right thing and risking the loss of their professional licenses. Explain how and under what circumstances Dodd-Frank enables accountants to report their observations.

20. "Give me the 'McFacts,' ma'am, nothing but the McFacts!" So argued the defense attorney for McDonald's Corporation as she questioned Stella Liebeck, an 81-year-old retired sales clerk, two years after her initial lawsuit against McDonald's claiming that it served dangerously hot coffee. Liebeck had bought a 49-cent cup of coffee at the drive-in window of an Albuquerque McDonald's, and while removing the lid to add cream and sugar, she spilled the coffee and suffered third-degree burns of the groin, inner thighs, and buttocks. Her suit claimed that the coffee was "defective." During the trial, it was determined that testing of coffee at other local restaurants found that none came closer than 20° to the temperature at which McDonald's coffee is poured (about 180°F). The jury decided in favor of Liebeck and awarded her compensatory damages of $200,000, which they reduced to $160,000 after determining that 20 percent of the fault belonged with Liebeck for spilling the coffee. The jury then found that McDonald's had engaged in willful, reckless, malicious, or wanton conduct, the basis for punitive damages. It awarded $2.7 million in punitive damages. That amount was ultimately reduced by the presiding judge to $480,000. The parties then settled out of court for an unspecified amount reported to be less than the $480,000.

For its part, McDonald's had suggested that Liebeck may have contributed to her injuries by holding the cup between her legs and not removing her clothing immediately. The company also argued that Liebeck's age may have made the injuries worse than they might have been in a younger individual, "since older skin is thinner and more vulnerable to injury."

Who is to blame for the McSpill? Be sure to support your answer with a discussion of personal responsibility, corporate accountability, and ethical reasoning.

## Endnotes

1. Craig E. Johnson, *Meeting the Ethical Challenges of Leadership,* 3d ed. (Thousand Oaks, CA: Sage Publications, Inc., 2009), p. 44.

2. Max H. Bazerman and Ann E. Trebrunsel, *Blind Spots: Why We Fail to Do What's Right and What to Do About It* (Princeton, NJ: Princeton University Press, 2011).

3. Marianne M. Jennings, *The Seven Signs of Ethical Collapse: How to Spot Moral Meltdowns in Companies Before It's Too Late* (New York: St. Martin's Press, 2006).

4. Jennings.

5. Jennings.

6. Jennings, pp. 138–139.

7. Andrew Crockett, Frederic S. Mishkin, and Eugene N. White, *Conflicts of Interest in the Financial Services Industry: What Should We Do about Them?* Centre for Economic Policy Research (January 2003) (Washington, DC: Center for Economic Policy Research, 2003).

8. Jennings, pp. 218–219.

9. Jennings.

10. Susan E. Fiske and Shelley E. Taylor, *Social Cognition* (New York: McGraw-Hill, 1991).

11. Thomas M. Jones, "Ethical Decsision Making by Individuals in Organizations: An Issue-Contingent Model," *The Academy of Management Review* 16, no. 2 (1991), pp. 366–395.

12. Mary Jo Burchard, "Ethical Dissonance and Response to Destructive Leadership: A Proposed Model," *Emerging Leadership Journeys* 4, no. 1, pp. 154–176.

13. Scott K. Jones and Kenneth M. Hiltebeitel, "Organizational Influence in a Model of the Moral Decision Process of Accountants," *Journal of Business Ethics* 14, no. 6 (1995), pp. 417–431.

14. Jones and Hiltebeitel.

15. Burchard.

16. Burchard, pp. 158–159.

17. Lawrence A. Pervin, "Performance and Satisfaction as a Function of Individual-Environment Fit," *Psychological Bulletin* 69, no. 1 (January 1968), pp. 56–68.

18. Burchard, pp. 162–163.

19. Hian Chye Koh and El'fred H. Y. Boo, "Organizational Ethics and Job Satisfaction and Commitment, *Management Decision* 4, nos. 5 and 6 (2004), pp. 677–693.

20. Burchard, pp. 163–164.

21. Art Padilla, Robert Hogan, and Robert B. Kaiser, "The Toxic Triangle: Destructive Leaders, Susceptible Followers, and Conducive Environments," *Leadership Quarterly* 18(3), (2007), pp. 176–194.

22. Burchard, pp. 164–165.

23. V. Lee Hamilton and Herbert Kelman, *Crimes of Obedience: Toward a Social Psychology of Authority and Responsibility* (New Haven, CT: Yale University Press, 1989).

24. Koh and Boo.

25. Randi L. Sims and Thomas L. Keon, The Influence of Ethical Fit on Employee Satisfaction, Commitment, and Turnover, *Journal of Business Ethics* 13, no. 12 (1994), 939–948.

26. O. C. Ferrell, John Fraedich, and Linda Ferrell, *Business Ethics: Ethical Decision Making and Cases.* 9th ed. (Mason: OH, South-Western, 2011).

27. Available at www.myspace.com/youdrinkcoffee/blog/289290652.

28. Available at http://ethisphere.com/ethisphere-institute-unveils-2012-worlds-most-ethical-companies/.

29. Johnson, p. 89.

30. Jennings, p. 45.

31. Russ McGuire, "WorldCom's Deadly Culture," Available at www.wnd.com/2003/06/19325/.

32. Institute of Internal Auditors (IIA). *Code of Ethics,* http//theiia.org.

33. John C. Maxwell, *There's No Such Thing as "Business" Ethics* (New York: Warner Business Books, 2003).

34. PBS Newshour interview with Paul O'Neill, July 9, 2002, Available at www.pbs.org/newshour/bb/business/julydec02/oneill_7-9.html.

35. Johnson & Johnson Credo, 333.jnj.com/our_company/our_credo/.

36. Tamara Kaplan, "The Tylenol Crisis: How Effective Public Relations Saved Johnson & Johnson," Pennsylvania State University, www.personal.psu.edu/users/w/x/wxk/116/tylenol/crisis.html.

37. Available at www.businessweek.com/ap/2012-07-19/report-j-and-j-will-pay-2-dot-2b-in-risperdal-settlement.

38. Ethics Resource Center (ERC), *2011 National Business Ethics Survey (NBES): Workplace Ethics in Transition,* www.ethics.org/nbes/files/FinalNBES-web.pdf.

39. NBES.

40. NBES, p. 14.

41. Win Swenson, "The Organizational Guidelines 'Carrot and Stick' Philosophy, and Their Focus on 'Effective Compliance'" in *Corporate Crime in America: Strengthening the "Good Citizenship," Corporation* (Washington, DC: U.S. Sentencing Commission, 1995), pp. 17–26.

42. Archie B. Carroll and Ann K. Buchholtz, *Business & Society: Ethics and Stakeholder Management* (Mason, OH: Cengage Learning, 2009).

43. Ferrell et al., p. 35.

44. Isabelle Maignan and O. C. Ferrell, "Corporate Social Responsibility: Toward a Marketing Conceptualization," *Journal of the Academy of Marketing Science* 32 (2004), pp. 3–19.

45. *United States v. Carroll Towing,* 159 F.2d 169 (2d Cir. 1947).

46. Douglas Birsch and John H. Fiedler, *The Ford Pinto Case: A Study in Applied Ethics, Business, and Technology* (Albany: State University of New York, 1994).

47. *Grimshaw v. Ford Motor Co.,* 1 19 Cal.App.3d 757, 174 Cal. Rptr. 348 (1981).

48. David De Cremer and Ann E. Tenbrunsel, *Behavioral Business Ethics: Shaping an Emerging Field* (New York: Routledge, 2012).

49. Association of Certified Fraud Examiners, *2012 Global Fraud Study: Report to the Nations on Occupational Fraud and Abuse,* www.acfe.com/uploadedFiles/ACFE_Website/Content/rttn/2012-report-to-nations.pdf.

50. ACFE, p. 6.

51. ACFE, p. 57.

52. Ernst & Young, *Detecting Financial Statement Fraud: What Every Manager Needs to Know,* www.ey.com/Publication/vwLUAssets/FIDS-FI_DetectingFinancialStatementFraud.pdf/$FILE/FIDS-FI_DetectingFinancialStatementFraud.pdf.

53. United States of America v. Quentin T. Wiles and Patrick J. Schleibaum, Nos. 94-1592, 95-1022. United States Court of Appeals, Tenth Circuit, December 10, 1996 *102 F.3d 1043,* www.bulk.resource.org/courts.gov/c/F3/102/102.F3d.1043.94-1592.95-1022.html.

54. Ferrell et al., p. 42.

55. Andrei Shleifer and Robert Vishny, "A Survey of Corporate Governance," *Journal of Finance* (1997).

56. J. E. Parkinson, *Corporate Power and Responsibility* (Oxford, UK: Oxford University Press, 1994).

57. R. I. Tricker, *Corporate Governance: Practices, Procedures and Powers in British Companies and Their Boards of Directors* (Aldershot, England: Gower Press, 1984).

58. Ferrell, p. 44.

59. W. Steve Albrecht, Conan C. Albrecht, and Chad O. Albrecht, "Fraud and Corporate Executives: Agency, Stewardship, and Broken Trust," *Journal of Forensic Accounting* 5 (2004), pp. 109–130.

60. Lex Donaldson and James H. Davis, "Stewardship Theory," *Australian Journal of Management* 16, no. 1 (June 1991).

61. Michael Jensen and William H. Meckling, "Theory of the Firm: Managerial Behavior, Agency Costs, and Ownership Structure, *Journal of Financial Economics* (1976), pp. 305–360.

62. Chamu Sundaramurthy and Marianne Lewis, "Control and Collaboration: Paradoxes and Government," *Academy of Management Review* 28, issue 3 (July 2003), pp. 397–416.

63. Donaldson and Davis.

64. James H. Davis, F. David Shoorman, and Lex Donaldson, "Toward a Stewardship Theory of Management," *The Academy of Management Review* 22, no. 1 (January 1997).

65. Economic Intelligence Unit (The Economist), "The Importance of Corporate Responsibility" (2005), www.graphics.eiu.com/files/ad_pdfs/eiuOracle_CorporateResponsibility_WP.pdf.

66. Economic Intelligence Unit (The Economist).

67. John A. Byrne with Louis Lavelle, Nanette Byrnes, Marcia Vickers, and Amy Borrus, "How to Fix Corporate Governance," *Business Week,* May 6, 2002, pp. 69–78.

68. Venkat Venkatasuvramanian, *What Is Fair Pay for Executives? An Information Theoretic Analysis of Wage Distributions,* www.mdpi.com/1099-4300/11/4/766.

69. Available at www.forbes.com/sites/tykiisel/2012/04/17/over-paid-ceos-are-they-really-worth-all-that-dough/.

70. DoddFrank Wall Street Reform and Consumer Protection Act (HR 4173), www.sec.gov/about/laws/wallstreetreform-cpa.pdf.

71. Robert E. Scully, J. "Executive Compensation, the Business Judgment Rule, and the Dodd-Frank Act: Back to the Future for Private Litigation?," *The Federal Lawyer,* January 2011.

72. Zabihollah Rezaee, *Corporate Governance and Ethics* (New York: Wiley, 2009).

73. Floyd Norris, "For Boards, S.E.C. Keeps the Bar Low," *The New York Times,* March 3, 2011, http://www.nytimes.com/2011/03/04/business/04norris.html?pagewanted=all&_r=0.

74. Sarbanes-Oxley Act of 2002 (HR 3763), www.sec.gov/about/laws/soa2002.pdf.

75. KPMG International, "Ten to-do's for Audit Committees in 2011," www.kpmg.com/Ca/en/IssuesAndInsights/ArticlesPublications/Documents/ACI-ten-to-do%27s-2011_Canada.pdf.

76. Available at www.corpgov.deloitte.com/site/sgeng/audit-committee/.

77. Rezaee, p. 130.

78. Report Available at http://www.coso.org/documents/Internal%20Control-Integrated%20Framework.pdf.

79. Available at www.businessweek.com/news/2012-04-02/groupon-revisions-highlight-new-model-s-risks.

80. National Commission on Fraudulent Financial Reporting (Treadway Commission Report), *Report of the National Commission on Fraudulent Financial Reporting,* October 1987.

81. www.reuters.com/article/2012/03/20/idUS106219+20-Mar-2012+PRN20120320

82. SEC, Release No. 34-61067; File No. SR-NYSE-2009-89, www.sec.gov/rules/sro/nyse/2009/34-61067.pdf.

83. Alison Frankel, "Sarbanes-Oxley's Lost Promise: Why CEOs Haven't been Prosecuted," July 27, 2012, www.blogs.reuters.com/alison-frankel/2012/07/27/sarbanes-oxleys-lost-promise-why-ceos-havent-been-prosecuted/.

84. Ethics and Compliance Officer Association (ECOA), www.eoa.org.

85. PricewaterhouseCoopers, "State on Compliance: 2012 Study, www.pwc.com/en_US/us/risk-management/assets/2012-compliance-study.pdf.

86. Kevin Dowd, "Moral Hazard and the Financial Crisis, Cato Institute, www.cato.org/pubs/journal/cj29n1/cj29n1-12.pdf.

87. The SEC Web site points out that a "Ponzi" scheme was named after Charles Ponzi, a crook who made his money by promising New England residents that he could provide 40 percent

returns on their investment, compared to the 5 percent return they could receive from banks at the time. Ponzi believed he could take advantage of the difference between the U.S. and foreign currencies used in buying and selling international mail coupons. In reality, he developed a pyramid scheme that used a "rob-Peter-to-pay-Paul" approach to make his money.

88. *Securities and Exchange Commission v. David G. Friehling, Friehling & Horowitz, CPA's, P.C.,* March 18, 2009, www.sec.gov/litigation/complaints/2009/comp20959.pdf.

89. SEC Web site, www.sec.gov/spotlight/secpostmadoffreforms.htm.

90. Securities and Exchange Commission (SEC), 17 CFR Parts 240 and 249 [Release No. 34-64545; File No. S7-33-10] Implementation of the Whistleblower Provisions of Section 21F of the Securities Exchange Act of 1934. www.sec.gov/rules/final/2011/34-64545.pdf.

91. Janet Near and Marcia Miceli, "Organizational dissidence: The case of whistle-blowing, *Journal of Business Ethics* 4, pp. 1–16.

92. Ferrell, p. 191.

93. Near and Miceli.

94. Ethics Resource Center (ERC), *Inside the Mind of a Whistleblower: A Supplement Report of the 2011 National Business Ethics Survey,* www.ethics.org/nbes/files/reportingFinal.pdf.

95. Kristy Mathewson, "Whistleblowing and Bystander Apathy: Connecting Ethics with Social Responsibility," The Corporate Social Responsibility Newswire, posted August 7, 2012, www.csrwire.com/blog/posts/494-whistleblowing-and-bystander-apathy-connecting-ethics-with-social-responsibility.

96. ERC, *Inside the Mind of a Whistleblower.*

97. www.whistleblowerlaws.com/whistleblower-protections-act/.

98. Sarbanes-Oxley Act of 2002.

99. "Stanford's Ponzi Scam: The System is Still Broken," www.forbes.com/sites/johnwasik/2012/03/07/stanfords-ponzi-scam-the-system-is-still-broken/print/.

100. "Whistle-blower Debate Heats Up," *CFO,* February 11, 2011, www.Cfo.com/article.cfm/145546017.

101. Khaled Asadi v. G. E. Energy, LLC, Civil Action No. 12-345, in the U.S. District Court for the Southern District of Texas, www.whistleblowingcompliancelaw.com/uploads/file/Asadi.pdf.

102. AICPA Code of Professional Conduct, Rule 301, www.aicpa.org/Research/Standards/CodeofConduct/Pages/et_300.aspx#et_301.

103. Ken Tysiac, "Hot tips: SEC fields 3,000 whistleblower complaints in 12 months," *Journal of Accountancy online,* November 15, 2012.

104. The Delaware Court of Chancery is widely recognized as the preeminent forum in the United States for the determination of disputes involving the internal affairs of thousands of Delaware corporations and other business entities, especially matters of board of director responsibilities. The court has jurisdiction to hear all matters related to equity. Its decisions can be appealed to the Delaware Supreme Court.

105. Arthur P. Brief and Stephen J. Motowidlo, "Prosocial Organizational Behaviors," *The Academy of Management Review* 11, no. 4, pp. 710–725.

106. www.nytimes.com/2009/10/31/business/31drug.html.

107. U.S. District Court for the District of Massachusetts, Case 1:06-cv-10972-WGY Document 238 Filed 05/27/10, http://freepdfhosting.com/4e9e317903.pdf.

## Appendix 1

# Ethical Decision-Making Model Analysis of Tylenol Poisoning

1. **Frame the ethical issue.** *How should the company react to the Tylenol crisis to protect the interests of those who rely on the product?*

   According to the company, its reaction was guided by the company's credo. If you read the credo, you'll notice how the company places the interests of the people who rely on the safety of the product ahead of its own self-interest. In fact, it links making a "fair profit" to its ethical action and social responsibility. The actions of Johnson & Johnson to the Tylenol crisis today are viewed as a model of business ethics.

2. **Gather all the facts.** Typically, these would be presented in summary or bullet form. Because the facts have already been described, they will not be repeated here.

3. **Identify the stakeholders and obligations.** This is arguably the most important step for Johnson & Johnson. The credo clarifies the stakeholders. In addition to the company's obligations to doctors, nurses, patients, and parents to provide a safe and reliable product, the company has an obligation to its employees to "walk the talk" of the credo. If it did not act in accordance with the company's written statement of core values, then employees might wonder about the company's commitment to its own credo. This would send a negative message concerning the tone at the top of the organization.

   The company also has an important obligation to its investors. As noted earlier, even though the company's stock price declined at first, it ultimately recovered all those losses. But the point is by acting ethically, the company retained the trust of its stockholders, many of whom are parents and can relate to the parents of children who might ingest a tainted product accidentally.

   Finally, Johnson & Johnson has an obligation to the government because the FDA regulates pharmaceutical products and is concerned about its role in protecting public health. The issue of product tampering is one that has grown in importance since the Tylenol event, as more and more companies have been questioned about the safety of products, including automobile manufacturers, tire manufacturers, and makers of silicone gel breast implants.

4. **Identify the relevant accounting ethics standards involved in the situation.** These are limited by the facts of the case. However, the manner of disclosing the facts of the situation relates to being honest and transparent in financial reporting.

5. **Identify the operational issues.** The application of Johnson & Johnson's credo in handling the Tylenol incident is an operational issue. The company indicated that it turned to its credo immediately for guidance. This means that it was guided operationally by one of its internal reporting controls—the credo—that enabled it to respond in an ethical manner.

   Additional facts of the Tylenol poisoning indicate that the company established a 1-800 hotline for consumers to call for any inquiries about the safety of Tylenol. Operationally, this was another positive step to assure the public of the company's concern for its safety.

   The company acted swiftly and responsibly to develop a safer packaging for Tylenol. It was a triple safety seal packaging—a glued box, a plastic seal over the neck of the bottle, and a foil seal over the mouth of the bottle. This is the industry standard today.

6. **Identify the technical accounting and auditing issues.** The main accounting issue was how to disclose information about the Tylenol poisonings and the ultimate legal liability of the company. Given that the Tylenol incident was the first of its kind, it would have been difficult for the accountants to determine the potential monetary liability in any lawsuit brought against the company. Still, the event itself should have been disclosed in the footnotes as a contingent liability because it was reasonably possible that there would have been a material liability for the company.

7. **List all the possible alternatives of what you can or cannot do.** In this case, the choices would be as follows:

   a. Ignore the poisonings and let the government dictate what the company should do.

   b. Do the minimum—recall the tainted product.

   c. Do all that the company can to assure the public by acting in a responsible and ethical manner.

   Undoubtedly, other alternatives can be identified. Of course, the company chose the last alternative, as already explained. Imagine the public outcry if the company had ignored or downplayed the severity of the situation as so many companies have since the Tylenol incident. Recall the way Ford reacted to safety concerns of its Pinto brand as discussed in this chapter by conducting a cost-benefit analysis of whether the company should fix the apparently unsafe placement of Pinto gas tanks behind the rear axle. Then there is the tobacco industry, which hid information from the public about studies it had conducted that showed nicotine was addictive. In that case, Jeffrey Wigand, the former vice president of research and development at Brown & Williamson, blew the whistle on the company's actions to hide the information and even enhance the addictive component of cigarettes. Wigand went so far as to inform the television show *60 Minutes,* which did an *exposé* on the tobacco industry. His story was ultimately told in the movie *The Insider.*

8. **Compare and weigh the alternatives.** Here are the key questions:

    - *Is it legal (in conformity with laws and rules)?* Johnson & Johnson is not obligated to recall product unless so ordered by the FDA. Its actions did not violate any laws.

    - *Is it consistent with professional standards?* The main issue is full disclosure and honest, reliable financial reporting.

    - *Is it consistent with in-house rules (i.e., codes of conduct)?* Yes, the "rules" in this instance reflect the company's credo, and they were diligently followed.

    - *Is it right?* This is the strength of the actions taken by Johnson & Johnson. The company respected the rights of the parties that used and relied on the safety of Tylenol in crafting a response to the crisis. Imagine if every company that faced a product tampering case did not act to assure the public of the safety of their product. All the public trust would be lost.

    - *What are the potential harms and benefits to the stakeholders?* It is difficult to see how a stakeholder would have benefited from a response other than the one developed by the company. The shareholders were harmed initially when the stock lost market value. However, in the long run, they were better off monetarily. From the perspective of employees working for Johnson & Johnson, they should have been proud to work for the company based on its handling of the Tylenol incident.

    - *Is it fair to the stakeholders?* The company acted in accordance with its credo, which emphasizes fair treatment for its stakeholders, especially the "doctors, nurses and patients, mothers and fathers, and all those who use [company] products and services."

    - *Is it consistent with virtue considerations?* Virtually all of Josephson's Six Pillars of Character are involved in the Tylenol situation. Honesty exists because the company has an obligation to fully disclose all the information that the public has a right or need to know. Integrity requires that the company have the courage to stand up for the values in its credo, regardless of the consequences. The company demonstrated accountability and responsibility by acting to remove the tainted form of Tylenol from the shelves of all supermarkets. At first, Johnson & Johnson acted only to remove the product from Chicago-area markets, but it eventually did a national recall of the capsule form of the product. By assuring the public that it would not allow a tainted product to be sold, the company earned its trust. Finally, because the company acted in a socially responsible manner, its commitment to citizenship was clearly established.

9. **Decide on a course of action.** We know what Johnson & Johnson did and why. Imagine if it had ignored the situation. The number of deaths may have risen before the government stepped in and forced a recall. The company's reputation might have suffered irreparable harm. The lawsuits would have been flowing.

10. **Reflect on your decision.** Johnson & Johnson's then-chair of the board of directors, James E. Burke, was quoted as saying with regard to questions about the survivability of the company after the poisonings were publicly reported: "It will take time, it will take money, and it will be very difficult; but we consider it a moral imperative, as well as good business, to restore Tylenol to its preeminent position."

---

## Appendix 2

# Microsoft Finance Code of Professional Conduct

Microsoft's code of conduct for finance professionals promotes professional conduct in the practice of financial management worldwide. Microsoft's CEO, CFO, corporate controller, and other employees of the finance organization hold an important and elevated role in corporate governance in that they are uniquely empowered to ensure (and capable of ensuring) that all stakeholders' interests are appropriately balanced, protected, and preserved. This Finance Code of Professional Conduct embodies principles that finance professionals are expected to adhere to and advocate. These principles of ethical business conduct encompass rules regarding both individual and peer responsibilities, as well as responsibilities to Microsoft employees, the public, and other stakeholders. The CEO, CFO, and Finance organization employees are expected to abide by this Code, as well as all applicable Microsoft business conduct standards and policies or guidelines in Microsoft's employee handbook relating to areas covered by the Code. Any violations of the Microsoft Finance Code of Professional Conduct may result in disciplinary action, up to and including termination of employment.

All employees covered by the Finance Code of Professional Conduct will

- Act with honesty and integrity, avoiding actual or apparent conflicts of interest in their personal and professional relationships.

- Provide stakeholders with information that is accurate, complete, objective, fair, relevant, timely, and understandable, including information in our filings with and other submissions to the U.S. Securities and Exchange Commission and other public bodies.

- Comply with rules and regulations of federal, state, provincial, and local governments, and of other appropriate private and public regulatory agencies.
- Act in good faith, responsibly, with due care, competence, and diligence, without misrepresenting material facts or allowing one's independent judgment to be subordinated.
- Respect the confidentiality of information acquired in the course of one's work except when authorized or otherwise legally obligated to disclose.
- Not use confidential information acquired in the course of one's work for personal advantage.
- Share knowledge and maintain professional skills important and relevant to stakeholders' needs.
- Proactively promote and be an example of ethical behavior as a responsible partner among peers, in the work environment, and the community.
- Exercise responsible use, control, and stewardship over all Microsoft assets and resources that are employed by or entrusted to us.
- Not coerce, manipulate, mislead, or unduly influence any authorized audit or interfere with any auditor engaged in the performance of an internal or independent audit of Microsoft's system of internal controls, financial statements, or accounting books and records.

If you are aware of any suspected or known violations of this Code of Professional Conduct, the Standards of Business Conduct, or other Microsoft policies or guidelines, you have a duty to report such concerns promptly to one of the following:

- Your manager
- Another responsible member of management
- A Human Resources representative
- A Legal and Corporate Affairs (LCA) contact

- The Director of Compliance
- The 24-hour Business Conduct Line:

  Within the United States (toll-free number): (877) 320-MSFT (6738)

  International toll-free number: (1) (704) 540-0139

The procedures to be followed for such a report are outlined in the Standards of Business Conduct and the Whistleblowing Reporting Procedure and Guidelines in the Employee Handbook.

If you have a concern about a questionable accounting or auditing matter, you can send a confidential email message to the Microsoft Office of Legal Compliance. If you want to submit your concern anonymously, you may use one of the following methods:

- Submit a report through the Microsoft Integrity Web site
- Call the Business Conduct Line
- Send a letter to the Director of Compliance at the following address:

  Microsoft Corporation
  Legal and Corporate Affairs
  One Microsoft Way
  Redmond, WA 98052
  USA
- Send a confidential fax to the Director of Compliance at (1) (425) 705-2985.

Microsoft will handle all inquiries discreetly and make every effort to maintain, within the limits allowed by law, the confidentiality of anyone requesting guidance or reporting questionable behavior and/or a compliance concern. It is Microsoft's intention that this Code of Professional Conduct be its written code of ethics under Section 406 of the Sarbanes-Oxley Act of 2002 complying with the standards set forth in Securities and Exchange Commission Regulation S-K Item 406.

## Appendix 3

# The False Claims Act ("FCA") in 31 U.S.C. 3729

The False Claims Act ("FCA"), in 31 U.S.C. 3729, provides, in pertinent part, that:

a. Any person who (1) knowingly presents, or causes to be presented, to an officer or employee of the United States Government or a member of the Armed Forces of the United States a false or fraudulent claim for payment or approval; (2) knowingly makes, uses, or causes to be made or used, a false record or statement to get a false or fraudulent claim paid or approved by the Government;

(3) conspires to defraud the Government by getting a false or fraudulent claim paid or approved by the Government; . . . or (7) knowingly makes, uses, or causes to be made or used, a false record or statement to conceal, avoid, or decrease an obligation to pay or transmit money or property to the Government, is liable to the United States Government for a civil penalty of not less than $5,000 and not more than $10,000, plus 3 times the amount of damages which the Government sustains because of the act of that person. . . .

b. For purposes of this section, the terms "knowing" and "knowingly" mean that a person, with respect to information (1) has actual knowledge of the information; (2) acts in deliberate ignorance of the truth or falsity of the information; or (3) acts in reckless disregard of the truth or falsity of the information, and no proof of specific intent to defraud is required.

While the False Claims Act imposes liability only when the claimant acts "knowingly," it does not require that the person submitting the claim have actual knowledge that the claim is false. A person, who acts in reckless disregard or in deliberate ignorance of the truth or falsity of the information, also can be found liable under the Act.

In sum, the False Claims Act imposes liability on any person who submits a claim to the federal government that he or she knows (or should know) is false. An example may be a physician who submits a bill to Medicare for medical services she knows she has not provided. The False Claims Act also imposes liability on an individual who may knowingly submit a false record in order to obtain payment from the government. An example of this may include a government contractor who submits records that he knows (or should know) are false and that indicate compliance with certain contractual or regulatory requirements. The third area of liability includes those instances in which someone may obtain money from the federal government to which he may not be entitled, and then uses false statements or records in order to retain the money. An example of this so-called "reverse false claim" may include a hospital that obtains interim payments from Medicare throughout the year, and then knowingly files a false cost report at the end of the year in order to avoid making a refund to the Medicare program.

In addition to its substantive provisions, the FCA provides that private parties may bring an action on behalf of the United States. These private parties, known as "*qui tam* relators," may share in a percentage of the proceeds from an FCA action or settlement.

The FCA provides, with some exceptions, that a *qui tam* relator, when the Government has intervened in the lawsuit, shall receive at least 15 percent but not more than 25 percent of the proceeds of the FCA action depending upon the extent to which the relator substantially contributed to the prosecution of the action. When the Government does not intervene, the Act provides that the relator shall receive an amount that the court decides is reasonable and shall be not less than 25 percent and not more than 30 percent.

The FCA provides protection to *qui tam* relators who are discharged, demoted, suspended, threatened, harassed, or in any other manner discriminated against in the terms and conditions of their employment as a result of their furtherance of an action under the FCA. Remedies include reinstatement with comparable seniority as the *qui tam* relator would have had but for the discrimination, two times the amount of any back pay, interest on any back pay, and compensation for any special damages sustained as a result of the discrimination, including litigation costs and reasonable attorneys' fees.

# Chapter 3 Cases

## Case 3-1

# The Parable of the Sadhu

*Bowen H. McCoy*

Reprinted with permission from "The Parable of the Sadhu," by Bowen H. McCoy, *Harvard Business Review.*
Copyright © Harvard Business Publishing.

Last year, as the first participant in the new six-month sabbatical program that Morgan Stanley has adopted, I enjoyed a rare opportunity to collect my thoughts as well as do some traveling. I spent the first three months in Nepal, walking 600 miles through 200 villages in the Himalayas and climbing some 120,000 vertical feet. My sole Western companion on the trip was an anthropologist who shed light on the cultural patterns of the villages that we passed through.

During the Nepal hike, something occurred that has had a powerful impact on my thinking about corporate ethics. Although some might argue that the experience has no relevance to business, it was a situation in which a basic ethical dilemma suddenly intruded into the lives of a group of individuals. How the group responded holds a lesson for all organizations, no matter how defined.

## The Sadhu

The Nepal experience was more rugged than I had anticipated. Most commercial treks last two or three weeks and cover a quarter of the distance we traveled.

My friend Stephen, the anthropologist, and I were halfway through the 60-day Himalayan part of the trip when we reached the high point, an 18,000-foot pass over a crest that we'd have to traverse to reach the village of Muklinath, an ancient holy place for pilgrims.

Six years earlier, I had suffered pulmonary edema, an acute form of altitude sickness, at 16,500 feet in the vicinity of Everest base camp–so we were understandably concerned about what would happen at 18,000 feet. Moreover, the Himalayas were having their wettest spring in 20 years; hip-deep powder and ice had already driven us off one ridge. If we failed to cross the pass, I feared that the last half of our once-in-a-lifetime trip would be ruined.

The night before we would try the pass, we camped in a hut at 14,500 feet. In the photos taken at that camp, my face appears wan. The last village we'd passed through was a sturdy two-day walk below us, and I was tired.

During the late afternoon, four backpackers from New Zealand joined us, and we spent most of the night awake, anticipating the climb. Below, we could see the fires of two other parties, which turned out to be two Swiss couples and a Japanese hiking club.

To get over the steep part of the climb before the sun melted the steps cut in the ice, we departed at 3.30 a.m. The New Zealanders left first, followed by Stephen and myself, our porters and Sherpas, and then the Swiss. The Japanese lingered in their camp. The sky was clear, and we were confident that no spring storm would erupt that day to close the pass.

At 15,500 feet, it looked to me as if Stephen was shuffling and staggering a bit, which are symptoms of altitude sickness. (The initial stage of altitude sickness brings a headache and nausea. As the condition worsens, a climber may encounter difficult breathing, disorientation, aphasia, and paralysis.) I felt strong—my adrenaline was flowing—but I was very concerned about my ultimate ability to get across. A couple of our porters were also suffering from the height, and Pasang, our Sherpa sirdar (leader), was worried.

Just after daybreak, while we rested at 15,500 feet, one of the New Zealanders, who had gone ahead, came staggering down toward us with a body slung across his shoulders. He dumped the almost naked, barefoot body of an Indian holy man—a sadhu—at my feet. He had found the pilgrim lying on the ice, shivering and suffering from hypothermia. I cradled the sadhu's head and laid him out on the rocks. The New Zealander was angry. He wanted to get across the pass before the bright sun melted the snow. He said, "Look, I've done what I can. You have porters and Sherpa guides. You care for him. We're going on!" He turned and went back up the mountain to join his friends.

I took a carotid pulse and found that the sadhu was still alive. We figured he had probably visited the holy shrines at Muklinath and was on his way home. It was fruitless to question why he had chosen this desperately high route instead of the safe, heavily traveled caravan route through the Kali Gandaki gorge. Or why he was shoeless and almost naked, or how long he had been lying in the pass. The answers weren't going to solve our problem.

Stephen and the four Swiss began stripping off their outer clothing and opening their packs. The sadhu was soon clothed from head to foot. He was not able to walk, but he was very much alive. I looked down the mountain and spotted the Japanese climbers, marching up with a horse.

Without a great deal of thought, I told Stephen and Pasang that I was concerned about withstanding the heights to come and wanted to get over the pass. I took off after several of our porters who had gone ahead.

On the steep part of the ascent where, if the ice steps had given way, I would have slid down about 3,000 feet, I felt vertigo. I stopped for a breather, allowing the Swiss to catch up with me. I inquired about the sadhu and Stephen. They said that the sadhu was fine and that Stephen was just behind them. I set off again for the summit.

Stephen arrived at the summit an hour after I did. Still exhilarated by victory, I ran down the slope to congratulate him. He was suffering from altitude sickness—walking 15 steps, then stopping, walking 15 steps, then stopping. Pasang accompanied him all the way up. When I reached them, Stephen glared at me and said: "How do you feel about contributing to the death of a fellow man?"

I did not completely comprehend what he meant. "Is the sadhu dead?" I inquired.

"No," replied Stephen, "but he surely will be!"

After I had gone, followed not long after by the Swiss, Stephen had remained with the sadhu. When the Japanese had arrived, Stephen had asked to use their horse to transport the sadhu down to the hut. They had refused. He had then asked Pasang to have a group of our porters carry the sadhu. Pasang had resisted the idea, saying that the porters would have to exert all their energy to get themselves over the pass. He believed they could not carry a man down 1,000 feet to the hut, reclimb the slope, and get across safely before the snow melted. Pasang had pressed Stephen not to delay any longer.

The Sherpas had carried the sadhu down to a rock in the sun at about 15,000 feet and pointed out the hut another 500 feet below. The Japanese had given him food and drink. When they had last seen him, he was listlessly throwing rocks at the Japanese party's dog, which had frightened him.

We do not know if the sadhu lived or died.

For many of the following days and evenings, Stephen and I discussed and debated our behavior toward the sadhu. Stephen is a committed Quaker with deep moral vision. He said, "I feel that what happened with the sadhu is a good example of the breakdown between the individual ethic and the corporate ethic. No one person was willing to assume ultimate responsibility for the sadhu. Each was willing to do his bit just so long as it was not too inconvenient. When it got to be a bother, everyone just passed the buck to someone else and took off. Jesus was relevant to a more individualistic stage of society, but how do we interpret his teaching today in a world filled with large, impersonal organizations and groups?"

I defended the larger group, saying, "Look, we all cared. We all gave aid and comfort. Everyone did his bit. The New Zealander carried him down below the snow line. I took his pulse and suggested we treat him for hypothermia. You and the Swiss gave him clothing and got him warmed up. The Japanese gave him food and water. The Sherpas carried him down to the sun and pointed out the easy trail toward the hut. He was well enough to throw rocks at a dog. What more could we do?"

"You have just described the typical affluent Westerner's response to a problem. Throwing money—in this case, food and sweaters—at it, but not solving the fundamentals!" Stephen retorted.

"What would satisfy you?" I said. "Here we are, a group of New Zealanders, Swiss, Americans, and Japanese who have never met before and who are at the apex of one of the most powerful experiences of our lives. Some years the pass is so bad no one gets over it. What right does an almost naked pilgrim who chooses the wrong trail have to disrupt our lives? Even the Sherpas had no interest in risking the trip to help him beyond a certain point."

Stephen calmly rebutted, "I wonder what the Sherpas would have done if the sadhu had been a well-dressed Nepali, or what the Japanese would have done if the sadhu had been a well-dressed Asian, or what you would have done, Buzz, if the sadhu had been a well-dressed Western woman?"

"Where, in your opinion," I asked, "is the limit of our responsibility in a situation like this? We had our own well-being to worry about. Our Sherpa guides were unwilling to jeopardize us or the porters for the sadhu. No one else on the mountain was willing to commit himself beyond certain self-imposed limits."

Stephen said, "As individual Christians or people with a Western ethical tradition, we can fulfill our obligations in such a situation only if one, the sadhu dies in our care; two, the sadhu demonstrates to us that he can undertake the two-day walk down to the village; or three, we carry the sadhu for two days down to the village and persuade someone there to care for him."

"Leaving the sadhu in the sun with food and clothing—where he demonstrated hand-eye coordination by throwing a rock at a dog—comes close to fulfilling items one and two," I answered. "And it wouldn't have made sense to take him to the village where the people appeared to be far less caring than the Sherpas, so the third condition is impractical. Are you really saying that, no matter what the implications, we should, at the drop of a hat, have changed our entire plan?"

## The Individual versus the Group Ethic

Despite my arguments, I felt and continue to feel guilt about the sadhu. I had literally walked through a classic moral dilemma without fully thinking through the consequences. My excuses for my actions include a high adrenaline flow, a superordinate goal, and a once-in-a-lifetime opportunity—common factors in corporate situations, especially stressful ones.

Real moral dilemmas are ambiguous, and many of us hike right through them, unaware that they exist. When, usually after the fact, someone makes an issue of one, we tend to resent his or her bringing it up. Often, when the full import of what we have done (or not done) hits us, we dig into a defensive position from which it is very difficult to emerge. In rare circumstances, we may contemplate what we have done from inside a prison.

Had we mountaineers been free of stress caused by the effort and the high altitude, we might have treated the sadhu differently. Yet isn't stress the real test of personal and corporate values? The instant decisions that executives make under pressure reveal the most about personal and corporate character.

Among the many questions that occur to me when I ponder my experience with the sadhu are: What are the practical limits of moral imagination and vision? Is there a collective or institutional ethic that differs from the ethics of the individual? At what level of effort or commitment can one discharge one's ethical responsibilities?

Not every ethical dilemma has a right solution. Reasonable people often disagree; otherwise there would be no dilemma. In a business context, however, it is essential that managers agree on a process for dealing with dilemmas.

Our experience with the sadhu offers an interesting parallel to business situations. An immediate response was mandatory. Failure to act was a decision in itself. Up on the mountain, we could not resign and submit our résumés to a headhunter. In contrast to philosophy, business involves action and implementation—getting things done. Managers must come up with answers based on what they see and what they allow to influence their decision-making processes. On the mountain, none of us but Stephen realized the true dimensions of the situation we were facing.

One of our problems was that as a group, we had no process for developing a consensus. We had no sense of purpose or plan. The difficulties of dealing with the sadhu were so complex that no one person could handle them. Because the group did not have a set of preconditions that could guide its action to an acceptable resolution, we reacted instinctively as individuals. The cross-cultural nature of the group added a further layer of complexity. We had no leader with whom we could all identify and in whose purpose we believed. Only Stephen was willing to take charge, but he could not gain adequate support from the group to care for the sadhu.

Some organizations do have values that transcend the personal values of their managers. Such values, which go beyond profitability, are usually revealed when the organization is under stress. People throughout the organization generally accept its values, which, because they are not presented as a rigid list of commandments, may be somewhat ambiguous. The stories people tell, rather than printed materials, transmit the organization's conceptions of what is proper behavior.

For 20 years, I have been exposed at senior levels to a variety of corporations and organizations. It is amazing how quickly an outsider can sense the tone and style of an organization and, with that, the degree of tolerated openness and freedom to challenge management.

Organizations that do not have a heritage of mutually accepted, shared values tend to become unhinged during stress, with each individual bailing out for himself or herself. In the great takeover battles we have witnessed during past years, companies that had strong cultures drew the wagons around them and fought it out, while other companies saw executives—supported by golden parachutes—bail out of the struggles.

Because corporations and their members are interdependent, for the corporation to be strong, the members need to share a preconceived notion of correct behavior, a "business ethic," and think of it as a positive force, not a constraint.

As an investment banker, I am continually warned by well-meaning lawyers, clients, and associates to be wary of conflicts of interest. Yet if I were to run away from every difficult situation, I wouldn't be an effective investment banker. I have to feel my way through conflicts. An effective manager can't run from risk either; he or she has to confront

risk. To feel "safe" in doing that, managers need the guidelines of an agreed-upon process and set of values within the organization.

After my three months in Nepal, I spent three months as an executive-in-residence at both the Stanford Business School and the University of California at Berkeley's Center for Ethics and Social Policy of the Graduate Theological Union. Those six months away from my job gave me time to assimilate 20 years of business experience. My thoughts turned often to the meaning of the leadership role in any large organization. Students at the seminary thought of themselves as antibusiness. But when I questioned them, they agreed that they distrusted all large organizations, including the church. They perceived all large organizations as impersonal and opposed to individual values and needs. Yet we all know of organizations in which people's values and beliefs are respected and their expressions encouraged. What makes the difference? Can we identify the difference and, as a result, manage more effectively?

The word *ethics* turns off many and confuses more. Yet the notions of shared values and an agreed-upon process for dealing with adversity and change—what many people mean when they talk about corporate culture—seem to be at the heart of the ethical issue. People who are in touch with their own core beliefs and the beliefs of others and who are sustained by them can be more comfortable living on the cutting edge. At times, taking a tough line or a decisive stand in a muddle of ambiguity is the only ethical thing to do. If a manager is indecisive about a problem and spends time trying to figure out the "good" thing to do, the enterprise may be lost.

Business ethics, then, has to do with the authenticity and integrity of the enterprise. To be ethical is to follow the business as well as the cultural goals of the corporation, its owners, its employees, and its customers. Those who cannot serve the corporate vision are not authentic businesspeople and, therefore, are not ethical in the business sense.

At this stage of my own business experience, I have a strong interest in organizational behavior. Sociologists are keenly studying what they call corporate stories, legends, and heroes as a way organizations have of transmitting value systems. Corporations such as Arco have even hired consultants to perform an audit of their corporate culture. In a company, a leader is a person who understands, interprets, and manages the corporate value system. Effective managers, therefore, are action-oriented people who resolve conflict, are tolerant of ambiguity, stress, and change, and have a strong sense of purpose for themselves and their organizations.

If all this is true, I wonder about the role of the professional manager who moves from company to company. How can he or she quickly absorb the values and culture of different organizations? Or is there, indeed, an art of management that is totally transportable? Assuming that such fungible managers do exist, is it proper for them to manipulate the values of others?

What would have happened had Stephen and I carried the sadhu for two days back to the village and become involved with the villagers in his care? In four trips to Nepal, my most interesting experience occurred in 1975, when I lived in a Sherpa home in the Khumbu for five days while recovering from altitude sickness. The high point of Stephen's trip was an invitation to participate in a family funeral ceremony in Manang. Neither experience had to do with climbing the high passes of the Himalayas. Why were we so reluctant to try the lower path, the ambiguous trail? Perhaps because we did not have a leader who could reveal the greater purpose of the trip to us.

Why didn't Stephen, with his moral vision, opt to take the sadhu under his personal care? The answer is partly because Stephen was hard-stressed physically himself and partly because, without some support system that encompassed our involuntary and episodic community on the mountain, it was beyond his individual capacity to do so.

I see the current interest in corporate culture and corporate value systems as a positive response to pessimism such as Stephen's about the decline of the role of the individual in large organizations. Individuals who operate from a thoughtful set of personal values provide the foundation for a corporate culture. A corporate tradition that encourages freedom of inquiry, supports personal values, and reinforces a focused sense of direction can fulfill the need to combine individuality with the prosperity and success of the group. Without such corporate support, the individual is lost.

That is the lesson of the sadhu. In a complex corporate situation, the individual requires and deserves the support of the group. When people cannot find such support in their organizations, they don't know how to act. If such support is forthcoming, a person has a stake in the success of the group and can add much to the process of establishing and maintaining a corporate culture. Management's challenge is to be sensitive to individual needs, to shape them, and to direct and focus them for the benefit of the group as a whole.

For each of us, the sadhu lives. Should we stop what we are doing and comfort him; or should we keep trudging up toward the high pass? Should I pause to help the derelict I pass on the street each night as I walk by the Yale Club en route to Grand Central Station? Am I his brother? What is the nature of our responsibility if we consider ourselves to be ethical persons? Perhaps it is to change the values of the group so that it can, with all its resources, take the other road.

## Questions

1. According to the Ethical Dissonance Model, the ethical person-organization fit helps to define the ethical culture of an organization and one's role in it. The ethics of an individual influences the values one brings to the workplace and decision making, while the ethics (through culture) of the organization influences that behavior. Throughout The Parable of the Sadhu, Bowen McCoy refers to the breakdown between the individual and corporate ethic. Explain what he meant by that and how, if we view the hikers on the trek up the mountain in Nepal as an organization, the ethical person-organization fit applied to the decisions made on the climb.

2. Evaluate the actions of McCoy and Stephen from the perspective of Kohlberg's model of moral development. At what stage did each reason throughout the trek? Do you think there was a bystander effect in how McCoy and the others acted?

3. What role did ethical fading have on the decision making of Bowen and other members of the group? How is utilitarian thinking involved in ethical fading?

4. McCoy concludes that the lesson of the sadhu is that "in a complex corporate situation, the individual requires and deserves the support of the group. When people cannot find such support in their organizations, they don't know how to act." What support in organizations do you think McCoy is referring to? If such support is not found, what should individuals do when they have an ethical dilemma such as that in the sadhu case?

5. What is the moral of the story of the sadhu from your perspective?

## Case 3-2

# Amgen Whistleblowing Case

Amgen, a Thousand Oaks, California–based company, has been dealing with lawsuits and whistleblower claims for years over its marketing tactics. The following describes the lawsuits, language from the legal filings against Amgen, and a statement made by the company on October 24, 2012, about its settlements in its earnings announcement for the third quarter of 2012.

## Whistleblower Shawn O'Brien

In 2009, the company was embroiled in lawsuits filed by 15 states alleging a Medicaid kickback scheme.[106] Two additional whistleblowing lawsuits were filed against the company in Ventura County. The whistleblowing complaints, which don't appear related to the fraud alleged by the group of states, were brought by former employees who said they had uncovered wrongdoing at the biotech giant and were terminated after they raised red flags to superiors. One employee alleged that the company violated federal law by underreporting complaints and problems with the company's drugs after they hit the market.

Former Amgen employee Shawn O'Brien sued Amgen for wrongful termination on October 9, 2009, alleging that he was laid off in October 2007 in retaliation for raising concerns about how the company reported complaints and problems with drugs already on the market. O'Brien worked as a senior project manager for Amgen's "Ongoing Change Program," according to the lawsuit filed in Ventura County Superior Court. His job was to improve Amgen's "compliance processes with high inherent risk to public safety, major criminal and civil liability, or both," according to the lawsuit.

The lawsuit alleged that in April 2007, Amgen's board of directors flagged the company's process for dealing with postmarket complaints about drugs as a potential problem. Federal law requires drug companies to track and report to the FDA any problems with their drugs after they hit the market. In June 2007, O'Brien was put on the case. He soon uncovered facts that Amgen was not adequately and consistently identifying phone calls or mail related to postmarket product complaints. That year, O'Brien warned the company about the seriousness of the issues but, he claims, the company would not take any action or offer any support. In August 2007, O'Brien took his complaint to a senior executive/corporate officer (unnamed) and warned that Amgen's process for dealing with postmarket problems wasn't adequate.

In early September 2007, O'Brien's managers instructed him to stop all work and not discuss the issues any further with anyone. Approximately four weeks later, he was informed that he was being terminated as part of Amgen's October 12, 2007, reduction in the workforce.

## Whistleblower Kassie Westmoreland

On October 22, 2012, Amgen announced it had set aside $780 million to settle various federal and state investigations and whistleblower lawsuits accusing it of illegal sales and marketing tactics. Amgen said it had reached an agreement in principle to settle criminal and civil investigations that had been under way for several years by the U.S. Attorney's offices in Brooklyn and Seattle. On December 18, 2012, the company pleaded guilty to a federal misdemeanor of misbranding its anemia drug Aranesp and has agreed to pay $762 million in fines and penalties. The information below describes the proceedings leading up to the legal action.

The federal investigations, according to Amgen, involved the marketing, pricing, and dosing of its anemia drugs, Aranesp and Epogen, and its dissemination of information about clinical trials on the safety and efficacy of those drugs. Numerous current and former executives had received civil and grand jury subpoenas.

One whistleblower lawsuit[107] that was unsealed accused the company of overfilling vials of Aranesp, essentially providing doctors with free amounts of the drug to give patients and then charge to Medicare, Medicaid, or private insurers. The lawsuit, filed by Kassie Westmoreland, a former Amgen sales representative and Aranesp product manager fired from Amgen, said that Amgen tried to persuade doctors to use Aranesp rather than Procrit, a rival drug sold by Johnson & Johnson, by pointing to the extra profits the doctors could make by using the overfill and billing for it. The federal government declined to join the lawsuit, but more than a dozen states did, including New York and California. Westmoreland is entitled to part of any settlement under whistleblower statutes. The court has not released the amount of the whistleblower award.

## Legal Filings

The filing in the Kassie Moreland case included the following statement by the court in response to how Amgen dealt with warnings of the FDA about the safety of its products:

In addition to causing damage to programs such as Medicare, Defendants' actions have also put patient safety and health at risk. The population of patients for whom Aranesp is indicated is especially vulnerable. Though Amgen was aware of issues earlier, beginning on or about March 9, 2007, the FDA issued a series of black box warnings for Aranesp when used in kidney and cancer patients, the most serious warning available on a drug's label. The black box warned of increased risk of death, of serious cardiovascular or thromboembolic events, and more rapid tumor progressions. The new warnings cautioned physicians to administer the *lowest dose possible* in order to bring red blood cell counts to the lowest level necessary to avoid blood transfusions. The FDA imposed a "Risk Evaluation and Mitigation Strategy" on Amgen for Aranesp in February 2010. This action resulted from concerns that, rather than helping patients, Aranesp can increase the risk of tumor growth and shorten survival in patients with cancer, and increase the risk of heart attack, heart failure, stroke, and blood clots in other patients.

One of Amgen's responses to the black box warnings appears to have been to treat them as humorous. A script for a July 2007 meeting of Amgen's Nephrology Business Unit from the files of Amgen Vice President of Sales Leslie Mirani included a joke about "black box warnings," following up on the FDA's February 2007 warning about potential harm from Aranesp.

## Questions

1. The following is from Amgen's values statement:

   Our Values form a deeply held belief system that guides our behavior, helps us make the right decisions and builds the framework for our daily interactions with each other. We value people, integrity, and results. This combination is essential in accomplishing our primary purpose of using science to dramatically improve people's lives. (www.amgen.com/about/compliance_summary.html).

   What is the role of a "values statement" in creating an ethical organization environment? Comment on the lawsuits described above and whistleblowing with respect to Amgen's values statement. What message do you get about what drives Amgen's operations when compared to a company like Alcoa and its values statement discussed in this chapter?

2. Evaluate the actions of Amgen and the two whistleblowers from an ethical perspective including motivation for action and ethical reasoning.

3. The following statement appears in Amgen's code of ethics with respect to "making ethical decisions" (http://www.ifpma.org/fileadmin/content/About%20us/2%20Members/Companies/Code-Amgen/Amgen-EN-Code.pdf):

   No code of conduct can cover every situation. When you face ethical issues which are difficult to resolve, ask yourself these questions to help you: Is it legal and ethical?; Is it consistent with Amgen's Code of Conduct and company policies?; Is it consistent with the Amgen Values?; Would I be comfortable explaining it to my family and friends, and if it appeared on television or in a newspaper?" The Code goes on to say if unsure about what to do, seek additional guidance about the ethics and legality of a matter before proceeding and "Do the Right Thing."

   What are the similarities between steps 8 and 10 of the Comprehensive Ethical Decision-Making Model discussed in chapter 2 and these statements in the Amgen Code? How does organizational dissonance relate to the actions taken by management of Amgen in light of these statements?

[1]www.oag.state.ny.us.

## Case 3-3

# United Thermostatic Controls

United Thermostatic Controls is a publicly owned company that engages in the manufacturing and marketing of residential and commercial thermostats. The thermostats are used to regulate temperature in furnaces and refrigerators. United sells its product primarily to retailers in the domestic market, with the company headquartered in San Jose, California. Its operations are decentralized according to geographic region. As a publicly owned company, United's common stock is listed and traded on the NYSE. The organization chart for United is presented in Figure 1.

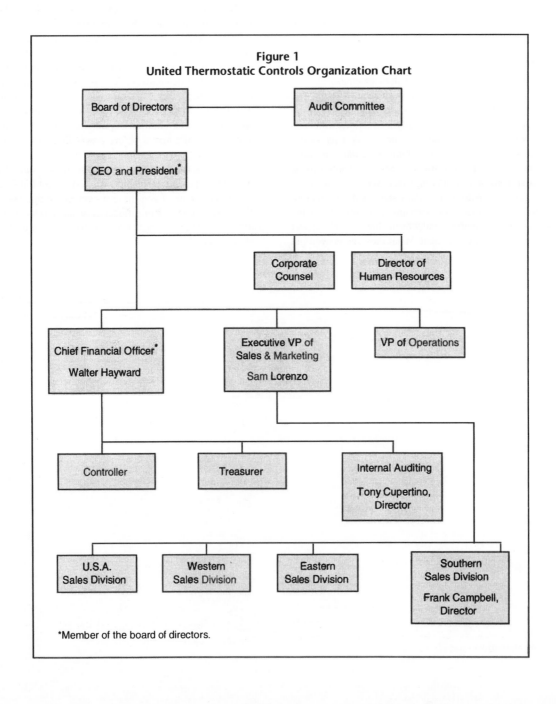

**Figure 1**
**United Thermostatic Controls Organization Chart**

Board of Directors — Audit Committee

CEO and President*

Corporate Counsel     Director of Human Resources

Chief Financial Officer*
Walter Hayward

Executive VP of Sales & Marketing
Sam Lorenzo

VP of Operations

Controller     Treasurer     Internal Auditing
Tony Cupertino, Director

U.S.A. Sales Division     Western Sales Division     Eastern Sales Division     Southern Sales Division
Frank Campbell, Director

*Member of the board of directors.

**Exhibit 1**
**United Thermostatic Controls**

**Budgeted and Actual Sales Revenue**
**First Three Quarters in 2013**

| Quarter Ended | U.S.A. Sales Division | | | Western Sales Division | | |
|---|---|---|---|---|---|---|
| | Budget | Actual | % Var. | Budget | Actual | % Var. |
| March 31 | $ 632,000 | $ 638,000 | .009% | $ 886,000 | $ 898,000 | .014% |
| June 30 | 640,000 | 642,000 | .003 | 908,000 | 918,000 | .011 |
| September 30 | 648,000 | 656,000 | .012 | 930,000 | 936,000 | .006 |
| Through September 30 | $1,920,000 | $1,936,000 | .008% | $2,724,000 | $2,752,000 | .010% |

| Quarter Ended | Eastern Sales Division | | | Southern Sales Division | | |
|---|---|---|---|---|---|---|
| | Budget | Actual | % Var. | Budget | Actual | % Var. |
| March 31 | $ 743,000 | $ 750,000 | .009% | $ 688,000 | $ 680,000 | (.012)% |
| June 30 | 752,000 | 760,000 | .011 | 696,000 | 674,000 | (.032) |
| September 30 | 761,000 | 769,000 | .011 | 704,000 | 668,000 | (.051) |
| Through September 30 | $2,256,000 | $2,279,000 | .010% | $2,088,000 | $2,022,000 | (.032)% |

Frank Campbell is the director of the Southern sales division. Worsening regional economic conditions and a reduced rate of demand for United's products have created pressures to achieve sales revenue targets set by United management nonetheless. Also, significant pressures exist within the organization for sales divisions to maximize their revenues and earnings for 2013 in anticipation of a public offering of stock early in 2014. Budgeted and actual sales revenue amounts, by division, for the first three quarters in 2013 are presented in Exhibit 1.

Campbell knows that actual sales lagged even further behind budgeted sales during the first two months of the fourth quarter. He also knows that each of the other three sales divisions exceeded their budgeted sales amounts during the first three quarters in 2013. He is very concerned that the Southern division has been unable to meet or exceed budgeted sales amounts. He is particularly worried about the effect this might have on his and the division managers' bonuses and share of corporate profits.

In an attempt to improve the sales revenue of the Southern division for the fourth quarter and for the year ended December 31, 2013, Campbell reviewed purchase orders received during the latter half of November and early December to determine whether shipments could be made to customers prior to December 31. Campbell knows that sometimes orders that are received before the end of the year can be filled by December 31, thereby enabling the division to record the sales revenue during the current fiscal year. It could simply be a matter of accelerating production and shipping to increase sales revenue for the year.

Reported sales revenue of the Southern division for the fourth quarter of 2013 was $792,000. This represented an 18.6 percent increase over the actual sales revenue for the third quarter of the year. As a result of this increase, reported sales revenue for the fourth quarter exceeded the budgeted amount by $80,000, or 11.2 percent. Actual sales revenue for the year exceeded the budgeted amount for the Southern division by $14,000, or 0.5 percent. Budgeted and actual sales revenue amounts, by division, for the year ended December 31, 2013, are presented in Exhibit 2.

During the course of their test of controls, the internal audit staff questioned the appropriateness of recording revenue of $150,000 on two shipments made by the Southern division in the fourth quarter of the year. These shipments are described as follows:

1. United shipped thermostats to Allen Corporation on December 31, 2013, and billed Allen $85,000, even though Allen had specified a delivery date of no earlier than February 1, 2014, to take control of the product. Allen intended to use the thermostats in the heating system of a new building that would not be ready for occupancy until March 1, 2014.
2. United shipped thermostats to Bilco Corporation on December 30, 2013, in partial (one-half) fulfillment of an order. United recorded $65,000 revenue on that date. Bilco had previously specified that partial shipments would not be accepted. Delivery of the full shipment had been scheduled for February 1, 2014.

**Exhibit 2**
**United Thermostatic Controls**

**Budgeted and Actual Sales Revenue**
**for the Year Ended December 31, 2013**

| Quarter Ended | U.S.A. Sales Division | | | Western Sales Division | | |
|---|---|---|---|---|---|---|
| | Budget | Actual | % Var. | Budget | Actual | % Var. |
| March 31 | $ 632,000 | $ 638,000 | .009% | $ 886,000 | $ 898,000 | .014% |
| June 30 | 640,000 | 642,000 | .003 | 908,000 | 918,000 | .011 |
| September 30 | 648,000 | 656,000 | .012 | 930,000 | 936,000 | .006 |
| December 31 | 656,000 | 662,000 | .009 | 952,000 | 958,000 | .006 |
| 2013 Totals | $2,576,000 | $2,598,000 | .009% | $3,676,000 | $3,710,000 | .009 % |

| Quarter Ended | Eastern Sales Division | | | Southern Sales Division | | |
|---|---|---|---|---|---|---|
| | Budget | Actual | % Var. | Budget | Actual | % Var. |
| March 31 | $ 743,000 | $ 750,000 | .009% | $ 688,000 | $ 680,000 | (.012)% |
| June 30 | 752,000 | 760,000 | .011 | 696,000 | 674,000 | (.032) |
| September 30 | 761,000 | 769,000 | .011 | 704,000 | 668,000 | (.051) |
| December 31 | 770,000 | 778,000 | .010 | 712,000 | 792,000 | .112 |
| 2013 Totals | $3,026,000 | $3,057,000 | .010% | $2,800,000 | $2,814,000 | .005% |

During their investigation, the internal auditors learned that Campbell had pressured United's accounting department to record these two shipments early to enable the Southern division to achieve its goals with respect to the company's revenue targets. The auditors were concerned about the appropriateness of recording the $150,000 revenue in 2013 in the absence of an expressed or implied agreement with the customers to accept and pay for the prematurely shipped merchandise. The auditors noted that, had the revenue from these two shipments not been recorded, the Southern division's actual sales for the fourth quarter would have been below the budgeted amount by $70,000, or 9.8 percent. Actual sales revenue for the year ended December 31, 2013, would have been below the budgeted amount by $136,000, or 4.9 percent. The revenue effect of the two shipments in question created a 5.4 percent shift in the variance between actual and budgeted sales for the year. The auditors felt that this effect was significant with respect to the division's revenue and earnings for the fourth quarter and for the year ended December 31, 2013. The auditors decided to take their concerns to Tony Cupertino, director of the internal auditing department. Cupertino is a licensed CPA and holds the CIA designation.

Cupertino discussed the situation with Campbell. Campbell informed Cupertino that he had received assurances from Sam Lorenzo, executive vice president of sales and marketing, that top management would support the recording of the $150,000 revenue because of its strong desire to meet or exceed budgeted revenue and earnings amounts. Moreover, top management is very sensitive to the need to meet financial analysts' consensus earnings estimates. According to Campbell, the company is concerned that earnings must be high enough to meet analysts' expectations because any other effect might cause the stock price to go down. In fact, Lorenzo has already told Campbell that he did not see anything wrong with recording the revenue in 2013 because the merchandise had been shipped to the customers before the end of the year and the terms of shipment were FOB shipping point.

At this point, Cupertino is uncertain whether he should take his concerns to Walter Hayward, the CFO, who is also a member of the board of directors, or take them directly to the audit committee. Cupertino knows that the majority of the members of the board, including those on the audit committee, have ties to the company and members of top management. Cupertino is not even certain that he should pursue the matter any further because of the financial performance pressures that exist within the organization. However, he is very concerned about his responsibilities and obligations to coordinate the work of the internal auditing department with that of the external auditors.

## Questions

1. Identify the stakeholders in this case. Identify their interests and United's obligations to satisfy those interests from an ethical perspective.

2. Describe the ethical responsibilities of Tony Cupertino as a CPA and CIA. How do these responsibilities effect whom Cupertino should approach in United based on the organization chart?

3. Assume that Tony Cupertino decides to delay contacting Walter Hayward. Instead, he contacts the CFO of Bilco Corporation and offers a 20 percent discount on the total $130,000 cost of merchandise if Bilco agrees to approve the partial shipment on December 30, 2013. Cupertino adds that the $26,000 would be deducted from the remaining $65,000 to be shipped during January 2014. Evaluate Cupertino's actions with respect to the following:

   a. Is the offer ethical or unethical? Why?

   b. Has Cupertino violated any of his reporting responsibilities in directly contacting the CFO of Bilco?

## Case 3-4

# Hewlett-Packard[1]

## Legal Settlement

On December 8, 2006, California's attorney general announced a settlement with Hewlett-Packard (HP) over its corporate spying scandal. The civil settlement involved a lawsuit that the state filed against the computer giant in Santa Clara County Superior Court. Under the agreement, HP paid $13.5 million to create a "privacy and piracy" fund to help state and local law enforcement fight privacy and intellectual property violations. The company also paid $650,000 in civil penalties and $350,000 to cover expenses of the investigation.

The scandal broke in September 2006 when HP acknowledged in an SEC filing that investigators probing internal HP leaks to the media had gained access to board members' personal phone records by impersonating the board members, a practice known as "pretexting." HP's investigators also conducted physical and electronic surveillance of board members and reporters, according to HP documents.

Pretexting violates a California criminal law banning the use of "false and fraudulent pretenses" to obtain confidential information from a phone company, stated Attorney General Bill Lockyer. California civil law also considers criminal acts unlawful business practices, which was the basis of the state's civil action.

Mark V. Hurd, HP's chair and chief executive, hailed the deal. "We are pleased to settle this matter with the attorney general and are committed to ensuring that HP regains its standing as a global leader in corporate ethics and responsibility," he said.

## The HP Investigation

An article in January 2006 by CNET reporter Dawn Kawamoto discussed confidential information available only to HP's board. The CNET article reignited the leak investigation. Recognizing the potential legal problems that board-level leaks could pose for HP, chairwoman Patricia Dunn immediately initiated a new investigation of the leak and expressed her urgency to HP's general counsel, Ann Baskins. The second and far more intrusive investigation extended from January through March and included the following:

- Reviewing the company email accounts, company phone records, and computer hard drives of every member of HP's "Executive Council"
- Hiring a private investigation firm, which in turn subcontracted the job of obtaining the private telephone records of select board members and nine journalists, including Kawamoto

[1]The case is *The 1199 SEIU Greater New York Pension Fund, et al. v. Patricia C. Dunn, et al.,* CA No. 06-071186, Santa Clara County Superior Court (San Jose).

- Surreptitiously following Kawamoto and suspected board members in public (and apparently searching through their trash)
- Setting up a "sting" in which investigators sent Kawamoto an email containing fake tips about HP and an attachment whose tracking software would trace the email's path after it reached Kawamoto's computer

## Insider Trading

HP investors sued some of the computer maker's directors, claiming they sold $38 million in company stock shortly before publicly acknowledging an internal probe into boardroom leaks. The directors, including CEO Mark Hurd, exercised options and sold shares during a 2½-week period beginning August 21, 2006. HP began its internal investigation after boardroom discussions about ex-CEO Carly Fiorina were quoted in news stories.

The flap over the probe cost chairwoman Dunn and two HP executives their jobs and sparked investigations by U.S. regulators. The company said on November 16 that the SEC stepped up its examination of the company's tactics and the Federal Communications Commission (FCC) had requested documents related to the leak probe.

California prosecutors had charged Dunn, HP's former CEO, with conspiracy and fraud for directing the boardroom spying. They also charged Kevin Hunsaker, an in-house lawyer and former director of ethics, as well as three private investigators who participated in the probe.

Board members, worried about negative publicity over the leak probe, took steps to protect the company's stock by approving a $6 billion share buyback program less than a month before the spying became public. That brought the amount of shares that HP was authorized to buy back to $11.7 billion, according to the complaint. The investors alleged that the share buybacks were prompted by defendants' illegal misconduct.

## Ethics Compliance Officer

Having a chief ethics officer didn't help HP. Chairwoman Dunn lost her job after hiring private investigators to find leakers on HP's board. The spying scandal that ensued led to Dunn's indictment and an investigation by the House Energy and Commerce Committee. Even Hurd, who had replaced Dunn as chair, has been implicated in the scandal. And it all happened under the watch of Kevin Hunsaker, HP's senior counsel and chief ethics officer. He resigned in September 2006.

## Corporate Governance and Ethics Issues

The original lawsuit claimed "breach of fiduciary responsibilities" by HP executives. It alleged that the executives' spy-like tactics to uncover boardroom leaks harmed the company, and that they engaged in insider trading just before news of the spying incident became public. Specifically, the suit claims that they sold off $41.3 million worth of stock two weeks before the scandal broke. The lawsuit also alleged that the executives approved stock buybacks in the months preceding the scandal in an effort "to keep the company's stock price propped up while insiders were selling."

HP also agreed to strengthen in-house monitoring to ensure that future investigations launched by HP or its contractors would comply with legal and ethical standards and protect privacy rights. HP further agreed to hire an independent director, expand the duties of its chief ethics officer and chief privacy officer, beef up staff ethics training, and create a compliance council to set policies for ethics programs.

In the lawsuit, Attorney General Bill Lockyer was quoted as saying:

> With its governance reforms, this settlement should help guide companies across the country as they seek to protect confidential business information without violating corporate ethics or privacy rights. The new fund will help ensure that when businesses cross the legal line they will be held accountable. Fortunately, Hewlett-Packard is not Enron. I commend the firm for cooperating instead of stonewalling, for taking instead of shirking responsibility, and for working with my office to expeditiously craft a creative resolution.

The settlement's corporate governance reforms aimed to strengthen in-house monitoring and oversight to ensure compliance with legal and ethical standards, and protection of privacy rights, during any investigations launched by HP or outside firms hired by HP. "This settlement creates a template for other companies seeking to protect confidential business information without violating corporate ethics or privacy rights," stated Lockyer.

## Major Governance Reforms

The major governance reforms included the following:

- A new independent director will serve as the board's watchdog on compliance with ethical and legal requirements. The director will have specific responsibilities in carrying out that oversight function and report violations to the board, other responsible HP officials, and the attorney general.
- HP's chief ethics and compliance officer (CECO) will have expanded oversight and reporting duties. The CECO will review HP's investigation practices and make recommendations to the board on how to improve the practices by July 31, 2007. The CECO, who previously reported only to the general counsel, now also will report to the board's audit committee. In addition, the CECO will have authority to retain independent legal advisors.

- HP will expand the duties and responsibilities of its chief privacy officer to include review of the firm's investigation protocols to ensure that they protect privacy and comply with ethical requirements.
- HP will establish a new Compliance Council, headed by the CECO and also comprised of the chief privacy officer, deputy general counsel for compliance, head of internal audit, and ethics and compliance liaisons. The council will develop and maintain policies and procedures governing HP's ethics and compliance program, and provide periodic reports to the CEO, audit committee, and board.
- HP will beef up the ethics and conflict-of-interest components of its training program. The training redesign will be directed and monitored by the CECO, Compliance Council, independent director, and chief privacy officer. HP also will create a separate code of conduct, for use by outside investigators that addresses privacy and business ethics issues.

The HP scandal ended on December 14, 2012, when Bryan Wagner, a player in the explosion of corporate drama that rocked HP, was sentenced to three months in jail. He had pleaded guilty in 2007 to charges of aggravated identity theft and faced a minimum sentence of two years in prison. Wagner was the only player in the pretexting scandal to see the inside of a prison cell. Others who were criminally sentenced received probation.

## Questions

1. The original lawsuit filed in the HP case claimed that the executives breached their fiduciary responsibilities. What are the fiduciary responsibilities of executives and members of the board of directors to shareholders? How were these obligations violated in the HP case?

2. Describe how ethical fading influenced the actions taken in the pretexting scandal, including those identified in the HP investigation. Are there similarities between the actions of management in the HP case and those in the Challenger Shuttle Disaster?

3. Recently, in 2011, Hewlett-Packard Vice President and Chief Ethics and Compliance Officer Jon Hoak talked about renewing HP's commitment to a culture of integrity at a meeting with members of the Business and Organizational Ethics Partnership at the Markkula Center for Applied Ethics at Santa Clara University. In his presentation that addressed the pretexting scandal, Hoak said "The people involved were only concerned about whether pretexting was legal. Nobody asked, 'Even if it's legal, is it the right thing to do?' What is the relationship between legality and what is the right thing to do in making business decisions?

## Case 3-5

# IRS Whistleblower and Informing on Tax Cheats

On October 4, 2012, the Internal Revenue Service (IRS) paid a $2 million reward to a whistleblower that exposed an alleged tax avoidance scheme by Illinois Tool Works Inc. (ITW) that cost the U.S. Treasury hundreds of millions of dollars. The scheme involved ITW enlisting a Swiss bank to fabricate unauthorized tax deductions by duplicating its own tax deductions in order for ITW, as a client and unrelated taxpayer, to claim the same deductions as an offset to ITW's otherwise taxable income. As a result of tax audits, ITW wrote down its deferred tax asset by $383 million.

Whether motivated by a sense of justice or the pursuit of a seven-figure reward, the Wall Street insider known only as "Mr. ABC" has demonstrated the huge return on investment available to IRS whistleblowers that provide information under a program that pays out between 15 percent to 30 percent of any recovery, without any monetary cap on the amount of the reward.

It was the third time that Mr. ABC had received an IRS whistleblowing award, including $1.1 million in 2004, when he provided information about abusive tax shelters that helped Enron avoid taxes on more than $600 million of taxable income, and $1.24 million in another case.

In testimony before the 2004 U.S. Senate Finance Committee, Mr. ABC proceeded to explain his motivation to blow the whistle by criticizing the government's ability to identify and investigate sophisticated tax shelters. "When I looked through all the financial engineering and big words, I believed it was just a fake deduction scheme," he testified.

The IRS refused to comment, noting confidentiality issues.

## Questions

1. Should we regard Mr. ABC as a new "caped crusader" or an opportunist? Explain the reasons for your response.

2. Is it ethical for a Wall Street insider to analyze financial data of an unrelated company in order to identify corporate wrongdoing, report it to the appropriate authorities, and then receive a whistleblowing reward?

3. Consider Mr. ABC's motivation for blowing the whistle in the ITW case and the fact that it was the third time he had engaged in whistleblowing to the IRS. Using Kohlberg's model of moral development, at what stage of ethical reasoning would you say Mr. ABC was at? Why?

## Case 3-6

# Bennie and the Jets

Bennie Gordon is a CPA and a member of the AICPA. Gordon works as an accounting manager at the division level at Jet Energy Company, a publicly owned company headquartered in South Carolina. Jet Energy is a regulated utility company by the state and provides electricity to 7 million customers in southern states. Jet Energy is allowed a rate of return on operating income at a maximum rate of 12.5 percent on electricity it sells. If the company is earning more than that, regulators can cut the rate that it charges to customers.

Gordon reports to Sarah Higgins, the controller of the division. Higgins holds the Certificate in Management Accounting (CMA) and is a member of the IMA. Higgins reports to Sam Thornton, the chief financial officer, who is a CPA. In turn, Thornton reports to Vanessa Jones, the CEO of the company. Joan Franks is the chief compliance officer. The company has an audit committee of three members, all of whom sit on the board of directors.

Gordon has identified irregular accounting entries dealing with the reclassification of some accounting items to make its returns lower so state regulators would not cut rates. One example is that Jet Energy often gets rebates from insurers of its nuclear plants based on safety records. Although the cost of the premiums is expensed to the electricity business, the rebates—approximately $26 million to $30.5 million each—were not booked back to the same accounts. On a number of occasions, they were booked below operating income in a nonoperating account. The moves kept Jet Energy from exceeding its allowable returns and kept the states from reducing electricity rates.

After two years of being silent, Gordon decided it was time to address the issue.

## Questions

1. What steps should Bennie Gordon take to ensure that the accounting matter is adequately addressed by the company? Why do you suggest those steps be taken? What are the ethical obligations of Bennie Gordon, Sarah Higgins, and Sam Thornton?

2. Assume that Gordon made a strong case that the accounting did not comply with GAAP, but his superiors said that the decisions already made were final. They never offered an explanation. What would you do next if you were Gordon? Would you blow the whistle and, if so, how would you do it? Explain your answer in terms of ethical reasoning.

## Case 3-7

# Exxon-XTO Merger

ExxonMobil Corporation (Exxon) is the world's largest corporation in terms of revenue and one of the largest in market capitalization. It had sales of $486 billion in 2011, giving it the number one position on the *Fortune* 500 list in that category. In recent years, Exxon has expanded its operations into hydraulic fracking. By pumping water, sand, and chemicals into a well at high pressure, cracks develop in the stone where gas is trapped, and the process allows it to flow out. There were more than 493,000 active natural-gas wells across 31 states in the United States in 2009, almost double the number in 1990. Around 90 percent have used fracking to get more gas flowing, according to the drilling industry. By 2015, the United States will produce more oil from unconventional methods like fracking than conventional means, according to a 2012 report from the economic forecasting firm IHS Global Insight.

Nationwide, residents living near fracked gas wells have filed over 1,000 complaints regarding tainted water, severe illnesses, livestock deaths, and fish kills. Fracking is controversial because the chemicals, mixed with water, may find their way into aquifers that supply drinking water. Oil companies say that fracking is safe and poses no threat to drinking water. Right now, few groups are calling for an outright ban on fracking. However, shareholders want companies to issue full disclosure about individual fracking operations and the chemicals used during the process. Some companies counter that they already abide by environmental laws and regulations and that further disclosure is not necessary.

On June 24, 2010, Exxon completed a $41 billion merger with XTO Energy, in large part to buy the company's hydraulic-fracking expertise and gain access to its 45 trillion cubic feet of gas. The terms of the merger called for Exxon to issue 0.7098 common shares for each common share of XTO. The merger augments Exxon's total production of energy resources by increasing natural gas production to 50 percent of the total, and its reserves will go up 50 percent as well.

## Breach of Fiduciary Duties

The merger was not without its critics, in part because of the way the deal was structured and the role of XTO's management and board of directors. On December 17, 2009, the Shareholders Foundation, Inc.,[1] filed a lawsuit in Tarrant County (Texas) District Court on behalf of current investors in XTO Energy who purchased their XTO shares before

[1] The Shareholders Foundation, Inc., is an investor advocacy group that does research related to shareholder issues and informs investors of securities class actions, settlements, judgments, and other legal related news to the stock/financial market. The group offers help, support, and assistance for every shareholder, and investors find answers to their questions and equitable solutions to their problems.

December 14, 2009, over alleged breach of fiduciary duty by the board of directors of XTO Energy.

The plaintiff alleged breaches of fiduciary duty by the board of directors of XTO Energy arising out of the company's attempt to sell XTO Energy to ExxonMobil. In addition, the plaintiff claims that the XTO management and directors agreed to sell the company through "an unfair process," and that XTO Energy is worth more because of likely future global warming regulations that could curtail carbon emissions.

Previous investigations by law firms examined the following: (1) whether the XTO Energy board of directors breached their fiduciary duties to XTO shareholders by agreeing to sell XTO at an unfair price, thereby harming the company and its shareholders; (2) whether the directors of XTO may have breached their fiduciary duties by not acting in XTO shareholders' best interests; and (3) whether the company may not have adequately shopped itself around before entering into this transaction and, pursuant to this proposed transaction, ExxonMobil may be underpaying for XTO, thereby unlawfully harming XTO shareholders. After the announcement, Exxon's shares fell 4.3 percent, to $69.69, while XTO shares jumped more than 15 percent, to $47.86 on the NYSE.

## Payments Made to Officers and Members of the Board of Directors of XTO

An important part of the merger agreement was payments made to officers and members of the board of directors at XTO. Given the distaste for large payout packages to corporate insiders during the period of the financial crisis in 2007–2008, there was some concern whether Congress would approve the merger. The issue was the arrangements detailed in Exhibit 1. At the end of its investigation, Congress approved the merger, although it raised concerns about disclosures to shareholders.

## SEC Financial Disclosures Rule

In 2011, shareholders of Exxon voted not to require company officials to disclose more information about fracking, although 30 percent of the shareholders voted to increase disclosures, indicating some concern whether investors receive sufficient information for their decision-making needs.

The SEC requires that publicly traded companies release and provide for the free exchange of all material facts that are relevant to their ongoing business operations. From an ethical perspective, the general need in business transactions is for both parties to tell the whole truth about any material issue pertaining to the transaction.

The SEC requires full disclosure from public companies that wish to be publicly traded on the major U.S. exchanges. By enforcing this rule, the SEC attempts to instill confidence in investors that the financial marketplace is efficient and

**Exhibit 1**
**Form 8-K Filing with the SEC on Officer/Board Member Payments**

## Consulting Agreements & Amendments to Share Grant Agreements

In connection with the Merger and pursuant to negotiations with ExxonMobil, Messrs. Simpson, Hutton, Vennerberg, Baldwin, and Petrus (each an "Officer" and collectively, the "Officers") have agreed to waive their employment and change in control protections under their existing arrangements with the Company and enter into consulting agreements with the Company and ExxonMobil which were executed on December 13, 2009, and will become effective at the time of the Merger. Pursuant to their existing employment agreements (for Messrs. Simpson, Hutton, and Vennerberg) or the Third Amended and Restated Management Group Employee Severance Protection Plan (for Messrs. Baldwin and Petrus), upon the occurrence of a change in control transaction, which would include the Merger, each of the Officers was entitled to receive a lump sum cash payment, within 45 days after the change in control, generally equal to three times (2.5 times for Messrs. Baldwin and Petrus) the sum of his (1) annual base salary, (2) annual cash bonus, and (3) for Mr. Simpson only, annual grant of the Company's common stock. Each Officer, other than Mr. Simpson, was also entitled to receive a gross-up payment for any excise taxes imposed under Section 280G of the Internal Revenue Code ("280G Excise Taxes"). In connection with entering into the Consulting Agreements, each Officer generally agreed to (i) waive his right to receive a portion of the Change in Control Payments; (ii) subject all or a portion of the remainder of his Change in Control Payments, as retention payments, to the continued performance of consulting services and continued compliance with agreed restrictive covenants (relating to confidentiality, noncompetition, and nonsolicitation) and (iii) relinquish his right to any Gross-Up Payment due.

The waiver of the existing arrangements and effectiveness of the new Consulting Agreements among the Officers, the Company, and ExxonMobil will be contingent on the closing of the Merger. Under the Consulting Agreements, the Officers will retire as employees of the Company upon completion of the Merger and continue to serve the Company thereafter as consultants on a full time basis. The initial term of the Consulting Agreements will end, unless earlier terminated, on the first anniversary of the Merger. The Consulting Agreements are each renewable for an additional one-year period upon the mutual agreement of the Officer and ExxonMobil, in consultation with the Company.

The Company will provide each Officer with an annual consulting fee equal to one-half of the Officer's current base salary. Each Officer will also be entitled to receive an annual cash bonus equal to one-half of the Officer's current base salary, generally subject to the Officer's continued service to the payment date (for reference, the Officers' current base salaries are: Simpson—$3,600,000; Hutton—$1,400,000; Vennerberg—$900,000; Baldwin—$500,000; Petrus—$475,000). Also under the Consulting Agreements, ExxonMobil has agreed to provide each Officer with a one-time grant of restricted ExxonMobil common stock or stock units having a grant date fair market value equal to 100% of the Officer's current base salary. One-half of the Restricted Equity will vest on the first anniversary of the Merger and one-half will vest on either the second anniversary of the Merger, or, if the Initial Term is extended, on the third anniversary of the Merger, in either case subject to service requirements and the Officer's continued compliance with the applicable restrictive covenants through the applicable vesting date.

In lieu of the payment Mr. Simpson otherwise would have received in connection with the Merger under his existing employment agreement, Mr. Simpson will receive a lump sum cash payment within five days after the Merger in an amount equal to $10,800,000 (which equals three times his current base salary). In addition, Mr. Simpson will be entitled to receive a retention payment, payable in equal installments at six and twelve months after the Merger, generally subject to Mr. Simpson's continued performance of consulting services through the payment date. Mr. Simpson's retention payment, which relates to his annual grant of the Company's common stock, will equal up to $24,750,000.

In lieu of payments each of the Officers, other than Mr. Simpson, would have received in connection with the Merger under either an existing employment agreement or the terms of the Third Amended and Restated Management Group Employee Severance Protection Plan, each of the Officers (other than Mr. Simpson and Mr. Petrus) will be entitled to receive a retention payment, payable in equal installments at six and twelve months after the Merger, generally subject to the Officer's continued performance of consulting services to the payment date. The payment for the Officers, which relates to the amount of the Change in Control Payments, will equal an amount up to the following: Mr. Hutton, $10,913,662; Mr. Vennerberg, $6,172,817; and Mr. Baldwin, $2,591,527. Mr. Petrus will not receive a retention payment.

Under pre-existing Amended and Restated Agreements with the Company, each of the Officers was entitled to certain additional lump sum cash payments in the event of a change in control transaction, which would include the Merger. On December 13, 2009, the Grant Agreements were amended to provide that the lump sum cash payments due thereunder in connection with the Merger will be made in the form of shares of the Company's common stock immediately prior to completion of the Merger. The number of shares is

*(Continued)*

---

**Exhibit 1** (*Continued*)

as follows: Mr. Simpson, 833,333 Shares; Mr. Hutton, 687,500 Shares; Mr. Vennerberg, 583,333 Shares; Mr. Baldwin, 166,667 Shares; and Mr. Petrus 156,250 Shares.

Each Officer has agreed pursuant to the terms of the Consulting Agreements and the Grant Agreement amendments that, instead of receiving a Gross-Up Payment for any 280G Excise Taxes that might apply to the amounts the Officer is entitled to receive in connection with the Merger, the combined amount of the Shares and the retention payment will be subject to an added reduction, if necessary, so that the total value of this combined amount, when added to the value of other equity awards granted to the Officer which are vesting in connection with the Merger and, for Mr. Simpson, his lump sum payment, does not exceed 90% of the amount that could be provided to the Officer without the imposition of 280G Excise Taxes.

Upon termination of an Officer's services as a consultant either by the Company without "Cause" or by the Officer with "Good Reason" (each as defined in the Consulting Agreements) or upon an Officer's death or disability, the Officer will be entitled to receive (1) a lump sum cash payment equal to the unpaid portion of the Consulting Fee, and the Completion Bonus for the current term, and the unpaid portion of the retention payment and (2) in the case of all Officers other than Mr. Simpson, accelerated vesting of any unvested equity awards which were granted prior to the Merger.

---

transparent so that individual investors can take part in it for material profit. The rule is often referred to as providing "full and fair disclosure."

## Waiver of Rights Under Outside Directors Severance Plan

The Outside Directors Severance Plan provides that, upon a change in control, each nonemployee director will receive a lump sum cash payment equal to three times the sum of the annual cash retainer and value of the company's common stock most recently granted to the nonemployee director. In February 2009, each nonemployee director received a grant of 4,166 fully vested shares of the company's common stock. The nonemployee directors received an annual cash retainer of $180,000 in respect of services performed in 2009.

On December 13, 2009, all nonemployee members of the company's board of directors voluntarily waived their rights to receive the payments that otherwise would have become payable to them upon the completion of the merger under XTO Energy. Absent such a waiver, based on the closing price of the company's common stock on December 1, 2009 ($42.93), each nonemployee director was entitled to receive a lump sum cash payment of approximately $1,000,000 upon completion of the merger.

## Questions

1. The lawsuit filed by the Shareholders Foundation alleged that the board of directors of XTO breached its fiduciary duties. What are the fiduciary duties of the board? Identify the duties allegedly violated in the XTO case. Do you think the board acted in accordance with a shareholder or stewardship perspective?

2. Much has been said during the recent financial crisis about top executive salaries being way too large, especially in those companies receiving a government bailout. The Obama administration sought to rein them in through threats of taxation or other forms of moral suasion. Do you believe that the government has an ethical right to intervene in a company's executive compensation program? Support your answer with reference to ethical reasoning. Review Exhibit 1. Do you believe that the agreement in the Form 8-K about payments to officers and board members raises any ethical issues? What is the role of the business judgment rule in such decisions?

3. One aspect of being an ethical corporation is to operate in a socially responsible way. The Corporate Social Responsibility Initiative at Harvard University[2] defines corporate social responsibility strategically: "Corporate social responsibility encompasses not only what companies do with their profits, but also how they make them. It goes beyond philanthropy and compliance and addresses how companies manage their economic, social, and environmental impacts, as well as their relationships in all key spheres of influence: the workplace, the marketplace, the supply chain, the community, and the public policy realm." The ethics of fracking is an issue raised in a number of articles and in the blog of one of the authors of this book. According to Mintz,[3] "From an ethical perspective, we might look at the harms and benefits of fracking. In other words, do the potential dangers of fracking, including contamination of water supplies, outweigh the potential benefits of producing badly needed oil and gas resources at a time when our national security may be in jeopardy because of our continued reliance on unreliable sources of energy? Is U.S. energy independence more important than the potential for harm to those affected by fracking procedures? Do jobs and economic growth trump health and safety concerns?"

4. Evaluate the ethics of fracking from a moral reasoning perspective using the methods discussed in Chapter 1. Going forward, do you believe that fracking should continue without regulation? Why or why not?

[2]www.hks.harvard.edu/m-rcbg/CSRI/init_define.html.
[3]www.ethicssage.com/2011/12/the-ethics-of-fracking.html

## Case 3-8

# Disclosure of Steve Jobs's Health as Apple CEO: A Public or Private Matter?

An important issue within the scope of corporate governance is whether a company should disclose the health problems of its CEO and how much information should be disclosed. The sensitivity of this issue is exemplified at Apple Inc., where CEO Steve Jobs faced numerous questions regarding his health and the impact that his sudden departure would have on the company.

In October 2003, Jobs was diagnosed with pancreatic cancer. No public announcement was made, although the board of directors was notified of his condition. The specific form of cancer was rare but considered treatable, with the majority of patients who undergo surgery experiencing a survival rate of more than 10 years. On July 31, 2004, Jobs entered Stanford Hospital for treatment.

The following day, Jobs sent an email to Apple employees stating, "This weekend I underwent a successful surgery to remove a cancerous tumor from my pancreas.... I will be recuperating during the month of August, and expect to return to work in September. While I'm out, I've asked Tim Cook [executive vice president of sales and operations] to be responsible for Apple's day-to-day operations, so we shouldn't miss a beat." A copy of the message was distributed to the Associated Press. It was the first public disclosure of his condition. Given Jobs's strategic and visionary role at Apple, it is perhaps not surprising that when trading resumed the next day, Apple stock fell 2.4 percent almost immediately.

The issue of Jobs's health resurfaced in June 2008, when he appeared noticeably thin at a public appearance.

A company spokeswoman responded to inquiries by stating that Jobs had "a common bug...He's been on antibiotics and getting better day by day and didn't want to miss [the event]. That's all there is to it." When analysts asked for more information during an earnings conference call, Apple CFO Peter Oppenheimer declined to elaborate: "Steve loves Apple. He serves as the CEO at the pleasure of Apple's board and has no plans to leave Apple. Steve's health is a private matter."

In January 2009, Apple released another letter from Jobs in which he explained that his recent weight loss was due to a "hormone imbalance." According to the letter, "The remedy for this nutritional problem is relatively simple and straightforward, and I've already begun treatment...I will continue as Apple's CEO during my recovery." Concurrently, the board of directors issued a statement that "[Jobs] deserves our complete and unwavering support during his recuperation. He most certainly has that from Apple and its Board."

However, the company announced 10 days later that Jobs would take another leave of absence. According to Jobs, "during the past week I have learned that my health-related issues are more complex than I originally thought. In order to take myself out of the limelight and focus on my health...I have decided to take a medical leave of absence until the end of June." No elaboration was offered. Cook, then chief operating officer (COO), would resume leadership of the company. In the two-week period surrounding these announcements, Apple stock fell 17 percent.

Jobs returned to work as scheduled six months later. Two weeks prior to his return, however, news leaked that Jobs had received a liver transplant at a Tennessee hospital the previous April. A company spokeswoman declined to comment other than to say, "Steve continues to look forward to returning at the end of June, and there's nothing further to say." Doctors unaffiliated with the case explained that tumors associated with the pancreatic cancer that Jobs was originally diagnosed with often metastasize in another organ, commonly the liver. The hospital where Jobs received the transplant stated that his prognosis was "excellent."

In January 2011, Jobs took a third leave of absence. In an email to employees, he explained that he would "continue as CEO and be involved in major strategic decisions" but that Cook would be responsible for "day-to-day operations." Jobs said he would be back with the company as soon as he could. "In the meantime, my family and I would deeply appreciate respect for our privacy." When asked for additional comment, an Apple spokeswoman replied, "We've said all we're going to say." Jobs died on October 5 of that year, due to complications from pancreatic cancer that led to respiratory arrest.

## Questions

1. Were the shareholders of Apple entitled to receive information about the health of Jobs? What about the general public? Of what value is such information? How might the company benefit from the disclosure of such information, and how might it suffer? How might the shareholders benefit, and how might they suffer?

2. From a corporate governance perspective, what issues are important in determining whether there should be disclosure of the health problems of a CEO? Is it an ethical matter?

3. Should information about the health of other senior managers, such as the five most highly compensated senior managers or the vice chair of the board of directors, be disclosed? Should other information be disclosed about the CEO of a public company, such as being involved in a contentious divorce that distracts from day-to-day management of the company?

## Case 3-9

# Bhopal, India: A Tragedy of Massive Proportions

We are citizens of the world. The tragedy of our times is that we do not know this.

*Woodrow T. Wilson (1856–1924),*
*28th president of the United States*

At five past midnight on December 3, 1984, 40 tons of the chemical methyl isocynate (MIC), a toxic gas, started to leak out of a pesticide tank at the Union Carbide plant in Bhopal, India. The leak was first detected by workers about 11:30 p.m. on December 2, 1984, when their eyes began to tear and burn. According to AcuSafe,[1] "in 1991 the official Indian government panel charged with tabulating deaths and injuries counted more than 3,800 dead and approximately 11,000 with disabilities." However, estimates now range as high as 8,000 killed in the first three days and over 120,000 injured.[2] There were 4,000 deaths officially recorded by the government, although 13,000 death claims were filed with the government, according to a United Nations report, and hundreds of thousands more claim injury as a result of the disaster.[3] On June 7, 2010, an Indian court convicted eight former senior employees of Union Carbide's Indian subsidiary to two years in jail each for causing "death by negligence" over their part in the Bhopal gas tragedy in which an estimated 15,000 people died more than 25 years ago. While the actual numbers may be debatable, there can be no doubt that the Bhopal incident raises a variety of interesting ethical questions, including:

- Did the company knowingly sacrifice safety at the Bhopal plant?
- Did the Indian government properly oversee the functioning of the plant consistent with its regulatory authority?
- Did the company react quickly enough to avoid sustained health problems to those injured by the leak of toxic fumes?
- In the aftermath of the disaster, were the disclosures made by Union Carbide sufficiently transparent to enable a concerned public to understand the causes of the leak and the steps that the company was taking to address all the issues?
- Did the company and the Indian government reach a fair resolution of the thousands of claims filed by Indian citizens?

- Is "business risk" a valid basis on which to make business decisions?

You make up your own mind as you read about the tragedy that is Bhopal.

## In the Beginning

On May 4, 1980, the first factory exported from the West to make pesticides using MIC began production in Bhopal, India. The company planned to export the chemicals from the United States to make the pesticide Sevin. The new CEO of Union Carbide came over from the United States especially for the occasion.[4]

As you might expect, the company seemed very concerned about safety issues. "Carbide's manifesto set down certain truths, the first being that 'all accidents are avoidable provided the measures necessary to avoid them are defined and implemented.'" The company's slogan was "Good safety and good accident prevention practices are good business."

## Safety Measures

The Union Carbide plant in Bhopal was equipped with an alarm system with a siren that was supposed to be set off whenever the "duty supervisor in the control room" sensed even the slightest indication that a possible fire might be developing "or the smallest emission of toxic gas." The "alarm system was intended to warn the crews working on the factory site." Even though thousands of people lived in the nearby bustees (shantytowns), "none of the loudspeakers pointed outward" in their direction. Still, they could hear the sirens coming from the plant. The siren went off so frequently that it seemed as though the population became used to it and weren't completely aware that one death and several accidental poisonings had occurred before the night of December 2, and there was a "mysterious fire in the alpha-naphtol unit."

In May 1982, three engineers from Union Carbide came to Bhopal to evaluate the plant and confirm that everything was operating according to company standards. However, the investigators identified more than 60 violations of operational and safety regulations. An Indian reporter managed to obtain a copy of the report that noted "shoddy workmanship," warped equipment, corroded circuitry, "the absence of automatic sprinklers in the MIC and phosgene production zones," a lack of pressure gauges, and numerous other violations. The severest criticism was in the area of personnel. There was "an alarming turnover of inadequately trained staff, unsatisfactory instruction methods, and a lack of rigor in maintenance reports."

[1]AcuSafe is an Internet resource for safety and risk management information that is a publication of AcuTech, a global leader in process safety and security risk management located in Houston, Texas; see www.acusafe.com/Incidents/Bhopal1984/incidentbhopal1984.htm.

[2]According to CorpWatch, www.corpwatch.org/.

[3]United Nations, *United Nations University Report (UNU Report) on Toxic Gas Leak*, www.unu.edu/unupress/unupbooks/uu21le/uu211eOc.htm.

[4]Dominique LaPierre and Javier Moro, *Five Past Midnight in Bhopal* (New York: Warner Books, 2002).

The reporter wrote three articles proclaiming the unsafe plant. The third article was titled "If You Refuse to Understand, You Will Be Reduced to Dust." Nothing seemed to matter in the end because the population was assured by Union Carbide and government representatives that no one need be concerned because the phosgene produced at the plant was not a toxic gas.

## The Accident

The accident occurred when a large volume of water entered the MIC storage tanks and triggered a violent chain reaction. Normally, water and MIC were kept separate, but on the night of December 2, "metal barriers known as slip blinds were not inserted and the cleaning water passed directly into the MIC tanks." It is possible that additional water entered the tanks later on in the attempts to control the reaction. Shortly after the introduction of water, "temperatures and pressures in the tanks increased to the point of explosion."

The report of consultants that reviewed the facts surrounding the accident indicates that workers made a variety of attempts to save the plant, including:[5]

- They tried to turn on the plant refrigeration system to cool down the environment and slow the reaction, but the system had been drained of coolant weeks before and never refilled as a cost-saving measure.
- They tried to route expanding gases to a neighboring tank, but the tank's pressure gauge was broken, indicating that the tank was full when it was really empty.
- They tried other measures that didn't work due to inadequate or broken equipment.
- They tried to spray water on the gases and have them settle to the ground, but it was too late as the chemical reaction was nearly completed.

## The Workers and Their Reaction

It was reported that the maintenance workers did not flush out the pipes after the factory's production of MIC stopped on December 2. This was important because the pipes carried the liquid MIC produced by the plant's reactors to the tanks. The highly corrosive MIC leaves chemical deposits on the lining of the tanks that can eventually get into the storage tanks and contaminate the MIC. Was it laziness, as suggested by one worker?

Another worker pointed out that the production supervisor of the plant left strict instructions to flush the pipes, but it was late at night and neither worker really wanted to do it. Still, they followed the instructions for the washing operation, but the supervisor had omitted the crucial step to place solid metal discs at the end of each pipe to ensure hermetically sealed tanks.

The cleansing operation began when one worker connected a hosepipe to a drain cock on the pipework and turned on the tap. After a short time, it was clear to the worker that the injected water was not coming out of two of the four drain cocks. The worker called the supervisor, who walked over to the plant and instructed the worker to clean the filters in the two clogged drain cocks and turn the water back on. They did that, but the water did not flow out of one drain. After informing the supervisor, who said to just keep the water flowing, the worker left for the night. It would now be up to the night shift to turn off the tap.

The attitude of the workers as they started the night shift was not good as Union Carbide had started to cut back on production and lay off workers. They wondered if they might be next. The culture of safety that Union Carbide tried to build up was largely gone, as the workers typically handled toxic substances without protective gear. The temperature readings in the tanks were made less frequently, and it was rare when anyone checked the welding on the pipework in the middle of the night.

Even though the pressure gauge on one of the tanks increased beyond the "permitted maximum working pressure," the supervisor ignored warnings coming from the control room because he was under the impression that Union Carbide had built the tanks with special steel and walls thick enough to resist even greater pressures. Still, the duty head of the control room and another worker went to look directly at the pressure gauge attached to the three tanks. They confirmed the excessive pressure in one tank.

The duty head climbed to the top of that tank, examined the metal casing carefully, and sensed the stirring action. The pressure inside was increasing quickly, leading to a popping sound "like champagne corks." Some of the gas then escaped, and a brownish cloud appeared. The workers returned to where the pipes had been cleaned and turned off the water tap. They smelled the powerful gas emissions, and they heard the fizzing, which sounded as if someone was blowing into an empty bottle. One worker had a cool enough head to sound the general alarm, but it was too late for most of the workers and many of those living in the shantytowns below the plant.

## The Political Response

Union Carbide sent a team to investigate the catastrophe, but the Indian government had seized all records and denied the investigators access to the plant and the eyewitnesses. The government of the state of Madhya Pradesh (where the plant was located) tried to place the blame squarely on the shoulders of Union Carbide. It sued the company for damages on behalf of the victims. The ruling Congress Party was facing national parliamentary elections three weeks after the accident, and it "stood to lose heavily if its partners in the state government were seen to be implicated, or did not deal firmly with Union Carbide."[6]

[5]Ron Graham, "FAQ on Failures: Union Carbide Bhopal," Barrett Engineering Consulting, www.tcnj.edu/rgraham/failures/UCBhopal.html.

[6]United Nations, *United Nations University Report (UNU Report) on Toxic Gas Leak*.

The government thwarted early efforts by Union Carbide to provide relief to the victims to block its attempt to gain the goodwill of the public. The strategy worked: the Congress Party won both the state legislative assembly and the national parliament seats from Madhya Pradesh by large margins.

## Economic Effects

The economic impact of a disaster like the one that happened in Bhopal is staggering. The $25 million Union Carbide plant in Bhopal was shut down immediately after the accident, and 650 permanent jobs were lost. The loss of human life means a loss of future earning power and economic production. The thousands of accident victims had to be treated and in many cases rehabilitated. The closure of the plant had peripheral effects on local businesses and the population of Bhopal. It is estimated that "two mass evacuations disrupted commercial activities for several weeks, with resulting business losses of $8 to $65 million."

In the year after the accident, the government paid compensation of about $800 per fatality to relatives of the dead persons. About $100 apiece was awarded to 20,000 victims. Beginning in March 1991, new relief payments were made to all victims who lived in affected areas, and a total of $260 million was disbursed. Overall, Union Carbide agreed to pay $470 million to the residents of Bhopal. By the end of October 2003, according to the Bhopal Gas Tragedy Relief and Rehabilitation Department, compensation had been awarded to 554,895 people for injuries received and 15,310 survivors of those killed. The average amount that families of the dead received was $2,200.

## Union Carbide's Response

Shortly after the gas release, Union Carbide launched what it called "an aggressive effort to identify the cause." According to the company, the results of an independent investigation conducted by the engineering consulting firm Arthur D. Little were that "the gas leak could only have been caused by deliberate sabotage. Someone purposely put water in the gas storage tank, causing a massive chemical reaction. Process safety systems had been put in place that would have kept the water from entering the tank by accident."[7]

A 1993 report prepared by Jackson B. Browning, the retired vice president of Health, Safety, and Environmental Programs at Union Carbide Corporation, stated that he didn't find out about the accident until 2:30 a.m. on December 3. He claims to have been told that "no plant employees had been injured, but there were fatalities—possibly eight or twelve—in the nearby community."

A meeting was called at the company's headquarters in Danbury, Connecticut, for 6 a.m. The chair of the board of directors of Union Carbide, Warren M. Anderson, had received the news while returning from a business trip to Washington, DC. He had a "bad cold and a fever," so Anderson stayed at home and designated Browning as his "media stand-in" until Anderson could return to the office.[8]

At the first press conference called for 1:00 p.m. on December 3, the company acknowledged that a disaster had occurred at its plant in Bhopal. The company reported that it was sending "medical and technical experts to aid the people of Bhopal, to help dispose of the remaining [MIC] at the plant and to investigate the cause of the tragedy." Notably, Union Carbide halted production at its only other MIC plant in West Virginia, and it stated its intention "to convert existing supplies into less volatile compounds."

Anderson traveled to India and offered aid of $1 million and the Indian subsidiary of Union Carbide pledged the Indian equivalent of $840,000. Within a few months, the company offered an additional $5 million in aid that was rejected by the Indian government. The money was then turned over to the Indian Red Cross and used for relief efforts.

The company continued to offer relief aid with "no strings attached." However, the Indian government rejected the overtures, and it didn't help the company to go through third parties. Union Carbide believed that the volatile political situation in India—Prime Minister Indira Gandhi had just been assassinated in October—hindered its relief efforts, especially after the election of Rajiv Gandhi shortly after the assassination on a government reform platform. It appeared to the company that Union Carbide was to be made an example of as an exploiter of Indian natural resources, and it suspected that the Indian government may have wanted to "gain access to Union Carbide's financial resources."

Union Carbide had a contingency plan for emergencies, but it didn't cover the "unthinkable." The company felt compelled to show its "commitment to employee and community safety and specifically, to reaffirm the safety measures in place at their operation." Anderson went to West Virginia to meet with the employees in early February 1985. At that meeting, as "a measure of the personal concern and compassion of Union Carbide employees," the workers established a "Carbide Employees Bhopal Relief Fund and collected more than $100,000 to aid the tragedy's victims."[9]

## Analysis of Union Carbide's Bhopal Problems

Documents uncovered in litigation[10] and obtained by the Environmental Working Group of the Chemical Industry Archives, an organization that investigates chemical company claims of product safety, indicate that Union Carbide "cut corners and employed untested technologies when building the Bhopal Plant." The company went ahead with

---

[7]After the leak, Union Carbide started a Web site, www.bhopal.com, to provide its side of the story and details about the tragedy. In 1998, the Indian state government of Madhya Pradesh took over the site.

[8]Jackson B. Browning, *The Browning Report*, Union Carbide Corporation, 1993, www.bhopal.com/pdfs/browning.pdf.
[9]*The Browning Report*, p. 8.
[10]*Bano et al. v. Union Carbide Corp & Warren Anderson*, 99cv11329 SDNY, filed on 11/15/99.

the unproven design even though it posed a "danger of polluting subsurface water supplies in the Bhopal area." The following is an excerpt from a document numbered UCC 04206 and included in the Environmental Working Group Report on Bhopal, India.[11] It also reveals the indifferent attitude of the Indian government toward environmental safety.

"The systems described have received provisional endorsement by the Public Health Engineering Office of the State of Madhya Pradesh in Bhopal. At present, there are no state or central government laws and/or regulations for environmental protection, though enactment is expected in the near future. It is not expected that this will require any design modifications."

## Technology Risks

"The comparative risk of poor performance and of consequent need for further investment to correct it is considerably higher in the [Union Carbide–India] operation than it would be had proven technology been followed throughout … the MIC-to-Sevin process, as developed by Union Carbide, has had only a limited trial run. Furthermore, while similar waste streams have been handled elsewhere, this particular combination of materials to be disposed of is new and, accordingly, affords further chance for difficulty. In short, it can be expected that there will be interruptions in operations and delays in reaching capacity or product quality that might have been avoided by adoption of proven technology.

[Union Carbide–India] finds the business risk in the proposed mode of operation acceptable, however, in view of the desired long-term objectives of minimum capital and foreign exchange expenditures. SO long as [Union Carbide-India] is diligent in pursuing solutions, it is their feeling that any shortfalls can be mitigated by imports. Union Carbide concurs."

As previously mentioned, there were one death and several accidental poisonings at the Bhopal plant before December 3, 1984. The International Environmental Law Research Center prepared a Bhopal Date Line showing that the death occurred on December 25, 1981, when a worker was exposed to phosgene gas. On January 9, 1982, 25 workers were hospitalized as a result of another leak. On October 5, 1982, another leak from the plant led to the hospitalization of hundreds of residents.[12]

It is worth noting that the workers had protested unsafe conditions after the January 9, 1982, leak, but their warning went unheeded. In March 1982, a leak from one of the solar evaporation ponds took place, and the Indian plant expressed its concern to Union Carbide headquarters. In May 1982, the company sent its U.S. experts to the Bhopal plant to conduct the audit previously mentioned.

Union Carbide's reaction to newspaper allegations that Union Carbide–India was running an unsafe operation was for the plant's works manager to write a denial of the charges as baseless. The company's next step was, to say the least, bewildering. It rewrote the safety manuals to permit switching off of the refrigeration unit and a shutdown of the vent gas scrubber when the plant was not in operation. The staffing at the MIC unit was reduced from 12 workers to 6. On November 29, 1984, three days before the disaster, Union Carbide completed a feasibility report and the company had decided to dismantle the plant and ship it to Indonesia or Brazil.

## India's Position

The Indian government has acknowledged that 521,262 persons, well over half the population of Bhopal at the time of the toxic leak, were "exposed" to the lethal gas.[13] In the immediate aftermath of the accident, most attention was devoted to medical recovery. The victims of the MIC leak suffered damage to lung tissue and respiratory functions. The lack of medical documentation affected relief efforts. The absence of baseline data made it difficult to identify specific medical consequences of MIC exposure and to develop appropriate medical treatment. Another problem was that malnourishment of the poor Indians affected by the tragedy added to the difficulty because they already suffered from many of the postexposure symptoms such as coughing, breathlessness, nausea, vomiting, chest pains, and poor sight.[14]

In a paper on the Bhopal tragedy written by Pratima Ungarala, a student at Hindu University, he analyzed the *Browning Report* and characterized the company's response as one of public relations. He noted that the report identified the media and other interested parties such as customers, shareholders, suppliers, and other employees as the most important to pacify. Ungarala criticized this response for its lack of concern for the people of Bhopal and the Indian people in general. Instead, the corporation saw the urgency to assure the people of the United States that such an incident would not happen here.[15]

Browning's main strategy to restore Union Carbide's image was to distance the company from the site of the disaster. He points out early in the document that Union Carbide had owned only 50.9 percent of the affiliate, Union Carbide India Ltd. He notes that all the employees in the company were Indians and that the last American employee had left two years before the leak.

The report contended that the company "did not have any hold over its Indian affiliate." This seems to be a contentious issue because while "many of the day-to-day details, such as staffing and maintenance, were left to Indian officials, the major decisions, such as the annual budget, had to be cleared with the American headquarters." In addition, according to both Indian and U.S. laws, a parent company

---

[11]Environmental Working Group, *Chemical Industry Archives,* www.chemicalindustryarchives.org/dirtysecrets/bhopal/index.asp.
[12]S. Muralidhar, "The Bhopal Date Line," International Environmental Law Research Centre, www.ielrc.org/content/n0409.htm.

[14]Paul Shrivastava, "Long-Term Recovery from the Bhopal Crisis," *The Long Road to Recovery: Community Responses to Industrial Disaster* (New York: United Nations University, 1996).
[15]Pratima Ungarala, *Bhopal Gas Tragedy: An Analysis,* Final Paper HU521/Dale Sullivan 5/19/98, www.hu.mtu.edu/hu_dept/tc@mtu/papers/bhopal.htm.

(United Carbide in this case) holds full responsibility for any plants that it operates through subsidiaries and in which it has a majority stake. Ungarala concluded that Union Carbide was trying to avoid paying the $3 billion that India demanded as compensation and was looking to find a "scapegoat" to take the blame.[16]

After the government of Madhya Pradesh took over the information Web site from Union Carbide, it began to keep track of applications for compensation. Between 1985 and 1997, over 1 million claims were filed for personal injury. In more than half of those cases, the claimant was awarded a monetary settlement. The total amount disbursed as of March 31, 2003, was about $345 million.[17] An additional $25 million was released through July 2004, at which time the Indian Supreme Court ordered the government to pay the victims and families of the dead the remaining $330 million in the compensation fund.

## Lawsuits

The inevitable lawsuits began in December 1984 and March 1985, when the government of India filed against Union Carbide–India and the United States, respectively. Union Carbide asked for the case filed in the Federal District Court of New York to be moved to India because that was where the accident had occurred and most of the evidence existed. The case went to the Bhopal District Court—the lowest-level court that could hear such a case. During the next four years, the case made "its way through the maze of legal bureaucracy" from the state high court up to the Supreme Court of India.

The legal disputes were over the amount of compensation and the exoneration of Union Carbide from future liabilities. The disputes were complicated by a lack of reliable information about the causes of the event and its consequences. The government of India had adopted the "Bhopal Gas Leak Disaster Ordinance—a law that appointed the government as sole representative of the victims." It was challenged by victim activists, who pointed out that the victims were not consulted about legal matters or settlement possibilities. The result was, in effect, to dissolve "the victims' identity as a constituency separate and differing from the government."[18]

In 1989, India had another parliamentary election, and it seemed a politically opportune time to settle the case and win support from the voters. It had been five years since the accident and the victims were fed up with waiting. By that time, "hundreds of victims had died and thousands had moved out of the gas-affected neighborhoods." Even though the Indian government had taken Union Carbide to court asking for $3 billion, the company reached a settlement with the government in January 1989 for $470 million; the agreement gave Union Carbide immunity from future prosecution.

In October 1991, India's Supreme Court upheld the compensation settlement but cancelled Union Carbide's immunity from criminal prosecution. The money had been held in a court-administered account until 1992 while claims were sorted out. By early 1993, there were 630,000 claims filed, of which 350,000 had been substantiated on the basis of medical records. The numbers are larger than previously mentioned because the extent of health problems grew continuously after the accident and hundreds of victims continued to die. Despite challenges by victims and activists to the settlement with Union Carbide, at the beginning of 1993, the government of India began to distribute the $470 million, which had increased to $700 million as a result of interest earned on the funds.[19]

## What Happened to Union Carbide?

Not surprisingly, the lawsuits and bad publicity affected Union Carbide's stock price. Before the disaster, the company's stock traded between $50 and $58 a share. In the months immediately following the accident, it traded at $32 to $40. In the latter half of 1985, the GAF Corporation of New York made a hostile bid to take over Union Carbide. The ensuing battle and speculative stock trading ran up the stock price to $96, and it forced the company into financial restructuring.

The company's response was to fight back. It sold off its consumer products division and received more than $3.3 billion for the assets. It took on additional debt and used the funds from the sale and borrowing to repurchase 38.8 million of its shares to protect the company from further threats of a takeover.

The debt burden had accounted for 80 percent of the company's capitalization by 1986. At the end of 1991, the debt levels were still high—50 percent of capitalization. The company sold its Linde Gas Division for $2.4 billion, "leaving the company at less than half its pre-Bhopal size."

The Bhopal disaster "slowly but steadily sapped the financial strength of Union Carbide and adversely affected" employee morale and productivity. The company's inability to prove its sabotage claim affected its reputation. In 1994, Union Carbide sold its Indian subsidiary, which had operated the Bhopal plant, to an Indian battery manufacturer. It used $90 million from the sale to fund a charitable trust that would build a hospital to treat victims in Bhopal.

Two significant events occurred in 2001. First, the Bhopal Memorial Hospital and Research Centre opened its doors. Second, the Dow Chemical Company purchased Union Carbide for $10.3 billion in stock and debt, and Union Carbide became a subsidiary of Dow Chemical.

Subsequent to the initial settlement with Union Carbide, the Indian government took steps to right the wrong and its aftereffects caused by the failure of management and the

---

[16]Ungarala.

[17]Madhya Pradesh Government, Bhopal Gas Tragedy Relief and Rehabilitation Department, www.mp.nic.in/bgtrrdmp/facts.htm.

[18]Michael R. Reich, *Toxic Politics: Responding to Chemical Disasters* (Ithaca, NY: Cornell University Press, 1991).

[19]United Nations Report.

systems at Union Carbide in Bhopal. On August 8, 2007, the Indian government announced that it would meet many of the demands of the survivors by taking legal action on the civil and criminal liabilities of Union Carbide and its new owner, Dow Chemical. The government established an "Empowered Commission" on Bhopal to address the health and welfare needs of the survivors, as well as environmental, social, economic, and medical rehabilitation.

On June 26, 2012, Dow Chemical Co. won dismissal of a lawsuit alleging polluted soil and water produced by its Union Carbide's chemical plant in Bhopal, India, injured area residents, one of at least two pending cases involving the facility known for the 1984 disaster that killed thousands.

U.S. District Judge John Keenan in Manhattan ruled that Union Carbide and its former chairman, Warren Anderson, weren't liable for environmental remediation or pollution-related claims made by residents near the plant, which had been owned and operated by a former Union Carbide unit in India.

## Questions

1. Evaluate the actions of the workers and management of Union Carbide in this case from the perspectives of System 1 and System 2 thinking that was discussed in Chapter 2.

2. The document uncovered by the Environmental Working Group Report refers to the acceptable "business risk" in the Bhopal operation due to questions about the technology. Is it ethical for a company to use business risk as a measure of whether to go ahead with an operation that may have safety problems? How would you characterize such a thought process from the perspective of ethical reasoning?

3. Evaluate management decision making in the Bhopal case from a corporate governance perspective. Compare the decision-making process used by Union Carbide to deal with its disaster with that of Ford Motor Co. in the Pinto case and Johnson & Johnson in the Tylenol incident as described in this chapter. How do you assess stakeholder responsibilities in each of these cases?

## Case 3-10

# Accountability of Ex-HP CEO in Conflict of Interest Charges

How could a CEO and chairperson of the board of directors of a major company resign in disgrace over a personal relationship with a contractor that led to a sexual harassment charge and involved a conflict of interests, a violation of the code of ethics? It happened to Mark Hurd on August 6, 2010. Hurd was the former CEO for Hewlett-Packard (HP) for five years and also served as the chair of the board of directors for four years. On departure from HP, Hurd said he had not lived up to his own standards regarding trust, respect, and integrity.

In 2006, Hurd led the company out of disgrace when it was found guilty of spying on its own members of the board of directors in a "pretexting case" where the company gained access to board members' personal phone records by impersonating the board members. The goal of obtaining information under false pretenses, was to plug leaks from the board by using private detectives to spy on directors, employees, and journalists who covered the company. The scandal resulted in the removal of then-chair Patricia Dunn and vaulted Hurd into the board chair position after assuming the CEO role in 2005. The facts of the pretexting situation are discussed in Case 3-4.

The board of directors of HP began an investigation of Hurd in response to a sexual harassment complaint by Jodie Fisher, a former contractor, who retained lawyer Gloria Allred to represent her. While HP did not find that the facts supported the complaint, they did reveal behavior that the board would not tolerate. Subsequent to Hurd's resignation, a severance package was negotiated granting Hurd $12.2 million, COBRA benefits, and stock options, for a total package of somewhere between $40 and $50 million.

In a letter to employees of HP on August 6, interim CEO Cathie Lesjak outlined where Hurd violated the "Standards of Business Conduct" and the reasons for his departure. Lesjak wrote that Hurd "failed to maintain accurate expense reports, and misused company assets." She indicated that each was a violation of the standards and "together they demonstrated a profound lack of judgment that significantly undermined Mark's credibility and his ability to effectively lead HP." The letter reminded employees that everyone is expected to adhere strictly to the standards in all business dealings and relationships and senior executives should set the highest standards for professional and personal conduct.

The woman who brought forward the sexual harassment complaint was a "marketing consultant" who was hired by HP for certain projects, but she was never an employee of HP. During the investigation, inaccurately documented expenses were found that were claimed to have been paid to the consultant for her services. Falsifying the use of company funds violated the HP Standards of Business Conduct.

On December 30, 2011, a letter from Allred about Fisher's responsibilities was leaked to the Associated Press during the trial in a Delaware court. The letter showed that in an effort to impress Fisher, who was hired as an event hostess (not a true marketing consultant), Hurd showed her his checking account balance holding over $1 million. The Delaware court had ruled that the disclosure of the letter did not violate Delaware laws. In rejecting efforts by Hurd's lawyers to keep it confidential, the court concluded that the letter did not contain trade secrets, nonpublic financial information, or third-party confidential information. The ruling said information that is only "mildly embarrassing" is not protected from public disclosure. Some sentences concerning Hurd's family were ordered redacted from the letter, however.[1]

Allred alleged in the letter that, while Fisher was ostensibly hired as an HP event hostess in late 2007, she was really brought on to accompany Hurd to HP events held out of town. In a serious corporate allegation, during a trip to Madrid in March 2008, Hurd allegedly called Fisher's room and told her about a then-undisclosed deal in the works, in which HP was going to acquire the tech consulting firm EDS. Fisher had heard of the company, having lived before in Dallas. Hurd told her to keep what she knew about the deal secret.

As for the sexual harassment claim, Allred alleged in the letter that Hurd harassed Fisher at meetings and dinners over a several year period during which time Fisher experienced a number of unwelcome sexual advances from Hurd including kissing and grabbing. Fisher said that this continual sexual harassment made her uncertain about her employment status.

## Questions

1. What is the role of trust in business? How does trust relate to stakeholder interests? How does trust engender ethical leadership? Evaluate Mark Hurd's actions in this case from a trust perspective.

2. Define conflict of interests in a business sense. How does Hurd's actions and relationship with Jodie Fisher in the case create a conflict of interest? Did the conflict of interest and trust issue contribute the possibility that sexual harassment may have existed? Why or why not?

3. Leo Apotheker, the former CEO of HP who succeeded Mark Hurd, resigned in September 2011, after just 11 months on the job—but he left with a $13.2 million severance package. Hurd left with a package between $40 million and $50 million. What is the role of a severance package in hiring a CEO? Do you think the size of the severance package given to Hurd was ethical? Does the Hurd case affect your views about the "say on pay" rule?

[1] The letter is Available at http://www.scribd.com/doc/76795283/Allred-Letter-Redacted-New.

# 4

# AICPA Code
# of Professional Conduct

First, it was the Big Eight CPA firms. Then, Arthur Young and Ernst & Whinney combined to form Ernst & Young (EY). This was followed by the merger of Deloitte Haskins & Sells and Touche Ross & Co. (Deloitte & Touche), and then Price Waterhouse and Coopers & Lybrand (PricewaterhouseCoopers). The Big Five, which also included KPMG, existed until the early 2000s, when Arthur Andersen (Andersen) was forced out of business as a result of the fallout from a criminal investigation of the firm by the U.S. Department of Justice that was triggered by the Enron fraud. Now, it's the Big Four certified public accounting (CPA) firms—the four largest firms in the world that audit major international companies.

In her book *Final Accounting*, which chronicles the rise and fall of Arthur Andersen, Barbara Ley Toffler describes Andersen's employees as "Androids." Toffler points to a culture at Andersen that led to a compromise of its ethical values by establishing a tone at the top for employees to live the mantra of "keep the client happy."[1]

The shortcomings of the Enron audit are generally credited with leading to the demise of Andersen. However, before that, the firm had reportedly settled more than a dozen cases over a 25-year period pertaining to claims that auditors concealed or failed to reveal material misstatements within financial reports. Multimillion-dollar settlements preceded the Enron scandal, which at that time was the largest bankruptcy case in the history of the United States.[2] Accounting frauds at Andersen clients, including Sunbeam, Waste Management, Enron, and WorldCom, typified Andersen's failure to act in the public interest.

On December 2, 2001, Enron filed for Chapter 11 bankruptcy, and two weeks later, it fired Andersen as its auditor.

On January 15, 2002, the main partner, David Duncan—who was responsible for the Enron audit—was fired by Andersen for his role in overseeing the mass destruction of Enron documents prior to the investigation of the firm by the Securities and Exchange Commission (SEC). On January 28, 2002, the U.S. Department of Justice filed a criminal obstruction-of-justice charge against Andersen for its shredding of documents in the Enron case. Andersen pleaded not guilty to a charge of obstructing justice and explained that the destruction of Enron documentation and e-mails was just part of routine company procedures of destroying confidential client documentation. On April 9, 2002, in an agreement with the Department of Justice, Duncan pleaded guilty to illegally shredding Enron documents. Just a day before, Andersen announced a massive layoff of 7,000 of its workforce. On June 15, 2002, after five weeks of hearing evidence and 10 days of deliberation, the jury found Andersen guilty of obstructing the course of justice.

In a surprise reversal, the U.S. Supreme Court reviewed the original jury instructions given by Judge Melinda Harmon, which defined the standards and hurdles that the jury had to clear to reach a guilty verdict. The court ruled that the instructions "failed to convey the requisite consciousness of wrongdoing," as Chief Justice William Rehnquist wrote in the unanimous opinion. "Indeed, it is striking how little culpability the instructions required."[3] Unfortunately for Andersen, it was too late; the firm had already closed its doors for good.

In this chapter we discuss a variety of terms that apply to varying services of CPAs and CPA firms. The ethical requirements in the AICPA Code are discussed as well. An assurance service is an independent professional service to improve the quality of information for decision makers.

An attestation service is a form of assurance service in which the CPA firm issues a report about the reliability of an assertion that is the responsibility of another party. Audit services are a form of attestation service in which the auditor expresses a written conclusion about the degree of correspondence between information and established criteria.

The most common form of audit service is an audit of historical financial statements, in which the auditor expresses a conclusion as to whether the financial statements are presented in conformity with generally accepted accounting principles. An example of an attestation service is a report on the effectiveness of an entity's internal control over financial reporting. There are many possible forms of assurance services, including services related to business performance measurement, health care performance, and information system reliability. For simplification purposes we use the term audit or attest services to refer to the examination of a client's financial statements and rendering of an independent opinion. The term nonaudit or nonattest services is then used when no opinion is rendered.

As you read this chapter, think about the following: (1) What are the ethical obligations of CPAs under the AICPA Code? (2) What is the role of independence in an audit, and how can CPAs manage the threats that exist to audit independence? (3) What are the professional and ethical obligations of CPAs in performing nonattest services including tax services?

> By certifying the public reports that collectively depict a corporation's financial status, the independent auditor assumes a public responsibility transcending any employment responsibility with the client. The independent public accountant performing this special function owes ultimate allegiance to the corporation's creditors and stockholders, as well as to the investing public. This "public watchdog" function demands that the accountant maintain total independence from the client at all times and requires complete fidelity to the public trust.[4]
>
> *Chief Justice Warren Burger, writing the unanimous opinion of the Supreme Court in United States v. Arthur Young & Co.*

This important ruling of the U.S. Supreme Court reminds us that the independent audit provides the foundation for the existence of the accounting profession in the United States. Even though independent audits were common before the passage of the landmark legislation of the Securities Act of 1933 and the Securities Exchange Act of 1934, there is no doubt that CPAs derive their franchise as a profession from these two pieces of legislation, which require independent audits of publicly owned companies.

The Burger Court opinion emphasizes the trust that the public places in the independent auditor. The accounting profession is the only profession where one's public obligation supersedes that to a client. The medical profession recognizes the primacy of the physician's responsibility to a patient. The legal profession emphasizes the lawyer's responsibility to the client. The Public Interest Principle in the Code of Professional Conduct of the American Institute of CPAs (AICPA Code) states, "In discharging their professional responsibilities, members (of the AICPA) may encounter conflicting pressures from each of these groups [clients, employers . . . ]. In resolving those conflicts, members should act with integrity, guided by the precept that when members fulfill their responsibility to the public, clients' and employers' interests are best served."[5]

# The Public Interest in Accounting: An International Perspective

We introduced the concept of "the public interest" in accounting in Chapter 1, pointing out that it primarily refers to the interests of investors and creditors. The interests of the client, an employer, and one's self-interest should not be placed ahead of the public interest.

Enron, WorldCom, Royal Dutch Shell, Parmalat, Satyam, and Cadbury Nigeria all were involved in major financial statement frauds during the dark days of the first decade of the 2000s. It was a disease that infected virtually every continent in the world and brought into question whether the public trust in accountants to produce accurate and reliable financial reports had been compromised. From special-purpose entities to improper capitalization of costs to disclosing unproven reserves to recording fictitious bank accounts to recording fictitious invoices for stock-buybacks, the dizzying array of transactions that created the frauds knew no bounds. A lack of internal controls, ineffective internal audits, and inattentive boards of directors all share blame for these frauds. In each case, a culture was established that made it easier for top management to perpetrate the fraud, and the accountants who were on the front lines of the fraud failed to act in the public interest and report and/or stop it.

Following the disclosure of numerous accounting scandals, the accounting profession and professional bodies turned their attention to examining how to rebuild the public trust and confidence in financial reporting. Stuebs and Wilkinson point out that restoring the accounting profession's public interest focus is a crucial first step in recapturing the public trust and securing the profession's future.[6] Copeland believes to regain the trust and respect that the profession enjoyed prior to the scandals of the early 2000s, the profession must rebuild its reputation on its historical foundation of ethics and integrity.[7]

The International Federation of Accountants (IFAC), a global organization that represents the accountancy profession, issued a research report, *Rebuilding Public Confidence in Financial Reporting: An International Perspective,* examining ways of restoring the credibility of financial reporting and corporate disclosure from an international perspective. The report reflects the views of accounting professionals from six countries: Australia, Canada, France, Japan, the United Kingdom, and the United States. It identifies several key weaknesses in corporate governance from a number of corporate failures worldwide. The findings of the study include a recommendation for more effective corporate ethics codes, as well as the provision of training and support for individuals within organizations to better prepare them to deal with ethical dilemmas.[8]

IFAC addresses the public interest dimension in its Policy Position Paper #4, entitled *A Public Interest Framework for the Accountancy Profession.* The framework is designed to enable IFAC and other professional bodies to better evaluate whether the public interest is being served through actions of the profession and its institutions. IFAC considers the "public interest" to represent the common benefits derived by stakeholders of the accounting profession through sound financial reporting. It links these benefits to responsibilities of professional accountants, including the application of high standards of ethical behavior and professional judgment.[9]

The International Ethics Standards Board for Accountants (IESBA) is an independent standard-setting body that serves the public interest by setting high-quality ethical standards for professional accountants and by facilitating the convergence of international and national ethical standards, including auditor independence requirements, through its *Handbook of the Code of Ethics for Professional Accountants* (IFAC Code) (IESBA 2012). The IESBA, along with the International Accounting Education Standards Board (IAESB), establish guidelines for 167 members and associates in 127 countries worldwide, representing approximately 2.5 million accountants in public practice, industry and commerce, the public sector, and education. No other accountancy body in the world, and few other professional organizations, have the broad-based international support that characterizes

IFAC. The IAESB and IESBA standards are authoritative pronouncements that have the same force as standards promulgated by other boards operating under the auspices of IFAC, such as the International Auditing and Assurance Standards Board (IAASB).

The ethical decision-making process explained in Chapter 2 includes consideration of the IFAC Code in step #8 of the comprehensive model and in step 1 of the condensed model. We also address international education standards using IES 4 in step #3, along with virtue considerations. Moreover, the decision-making process incorporates elements of the IFAC framework and includes ethical reasoning and the application of core values, ethics, and attitudes that are, for the most part, similar to those in the United States. As a member body of IFAC, the AICPA agrees to have ethics standards that are at least as stringent as the IESBA standards. Since 2001, the AICPA Professional Ethics Executive Committee has undertaken certain convergence projects to align the AICPA Code with the IFAC Code. Efforts are ongoing and currently include the initiation of a task force to evaluate the IFAC provisions for members in business and industry and another to review the application of independence rules to affiliates of an attest client.[10]

The fundamental principles of professional ethics for professional accountants identified by the IESBA include integrity, objectivity, professional competence and due care, confidentiality, and professional behavior, including compliance with laws and regulations. These principles are similar to those in the AICPA Code, state board of accountancy rules in the United States, and the codes of conduct in the United Kingdom and Australia, as well as most of the developed world.[11]

Support exists among professional bodies for education in professional values, ethics, and attitudes. A survey of IFAC member bodies reported in the IAESB's information paper notes that member bodies agree that ethics education is necessary to do all of the following:[12]

- Develop a sense of ethical responsibility in accountants.
- Improve the moral standards and attitudes of accountants.
- Develop the problem-solving skills that have ethical implications.
- Develop a sense of professional responsibility or obligation.

The report considers the term *ethics* as an overarching term for values, ethics, and attitudes. Professional values, ethics, and attitudes include the ethical principles of conduct that are found in professional codes of ethics. Collectively, the values, ethics, and attitudes include technical competence; core values of integrity, objectivity, independence, and confidentiality; professionalism of respect, reliability, responsibility, timelines, due care, and courteousness; commitment to continuous improvement and lifelong learning; and social responsibility.

Our discussion of ethics, core values, behaviors, and attitudes recognizes the importance of establishing consistent professional ethics standards in countries throughout the world. We have a global economic system that relies on accurate financial reporting and efficient audits to assure the public of the reliability of financial statements. We build on this discussion in Chapter 8 and include the role of ethics in establishing International Financial Reporting Standards (IFRS). Finally, note that state boards of accountancy (i.e., California and Texas) have recognized the need to incorporate behaviors and attitudes with ethics and ethical reasoning in developing ethics courses that prepare accounting students to take the CPA Exam.

## Investigations of the Profession: Where Were the Auditors?

The auditing profession in the United States has come under periodic scrutiny from Congress during the past 40 years. The questions that are consistently asked are: Where were the auditors? Why didn't auditing firms detect and report the many frauds that occurred during this time period? Was it a matter of bending to the wishes of the client that hires (and can fire) the firm, and pays its fee? Were these failures due to inadequate and sometimes sloppy audits by firms that may have been trying to cut corners because they lowballed their audit fees to lure clients, with the hope of gaining lucrative tax advice and consulting fees down the road? In the case of Andersen's treatment of Enron, it seems all of the factors were present, as well as the cozy relationship that the auditor had with Enron that influenced the firm's ability to be independent in making decisions regarding the audits.

The rules of conduct in the AICPA Code are best understood in light of the investigations of the accounting profession that followed high-profile frauds during the past 40 years. Congressional concern was that auditors were not living up to their ethical and professional responsibilities (as stated in the Burger Court opinion). The major themes of these investigations were (1) whether nonauditing services impair auditor independence, (2) the need for management to report on internal controls, (3) the importance of developing techniques to prevent and detect fraud, and (4) the need to strengthen the role of the audit committee and communications between the auditor and audit committee.

## Metcalf Committee and Cohen Commission: 1977–1978

As CPA firms have become global entities, the profession's concern about ethics and regulation has grown. In 1977, a major study examined the relationship between auditors and clients and the provision of nonauditing services for those clients. The Metcalf (Moss) Report was the first real investigation of the accounting profession since the 1930s. An investigation was conducted between 1975 and 1977 by Senator Lee Metcalf (D-MT) and, on the House side, Representative John Moss (D-CA).[13] The Metcalf Report issued four recommendations, two of which are described here. The report did not lead to any new legislation at the time, although in the aftermath of the frauds at Enron and WorldCom, changes were made to enhance audits and financial reporting.

The first recommendation of the Metcalf Committee was to establish a self-regulatory organization of firms that audit publicly owned companies. It led to the AICPA's formation of a two-tier voluntary peer review program in 1977: one for firms with public-company clients and one for smaller firms with only private companies. In 2004, the Public Company Accounting Oversight Board (PCAOB) assumed the AICPA's responsibilities relating to firms that audit public clients ending the period of self-regulation by the profession, at least for public companies.* PCAOB instituted a mandatory quality inspection program for CPA firms that audit public companies. The AICPA continued its two-tier program to assist firms in meeting state licensing and AICPA membership requirements. We discuss the PCAOB audit inspection program in Chapter 5.[14]

The second recommendation of the Metcalf Committee was to limit types of management services to those relating directly to accounting. The accounting profession was upset at the implication that the provision of management consulting services somehow tainted the audit. It was left to the Cohen Commission to conduct an in-depth study of the issue. In the meantime, the SEC followed up the concern with a requirement that public companies

---

*In *Free Enterprise Fund v. Public Company Accounting Oversight Board*, No. 08-861, 2010 WL 2555191 (June 28, 2010), the United States Supreme Court held that the provisions of Sarbanes-Oxley (SOX) that restrict the removal of the members of the five member Public Company Accounting Oversight Board (PCAOB) violate the Constitution's separation of legislative and executive powers. The Court held, however, that the unconstitutional removal provision was severable from the remainder of SOX. Pursuant to SOX, the Board has extensive authority to promulgate auditing standards and conduct investigative and disciplinary proceedings. Violations of Board rules are treated as violations of the Securities Exchange Act of 1934. Although subject to SEC oversight, members of the Board can only be removed by formal SEC Order "for good cause shown" based on certain specified misconduct, which is subject to judicial review.

disclose in their annual reports the aggregate fees that they paid to their accountants for nonauditing services.

The profession's own Cohen Commission Report on auditors' responsibilities examined a variety of issues that are still debated today, including the auditor's responsibility for detecting fraud and the expectation gap that exists between the profession's goals for the audit and what the public expects an audit to accomplish.[15] Beyond that, the commission recommended that management report on its internal controls to the users of the financial statements and that the auditor should evaluate management's report. This recommendation was ultimately enacted into legislation as part of the Sarbanes-Oxley (SOX) Act of 2002.

The events that eventually led to change were two rounds of major scandals—one in the 1980s that included the failures of savings and loan institutions, and the second in the late 1990s and early 2000s, led by Enron and WorldCom. After Enron and WorldCom, the profession agreed to go along with change in the form of the provisions passed by SOX and the creation of PCAOB.

The Cohen Commission headed by Manny Cohen, a former SEC commissioner, was important for two reasons. First, its final report included an instance that demonstrates the potential conflict when providing nonauditing services for an audit client. It was discovered that the audit of Westec Corporation had been compromised because of a consulting project. Second, it decried the lowballing of audit fees that raised the possibility of a decline in audit quality.[16] The latter concern, along with opinion shopping, have contributed over the years to a shift in the environment of professionalism that has existed in the accounting profession to one emphasizing the commercialization of accounting services.

The practice of lowballing consists of deliberately underbidding for an audit engagement to obtain the audit client and with the hope of securing more lucrative management advisory or other consulting services from that client in the future. To a large extent, the practice became less prevalent after the passage of SOX, which restricts providing certain nonauditing services for audit clients. Opinion shopping occurs when a client seeks out the views of various accountants until finding one that will go along with the client's desired—if not necessarily most ethical—accounting treatment. This practice can lead to pressure being applied on the auditor to remain silent or risk losing the account, an intimidation threat to independence.

## House Subcommittee on Oversight and Investigations: 1986

Representative Ron Wyden (D-OR) had introduced a bill in May 1986 to hold the accounting profession responsible for the detection of fraud in light of the failure at ESM Government Securities and bank failures in the early 1980s at Continental Illinois National Bank and Trust and Penn Square Bank.[17] Even though Continental Illinois had received a $4.5 billion federal bailout, the company ultimately was liquidated by the Federal Deposit Insurance Corporation (FDIC) just four months after receiving an unqualified opinion on its audit by Peat Marwick (now KPMG). This was the first time we heard the refrain in Congress, "Where were the auditors?"

Wyden eventually changed his proposed legislation because of criticisms by the AICPA and SEC, the latter under then-chair John Shad, who believed the system was "working well" to protect the public from major financial fraud. The new legislation called once again for internal control reports and emphasized the need for auditors to detect material illegalities or irregularities.

Representative John Dingell (D-MI) was chair of both the House Committee on Energy and Commerce and its Subcommittee on Oversight and Investigations. In January and February 1988, the subcommittee held two hearings concerning the failure of ZZZZ Best Company, a corporation that had "created" 80 percent or more of its total revenue in the form of fictitious revenue from the restoration of carpets, drapes, and other items in office buildings after fires and floods. Chair Dingell characterized the fraud as follows:[18]

> The fact that auditors and attorneys repeatedly visited make-believe job sites and came away satisfied does not speak well for the present regulatory system. The fact that the auditing firm discovering the fraud resigned the engagement without telling enforcement authorities is even more disturbing. . . . Cases such as ZZZZ Best demonstrate vividly that we cannot afford to tolerate a system that fails to meet the public's legitimate expectations in this regard.

### Savings and Loan Industry Failures: Late 1980s–Early 1990s

By the late 1980s, the savings and loan (S&L) industry failures became the focus of the congressional hearings as a $300 million failure at Beverly Hills Savings & Loan and a $250 million failure at Sunrise Savings, a Florida S&L, engulfed Deloitte & Touche. Arthur Young, the firm that was to merge with Ernst & Whinney to form Ernst & Young, had run into deep trouble in its S&L audits. In particular, it certified the financial statements of the Western Savings Association in 1984 and 1985, which were overstated by $400 million. If Arthur Young had not merged with Ernst & Whinney, the firm may have been forced out of business. Eventually the firm paid the federal government $400 million to settle claims that the company's auditors failed to warn of disastrous financial problems that caused some of the nation's biggest thrift failures.

Perhaps the most publicized failure is that of Lincoln Savings & Loan. Thousands of California retirees lost their life savings after buying uninsured subordinated debentures issued by Lincoln's parent company, American Continental, and sold through Lincoln branches. Arthur Young, the auditors of American Continental, issued unqualified opinions on the entity's financial statements for fiscal years 1986 and 1987. The audit opinions were part of the annual reports of American Continental that were furnished to prospective buyers of the worthless debentures.

The cost to the public to clean up 1,043 failed thrift institutions with total assets of over $500 billion during the 1986–1995 period was reported to be $152.9 billion, including $123.8 billion of U.S. taxpayer losses. The balance was absorbed by the thrift industry itself. It was the greatest collapse of U.S. financial institutions since the Great Depression.[19] Little did we know that 20 years later, banks and financial institutions would be embroiled in a scandal that involved risky investments, including derivatives and worthless mortgage-backed securities, and some institutions would need federal bailout funds to stay in business, while others were taken over by the government or other institutions.

The accounting issues in failed S&Ls centered on three issues: (1) the failure to provide adequate allowances for loan losses, (2) the failure to disclose dubious deals between the S&Ls and some of their major customers, and (3) the existence of inadequate internal controls to prevent these occurrences. The profession was already considering ways to address the large number of business failures in the 1980s when the S&L debacle occurred. The profession's response to deal with this new pressure was to form the Treadway Commission, and its work was given a new sense of urgency.

## Treadway Commission Report: 1985; COSO: 1992; and Enterprise Risk Management: 2004

The National Commission on Fraudulent Financial Reporting, referred to as the Treadway Committee after its chair James C. Treadway, was formed in 1985 to study and report on the factors that can lead to fraudulent financial reporting. The Committee of Sponsoring Organizations of the Treadway Commission (COSO) is a joint initiative of five private sector organizations, established in the United States, that provides leadership on organizational governance, business ethics, internal control, enterprise risk management, fraud, and financial reporting. COSO has established a common internal control model against which companies and organizations may assess their control systems.

COSO has emphasized the need to change the corporate culture and establish the systems necessary to prevent fraudulent financial reporting. It starts with the "tone at the top"; that is, top management should set an ethical tone that filters throughout the organization and influences everything and everyone.

While Metcalf and Moss, Dingell, and Wyden focused mainly on the role of the external auditor (including independence), COSO extended the review to include the role and responsibilities of internal accountants and auditors and the board of directors in preventing and detecting fraud. An important part of the COSO framework is to stress the importance of a strong control environment so that the internal auditors can have direct and unrestricted access to the audit committee of the board of directors (refer back to Exhibit 3.10 in Chapter 3).[20] If top management, such as the chief executive officer (CEO) and chief financial officer (CFO), attempts to manipulate earnings or use company assets for inappropriate reasons, then the internal auditors supported by strong internal controls should detect and report the wrongdoing to the audit committee. The audit committee's responsibility is to do whatever is necessary to reverse top management's action.

In an interview with *The CPA Journal* on April 20, 2005, former COSO chairman Larry Rittenberg identified the contributions of the Treadway Report and follow-up work in creating a sounder ethical culture in organizations. According to Rittenberg, "One of its most consequential recommendations was for the development of a conceptual framework for implementing and evaluating internal controls. Prior to the 1992 issuance of COSO's *Internal Control–Integrated Framework,* internal control guidance consisted primarily of ad hoc checklists. The COSO framework developed all aspects of the organization: financial reporting, operational activities, and compliance issues. As a result, it has been widely accepted over time. In terms of overall impact on businesses, the 1992 internal control project is COSO's most significant contribution to date."[21]

In the years following the COSO report, the audit profession experienced a heightened concern and focus on risk management, and it became increasingly clear that a need existed for a robust framework to identify, assess, and manage risk effectively. In 2001, COSO initiated a project to develop a framework that would be readily usable by managements to evaluate and improve their organizations' enterprise risk management. PricewaterhouseCoopers was the firm engaged for this task.

The period of the framework's development was marked by a series of high-profile business scandals and failures, including Enron and WorldCom, where investors, company personnel, and other stakeholders suffered major losses. This led to calls for enhanced corporate governance and risk management, with new laws, regulations, and listing standards. The need for an enterprise risk management framework that provided key principles and concepts, a common language, and clear direction and guidance, became even more compelling. The result was the issuance of a study titled *Enterprise Risk Management–Integrated Framework.* COSO believes that the recommendations of the study fill this need and expects that it will become widely accepted by companies and other organizations over time and gain the support of all stakeholders and interested parties.[22]

Rittenberg explained the role of "enterprise risk management (ERM)" as broader than internal controls. He stated that controls exist only to mitigate risks that are part of organizational behavior. So every internal control framework has to start with a systematic approach to identifying risk. Management and boards have to determine their risk "appetites" and their risk tolerances and discuss these at the highest levels of an organization.

In the ERM framework, controls are designed to manage the risks within the organization's tolerances. There are a variety of ways to manage risk: one way is to control the risk, perhaps through diversification; another way is to insure against the risk. The ERM framework is an enhanced, proactive approach to managing organizational risk. More will be said about internal controls and risk management in Chapter 5, when we discuss audit standards and fraud detection and prevention.

### A Final Word About the Internal Control Environment: Armadillo Foods, Inc.

Let's assume that you are a CPA and the controller of Armadillo Foods, Inc., a large southwestern processor of armadillo-based food products. One day, the CFO comes to you and says the earnings results for the quarter ending June 30, 2013, are 20 percent below the financial analysts' estimates. Because Armadillo is a public company, you know that the stock price is likely to decline—perhaps significantly—after public disclosure of the earnings reduction for the second straight quarter in 2013. You also know that bonuses to top management depend on increasing reported earnings. The CFO tells you that the CEO insists the company must "make the numbers" this quarter, and you need to find a way to make that happen. What would you do? Why?

This is a hypothetical situation but one that occurred all too often during the accounting scandals of the 1990s and 2000s. The pressure applied by the CFO and CEO on the controller tests that person's commitment to act with objectivity and integrity. The controller is probably quite aware of her ethical obligations to act in accordance with the public interest. She also knows that integrity requires that she not subordinate her judgment and give in to the pressure to go along with materially misstated financial statements. Recall that AICPA Code Interpretation 102-4, which was discussed in Chapter 1, outlines the steps to be taken by internal accountants to avoid subordinating judgment. The controller has an ethical dilemma that challenges her ability and willingness to take ethical action. Interpretation 102-4 requires that she bring her concerns to higher-ups in the organization, including the audit committee, and prepare an informative memorandum that summarizes the various positions, including those of top management. The memo should help provide a defense of due care and the compliance with ethical standards in case it becomes a regulatory or legal matter.

If all parties refuse to support the controller, then the question is whether to inform the external auditors who, after all, rely on the objectivity and integrity of the controller in performing external auditing services. The relationship of trust that exists between the controller and the external auditors may be compromised if the controller is silent. Beyond informing the external auditors, the controller has no responsibility to bring accounting matters of concern to outsiders—not only that, to do so violates confidentiality under the AICPA Code. However, under the Dodd-Frank Financial Reform Act that was discussed in Chapter 3, individuals with internal compliance or audit responsibilities at an entity, including CPAs, are expected to disclose improper accounting practices to the SEC to prevent "substantial injury" to the financial interest of an entity or its investors.

# The Role of the Accounting Profession in the Financial Crisis of 2007–2008

The financial crisis that started in 2007 and accelerated in 2008, ushered in a period of reflection about how the United States could have been pushed into a recession brought on by excessive risk taking and a mortgage meltdown. Some have blamed moral hazard as a major contributing factor. *Moral hazard* occurs where one party is responsible for the interests of another, but has an incentive to put her own interests first. Research by Atif Mian and Amir Sufi of the University of Chicago's business school provides hard evidence that securitization of mortgages fostered moral hazard among mortgage originators, which led them to issue loans to uncreditworthy borrowers. They were motivated to do so by moral hazard effects, in that the securitized assets were sold off to unsuspecting investors and so the risk of default transferred to these parties, not the originating banks.[23]

For two and a half years, the U.S. Senate focused on the role of financial institutions in the financial crisis of 2007–2008 that started with the failure of Lehman Brothers. A bankruptcy examiners report[24] issued on April 12, 2011, shed light on the role of auditing firms in the financial meltdown. The report was written by Jenner & Block chairman Anton Valukas. The details of Lehman's financial activities that vaulted the company into bankruptcy are too complicated to discuss in detail, but we provide a summary in Exhibit 4.1.

**EXHIBIT 4.1**

**Lehman's Financial Transactions and Accounting Disclosures**

Despite the profession's efforts to control for risk and improve corporate culture, the United States experienced its worst recession that began in 2007 in part due to risky financial activities and improper accounting practices. It started when the investment banking firm of Lehman Brothers failed because it was unable to retain the confidence of its lenders and counterparts and because it did not have sufficient liquidity to meet its current obligations. Lehman engaged in a series of business decisions and transactions using a device known as "Repo 105" that had left it with heavy concentrations of illiquid assets with deteriorating values such as residential and commercial real estate.

Confidence eroded when Lehman reportedly had two consecutive quarters of huge reported losses, $2.8 billion in the second quarter of 2008 and $3.9 billion in the third quarter of that year.

The business decisions that had brought Lehman to its crisis of confidence may have been in error but were deemed by the bankruptcy examiner to be largely within the business judgment rule. But the decision not to disclose the effects of those judgments created a valid claim against the senior officers who oversaw and certified misleading financial statements. Legal claims of failing to meet professional responsibilities were charged against Lehman's CEO, Richard Fuld, and its CFOs, Christopher O'Meara, Erin M. Callan, and Ian Lowitt. A valid claim also existed against its external auditor, Ernst & Young, for its failure to question and challenge improper or inadequate disclosures in those financial statements, among other things.

Lehman had used an accounting device (known within Lehman as "Repo 105") to manage its balance sheet by temporarily removing approximately $50 billion of assets from the balance sheet at the end of the first and second quarters of 2008.

In an ordinary "repo," Lehman raised cash by selling assets with a simultaneous obligation to repurchase them the next day or several days later; such transactions were accounted for as financings, and the assets remained on Lehman's balance sheet. In a Repo 105 transaction, Lehman did exactly the same thing, but because the assets were 105 percent or more of the cash received, accounting rules permitted the transactions to be treated as sales rather than financings, so that the assets could be removed from the balance sheet. With Repo 105 transactions, Lehman's reported net leverage was 12.1 at the end of the second quarter of 2008, but if Lehman had used ordinary repos, net leverage would have been reported at 13.9.

Lehman did not disclose its use—or the significant magnitude of its use—of Repo 105 to the federal government, to the rating agencies, to its investors, or to its own board of directors. Ernst & Young was aware of its use but did not question it or the nondisclosure of the Repo 105 accounting transactions. It took Lehman until September 2008, several months into the financial meltdown, to publicly disclose the liquidity issues. On September 10, 2008, the company announced that it was projecting a $3.9 billion loss for the third quarter of 2008. By the close of trading on September 12, its stock price had declined to $3.65 a share, a 94 percent drop from the $62.19 price on January 2, 2008.

Over the weekend of September 12–14, 2008, a series of meetings were held by U.S. Treasury Secretary Henry Paulson, president of the Federal Reserve Bank of New York Timothy Geithner, SEC chairman Christopher Cox, and the chief executives of leading financial institutions. The government made a decision that many believe ushered in the financial crisis. It refused to fund a solution to the Lehman problem, stating that it did not have the legal authority to make a direct capital investment in Lehman, and Lehman's assets were insufficient to support a loan large enough to avoid its collapse.

As an alternative to government intervention, Lehman approached Barclays, a British bank, and it appeared a deal had been reached on September 14 that would save Lehman from collapse, but later that day, the deal fell apart when it was learned that the Financial Services Authority, the United Kingdom's bank regulator, refused to waive U.K.-shareholder-approval requirements. Clearly, that would take too long. Meanwhile, Lehman could no longer fund its operations. The bank collapsed on September 15, when it filed for bankruptcy protection. The filing remains the largest bankruptcy filing in U.S. history, with Lehman holding over $600 billion in assets.

At the Senate Banking Committee hearings on the Lehman failure and subsequent financial crisis, Jenner & Block chairman Anton Valukas spoke about the general principle that auditors play a critical role in the proper functioning of public companies and financial markets. He said:

> Boards of directors and audit committees are entitled to rely on external auditors to serve as watchdogs—to be important gatekeepers who provide an independent check on management. And the investing public is entitled to believe that a "clean" report from an independent auditor stands for something. The public has every right to conclude that auditors who hold themselves out as independent will stand up to management and not succumb to pressure to avoid rocking the boat. I found that [valid] claims exist against Lehman's external auditor in connection with Lehman's issuance of materially misleading financial reports.[25]

Also at the hearing before the Senate Banking Committee, SEC chief accountant James Kroeker was called on to answer questions that the SEC had information about problems at Lehman (specifically, concerns about liquidity pools) and failed to take adequate action.

The Valukas report suggested that the now-defunct Trading and Markets unit at the SEC knew about problems and did not inform officials at other divisions of the commission. Kroeker said that the SEC took the report seriously and responded: "It is a very serious observation, but it has been addressed."[26] It was not explained exactly how the problem was addressed, beyond the fact that the SEC went through a reorganization of divisions in late 2008.

In addition to Valukas and Kroeker, the chairman of PCAOB, James Doty, was called on to testify. Doty admitted that auditors should have been more vigilant—not just at Lehman, but across the board. "There were a number of areas where auditors should have delved more deeply," Doty said. He pointed to serious ongoing problems with valuations and end-of-period transactions.[27]

The findings of the committee will likely have a serious impact on the oversight of the auditing industry as a whole. The SEC requires mandatory rotation of key auditing personnel within a firm every five years in keeping with that requirement in SOX. Now, the government is examining various aspects of the way auditing firms are regulated and their level of accountability to companies and investors who rely on their assessments. One controversial proposal is to institute a mandatory auditor rotation policy whereby every few years (i.e., 5 or 10 years), there would be a required change in the auditing firm.

On October 19, 2012, the PCAOB held a public meeting in Houston to hear feedback on its proposals for mandatory auditing firm rotation and auditor independence. The PCAOB heard from a variety of speakers, including a representative from the European Commission, who described the proposal for mandatory firm rotation in the European Union (EU). Nathalie Berger, head of the European Commission's audit and credit-rating agencies unit, told the PCAOB that it is seeing support in the European Parliament for mandatory firm rotation. "There are obvious reasons and good grounds on which the introduction of mandatory auditing firm rotation can be based," she said. "It would strengthen the independence of auditors by mitigating the familiarity threat."[28]

The other side of the issue was presented by W. David Rook, partner-in-charge of firm assurance and advisory services at Weaver & Tidwell in Houston. Weaver & Tidwell does root cause analysis after a CPA firm receives an negative inspection report from the PCAOB to see what went wrong. While Rook agreed that independence, objectivity, and professional skepticism are critical to the viability of auditing, he said that the firm opposed mandatory rotation.

"While we support the board's ongoing efforts to improve independence, objectivity, and audit quality, we do not believe that mandatory auditing firm rotation is a concept that will work and, if enacted, could raise significant risks and result in unintended consequences," he said. "We have always believed that the danger of a failed audit is greater when the auditor does not fully understand the client's business than from the auditor being too familiar with the client's business."[29]

On April 25, 2013, the Legal Affairs Committee of the European Parliament, the legislative arm of the EU, voted to require public companies to change audit firms after up to 14 years. The proposed law was scheduled to be voted on in later 2013. On July 8, 2013, the U.S. House of Representatives approved a bill that prohibits the Public Company Accounting Oversight Board from forcing public companies to automatically change or rotate their independent auditing firm.[30]

Reflecting on the years of investigations after business and audit failures and important changes in the landscape of audit regulation, we believe that there will continue to be instances of audit independence violations because of the growing personal and business relationships between auditing firms, the client, and client management. A culture of ethics and professionalism that existed for so many years has been replaced by an emphasis on marketing of professional services. Growth and revenue enhancement now rules the day rather than providing services in the public interest.

# AICPA Code of Professional Conduct and State Board Requirements

The AICPA Code is generally recognized as a model for the accounting profession. Each of the 50 states as well as Washington, DC, and U.S. territories—Puerto Rico, the Virgin Islands, Guam, and the Commonwealth of the Northern Mariana Islands—have independent professional societies for CPAs. The state CPA societies also have codes of conduct for their membership that often mirror the AICPA Code. Even though only members of these voluntary organizations are bound by the codes, the provisions are generally similar to those of state boards of accountancy, so we use the AICPA Code as the model of ethical standards to be followed by CPAs.

We urge students to become familiar with their state board regulations and rules of conduct because differences may exist with the AICPA Code; licensed CPAs in a given state are expected to follow that state's requirements in such cases. From time to time in this text, we refer to the rules of conduct in California and Texas. The reason is that, as discussed in Chapter 1, these two states require ethics education as part of the university coursework of accounting students. Moreover, well over 100,000 CPAs are licensed in these two states alone.

A good example of a difference between AICPA and state board rules is the ethical obligation of a licensed CPA to return client books and records. The rules in most states include a requirement that a licensee cannot refuse to return client books and records solely because there are unpaid fees. While the AICPA permits withholding client books and records with respect to specific work product under these circumstances, most state boards consider it to be a violation of the rules of conduct. An example is Section 68 of the California regulations, which provides as follows:[31]

> A licensee, after demand by or on behalf of a client, for books, records or other data, whether in written or machine sensible form, that are the client's records shall not retain such records. *Unpaid fees do not constitute justification for retention of client records.* Although, in general, the accountant's working papers are the property of the licensee, if such working papers include records which would ordinarily constitute part of the client's

books and records and are not otherwise available to the client, then the information on those working papers must be treated the same as if it were part of the client's books and records.

A similar requirement exists in Texas under Rule Section 501.76[32]

A person [licensee] shall return original client records to a client or former client within a reasonable time (promptly, not to exceed 10 business days) after the client or former client has made a request for those records. Client records are those records provided to the person by the client or former client in order for the person to provide professional accounting services to the client or former client. Client records also include those documents obtained by the person on behalf of the client or former client in order for the person to provide professional accounting services to the client or former client. Client records include only the original client documents and do not include the electronic and hard copies that the firm produces. The person shall provide these records to the client or former client, regardless of the status of the client's or former client's account and cannot charge a fee to provide such records. Such records shall be returned to the client or former client in the same format, to the extent possible, that they were provided to the person by the client or former client. The person may make copies of such records and retain those copies.

One of the most frequently violated rules of conduct is records retention. The failure to return client books and records in all likelihood would lead to a disciplinary action against the licensee by the state board of accountancy. Always remember that your state board issues your license to practice public accounting in the state as a CPA, and the state board can impose disciplinary action for violating the rules. Disciplinary action might include requiring specific continuing professional education hours.** Disciplinary action also might include the suspension or revocation of the license to practice.

## National Association of State Boards of Accountancy

We briefly introduced the National Association of State Boards of Accountancy (NASBA) in Chapter 1. Founded in 1908, NASBA has served as an association dedicated to enhancing the effectiveness of the country's 55 state boards of accountancy for more than 100 years. NASBA and its Member Boards are responsible for the nearly 700,000 accounting professionals licensed in the 55 U.S. jurisdictions. NASBA creates a forum for accounting regulators and practitioners to address issues relevant to the accounting profession. One way it accomplishes its goal is through the Uniform Accountancy Act (UAA). Recall that in 2009, NASBA revised its Rule 5.2 on education and set an either/or approach that recommends either the integration of ethics course material throughout the undergraduate and/or graduate curriculum or a three-hour stand-alone course in ethics.

Students should be aware that their ability to move from state to state and practice public accounting as a licensed CPA without meeting additional requirements may be constrained by whether state board rules in your state of licensure are equal to or require more than another state you might move into. Under Section 23 of the UAA, a CPA with a license in good standing from a jurisdiction with CPA licensing requirements essentially

---

**Most states require as a condition of license renewal 40 hours of continuing education each year; 80 hours every two years; or 120 hours every three years. The majority of states also require that licensed CPAs complete a course in ethics and professional responsibility as part of the continuing education requirement.

equivalent to those outlined in the UAA is deemed to be "substantially equivalent," or a licensee who individually meets the requirements of:

- Obtaining 150 semester credit-hours (225 quarter-hours) with a baccalaureate degree
- Minimum 1 year of CPA experience
- Passing the Uniform CPA Examination

Uniform adoption of the UAA's substantial equivalency provision creates a system similar to the nation's driver's license program by providing CPAs with mobility while retaining and strengthening state boards' ability to protect the public interest. The system enables consumers to receive timely services from the CPA best suited to the job, regardless of location, and without the hindrances of unnecessary filings, forms, and increased costs that do not protect the public interest.

As of May 2013, a total of 49 states and the District of Columbia have passed mobility laws and are now in the implementation and navigation phases. Only the Commonwealth of the Northern Mariana Islands, the Virgin Islands, Hawaii, Puerto Rico, and Guam have not passed mobility laws.

## Professional Services of CPAs

Rules of professional conduct, whether issued by the AICPA or a state board of accountancy, apply to CPAs in public accounting, private industry, government, and education. The rules apply to a variety of professional services, including accounting, auditing and other assurance services, taxation, financial advisory services, and consulting services.

The *practice of public accounting*[33] is defined under the AICPA Code as the performance for a client, by a member or member's firm, while holding out as CPA(s) of the professional services of accounting, tax, personal financial planning, litigation support services, and those professional services for which standards are established by bodies designated by the AICPA ruling Council. Such standards include:

- Financial Accounting Standards, established by the Financial Accounting Standards Board (FASB)
- Statements on Auditing Standards, established by the AICPA for non-public companies
- Auditing standards of the PCAOB for public company audits
- Statements on Standards for Accounting and Review Services
- Statements on Standards for Consulting Services
- Statements of Governmental Accounting Standards
- International Financial Reporting Standards (IFRS) and International Accounting Standards set by the International Accounting Standards Board (IASB)
- Statements on Standards for Attestation Engagements
- Statements on Standards for Valuation Services

The cornerstone ethical obligation of a CPA to society is to render an opinion on the financial statements of an entity. An opinion is rendered after auditing or examining the financial statements of that entity. All publicly owned companies that sell stock on an established exchange such as the New York Stock Exchange (NYSE) and National Association of Securities Dealers (NASDAQ) are required by the SEC to have their financial statements audited annually and their interim financial information reviewed. A review provides only limited assurance that there are no material modifications that should be made to the financial statements in order for them to be in conformity with generally accepted accounting principles (GAAP), whereas an audit provides "reasonable assurance" that the financial statements are free of material misstatements. We explore auditing standards in Chapter 5.

A CPA also might compile financial statements based on data provided by the client. Because a compilation entails putting together the statements from accounting data, both internal and external accountants can perform this service. Unlike the audit and review service, which cannot be performed by an external CPA unless that person is independent of the client, a compilation can be performed when independence is lacking, so long as there is disclosure of that fact to the client and any third-party users. The reason for not requiring independence with a compilation is that the CPA does not render an opinion along with the compiled statements.

SOX prohibits the performance of certain services for audit clients because it may create the appearance in the mind of a reasonable third party that independence is lacking. For example, bookkeeping services cannot be provided for audit clients. Auditors should not record transactions or prepare the financial statements for an entity under audit. To do so would create a conflict of interests that impairs independence because the auditor would be placed in the position of examining and reporting on his or her own work. The client's management should prepare the financial statements. Typically, this means the accounting department prepares the statements with oversight by the controller. In most publicly owned companies, the controller reports to the CFO. Recall that AICPA Interpretation 102-4 requires that when there is a difference of opinion between a controller and the CFO, specific steps should be taken to explore all avenues of change, including taking the matter to the audit committee of the board of directors.

The situation is a bit more complicated with respect to internal audit outsourcing services. SOX prohibits these services for audit clients because it might appear that the CPA is rendering an independent opinion on work performed internally for the client in the form of internal auditing services. We might conclude that it is reasonable to expect a CPA firm that performs internal auditing services for an audit client to point out deficiencies in some area of the internal audit as part of the external examination—but will the CPA do so? The fact is that it doesn't matter; the appearance that the CPA might not do it is enough to impair independence. A similar restriction exists for public companies reporting to the SEC. However, the AICPA is more lenient on these services and, instead of an outright ban, provides guidelines when such services can and cannot be provided. To perform internal audit assistance for a client and maintain independence, the CPA/CPA firm may not act—or appear to act—as a member of the client's management. For example, the CPA/firm may not do the following:[34]

- Make decisions on the client's behalf
- Report to the client's governing body

  To maintain independence, the client must do the following:

- Designate an individual or individuals who possess suitable skill, knowledge, and experience to oversee the internal audit function
- Determine the scope, risk, and frequency of internal audit activities
- Evaluate the findings and results of internal audit activities
- Evaluate the adequacy of the audit procedures performed and related findings

The PCAOB oversees the audits of public companies in order to protect the interests of investors and further the public interest in the preparation of informative, accurate, and independent audit reports. The PCAOB establishes audit standards, ethics rules, independence requirements, quality controls for registered firms, and attestation standards. Under Rule 2100, each public accounting firm that (1) prepares or issues any audit report with respect to any issuer, or (2) plays a substantial role in the preparation or furnishing of an audit report with respect to any issuer must be registered with the board.[35] We discuss PCAOB ethics standards later in this chapter and auditing standards in Chapter 5.

# AICPA and IFAC Principles of Professional Conduct

We discussed the Principles of the AICPA Code of Professional Conduct in Chapter 1. The principles include independence, integrity and objectivity, due care, and acting in the public interest. The ethical reasoning methods discussed in Chapters 1 and 2 help accounting professionals to reason through conflict situations, such as when the public interest conflicts with the interests of the client, and come to a decision consistent with the profession's ethical standards. Ethical reasoning and judgment are critical components of ethical decision making. These skills can be learned through the application of philosophical reasoning methods. CPAs should use these techniques when the accounting rules are unclear, where there is a difference of opinion with an employer or client on an accounting issue, and when there are conflicts between the interests of stakeholder groups. The Integrity Principle best illustrates the link between ethical reasoning and professional judgment.

According to the AICPA Code, "[Integrity] is measured in terms of what is right and just. In the absence of specific rules, standards, or guidance, or in the face of conflicting opinions, a [CPA] should test decisions and deeds by asking: "Am I doing what a person of integrity would do? Have I retained my integrity?" Integrity requires a [CPA] to observe both the form and the spirit of technical and ethical standards; circumvention of those standards constitutes subordination of judgment."[36]

The *Handbook of the Code of Ethics for Professional Accountants* (IFAC Code) issued by the IESBA in 2012 previously mentioned in this chapter provides what we believe to be a more foundational approach to defining the principles of professional behavior. These fundamental principles include Integrity, Objectivity, Professional Competence and Due Care, Confidentiality, and Professional Behavior. While the IFAC Code Principles may appear to be virtually the same as those in the AICPA Code, basic differences exist. Exhibit 4.2 summarizes the IFAC Principles.

**EXHIBIT 4.2**
**IFAC Code Foundational Principles**

---

### Fundamental Principles[37]

A professional accountant shall comply with the following fundamental principles:

a. Integrity—to be straightforward and honest in all professional and business relationships.

b. Objectivity—to not allow bias, conflict of interest, or undue influence of others to override professional or business judgments.

c. Professional Competence and Due Care—to maintain professional knowledge and skill at the level required to ensure that a client or employer receives competent professional services based on current developments in practice, legislation and techniques and act diligently and in accordance with applicable technical and professional standards.

d. Confidentiality—to respect the confidentiality of information acquired as a result of professional and business relationships and, therefore, not disclose any such information to third parties without proper and specific authority, unless there is a legal or professional right or duty to disclose, nor use the information for the personal advantage of the professional accountant or third parties.

e. Professional Behavior—to comply with relevant laws and regulations and avoid any action that discredits the profession.

One difference is the explicit recognition of a standard for professional behavior that includes compliance with relevant laws and regulations and avoiding actions that bring discredit on the profession. Perhaps the AICPA took it for granted that the Principles in the AICPA Code implicitly addresses following laws and regulations, and these issues are addressed elsewhere, such as in the definition of the practice of public accounting. Nevertheless, explicit recognition highlights the point that ethical behavior is a combination of following laws and exercising ethical and professional judgment as recognized in the IFAC Objectivity principle.

Another difference is the explicit recognition of a Confidentiality principle, rather than its treatment as a rule of conduct in the AICPA Code that tries to identify virtually all situations where disclosure of confidential client information may be an issue. The important point here is, unlike a rule of conduct that defines what can and cannot be done, a principles-based approach establishes the guidelines within which decisions are made about disclosure with the use of professional judgment to support that decision.

# Conceptual Framework for AICPA Independence Standards

The AICPA uses a risk-based approach to assess whether a CPA's relationship with a client would pose an unacceptable risk to the member's independence. In the following discussion, we refer to "CPA" to replace the AICPA's reference to "member."

Risk is unacceptable if the relationship would compromise (or would be perceived as compromising by an informed third party knowing all the relevant information) the CPA's professional judgment when rendering an attest service to the client (i.e., audit, review, or attestation engagement). Key to that evaluation is identifying and assessing the extent to which a threat to the CPA's independence exists, and if it does, whether it would be reasonable to expect that the threat would compromise the CPA's professional judgment and, if so, whether it can be effectively mitigated or eliminated. Under the risk-based approach, steps are taken to prevent circumstances that threaten independence from compromising the professional judgments required in the performance of an attest engagement.[38]

The risk-based approach involves the following steps:[39]

1. Identifying and evaluating threats to independence.
2. Determining whether safeguards already eliminate or sufficiently mitigate identified threats and whether threats that have not yet been mitigated can be eliminated or sufficiently mitigated by safeguards.
3. If no safeguards are available to eliminate an unacceptable threat or reduce it to an acceptable level, independence would be considered impaired.

## Threats to Independence

*Independence in fact* is defined as the state of mind that permits the performance of an attest service without being affected by influences that compromise professional judgment, thereby allowing an individual to act with integrity and professional skepticism. To *appear to be independent,* the CPA should avoid circumstances that might cause an informed third party to reasonably conclude that the integrity, objectivity, or professional skepticism of a firm or member of the audit (attest) engagement team has been compromised.

Threats to independence include a self-review threat, advocacy threat, adverse interest threat, familiarity threat, intimidation threat, financial self-interest threat, and management participation threat. A brief description of each threat is given below, and Exhibit 4.3 provides examples of each threat.

**EXHIBIT 4.3**
**Examples of Threats to Independence**

| Threat | Example |
|---|---|
| Self-Review Threat | Preparing source documents used to generate the client's financial statements. |
| Advocacy Threat | Promoting the client's securities as part of an initial public offering or representing a client in U.S. tax court. |
| Adverse Interest Threat | Commencing, or the expressed intention to commence, litigation by either the client or the CPA against the other. |
| Familiarity Threat | A CPA on the attest engagement team whose spouse is the client's CEO. |
| Undue Influence Threat | A threat to replace the CPA or CPA firm because of a disagreement with the client over the application of an accounting principle. |
| Financial Self-Interest Threat | Having a loan from the client, from an officer or director of the client, or from an individual who owns 10 percent or more of the client's outstanding equity securities. |
| Management Participation Threat | Establishing and maintaining internal controls for the client. |

### Self-Review Threat

A self-review threat occurs when a CPA reviews evidence during an attest engagement that is based on her own or her firm's nonattest work. An example would be preparing source documents used to generate the client's financial statements.

### Advocacy Threat

An advocacy threat occurs when a CPA promotes an attest client's interests or position in such a way that objectivity may be, or may be perceived to be, compromised.

### Adverse Interest Threat

An adverse interest threat occurs when a CPA takes actions that are in opposition to an attest client's interests or positions.

### Familiarity Threat

A familiarity threat occurs when a close relationship is formed between the CPA and an attest client or its employees, members of top management, or directors of the client entity, including individuals or entities that performed nonattest work for the client (i.e., tax or consulting services).

### Undue Influence Threat

An undue influence threat results from an attempt by the management of an attest client or other interested parties to coerce the CPA or exercise excessive influence over the CPA.

### Financial Self-Interest Threat

A financial self-interest threat occurs when there is a potential benefit to a CPA from a financial interest in, or from some other financial relationship with, an attest client.

### Management Participation Threat

A management participation threat occurs when a CPA takes on the role of client management or otherwise performs management functions on behalf of an attest client.

## Safeguards to Counteract Threats

*Safeguards* are controls that eliminate or reduce threats to independence. These range from partial to complete prohibitions of the threatening circumstance to procedures that counteract the potential influence of a threat. The nature and extent of the safeguards to be applied depend on many factors, including the size of the firm and whether the client is a public interest entity. To be effective, safeguards should eliminate the threat or reduce to an acceptable level the threat's potential to impair independence.[40]

There are three broad categories of safeguards. The relative importance of a safeguard depends on its appropriateness in light of the facts and circumstances.

1. *Safeguards created by the profession, legislation, or regulation.* For example, continuing education requirements on independence and ethics and external review of a firm's quality control system.
2. *Safeguards* implemented by the attest client, such as a tone at the top that emphasizes the attest client's commitment to fair financial reporting and a governance structure, such as an active audit committee, that is designed to ensure appropriate decision making, oversight, and communications regarding a firm's services.
3. *Safeguards* implemented by the firm, including policies and procedures to implement professional and regulatory requirements.

## Financial Relationships That Impair Independence

To avoid violating the independence standard, a CPA should not own a direct or material indirect financial interest in the client. This would create a financial self-interest threat. The ownership of even one share of stock precludes independence. The CPA also should not own a material indirect financial interest in a client, such as through ownership of a mutual fund that includes the client entity's stock. The problem with owning direct and material indirect financial interests is that these arrangements might create the impression in the mind of an outside observer that the CPA cannot make decisions without being influenced by the stock ownership, even if that is not the case for any specific CPA. The logical conclusion is that the auditor's opinion would be tainted by the existence of these relationships.

Another example of a financial self-interest threat is when a CPA becomes involved in a loan transaction to or from a client, including home mortgage loans from financial institution clients. This type of loan is prohibited under Interpretation 101-5. According to 101-5, independence is considered to be impaired if during the period of the professional engagement, a covered member, such as a CPA on the attest engagement team or an individual in a position to influence the attest engagement team, has any loan to or from a client, any officer or director of the client, or any individual owning 10 percent or more of the client's outstanding equity securities or other ownership interests.

Examples of permitted loans include automobile loans and leases collateralized by the automobile, loans fully collateralized by cash deposits at the same financial institution (e.g., "passbook loans"), and aggregate credit card balances from credit cards and overdraft reserve accounts that are reduced to $10,000 or less on a current basis, taking into consideration the payment due and any available grace period.[41]

Perhaps no other situation illustrates the danger of a CPA accepting loans from a client more than that of Jose Gomez, the lead partner of Alexander Grant (now Grant Thornton) during its audit of ESM Government Securities from 1977 to 1984. Over the eight-year period, ESM committed fraud and, in the process, used its leverage against Gomez from $200,000 in loans to him so he would keep silent about the fact that ESM's financial statements did not present fairly financial position and the results of operations. Top management of ESM also threatened to pull the audit from Gomez's firm if he spoke out about the fraud. Gomez compromised his integrity, and the event ruined his reputation. Ultimately, Gomez was sentenced to a 12-year prison term and served 4½ years, and the firm paid approximately $175 million in civil payments.[42]

AICPA Interpretation 101-1 extends the Independence rule to certain family members of the CPA. The detailed provisions of this Interpretation are beyond the scope of this book, but we do want to emphasize two points to provide examples of familiarity threats to independence. First, when a CPA is part of the attest engagement team, which includes employees and contractors directly involved in an audit and those who perform concurring and second partner reviews, the rules extend to that CPA's immediate family members and close relatives. The former include the CPA's spouse, spousal equivalent, and dependents (whether or not they are related). These family members come under the Independence rules. The rules also extend to the CPA's close relatives, including parents, siblings, or nondependent children if they hold a key position with the client (that is, one that involves direct participation in the preparation of the financial statements or a position that gives the CPA the ability to exercise influence over the contents of the financial statements). Close relatives are subject to the Independence rule if they own a financial interest in the client that is material to that person's net worth and of which the CPA has knowledge, or if they own a financial interest in the client that enables the close relative to exercise significant influence over the client. The potential danger in these family relationships is that the family member's financial or employment relationship with the client might influence the perception that the CPA can be independent in fact or appearance. One problem with the rule is that the CPA might feign ignorance of the ownership interest even though he is aware of it—an unethical act.

There are other relationships that will bring a CPA under the Independence rules, including when a partner or manager provides 10 hours or more of nonattest services to the attest client. The problem is it may appear to an outside observer that the partner or manager may be able to influence the attest work because of the significant number of hours devoted to the nonattest services.

Let's stop at this point and consider that the Independence rule is a challenging standard for the CPA and family members to meet, and it might present some interesting dilemmas. For example, imagine if a CPA knows that his or her father owns a financial interest in a client entity but does not know if that interest is material to the father's net worth. Should the CPA contact the father to find out? Or, might the CPA reason that it is better not to know because the Independence rule applies only if the CPA has knowledge of the extent of the father's financial interest in the client? From an ethical perspective, the CPA should make a good-faith effort to determine the extent of the father's financial interest in the client entity.

## Providing Nonattest Services to an Attest Client

As previously mentioned in our review of congressional investigations, the issue of when should a CPA be permitted to provide nonattest services to an attest client has been examined for many years. The concern is that by providing certain nonattest services for an attest client, the CPA risks creating a conflict of interest that gives the client leverage over the CPA firm and its audit opinion. An example of a prohibited activity under AICPA and SEC rules is that a CPA should not perform management functions or make management decisions for an attest client. The relationship creates a management participation threat that places the CPA in the compromising position of making decisions for the client and then auditing those decisions. On the other hand, the CPA may provide advice, research materials, and recommendations to assist the client's management in performing its functions and making decisions.

Interpretation 101-3 establishes requirements that must be met during the period covered by the financial statements and the period of the attest engagement by the CPA in order to conduct nonattest services for the client without impairing audit independence. The client must agree to perform the following functions in connection with the nonattest engagement: (1) make all management decisions and perform all management functions; (2) designate an individual who possesses suitable skill, knowledge, and/or experience, preferably within senior management, to oversee the services; (3) evaluate the adequacy and results of the services performed; and (4) accept responsibility for the results of the services.[43]

# SEC Position on Auditor Independence

Publicly owned companies have been obligated to follow SEC rules since the passage of the Securities Act of 1933 and the Securities and Exchange Act of 1934. The PCAOB has taken some of that responsibility away from the SEC, while at the same time requiring the SEC to adopt final rules on auditor independence. We will examine the PCAOB rules later in this chapter.

The SEC approach to independence emphasizes independence in fact and appearance in three ways: (1) proscribing certain financial interests and business relationships with the audit client, (2) restricting the provision of certain nonauditing services to audit clients, and (3) subjecting all auditor conduct to a general standard of independence. The general standard of independence is stated as follows: "The Commission will not recognize an accountant as independent, with respect to an audit client, if the accountant is not, or a reasonable investor with knowledge of all relevant facts and circumstances would conclude that the accountant is not, capable of exercising objective and impartial judgment on all issues encompassed within the accountant's engagement."

The general standard of independence is evaluated by applying four principles that are similar to the AICPA's conceptual framework and that indicate when auditor independence may be impaired by a relationship with the audit client. If a situation results in any of the following, the auditor's independence may be impaired: (1) creates a mutual or conflicting interest between an accountant and his audit client, (2) places an accountant in the position of auditing her own work, (3) results in an accountant acting as management or an employee of the audit client, and (4) places an accountant in a position of being an advocate for the audit client.[44]

The SEC believes that these principles are "general guidance and their application may depend on particular facts and circumstances . . . [but they do] provide an appropriate framework for analyzing auditor independence issues." To provide further guidance on implementing the principles, the SEC identified three basic overarching principles that underlie auditor independence: (1) an auditor cannot function in the role of management, (2) an auditor cannot audit her own work, and (3) an auditor cannot serve in an advocacy role for his client.

## SEC Actions Against Auditing Firms

Over the years, the SEC has brought actions against auditing firms for violating the independence rules. The cases are instructive and illustrate the failure of the auditing profession to adhere to both the form and the spirit of the independence rules, and therefore violate the public trust. We use the PeopleSoft case and an insider trading case as illustrations.

## The PeopleSoft Case

On April 16, 2004, the SEC sanctioned Ernst & Young LLP (EY) because it was not independent in fact or appearance when it audited the financial statements of PeopleSoft for fiscal years 1994–1999. The SEC's sanctions included a six-month suspension from accepting new SEC audit clients, disgorgement of audit fees (more than $1.6 million), an injunction against future violations, and an independent consultant report on its independence and internal quality controls.[45]

The SEC found independence violations arising from EY's business relationships with PeopleSoft while auditing the company's financial statements. These relationships created a mutuality of interests between the firm and PeopleSoft, resulting in a financial self-interest threat.

The SEC action against EY states that the firm violated independence standards in its business dealings with PeopleSoft as a result of the relationship that developed between the two entities with respect to EY's Global Expatriate Management System (EY/GEMS). EY's Tax Group developed this in-house software program for assisting clients with the tax consequences of managing employees with international assignments. The EY/GEMS system was enhanced with the use of PeopleTools, a software product created by EY's audit client, PeopleSoft. A business relationship was created whereby a license to use PeopleTools was granted to EY in return for a payment to PeopleSoft of 15 percent of each licensee fee that EY received from outside customers purchasing the new software, 30 percent of each license renewal fee, and a minimum royalty of $300,000, payable in 12 quarterly payments of $25,000 each.

The licensing agreement provided that EY would make PeopleSoft a third-party beneficiary of each sublicense. PeopleSoft agreed to assist EY's efforts by providing technical assistance for a $15,000 quarterly fee. The agreement provided that EY could not distribute the derivative software to PeopleSoft's direct competitors. The agreement permitted EY to use PeopleSoft trademarks and trade names in marketing materials. PeopleSoft maintained a degree of control over the product by restricting EY's distribution rights and requiring the firm to work closely with PeopleSoft to ensure the quality of the product.

The SEC found that EY and PeopleSoft had a "symbiotic relationship" engaging in joint sales and marketing efforts and sharing considerable proprietary and confidential business information, and that EY partnered with PeopleSoft to accomplish increased sales and boost consulting revenues for EY. The findings of the SEC indicate that EY and PeopleSoft entered into a direct business relationship and shared a mutual interest in the success of EY/GEMS for PeopleSoft and acted together to promote the product so that a reasonable investor with knowledge of all the facts would conclude that EY was closely identified in fact and appearance with its audit client.

Brenda P. Murray, the chief administrative law judge at the SEC, wrote in her opinion that "Ernst's day-to-day operations were profit-driven and ignored considerations of auditor independence." She pointed out some failings in EY's quality control monitoring system, including that (1) EY did not give its employees any formal training on a regular basis concerning the independence rules on business dealings with an audit client; (2) EY had no procedures in place that could reasonably be expected to deter violations and ensure compliance with the rules on auditor independence with respect to business dealings with audit clients; and (3) EY maintained a self-reporting system for firm partners and employees to report whether they abided by the firm's independence policies. There was no threat of random verification, a control that the SEC believes is essential to an effective independence compliance system.

## Insider Trading Scandals Damage the Reputation of the Accounting Profession: Former KPMG Audit Partner, Scott London

What possesses an audit partner to trade on inside information and violate the accounting profession's most sacred ethical standard of audit independence? Is it carelessness, greed, or ethical blindness? In the case of Scott London, the former partner in charge of the KPMG's Southern California's regional audit practice, it was a bit of each fueled by egoistic behavior that motivated him to violate ethical standards and, in the course of doing so, causing the audit opinions signed by London on Skechers and Herbalife to be withdrawn by the accounting firm.

On April 11, 2013, the SEC charged London with leaking confidential information to his friend, Brian Shaw, about Skechers, and Herbalife. The leak of information about quarterly earnings information led to Shaw's unjust enrichment of $1.27 million. Shaw, a jewelry store owner and country club friend of London, repaid London with $50,000 in cash and a Rolex watch, according to legal filings. Shaw was also charged in the case.[46]

It did not take long for both Shaw and London to admit their guilt in the insider trading matter. On May 21, 2013, Shaw pleaded guilty to a conspiracy charge and agreed to turn over $1.27 million of ill-gotten stock gains. Just one week later on May 28, London pleaded guilty to securities fraud for providing confidential information about KPMG clients to Shaw.

The leaking of financial information about a company to anyone prior to its public release affects the level playing field that should exist with respect to personal and business contacts of an auditor and the general public. It violates the fairness doctrine in treating equals, equally, and it violates basic integrity standards. Such actions cut to the core values of integrity and trust—the foundation of our free enterprise system.

## Former Deloitte & Touche Management Advisory Partner, Thomas Flannigan

In 2010, Deloitte and Touche found itself involved in an SEC investigation of repeated insider trading by Thomas P. Flanagan, a former management advisory partner and a vice chairman at Deloitte and Touche LLP. Flanagan traded in the securities of multiple Deloitte clients on the basis of inside information that he learned through his duties as a Deloitte partner. The inside information concerned market-moving events such as earnings results, revisions to earnings guidance, sales figures and cost cutting, and an acquisition. Flanagan's illegal trading resulted in profits of more than $430,000.

Flanagan also tipped his son, Patrick, to certain of this material nonpublic information. Patrick then traded based on that information. Patrick's illegal trading resulted in profits of more than $57,000. Here is a summary of the facts of the filing by the SEC:[47]

- Defendants Thomas and Patrick Flanagan directly and indirectly engaged in transactions, acts, practices, and courses of business that violated Section 10(b) of the Securities Exchange Act of 1934.
- The commission brought the action seeking a permanent injunction, disgorgement of trading profits plus prejudgment interest, and civil penalties.
- Between 2003 and 2008, Thomas Flanagan made 71 purchases of stock and options in the securities of Deloitte audit clients. Flanagan made 62 of these purchases in the securities of Deloitte audit clients while serving as the advisory partner on those audits.
- On at least nine occasions between 2005 and 2008, Thomas Flanagan traded on the basis of material nonpublic information of Deloitte clients, including Best Buy, Motorola, Sears, and Option Care.

The SEC charged that Thomas and Patrick Flanagan, in connection with the purchase and sale of the securities of these Deloitte clients, "by use of the means and instrumentalities of interstate commerce and of the mails, directly and indirectly employed devices, schemes, and artifices to defraud, made untrue statements of material facts, and omitted to state material facts necessary in order to make the statements made, in the light of the circumstances under which they were made, not misleading; and engaged in acts, practices, and courses of business which operated as a fraud and deceit upon the purchasers and sellers of such securities."[48]

These cases illustrate the risk to audit independence when audit engagement team members, including partners, trade on information that is not publicly available. Beyond that, the use of sensitive financial information about a client for personal reasons violates the independence requirement because it creates a financial self-interest relationship between the partner and the client.

# SOX Provisions

Similar to AICPA and SEC rules, SOX prohibits CPAs and CPA firms from providing certain nonattest services for public company attest clients. The potential for a conflict of interest exists because of a self-review threat to independence that occurs when a CPA reviews, as part of an attest engagement, evidence that results from the CPA's own nonattest services.[49]

As previously discussed, the accounting profession had successfully fought challenges to restrict nonattest services for attest clients up until the passage of SOX in 2002. The Enron scandal was the tipping point in the relationship between auditors and their clients. Andersen's revenue from Enron in its last year was $25 million in audit fees and $27 million in nonaudit fees. The firm had performed significant internal auditing work for Enron, creating a self-review threat. Given that the firm seemed to have adopted a hands-off approach on certain accounting issues, the impression was that the firm had lost its independence. Perhaps the close relationship between Andersen professionals and Enron employees was attributable to the internal audit services. If so, the relationship may have affected Andersen's ability to approach audit issues with the professional skepticism required by audit standards and essential in making ethical judgments. It didn't help that dozens of former Andersen employees worked for Enron, or that both entities had offices in the same building.

## Restrictions on Nonattest Services

Section 201 of SOX provides that the following nonattest services may not be performed for attest clients in addition to bookkeeping or other services related to the accounting records or financial statements of the audit client:

1. Financial information systems design and implementation
2. Appraisal or valuation services, fairness opinions, or contribution-in-kind reports
3. Actuarial services
4. Internal audit outsourcing services
5. Management functions or human resources
6. Broker or dealer, investment adviser, or investment banking services
7. Legal services and expert services unrelated to the audit
8. Any other service that the board of directors determines, by regulation, is impermissible

The Act also requires that tax services provided for the audit client should be preapproved by the audit committee. Tax services are not restricted under the Act, but an audit committee may decide to help gain the public trust by not permitting the auditing firm to do taxes. As will be mentioned later in the chapter, the PCAOB restricts certain kinds of tax services and fee payment arrangements.

### Corporate Responsibility for Financial Reports Under SOX

At the conclusion of an audit, it has been customary for the CEO and CFO to sign a letter of representation or other communication to the external auditor on behalf of the client about the GAAP conformity of the financial statements. This management representation is similar to the requirement in Section 302 of SOX that the CEO and CFO certify the financial statements filed with the SEC. The certification states that "based on the officer's knowledge, the report does not contain any untrue statement of a material fact or omit to state a material fact necessary in order to make the statements, in light of the circumstances under which such statements were made, not misleading." Section 906 of SOX establishes penalties for the false certification of financial statements under Section 302. The maximum fine is $1 million and maximum imprisonment is 10 years, or both. If the false certification was made willfully, the penalties go up to $5 million and 20 years, or both.[50] An officer who signs such a compliance statement while knowing that the financial statements contain a material misstatement compromises the relationship of trust that should exist between top management and the external auditor.

An important issue to consider is whether SOX's certification requirement serves as a deterrent to fraudulent financial statements. Karen Seymour was the chief of the criminal division of the U.S. Attorney's Office in Manhattan in 2002 when SOX was passed by Congress. The U.S. Attorney's Office in Manhattan is regarded as the country's most prolific prosecutor of financial crimes. Seymour had high hopes for the Act when it was passed. In an interview with Reuters news agency on July 27, 2012, about the effectiveness of the Act during the 10-year period since it became law, Seymour shared that when she read SOX's certification provisions, which specify that CEOs and CFOs can be sent to prison for falsely certifying corporate financial reports and reports on internal controls, she thought she finally had a way of getting at wrongdoing by top officials. "I thought it was going to be a really good tool, but it never really developed," she said.[51]

Seymour stated that in practice, exceedingly few defendants have even been charged with false certification, and fewer still have been convicted. The most notorious SOX criminal case, against former HealthSouth CEO Richard Scrushy that is discussed below (and was covered to some extent in Chapter 3 as well), ended in an acquittal in 2005. In 2007, the former CFO of a medical equipment financing company called DVI pleaded guilty to mail fraud and false certification and was sentenced to 30 months in prison. In a more recent case, a SOX false certification charge against former Vitesse CEO Louis Tomasetta was dismissed. (Tomasetta's trial on other charges ended in a mistrial in April 2012.)[52] The Justice Department doesn't directly track SOX prosecutions, so there may be other cases. Nevertheless, with only four or five criminal cases in 10 years, we have to wonder about the effectiveness of the law.

### HealthSouth: The Case of Richard Scrushy

The first major test case of Section 302 occurred in 2003 when the SEC charged the CEO of HealthSouth Corporation, Richard Scrushy, and the CFO, William T. Owens, with certifying financial statements filed with the SEC on August 14, 2002, that they knew (or were reckless in not knowing) contained materially false and misleading information. Other accounting personnel also were charged with participating in the falsification of HealthSouth's financial statements during the 1999–2002 reporting periods. The alleged fraud led to an earnings restatement of about $2.7 billion.[53]

The HealthSouth story is a sad one, in that Scrushy was acquitted of all charges that he participated in the fraud and cover-up. Scrushy served as chair of the board at HealthSouth from 1984 through early 2003. He also served as CEO during that time, except for periods in late 2002 and early 2003. Still, the jury chose to believe Scrushy's claims of ignorance, even though five HealthSouth financial and accounting officers (including William Owens) had admitted to their roles in the fraud and had accused Scrushy of knowing about it. As U.S. District County Judge Sharon Lovelace Blackburn stated on December 9, 2005, before sentencing Owens to five years in prison for his part in the financial scandal, "life is not always fair" and the sentence "should be sufficient to serve as a deterrent and provide just punishment."[54]

Even though Scrushy was acquitted in state court, the SEC brought a federal action against him that was successful and that led to the following sanctions/penalties:

- Permanently barred Scrushy from serving as an officer or director of a public company
- Permanently enjoined Scrushy from committing future violations of the antifraud and other provisions of the federal securities laws
- Required Scrushy to pay $81 million in disgorgement and civil penalties[55]

The HealthSouth case is discussed in greater detail in Case 4-8 at the end of this chapter.

# Integrity and Objectivity

We discussed the Integrity and Objectivity Principles in Chapter 1. Rules of conduct exist to describe the requirements of these standards and when they might be violated under AICPA Code Section 100. Rule 102 of the Code provides that in the performance of any professional service, a CPA should maintain objectivity and integrity, be free of conflicts of interest, and not knowingly misrepresent facts or subordinate her judgment to others. Recall that Interpretation 102-4 provides specific steps to be taken by internal accountants and auditors who are CPAs and members of the AICPA when differences exist over the proper reporting of financial statement items to avoid subordinating judgment to a superior and top management, a violation of integrity. The Standards of Ethical Professional Practice of the Institute of Management Accountants, which was also discussed in Chapter 1, provides a procedure to resolve ethical conflict that mirrors the steps in Interpretation 102-4. The Code of Ethics of the Institute of Internal Auditors, which was discussed in Chapter 3, also includes the ethical requirements of integrity and objectivity.

Interpretations of the Integrity and Objectivity rules in the AICPA Code identify specific instances when the integrity and objectivity standards may be violated, including:

*Interpretation 102-1.*
- Knowingly misrepresenting facts by making, or permitting or directing others to make, materially false and misleading entries in an entity's financial statements or records; failing to correct an entity's financial statements or records that are materially false and misleading when authority exists to record an entry; or signing, or permitting or directing another to sign, a document containing materially false and misleading information.[56] A good example is the knowing certification of financial statements by the CEO and CFO of financial statements in violation of Rule 302 of SOX.

*Interpretation 102-2.*
- Becoming involved in a conflict of interest relationship with another party, such as when a CPA performs a professional service for a client or employer and the CPA or his or her firm has a relationship with another person, entity, product, or service that could, in the CPA's professional judgment, be viewed by the client, employer, or other appropriate parties as impairing the member's objectivity. If the CPA believes that the professional service can be performed with objectivity, and the relationship is disclosed

to and consent is obtained from such client, employer, or other appropriate parties, the professional service can be performed.[57] One example is when a CPA is asked to perform litigation services for the plaintiff in connection with a lawsuit filed against a client of the member's firm. This would create an adverse interest threat to objectivity and independence, if audit services are provided. Another example is when a CPA recommends or refers a client to a service bureau in which the CPA or partner(s) in the CPA firm hold material financial interest(s). This type of relationship creates a financial self-interest threat because of the material joint business arrangement with the client.

*Interpretation 102-3.*

- This interpretation relates to Interpretation 102-4 that has been discussed previously in Chapter 1 in this chapter and provides that in dealing with an employer's external accountant, an internal accountant and internal auditor must be candid and not knowingly misrepresent facts or knowingly fail to disclose material facts.[58] This would include, for example, responding to specific inquiries for which his or her employer's external accountant requests written representation. The failure of an internal accountant to respond truthfully to requests for information from the external auditor makes it extremely difficult for the external auditor to carry out her professional responsibilities in accordance with the profession's ethical standards.

Let's pause for a moment and return to the ethical standards of the IESBA. In describing its conceptual framework approach, the IESBA takes a broader view than the AICPA, stating that "the circumstances in which professional accountants operate may create specific threats *to compliance with fundamental principles.*[59] The IESBA takes a broader approach to these threats linking their existence to basic principles, not just independence. This makes more sense to us because threats to objectivity may exist when certain relationships exist between auditor and client, or when client management creates conflicts of interest. Even though auditing services may not be performed for the client and independence is not required, a possible impairment of objectivity (and integrity) exists because of these conflicting relationships.

# Principles of Professional Practice

Section 200 of the AICPA Code defines the basic principles that establish requirements to follow professional standards in the practice of public accounting. By following these requirements, the CPA can demonstrate adherence to the technical standards of the profession including GAAP, generally accepted auditing standards (GAAS), standards for accounting and review services (SSARS), and the AICPA Statements on Standards for Tax Services (SSTS).

### Due Care in the Performance of Professional Responsibilities

Underlying the requirement to follow technical and professional standards is the Due Care requirement under Rule 201. Exercising due care means to perform services competently, accurately, and completely. It relates to the quality of an audit and is a critical component of virtue because the pursuit of excellence relies on a careful, thoughtful process of decision making when forming professional judgments.

Whereas independence, integrity, and objectivity relate to the quality of the individual CPA who performs professional services, the Principle of Due Care addresses the quality of services performed by the CPA. The codes of the Institute of Management Accountants (IMA) and Institute of Internal Auditors (IIA) that were first discussed in Chapters 1 and 3 contain competency standards that are similar to the AICPA's Due Care standard.

Rule 201 of the AICPA Code establishes standards for professional competence, due professional care, planning and supervision, and obtaining of sufficient relevant data. Interpretation 201-1 of the rule also requires that a CPA gain the competence to perform services, if necessary, by consulting with experts in the area of those services. If a CPA is unable to gain sufficient competence, then an option exists, "in fairness to the client and the public," to engage "someone competent to perform the needed professional service, either independently or as an associate."[60]

CPAs should be sensitive to situations when one's capabilities are limited and the conservative action is to recommend another practitioner to perform the services. For example, a CPA or CPA firm should not undertake an audit of a school district without sufficient knowledge of generally accepted government accounting and auditing standards. Think of it this way: An accounting student who works on a group project with other students to develop a business plan might feel comfortable working on the financial plan, but presumably that student would not want to be responsible for developing the marketing plan. He would expect a marketing student to assume that responsibility. Professional and technical standards address a variety of services performed by CPAs including audits, reviews and compilations, consulting and tax standards.

Rule 202 obligates a CPA to follow the technical standards of the profession previously mentioned. Rule 203 obligates CPAs to ensure that the financial statements and disclosures conform to GAAP before rendering an opinion that the statements comply with those accounting standards. On July 1, 2009, the FASB issued the FASB Standards Codification, which became the official source of authoritative, nongovernmental GAAP. A new research structure to access GAAP exists. There are now two sources of GAAP: (1) authoritative standards (i.e., FASB Standards and Interpretations and Technical Bulletins), represented by the Codification; and (2) nonauthoritative standards, represented by all other literature.

Interpretation 203-1 emphasizes that there is a strong presumption that adherence to GAAP would, in nearly all instances, result in financial statements that are not misleading. Rule 203 recognizes that, in some (limited) cases, there may be unusual circumstances when the literal application of GAAP would have the effect of making financial statements misleading. In such cases, the CPA should choose an accounting treatment that will render the financial statements not misleading. The question then becomes what constitutes "unusual circumstances." According to Rule 203, the decision is a matter of "professional judgment involving the ability to support the position that adherence to a promulgated principle within GAAP would be regarded generally by reasonable persons as producing misleading financial statements."[61]

An interesting element of this non-GAAP compliance exception is that it relies on professional judgment. Recall our discussions about professional judgment and its link to ethical behavior. In Rest's model, discussed in Chapter 2, the ability to make ethical, professional judgments by applying moral reasoning methods is an essential component of ethical decision making. So, here is another link between our discussion of the philosophy of ethics and the ethical behavior of accountants.

Interpretation 203-4 emphasizes that GAAP requirement applies equally to internal and external accountants.[62] Rule 203 provides, in part, that a CPA shall not state affirmatively that financial statements or other financial data of an entity are presented in conformity with GAAP if such statements or data contain any departure from an accounting principle promulgated by a body designated by the AICPA Council to establish such principles that has a material effect on the statements or data taken as a whole (i.e., FASB).

Rule 203 applies to all CPAs with respect to any statement that financial statements or other financial data are presented in conformity with GAAP. Representation regarding GAAP conformity included in a letter or other communication from a client entity to its auditor or others related to that entity's financial statements is subject to Rule 203 and may be considered an affirmative statement within the meaning of the rule with respect to CPAs who signed the letter or other communication (for example, signing reports to regulatory authorities, creditors, and auditors). This would include SOX certifications under Section 302 of the Act previously discussed.

Interpretation 203-5 recognizes the importance of international accounting standards in preparing financial reports. We discuss IFRS further in Chapter 8. This interpretation does not preclude a CPA from preparing or reporting on financial statements that have been prepared pursuant to financial reporting frameworks other than GAAP, such as (1) financial reporting frameworks generally accepted in another country, including jurisdictional variations of IFRSs such that the entity's financial statements do not meet the requirements for full compliance with IFRSs as promulgated by the IASB; (2) financial reporting frameworks prescribed by an agreement or a contract; or (3) another comprehensive basis of accounting, including statutory financial reporting provisions required by law or a U.S. or foreign governmental regulatory body to whose jurisdiction the entity is subject. When financial statements are prepared under a non-GAAP reporting framework, the CPA should not indicate in any way that those statements are GAAP-compliant, and it should be made clear which financial reporting framework(s) have been used.[63]

# Responsibilities to Clients

Section 300 of the AICPA Code establishes important standards that directly address a CPA's responsibilities to clients. The first, Rule 301 on confidential client information, emphasizes the CPA's obligation not to divulge client information. The second, Rule 302 on contingent fees, clarifies when contingent fees can and cannot be accepted as a form of payment for services.[64]

### Confidentiality of Client Information

Generally, a CPA should not divulge confidential client information unless the client specifically agrees. The client may consent, for example, when there is a change of auditor and the successor auditor approaches the client for permission to discuss matters related to the audit with the predecessor. This step is required by GAAS. Of course, the client can always deny permission and cut off any such contact, in which case the successor auditor probably should run in the opposite direction of the client as quickly as possible. In other words, the proverbial "red flag" will have been raised. The CPA should be skeptical and wonder why the client may have refused permission.

Rule 301 also permits the CPA to discuss confidential client information without violating the rule in the following situations: (1) in response to a validly issued subpoena or summons, or to adhere to applicable laws and government regulations (i.e, Dodd-Frank Financial Reform Act); (2) to provide the information necessary for a review of the CPA's professional practice (inspection/quality review) under PCAOB, AICPA, state CPA society, or board of accountancy authorization; and (3) to provide the information necessary for one's defense in an investigation of the CPA in a disciplinary matter.[65]

Conflicts of interest can arise in the course of deciding confidentiality issues. A classic case occurred in the early 1980s—*Fund of Funds Ltd. v. Arthur Andersen & Co.* In that case, Arthur Andersen had issued an unqualified opinion on the audit of Fund of Funds, and then essentially the same audit team began the audit of King Resources, a natural resource company whose stock was part of the mutual funds holdings of Fund of Funds. Andersen had learned during its audit of King Resources that King's natural resource holdings were overvalued, which affected the investment's value as it related to Fund of Funds. Rather than withdrawing from the audit upon learning that there was a relationship between two of Andersen's clients, the firm decided not to tell Fund of Funds. Andersen was probably concerned about a lawsuit if it had told the mutual fund company; instead, the firm gambled that the company would not find out that King's natural resource properties were overstated, thereby rendering the company's investment much less valuable.[66]

King Resources went bankrupt, and the investors in Fund of Funds sued Andersen, claiming that the auditors should have disclosed that the properties were overvalued. The firm claimed a confidentiality obligation to King Resources in its defense, but the court did not buy it. The court found that the auditors were liable of, among other things, failing to use information that they had obtained from another client (King) to determine which of the two clients' financial statements accurately portrayed the facts of the same transaction.[67] At the time, it was thought that a legal precedent might exist for holding an auditor liable for failing to disclose and use information obtained from services rendered to one client that is relevant to the audit of another client.

While the above case illustrates where silence was deemed inappropriate, Cashell and Fuerman[68] point out there have been several cases that support the CPA's lack of obligation to disclose fraud to outsiders. One common characteristic in these cases is that the CPA was either not engaged to, or did not, report on the fraudulent financial information. Two such cases of note are *Fischer v. Kletz and Gold v. DCL.*

In *Fischer v. Kletz,*[69] Peat, Marwick, Mitchell, & Co. (now KPMG), subsequent to issuing its audit report on the 1963 annual financial statements of Yale Express System, Inc., discovered that they were substantially false and misleading. The firm also discovered that several 1964 interim statements, with which it was not associated, were also false and misleading. The firm delayed disclosing its findings to the SEC and the public until May 1965.

One of the plaintiff's claims against Peat Marwick was that it aided and abetted Yale's scheme to defraud with respect to the interim statements. The court reasoned that there was no basis in law for imposing a duty upon the firm to disclose its knowledge of the misleading interim statements because it was not associated with the statements.[†] In the second case, *Gold v. DCL Inc.,*[70] Price Waterhouse, & Co. (now PricewaterhouseCoopers) informed DCL in December 1971 that it intended to qualify its audit report on DCL's 1971 financial statements. DCL was in the business of leasing computers, and the firm believed that DCL's ability to recover their computer equipment costs was impaired due to the impending release of a new line of more powerful computers by IBM. On February 8, 1972, DCL announced earnings without mentioning Price Waterhouse's concern, and on February 15, prior to issuing their opinion, the firm was replaced.

In this case, the plaintiff claimed Price Waterhouse failed to inform the public that the financial information released by DCL on February 8 was, in its opinion, incomplete and misleading. The court, in dismissing this claim, ruled that there is no basis in principle or authority for extending an auditor's duty to disclose beyond cases where the auditor is giving or has given some representation or certification, and the silence and inaction of the defendant auditors did not make them culpable. In holding that the auditors had no duty to disclose, the court reasoned that because the auditors had issued no public opinion, rendered no certification, and in no way invited the public to rely on their financial judgment, there was no special relationship that imposed a duty of disclosure.

---

[†]For reviews of interim periods ending before November 15, 2007, the SEC now requires a registrant (publicly owned company) to engage an independent accountant to review the registrant's interim financial information before the registrant files its quarterly report with the commission. The SEC also requires management, with the participation of the principal executive and financial officers (the certifying officers) to make quarterly certifications (similar to annual ones under SOX Section 302) with respect to the company's internal control over financial reporting. Although an accountant is not required to issue a written report on a review of interim financial information, the SEC requires that an accountant's review report be filed with the interim financial information if, in any filing, the entity states that the interim financial information has been reviewed by an independent public accountant.

Accountants' legal liability cases can raise complex issues about confidentiality, duty to disclose, and whether professional standards have been followed. More will be said about these issues in Chapter 6.

### Confidentiality and Whistleblowing

In Chapter 1, we pointed out that while internal whistleblowing is the expected standard of behavior under AICPA Interpretation 102-4 and the IMA ethical standards to resolve ethical conflicts, to go outside the company and externally blow the whistle on wrongdoing violates the confidentiality obligation to the client. If a CPA even contemplates such an action, legal advice should be sought out before making a final decision. However, this does not mean that a CPA should never go outside the company and bring certain matters to the attention of the SEC. For example, when the auditor believes a client has committed an illegal act that has a material effect on the financial statements, the matter must be reported to the audit committee. The board then has one business day to inform the SEC. If the board decides not to inform the SEC, the auditor must provide the same report to the SEC within one business day or resign from the engagement. A brief explanation follows, and more will be said about illegal acts in Chapter 5.

Louwers et al. provide useful guidelines with respect to the auditors' obligations to blow the whistle about clients' illegal practices under auditing standards. If a client refuses to accept an auditors' report that has been modified in any of the following situations, the public accounting firm should withdraw from the engagement and give its reasons in writing to the board of directors: (1) the inability to obtain sufficient appropriate evidence about a suspected illegal act; (2) failure to account for or disclose properly a material amount connected with an illegal act; or (3) the inability to estimate amounts involved in an illegal act. As the authors point out, the information in these cases is not considered confidential if its disclosure is necessary to prevent financial statements from being misleading.[71]

Louwers also points out that while auditors are not legally obligated to blow the whistle on clients in general, there are circumstances in which auditors are legally *justified* in making disclosures to a regulatory agency or a third party. As pointed out above, such action is allowed for under Rule 301. A good example is the requirement under Dodd-Frank discussed in Chapter 3 that specifically permits disclosure to the SEC to prevent "substantial injury" to the financial interest of an entity or its investors. Disclosure also is justified when the whistleblower reasonably believes that the entity is impeding investigation of the misconduct, or when the whistleblower has first reported the violation internally and at least 120 days have passed.

Additional examples where disclosure may be justified as noted by Louwers include (1) when a client has, intentionally and without authorization, associated or involved a CPA in its misleading conduct, such as by using the CPA's name on financial statements; (2) when a client has distributed misleading draft financial statements prepared by a CPA for internal use only; or (3) when a client prepares and distributes in an annual report or prospectus misleading information for which the CPA has not assumed any responsibility.[72]

### Contingent Fees

Years ago in the accounting profession, it was a violation of the rules of conduct for a CPA to accept a contingent fee for services performed for a client or for recommending a product or service to the client. These forms of payment were thought to be "unprofessional" and could potentially compromise the CPA's professional judgment. Over the years, however, professional accountants have become more involved in performing nonattest services (i.e., advisory services) in which, unlike audits, reviews, and other attestation services where an independent opinion is provided to third parties, the nonattest services are provided solely for the client's benefit. Thus, there is no third-party reliance on the work of the accountant. Moreover, CPAs who provide these nonattest services to clients are competing with non-CPAs who perform similar services and are not bound by a professional code of conduct such as the AICPA Code. The result has been a loosening of the rules to permit the acceptance of contingent fees and commissions when performing advisory-type services for a non-audit client. Certain restrictions do apply, as discussed next.

Under Rule 302 of the AICPA Code, a CPA is prohibited from performing for a contingent fee any professional services for, or to receive such a fee from, a client for whom the CPA or CPA firm performs any of the following services: (1) an audit or review of a financial statement; (2) a compilation of a financial statement when the CPA expects, or reasonably might expect, that a third party will use the financial statement and the compilation report does not disclose a lack of independence; or (3) an examination of prospective financial information.[73]

The reason for prohibiting contingent fee payments in these instances is the requirement for independence in each case when also performing attest services (i.e., audit) for the client. This raises the bar with respect to not becoming involved in any relationship with the client or a third party that may threaten independence, such as when a financial self-interest exists as a result of the contingent fee arrangement. For example, if an accounting firm and audit client were to agree that the firm would receive 30 percent of any tax savings to the client resulting from tax advice provided by the firm, the fee would be a contingent fee and impair the auditor's independence, notwithstanding an expectation that a government agency would consider issues related to the client's taxes as explained below. In the tax-savings case, the firm and client, not a court or government agency, would have agreed to the determination of the fee. The fact that a government agency might challenge the amount of the client's tax savings, and thereby alter the final amount of the fee paid to the firm, heightens rather than lessens the mutuality of interest between the firm and client. Accordingly, such fees impair an auditor's independence. Contingent fees for preparation of amended tax returns or refund claims are permitted as long as the CPA has a reasonable expectation the claim would be the subject of a substantive review by the taxing authority. Finally, a contingent fee can be accepted when filing an amended federal or state income tax return (or refund claim) claiming a tax refund in an amount greater than the threshold for review by the Joint Committee on Internal Revenue Taxation ($1 million at March 1991) or state taxing authority.[74] In these instances, the fee is determined not by the parties but by courts or government agencies acting in the public interest so that it is less likely that such fees would be used to create a mutual financial interest between the auditor and audit client.

# Other Responsibilities and Practices

## Commissions and Referral Fees

Section 500 of the AICPA Code establishes rules for commissions and referral fees that are similar to those for contingent fees. Unlike a contingent fee, which is conditioned on the outcome of a service, a commission is typically paid to a CPA for recommending or referring to a client any product or service of another party, such as an investment product whereby the CPA receives a commission from the investment company if the client purchases the product. A similar arrangement exists when a CPA, for a commission, recommends or refers any product or service to be supplied by a client to another party. The restricted services identified under Rule 302 apply to Rule 503 on commissions and referral fees. The same independence concerns as with contingent fee payments apply when accepting a commission or referral fee for products or services provided to a client or of the client to another party.[75]

Imagine, for example, that a CPA is engaged to perform financial planning services for a client and to recommend a financial product or products based on the service. Now, if one of three products pays a commission to the CPA, assuming that the client purchases the product, while the other two do not, it may appear that the CPA can no longer be independent with respect to providing audit or other attest services for the client. The key point is that it doesn't matter if the CPA can, in fact, make independent decisions. The perception may be in the mind of a reasonable observer that such an independent mindset is no longer possible because of the commission arrangement. What if, for example, during the course of the audit and valuation of the investment product, the CPA discovers a flaw in the logic used to recommend the commission-based product to the client? Would the CPA disclose that fact to the client?

One requirement under the commission and referral fee rule that does not exist for contingent fees is to disclose permitted commissions and referral fees to any person or entity to whom the CPA recommends or refers a product or service to which the commission relates. In other words, the disclosure meets the CPA's ethical obligation when accepting such forms of compensation, and the objectivity rule applies in making product and service recommendations.

Once again we point out that students should be informed of their state board rules of conduct in the commissions area because there may be more restrictive requirements that must be followed such as exists in Texas. The Texas State Board of Public Accountancy's commissions rule requires that a "person [licensed CPA] who receives, expects or agrees to receive, pays, expects, or agrees to pay other compensation in exchange for services or products recommended, referred, or sold by him shall, *no later than the making of such recommendation, referral, or sale, disclose to the client in writing the nature, source, and amount, or an estimate of the amount when the amount is not known, of all such other compensation.*

## Advertising and Solicitation

Rule 502 of the AICPA Code establishes guidelines when a CPA can advertise professional services or solicit clients. While advertising and solicitation is permitted, these forms of communication cannot be done in a manner that is false, misleading, or deceptive. Solicitation by the use of coercion, overreaching, or harassing conduct is prohibited under the rule.[76]

Advertising and solicitation practices of CPAs should never cross the line, as might occur if they (1) create false or unjustified expectations of favorable results; (2) imply the ability to influence any court, tribunal, regulatory agency, or similar body or official; (3) contain a representation that specific professional services in current or future periods will be performed for a stated fee, estimated fee, or fee range when it was likely at the time of the representation that such fees would be substantially increased and the prospective client was not advised of that likelihood; and (4) contain any other representations that would be likely to cause a reasonable person to misunderstand or be deceived.

A final observation about advertising practices is to emphasize that the rules also apply to advertising and public communications on CPA and CPA firm websites, e-mails, and other electronic or Internet marketing, as well as all other forms of advertising, marketing, and public communications. In recent years, like so many professional service providers, CPAs have increasingly used the Internet and developed CPA firm websites. Prior to the advent of the Internet and universal access to marketing and advertising information, such information may have been in brochures or other printed material. Traditionally, such material was disseminated only by hand or mail and was not as available for general reference or scrutiny. Now, the information is available with one click, so the rules have had to catch up with the technology.

We have observed that state boards have become concerned in recent years with the proliferation of advertisements and public communications that contain false, fraudulent, misleading, deceptive, or unfair statements or claims. The Louisiana Board of Accountancy issued a "Statement of Position" on such matters to guide licensed CPAs in that state. Basically, the statement reminds licensees that

> "[the] Board's Rules of Professional Conduct relative to advertising and public communications apply to all forms of marketing, advertising and public communication . . . inclusive of the content on a licensee's website, or other marketing content, disseminated by or on behalf of a licensee, by e-mail or otherwise through the Internet. The Rules apply to printed advertisements, verbal communications, letterhead stationery, business cards, telephone directory advertisements, brochures, letters, radio and television advertisements, websites, e-mails, other electronic or Internet marketing or advertisement, and any other form of advertisement or public communications disseminated by or on behalf of a licensed CPA or CPA Firm."[77]

Perhaps it is not surprising to learn that CPAs are "pushing the envelope" with respect to advertising and soliciting clients. The competition for professional services has increased dramatically over the past 40 years or so as CPAs have entered new areas of professional service such as consulting, advisory, financial planning, and other nonattest service areas. CPAs now routinely compete with non-CPAs for the same clients; the latter are not constrained by a strict code of conduct. Moreover, the new forms of media to advertise services create additional challenges to the ethics of CPAs, who may erroneously assume that state boards are having difficulty keeping up with the new technology. As we have said throughout the book, a commitment to ethics in one's professional services should also apply to other areas, including ethical advertising practices. The initial contact between a CPA and prospective client often sets the tone for the relationship and establishes a basis of trust that should carry over to those services.

## Form of Organization and Name

Ethics rules apply not only to individual CPAs who are licensed by state boards but also to accounting firms and certain members of alternative practice structures, networks, and affiliate firms. The forms of organization used by CPA firms over the years have changed to recognize the importance of nonattest services to the revenue flow of firms and competition with non-CPA firms in providing such services. Years ago, CPAs had to own 100 percent of a firm's equity interests. Today, most states simply require a majority ownership in the hands of CPA firms. The rules now accommodate non-CPA owners who perform a variety of advisory services and want a partial ownership interest in the firm. Toffler, in her book on the demise of Arthur Andersen that was mentioned in the opening section of this chapter, laid blame on the proliferation of nonattest services at Andersen and non-CPA-consultants, who operated under a less strict culture of ethical behavior than their CPA-attest colleagues. She claims that corners were cut and decisions were made that were in the interests of the client and firm, at the sacrifice of the public interest, as a result of compromises to independence and objectivity in audit services so as not to upset clients and possibly lose lucrative consulting services.

State boards need to have regulatory authority over practice units as well as CPAs because the members of a CPA firm might pressure an individual CPA within that firm to do something unethical. The firm should be sanctioned for the inappropriate behavior, and so should the CPA if she gives in to the pressure. For example, let's assume that you are working for a CPA firm in your hometown and your supervisor-CPA tells you to ignore a material sales return at year-end and wait to record it as a reduction of revenue until the first of next year. It seems that the client needs that revenue to meet targeted amounts that trigger bonuses to top management. If you go along with your supervisor, then you, the supervisor, and the firm itself can be cited for violating the ethics rules.

Rule 505 of the Code provides that CPAs may practice public accounting only in a form of organization permitted by state law or regulation.[78] For example, in Texas, the legal forms of ownership must contain the names of a corporation, professional corporation, limited liability partnership, or professional limited liability company. A sole-proprietor CPA firm must contain the name of the sole proprietor. The AICPA and virtually all state board rules prohibit the use of a firm name that is misleading.

In recent years, the AICPA has become concerned over the different ways that state boards interpret the term *misleading*. These concerns prompted the AICPA to issue guidance about CPA firm names by issuing Interpretation 505-4. According to the Interpretation, a firm name would be considered misleading if the name contains any representation that would be likely to cause a reasonable person to misunderstand, or be confused about, the legal form of the firm or who the owners or members of the firm are, such as a reference to a type of organization or an abbreviation of the name that does not accurately reflect the form under which the firm is organized.[79]

The overarching principle set forth is that a CPA firm's name should allow the users of the firm's services, as well as the public at large, to recognize the firm's identity. The reason that this is a problem today is the varying ways in which a firm is established, including intertwined networks and affiliates that may perform different services for the same client, and alternative business structures, where one firm performs audit services and the other entity performs nonattest services for the same client. Additional concerns include the manner in which a CPA firm markets or advertises its services and capabilities to the public, the responsibilities of the public to consider the CPA firm's attributes other than its name, or any potential legal implications related to the use of a CPA firm name.[77] For example, states generally require firms to have at least two partners in order to be called "CPA and Company" or "CPA and Associate," and at least three partners in order to be called "CPA and Associates."

One major shift in the form and organization of providing accounting and auditing services to the public in the last 20 years has been to provide professional services through the formation of alternative practice structures (APSs). Typically, a CPA firm is purchased by an entity that is not majority owned by CPAs, a so-called APS. The latter assumes the nonattest services, while the CPA firm continues to provide attest services (sometimes as a shell entity). The CPA firm may be making payments to the APS, such as for leasing space and payments for the use (in audit work) of former CPA firm members who now perform nonattest services for the APS.[80]

Imagine, for example, that a tax preparation entity purchased a small CPA firm. The tax entity (now called an APS) cannot do audit work because it is not majority CPA owned. It can, however, perform all nonattest services while the original CPA firm does the audit work. The CPA firm and the APS have a relationship as a result of the sale, and that may cause some problems. A potential danger is when the APS performs its services for the same client who uses the related CPA firm for audit services. Independence of CPA firm members may be impaired by virtue of the relationship because the APS has some control over the CPA firm and its members as a result of the acquisition.

To control for the possibility that a top management official of the APS may attempt to influence the decision making of a member of the CPA firm, the AICPA rules extend to direct superiors of the APS, who can directly control the activities of those in the CPA firm, and indirect superiors, who might influence the decisions made by the CPA in its audit work for mutual clients. Interpretation 101-14 subjects direct superiors to Rule 101 and its interpretations while indirect superiors are included only if they have material financial relationships as defined under Rule 101 and its interpretations.[81]

AICPA Interpretations 101-17 and 101-18 recognize network and affiliate forms of organization and the potential for independence impairments. While these standards go beyond the scope of this chapter, we do want to make certain important points because students may find themselves working for one of these non-traditional CPA firms. Perhaps most important is to recognize the size and scope of these organizations.

CBIZMHM, LLC (CBIZ) is the largest non–Big Four firm in size of revenues that provides management advisory services according to a 2012 survey by *Accounting Today.*[82] On its website, CBIZ describes itself as providing a wide range of accounting and business management services to assist both individuals and small to medium-sized businesses in meeting all their diverse needs. CBIZ has over 140 offices and 6,000 associates in major metropolitan and suburban cities throughout the United States.

Interpretation 101-17[83] points out that a firm may join a larger group to enhance its ability to provide professional services. These may be membership associations that are separate legal entities that are otherwise unrelated to their members. The associations facilitate their members' use of association services and resources; they do not themselves typically engage in the practice of public accounting or provide professional services to their members' clients or to other third parties. For example, a firm may become a member of an association in order to refer work to, or receive referrals from, other association members.

A network firm is required to be independent of financial statement audit and review clients of the other network firms if the use of the audit or review report for the client is not restricted, as defined by professional standards. For all other attest clients, consideration should be given to any threats that the firm knows or has reason to believe may be created by network firm interests and relationships. If those threats are not at an acceptable level, safeguards should be applied to eliminate the threats or reduce them to an acceptable level. The independence requirements apply to any entity within the network that meets the definition of a *network firm*.[84]

The characteristics of a network include sharing common brand name, sharing common control, sharing profits or costs, sharing common business strategy, sharing significant professional resources, and sharing common quality control policies and procedures.

Interpretation 101-18 defines *affiliates* as entities with financial interests in, and other relationships with, entities that are related in various ways to a financial statement attest client that may impair independence. This interpretation provides guidance on which entities should be considered an affiliate of a financial statement attest client and subject to the independence provisions of the AICPA Code of Professional Conduct.[85]

## Acts Discreditable—Client Books and Records; CPA Workpapers

A variety of acts discreditable are considered to be a violation of Rule 501. In general, the acts discreditable rule is designed to hold CPAs accountable for personal and professional actions that bring disrepute on the individual and profession.

Interpretation 501-1 establishes the standards of behavior for CPAs when responding to requests by clients and former clients for records. First, we review important definitions under the interpretation:[86]

- *Client-provided records* are accounting or other records belonging to the client that were provided to the member [CPA] by or on behalf of the client, including hardcopy or electronic reproductions of such records.

- *Member-prepared records* are accounting or other records that the member was not specifically engaged to prepare and that are not in the client's books and records or are otherwise not available to the client, with the result that the client's financial information is incomplete. Examples include adjusting, closing, combining, or consolidating journal entries (including computations supporting such entries) and supporting schedules and documents that are proposed or prepared by the member as part of an engagement (e.g., an audit).

- *Member's work products* are deliverables as set forth in the terms of the engagement, such as tax returns.
- *Member's working papers* are all other items prepared solely for purposes of the engagement and include items prepared by the CPA, such as audit programs, analytical review schedules, and statistical sampling results and analyses.

Licensed CPAs must comply with the rules and regulations of authoritative regulatory bodies, such as the state board of accountancy. For example, as previously mentioned, the state board may not permit a licensed CPA to withhold certain records pending fee payment from the client for the work performed. Failure to comply with the more restrictive provisions contained in the rules and regulations of the applicable regulatory body concerning the return of certain records would constitute a violation of this interpretation.

The rules are summarized as follows:[87]

1. Client-provided records in the custody or control of the CPA should be returned to the client at the client's request.
2. Unless a CPA and the client have agreed to the contrary, when a client makes a request for member-prepared records, or a member's work products that are in the custody or control of the member or the member's firm (member) that have not previously been provided to the client, the member should respond to the client's request as follows:
   a. Member-prepared records relating to a completed and issued work product should be provided to the client, except that such records may be withheld if there are fees due to the member for the specific work product.
   b. Member's work products should be provided to the client, except that such work products may be withheld in any of the following circumstances:
      - If there are fees due to the member for the specific work product
      - If the work product is incomplete
      - For purposes of complying with professional standards (for example, withholding an audit report due to outstanding audit issues)
      - If threatened or outstanding litigation exists concerning the engagement or member's work
      - For purposes of complying with professional standards (for example, withholding an audit report due to outstanding audit issues)
      - If threatened or outstanding litigation exists concerning the engagement or member's work

State board rules on these matters can be confusing. The New York State Rules of the Board of Regents provide that certain information should be provided to a client upon request, such as: copies of tax returns, copies of reports, or other documents that were previously issued to or for such client; copies of information that are contained in the accountant's working papers, if the information would ordinarily constitute part of the client's books and records and is not otherwise available to the client including client-owned records or records that the licensee receives from a client, and any records, tax returns, reports, or other documents and information that are contained in an accountant's working papers that were prepared for the client by the accountant and for which the accountant *has received payment from the client.*[88] Thus, it can be assumed the information can be withheld if payment has not been received. On the other hand, we previously mentioned that Texas State Board Rule 501.76 provides that a person's work papers (to the extent that such work papers include records that would ordinarily constitute part of the client's or former client's books and records and are not otherwise available to the client or former client) *should be furnished to the client within a reasonable time* (promptly, not to exceed 20 business days) after the client has made a request for those records. The person can charge a reasonable fee for providing such work papers.[89] The question is whether a "reasonable fee" precludes withholding working papers that constitute client books and records due to nonpayment of *client service fees.* As the saying goes, a word to the wise should be sufficient. Check with your state board rules on these matters once you become a licensed CPA.

The complexities of work-product privilege were brought to the forefront in a U.S. Supreme Court decision on May 24, 2010. In *United States v. Textron Inc.,* the Supreme Court declined to review a lower court opinion and let stand the decision by the First Circuit Court of Appeals that a corporation's tax accrual workpapers were not protected from an IRS summons by the work product privilege.[90] Exhibit 4.4 summarizes the facts of this case.

## Acts Discreditable—Negligence in the Preparation of Financial Statements or Records

Briefly, other discreditable acts that can lead to disciplinary action include discrimination and harassment in employment practices; failure to follow standards and/or procedures or other requirements in governmental audits; failure to follow requirements of governmental bodies, commissions, or other regulatory agencies; negligence in the preparation of financial statements or records; solicitation or disclosure of CPA examination questions and answers; failure to file tax returns or pay tax liability (i.e., personal tax returns); and false, misleading, or deceptive acts in promoting or marketing professional services.[91]

**EXHIBIT 4.4**
**Supreme Court Declines to Hear *Textron* Work Product Privilege Case**

The case results from an IRS administrative summons for Textron's tax accrual workpapers with respect to the company's 1998–2001 tax returns. The workpapers were spreadsheets prepared by persons (some of whom were lawyers) in Textron's tax department to support Textron's calculation of its tax reserves for its audited financial statements. Textron refused to supply the workpapers to the IRS, and the dispute ended up in litigation.

In district court, Textron argued that its tax accrual workpapers were protected by either the attorney-client privilege, the tax practitioner privilege, or the work product privilege. Textron acknowledged at trial that the documents' primary purpose was to support its reserve amounts for contingent tax liabilities, but it argued that they also analyzed the prospects for litigation over individual tax positions. The district court rejected Textron's attorney-client and tax practitioner privilege claims, saying that Textron waived those privileges by showing the documents to its outside accountants ; however, it held that Textron's tax accrual workpapers were protected by the work product privilege (*Textron Inc. v. United States,* 507 F. Supp. 2d 138 (D.R.I. 2007)).

A contentious issue in the case was whether Textron created the workpapers "in anticipation of litigation," because the work product privilege does not protect documents prepared in the ordinary course of business. The district court concluded that although Textron undeniably created the workpapers to satisfy its financial audit requirements, but for the prospect of litigation, the documents would not have been created at all, and therefore they were protected by the work product privilege.

On appeal, a three-judge panel of the First Circuit affirmed the district court. The court then granted an IRS petition to hear the case. The full court reversed the district court and held that the work-product privilege did not apply to Textron's tax accrual workpapers because the documents sought were prepared not for litigation, but for a statutorily required purpose of financial reporting, and so were prepared in the ordinary course of business; therefore, they were not protected by the privilege.

The Supreme Court decided not to review the case by denying a writ of certiorari.

Interpretation 501-4, Negligence in the Preparation of Financial Statements or Records, merits additional discussion. According to the interpretation, it is an act discreditable to the profession if a CPA does any of the following:[92]

- Makes, or permits or directs another to make, materially false and misleading entries in the financial statements or records of an entity
- Fails to correct an entity's financial statements that are materially false and misleading when the member has the authority to record an entry
- Signs, or permits or directs another to sign, a document containing materially false and misleading information

These provisions of 501-4 tie into those of Interpretations 102-4 on subordination of judgment and 203-4 on statements about the GAAP-conformity of financial statements.

This completes our discussion of the rules of conduct and interpretations of the AICPA Code. The key point is that professional judgments and ethical behavior are integral parts of adhering to both the form and substance of the requirements under the AICPA Code. Ethical decision making does not occur in a vacuum. Accounting professionals are part of an organization and should adhere to its standards and policies, including codes of ethics (as discussed in Chapter 3). They also belong to the accounting profession, and as such, are expected to follow rules of conduct of state boards of accountancy that grant licenses to practice public accounting, as well as the AICPA Code of Professional Conduct. Even if CPAs decide not to join the AICPA, their standards of conduct are similar to most rules of conduct of state boards and in many states, the boards refer to the AICPA Code as providing authoritative statements on ethical conduct.

# Ethics and Tax Services

Students who graduate from college and take positions with accounting and professional services firms might end up providing tax advice for a client at some time in their careers. While the discussion below emphasizes the AICPA Statements on Standards for Tax Services (SSTS) that establish required standards of practice in the tax area, we start by briefly discussing U.S. Treasury Department Circular No. 230 (Circular 230). Circular 230 contains the U.S. Department of the Treasury regulations that govern a CPA's practice before the IRS. Those who practice before the IRS include attorneys, CPAs, and those meeting the requirements to become an enrolled agent.[93]

Essentially, the IRS is concerned with practices in providing advice to clients and in preparing, or assisting in the preparation of, information submitted to the IRS. They include:

- Communicating clearly with the client regarding the terms of the engagement
- Establishing the facts, determining their relevance, evaluating the reasonableness of assumptions and representations, relating the applicable law to the relevant facts, and arriving at a conclusion supported by the law and facts
- Advising the client of the importance of the conclusions reached under the IRS Code
- Acting fairly and with integrity in practice before the IRS

Recall that the rules of professional conduct in the AICPA Code apply to CPAs in the performance of all professional responsibilities, including tax services. The relevant AICPA rules are discussed in the next sections.

## Rule 101—Independence

A tax practitioner must adhere to requirements in Rule 101 because audit independence may be impaired by performing certain tax services. An example would be when a CPA performs year-end tax planning and prepares the tax returns for an attest client. Such services would be considered nonattest services and therefore subject to the requirements of Interpretation 101-3, including the CPA's understanding with the client with respect to the tax services and documentation of understandings with the client with respect to the objectives of the engagement, services to be performed, client's acceptance of its responsibilities, CPA's responsibilities, and any limitations of the engagement.

### Rule 102—Integrity and Objectivity

Interpretation 102-6, Professional Services Involving Client Advocacy, recognizes that tax services involve acting as an advocate for the client. An advocacy threat to independence may exist when representing a client in U.S. tax court. However, this does not preclude providing tax services for an attest client. Instead, CPAs are cautioned to follow Rules 101, 102, 201, 202, and 203 when providing tax services.

### Rule 201—Professional Competence and Due Care

CPA-tax practitioners should understand the requirements of the SSTS and perform tax services with care, including proper planning and supervision of those involved in performing such services. Knowledge of the tax law is a challenging element of providing tax services for a client. Rule 201 includes keeping up with changes in the law, tax court decisions in relevant situations, city, state, and federal tax laws, and participation in continuing education in the tax area.

### Rule 202—Compliance with Professional Standards

Rule 202 obligates CPAs to follow professional standards, including SSTS.

Other rules apply as well, including confidentiality requirements (Rule 301) and the acceptance of contingent fees in performing tax services (Rule 302).

### Tax Compliance Services

Interpretation 101-3 establishes rules when providing tax compliance services,[94] which include preparation of a tax return, transmittal of a tax return and transmittal of any related tax payment to the taxing authority, signing and filing of a tax return, and authorized representation of clients in administrative proceedings before a taxing authority. Preparing a tax return and transmitting the tax return and related tax payment to a taxing authority, whether in paper or electronic form, would not impair a CPA's independence provided that she does not have custody or control over the client's funds and the individual designated by the client to oversee the tax services (1) reviews and approves the tax return and related tax payment; and (2) if required for filing, signs the tax return prior to the member transmitting the return to the taxing authority.

Authorized representation of a client in administrative proceedings before a taxing authority would not impair a member's independence provided that the CPA obtains client agreement prior to committing the client to a specific resolution with the taxing authority. However, representing a client in a court or in a public hearing to resolve a tax dispute would impair audit independence because it establishes an advocacy relationship between the CPA and the client that may create the appearance of a loss of independence with respect to the audit of a client's financial statements.

### Statements on Standards for Tax Services (SSTS)

The AICPA has issued seven *Statements on Standards for Tax Services (SSTS)* that explain CPAs' responsibilities to their clients and the tax systems in which they practice.[95] The statements demonstrate a CPA's commitment to tax practice standards that balance advocacy and planning with compliance.

Tax services differ from audit services in two important respects. First, the independence requirement for an auditor does not generally pertain to the tax practitioner, although a CPA firm that performs both services would be required to be independent to conduct the audit. Under SOX requirements, the audit committee of a public client must approve the tax services. This is a check in the system to ensure that the board of directors is comfortable with the auditing firm also performing tax services.

The second difference is due to the way in which objectivity relates to tax services. Auditors must maintain an unbiased attitude in conducting the audit. An auditor should never do what the client asks just because the client asks it. The final decision must be made by the CPA based on ethical considerations and using her professional judgment informed by ethical reasoning. Generally speaking, when a CPA serves as an advocate for the client's tax position, she must be sure that a reasonable level of support exists for that position, as discussed below. The tax practitioner still has to be objective in determining the supportability of that position. However, once supportability has been affirmed, the CPA can advocate that position in tax and legal proceedings.

The SSTSs establish required ethics rules for tax practitioners. Given the complexity of the area, we focus on the most important standards under SSTS No. 1, as well as some related issues, such as requirements for taking a tax position and tax-planning issues.

### SSTS No. 1—Tax Return Positions

This statement sets forth the applicable standards for members (i.e., CPAs) when recommending tax return positions or preparing or signing tax returns (including amended returns, claims for refund, and information returns) filed with any taxing authority. The following definitions apply:

- A *tax return position* is a position reflected on a tax return on which a CPA has specifically advised a taxpayer, or a position about which a CPA has knowledge of all material facts and, on the basis of those facts, has concluded whether the position is appropriate.
- A *taxpayer* is a client, a CPA's employer, or any other third-party recipient of tax services.

This statement also addresses a CPA's obligation to advise a taxpayer of relevant tax return disclosure responsibilities and potential penalties. In addition to the AICPA and IRS tax regulations, various taxing authorities at the federal, state, and local levels may impose specific reporting and disclosure standards with regard to recommending tax return positions or preparing or signing a tax return. A CPA should determine and comply with the standards, if any, that are imposed by the applicable taxing authority with respect to recommending a tax return position, or preparing or signing a tax return.

If the applicable taxing authority has no written standards with respect to recommending a tax return position or preparing or signing a tax return, or if its standards are lower than the standards set forth in this paragraph, the following standards will apply.

A CPA should not recommend a tax return position or prepare or sign a tax return taking a position unless he has a good-faith belief that the position has at least a realistic possibility of being sustained administratively or judicially on its merits if challenged. This is known as the *realistic possibility of success* standard under SSTS Interpretation No. 101-1. It requires that the tax return position should not be recommended unless the position satisfies applicable reporting and disclosure standards.

Notwithstanding the previous statement, a CPA may recommend a tax return position if she concludes that there is a reasonable basis for the position and advises the taxpayer to disclose that position appropriately. An interesting aspect of the standard is the prohibition against recommending a tax return position or preparing or signing a tax return reflecting a position that the CPA knows exploits the "audit selection process of a taxing authority," or serves as a mere arguing position advanced solely to obtain leverage in a negotiation with a taxing authority. The former refers to the fact that a tax practitioner might recommend an overly aggressive position to a client hoping that the IRS does not choose to examine the client's tax return. Clearly, that would be a violation of basic ethical standards, including honesty (non-deceptiveness) and integrity.

### SSTS Interpretation No. 1-1—Reporting and Disclosure Standards[‡]

SSTS No. 1-1 describes various tax reporting standards to provide a context for making determinations with respect to the realistic possibility of success standard. After all, what one tax practitioner decides might meet that standard could be different from another practitioner. In an effort to satisfy the objectivity standard in the AICPA Code, the following definitions of tax positions are provided in 1-1.

### More Likely Than Not

The *more likely than not* standard generally is satisfied if it is reasonable to conclude in good faith that there is a greater than 50 percent likelihood that the position will be upheld on its merits if it is challenged.

## Substantial Authority

The *substantial authority* standard is an objective standard and is satisfied if the weight of the authorities supporting the position is substantial compared to the weight of authorities supporting a contrary treatment. In practice, the substantial authority standard generally is interpreted as requiring approximately a 40 percent likelihood that the position will be upheld on its merits if it is challenged.

## Realistic Possibility of Success

The *realistic possibility of success* standard is generally satisfied if there is approximately a one-in-three (33 percent) likelihood that the position will be upheld on its merits if it is challenged.

## Reasonable Basis

The *reasonable basis* standard is satisfied if the position is reasonably based on one or more authorities, taking into account the relevance and persuasiveness of those authorities. The reasonable basis standard is lower than the realistic possibility of success standard but is significantly higher than not frivolous or not patently improper, and it is not satisfied by a return position that is merely arguable or that is merely a colorable claim. In practice, the reasonable basis standard generally is interpreted as requiring that there be approximately a 20 percent likelihood that the position will be upheld on its merits if it is challenged.

Now, these standards may seem as though tax return positions are decided using a "casino-based" mentality. There is no doubt that a strong sense of right and wrong—that is, what constitutes ethical behavior—is essential for not abusing these rather loosely defined standards. From an ethical perspective, it would be wrong to recommend a tax position to a client that one knows is not supportable, regardless of the chances of prevailing in a tax matter with the IRS. Still, we recognize the difficulty of establishing a right and wrong position in tax matters, especially when the rules are nonexistent or unclear and no precedents might be set for a client's specific return situation.

---

[‡]SSTS No. 1-1 and 1-2 were undergoing a thorough review at the time of writing and will be changed.

## SSTS Interpretation No. 1-2—Tax Planning[§]

*Tax planning* encompasses a wide variety of situations. It includes situations in which the CPA provides advice on prospective or completed transactions, whether the advice reflects favorable or unfavorable treatment to the taxpayer. When providing professional services that include tax planning, a CPA should determine and comply with any applicable standards for reporting and disclosing tax return positions or for providing written tax advice.

For purposes of this Interpretation, *tax planning* includes, both with respect to prospective and completed transactions, recommending or expressing an opinion (whether written or oral) on a tax return position or a specific tax plan developed by the CPA, the taxpayer, or a third party. The realistic possibility standard in these matters provides that a CPA may still recommend a position that does not satisfy the realistic possibility standard if all of the following are true:

- A reasonable basis exists for the position.
- The CPA recommends appropriate disclosure.
- A higher standard is not required under applicable taxing authority rules.

When issuing an opinion to reflect the results of the tax planning service, a CPA should do all of the following:

1. Establish the relevant background facts.
2. Consider the reasonableness of the assumptions and representations.
3. Consider applicable regulations and standards regarding reliance on information and advice received from a third party.
4. Apply the pertinent authorities to the relevant facts.
5. Consider the business purpose and economic substance of the transaction, if relevant to the tax consequences of the transaction (mere reliance on a representation that there is a business purpose or economic substance generally is insufficient).
6. Consider whether the issue involves a *listed transaction* or a *reportable transaction* (or their equivalents) as defined by the applicable taxing authority.
7. Consider other regulations and standards applicable to written tax advice promulgated by the applicable taxing authority.
8. Arrive at a conclusion supported by the authorities.

A listed transaction is defined by the IRS as a transaction that is the same as or substantially similar to one of the types of transactions that the IRS has determined to be a tax avoidance transaction. Such actions are identified by notice, regulation, or other form of published guidance as listed transactions. Tax avoidance transactions are sometimes labeled *tax shelters*. It is complicated, but basically the term *prohibited tax shelter transaction* means listed transactions, transactions with contractual protection, or confidential transactions.

The IRS guidelines for listed transactions identify participation in any of the following:

- A tax return reflects tax consequences or a tax strategy described in published guidance that lists the transaction.
- The CPA knows or has reason to know that tax benefits reflected on the tax return are derived directly or indirectly from such tax consequences or tax strategy.
- The client is in a type or class of individuals or entities that published guidance treats as participants in a listed transaction.

In other words, under IRS rules, any transaction that is the same or "substantially similar" to a transaction identified as a tax avoidance transaction by IRS notice, regulation, or other published guidance is a reportable transaction—it must be reported to the IRS.

---

[§]SSTS No. 1-1 and 1-2 were undergoing a thorough review at the time of writing and will be changed.

## Tax Shelters

One of the most controversial aspects of the Enron collapse was the alleged involvement of Andersen in marketing aggressive tax planning ideas that the IRS and the courts subsequently found to be abusive. After the Enron scandal, the accounting profession received a second serious blow in 2005, when KPMG settled a criminal tax case with the Department of the Treasury and the IRS for $456 million to prevent the firm's prosecution over tax shelters sold between 1996 and 2002. This is the largest criminal tax case ever filed.

The creation of tax shelter investments to help wealthy clients avoid paying taxes has been part of tax practice for many years. The difference in the KPMG case, according to the original indictment, is that tax professionals in the firm prepared false documents to deceive regulators about the true nature of the tax shelters. There appeared to be a clear intent to deceive the regulators, and that makes it fraud.[96]

The indictment claimed that the tax shelter transactions broke the law because they involved no economic risk and were designed solely to minimize taxes. The firm had collected about $128 million in fees for generating at least $11 billion in fraudulent tax losses, and this resulted in at least $2.5 billion in tax evaded by wealthy individuals. On an annual basis, KPMG's tax department was bringing in for the firm nearly $1.2 billion of its $3.2 billion total U.S. revenue. Ultimately, the $128 million in fees were forfeited as part of the $456 million settlement.[97]

Perhaps the most interesting aspect of the KPMG tax shelter situation is the culture that apparently existed in the firm's tax practice during the time the shelters were sold. In 1998, the firm had decided to accelerate its tax services business. The motivation probably was the hot stock market during the 1990s and increase in the number of wealthy taxpayers. The head of the KPMG's tax department, Jeffrey M. Stein, and its CFO, Richard Rosenthal, created an environment that treated those who didn't support the "growth at all costs" effort as not being team players. From the late 1990s, KPMG established a telemarketing center in Fort Wayne, Indiana, that cold-called potential clients from public lists of firms and companies. KPMG built an aggressive marketing team to sell tax shelters that it created with names like Blips, Flip, Opis, and SC2.[98]

In an unusual move, the Justice Department brought a lawsuit against two former KPMG managers on 12 counts of tax evasion using illegal tax shelters. On April 1, 2009, John Larson, a former senior tax manager, was sentenced to more than 10 years and ordered to pay a fine of $6 million. Robert Plaff, a former tax partner at KPMG, was sentenced to more than 8 years and fined $3 million. A third person convicted in the case, Raymond J. Ruble, a former partner at the law firm Sidley Austin, was sentenced to 6 years and 7 months. In handing down the ruling in the U.S. District Court in Manhattan, Judge Lewis A. Kaplan stated: "These defendants knew they were on the wrong side of the line," adding later that they had cooked up "this mass-produced scheme to cheat the government out of taxes for the purposes of enriching themselves." The losses through the scheme were estimated at more than $100 million.

In a more recent case that illustrates the danger for CPAs of developing tax shelter arrangements for their clients, on June 18, 2012, BDO USA LLP (BDO), the seventh-largest U.S. accounting firm, agreed to pay a civil penalty of $34.4 million to the IRS and forfeit $15.6 million to the U.S. government as part of a deferred prosecution agreement. BDO admitted that it helped U.S. citizens evade about $1.3 billion in income taxes from 1997 to 2003 by failing to register various tax shelters, as required by law, in an effort to conceal them from the IRS. Some of these tax shelters were deemed abusive and fraudulent.

The settlement and payment resulted from the following determinations, according to the IRS:[99]

- Between 1997 and 2003, BDO violated federal tax laws concerning the registration and maintenance and turning over to the IRS of tax shelter investor lists involving abusive and fraudulent tax shelters.

- Primarily through a group within the firm known as the Tax Solutions Group, BDO developed, marketed, sold, and implemented fraudulent tax shelter products to high-net-worth individuals, who had, or expected to have, reportable income or gains in excess of $5 million.
- These fraudulent tax shelters, although designed to appear to the IRS to be investments, in fact were a series of preplanned steps that assisted BDO's high-net-worth clients to evade individual income taxes of approximately $1.3 billion.
- The fraudulent tax shelters were sometimes known under the following names: SOS, Short Sale, BEST, BEDS, Spread Options, Currency Option Investment Strategy (COINS), Digital Options, G-1 Global Fund, FC Derivatives, Distressed Asset Debt, POPS, OPIS, Roth IRA, and OID Bond.

The tax shelter case against KPMG and insider trading scandal that was discussed earlier in the chapter raise questions about the quality controls in existence at the firm to prevent violations of ethical standards.

Perhaps Yogi Berra said it best: "It's déjà vu all over again." One more time, as with the audit investigations mentioned earlier, the government had to step in to right a wrong. We would like to see the day when the profession truly regulates itself and operates at the highest ethical standards. Admittedly, what we read about most are firms that get caught after the fact of an accounting or tax fraud, while the vast majority of firms operate honestly and in the public interest. Nevertheless, the accounting profession, now known as the accounting industry, may have lost sight of why the SEC entrusted it with the independent audit and sole responsibility to protect the public interest.

# PCAOB Rules

The PCAOB has issued a variety of standards that pertain to ethics and independence. We briefly review them below.[100]

## Rule 3520—Auditor Independence

Rule 3520 establishes the requirement for the accounting firm to be independent of its audit client throughout the audit and professional engagement period, as a fundamental obligation of the auditor. Under Rule 3520, a registered public accounting firm or an associated person's independence obligation with respect to an audit client that is an issuer encompasses not only an obligation to satisfy the independence criteria set out in the rules and standards of the PCAOB, but also an obligation to satisfy all other independence criteria applicable to the engagement, including the independence criteria set out in the rules and regulations of the commission under the federal securities laws.

## Rule 3521—Contingent Fees

Rule 3521 treats registered public accounting firms as not independent of their audit clients if the firm, or any affiliate of the firm, during the audit and professional engagement period, provides any service or product to the audit client for a contingent fee or a commission, or receives from the audit client, directly or indirectly, a contingent fee or commission. This rule mirrors Rules 302 and 503 of the AICPA Code that prohibits contingent fees, commissions, and referral fees for any service provided to an attest client.

## Rule 3522—Tax Transactions

Under Rule 3522, a rule that was issued in the aftermath of the tax shelter transactions, a registered public accounting firm is not independent of its audit client if the firm, or any affiliate of the firm, during the audit and professional engagement period, provides any non-auditing service to the audit client related to marketing, planning, or opining in favor of the tax treatment of either a confidential transaction or an "aggressive tax position" transaction. An aggressive tax position transaction is one that was initially recommended, directly or indirectly, by the registered public accounting firm and a significant purpose of which is tax avoidance, unless the proposed tax treatment is at least more likely than not to be allowable under applicable tax laws.

## Rule 3523—Tax Services for Persons in Financial Reporting Oversight Roles

Rule 3523 treats a registered public accounting firm as not independent if the firm provides tax services to certain members of management who serve in *financial reporting oversight roles* at an audit client or to immediate family members of such persons unless any of the following apply:

1. The person is in a financial reporting oversight role at the audit client only because she serves as a member of the board of directors or similar management or governing body of the audit client.
2. The person is in a financial reporting oversight role at the audit client only because of the person's relationship to an affiliate of the entity being audited:
   a. Whose financial statements are not material to the consolidated financial statements of the entity being audited
   b. Whose financial statements are audited by an auditor other than the firm or an associated person of the firm
3. The person was not in a financial reporting oversight role at the audit client before a hiring, promotion, or other change in employment and the tax services are provided pursuant to an engagement in process before the hiring, promotion, or other change in employment completed not after 180 days after the hiring or promotion event.

We are skeptical of ethics rules that build in exceptions, such as for members of the board of directors. From an ethical perspective, a practice is wrong if it violates certain standards of behavior, and it doesn't matter if the relationship with the other party is not deemed to be significant. After all, members of the board of directors at most companies today have ratcheted-up responsibilities under SOX and NYSE listing requirements. There does not appear to be a reasonable basis to exclude board members from the rule that prohibits providing tax services for persons in financial reporting oversight roles.

## Rule 3524—Audit Committee Pre-Approval of Certain Tax Services

In connection with seeking audit committee pre-approval to perform for an audit client any permissible tax service, a registered public accounting firm should do all of the following:

1. Describe, in writing, to the audit committee of the issuer
   1. The scope of the service, the fee structure for the engagement, and any side letter or other amendment to the engagement letter, or any other agreement (whether oral, written, or otherwise) between the firm and the audit client, relating to the service
   2. Any compensation arrangement or other agreement, such as a referral agreement, a referral fee, or a fees-sharing arrangement, between the registered public accounting firm (or an affiliate of the firm) and any person (other than the audit client) with respect to the promoting, marketing, or recommending of a transaction covered by the service
2. Discuss with the audit committee of the issuer the potential effects of the services on the independence of the firm.
3. Document the substance of its discussion with the audit committee of the issuer.

## Rule 3525—Audit Committee Pre-Approval of Nonauditing Services Related to Internal Control over Financial Reporting

Rule 3525 provides that when seeking audit committee pre-approval to perform for an audit client any permissible nonauditing service related to internal control over financial reporting, a registered public accounting firm should describe, in writing, to the audit committee the scope of the service, discuss with the committee the potential effects of the service on the independence of the firm, and document the substance of its discussion with the audit committee of the issuer.

## Rule 3526—Communication with Audit Committees Concerning Independence

Rule 3526 establishes guidelines when an accounting firm should discuss with the audit committee of the client information with respect to any relationships between the firm and the entity that might bear on auditor independence. Under the rule, a registered public accounting firm must do the following:

1. Prior to accepting an initial engagement, pursuant to the standards of the PCAOB, describe in writing, to the audit committee of the issuer, all relationships between the registered public accounting firm or any affiliates of the firm and the potential audit client or persons in financial reporting oversight roles at the potential audit client that, as of the date of the communication, may reasonably be thought to bear on independence.

2. Discuss with the audit committee the potential effects of the relationships on the independence of the firm, should it be appointed as the entity's auditor.

3. Document the substance of its discussion with the audit committee.

These requirements would also apply annually subsequent to being engaged as the auditor. An additional requirement annually is to affirm to the audit committee of the issuer of the communication that the registered public accounting firm is still independent in compliance with Rule 3520.

An important question is whether the PCAOB has made a difference in reducing auditing failures. Perhaps the most valuable part of the PCAOB's work has been in the audit inspections of registered auditing firms. Prior to establishing the PCAOB under SOX, these inspections were conducted as part of the accounting profession's own peer review program. Once it was determined that firms such as Andersen that conducted audits at companies like Enron and WorldCom had been given clean reviews by other public accounting firms, the SEC realized that the inspection process had to be carried out by an independent body such as the PCAOB. The answer to this question has yet to be determined, although we have observed that the process seems to be more rigorous and is helping to identify deficient audit procedures at CPA firms, as we will discuss in Chapter 5.

---

**Concluding Thoughts**

Independence is the backbone of the accounting profession. The usefulness of the audit opinion depends on it. Yet, auditors are subjected to pressures that threaten to compromise independence. The key is to never lose sight of the fact that the public interest must come before all others, including that of an employer, client, or one's own self-interest. If accountants and auditors allow themselves to be influenced by employer and client demands, then they place the public trust at risk, as occurred for Andersen in their audits of Enron and WorldCom.

Auditors must be independent in appearance as well as in fact because factual independence is difficult to assess. Threats to independence caused by relationships with a client must be managed carefully. The marketing of professional services creates other challenges that may lead to accepting forms of payment such as commissions and contingent fees that may, under certain circumstances, impair objectivity and threaten audit independence. Alternative business structures have created a new culture in the accounting industry that threatens to place profits, client retention, and a never-ending appetite for new forms of service ahead of serving the public interest. The growth of tax services and expansion into providing tax-advantaged investments, such as tax shelters, tests the commitment of accounting professionals to make ethical decisions.

The profession has been investigated by Congress on a number of occasions following a series of financial frauds accompanied by audit failures. Recently, there have been calls for Congress to begin a new investigation of the industry's role in the financial meltdown of 2007–2008. On April 6, 2011, Congress held a hearing on the role of the accounting profession in preventing another financial crisis, listening to testimony from accounting regulators, standard-setters, and critics.

In his testimony before the Subcommittee on Securities, Insurance, and Investment of the Senate Committee on Banking, Housing, and Urban Affairs, SEC chief accountant James Kroeker said:

> There is reason to consider the extent to which improper, fraudulent, or inadequate financial reporting relating to GAAP reported results or to disclosures outside of the audited financial statements played a role in the financial crisis. SEC enforcement teams continue to pursue cases stemming from actions that contributed to the financial crisis, following settled enforcement actions involving Countrywide Financial, American Home Mortgage, New Century, IndyMac Bancorp, and Citigroup. When poorly performed audits contribute to or fail to detect financial reporting abuses, there are existing mechanisms for dealing with such misconduct, including SEC or PCAOB enforcement actions. For our part, we will continue to prosecute those who fail to comply with their obligations.[101]

Anton Valukas, the examiner in the Lehman Brothers bankruptcy, told the committee about his report on Ernst & Young's audits of the failed investment bank, but he cautioned, "I want to emphasize at the outset that I did not make any finding as to whether regulators or auditors necessarily could have prevented Lehman's collapse. Lehman failed in part because it was unable to retain the confidence of its lenders and counterparties and because it did not have sufficient liquidity."[102]

Perhaps that is the moral of the story for CPAs and their ethical obligations to clients: It is sometimes difficult to know whether a business failure is caused by the abusive business practices and fraudulent financial reporting of transactions entered into by management or because auditing firms failed in their responsibilities to raise the red flag about these practices in a timely manner to stop them in their tracks, or at least before so many innocent shareholders, employees of failed entities, and the general public are harmed.

We conclude by citing Valukas's statement to Congress:

> Nevertheless, and wholly apart from the claims involving Lehman's auditors, we must recognize the general principle that auditors serve a critical role in the proper functioning of public companies and financial markets. Boards of directors and audit committees are entitled to rely on external auditors to serve as watchdogs—to be important gatekeepers who provide an independent check on management. And the investing public is entitled to believe that a "clean" report from an independent auditor stands for something. The public has every right to conclude that auditors who hold themselves out as independent will stand up to management and not succumb to pressure to avoid rocking the boat.[103]

All we can say is "Amen to that."

## Discussion Questions

1. It has been said that independence is the cornerstone of the accounting profession. Explain what this means. How do auditors protect against impairments of independence?

2. Do you think independence with respect to a client would be impaired if a partner leaves a CPA firm and is subsequently employed by a client of the firm that the partner audited? Why or why not? Are there any procedures that might be put into place to deal with any identified threat to independence? If so, what are these procedures?

3. Comment on the statement, "Independence is not easily achieved where an auditor is hired, paid, and fired by the same corporate managers whose activities are the subject of the audit." How might financial incentives in the form of client services unconsciously introduce auditor bias into the independent audit function?

4. Assume that a CPA serves as an audit client's business consultant and performs each of the following services for the client. Discuss whether independence would be impaired in each instance and why.

   a. Advising on how to structure its business transactions to obtain specific accounting treatment under GAAP

b. Advising and directing the client in the accounting treatment that the client employed for numerous complex accounting, apart from its audit of the client's financial statements

c. Selecting the audit client's most senior accounting personnel by directly interviewing applicants for those positions

5. States require accounting students, CPA candidates, and licensed CPAs to complete different forms of ethics education. Go to the Internet and look up the rules and regulations of the state board of accountancy in your state. Does your state have a requirement to complete a specified number of hours in ethics education prior to taking the CPA Exam? Is there a separate examination in ethics given after passing the Uniform CPA Exam prior to licensing? What are your state's requirements with respect to continuing education in ethics? What is the purpose of ethics requirements in each area?

6. Assume that you complete tax returns for clients. You were engaged to file the 2013 individual and corporate tax returns for a client. The client provided her records and other tax information to you on February 1, 2014, to help prepare the 2013 tax return. Your client paid you $12,000 to prepare those returns. On April 1, 2014, after repeated requests by the client to return her records, you informed the client that her tax returns for 2013 were soon to be completed. However, you did not complete the returns by April 15. Consequently, your client paid another accountant $6,000 to complete the returns after the deadline. Your failure to complete the 2013 individual and corporate tax returns for the client caused her to incur substantial federal and state tax penalties. In retrospect, do you believe that you violated any of the rules of conduct in the AICPA Code? Explain which rules were violated and why. If you do not believe that any rules were violated, explain your reasons for reaching this conclusion.

7. In the fall of 2012, KPMG's Columbus, Ohio office was auditing JobsOhio's books while, at the same time, an out-of-state office of the firm was seeking $1 million in taxpayer money from JobsOhio for an unnamed client. As the state's lead economic-development agency, JobsOhio is charged with recommending financial incentives for companies seeking to relocate in the state. On November 5, 2012, about the time that the audit was being conducted, KPMG was also listed on a sheet of eight pending grant commitments from the state for fiscal year 2013, one of which was for the unnamed client.[104] Do you think KPMG violated any independence standards in this situation? Be specific about the standards and any threats to independence that may have existed.

8. It has been said that ethical people try to observe both the form and spirit of ethical standards in making professional judgments. What does this mean? How does this relate to the realistic possibility of success standard in tax practice?

9. In the course of researching whether a particular tax position of your tax client satisfies the realistic possibility of success standard, you discover that another taxpayer took the same position on a tax return several years ago and that the return was audited by the IRS. You discover that the IRS agent who conducted the audit was aware of the position and decided the treatment on the return was correct. The revenue agent's report, however, made no mention of the position. Do you believe the determination by the revenue agent provides sufficient authority for purposes of the realistic possibility of success standard with respect to your client's tax position? Explain why or why not, in light of SSTS No. 1. Assume you adopt that position, what should your tax client do as a result and why?

10. Assume that the CPA firm of Giants & Jets LLP audits Knickerbocker Systems Inc. (the Knicks). The controller of the Knicks happens to be a tax expert. During the current tax season, Giants & Jets gets far behind in processing tax returns for wealthy clients. It does not want to approach clients and ask permission to file for an extension to the April 15 deadline. One alternative is for the firm to hire the Knicks controller as a consultant just for the tax season. Discuss the ethical issues that should be considered by Giants & Jets before deciding whether to hire the controller of a client, including possible threats to independence.

11. The managing partner of a CPA firm is approached by the CEO of a major client in the firm's headquarters in New York City. The CEO can't use two tickets to the Super Bowl between the Denver Broncos and the New York Giants. The CEO knows that the partner is a huge New York Giants football fan and is looking forward to the Peyton Manning versus Eli Manning matchup. While both quarterbacks have won the Super Bowl in different years, the Manning brothers have never played against each other in the Super Bowl. In a gesture of gratitude for

services rendered, the CEO offers the tickets to the partner. At first, the partner is excited about the prospects of going to the Super Bowl but she also realizes that there may be some ethical issues to consider before deciding whether to accept the tickets. Assume that the partner asks for your help. You are a CPA and a longtime friend of the partner. You hate football, so your advice will be completely objective. What are the ethical issues that you would raise with the partner to help in deciding whether to accept the Super Bowl tickets? Would your advice be different with respect to accepting the tickets if the firm provides only nonauditing services to the client? What if it provides both nonauditing and auditing services? Be sure to cite specific ethics rules in the AICPA Code of Professional Conduct that would guide your actions.

12. Can a CPA be independent without being objective? Why or why not? Can a CPA be objective without being independent? Why or why not? Does your answer matter, assuming that you provide only nonauditing services to the client? What if you provide both audit and nonauditing services?

13. With respect to the Armadillo Foods case in this chapter, let's assume that the controller is being instructed by the CFO that to "make the numbers," the company must increase earnings per share (EPS) by $.02. This sounds innocent enough, and it is only a 5 percent increase. Does the relative size of the increase make any difference in deciding whether to increase EPS by $.02? Would you go along with the demand of the CFO? What ethical issues should you consider in deciding on a course of action? Assume that you discover that top management supports the CFO's position because it would lead to bonuses for themselves. Under what circumstances might you consider blowing the whistle in this case?

14. What is the danger from an ethical perspective of having a CPA firm that conducts the audit of a public company also engaged in consulting with the company on the installation of a new financial information system? What about giving tax advice to an audit client? What are the possible ethical dangers of having the tax practitioners at a CPA firm that audits a client entity prepare the tax return for members of management of the client who have a financial reporting oversight role?

15. In 2004, the Government Accountability Office (GAO) conducted an investigation of the tax shelters of 61 Fortune 500 users of tax shelters provided by accounting firms that were their external auditors covering more than one year between 1998–2003. In each case, the company received benefits from the tax shelter: 61 companies had 82 transactions worth about $3.4 billion in estimated potential tax losses generally reportable to the IRS.

    What are the potential ethical dangers for an auditing firm that provides tax shelters for an audit client? Is it ethically appropriate to do so under the profession's ethical standards?

16. The IRS contacted your client as part of an examination of its tax return and proposed that the client owes an extra $100,000. As the client's tax accountant and a CPA, can you agree to handle the matter with respect to deliberations with the IRS for 40 percent of what you save the client? Under what circumstances might this be an acceptable form of payment for services rendered, and when might it be unacceptable and in violation of the AICPA rules of conduct and/or SSTS? Notwithstanding the AICPA rules and SSTS, is there anything ethically improper with agreeing to handle the matter for 40 percent of what you save the client?

17. A large, national accounting firm decides that it is time to outsource the preparation of income tax returns to an organization in India that has performed outsourced services for other U.S. CPA firms. The firm will transmit income tax information necessary to prepare the returns electronically and staff accountants in India will prepare the return. The return will then be transmitted back to the United States for final review and approval and then given to clients. Assume that the cost savings for the CPA firm are significant because of the lower salaries paid to chartered accountants in India, and that the quality of work in India is as good as or better than that of U.S. tax accountants. Would you recommend that the firm outsource? Why or why not? Be sure to address ethical considerations with respect to the AICPA Code.

18. In August 2008, Ernst & Young LLP (EY) agreed to pay more than $2.9 million to the SEC to settle charges that it violated ethics rules by coproducing a series of audio CDs with a man who was also a director at three of EY's audit clients. According to the SEC, EY collaborated with Mark C. Thompson between 2002 and 2004 to produce a series of audio CDs called *The Ernst & Young Thought Leaders Series*. Thompson served on the boards at several of EY's clients during the period when the CDs were produced. What threat to independence existed in the relationship between EY and Thompson? What are the potential harms of EY or any other accounting firm of engaging in this kind of relationship?

19. On January 16, 2008, the SEC charged two former employees of PricewaterhouseCoopers (PwC) LLP with insider trading. According to the SEC's complaint, Gregory B. Raben, a former PwC auditor, and William Patrick Borchard, a former senior associate in PwC's Transaction Services Group, used their access to sensitive information about PwC's clients to allow Raben to buy stock ahead of a series of corporate takeovers. According to the complaint, Raben netted trading profits of more than $20,000 by buying stock ahead of public announcements disclosing the acquisitions and then selling his shares. Assume that the actions of Raben and Borchard had no effect on the client or its operations. What is wrong with allowing the actions of Raben and Brochard from an ethical perspective? Would disclosure of the acquisition of client stock to the client solve the problem that you identified? What about disclosing it to the public?

20. In the aftermath of the collapse of financial institutions like Lehman Brothers and audit deficiencies of investment banking firms, a great deal of attention has been devoted to requiring mandatory auditor rotation. Some critics of the audit profession are concerned about a breakdown in external auditor independence, objectivity, and professional skepticism. Others point out the inherent conflict of interests in the "issuer pays" model for auditing firms.

Kenneth Daly, president and CEO of the National Association of Corporate Directors (NACD), told the PCAOB in its hearings on these matters that there should be a rigorous annual evaluation of the external auditor led by the audit committee, endorsed by the board, and communicated to shareholders.

Do you think such an annual process negates the need to consider mandatory auditor rotation? What are some of the possible unintended consequences of instituting a mandatory auditor rotation requirement? What are the costs and benefits of mandatory auditor rotation from an ethical perspective? Do you believe auditors should be required to rotate off a client's audit engagement after a specific period of time? Why or why not?

## Endnotes

1. Barbara Ley Toffler with Jennifer Reingold, *Final Accounting: Ambition, Greed, and the Fall of Arthur Andersen* (New York: Broadway Books, 2003).

2. The description of Andersen's demise is taken from an online document titled "The Demise of Arthur Andersen," www.utminers.utep.edu/.../Final%20Arthur%20Andersen%20Paper.doc.

3. U.S. Supreme Court, No. 04-368, *Arthur Andersen LLP v. U.S. on Writ of Certiorari to the U.S. Court of Appeals for the Fifth Circuit* (May 31, 2005), www.law.cornell.edu/supct/html/04-368.ZO.html.

4. *United States v. Arthur Young,* 465 U.S. 805, www.caselaw.lp.findlaw.com.

5. American Institute of CPAs, *AICPA Professional Standards. Volume 2 as of June 1, 2012,* AICPA Code of Professional Conduct (New York: AICPA, 2012).

6. Marty J. Stuebs and Brett M. Wilkinson, "Restoring the profession's public interest role," *The CPA Journal* (2009) 79(11), pp. 62–66.

7. James E. Copeland Jr. "Ethics as an imperative," *Accounting Horizons* (2005) 19(1), pp. 35–43.

8. International Federation of Accountants (IFAC), *Rebuilding Public Confidence in Financial Reporting: An International Perspective.* (New York: IFAC, 2003).

9. International Federation of Accountants (IFAC), *A Public Interest Framework for the Accountancy Profession.* IFAC Policy Position Paper #4. (New York: IFAC, 2010).

10. Catherine Allen, "Comparing the ethics codes: AICPA and IFAC," *Journal of Accountancy* (October 2010), http://www.journalofaccountancy.com/Issues/2010/Oct/20103002.htm.

11. International Accounting Education Standards Board (IAESB), *Proposed Revised International Education Standard IES 4, Professional Values, Ethics, and Attitudes* (New York: IFAC, 2011).

12. IAESB, *Approaches to the Development and Maintenance of Professional Values, Ethics and Attitudes in Accounting Education Programs. Information Paper* (New York: IFAC, 2006).

13. Mike Brewster, *Unaccountable: How the Accounting Profession Forfeited a Public Trust* (Hoboken, NJ: Wiley, 2003).

14. William F. Messier Jr., Steven M. Glover, and Douglas F. Prawitt, *Auditing & Assurance Services: A Systematic Approach* (New York: McGraw-Hill Irwin, 2010).

15. American Institute of CPAs, *Journal of Accountancy: AICPA Centennial Issue 1987,* May 1987.

16. Brewster, pp. 153–154.

17. Jeff Baily, "Continental Illinois Dismisses Ernst & Whinney," *Wall Street Journal,* November 2, 1984, D1.

18. "Hearings Focus on ZZZZ Best," *Journal of Accountancy,* April 1988.

19. Timothy Curry and Lynn Shibut, "The Cost of the Savings and Loan Crisis: Truth and Consequences," www.fdic.gov/bank/analytical/banking/2000dec/brv13n2_2.pdf.

20. National Commission on Fraudulent Financial Reporting (Treadway Commission Report), *Report of the National Commission on Fraudulent Financial Reporting,* October 1987.

21. Donald E. Tidrick, "A Conversation with COSO Chairman Larry Rittenberg," *The CPA Journal* (November 2005); www.nysscpa.org/printversions/cpaj/2005/1105/special_issue/essentials/p22.htm.

22. Tidrick.

23. Alison Frankel, "Sarbanes-Oxley's Lost Promise: Why CEOs Haven't been Prosecuted," July 27, 2012, www.blogs.reuters.com/alison-frankel/2012/07/27/sarbanes-oxleys-lost-promise-why-ceos-havent-been-prosecuted/.

24. www.jenner.com/lehman/VOLUME%203.pdf.

25. www.jenner.com/lehman/VOLUME%203.pdf.

26. www.jenner.com/lehman/VOLUME%203.pdf.

27. www.jenner.com/lehman/VOLUME%203.pdf.

28. www.kpmg.com/Global/en/services/Audit/EU-Audit-Reform/Documents/further-ec-audit-reform-proposals-in-the-headlines.pdf.

29. www.kpmg.com/Global/en/services/Audit/EU-Audit-Reform/Documents/further-ec-audit-reform-proposals-in-the-headlines.pdf.

30. Tammy Whitehouse, "House Vote Blocks PCAOB Action on Auditor Rotation," July 9, 2013, Available at: http://www.complianceweek.com/house-vote-blocks-pcaob-action-on-auditor-rotation/article/302191/.

31. California Board of Accountancy, *California Code of Regulations. Title 16.* Section 68 Retention of Client Records, www.dca.ca.gov/cba/laws_and_rules/regs.shtml.

32. Texas State Board of Public Accountancy, Texas Administrative Code, Title 22, Part 22, Chapter 501, *Rules of Professional Conduct, Subchapter C Responsibilities to Clients,* Rule Section 501.76, Records and Work Papers; www.info.sos.state.tx.us/pls/pub/readtac$ext.TacPage?sl=R&app=9&p_dir=&p_rloc=&p_tloc=&p_ploc=&pg=1&p_tac=&ti=22&pt=22&ch=501&rl=76.

33. AICPA, Professional Standards Volume 2.

34. AICPA, "AICPA Plain English Guide to Independence," July 1, 2009; www.aicpa.org/Interest Areas/ProfessionalEthics/.../plainenglish.doc.

35. Public Company Accounting Oversight Board (PCAOB), Rule 2100, "Registration Requirements for Public Accounting Firms, www.pcaobus.org/Rules/PCAOBRules/Pages/Section_2.aspx#rule2100.

36. AICPA, *Professional Standards Volume 2,* AU Sections 101.06–07.

37. International Ethics Standards Board for Accountants, *Handbook of the Code of Ethics for Professional Accountants,* 2012 Edition (New York: IFAC, 2012).

38. AICPA, Professional Standards Volume 2, ET Section 100-1 Conceptual Framework for AICPA Independence Standards, New York: AICPA, 2012).

39. AICPA, Professional Standards Volume 2, ET Section 100-1.

40. AICPA, Professional Standards Volume 2, ET Section 100-1.

41. AICPA, Professional Standards Volume 2, AU Section 101.5.

42. Association of Certified Fraud Examiners, "Cooking the Books: What Every Accountant Should Know About Fraud," www.acfe.org.

43. AICPA, Professional Standards, Volume 2, ET Section 101-3.

44. SEC, Final Rule: Revision of the Commission's Auditor Independence Requirements, February 5, 2001, www.sec.gov/rules/final/33-7919.htm.

45. SEC, Release No. 249, File No. 3-10933, *In the Matter of Ernst & Young LLP: Initial Decision,* April 16, 2004, www.sec.gov/litreleases.

46. Securities and Exchange Commission (SEC), Case CV 13-02558. Filed 04/11/13, United States District Court Central District of California, *SEC v. Scott London and Bryan Shaw,* http://www.sec.gov/litigation/complaints/2013/comp-pr2013-58.pdf.

47. Securities and Exchange Commission (SEC), Case 1:10 cv-04885. Filed 09/04/10, United States District Court Northern District of Illinois Eastern Division, *SEC v. Thomas P. Flanagan and Thomas T. Flanagan,* http://www.sec.gov/litigation/complaints/2010/comp21612.pdf.

48. Securities and Exchange Commission (SEC), Case 1:10 cv-04885.

49. HR 3763, One Hundred Seventh Congress of the United States of America: The Sarbanes-Oxley Act, www.findlaw.com.

50. HR 3763,

51. Alison Frankel, "Sarbanes-Oxley's Lost Promise," Reuters News Agency interview with Karen Seymour, July 27, 2012, www.reuters.com/article/2012/07/27/us-financial-sarbox-idUSBRE86 Q1BY20120727.

52. SEC, Accounting and Auditing Enforcement Release (AAER) No. 1744, March 20, 2003, www.sec.gov/litigation/litreleases/lr18044.htm.

53. Michael Tomberlin, "Owens Sentenced to 5 Years in Prison," *The Birmingham News,* December 10, 2005. www.litigation-essentials.lexisnexis.com/.../app?.

54. AAER No. 1744.

55. International Ethics Standards Board for Accountants (IESBA), *Handbook of the Code of Ethics for Professional Accountants* (New York: IFAC, 2012).

56. AICPA, *Professional Standards Volume 2,* AU Section 102.02.

57. AICPA, *Professional Standards Volume 2,* AU Section 102.03.

58. AICPA, *Professional Standards Volume 2,* AU Section 102.04.

59. AICPA, *Professional Standards Volume 2,* AU Section 203.06

60. AICPA, *Professional Standards Volume 2,* AU Section 201.

61. AICPA, *Professional Standards Volume 2,* AU Section 301.01.

62. AICPA, *Professional Standards Volume 2,* AU Section 203.02.

63. AICPA, *Professional Standards Volume 2,* AU Section 203.06.

64. AICPA, *Professional Standards Volume 2,* AU Section 301.

65. AICPA, *Professional Standards Volume 2,* AU Section 301.01.

66. Louwers, pp. 610–611.

67. James D. Cashell and Ross D. Fuerman, "The CPA's Responsibility for Client Information," *The CPA Journal* (online), September 1995, www.nysscpa.org/cpajournal/1995/SEP95/aud0995.htm.

68. James D. Cashell and Ross D. Fuerman, "The CPA's Responsibility for Client Information," *The CPA Journal* (online), September 1995, www.nysscpa.org/cpajournal/1995/SEP95/aud0995.htm.

69. *Fischer v. Kletz,* 266 F.Supp. 180 (1967), www.leagle.com/xmlResult.aspx?xmldoc=196744626 6FSupp180_1405.xml&docbase=CSLWAR1-1950–1985.

70. *Gold v. DCL Incorporated, 399 F.Supp. 1123 (1973).*

71. Timothy J. Louwers, Robert J. Ramsey, David H. Sinason, Jerry R. Strawser, and Jay C. Thibodeau, *Auditing and Assurance Services,* 5th edition (New York: McGraw-Hill Irwin, 2013).

72. Louwers, pp. 610–611.

73. AICPA, *Professional Standards Volume 2,* AU Section 302.02.

74. AU Section 302.02.

75. AICPA, *Professional Standards Volume 2,* AU Section 503.01

76. AICPA, *Professional Standards Volume 2*, AU Section 502.01

77. Louisiana Board of Accountancy, "Statement of Position: Advertising and Public Communication, Revised January 2007, www.cpaboard.state.la.us/blog/wp-content/uploads/2010/10/SOP-Advertising_Jan-20073.pdf.

78. AICPA, *Professional Standards Volume 2*, AU Section 505.3.

79. AICPA, *Professional Standards Volume 2*, AU Section 505.4

80. AICPA, *Professional Standards Volume 2*, AU Section 505.3.

81. AICPA, *Professional Standards Volume 2*, AU Section 101.14.

82. www.cpat-jacksonwhelan.netdna-ssl.com/wp-content/uploads/2012/04/Accounting-Today-Top-100-Firms-2012.pdf.

83. AICPA, *Professional Standards Volume 2*, AU Section 101.17.

84. AU Section 101-17

85. AICPA, *Professional Standards Volume 2*, AU Section 101.18.

86. AICPA, *Professional Standards Volume 2*, AU Section 501.01.

87. AU Section 501.01.

88. New York State Board of Regents, Rules of the Board of Regents, Part 29, Unprofessional Conduct, www.op.nysed.gov/title8/part29.htm#cpa.

89. Texas State Board of Public Accountancy, Rule 501.76, www.info.sos.state.tx.us/pls/pub/readtac$ext.TacPage?sl=R&app=9&p_dir=&p_rloc=&p_tloc=&p_ploc=&pg=1&p_tac=&ti=22&pt=22&ch=501&rl=76.

90. *United States v. Textron Inc.*, Docket no. 07-2631 (1st Cir., 8/13/09).,www.ca1.uscourts.gov/pdf.opinions/07-2631EB-01A.pdf.

91. AICPA, *Professional Standards Volume 2*, AU Section 501.04.

92. AU Section 501.04.

93. IRS Circular No. 230, www.irs.gov/pub/irs-utl/pcir230.pdf.

94. AICPA, *Professional Standards Volume 2*, AU Section 101-3.

95. The following discussion of tax standards comes from *Statements on Standards for Tax Services Nos 1–7*, issued by the Tax Executive Committee of the AICPA in November 2009, and can be found at www.aicpa.org/InterestAreas/Tax/Resources/StandardsEthics/StatementsonStandardsforTaxServices/DownloadableDocuments/SSTS,%20Effective%20January%201,%202010.pdf.

96. "KPMG Superseding Indictment: In Criminal Tax Case Related to KPMG Tax Shelters," www.justice.gov/usao/nys/pressreleases/.../kpmgsupersedingindictmentpr.pdf.

97. "KPMG to Pay $456 Million for Criminal Violations," Statement by IRS Commissioner Mark W. Everson, IR-2005-83, August 29, 2005

98. KPMG Superseding Indictment.

99. These standards can be found on the PCAOB website at www.pcaobus.org/Standards/EI/Pages/default.aspx.

100. These standards can be found on the PCAOB website at www.pcaobus.org/Standards/EI/Pages/default.aspx.

101. Michael Cohn, "Congress Probes Accountants' Role in Financial Crisis," *Accounting Today*, April 6, 2011, www.accountingtoday.com/news/Congress-Probes-Accountants-Role-Financial-Crisis-57948-1.html.

102. Cohn.

103. Cohn.

104. Joe Vardon, "Accounting firm faces claim of conflict of interest in audit of development agency," *The Columbus Ohio Dispatch*, May 1, 2013, www.cpapracticeadvisor.com/news/10932168/accounting-firm-faces-claim-of-conflict-of-interest-in-audit-of-development-agency.

# Chapter 4 Cases

## Case 4-1

# America Online (AOL)

## Background[1]

In May 2000, America Online Inc. (AOL), the world's biggest Internet service provider (ISP) at the time, settled charges that it improperly accounted for certain advertising costs. This was the first time that the SEC had brought such an enforcement case against a public company for improper capitalization of advertising related to soliciting new customers, and it was meant as a warning to Internet start-up companies trying to draw in new customers.

The company reported profits for six of eight quarters during fiscal 1995 and 1996 instead of the losses that it would have reported had advertising costs associated with acquiring new customers been accounted for as expenses instead of being deferred, according to the SEC. "This action reflects the commission's close scrutiny of accounting practices in the technology industry to make certain that the financial disclosure of companies in this area reflects present reality, not hopes for the future," said Richard Walker, head of the agency's enforcement division.

## AOL Subscribers

During fiscal year 1996, AOL had nearly $1.1 billion in revenues, and at June 30, 1996, had approximately 6.2 million subscribers worldwide. AOL's common stock was registered with the SEC pursuant to Section 12(b) of the Exchange Act and was listed on the NYSE.

During its fiscal years ended June 30, 1995, and June 30, 1996, AOL rapidly expanded its customer base as an ISP through extensive advertising efforts. These efforts involved, among other things, distributing millions of computer disks containing AOL start-up software to potential AOL subscribers, as well as bundling AOL software with computer equipment. Largely as a result of its extensive advertising expenditures, this period was characterized by negative cash flows from operations.

For fiscal years 1995 and 1996, AOL capitalized most of the costs of acquiring new subscribers as "deferred membership acquisition costs" (DMAC)—including the costs associated with sending disks to potential customers and the fees paid to computer equipment manufacturers that bundled AOL software onto their equipment—and reported those costs as an asset on its balance sheet, instead of expensing the costs as incurred. Substantially all customers were derived from this direct marketing program. For fiscal years 1993, 1994, and 1995, AOL (generally) amortized DMAC on a straight-line

[1]Additional materials available on the AOL case can be found in Litigation Release No. 16552, www.sec.gov/litigation/litreleases/lr16552.htm.

basis over a 12-month period. Beginning July 1, 1995, the company increased that amortization period to 24 months.

During fiscal year 1996, while the amount of DMAC reported on AOL's balance sheet grew from $77 million to $314 million, the uncertainties in the Internet marketplace became more pronounced. First, AOL's costs of subscriber acquisition increased substantially, as the response rate to its disk mailings decreased. Moreover, AOL's competition continued to increase, including competition from ISPs offering unlimited Internet access for a flat monthly fee. To increasing numbers of Internet users, this unlimited access pricing was an attractive alternative to AOL's pricing plan, which charged customers on an hourly basis, and AOL's senior management was actively considering adoption of some variant of unlimited access pricing. In part as a result of this competition, AOL experienced declining rates of customer retention throughout fiscal year 1996. AOL introduced a modification to its pricing plan, offering a lower hourly rate for heavy users, on July 1, 1996, in hopes of improving customer retention. But AOL disclosed in its 1996 Form 10-K filed with the SEC: "The Company cannot predict the overall future rate of retention."

## Accounting for Advertising Costs

At July 1, 1994, the beginning of AOL's 1995 fiscal year, June 30, 1995, and June 30, 1996, the DMAC on AOL's balance sheets were $26, $77, and $314 million, respectively, or 17, 19, and 33 percent of total assets and 26, 35, and 61 percent of shareholders' equity. Had these costs been properly expensed as incurred, AOL's 1995 reported pretax loss would have increased from $21 to $98 million (including the write-off of DMAC that existed as of the end of fiscal year 1994), and AOL's 1996 reported pretax income of $62 million would have been decreased to a pretax loss of $175 million. On a quarterly basis, the effect of capitalizing DMAC was that AOL reported profits for six of eight quarters in fiscal years 1995 and 1996, rather than losses that it would have reported had the costs been expensed as incurred.

On October 29, 1996, AOL announced that as of September 30, 1996, it would write off all capitalized costs of membership acquisition carried as an asset at September 30, 1996, and would expense as incurred all such costs going forward from October 1, 1996. AOL charged retained earnings in a one-time charge for all improperly capitalized costs through September 30, 1996 in the amount of $385 million to write off the DMAC asset. The company stated that the write-off was necessary to reflect changes in its evolving business model, including reduced reliance on subscribers' fees as the company developed other revenue sources. AOL had responded to competitive pressure by adopting an unlimited-use pricing plan and, by writing off DMAC, acknowledged that it could not rely on its revenue history under a different pricing model as support for the recoverability of DMAC. But the increasing competition and rapid changes in AOL's marketing merely confirmed that AOL, given its volatile business environment, could not comply with the requirements of AICPA *Statement of Position (SOP) 93-7.*[2]

The general rule as set forth in *SOP 93-7* is that "the costs of advertising should be expensed either as incurred or the first time the advertising takes place." To meet the requirements of the narrow exception to this general rule (allowing capitalization), an entity must operate in a sufficiently stable business environment that the historical evidence upon which it bases its recoverability analysis is relevant and reliable.[3] AOL did not meet the essential requirements of *SOP 93-7* because the unstable business environment precluded reliable forecasts of future net revenues. AOL was not operating in a stable environment, and its business was characterized during the relevant period by the following factors:

- AOL was operating in a nascent business sector characterized by rapid technological change.
- AOL's business model was evolving.
- Extraordinarily rapid growth in AOL's customer base caused significant changes to its customer demographics.
- AOL's customer retention rates were unpredictable.
- AOL's product pricing was subject to potential change.
- AOL could not reliably predict future costs of obtaining revenues.
- AOL's competition was increasing.
- AOL was experiencing negative cash flow.

## SEC Ruling

Due to the previously mentioned factors, AOL did not have sufficient reliable evidence that its DMAC asset was recoverable, and therefore AOL did not satisfy the capitalization and amortization requirements of *SOP 93-7.* As a consequence, AOL's financial statements as filed with the commission in quarterly reports on Form 10-Q and annual reports on Form 10-K, from the quarter that began July 1, 1994, through the quarter beginning July 1, 1996, were rendered inaccurate by AOL's accounting treatment for DMAC. Therefore, AOL violated Section 13(a) of the Exchange Act that requires issuers of registered securities to file with the commission factually accurate annual and quarterly reports. Financial statements incorporated in commission filings must comply with Regulation S-X, which in turn requires conformity with

[2]AICPA Statements of Position are part of the authoritative literature in the GAAP Codification.
[3]American Institute of CPAs, Accounting Standards Executive Committee, *Statement of Position (SOP) 93-7*, Reporting on Advertising Costs, www.aicpa.org.

GAAP. The filing of a periodic report containing inaccurate information constitutes a violation of these regulations.

Registered companies are also required to make and keep books, records, and accounts that accurately reflect the transactions and disposition of their assets. AOL violated Section 13(b) of the Exchange Act during its fiscal years 1995 and 1996, and the quarter beginning July 1, 1996, by recording as an asset advertising costs that could not be capitalized in accordance with the requirements of *SOP 93-7.*

In settlement of the matter in a cease-and-desist order with the SEC, AOL agreed to pay $3.5 million to settle financial reporting violations. AOL ultimately combined with Time Warner in January 2001.

## Questions

1. From an accounting principles perspective, why was it wrong to capitalize the advertising costs? What do you think was the motivation for AOL's original treatment of those costs?

2. Using Kohlberg's Six Stages of Moral Development, at which stage was AOL at when it made the decision to capitalize the advertising costs? Explain why. Include in your discussion what would it have done if it reasoned at stages 2 through 5.

3. Assume that the external auditors for AOL went along with the accounting for capitalized costs right up to the company's announcement on October 29, 1996. Explain what AICPA rules of conduct would have been violated by the auditors.

### *Optional Question*

4. On March 21, 2005, the SEC charged Time Warner, Inc. (formerly known as AOL Time Warner) with materially overstating online advertising revenue and the number of its Internet subscribers by employing fraudulent round-trip transactions that boosted its online advertising revenue to mask the fact that it also experienced a business slowdown. With the round-trip transactions, the company effectively funded its own online advertising revenue by giving the counterparties the means to pay for advertising that they would not otherwise have purchased from Time Warner. To conceal the true nature of the transactions, the company typically structured and documented round-trips as if they were two or more separate, bona fide transactions, conducted at arm's length and reflecting each party's independent business purpose. The company delivered mostly untargeted, less desirable, remnant online advertising to the round-trip advertisers, and the round-trip advertisers often had little or no ability to control the quantity, quality, and sometimes even the content of the online advertising they received. Because the round-trip customers effectively were paying for the online advertising with the company's funds, the customers seldom, if ever, complained. Review Accounting and Auditing Enforcement Release No. 2829 issued on May 19, 2008, by the

SEC that explains the commissions findings in its action against four officers of AOL,[4] and answer the following questions:

a. Explain what is meant by a "round-trip" transaction.

b. The original complaint against the company (http://www.sec.gov/litigation/complaints/comp19147.pdf) cites three round-trip transactions between AOL and other parties. Choose one and explain why AOL's accounting did not conform to GAAP.

c. The SEC filings do not address corporate governance failings at AOL in any meaningful way. With respect to the round-trip transactions, the complaint states that "senior finance managers (i.e., CEO and CFO) at AOL signed client representation letters to Ernst & Young claiming that the advertising revenues were being properly recognized." Given that the falsification of certifications in the representation letter occurred prior to passage of SOX, do you think the managers did anything wrong? How might the false certifications affect audit work?

[4]U.S. District Court of Southern District of New York, *Securities and Exchange Commission v. David M. Colburn, Eric L. Keller, James F. MacGuidwin, and Jay B. Rappaport,* 08 CV 4611, www.sec.gov/litigation/complaints/2008/comp20586_colburn.pdf.

## Case 4-2

# Beauda Medical Center

Lance Popperson woke up in a sweat, with an anxiety attack coming on. Popperson popped two anti-anxiety pills, lay down to try to sleep for the third time that night, and thought once again about his dilemma. Popperson is an associate with the accounting firm of Hodgins and Gelman LLP. He recently discovered, through a casual conversation with Brad Snow, a friend of his on the audit staff, that one of the firm's clients managed by Snow recently received complaints that its heart monitoring equipment was malfunctioning. Cardio-Systems Monitoring, Inc. (CSM), called for a meeting of the lawyers, auditors, and top management to discuss what to do about the complaints from health care facilities that had significantly increased between the first two months of 2013 and the last two months of that year. Doctors at these facilities claimed that the systems shut off for brief periods, and in one case, the hospital was unable to save a patient who went into cardiac arrest.

Popperson tossed and turned and wondered what he should do about the fact that Beauda Medical Center, his current audit client, plans to buy 20 units of Cardio-Systems heart monitoring equipment for its brand-new medical facility in the outskirts of Beauda.

## Questions

1. Assume that both Popperson and Snow are CPAs. Do you think that Snow violated his confidentiality obligation under the AICPA Code by informing Popperson about the faulty equipment at CSM? Why or why not? As a licensed CPA firm, do you think Hodgins and Gelman has any ethical responsibilities in this regard?

2. Popperson has not told anyone connected to the Beauda Medical Center audit about the situation at CSM. What do you think he should do with the information? Be sure to consider Popperson's ethical obligations in answering this question. How might Hodgins and Gelman be affected by what Popperson decides to do?

    Assume that Popperson informs the senior auditor in charge of the Beauda Medical audit, and the senior

informs the manager, Kelly Kim. A meeting is held the next day with all parties in the office of Ben Smith, the managing partner of the firm. Here's how it goes:

**Ben:** If we tell Beauda about the problems at CSM, we will have violated our confidentiality obligation as a firm to CSM. Moreover, we may lose both clients.

**Kelly:** Lance, you are the closest to the situation. How do you think Beauda's top hospital administrators would react if we told them?

**Lance:** They wouldn't buy the equipment.

**Ben:** Once we tell them, we're subject to investigation by our state board of accountancy for violating confidentiality. We don't want to alert the board and have it investigate our actions. What's worse, we may be flagged for the confidentiality violation in our next peer review.

**Kelly:** Who would do that? I mean, CSM won't know about it, and the Beauda people are going to be happy we prevented them from buying what may be faulty equipment.

**Senior:** I agree with Kelly. They are not likely to say anything.

**Ben:** I don't like it. I think we should be silent and find another way to warn Beauda Medical without violating confidentiality.

**Lance:** What about contacting the state board for advice?

3. Using Kohlberg's model of moral development, explain what actions should be taken by the firm, assuming that it reasons at levels 2 through 5. What would you recommend the firm do in this matter? Why?

4. What do you think about Lance's suggestion to contact the state board for advice on the matter? Is that the function of a state board of accountancy? Are there any other parties that might be contacted to provide guidance on this matter?

## Case 4-3

# Family Games, Inc.

"Yeah, I know all of the details weren't completed until January 2, 2014, but we agreed on the transaction on December 30, 2013. By my way of reasoning, it's a continuation transaction and the $12 million revenue belongs in the results for 2013." This comment was made by Carl Land, the CFO of Family Games, Inc. The company has annual sales of about $50 million from a variety of manufactured board and electronic games that are designed for use by the entire family. However, during the past two years, the company reported a net loss due to cost-cutting measures that were necessary to compete with overseas manufacturers and distributors.

Land made the previous comment to Helen Strom, the controller of Family Games, after Strom had expressed her concern that because the lawyers did not sign off on the transaction until January 2, the revenue should not be recorded in 2013. Strom emphasized that the product was not shipped until January 2 and there was no way of justifying its inclusion in the previous year's operating results.

Land felt that Strom was being hypertechnical because the merchandise had been placed on the carrier (truck) on December 31, 2013. The items weren't shipped until January 2 because of the holiday. "Listen, Helen, this comes from the top," Land said. "The big boss said we need to have the $12 million recorded in the results for 2013."

"I don't get it," Helen said to Land. "Why the pressure?"

"The boss wants to increase his performance bonus by increasing earnings in 2013. Apparently, he lost some money in Vegas over the Christmas weekend and left a sizable IOU at the casino," Land responded.

Helen shook her head in disbelief. She didn't like the idea of operating results being manipulated based on the personal needs of the CEO. She knows that the CEO has a gambling problem. This sort of thing had happened before. The difference this time is that it has the prospect of affecting the reported results, and she is being asked to do something that she knows is wrong.

"I can't change the facts," Helen said.

"All you have to do is backdate the sales invoice to December 30, when the final agreement was reached," Land responded. "As I said before, just think of it as a revenue-continuation transaction that started in 2013 and, but for one minor technicality, should have been recorded in 2014."

"You're asking me to 'cook the books,'" Helen said. "I won't do it."

"I hate to play hardball with you, Helen, but the boss authorized me to tell you he will stop reimbursing you in the future for child care costs so that your kid can have a live-in nanny 24-7 unless you are a team player on this issue. Remember, Helen, this is a one-time request only." Land said.

Helen was surprised by the threat and dubious of the "one-time-event" explanation. She sat down and reflected on the fact that the reimbursement payments for her child care were $35,000, 35 percent of her annual salary. She is a single working mother. Helen knows that there is no other way that she can afford to pay for the full-time care needed by her autistic son.

## Questions

1. Briefly discuss the rules for revenue recognition in accounting and how they pertain to this case. Does the proposed handling of the $12 million violate those rules? Be specific.

2. Assume Carl Land is a CPA and Helen Strom holds the Certificate in Management Accounting (CMA). What ethical issues exist for them in this situation? Identify the stakeholders in this case and Strom's ethical obligations to them.

3. To what extent should Helen consider the gambling problems of her boss in deciding on a course of action? To what extent should Helen consider her child care situation and the threatened cutoff of reimbursements? If you were Helen, what would you do given the directions from Carl Land. Why?

## Case 4-4

# First Community Church

First Community Church is the largest church in the city of Perpetual Happiness. (Yes, it's in California!)

A meeting was held on Friday, November 16, to address the fact that money has been stolen from the weekly collection box during the course of the year and church leaders were getting quite concerned. At first, no one paid much attention, as the amounts were small and could have been attributed to inadvertent errors due to discrepancies between the actual count and what really was collected. However, after 45 weeks of the continuous discrepancies, the total amount of the differences had become alarming. Eddie Wong, the controller for the church, estimated the current total as $23,399. That represents well over 5 percent of their annual collections from church members, which total about $400,000.

The meeting began at 9 a.m., a time that was early for the church leaders, who often had late evening calls to make. The church staff brought doughnuts, bagels, and coffee to help get the meeting off to a good start, but it didn't work.

"I want an explanation," said Allen Yuen, the executive director of the church. The board of trustees is on my back on this matter. Some of them talk about this Sarbanes-Oxley Act and our lack of internal controls. It's all foreign to me, but I know indignation when I see it!"

"I can't explain it, Allen," responded Eddie Wong.

"Jennie. How about you?" Yuen asked. He was addressing Jennie Lin, the member of the executive committee of the board of trustees who was directly responsible for the count each week.

Jennie seemed uncomfortable. She hesitated before saying: "I think my count is correct. I take the money given to me by Joey, put it in the safe, and then Eddie opens the safe on Monday morning. He records the cash receipts and makes a bank deposit."

Eddie said, "That's right. My deposit always matches the amount of money reported by Jennie."

"That doesn't make sense," Yuen said. "Someone is getting his or her hands on the money between the collection process and recording of the amount. I trust you, Jennie, to watch over these things and the internal control matter."

"Perhaps the recorded tally amount independently submitted by the church volunteers has been overstated," Jennie said.

"Why would that happen?" Yuen asked. "I mean, while it could happen and it would be an honest mistake, it seems unlikely."

Jennie was starting to sweat. She decided that a diversion was in order. "Maybe someone gets their hands on the money between the collection box after the tally and before Joey gives it to me." Joey Chang was the accounting manager, who delivers the collection box and tally sheet to Jennie after each service. Joey goes to church on a regular basis and had volunteered to do the job in order to establish some level of control over the process.

At this point, Jennie lowered her head while she waited for a response. It came from Allen Yuen. "Jennie, are you accusing Joey of stealing money from the church collection box?"

Jennie shook her head no. She was visibly upset. A phone call came in for Yuen, and the meeting had to break up. The group agreed to continue the discussion in two days. In the meantime, Jennie went back to her office, closed the door, and started to reflect on what she had just done. The truth is that Jennie has been taking the money each week and giving it to a homeless shelter two blocks from the church. Some of the homeless attend church services, and Jennie has befriended many of them. She knew that it was wrong to take money from the collection box, but she thought it was for a very good cause and that the church clergy would approve. She never thought about getting caught because she told the bookkeeper to record the lower amount. Now, she feels guilty about bringing Joey into the picture.

## Questions

1. Assume that Jennie Lin is a CPA. Evaluate her actions from an ethical perspective with respect to the rules of conduct of the AICPA.

2. Jennie believes that her actions were proper because taking the money from the church and giving it to the homeless served a greater good. Do you agree with her position from an ethical perspective?

3. As a member of the board of trustees of the church, what are Jennie's ethical obligations to the church? Do you think that it is more difficult to establish strong internal controls in a nonprofit such as the First Community Church, as opposed to a public or private company? Why or why not? Do nonprofits such as churches come under the rules of SOX?

4. Assume that Jennie explains why she did what she did, and, after due deliberation, Yuen fires Jennie and tells her that she must replace the money she stole from the collection box. Moreover, Yuen threatens to report Jennie to the state board of accountancy for violating its ethics rules. How would you evaluate Yuen's actions from an ethical perspective?

## Case 4-5

# Lee & Han, LLC

Joe Kang is an audit partner for Lee & Han, LLC. Joe is a CPA in the state of Florida and a member of the AICPA. He recently met with Kate Boller, the CFO of Frost Systems, an audit client of the firm, about the market value of their inventory. Joe told Boller that a write-down of 50 percent had to be made because the net realizable value of the inventory was 50 percent less than the original cost recorded on its books. That meant the earnings for the year would be reduced by $10 million and the client would show a $2 million loss for fiscal year 2013 rather than the current $8 million profit. In a heated exchange with Boller, Joe was instructed not to record any write-down for the year and to wait until 2014 to see if, in fact, the value of the inventory was 50 percent of its cost. Boller argued that the demand for the inventory would pick up next year because the economy in Florida was finally recovering from the recession of 2007–2008. Boller told Joe that her boss, Judy Preston, the CEO, had given the order not to write down the inventory. Joe was told to submit the final financial statements to Boller by the end of the week because the company was going to use the statements to support a $20 million loan for market expansion.

Joe spent the next few hours thinking about the situation. He was under a great deal of pressure from firm management to grow the business. Joe knew he would never advance from his junior partner status unless he maintained the current clients under his control and brought in new business. Joe worried what might happen if he took a tough position with Boller and Frost Systems and insisted on the write down. What Joe did next troubled him deeply but he felt there was no other option for him short of jeopardizing the relationship he had built over many years with one of the largest clients in the West Palm Beach office of the firm.

Joe contacted Barbara Simon, the audit manager on the engagement who is a CPA, and instructed Barbara to change the audit work papers to not reflect a market decline in the value of inventory. Barbara was shocked by the request as she always thought of Joe as an honest professional. Even after Joe explained his reasons, Barbara said she did not feel comfortable making the change. In the end, Joe ordered her to change the work papers or he would see to it that she received a bad performance review and it would negatively affect her future with the firm.

## Questions

1. Evaluate Joe's actions and motives using ethical reasoning and with reference to the AICPA Code of Professional Conduct.

2. Evaluate Joe's actions from a cognitive development perspective.

3. What would you do if you were in Barbara's position? Use ethical reasoning to support your action including your responsibilities as an accounting professional.

4. Assume Barbara speaks to the managing partner of the firm about the inventory matter and she tells Barbara to forget about it and just be a team player in this instance. Does Barbara have any whistleblowing obligations at this point? What ethical issues should be of concern to Barbara in deciding whether to blow the whistle on Frost Systems and the accounting firm?

## Case 4-6

# Gee Wiz

Wanda David, a licensed CPA, works for Gee, LLC, a professional accountancy corporation with offices in Wisconsin and Illinois, in the audit department and she also has some small business clients that she provides tax services to in her spare time—generally on weekends. Her employer does not know that she does this. Wanda never thought about a conflict of interests because the firm does no tax work.

One of Wanda's small business clients, Wiz Inc., was also an audit client of Gee and had fallen more than 90 days past due on paying bills. In her position with Gee, Wanda was assigned to the audit of Wiz and is responsible for preparing and estimating the Allowance for Doubtful Accounts. During the audit of Wiz's financial statements during the week ending March 1, 2013, her boss asks her for justification for not including Wiz Inc. in the 90+ day aging report. It seems there are some audit-related questions about the collectible of the Wiz account. Wanda came up with an explanation for not including the Wiz account in the estimated allowance and her boss was satisfied. Within a week of this request, Wanda is given a nice promotion and raise, but she has to transfer to the office of Gee in Chicago for the new job. Wanda accepts the promotion, leaves immediately, and decides to quit doing accounting on the side. In moving, Wanda does not complete the corporate tax return for Wiz on Form 1120, which should be filed with the IRS by March 15. She also fails to inform Wiz of her relocation. In trying to locate Wanda given the impending tax filing deadline, Wiz contacts the managing partner at Gee and discloses Wanda's side business.

## Questions

1. Do you think it is ethically appropriate for Wanda David to provide tax services to Wiz, an audit client of her employer, Gee, LLC, at the same time that she works for the audit firm and is part of the audit engagement team on the Wiz audit? Why or why not?

2. Has David violated any of her ethical responsibilities to Wiz? How about her ethical responsibilities to Gee, LLC? Be specific and reference the AICPA Code of Professional Conduct in answering the question.

3. Assume that you are David's new boss in Chicago and just found out about her dual role as the tax accountant for Wiz and auditor for the firm on the Wiz audit. What would you do at this point?

## *Optional Question*

4. Review the accountancy law and rules of conduct in your state and explain whether David has violated any ethical standards with respect to the facts of this case.

## Case 4-7

# Family Outreach

Yimei is a senior state auditor in Michigan and licensed CPA. She has been assigned the audit of Family Outreach (FO), a nonprofit social services organization that helps about 32,000 families a year with child-raising and child-development issues, especially those considered "at-risk" families. The organization holds workshops and programs for parents, teachers, and child-care providers. The organization has an annual budget of $3.1 million. FO employs about 30 employees and receives funds from a variety of private, city, state, and federal grants. Yimei was in charge of the audit of FO for the city, state, and federal grants for 2013. She reports to Kwami, her supervisor in the Michigan state auditor's office.

In reviewing the audit papers so far, Yimei noticed that $200,000 appeared in three expense accounts that she never had seen before on the books of a nonprofit: parent reimbursements, entertainment expenses, and reconciling costs. Together, the $200,000 was a material amount.

## Questions

1. If you were Yimei, what ethical concerns would exist for you upon discovering the three accounts? What is the first thing you would do upon discovering the three accounts?

2. Assume that FO provides invoices to justify the amounts in each account. You review the documentation and notice that each one has the same font, font size, and exact format. Being a skeptical auditor, you are suspicious about the validity of the audit evidence. What are your ethical and professional responsibilities given the questionable nature of the audit evidence and your role as the lead auditor?

3. We discussed the issues of accountability and transparency with respect to corporate governance in Chapter 3. In the public sector, the chief investigative officer is the Inspector General (IG) who is accountable to the taxpayers. IG's are supposed to detect and prevent waste, fraud and abuse and thereby build trust in government. What would you do if you were Yimei and were told by Kwami to drop the matter because the chief operating officer of FO is the sister of the IG? Do you have any whistle-blowing obligations in this matter?

## *Optional Question*

4. Review the accountancy law and rules of conduct in your state, and discuss Yimei's ethical responsibilities with respect to the facts of this case.

## Case 4-8

# HealthSouth Corporation

The HealthSouth case is unique because the CEO, Richard Scrushy, was initially acquitted on all accounts, while five former HealthSouth employees were sentenced by a federal judge for their admitted roles in a scheme to inflate revenues and reported earnings of the company from 1999 through mid-2002. These amounts are presented in Exhibit 1.

HealthSouth is one of the nation's largest providers of outpatient surgery, diagnostic imaging, and rehabilitative services. In 2003, the SEC filed a complaint against the company and Scrushy for violating provisions of the Securities Act of 1933 and the Securities Exchange Act of 1934.[1] The complaint alleged that HealthSouth, under Scrushy's direction and with the help of key employees, falsified its revenue to inflate earnings and "meet their numbers." Specifically, false accounting entries were made to an account called "contractual adjustment." The contractual adjustment account is a revenue allowance account that estimates the difference between the gross amount billed to the patient and the amount that various health care insurers will pay for a specific treatment. HealthSouth deducted this account from gross revenues to derive net revenues, which were disclosed on the company's periodic reports filed with the SEC. The allowances were deliberately understated to help meet financial analyst earnings estimates.

The SEC contended that in mid-2002, certain senior officers of HealthSouth discussed with Scrushy the impact of the scheme to inflate earnings because they were concerned about the consequences of the August 14, 2002, financial statement certification required under Section 302 of SOX. Allegedly, "Scrushy agreed that, going forward, he would not insist that earnings be inflated to meet Wall Street analysts' expectations."

The filing also alleged that Scrushy received at least $6.5 million from HealthSouth during 2001 in "Bonus/Annual Incentive Awards." Also, from 1999 through 2002, HealthSouth paid Scrushy $9.2 million in salary. Approximately $5.3 million

of this salary was based on the company's achievement of certain budget targets. On December 10, 2003, U.S. District Judge Inge P. Johnson sentenced former vice president of finance Emery Harris, who pleaded guilty in March 2003 to a charge of conspiracy and willfully falsifying books and records, to a term of five months in prison on each count (to run concurrently), three years of supervised release with five months of unsupervised house detention, and payment of a $3,000 fine and a $200 special assessment. Harris was also ordered to pay $106,500 in forfeiture.[2]

On June 28, 2005, Scrushy was acquitted on all charges despite the testimony of more than a half-dozen former lieutenants who said that he had presided over a $2.7 billion accounting fraud while running the HealthSouth national hospital chain. The jury had even heard secretly recorded conversations between Scrushy and the CFO, William T. Owens, in March 2003 discussing balance sheet problems, with Scrushy asking, "You're not wired, are you?"

In an ironic twist in the HealthSouth saga, Owens, who was the key prosecution witness in the government's case against Scrushy, was sentenced on December 9, 2005, to five years in prison for his role in the accounting fraud at HealthSouth. Owens had manipulated the company's books and instructed subordinates to make phony accounting entries. He also falsely certified the 2002 financial statements filed with the 10-K report to the SEC.

U.S. District Judge Sharon Lovelace Blackburn knocked three years from the prosecutor's sentencing request, stating to Owens, "I believe you told the truth." Blackburn called Scrushy's acquittal a "travesty." Nonetheless, Blackburn said that white-collar criminals merit stiff sentences, if only to send a message of deterrence to other business executives. "Corporate offenders are nothing more than common thieves wearing suits and wielding pens," Blackburn said.[3]

---

[1] Securities and Exchange Commission, Civil Action No. CV-03-J-0615-S, U.S. District Court Northern District of Alabama, *Securities and Exchange Commission v. HealthSouth Corporation and Richard M. Scrushy, Defendants.*

[2] Department of Justice, "Five Defendants Sentenced in HealthSouth Fraud Case," www.usdoj.gov.

[3] Carrie Johnson, "5 Years for HealthSouth Fraud: Former Chief Financial Officer Was Key Witness," *Washington Post*, December 10, 2005, D1.

---

**EXHIBIT 1**
**Misstatement of Net Income by HealthSouth Corporation**

| Net Income (in millions) | 1999 Form 10-K | 2000 Form 10-K | 2001 Form 10-K | For Six Months Ended June 30, 2002 |
|---|---|---|---|---|
| Actual | $(191) | $194 | $9 | $157 |
| Reported | $230 | $559 | $434 | $340 |
| Misstated amount | $421 | $365 | $425 | $183 |
| Misstated percentage | 220% | 188% | 4,722% | 119% |

# The Fraud Investigation—
# Implications of Whistleblowing

HealthSouth said that a forensic audit by PwC found fraudulent entries to raise the total to a range of $3.8 to $4.6 billion, up from $3.5 billion, which had been the government's original estimate. The fraud included $2.5 billion in fraudulent accounting entries from 1996 to 2002, $500 million in incorrect accounting for goodwill and other items involved in acquisitions from 1994 to 1999, and $800 million to $1.6 billion in "aggressive accounting" from 1992 to March 2003.

Allegedly, HealthSouth's auditors—and maybe even government regulators—were tipped off to a possible massive accounting fraud at the company five years before it became public knowledge. At least that's the takeaway from a shareholder's memo that was released by a congressional committee during its investigation. The memo, dated November 1998, was apparently written by an anonymous HealthSouth shareholder and sent to auditor Ernst & Young (EY). In it, the shareholder alerts the auditing firm to alleged bookkeeping violations at the rehabilitation-services company. Reportedly HealthSouth's top lawyer assured its independent auditor that it would conduct an internal investigation of the allegations. The committee notes no record of such an inquiry, however. "You bring the smoke, I'll bring the mirrors," the unnamed shareholder wrote in the memo.

The shareholder's list of alleged violations at HealthSouth included an assertion that the company booked charges to outpatient clinic patients before checking that insurers would reimburse the claims. The shareholder also alleged that HealthSouth continued to record these charges as revenue even after payments were denied. "How can the company carry tens of millions of dollars in accounts receivable that are well over 360 days?" the shareholder asked in the letter.

More questions followed: "How can some hospitals have *no* bad debt reserves? How did the EY auditors in Alabama miss this stuff? Are these clever tricks to pump up the numbers, or something that a novice accountant could catch?" In a statement issued by EY, the firm stated that it had conducted a review at the time the allegations were made and determined the issues raised did not affect the presentation of HealthSouth's financial statements. "You people and I have been hoodwinked," the shareholder concluded in the memo. "This note is all that I can do about it. You all can do much more, if all you do is look into it to see if what I say is true." At 10:06 a.m. on February 13, 2003, someone made a sensational claim on the Yahoo bulletin board devoted to discussion of HealthSouth to this effect: "What I know about the accounting at HealthSouth will be the blow that will bring the company to its knees."

Michael Vines, a former bookkeeper in HealthSouth's accounting department, tried to spread the word about alleged questionable practices while at HealthSouth but was turned away everywhere he went. According to Vines's testimony at the April 2002 federal court hearing, he came to believe that people in the department were falsifying assets on the balance sheet. The accountants, he testified, would move expenses from the company's income statement—where the expenses would have to be deducted from profits immediately—to its balance sheet, where they wouldn't have to be deducted all at one time. Thus, the company's expenses looked lower than they should have been, which helped artificially boost net income.

The individual expenses were relatively small—between $500 and $4,999 apiece, according to Vines's testimony—for the express reason that EY examined expenses over $5,000. Overall, according to the SEC complaint, about $1 billion in fixed assets were falsely entered. In his testimony, Vines identified about $1 million in entries that he believed were fraudulent. He told his immediate superior, Cathy C. Edwards, a vice president in the accounting department, that he wouldn't make such entries unless she first initialed them. "I wanted her signature on it," Vines testified. Edwards, according to Vines's testimony, signed off on the entries, and he logged them. Vines also testified that he saw Edwards falsifying an invoice, which according to his testimony was a way to cover up the larger fraud involving the accounts. On April 3, Edwards pleaded guilty to conspiracy to commit wire and securities fraud. As part of the plea, she admitted to falsifying records, although the plea didn't mention specific incidents.

Over time, Vines had grown more concerned about accounting practices, particularly in light of the scandal that had recently erupted at Enron. He quit his job and moved to the accounting office of a Birmingham country club. Not long afterward, he sent an e-mail to EY alleging fraudulent transactions and identified three account numbers that Ernst should investigate. The accounts covered expenses for "minor equipment," "repairs and maintenance," and "public information," which included costs for temporary workers and advertising job openings, he said in an interview and in court testimony.

Vines's e-mail was passed on to James Lamphron, a partner in EY's Birmingham office. Lamphron testified that he had contacted Owens, who was then president and chief operating officer at HealthSouth, and George Strong, who served as chair of the audit committee of HealthSouth's board. A HealthSouth spokesperson said that Strong felt the matter was being resolved. According to Lamphron's testimony, Owens defended the company's accounting practices. He acknowledged that the company had moved expenses from one category to another, but he argued that the company had done it for several years and that it was an acceptable practice. Lamphron testified that Owens called Vines a "disgruntled employee." On March 26, 2004, Owens pleaded guilty to wire and securities fraud and certifying a false financial report to the SEC.

Lamphron testified that EY had conducted "audit-related procedures" with the accounts that Vines pointed out. The result: EY "reached a point where we were satisfied with the explanation that the company had provided to us. . . . We then closed the process." According to Lamphron's testimony, Vines never specified that invoices were being falsified—only that there was a problem with the three accounts he mentioned. So EY never investigated the falsified invoices and didn't find any evidence of fraud. EY defended itself by stressing the difficulty of detecting accounting fraud in the midst of a conspiracy involving senior executives and allegedly false documentation. EY wasn't named or charged as a defendant in the government cases, and the firm cooperated with investigators.

## What Happened to Scrushy?

Four months after his acquittal in Birmingham, Scrushy was indicted on October 28, 2005, by a federal grand jury in Montgomery, Alabama on charges of money laundering, extortion, obstruction of justice, racketeering, and bribery. He was found guilty of these charges. However, his 82-month sentence was cut short after the Eleventh Circuit Court of Appeals threw our Scrushy's convictions on "honest services fraud," a concept that says executives and government officials can be found guilty of crimes when they deny the people they serve the intangible right to honest services. Thus, the court decided Scrushy did not deny that right to the shareholders and reduced his term to 70 months.

While in jail, on June 18, 2009, Judge Allwin E. Horn ruled that Scrushy was responsible for HealthSouth's fraud and ordered him to pay $2.87 billion. On July 25, 2012, Scrushy was released from federal custody.

## Forensic Audit of HealthSouth

It's hindsight now, but Craig Greene, a certified fraud examiner from Chicago who has investigated accounting scandals nationwide, says that the government's lawsuit against HealthSouth points to many red flags in the company's financial statements that he believes auditor EY "should have picked up on." Greene investigated the HealthSouth fraud and concluded that officials at the company manipulated revenue figures, created phony invoices, and inflated the value of assets to overstate earnings by $1.4 billion between 1999 and mid-2002. Greene said that there were signs of a fraud that should have set off "alarm bells."

One example: HealthSouth's reported net income rose almost 400 percent from 1999 to 2000, yet cash on hand only increased by 40 percent. "The old story is follow the money," said Greene. "Was cash really tracking earnings?"

Greene also noted HealthSouth reported a $342 million adjustment in 1999 to an allowance for doubtful accounts, followed by only $98 million in 2000. "I believe this is the account that was manipulated for revenues," Greene said. "Why such a drastic change?"

Moreover, HealthSouth reported significant capital expenditures between 1998 and 2001, but that did not translate into additional sales, as one might expect, he said. "That is more equipment and property to treat more patients, which results in more revenue," Greene said.

Yet another red flag: the U.S. economy began to sour at the end of 1999, yet HealthSouth's books showed strong profit growth in 2000 and 2001.

## Questions

1. What is the nature of the contractual allowance account? Can you equate it to other allowance accounts? Explain the rules under GAAP to account for such allowances and why.

2. Personal morality and ethics make up the collective morality and ethics of a corporation. Given our discussion about the ethics of organizations in Chapter 3, evaluate the ethical climate at HealthSouth and the tone at the top established by key officers and company decisions.

3. Small concessions lead to greater compromises and, unchecked, will lead to serious ethical lapses and even crimes. Nobody sets out to end up in prison, but as detailed in the case, several people from HealthSouth in fact did end their careers that way; it all started with small, seemingly insignificant, compromises. Comment on these statements from the perspective of ethical decision making.

4. Looking at the findings of Craig Greene, the certified fraud examiner who investigated the HealthSouth fraud, explain why so-called red flags are important in an independent audit. In other words, what is the purpose of an auditor looking for financial information to sense the "alarm bells" that warn of danger ahead?

## Case 4-9

# Healthcare Fraud and Accountants' Ethical Obligations

Sue Kolb has been associated with the Valley View Hospital in Highlands Ranch, a small town in Colorado. Sue is a CPA licensed in Colorado and handles the hospital's financial affairs; eventually, she climbed the ladder to CFO after 10 years in the accounting department.

In 2012, Valley View's Board of Trustees hired Denver-based Bronco Resources, Inc. to manage the hospital's operations. Bronco, formerly a division of Hospital Corporation of America (HCA), claimed that they could maximize the federal government's reimbursement for hospital expenses.

Kolb found out that Bronco was using a secret accounting system devised by HCA to cheat the government out of Medicare payments. Bronco, and similar companies around the country, had been keeping two sets of accounting records for reporting the healthcare costs of Medicare patients. One set inflated the costs that were charged to the federal government.

The other set, for internal use, listed the actual costs of hospital operations.

Kolb questioned the company's accounting methods and threatened not to go along with the fraud. She was told by the CEO that she would be fired if she followed through on the threat.

## Questions

1. Who are the stakeholders in this case, and what are their interests?

2. What are Kolb's ethical obligations with respect to the Medicare fraud and her reporting it within Valley View under the AICPA Code of Professional Conduct?

3. What would you do at this point if you were Sue Kolb, and why?

## Case 4-10

# Independence Violations at PwC

PricewaterhouseCoopers (PwC) was involved in a series of independence violations in the late 1990s and early 2000s that resulted in strengthening the independence rules for auditors. We discuss these situations in two parts.

## Part I

On January 6, 2000, the SEC made public a report by independent consultant Jess Fardella, who was appointed by the commission in March 1999 to conduct a review of possible independence rule violations by PwC arising from ownership of client-issued securities. The report found significant violations of the firm's, the profession's, and the SEC's auditor independence rules.

## Background

On January 14, 1999, the commission issued an Opinion and Order Pursuant to Rule 102(e) of the commission's Rules of Practice, *In the Matter of PricewaterhouseCoopers LLP* (Securities Exchange Act of 1934, Release No. 40945) ("Order"),[1] which censured PwC for violating auditor independence rules and improper professional conduct. Pursuant to the settlement reached with the commission, PwC agreed, among other things, to complete an internal review by Fardella to identify instances in which the firm's partners or professionals owned securities of public audit clients of PwC in contravention of applicable rules and regulations concerning independence.

The independent consultant's report discloses that a substantial number of PwC professionals, particularly partners, had violations of the independence rules, and that many had multiple violations. The review found excusable mistakes, but it also attributed the violations to laxity and insensitivity to the importance of independence compliance. According to Fardella's report, PwC acknowledged that the review disclosed widespread independence noncompliance that reflected serious structural and cultural problems in the firm.

## Results of the Independent Consultant's Report

The report summarizes results of the internal review at PwC, which included two key parts: PwC professionals were requested in March 1999 to self-report independence violations; and the independent consultant randomly tested a sample of the responses for completeness and accuracy. The results are as follows:

1. Almost half of the PwC partners—1,301 out of a total of 2,698—self-reported at least one independence violation.

[1]Available at www.sec.gov/pdf/pwclaw.pdf.

The 1,301 partners who reported a violation reported an average of 5 violations; 153 partners had more than 10 violations each. Of 8,064 reported violations, 81.3 percent were reported by partners and 17.4 percent by managers; 45.2 percent of the violations were reported by partners who perform services related to audits of financial statements.

2. Almost half of the reported violations involved direct investments by PwC professionals in securities, mutual funds, bank accounts, or insurance products associated with a client. Almost 32 percent of reported violations, or 2,565 instances, involved holdings of a client's stock or stock options.

3. A total of 6 of 11 partners at the senior management level who oversaw PwC's independence program self-reported violations. Each of the 12 regional partners who helped administer PwC's independence program reported at least 1 violation; one reported 38 violations and another reported 34 violations.

4. In addition, 31 of the 43 partners who comprise PwC's Board of Partners and its U.S. Leadership Committee self-reported at least 1 violation. Four of these had more than 20 violations; one of these partners had 41 violations and another had 40 violations.

These random tests of the self-reporting process indicated that a far greater percentage of individuals had independence violations than was reported. Despite clear warnings that the SEC was overseeing the self-reporting process, the random tests of those reports indicated that 77.5 percent of PwC partners failed to self-report at least one independence violation. The combined results of the self-reporting and random tests of those reports indicated that approximately 86.5 percent of PwC partners and 10.5 percent of all other PwC professionals had independence violations.

The independent consultant's report identifies key weaknesses in the systems PwC had used to prevent or detect independence violations:

1. Reporting systems relied on the individuals themselves to sort through their own investments and interests for violations.

2. Efforts to educate professionals about the independence rules and their responsibilities to the client to comply with the rules were insufficient.

3. Resolution of reported violations was not documented adequately.

4. Reporting systems did not focus on the reporting of violations that were deemed to be resolved before annual confirmations were submitted.

The consultant's report concludes that the numbers of violations alone, as PwC acknowledged, reflect serious structural and cultural problems that were rooted in both its legacy firms (Price Waterhouse and Coopers & Lybrand). Although a large percentage of the reported and unreported violations is attributable solely to the merger, an even larger portion is not; thus, the situation revealed by the internal investigation is not a one-time breakdown explained solely by the merger. Nor can the magnitude of the reported and unreported violations be attributed simply to less familiar independence rules such as those pertaining to brokerage, bank, and sweep accounts. At least half of the reported and unreported violations consisted of interests held by a reporting PwC professional himself or herself, and most of the violations arose from either mutual fund or stock holdings. Independence compliance at PwC and its legacy firms was dependent largely on individual initiative. This system failed, as PwC has acknowledged.

## Changes Needed

As accounting firms have grown larger, acquired more clients, and provided more services, and as investment opportunities and financial arrangements have increased in number and complexity, well-designed and extensive controls are needed both to facilitate independence compliance and to discourage and detect noncompliance. The violations discussed in the consultant's report had come to light as a result of a commission-ordered review after professional self-regulatory procedures failed to detect such violations. As a result, the SEC requested the then-current Public Oversight Board (largely replaced by the PCAOB) to sponsor similar independent reviews at other firms and oversee development of enhancements to quality control and other professional standards. The firm also agreed in a settlement to conduct the review and create a $2.5 million education fund after the SEC alleged that some of its accountants compromised their independence by owning stock in corporations that they audited.

PwC promised at the time to take steps to ensure that this didn't happen again. As a result of the inquiry, five partners of the firm and a slightly larger number of other employees had been dismissed, and other employees were disciplined, but not fired.

Two changes that resulted from the problems at PwC were (1) to define clearly family members and other close relatives of members of the attest engagement team that might create an independence impairment for the auditors because of the formers' ownership interests in a client and/or their position within the client, including having a financial reporting oversight role (Interpretation 101-1); and (2) to restrict the ability of audit personnel from having loans to or from banks and other financial institution clients (Interpretation 101-5).

## Questions

1. In commenting on the findings in the consultant's report, the then-chief accountant of the SEC, Lynn E. Turner, said, "This report is a sobering reminder that accounting professionals need to renew their commitment to the fundamental principle of auditor independence." Why is it so important for auditors to be independent of their clients? Explain the nature of the independence impairments at PwC with respect to the threats to independence discussed in the chapter.

2. Review question 19 in the "Discussion Questions" section at the end of the chapter. What are the commonalities between the facts of these two cases with respect to independence violations at PwC? How might the independence violations in these cases negatively affect the ability of an auditor to be objective in performing professional services and maintain her integrity?

## Part II

On July 17, 2002, the SEC announced a settlement with PwC and its broker-dealer affiliate, PricewaterhouseCoopers Securities LLC, for violations of the auditor independence rules. The auditor independence violations spanned a five-year period from 1996 to 2001 and arise from (1) PwC's use of prohibited contingent fee arrangements with 14 different audit clients for which PwC provided investment banking services, and (2) PwC's participation with two other audit clients, Pinnacle Holdings Inc. and Avon Products Inc., in the improper accounting of costs, including PwC's own consulting fees.

The SEC's order found that, by virtue of PwC's independence violations, the firm caused 16 PwC public audit clients to file financial statements with the SEC that did not comply with the reporting provisions of the federal securities laws. The order also found that, in connection with the improper accounting of its consulting fees, PwC caused two of those clients to violate the reporting, recordkeeping, and/or internal controls provisions of the federal securities laws. PwC and the firm agreed to pay a total of $5 million and PwC agreed to comply with significant remedial undertakings as a result of its settlement with the SEC. PwC also agreed to cease and desist from violating the auditor independence rules and to be censured for engaging in improper professional conduct.

The SEC's order found that PwC's independence violations involved 16 separate audits of 16 public companies, as follows:

- From 1996 to 2001, PwC and one of its predecessors, Coopers & Lybrand, entered into impermissible contingent fee arrangements with 14 public audit clients. In each instance, the client hired the auditing firm's investment bankers, either PricewaterhouseCoopers Securities LLC or Coopers & Lybrand Securities, to perform financial advisory services for a fee that depended on the success of the transaction the client was pursuing. These fee arrangements violated the accounting professions' own prohibition against contingent fee arrangements with audit clients and violated the SEC's independence rules. As a result, the SEC found that PwC lacked the requisite independence when it performed audits for these 14 public companies.

- In 1999 and 2000, PwC participated in and approved of the improper accounting of its own non-audit fees by two public audit clients, Pinnacle and Avon:
  - In 1999 and 2000, while accounting for a 1999 acquisition of certain assets of Motorola, Inc., PwC assisted Pinnacle in establishing more than $24 million in improper reserves and in improperly capitalizing approximately $8.5 million in costs, including $6.8 million in fees paid to PwC for consulting and other non-auditing services that should have been expensed. In April and May 2001, Pinnacle restated its accounting for the 1999 acquisition, and in December 2001, the SEC issued a settled cease and desist order against Pinnacle. See *In the Matter of Pinnacle Holdings, Inc.,* Exchange Act Release No. 45135 (Dec. 6, 2001).
  - In the first quarter of 1999 and in its 1999 audit of Avon's financial statements, PwC assisted in and approved of Avon's improper accounting of an impaired asset that included PwC's non-audit consulting fees. In April 1999, after nearly three years and an investment of approximately $42 million, Avon stopped an uncompleted order-management software project that PwC consultants had attempted to develop for Avon's internal use. Instead of writing off all of the project's costs in the first quarter of 1999, however, Avon improperly retained $26 million, which was comprised mostly of PwC's own consulting fees. PwC participated in and approved of Avon's improper accounting, and also contributed to Avon's misleading disclosures concerning the accounting.
- For both Pinnacle and Avon, the SEC found that PwC failed to exercise the objective and impartial judgment required by the independence rules.

## Questions

1. What are the dangers of accepting contingent fees from audit clients for performing non-auditing services? Assume that in such situations the auditor can, in fact, make independent auditing decisions regardless of the contingent fee arrangements. Would independence be impaired in such situations?

2. How did Avon's accounting for the project costs on the abandoned order-management software project violate GAAP? How did PwC's role in the capitalized costs for consulting services violate its ethical obligations?

# Chapter 5

# Fraud in Financial Statements and Auditor Responsibilities

## Ethics Reflection

In Chapter 3, we addressed the issue of occupational fraud and how to create an organization environment that supports ethical behavior. In this chapter, we focus on financial statement fraud and discuss audit-related responsibilities. The 2012 *Global Fraud Survey* published by the Association of Certified Fraud Examiners (ACFE),[1] which covers the 2008–2012 period, indicates that on average, a financial statement fraud lasts twenty-seven months prior to being detected. Financial statement fraud schemes occur when an employee (i.e., the controller or chief financial officer/CFO) *intentionally* causes a misstatement or omission of material information in the organization's financial reports (e.g., recording fictitious revenues, understating reported expenses, artificially inflating reported assets, or failing to record liabilities). A key point is that fraud is a deliberate act and it is designed to deceive another party or parties, such as investors and creditors. The ACFE survey found that while financial statement fraud made up only 8 percent of the fraud cases examined, the median loss of $1 million was the greatest of all types of fraud. A financial statement fraud can lead to whistleblower actions under both the Federal False Claims Act and the Dodd-Frank Financial Reform Act.

Financial statement fraud undermines the reliability, quality, transparency, and integrity of the financial reporting process and jeopardizes the integrity and objectivity of auditors and auditing firms. Financial statement fraud diminishes the confidence of the capital markets, as well as market participants, in the reliability of financial information, and as a consequence, makes the capital markets less efficient. It causes devastation in the normal operations and performance of alleged companies and erodes public confidence and trust in the accounting and auditing professions. Ultimately, financial statement fraud translates to massive stockholder losses and debts to creditors, not to mention emotional trauma to employees who lose their jobs and retirement funds.

Financial statement fraud may be committed by the senior and mid-level management of an organization to fraudulently enhance the financial health of a business and enrich one's own net worth. Senior management may indulge in fraudulent cover-ups motivated by the desire to exceed the earnings or revenue growth expectations of financial analysts, to comply with loan agreements, to increase the amount of financing available from asset-based loans, and to meet a lender's criteria for granting/extending loan facilities. They may also fudge the statements to create a rosy picture for the shareholders.

Students should understand the nature and scope of an audit in accordance with generally accepted auditing standards because the professional and ethical responsibilities of auditors are directly linked to the proper conduct of an audit. As you read this chapter, reflect on the following: (1) What are the red flags that are indicators fraud may exist? (2) What is the difference between an error, a fraud, and an illegal act and related audit responsibilities? (3) What are the auditor's responsibilities to detect and report fraud? (4) What is the role of internal controls and risk assessment in preventing and detecting fraud?

I would want [the auditor], on the basis of his credentials, his professional responsibility and integrity, to assert that, from the alternatives in GAAP, he has determined the options and the particular alternatives that he deemed to be most appropriate and fairest under the circumstances. Note the superlatives "most appropriate" and "fairest." . . . At present, the words used by the auditor when he "certifies" the financial statements make it appear that this is precisely what he is presently doing; but those of us who are sophisticated know that the words in the auditor's certificate about the statements presenting the financial condition and operations fairly [present fairly] are specious. I am presently urging that this appearance become reality. While our profession usually prefers to gloss over this condition, namely, the auditor's abdication of primary responsibility for the statements, when it suits the profession's purposes the condition is permitted to surface. This usually occurs in the process of litigation, when an accountant is found with his procedures down.

*Abraham Briloff, a frequent critic of the accounting profession and a well-regarded academician, commenting on whether responsibility for financial statements should be shifted from management to the independent auditor.*

## Fraud in Financial Statements and the Audit Function

Abe Briloff made these prescient comments in 1978. They ring as true today as they did more than 30 years ago. The series of congressional investigations of the accounting profession that were discussed in Chapter 4 seem to indicate that auditors may not have learned their lesson over the years, as accounting frauds rear their ugly head about once every 10 years.

An *audit* is an examination of the financial statements prepared by management and the rendering of an independent opinion that the statements have been prepared in accordance with generally accepted accounting principles (GAAP). Securities and Exchange Commission (SEC) rules require that publicly owned companies have an audit.

The Public Company Accounting Oversight Board (PCAOB) establishes audit standards for the independent auditors and ethics standards for companies issuing stock on established exchanges [i.e., the New York State Exchange (NYSE) and NASDAQ]. The American Institute of Certified Public Accountants (AICPA) issues generally accepted auditing standards (GAAS),* some of which have been adopted by PCAOB and some pertain solely to private companies.

---

*The meaning of GAAS was changed on June 1, 2012, when the AICPA completed its clarity project. At that time the Auditing Standards Board of the AICPA redrafted almost all of the auditing sections in Codification of Statements on Auditing Standards (contained in *AICPA Professional Standards*). The purpose of the change is for GAAS to more clearly state the objectives of the auditor and the requirements with which the auditor has to comply when conducting an audit in accordance with GAAS.

The independent auditor's responsibility is to audit and report on the financial statements prepared by management. Perceptions of the shortcomings in the effectiveness of independent audits erode public confidence in the integrity of the financial reporting system. In the past, an "expectations gap" existed—that is, the difference between what the public and the users of financial statements perceive as the responsibilities of accountants and auditors and what accountants and auditors themselves see as their responsibilities. A survey of investor views of audit assurance going back to 1994 by Epstein and Geiger indicates that the investing public holds auditors to a much higher level of accountability for detecting material misstatements due to error and fraud than the profession has assumed. The authors conclude that the profession's perception that an audit should provide only *reasonable assurance* of financial statement accuracy is held by a minority of investors. The majority of investors expect an audit to provide absolute assurance that the financial statements are free of all types of material misstatements, thereby confirming the existence of the gap.[2]

The auditing profession recognizes its obligation to look for fraud by being alert to certain red flags, assessing the control environment of the organization, passing judgment on internal controls, and considering audit risk and materiality when performing an audit of financial statements in accordance with generally accepted auditing standards. However, this is a far cry from guaranteeing that fraud will be detected, especially when top management goes to great lengths to hide it from the auditors.

The audit standard titled *Consideration of Fraud in a Financial Statement Audit* (AU 240), addresses ethics in an organization by identifying the organization's responsibility to create a culture of honesty and ethics and to communicate acceptable behavior and expectations of each employee clearly. The culture is rooted in a strong set of core values that provide the foundation for employees as to how the organization conducts its business. It also allows an entity to develop an ethical framework that covers (1) fraudulent financial reporting, (2) misappropriation of assets, and (3) corruption.[3] The ethical values discussed in Chapters 1 and 2 provide the basis for such a culture, including honesty, trustworthiness, reliability, responsibility, and integrity.

Recent attempts by the auditing profession to close the gap have focused on better defining audit risk. *Materiality in Planning and Performing an Audit* (AU 320) defines audit risk as the risk that the auditor may unknowingly fail to modify appropriately his opinion on financial statements that are materially misstated. In other words, when the statements are materially misstated, the auditor should not give an unqualified (now referred to as unmodified) opinion but should modify the opinion as either qualified because of that matter or an adverse opinion if the material misstatement leads to the conclusion that the financial statements, taken as a whole, do not present fairly the financial position, results of operations, and cash flows.[4]

Fraudulent financial reporting involves either intentional misstatements or omissions of amounts or disclosures in financial statements to deceive financial statement users. Fraudulent financial reporting generally occurs in one of three ways: (1) Deception such as manipulation, falsification, or alteration of accounting records or supporting documents from which the financial statements are prepared; (2) misrepresentation in, or intentional omission from, the financial statements of events, transactions, or other significant information; and (3) intentional misapplication of accounting principles relating to measurement, recognition, classification, presentation, or disclosure. Accountants and auditors who go along with the fraud fail in their ethical obligation to place the public interest above all else. Because fraud involves an intentional act, the perpetrator of the falsehood knows, or should know, that what she proposes to do is wrong. It is dishonest and fails to consider stakeholder obligations. Once financial statements have been falsified, the trust relationship between an auditor and the public breaks down.

The audit of financial statements and auditor assessment of internal controls are the primary methods of detecting fraudulent financial statements. We begin the chapter with a discussion of errors, fraud, and illegal acts and address the auditor's obligations. Later on, we will examine the audit report and audit opinions. Finally, we review internal control requirements under the *Internal Control—Integrated Framework* of the Committee of Sponsoring Organizations of the Treadway Commission (COSO).

# Nature and Causes of Misstatements

The auditor has a responsibility to plan and perform the audit to obtain reasonable assurance about whether the financial statements are free of material misstatement, whether caused by error or fraud. Because of the nature of audit evidence and the characteristics of fraud, the auditor is able to obtain reasonable, but not absolute, assurance that material misstatements are detected. The auditor has no responsibility to plan and perform the audit to obtain reasonable assurance that misstatements, whether caused by errors or fraud, that are not material to the financial statements are detected.

According to AU450, *Forming an Opinion and Reporting on Financial Statements,* the representation in the auditor's standard report regarding fair presentation, in all material respects and in conformity with GAAP, indicates the auditor's belief that the financial statements, taken as a whole, are not materially misstated.[5] Misstatements can result from errors or fraud and may consist of any of the following:

1. An inaccuracy in gathering or processing data from which financial statements are prepared
2. A difference between the amount, classification, or presentation of a reported financial statement element, account, or item and the way that it should have been reflected under GAAP
3. The omission of a financial statement element, account, or item
4. A financial statement disclosure that is not presented in conformity with GAAP
5. The omission of information required to be disclosed in conformity with GAAP
6. An incorrect accounting estimate due to oversight, misrepresentation of facts, or fraud
7. Management's judgments concerning an accounting estimate or the selection or application of accounting policies that the auditor may consider unreasonable or inappropriate

## Errors, Fraud, and Illegal Acts

Material errors, fraud, and illegal acts represent situations where the financial statements should be restated. The following briefly describes the nature and effects of such acts.

### Errors

An *error* can occur due to unintentional misstatements or omissions of amounts or disclosures in the financial statements. Errors may involve mistakes in gathering or processing data, unreasonable accounting estimates arising from oversight or misinterpretation of facts, or mistakes in the application of GAAP. Auditors are responsible for detecting errors that have a material effect on the financial statements and reporting their findings to the audit committee. Errors are typically recorded by adjusting the opening balance of retained earnings for the prior period adjustment to net income.

### Fraud

*Fraud,* as the term is used in *AU 240,* relates to intentional acts that cause a misstatement of the financial statements.[6] Misstatements due to fraud may occur due to either (1) fraudulent financial reporting or (2) misappropriation of assets. It is important to remember that fraud does not occur by accident. Fraud exists when there is a deliberate decision made to deceive another party, such as the investors and creditors. As will be discussed in Chapter 6, the auditor has a legal liability for fraud to both the client and third parties who may have relied on the misstatement to their detriment.

Financial statement fraud can also be viewed as management fraud and is distinguished from other types of fraud both by the nature of the perpetrators and by the method of deception. In its most common form, management fraud involves top management's deceptive manipulation of financial statements.[7]

Let's assume that Risky Software, Inc., records revenue from the sale of software of $1 million on December 28, 2013. The sale requires Risky to provide support services, including a 24-hour help desk, for three years. Risky records all the $1 million of revenue in 2013. However, GAAP requires that the company should separate from the sale price the relevant amount that represents support services and record it as deferred revenue. This is known as *accounting for the multiple elements of a transaction.* The deferred amount would then be matched with the support services provided over the next three years.

The intent of management determines whether the misapplication of GAAP is an error in judgment or a deliberate decision to inflate revenues. In a court of law, it typically comes down to the credibility of the CFO and chief executive officer (CEO) who are charged with fraud. Absent a "smoking gun," the court might look for parallel actions by these top officers, such as selling their own shares of corporate stock after the fraudulent act but before it becomes public knowledge, as occurred at Enron and WorldCom.

### Illegal Acts

*Consideration of Laws and Regulations in an Audit of Financial Statements* (AU 250), defines illegal acts as violations of laws or governmental regulations. For example, a violation of the Foreign Corrupt Practices Act (FCPA) that prohibits bribery constitutes an illegal act. *AU 250* discusses illegal acts in the context of compliance with laws and regulations and would include acts attributable to the entity whose financial statements are under audit or as acts by management or employees acting on behalf of the entity. Such acts expose the company to both legal liability and public disgrace. The auditor's responsibility is to determine the proper accounting and financial reporting treatment of a violation once it has been determined that a violation has in fact occurred.[8]

The auditor's responsibility is to detect and report misstatements resulting from illegal acts that have a direct and material effect on the determination of financial statement amounts (i.e., they require an accounting entry). The auditors' responsibility for detecting direct and material effect violations is greater than their responsibility to detect illegal acts arising from laws that only indirectly affect the client's financial statements.[9] An example of the former would be violations of tax laws that affect accruals and the amount recognized as income tax liability for the period. Tax law would be violated, triggering an adjustment in the current period financial statements if, say, a company, for tax purposes, were to expense an item all in one year that should have been capitalized and written off over three years. Examples of items with an indirect effect on the statements include the potential violation of other laws such as occupational safety and health, environmental protection, and equal employment regulations. The events are due to operational, not financial, matters and their financial statement effect is indirect, such as a possible contingent liability that should be disclosed in the notes to the financial statements.

The auditor's obligation when she concludes that an illegal act has or is likely to have occurred is first to assess the impact of the actions on the financial statements including materiality considerations. This should be done regardless of any direct or indirect effect on the statements. The auditor should consult with legal counsel and any other specialists in this regard. Illegal acts should be reported to those charged with governance such as the audit committee. The auditor should consider whether the client has taken appropriate remedial action concerning the act. Such remedial action may include taking disciplinary actions, establishing controls to safeguard against recurrence, and, if necessary, reporting the effects of the illegal acts in the financial statements. Ordinarily, if the client does not take the remedial action deemed necessary by the auditor, then the auditor should withdraw from the engagement.[10] This action on the part of the auditor makes clear that she will not be associated in any way with illegal activities.

## Reporting an Illegal Act

The auditor should assure herself that the audit committee is informed as soon as practicable and prior to the issuance of the auditor's report with respect to illegal acts that come to the auditor's attention. The auditor need not communicate matters that are clearly inconsequential and may reach agreement in advance with the audit committee on the nature of such matters to be communicated. *AU 250* requires that the communication should describe the act, the circumstances of its occurrence, and the effect on the financial statements.[11]

The standards for reporting illegal acts differ for material and inconsequential items. These standards seem to err on the side of protecting the auditor's position in a legal matter rather than strict honesty because certain items can be ignored even though they violate the law. As discussed in Chapter 1, honesty requires that we should express the truth as we know it and without deception. By leaving out truthful (inconsequential) information in auditor communications, *AU 250* sanctions unethical behavior. Some may view our perspective as being too harsh given the perceived lack of a material monetary effect on the financial statements. Others may find it impractical given the realities of auditing. But we believe that it is a slippery slope once distinctions are made as to whether acts that are inherently wrong by their nature are not reported. Moreover, even inconsequential items can become consequential if the pattern of misstatement persists.

The Private Securities Litigation Reform Act (PSLRA) of 1995 places additional requirements upon public companies registered with the SEC and their auditors when (1) the illegal act has a material effect on the financial statements, (2) senior management and the board of directors have not taken appropriate remedial action, and (3) the failure to take remedial action is reasonably expected to warrant departure from a standard (i.e., unmodified audit report) or to warrant resignation.

When the auditor believes that the illegal act has a material effect on the financial statements and the matter has been reported to the client, the board of directors has one business day to inform the SEC. If the board decides not to inform the SEC, the auditor must provide the same report to the SEC within one business day or resign from the engagement within one business day.[12] In either case, the ethical obligation of confidentiality is waived so that the auditor can provide the necessary information and the SEC can live up to its responsibility to protect investor interests. If auditors do not fulfill this legal obligation, the SEC can impose a monetary fine on them.

Notwithstanding the reporting obligations described above, disclosure of an illegal act to parties other than the client's senior management and its audit committee or board of directors is not ordinarily part of the auditor's responsibility, and such disclosure would be precluded by the auditor's ethical or legal obligation of confidentiality, unless the matter affects his opinion on the financial statements. The auditor should recognize, however, that in the following circumstances, a duty to notify parties outside the client may exist:[13]

- When the entity reports an auditor change under the appropriate securities law on Form 8-K

- To a successor auditor when the successor makes inquiries in accordance with *Terms of Engagement* (AU 210)

**EXHIBIT 5.1**    Auditors' Responsibility to Detect Errors, Illegal Acts, and Fraud

| | Responsible for Detection | | Required to Communicate Findings | |
|---|---|---|---|---|
| | **Material** | **Immaterial** | **Material** | **Immaterial** |
| **Errors** | Yes | No | Yes (audit committee) | No |
| **Illegal acts** | Yes (direct effect) | No | Yes (audit committee) | Yes (one level above) |
| **Fraud** | Yes | No | Yes (audit committee) | Yes (by low-level employee, to one level above) (by management-level employee, to audit committee) |

- In response to a subpoena
- To a funding agency or other specified agency in accordance with requirements for the audits of entities that receive financial assistance from a government agency

Because potential conflicts with the auditor's ethical and legal obligations for confidentiality may be complex, the auditor may wish to consult with legal counsel before discussing illegal acts with parties other than the client.

## Auditors' Responsibilities for Fraud Prevention, Detection, and Reporting

Auditors are responsible for detecting material fraud and reporting it to the board of directors. The requirements are similar to those for illegal acts with a direct effect on the financial statements. Louwers et al. provide a useful summary of the auditor's responsibility to detect errors, illegal acts, and fraud.[14] The summary appears in Exhibit 5.1.

The first line of defense against fraud is to have an effective system of internal controls and an independent internal audit function. As described in Chapter 3, the internal auditors should have direct and unrestricted access to the audit committee. The head of internal auditing should not have to discuss matters pertaining to the existence of material misstatements in the financial statements with the CFO and CEO, both of whom may be responsible for the fraud. Recall that at WorldCom, Cynthia Cooper eventually bypassed Scott Sullivan, the CFO, after she concluded that he was not about to do anything about the fraud—which wasn't surprising because it was a fraud that he himself had initiated. Instead, she approached the chair of the audit committee with her concerns and, after dealing with some resistance and soliciting help from the external auditors, she was successful in getting the company to come clean about its improper accounting.

## The Fraud Triangle

*AU 240* defines *fraudulent financial reporting* as "intentional misstatements or omissions of amounts or disclosures in financial statements designed to deceive financial statement users where the effect causes the financial statements not to be presented, in all material respects, in conformity with GAAP." The reasons for the deception are many and are identified by this auditing standard as part of "the Fraud Triangle" depicted in Exhibit 5.2.

Three conditions generally are present when fraud occurs. First, management or other employees have an incentive or are under pressure, which provides the motivation for the fraud. Second, circumstances exist that provide an opportunity for a fraud to be perpetrated. Examples include the absence of or ineffective internal controls and management's override of internal controls. Third, those involved are able to rationalize committing a fraudulent act. Recall that in the WorldCom case, Betty Vinson rationalized that it would be a one-time request by higher-ups to falsify accounting information.

**EXHIBIT 5.2**
**The Fraud Triangle**

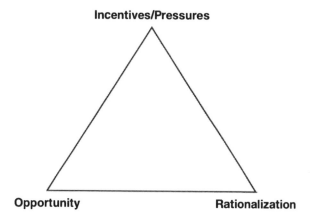

As noted in *AU 240,* some individuals possess an attitude, character, or set of ethical values that allow them to commit a dishonest act knowingly and intentionally. For the most part, this is the exception rather than the rule. However, even honest individuals can commit fraud in an environment that imposes sufficient pressure on them. The greater the incentive or pressure, the more likely that an individual will be able to rationalize the acceptability of committing fraud.[15]

## Incentives/Pressures to Commit Fraud

The incentive to commit fraud typically is a self-serving one. Egoism drives the fraud in the sense that the perpetrator perceives some benefit by committing the fraud, such as a higher bonus or promotion. The fraud may be caused by internal budget pressures or financial analysts' earnings expectations that are not being met. Personal pressures also might lead to fraud if, for example, a member of top management is deep in personal debt or has a gambling or drug problem. In a 60-Minutes interview (http://www.youtube.com/watch?v=MYmLaVYsyHw) with Dennis Kozlowski, the former CEO of Tyco who was sentenced to a jail term of 8 1/3–25 years, Kozlowski said his motivation to steal from the company was to keep up with "the masters of the universe." This meant keeping up with other CEOs of large and successful companies that had pay packages in the hundreds of millions. In 2005, the jury, in New York State Supreme Court in Manhattan, found that Kozlowski and ex-Chief Financial Officer Marc Swartz stole about $137 million from Tyco in unauthorized compensation and made $410 million from the sale of inflated stock.

### Techniques Used to Falsify Financial Information

The techniques used to falsify financial information range from the basic to the exotic. The Waste Management fraud involved the arbitrary lengthening of the useful lives of trash hauling equipment to reduce annual depreciation charges and increase earnings. The Enron fraud involved financially structured transactions that created special-purpose entities (SPEs) that borrowed funds and then shifted the amounts to Enron in return for some under-performing asset. The liability was kept off Enron's books, a form of off-balance-sheet financing. The Enron saga will be discussed in full in Chapter 7.

Financial results can be manipulated through the use of bogus invoices to record revenue, as was the case at ZZZZ Best. In some instances, a company might manipulate its own accounting records to achieve its goal. MicroStrategy is a company that backdated sales agreements to push revenue back into the preceding period, such as by back dating a transaction to December 31 that wasn't legally approved until January of the following year.

### Misappropriation of Assets

The misappropriation of assets involves the theft of company assets where the action leads to financial statements that do not conform to GAAP. For example, an employee might write company checks payable to himself for personal expenses. The diversion of company funds for personal purposes understates cash and overstates expenses. Often, the guilty employee tries to "bury" the personal expense in an innocuous account such as miscellaneous or sundry expenses. The audit procedure that should catch such activities is to prepare a bank reconciliation or proof of cash and examine each check for proper authorization and recording.

Some fraudsters seem to have no shame. In the ZZZZ Best fraud, Barry Minkow set up front companies as clients that issued checks from its bank account to pay for services never performed. The checks were then deposited into the ZZZZ Best account and revenue was recorded. Minkow would then use some of the money to pay for personal expenses and would bury the expenses in miscellaneous accounts. The original funds paid by the fictitious company to ZZZZ Best came from funds diverted by Minkow and his cohorts to create the illusion of the front company.

## Opportunity to Commit Fraud

The second side of the Fraud Triangle connects the pressure or incentive to commit fraud with the opportunity to carry out the act. Employees who have access to assets such as cash and inventory should be monitored closely through an effective system of internal controls that helps safeguard assets. For example, the company should segregate cash processing responsibilities, including the opening of mail that contains remittance advices, along with checks for the payment of services; the recording of the receipts as cash and a reduction of receivables; the depositing of the money in the bank; and the reconciling of the balance in cash on the books with the bank statement balance. Obviously, when the fraud is perpetrated by the CEO and CFO, as was the case with Tyco, access is a given.

The opportunity to commit fraud also can be seen when top management backdates stock options to increase the potential gain for those executives receiving the options. For example, if a company's stock price is rapidly increasing and top management wants to attract new employees to the company, management may agree to set a strike (exercise) price that is dated weeks or months prior to the grant date. The executive gains because of the increased spread between the exercise price and future market price, assuming that the stock price continues to rise. The backdating options problem first became public in the summer of 2006 and was investigated throughout the decade of the 2000s. The SEC Web site describes dozens of such cases, including that of Monster Worldwide Inc.,[16] which is described next.

### Backdating Stock Options—Monster Worldwide, Inc.

On May 18, 2009, the SEC charged that employment search company Monster Worldwide, Inc., schemed to secretly backdate stock options granted to thousands of Monster officers, directors, and employees. Monster agreed to pay a $2.5 million penalty to settle the SEC's charges that the company defrauded investors by granting backdated, undisclosed, "in-the-money" stock options (where current market value exceeds option price) while failing to record required noncash charges for option-related compensation expenses.[17]

According to the SEC, "Monster misled investors by failing to report hundreds of millions of dollars of expenses. Backdating stock options made the company look like it had more money than it really did." The SEC's complaint alleged that in connection with this scheme, Monster filed false and materially misleading statements concerning the true grant date and exercise price of stock options in its annual, quarterly, and current reports, proxy statements, and registration statements. Many of these documents also falsely represented that stock options were being granted at fair market value. Further, Monster failed to record and disclose the compensation expense associated with the in-the-money portion of stock option grants. As a result, Monster materially overstated its quarterly and annual earnings in its financial statements and was required to restate its historical financial results for 1997–2005 in a cumulative pretax amount of approximately $339.5 million and to record additional noncash charges for option related compensation expenses.

## Rationalization for the Fraud

Fraud perpetrators typically try to explain away their actions as acceptable. For corporate executives, rationalizations to commit fraud might include thoughts such as "We need to protect our shareholders and keep the stock price high," "All companies use aggressive accounting practices," "It's for the good of the company," or "The problem is temporary and will be offset by future positive results."[18] In the Tyco case, Kozlowski stated in his 60-Minutes interview that he wasn't doing anything different from what was done by his predecessor. He took the low road of ethical behavior and rationalized his actions by essentially claiming that everyone (at least at Tyco) does what he did by misappropriating company resources for personal purposes.

Other rationalizations might include "My boss doesn't pay me enough" or "I'll pay the money back before anyone notices it's gone." The underlying motivation for the fraud in these instances may be dissatisfaction with the company and/or personal financial need. *AU 240* provides an extensive list of examples of the elements of fraud that can lead to fraudulent financial reporting. These are presented in Exhibit 5.3.

## Tyco Fraud

### *Failure of the Corporate Governance System*

Returning to the Tyco fraud, the corporate governance system at Tyco completely broke down. Most members of Tyco's board of directors benefited personally as a result of Tyco's practices. For example, one board member worked for a law firm that "just happened" to receive as much as $2 million in business from Tyco. This person's pay at the law firm was linked to the amount of work that he helped bring in from Tyco. Another director received a $10 million payment for help in engineering an acquisition for Tyco. The problem here was (1) Tyco board members did business with the company, (2) directors and officers borrowed money from the company, and (3) related-party disclosures were not made in the financial statements. Clearly, board members lacked independence from management and the company, and their own greed contributed to the lax oversight at Tyco.

Exhibit 5.4 applies the Fraud Triangle concept to Tyco. Notice how the opportunities to commit fraud because of lax oversight and the complicity of those in corporate governance enabled the fraud. Also, Kozlowski seemed to come up with every excuse imaginable to rationalize the fraud.

The Tyco fraud serves as a shocking example of what can happen when all systems involved in the governance of a corporation fail at the same time. Kozlowski sold $258 million of Tyco stock back to the company, on top of salary and other compensation valued near $30 million. By the time Kozlowski quit under indictment for sales tax fraud in 2002, $80 billion of Tyco's shareholder wealth had evaporated.

**EXHIBIT 5.3**

**Risk Factors Relating to Misstatements Arising from Fraudulent Financial Reporting**

## Incentives/Pressures

a. *Incentives* exist because financial stability or profitability is threatened by economic, industry, or entity operating conditions, such as (or as indicated by):

- High degree of competition or market saturation, accompanied by declining margins
- High vulnerability to rapid changes, such as changes in technology, product obsolescence, or interest rates
- Significant declines in customer demand and increasing business failures in either the industry or overall economy
- Operating losses making the threat of bankruptcy, foreclosure, or hostile takeover imminent
- Recurring negative cash flows from operations and an inability to generate cash flows from operations while reporting earnings and earnings growth
- Rapid growth or unusual profitability, especially compared to that of other companies in the same industry
- New accounting, statutory, or regulatory requirements

b. Excessive *pressure* exists for management to meet the requirements or expectations of third parties due to the following:

- Profitability or trend level expectations of investment analysts, institutional investors, significant creditors, or other external parties (particularly expectations that are unduly aggressive or unrealistic), including expectations created by management in, for example, overly optimistic press releases or annual report messages
- Need to obtain additional debt or equity financing to stay competitive—including financing of major research and development or capital expenditures
- Marginal ability to meet exchange listing requirements or debt repayment or other debt covenant requirements
- Perceived or real adverse effects of reporting poor financial results on significant pending transactions, such as business combinations or contract awards

c. Information available indicates that management's or those charged with governance's personal financial situation is threatened by the entity's financial performance arising from the following:

- Significant financial interests in the entity
- Significant portions of their compensation (for example, bonuses, stock options, and -earn-out arrangements) being contingent upon achieving aggressive targets for stock price, operating results, financial position, or cash flow
- Personal guarantees of debts of the entity

d. There is excessive pressure on management or operating personnel to meet financial targets set up by those charged with governance or management, including sales or profitability incentive goals.

## Opportunities

a. The nature of the industry or the entity's operations provides opportunities to engage in fraudulent financial reporting that can arise from the following:

- Significant related-party transactions not in the ordinary course of business or with related entities not audited or audited by another firm
- A strong financial presence or ability to dominate a certain industry sector that allows the entity to dictate terms or conditions to suppliers or customers that may result in inappropriate or non-arm's-length transactions
- Assets, liabilities, revenues, or expenses based on significant estimates that involve subjective judgments or uncertainties that are difficult to corroborate
- Significant, unusual, or highly complex transactions, especially those close to period end that pose difficult "substance over form" questions
- Significant operations located or conducted across international borders in jurisdictions where differing business environments and cultures exist
- Significant bank accounts or subsidiary or branch operations in tax-haven jurisdictions for which there appears to be no clear business justification

b. There is ineffective monitoring of management as a result of the following:

- Domination of management by a single person or small group (in a nonowner-managed business) without compensating controls
- Ineffective oversight **over** the financial reporting process **and** internal **control** by those charged with governance

c. There is a complex or unstable organizational structure, as evidenced by the following:
- Difficulty in determining the organization or individuals that have controlling interest in the entity
- Overly complex organizational structure involving unusual legal entities or managerial lines of authority
- High turnover of senior management, counsel, or board members

d. Internal control components are deficient as a result of the following:
- Inadequate monitoring of controls, including automated controls and controls over interim financial reporting (where external reporting is required)
- High turnover rates or employment of ineffective accounting, internal audit, or information technology staff
- Ineffective accounting and information systems, including situations involving significant deficiencies or material weaknesses in internal control

### Attitudes/Rationalizations

Risk factors reflective of attitudes/rationalizations by those charged with governance, management, or employees that allow them to engage in and/or justify fraudulent financial reporting, may not be susceptible to observation by the auditor. Nevertheless, the auditor who becomes aware of the existence of such information should consider it in identifying the risks of material misstatement arising from fraudulent financial reporting. For example, auditors may become aware of the following information that may indicate a risk factor:

- Ineffective communication, implementation, support, or enforcement of the entity's values or ethical standards by management or the communication of inappropriate values or ethical standards
- Nonfinancial management's excessive participation in or preoccupation with the selection of accounting principles or the determination of significant estimates
- Known history of violations of securities laws or other laws and regulations, or claims against the entity, its senior management, or board members alleging fraud or violations of laws and regulations
- Excessive interest by management in maintaining or increasing the entity's stock price or earnings trend
- A practice by management of committing to analysts, creditors, and other third parties to achieve aggressive or unrealistic forecasts
- Management failing to correct known significant deficiencies or material weaknesses in internal control on a timely basis
- An interest by management in employing inappropriate means to minimize reported earnings for tax-motivated reasons

Kozlowski bought off the board of directors by providing personal favors. The audit committee was irrelevant. The company and its top officers violated its duty of care and loyalty to shareholder interests, which is the foundation of good governance. The external auditors for their part either didn't look too hard to find the fraud or looked the other way when it should have been detected.

### Auditor Failure

The news was not any better for PricewaterhouseCoopers LLP (PwC), the auditors for Tyco. On August 13, 2003, the SEC issued a cease-and-desist order against Richard P. Scalzo, the PwC engagement partner for the firm's audits of Tyco's financial statements for fiscal years 1997 through 2001. The commission's order found that Scalzo recklessly violated the antifraud provisions of the federal securities laws and engaged in improper professional conduct. On July 7, 2007, PwC agreed to pay $225 million to settle audit malpractice claims arising from the criminal misdeeds of top executives at Tyco, marking the largest single legal payout ever made by that firm and one of the biggest ever by an auditor.[19]

Of particular note with respect to the culture at Tyco that enabled the fraud to occur is the finding by the SEC that both PwC and its lead engagement partner failed to follow

**EXHIBIT 5.4**  Application of the Fraud Triangle to Tyco

| Incentive | Pressure | Opportunity | Rationalization |
|---|---|---|---|
| *Pursuit of self-interest:* Keeping up with the "masters of the universe" | Keep up with Wall Street expectations that were enamored with Kozlowski's aggressive management style. | There was lack of internal controls to support growth. | Claimed to need to "push the company," to continue to grow without putting into place the infrastructure to support some of that growth. |
| *Pursuit of self-interest:* Use of corporate funds for personal purposes | | Kozlowski was in a position to sign off on home purchases and elaborate use of corporate funds for personal purposes. | Victim of Enronitis and the jury's alleged distaste for the $100 million man; actions did not negatively affect employees as was the case with Enron's share price decline in 401(k) employee retirement funds. |
| *Pursuit of self-interest:* What's in it for me? | Mark Swartz (CFO) wanted in on the action. | Swartz benefited from the misuse of corporate assets for personal purposes so one element of oversight was compromised. | Did everything the way the "programs" were authorized to operate; did the same things as his predecessors. |
| *Pursuit of self-interest:* What's in it for me? | Concessions to get the board to buy into the fraud. | Members of the board also benefited; some misused corporate resources for personal purposes, thereby compromising this element of governance. | Did everything the way the "programs" were authorized to operate. |
| *Pursuit of self-interest:* Go along to get along | Auditors didn't want to lose Tyco as a client. | Auditors failed to assess the culture at Tyco (control environment) properly. | Activities were approved at the top management and board level. |

GAAS and failed in their professional obligations. *Accounting and Auditing Enforcement Release No. 1839* notes:

> Multiple and repeated facts provided notice to Scalzo regarding the integrity of Tyco's senior management and that Scalzo was reckless in not taking appropriate audit steps in the face of this information. By the end of the Tyco annual audit for its fiscal year ended September 30, 1998, if not before, those facts were sufficient to obligate Scalzo, pursuant to GAAS, to reevaluate the risk assessment of the Tyco audits and to perform additional audit procedures, including further audit testing of certain items (most notably, certain executive benefits, executive compensation, and related party transactions).

### Ethical Issues in Tyco Fraud

In addition to the illegal behavior and corporate governance failings, the bad actors in the Tyco fraud violated basic ethical standards of behavior. Kozlowski and his cohorts stole money from the company (and, therefore, the shareholders). Their actions were dishonest in that they told investors they had not sold their shares, even though they had done so while the fraud was unraveling.

Kozlowski didn't seem to care about the consequences of his actions as required under teleological methods of ethical reasoning. He may have thought Tyco's actions would somehow benefit the shareholders, but that was just a rationalization for his self-serving actions. There is no evidence that he considered the harms that his actions caused others.

Deontological ethics focuses on one's duty to others. As CEO of Tyco, Kozlowski had a fiduciary responsibility to protect the assets of the company. His misuse of those assets for personal purposes violated his obligations to the company and its shareholders.

Rawlsian justice theory was ignored by Kozlowski. He cared about no one but himself and what he could achieve. As previously mentioned, he needed to keep up with the masters of the universe, as stated by Morley Safer in his *60-Minutes* interview. Fairness to others was nowhere on Kozlowski's radar. The fact that shareholders lost millions in stock value did not even seem to bother him.

Ethical relativism is what drove Kozlowski's actions. He created his own rules and governed his own ethics. We believe that this is why he never saw anything wrong with the things that he was doing. Even to the end, he maintained that he didn't do anything wrong. Kozlowski was judging himself by his own standard, which was created by him, and because he thought that he had not broken any of the preestablished rules, he felt innocent. He had no stakeholder interest in mind when doing the things that he did, and he cared only for himself.

# Fraud Considerations in the Audit

*AU 240* details ten areas of fraud considerations that should improve the auditor's ability to detect and report fraud: (1) describing the characteristics of fraud; (2) exercising professional skepticism; (3) discussing with engagement personnel the risks of material misstatement due to fraud; (4) obtaining the information needed to identify the risks of material misstatement due to fraud; (5) identifying the risks that may result in a material misstatement due to fraud; (6) assessing the identified risks after taking into account an evaluation of the entity's programs and controls; (7) responding to the results of the assessment; (8) evaluating audit evidence; (9) communicating about fraud to management, the audit committee, and others; and (10) documenting the auditor's consideration of fraud.[20]

## Fraud Risk Assessment

Most of the requirements of *AU 240* call for the auditor to engage in risk assessment during the audit. Actually, the assessment of risk starts with an evaluation of evidence about the potential client before agreeing to do the audit. One important step is to communicate with the predecessor auditor to find out the reasons for the firing or the reasons for no longer servicing the client. Of particular importance is assessing the integrity of the top management and key accounting personnel. The successor auditor also should clarify with the predecessor whether there were any differences of opinion with management over the application of accounting principles and how these were handled, including the role of the audit committee.

To support risk assessment, the auditor should approach each engagement with a healthy dose of skepticism. This means to approach the audit with a questioning mind and be skeptical of the truth in gathering information, asking questions, and evaluating the corporate culture. In making the assessment, of course, the auditor should not approach the audit with an attitude toward management of "You are crooks. Prove me wrong." Instead, a healthy attitude is one that informs management in word and deed that the auditor's responsibility is to ask the tough questions, thoroughly examine relevant documentation, and probe to determine whether the organization culture promotes ethical decision making and whether there is support for financial statement amounts and disclosures. Professional skepticism is part of the due care ethics standard discussed in Chapter 4.

The auditor should obtain information needed to identify the risk of material misstatement due to fraud. According to *AU 240,* the goal should be to (1) make inquiries of management and others within the organization to obtain their views about the risks of fraud and how they are addressed; (2) consider any unusual or unexpected relationships that have been identified in performing analytical procedures (i.e., financial statement comparisons over time and ratio analysis) in planning the audit; (3) consider whether one or more fraud risk factors exist; and (4) consider other information (i.e., interim financial results and factors associated with the acceptance of the client) that may be helpful in identifying risks of material misstatement due to fraud.[21]

Fraud risk factors are explained in *AU 240* by linking them to one of the three sides of the Fraud Triangle. Essentially, they represent red flags that should serve as a warning to the auditor that financial stability, operating, and/or corporate culture factors exist that may be a precursor to fraud or indicate that fraud has occurred. The auditor's role is to follow up on these warning signs by asking the tough questions, gathering the necessary information to support or refute the signs, and not to give in to client pressures to look the other way. For example, Andersen, the auditor of Waste Management, was satisfied with explanations of highly questionable transactions and the related accounting, and the auditors accepted management's promise to "clean up its act" in the future. In retrospect, that made no sense because the firm was choosing to accept the word of those who had already committed fraud.

## Fraud Associated with Management Override of Controls

*AU 240* recognizes that management has a unique ability to perpetrate fraud as a result of being in a position to manipulate accounting records and present fraudulent financial information, whether directly or indirectly.[22] To address the risk of management override of controls, the standard requires auditors to perform certain procedures, such as checking journal entries and other adjustments and reviewing accounting estimates for possible biases that could result in material misstatement due to fraud.[23]

To some extent, U.S. standards are lagging those of other countries, such as Canada, in providing specific guidance with respect to assessing the possibility of management override of internal controls. The Auditing and Assurance Standards Board in Canada has issued a standard related to the auditor's responsibility to consider fraud and error (Handbook Section 5135)[24] that builds on its professional skepticism requirement in three areas. The standard was recently reissued to conform to International Standards on Auditing (ISA) 240, issued by the International Auditing and Assurances Board (IAASB) of the International Federation of Accountants (IFAC). We discuss international accounting and auditing issues in Chapter 8.

The first requirement is to recognize that the risk of management override of internal controls is such that it cannot be addressed adequately without mandatory substantive procedures. Required procedures are:

- Testing the appropriateness of journal entries and other adjustments
- Identifying bias in management's accounting estimates, including a retrospective review of management's judgments and significant assumptions reflected in the financial statements of the prior year
- Understanding the business rationale for significant transactions and considering whether the rationale (or lack thereof) suggests that the transactions may have been entered into to engage in fraudulent financial reporting or to conceal misappropriation of assets

The second key feature responds to the many high-profile problems that have occurred due to improper revenue recognition. Section 5135 requires auditors to presume there is a risk of fraudulent revenue recognition. Auditors are specifically required to perform analytical procedures when planning the audit that are aimed at identifying unusual or unexpected relationships that may indicate risks of fraud due to improper revenue recognition. When auditors identify such risks, they are required to consider the design of the entity's policies and procedures to prevent and detect fraud and whether they have been implemented. They are also required to design further audit procedures that are responsive to those risks.

The third key feature is expanded requirements and guidance for discussions among the engagement team on the susceptibility of the client's financial statements to material misstatement due to fraud. These discussions will provide the engagement team with a good understanding of:

- Information that experienced engagement team members have about their experiences with the client
- How a fraud might be perpetrated and concealed at the entity
- The procedures the team might perform to detect any material misstatements that result

Other changes to Section 5135 include:

- Greater emphasis on inquiries of the audit committee concerning its knowledge of fraud risks and actual fraud
- Expanded guidance in the appendices on fraud risk factors and responses to the risk, with particular emphasis on revenue recognition, inventory quantities, and management estimates
- Classification of fraud risk factors into those relating to incentives or pressures to commit fraud, perceived opportunity to do so without getting caught, and ability to rationalize the act

While standards issued by the AICPA in the United States address many of these issues, the guidance for auditors is less specific than that provided by the Canadian Institute of Chartered Accountants' Auditing and Assurances Board and International Auditing and Assurances Board of IFAC.

## Rite Aid Fraud and Failure of Internal Controls

Apostolou and Crumbley point out that in the Rite Aid fraud, management directed its staff to make improper adjusting entries to reduce the cost of goods sold and accounts payable in every quarter from the first quarter of fiscal 1997 through the first quarter of fiscal year 2000. These entries could not be substantiated; they were intended solely to manipulate Rite Aid's reported earnings. As a result of these entries alone, Rite Aid overstated pretax income by $100 million in the second quarter of fiscal year 1999.[25]

According to the SEC action against Rite Aid, its fraudulent practices inflated reported pretax income by the amounts shown in Exhibit 5.5.[26]

In its examination of the work of KPMG, the auditors of Rite Aid, the SEC noted that Rite Aid failed to devise and maintain a system of internal accounting controls sufficient to provide reasonable assurances that transactions were recorded as necessary to permit preparation of financial statements in conformity with GAAP or other relevant criteria, or to maintain accountability for assets. The commission assigned blame to top management for failing to develop an internal control system that would promote accurate and reliable financial reports while, at the same time, circumventing the internal controls Rite Aid did have.[27]

## Communicating About Possible Fraud to Management and Those Charged with Governance

Whenever the auditor has determined that there is evidence that fraud may exist, the matter should be brought to the attention of the appropriate level of management. *AU 240* requires such communication even if the matter might be considered inconsequential, such as a minor misappropriation by an employee. Fraud (whether caused by senior management or other employees) that causes a material misstatement of the financial statements should be reported directly to those charged with governance. In addition, the auditor should reach an understanding with those charged with governance regarding the nature and extent of communications with them about misappropriations perpetrated by lower-level employees.[28]

If the auditor, as a result of the assessment of the risks of material misstatement, has identified such risks due to fraud that have continuing control implications the auditor should consider whether these risks represent significant deficiencies or material weaknesses in the entity's internal control that should be communicated to management and those charged with governance. The auditor should also consider whether the absence of or deficiencies in controls to prevent, deter, and detect fraud represent significant deficiencies or material weaknesses that should be communicated to management and those charged with governance.[29] More will be said about the auditor's responsibility to communicate deficiencies in internal controls later on.

**EXHIBIT 5.5**
**Rite Aid's Percentage Misstatement of Pretax Income by Quarter and Year**

| | |
|---|---|
| 1Q98 | 38% |
| 2Q98 | 66% |
| 3Q98 | 16% |
| FY98 | 9% |
| 1Q99 | 71% |
| 2Q99 | 5,533% |
| 3Q99 | 94% |
| FY99 | Percentage not mathematically calculable—reported pre-tax income of $199.6 million, when actual results were *loss* of $14.7 million |
| 1Q00 | 54% |

### Audit Committee Responsibilities for Fraud Risk Assessment

*AU 240* addresses the responsibilities of the audit committee with respect to fraud risk assessment. Specifically, "the audit committee or those charged with governance where no audit committee exists should evaluate management's identification of fraud risks, implementation of antifraud measures, and creation of the appropriate tone at the top." Active oversight by the audit committee can help reinforce management's commitment to create a culture with "zero tolerance" for fraud. An entity's audit committee also should ensure that senior management (in particular, the CEO) implements appropriate fraud deterrence and prevention measures to better protect investors, employees, and other stakeholders.

The audit committee's evaluation and oversight not only helps ensure that senior management fulfills its responsibility, but also can serve as a deterrent to senior management engaging in fraudulent activity (that is, by ensuring an environment is created whereby any attempt by senior management to involve employees in committing or concealing fraud would lead promptly to reports from such employees to appropriate persons, including the audit committee).

The audit committee also plays an important role in helping those charged with governance fulfill their oversight responsibilities with respect to the entity's financial reporting process and the system of internal control. In exercising this oversight responsibility, the audit committee should consider the potential for management override of controls or other inappropriate influence over the financial reporting process. Some examples follow:

- The audit committee should solicit the views of the internal auditors and independent auditors with respect to management's involvement in the financial reporting process and, in particular, the ability of management to override information processed by the entity's financial reporting system (for example, the ability of management or others to initiate or record nonstandard journal entries).
- The audit committee should consider reviewing the entity's reported information for reasonableness compared with prior or forecasted results, as well as with peers or industry averages.
- Information received in communications from the independent auditors can assist the audit committee in assessing the strength of the entity's internal control and the potential for fraudulent financial reporting.

As part of its oversight responsibilities, the audit committee should encourage management to provide a mechanism for employees to report concerns about unethical behavior, actual or suspected fraud, or violations of the entity's code of conduct or ethics policy. The committee should then receive periodic reports describing the nature, status, and eventual disposition of any fraud or unethical conduct. A summary of the activity, follow-up, and disposition also should be provided to all of those charged with governance.

## Management Representations and Financial Statement Certifications

The responsibility for preventing and detecting fraud rests with the management of entities. The auditor has a responsibility to plan and perform the audit to obtain reasonable assurance about whether the financial statements are free of material misstatement, whether caused by error or fraud. The auditor should plan and perform the audit with an attitude of professional skepticism, recognizing that conditions or events may be found that indicate that fraud or error may exist. Based on the audit risk assessment, the auditor should develop programs and audit procedures to obtain reasonable assurance that all significant errors and fraud have been identified. The auditor should communicate with management and inquire whether any significant fraud or error has been detected, in part to adjust audit procedures accordingly. However, the auditor faces the inevitable risk that some significant errors will not be detected, even if the audit is planned and done properly. Management can override internal controls and create deceptive accounting for transactions that makes identifying fraud difficult at best.

One way to deal with the problem, although not foolproof, is to obtain written representations (also known as *management representations* or *client representations*) to confirm certain matters and support other evidence obtained during the audit. The representations are made by the CEO, the CFO, and other appropriate officers. The management letter generally includes:[30]

- A statement that the client has provided access to all known information that bears on the fair presentation of the financial statements
- Confirmation that management has performed an assessment of the effectiveness of internal control over financial reporting based on criteria established in the *Internal Control—Integrated Framework* issued by COSO
- Conclusions as to whether the company has maintained an effective internal control over financial reporting
- Disclosure of any deficiencies in the design or operation of internal control over financial reporting

Under Section 302 of the Sarbanes-Oxley Act (SOX), all quarterly (10-Q) and annual (10-K) filings with the SEC are required to include certifications from the CEO and CFO related to the fairness of the financial statements and the effectiveness of the internal control over financial reporting. In addition to the statements made in traditional management representations as explained above, Section 302 requires a statement whether the report contains any material untrue statements or material omission or be considered misleading.[31] The experience to date with enforcing Section 302 by the SEC has been disappointing. The most notorious SOX criminal case, against former HealthSouth CEO Richard Scrushy, ended in an acquittal in 2005, as discussed in in Chapter 4.

# Contents of the Audit Report

## Background

Much attention has been given in the last few years to the convergence of U.S. accounting standards with International Financial Reporting Standards (IFRS). Recently, the Auditing Standards Board of the AICPA has turned its attention to the convergence of U.S. auditing standards with its international counterpart; namely, ISAs, as issued by the International Auditing and Assurance Standards Board (IAASB) of the IFAC. We discuss international accounting and auditing standards in Chapter 8.

To accomplish the auditing convergence goal, the Auditing Standards Board undertook the Clarity Project to redraft and recodify U.S. GAAS to make them easier to read, understand, and implement. The revised standards more clearly state the objectives of the auditor and the requirements with which the auditor has to comply when conducting an audit in accordance with GAAS. The redrafted standards are principles-based in nature and went into effect on December 15, 2012.[32]

Of particular note is the new requirement for auditors to perform procedures to identify instances of noncompliance with those laws and regulations that may have a material effect on the financial statements. Specifically, an auditor is required to inspect any correspondence with relevant licensing or regulatory authorities. In addition, auditors are now required to obtain written representation from management concerning the absence of noncompliance with laws and regulations.

The new standards make explicit the following requirements, which have been implied under GAAS for years:

- Determine whether, on the basis of the audit work performed, the auditor has identified one or more deficiencies in internal control
- Include specific matters in a written communication stating that no material weaknesses were identified during the audit

These changes most directly affect how U.S. auditors of privately held entities conduct their audits because the PCAOB establishes standards for public entities under SOX. However, members of management of private entities, audit committees, and those charged with governance need to have an understanding of the potential impact of the changes to their organization's auditing of financial statements in upcoming and future audits. The PCAOB is in the process of considering how such changes will affect its standards for public companies, including the content and form of the audit report.

The examination of the financial statements and assessment of internal controls by the external auditor provides the basis for fraud detection. In order to form an opinion, the auditor should draw a conclusion whether she has obtained "reasonable assurance" about whether the financial statements as a whole are free from "material" misstatement, whether due to fraud or error. These terms will be discussed later in this chapter.

Students should understand the auditing process and how audit opinions might change based on material differences with the client on accounting and financial reporting issues. Given that many students may have already completed an auditing course, we focus on the most important conceptual issues here and leave most of the details about audit report wording to the appendices of this chapter.

The exact wording of the unmodified audit report (formerly known as *unqualified*) for public companies appears in Exhibit 5.6.

## Introductory Paragraph

The introductory paragraph identifies the entity, the financial statements being examined, the period covered by each financial statement, and that the statements have been audited. Typically, the audit report references two or three years since auditors tend to be engaged to conduct an audit of a client for more than just the current year.

## Management's Responsibility

This section includes a description of management's responsibility for the preparation and fair presentation of the financial statements in accordance with GAAP, including responsibility for the design, implementation, and maintenance of internal controls necessary to the preparation and fair presentation of financial statements that are free of misstatements, whether due to error or fraud.

## Auditor's Responsibility

This section includes a heading that expresses the auditor's responsibility to express an opinion on the financial statements based on the audit. It also includes reference to GAAS as established in the U.S. as the basis for the audit. Other matters addressed include (1) an explicit discussion of how an audit involves performing procedures to obtain audit evidence about the amounts and disclosures in the financial statements; (2) the procedures selected depend on the auditor's judgment and risk assessments of the likelihood of material misstatements in the financial statements, whether due to error or fraud; (3) risk assessments involve consideration of internal control relevant to the entity's preparation and fair presentation

**EXHIBIT 5.6**
Unmodified Opinion
of Mintz & Morris
LLP, Independent
Registered Public
Accounting Firm

**Independent Auditor's Report**
**To the Board of Directors and Stockholders, XYZ Company**
**Introductory Paragraph**

We have audited the accompanying consolidated financial statements of XYZ Company and its subsidiaries, which comprise the consolidated balance sheets as of December 31, 2013 and 2012, and the related consolidated statements of income, changes in stockholders' equity, and cash flows for the years then ended, and the related notes to the financial statements.

**Management's Responsibility for the Financial Statements**

Management is responsible for the preparation and fair presentation of these consolidated financial statements in accordance with accounting principles generally accepted in the United States of America; this includes the design, implementation, and maintenance of internal control relevant to the preparation and fair presentation of consolidated financial statements that are free from material misstatement, whether due to fraud or error.

**Auditor's Responsibility**

Our responsibility is to express an opinion on these consolidated financial statements based on our audits. We conducted our audits in accordance with auditing standards generally accepted in the United States of America. Those standards require that we plan and perform the audit to obtain reasonable assurance about whether the consolidated financial statements are free of material misstatement.

An audit involves performing procedures to obtain audit evidence about the amounts and disclosures in the consolidated financial statements. The procedures selected depend on the auditor's judgment, including the assessment of the risks of material misstatement of the consolidated financial statements, whether due to fraud or error. In making those risk assessments, the auditor considers internal controls relevant to the entity's preparation and fair presentation of the consolidated financial statements in order to design audit procedures that are appropriate in the circumstances, but not for the purpose of expressing an opinion on the effectiveness of the entity's internal controls. Accordingly, we express no such opinion. An audit also includes evaluating the appropriateness of accounting policies used and the reasonableness of significant accounting estimates made by management, as well as evaluating the overall presentation of the consolidated financial statements.

We believe that the audit evidence we have obtained is sufficient and appropriate to provide a basis for our audit opinion.

**Opinion**

In our opinion, the consolidated financial statements referred to above present fairly, in all material respects, the financial position of XYZ Company and its subsidiaries as of December 31, 2013, and 2012, and the results of its operations and its cash flows for the years then ended in accordance with accounting principles generally accepted in the United States of America.

**Optional Paragraph**

**Report on Other Legal and Regulatory Requirements** *[This section usually won't apply unless the auditor has other reporting responsibilities. If so, then the opening paragraph after the salutation should be titled Report on the Financial Statements]*

[Auditor's signature]

[Auditor's city and state]

[Date of the auditor's report]

of the financial statements in order to design audit procedures that are appropriate in the circumstances; (4) the audit includes evaluating the appropriateness of accounting policies used and reasonableness of significant accounting estimates made by management; and (5) whether the auditor believes that the audit evidence gathered is sufficient and appropriate to provide a basis for the opinion. It is important to note that the consideration of internal controls is not for the purpose of expressing an opinion on the effectiveness of the entity's internal controls.

## Opinion

A section with the heading of "Opinion" should be included. If an unmodified opinion is expressed, the opinion should state that the financial statements present fairly, in all material respects, the financial position of the entity for the years examined in accordance with GAAP for the relevant country (i.e., U.S. GAAP).

This new audit report has an effective date of audits of financial statements for periods ending on or after December 15, 2012.

## Types of Audit Opinions

Auditors can express an unmodified opinion, an unmodified opinion with an emphasis-of-matter or other-matter paragraph, a qualified opinion, an adverse opinion, or a disclaimer. An auditor also can withdraw from the engagement under restricted circumstances. The qualified opinion, adverse opinion, or disclaimer of opinion is a "modified" opinion. At one time, an additional paragraph added to the unqualified opinion was considered an "explanatory" paragraph; that term has been removed from U.S. GAAS.

### Opinion Paragraph—Unmodified

An auditor should give an unmodified opinion when the financial statements "present fairly" financial position, results of operations, and cash flows. Certain situations may call for adding an additional paragraph: either an emphasis-of-matter or other-matter paragraph.

An emphasis-of-matter paragraph is a paragraph in the auditor's report that refers to a matter appropriately presented or disclosed in the financial statements (e.g., going concern, litigation uncertainty, subsequent events, etc.). It is added when, in the auditor's professional judgment, the item is of such importance that it is fundamental to users' understanding of the financial statements. Some emphasis-of-matter paragraphs are required by the Clarified Statements on Auditing Standards (SASs), and others are added at the discretion of the auditor.

An other-matter paragraph is a paragraph included in the auditor's report that refers to a matter other than those presented or disclosed in the financial statements that, in the auditors' professional judgment, is relevant to users' understanding of the audit, the auditor's responsibilities, or the auditor's report (e.g., supplemental information).

An emphasis-of-matter or other-matter paragraph follows the opinion paragraph and has a section heading of "Emphasis-of-Matter" or "Other-Matter."

*AU 706, Emphasis-of-Matter Paragraphs and Other-Matter Paragraphs in the Independent Auditor's Report,* requires that the auditor evaluate whether there is substantial doubt about the entity's ability to continue as a going concern for a reasonable period of time (not to exceed one year beyond the financial statement audit date). Auditors are not required to perform procedures specifically designed to test the going-concern assumption; they must evaluate the assumption in relation to the results of the normal auditing procedures.[33] Conditions that may cause the auditors to question the going-concern assumption include negative cash flows from operations, defaults on loan agreements, restructuring of debt, and adverse financial ratios. When such conditions or events are identified, the auditors should gather additional information and consider whether management's plans for dealing with the conditions are likely to mitigate the adverse effects for a reasonable period of time and that such plans can be implemented effectively. If the auditors conclude that the substantial doubt is resolved, they may issue the unmodified report. On the other hand, if the auditors conclude that substantial doubt still exists about the company's ability to continue as a going concern for a period of one year from the balance sheet date, then the auditors should include an emphasis-of-matter paragraph in their report. Appendix 1 shows the language of this paragraph.

A going-concern issue may exist where the entity's ability to survive is attributable to continuing operating losses and/or the projected excess of cash outflows over cash inflows over an extended period of time and/or the inability of the company to raise needed funds to continue operations. Start-up companies sometimes have these kinds of problems, as would a company facing bankruptcy. During the 2007–2008 financial crisis, well-established companies like General Motors faced going-concern problems.

If a company makes a change in accounting principle, the nature of, justification for, and effect of the change are reported in a note to the financial statements for the period in which the change is made. To determine general acceptance of the new principle, the auditor should evaluate whether (1) the newly adopted principle is generally accepted, (2) the method of accounting for the effect of the change is in conformity with GAAP, and (3) management's justification for the change is reasonable. When the auditors believe that the new principle is generally accepted, the accounting is proper, and the change is justified, the audit report includes an emphasis-of-matter paragraph to highlight the lack of consistent application of acceptable accounting principles, but the opinion remains unmodified. An example of such a paragraph in the audit report under these circumstances appears in Appendix 2.

### Opinion Paragraph—Modified

Recall that Rule 203 of the AICPA Code of Professional Conduct precludes rendering an opinion that states that the financial statements have been prepared in accordance with GAAP or any statement that the auditor is not aware of any material modifications that should be made to such statements or data to make them conform with GAAP, if such statements or data contain any departure from an accounting principle that has a material effect on the statements or data taken as a whole. The result would be the issuance of a modified opinion on the matter that creates a deviation from GAAP.

The auditor should modify the opinion in the auditor's report when (1) the auditor concludes, based on the audit evidence obtained, the financial statements as a whole are *materially misstated;* or (2) the auditor is unable to obtain sufficient appropriate audit evidence to conclude that the financial statements as a whole are free from material misstatement. A modified opinion includes a qualified opinion, an adverse opinion, or a disclaimer of opinion. The circumstances when each opinion is proper are discussed next.

A qualified opinion would be appropriate when (1) the auditor, having obtained sufficient appropriate audit evidence, concludes that misstatements, individually or in the aggregate, are material but not pervasive to the financial statements; or (2) the auditor is unable to obtain sufficient appropriate audit evidence on which to base the opinion, but the auditor concludes that the possible effects on the financial statements of undetected misstatements, if any, could be material but not pervasive.

An adverse opinion is proper when the auditor, having obtained sufficient appropriate audit evidence, concludes that misstatements, individually or in the aggregate, are both material and pervasive to the financial statements. *Pervasive* is a term used in the context of misstatements to describe the effects on the financial statements of misstatements, if any, that are undetected due to an inability to obtain sufficient appropriate audit evidence. Pervasive effects on the financial statements require professional judgment by the auditor and are not generally confined to specific elements, accounts, or items of the financial statements, but if they are, they would represent or could represent a substantial proportion of the financial statements.

A disclaimer of opinion is warranted when the auditor is unable to obtain sufficient appropriate audit evidence on which to base the opinion, and the auditor concludes that the possible effects on the financial statements of undetected misstatements, if any, could be both material and pervasive.

### Basis for Modification and Types of Opinions

The auditor should include a separate paragraph in the audit report that describes the matter giving rise to the modification. This paragraph should be placed immediately before the opinion paragraph in the auditor's report and include a heading such as "Basis for Qualified Opinion," "Basis for Adverse Opinion," or "Basis for Disclaimer of Opinion," as appropriate.

If there is a material misstatement of the financial statements that relates to specific amounts in the financial statements, the auditor should include in the "Basis for Modification" paragraph a description and quantification of the financial effects of the misstatement unless doing so is impracticable, in which case the auditor should so state.

When the auditor modifies the audit opinion, the auditor should use a heading for the "Opinion" paragraph that includes "Qualified Opinion," "Adverse Opinion," or "Disclaimer of Opinion." Appendix 3 (Qualified Opinion), Appendix 4 (Adverse Opinion), and Appendix 5 (Disclaimer of Opinion) illustrate the appropriate language when modifying the auditor's report.

When the auditor expresses a qualified opinion due to a material misstatement in the financial statements, the auditor should state in the opinion paragraph that, in the auditor's opinion, except for the effects of the matter(s) described in the "Basis for Qualified Opinion" paragraph, the financial statements are presented fairly, in all material effects, in accordance with GAAP.

When the auditor expresses an adverse opinion, the auditor should state in the opinion paragraph that, in the auditor's opinion, because of the significance of the matter(s) described in the "Basis for Adverse Opinion" paragraph, the financial statements are not presented fairly in accordance with GAAP.

When the auditor disclaims an opinion due to an inability to obtain sufficient appropriate evidence, the auditor should so state in the "Disclaimer of Opinion" paragraph and include the statement that, accordingly, the auditor does not express an opinion on the financial statements. Exhibit 5.7 includes a summary of various paragraphs that can be included in the standard audit report and modified opinions.

### Withdrawal from the Engagement

From time to time, an auditor might consider withdrawing from an engagement. Withdrawal generally is not appropriate because an auditor is hired by the client to do an audit and render an opinion, not walk away from one's obligations when the going gets tough. However, if a significant conflict exists with management or the auditor decides that management cannot be trusted, then a withdrawal may be justified. Factors that affect the auditor's conclusion include the implication of the involvement of a member of management or those charged with governance in any misconduct. Trust issues are a matter of ethics. Once pressure builds up in the auditor-client relationship and it boils over, the auditor must consider whether the breakdown in the relationship has advanced to the point that any and all information provided by the client is suspect. An auditor should not allow himself to be in the position of questioning the client's motives with every statement made and piece of evidence gathered. Withdrawal triggers the filing of the SEC's 8-K form by management.

## Generally Accepted Auditing Standards (GAAS)—Overview

For many years, the AICPA had sole responsibility for GAAS through its Auditing Standards Board. Following the passage of SOX, the SEC established the PCAOB to set auditing standards for public companies that file 10-K reports with the commission. PCAOB reports to the SEC in carrying out its responsibilities. The AICPA's Auditing Standards Board continues to set auditing standards for privately owned businesses. GAAS have traditionally referred to general, field work, and reporting standards. Recently, the AICPA redrafted these standards to more clearly state the objectives of the auditor and the requirements with which the auditor has to comply when conducting an audit.

**EXHIBIT 5.7** Examples of Paragraphs in the Audit Report

| Type of Report/Opinion | Management's Responsibility | Auditor's Responsibility | Opinion | Emphasis-of-Matter OR Other-Matter |
|---|---|---|---|---|
| **Unmodified Opinion** | Standard | Standard | Standard | |
| *Emphasis of Matter* | | | | |
| Going Concern Issue | Standard | Standard | Standard | Description |
| Consistent GAAP Application | Standard | Standard | Standard | Description |
| **Modified Opinions** | | | | |
| *Qualified* | Standard | Include departure from GAAP or scope limitation | "Except for the [GAAP departure or effects of scope limitation] . . . the financial statements present fairly . . ." | |
| *Adverse* | Standard | Include substantial reasons for adverse opinion | ". . . the financial statements do not present fairly . . ." | |
| *Disclaimer* | Omitted | Omitted | Changed to indicate that an opinion cannot be expressed on the financial statements and why | |

This two-tier system can be confusing because the traditional GAAS (i.e., general, field work, and reporting standards) that existed before PCAOB was established have been incorporated by PCAOB as its standards effective on April 16, 2003. Therefore, GAAS still has widespread applicability to the audits of public companies (incorporated into PCAOB standards), and nonpublic companies and not-for-profit entities. PCAOB now establishes its own auditing standards for public companies. PCAOB audit standards are considered to be required, not "generally accepted." PCAOB's position is that its standards should be used regardless of what might be "generally accepted" in practice.

PCAOB also establishes independence rules and quality control standards for registered CPA firms. The board conducts an inspection program whereby its representatives review the quality controls in effect at registered firms and issue an opinion to firm management. The opinion can be unmodified if the quality control system provides the firm with reasonable assurance of complying with professional standards. A modified report means the quality control system fails to provide reasonable assurance. An adverse report identifies significant deficiencies in the control system. More will be said about the specific PCAOB standards later on. For now we focus on the GAAS adopted by PCAOB.

## GAAS Requirements

An independent auditor plans, conducts, and reports the results of an audit in accordance with GAAS. *Auditing standards* provide a measure of audit quality and the objectives to be achieved in an audit. Auditing standards differ from auditing procedures because the procedures are steps taken by the auditor during the course of the audit to comply with GAAS.

The PCAOB requires the ten basic standards developed by the Auditing Standards Board of the AICPA as divided into the general standards, standards of fieldwork, and standards of reporting. The AICPA, also identifies three fundamental principles underlying an audit. Those fundamental principles are responsibilities, performance, and reporting. The principles are very similar in nature to the ten basic standards. The responsibility principle relates to the general standards and defines objectivity. The performance principles relates to the standards of fieldwork and defines reasonable assurance, planning the work, obtaining and evaluating evidence, assessing risk of material misstatement, and gathering sufficient appropriate evidence. The reporting principle relates to the standards of reporting and provides guidance on communicating audit results. The ten basic standards required by the PCAOB are discussed next. Recall that the AICPA has taken this material and repositioned it as part of the objectives of audit standards.

### General Standards

There are three general standards that relate to the quality of the professionals who perform the audit. These include (1) adequate technical training and proficiency, (2) independence in mental attitude, and (3) due care in the performance of the audit and preparation of the report. Independence is a basic standard in the AICPA Code of Professional Conduct. As discussed in Chapter 4, to be independent means to avoid all appearances that one's judgment may be clouded by events and relationships. Due care in performing an audit is also included in the Code; it requires diligence and competence.

### Standards of Fieldwork

Standards of fieldwork establish the criteria for judging whether the audit has met quality requirements. These standards should guide the auditor in meeting the expectations for a high-quality examination. The standards include (1) to adequately plan the audit work and supervise assistants so that the audit is more likely to detect a material misstatement; (2) to obtain a sufficient understanding of the entity and its internal control, to assess the risk of material misstatement of the financial statements, whether due to error or fraud, and to plan effectively the nature, timing, and extent of further audit procedures; and (3) to gather sufficient competent evidential matter through audit procedures including inspection, observation, inquiries, and confirmations to provide a reasonable basis (support) for an opinion regarding the financial statements under audit.

The standards of fieldwork provide the basis for determining whether the audit has been carried out with the level of care expected by the public. It is an integral part of providing the degree of support needed to make a statement that the audit provides a "reasonable basis" for the opinion and that the opinion provides "reasonable assurance" that the financial statements are free of material misstatement.

### Standards of Reporting

Just as the financial statements are the end product of the accountants' work, the audit report is the end product of an auditor's work. The audit report carries particular significance for investors and creditors, who rely on financial statements to help make decisions such as buying or selling stock and granting loans. Moreover, the report can be used to identify red flags that create questions about the entity's ability to continue as a going concern and point out any material nonconformity with GAAP.

There are three reporting standards that guide auditors in rendering an audit report and in determining the degree of responsibility that the auditor is taking with respect to the expression of an opinion of the financial statements. They include (1) determination of whether the statements have been prepared in conformity with GAAP, (2) identification of situations where the accounting principles have not been observed consistently in the current period in relation to the preceding period, and (3) discussion in the report of any situation identified in the footnotes to the financial statements where informative disclosures are inadequate.

## Audit Evidence

Gathering and objectively evaluating audit evidence requires the auditor to consider the competency and sufficiency of the evidence. Representations from management, while part of the evidential matter the auditor obtains, are not a substitute for the application of those auditing procedures necessary to afford a reasonable basis for an opinion regarding the financial statements under audit.

Audit risk and materiality need to be considered together in determining the nature, timing, and extent of auditing procedures and in evaluating the results of those procedures. According to *AU 315* the auditor should consider audit risk and materiality both in (a) planning the audit and designing auditing procedures and (b) evaluating whether the financial statements taken as a whole are presented fairly, in all material respects, in conformity with GAAP.[34]

The auditor's response to the risks of material misstatement due to fraud involves the application of professional skepticism when gathering and evaluating audit evidence. Examples of the application of professional skepticism in response to the risks of material misstatement due to fraud are obtaining additional corroboration of management's explanations or representations concerning material matters, such as through third-party confirmation, the use of a specialist, analytical procedures, examination of documentation from independent sources, or inquiries of others within or outside the entity. The independent auditor's direct personal knowledge, obtained through physical examination, observation, computation, and inspection, is more persuasive than information obtained indirectly.

*Audit procedures* are specific acts performed by the auditor to gather evidence about whether specific assertions are being met. For example, the client may state that the inventory value is $1 million. That is a specific assertion. The auditor then uses the procedure of observing the physical count of inventory to assess inventory quantity and traces certain year-end purchases and sales of inventory to invoices and other documentation as part of the cutoff process to determine whether year-end transactions should be part of the inventory. Typically, the auditor also tests the pricing of the inventory to assess the application of methods such as first-in, first-out (FIFO); last-in, first-out (LIFO); and the weighted average methods. The current market value of the inventory also has to be assessed.

Audit procedures help obtain an understanding of the entity and its environment, including its internal controls, to assess the risks of material misstatements. Such audit procedures are referred to as *risk assessment procedures.* Audit procedures also test the operating effectiveness of controls in preventing or detecting material misstatements.

## Limitations of the Audit Report

Three phrases in the audit report are critical to understanding the limits of the report: (1) *reasonable assurance,* (2) *material,* and (3) *present fairly.* These expressions are used to signal the reader about specific limitations of the audit report.

## Reasonable Assurance

The term *reasonable* is often used in law to define a standard of behavior to decide legal issues. For example, an auditor should exercise a *reasonable* level of care (due care) to avoid charges of negligence and possible liability to the client. The *reasonable* (prudent) person standard typically is used to judge whether an uninvolved individual looking at the behavior of an auditor, perhaps in relation to independence and client relationships, can conclude that the auditor has maintained the appearance of independence. This appearance standard is used because oftentimes it is difficult to know whether the auditor truly is independent in fact in making audit decisions because independence in fact relies on what was in the mind of the auditor at the time she decided to either include or exclude certain audit evidence.

Reasonable assurance is not an absolute guarantee that the financial statements are free of material misstatement. Auditors do not examine all of a company's transactions. The transactions selected for examination are determined based on materiality considerations and risk assessment. Even then, only a small percentage of transactions are selected, often by statistical sampling techniques.

The auditor makes the reasonable assurance statement in the context of GAAS. It means that the auditor has followed GAAS in carrying out audit responsibilities, including gathering sufficient competent evidential matter. The auditor uses professional judgment to decide whether available evidence is sufficient to justify an opinion. If the auditor fails to follow GAAS in making that decision, then an allegation of negligence is supportable. If the auditor was to ignore purposefully justified audit procedures or evidence that, for example, has negative implications for the client, then a charge of constructive fraud or fraud may be sustained in a court of law. These charges can be brought by clients as well as third parties, as will be discussed in Chapter 6.

The auditor obtains and evaluates audit evidence to obtain reasonable assurance about whether the financial statements are presented fairly, in all material respects, in accordance with GAAP. The concept of reasonable assurance acknowledges that there is a risk that the audit opinion is inappropriate. The risk that the auditor expresses an inappropriate audit opinion when the financial statements are materially misstated is known as *audit risk.*

## Materiality

The concept of *materiality* recognizes that some matters are important to the fair presentation of financial statements, while others are not. The materiality concept is fundamental to the audit because the audit report states that an audit is performed to obtain reasonable assurance about whether the financial statements are free of material misstatement.

Materiality judgments require the use of professional judgment and are based on management and auditor perceptions of the needs of a reasonable person who will rely on the financial statements. *Materiality* is defined in the glossary of *Statement of Financial Accounting Concepts (SFAC) 2, Qualitative Characteristics of Accounting Information,*[35] as: *The magnitude of an omission or misstatement of accounting information that, in the light of surrounding circumstances, makes it probable that the judgment of a reasonable person relying on the information would have been changed or influenced by the omission or misstatement.*

*AU 240* notes that "the auditor has a responsibility to plan and perform the audit to obtain reasonable assurance about whether the financial statements are free of material misstatement, whether caused by error or fraud."[36] The concept of materiality is perhaps one of the most challenging in accounting. The application of professional judgment to the surrounding circumstances in which materiality is at issue provides the setting to assess whether an item or event is either quantitatively or qualitatively significant enough to warrant financial reporting or disclosure.

### Judging Materiality

Materiality in the context of an audit reflects the auditor's judgment of the needs of users in relation to the information in the financial statements and the possible effect of misstatements on user decisions as a group. Materiality is judged by assessing whether the omissions or misstatements of items in the statements could, individually or collectively, influence the economic decisions of users taken on the basis of financial statements. Materiality depends on the size and nature of the omission or misstatement judged in the surrounding circumstances.

Each *FAS* statement adopted by FASB says, "The provisions of this Statement need not be applied to immaterial items." The SEC has ruled in *Staff Accounting Bulletin (SAB) 99* that this does not mean that a public company filing financial statements with the commission, or its auditor, may rely solely on a quantitative threshold as a "rule of thumb" to determine materiality.[37] Typically, an auditor might use a percentage for the numerical threshold, such as 5 percent. Materiality is then judged by comparing an item in question to some amount such as total assets or net income. If the questionable item is equal to or greater than 5 percent of the comparison amount, then it is material and must be reported in the financial statements.

Assume that a company has one item in inventory that cost $400,000. The auditor believes the current market value is $381,000, or $19,000 (4.75 percent) below cost. Under the 5 percent rule, the item may be judged immaterial and the write-down ignored. However, what if the net income for the year is only $300,000? Then the $19,000 write-down becomes material because it equals 6.33 percent of net income.

One unintended consequence of the accounting profession's approach to materiality is that a controller—knowing the 5 percent rule is in effect—may attempt to decrease expenses or increase revenues by an amount less than 5 percent to increase earnings by an amount that will not be challenged by the auditor. It is somewhat ironic that the auditor can let the difference go unchallenged, even though it may be due to the misapplication of GAAP, simply because it is not "material" in amount. A good example is at North Face Inc. where the company engaged in barter transactions in the late 1990s. The CFO knew the materiality criteria used by the auditors, Deloitte & Touche, and he structured a transaction to produce gross profit ($800,000) below the materiality amount. The auditors had recommended an adjustment for that amount, which was part of a $1.64 million revenue transaction. The auditors passed on the adjustment using materiality as the explanation.

*AU 240* provides that a percentage test may be used to form a preliminary assumption that—without considering all relevant circumstances—a "deviation of less than the specified percentage with respect to a particular item on the registrant's financial statements is unlikely to be material." However, the auditor must go beyond using such a "bright line" test based on the magnitude of misstatement as the sole source of judgment about materiality. According to the standard, "It cannot be used as a substitute for a full analysis of all relevant considerations."

The U.S. Supreme Court noted in *TSC Industries v. Northway, Inc.* that judgments of materiality require "delicate assessments of the inferences a 'reasonable shareholder' would draw from a given set of facts and the significance of those inferences to him."[38] In other words, the Court and the accounting profession have similar interpretations: a fact is material if there is a substantial likelihood that it would have been viewed by the reasonable investor as having significantly altered the "total mix" of information made available.

*AU 240* greatly advances the accounting profession's assessment of materiality by linking it to the obtaining of information needed to identify the risks of material misstatement due to fraud. This standard provides guidance to auditors in fulfilling their responsibilities to plan and perform the audit to obtain reasonable assurance about whether the financial statements are free of material misstatement, whether caused by error or fraud.[39]

## What Is Meant by "Present Fairly"?

Without an understanding of the term *present fairly,* the users of a financial statement would be unable to assess its reliability. For the purposes of our discussion about fair presentation, we will proceed with the following guideline: that the auditor's assessment of fair presentation depends on whether (1) the accounting principles selected and applied have general acceptance; (2) the accounting principles are appropriate in the circumstances; (3) the financial statements, including the related notes, are informative of matters that may affect their use, understanding, and interpretation; (4) the information presented in the statements is classified and summarized in a reasonable manner—that is, neither too detailed nor too condensed; and (5) the financial statements reflect transactions and events within a range of reasonable limits.

*SAS 122,*[40] addresses the issue of a "fair presentation" in the financial statements in the context of the applicable financial reporting framework. A *financial reporting framework* is a set of criteria (such as U.S. GAAP and IFRS) used to determine the measurement, recognition, presentation, and disclosure of all material items appearing in the financial statements.

The term *fair presentation framework* is used to refer to a financial reporting framework that requires compliance with the requirements of the framework and (1) acknowledges explicitly or implicitly that, to achieve fair presentation of the financial statements, it may be necessary for management to provide disclosures beyond those specifically required by the framework; or (2) acknowledges explicitly that it may be necessary for management to depart from a requirement of the framework to achieve a fair presentation of the financial statements. Such departures are expected to be necessary only in extreme cases.

The preparation and fair presentation of the financial statements by management and, when appropriate, those charged with governance require:

- The identification of the applicable financial reporting framework, in the context of any relevant laws or regulations
- The preparation and fair presentation of the financial statements in accordance with the framework
- The inclusion of an adequate description of that framework in the financial statements

An example of when the financial statements would not be fairly presented is provided in Exhibit 5.8. It deals with lease accounting rules that require, among other things, that

**EXHIBIT 5.8**
**Lease Accounting
and "Present Fairly"**

A *lease* is a form of property rental where the party using the asset (lessee) makes periodic payments to the legal owner of the asset (lessor). GAAP for leases comes from a variety of FASB statements, but *Statement of Financial Accounting Standards (FAS 17), Accounting for Leases*, establishes the lease standards in accounting. *FAS 17* provides that the lessee (user of the property) determine the present value (PV) of future lease payments and record an asset and liability if any one of four criteria exists.

The capital lease criteria include (1) transfer of ownership to the lessee at the end of the lease term, (2) bargain purchase option for the lessee, (3) lease life of 75 percent or more of the economic life of the leased asset, and (4) the PV equals 90 percent or more of the fair value of the leased asset (plus any guaranteed residual value) at the date of the lease.[41] Only one of the four criteria needs to be met to treat the lease as a capital item, thereby recording an asset and liability at PV. Absent all four criteria, the lease is treated as an operating lease, and each lease payment is debited to an expense account, offset by a credit to cash, and the asset remains on the books of the lessor, the legal owner of the leased asset. Operating leases lead to "off-balance sheet financing" because the amount due to the lessor over the lease contract is not recorded on the lessee's balance sheet. This creates a potentially troublesome practice from the perspective of the user of the financial statements, who might be interested in knowing the company's future cash obligations. GAAP deals with this issue by requiring the lessee to disclose the scheduled lease payments for the next five years.

In a capital lease, the lessor essentially finances the acquisition for the lessee by allowing a period of time for the lessee to make lease payments. Each payment includes an amount representing interest, and the difference between the total amount and the interest portion decreases the lease liability. Capital lease information in the balance sheet should reflect the carrying value of the leased asset and a breakdown of the current lease liability and long-term balance. Users would be misled if a company were to combine those numbers and just present the total as a *long-term lease liability*. The combined number also affects liquidity analysis such as the current ratio. The result of combining the liability amounts into one number is that the financial statements would not "present fairly" financial position.

The capital lease treatment of the discounted future lease payments as an asset on the balance sheet of the lessee (and removal of the asset and liability from the lessor's books) exemplifies putting the economic substance of a transaction over its legal form. Legally, the lessor owns the asset. There has been no sale. However, if any one of the four criteria is met, the accounting treatment reflects the conclusion that, for all intents and purposes, the lessee effectively owns the asset and is merely being given a fixed period of time to pay for it.

the current portion of the lease liability be separated out from the long-term amount. Lease accounting rules in the United States create "bright line rules" to determine proper accounting, whereas the rules under IFRS are more principle-based and rely on the interpretation of the economic substance of a transaction over its legal form in determining proper accounting.

The notion of "fair presentation" is generally thought to mean that the financial statements are presented in accordance with GAAP and are "not misleading." These terms seem to be somewhat contradictory. Zeff points out that fair presentation means that the financial statements meet a positive standard of informativeness and do not lead readers astray. According to Zeff, the objective of financial reporting is to convey useful financial information, not merely to avoid a deception.[42]

Mautz and Sharaf have written: that "an approach sometimes followed is one that finds acceptable any [accounting] method that is 'not misleading'. Such a negative attitude should not be condoned and certainly does not satisfy the concept of accounting propriety. Surely the auditor should insist upon something more constructive than the mere absence of injury; unless a practice actually aids and furthers understanding, it should be held deficient."[43]

We wonder how the term *fair* in *fair presentation* relates to the traditional ethics notion of fairness as justice. Does this mean that financial statements that present fairly are just statements? We think not, because justice means, in part, to treat equals equally and unequals unequally. There is no such distinction in accounting to provide a different level of information for different user groups that might have different needs for information to assist decision making.

Outside the United States, in European and other countries that have adopted IFRS, the term *true and fair view* replaces *fair presentation*. The former is associated with a higher degree of professional judgment, while the latter is more rules-based. This is a complicated matter that will be explored in greater detail in Chapter 8.

It has been said that fairness lies in the eyes of the beholder. If that were true in accounting, then no objective standard would exist to record and report financial information. On the other hand, financial reports that are true (truthful) clearly denote a level of honesty that, at least on the surface, implies a greater degree of reliability.

## Audit Risk Assessment

In March 2006, the AICPA's Auditing Standards Board issued eight *Statements on Auditing Standards (SAS 104–111)* relating to the assessment of risk in an audit of financial statements. These statements establish standards and provide guidance concerning the auditor's assessment of the risks of material misstatement (whether caused by error or fraud) in a financial statement audit, and the design and performance of audit procedures whose nature, timing, and extent are responsive to the assessed risks. The statements also establish standards and provide guidance on planning and supervision, the nature of audit evidence, and the evaluation of whether the audit evidence obtained affords a reasonable basis for an opinion regarding the financial statements under audit.[44]

The audit risk assessment standards are addressed in six new audit sections (AU 300, 315, 320, 330, 402, and 450) in the Clarified Standards.

There is no doubt that these standards were motivated by the continuing expectation gap between the public's perception of auditors' responsibilities to ferret out fraud and the accounting profession's traditional role of providing only reasonable assurance that the financial statements are free of material misstatement due to fraud.

The goal of the eight risk assessment standards is to enhance auditors' evaluation of audit risk by specifying, among other things:

1. More in-depth understanding of the entity and its environment, including its internal controls, to identify the risks of material misstatement in the financial statements and what the entity is doing to mitigate them
2. More rigorous assessment of the risk of material misstatement of the financial statements based on that understanding
3. Improved linkage between the assessed risks and the nature, timing, and extent of audit procedures performed in response to those risks

Of particular note is the distinction between two types of misstatements: known and likely, defined as follows:

- *Known misstatements.* These are specific misstatements identified during the audit arising from the incorrect selection or misapplication of accounting principles or misstatements of facts identified, including, for example, those arising from mistakes in gathering or processing data and the overlooking or misinterpretation of facts.
- *Likely misstatements.* (1) These arise from differences between management's and the auditor's judgments concerning accounting estimates that the auditor considers unreasonable or inappropriate (for example, because an estimate included in the financial statements by management is outside the range of reasonable outcomes the auditor has determined). (2) The auditor considers the differences likely to exist based on an extrapolation from audit evidence obtained (for example, the amount obtained by projecting known misstatements identified in an audit sample to the entire population from which the sample was drawn).

Taken together, the misapplication of accounting principles, misstatement of facts, and differences in judgment with respect to accounting estimates create conditions whereby the risk of material misstatement in the financial statements increases. The auditor should be sensitive to these events, as they bear directly on the type of audit opinion to be given.

The risk assessment standards were issued by the AICPA after its responsibilities for setting auditing standards for public companies ended. Still, the AICPA does set auditing standards for nonpublic companies. Moreover, the PCAOB has adopted standards that include much of the risk assessment requirements of AICPA including PCAOB Auditing Standard 12, *Identifying and Assessing Risks of Material Misstatement,* and PCAOB Auditing Standard 13, *The Auditor's Responses to the Risks of Material Misstatement.* We discuss the PCAOB standards later in this chapter.

## Internal Control Assessment

The risk that internal controls will not help prevent or detect a material misstatement in the financial statements is a critical evaluation to provide reasonable assurance. The system of internal controls and whether it operates as intended enables the auditor to gain either confidence about the internal processing of transactions, which is fine, or doubt, which the auditor should pursue.

## Internal Control—Integrated Framework

The accounting profession's standards for internal control are embedded in *Internal Control—Integrated Framework,* published by the COSO. The framework defines *internal control* as a process effected by an entity's board of directors, management, and other personnel that is designed to provide reasonable assurance regarding the achievement of the following objectives: (1) effectiveness and efficiency of operations, (2) reliability of financial reporting, and (3) compliance with applicable laws and regulations.[45] COSO emphasizes the roles and responsibilities of management, the board of directors, internal auditors, and other personnel in creating an environment that supports the objectives of internal control. COSO notes that if members of the board and audit committee do not take their responsibilities seriously, then the system will likely break down, as occurred in the accounting frauds of the 1990s and 2000s.

An important development in the internal control landscape was completed in May 2013 with the release of an update to the integrated framework of COSO. The update acknowledges recent changes in internal control requirements due in part by the changing business and operating environments and the need to develop systems of internal controls and support mechanisms such as governance of the organization that can adapt to the changes. According to this COSO report, an effective system of internal control demands more than rigorous adherence to policies and procedures: it requires the use of judgment. Management and boards of directors use judgment to determine how much control is enough. Management and internal auditors apply judgments as they monitor and assess the effectiveness of the system of internal control.[46] The judgment-based approach links to ethics through principles such as objectivity, integrity, due care, and professional skepticism. Judgments should be made through ethical reasoning about the rights of investors and creditors to receive accurate and reliable financial information, supported by internal controls that account for the control environment and risk assessment, and the need to prevent and detect material misstatements in financial statements including fraud and illegal acts.

The COSO *Internal Control—Integrated Framework* is a widely used tool to assess internal controls, and is recognized by the PCAOB as an appropriate internal control framework in *Auditing Standard (AS) 5,* An Audit of Internal Control over Financial Reporting Performed in Conjunction with an Audit of Financial Statements.[47] According to *AS 5,* the COSO framework "provides a suitable and available framework" for assessing a company's internal controls and financial reporting.

Additional professional guidance may be found in *AU 315* and *AU 320* that were previously mentioned. These standards deal with an auditor's understanding of internal control. The standard specifically includes the five interrelated components of internal control identified in the COSO framework. A survey of members of the Institute of Management Accountants and the Institute of Internal Auditors reports that approximately 90 percent of respondents rely to some extent on the COSO framework to evaluate controls.

### COSO Findings on Financial Statement Fraud

COSO analyzed the financial reporting by public companies from 1987 to 1997, a period during which business failures were high due to accounting fraud at companies such as ZZZZ Best. It is noteworthy that most of its findings were precursors to what happened during the business frauds and accounting failures of the 1998–2003 period. The result was the issuance in 1999 of *Fraudulent Financial Reporting: 1987–1997.*[48]

COSO examined 200 cases of financial statement fraud and found the following:

1. Some companies committing the fraud were experiencing net losses or were in close to breakeven positions in periods before the fraud. These pressures may have led some companies to commit fraud to reverse downward spirals, while others may have been motivated to preserve upward trends.
2. Top senior executives were frequently involved. In the SEC investigation and subsequent actions as reflected in the Accounting and Auditing Enforcement Releases (AAERs), 72 percent named the CEO and 43 percent the CFO. When considered together, in 83 percent of the cases, the AAERs named one or the other officer, or both of them.
3. Most audit committees met infrequently or not at all; and 25 percent of the companies did not even have an audit committee. Not only that, but 65 percent of the committees did not have a member with expertise in accounting or finance.
4. Boards were dominated by insiders and "gray" directors (outsiders with special ties to the company or management) with significant equity ownership and little experience. Collectively, the directors and officers owned nearly one-third of the companies' stock, with the CEO/president personally owning about 17 percent.
5. Family relationships among directors and officers were fairly common, as were individuals who seemed to have significant power. The founder and current CEO were the same person or the original CEO/president in nearly half of the companies.
6. A majority of the audit reports were issued during the fraud period; 55 percent of reports in the last year of the fraud contained unqualified opinions.
7. The remaining 45 percent of the reports issued in the last year contained departures from the unqualified opinion. The reasons were substantial doubt about the entity's ability to continue as a going concern, litigation and other uncertainties, changes in accounting principles, and changes in auditors between fiscal years comparatively reported. A total of 3 percent of the audit reports were qualified (i.e., modified) due to a GAAP departure during the fraud period.
8. Financial statement fraud occasionally implicated the external auditor. Auditors were explicitly named in 29 percent of the fraud cases. Auditors were also named for alleged involvement in the fraud (30 of 56 cases) or for negligent auditing (26 of 56 cases).
9. Some of the companies changed auditors during the fraud period. Just over 25 percent changed auditors during the time frame between the beginning of the last clean financial statement period and ending with the last fraudulent financial statement period. A majority of the auditor changes occurred during the fraud period.

One obvious conclusion from the findings is the link between SOX provisions and the deficiencies noted by COSO, in particular strengthening the role of the audit committee and board of directors through independence requirements.

COSO sponsored a study to update its understanding of fraud by providing an analysis of fraudulent financial reporting occurrences investigated by the U.S. SEC between January 1998 and December 2007. The findings in the study were issued in 2010 in *Fraudulent Financial Reporting: 1998–2007*:[49]

- There were 347 alleged cases of public company fraudulent financial reporting from 1998 to 2007, versus 294 cases from 1987 to 1997. Consistent with the high-profile frauds at Enron, WorldCom, etc., the dollar magnitude of fraudulent financial reporting soared in the last decade, with total cumulative misstatement or misappropriation of nearly $120 billion across 300 fraud cases with available information (with a mean of nearly $400 million per case). This compares to a mean of $25 million per sample fraud in COSO's 1999 study. While the largest frauds of the early 2000s skewed the 1998–2007 total and mean cumulative misstatement or misappropriation upward, the median fraud of $12.05 million in the present study also was nearly three times larger than the median fraud of $4.1 million in the 1999 COSO study.

- The companies allegedly engaging in financial statement fraud had median assets and revenues just under $100 million. These companies were much larger than fraud companies in the 1999 COSO study, which had median assets and revenues under $16 million.

- The SEC named the CEO and/or CFO for some level of involvement in 89 percent of the fraud cases, up from 83 percent of cases in 1987–1997. Within two years of the completion of the SEC's investigation, about 20 percent of CEOs/CFOs had been indicted, and over 60 percent of those indicted were eventually convicted.

- The most common fraud technique involved improper revenue recognition, followed by the overstatement of existing assets or capitalization of expenses. Revenue frauds accounted for over 60 percent of the cases, versus 50 percent in 1987–1997.

- Relatively few differences in board of director characteristics existed between firms engaging in fraud and similar firms not engaging in fraud. Also, in some instances, noted differences were in directions opposite of what might be expected. These results suggest the importance of research on governance processes and the interaction of various governance mechanisms.

- A total of 26 percent of the fraud firms changed auditors between the last clean financial statements and the last fraudulent financial statements, whereas only 12 percent of no-fraud firms switched auditors during that same time. In addition, 60 percent of the fraud firms that changed auditors did so during the fraud period, while the remaining 40 percent changed in the fiscal period just before the fraud began.

- Initial news in the press of an alleged fraud resulted in an average 16.7 percent abnormal stock price decline in the two days surrounding the news announcement. In addition, news of an SEC or Department of Justice investigation resulted in an average 7.3 percent abnormal stock price decline.

- Long-term negative consequences of fraud were apparent. Companies engaged in fraud often experienced bankruptcy, delisting from a stock exchange, or material asset sales following discovery of fraud at rates much higher than those experienced by no-fraud firms.

A disturbing result of the two studies is the increase in CEO/CFO involvement in the fraud from the 1999 study (83 percent) to the 2010 study (89 percent). Given that SOX passed in 2002 and imposed increased responsibilities on the CEO and CFO, including financial statement certifications, we have to wonder whether top management is really taking the problem of financial statement fraud seriously.

Another disturbing result is that 26 percent of the fraud firms in the 2010 study changed auditors between the last clean opinion on financial statements and the fraudulent statements, while only 12 percent of no-fraud firms did the same. One possible conclusion is that the fraud firms changed auditors to look for an auditing firm that might provide less resistance to going along with the fraudulent statements raising the possibility of opinion shopping. It is also possible that some auditing firms withdrew from the engagement when fraudulent statements existed.

"Opinion shopping" occurs when management threatens an auditor with putting up the engagement for competitive bidding when the auditor refuses to support management's position. The goal of opinion shopping is to seek out a different (more favorable) opinion from the auditors. There is nothing (ethically) wrong with a client exercising its due diligence and putting out an audit for competitive bids, especially if a concern exists about the quality of work or size of the audit fees. However, when the client seeks other views until finding an auditor who will go along with the client's desired—not necessarily most ethical—accounting treatment, we have the classic example of opinion shopping. In this case, management might threaten to change auditors because of the disagreement. If a change occurs, then an 8-K report is filed with the SEC explaining the reason for the change in auditor. The filing of an 8-K may trigger an SEC investigation.

### Enterprise Risk Management—Integrated Framework

In 2001, COSO initiated a project to develop a framework that would be readily usable by managements to evaluate and improve their organizations' enterprise risk management (ERM). The framework incorporates internal control principles that enhance corporate governance and risk management. *ERM* is defined as a process, effected by an entity's board of directors, management, and other personnel and applied in strategy setting and across the enterprise, designed to identify potential events that may affect the entity and to manage risk within its risk appetite.[50]

According to COSO, ERM encompasses six elements:

1. *Aligning risk appetite and strategy.* Risk appetite is considered by management in evaluating strategic alternatives, setting related objectives, and developing mechanisms to manage related risks.
2. *Enhancing risk response decisions.* ERM provides the discipline to identify and select among alternative risk responses—risk avoidance, reduction, sharing, and acceptance.
3. *Reducing operational surprises and losses.* ERM provides the capability to identify potential events and establish responses, reducing surprises and associated costs or losses.
4. *Identifying and managing multiple and cross-enterprise risks.* ERM facilitates effective responses to interrelated aspects of risk that affect different parts of the organization, and integrated responses to multiple risks.
5. *Seizing opportunities.* ERM allows management to consider a full range of potential events, positioning it to identify and proactively realize opportunities.
6. *Improving deployment of capital.* The risk information provided by ERM enables management to assess effectively overall capital needs and enhance capital allocation.

COSO's ERM is designed to help an entity get where it wants to go and avoid pitfalls and surprises along the way. ERM adds a number of strategic issues, including objective setting by management, identification of risks and opportunities affecting achievement of an entity's objectives, and risk responses selected by management to align risk tolerance and risk appetite.[51]

In 2009, COSO issued *Guidance on Monitoring Internal Control Systems,* an integral part of its framework. Monitoring should be done to assess the quality of internal control performance over time. To provide reasonable assurance that an entity's objectives will be achieved, management should monitor controls to determine whether they are operating effectively and whether they need to be redesigned when risks change.[52]

According to COSO's *Guidance,* effective monitoring involves (1) establishing a baseline for control effectiveness, (2) designing and executing monitoring procedures that are based on the significance of business risks relative to the entity's objectives, and (3) assessing and reporting results, including follow-up on corrective actions.[53]

Monitoring can be done through ongoing activities or separate evaluations that are built into the normal, recurring activities of the entity and include regular management and supervisory activities. Management can use internal auditors or personnel performing similar functions to monitor the operating effectiveness of internal control. For example, management might review whether bank reconciliations are being prepared on a timely basis and reviewed by the internal auditors.[54]

The success of COSO's efforts to strengthen internal controls and ERM systems depends on changing the culture of most organizations. Shifting employees' attitudes about risk management will happen only after they see senior management and the board of directors adopting the procedures. As the risk management culture develops throughout the organization, each aspect of the ERM framework can be incorporated efficiently into day-to-day operations. To create a risk management culture requires a commitment to integrity and ethical values in all aspects of an entity's operations.

The ERM framework represents the accounting profession's response to the increased need to manage risk in the aftermath of the accounting scandals and business failures that caused substantial harm to investors, company personnel, and other stakeholders. The framework adopts the position that management should determine its risk appetite and align it with strategic objectives. Unfortunately, ERM seems to place emphasis in the wrong areas by focusing on risk appetite. The usefulness of the ERM framework in establishing an ethical culture can be questioned because it does not place any emphasis on the ethical dimensions of making strategic decisions. Instead, the focus is on the company's "hunger" for risk in terms of its strategic objectives.

# PCAOB Standards

PCAOB issues standards for the audit of public companies by registered CPA firms. In its standards, PCAOB recognizes the importance of internal control over financial reporting as the foundation for the financial statement audit. The usefulness of financial statement amounts can be questioned if the underlying system that produced the numbers is not reliable. PCAOB requires auditors to examine the design and effectiveness of internal control sufficient to render an opinion on its effectiveness.

Students should become familiar with PCAOB standards because many of you will work for accounting firms that have publicly-owned clients and must adhere to the standards. Knowledge of PCAOB auditing standards also helps to understand the context of reporting on whether material misstatements exist in a client's financial statements and whether the internal controls are operating as intended. We discuss selected PCAOB standards below.

The PCAOB issues ethics and independence standards that apply to public companies. Rule 3526, *Communication with Audit Committees Concerning Independence,* requires that a registered public accounting firm must, prior to accepting an initial engagement pursuant to the standards of the PCAOB, describe to the audit committee of the issuer, in writing, all relationships between the registered public accounting firm or any affiliates of the firm and the potential audit client or persons in financial reporting oversight roles at the potential audit client that, as of the date of the communication, may reasonably be thought to bear on independence. The communication should address the potential effects of the relationships on the independence of the registered public accounting firm, should it be appointed the issuer's auditor, and document the substance of its discussion with the audit committee of the issuer. The firm also must affirm to the audit committee of the issuer, in writing, that, as of the date of the communication, the registered public accounting firm is independent in compliance with Rule 3520.[55]

## AS 4: Reporting on Previously Reported Material Weakness

*AS 4* describes the steps to be used by auditors when a company voluntarily engages them to report on whether a material weakness, previously identified in SOX Section 404 report on internal controls, is no longer present. The auditor's objective in performing work under *AS 4* is to obtain reasonable assurance as to whether the previously reported material weakness still exists. The auditor focuses on whether the controls specified by management as addressing the material weakness were designed and operating effectively as of the date chosen by management. The auditor's opinion is not an opinion on the effectiveness of internal controls over financial reporting overall, nor is it an update to a previous opinion on internal control over financial reporting.

*AS 4* establishes the following steps to be taken by auditors engaged to report on whether a previously reported material weakness still exists:

1. Evaluate whether conditions for engagement performance have been met, including the following:
   a. Management accepts responsibility for the effectiveness of internal controls.
   b. Management has evaluated controls that it believes have addressed the material weakness.
   c. Management asserts that the controls are effective in correcting the material weakness.
   d. Management has obtained sufficient evidence, including documentation, that supports its assessment.
   e. Management presents a report to accompany the auditor's report.
2. Plan the engagement.
3. Evaluate whether to use the work of others.
4. Obtain evidence about the effectiveness of controls.
5. Obtain written representations from management and evaluate management's report.
6. Form a conclusion and report.
7. Communicate with the audit committee.

## AS 5: An Audit of Internal Control over Financial Reporting That Is Integrated with an Audit of Financial Statements

*AS 5* establishes requirements and provides direction that applies when an auditor is engaged to perform an audit of management's assessment of the effectiveness of internal control over financial reporting. It provides that "effective internal control over financial reporting [ICFR] provides reasonable assurance regarding the reliability of financial reporting and the preparation of financial statements for external purposes. If one or more material weaknesses exist, the company's ICFR cannot be considered effective." The standard emphasizes that the general standards are applicable to an audit of ICFR. Those standards require technical training and proficiency as an auditor, independence, and the exercise of due professional care, including professional skepticism. The standard also establishes fieldwork and reporting standards applicable to an audit of ICFR.

The audit of ICFR should be integrated with the audit of financial statements. While the objectives of the audits are not identical, the auditor must plan and perform the work to achieve the objectives of both audits. In an integrated audit, the auditor should design testing procedures for internal controls to accomplish the objectives of both audits simultaneously: (1) to obtain sufficient evidence to support the auditor's opinion on ICFR at year-end, and (2) to obtain sufficient evidence to support the auditor's control risk assessments for purposes of the auditing of financial statements.

*AS 5* standards include obtaining reasonable assurance about whether the financial statements are free of material misstatement, whether caused by error or fraud, and whether management's assessment of the effectiveness of the company's ICFR is fairly stated in all material respects. Accordingly, there is some risk that a material misstatement of the financial statements or a material weakness in internal control over financial reporting would remain undetected. Although not absolute, reasonable assurance is, nevertheless, a high level of assurance. Also, an integrated audit is not designed to detect error or fraud that is immaterial to the financial statements or deficiencies in internal control over financial reporting that, individually or in combination, are less severe than a material weakness. If, for any reason, the auditor is unable to complete the audit or is unable to form or has not formed an opinion, she may decline to express an opinion or decline to issue a report as a result of the engagement.

### *AS 6:* **Evaluating Consistency of Financial Statements**

*AS 6* establishes requirements and provides direction for the auditor's evaluation of the consistency of the financial statements, including changes to previously issued financial statements, and the effect of that evaluation on the auditor's report on the financial statements. The comprehensive and far-reaching nature of the standard precludes complete coverage. Therefore, what follows is a description of its major provisions with respect to restatements of the financial statements due to errors and misstatements.

*AS 6* states that a change in accounting principle is a change from one GAAP to another GAAP when (1) there are two or more GAAPs that apply, or when (2) the accounting principle formerly used is no longer generally accepted.

Second, according to *AS 6,* a change in the method of applying an accounting principle also is considered a change in accounting principle. A change from an accounting principle that is not generally accepted to one that is generally accepted is a *correction of a misstatement.* The term *error,* as used in *FAS 154,* is equivalent to *misstatement,* as used in the auditing standards. Recall that such errors are recorded as an adjustment to the beginning balance of retained earnings, and prior years' income amounts would be restated.

Third, *AS 6* states that the correction of a material misstatement in previously issued financial statements should be recognized in the auditor's report on the audited financial statements through the addition of an explanatory paragraph i.e., emphasis-of-matter. The accounting pronouncements generally require certain disclosures relating to restatements to correct misstatements in previously issued financial statements. If the financial statement disclosures are inadequate, the auditor should address the inadequacy of disclosure and decide on the proper course of action with respect to the audit opinion.

Finally, *AS 6* says that changes in classification in previously issued financial statements do not require recognition in the auditor's report unless the change represents the correction of a material misstatement or a change in accounting principle. Accordingly, the auditor should evaluate a material change in financial statement classification and the related disclosure to determine whether such a change also is a change in accounting principle or a correction of a material misstatement. For example, certain reclassifications in previously issued financial statements, such as reclassifications of debt from long-term to short-term or reclassifications of cash flows from the operating activities category to the financing activities category, might occur because those items were incorrectly classified in the previously issued financial statements. In such situations, the reclassification also is the correction of a misstatement. If the auditor determines that the reclassification is a change in accounting principle or if the auditor determines that the reclassification is a correction of a material misstatement in previously issued financial statements, he should address the matter as required by reporting standards.

### PCAOB Risk Assessment Standards

In order to establish stricter standards for risk assessment, the PCAOB adopted eight auditing standards related to the auditor's assessment of, and response to, risk for audits of fiscal years beginning on or after December 15, 2010.

The risk assessment standards, *AS 8–15,* set forth requirements that enhance the effectiveness of the auditor's assessment of, and response to, the risks of material misstatement in the financial statements.

The risk assessment standards address audit procedures performed throughout the audit, from the initial planning stages through the evaluation of the audit results. A brief summary of the standards follows.

## AS 8—Audit Risk[56]

This standard discusses the auditor's consideration of audit risk in an audit of financial statements as part of an integrated audit including internal controls or an audit of financial statements only. It describes the components of audit risk and the auditor's responsibilities for reducing audit risk to an appropriately low level in order to obtain reasonable assurance that the financial statements are free of material misstatement. To form an appropriate basis for expressing an opinion on the financial statements, the auditor must plan and perform the audit to obtain reasonable assurance about whether the financial statements are free of material misstatement due to error or fraud. Reasonable assurance is obtained by reducing audit risk to an appropriately low level through applying due professional care, including obtaining sufficient appropriate audit evidence.

## AS 9—Audit Planning[57]

This standard establishes requirements regarding planning an audit, including assessing matters that are important to the audit and establishing an appropriate audit strategy and audit plan. The auditor should perform the following activities at the beginning of the audit:

1. Perform procedures regarding the continuance of the client relationship and the specific audit engagement.
2. Determine compliance with independence and ethics requirements in the preliminary engagement and reevaluate independence with changes in circumstances.
3. Establish an understanding of the terms of the audit engagement with the audit committee in accordance with *AS 16, Communications with Audit Committees.*

## AS 10—Supervision of the Audit Engagement[58]

This standard sets forth requirements for supervision of the audit engagement, including, in particular, supervising the work of engagement team members. It applies to the engagement partner and to other engagement team members who assist the engagement partner with supervision. The engagement partner and, as applicable, other engagement team members performing supervisory activities, should inform engagement team members of their responsibilities, including (1) the objectives of the procedures that they are to perform, (2) the nature, timing, and extent of procedures they are to perform, and (3) matters that could affect the procedures performed or the evaluation of the results of those procedures, including relevant aspects of the company, its environment, and its internal control over financial reporting, and possible accounting and auditing issues.

## AS No. 11—Consideration of Materiality in Planning and Performing an Audit[59]

This standard describes the auditor's responsibilities for consideration of materiality in planning and performing an audit. AS 11 provides a definition of materiality that has been used in resolving legal cases. In interpreting the federal securities laws, the Supreme Court of the United States has held that a fact is material if there is "a substantial likelihood that the . . . fact would have been viewed by the reasonable investor as having significantly altered the 'total mix' of information made available." As the Supreme Court has noted, determinations of materiality require "delicate assessments of the inferences a 'reasonable shareholder' would draw from a given set of facts and the significance of those inferences to him. . . ."

To obtain reasonable assurance about whether the financial statements are free of material misstatement, the auditor should plan and perform audit procedures to detect misstatements that, individually or in combination with other misstatements, would result in material misstatement of the financial statements. This includes being alert while planning and performing audit procedures for misstatements that could be material due to *quantitative or qualitative factors.*

## AS No. 12—Identifying and Assessing Risks of Material Misstatement[60]

This standard establishes requirements regarding the process of identifying and assessing risks of material misstatement of the financial statements. The risk assessment process discussed in the standard includes information-gathering procedures to identify risks and an analysis of the identified risks. This standard discusses the following risk assessment procedures:

- Obtaining an understanding of the company and its environment
- Obtaining an understanding of internal control over financial reporting
- Considering information from the client acceptance and retention evaluation, audit planning activities, past audits, and other engagements performed for the company
- Performing analytical procedures
- Conducting a discussion among engagement team members regarding the risks of material misstatement
- Inquiring of the audit committee, management, and others within the company about the risks of material misstatement.

## AS No. 13—The Auditor's Responses to the Risks of Material Misstatement[61]

This standard establishes requirements for responding to the risks of material misstatement in financial statements through the general conduct of the audit and performing audit procedures regarding significant accounts and disclosures. The auditor must design and implement audit responses that address the risks of material misstatement that are identified and assessed in accordance with *AS 12, Identifying and Assessing Risks of Material Misstatement.*

## AS No. 14—Evaluating Audit Results[62]

This standard establishes requirements regarding the auditor's evaluation of audit results and determination of whether the auditor has obtained sufficient appropriate audit evidence. The evaluation process set forth in this standard includes, among other things, evaluation of misstatements identified during the audit; the overall presentation of the financial statements, including disclosures; and the potential for management bias in the financial statements.

In forming an opinion on whether the financial statements are presented fairly, in all material respects, in conformity with the applicable financial reporting framework, the auditor should take into account all relevant audit evidence, regardless of whether it appears to corroborate or to contradict the assertions in the financial statements.

In the audit of financial statements, the auditor's evaluation of audit results should include the following:

- The results of analytical procedures performed in the overall review of the financial statements ("overall review")
- Misstatements accumulated during the audit, including, in particular, uncorrected misstatements
- The qualitative aspects of the company's accounting practices
- Conditions identified during the audit that relate to the assessment of the risk of material misstatement due to fraud ("fraud risk")
- The presentation of the financial statements, including disclosures
- The sufficiency and appropriateness of the audit evidence obtained

## AS No. 15—Audit Evidence[63]

This standard explains what constitutes audit evidence and establishes requirements for designing and performing audit procedures to obtain sufficient appropriate audit evidence to support the opinion expressed in the auditor's report. *Audit evidence* is all information, whether obtained from audit procedures or other sources, that is used by the auditor in arriving at the conclusions on which the auditor's opinion is based. It consists of both information that supports and corroborates management's assertions regarding the financial statements or internal control over financial reporting and information that contradicts such assertions.

The auditor must plan and perform audit procedures to obtain sufficient appropriate audit evidence to provide a reasonable basis for her opinion. Sufficiency is the measure of the quantity of audit evidence. The quantity of audit evidence needed is affected by the following:

- *Risk of material misstatement (in the audit of financial statements) or the risk associated with the control (in the audit of internal control over financial reporting).* As the risk increases, the amount of evidence that the auditor should obtain also increases. For example, ordinarily more evidence is needed to respond to significant risks.
- *Quality of the audit evidence obtained.* As the quality of the evidence increases, the need for additional corroborating evidence decreases. Obtaining more of the same type of audit evidence, however, cannot compensate for the poor quality of that evidence.

Appropriateness is the measure of the quality of audit evidence (i.e., its relevance and reliability). To be appropriate, audit evidence must be both relevant and reliable in providing support for the conclusions on which the auditor's opinion is based.

*AS 8–15* establish requirements that enhance the effectiveness of the auditor's assessment of and response to the risks of material misstatement in an audit. As previously discussed, the "present fairly" statement depends on the financial statements being free of material misstatements caused by error, fraud, or illegal acts. An audit in accordance with GAAS should be designed to detect the risk of material misstatement and act accordingly to reduce the risk to acceptable levels. Most important, audit standards establish the framework in which auditors rely on professional judgment and ethical decision-making to meet their public interest obligations.

## Communications with Audit Committees

*AS 16, Communications with Audit Committees,* requires the auditor to communicate with the company's audit committee regarding certain matters related to the conduct of an audit and to obtain certain information from the audit committee relevant to the audit.[64]

The objectives of the auditor are to:

1. Communicate to the audit committee the responsibilities of the auditor in relation to the audit and establish an understanding of the terms of the audit engagement with the audit committee.
2. Obtain information from the audit committee relevant to the audit.
3. Communicate to the audit committee an overview of the overall audit strategy and timing of the audit.
4. Provide the audit committee with timely observations arising from the audit that are significant to the financial reporting process.

The auditor should discuss with the audit committee any significant issues that the auditor discussed with management in connection with the appointment or retention of the auditor, including significant discussions regarding the application of accounting principles and auditing standards.

The auditor should establish an understanding of the terms of the audit engagement with the audit committee. This understanding includes communicating to the audit committee the following:

1. The objective of the audit
2. The responsibilities of the auditor
3. The responsibilities of management

The auditor should inquire of the audit committee about whether it is aware of matters relevant to the audit, including, but not limited to, violations or possible violations of laws or regulations.

The auditor should communicate to the audit committee the following matters:

1. *Significant accounting policies and practices.* Significant accounting policies include management's initial selection of, or changes in, significant accounting policies or the application of such policies in the current period and the effect on financial statements or disclosures of significant accounting policies in controversial areas or areas for which there is a lack of authoritative guidance or consensus, or diversity in practice.
2. *Critical accounting policies and practices.* All critical accounting policies and practices to be used should be communicated to the audit committee, including the reasons certain policies and practices are considered critical and how current and future events might affect the determination of whether certain policies are considered critical.
3. *Critical accounting estimates.* A description of the process management used to develop critical accounting estimates should be communicated, along with management's significant assumptions used in critical accounting estimates that have a high degree of subjectivity. Additional communications include any significant changes that management made to the processes used to develop critical accounting estimates or significant assumptions, a description of management's reasons for the changes, and the effects of the changes on the financial statements.
4. *Significant unusual transactions.* Significant unusual transactions include those that are outside the normal course of business for the company or that otherwise appear to be unusual due to their timing, size, or nature; and the policies and practices management used to account for significant unusual transactions.

## Auditor's Evaluation of the Quality of the Company's Financial Reporting

The auditor should communicate to the audit committee the following matters:

- Qualitative aspects of significant accounting policies and practices, including situations in which the auditor identified bias in management's judgments about the amounts and disclosures in the financial statements

- The results of the auditor's evaluation of the differences between estimates best supported by the audit evidence and estimates included in the financial statements, which are individually reasonable but that indicate a possible bias on the part of the company's management

- The auditor's assessment of management's disclosures related to the critical accounting policies and practices, along with any significant modifications to the disclosure of those policies and practices proposed by the auditor that management did not make

- The basis for the auditor's conclusions regarding the reasonableness of the critical accounting estimates

- The auditors' understanding of the business rationale for significant unusual transactions

- The results of the auditor's evaluation of whether the presentation of the financial statements and the related disclosures are in conformity with the applicable financial reporting framework, including the auditor's consideration of the form, arrangement, and content of the financial statements (including the accompanying notes), encompassing matters such as the terminology used, the amount of detail given, the classification of items, and the bases of amounts set forth

- Situations in which, as a result of the auditor's procedures, the auditor identified a concern regarding management's anticipated application of accounting pronouncements that have been issued but are not yet effective and might have a significant effect on future financial reporting

- Alternative treatments permissible under the applicable financial reporting framework for policies and practices related to material items that have been discussed with management, including the ramifications of the use of such alternative disclosures and treatments and the treatment preferred by the auditor

### Difficult or Contentious Matters

The auditor should communicate to the audit committee matters that are difficult or contentious for which the auditor consulted outside the engagement team and that the auditor reasonably determined are relevant to the audit committee's oversight of the financial reporting process.

### Going Concern

The auditor should communicate to the audit committee, when applicable, the following matters relating to the auditor's evaluation of the company's ability to continue as a going concern:

- If the auditor believes there is substantial doubt about the company's ability to continue as a going concern for a reasonable period of time, the conditions and events that the auditor identified that, when considered in the aggregate, indicate that there is substantial doubt

- If the auditor concludes, after consideration of management's plans, that substantial doubt about the company's ability to continue as a going concern is alleviated, the basis for the auditor's conclusion, including elements the auditor identified within management's plans that are significant to overcoming the adverse effects of the conditions and events

- If the auditor concludes, after consideration of management's plans, that substantial doubt about the company's ability to continue as a going concern for a reasonable period of time remains, then the effects, if any, on the financial statements and adequacy of related disclosures should be communicated, along with the effects on the auditor's report

### Uncorrected and Corrected Misstatements

The auditor should provide the audit committee with the schedule of uncorrected misstatements related to accounts and disclosures that the auditor presented to management and discuss with the audit committee, or determine that management has adequately discussed with the audit committee, the basis for the determination that the uncorrected misstatements were immaterial, including the qualitative factors considered.

The auditor also should communicate that uncorrected misstatements or matters underlying those uncorrected misstatements could potentially cause future-period financial statements to be materially misstated, even if the auditor has concluded that the uncorrected misstatements are immaterial to the financial statements under audit.

The auditor should communicate to the audit committee those corrected misstatements (other than those that are clearly trivial) related to accounts and disclosures that might not have been detected except through the auditing procedures performed, and discuss with the audit committee the implications that such corrected misstatements might have on the company's financial reporting process.

### Departure from the Auditor's Standard Report

The auditor should communicate to the audit committee the following matters related to the auditor's report:

- When the auditor expects to modify the opinion in the auditor's report, the reasons for the modification, and the wording of the report
- When the auditor expects to include explanatory language or an explanatory paragraph in the auditor's report (i.e., emphasis of matter), the reasons for the explanatory language or paragraph, and the wording of the explanatory language or paragraph

### Disagreements with Management

The auditor should communicate to the audit committee any disagreements with management about matters, whether or not satisfactorily resolved, that individually or in the aggregate could be significant to the company's financial statements or the auditor's report. Disagreements with management do not include differences of opinion based on incomplete facts or preliminary information that are later resolved by the auditor obtaining additional relevant facts or information prior to the issuance of the auditor's report.

### Difficulties Encountered in Performing the Audit

The auditor should communicate to the audit committee any significant difficulties encountered during the audit. Significant difficulties encountered during the audit include, but are not limited to:

- Significant delays by management, the unavailability of company personnel, or an unwillingness by management to provide information needed for the auditor to perform her audit procedures
- An unreasonably brief time within which to complete the audit

- Unexpected extensive effort required by the auditor to obtain sufficient appropriate audit evidence

- Unreasonable management restrictions encountered by the auditor on the conduct of the audit

- Management's unwillingness to make or extend its assessment of the company's ability to continue as a going concern when requested by the auditor

### Form and Documentation of Communications

The auditor should communicate to the audit committee the matters in this standard, either orally or in writing and document the communications in the work papers.

The PCAOB's primary objectives in issuing a new standard on audit committee communications are to (1) enhance communications between auditors and audit committees and (2) improve audits by fostering constructive dialogue between the auditor and the audit committee.

*AS 16* should improve auditors' communications with audit committees by expanding on and adding to previously required communications, including those related to significant accounting policies, practices, and estimates; significant unusual transactions; and the auditor's evaluation of the quality of the company's financial reporting. Audit committee communications are an essential part of an effective governance system and a key ingredient in creating an ethical organization environment.

Open communications between the auditor and audit committee are essential to supporting the financial reporting oversight role assigned to the audit committee under SOX. The audit committee plays a critical role in resolving differences between the auditor and management and supporting the goal of a fair presentation of the financial statements and efficient and effective internal controls over financial reporting.

## Financial Statements Restatements

The risk of financial restatements is directly related to the quality of corporate governance, risk management, and compliance systems. DeZoort points out that financial restatements increased consistently after SOX until 2007, when the number and magnitude of restatements started to decrease.[65]

Early results seemed to have supported that perspective because 15 percent of public companies that file financial statements with the SEC in the first full year of implementation of *AS 2* (which was superseded by *AS 5*) restated their financial statements. This is double the number in 2004. In fact, an estimated range of 11 to 15 percent of public companies have identified in their filings with the SEC at least one material weakness in the internal controls over financial reporting.

In 2007, the number of restatements declined by 31.4 percent (from 1,800 to 1,235). This decline continued in 2008, during which a total of 869 restatements were filed by 778 unique companies. These figures represent a 31.4 percent drop in the amount of restatements (1,235 down to 869) and a 30 percent drop in the number of unique filers (1,111 down to 778). The downward trend appears to be attributable to the improved reliability of internal control over financial reporting implemented in response to SOX, but some observers suggest that the drop in restatements, at least to some extent, is due to a more relaxed approach adopted by the SEC regarding materiality and the need to file restatements. In addition to a drop in quantity, calendar year 2008 experienced an equivalence or drop in the severity of restatements compared to prior years. Restatements are also taking a smaller cut out of profits. The typical reduction to net income for a company restating financials in 2008 was only $6.1 million, compared to $7.4 million in 2007 and $20 million in both 2006 and 2005. Restatements also took less time to file and cited fewer accounting problems.

Restatements and material weaknesses took a sharp drop in 2009, but it is difficult to know whether that means companies are making fewer mistakes or just catching and reporting fewer mistakes. In 2009, only 75 companies with market capitalizations of at least $250 million restated their financial statements, according to data from Glass Lewis & Co. That is fewer than half the 172 companies that restated in 2008—and even that was a steep drop from the 334 that restated in 2007. Glass Lewis said the 2009 figure represents the lowest restatement rate since 2001, when massive corporate frauds at Enron, WorldCom, and others began a flood of restatements.[66]

The number of companies reporting material weaknesses also dropped considerably, to 69 in 2009 as opposed to 193 in 2008 and 325 in 2007. Only 87 companies in 2009 received adverse opinions on internal controls from their external auditors, down from 202 in 2008 and 263 in 2007.[67]

Financial restatements undermine shareholder confidence in the reliability of financial statements. The research literature in accounting and finance provides useful evidence about the leading causes of financial restatements, including accounting and transaction complexity, human error, and fraud. The effects of the restatements include negative market reactions, reduced credit access, and turnover within management and the board of directors.[68]

If we examine the ethical implications of financial restatements, what stands out is the lack of reliability of the financial information, which is a primary qualitative characteristic necessary to make accounting information useful to users making economic judgments and decisions. *Reliability* in this context refers to a quality of financial reporting that makes it a verifiable, faithful representation of transactions and events that have occurred within an organization.[69] Recall that in our discussion in Chapter 1 we pointed out that reliability was a virtuous character trait and part of the trustworthiness pillar of character.

Looking at the research more closely, the causes of financial restatements vary considerably across cases. Plumlee and Yohn highlight a number of potential causes of restatements, including the following:[70]

- Complexity of accounting standards and/or transactions driven by a highly technical rules-based system of accounting standards in the United States.
- Weak financial governance and controls (i.e., board of directors, audit committee, and internal control over financial reporting) that increase the likelihood of financial reporting failure and restatement.
- Increased auditor and audit committee conservatism driven by SOX and the number of new demands on auditors and audit committees. Increased regulation, scrutiny, and legal exposure for auditors and audit committees increase their motivation to be conservative and revisit management's judgments when evaluating financial reporting and specific accounting issues.
- Broad application of materiality. The SEC Advisory Committee on Improvements in Financial Reporting expressed concern that restatements result from overly strict materiality assessments, where restatements occur to correct misstatements that investors might not find important.
- Earnings management driven by pressure to meet or beat expectations established by various groups (e.g., analysts, directors).
- Lack of transparency that leads to the failure to provide disclosures that are complete and understandable in compliance with GAAP.
- Fraud due to financial reporting schemes where individuals intentionally misstate companies' financial statements.

Plumlee and Yohn conducted an empirical study of over 3,700 restatements during the period 2003–2006 to identify the leading causes of financial restatements. They classified restatement causes as due to either a basic company error, an intentional manipulation, a transaction complexity, or some characteristic of an accounting standard. Their results revealed that over half of the restatements analyzed during the four-year period were due to "basic internal company errors" rather than to the complexity of the transaction or accounting standard.[71]

## PCAOB Enforcement Program[72]

In addition to authorizing the PCAOB to inspect and set professional standards for public accounting firms, SOX conferred broad discretion on the board to investigate and discipline firms and their "associated persons" for violations of the federal securities laws governing the preparation and issuance of audit reports, as well as other professional standards. SOX did so, however, without curtailing the existing enforcement authority of the SEC over public company auditors.

The PCAOB announced its first settled enforcement action against a registered public accounting firm in 2005 and, as of December 2011, has publicly announced the resolution of 45 enforcement actions. Under SOX and the board's rules, PCAOB enforcement proceedings are non-public unless (1) the parties consent to a public hearing, (2) the board has imposed sanctions and the time to file an appeal with the SEC has expired, or (3) the SEC, on appeal, issues an order regarding the sanctions imposed. Because a respondent in a PCAOB proceeding has little incentive to consent to a public hearing, and the appeals process can take years to complete, there are enforcement actions brought by the PCAOB that are not yet—and may never be—known to the public. Moreover, if a formal or informal investigation is conducted but no disciplinary proceeding is instituted, or if a disciplinary proceeding is instituted but no sanctions are imposed by a hearing officer (or, on appeal, by the board), the public is unlikely to learn of the existence of the investigation or the proceeding.

Of the PCAOB's 45 public enforcement actions, 41 are settled disciplinary orders. A review of the board's publicly disclosed actions indicates that, in broad terms, the board's enforcement activities have focused principally on two objectives: (1) responding to perceived failures by PCAOB-registered firms or their associated persons to comply with professional standards during audit engagements, and (2) addressing improper conduct by registered firms or their associated persons during board inspections or enforcement investigations.

Specifically, 26 of the board's 45 publicly announced enforcement actions allege failures by firms or individual auditors to have complied with professional auditing standards during the course of an audit. The alleged violations that gave rise to such enforcement actions include, for example:

- Excessive reliance by auditors on management representations without performing sufficient audit procedures
- The failure to perform sufficient audit procedures with respect to key financial statement items, such as significant assets and sources of revenue
- The failure to evaluate whether information obtained during an audit represented fraud risks that warranted further inquiry
- Excessive reliance on audit staff that did not have the degree of technical training or proficiency required under the circumstances
- Reliance by registered firms on work performed by other auditors without performing sufficient procedures to determine whether such reliance was appropriate
- The failure to take steps to prevent further reliance on a prior audit opinion after having concluded that a client's previously issued financial statements were misleading
- The failure to exercise due care and objectivity in the performance of a concurring partner review
- The failure to assemble and maintain sufficient audit documentation

While most PCAOB proceedings alleging audit deficiencies have confined the claims to violations of professional standards, in a few cases the board has taken the additional step of asserting that the conduct of registered firms was so egregious that it violated the

Securities Exchange Act of 1934. Two such cases involved allegations that auditors violated the antifraud provisions of Section 10(b) of the Exchange Act and Rule 10b-5 thereunder by issuing audit reports representing that audits had been conducted in accordance with PCAOB standards, when the auditors knew, or were reckless in not knowing, that such representations were false. In addition, the PCAOB has alleged in four proceedings that registered firms failed to comply with their responsibilities under Section 10A of the Exchange Act, which prescribes the steps that outside auditors must take when they become aware that a client may have engaged in illegal conduct.[73] We discuss legal liability issues in Chapter 6.

The PCAOB has also brought four public enforcement actions alleging that registered firms and associated persons violated auditor independence requirements. These violations included, among other things, purchasing the audit client's securities while serving as a member of the engagement team and accepting an offer to serve on the audit client's board of directors, and commencing service in that role, during the audit engagement period.[74]

To date, 11 of the board's public enforcement actions—approximately 24 percent of the total—have been brought against one of the "Big Four" accounting firms or their associated persons. The remainder of the PCAOB's proceedings have been brought against smaller firms or individual practitioners. The nature and extent of PCAOB disciplinary actions raise the question whether CPAs are living up to their professional responsibilities and best serving the public interest.

## Concluding Thoughts

**Financial statement fraud** threatens the foundation of the financial reporting process and jeopardizes the integrity of the auditing function. An audit opinion provides reasonable assurance that the financial statements are free of material misstatements, including fraud. The basis for making that assertion is compliance with established auditing standards including those of the PCAOB.

Audit standards have come a long way in the last twenty years. In particular, the standards today provide a framework to evaluate internal controls and assess audit risk, and they do a better job of identifying the red flags indicating that fraud may be present. COSO guidelines provide that internal controls are an integral part of the reasonable assurance given in an audit report and that an entity's objectives will be achieved.

The Fraud Triangle provides a framework to evaluate risks of fraud and better understand how to prevent and detect it from occurring. A strong corporate governance system, including an independent audit committee, effective internal controls over financial reporting, and audit risk assessment procedures, is the best way to prevent fraud. The external auditors should communicate with the audit committee about accounting irregularities, weaknesses in control, and management override of the internal controls. The foundation of an effective corporate governance system is to create an ethical organization environment and build integrity into the financial reporting process.

From time to time, accountants seem to lose sight of the critical role that the independent audit plays in our free market economic system. Shareholders must be reassured that the financial statement numbers present fairly a company's financial position and the results of operations. Creditors need to know that the financial results accurately portray liquidity and profitability. All parties expect that the financial statements are in conformity with GAAP and the audit has been conducted in accordance with established standards.

Ethical conduct and successful audits go hand in hand. An auditor must consider the rights of shareholders and creditors to receive accurate and reliable information about the client's financial statements to assist these users to make decisions regarding buying, selling, or holding stock and making or not making loans.

This is a good time to remind you of the whistleblower provisions of the Dodd-Frank Financial Reform Act that restricts whistleblower rewards to accountants because of their preexisting legal duty to report securities violations. Individuals with internal compliance or audit responsibilities at an entity who receive information about potential violations cannot receive whistleblower awards because it is part of their job responsibilities to report suspicion of illegal acts to management. However, these individuals will not be excluded from receiving a whistleblower award in the following situations: (1) disclosure to the SEC is needed to prevent "substantial injury" to the financial interest of an entity or its investors, (2) the whistleblower reasonably believes the entity is impeding investigation of the misconduct, or (3) the whistleblower has first reported the violation internally and at least 120 days have passed.

CPAs who receive information about potential violations of a client or its directors or officers through an audit or other engagement required under the federal securities laws are not eligible to receive whistleblower awards. The SEC included this exclusion so as not to undermine the legal duty that auditors have under Section 10A of the Securities and Exchange Act of 1934 to report illegal acts by officers, directors, and other client personnel up the chain of command. If the issues are not addressed adequately by management, the auditor must then resign from the engagement and file a 10-K report with the SEC.

Accounting professionals are subject to legal liability if they fail to follow GAAP and GAAS and are unable to meet their ethical and professional obligations. In Chapter 6, we will look at a variety of classic cases that have established precedents for the legal liabilities of accountants and auditors to clients and third parties. We conclude this chapter by reiterating the need for a strong set of ethical values, including due care, professional skepticism, and the ethical judgment necessary to assess risk and detect fraud in the financial statements. Auditors meet their professional and ethical responsibilities in this regard by maintaining their integrity when client pressure exists to go along with materially misstated financial statements.

## Discussion Questions

1. What is the purpose of audit "risk assessment"? What are its objectives, and why is it important in assessing the likelihood that fraud may occur?

2. Distinguish between an auditor's responsibilities to detect and report errors, illegal acts, and fraud. What role does materiality have in determining the proper reporting and disclosure of such events?

3. *AU 240* points to three conditions that enable fraud to occur. Briefly describe each condition. How does one's propensity to act ethically, as described by Rest's model of morality, influence each of the three elements of the Fraud Triangle?

4. Explain the content of each section of the audit report. Evaluate the importance of each section with respect to the users of financial reports.

5. Give one example each of when an auditor might render an unmodified opinion and include an emphasis-of-matter paragraph and an other-matter paragraph. What is the value of such paragraphs in the audit report?

6. The following statement expresses the conclusion of XYZ auditors with respect to the company's investment in ABC. Assume that all amounts are material. What type of audit opinion should be rendered given this statement? Explain the reasoning behind your answer.

   XYZ's investment in ABC, a foreign subsidiary acquired during the year and accounted for by the equity method, is carried at xxx on the statement of financial position as at December 31, 2013, and XYZ's share of ABC's net income of xxx is included in XYZ's income for the year then ended. We were unable to obtain sufficient appropriate audit evidence about the carrying amount of XYZ's investment in ABC as at December 31, 2013, and XYZ's share of ABC's net income for the year because we were denied access to the financial information, management, and the auditors of ABC. Consequently, we were unable to determine whether any adjustments to these amounts were necessary.

7. Rationalization for fraud can fall under two categories: "no harm" and "no responsibility." Assume an employee is directed by management to reduce recorded expenses at year-end by insignificant amounts individually, but which are material in total. How might the employee justify her actions if questioned by the auditor with respect to no harm and no responsibility? What stage of moral development in Kohlberg's model is best illustrated by the employee's actions? Why?

8. Some criticize the accounting profession for using expressions in the audit report that seem to be building in deniability should the client commit a fraudulent act. What expressions enable the CPA to build a defense should the audit wind up in the courtroom? How does your analysis relate to the opening statement in the chapter by Abe Briloff?

9. The audit report on General Motors for 2008 issued by Deloitte & Touche included the following statement: "The corporation's recurring losses from operations, stockholders' deficit, and

inability to generate sufficient cash flow to meet its obligations and sustain its operations raise substantial doubt about its ability to continue as a going concern." Are you surprised to learn of this going-concern alert at a company such as General Motors? What signs might the auditors look for prior to issuing their report on the 2009 financial statements that help them reevaluate the going-concern assessment?

10. Do you think the concept of materiality is incompatible with ethical behavior? Why or why not?

11. How do materiality judgments affect risk assessment in an audit of financial statements?

12. According to GAAS, the auditor must evaluate the control deficiencies that he has become aware of to determine whether those deficiencies, individually or in combination, are significant deficiencies or material weaknesses. What is the purpose of the auditor's evaluation of internal controls in these contexts with respect to conducting an audit in accordance with established auditing standards?

13. In 2005, the IMA reported the results of a survey of business, academic, and regulatory leaders conducted by the Center for Corporate Change that found the corporation's culture to be the most important factor influencing the attitudes and behavior of executives. The results indicate that 88 percent of the representatives who took part in the survey believe that companies devote little management attention to considering the effect of the culture on their executives. What are the elements of the corporate culture? How do the standards in COSO's *Integrated Framework* help define a strong control environment?

14. Kinetics, Inc., included the following footnote in its December 31, 2013, financial statements:

> We corrected the misstatement of capitalized advertising costs recorded in 2012 by adjusting operating expenses for 2013, and crediting the asset account. The result of this correction is to reduce income by $500,000 for 2013 [a material amount] and reduce recorded assets by a like amount.

How would you determine whether to include reference to the correction in the audit report? If reference is needed, how should it affect the type of audit opinion given?

15. What do you think is meant by the term ethical auditing with respect to the principles and rules of professional conduct in the AICPA Code?

16. Mr. Arty works for Smile Accounting Firm as a senior accountant. Currently, he is doing a review of rental property compliance testing completed by the staff accountants. He is testing rental receipts and expenses of the property owned by the client. Arty realizes that the staff accountants tested only two tenants per property, instead of the three required by the audit program based on materiality considerations. However, to request more information from the client would cause massive delays, and the manager on the engagement is pressing hard for the information before Christmas vacation. Assume that the manager approaches the client, who states that she does not want any additional testing: "I needed the report yesterday." The manager points out to Arty that no problems were found from the testing of the two properties. Moreover, the firm has never had any accounting issues with respect to the client. Assume that the firm decides that it is not necessary to do the additional testing. What would you do if you were Arty? Consider in your answer the ethics of the situation, your ethical obligations as a CPA, and the reporting obligations of the firm.

17. What are the auditor's responsibilities to communicate information to the audit committee under PCAOB standards? If the auditor discovers that the audit committee routinely ignores such communications especially when they are critical of management's use of GAAP in the financial statements, what step(s) might the auditor take at this point?

18. In Europe, the audit reports use the expression "true and fair view" to characterize the results of the audit. Do you think there is a meaningful difference between that language and the "present fairly" statement made in U.S. audit reports? As a user of the financial statements in each instance, does one expression more than the other give you a greater comfort level with respect to the conformity of the financial statements with GAAP? Why or why not?

19. "Accounting firms and their personnel must continually evaluate their clients' accounting and related disclosures, putting themselves in investors' shoes." This statement was made on February 8, 2012, by Claudius B. Modesti, director of the PCAOB Division of Enforcement and Investigations, in reporting on PCAOB's audits of Medicis Pharmaceutical Corporation's fiscal 2005 through 2007 financial statements. Medicis was a client of Ernst & Young that was

undergoing an inspection in accordance with PCAOB's enforcement program. The board found that EY and its partners failed to audit key assumptions sufficiently and placed undue reliance on management's representation that those assumptions were reasonable. Further, the firm failed to evaluate properly a material departure from GAAP in the company's financial statements—its sales returns reserve.[75]

PCAOB chairman James R. Doty was quoted as saying: "The auditor's job is to exercise professional skepticism in evaluating a public company's accounting and in conducting its audit to ensure that investors receive reliable information, which did not happen in this case."

Following the audits and PCAOB inspection of EY's audit of Medicis, the company corrected its accounting for its sales returns reserve and filed restated financial statements with the SEC.

What is the link between professional skepticism and Josephson's Six Pillars of Character that were discussed in Chapter 1? Given the limited information, which rules of professional conduct in the AICPA Code were violated by EY? Explain why.

20. Audit morality includes moral sensitivity, moral judgment, moral motivation, and moral character. Explain how audit morality plays a key role in determining best audit practice that influences audit performance.

## Endnotes

1. Association of Certified Fraud Examiners, *2012 Global Fraud Study: Report to the Nations on Occupational Fraud and Abuse,* www.acfe.com/uploadedFiles/ACFE_Website/Content/rttn/2012-report-to-nations.pdf.

2. Marc J. Epstein and Marshall Geiger, "Investor Views of Audit Assurance: Recent Evidence of the Expectations Gap," *Journal of Accountancy,* January 1994.

3. American Institute of CPAs, *AICPA Professional Standards. Volume 1 as of June 1, 2012, Consideration of Fraud in a Financial Statement Audit* (New York: AICPA, 2009), AU Section 240.

4. American Institute of CPAs, *AICPA Professional Standards. Volume 1 as of June 1, 2012, Audit Risk and Materiality in Conducting an Audit* (New York: AICPA, 2009), AU Section 320.

5. *AU 320 and 450.*

6. *AU 240.*

7. Association of Certified Fraud Examiners (ACFE). *ACFE Report to the Nation on Occupational Fraud and Abuse* (Austin, TX: ACFE, 2006).

8. American Institute of CPAs, *AICPA Professional Standards. Volume 1 as of June 1, 2012, Statement on Auditing Standards (SAS) No. 54, Illegal Acts* (New York: AICPA, 2012), AU Section 250.

9. Timothy J. Louwers, Robert J. Ramsay, David H. Sinason, Jerry R. Strawser, and J.C. Thibodeau, *Auditing and Assurance Services* (New York: McGraw-Hill Irwin, 2013).

10. Louwers, pp. 77–78.

11. *AU 250.*

12. *AU 250.*

13. *AU 250.*

14. Timothy J. Louwers, Robert J. Ramsay, David H. Sinason, and Jerry R. Strawser, *Auditing and Assurance Services* (New York: McGraw-Hill Irwin, 2008).

15. *AU 240.*

16. Available at www.sec.gov/spotlight/optionsbackdating.htm.

17. SEC, Litigation Release No. 21042, May 18, 2009, Accounting and Auditing Release No. 2970, May 18, 2009, *SEC v. Monster Worldwide, Inc.,* U.S. District Court for the Southern District of New York, Civil Action No. 09 CV 4641 (S.D.N.Y. May 18, 2009), www.sec.gov/litigation/litreleases/2009/lr21042.htm.

18. Available at www.sec.gov/news/press/2009/2009-113.htm.

19. Securities and Exchange Commission, *SEC v. Tyco International Ltd.,* Litigation Release No. 19657, April 17, 2006, www.sec.gov/litigation/litreleases/2006/lr19657.htm.

20. Available at http://www.gelaw.com/tyco-international/tyco-in-the-news.

21. AICPA, AU Sections 240.06.07.

22. *AU 240.*

23. Nicholas Apostolou and D. Larry Crumbley, "Auditors' Responsibilities with Respect to Fraud: A Possible Shift," *The CPA Journal,* February 2008. Available at http://www.nysscpa.org/cpajournal/2008/208/essentials/p32.htm.

24. AU Section 240.

25. CA Magazine, January–February 2013, Available at http://www.camagazine.com/archives/print-edition/2002/aug/regulars/camagazine24193.aspx.

26. Apostolou and Crumbley.

27. SEC, Litigation Release No. 18728, May 24, 2004, Accounting and Enforcement Release No. 2024, May 24, 2004, *SEC v. Frank M. Bergonzi, Martin L. Grass, and Franklin C. Brown, http://www.sec.gov/litigation/litreleases/lr18728.htm*

28. *SEC vs. Bergonzi et al.*

29. AU Section 240.79-82.

30. AU Section 240.80.

31. Louwers, pp. 463–465.

32. U.S. House of Representations, H. R. 3763, Sarbanes-Oxley Act of 2002, www.findlaw.com.

33. AICPA, Clarified Statements on Auditing Standards, effective December 15, 2002. Available at www.aicpa.org/Research/Standards/AuditAttest/Pages/clarifiedSAS.aspx.

34. American Institute of CPAs, *AICPA Professional Standards. Volume I as of June 1, 2012,* Audit Documentation (New York: AICPA, 2012), AU Section 230.

35. American Institute of CPAs, *AICPA Professional Standards. Volume 1 as of June 1, 2012 Statement on Auditing Standards (SAS) No. 107,* Audit Risk and Materiality in Conducting an Audit (New York: AICPA, 2012), AU Section 570.

36. Financial Accounting Standards Board, *Statement of Financial Accounting Concepts (SFAC) No. 2,* Qualitative Characteristics of Accounting Information (Stamford, CT: FASB, May 1980).

37. *AU 240.*

38. Securities and Exchange Commission, *SEC Staff Accounting Bulletin: No. 99—Materiality,* www.sec.gov/interps/account/sab99.htm.

39. TSC Industries, Inc. v. Northway, Inc. - 426 U.S. 438 (1976), http://caselaw.lp.findlaw.com/scripts/getcase.pl?court5us.

40. *AU 240.*

41. AICPA, *Statement on Auditing Standards (SAS) No. 122* (part of AICPA's "Clarification Project)"; Available at www.aicpa.org/Research/Standards/AuditAttest/Pages/clarifiedSAS.aspx.

42. Financial Accounting Standards Board, *Statement of Financial Accounting Standards (FAS) No. 17,* Accounting for Leases (Stamford, CT: FASB, November 1977).

43. Stephen A. Zeff, "The Primacy of 'Present Fairly' in the Auditor's Report," Available at http://www.ruf.rice.edu/~sazeff/PDF/Primacy%20AP%20pdf.pdf.

44. Robert Kuhn Mautz, Hussein Amer Sharaf, *The Philosophy of Auditing* (New York: Sarasota, FL: American Accounting Association, 1961).

45. AICPA, *Statement on Auditing Standards (SAS) No. 104–No.111,* Risk Assessment Standards, March 2006, www.aicpa.org/audit and attest standards/risk assessmentstandards.html.

46. Committee of Sponsoring Organizations of the Treadway Commission (COSO), *Internal Control—Integrated Framework* (New York: AICPA, 1992).

47. COSO, *Internal Control—Integrated Framework.* May 2013. http://www.coso.org/documents/COSO%202013%20ICFR%20Executive_Summary.pdf.

48. PCAOB, *AS No. 5,* An Audit of Internal Control over Financial Reporting That Is Integrated with an Audit of Financial Statements. Available at http://pcaobus.org/Standards/Auditing/Pages/Auditing_Standard_5.aspx.

49. COSO, *Fraudulent Financial Reporting: 1987–1997.* March 1999. Available at http://www.coso.org/publications/ffr_1987_1997.pdf.

50. COSO, *Fraudulent Financial Reporting: 1987–1997.* May 2010. Available at http://www.coso .org/documents/COSOFRAUDSTUDY2010_001.pdf.

51. COSO, *Enterprise Risk Management (ERM)—Integrated Framework: Executive Summary* (New York: AICPA, September 2004).

52. COSO, *Enterprise Risk Management (ERM).*

53. COSO, *Guidance on Monitoring Internal Control Systems,* Vol. 1, p. 4, 2009.

54. COSO, *Guidance on Monitoring Internal Control Systems,* Vol. 1.

55. PCAOB, Rule 3526, *Communication with Audit Committees Concerning Independence,* August 22, 2008. http://pcaobus.org/Rules/PCAOBRules/Pages/Section_3.aspx#rule3526.

56. PCAOB, *Auditing Standard No. 8, Audit Risk,* December 15, 2010, www.pcaobus.org/Standards.html.

57. PCAOB, *Auditing Standard No. 9, Audit Planning,* December 15, 2010, www.pcaobus.org/ Standards.html.

58. PCAOB, *Auditing Standard No. 10, Supervision of the Audit Engagement,* December 15, 2010. www.pcaobus.org/Standards.html.

59. PCAOB, *Auditing Standard No. 11, Consideration of Materiality in Planning and Performing an Audit,* December 15, 2010. www.pcaobus.org/Standards.html.

60. PCAOB, *Auditing Standard No. 12, Identifying and Assessing Risks of Material Misstatement,* December 15, 2010. www.pcaobus.org/Standards.html.

61. PCAOB, *Auditing Standard No. 13, The Auditor's Responses to the Risks of Material Misstatement,* December 15, 2010. www.pcaobus.org/Standards.html.

62. PCAOB, *Auditing Standard No. 14, Evaluating Audit Results,* December 15, 2010. www .pcaobus.org/Standards.html.

63. PCAOB, *Auditing Standard No. 15, Audit Evidence,* December 15, 2010. www.pcaobus.org/ Standards.html.

64. PCAOB, *Auditing Standard 16, Communications with Audit Committees,* December 15, 2012. www.pcaobus.org/Standards.html.

65. Todd DeZoort, "What Are the Leading Causes of Financial Restatements?" *QFinance,* Available at http://www.qfinance.com/accountancy-best-practice/what-are-the-leading-causes-of-financial-restatements?page=1.

66. Tammy Whitehouse, "Restatements, Weaknesses Drop Again in 2009," *Compliance Week,* February 2, 2010, http://www.complianceweek.com/restatements-weaknesses-drop-again-in-2009/article/ 189499/.

67. Whitehouse.

68. DeZoort.

69. Financial Accounting Standards Board. FASB Concepts Statement No. 2, *Qualitative Characteristics of Accounting Information,* May 1980.

70. Plumlee, M., and T. L. Yohn. "An analysis of the underlying causes of restatements." Working paper, March 1, 2008. Available at http://papers.ssrn.com/sol3/papers.cfm?abstract_id=1104189.

71. Plumlee and Yohn.

72. The following paragraphs are taken from *Observations from 2010 Inspections of Domestic Annually Inspected Firms Regarding Deficiencies in Audits of Internal Control over Financial Reporting,* PCAOB Release No. 2012-006, December 10, 2012; Available at http://pcaobus.org/ Inspections/Documents/12102012_Release_2012_06.pdf.

73. Section 10A(k) of the Exchange Act, 15 U.S.C. § 78j-1(k), and Rule 2-07(a)(1) of Regulation S-X, 17 C.F.R. § 210.2-07(a)(1).

74. *See* AU sec. 540, *Auditing Accounting Estimates,* which discusses the auditor's responsibilities to obtain and evaluate sufficient appropriate audit evidence to support significant accounting estimates in an audit of financial statements.

75. Available at http://goingconcern.com/post/ernst-young-settles-2-million-slap-hand-pcaob.

## Appendix 1

# Unmodified Opinion with an Emphasis-of-Matter Paragraph— Going-Concern Issue[1]

The accompanying consolidated financial statements have been prepared assuming that the Company will continue as a going concern. As discussed in note 1 to the consolidated financial statements, the Company has suffered negative cash flows from operations and has an accumulated deficit that raise substantial doubt about its ability to continue as a going concern. Management's plans in regard to these matters are also described in note 1. The consolidated financial statements do not include any adjustments that might result from the outcome of this uncertainty. Our opinion is not modified with respect to this matter.

[1]American Institute of CPAs, *AICPA Professional Standards. Volume 1 as of June 1, 2012, Statement on Auditing Standards (SAS) No. 59,* Internal Control in a Financial Statement Audit (New York: AICPA, 2012), AU Section 341·

## Appendix 2

# Unmodified Opinion with an Emphasis-of-Matter Paragraph— Change in Accounting Principle[2]

As discussed in note 2 to the consolidated financial statements, the Company adopted Accounting Standards Update No. 2013-02—Comprehensive Income—issued by the Financial Accounting Standards Board in February 2013 (Reporting of Amounts Reclassified Out of Accumulated Other Comprehensive Income) as of December 31, 2012.

[2]American Institute of CPAs, *AICPA Professional Standards. Volume 1 as of June 1, 2012, Statement on Auditing Standards (SAS) No. 50* Reports on the Application of Accounting Principles (New York: AICPA, 2012), AU Section 625.

## Appendix 3

# Qualified Opinion Due to Material Misstatement of the Financial Statements[3]
*Basis for Qualified Opinion*

The Company has excluded from property and debt in the accompanying balance sheets certain lease obligations that should be capitalized in order to conform to accounting principles generally accepted in the United States. If these lease obligations were capitalized, property would be increased by $15,000,000, long-term debt by $14,500,000, and retained earnings by $500,000 as of December 31, 2013. Additionally, net income would be increased by $500,000 and earnings per share would be increased by $1.22 for the year then ended.

## Qualified Opinion

In our opinion, except for the effects of not capitalizing certain lease obligations described in the Basis for Qualified Opinion paragraph, the financial statements referred to above present fairly, in all material respects, the financial position of XYZ Company as of December 31, 2013, and the results of its operations and its cash flows for the year then ended in conformity with accounting principles generally accepted in the United States.

[3]American Institute of CPAs, *AICPA Professional Standards. Volume 1 as of June 1, 2012, Statement on Auditing Standards (SAS) No. 58* Reports on Audited Financial Statements (New York: AICPA, 2012), AU Section 508.

## Appendix 4

# Adverse Opinion Due to Material Misstatement of the Financial Statements[4]

## Basis for Adverse Opinion

As described in note 3, losses expected to arise on certain long-term contracts currently in progress have been offset against amounts recoverable on other long-term contracts. Under accounting principles generally accepted in the United States, the losses should have been recognized as expenses. Had these amounts been so recognized, the financial statements would have been materially affected.

## Adverse opinion

In our opinion, because of the significance of the matters discussed in the Basis for Adverse Opinion paragraph, the financial statements referred to above do not present fairly the financial position of XYZ Company as of December 31, 2013, or the results of operations or their cash flows for the year then ended.

[4]American Institute of CPAs, *AICPA Professional Standards. Volume 1 as of June 1, 2012, Statement on Auditing Standards (SAS) No. 58* Reports on Audited Financial Statements (New York: AICPA, 2012), AU Section 508.

## Appendix 5

# Disclaimer of Opinion Due to the Auditor's Inability to Obtain Sufficient Appropriate Audit Evidence about a Single Element of the Financial Statements[5]

## Basis for Disclaimer of Opinion

We were not engaged as auditors of XYZ Company until after December 31, 2013, and, therefore, did not observe the counting of physical inventories at the beginning or end of the year. We were unable to satisfy ourselves by other auditing procedures concerning the inventory held at December 31, 2013, which is stated in the balance sheet at $100,000,000. As a result of this matter, we were unable to determine whether any adjustments might have been found necessary in respect of recorded or unrecorded inventories and the elements making up the statements of income, changes in stockholders' equity, and cash flows.

## Disclaimer of Opinion

Because of the significance of the matters described in the Basis for Disclaimer of Opinion paragraph, we have not been able to obtain sufficient appropriate audit evidence to provide a basis for an audit opinion. Accordingly, we do not express an opinion on these financial statements.

[5]American Institute of CPAs, *AICPA Professional Standards. Volume 1 as of June 1, 2012, Statement on Auditing Standards (SAS) No. 58* Reports on Audited Financial Statements (New York: AICPA, 2012), AU Section 508.

# Chapter 5 Cases

## Case 5-1

# Computer Associates

Computer Associates (CA) is a business consulting and software development company that designs, markets, and licenses computer software products that allow businesses to run and manage critical aspects of their information technology efficiently. CA's stock trades on the NYSE and is registered pursuant to Section 12(b) of the Exchange Act, 15 U.S.C. §78l(b).

Between about the fourth quarter of fiscal year (FY) 1998 through the second quarter of FY2001, CA engaged in a widespread practice that allowed for the premature recognition of revenue from software licensing agreements. CA personnel recorded, into the just-elapsed fiscal quarter, revenue from software contracts that were not finalized and signed by both CA and its customers until days or weeks after that quarter ended. The reported revenue was improper because it violated GAAP, which required that license agreements be fully executed by both CA and its customers by quarter end before recognizing revenue. CA's reported revenue and earnings per share (EPS) appeared to meet or exceed Wall Street analysts' expectations, when—in truth and fact—those results were based in part on revenue that CA recognized prematurely and in violation of GAAP.[1]

## Audit Committee Investigation

In 2003, CA announced that the Audit Committee of its Board of Directors was conducting an investigation into the timing of revenue recognition at the company. On April 26, 2004, CA filed with the SEC a Form 8-K ("Form 8-K") stating, among other things, that:

> "The Audit Committee's investigation found accounting irregularities that led to material misstatements of the Company's financial reports for fiscal years 2000 and 2001, and prior periods. The effect of prior period errors which have an impact on fiscal year 2000 have been considered as part of this restatement. The Audit Committee believes that several factors contributed to the improper recognition of revenue in these periods, including a practice of holding the financial period open after the end of the fiscal quarters, providing customers with contracts with preprinted signature dates, late countersignatures by Company personnel, backdating of contracts, and not having sufficient controls to ensure the proper accounting. In addition, the Audit Committee found that certain former executives and other personnel were engaged in the practice of "cleaning up" contracts by, among other things, removing fax time stamps before providing agreements to the outside auditors. These same executives and personnel also misled the Company's outside counsel, the Audit Committee and its counsel and accounting advisers regarding these accounting practices."

[1] The material in this case is taken from the SEC complaint against CA that can be found at http://www.sec.gov/litigation/complaints/comp18891-cai.pdf.

Also in the Form 8-K, CA announced that it was restating over $2.2 billion in revenue that CA had recognized improperly in FY2000 and FY2001.

## Improper Revenue Recognition at CA

From at least the fourth quarter of FY1998 through the second quarter of FY2001, CA derived its income primarily from licensing software and providing maintenance for that software. CA's software operated and maintained powerful "mainframe" computers, those generally used by businesses and other organizations. Prior to October 2000, CA's contract and licensing model involved entering into long-term licensing contracts, some as long as seven years in duration. Under that business model, customers paid an initial licensing fee for the software, plus subsequent licensing fees for the right to use the software in subsequent years. In addition, customers paid CA for ongoing maintenance, such as technical support. Customers often entered into long-term contracts and spread out the licensing and maintenance fees over the term of the contract.

For contracts under its pre-October 2000 business model, GAAP allowed CA to recognize all the license revenue called for during the duration of the contract up front, during the fiscal quarter in which the software was shipped and the contract was executed and final.

*SOP 97-2,*[2] which the AICPA adopted in October 1997, requires the following before revenue can be recognized from a software sale:

- Evidence of an arrangement
- Delivery
- Fixed and determinable fees
- Ability to collect

When a software company uses contracts requiring signatures by the software company and its customer, then *SOP 97-2* provides that both signatures—the software company and the customer—are required as "evidence of an arrangement" before the software company may recognize revenue. During the period in question, all CA's license agreements required signatures by both CA and the customer.

## Materially False Statements and Omissions in Filings with the SEC

During at least the fourth quarter of FY1998 through the second quarter of FY2001, CA violated GAAP, including *SOP 97-2,* by backdating software contracts into prior

[2] SOPs are pronouncements on specific accounting matters that had been issued by the AICPA's Accounting Standards Division from 1974 to 2009. The FASB GAAP Codification of authoritative accounting standards issued in 2009 supersedes existing sources of US GAAP including Statements of Position.

fiscal quarters expired software contracts that were not executed—and for which "evidence of an arrangement" did not exist—until a subsequent quarter. This extended quarters practice resulted in CA's premature recognition of revenue. As a consequence, CA made material misrepresentations and omissions of fact concerning CA's revenues and earnings for the fourth quarter of FY1998 through the second quarter of FY2001 in various public documents and in connection with the offer, purchase, and sale of securities. CA's reported results for at least the fourth quarter of FY1998 through the

fourth quarter of FY2000 appeared to meet or exceed the revenue and earnings estimates of outside analysts when, in fact, those reported results did not comply with GAAP and were false and misleading.

In its Form 8-K, which was not an audited restatement, CA admits that the extended quarters practice resulted in CA prematurely recognizing substantial percentages of revenue for all quarters of FY2000 and the first two quarters of FY2001. The following chart illustrates the impact of the premature revenue recognition in each fiscal quarter:

| Fiscal Quarter | GAAP Value of Revenue Properly Recorded | GAAP Value of Contracts that CA Signed After Quarter End | GAAP Value of Contracts that Clients Signed After Quarter End | GAAP Value of Revenue Improperly Accelerated and Recorded | Percentage that Properly Recorded Revenue was Inflated by Improperly Accelerated Revenue |
|---|---|---|---|---|---|
| Q1 FY2000 | $977,165,281 | $122,230,689 | $122,604,030 | $244,834,719 | 25% |
| Q2 FY2000 | $1,047,256,904 | $90,099,723 | $467,643,373 | $557,743,096 | 53% |
| Q3 FY2000 | $1,239,902,741 | $170,450,718 | $401,646,541 | $572,097,259 | 46% |
| Q4 FY2000 | $1,748,131,031 | $179,493,620 | $199,375,348 | $378,868,969 | 22% |
| Q1 FY2001 | $1,135,600,000 | $126,740,000 | $15,660,000 | $142,400,000 | 13% |
| Q2 FY2001 | $1,462,040,000 | $214,720,000 | $4,240,000 | $218,960,000 | 15% |

The greatest amount of prematurely recognized revenue as a result of the extended quarters practice occurred in FY2000, particularly in the third quarter, followed by the second, fourth and first quarters of that fiscal year. If CA had not improperly recognized revenue in each of those fiscal quarters, CA would not have met analysts' revenue and earnings estimates.

The following is a chart which shows the impact of the extended quarters practice on CA's earnings per share in the four quarters of FY2000 and the extent of the material misstatements and misrepresentations in the Forms 10-Q and Form 10-K that CA filed with the SEC which reported each quarterly result, and related public statements made by CA:

| Quarter | Total Revenue Properly Recorded | Total Revenue Improperly Recorded | Analyst EPS Estimate | Announced EPS | EPS without Improper Revenue | Overstatement of EPS |
|---|---|---|---|---|---|---|
| Q1 FY2000 | $977 million | $244 million | $0.47 | $0.49 | $0.29 | $0.20 |
| Q2 FY2000 | $1.047 billion | $557 million | $0.59 | $0.60 | $0.05 | $0.55 |
| Q3 FY2000 | $1.240 billion | $572 million | $0.90 | $0.91 | $0.31 | $0.60 |
| Q4 FY2000 | $1.748 billion | $378 million | $1.13 | $1.13 | $0.82 | $0.31 |

## A Systemic and Intentional Practice

The premature recognition of revenue at CA during at least the fourth quarter of FY1998 through the second quarter of FY2001 was the result of a systemic, intentional practice by certain CA personnel. To implement and conceal this extended quarters practice, CA personnel employed a variety

of improper techniques, many of which rendered the company's books and records false and misleading, including:

• Some employees at CA called the extended quarters practice the "35-day month" practice, because generally most quarters were extended by at least 3 business days, although some quarterly extensions lasted longer.

• Sometimes CA had its customers execute contracts bearing preprinted dates from the just-expired quarter, even though the customer did not actually sign the contract until days or weeks into the new quarter.

CA substantially stopped prematurely recognizing revenue for software contracts signed after quarter end by CA's customers during the first quarter of FY2001 (quarter ended June 30, 2000). That quarter, CA missed its Wall Street earnings estimates. CA issued a press release on July 3, 2000, stating that it would miss the analysts' estimates, specifically citing the fact that the company did not complete several large contracts that they had hoped to conclude before the close of the quarter. This was only the second time in CA's then-recent history that CA missed Wall Street's estimates. The next trading day, July 5, 2000, CA's share price dropped over 43 percent, from $51.12 to $28.50, as the market reacted to the news. The share price has not recovered and closed at $26.26 on June 14, 2013.

CA continued to recognize revenue prematurely from contracts that CA signed after quarter end (although, with a few exceptions, the customer did sign the contract by quarter end) for the first two quarters of FY2001, after which that practice substantially stopped.

## Legal Matters Resolved

In September 2004, CA agreed to pay $225 million in restitution to shareholders to settle the civil case brought by the SEC and to defer criminal charges by the U.S. Department of Justice. At the same time, a federal grand jury brought criminal charges against former CA chairman and CEO Sanjay Kumar. Kumar resigned in April 2004 following an investigation into securities fraud and obstruction of justice at CA. A federal grand jury in Brooklyn indicted him on fraud charges on September 22, 2004. Kumar pled guilty to obstruction of justice and securities fraud charges on April 24, 2006. On November 2, 2006, he was sentenced to 12 years in prison and fined $8 million for his role in the massive accounting fraud at CA. Kumar is currently housed at the Federal Correctional Institution in Miami, Florida, with a projected release date of January 25, 2018.

## Questions

1. Analyze each revenue recognition technique identified in the audit committee investigation and explain whether each technique violates revenue recognition rules in accounting. Evaluate the practices followed by CA from an ethical perspective.

2. CA executives were not accused of reporting nonexistent deals or hiding major flaws in the business. The contracts that were backdated by a few days were real. Was this really a crime, or should it fall under the heading of "no harm, no foul"? Be sure to use ethical reasoning in responding to the question.

3. In her "Seven Signs of Ethical Collapse," which were discussed in Chapter 3, Marianne Jennings listed "pressure to maintain the numbers" as the number one sign. How can a company like CA resist such pressure?

## Case 5-2
# ZZZZ Best[1]

The story of ZZZZ Best is one of greed and audaciousness. It is the story of a 15-year-old boy from Reseda, California, who was driven to be successful regardless of the costs. His name is Barry Minkow.

Minkow had high hopes to make it big—to be a millionaire very early in life. He started a carpet cleaning business in the garage of his home. But Minkow realized early on that he was not going to become a millionaire cleaning other people's carpets. He had grander plans than that. Minkow was going to make it big in the insurance restoration business. In other words, ZZZZ Best would contract to do carpet and drapery cleaning jobs after a fire or flood. Because the damage from the fire or flood probably would be covered by insurance, the customer would be eager to have the work done, and perhaps not be all that concerned with how much it would cost. The only problem with Minkow's insurance restoration idea was that it was all a fiction. There were no insurance restoration jobs—at least not for ZZZZ Best. Allegedly, over 80 percent of his revenue was from this work. In the process of creating the fraud, Minkow was able to dupe the auditors, Ernst & Whinney (one of the predecessor firms of Ernst & Young), into thinking the insurance restoration business was real. The auditors never caught on until it was too late.

## How Barry Became a Fraudster

Minkow wrote a book, *Clean Sweep: A Story of Compromise, Corruption, Collapse, and Comeback,*[2] that provides some insights into the mind of a 15-year-old kid who was called a "wonder boy" on Wall Street until the bubble burst. He was trying to find a way to drum up customers for his fledgling carpet cleaning business. One day, while he was alone in his garage-office, Minkow called Channel 4 in Los Angeles. He disguised his voice so he wouldn't sound like a teenager and told a producer that he had just had his carpets cleaned by the 16-year-old owner of ZZZZ Best. He sold the producer on the idea that it would be good for society to hear the success story about a high school junior running his own business. The producer bought it lock, stock, and carpet cleaner. Minkow gave the producer the phone number of ZZZZ Best and waited. It took less than five minutes for the call to come in. Minkow answered the phone and when the producer asked to speak with Mr. Barry Minkow, Minkow said: "Who may I say is calling?" Within days, a film crew was in his garage shooting ZZZZ Best at work. The story aired that night, and it was followed by more calls from radio stations and other

television shows wanting to do interviews. The calls flooded in with customers demanding that Barry Minkow personally clean their carpets.

As his income increased in the spring of 1983, Minkow found it increasingly difficult to run the company without a checking account. He managed to find a banker that was so moved by his story that the banker agreed to allow an underage customer to open a checking account. Minkow used the money to buy cleaning supplies and other necessities. Even though his business was growing, Minkow ran into trouble paying back loans and interest when due.

Minkow developed a plan of action. He was tired of worrying about not having enough money. He went to his garage—where all his great ideas first began—and looked at his bank account statement, which showed that he had more money than he thought he had based on his own records. Minkow soon realized it was because some checks he had written had not been cashed by customers, so they didn't yet show up on the bank statement. Voilá! Minkow started to kite checks between two or more banks. He would write a check on one ZZZZ Best account and deposit it into another. Because it might take a few days for the check written on Bank #1 to clear that bank's records (back then, checks weren't always processed in real time the way they are today), Minkow could pay some bills out of the second account and Bank #1 would not know—at least for a few days—that Minkow had written a check on his account when, in reality, he had a negative balance. The bank didn't know it because some of the checks that Minkow had written before the visit to Bank #2 had not cleared his account in Bank #1.

It wasn't long thereafter that Minkow realized he could kite checks big time. Not only that, he could make the transfer of funds at the end of a month or a year and show a higher balance than really existed in Bank #1 and carry it onto the balance sheet. Because Minkow did not count the check written on his account in Bank #1 as an outstanding check, he was able to double-count.

## Time to Expand the Fraud

Over time, Minkow moved on to bigger and bigger frauds, like having his trusted cohorts confirm to banks and other interested parties that ZZZZ Best was doing insurance restoration jobs. Minkow used the phony jobs and phony revenue to convince bankers to make loans to ZZZZ Best. He had cash remittance forms made up from nonexistent customers with whatever sales amount he wanted to appear on the document. He even had a co-conspirator write on the bogus remittance form, "Job well done." Minkow could then show a lot more revenue than he was really making.

Minkow's phony financial statements enabled him to borrow more and more money and expand the number of carpet cleaning outlets. However, Minkow's personal tastes had

---

[1]The facts are derived from a video by the ACFE, *Cooking the Books: What Every Accountant Should Know about Fraud.*
[2]Barry Minkow, *Clean Sweep: A Story of Compromise, Corruption, Collapse, and Comeback* (Nashville, TN: Thomas Nelson, 1995).

become increasingly more expensive, including purchasing a Ferrari with the borrowed funds and putting a down payment on a 5,000-square-foot home. So, the question was: How do you solve a perpetual cash flow problem? You go public! That's right, Minkow made a public offering of stock in ZZZZ Best. Of course, he owned a majority of the stock to maintain control of the company.

Minkow had made it to the big leagues. He was on Wall Street. He had investment bankers, CPAs, and attorneys all working for him—the now 19-year-old kid from Reseda, California, who had turned a mom-and-pop operation into a publicly owned corporation.

## Barry Goes Public

Minkow's first audit was for the 12 months ended April 30, 1986. A sole practitioner performed the audit. (There are eerie similarities in the Madoff fraud, with its small practitioner firm—Friehling & Horowitz—conducting the audit of a multibillion-dollar operation, and that of the sole practitioner audit of ZZZZ Best.)

Minkow had established two phony front companies that allegedly placed insurance restoration jobs for ZZZZ Best. He had one of his cohorts create invoices for services and respond to questions about the company. There was enough paperwork to fool the auditor into thinking the jobs were real and the revenue was supportable. However, the auditor never visited any of the insurance restoration sites. If he had done so, there would have been no question in his mind that ZZZZ Best was a big fraud.

Pressured to get a big-time CPA firm to do his audit as he moved into the big leagues, Minkow hired Ernst & Whinney to perform the April 30, 1987, fiscal year-end audit. Minkow continued to be one step ahead of the auditors—that is, until the Ernst & Whinney auditors insisted on going to see an insurance restoration site. They wanted to confirm that all the business—all the revenue—that Minkow had said was coming in to ZZZZ Best was real.

The engagement partner drove to an area in Sacramento, California, where Minkow did a lot of work—supposedly. He looked for a building that seemed to be a restoration job. Why he did that isn't clear, but he identified a building that seemed to be the kind that would be a restoration job in progress.

Earlier in the week, Minkow had sent one of his cohorts to find a large building in Sacramento that appeared to be a restoration site. As luck would have it, Minkow's associate picked out the same site as had the partner later on. Minkow's cohorts found the leasing agent for the building. They convinced the agent to give them the keys so that they could show the building to some potential tenants over the weekend. Minkow's helpers went up to the site before the arrival of the partner and placed placards on the walls that indicated ZZZZ Best was the contractor for the building restoration. In fact, the building was not fully constructed at the time, but it looked as if some restoration work was going on at the site.

Minkow was able to pull it off in part due to luck and in part because the Ernst and Whinney auditors did not want to lose the ZZZZ Best account. It had become a large revenue producer for the firm, and Minkow seemed destined for greater and greater achievements. Minkow was smart and used the leverage of the auditors not wanting to lose the ZZZZ Best account as a way to complain whenever they became too curious about the insurance restoration jobs. He would even threaten to take his business from Ernst and Whinney and give it to other auditors.

Minkow also took a precaution with the site visit. He had the auditors sign a confidentiality agreement that they would not make any follow-up calls to any contractors, insurance companies, the building owner, or other individuals involved in the restoration work. This prevented the auditors from corroborating the insurance restoration contracts with independent third parties. The auditors clearly dropped the ball here as the firm failed to gather the evidence necessary to support the existence of the work and revenue-production from the insurance restoration contracts.

## The Fraud Starts to Unravel

It was a Los Angeles housewife who started the problems for ZZZZ Best that would eventually lead to the company's demise. Because Minkow was a well-known figure and flamboyant character, the *Los Angeles Times* did a story about the carpet cleaning business. The Los Angeles housewife read the story about Minkow and recalled that ZZZZ Best had overcharged her for services in the early years by increasing the amount of the credit card charge for its carpet cleaning services.

Minkow had gambled that most people don't check their monthly statements, so he could get away with the petty fraud. However, the housewife did notice the overcharge and complained to Minkow, and eventually he returned the overpayment. She couldn't understand why Minkow would have had to resort to such low levels back then if he was as successful as the *Times* article made him out to be. So, she called the reporter to find out more, and that ultimately led to the investigation of ZZZZ Best and future stories that weren't so flattering.

Because Minkow continued to spend lavishly on himself and his possessions, he always seemed to need more and more money. It got so bad over time that he was close to defaulting on loans and had to make up stories to keep the creditors at bay, and he couldn't pay his suppliers. The complaints kept coming in, and eventually the house of cards that was ZZZZ Best came crashing down.

During the time that the fraud was unraveling, Ernst and Whinney decided to resign from the ZZZZ Best audit. The firm never did issue an audit report. It had started to doubt the veracity of Minkow and his business at ZZZZ Best.

The procedure to follow when a change of auditor occurs is for the company being audited to file an 8-K form with the SEC and the audit firm to prepare an exhibit commenting on the accuracy of the disclosures in the 8-K. The exhibit is attached to the form that is sent to the SEC within 30 days of the change.[3] Ernst & Whinney waited the full 30-day period, and the SEC released the information to the public 45 days after the change had occurred. Meanwhile, ZZZZ Best filed for bankruptcy. During the period of time that had elapsed, Minkow had borrowed more than $1 million, and the lenders never were repaid. Bankruptcy laws protected Minkow and ZZZZ Best from having to make those payments.

## Legal Liability Issues

The ZZZZ Best fraud was one of the largest of its time. ZZZZ Best reportedly settled a shareholder class action lawsuit for $35 million. Ernst & Whinney was sued by a bank that had made a multimillion-dollar loan based on the financial statements for the three-month period ending July 31, 1986. The bank claimed that it had relied on the review report issued by Ernst & Whinney in granting the loan to ZZZZ Best. However, the firm had indicated in its review report that it was not issuing an opinion on the ZZZZ Best financial statements. The judge ruled that the bank was not justified in relying on the review report because Ernst & Whinney had expressly disclaimed issuing any opinion on the statements.

Barry Minkow was charged with engaging in a $100 million fraud scheme. He was sentenced to a term of 25 years.

## Questions

1. Do you believe that auditors should be held liable for failing to discover fraud in situations such as ZZZZ Best, where top management goes to great lengths to fool the auditors? Answer this question with respect to the ethical and professional responsibilities of audit professionals when conducting an audit.

2. Discuss the red flags that existed in the ZZZZ Best case and evaluate Ernst & Whinney's efforts with respect to fraud risk assessment. Do you think Ernst & Whinney's relationship with ZZZZ Best influenced risk assessment and the work done on the audit?

3. These are selected numbers from the financial statements of ZZZZ Best for fiscal years 1985 and 1986:

| | 1985 | 1986 |
|---|---|---|
| Sales | $1,240,524 | $4,845,347 |
| Cost of goods sold | 576,694 | 2,050,779 |
| Accounts receivable | 0 | 693,773 |
| Cash | 30,321 | 87,014 |
| Current liabilities | 2,930 | 1,768,435 |
| Notes payable—current | 0 | 780,507 |

4. Evaluate Minkow's actions using the fraud triangle.

[3]Under current SEC rules, Item 4.01 of Form 8-K requires a company to request the former accountant to furnish a letter stating whether the former accountant agrees with the company's statements concerning the reasons for the change. Where the former accountant declines to provide such a letter, the company should indicate that fact in the Form 8-K. The company must file the 8-K report for the change in accountant within five business days of notification.

What calculations or analyses would you make with these numbers that might help you assess whether the financial relationships are "reasonable"? Given the facts of the case, what inquiries might you make of management based on your analysis?

## Barry: The Afterlife

After being released from jail in 1995, Minkow became a preacher and a fraud investigator, and he spoke at schools about ethics. This all came to an end in 2011, when he admitted to helping deliberately drive down the stock price of Lennar, a home-building company, and was sent back to prison. The facts below explain what happened to Barry since 1995.

In 1997, Minkow became the senior pastor of Community Bible Church in San Diego. Soon after his arrival, a church member asked him to look into a money management firm in nearby Orange County. Suspecting something was not right, Minkow used his "fraud-sniffing" abilities to alert federal authorities, who discovered the firm was a $300 million pyramid scheme. This was the beginning of the Fraud Discovery Institute, a for-profit investigative firm. Minkow managed to dupe the investment community again; several Wall Street investors liked what they saw and sent him enough money to go after bigger targets. By Minkow's estimate, he had uncovered $1 billion worth of fraud over the years.

We assume that Minkow missed the adrenalin rush of committing fraud that kept him going for so long in the 1990s, and in 2009 he issued a report accusing the major homebuilder Lennar of massive fraud. Minkow claimed that irregularities in Lennar's off-balance-sheet debt accounting were evidence of a massive Ponzi scheme. He accused Lennar of not disclosing enough information about this to its shareholders, and also claimed that a Lennar executive took out a fraudulent personal loan. Minkow denounced Lennar as "a financial crime in progress" and "a corporate bully." From January 9, 2009 (when Minkow first made his accusations) to January 22, Lennar's stock tumbled from $11.57 a share to only $6.55. Minkow issued the report after being contacted by Nicholas Marsch, a San Diego developer who had filed two lawsuits against Lennar for fraud. One of Marsch's suits was summarily thrown out of court, while the other ended with Marsch having to pay Lennar $12 million in counterclaims.

Lennar responded by adding Minkow as a defendant in a libel-and-extortion suit against Marsch. According to court records, Minkow had shorted Lennar stock, buying $20,000 worth of options in a bet that the stock would fall. Minkow also forged documents alleging misconduct on Lennar's part. He went forward with the report even after a private investigator he had hired for the case could not substantiate Marsch's claims. (In an unrelated development, it was also revealed that Minkow operated the Fraud Discovery Institute out of the offices of his church and even used church money to fund it—something which could have potentially jeopardized his church's tax-exempt status.)

On December 27, 2010, Florida circuit court judge Gill Freeman issued terminating actions against Minkow in response to a motion by Lennar. Freeman found that Minkow had repeatedly lied under oath, destroyed or withheld evidence, concealed witnesses, and deliberately tried to "cover up his misconduct." According to Freeman, Minkow had even lied to his own lawyers about his behavior. Freeman determined that Minkow had perpetuated "a fraud on the court" that was so egregious that letting the case go any further would be a disservice to justice. In her view, "no remedy short of default" was appropriate for Minkow's lies. She ordered Minkow to reimburse Lennar for the legal expenses it incurred while ferreting out his lies. Lennar estimates that its attorneys and investigators spent hundreds of millions of dollars exposing Minkow's lies.

On March 16, 2011, Minkow announced through his attorney that he was pleading guilty to one count of insider trading. According to his lawyer, Minkow had bought his Lennar options using "nonpublic information." The plea, which was separate from the civil suit, came a month after Minkow learned that he was the subject of a criminal investigation. Minkow claimed not to know at the time that he was breaking the law. The SEC had already been probing Minkow's trading practices. On the same day, Minkow resigned his position as senior pastor, saying in a letter to his flock that because he was no longer "above reproach," he felt that he was "no longer qualified to be a pastor." Six weeks earlier, $50,000 in cash and checks was stolen from the church during a burglary. Though unsolved, it was noted as suspicious due to Minkow's admitted history of staging burglaries to collect insurance money.

The nature of the "nonpublic information" became clear a week later, when federal prosecutors filed a criminal information action against Minkow, with one count of conspiracy to commit securities fraud. Prosecutors charged that Minkow and Marsch conspired to extort money from Lennar by driving down its stock. The complaint also revealed that Minkow had sent his allegations to the Federal Bureau of Investigation (FBI), Internal Revenue Service (IRS), and SEC, and that the three agencies found his claims credible enough to open a formal criminal investigation into Lennar's practices. Minkow then used confidential knowledge of that investigation to short Lennar stock, even though he knew he was barred from doing so. Minkow opted to plead guilty to the conspiracy charge rather than face charges of securities fraud and market manipulation, which could have sent him to prison for life.

On March 30, 2011, Minkow pleaded guilty and was eventually sent to jail for five years and ordered to pay Lennar $584 million in damages—roughly the amount the company lost as a result of the bear raid. The ruling stated that Minkow and Marsch had entered into a conspiracy to wreck Lennar's stock in November 2008. With interest, the bill could easily approach $1 billion—far more than he stole in the ZZZZ Best scam.

## Questions *(continued)*

5. What factors do you think motivated Minkow to return to his evil ways after becoming a respected member of the community following his release from prison in the ZZZZ Best fraud?

6. Using Kohlberg's stages of moral development, how would you characterize Minkow's actions after being released from prison in the ZZZZ Best fraud? Explain the effects of Minkow's actions on the stakeholders who relied on him to act in a professional manner.

## Case 5-3

# Imperial Valley Thrift & Loan

Bill Stanley, of Jacobs, Stanley & Company, started to review the working paper files on his client, Imperial Valley Thrift & Loan, in preparation for the audit of the client's financial statements for the year ended December 31, 2013. The bank was owned by a parent company, Nuevo Financial Group, and it serviced a small western Arizona community near Yuma that reached south to the border of Mexico. The bank's preaudit statements are presented in Exhibit 1.

Bill Stanley knew there were going to be some problems to contend with during the course of the audit, so he decided to review several items in the file in order to refresh his memory about the client's operations.

---

**EXHIBIT 1**
**IMPERIAL VALLEY THRIFT & LOAN**
**Balance Sheet (preaudit) December 31, 2013**

### Assets

| | |
|---|---:|
| Cash and cash equivalents | $1,960,000 |
| Loans receivable | 6,300,000 |
| Less: Reserve for loan losses | (25,000) |
| Unearned discounts and fees | (395,000) |
| Accrued interest receivable | 105,000 |
| Prepayments | 12,000 |
| Real property held for sale | 514,000 |
| Property, plant, and equipment | 390,000 |
| Less: Accumulated depreciation | (110,000) |
| Contribution to Thrift Guaranty Corp. | 15,000 |
| Deferred start-up costs | 44,000 |
| Total assets | $8,810,000 |

### Liabilities & Equity

| | |
|---|---:|
| **Liabilities** | |
| Regular and money market savings | $2,212,000 |
| T-bills and CDs | 5,180,000 |
| Accrued interest payable | 190,000 |
| Accounts payable and accruals | 28,000 |
| Total liabilities | $7,610,000 |
| **Equity** | |
| Capital stock | $ 700,000 |
| Additional paid-in capital | 1,120,000 |
| Retained earnings (deficit) | (620,000) |
| Total equity | $1,200,000 |
| Total liabilities and equity | $8,810,000 |

**Statement of Operations (preaudit) for the Year Ended December 31, 2013**

### Revenues

| | |
|---|---:|
| Interest earned | $ 820,000 |
| Discount earned | 210,000 |
| Investment income | 82,000 |
| Fees, charges, and commissions | 78,000 |
| Total revenues | $1,190,000 |

*(continued)*

**EXHIBIT 1** *(continued)*
**IMPERIAL VALLEY THRIFT & LOAN**
Statement of Operations (preaudit) for the Year Ended December 31, 2013

### Expenses

| | |
|---|---|
| Interest expense | $   815,000 |
| Provision for loan losses | 180,000 |
| Salary expense | 205,000 |
| Occupancy expense including depreciation | 100,000 |
| Other administrative expense | 160,000 |
| Legal expense | 12,000 |
| Thrift Guaranty Corp. payment | 48 ,000 |
| Total expenses | $ 1,520,000 |
| Net loss for the year | $   (330,000) |

## Background

The first item Stanley reviewed was the planning memo that he had prepared about two months earlier. This memo is summarized in Exhibit 2.

The next item he reviewed was an internal office communication on potential audit risks. This communication described three areas of particular concern:

1. The client charged off $420,000 in loans in 2012 and had already charged off $535,000 through July 31, 2013. Assuming that reserve requirements by law are a minimum of 1.25 percent of loans outstanding, this statutory amount probably would not be large enough for the loan loss reserve. This, in combination with the prior auditors' concerns about proper loan underwriting procedures and documentation, indicates that the audit engagement team should carefully review loan quality.

2. The audit report issued on the 2012 financial statements contained an unmodified opinion with an emphasis-of-matter paragraph describing the uncertainty about the client's ability to continue as a going concern. The concern was caused by the "capital impairment" declaration by the Arizona Department of Corporations.

3. The client had weak internal controls according to the prior auditors. Some of the items to look out for, in addition to proper loan documentation, were whether the preaudit financial statement information provided by the client was supported by the general ledger, whether the accruals were appropriate, and whether all transactions were properly authorized and recorded on a timely basis.

## Audit Findings

Stanley conducted the audit during January and February 2014. Based on information gathered during the audit, the following were the areas of greatest concern to him:

1. **Adequacy of Loan Collateral.** A review of 30 loan files representing $2,100,000 of total loans outstanding (33.3 percent of the portfolio) indicated that much of the collateral for the loans was in the form of second or third mortgages on real property. This gave the client a potentially unenforceable position due to the existence of very large senior liens. For example, if foreclosure became necessary to collect Imperial Valley's loan, the client would have to pay off these large senior liens first. Other collateral often consisted of personal items such as jewelry and furniture. In the case of jewelry, often there was no effort made by the client after granting the loan to ascertain whether the collateral was still in the possession of the borrower. The jewelry could have been sold without the client's knowledge. It was difficult to obtain sufficient audit evidence about these amounts.

2. **Collectibility of Loans.** Many loans were structured in such a way as to require interest payments only for a small number of years (two or three years), with a balloon payment for principal due at the end of this time. This structure made it difficult to evaluate the payment history of the borrower properly. Although the annual interest payments may have been made for the first year or two, this was not necessarily a good indication that the borrower would come up with the cash needed to make the large final payment, and the financial statements provided no additional disclosures about this matter.

3. **Weakness in Internal Controls.** Internal control weaknesses were a pervasive concern. The auditors recomputed certain accruals and unearned discounts, confirmed loan and deposit balances, and reconciled the preaudit financial information provided by the client to the general ledger. Some adjustments had to be made as a result of this work. A material weakness in the lending function was identified. Loans were too frequently granted merely because the borrowers were well known to Imperial Valley officials, who believed that they could be counted on to repay their outstanding loans. An ability to repay these loans was based too often on "faith" rather than on clear indications that the borrowers would have the necessary cash available to repay their loans when they came due. This was of great concern to the auditors, especially

---

**EXHIBIT 2**
**Planning Memo**

1. The firm of Jacobs, Stanley, & Co. succeeded the firm of Nelson, Thomas, & Co. as auditors for Imperial Valley Thrift & Loan. The prior auditors conducted the 2011 and 2012 audits. Jacobs, Stanley, & Co. communicated in writing with Nelson, Thomas, & Co. prior to accepting the engagement. In addition, authorization was given by the client for a review of the predecessor auditors' working papers. The findings of these inquiries are summarized in item 6 below and the previously discussed internal office communication.

2. Imperial Valley Thrift & Loan was incorporated in Arizona on June 12, 1997. It is a wholly owned subsidiary of Nuevo Financial Group, S.A., a Mexican corporation. As an industrial loan company, it is restricted to certain types of business, including making real estate and consumer loans and certain types of commercial loans.

3. Imperial Valley accepts deposits in the form of interest-bearing passbook accounts and investment certificates. Most of the depositors are of Spanish descent. The client primarily services the Spanish-speaking community in the Imperial Valley of southern Arizona, which is a rural community located on the Mexican border.

4. The principal officers of Imperial Valley are Jose Ortega and his brother, Arturo. They serve as the CEO and the CFO, respectively. Two cousins serve as the Chief Operating Officer (COO) and chief compliance officer.

5. Imperial Valley is subject to the regulations of the Arizona Industrial Loan Law and is examined by the Department of Corporations. It was last examined in December 2012 and was put on notice as "capital impaired." Additional capital was being sought from local investors.

6. Based on review of the prior auditors' working papers, the following items were noted:

   a. The client's lack of profitability was due to a high volume of loan losses resulting from poor underwriting procedures and faulty documentation.

   b. Imperial Valley has a narrow net interest margin due to the fact that all deposits are interest bearing and it pays the highest interest rates in the area.

   c. Due to the small size of the client and its focus on handling day-to-day operating problems, the internal controls are marginal at best. There were material weaknesses in its loan underwriting procedures and documentation, as well as in compliance with regulatory requirements.

   d. There are no reports issued by management on the internal controls.

   e. Audit evidence was frequently unavailable to the prior auditors, and they expressed their concerns about this matter in an internal memo.

---

in light of the inadequacy of the loan reserve, as detailed in item 5 that follows.

4. **Status of Additional Capital Infusion.** The audit engagement team is working under the assumption that under Arizona regulatory requirements, a thrift and loan institution must maintain a 6:1 ratio of thrift certificates to net equity capital. Based on the financial information provided by Imperial Valley, the capital deficiency was only $32,000 below capital requirements (preaudit), as follows:

| | |
|---|---|
| Thrift certificates ratio | $7,392,000 |
| | 6 |
| Net equity capital required | $1,232,000 |
| Net equity capital reported | $1,200,000 |
| Deficiency | $    32,000 |

Audit adjustments explained in Exhibit 3 increased the capital deficiency to $622,000, as follows:

| | |
|---|---|
| Net equity capital required | $1,232,000 |
| Net equity capital (postaudit) | $  610,000 |
| (1,200,000–$590,000) | |
| Deficiency | $  622,000 |

There was a possibility that the parent company, Nuevo Financial Group, would contribute the additional equity capital. Also, management had been in contact with a potential outside investor about the possibility of investing $600,000. This investor, Manny Gonzalez, has strong ties to the Imperial Valley community and to the family ownership of Imperial Valley.

5. **Adequacy of General Reserve Requirement.** The general reserve requirement of 1.25 percent had not been met.

**EXHIBIT 3**

**Audit Adjustments**

| | | | |
|---|---|---|---|
| AJE #1 | Reserve for loan losses | $ 200,000 | |
| | Loans receivable | | $ 200,000 |
| | To write down loans to net realizable value | | |
| AJE #2 | Reserve for loan losses | $ 300,000 | |
| | Unearned discounts & fees | 80,000 | |
| | Loans receivable | | $ 380,000 |
| | To write off loans more than 180 days past due in compliance with statutes | | |
| AJE #3 | Provision for loan losses | $ 590,000 | |
| | Reserve for loan losses | | $ 590,000 |
| | To increase the reserve balance to 2 percent of outstanding loans as follows: | | |
| | Reserve balance (preaudit) | | $ (25,000) |

| | | |
|---|---|---|
| Less adjusting entry | | |
| #1 | $ 200,000 | |
| #2 | 300,000 | |
| | | $ 500,000 |
| Subtotal | | $ 475,000 |
| Add: Desired balance | | |
| Loan balance (preaudit) | $ 6,300,000 | |
| Less: AJE #1 | (200,000) | |
| #2 | (380,000) | |
| Loan balance (postaudit) | $ 5,720,000 | |
| Reserve requirement | 2% | |
| Desired balance (approx.) | | 115,000 |
| Adjustment required | | $ 590,000 |

Based on the client's reported outstanding loan balance of $6,300,000, a reserve of $78,750 would be necessary. However, audit adjustments for the charge-off of uncollectible loan amounts significantly affected the amount actually required. In addition, the auditors felt that a larger percentage would be necessary because of the client's history of problems with loan collections; initially, a 5 percent rate was proposed. Management felt this was much too high, arguing that the company had improved its lending procedures in the last few months and that it expected to have a smaller percentage of charge-offs in the future. A current delinquent report received in February 2014 showed only two loans from 2013 still on the past due list. The auditors agreed to a 2 percent reserve, and an adjusting entry (AJE #3, shown in Exhibit 3) was made.

## Regulatory Environment

Imperial Valley Thrift & Loan was approaching certain regulatory filing deadlines during the course of the audit. Stanley had a meeting with the regulators at which representatives of management were present. Gonzalez also attended the meeting because he had expressed some interest in possibly making a capital contribution. There was a lot of discussion about the ability of Imperial Valley to keep its doors open if the loan losses were recorded as proposed by the auditors. This was a concern because the proposed adjustments would place the client in a position of having net equity capital significantly below minimum requirements.

The regulators were concerned about the adequacy of the 2 percent general reserve because of the prior collection problems experienced by Imperial Valley. The institution's solvency was a primary concern. At the time of the meeting, the regulators were quite busy trying to straighten out problems caused by the failure of two other savings and loan (S&L) institutions in Arizona. Many depositors had lost money as a result of the failure of these S&Ls. The regulators were concerned that a domino effect might occur, as had happened in the early 1990s, and that Imperial Valley would get caught up in the mess. Also, the regulators were unable to make a thorough audit of the company on their own, so they relied quite heavily on the work of Jacobs, Stanley, & Company. In this sense, the audit was used as leverage on the institution to get more money in as a cushion to protect depositors. The regulators viewed this as essential in light of the other S&L failures and the fact that the insurance protection mechanism for thrift and loan depositors was less substantial than depository insurance available through the Federal Deposit Insurance Corporation (FDIC) in commercial banks and in S&Ls.

## Summary of the Client's Position

The management of Imperial Valley Thrift & Loan placed a great deal of pressure on the auditors to reduce the amount of loan write-offs. It maintained that the customers were "good for the money." Managers pointed out the payments to date on most of the loans had been made on a timely basis. The client felt that the auditors did not fully understand the nature of its business. Managers contend that a certain amount of risk had to be accepted in their business because they primarily made loans that commercial banks and S&Ls did not want to make. "We are the bank of last resort for many of our customers," commented bank president Eddie Salazar. Salazar then commented that the auditors' inability to understand and appreciate this element of the thrift and loan business was the main reason why the auditors were having trouble evaluating the collectibility of the outstanding loans. Management informed the auditors that they vouched for the collectibility of the outstanding loans.

## Outstanding Loans

The auditors' contended that the payments to date, which were mostly annual interest amounts, were not necessarily a good indication that timely balloon principal payments would be made. They felt it was very difficult to evaluate the collectibility of the balloon payments adequately, primarily because the borrowers' source of cash for loan repayment had not been identified. They could not objectively audit or support borrowers' good intentions to pay or undocumented resources as represented by client management.

To ensure that they were not being naïve about the thrift and loan industry, the auditors checked with colleagues in another office of the firm who knew more about this type of business. One professional in this office explained that the real secret of this business is to follow up ruthlessly with any nonpayer. The auditors certainly did not believe that this was being done by Imperial Valley management.

The auditors knew that Manny Gonzalez was a potential source of investment capital for Imperial Valley. They believed it was very important to give Gonzalez an accurate picture because if a rosier picture were painted than actually existed, and Gonzalez made an investment, then the audit firm would be a potential target for a lawsuit.

### Board of Trustees

The auditors approached the nine-member board of trustees that oversaw the operations of Imperial Valley, three of whom

also served on the audit committee. Of the nine board members, four were officers with the banks and five were outsiders. All members of the audit committee were outsiders. The auditors had hoped to solicit the support of the audit committee in dealing with management over the audit opinion issue, as detailed in the next section. However, the auditors were concerned about the fact that all five outsiders had loans outstanding from Imperial Valley that carried 2 percent interest payments until the due date in two years. Perhaps not coincidentally, all five had supported management with respect to the validity of collateral and loan collectibility issues with customers.

## Auditor Responsibilities

The management of Imperial Valley Thrift & Loan was pressuring the auditors to give an unmodified opinion. If the auditors decided to modify the opinion, then in the client's view, this would present a picture to their customers and the regulators that their financial statements were not accurate. The client maintained that this would be a blow to its integrity and would shake depositors' confidence in the institution.

On one hand, the auditors were very cognizant of their responsibility to the regulatory authority, and they were also concerned about providing an accurate picture of Imperial Valley's financial health to Manny Gonzalez or other potential investors. On the other hand, they wondered whether they were holding the client to standards that were too strict. After all, the audit report issued in the preceding year was unmodified with an emphasis-of-matter paragraph on the capital impairment issue. They also wondered whether the doors of the institution would be closed by the regulators if they gave a qualified or adverse opinion. What impact could this action have on the depositors and the economic health of the community? Bill Stanley wondered whose interests they were really representing—depositors, shareholders, management, the local community, or regulators, or all of these.

Stanley knew that he would soon have to make a recommendation about the type of audit opinion to be issued on the 2013 financial statements of Imperial Valley Thrift & Loan. Before approaching the advisory partner on the engagement, Stanley drafted the memo on the next page to file.

## Questions

1. What is the role of professional skepticism in auditing financial statements? Do you think that the auditors were skeptical enough in evaluating the operations of Imperial Valley?

2. a. Assume that the auditors decide to support management's position and reduce the amount of loan write-offs. The decision was made in part because of concerns that regulators might force the bank to close its doors, and then many customers would have nowhere else to go to borrow money. Evaluate the auditors' stage of moral reasoning in making this decision.

   b. Assume instead that the auditors *insist* on a higher level of loan write-offs and allowance for uncollectibles to reserve for loan losses. What level of reasoning are they at in making this decision?

3. Evaluate the facts of the case from the perspective of materiality and risk assessment. How does your evaluation help in determining the appropriate audit opinion to give in the Imperial Valley case? What opinion do you think is appropriate in this case? Why?

## Optional Question

4. Assume that you were asked to review the information in this case as the advisory partner on the audit of Imperial Valley Thrift & Loan. Using the relevant steps in the Integrated Ethical Decision-Making Process explained in Chapter 2, analyze the case and come up with a decision on what type of opinion to recommend to management.

---

### Memo: Going-Concern Question

The question of the going-concern status of Imperial Valley Thrift & Loan is being raised because of the client's continuing operating losses and high level of loan losses that has resulted in a "capital impairment" designation by the Arizona Department of Corporations. The client lost $920,000 after audit adjustments in 2013. This is in addition to a loss of $780,000 in 2012. Imperial Valley has also reported a loss of $45,000 for the first two months of 2014.

Imperial Valley is also out of compliance with regulatory capital requirements. After audit adjustments, the client has net equity capital of $610,000 as of December 31, 2013. The Arizona Department of Corporations requires a 6:1 ratio of thrift certificates to capital. As of December 31, 2013, these regulations would require net equity capital of $1,232,000. Imperial Valley was therefore undercapitalized by $622,000 at that date, and no additional capital contributions have been made subsequent to December 31. It is possible, however, that either the parent company, Nuevo Financial Group, or a private investor, Manny Gonzalez, will contribute additional equity capital.

We have been unable to obtain enough support for the value of much of the collateral backing outstanding loans. We also have concluded that there is a substantial doubt about the bank's ability to continue in business. The reasons for this conclusion include the following:

- The magnitude of losses, particularly loan losses, implies that Imperial Valley is not well managed.
- The losses are continuing in 2014. Annualized losses to date, without any provision for loan losses, are $270,000.
- Additional equity capital has not been contributed to date, although Gonzalez has $600,000 available.
- Our review of client loan files and lending policies raises an additional concern that loan losses may continue. If this happens, it would only exacerbate the conditions mentioned herein.

We also believe that it is not possible to test the liquidation value of the assets at this time should Imperial Valley cease to operate. The majority of client assets are loans receivable. These would presumably have to be discounted in order to be sold. In addition, there is some risk that the borrowers will simply stop making payments.

In conclusion, it is our opinion that a going-concern question exists for Imperial Valley Thrift & Loan at December 31, 2013.

## Case 5-4

# Audit Client Considerations and Risk Assessment

Lanny Beaudean joined Cardinal & Coyote LLP in 2011 after working for two years for the IRS in Phoenix, Arizona. Cardinal & Coyote is a second-tier CPA firm just below the Big Four in size. Beaudean had passed all four parts of the CPA Exam in Arizona and decided to work for a locally based CPA firm with international clients to gain a broad base of experience that might help him become a CFO at a public company in the future. Beaudean has been advancing rapidly and just became a senior auditor at Cardinal & Coyote.

Yancy Corliss is a new audit partner at Cardinal & Coyote. One day, Corliss was summoned to the office of Sharon Rules, the managing partner of the firm. Rules told Corliss that she had been approached by a new client, Jerry Jost of Jost Furniture International. Jost Furniture (Jost) is a large chain of home furniture rental companies in the Southwest catering to young, upscale individuals who might live in a city for two years or so and then move on. It recently opened an office in Canada and plans to expand to Europe in the not-too-distant future. Top management at Jost seemed to imply that the firm would get the audit so long as it submitted a reasonable bid.

Rules asked Corliss to do background checks on Jost and make whatever inquiries were necessary to assess the potential business risk of Jost as a future client, including an assessment of the integrity of management. Corliss was given three days to do the work and report back to Rules with a recommendation. If the decision was to go ahead, then Cardinal & Coyote would submit a bid and compete with one other CPA firm for the account. The firm believes that it will be a lucrative account, especially because the company has been in expansion mode and will require advisory services in the future including advice on acquisitions and other consulting services.

Corliss assembled his team to review the background and other information about Jost, and he asked Beaudean to head up the assessment and report back to Corliss in two days. During that time, Beaudean would have two other staff members to help with the assignment. Beaudean was excited about his first opportunity to work on new client assessment.

Beaudean met with Vinnie Gabelli, a transplanted Brooklyn native who had graduated from Arizona State University (ASU) at Phoenix. Gabelli was like a fish out of water in Arizona, even though he had spent 16 months in the Master's of Accounting program at ASU. Gabelli thought a prickly pear was someone who could not make it in Staten Island and moved to Brooklyn for a better life.

Gabelli told Beaudean that he welcomed the opportunity to work with a native of Phoenix and learn about its colorful history. Beaudean also asked Jackie Oloff, a native of Minneapolis, to join the team. Jackie had moved to Phoenix two years ago with her husband, who is a professor of accounting at ASU. The team discussed mutual responsibilities, data

sources for the information, and key areas of risk, and then they broke up to start their work. At the end of the day, the team reassembled to share information. Here is a brief list of the findings:

1. The predecessor audit firm had helped Jost Furniture with its initial public offering (IPO) and audited the financial statements of the company for five years. The firm resigned the account in 2010 following the issuance of a qualified (i.e., modified) opinion on the 2009 financial statements. The firm had issued this opinion because of differences with management over the proper accounting for inventories.

2. A second firm audited the financial statements for 2010. That firm also issued a qualified opinion.

3. Jost's financial statements for 2011 and 2012 were audited by a third firm, which was dismissed after two years for reasons that were unclear.

4. The financial statements for 2013 had not been audited, and on March 19, 2014, the CEO of Jost Furniture, Jerry Jost, approached Sharon Rules at a community event and asked her to submit a bid for the Jost audit. Jost asked that the bid be submitted by March 23.

5. A memorandum to the file prepared by Rules indicated that Jost had admitted to Rules that the company had past problems with various auditors, but Jost assured Rules that the accounting issues had been resolved. He also told Rules that the company's controller had recently quit—the third time in four years there had been a turnover in that position. Jost told Rules that the company had two candidates to replace the controller, and he wanted her to help with the final decision because the CPA firm would work closely with the controller.

6. Beaudean, with the help of Gabelli and Oloff, reviewed the financial statements of Jost Furniture for the past four years, during which time the qualified opinions had been issued. They went through a checklist of risk assessment issues for new clients and stopped when they came to the following: Verify the circumstances of any prior auditor dismissal or withdrawal by first asking the client for permission to approach the predecessor auditor(s).

One final discovery that gave the auditors pause with respect to taking on Jost Furniture as a client was a statement in the report on internal control over financial reporting for 2012. That statement indicated the existence of a material weakness in internal control that had not been mentioned in management's internal control assessment.

At the meeting at the end of the first day, the auditors discussed the unusual number of auditor changes in a short period of time, apparently due to the accounting differences that were raised in the audit reports for the years 2009 through

2012. Beaudean asked Gabelli to contact Jerry Jost and ask permission to speak with the auditors for the 2011 and 2012 financial statements. Gabelli was also asked to contact the two banks where the company does business and check into its payment record. Oloff had a past business relationship with Miles Frazer, the attorney for Jost Furniture. Oloff agreed to contact Frazer to determine whether there are any outstanding litigation issues or other legal matters that the firm should know about. They all agreed to get these matters done by the end of the second day, and a meeting was set for 5:00 p.m. With respect to the material weakness in internal controls, the decision was made to ask Sharon Rules to discuss the matter directly with Jerry Jost.

Gabelli found out that a $1 million loan payable to Phoenix Second National Bank had been overdue before payment was made on March 15, 2014. The president of the bank told Gabelli that Jost had been in violation of a debt covenant agreement that obligated Jost to maintain a current ratio of 1.5:1 at all times, and that the bank was concerned about Jost's ability to continue as a going concern, pointing out that Jost had gone below the ratio twice. The first time that Jost violated the covenant, the bank accepted the explanation of a temporary cash flow problem. The bank granted the company a three-month extension to meet the requirements of the debt covenant. It subsequently found out that the cash flow problem had happened because Jerry Jost withdrew $500,000 from the Jost Furniture cash account at Second National Bank to help put a down payment on a mortgage to buy an upscale house in Scottsdale. The second time that it occurred, the bank began foreclosure on the loan on January 31, 2014, but by the time the process completed, Jost had paid off the entire $1 million balance.

Oloff had no luck with Frazer, the attorney for Jost. When she called his office, the secretary always told Oloff that Frazer was on another line and she'd take a message. When Oloff asked to leave a voicemail message, she was told Frazer did not have voicemail. How about leaving an e-mail message? She asked. No, the secretary said, no e-mail either. Can I text him, tweet him, or just do it the old-fashioned way and set up an appointment? No, no, and no were the answers.

Oloff had left five messages for Frazer by the time of the team's second meeting, and she had nothing to report except to make an editorial comment about lawyer responsiveness (or lack thereof).

As for permission to speak with the predecessor auditor, Jerry Jost was indignant with the request. Gabelli wasn't sure why or whether it meant problems existed with the 2011–2012 audits. He reported to the audit team that Jost asked for more time to consider the request.

At 5:00 p.m. on March 22, the auditors met in the firm's conference room to discuss their findings. After hearing about Gabelli's concerns, the internal control issue, and Oloff's lack of success with Frazer, Beaudean expressed serious concerns about taking on Jost as a client.

## Questions

1. From an ethical perspective, why do auditors evaluate business risk before deciding whether to accept a new client?

2. Integrity is an essential element in the relationship between client management and the auditor. Evaluate the issue of integrity from the perspective of possibly taking on Jost Furniture as a new client. Use Josephson's Six Pillars of Character to support your decision whether to submit a bid for the Jost Furniture audit.

3. Some CPA firms have started to add an indemnification clause to their engagement letters that provides that the client would release, indemnify, defend, and hold the auditor harmless from any liability and costs resulting from knowing misrepresentations by management. Would inclusion of such an indemnification clause in engagement letters impair independence? Why or why not? What if, as a condition to retaining an auditor to perform an audit engagement, a prospective client requests that the firm enter into an agreement providing that the firm indemnify the client for damages, losses, or costs arising from lawsuits, claims, or settlements that relate directly or indirectly to client acts. Would entering into such an agreement impair independence?

## Case 5-5

# Krispy Kreme Doughnuts, Inc.[1]

On March 4, 2009, the SEC reached an agreement with Krispy Kreme Doughnuts, Inc., and issued a cease-and-desist order to settle charges that the company fraudulently inflated or otherwise misrepresented its earnings for the fourth quarter of its FY2003 and each quarter of FY2004. By its improper accounting, Krispy Kreme avoided lowering its earnings guidance and improperly reported earnings per share (EPS) for that time period; these amounts exceeded its previously announced EPS guidance by 1 cent.[2]

The primary transactions described in this case are "round-trip" transactions. In each case, Krispy Kreme paid money to a franchisee with the understanding that the franchisee would pay the money back to Krispy Kreme in a pre-arranged manner that would allow the company to record additional pretax income in an amount roughly equal to the funds originally paid to the franchisee.

There were three round-trip transactions cited in the SEC consent agreement. The first occurred in June 2003, which was during the second quarter of FY2004. In connection with the reacquisition of a franchise in Texas, Krispy Kreme increased the price that it paid for the franchise by $800,000 (i.e., from $65,000,000 to $65,800,000) in return for the franchisee purchasing from Krispy Kreme certain doughnut-making equipment. On the day of the closing, Krispy Kreme debited the franchise's bank account for $744,000, which was the aggregate list price of the equipment. The additional revenue boosted Krispy Kreme's quarterly net income by approximately $365,000 after taxes.

The second transaction occurred at the end of October 2003, four days from the closing of Krispy Kreme's third quarter of FY2004, in connection with the reacquisition of a franchise in Michigan. Krispy Kreme agreed to increase the price that it paid for the franchise by $535,463, and it recorded the transaction on its books and records as if it had been reimbursed for two amounts that had been in dispute with the Michigan franchisee. This overstated Krispy Kreme's net income in the third quarter by approximately $310,000 after taxes.

The third transaction occurred in January 2004, in the fourth quarter of FY2004. It involved the reacquisition of the remaining interests in a franchise in California. Krispy Kreme owned

a majority interest in the California franchise and, beginning on or about October 2003, initiated negotiations with the remaining interest holders for acquisition of their interests. During the negotiations, Krispy Kreme demanded payment of a "management fee" in consideration of Krispy Kreme's handling of the management duties since October 2003. Krispy Kreme proposed that the former franchise manager receive a distribution from his capital account, which he could then pay back to Krispy Kreme as a management fee. No adjustment would be made to the purchase price for his interest in the California franchise to reflect this distribution. As a result, the former franchise manager would receive the full value for his franchise interest, including his capital account, plus an additional amount, provided that he paid back that amount as the management fee. Krispy Kreme, acting through the California franchise, made a distribution to the former franchise manager in the amount of $597,415, which was immediately transferred back to Krispy Kreme as payment of the management fee. The company booked this fee, thereby overstating net income in the fourth quarter by approximately $361,000.

Additional accounting irregularities were unearthed in testimony by a former sales manager at a Krispy Kreme outlet in Ohio, who said a regional manager ordered that retail store customers be sent double orders on the last Friday and Saturday of FY2004, explaining "that Krispy Kreme wanted to boost the sales for the fiscal year in order to meet Wall Street projections." The manager explained that the doughnuts would be returned for credit the following week—once FY2005 was under way. Apparently, it was common practice for Krispy Kreme to accelerate shipments at year end to inflate revenues by stuffing the channels with extra product, a practice known as "channel stuffing."

Some could argue that Krispy Kreme auditors—PwC—should have noticed a pattern of large shipments at the end of the year with corresponding credits the following fiscal year during the course of their audit. Typical audit procedures would be to confirm with Krispy Kreme's customers their purchases. In addition, monthly variations analysis should have led someone to question the spike in doughnut shipments at the end of the fiscal year. However, PwC did not report such irregularities or modify its audit report.

In May 2005, Krispy Kreme disclosed disappointing earnings for the first quarter of FY2005 and lowered its future earnings guidance. Subsequently, as a result of the transactions already described, as well as the discovery of other accounting errors, on January 4, 2005, Krispy Kreme announced that it would restate its financial statements for 2003 and 2004. The restatement reduced net income for those years by $2,420,000 and $8,524,000, respectively.

In August 2005, a special committee of the company's board issued a report to the SEC following an internal investigation of

---

[1]An article that deals with the intangible asset aspect of the case can be found at Lori Holder-Webb and Mark Kohlbeck, "The Hole in the Doughnut: Accounting for Acquired Intangibles at Krispy Kreme," *Issues in Accounting Education*, August 2006, Vol. 21, No. 3, pp. 297–312. Available at http://dx.doi.org/10.2308/iace.2006.21.3.297.

[2]Securities and Exchange Commission, Accounting and Auditing Enforcement Release No. 2941, *In the Matter of Krispy Kreme Doughnuts, Inc.,* March 4, 2009, www.sec.gov/litigation/admin/2009/34-59499.pdf.

the fraud at Krispy Kreme. The report states that every Krispy Kreme employee or franchisee who was interviewed "repeatedly and firmly" denied deliberately scheming to distort the company's earnings or being given orders to do so; yet, in carefully nuanced language, the Krispy Kreme investigators hinted at the possibility of a willful cooking of the books. "The number, nature, and timing of the accounting errors strongly suggest that they resulted from an intent to manage earnings," the report said. "Further, CEO Scott Livengood and COO John Tate failed to establish proper financial controls, and the company's earnings may have been manipulated to please Wall Street." The committee also criticized the company's board of directors, which it said was "overly deferential in its relationship with Livengood and failed to adequately oversee management decisions."

Krispy Kreme materially misstated its earnings in its financial statements filed with the SEC between the fourth quarter of FY2003 and the fourth quarter of FY2004. In each of these quarters, Krispy Kreme falsely reported that it had achieved earnings equal to its EPS guidance plus 1 cent in the fourth quarter of FY2003 through the third quarter of FY2004 or, in the case of the fourth quarter of FY2004, earnings that met its EPS guidance.

The SEC cited Krispy Kreme for violations of Section 13(a) of the Exchange Act and Rules 12b-20, 13a-1, and 13a-13 thereunder, which require every issuer of a security registered pursuant to Section 12 of the Exchange Act to file with the commission all the necessary information to make the financial statements not misleading. The company was also sanctioned for its failure to keep books, records, and accounts that, in reasonable detail, accurately and fairly reflect their transactions and dispositions of their assets. Finally, Krispy Kreme was cited for failing to devise and maintain a system of internal accounting controls sufficient to provide reasonable assurances that transactions are recorded as necessary to permit preparation of financial statements in accordance with GAAP.

On March 4, 2009, the SEC reached agreement with three former top Krispy Kreme officials, including onetime chair, CEO, and president Scott Livengood. Livengood, former COO John Tate, and CFO Randy Casstevens all agreed to pay more than $783,000 for violating accounting laws and fraud in connection with their management of the company.

Livengood was found in violation of fraud, reporting provisions, and false certification regulations. Tate was found in violation of fraud, reporting provisions, recordkeeping, and internal controls rules. Casstevens was found in violation of fraud, reporting provisions, recordkeeping, internal controls, and false certification rules. Livengood's settlement required him to pay about $542,000, which included $467,000 of what the SEC considered as the "disgorgement of ill-gotten gains and prejudgment interest" and $75,000 in civil penalties. Tate's settlement required him to return $96,549 and pay $50,000 in civil penalties, while Casstevens had to return $68,964 and pay $25,000 in civil penalties. Krispy Kreme itself was not required to pay a civil penalty because of its cooperation with the SEC in the case.

## Questions

1. Why did the round-trip transactions engaged in by Krispy Kreme and its franchisees violate revenue recognition rules? How should they have been recorded under GAAP?

2. Evaluate the corporate governance at Krispy Kreme during its financial statement fraud including management's stewardship responsibility to owners.

3. Krispy Kreme had materially misstated its financial results in an effort to manage its earnings. Subsequently, after the fraud was detected, the company restated its net income for 2003 and 2004. What are an auditor's responsibilities to detect material misstatements in the financial statements? What should an auditor do after discovering material accounting irregularities? In other words, how should an auditor correct for the fact that in the current year it was discovered that a previous years' financial statements were materially misstated?

## Optional Question

4. Prime accounting issues with respect to accounting for franchise activities include how to recognize revenue on the individual sale of franchise territories and on the transactions that arise in connection with the continuing relationship between the franchisor and franchisee. The Krispy Kreme case describes three transactions between the company and its franchisees that created false earnings. Review *FAS 45, Accounting for Franchise Fee Revenue*, and explain specifically how Krispy Kreme's transactions violated *FAS 45*. (See www.fasb.org/pdf/fas45.pdf.)

## Case 5-6

# Dunco Industries

## The following two cases deal with accounting issues at Dunco Industries.

### Part 1—Marcus Yamabuto

Marcus Yamabuto graduated from Washington State University in June 2013. He began his career working for Dunco Industries, a public company that manufactures full HD plasma televisions. Frank Johnson is the CEO of Dunco, and Karen Gross is the CFO. Dunco has a three-person audit committee whose chair is Ken Holden.

Dunco is the original equipment manufacturer (OEM) of 42- through 64-inch plasma screens. The company sells its monitors to major manufacturers in the United States and overseas. Marcus was hired directly by the internal audit department and reports to Francey Gordon, the director of internal auditing. Both Marcus and Gordon are CPAs.

Marcus was assigned to review sale documents and freight bills to determine the amount of freight, the terms of the sale, and the proper cutoff treatment. During the course of his examination, Marcus discovered $2.4 million that was prematurely recognized as revenue by the accountants for the year ended December 31, 2013. He identified the problem by matching the invoices with corresponding freight bills and found that the shipping date of the transaction was January 2, 2014. However, there was a note signed by the freight forwarder: "Picked up for shipment at Dunco warehouse on December 31, 2013."

Marcus went to see Gordon to discuss the matter. They determined that the $2.4 million was material and should have been recorded in 2014. They were concerned about the premature revenue recognition given the impending external audit that will begin next week.

### Question

Assume that Francey Gordon goes to Karen Gross and Frank Johnson to discuss the matter. Gordon tells Gross and Johnson that just because the freight forwarder indicates the merchandise is picked up on December 31, that doesn't justify reporting the revenue until the goods are on its way to customers. Gross and Johnson disagree and instruct Gordon to leave the matter alone. What would you do if you were Francey Gordon at this point? Be sure to include your ethical obligations in the discussion.

### Part 2—Sandy Cole

Sandy Cole is a staff auditor of Lyons & Co., CPAs. She just completed her review of various accrual accounts during a routine audit of one of the firm's clients, Dunco Industries. Sandy uncovered ten manual entries made after the quarter's close that lacked sufficient supporting documentation and that significantly reduced the reserve balance for each account. She reviewed the entries in the system and found the same explanation for each reduction: "Reduce accrual by $1.5 million, per Jim Benson, corporate controller." The total amount of reductions came to $15 million and was material to the financial statements of Dunco.

Sandy brought this information to Joan Franks, the audit manager who was in charge of the engagement. Franks advised Sandy to discuss the entries with the corporate controller. The controller provided verbal support for each entry. Sandy had no reason to disbelieve the controller, so she cited the lack of supporting documentation as an audit finding and completed the report.

Six months later, news came out that the controller was adjusting various accrual accounts to manipulate earnings. Sandy, distraught about the situation, questioned her conduct and the audit procedures. Joan Franks was asked by Grace Wong, the audit partner in charge of the engagement, to explain why the audit team did not pursue the findings and press for supporting documentation.

The controller was terminated, and the company underwent an investigation by the SEC. Sandy continued to wrestle with her conscience: "I'm an auditor, not an investigator . . . right?" she thought.

### Questions

1. What is the role of an external auditor? Is it to simply examine the client's financial statements, or does it involve more—to be an investigator in conducting and completing the audit?

2. Evaluate the actions taken by Sandy Cole and Joan Franks in this case. Were their actions in accordance with ethical and professional standards? Why or why not?

## Case 5-7

# First Community Bank

This case involves the valuation of loan loss estimates of First Community Bank (FCB) and the examination of relevant accounts by the CPA firm of Howard & Stacey LLP.

FCB provided mostly residential loans to customers in Las Vegas, Florida, and Arizona. Beginning in about 2004, FCB expanded into high-risk types of lending that were experiencing unusual, rapid escalation in market values. This strategy made the bank particularly vulnerable to the fallout from the financial crisis, as these areas were hardest hit by the precipitous fall in real estate prices, which began in late 2006 and early 2007.

Throughout 2008, FCB was experiencing a dramatic rise in high-risk problem loans, including land and land development and residential construction. Certain of these problem loans were deemed "impaired" pursuant to Statement on Financial Accounting Standards (FAS) No. 114, meaning that it was probable the bank would not recover all amounts as contractually due. FCB reported FAS 114 impaired loan balance had increased from less than $4 million as of December 31, 2006, to nearly $186 million as of December 31, 2008.

In June 2008, Office of Community Bank Regulator (OCBR), the bank regulator, conducted a "risk-focused examination" of the bank that focused on asset quality, credit administration, management, earnings, and the adequacy of all items. As a result of that examination, OCBR downgraded the bank's credit rating from a 1 (indicating a financial institution that was "sound in every respect") to a 4 (indicating a financial institution with "serious financial or managerial deficiencies" that require close supervisory attention).

OCBR provided the bank with a report that deemed the institution to be in troubled condition and board and management performance to be exceptionally poor. OCBR concluded that FCB had experienced a significant deterioration in asset quality due to eroding real estate values in Nevada and Florida, and that poor board and management oversight had exacerbated the problem. OCBR directed FCB to maintain higher minimum capital ratios. Failure to correct the problems identified by OCBR or to meet the heightened capital requirements would result in additional enforcement action by the regulator.

The bank's FAS 114 loans had a negative effect on FCB's ability to meet the heightened capital requirements mandated by the OCBR. Under GAAP, FCB was required to assess probable losses associated with its impaired loans and record those losses. The bank applied the rules in FAS 114, *Accounting by Creditors for Impairment of a Loan,* and decided to measure impairment using the fair value of the loans in the marketplace.

As loan losses increased, the bank's capital was further eroded, directly affecting the OCBR capital requirements. In order to assess the loan losses for the bank's FAS 114 loans, FCB prepared loan-by-loan spreadsheets that contained estimates of collateral values and loan impairment determinations. The auditors generally based the valuation on the most recent appraisal in FCB's loan files. If the appraisal was aged, as it typically was, FCB would sometimes apply a discount to the appraised value. The rationale for applying any particular discount—or for not discounting an appraisal at all—was not documented. In the limited instances where FCB did get updated appraisals or valuations on the bank's FAS 114 loans during 2008, the collateral value typically showed a significant decline from the amount used by management in the immediately preceding quarter. The auditors' review of the appraisals showed that management's estimates were inflated by twenty to almost fifty times.

With respect to the audit of FCB, Howard was the engagement partner and was responsible for the audit engagement and its performance, for proper supervision of the work of the engagement team members, and for compliance with PCAOB standards. Stacey was more of a hands-on partner and contributed significantly to the planning of the audit, the design of tests of controls, and the design and implementation of substantive procedures. In addition, Stacey was responsible for executing the audit, including directing the audit engagement team on how to conduct the audit. She reviewed the audit work papers and was responsible for on-site supervision of the audit engagement team. She also played a significant role in gathering and evaluating evidential matter to support the loan loss reserve, and specifically the valuation of collateral underlying the bank's FAS 114 loans. Both partners were responsible for compliance with PCAOB standards with respect to the supervisory responsibilities that were assigned to Stacey.

Prior to and during their 2008 audit of FCB, Howard & Stacey auditors were aware of the valuation issues with the bank's loan loss reserve. The FCB loans subject to impairment were individually material to the financial statements and presented a significant risk of material misstatement. It far exceeded the $1.9 million materiality threshold established for the 2008 audit. It was reasonably possible that even a relatively small change in the value of the bank's FAS 114 loans would cause a material error in the financial statements. The audit planning document mentioned the significant risk, including a risk of fraud.

At the completion of the audit, both Howard and Stacey signed off that "all necessary auditing procedures were completed," that "support for conclusions was obtained," and that "sufficient appropriate audit evidence was obtained." Further, Howard specifically signed off on the audit checklist's requirement that the audit engagement team had "performed and documented its work in compliance with . . . applicable auditing standards . . . and the working papers demonstrate this compliance."

In the summer of 2009, when the OCBR began its annual exam, the bank was forced to get a significant number of updated appraisals and to use those appraisals in its loan loss calculations. In the fall of 2009, FCB disclosed over $130 million in additional loan loss provisions. FCB was shut down by bank regulators on June 4, 2010 and filed for bankruptcy later that month.

In April 2010, Howard & Stacey LLP resigned as FCB's auditor. Howard & Stacey withdrew its audit opinion relating to FCB's 2008 financial statements on the basis that they were materially misstated with respect to certain out-of-period adjustments for loan loss reserves. The firm also withdrew its opinion relating to FCB's internal control over financial reporting as of year-end 2008 due to a material weakness in internal control over financial reporting related to the material misstatements.

In the aftermath of the FCB fraud, a forensic auditor was called in to look at the work of the auditors. A review of the audit documents showed concerns on the part of Howard & Stacey after receiving the report from OCBR indicating an inadequacy in the loan loss reserve of $5 million, a material amount. Concern also existed about the value of the collateral supporting the outstanding loans.

The forensic auditor also discovered that valuation adjustments on the collateral underlying the bank's FAS 114 loans were inconsistent with independent market data. Third-party market data indicated that real estate values were declining precipitously in many of the markets where the bank's FAS 114 collateral was located, including Las Vegas, Nevada, and Phoenix, Arizona. At year-end 2008, FCB had prepared spreadsheets analyzing more than fifty borrower relationships, totaling approximately $255 million in loans, for evaluation for impairment under FAS 114. Approximately $186 million of these loans were actually deemed impaired by the bank. The majority of the loans that the bank evaluated for impairment under FAS 114 were collateralized by property with appraisals more than a year old; over half of those stale appraisals were not discounted. Critically, when management did discount appraisals, those discounts were typically inconsistent with—and more favorable to the bank than—the declines indicated by the independent market data.

## Questions

1. Explain the rules for accounting for impairment of loans under Statement of Financial Accounting Standards (FAS) No. 114, *Accounting by Creditors for Impairment of a Loan.* Did FCB apply these rules properly?

2. Evaluate the audit work of Howard & Stacey with respect to PCAOB audit standards discussed in the text and any other standards you choose to review. In particular comment on the auditors risk assessment in the audit of First Community Bank.

3. Evaluate the actions of the auditors using the AICPA ethics rules discussed in Chapter 4 and the GAAS discussed in this chapter.

## Case 5-8

# Fannie Mae: The Government's Enron

## Background

The Federal National Mortgage Association (Fannie Mae) and the Federal Home Loan Mortgage Corporation (Freddie Mac) are government-sponsored entities (GSEs) that operate under congressional charters to "help lower- and middle-income Americans buy homes." Both entities receive special treatment aimed at increasing home ownership by decreasing the cost for homeowners to borrow money. They do this by purchasing home mortgages from banks, guaranteeing them, and then reselling them to investors. This helps the banks eliminate the credit and interest rate risk, as well as lengthen the mortgage period. Fannie Mae and Freddie Mac receive advantages over commercial banks, including the following: (1) the U.S. Treasury can buy $2.25 billion of each company's debt; (2) Fannie Mae and Freddie Mac receive exemption from state and local taxes; and (3) the implied government backing gives them the ability to take on large amounts of home loans without increasing their low cost of capital.

Fannie Mae makes money either by buying, guaranteeing, and then reselling home mortgages for a fee or by buying mortgages, holding them, and then taking on the risk. By selling the mortgages, Fannie Mae eliminates the interest rate risk. There is less profit from this conservative approach than by holding the mortgages they buy. By holding the mortgages, Fannie Mae can make money on the spread because it has such a low cost of capital. In 1998, Fannie Mae's holdings hit a peak of $375 billion of mortgages and mortgage-backed securities on its own books, not to mention the more than $1 trillion of mortgages that it guaranteed. This process of holding mortgages on its books helped Fannie Mae expand rapidly. It also stimulated unprecedented profit growth because there was more profit to be made by keeping the mortgages than by guaranteeing them and then reselling them to other investors.

The reasons for growth in the telecommunications sector in the 1990s were, in part, the building of overcapacity in telecommunications equipment inventory based on the belief the economic growth bubble of the early 1990s would never end. Fannie Mae was similarly affected by the bubble in making and holding home mortgage loans. Just as telecommunication companies such as Global Crossing and Qwest were motivated to keep revenue and net income increasing quarter after quarter, the pressure also was on the top management of Fannie Mae to keep up the pace of growth. Fannie Mae's CEO, Franklin Raines, was so optimistic that he claimed at an investor conference in May 1999, "The future is so bright that I am willing to set as a goal that our earnings per share will double over the next five years."[1]

[1] Bethany McLean, "Fannie Mae: The Fall of Fannie Mae," *Fortune,* January 10, 2005.

As growth pressures continued, Fannie Mae began to use more derivatives to hedge interest rate risk. Critics looked at Fannie Mae's portfolio and expressed concern that with the risk involved in using derivatives, it may be at risk of defaulting. They pointed out that unlike federally guaranteed commercial bank deposits and the partial government guarantee of pension obligations through the Pension Benefit Guaranty Corporation (PBGC), there was no federal guarantee of Fannie Mae. Behind the scenes, Fannie Mae encouraged the concept that if it did default, the government would back it. This belief in the government as a back-stop if Fannie Mae got into financial trouble raised the specter of "moral hazard." Moral hazard is the idea that a party that is protected in some way from risk will act differently than if they didn't have that protection. This "too big to fail" philosophy turned out to be true later on, after the initial crisis in the 1990s, when the government bailed out Fannie Mae during the 2007–2008 financial crisis.[2]

In the 1990s, Fannie Mae was growing, and the market loved it. Top executives were receiving large bonuses for the growing profits. The growth was due to increased risk but people believed that, at the end of the day, the government would come to the rescue of Fannie Mae if that became necessary.

## The Accounting Scandal

The discovery of Fannie Mae's accounting scandal began in 2001, when Freddie Mac fired its auditor, (Arthur) Andersen, right after Enron's scandal exploded and the firm's existence seemed untenable. Freddie Mac then hired PwC.

PwC looked very closely at Freddie Mac's books and found that it had understated its profits in an attempt to smooth earnings. Freddie Mac agreed to a $5 billion restatement and fired many of its top executives. Meanwhile, Fannie Mae continued on its course and accused Freddie Mac of causing "collateral damage." The Fannie Mae Web site even included the statement, "Fannie Mae's reported financial results follow [GAAP] to the letter. There should be no question about our accounting." To a cynic, that statement may have had the unintended consequence of raising suspicion about Fannie Mae's accounting. After all, the markets had already been through it with Enron.

The government agency that regulated Fannie Mae and Freddie Mac at the time, the Office of Federal Housing Enterprise Oversight (OFHEO), had stated days before Freddie Mac's restatement that its internal controls were

[2] With a growing sense of crisis in U.S. financial markets, Fannie Mae and Freddie Mac were placed into conservatorship and the U.S. government committed to backstop the two-government-sponsored enterprises (GSEs) with up to $200 billion in additional capital.

"accurate and reliable." Once the restatement was made public, OFHEO had no choice but to look deeper into Fannie Mae's accounting to make sure that such a serious misjudgment did not happen again.

OFHEO was much weaker than most regulatory agencies such as the SEC and Justice Department that went after Enron in the obstruction of justice case. Fannie Mae essentially established OFHEO in 1992 as the regulatory agency that oversaw its operations and accounting. Fannie Mae was able to control its own regulator because it had enough influence in Congress to have OFHEO's budget cut. Fannie Mae had political influence because of its connections with realtors, homebuilders, and trade groups. Fannie Mae also made large contributions to various organizations and gained political clout.

After the Enron debacle, the White House wanted to make sure to avoid another scandal. The government provided the funding needed to bring in an independent investigator, Deloitte & Touche, that uncovered massive accounting irregularities. In September 2004, OFHEO released results of its investigation and "accused Fannie of both willfully breaking accounting rules and fostering an environment of 'weak or nonexistent' internal controls."

The investigation focused on the use of derivatives and Fannie Mae's deferring derivative losses on the balance sheet, thus inflating profits. OFHEO and Deloitte believed that the derivative losses should be recorded on the income statement. The dispute involved the application of *FAS 133, Accounting for Derivative Instruments and Hedging Activities.* The SEC's chief accountant determined that Fannie Mae failed to comply with the requirements for hedge accounting—including *FAS 133*'s rigorous documentation requirements. Fannie Mae was required by law to document its derivative use and file with the SEC. But "Fannie Mae's application of *FAS 133* (and its predecessor standards, *FAS 91*) did not comply in material respects with the accounting requirements" of GAAP. In particular, Fannie Mae's practice of putting losses on the balance sheet rather than on the income statement resulted in overstated earnings and excess executive compensation.[3]

OFHEO issued a report charging that in 1998, Fannie Mae recognized only $200 million in expenses when it was supposed to recognize $400 million. The underreporting of expenses led to an earnings per share (EPS) value of $3.23 and a total of $27 million in executive bonuses. These charges prompted investigations by the SEC and the Justice Department.[4]

Two weeks after the OFHEO report and charges against Fannie Mae, the House of Representatives Subcommittee on Capital Markets called a hearing. Raines initially deflected criticisms by saying, "These accounting standards are highly complex and require determinations on which experts often disagree." Raines was quite convincing in his defense of OFHEO charges that Fannie Mae executives had manipulated earnings in an attempt to increase bonuses. In the end, Raines won because the tone of the OFHEO reports made it seem as though the regulator was out to get Fannie Mae.

Perhaps feeling his oats after the victory in the House, Raines demanded that the SEC review OFHEO's findings. On December 15, 2004, the SEC announced that "Fannie did not comply 'in material respects' with accounting rules, and that as a result, Fannie would have to restate its results by more than $9 billion." Other than the $11–13 billion WorldCom fraud, the Fannie Mae fraud has the "dubious" honor of being the next largest fraud during the dark days of the late 1990s and early 2000s.

The OHFEO had been vindicated. The Fannie Mae board was told that both Raines and CFO Tim Howard had to be fired. Soon after, both resigned, and Fannie Mae fired KPMG and appointed Deloitte & Touche as the new auditor. Deloitte was asked to audit the 2004 statements of Fannie Mae and reaudit previous statements from 2001.

## OFHEO Report of May 23, 2006

On May 23, 2006, OFHEO issued a more extensive report of a comprehensive three-year investigation that officially charged senior executives at Fannie Mae with manipulating accounting to collect millions of dollars in undeserved bonuses and to deceive investors. The fraud led to a $400 million civil penalty against Fannie Mae, more than three times the $125 million penalty imposed on Freddie Mac for understating its earnings by about $5 billion from 2000 to 2002 to minimize large profit swings. The $400 million is one of the largest penalties ever in an accounting fraud case. Of this amount, $350 million will be returned to investors damaged by the alleged violations as required by the Fair Funds for Investors provision of SOX.[5]

The OFHEO review involves nearly 8 million pages of documents and details what the agency calls an arrogant and unethical corporate culture. The report, which concluded an 18-month investigation led by former senator Warren Rudman, was commissioned by Fannie Mae's board of directors. The final 2,600 page report charges Fannie Mae executives with perpetrating an $11 billion accounting fraud in order to meet earnings targets that would trigger $25 million in bonuses for top executives. The report charged former CFO Tim Howard and former controller Leanne G. Spencer as the chief culprits. Along with former chair and CEO Franklin Raines, who earned $20 million (including $3 million in stock options) in 2003 and $17.7 million in 2002, these executives created a "culture that improperly stressed stable earnings growth."

[3]Securities and Exchange Commission, SEC Form 8-K for Federal National Mortgage Association (Fannie Mae), December 28, 2004.

[4]Office of the Federal Housing Oversight, *Report of the Findings to Date: Special Examination of Fannie Mae,* September 17, 2004, www.ofheo.gov/media/pdf/FNMfindingstodate17septo4 .pdf.

[5]OFHEO, *Report of the Findings to Date: Special Examination of Fannie Mae,* September 17, 2004, www.fanniemae.com/media/pdf/newsreleases/FNMSPECIALEXAM.pdf.

Rudman told reporters that the management team Raines hired was "inadequate and in some respects not competent."[6]

## Criticisms of Internal Environment

From 1998 to mid-2004, the smooth growths in profits and precisely hit earnings targets each quarter reported by Fannie Mae were illusions deliberately created by senior management using faulty accounting. The report shows that Fannie Mae's faults were not limited to violating accounting standards but included inadequate corporate governance systems that failed to identify excessive risk taking and poor risk management. Randal Quarles, U.S. Treasury undersecretary for domestic finance at the time, said in a statement, "OFHEO's findings are a clear warning about the very real risk the improperly managed investment portfolios of [Fannie Mae and Freddie Mac] posed to the greater financial system."[7]

Fannie Mae agreed to make these changes in its operations:

- Limit the growth of its multibillion-dollar mortgage holdings, capping them at $727 billion.
- Make top-to-bottom changes in its corporate culture, accounting procedures, and ways of managing risk.
- Replace the chair of the board's audit committee. The board named accounting professor Dennis Beresford to replace audit committee chair Thomas Gerrity.

The report also faulted Fannie Mae's board of directors for failing to discover "a wide variety of unsafe and unsound practices" at the largest buyer and guarantor of home mortgages in the country. It signaled out senior management for failing to make investments in accounting systems, computer systems, other infrastructure, and staffing needed to support a sound internal control system, proper accounting, and GAAP-consistent financial reporting.

## KPMG's Audits

As for the role of KPMG as Fannie Mae's auditors, the report alleges that external audits performed by the firm failed to include an adequate review of Fannie Mae's significant accounting policies for GAAP compliance. KPMG also improperly provided unqualified opinions on financial statements even though they contained significant departures from GAAP. The failure of KPMG to detect and disclose the serious weaknesses in policies, procedures, systems, and controls in Fannie Mae's financial accounting and reporting, coupled with the failure of the board of directors to oversee KPMG properly, contributed to the unsafe and unsound conditions at Fannie Mae.

## SEC Civil Action

The SEC filed a civil action against Fannie Mae on May 23, 2006, charging that it engaged in a financial fraud involving multiple violations of GAAP in connection with the preparation of its annual and quarterly financial statements. These violations enabled Fannie Mae to show a stable earnings growth and reduced income statement volatility, and—as of year-end 1998—Fannie Mae was able to maximize bonuses and meet forecasted earnings. The SEC action thoroughly details a variety of deficiencies in accounting and financial reporting. Four of the more serious situations are described below.[8]

## Improper Accounting for Loan Fees, Premiums, and Discounts

*FAS 91* requires companies to recognize loan fees, premiums, and discounts as an adjustment over the life of the applicable loans, to generate a "constant effective yield" on the loans. Because of the possibility of loan prepayments, the estimated life of the loans may change with changing market conditions. *FAS 91* requires that any changes to the amortization of fees, premiums, and discounts caused by changes in estimated prepayments be recognized as a gain or loss in its entirety in the current period's income statement. Fannie Mae referred to this amount as the "catch-up adjustment." In the fourth quarter of 1998, Fannie Mae's accounting models calculated an approximate $439 million catch-up adjustment, in the form of a decrease to net interest income. Rather than book this amount consistent with *FAS 91,* senior management of Fannie Mae directed employees to record only $240 million of the catch-up amount in that year's income statement. By not recording the full catch-up adjustment, Fannie Mae understated its expenses and overstated its income by a pretax amount of $199 million. The unrecorded catch-up amount represented 4.3 percent of the 1998 earnings before taxes and 4.9 percent of 1998 net interest income for the fiscal year 1998.[9]

## Improper Hedge Accounting

Fannie Mae used debt to finance the acquisition of mortgages and mortgage securities and it turned to derivative instruments to hedge against the effect of fluctuations in interest rates on its debt costs. Application of *FAS 133* required that Fannie Mae adjust the value of its derivatives to changing market values. Critics contended that this standard opened

[6]Stephen Labaton and Eric Dash, "Report on Fannie Mae Cites Manipulation to Secure Bonus," *New York Times*, February 23, 2006, www.nytimes.com/2006/02/23/business/23cnd-fannie .htm.

[7]*Under Secretary Randal K. Quarles Statement on Treasury Reaction to OFHEO Report*, May 23, 2006, www.ustreas.gov/press/ releases/js4278.htm.

[8]Securities and Exchange Commission, Case Number 1:06CV00959, *Securities and Exchange Commission v. Federal National Mortgage Association*, May 23, 2006.

[9]Financial Accounting Standards Board, *Statement of Financial Accounting Standards (FAS) No. 91*, Accounting for Nonrefundable Fees and Costs Associated with Origination or Acquiring Loans and Initial Direct Costs of Leases (Norwalk, CT: FASB, 1982).

the door to earnings volatility, and it would appear that Fannie's desire to create earnings stability was used as the motivation for the application of the standards in *FAS 133*.[10]

## Accounting for Loan Loss Reserve

During the period 1997 through 2003, management failed to provide any quantitative estimate of losses in their loan portfolio, instead relying on a qualitative judgment. The failure to establish and implement an appropriate model for determining the size of the loan loss reserve was a violation of the GAAP rules in *FAS 5*.[11]

Fannie Mae maintained an unjustifiably high level of loan loss reserve in case it was needed to compensate for possible future changes in the economic environment. This violates the GAAP requirement that the estimate of loss reserves should be based on losses currently inherent in the loan portfolio. At year-end 2002, Fannie Mae's reserve was overstated by at least $100 million. This overstatement resulted in a $100 million understatement of earnings before tax, which represented 1.6 percent of the earnings before tax and $.08 of additional EPS on the year-end 2002 figure of $4.52.

## Classifications of Securities Held in Portfolio

*FAS 115* requires the classification of securities acquired as either trading, available for sale, or held to maturity at the time of acquisition. Rather than follow the *FAS 115* rules, Fannie Mae initially classified the securities that it acquired as held to maturity and then, at the end of the month of acquisition, decided on the ultimate classification.[12]

GAAP requires that the accounting classification be made at the time of acquisition. Once a security is classified, it can be reclassified only in narrow circumstances. Both trading and available-for-sale securities are valued at current market value, with any declines over time (or recaptures) in trading securities reported as a loss (or gain) in the income statement and as other comprehensive income in the equity section of the balance sheet for available-for-sale securities.

## Postscript

On October 27, 2008, Congress formed the Federal Housing Finance Agency (FHFA) by a legislative merger of OFHEO, the Federal Housing Finance Board (FHFB), and the U.S.

[10]Financial Accounting Standards Board, *Statement of Financial Accounting Standards (FAS) No. 133*, Accounting for Derivatives Instruments and Hedging Activities (Norwalk, CT: FASB, 1998).

[11]Financial Accounting Standards Board, *Statement of Financial Accounting Standards (FAS) No. 5*, Accounting for Contingencies (Norwalk, CT: FASB, 1975).

[12]Financial Accounting Standards Board, *Statement of Financial Accounting Standards (FAS) No. 115*, Accounting for Certain Investments in Debt and Equity Securities (Norwalk, CT: FASB, 1993).

Department of Housing and Urban Development (HUD) government-sponsored enterprise mission team. FHFA now regulates Fannie Mae, Freddie Mac, and the 12 Federal Home Loan Banks.

The meltdown in the mortgage-backed securities market that occurred during the financial crisis of 2007–2008 took place after the facts of this case. One can only wonder how bad things would have been for Fannie Mae had the entity been exposed to huge market losses in the mortgages that it held in addition to the financial fraud discussed in the case.

During the financial crisis, the market prices of many securities, particularly those backed by subprime home mortgages, had plunged to fractions of their original prices. That forced banks to report hundreds of billions of dollars in losses during 2008. The business community turned its attention to the accounting standards established by FASB for some relief. Bankers bitterly complained that the current market prices were the result of distressed sales and that they should be allowed to ignore those prices and value the securities instead at their value in a normal market.

At first, FASB resisted making changes, but that changed within a few days of a congressional hearing at which legislators from both parties demanded that the board act. FASB approved three changes to the rules, one of which would allow banks to keep some declines in asset values off their income statements. Reluctant FASB board members rationalized going along with this change by stating that improved disclosures would help investors. The American Bankers Association, which pushed legislators to demand the board make changes, praised the board stating that the "decision should improve information for investors by providing more accurate estimates of market values." The change that met with the most dissent was to allow banks to write down these investments to market value only if they conclude that the decline is "other than temporary." This change will now enable banks to keep many losses off the income statements, although the declines will still show up in the institutions' balance sheets.

A class action lawsuit was filed in 2005 on behalf of approximately 1 million Fannie Mae shareholders who incurred losses after regulators identified pervasive accounting irregularities at the company. Government investigators found that between 1998 and 2004, senior executives at Fannie had manipulated its results to hit earnings targets and generate $115 million in bonus compensation. The company had to restate its earnings, reducing them by $6.3 billion.

In 2006, the government sued three former executives, seeking $100 million in fines and $115 million in restitution from bonuses that it maintained they had not earned. Without admitting wrongdoing, former CEO Franklin Raines and two other members of top management paid $31.4 million to settle the matter in 2008. In September of that year, the federal government stepped in to rescue Fannie Mae, which was struggling under a mountain of bad mortgages.

Costs spent defending the three former executives against the shareholder suit recently totaled almost $100 million, according to a report in February 2012 by the inspector general of the FHFA. Since Fannie was taken over by the government in September 2008, the inspector general said, taxpayers have borne $37 million in legal outlays on behalf of the three executives.

On September 21, 2012, the federal judge overseeing the class action against Fannie Mae and its management ruled that the investors' lawyers had not proved that Raines knowingly misled shareholders about the company's accounting and internal controls, a necessary hurdle for the case against him to continue. The judge ruled that at best, evidence submitted by the shareholders showed that Raines "acted negligently in his role as the company's chief executive and negligently in his representations about the company's accounting and earnings management practices."

## Questions

1. An eight-month investigation by OFHEO concluded that slack standards at Fannie Mae created a corporate culture "that emphasized stable earnings at the expense of accurate financial disclosures." What is wrong with having stable earnings over time? Answer this question with respect to stakeholder interests.

2. Fannie Mae's corporate governance system failed to identify excessive risk taking. Describe those risks and the mechanisms that should have been used by Fannie Mae and KPMG to enhance risk assessment. To what extent do you think the risk taking at Fannie Mae was due to moral hazard?

3. According to the case, KPMG failed to review Fannie Mae's significant accounting policies for GAAP compliance. One item in particular was the failure of Fannie Mae to make a quantitative estimate of losses on its loan portfolio. In the end, KPMG gave an unqualified (now unmodified) opinion even though the financial statements contained significant departures from GAAP. What ethical and professional standards did KPMG violate in taking that position?

## Case 5-9

# Royal Ahold N.V. (Ahold)

## Summary of the Charges against Ahold

On October 13, 2004, the SEC charged Royal Ahold N.V. (Ahold) with multiple violations of Section 17(a) of the Securities Act, Section 10(b) of the Exchange Act, and Exchange Act Rule 10b-5. Charges were also filed against three former top executives: Cees van der Hoeven, the former CEO and chair of the executive board; A. Michael Meurs, the former CFO and executive board member; and Jan Andreae, the former executive vice president and executive board member. The commission also filed a related administrative action charging Roland Fahlin, a former member of Ahold's supervisory board and audit committee, with causing violations of the reporting, books and records, and internal control provisions of the securities laws.[1]

As a result of two frauds and other accounting errors and irregularities that are described in the following text, Ahold made materially false and misleading statements in SEC filings and in other public statements for at least fiscal years 1999 through 2001 and for the first three quarters of 2002. The company failed to adhere to the requirements of the Exchange Act and related rules that require each issuer of registered securities to make and keep books, records, and accounts that, in reasonable detail, accurately and fairly reflect the business of the issuer. The company also failed to devise and maintain a system of internal controls sufficient to provide reasonable assurances that, among other things, transactions are recorded as necessary to permit preparation of financial statements and to maintain the accountability of accounts.

## About the Company

Ahold is a publicly held company organized in the Netherlands with securities registered with the SEC pursuant to Section 12(b) of the Exchange Act. Ahold's securities trade on the NYSE and are evidenced by American Depositary Receipts (ADRs).[2]

As a foreign issuer, Ahold prepared its financial statements pursuant to Dutch accounting rules and included, in its filings with the commission, a reconciliation to U.S. GAAP and condensed financial statements prepared pursuant to U.S. GAAP.[3]

U.S. Foodservice (USF), a food service and distribution company with headquarters in Columbia, Maryland, is a wholly owned subsidiary of Ahold. USF was a publicly held company with securities registered with the SEC pursuant to Section 12(b) of the Exchange Act prior to being acquired by Ahold in April 2000.

## Summary of Complaint

The SEC's complaints, filed in the U.S. District Court for the District of Columbia, alleged that, as a result of the fraudulent inflation of promotional allowances at USF, the improper consolidation of joint ventures through fraudulent side letters, and other accounting errors and irregularities, Ahold's original SEC filings for at least fiscal years 2000 through 2002 were materially false and misleading. For fiscal years 2000 through 2002, Ahold overstated net sales by approximately $30 billion. Ahold overstated its operating income and net income by approximately $3.3 billion and $829 million, respectively, in total for fiscal years 2000 and 2001 and the first three quarters of 2002.

Ahold agreed to settle the commission's action, without admitting or denying the allegations in the complaint, by consenting to the entry of a judgment permanently enjoining the company from violating the antifraud and other provisions of the securities laws. Various officers of the company also settled charges, without admitting or denying the allegations in the complaint, by consenting to permanent injunctions and officer and director bars.

The SEC did not seek penalties in the enforcement actions because the Dutch Public Prosecutor's Office, which conducted a parallel criminal investigation in the Netherlands, requested that the commission not seek penalties against the

---

[1]U.S. Securities and Exchange Commission, Litigation Release No. 18929, October 13, 2004, www.sec.gov/litigation/litreleases/lr18929.htm.

[2]An ADR represents ownership in the shares of a non-U.S. company and trades in U.S. financial markets. The stocks of many non-U.S. companies trade on U.S. stock exchanges through the use of ADRs. ADRs enable U.S. investors to buy shares in foreign companies without the hazards or inconveniences of cross-border and cross-currency transactions. ADRs carry prices in U.S. dollars, pay dividends in U.S. dollars, and can be traded like the shares of U.S.-based companies.

[3]Starting in 2005, members of the European Union (EU), including the Netherlands, adopted IFRS as the only acceptable standards for EU companies when filing statements with securities commissions in the European Union. Subsequent to the adoption, the SEC in the United States announced it would accept IFRS-based financial statement filings for foreign companies listing their stock on the NYSE and NASDAQ without reconciliation to U.S. GAAP. The United States has not adopted IFRS, although the SEC has established a method known as "condorsement" that calls for IFRS to be examined for conformity with U.S. GAAP and determination whether to endorse IFRS as a part of GAAP. These issues are discussed in Chapter 8.

individuals because of potential double jeopardy issues under Dutch law. Because of the importance of this case in the Netherlands and the need for continued cooperation between the SEC and regulatory authorities in other countries, the commission agreed to the Dutch prosecutor's request.

The commission did not seek a penalty from Ahold because of, among other reasons, the company's extensive cooperation with the commission's investigation. Ahold self-reported the misconduct and conducted an extensive internal investigation. On its own initiative, Ahold expanded its internal investigation beyond the fraud at USF and the improper joint venture accounting to analyze accounting practices and internal controls at 17 operating companies. Ahold promptly provided the staff with the internal investigative reports and the supporting information and waived the attorney-client privilege and work product protection with respect to its internal investigations. Ahold also made its current personnel available for interviews or testimony and significantly assisted the staff in arranging interviews with, or testimony from, former Ahold personnel located in the United States and (of even greater importance) abroad. Ahold promptly took remedial actions including, but not limited to, revising its internal controls and terminating employees responsible for the wrongdoing.

In a separate action, on June 17, 2009, Ahold reached a final settlement with plaintiffs in a class action securities lawsuit that requires the company to pay the lead plaintiffs $1.1 billion to resolve all claims against Ahold. The settlement applies to all qualifying common shareholders around the world and covers Ahold, its subsidiaries and affiliates, the individual defendants, and the underwriters.[4]

## Statement of Facts

The following summarizes the main facts of the case with respect to transactions between Ahold and USF.

### Budgeted Earnings Goals

From the time that it acquired USF in April 2000, Ahold and USF budgeted annual earnings goals for USF. Compensation for USF executives was based on, among other things, USF's meeting or exceeding budgeted earnings targets. USF executives each received a substantial bonus in early 2002 because USF purportedly satisfied earnings goals for FY2001. USF executives were each eligible for a substantial bonus if USF met earnings targets for FY2002. Certain USF executives engaged in or substantially participated in a scheme whereby USF reported earnings equal to or greater than the targets, regardless of the company's true performance.

### Promotional Allowances

A significant portion of USF's operating income was based on payments by its vendors, referred to in various ways such

as "promotional allowances," "rebates," "discounts," and "program money" (referred to below only as "promotional allowances"). During at least FY2001 and FY2002, USF made no significant profit on most of its end sales to its customers. Instead, the majority of USF's operating income was derived from promotional allowances.

In a typical promotional allowance agreement, USF committed to purchasing a minimum volume from a vendor. The vendor in turn paid USF a per-unit rebate of a portion of the original price that it charged USF, according to an agreed-upon payment schedule.

Sometimes the volume-based promotional allowances were paid as they were earned, but it was a common practice for the vendor to "prepay" on multiyear contracts at least some portion of the amounts that would be due if USF met all the projected purchase volume targets in the contract. Promotional allowances were critical to USF's financial results—without them, USF's operating income for FY2001 and FY2002 would have been materially reduced.

## False Confirmations and Statements to Auditors

USF executives engaged in or substantially participated in a scheme whereby USF reported earnings equal to or greater than its earnings targets, regardless of the company's true performance. The primary method used to carry out this fraudulent scheme to "book to budget" was to inflate USF's promotional allowance income improperly. USF executives booked to budget by, among other things, causing USF to record completely fictitious promotional allowances that were sufficient to cover any shortfall to budgeted earnings.

USF executives covered up the false earnings by making it appear that the inflated promotional allowance income had been earned by (1) inducing vendors to confirm false promotional allowance income, payments, and receivable balances; (2) manipulating the promotional allowance accounts receivable from vendors and manipulating and misapplying cash receipts; and (3) making false and misleading statements and material omissions to the company's independent auditors, other company personnel, and/or Ahold personnel.

USF executives falsely represented to the company's independent auditors that there were no written promotional allowance contracts for the vast majority of promotional allowance agreements when in fact they knew, or were reckless in not knowing, that such written contracts existed. These executives falsely represented that USF had only handshake deals with its vendors that a USF executive would renegotiate at the end of each year to arrive at a mutually agreed-upon final amount due from each vendor for the year. They knew, or were reckless in not knowing, that these representations were false when they were made.

## Nonexistent Internal Controls

USF had no comprehensive, automated system for tracking the amounts owed by the vendors pursuant to the promo-

[4]Securities and Exchange Commission, U.S. District of Columbia, December 5, 2009, www.sec.gov/litigation/complaints/comp 19034-6.pdf.

tional allowance agreements. Instead, USF, for purposes of interim reporting, purported to estimate an overall "promotional allowance rate" as a percentage of sales and recorded periodic accruals based on that rate. Information provided by USF executives caused the estimated rate to be inflated. The intended and actual result of inflating USF's promotional allowance income was that USF, and Ahold, materially overstated their operating incomes.

## Corrupting the Audit Process

USF executives participated in a systematic effort to corrupt the audit process to keep the fraud from being discovered. Ahold's auditors attempted at the end of each fiscal year to confirm with the vendors that they actually paid, or still owed, the promotional allowances recorded by USF. To satisfy the auditors, USF executives successfully convinced vendors to sign audit confirmation letters even though they knew that the letters were false.

For each vendor subject to the confirmation process, USF executives prepared a schedule purportedly reflecting the promotional allowances earned by USF for the year, the amount paid by the vendor, and the balance due. USF executives grossly inflated the figures contained in these schedules. The schedules were used both by USF to support the related amounts recorded in its financial statements and by its auditors to perform the year-end audit.

USF executives provided information used to prepare confirmation request letters that they signed and that were sent to major vendors reflecting the inflated aggregate promotional allowances purportedly paid or owed to USF during the year. The promotional monies earned, paid, and receivable that were stated in the confirmations were grossly inflated and in many cases were simply fictitious, having no relationship to the actual promotional allowances earned, paid, or receivable.

## Fraudulent Acts by Management

As a further part of the fraud, USF executives contacted or directed subordinates to contact vendors to alert them that they would receive confirmation letters and to ask them to sign and return the letters without objection. If a vendor balked at signing the fraudulent confirmation, USF executives pressed the vendor by, for example, falsely representing that the confirmation was just "an internal number" and that USF did not consider the receivable reflected in the confirmation to be an actual debt that it would seek to collect. USF executives sent, or directed subordinates to send, side letters to vendors who continued to object to the fraudulent confirmations. The side letters assured the vendors that they did not, in fact, owe USF amounts reflected as outstanding in the confirmation letters.

USF executives attempted to prevent the discovery of the fraudulent scheme by making accounting entries that unilaterally deducted material amounts from the balances that USF owed to certain vendors for the products USF had purchased, and simultaneously credited the promotional allowance receivable balance for the amount of such deductions. These "deductions" were made at the end of the year and had the net effect of making it appear that USF had made material progress in collecting promotional allowance payments allegedly due.

The large year-end deductions facilitated the fraudulent recording of promotional allowance income because these deductions made it appear that the amounts recorded had been earned and paid. The USF executives concealed the fact that the deductions were not authorized, were not legitimate, and that a substantial percentage of the deductions were reversed in the early part of the following fiscal year.

USF executives also knew, or were reckless in not knowing, that the amounts paid by some vendors included prepayments on multiyear contracts. But they falsely represented to USF personnel, Ahold personnel, and/or the company's independent auditors that none of the promotional allowance agreements included such prepayments. As a result, USF treated the prepayments by vendors as if they were payments for currently owed promotional allowances. This made it falsely appear that USF was making material progress in collecting the inflated promotional allowance income that it had recorded.

## Role of the Auditors

Deloitte & Touche had been Ahold's group (the consolidated entity) auditor since the company went public. A few years after Ahold had acquired USF and the accounting fraud surfaced, investors sued the firm for engaging in deceptive conduct and recklessly disregarding misstatements in Ahold's financial statements. The charges were dismissed because it was concluded that Deloitte was being deceived by Ahold executives, many of whom went to great lengths to conceal the fraud.

When Deloitte took over the auditing of USF after being taken over by Ahold, the firm uncovered multiple accounting errors that not only had a material effect on USF's profits, but materially distorted the net income of Ahold as well.

## Financial Statement Misstatements and Restatements

As a result of the schemes already described, USF materially overstated its operating income during at least FY2001 and FY2002. On February 24, 2003, Ahold announced that it would issue restated financial statements for previous periods and would delay filing its consolidated 2002 financial statements as a result of an initial internal investigation based, in part, on the overstatement of income at USF. Ahold announced in May 2003 that USF's income had been overstated by more than $800 million since April 2000. Ahold's stock price plummeted from approximately $10.69 per share to $4.16 per share.

On or about October 17, 2003, Ahold filed its Form 20-F (filing with the SEC for foreign entities) for the fiscal year ended December 29, 2002, which contained restatements for FY2000 and FY2001, corrected accounting adjustments for FY2002, and restated amounts for FY1998 and FY1999 included in the five-year summary data. The restatements indicated that in its original SEC filings and other public statements, Ahold had overstated (1) net income by approximately 17.6, 32.6, and 88.1 percent for FY2000, FY2001, and the first three quarters of FY2002, respectively; (2) operating income by approximately 28.1, 29.4, and 51.3 percent for FY2000, FY2001, and the first three quarters of FY2002, respectively; and (3) net sales by approximately 20.8, 18.6, and 13.8 percent for FY2000, FY2001, and the first three quarters of FY2002, respectively. Ahold and three of the individual defendants agreed to settlements with the commission.

## Ahold Today

Ahold operates a number of grocery chains throughout the United States and Europe. Its common shares are listed and traded on the NYSE Euronext.[5]

[5]NYSE Euronext is the result of a merger on April 4, 2007, between the NYSE and stock exchanges in Paris, Amsterdam, Brussels, and Lisbon, as well as the NYSE Liffe derivatives markets in London, Paris, Amsterdam, Brussels, and Lisbon. NYSE Euronext is a U.S. holding company that operates through its subsidiaries. NYSE Euronext is a listed company. NYSE Euronext common stock is dually listed on the NYSE and Euronext Paris under the symbol "NYX." Each of the Euronext exchanges holds an exchange license granted by the relevant national exchange regulatory authority and operates under its supervision. Each market operator is also subject to national laws and regulations in its jurisdiction in addition to the requirements imposed by the national exchange authority and, in some cases, the central bank and/or the finance ministry in the relevant European country. Regulation of Euronext and its constituent markets is conducted in a coordinated fashion by the respective national regulatory authorities pursuant to memoranda of understanding relating to the cash and derivatives markets.

## Questions

1. Explain how Ahold used promotional allowances to manipulate earnings. Refer to the Fraud Triangle described in this chapter and analyze the incentives, pressures, and opportunities to commit fraud at Ahold.

2. Use the COSO *Integrated Framework* and discussion of risk assessment in the chapter and evaluate the deficiencies in the internal control system at Ahold. Include in your discussion whether you believe Ahold adequately monitored its internal controls as suggested in COSO's *Guidance on Monitoring Internal Control Systems* discussed earlier in this chapter.

3. The court ruled that Deloitte was not responsible for the fraud at Ahold because its management deceived the auditors and hid information from the firm. How does such deception relate to the Deloitte auditors' obligations to identify material misstatements in the financial statements of Ahold and provide an opinion that the statements present fairly financial position, results of operations, and changes in cash flows? Do you believe auditors should be left off the hook with respect to their ethical and professional obligations because of management deception?

## Optional Questions

4. In addition to the deficiencies in accounting for promotional allowances, Ahold engaged in joint venture transactions that materially misstated the financial statements. Review the litigation referred to in the case and the nature and scope of the joint venture transactions and the problems that existed with the company's accounting and financial reporting and answer the following two questions.

a. Evaluate the operation of internal controls with respect to accounting for the joint venture transactions. How might the company have strengthened its controls?

b. From a corporate governance perspective, what were the deficiencies that seem to have contributed to the fraud in accounting for and reporting the joint venture transactions? Can you identify corporate governance mechanisms that might have helped prevent or detect the fraud at Ahold but that were nonexistent?

## Case 5-10

# Groupon

## Introduction

The Groupon case was first discussed in Chapter 3. Here, we expand on the discussion of internal controls and the risk of material misstatement in the financial statements. Groupon is a deal-of-the-day recommendation service for consumers. Launched in 2008, Groupon—a fusion of the words *group* and *coupon*—combines social media with collective buying clout to offer daily deals on products, services, and cultural events in local markets. Promotions are activated only after a certain number of people in a given city sign up.

Groupon pioneered the use of digital coupons in a way that created an explosive new market for local business. Paper coupon use had been declining for years. But when Groupon made it possible for online individuals to obtain deep discounts on products in local stores using emailed coupons, huge numbers of people started buying. Between June 2009 and June 2010, revenues grew to $100 million. Then, between June 2010 and June 2011, revenues exploded tenfold, reaching $1 billion. In August 2010, *Forbes* magazine labeled Groupon the world's fastest growing corporation. And that did not hurt the company's valuation when it went public in November 2011.

On November 5, 2011, Groupon took its company public with a buy-in price of $20 per share. Groupon shares rose from that IPO price of $20 by 40 percent in early trading on NASDAQ, and at the 4 p.m. market close, it was $26.11, up 31 percent. The closing price valued Groupon at $16.6 billion, making it more valuable than companies such as Adobe Systems and nearly the size of Yahoo!

But after trading up for a couple of months, at the beginning of March 2012, Groupon's stock price turned downward, and the company has since lost 75 percent of its market capitalization. Groupon is now valued at about $3.6 billion—approaching half of what Google offered to pay for the company in 2011 before Groupon leadership decided to go public.

The problem seems to be growing competition from sites such as LivingSocial and AmazonLocal. Also, the leadership of the company has come under scrutiny for some of their practices. But the main reason Groupon seems to be struggling is concern over its reported numbers.

## Problems with Financial Results

Less than five months after its IPO on March 30, 2012, Groupon announced that it had revised its financial results, an unexpected restatement that deepened losses and raised questions about its accounting practices. As part of the revision, Groupon disclosed a "material weakness" in its internal controls saying that it had failed to set aside enough money to cover customer refunds. The accounting issue increased the company's losses in the fourth quarter to $64.9 million from $42.3 million. These amounts were material based on revenue of $500 million in the prior year. The news that day sent shares of Groupon tumbling 6 percent, to $17.29. Shares of Groupon had fallen by 30 percent since it went public, and the downward trend continues today.

In its announcement of the restatement, Groupon explained that it had encountered problems related to certain assumptions and forecasts that the company used to calculate its results. In particular, the company said that it underestimated customer refunds for higher-priced offers such as laser eye surgery.

Groupon collects more revenue on such deals, but it also carries a higher rate of refunds. The company honors customer refunds for the life of its coupons, so these payments can affect its financials at various times. Groupon deducts refunds within 60 days from revenue; after that, the company has to take an additional accounting charge related to the payments.

Groupon's restatement is partially a consequence of the "Groupon Promise" feature of its business model. The company pledges to refund deals if customers aren't satisfied. Because it had been selling those deals at higher prices—which leads to a higher rate of returns—it needed to set aside larger amounts to account for refunds, something it had not been doing. It is an example of Groupon failing to account accurately for a part of its business that reduces its financial performance.

The financial problems escalated after Groupon released its third-quarter 2012 earnings report, marking its first full-year cycle of earnings reports since its IPO in November 2011. While the net operating results showed improvement year-to-year, the company still showed a net loss for the quarter. Moreover, while its revenue had been increasing in fiscal 2012, its operating profit had declined over 60 percent. This meant that its operating expenses were growing faster than its revenues, a sign that trouble may be lurking in the background. The company's stock price on NASDAQ went from $26.11 per share on November 5, 2011, the end of the IPO day, to $4.14 a share on November 30, 2012, a decline of more than 80 percent in one year. The company did not meet financial analysts' expectations for the third quarter of 2012.

Groupon's fourth quarter 2012 results show a revenue increase to $638.8 million but with an operating loss of $12.9 million and a loss per share of 12 cents, falling short of analyst expectations on the EPS front—they had predicted $638.41 million in revenue and EPS of $0.03. The Groupon share price has recovered somewhat to $7.65 per share on June 14, 2013.

Groupon blamed the disappointing results on its European operations. Some analysts took solace in the fact that Groupon reported that it has 39.5 million active customers, an increase of 37 percent from the previous year. But what good does it do to have a larger customer base if it also leads to larger-than-expected operating costs?

# Problems with Internal Controls

As Groupon prepared its financial statements for 2011, its independent auditor, Ernst & Young (EY), determined that the company did not accurately account for the possibility of higher refunds. By the firm's assessment, that constituted a "material weakness." Groupon said in its annual report, "We did not maintain effective controls to provide reasonable assurance that accounts were complete and accurate." This means other transactions may be at risk because poor controls in one area tend to cause problems elsewhere. More important, the internal control problems raise questions about the management of the company and its corporate governance. But Groupon blamed EY for the admission of the internal control failure to spot the material weakness.

In a related issue, on April 3, 2012, a shareholder lawsuit was brought against Groupon accusing the company of misleading investors about its financial prospects in its IPO and concealing weak internal controls. According to the complaint, the company overstated revenue, issued materially false and misleading financial results, and concealed the fact that its business was not growing as fast and was not nearly as resistant to competition as it had suggested. These claims bring up a gap in the sections of SOX that deal with companies' internal controls. There is no requirement to disclose a control weakness in a company's IPO prospectus.

The red flags had been waving even before the company went public in 2011. In preparing its IPO, the company used a financial metric that it called "Adjusted Consolidated Segment Operating Income." The problem was that that figure excluded marketing costs, which make up the bulk of the company's expenses. The net result was to make Groupon's financial results appear better than they actually were. After the SEC raised questions about the metric—which *The Wall Street Journal* called "financial voodoo"—Groupon downplayed the formulation in its IPO documents.

In an updated filing with the SEC, Groupon said that it is working to "remediate the material weakness," in its internal financial reporting controls, and will hire "additional finance personnel." But it warned: "If our remedial measures are insufficient to address the material weakness, or if additional material weaknesses or significant deficiencies in our internal control over financial reporting are discovered or occur in the future, our consolidated financial statements may contain material misstatements and we could be required to restate our financial results."

## Questions

1. What is the responsibility of management and the auditor with respect to the internal controls of a client?

2. Groupon disclosed a "material weakness" in its internal controls saying that it had failed to set aside enough money to cover customer refunds. Do you believe the company engaged in fraud with respect to customer refunds? Why or why not?

3. Groupon blamed EY for the admission of the internal control failure to spot the material weakness. Do you agree that EY should have spotted the internal control weakness earlier and taken appropriate action? Include in your response the role that risk assessment should have played in EY's actions.

## Optional Question

4. According to Groupon, the merchants are responsible for fulfilling the obligation to deliver the goods and services. Groupon disclosed that fact and the following statement in its restated financial statements:"We record the gross amount received from Groupon, excluding taxes where applicable, as the Company is the primary obligor in the transaction, and records an allowance for estimated customer refunds on total revenue primarily based on historical experience . . . the Company also records costs related to the associated obligation to redeem the award credits granted as issuance as an offset to revenue."

Review SEC Staff Accounting Bulletin 101 (Question 10) and Emerging Issues Task Force (EITF) pronouncement 99-19 using the links provided below and evaluate whether Groupon's accounting for the allowance referred to in this scenario met GAAP requirements.

**Staff Accounting Bulletin 101—*Revenue Recognition in Financial Statements***
http://www.sec.gov/interps/account/sab101.htm

***EITF No. 99-19 Reporting Revenue Gross as a Principal versus Net as an Agent***
http://www.fasb.org/cs/BlobServer?blobkey=id&blobwhere
=1175820914023&blobheader=application%2Fpdf&blobcol
=urldata&blobtable=MungoBlobs

# 6

# Legal, Regulatory, and Professional Obligations of Auditors

From time to time, external auditors are sued by shareholders in a class action lawsuit for violations of Section 10 and Rule 10b-5 of the Securities Exchange Act of 1934. The auditors' liability under these provisions makes it unlawful for a CPA to be engaged in a fraudulent act, including making an untrue statement of material fact or omitting a material fact. The guilt or innocence of an auditor depends on the plaintiff's ability to prove that a material misrepresentation has occurred in the financial statements that was relied on by the plaintiff to her detriment and that the auditor intended to deceive, manipulate, or defraud.

In addition to statutory law violations, such as Rule 10b-5 of the Securities and Exchange Act of 1934, auditor liability is subject to common law that evolves from legal opinions decided by judges in cases that set precedents and guide judges in deciding future cases. In *Ernst & Ernst v. Hochfelder*, the Supreme Court held that actions under Section 10(b) of the Exchange Act and Rule 10b-5 require an allegation of scienter, or knowledge of the falsehood by the auditor.

Bear Stearns was a large investment bank, securities trader, and brokerage firm operating globally with headquarters in New York. The firm had been in operation for 85 years when its outsized position in subprime mortgages raised questions from investors, clients, and counterparties about the bank's balance sheet and the quality of its assets. A failed hedge fund sponsored by a subsidiary of the bank in 2007 had brought unwanted questions about subprime

loans in general in an increasingly wary market. Legal action against the bank and its auditor ushered in a period of doubt about the role of auditing firms in the financial crisis of 2007–2008.

On November 9, 2012, Judge Robert W. Sweet of the U.S. District Court of New York granted final approval to two settlements in class actions against (1) Bear Stearns and its management and (2) Deloitte & Touche LLP, the external auditors for Bear Stearns. The complaint alleged that defendants issued materially false and misleading statements regarding the business and financial results of Bear Stearns. It also was alleged that the defendants failed to inform the market of the problems with the company's hedge funds due to the deteriorating subprime mortgage market and liquidity issues related thereto.

The shareholder case against Deloitte resulted from its role as auditor of Bear Stearns. In *Re: Bear Stearns Companies, Inc. Securities Litigation*,[1] the plaintiffs' attorneys successfully pled recklessness equivalent to scienter by identifying as a red flag the fact that Deloitte knew or should have known about the risk factors inherent in the industry, such as declining housing prices, relaxation of credit standards, excessive concentration on lending, and increasing default rates. The court ruled that Deloitte should have identified losses in the value of Bear Stearns mortgage-backed assets. Deloitte failed to properly assess the risk of fraud, a concept we discussed in Chapter 5. Deloitte violated ethical standards

*(Continued)*

of the profession by failing to exercise the degree of care required in conducting an audit of client financial statements and professional skepticism was nowhere in sight.

The precipitous decline in the share price of Bear Stearns once news of its financial disclosure failings became public was a harbinger of things to come for the financial services industry. The stock price of Bear Stearns had reached a peak of $172.61 prior to the financial meltdown. At the end of the meltdown, the price had declined to $30 per share. Ultimately, JP Morgan Chase Bank bought Bear Stearns for $2 per share.

The investors in the lawsuit, led by the State of Michigan Retirement Systems, settled with Bear Stearns execu-

tives for $275 million and Deloitte for a cash payment of $19.9 million.

Students should become informed about the legal liability of auditors because their failure to follow proper auditing standards and ethics rules can lead to claims of unprofessional work. As you read this chapter, consider the following: (1) What are the common law and statutory obligations of auditors under the Securities Acts? (2) Why is it important for auditors to show that they have adhered to the standards of the profession, both ethical and professional, to defend against a lawsuit alleging the failure to detect material misstatements in the financial statements and fraud? (3) How do auditor legal liabilities relate to the ethical standards discussed in this text?

---

U.S. District Judge Shira Scheindlin issued a 72-page opinion on April 8, 2013, dismissing allegations that the Chinese unit of Deloitte & Touche failed investors in its audits of the Chinese financial software firm Longtop Financial Technologies, which admitted in 2011 to cooking its books and was subsequently sued by the SEC. Scheindlin concluded that Deloitte may have been lazy, at worst, but under U.S. laws and accounting standards, the audit firm should be considered a victim of Longtop's fraud, not an abetter of it. Scheindlin went on to say that in the standard for scienter shareholders would have had to show Deloitte's audits were so deficient that they fell outside any acceptable bounds. It's easy in retrospect, she said, to say that "an audit firm should have followed up on one concern or another, but U.S. laws require evidence that fraud is the most plausible explanation for an auditor's failures. As long as the auditor can offer an equally reasonable explanation for its conduct, it's off the hook."[2]

---

The legal opinion by Judge Scheindlin illustrates the challenges of determining legal liability and when auditors are willing participants in fraud or failed to identify it through proper audit procedures.

Dr. Herbert W. Snyder, a certified fraud examiner and associate professor at North Dakota State University, makes an important observation in an article titled "Client Confidentiality and Fraud: Should Auditors Be Able to Exercise More Ethical Judgment?" in the January/February 2011 issue of the *Fraud Magazine*.[3] Snyder points out that the audit profession has come under significant criticism during the past decade about the ethical conduct of auditors and their roles in a variety of financial scandals, such as Enron, Tyco, and WorldCom. This heightened attention led to the creation of the Sarbanes-Oxley Act of 2002 (SOX) and professional standards, such as the fraud triangle which provides better guidance for the consideration of fraud during an audit. Notably, at the same time that legislators (and the accounting profession) are attempting to guide auditors' behavior toward detecting financial statement fraud, the profession's own standards of client confidentiality might be working to limit the ethical choices of accountants.

The concept of accountant-client privilege has never been supported by the federal courts, including a number of U.S. Supreme Court decisions, which failed to find such a right. In *Couch v. United States,* the Supreme Court ruled that "no confidential accountant-client privilege exists under federal law, and no state-created privilege has been recognized in federal cases."[4]

This does not mean that the confidentiality standard in the American Institute of Certified Public Accountants (AICPA) Code of Professional Conduct (Rule 301) should be abolished. However, such pledges of confidentiality might constrain the full disclosure of company information, which can include sensitive and/or proprietary information. Snyder believes that disclosure in limited circumstances, such as when a fraud is discovered, might help to prevent future harm without compromising the quality of financial audits.[5]

# Client Confidentiality, Fraud, and Whistleblowing

## Confidentiality Obligation and Fraud

Accountants have traditionally asserted the right of confidentiality under Rule 301 of the AICPA Code to restrict the disclosure of fraud outside the entity without the specific consent of the client. As we learned in Chapter 5, when auditors detect fraud or illegal acts and deem them material, they must report the misconduct to the audit committee or full board of directors. Under AU 240, the disclosure of fraud to parties other than the client and its audit committee . . . would be precluded by the auditor's ethical and legal obligations of confidentiality.[6]

Snyder challenges the assertion of a privileged accountant-client relationship with respect to the audit function when fraud has been uncovered. He cites the ruling in *U.S. v. Arthur Young*[7] that was discussed in Chapter 4. The Court ruled that an accountant's "public watchdog" function demands that the accountant maintain total independence from the client at all times and requires complete fidelity to the public trust. It is difficult to see how an auditor can justify withholding important information about material misstatements of the financial statements or fraud from the public given this watchdog function.[8] Moreover, the AICPA Code and Public Company Accounting Oversight Board (PCAOB) ethics standards require auditors to act with integrity and consider their duty to the public to be their primary responsibility.

The "confidentiality gap" seems to have been filled with the passage of the Dodd-Frank Financial Reform Act of 2010. Dodd-Frank is a federal law so it preempts state laws, such as statutes that govern licensed certified public accountant (CPA) behavior in jurisdictions. So, state laws that might have kept CPAs from reporting confidential information have been overtaken by Dodd-Frank, which has given CPAs increased protections to better fulfill their responsibilities to society and, when justified, blow the whistle on one's employer for financial fraud. Relatedly, AICPA Rule 301 recognizes the CPA's legal obligations with respect to the confidentiality rule in that Rule 301 should not be construed to prohibit a member's compliance with applicable laws and government regulations.[9]

## Dodd-Frank and Whistleblowing

One of Dodd-Frank's key provisions requires the Securities and Exchange Commission (SEC) to establish a whistleblower program offering significant protections and report possible violations of the federal securities laws, including misrepresenting or omitting important information in a company's financial statements. Dodd-Frank and the SEC's implementing rules broadly define a whistleblower and expressly permit accountants to participate in the program so that a whistleblower would be acting in "compliance with applicable laws and regulations." Therefore, the accountant would not be violating confidentiality rules.

The Dodd-Frank Act requires the SEC to pay whistleblowers 10 percent to 30 percent of the monetary sanctions collected as a result of a successful SEC enforcement action in excess of $1 million. While accountants can participate in the program, their ability to receive rewards for reporting information to the SEC is limited as we discussed in Chapter 3. To review, internal accountants and auditors are eligible only under the following conditions: (1) the whistleblower has a reasonable basis to believe that the disclosure is necessary to prevent the relevant entity from engaging in conduct that is likely to cause substantial injury to the entity or investors; (2) the whistleblower has a reasonable basis to believe the relevant entity's conduct will impede an investigation of the misconduct; or (3) the whistleblower reported the information to the relevant entity's audit committee, chief legal or compliance officer, the whistleblower's supervisor, or the whistleblower received the information under circumstances indicating that these individuals were already aware of it, and more than 120 days have elapsed.

The rules prohibit an award to an accountant who gains information during "an audit of financial statements required under the securities laws and for whom such submission would be contrary to the requirements of Section 10A of the Securities Exchange Act"; that is, an accountant who gains information about wrongdoing during the audit of a public company. Section 10A of the Securities Exchange Act provides that if an auditor of a public company becomes aware of information indicating that an illegal act has or may have occurred, the auditor must investigate the financial materiality of the illegal act and inform management and the company's audit committee. If the company fails to take appropriate remedial action, the auditor must report its conclusions to the company's board of directors, which is then obligated to inform the SEC. If the board of directors fails to inform the SEC within the required time period, the auditor must report its conclusions directly to the SEC. Accordingly, this rule prevents an auditor who is already obligated to report information to the SEC from personally profiting from reporting that same information as a whistleblower.

For accountants and accounting firms, perhaps the most important aspect of the whistleblower rule is the fact that an employee of (or any person associated with) an independent auditor of a public company can make a whistleblower submission alleging that the auditor/audit firm failed to assess, investigate, or report wrongdoing in accordance with Section 10A, or that the auditor failed to follow other professional standards. Moreover, if the whistleblower makes such a 10A submission, the whistleblower will be able to obtain an award not only from a successful enforcement action against the auditing firm, but also from any successful enforcement action against the firm's engagement client.

In allowing such claims, the goal of the SEC is to "help insure that wrongdoing by the [accounting] firm (or its employees) is reported in a timely fashion." According to the SEC, this goal is paramount "because of the important gatekeeper role that auditors play in the securities markets."[10]

Taylor and Thomas* point out that contrary to popular belief, accountants are not prohibited from reporting fraud and other violations externally. Instead, under Dodd-Frank, they are called upon to make ethical choices about what to do when they identify possible violations of the federal securities laws. In most cases, the proper approach is first to report the securities violations to their employers or clients in accordance with relevant rules and regulations, and then work together to uncover the extent of wrongdoing and ensure that those responsible are held accountable.[11] Potential whistleblowers should attempt to confirm the existence of a violation of the securities laws before reporting to the SEC.

---

*The authors provide useful exhibits that describe the steps to be taken by accountants and auditors in reporting wrongdoing and whistleblowing obligations. See endnote 12 for the reference.

The confidentiality obligation in the AICPA Code should not be used to mask a CPA's duties to the public and to investors. An ethical perspective requires that CPAs should question whether complete confidentiality is essential to the accountant-client relationship. Given the public reporting responsibilities of auditors and the audit report, the accountant's primary duty is to protect the public from improper reporting rather than to protect the client from disclosure of wrongdoing.

# Ethical and Legal Responsibilities of Officers and Directors

## Duty of Care—Managers and Directors

Directors and officers are deemed fiduciaries of the corporation because their relationship with the corporation and its shareholders is one of trust and confidence. As fiduciaries, directors and officers owe ethical—and legal—duties to the corporation and to the shareholders. These fiduciary duties include the duty of care and the duty of loyalty. We briefly introduced these concepts in Chapter 3 in the discussion of corporate governance and elaborate on them in this chapter because of the legal implications of director and officer fiduciary responsibilities.

Directors and officers must exercise due care in performing their duties. The standard of *due care* provides that a director or officer act in good faith, exercise the care that an ordinarily prudent person would exercise in similar circumstances, and act in the way that she considers to be in the best interests of the corporation. Directors and officers who have not exercised the required duty of care can be held liable for the harms suffered by the corporation as a result of their negligence.

The duty of due care specifies the manner in which directors must discharge their legal responsibilities, not the substance of director decisions. Directors, due to their statutory responsibilities to direct the business and affairs of a corporation, also have a duty to monitor and oversee the business affairs of a corporation properly. Failure to do so may constitute a breach of the duty of care.

## Duty of Loyalty

The duty of loyalty requires directors to act in the best interests of the corporation. *Loyalty* can be defined as faithfulness to one's obligations and duties. In the corporate context, the duty of loyalty requires directors and officers to subordinate their personal interests to the welfare of the organization. For example, directors must not use corporate funds or confidential corporate information for personal advantage. They must also refrain from self-dealing, such as when a director opposes a stock tender offer that is in the corporation's best interest simply because its acceptance may cost the director her position.

## Director Duty of Good Faith

The obligation of good faith has long been important to fiduciary analysis in corporate law, but its meaning has been somewhat nebulous. Recently, good faith has been receiving a great deal of attention. A statement by former Delaware Chancery Court** Chief Justice Veasey helps to understand its scope and purpose. Veasey said that good faith requires an honesty of purpose that leads to caring for the well-being of the constituents of the fiduciary.[12]

Vice Chancellor Leo Strine linked good faith to fiduciary analysis in the Enron fraud by suggesting that the Enron case might influence courts to look more carefully at whether

---

**The Chancery Court, located in Delaware, is the preeminent forum for the resolution of commercial business litigation matters, including the duties of officers and directors. Many matters that involve the management of a corporation's inner workings are within the jurisdiction of Chancery Court. The Chancery Court is a court of equity, as opposed to a court of law. Most states do not separate the types of legal remedies available to litigants into equity and law the way that Delaware does. An equity court is the type that can issue temporary injunctions and declaratory judgments.

directors have made a good faith effort to accomplish their duties.[13] He connected good faith with directors' "state of mind." Strine identified certain kinds of director conduct that may call good faith into question. These include "a failure to monitor if [the directors'] laxity in oversight was so persistent and substantial that it evidence bad faith." It can also arise in situations where "committee members knew that their inadequate knowledge disabled them from discharging their responsibilities with fidelity."[14]

## Business Judgment Rule

A corporate director or officer may be able to avoid liability to the corporation or to its shareholders for poor business judgments under the *business judgment rule.* Directors and officers are expected to exercise due care and to use their best judgment in guiding corporate management, but they are not insurers of business success. Honest mistakes of judgment and poor business decisions on their part do not make them liable to the corporation for resulting damages.

To obtain the business judgment rule's protection, directors must be independent and disinterested as to the matter acted upon. Directors must act with due care and good faith. The due care inquiry is process-oriented, and due care is measured by a standard of gross negligence, not simple negligence. The burden of proof is on the party challenging the board's decision, to establish facts rebutting the presumption in favor of upholding the decision. Unless a plaintiff succeeds in rebutting the rule, the court will not substitute its views for those of the board's if the latter's decision can be "attributed to any rational business purpose." The last point reflects the well-known substantive deference shown by courts to board decisions. As a result of this "hands-off" approach, plaintiffs rarely win duty of care cases.[15]

The business judgment rule generally immunizes directors and officers from liability for the consequences of a decision that is within managerial authority, so long as the decision complies with management's fiduciary duties and so long as acting on the decision is within the powers of the corporation. Therefore, if there is a reasonable basis for a business decision, it is unlikely that a court will interfere with that decision, even if the corporation suffers as a result.

## Caremark Opinion

The Caremark International investigation was a precedent setting case on directors' obligations. In 1991, Caremark was investigated by state and federal authorities for alleged violations of Medicare's anti-referral law. The investigations led to indictments, substantial fines, and a shareholder's derivative suit alleging that the company directors had breached their fiduciary duty of care.

When the proposed settlement of the derivative action reached the Delaware Court of Chancery, it ruled in *Caremark International Derivative Legislation* that directors have an affirmative fiduciary obligation to ensure that adequate information and reporting systems exist in a corporation to provide timely and accurate information to the board and management about compliance with legal requirements.[16] The *Caremark* view of this duty of care goes beyond the more passive standard, which allows a board to rely on the integrity of employees to comply with legal and regulatory requirements.

## Shareholder Derivative Suit—Citigroup Subprime Lending

On February 25, 2009, Chancellor William B. Chandler III dismissed all but one of the claims in a shareholder suit in the Delaware Chancery Court against the board of Citigroup. The shareholders principally alleged that the board had breached its fiduciary duties by allowing the company to invest in the subprime lending market, and subsequently sustained significant losses.

The decision is important for two reasons. First, it shows that attempts to hold boards liable for some extremely bad decisions (bad in hindsight, at least) made prior to the financial crisis are going to be met with heavy skepticism by the Delaware courts. Here is one of the quotes from the opinion on this point: "Oversight duties under Delaware law are not designed to subject directors, even expert directors, to personal liability for failure to predict the future and to properly evaluate business risk."

Second, Chancellor Chandler dismissed the plaintiffs' breach of fiduciary duty claim. The plaintiffs had phrased this claim as a failure of the board "to properly monitor and manage the risks [Citigroup] faced from problems in the subprime lending market and for failing to properly disclose Citigroup's exposure to subprime assets."

The court ruled that the Citigroup case is a *Caremark* claim. Chandler's opinion notes the high standard under *Caremark:*

> To establish oversight liability, a plaintiff must show that the directors knew they were not discharging their fiduciary obligations or that the directors demonstrated a conscious disregard for their responsibilities such as by failing to act in the face of a known duty to act. The test is rooted in concepts of bad faith; indeed, a showing of bad faith is a necessary condition to director oversight liability.[17]

Chancellor Chandler went on to distinguish regular *Caremark* duties to prevent fraud and wrongdoing from business decisions, such as those in the Citigroup case, stating:

> Such oversight programs allow directors to intervene and prevent frauds or other wrongdoing that could expose the company to risk of loss as a result of such conduct. While it may be tempting to say that directors have the same duties to monitor and oversee business risk, imposing Caremark-type duties on directors to monitor business risk is fundamentally different. Citigroup was in the business of taking on and managing investment and other business risks. To impose oversight liability on directors for failure to monitor "excessive" risk would involve courts in conducting hindsight evaluations of decisions at the heart of the business judgment of directors.

## Clawback of Incentive Compensation from Executive Officers

Under the provisions of Dodd-Frank, public companies have an increased obligation in most instances to recover, or "claw back," some portion of incentive-based compensation from senior executives in the event of a financial restatement. Public companies—as a condition to list on a national securities exchange—will be required to develop and implement policies:

- For disclosure of the company's policy on incentive-based compensation based on financial information required to be reported under applicable securities laws
- For recovery from current or former executive officers of incentive-based compensation in the event that the company is required to prepare an accounting restatement due to material noncompliance with any financial reporting requirements under the securities laws

Dodd-Frank specifies that the clawback requirement will apply to incentive-based compensation received during the three-year period preceding the date on which the company is required to prepare the restatement and which is in excess of the amount that would have been paid to the executive using the restated financial components. Dodd-Frank also requires the stock exchanges to develop rules that a company must have clawback policies to qualify for listing on that exchange.[18]

The clawback requirement under Dodd-Frank is both broader and narrower than the one under SOX. The Dodd-Frank requirement extends to current or former executive officers, unlike the clawback requirement under SOX, which applies only to the chief executive officer (CEO) and chief financial officer (CFO) of an issuer. The three-year clawback period is also broader than the one-year period under SOX. Finally, the Dodd-Frank clawback applies to any restatement as a result of material noncompliance with the financial reporting requirements, whereas SOX's requirement applies only to restatements caused by "misconduct." However, unlike SOX Section 304, which requires the CEO and CFO to repay both incentive compensation and stock sale profits, Dodd-Frank limits the clawback to incentive-based compensation.

On November 14, 2012, U.S. District Judge Sam Sparks issued a precedent-setting ruling in the case of *SEC v Michael A. Baker and Michael T. Gluk,* which stated that under Section 304 of SOX, the SEC can force the CEOs and CFOs of companies that violated securities laws to surrender their bonuses and stock options. In this case, the SEC had charged that two former top officials of a company called Arthrocare failed in their duties to shareholders and should return to the company the unspecified bonuses, stock options, and stock-sale profits they received in 2006 and 2007—even though Baker and Gluk were not involved in the accounting misconduct that forced Arthrocare to restate its financials in those years. The judge ruled: "Apologists for the extraordinarily high compensation given to corporate officers have long justified such pay by asserting CEOs take 'great risks,' and so deserve great rewards. For years, this has been a vacuous saw, because corporate law, and private measures such as wide-spread indemnification of officers by their employers, and the provision of Directors & Officers insurance, have ensured any 'risks' taken by these fearless captains of industry almost never impact their personal finances. In enacting Section 304 of Sarbanes-Oxley, Congress determined to put a modest measure of real risk back into the equation."[19]

Since its passage in 2002, federal prosecutors have been reluctant to bring criminal cases under SOX against CEOs and CFOs who certify financial reports that turn out to be materially false. Section 304 imposes a financial penalty on corporate officials who certify inaccurate SEC filings. By demanding that they return bonuses and other incentive compensation to the company, the provision "creates an incentive for (officials) to be diligent in carrying out those (certification) duties," Judge Sparks wrote, noting that Congress deliberately drafted the law to apply to officials who weren't involved directly in cooking the books. "The absence of any requirement of personal misconduct is in furtherance of that purpose: It ensures corporate officers cannot simply keep their own hands clean, but must instead be vigilant in ensuring there are adequate controls to prevent misdeeds by underlings."

The implications of the ruling are widespread. Defense lawyers have typically asserted that the SOX provision requires proof of scienter (i.e., knowledge of wrongdoing). According to the attorney for the defendants, "An innocent executive should not be forced to forfeit his compensation because of the actions of others. We believe that Section 304 requires a showing of misconduct by any executive whose compensation is to be forfeited.

Judge Sparks's decision should prompt corporate CEOs and CFOs to sit up and take notice that their legal liability may not be fully protected by asserting a lack of knowledge of fraud when their oversight obligations dictate a more careful review of financial reporting, including internal controls.

## Audit Committee and Business Judgment Rule

The business judgment rule applies to audit committee acts when they relate to business judgments. Examples would include committee decisions to hire an auditor, approving audit services, preparing audit committee reports, and deciding how to respond to deficiencies in the internal controls or elsewhere in the audit oversight area, including those revealed by CEO and CFO certifications.[20] Where the audit committee has responsibilities but does not exercise business judgment, the business judgment rule is inapplicable. Examples may include supervision of the auditor and reviewing information prepared by management or by the independent auditor. Fiduciary duties continue to govern conduct by the audit committee in these areas. There is relatively little case law on the liability of audit committee members, and much of that law deals with liability under the federal securities laws.[21]

The Delaware Chancery Court has considered whether a plaintiff can use Section 220 of the Delaware corporate statute (the "books and records" statute)[22] to obtain the results of an audit committee's investigation into possible wrongdoing, where the committee used legal counsel and asserted attorney-client privilege and work product protection. In *Chinn v. Endocare, Inc.,* the Chancery Court held that a forensic accounting report prepared for the audit committee at the direction of the committee's legal counsel was not protected because it was shared with the outside accounting firm that was under investigation.[23] In *Saito v. McKesson HBOC, Inc.,* disclosure under section 220 was denied as to materials given to the SEC under a confidentiality agreement.[24]

# Legal Liability of Auditors: An Overview

Legal liability is an important consideration for auditors and accounting firms as they conduct business. Louwers et al. point out that recent settlements that can result from unprofessional conduct involving the largest accounting firms reveal the size of the settlements, including:[25]

- **Deloitte & Touche:** Fortress ($250 million in 2005); Adelphia Communications ($167.5 million in 2007); Delphi ($38 million in 2008); General Motors ($26 million in 2008); and the Italian Company Parmalat, SpA ($159 million in 2007).
- **Ernst & Young:** Cendant ($335 million in 1999); Bank of New England ($84 million in 2005); HealthSouth ($143 million in 2009); and the Chinese company Sino-Forest ($117 million in 2012).
- **KPMG:** Xerox ($80 million in 2008); Countrywide ($24 million in 2010); and Wells Fargo ($627 in 2011).
- **PricewaterhouseCoopers (PwC):** Tyco ($225 million in 2007); American International group (AIG) ($97.5 million in 2008); and the Australian company the Centro Group ($200 million in 2011).

Zoe-Vonna Palmrose, a professor at the University of Southern California, identifies the four general stages in an audit-related dispute: (1) the occurrence of events that result in losses for users of the financial statements, (2) the investigation by plaintiff attorneys before filing, to link the user losses with allegations of material omissions or misstatements of financial statements, (3) the legal process, which commences with the filing of the lawsuit, and (4) the final resolution of the dispute.[26] The first stage comes about as a result of some loss-generating event, including client bankruptcy, fraudulent financial reporting, and the misappropriation of assets. The latter two events will be discussed later in the chapter.

Auditors can be sued by clients, investors, creditors, and the government for failure to perform services adequately and in accordance with the profession's ethics standards. Auditors can be held liable under two classes of law: (1) common law and (2) statutory law. Common-law liability evolves from legal opinions issued by judges in deciding a case. These opinions become legal principles that set a precedent and guide judges in deciding similar cases in the future. Statutory law reflects legislation passed at the state or federal level that establishes certain courses of conduct that must be adhered to by covered parties.[27]

Exhibit 6.1 summarizes the types of liability and auditors' actions that result in liability.

## Common-Law Liability

Common-law liability requires the auditor to perform professional services with due care. Recall that due care is a basic principle and rule of conduct in the AICPA Code. Evidence of having exercised due care exists if the auditor can demonstrate having performed services with the same degree of skill and judgment possessed by others in the profession. Typically, an auditor would cite adherence to generally accepted auditing standards as evidence of having exercised due care in conducting the audit.

Breach of contract is a claim that accounting and auditing services were not performed in a way consistent with the terms of a contract. Although auditors may have contractual relationships with third parties, cases involving breach of contract are brought most frequently against auditors by their clients.[28]

**EXHIBIT 6.1**
**Summary of Types of Liability and Auditors' Actions Resulting in Liability**

Source: William F. Messier Jr., Steven M. Glover, and Douglas F. Prawitt, *Auditing and Assurance Services: A Systematic Approach* (New York: McGraw-Hill Irwin, 2010), p. 686.

| Types of Liability | Auditors' Actions Resulting in Liability |
| --- | --- |
| Common law—clients | Breach of contract (privity relationship)<br>Negligence<br>Gross negligence/constructive fraud<br>Fraud |
| Common law—third parties | Negligence<br>Gross negligence/constructive fraud<br>Fraud |
| Federal statutory law—civil liability | Negligence<br>Gross negligence/constructive fraud<br>Fraud |
| Federal statutory law—criminal liability | Willful violation of federal statutes |

Tort actions (for wrongdoings) cover other civil complaints (e.g., fraud, deceit, and injury) arising from auditors' failure to exercise the appropriate level of professional care sometimes referred to as substantiated performance. Clients or users of financial statements can bring tort actions against auditors.[29]

Lawsuits for damages under common law usually result when someone suffers a financial loss after relying on financial statements later found to be materially misstated. Plaintiffs in legal actions involving auditors, such as clients or third-party users of financial statements, generally assert all possible causes of action, including breach of contract, tort, deceit, fraud, and anything else that may be relevant to the claim. These cases are often referred to as "audit failures" in the financial press.

## Liability to Clients—Privity Relationship

An accountant has a contractual obligation to the client that creates a *privity relationship*. A client can bring a lawsuit against an accountant for failing to live up to the terms of the contract, asserting breach of contract, and other tort actions. When privity exists, plaintiffs must demonstrate all of the following:[30]

1. They suffered an economic loss.
2. Auditors did not perform in accordance with the terms of the contract, thereby breaching that contract.
3. Auditors failed to exercise the appropriate level of professional care related to tort actions.
4. The breach of contract or failure to exercise the appropriate level of care caused the loss.

In addition to breach of contract, auditors may be liable to clients for tort liability that range from simple ordinary negligence to the more serious case of fraud. In the case of ordinary negligence, the auditor failed to exercise due care or the standard of care that other accountants would have done in similar situations. Notice the link to ethical responsibilities of accountants and auditors through the due care ethics rule and the *universality perspective*. The legal interpretation of the due care rule is linked to what accountants would have done in similar situations (for similar reasons) through the *categorical imperative* (Kantian) ethical reasoning method. Finally, legal liability between the ordinary negligence responsibility and fraud includes gross negligence or constructive fraud that represents an extreme or reckless departure from professional standards of care.

### Ultramares v. Touche

In the 1933 landmark case, *Ultramares v. Touche,* the New York State Court of Appeals held that a cause of action based on negligence could not be maintained by a third party who was not in contractual privity. The court did leave open the possibility that a third party could successfully sue for gross negligence that constitutes fraud (constructive fraud) and fraud.[31]

Ultramares had lent $100,000 to Fred Stern & Company. Before making the loan, the company had asked Stern to provide an audited balance sheet, and Stern had its auditor, Touche Ross & Co. (now Deloitte & Touche), do so. The firm issued an unqualified (i.e., unmodified) audit report. Subsequently, the company went bankrupt, and it was alleged that false accounting entries had been made to conceal the company's problems. Ultramares alleged that Touche had been both negligent and fraudulent in its audit of Stern. Because the privity relationship did not exist for Ultramares and Stern, the fraud charges against Touche were dismissed. However, the jury ruled that Touche had been negligent and awarded Ultramares about $186,000 in damages.

The importance of the *Ultramares* decision is that third parties (i.e., Ultramares) without privity could sue if negligence was so great as to constitute gross negligence. The opinion of the New York Court of Appeals was written by Judge Benjamin Cardozo:

> If a liability for negligence exists, a thoughtless slip or blunder, the failure to detect a theft or forgery beneath the cover of deceptive entries, may expose accountants to a liability in an indeterminate amount for an indeterminate time to an indeterminate class [third parties]. The hazards of a business on these terms are so extreme as to [raise] doubt whether a flaw may not exist in the implication of a duty that exposes to these circumstances.

The *Ultramares* decision was the first of three different judicial approaches to deciding the extent of an accountant's liability to third parties. The other two are the *Restatement (Second) of the Law of Torts* approach and the foreseeable third-party approach. Both are described in the following text.

## Liability to Third Parties

### Near-Privity Relationship

While the *Ultramares* decision established a strict privity standard, a number of subsequent court decisions in other states had moved away from this standard over time. Following years of broadening the auditor's liability to third parties to include those that were "foreseen" and "reasonably foreseeable" (which we will discuss shortly), in a 1985 decision, the court seemed to move the pendulum back in favor of limiting the liability of accountants to third parties based on the privity standard. The New York Court of Appeals expanded the privity standard in the case of *Credit Alliance v. Arthur Andersen & Co.*[32] to include a *near-privity relationship* between third parties and the accountant. In the case, Credit Alliance was the principal lender to the client and demonstrated that Andersen had known Credit Alliance was relying on the client's financial statements prior to extending credit. The court also ruled that there had been direct communication between the lender and the auditor regarding the client.

The *Credit Alliance* case establishes the following tests that must be satisfied for holding auditors liable for negligence to third parties: (1) knowledge by the accountant that the financial statements are to be used for a particular purpose; (2) the intention of the third party to rely on those statements; and (3) some action by the accountant linking him or her to the third party that provides evidence of the accountant's understanding of intended reliance. The 1992 New York Court of Appeals decision in *Security Pacific Business Credit, Inc. v. Peat Marwick Main & Co.*[33] sharpens the last criterion in its determination that the third party must be known to the auditor, who directly conveys the audited report to the third party or acts to induce reliance on the report.

## Actually Foreseen Third Parties

The "middle ground" approach followed by the vast majority of states (and federal courts located within those states) expands the class of third parties that can sue successfully an auditor for negligence beyond near-privity to a person or limited group of persons whose reliance is (*actually*) *foreseen,* even if the specific person or group is unknown to the auditor.[34]

The courts have deviated from the *Ultramares* principle through a variety of decisions. For example, a federal district court in Rhode Island decided a case in 1968, *Rusch Factors, Inc. v. Levin,*[35] that held an accountant liable for negligence to a third party that was not in privity of contract. In that case, Rusch Factors had requested financial statements prior to granting a loan. Levin audited the statements, which showed the company to be solvent when it was actually insolvent. After the company went into receivership, Rusch Factors sued, and the court ruled that the *Ultramares* doctrine was inappropriate. In its decision, the court relied heavily on the *Restatement (Second) of the Law of Torts.*

### Restatement (Second) of the Law of Torts

The Restatement (Second) of the Law of Torts approach, sometimes known as Restatement 552,[36] expands accountants' legal liability exposure for negligence beyond those with near privity (actually foreseen) to a small group of persons and classes who are or *should be* foreseen by the auditor as relying on the financial information. This is known as the *foreseen third-party* concept because even though there is no privity relationship, the accountant knew that that party or those parties would rely on the financial statements for a specified transaction.

Section 552 states: "The liability . . . is limited to loss (a) suffered by the person or one of the persons for whose benefit and guidance he or she intends to supply the information, or knows that the recipient [client] intends to supply it; and (b) through reliance upon it in a transaction which he or she intends the information to influence, or knows that the recipient so intends." For example, assume that a client asks an accountant to prepare financial statements and the accountant knows that those statements will be used to request a loan from one or more financial institutions. The accountant may not know the specific bank to be approached, but he or she does know the purpose for which the statements will be used. Thus, the third parties as a class of potential users can be foreseen.

A majority of states now use the modified privity requirement imposed by Section 552 of the *Restatement (Second) of the Law of Torts.* The *Restatement* modifies the traditional rule of privity by allowing nonclients to sue accountants for negligent misrepresentation, provided that they belong to a "limited group" and provided that the accountant had actual knowledge that his or her professional opinion would be supplied to that group. In some state court decisions, a less restrictive interpretation of Section 552 has been made. For example, a 1986 decision by the Texas Court of Appeals in *Blue Bell, Inc. v. Peat, Marwick, Mitchell & Co.* held that if an accountant preparing audited statements knows or should know that such statements will be relied upon, the accountant may be held liable for negligent misrepresentation.[37]

## Reasonably Foreseeable Third Parties

A third judicial approach to third-party liability expands the legal liability of accountants well beyond *Ultramares.* The *reasonably foreseeable third-party* approach results from a 1983 decision by the New Jersey Supreme Court in *Rosenblum, Inc. v. Adler.*[38] In that case, the Rosenblum family agreed to sell its retail catalog showroom business to Giant Stores, a corporation operating discount department stores, in exchange for Giant common stock. The Rosenblums relied on Giant's 1971 and 1972 financial statements, which had been audited by Touche. When the statements were found to be fraudulent and the stock was deemed worthless, the investors sued Touche. The lower courts did not allow the Rosenblums' claims against Touche on the grounds that the plaintiffs did not meet either the *Ultramares* privity test or the *Restatement* standard. The case was taken to the New Jersey Supreme Court, and it overturned the lower courts' decision, ruling that auditors can be held liable for ordinary negligence to all *reasonably foreseeable third parties* who are recipients of the financial statements for routine business purposes. In finding for

Rosenblum on certain motions, the Court held, "Independent auditors have a duty of care to all persons whom the auditor should reasonably foresee as recipients of the statements from the company for proper business purposes, provided that the recipients rely on those financial statements. It is well recognized that audited financial statements are made for the use of third parties who have no direct relationship with the auditor. Auditors have responsibility not only to the client who pays the fee but also to investors, creditors, and others who rely on the audited financial statements."

Another important case that followed this approach was *Citizens State Bank v. Timm, Schmidt, & Company*.[39] In this case, the bank sued the public accounting firm after relying on financial statements for one of its debtors that had been audited by Timm. The Wisconsin court used a number of reasons for extending auditors' liability beyond privity. The following quote from the case demonstrates the court's rather liberal leanings with respect to auditor legal liability to third parties: "If relying third parties, such as creditors, are not allowed to recover, the cost of credit to the general public will increase because creditors will either have to absorb the cost of bad loans made in reliance on faulty information or hire independent accountants to verify the information received."

Since 1987, no state high court has adopted this foreseeability approach to accountants' legal liability, while a large number have approved or adopted one of the narrower standards.[40] For example, in its 1992 ruling in *Bily v. Arthur Young* (now Ernst & Young), the California Supreme Court expressly rejected the foreseeability approach in favor of the *Rusch Factors* or *Restatement* standard. The court gave a number of reasons for rejecting the *Rosenblum* foreseeability approach, including that the foreseeability rule exposes auditors to potential liability in excess of their proportionate share and the sophisticated plaintiffs have other ways to protect themselves from the risk of inaccurate financial statements (e.g., they can negotiate improved terms or hire their own auditor).[41]

However, in its 2003 ruling in *Murphy v. BDO Seidman, LLP*, the California Court of Appeals ruled that "grapevine plaintiffs," who alleged indirect reliance based on what others (e.g., stockholders and stockbrokers) told them about the financial statements, had legal claims for ordinary negligence against the auditors so long as the auditor would have reasonably foreseen that stockholders or stockbrokers would tell other people of the content of the financial statements and that the other people would rely upon the misrepresentations in purchasing the corporate stock. The court ruled that nothing in the *Bily* decision precludes indirect reliance.[42]

The *Murphy* ruling seems to stretch auditors' legal liability to third parties beyond reasonable bounds. Imagine, for example, that you are watching Jim Cramer's television show *Mad Money* on CNBC, and Cramer recommends a stock that you then purchase online. Shortly thereafter, news breaks of an accounting fraud. You sue the auditors based on your belief that the auditors should have known the public would buy the stock after Cramer recommended it. It makes little sense to conclude that a plaintiff may be successful in a lawsuit against the auditors based on a claim of ordinary negligence in this situation, given that auditors cannot control every use of audit information.

The conflicting common-law rulings can be confusing in trying to apply legal precedent to current court cases. To assist students, we have developed a summary in Exhibit 6.2 of the primary legal issues and guiding principles addressed in important court cases in deciding the auditor's liability to third parties.

Liability for fraud is not restricted to cases where the auditor had knowledge of the deceit. Some courts have interpreted gross negligence (i.e., constructive fraud) as an instance of fraud. Such fraud occurs when the auditor acts so carelessly in the application of professional standards that it implies a reckless disregard for the standards of due care. Examples are if the auditor failed to observe the physical count of inventory at year-end or to confirm accounts receivable.

The legal liability of accountants is not limited to audited statements. In the 1967 case *1136 Tenants Corp. v. Max Rothenberg & Co.*,[43] an accounting firm was sued for negligent

**EXHIBIT 6.2** **Auditor Legal Liability to Third Parties**

| Legal Approach | Case | Legal Principle | Legal Liability to Third Parties |
|---|---|---|---|
| *Ultramares* | *Ultramares v. Touche* | Privity (only clients can sue) | Possibly gross negligence that constitutes (constructive) fraud |
| Near-privity relationship | *Credit Alliance* | Three-pronged approach: knowledge of accountant that the statements will be used for a particular purpose; intention of third party to rely on those statements; some action by third party that provides evidence of the accountant's understanding of intended reliance | Ordinary negligence |
| *Restatement (Second) of the Law of Torts* | *Rusch Factors* | Actually foreseen third-party users | Ordinary negligence beyond near-privity |
| Foreseeable third party | *Rosenblum* | Reasonably foreseeable third-party users | Ordinary negligence with reliance on the statements |

failure to discover embezzlement by the managing agent who had hired the firm to "write up" the books, which did not include any audit procedures. The firm was held liable for failure to inquire or communicate about missing invoices, despite a disclaimer on the financial statements informing users that "No independent verifications were undertaken thereon." The firm moved to dismiss the case, but the court denied the motion and held that even if a CPA "acted as a robot, merely doing copy work," there was an issue as to whether there were suspicious circumstances relating to missing invoices that imposed a duty on the firm to warn the client. When the case went to trial, the court found there to be an engagement to audit and entered a judgment for more than $237,000 despite the firm's oral evidence that it was employed for $600 annually to write up the books.

The *1136* case affected auditing standards in two notable areas. First, the engagement letter was developed to clarify the responsibilities of accountants and auditors in performing professional services. The engagement letter formalizes the relationship between the auditor and the client. It serves as a contract detailing the responsibilities of the accountant or auditor and expectations for management. While engagement letters are not required by accounting or auditing standards, it does help clarify the obligations of professionals and any legal matters.

A second result was that the Accounting and Review Services Committee of the AICPA, a senior technical committee, was formed to formulate standards to be followed by accountants who perform two levels of service—a compilation and a review. A *review* provides limited assurance that the financial statements are free of material misstatements (a lower standard than the reasonable assurance requirement in the audit), while a *compilation* provides no assurance because the only services provided are of a bookkeeping nature.

## Auditor Liability to Third Parties

### Plaintiff Claims for Action

Common-law liability for fraud is available to third parties in any jurisdiction. The plaintiff (third party) must prove (1) a false representation by the accountant, (2) knowledge or belief by the accountant that the representation was false, (3) that the accountant intended to induce the third party to rely on false representation, (4) that the third party relied on the false representation, and (5) that the third party suffered damages.[44]

Courts have held that fraudulent intent or scienter may be established by proof that the accountant acted with knowledge of the false representation. However, liability for fraud is not limited to cases where the auditor was knowingly deceitful. Some courts have interpreted gross negligence or constructive fraud as an instance of fraud. An important case in this area is *State Street Trust Co. v. Ernst*.[45] In this case, the auditors issued an unqualified (i.e., unmodified) opinion on their client's financial statements, knowing that State Street Trust Company was making a loan based on those financial statements. A month later, the auditors sent a letter to the client indicating that receivables had been overstated. The auditors, however, did not communicate this information to State Street, and the client subsequently went bankrupt. The New York court ruled that the auditor's actions appeared to be grossly negligent and that "reckless disregard of consequences may take the place of deliberate intention." In such cases, while fraudulent intent may not be present, the court "constructs" fraud due to the grossness of the negligence.[46]

In *Phar-Mor v. Coopers & Lybrand* (now PricewaterhouseCoopers), the auditors were found guilty of fraud under both common and statutory law, even though the plaintiffs acknowledged that the auditors had no intent to deceive. Instead, the plaintiff successfully argued reckless disregard for the truth (i.e., gross negligence or constructive fraud), which gives rise to an inference of fraud. An important part of this ruling is that plaintiffs who are barred from suing for ordinary negligence because they lack a privity relationship or are not foreseen users can choose to sue the auditor for fraud because to find an auditor guilty of fraud, the plaintiffs need only prove gross negligence.[47]

In more recent cases, the court ruled in *Houbigant, Inc. v. Deloitte & Touche LLP*[48] and *Reisman v. KPMG Peat Marwick LLP*[49] that for an auditor to be found guilty of fraud, the plaintiffs must prove only that the auditor was aware that its misrepresentations might reasonably be relied upon by the plaintiff, not that the auditor intended to induce the detrimental reliance. The court referred to recent audit failures in its *Houbigant* decision: "It should be sufficient that the complaint contains some rational basis for inferring that the alleged misrepresentation was knowingly made. Indeed, to require anything beyond that would be particularly undesirable at this time, when it has been widely acknowledged that our society is experiencing a proliferation of frauds perpetrated by officers of large corporations . . . unchecked by the 'impartial' auditors they hired."[50]

### Auditor Defenses

The auditor's defense against third-party lawsuits for negligence that claim the auditor did not detect a misstatement or fraud requires proof that (1) the auditor did not have a duty to the third party, (2) the third party was negligent, (3) the auditor's work was performed in accordance with professional standards, (4) the third party did not suffer a loss, (5) any loss to the third party was caused by other events, or (6) the claim is invalid because the statute of limitations has expired.[51] Here are examples of the various defenses that an auditor can use:

1. Auditors can defend a common law action by presenting arguments and evidence to rebut third-party plaintiffs' claims and evidence. Once a plaintiff has demonstrated an economic loss and materially misstated financial statements, defenses available to auditors against third parties include the following:[52] The third party lacked standing to sue in a particular jurisdiction, as would be the case when bringing a lawsuit for ordinary negligence; and the appropriate relationship between the auditor and third party did not exist (i.e., a privity relationship).
2. The third party's loss was due to events other than the financial statements and auditors' examination, as might be the case if poor business practices or stock market declines caused the loss.
3. Auditors' work was performed in accordance with accepted auditing standards (e.g., AICPA or PCAOB standards), which is generally interpreted to mean that auditors were not negligent (ordinary negligence).

*Grant Thornton LLP v. Prospect High Income Fund, et al.*

A Texas Supreme Court decision in 2010 in the case of *Grant Thornton LLP v. Prospect High Income Fund, et al.* has strengthened defenses available to auditors brought by third parties for negligent misrepresentation and fraud. The Court overruled what had been a broader standard for establishing liability in negligent misrepresentations when financial failings of their clients exist. The ruling also sets new limitations on "holder" claims, wherein investors contend that they were put at a disadvantage because they held securities based on an auditor's report that they otherwise would have sold.[53] Given the potential importance of the case, we present a summary of the ruling in Exhibit 6.3.

The good news for accountants and other defendants is that this ruling sets forth a strong defense to the otherwise difficult-to-defend claim that "if I had known, I would have sold or taken other action to protect myself." Up until now, defendants have had little ability to defend holder claims because there is rarely any proof other than the plaintiff's testimony of what he did not do or would have done. This unfairness was recognized by the U.S. Supreme Court when it refused to allow holder claims under Rule 10b-5, but that decision left open the possibility that there could be state law causes of action. *Prospect* significantly closes that door. The decision could influence other courts to deny the open-ended holder claims.

# Statutory Liability

The most relevant sources of statutory liability for auditors are (1) the Securities Act of 1933; (2) the Securities Exchange Act of 1934; (3) Insider Trading and Securities Fraud Enforcement Act of 1988; (4) Private Securities Litigation Reform Act of 1995; (5) the Sarbanes-Oxley Act of 2002; and (6) Dodd-Frank Wall Street Reform and Consumer Protection Act of 2010. We have previously discussed SOX and Dodd-Frank in this and prior chapters. The regulations in items 1–4 create potential civil liabilities for auditors for failing to adhere to the requirements of the laws in carrying out professional obligations. Criminal liability exists when an auditor defrauds a third party through knowingly being involved with falsifications in financial statements.

An individual who engages in conduct proscribed by the Securities Act of 1933 or the Securities Exchange Act of 1934 may be convicted of a crime, provided her conduct was "willful." Given the centrality of the concept of "willfulness" in our criminal juris-prudence and the fact that numerous individuals have been prosecuted, convicted and imprisoned for "willfully" violating the federal securities laws, we might expect that the standard for when a "willful" violation has occurred would by now be well-settled. There is, however, a surprising paucity of case law interpreting the willfulness standard in the securities arena, and those courts that have addressed the issue have not always been uniform in defining a standard for when conduct proscribed by the statutes is criminal.

The term "willful" and its application in criminal securities law cases often is influenced by the context of the situation. Section 32(a) of the Exchange Act provides that any person who "willfully" violates any provision of the Act can be charged with a crime, while Section 15(b)(4) of the same Act authorizes the SEC to seek civil administrative penalties against any person who "willfully" violates certain provisions of the securities laws.

In 1970, the first Court of Appeals addressed the "willfulness" issue in *United States* v. *Peltz,* 433 F.2d 48.[54] In that decision the court held that, in order to sustain a criminal conviction, the prosecution had to establish "a realization on the defendant's part that he was doing a wrongful act."

In 1972, the Court of Appeals in *United States* v. *Schwartz,* 464 F.2d 499,[55] under a different panel of judges addressed the meaning of the term "willfully" and stated that a criminal conviction under Section 32(a) for willfully violating a provision of the Exchange Act would be sustained upon "satisfactory proof . . . that the defendant intended to commit the act prohibited."

**EXHIBIT 6.3**

*Grant Thornton LLP v. Prospect High Income Fund, et al.*

### Background

Epic Resorts, a timeshare operator, issued $130 million in corporate bonds in 1998 and sold them in the open market. Epic was required to make semiannual interest payments of $8.45 million to bondholders. To secure the interest payments, it was also required to maintain $8.45 million in an escrow account at U.S. Trust, which served as both the indenture trustee and escrow agent, for the benefit of the bondholders. Epic was required to provide annual audited financial statements, as well as a negative assurance statement from its auditors confirming that Epic was in compliance with the financial conditions of the indenture and related agreements.

Grant Thornton was engaged as Epic's auditor in March 2000, and subsequently audited Epic's financial statements for both 1999 and 2000. In the course of its 1999 audit, Grant discovered that Epic did not have the minimum required amount in the U.S. Trust account. Despite this deficiency, in April 2000, Grant issued an unqualified opinion on Epic's 1999 financial statements and confirmed in its negative assurance letter that Epic was in compliance with the escrow requirement. Grant's opinion and negative assurance were based, in part, upon representations from Epic that it was allowed to use more than one account to meet its escrow responsibilities, and the combined balances of escrow funds that it held never totaled less than the required minimum. U.S. Trust never objected to the lack of sufficient funds in the account that it maintained. In April 2001, Grant issued an unqualified opinion on Epic's 2000 financial statements, despite a continuing shortfall of funds in the U.S. Trust account, but it did not issue a negative assurance letter to the trustee.

The plaintiffs in this case were hedge funds that over several years purchased Epic bonds. Prospect had made three purchases before Grant was hired to perform its first audit. Thereafter, Highland Capital Management Corporation and its portfolio manager, Davis Deadman, began managing Prospect's investments and, as a result, became familiar with Epic's bonds. Deadman, on behalf of the Cayman Fund, a second fund, purchased more Epic bonds in December 2000, two days before Epic made its semiannual interest payment. At about the same time, Epic's primary lender, Prudential, told Epic that it would not renew its credit arrangement. This credit was critical to Epic's survival and its ability to meet its obligations to bondholders. Deadman learned of Prudential's decision sometime in the first quarter of 2001 but continued to buy Epic bonds throughout the spring of 2001.

In June 2001, Epic defaulted on its interest payment to bondholders, claiming that Prudential's failure to renew the credit arrangement forced the timeshare operator to use that money to fund operations. Four days after this default, the hedge funds purchased more bonds and forced Epic into bankruptcy. The hedge funds then sued Grant Thornton, alleging that the audit reports misrepresented the status of the escrow account.

### Procedural History

The plaintiff hedge funds sued Grant for negligent misrepresentation, direct negligence, fraud, conspiracy to commit fraud, aiding and abetting fraud, and third-party beneficiary breach of contract. They sought damages equal to the par value of the bonds, plus five years' interest. The trial court, two months before trial in August 2004, granted summary judgment to Grant Thornton on all counts. In October 2006, the Dallas Court of Appeals affirmed the judgment on certain claims, but reversed the judgment on the negligent misrepresentation, fraud, conspiracy, and aiding and abetting claims, finding genuine issues as to material facts.

Grant Thornton filed its petition for review with the Texas Supreme Court in January 2007. The petition argued that the Court of Appeals erred in not holding the following: (1) there was no evidence of a causal connection between Grant's alleged misrepresentation and the funds' alleged injury; (2) there was no evidence of actual and justifiable reliance; and (3) that liability for fraudulent misrepresentations runs only to those whom the auditor knows and intends to influence, all of which was not present. The hedge funds responded that Grant's misrepresentations caused them to fail to take action to protect themselves earlier and to refrain from selling their bonds ("holder" claims). The petition was granted in August 2008. In a victory for the auditing profession, in July 2010, the Texas Supreme Court ruled the law does not impose on auditors an obligation to provide an accurate accounting to anyone who reads and relies upon an audit report.

Other cases have led to somewhat different decisions in the same way that legal rulings involving the civil liability of auditors to third parties for ordinary negligence has changed over time.

## Securities Act of 1933

The Securities Act of 1933 regulates the disclosure of information in a registration statement for a new public offering of securities (i.e., an initial public offering, or IPO). Companies must file registration statements (S-1, S-2, and S-3 forms) and prospectuses that contain financial statements that have been audited by an independent CPA. Accountants who assist in the preparation of the registration statement are civilly liable if the registration statement (1) contains untrue statements of material facts, (2) omits material facts required by statute or regulation, or (3) omits information that if not given makes the facts stated misleading.[56]

Section 11 of the Securities Act of 1933 imposes a liability on issuer companies and others, including auditors, for losses suffered by third parties when false or misleading information is included in a registration statement. Any purchaser of securities may sue: the purchaser generally must prove that (1) the specific security was offered through the registration statements, (2) damages were incurred, and (3) there was a material misstatement or omission in the financial statements included in the registration statement. The plaintiff need not prove reliance on the financial statements unless the purchase took place after one year of the offering.

If items (2) and (3) are proven, it is a *prima facie* case (sufficient to win against the CPA unless rebutted) and shifts the burden of proof to the accountant, who may escape liability by proving the following: (1) after reasonable investigation, the CPA concludes that there is a reasonable basis to believe that the financial statements were true and there was no material misstatement (the materiality defense); (2) a "reasonable investigation" was conducted (the due diligence defense); (3) the plaintiff knew that the financial statements were incorrect when the investment was made (the knowledge of falsehood defense); or (4) the loss was due to factors other than the material misstatement or omission (the lack of causation defense).

### Materiality Defense

An accountant might argue that the false or misleading information is not material and thus should not have had an impact on the purchaser's decision-making process. The SEC and the courts have attempted to define materiality. The term *material* describes the kind of information that an average prudent investor would want to have so that he can make an intelligent, informed decision whether or not to buy the security. Thus, it is linked to the objectivity ethical standard discussed in Chapter 4. A material fact is one that, if correctly stated or disclosed, would have deterred or tended to deter the average prudent investor from purchasing the securities in question. The term does not cover minor inaccuracies or errors in matters of no interest to investors. Facts that tend to deter a person from purchasing a security are those that have an important bearing upon the nature or condition of the issuing corporation or its business.[57]

### Due Diligence Defense

To establish a due diligence defense, the defendant must prove that a reasonable investigation of the financial statements of the issuer and controlling persons was conducted. As a result, there was no reason to believe any of the information in the registration statement or prospectus was false or misleading. To determine whether a reasonable investigation has been made, the law provides that the standard of *reasonableness* is that required of a prudent person in the management of his own property. The burden of proof is on the defendant, and the test is as of the time the registration became effective. The due diligence defense, in effect, requires proof that a party was not guilty of fraud or negligence.[58] Notice the link to the due care/competence ethical standard discussed in Chapter 4.

The due diligence defense available to the auditor under Section 11 requires that the auditor has made a reasonable investigation of the facts supporting or contradicting the information included in the registration statement. The test is whether a "prudent person" would have made a similar investigation under similar circumstances. There is a link to be made between the legal notion of a prudent person test and rights theory. Recall that the universality principle in rights theory posits that an ethical action is one in which, based on the judgment of the decision maker, others would take in similar circumstances for similar reasons, thereby linking back to the due care standard as well.

## Key Court Decisions

Two court decisions illustrate the application of Section 11 to securities registration matters: *Escott v. Bar Chris Construction Corp.* and *Bernstein v. Crazy Eddie, Inc.* These cases are summarized in Exhibits 6.4 and 6.5, respectively.

**EXHIBIT 6.4**
*Escott v. Bar Chris Construction Corp.*

In *Escott v. Bar Chris Construction Corp.*, the company issued a registration statement in 1961 in connection with its public offering of convertible bonds. The statements included audited financial statements by Peat, Marwick, Mitchell, & Co. (now KPMG). The financial statements included material overstatements of revenues, current assets, gross profit, and backlog of sales orders and material understatements of contingent liabilities, loans to company officers, and potential liability for customer delinquencies. Bar Chris's worsening financial position resulted in a default on interest payments and the company eventually declared bankruptcy. Barry Escott and other investors sued Bar Chris's executive officers, directors, and the auditors under Section 11 of the Securities Act, citing a lack of appropriate professional care during the conduct of the audit. The judge ruled that the auditor's actions in reviewing events subsequent to the balance sheet date (subsequent events) were not conducted with due diligence because the senior auditor in charge of reviewing these events had not spent sufficient time and accepted unconvincing answers to key questions. The court determined that there had been sufficient warning signs that further investigation was necessary. The auditors' failure to perform a reasonable investigation of subsequent events did not satisfy Section 11(b) and resulted in their liability to investors in Bar Chris's bonds.[59]

**EXHIBIT 6.5**
*Bernstein v. Crazy Eddie, Inc.*

New Yorkers might remember television commercials of an electronics company called Crazy Eddie that aired during the mid- and late-1980s. The former chair and CEO, Eddie Antar, advertised that his prices were lower than the competition. An actor would come on the screen, act like a madman, and scream: "Our prices are insane." In the aftermath of the fraud at Crazy Eddie, cynics might claim that Eddie Antar was insane.

Crazy Eddie made several public offerings of securities from 1984 through 1987, during which time the prospectuses wrongly gave the impression that the company was a growing concern. The financial statements had been misstated by a number of schemes, including inflated inventory and net income. The plaintiffs in the case were purchasers of the company's stock prior to the disclosure of the fraudulent financial statements. They sued Peat Marwick, the board of directors, and others, alleging that the accounting firm had violated generally accepted auditing standards (GAAS) and generally accepted accounting practices (GAAP) by failing to uncover the company's fraudulent and fictitious activities. The plaintiffs were able to show that they suffered a loss and that the certified financial statements in the registration statements and prospectuses had been false and misleading, in violation of Sections 11 and 12 of the Securities Acts of 1933. The court decided the plaintiffs did not have to prove fraud or gross negligence, only that any material misstatements in the registration statements were misleading and that they had suffered a loss. In this case, the auditor was unable to prove that they had exercised appropriate due professional care to rebut the claim.

An interesting element of the due care failing was that Peat Marwick charged a relatively modest audit fee and, allegedly, the firm lowballed the engagement to obtain Crazy Eddie as an audit client, realizing that it could make up for lost audit revenue by selling the company consulting services. If this were true, Peat Marwick risked compromising its independence and objectivity because the firm may have been reluctant to go against top management when a difference of opinion on an accounting issue existed. The firm would know that the client might hold back on the consulting services pending the firm's acquiescence to the demands of top management.[60]

Auditors are considered to be experts regarding the fairness of the financial statements and must perform a "reasonable investigation" (an audit in accordance with GAAS). Section 11(b) requirements impose a liability for auditors for acts representing ordinary negligence. The Securities Act of 1933 shifts the burden of proof from the plaintiff (investor) to the auditors. To be successful in a legal action against the auditors, the plaintiffs must prove that they suffered an economic loss and that the financial statements contained a material misstatement that directly led to the loss.

## Securities Exchange Act of 1934

The Securities Exchange Act of 1934 regulates the ongoing reporting by companies whose securities are listed and traded on a stock exchange such as the New York Stock Exchange (NYSE) and National Association of Securities Dealers (NASDAQ). The act requires ongoing filing of quarterly (10-Q) and annual (10-K) reports and the periodic filing of an 8-K form whenever a significant event takes place affecting the entity, such as a change in auditors. Entities having total assets of $10 million or more and 500 or more stockholders are required to register under the Securities Exchange Act. The form and content of 10-K and 10-Q filings are governed by the SEC through Regulation S-X (which covers annual and interim financial statements) and Regulation S-K (which covers other supplementary disclosures).[61]

In addition to these two regulations, auditors must be familiar with Financial Reporting Releases (FRRs), which express new rules and policies about disclosure, and Staff Accounting Bulletins (SABs), which provide unofficial, but important, interpretations of Regulations S-X and S-K. Taken together, these four pronouncements provide the authoritative literature for information that must be filed with the SEC.[62]

Section 18 of the Act imposes liability on any person who makes a material false or misleading statement in documents filed with the SEC. The auditor's liability can be limited if the auditor can show that she "acted in good faith and had no knowledge that such statement was false or misleading." However, a number of cases have limited the auditor's good-faith defense when the auditor's action has been judged to be grossly negligent.[63]

The liability of auditors under the act often centers on Section 10 and Rule 10b-5. These provisions make it unlawful for a CPA to (1) employ any device, scheme, or artifice to defraud; (2) make an untrue statement of material fact or omit a material fact necessary in order to make the statement made, in the light of the circumstances under which they were made, not misleading; or (3) engage in any act, practice, or course of business to commit fraud or deceit in connection with the purchase or sale of the security.[64]

Once a plaintiff has established the ability to sue under Rule 10b-5, the following elements must be proved: (1) a material, factual misrepresentation or omission, (2) reliance by the plaintiff on the financial statements, (3) damages suffered as a result of reliance on the financial statements, and (4) the intent to deceive, manipulate, or defraud (scienter).[65]

### Reliance by Plaintiff

The first element can include materially misleading information or the omission of material information. Reliance cannot be established if the damages or loss suffered by the plaintiff would have occurred regardless of whether the audited financial statements were misstated. A good example of the failure to establish direct causation between the audited financial statements, reliance thereon and damages to the plaintiff is the court ruling in *Maxwell v. KPMG LLP.* In this case, the court ruled that even if the other elements necessary to sue under Rule 10b-5 could be established, Maxwell's alleged reliance on the audited financial statements of an acquiring entity was irrelevant, as the business model of that entity was bound to fail because of the dot.com collapse, and thus Maxwell's harm was not caused by KPMG's audit.[66]

This ruling stands as an example of non-accounting events that are the proximate cause of a failed business being given more weight than audited statements. The necessary conditions for the audit client's demise (Whittman-Hart) were first, its decision to buy U.S.

Web, and second, the precipitate decline of the dot.com business. The decision to buy U.S. Web was not influenced by KPMG's approving Whittman-Hart's accounting decisions, and neither were the dot.com troubles. U.S. Web's agreement to be bought may have been influenced by KPMG's advice to Whittman-Hart, but that is irrelevant because U.S. Web was doomed by the coming collapse of its market and thus was not harmed by the advice. Exhibit 6.6 contains a summary of the case.

### Intent to Deceive or Defraud (Scienter)

Under Rule 10b-5, auditor liability is linked to scienter, or the intent to deceive, manipulate, or defraud. It is not enough to assert the failure to exercise the appropriate level of care to cause liability. The *Hochfelder* case that appears in Exhibit 6.7 illustrates the need for purchasers and sellers of securities to prove scienter on the part of the auditors and confirm the inability for these parties to bring suit against auditors for ordinary negligence. The case was also significant in providing exposure for auditors in cases of gross negligence, even in the absence of scienter.

**EXHIBIT 6.6**
*Maxwell v. KPMG LLP*

KPMG was the auditor of a firm called Whittman-Hart, which offered consulting services in information technology. In the fall of 1999, Whittman-Hart became interested in buying a firm larger than itself called U.S. Web/CKS, which provided consulting services primarily to companies that used the Internet to sell goods or services. The purchase was consummated on March 1, 2000, and the new name of the combined company became marchFIRST, Inc. Whittman-Hart paid the owners of U.S. Web more than $7 billion. It paid entirely in the form of stock, a risky currency. Beginning the next month, many Internet-related ("dot.com") businesses experienced deep, often terminal, reverses. By virtue of the acquisition of U.S. Web, marchFIRST was such a business, and the following April, thirteen months after the acquisition, it declared bankruptcy.

The bankruptcy trustee argued that while the acquisition was being negotiated, KPMG approved a statement of Whittman-Hart's fourth-quarter 1999 earnings that it should have known was false. It should have known, the trustee argued, that Whittman-Hart had engaged in a form of what is called *round-tripping*. In this practice, a company makes a loan to a firm controlled by it, with the understanding that the borrower will purchase services from the lender in an amount equal to the amount of the loan, though the services may never be performed, or if performed, they may have little value and thus cost the lender little or nothing. In effect, the loan is reclassified from an account receivable by the lender to operating income.

Causation is the issue here and the same conclusion about the lack of a proximate cause can be reached, by a different route, by asking what duty, enforceable by tort law, was assumed by KPMG as Whittman-Hart's auditor. It was the duty to protect creditors of and investors in Whittman-Hart from being misled to their harm by financial statements issued by Whittman-Hart that contained errors that would be material to a creditor or an investor. It was not a duty to give the company business advice, such as advice on whether to acquire another company. The knowledge required to give such advice is possessed by the business itself and by business-consulting firms, as distinct from auditors. The auditors' concern is with the accuracy of the company's books, not with the demand for the company's products or services or the attractiveness of its investment opportunities. It is true that many accounting firms offer business consulting as well as auditing services, and that KPMG was one of them and did some consulting for Whittman-Hart (and hoped to continue doing so for marchFIRST). But the suit complains only about KPMG's auditing services, and there is no contention that they were influenced by the firm's consulting wing.

The failure to state Whittman-Hart's fourth-quarter earnings accurately, insofar as that was KPMG's fault, may have been a wrong to U.S. Web (though a wrong that did no harm if indeed that firm was doomed), but it was not a wrong to Whittman-Hart, as the auditor neither was asked to advise nor did advise Whittman-Hart to buy U.S. Web. By swallowing a larger company, and one concentrated in the dot.com business, Whittman-Hart assumed the risk of being injured—fatally, as it turned out—by a downturn in that business. In this case, Whittman-Hart wanted to make its auditor the insurer against the ill-informed business decision (the decision to try to acquire U.S. Web) unrelated to what an auditor is hired to do.

**EXHIBIT 6.7**
*Ernst & Ernst v. Hochfelder*

An important case that strengthens the scienter requirement is the 1976 U.S. Supreme Court reversal in *Ernst & Ernst v. Hochfelder*. The U.S. Court of Appeals had ruled in favor of Hochfelder and reversed the lower court opinion. The court decision includes this statement: "One who breaches a duty of inquiry and disclosure owed another is liable in damages for aiding and abetting a third party's violation of Rule 10b-5 if the fraud would have been discovered or prevented but for the breach, and that there were genuine issues of fact as to whether [Ernst] committed such a breach, and whether inquiry and disclosure would have led to discovery or prevention of the . . . fraud."[67]

The *Hochfelder* case involves the president of a brokerage firm who induced Hochfelder to invest in "escrow" accounts that the president represented would yield a high rate of return. The president converted those funds to personal use. The fraud came to light after the president committed suicide, leaving a note that described the brokerage as bankrupt and the escrow accounts as "spurious." Hochfelder's cause of action rested on a theory of negligent nonfeasance. The premise was that Ernst had failed to utilize "appropriate auditing procedures" in its audits of the brokerage, thereby failing to discover internal practices of the firm said to prevent an effective audit. The practice principally relied on the president's rule that only he could open mail addressed to him or to his attention at the brokerage, even if it arrived in his absence. Hochfelder argued that had Ernst conducted a proper audit, it would have discovered this "mail rule."

The U.S. Supreme Court reversed the decision, ruling that a private cause of action for damages does not come under Rule 10b-5 in the absence of any allegation of scienter. The Court cited the language in Section 10 that it is unlawful for any person to use or employ any manipulative or deceptive device or contrivance in contravention of SEC rules. The Court ruled that the use of those words clearly shows that it was intended to prohibit a type of conduct quite different from negligence. The term *manipulative* connotes intentional or willful conduct designed to deceive or defraud investors, a type of conduct that did not exist in the case.

In a footnote to the decision, the Court recognized that in certain areas of the law, recklessness is considered to be a form of intentional conduct for the purpose of imposing liability for some act, thereby providing potential exposure to auditors for gross negligence under the Securities Exchange Act.

## Interaction of Ethics and Legal Liability

Auditors typically will not be sued unless they have (allegedly) violated the ethical and professional standards. Auditor defenses under the Securities Exchange Act of 1934 include, in addition to a lack of scienter, nonnegligent performance of services, a lack of duty to the third party, and the absence of any casual connection that demonstrates that the third party relied on the audit and suffered damages as a result. The best defense for an auditor is to view professional responsibilities as going beyond mere adherence to the technical requirements of GAAS. The standards cannot cover every situation. Recall that when the rules are unclear or provide only vague guidance on an auditing matter, the auditor should act in accordance with the ethical standards described in Chapters 1 and 2, including the ethical reasoning methods, and the principles and rules of conduct in the AICPA Code that were discussed in Chapter 4.

The law establishes a minimum standard of conduct as well as the legal consequences for failing to adhere to relevant legal provisions. However, the law cannot completely address all matters and in all instances. When the situation is unclear and application of legal rules in doubt, the accounting professional should follow these ethical standards in resolving uncertain situations.

The standard under Rule 10b-5 that requires an intent to deceive is illustrative of the link between ethical conduct and legal liability. As discussed in Rest's model in Chapter 2, ethical intent is an element of moral decision making. We might evaluate one's ethical intent in making a decision against the scienter provision. Ethical action would then be tested by assessing whether the accountant carried through ethical decision making with integrity.

Legal principles and ethical values are closely interwoven, but ethical duties exceed legal requirements. A good example of how the profession's ethical standards address this issue is the *Integrity* principle in the AICPA Code of Conduct:

> *Integrity is measured in terms of what is right and just. In the absence of specific rules, standards, or guidance, or in the face of conflicting opinions, a member should test decisions and deeds by asking: "Am I doing what a person of integrity would do? Have I retained my integrity?" Integrity requires a member to observe both the form and the spirit of technical and ethical standards; circumvention of those standards constitutes subordination of judgment.*

# Court Decisions and Auditing Procedures

From time to time, court decisions lead to establishing new audit standards, policies, and procedures in reaction to a court ruling. The cases described below illustrate the point: McKesson & Robbins (Exhibit 6.8) and Equity Funding (Exhibit 6.9).

The McKesson & Robbins case involved audit failings in the area of accounts receivable and inventory, while the Equity Funding case addressed the inspection of assets and confirming customer insurance policies. In both cases, the auditors failed to exercise the level of care required in audit examinations.

**EXHIBIT 6.8**

*United States v. McKesson & Robbins*

The McKesson & Robbins case in 1939 was the first instance in which auditing practices were subject to significant public scrutiny. The case involved a conspiracy to defraud the company by its former president, Donald Coster. Coster and his brothers undertook an elaborate scheme that included dummy trading companies, fictitious warehouses, and forged documents. A cynic might contend that Coster's actions served as a (negative) role model for Barry Minkow in ZZZZ Best some 40-plus years later.

A 1939 investigation by the SEC revealed that Coster and his confidants had stolen around $2.9 million of McKesson & Robbins's cash in the previous 12 years. However, due to the lack of two "then-not-required" audit procedures, physical observation of inventory and direct confirmation of accounts receivable, Price Waterhouse failed to detect $19 million nonexistent assets (out of a total assets of over $87 million) and $1.8 million gross profit on fictitious sales of $18 million that were included in McKesson's 1937 certified financial statements.[68]

Up until 1940, the auditor was allowed to rely on the representations of management concerning the accuracy of physical quantities and the costs of its inventory. The SEC criticized the accountants for inaccuracies in the corporation's audited financial statements and set forth several findings in the McKesson & Robbins case:[69]

1. The accounting firm "'failed to employ that degree of vigilance, inquisitiveness, and analysis of the evidence available that is necessary in a professional undertaking and is recommended in all well-known and authoritative works on auditing."

2. Although the accounting profession claims that the auditor is not a guarantor and should not be liable for fraud, the SEC ruled that "the discovery of gross overstatements in the accounts is a major purpose of such an audit even though it [may] be conceded that [the audit] might not disclose every minor defalcation."

3. The SEC advised the accounting profession to take physical inventories and to require confirmations of accounts and notes receivable.

4. The SEC recommended that the board of directors nominate the auditors and that the activities of management be included in the audit.

The SEC made additional recommendations to the AICPA, including to distinguish auditing "standards" from auditing "procedures." Also, the auditor's certificate should state whether "the audit was made in accordance with generally accepted auditing standards applicable in the circumstances." Subsequently, the AICPA adopted these procedures and eventually codified them in the *Statement on Auditing Standards*. As discussed in Chapter 5, these standards have been recodified as a result of the Clarity Project.

**EXHIBIT 6.9**

*In re Equity Funding
Corporation of
America Securities
Litigation*

The Equity Funding case changed the way that CPA firms audited lients, and it brought attention to the red flags that might indicate fraud. Equity Funding's principal line of business was to create "funding programs" that included the sale of life insurance combined with mutual fund investment. Equity Funding derived its income from commissions on the sales. The fraud started just prior to the company's going public, and it was motivated by an attempt to increase the earnings of the company. Equity Funding inflated its earnings by recording fictitious commissions from the sale of its product that the company called "reciprocals." The company also borrowed funds without recording them as liabilities; instead, the cash was recorded as payments on the loan receivable by participants in the program. By reducing the loans receivable, Equity Funding could record more fictitious commissions. The last part of the fraud involved creating fictitious insurance policies, which were then reinsured with other insurance companies. This enabled the company to obtain additional cash to pay premiums on policies, which in turn required that more fictitious policies be created on their books.[70]

Equity Funding collapsed in 1973 when a former employee disclosed the existence of the massive fraud. During the period of the fraud, Equity Funding was audited first by Wolfson Weiner, which ultimately was taken over by the CPA firm Seidman & Seidman. A lengthy audit by Touche during the bankruptcy proceedings disclosed that the company had generated more than $2 billion of fictitious insurance policies.

On November 1, 1973, a federal grand jury in California indicted twenty-two executives and employees of Equity Funding, including Stanley Goldblum, the chair and CEO of the company. According to the indictment, Goldblum wanted to achieve a level of growth that was not attainable through legitimate business operations. He arranged for various officers and employees to make fictitious bookkeeping entries to inflate the company's income and assets. He also directed employees to create fictitious insurance policies. On November 2, 1970, an employee was instructed to write a computer program creating fictitious policies with a face value of $430 million and a total yearly premium of $5.5 million. In 1971, some phony policies were reinsured, and some employees were instructed to create death claims on the policies.[71]

Creating phony accounting entries is relatively easy, but creating the documentation for 64,000 phony policies was a big challenge, even at Equity Funding. Management wanted to be able to satisfy the auditors, who would ask to see a sample of policies for review. The auditors would examine the policies' documentation on file, and then cross-check for premium receipts and reserve policy information. However, in all but a handful of cases, there were no policy files available. To solve this problem, management created an in-house institution—the "forgery party."

At Equity Funding, policy files the auditors requested would often be "temporarily unavailable." Employees would work at night to forge the missing files to have them ready for auditor review the next day. The fact that the auditors were duped was the least of their embarrassment. One night when the auditor left his briefcase unlocked, an Equity Funding executive, in full sight of others, opened the case and took the audit plan and was able to anticipate next steps. Another time, an auditor wanted to send out policy confirmations to a sample of policyholders. Equity Funding officials, eager to help, did some clerical chores for the auditor. The result was letters addressed to branch sales managers and agents, who dutifully filled out the forms for the fictitious policyholders.[72]

An AICPA committee studied the Equity Funding scandal and concluded that "customary audit procedures properly applied" would have reasonably ensured detection of the fraud. There is no way to know if this is true. However, we can examine some of the ethical issues confronting the auditors at Equity Funding including independence and professional skepticism.

The auditors at Equity Funding compromised their independence in a number of instances. For example, one of the auditors earned $130,000 to $150,000 a year, largely because this company was his firm's largest client. Equity Funding paid the auditing firm $300,000 in 1970, more than twice the amount paid by the firm's next three largest clients. The second auditor was given 300 shares of Equity Funding in 1965, which he kept in his wife's former name until he sold them in 1967. The third auditor received a $2,000 loan from an Equity Funding officer. Finally, these auditors (who were subsequently found guilty of fraudulent activities) were allowed to continue auditing Equity Funding—at the insistence of Stanley Goldblum—when another accounting firm bought out their firm.[73]

When auditors allow management extended periods of time to pull the records needed for the audit, it allows management to selectively choose the records, add data that didn't exist, clear out data that is harmful, and generally sanitize the information going to the auditors.

Another red flag that the auditors did not seem to pursue was the rapidly increasing revenue and accounts receivable accounts. The auditors missed the ongoing fraud, not because they lacked technical know-how, but because they did not follow the basics of auditing. Beyond analytical reviews and examining documentation, a fundamental tenet of auditing is to verify the existence of the asset. If the auditors missed 64,000 phony insurance policies, $25 million in counterfeit bonds, and $100 million in missing assets, they simply weren't doing their job.

# Liability for Securities Violations

An accountant may be found criminally liable for violations of the Securities Acts of 1933 and the Securities Exchange Act of 1934. Under both the 1933 and 1934 acts, accountants may be subject to criminal penalties for willful and knowing violations. Therefore, to be subject to criminal liability, auditors must be shown to be guilty of fraud. SOX increased the criminal penalties for violating the Securities Exchange Act to $5 million and imprisonment for a maximum of 25 years. The following is a summary of jail time sentences imposed on CEOs responsible for fraud in some of the cases discussed in this book.

| CEO | Company | Jail Time |
| --- | --- | --- |
| Bernie Ebbers | WorldCom | 25 years |
| Dennis Kozlowski | Tyco | 8 1/3 to 25 years |
| Richard Scrushy | HealthSouth | 6 years, 10 months |
| Jeff Skilling | Enron | 24 years, 4 months |

## Honest Services Assessment in Criminal Matters

Jeff Skilling was originally sentenced to a 24-year jail sentence for fraud and insider trading, but the former Enron chief executive continues to push his case for innocence through the U.S. legal system. His latest challenge came in September 2011, when lawyers filed an appeal against an April 2011 ruling that upheld a potential error in the guidance that led to his 2006 conviction.

He had appealed the 19 out of 28 charges that he was sentenced for in 2006 all the way up to the U.S. Supreme Court. His lawyers challenged the ruling based on the instructions given to the jury, which asked them to consider whether he had deprived his company of intangible honest services. The U.S. Supreme Court found on June 24, 2010, that he had not violated the honest services rule, as he had not solicited or accepted bribes or kickbacks; rather, he conspired to defraud Enron's shareholders by other means.

In its decision, the U.S. Supreme Court ruled that the federal government's "honest services" law could be constitutionally applied only to cases involving bribery and kickbacks. With regard to Enron's Skilling, Justice Ginsburg wrote: "The Government charged Skilling with conspiring to defraud Enron's shareholders by misrepresenting the company's fiscal health to his own profit, but the Government never alleged that he solicited or accepted side payments from a third party in exchange for making these misrepresentations . . . Because Skilling's alleged misconduct entailed no bribe or kickback, it does not fall within the Court's confined definition of what is proscribed by the law."[74]

The U.S. Supreme Court then passed its ruling down to the U.S. Court of Appeals for the Fifth Circuit to consider whether this should alter his conviction. The U.S. Court of Appeals for the Fifth Circuit ruled in April 2012 that it should not alter his conviction. Skilling's lawyers are currently appealing this ruling. Perhaps the legal system is growing weary of dealing with Skilling's appeals because on May 8, 2013, it was announced by the U.S. Department of Justice (DOJ) that Skilling might be freed ten years early. This means he would spend a total of 14 years in jail. In return for the lighter sentence, Skilling agreed to stop appealing his conviction. The agreement would also allow more than $40 million seized from him to be freed up for distribution to Enron fraud victims.

## Is There a Difference Between Lying and Stealing in Securities Fraud?

On some level, the whole tale of Enron is, in many ways, a tale of self-delusion and of the power of rationalization. In his trial, Skilling sounded like a man who believed he had done nothing illegal. Wrong, risky, mistaken, yes; but was it illegal?

The jury in the Skilling trial found that he did lie, but his case is different from that of other high-profile CEOs during the past ten years. The ethical question is whether Skilling's lies are the same or different from stealing by other CEOs. Is there a difference between lying—telling an untruth—and stealing, or taking something that does not belong to you? Is lying different from stealing in matters of securities fraud?

In a 2007 *New Yorker* article, Malcolm Gladwell controversially argued that much of the information that constituted this lie was already in the public domain, such that the problems of Enron were discoverable had someone only looked hard enough.[75] We suppose that that means in Gladwell's mind that lying it is no big deal because investors could have discovered the truth by diligent examination of the financial records of Enron. This is a dangerous position from an ethical perspective because it places the burden on those whose interests are supposed to be protected—the investors—to ferret out information that should willingly be provided by the overseers of the financial records. Recall our discussion in Chapter 3 about agency theory. Clearly, Skilling failed in his responsibilities to the shareholders to act in their best interests.

However, Skilling's crimes could be seen as different from the kind committed by Bernie Madoff. Madoff deliberately stole to benefit himself. He received a 150-year sentence for taking billions. Madoff's sentence was dictated by the federal sentencing guidelines, which specify sentences that increase rapidly depending on the size of the loss. In a multibillion-dollar public company, these numbers quickly escalate to a life sentence. In Enron's case, the guidelines recommended a minimum sentence of 24 years for Skilling.

The question about lying versus stealing can be considered in the following context: To what degree are CEOs responsible for *not* preventing ethical misconduct and illegal activities within the organization? Skilling was part of the infected culture at Enron that believed in making the deal at any cost, showing an increased rate of profitability, and increasing share prices regardless of what had to be done to keep up the charade of success. The investors and employees became collateral damage along the way. The bottom line is that Skilling lied to the investing public about the true condition of the company; and no matter how you slice it, that's against the law.

# Insider Reporting and Trading

Officers, directors, and stockholders owning 10 percent of the class of equity securities registered under Section 12 of the 1934 Securities Exchange Act must file reports with the SEC concerning their ownership and trading of the corporations' securities.[76] The SEC defines an officer for insider trading purposes as the executive officers, accounting officers, CFOs, and controllers. Section 16 and the SEC regulations require that insiders file, at the time of the registration or within ten days after becoming an insider, a statement of the amount of such issues of which they are owners. The regulations also require filing within ten days after the close of each calendar month thereafter if there has been any change in such ownership during that month. SOX shortens the time period for filing information about insider transactions. Now these filings with the SEC must be made electronically within two business days of the insider's transactions.

The reason for prohibiting insiders from trading for profit is to prevent the use of information that is available to an insider but not to the general public. Because the SEC cannot determine for certain when nonpublic information is improperly used, Section 16 creates a presumption that any profit made within a six-month time period is illegal. These profits are referred to as *short-swing profits*. Thus, if a director, officer, or principal owner realizes profits on the purchase and sale of a security within a six-month period, the profits legally belong to the company or to the investor who purchases it from or sold it to an insider, resulting in the insider's profit and the investor's loss. The order of the purchase and sale is immaterial. The short-swing rule does not depend of any misuse of information.[77]

When most people hear the term *insider trading,* they think of the illegal version. However, insider trading can also mean the perfectly legal buying and selling of stock by a company's corporate insiders. Insider trading is legal when these corporate insiders trade stock of their own company and report these trades to the SEC. That way, the insider trading is not kept a secret and anyone can find out a corporate insider's opinion of his or her company. Insider trading is illegal only when a person bases his trade of stocks in a public company on information that the public does not know. It is illegal to trade your own stock in a company based on this information, but it is also illegal to give someone that information—a tip—so he or she can trade the stock.

## Leaking Nonpublic Information

A *tippee* is a person who learns of nonpublic information from an insider. A tippee is liable for the use of nonpublic information because an insider should not be allowed to do indirectly what he or she cannot do directly. In other words, a tippee is liable for trading or passing on information that is nonpublic. The use of nonpublic information for financial gain has not been prohibited entirely. For example, in one case, the U.S. Supreme Court narrowed a tippee's liability by ruling that a tippee becomes liable under Section 10(b) only if the tipper breaches a fiduciary duty to the business organization or fellow shareholders. Therefore, if the tipper communicated nonpublic information for reasons other than personal gain, neither the tipper nor the tippee could be liable for securities violation.

Insider trading continues to be a high-priority area for the SEC's enforcement program. The SEC brought 58 insider trading actions in fiscal year 2012 against 131 individuals and entities. Between 2010 and 2012, the SEC had filed more insider trading actions (168 total) than in any three-year period in the agency's history. These insider trading actions were filed against nearly 400 individuals and entities, with illicit profits or losses avoided totaling approximately $600 million. Many of these actions involved financial professionals, hedge fund managers, corporate insiders, and attorneys who unlawfully traded on material nonpublic information, undermining the level playing field that is fundamental to the integrity and fair functioning of the capital markets.[78]

A good example of the SEC's activities in the insider trading arena occurred on September 20, 2012, when the commission obtained an emergency court order to freeze the assets of a stockbroker who used nonpublic information from a customer and engaged in insider trading ahead of Burger King's announcement that it was being acquired by a New York private equity firm.

The SEC alleged that Waldyr Da Silva Prado Neto, a citizen of Brazil who was working for Wells Fargo in Miami, learned about the impending acquisition from a brokerage customer who invested at least $50 million in a fund managed by private equity firm 3G Capital Partners Ltd. and used to acquire Burger King in 2010. Prado misused the confidential information to trade illegally in Burger King stock for $175,000 in illicit profits, and he tipped off others living in Brazil and elsewhere who also traded on the nonpublic information.[79]

Perhaps the most celebrated case of insider trading was that of Martha Stewart selling shares of ImClone Systems ahead of an announcement by the U.S. Food and Drug Administration (FDA) that it had rejected the company's cancer drug before this information was made public. In 2001, Stewart sold $228,000 worth of ImClone stock the day after her friend and founder of ImClone, Sam Waksal, sold his shares and told his family to sell out too. A summary of the case appears in Exhibit 6.10.

Insider cases took on new importance on October 24, 2012, when the well-respected Raj Gupta, a former Goldman Sachs director who once ran top consulting firm McKinsey & Co., was sentenced to two years in prison and fined $5 million for leaking tips to Raj Rajaratnam, a former hedge fund manager who was sentenced for 11 years for insider trading. Rajaratnam, the founder of Galleon Group, has already paid $63.8 million in criminal penalties, and a judge had earlier ordered him to pay $92.8 million in a civil case brought by the SEC. On December 27, 2012, he agreed to pay disgorgement of about $1.5 million in a civil lawsuit filed by the SEC and to waive his right to appeal the judgment.

**EXHIBIT 6.10**

*United States v. Martha Stewart and Peter Bacanovic*

Samuel Waksal, the CEO of ImClone Systems, Inc., a biotechnology company, was a client of stockbroker Peter Bacanovic. Bacanovic's other clients included Martha Stewart, then the CEO of Martha Stewart Living Omnimedia (MSLO). On December 27, 2001, Waksal began selling his ImClone shares. The next day, ImClone announced that the FDA had rejected the company's application for approval of its leading product, a medication called Erbitux. The government began to investigate Stewart's ImClone trades, the media began to report on the investigation, and the value of MSLO stock began to drop.[80]

In June 2002, at a mid-year media review conference attended by investment professionals and investors, Stewart said that she had previously agreed with Bacanovic to sell her ImClone stock if the price fell to $60 per share. "I have nothing to add on this matter today. And I'm here to talk about our terrific company." Her statements were followed by a 40-minute presentation on MSLO.

Subsequently, Stewart was charged with, among other things, fraud in connection with the purchase and sale of MSLO securities in violation of the SEC Act of 1934. She filed a motion for acquittal of this charge. The court granted Stewart's motion. The court reasoned that "to find the essential element of criminal intent beyond a reasonable doubt" and conclude that Stewart lied to influence the market for the securities of her company, "a rational juror would have to speculate."

Unfortunately for Stewart, that was not the end of the story. In 2004, she was convicted on other charges related to her sale of ImClone stock, including obstruction of justice and lying to federal officials. Stewart served five months in prison and five months and three weeks of house arrest. In 2006, as part of a settlement with the regulatory agency, Stewart agreed to a five-year ban from serving as a director of a public company and a five-year limitation of the scope of her service as an officer or employee of a public company. That ban ended on September 28, 2011, and she was then reinstated as a board member of MSLO.[81]

Until his indictment in 2011, Gupta was considered one of the world's leading business advisors. He was managing director of McKinsey until he retired in 2007, and served on boards of leading companies, including Goldman Sachs. The presiding judge in Gupta's trial, Judge Jed S. Rakoff, said after pronouncing sentence: "He is a good man. But the history of this country and the history of the world are full of examples of good men who did bad things." A summary of the facts of the Gupta case appears in Exhibit 6.11.

## Auditor Betrayal of Client Confidences and Insider Trading

No Big-4 audit firms or their partners have been named in the insider trading scandal surrounding the now-defunct hedge fund Galleon Management. However, some firms have got caught up in insider-trading allegations and violations of client confidentiality. In Chapter 4 we discussed the case of Scott London, an audit partner with KPMG, who gave inside tips about two audit clients—Skechers and Herbalife—to his friend Bryan Shaw. Shaw pleaded guilty on May 21, 2013, to conspiring with London to trade in stocks of the accounting firm's clients and agreed to return nearly $1.27 million in stock-trading gains. Shaw also faces a maximum of five years in federal prison for his insider trading crime. On May 28, 2013, London pleaded guilty to securities fraud for providing confidential information about KPMG clients to Shaw. KPMG admitted that London violated the firm's independence rules and it resigned from the engagements and withdrew its audit opinions.

**EXHIBIT 6.11**
**Rajat Gupta and Raj Rajaratnam Insider Trading Scandal**

On October 24, 2012, Rajat Gupta was sentenced to two years in prison and ordered to pay a $5 million fine for leaking tips to convicted hedge-fund billionaire Raj Rajaratnam.

Gupta, a former Goldman Sachs director who once ran top consulting firm McKinsey & Co., was convicted in June 2012 of three counts of securities fraud and one count of conspiracy, including tipping Rajaratnam to Warren Buffett's $5 billion investment in Goldman Sachs at the height of the financial crisis.

Gupta had been indicted in October 2011 with one count of conspiracy to commit securities fraud and five counts of securities fraud, all related to tips in 2008. The jury found Gupta guilty of leaking confidential information about Goldman to his former friend and business associate, Rajaratnam, on three different occasions in 2008. He was also convicted of conspiring in an insider trading scheme with Rajaratnam.

Rajaratnam, the former head of the Galleon Group hedge fund, was convicted in 2011 of orchestrating an insider trading conspiracy that reaped at least $63 million in illegal gains, and was sentenced to an 11-year prison term, the longest sentence ever given for insider trading. Prosecutors contended that Rajaratnam illegally traded on the tips that he got from Gupta.

Gupta's arrest in October 2011 stunned the business world. He had come to the United States from his native India to earn a graduate degree and finished in the top of his class at Harvard Business School. He landed a job at McKinsey and rose quickly through the ranks. In 1994, his partners elected him global head of the firm, the first non-American to hold that position.

After ten years running McKinsey, Gupta assumed the role of corporate wise man, joining the boards of many corporations and nonprofit organizations. In addition to Procter & Gamble and Goldman, he was a director of the AMR Corporation, the parent company of American Airlines. The Rockefeller Foundation appointed him a trustee; he was named an adviser to Bill Clinton and Bill Gates on their global health initiatives.

Around the time he became a Goldman director, Gupta struck up a relationship with Rajaratnam, a native of Sri Lanka whom he had met through philanthropic work. Together, they helped start New Silk Route Partners, a private equity firm focused on investments in India. Gupta invested—and lost—$10 million in a Galleon-sponsored vehicle called the Voyager Fund. He also considered becoming chairman of a Galleon international investment vehicle.

According to testimony from Rajaratnam's trial, Gupta became fixated on the extraordinary wealth showered on hedge fund managers and private equity chiefs. Gupta periodically visited Rajaratnam's hedge fund, Galleon, in midtown Manhattan. Gupta became an investor in Galleon's hedge funds. By all accounts, he seemed enamored with the hedge fund industry and wanted to be in the "billionaire's" circle.

In another case discussed in Chapter 4, Thomas Flanagan, a Deloitte & Touche vice chairman, was accused of insider trading and settled with the SEC on August 8, 2012. Flanagan pleaded guilty to one count of criminal securities fraud for engaging in insider trading after he obtained material, nonpublic information about several Deloitte clients. Flanagan used that information himself and shared it with a relative to make illegal trading profits. On October 26, 2012, the SEC announced that Flanagan would serve 21 months of incarceration, followed by supervised release of 12 months; in addition, he was ordered to pay a $100,000 penalty.

In the fall of 2004, a rather bizarre case was announced by the SEC in *SEC v. James E. Gansman, et al.* Investment banker Donna Murdoch logged onto a discreet dating Web site called Ashley Madison, which married people visit when divorce is not an option for personal reasons. Murdoch introduced herself to James Gansman, a partner at Ernst & Young (EY) in New York. The two struck up a relationship, meeting occasionally in hotels in Philadelphia, New York, and California, and talking on the phone about their lives. As the friendship flourished, the conversations about business matters came to the forefront. Gansman would lead Murdoch through a guessing game about which deals he was working on, and eventually Gansman became more direct about upcoming deals of EY clients.

In one case, Gansman learned that EY had been retained by Blackstone Group in connection with a possible acquisition of Freescale Semiconductor by an investment consortium led by Blackstone. At that time, Gansman was informed that Blackstone wanted the transaction to be "treated superconfidential," and was told in an internal EY e-mail message, "[d]o not breathe the name of the target outside of team." Nonetheless, he provided Murdoch with inside information about the impending transaction.

The pair communicated over 400 times via telephone and text message from the time that Gansman learned of the acquisition to the time, less than four weeks later, when Murdoch began buying options to purchase Freescale stock, according to a press release. Murdoch made about $158,000 from her trades.

According to the SEC complaint,[82] Murdoch used the nonpublic information to trade in the securities of the target companies; to tip her father, Gerald Brodsky, who also traded; and to make recommendations to two others, who traded as well.

On August 18, 2010, Gansman settled insider trading charges of tipping off his stock-broker girlfriend about at least seven different acquisition targets that happened to be his firm's clients. To settle the commission's charges, Gansman and Murdoch each consented, without admitting or denying the allegations in the complaint, to a separate final judgment that permanently enjoined each from violating Securities Exchange Act Sections 10(b) and 14(e) and Rules 10b-5 and 14e-3. The final judgment to which Gansman consented further ordered him to pay disgorgement of $233,385, together with $16,470 in prejudgment interest and $145 in post-judgment interest. In addition, Gansman and Murdoch each consented, in related administrative proceedings, to the entry of an SEC order that, in the case of Gansman, suspended him from appearing or practicing before the commission as an attorney, and in the case of Murdoch, barred her from association with any professional broker or dealer.

A gross lack of common judgment and indifference to client needs characterize the behavior and actions of James Gansman. He breached his ethical obligations to his clients and violated Rule 301 of the AICPA Code of Professional Conduct on client confidential information. A case also can be made that he violated Rule 501 by committing an act discreditable to the profession.

Unfortunately, we find that some members of the accounting profession are not immune from engaging in ill-thought-out, self-serving acts that bring into question their professionalism and lead us to ask: "What could they have been thinking?"

# Private Securities Litigation Reform Act (PSLRA)

The Private Securities Litigation Reform Act (PSLRA) of 1995 amends the Securities Exchange Act of 1934 by adding Section 10A, "Audit Requirements," which specified that each independent auditor of an issuer under the Act must include "Procedures designed to provide reasonable assurance of detecting illegal acts that would have a direct and material effect on the determination of financial statements amounts." The Act also includes in federal law the auditor's responsibility to detect fraud and requires auditors to promptly notify the audit committee and board of directors of illegal acts. We have already discussed the reporting requirements of illegal acts in Chapter 5, and we will review the key points here. We also explain the proportionate liability standard for auditor legal liability under the PSLRA.

## Reporting Requirements

Section 10A(b), "Required Response to Audit Discoveries," establishes the independent auditor's duties when she detects or otherwise becomes aware of information indicating that an illegal act has or may have occurred. Basically, the auditor must first assess materiality to move on with reporting requirements. Next, the auditor needs to assess whether an illegal act has occurred and, if so, determine the possible effects of the illegal act on the client's financial statements. Finally, the auditor should inform the appropriate level of management and assure the audit committee or the board of directors has been informed, unless such illegal act is clearly inconsequential.[83]

If the auditor concludes that an illegal act with a material effect on the financial statements has not been dealt with by senior management in a timely manner and with appropriate remedial actions, then the auditor should report her conclusions directly to the board of directors. The report should indicate that (1) the illegal act has a material effect on the financial statements of the issuer; (2) the senior management has not taken, and the board of directors has not caused senior management to take, timely and appropriate remedial actions with respect to the illegal act; and (3) the failure to take remedial action is reasonably expected to warrant departure from the standard audit report (i.e., unmodified opinion) of the auditor, when made, or warrant resignation from the audit engagement. If a board of directors receives such a report from its auditors, then management has one business day from the receipt of such a report to inform the SEC and furnish a copy to the auditors. If the issuers fail to provide the SEC and the independent auditors with the required notice, the audit firm is required to resign from the engagement or furnish to the commission a copy of its report not later than one business day following such failure of the issuer to give proper notice. If the independent auditors resign, they still are required to provide the SEC with a copy of their report to the board of directors of the issuer.[84]

Recall that Rule 301 of the AICPA Code of Professional Conduct prohibits CPAs from directly disclosing information to outside parties, including illegal acts, unless the auditors have a legal duty to do so. Therefore, Rule 301 does permit the CPA to discuss confidential client information without violating the rule to adhere to applicable laws and government regulations. Compliance with the PSLRA would qualify as an exception to the bar on disclosing confidential client information as would compliance with SOX and Dodd-Frank provisions. Auditors are also required to communicate illegal acts in other situations. When illegal activities cause the auditors of a public company to lose faith in the integrity of senior management, they should resign and a Form 8-K, which discloses the reasons for the auditors' resignation, should be filed with the SEC by management. The auditors must file a response to the filing indicating whether they agree with management's reasons and providing the details when they disagree.

### Xerox case: SEC v. KPMG

A good example of the application of Section 10A is the litigation in the Xerox fraud. The accounting issues are discussed in Chapter 7; here, we look at the reporting requirements for fraud and illegal acts and whether KPMG met those standards with regard to its client, Xerox.

In *SEC v. KPMG LLP, Joseph T. Boyle, Michael A. Conway, Anthony P. Dolanski, and Ronald A. Safran,* the SEC alleged, among other claims, violations of Section 10A by KPMG and four of its partners. On January 29, 2003, the SEC filed an action against the firm and its partners, claiming as follows:

> "Defendants KPMG . . . and certain KPMG partners permitted Xerox Corporation to manipulate its accounting practices and fill a $3 billion "gap" between actual operating results and results reported to the investing public from 1997 through 2000. Instead of putting a stop to Xerox's fraudulent conduct, the KPMG defendants themselves engaged in fraud by falsely representing to the public that they had applied professional auditing standards to their review of Xerox's accounting, that Xerox's financial reporting was consistent with GAAP and that Xerox's reported results fairly represented the financial condition of the company. . . . Section 10A of the Exchange Act requires a public accountant conducting an audit of a public company such as Xerox to: (1) determine whether it is likely that an illegal act occurred and, if so, (2) determine what the possible effect of the illegal act is on the financial statements of the issuer; and (3) if the illegal act is not clearly inconsequential, inform the appropriate level of management and assure that the Audit Committee of the client is adequately informed about the illegal act detected. If neither management nor the Audit Committee takes timely and appropriate remedial action in response to the auditor's report, the auditor is obliged to take further steps, including reporting the likely illegal act to the Commission."[85]

> In November 2004, KPMG reached a settlement with the SEC. KPMG consented to a finding that it violated Section 10A of the Securities Exchange Act of 1934; to pay disgorgement of $9,800,000, plus prejudgment interest; to pay a civil penalty of $10 million; and to implement a number of internal reforms. A final judgment against KPMG was issued on April 20, 2005.

## Proportionate Liability

The attempts to reform auditor liability in the United States focused on the argument that the tort system was out of control, partly as a consequence of the 1933 Securities Act, which placed auditors under a joint and several liability regime and made them, not the plaintiffs, carry the burden of proof. The accounting profession had fought over time to effectuate this change because of what the profession perceived to be frivolous lawsuits that included the auditors as defendants primarily because the plaintiffs counted on out-of-court settlement by the auditors who had "deep pockets"; auditors also carry large amounts of professional liability insurance for such matters. The senior partners in the large firms argued that SEC Rule 10-b permits class action claims against companies and auditors where share prices have fallen. Because there is no provision in U.S. law for recovery of costs by successful defendants, auditors felt compelled to settle even meritless legal claims in order to avoid high costs of litigation. Prior to enactment of the PSLRA in 1995, the average claim in 1991 was $85 million; the average settlement was $2.6 million, with legal costs of $3.5 million. The audit firms claimed that legal costs represented 9 percent of their revenues in 1991.[86]

The PSLRA changes the legal liability standard of auditors from joint and several liability to proportionate liability. The Act adopts proportionate liability for all unknowing securities violations under the Exchange Act. (It adopts the same rule for non-officer directors under Section 11 of the Securities Act.) This provision is particularly important for underwriters, venture capital firms, outside directors, accounting firms, and others pulled into securities cases as deep-pocketed defendants. Plaintiffs will no longer have the hammer of joint and several liability to coerce peripheral defendants into settlements because the risk to those defendants of defending the action is unacceptable and they fear being charged with the entire responsibility for the fraud rather than only their share of it. Only those whom the trier of fact finds to have committed "knowing" securities fraud—that is, had actual knowledge that (1) a statement was false and/or that an omission led to a misleading statement, and (2) investors were reasonably likely to rely on the misrepresentation or omission—will suffer joint and several liability.

# Sarbanes Oxley (SOX) Legal Liabilities

Some of the most important provisions of SOX are aimed at increasing the responsibility of corporate officers and directors for the reliability of their company's financial statements. Section 302 requires the certification of financial statements by the CEO and CFO. Section 906 addresses criminal penalties for certifying a misleading or fraudulent financial report. These penalties can be upward of $5 million in fines and 20 years in prison. As for the auditors, Section 802 stipulates that audit firms must retain their audit documentation for a period of five years, while the SEC's final ruling on this section extended the period to seven years. Failure to retain audit documentation can result in fines and imprisonment for up to 10 years.[87] SOX makes it a felony to destroy or create documents to impede or obstruct a federal investigation. Obstruction of justice charges were brought against Andersen in its audit of Enron, and the charge itself led to a parade of clients abandoning the firm, and ultimately to its demise.

We have already addressed four important provisions of SOX, including Section 201 restricting certain nonaudit services for audit clients (Chapter 4); Section 302 requiring the certification of a company's financial statements by the CEO and CFO (Chapter 4); Section 404 and the related PCAOB *Auditing Standard No. 5* on conducting an audit of internal controls along with the audit of financial statements (Chapter 5); and Section 806 on whistleblowing provisions under SOX (Chapter 3). We now review legal liability issues related to false certifications under Section 302.

## Section 302. *Corporate Responsibility for Financial Reports*

Section 302 requires the certification of periodic reports filed with the SEC by the CEO and CFO of public companies. The certification states that "based on the officer's knowledge, the report does not contain any untrue statement of a material fact or omit to state a material fact necessary in order to make the statements, in light of the circumstances under which such statements were made, not misleading." The HealthSouth fraud was the first case where the SEC brought action against company officers for a false certification.

The following is a summary of key provisions:

- The signing officers have reviewed the report.
- The report does not contain any material untrue statements or material omission or be considered misleading.
- The financial statements and related information fairly present the financial condition and the results in all material respects.
- The signing officers are responsible for internal controls and have evaluated these internal controls within the previous ninety days and have reported on their findings.
- A list of all deficiencies in the internal controls and information on any fraud that involves employees who are involved with internal activities has been created.
- Any significant changes in internal controls or related factors that could have a negative impact on the internal controls have been made.

## Section 302. *Liability in Private Civil Actions*

The first reported case dealing with 302 certifications was *Higginbotham v. Baxter Int'l.,* in 2005. The plaintiffs argued that the 302 certifications concerning the adequacy of the company's internal controls were false, and accordingly, the court could infer that Section 10(b)'s scienter requirement was met as to the individuals signing those certifications. The *Higginbotham* court rejected this argument because plaintiffs provided "no specific allegations as to what the deficiencies in the controls were, nor [did they provide] any specific allegations as to [the certifying executives'] awareness of those deficiencies."[88] The ruling does not mean that a false statement with regard to internal controls is not an actionable offense. Instead, the conclusion to be drawn is that claims of scienter require more than just an assertion; specific proof of such knowledge must exist.

The next such case was *In re Lattice Semiconductor Corp.* In *Lattice Semiconductor,* plaintiffs alleged a series of accounting errors that resulted in materially misstated financial statements. In this case, plaintiffs argued that false 302 certifications raised a strong inference that the CEO and CFO were, at a minimum, deliberately reckless, thereby satisfying Section 10(b)'s scienter requirement. Defendants responded by arguing that if "these certifications raised a strong inference of *scienter,* every corporate officer who signed a certification for a Form 10-Q or 10-K filing that was later found to be incorrect would be subject to a securities fraud action."[89]

The *Lattice Semiconductor* court sided with plaintiffs, holding that the 302 certifications in that case did, in fact, give rise to an inference of scienter "because they provide evidence either that defendants knew about the improper journal entries and unreported sales credits that led to the over-reporting of revenues (because of the internal controls they said existed) or, alternatively, knew that the controls they attested to were inadequate."

Soon after *Lattice Semiconductor,* the court in *In re WatchGuard Secs. Litig.* considered allegedly false 302 certifications in the context of a private Section 10(b) action. In *WatchGuard,* plaintiffs alleged that the defendant company had made material misstatements about interest expenses and revenue recognition in its financial statements. Plaintiffs also contended that WatchGuard's quarterly 302 certifications were themselves actionable misstatements on which they could base a Section 10(b) and Rule 10b-5 claim. Plaintiffs also argued that the certifications demonstrated scienter under the "deliberate recklessness" standard because the certifying individual defendants either knew about WatchGuard's revenue recognition problems or were "deliberately reckless in not obtaining the information or conducting the investigations described in their certifications prior to publishing the false financial statements."[90]

The *WatchGuard* court rejected plaintiffs' arguments, holding that the individual defendants' 302 certifications were, by themselves, inadequate to support a strong inference of scienter. In so holding, the court stressed that the failure of plaintiffs to plead scienter adequately is what doomed their 302 argument. "In a case like this one, however, where the court finds no strong inference that any defendant was at least deliberately reckless in issuing corporate earnings statements, the court has no basis for a strong inference that the Sarbanes-Oxley certifications were culpably false."[91]

It is safe to say the courts are still finding their way with respect to legal liability issues and alleged violations of SOX under Section 302. However, based upon the reported private securities cases thus far, it appears that that Section 302 certifications that turn out to be inaccurate do not give rise to independent private claims under the securities laws, nor do they appear to alter the fundamental standards that are applied in Section 10(b) actions. Rather, they are viewed by courts in the overall context of a case and bear on civil liability only when other pleaded facts create a strong inference of scienter against the 302 certifier.[92]

### Section 302. *Liability in Civil and Criminal Government Actions*

The first notable prosecution for filing a false certification was based upon Section 302 and the related Section 906. Federal prosecutors in the HealthSouth case obtained an indictment of Richard Scrushy for, among other things, filing false 302/906 certifications. In this case, which was discussed in Chapter 4, Scrushy was charged based upon two statutes: 18 U.S.C. § 1001(2) (making materially false statement to government) and 18 U.S.C. § 1350(c)(2) (criminal liability under SOX for 906 certification).[93] Although the prosecutors did not convince the jury to convict Scrushy, additional cases have followed where the results were better.

With respect to 302 certifications, both the SEC and the DOJ have used such certifications as a basis for civil and criminal liability for financial fraud under Section 906 ($5 million in fines and 20 years in prison). On June 7, 2006, the SEC announced the filing of a settled civil injunctive action against Joseph P. Micatrotto, Sr., the former CEO of Buca, Inc. Two weeks later, the U.S. Attorney's Office for the District of Minnesota announced that it had reached a plea agreement with Micatrotto in which he agreed to plead guilty to certain felonies, including, among other things, filing a false 302 certification. The *Micatrotto* case provides some clues as to potential theories of administrative and criminal liability stemming from the filing of false 302 certifications.[94]

According to the SEC complaint and the indictment by the U.S. Attorney, Buca's 10-K reports and proxy statements which were incorporated by reference into Buca's 10-Ks, for several years materially understated Micatrotto's annual compensation and several related-party transactions which benefited Micatrotto. Micatrotto, among other things, used company funds to purchase and renovate a villa in Italy that was titled in the name of himself and his wife, and he obtained company reimbursement for his personal and business expenses, sometimes receiving reimbursement for the same expense multiple times.

The basis of the SEC complaint alleged that Micatrotto knew that the 10-K reports that he certified contained untrue statements of material fact or material omissions, but not that those untrue statements caused Buca's financial statements to no longer fairly present the financial condition of the company.

The SEC's allegations are based on inadequate internal controls, rather than misstatements in the financial statements of the company. Nevertheless, both the SEC and the U.S. Attorney chose to seek severe penalties against Micatrotto for knowingly certifying untrue statements in Buca's 10-Ks. In this settled matter, Micatrotto consented to a fine, an order of disgorgement, and a permanent ban on being a director and officer of a public company.

Looking at the emerging case law, it appears that 302 certifications do not substantially change the potential liabilities of certifying CEOs and CFOs, with two important exceptions. The first exception is that CEOs and CFOs are now required to review and evaluate internal controls for financial reporting and disclosure controls. Thus, a certifier who can prove a thorough evaluation done in good faith is more likely to avoid being charged with filing a false 302 certification than a certifier who cannot do so. The second exception is that a 302 certification of *immaterial* misstatements or omissions may subject a certifier to liability to the extent that they are part of a larger fraudulent scheme. In such a case, a false 302 certification may constitute evidence supporting charges of criminal securities fraud or criminal mail or wire fraud.[95]

### Perspective on Accomplishments of SOX

SOX is sometimes faulted for not preventing the financial crisis and the great recession from which the U.S. economy is still recovering. But defenders argue that it wasn't designed to do more than ensure that accounting rules were followed.

"If you've got employees who are stealing stuff out the back door of the warehouse, Sarbanes-Oxley would tell you whether you have inventory controls in place, not whether the door is locked," according to Gary Kabureck, vice president and chief accounting officer (CAO) at Xerox Corp.

However, Sherron Watkins, the whistleblower at Enron, questions why, for example, charges weren't brought under SOX against top executives at the banks, mortgage lenders, and Wall Street firms playing fast and loose with the law. "Dick Fuld of Lehman Brothers Holdings Inc. was signing off on the financial statements," she notes. "I fear that the DOJ was politicized."

One consolation, says Lynn Turner, former chief accountant for the SEC, is that SOX no doubt mitigated the force of the financial crisis, which could have been worse. "We didn't see the huge rash of fraudulent reporting like we saw in the 1996–2002 time period," he says. "So that would tell you, 'Yes, the legislation did accomplish its goal.' "

Les Brorsen, EY's vice-chair for corporate policy, sees the creation of the PCAOB to police the auditing profession—coupled with corporate governance rules that put a public company's board-level audit committee, rather than company management, in charge of the auditing process—as "the top two fundamental changes" brought about by the act. He believes improved corporate governance is one of the hallmarks of the legislation.[96]

Looking at the potential for SOX to have a permanent effect on reducing instances of financial fraud, our concern is that the SEC has had an arsenal of laws at its disposal for many years, and that does not seem to have made a great deal of difference with respect to periodic outbreaks of financial fraud "flu." Perhaps Section 302 enforcement will stem the tide of financial fraud in the future. We believe that the jury is still out on that one.

As described in Chapter 4, the history of accounting frauds is as old as the commission's tenure. The "bottom line" may be that the government will not be successful in its effort to control fraud because you cannot legislate ethics. This is no surprise, because being ethical comes from one's desire to do the right thing and courage to carry out an ethical action in the face of pressure and resistance from one's superiors. Still, a set of civil and criminal deterrents is an important part of a healthy securities regulatory system.

# Other Laws Affecting Accountants and Auditors

In addition to the PSLRA and SOX, two other laws have influenced audit procedures, legal liability, and ethics requirements under the due care principle. These include the Foreign Corrupt Practices Act and the U.S. Federal Sentencing Guidelines.

## Foreign Corrupt Practices Act (FCPA)

The Foreign Corrupt Practices Act (FCPA) establishes standards for the acceptability of payments made by U.S. multinational entities or their agent to foreign government officials. The act was motivated when, during the period of 1960 to 1977, the SEC cited 527 companies for bribes and other dubious payments that were made to win foreign contracts. Lockheed Corporation was one of the companies caught in this scandal. It was determined that Lockheed had made about $55 million in illegal payments to foreign governments and officials. One such payment, $1.7 million to Japanese premier Kukuei Tanaka, led to his resignation in disgrace in 1974.

The FCPA makes it a crime to offer or provide payments to officials of foreign governments, political candidates, or political parties for the purpose of obtaining or retaining business. It applies to all U.S. corporations, whether they are publicly or privately held, and to foreign companies filing with the SEC. The DOJ is responsible for all criminal enforcement and for civil enforcement of the antibribery provisions with respect to domestic entities and foreign companies and nationals. The SEC is responsible for civil enforcement of the antibribery provisions with respect to registrants.

Under the FCPA, a corporation that violates the law can be fined up to $1 million, while its officers who directly participated in violations of the act or had "reason to know" of such violations can be fined up to $10,000, imprisoned for up to five years, or both. The act also prohibits corporations from indemnifying fines imposed on directors, officers, employees, or agents. FCPA does not prohibit "grease payments" (i.e., *permissible facilitating payments*) to foreign government employees whose duties are primarily ministerial or clerical because such payments are sometimes required to persuade recipients to perform their normal duties.[97]

As a result of the criticisms of the antibribery provisions of the 1977 FCPA, Congress amended the act as part of the Omnibus Trade and Competitiveness Act of 1988 to clarify when a payment is prohibited, as follows:[98]

1. A payment is defined as illegal if it is intended to influence a foreign official to act in a way that is incompatible with the official's legal duty.
2. The "reason to know" standard is replaced by a "knowing" standard, so that criminal liability for illegal payments to third parties applies to individuals who "knowingly" engage in or tolerate illegal payments under the act.
3. The definition of "grease" payments is expanded to include payments to any foreign official that facilitates or expedites securing the performance of a routine governmental action.
4. Examples of acceptable payments include (1) obtaining permits, licenses, and the official documents to qualify a person to do business in a foreign country; (2) processing governmental papers, such as visas or work orders; (3) providing police protection, mail pickup, and delivery, or scheduling inspections associated with contract performance or inspections related to the transit of goods across country; (4) providing telephone service, power, and water, unloading and loading cargo, or protecting perishable product or commodities from deterioration; and (5) performing actions of a similar nature.

Two affirmative defenses for those accused of violating the act are that the payment is lawful "under the written laws" of the foreign country, and that the payment can be made for "reasonable and bona fide expenditures." These include lodging expenses incurred by or for a foreign official to promote products or services or execute the performance of a contract.

Individuals can be prosecuted under the 1988 amendment even if the company for which they work is *not* guilty. Penalties for violations were raised to $2 million for entities and $100,000 for individuals. The maximum term of imprisonment is kept at five years. A new $10,000 civil penalty was enacted.

## SEC Charges Pfizer with FCPA Violations

The health-care industry has been under increased SEC and DOJ scrutiny lately for potential FCPA violations. What has been described as an "industry sweep" has focused primarily on medical device and pharmaceutical companies. Exhibit 6.12 summarizes the SEC and DOJ settlement with Pfizer for violations of the FCPA on August 7, 2012.

The enforcement action against Pfizer arose in part out of improper payments, including hospitality and travel expenses, made to doctors and health-care professionals employed by government-controlled or owned health-care providers in countries such as Bulgaria, Croatia, Kazakhstan, Italy, China, Serbia, and Russia.

**EXHIBIT 6.12**

**The SEC Case Against Pfizer**

A recent allegation by the SEC against Pfizer Inc. illustrates the vast global nature of foreign bribery. On August 7, 2012, the SEC charged Pfizer Inc. with violating the FCPA when its subsidiaries bribed doctors and other health-care professionals employed by foreign governments in order to win business.[99]

The SEC alleged that employees and agents of Pfizer's subsidiaries in Bulgaria, China, Croatia, Czech Republic, Italy, Kazakhstan, Russia, and Serbia made improper payments to foreign officials to obtain regulatory and formulary approvals, sales, and increased prescriptions for the company's pharmaceutical products. They tried to conceal the bribery by improperly recording the transactions in accounting records as legitimate expenses for promotional activities, marketing, training, travel and entertainment, clinical trials, freight, conferences, and advertising.

The SEC separately charged another pharmaceutical company that Pfizer acquired a few years ago—Wyeth LLC—with its own FCPA violations. Pfizer and Wyeth agreed to separate settlements in which they will pay more than $45 million combined to settle their respective charges. In a parallel action, the DOJ announced that Pfizer H.C.P. Corporation, an indirectly wholly-owned subsidiary of Pfizer, agreed to pay a $15 million penalty to resolve its investigation of FCPA violations.

"Pfizer subsidiaries in several countries had bribery so entwined in their sales culture that they offered points and bonus programs to improperly reward foreign officials who proved to be their best customers," said Kara Brockmeyer, chief of the SEC Enforcement Division's FCPA Unit. "These charges illustrate the pitfalls that exist for companies that fail to appropriately monitor potential risks in their global operations."

According to the SEC's complaint against Pfizer filed in U.S. District Court for the District of Columbia, the misconduct dated back as far as 2001. Employees of Pfizer's subsidiaries authorized and made cash payments and provided other incentives to bribe government doctors to use Pfizer products. In China, for example, Pfizer employees invited "high-prescribing doctors" in the Chinese government to clublike meetings that included extensive recreational and entertainment activities to reward doctors' past product sales or prescriptions. Pfizer China also created various "point programs," under which government doctors could accumulate points based on the number of Pfizer prescriptions that they wrote. The points were redeemed for various gifts ranging from medical books to cell phones, tea sets, and reading glasses. In Croatia, Pfizer employees created a "bonus program" for Croatian doctors who were employed in senior positions in Croatian government health-care institutions. Once a doctor agreed to use Pfizer products, a percentage of the value purchased by a doctor's institution would be funneled back to the doctor in the form of cash, international travel, or free products.

According to the SEC's complaint, Pfizer made an initial voluntary disclosure of misconduct by its subsidiaries to the SEC and DOJ in October 2004 and fully cooperated with SEC investigators. Pfizer took extensive remedial actions, such as undertaking a comprehensive worldwide review of its compliance program.

The SEC further alleged that Wyeth subsidiaries engaged in FCPA violations primarily before but also after the company's acquisition by Pfizer in late 2009. Starting at least in 2005, subsidiaries marketing Wyeth nutritional products in China, Indonesia, and Pakistan bribed government doctors to recommend their products to patients by making cash payments, or in some cases, providing BlackBerrys and cell phones or travel incentives. They often used fictitious invoices to conceal the true nature of the payments. In Saudi Arabia, Wyeth's subsidiary made an improper cash payment to a customs official to secure the release of a shipment of promotional items used for marketing purposes. The promotional items were held in port because Wyeth Saudi Arabia had failed to secure a required Saudi Arabian Standards Organization Certificate of Conformity. (This could have been deemed a facilitating payment under FCPA.)

Following Pfizer's acquisition of Wyeth, Pfizer undertook a risk-based FCPA due diligence review of Wyeth's global operations and voluntarily reported the findings to the SEC staff. Pfizer diligently and promptly integrated Wyeth's legacy operations into its compliance program and cooperated fully with SEC investigators.

Pfizer consented to the entry of a final judgment ordering it to pay disgorgement of $16,032,676 in net profits, as well as prejudgment interest of $10,307,268, for a total of $26,339,944. Wyeth also is required to report to the SEC on the status of its remediation and implementation of compliance measures over a two-year period, and is permanently enjoined from further violations of Sections 13(b)(2)(A) and 13(b)(2)(B) of the Securities Exchange Act of 1934.

Importantly, Pfizer had a preexisting compliance program in place, it self-reported potential violations, and it undertook extensive remedial efforts to assess and investigate the company's relationships with doctors and employees of government-owned hospitals and health-care providers. Nonetheless, the DOJ's Deferred Prosecution Agreement with Pfizer imposed specific and detailed requirements to bolster Pfizer's compliance programs.

For example, Pfizer is required to improve its existing compliance procedures to prevent potential FCPA violations, such as by conducting biannual training of employees and executives, as well as triennial training of third parties whose activities may bring them under the reach of the FCPA. Similarly, Pfizer is required to continue to maintain controls over its compliance policies, such as those addressing gift-giving and hospitality expenditures to government officials and to monitor compliance with these policies closely. Pfizer is also required to conduct periodic testing of compliance efforts and institute due diligence procedures for acquisition targets and third parties.

The FCPA violations at Pfizer clearly illustrate the importance of an effective system of internal controls, strong corporate governance, and a tone at the top that filters throughout the organization and strengthens compliance with regulations and ethical behavior. FCPA compliance is important for accountants and auditors who are charged with disclosing illegal acts and evaluating internal controls.

### *Internal Accounting Control Requirements*

The FCPA requires all SEC registrants to maintain internal accounting controls to ensure that all transactions are authorized by management and recorded properly. The FCPA requires issuers to maintain adequate books and records and makes it unlawful to offer, promise, or pay anything of value to a foreign government official (including employees of state-controlled organizations) in order to obtain an improper business advantage. As discussed in earlier chapters, Section 404 of SOX requires management to prepare a report on its internal controls, and auditors must assess that report and issue their own opinion along with a separate audit opinion or combined opinion (integrated audit).

In recent deferred and nonprosecution agreements, 13 elements repeatedly show up as part of an effective compliance program, including demonstrated support for compliance efforts from the top down; oversight of a compliance program, including a direct reporting line between the monitoring body or individual and the board of directors; the inclusion of third-party business partners in the compliance process; accounting controls; a system where employees can report suspected compliance violations and where employees can receive urgent advice when confronting potential violations in foreign countries; and periodic reviews to evaluate the effectiveness of a compliance program.

A recent white paper, entitled "Staying out of the Headlines: Strategies to Combat Corruption Risk" and jointly produced by the consulting firm of Protiviti and the law firm of Covington and Burling, reviewed 286 FCPA cases and analyzed the internal control weaknesses that led to FCPA enforcement actions. From this review, the authors derived a top five list of control weaknesses.[100]

### *1. Inadequate Contract Pricing Review*

The authors found that in 110 cases they reviewed, the internal controls were insufficient to confirm whether contract pricing was artificially inflated or otherwise altered. This enhanced the risk that a foreign business representative could inflate the price of goods and either keep the spread or use it to bribe a foreign governmental official. The types of internal controls weaknesses noted by the authors included:

- Inflated contract prices were used to generate and conceal kickbacks.
- Commissions were disguised as legitimate business expenses.
- Unwarranted additional fees were added to contract prices.

### 2. Inadequate Due Diligence and Verification of Foreign Business Representative

It is well known that companies are responsible for the actions of their business representatives and that this is a large source of FCPA exposure. Based upon their review, the authors found several examples of weaknesses in internal controls leading to FCPA enforcement actions, including:

- Monthly payments made to foreign business representatives where no written contract was in place
- Contracts with foreign business representatives with prior histories of improper payments
- Lack of vigorous due diligence based upon a valid risk analysis

### 3. Ineffective Accounts Payable Payment and Review

This area involves the review and appropriate authorization of funds prior to disbursement. The authors noted that vendor setup and management procedures were not well documented in the cases they reviewed, and that company processes across wide geographic areas may not have the appropriate "checks and balances." The authors found the following internal control weaknesses in this area:

- Inappropriate payments made to agents under the guise of commissions, fees, or legal services
- Payments for professional services where no backup was provided by the vendor
- Services were paid under contracts where such services were not addressed

### 4. Ineffective Financial Account Reconciliation and Review

The books and records component of the FCPA, together with the accounting control provisions, mandate that documentation on transactions must not only record the transaction, but also adequately describe it to alert the reviewer to possible violations. In their analysis, the authors found several examples of ineffectual financial account reconciliation and review, which included:

- Inflated revenues through improper schemes
- Recording of false entries by a subsidiary that was rolled up to a parent
- False invoices being paid
- Improper recording of payments in various ledger accounts
- Lack of appropriate documentation for disbursements

### 5. Ineffective Commission Payment Review and Authority

The authors noted instances of the lack of procedures to verify the payments of commissions to foreign business partners. These failures led to instances of bribery of a foreign governmental official by the foreign business partner. In their review, the authors noted some of the following internal control weaknesses, which led to a high number of enforcement cases in this area:

- Mission creep by foreign business partners, in that the duties they carried out were not assigned within or by the contract
- Misleading information presented to company internal auditors regarding the amount of commissions paid by foreign business partners
- Commission payments being inflated so that foreign business partners could provide kickbacks to foreign government officials

### FCPA Violations and Tyco

Our friends at Tyco have been at it again. Recall that in Chapter 5, we described the misappropriation of assets by former CEO Dennis Kozlowski. Tyco seems to be a recidivist offender. In 2006, the SEC charged the company with using various improper accounting practices and a scheme involving transactions with no economic substance to overstate its reported financial results by at least $1 billion. This was on top of the misappropriation case against Kozlowski. The complaint also alleged that Tyco violated the antibribery provisions of the FCPA when employees or agents of its Earth Tech Brasil Ltda. subsidiary made payments to Brazilian officials for the purpose of obtaining or retaining business for Tyco. Between 1996 and 2002, as a result of these various practices, Tyco made false and misleading statements or omissions in its filings with the commission and its public statements to investors and analysts.[101]

On September 24, 2012, the SEC charged Tyco in another FCPA case that alleges schemes typically involving illegal payments that were falsely recorded as "commissions" in Tyco's books and records, when they were in fact bribes to pay off government customers. Tyco's benefit as a result of these illicit payments was more than $4.6 million. The Tyco FCPA case is described in greater detail in Exhibit 6.13.

### FCPA and Whistleblowing

Lawsuits claiming retaliatory discharge for internally reporting FCPA violations are a particularly likely avenue for follow-up legislation, especially in light of the Dodd-Frank's whistleblower provisions. The SEC's Office of the Whistleblower published its first list of enforcement actions that might be eligible for whistleblower rewards in November 2011, and the list included FCPA-related cases. In the typical case, a discharged employee sues the company for wrongful discharge, claiming that he was fired in retaliation for reporting unlawful conduct that violated the FCPA.

According to a 2012 study by the international law firm of Shearman & Sterling LLP, over $260 million in FCPA-violation penalties were paid to the U.S. government. However, the number of cases were down from 20 in 2010 and 16 in 2011 to just 12 in 2012.[103] This does not mean there are fewer instances of FCPA violations. Instead, the decline reflects the increasing complexity of such cases and possible whistleblower lawsuits that may follow if a complaining employee is fired or otherwise retaliated against.

## Federal Sentencing Guidelines for Organizations

In response to the savings and loan crises of the later 1980s and early 1990s and to the general perception that corporate crime is too often inadequately punished, the U.S. Sentencing Commission adopted the 1991 Federal Sentencing Guidelines for Organizations (FSGFO). These guidelines prescribe formulas for levying fines and probation on organizations.[104]

One of the most important parts of the FSGFO from the standpoint of the corporation and SOX is Section 8B2.1, which reduces the prescribed punishment if the company has "an effective ethics and compliance program." Section 8B2.1 sets minimal criteria for organizations to qualify for the reduction:

- The organization shall establish standards and procedures to prevent and detect criminal conduct.
- The organization must have an adequately organized and funded ethics and compliance program with a knowledgeable high-level person in charge.

**EXHIBIT 6.13**
SEC Charges Tyco
for Illicit Payments
to Foreign Officials

On September 24, 2012, the SEC charged Tyco in an FCPA case that alleges schemes that typically involved payments of fake "commissions" or the use of third-party agents to funnel money improperly to obtain lucrative contracts. Overall, Tyco reaped illicit benefits amounting to more than $10.5 million as a result of their paying to win business.[102]

Tyco agreed to pay more than $26 million to settle the SEC's charges and resolve a criminal matter with the DOJ. "Tyco's subsidiaries operating in Asia and the Middle East saw illicit payment schemes as a typical way of doing business in some countries, and the company illicitly reaped substantial financial benefits as a result," said Scott W. Friestad, associate director of the SEC's Division of Enforcement.

The SEC alleges that Tyco subsidiaries operated 12 different illicit payment schemes around the world starting before 2006 and continuing until 2009. The most profitable scheme occurred in Germany, where agents of a Tyco subsidiary paid third parties to secure contracts or avoid penalties or fines in several countries. These payments were falsely recorded as "commissions" in Tyco's books and records, when they were actually bribes to pay off government customers. Tyco's benefit as a result of these illicit payments was more than $4.6 million.

According to the SEC's complaint, Tyco's subsidiary in China signed a contract with the Chinese Ministry of Public Security for $770,000 but reportedly paid approximately $3,700 to the "site project team" of a state-owned corporation so it could obtain that contract. This amount was improperly recorded as a commission. Tyco's subsidiary in France recorded payments to individuals from 2005 to 2009 for "business introduction services." However, one of the individuals receiving payments was a security officer at a government-owned mining company in Mauritania, and many of the earlier payments were deposited in the official's personal bank account in France. In Thailand, Tyco's subsidiary had a contract to install a closed-circuit TV (CCTV) system in the Thai Parliament House in 2006 and paid more than $50,000 to a Thai entity that acted as a consultant. The invoice for the payment refers to "renovation work," but Tyco is unable to ascertain what work was actually done, if any.

The SEC alleges that another scheme occurred in Turkey, where Tyco's subsidiary retained a New York City–based sales agent who made illicit payments involving the sale of microwave equipment in September 2006 to an entity controlled by the Turkish government. Employees at Tyco's subsidiary were well aware that the agent was paying foreign government customers to obtain orders. One internal e-mail stated, "Hell, everyone knows you have to bribe somebody to do business in Turkey. Nevertheless, I'll play it dumb if [the sales agent] should call." The benefit obtained by Tyco as a result of the September 2006 deal was $44,513.

The SEC's complaint alleges that Tyco's books and records were misstated as a result of the misconduct, and Tyco failed to devise and maintain internal controls sufficient to detect the violations. The complaint also alleges that the payments by the sales agent to Turkish government officials violated the antibribery provisions of the FCPA.

In arriving at the settlement, the commission considered Tyco's extensive efforts to identify and remediate its wrongdoing. Tyco conducted a global review and internal investigation for potential FCPA violations and voluntarily disclosed its findings to the SEC, while implementing significant, broad-spectrum remedial measures. Tyco consented to a proposed final judgment that orders the company to pay $10,564,992 in disgorgement and $2,566,517 in prejudgment interest. Tyco also agreed to be permanently enjoined from violating Section 13(b)(2)(A), Section 13(b)(2)(B), and Section 30A(a) of the Securities Exchange Act of 1934.

- The organization must exercise due diligence to ensure that those with substantial authority in the organization have not engaged in illegal activities or other conduct inconsistent with an effective compliance and ethics program.
- The organization must have an effective training program in place to communicate the organization's ethics and compliance program to all employees.
- The organization must have a monitoring and auditing system in place that includes consistent disciplinary measures and ensures compliance with its ethics and compliance programs.
- The organization must follow up on criminal conduct to prevent it from recurring. Preventative steps must include changing the ethics and compliance programs as needed.

Organizations can be denied penalty reductions if they fail to satisfy any one of the minimal criteria. They can also be denied for a delay in reporting offenses to authorities or if any high-level officials participate in, condone, or willfully ignore offenses.

The most important point about the FSGFO compliance measures is that they establish a foundation for an organization to build an ethical culture. An ethical culture starts with top management and permeates every aspect of the organization. All the stakeholders have to enjoy the highest ethical climate—employees, customers, suppliers, the community, the environment, and, of course, the lenders and shareholders.

A code of conduct is a part of ethical behavior, but it helps to have the rules in writing. A written code of ethics is important; however, Enron had the most elegant code of ethics ever. A code is no better than the paper it is written on. To have an effective code, top management must set the proper tone at the top, develop a compliance system that is enforced, and walk the talk of ethics.

While an ethical business model is its own reward, an organization's standing under SOX and FSGFO benefits as well. Most important is the simple fact that businesses that choose an ethical business model are more profitable. Since 2007, Ethisphere has published an annual list of the World's Most Ethical Companies within each industry. They have also tracked the performance of the public companies that have made their list against the performance of the S&P 500. Ethisphere has found that companies that take ethics seriously enough to make their list outperform the S&P 500 with better returns.[105]

The moral here is fairly simple: When a company's ethical compass is pointing true north, everything else falls into line, and legal liability issues are controlled. This isn't to say that companies with great ethics don't fail. But it does seem to indicate that companies without good ethics are far more likely to fail because they fail to nurture an environment of honesty, trustworthiness, responsibility, accountability, and integrity.

## Concluding Thoughts

The primary sources of CPA liability under common law are breach of contract, negligence—ordinary and gross—and fraud. Statutory liability exists under the Securities Act of 1933 and the Securities Exchange Act of 1934. Under common law, a client must prove that the CPA breached a duty of care and it was the proximate cause of losses. Third-party liability can occur when proof exists that losses resulted from the CPA's performance and that the CPA breached a duty of due professional care.

Auditor ethical and legal obligations require adherence to the standards discussed in Chapters 4–6. Auditors are expected to report illegal acts by clients to the SEC if the client fails to report them. We believe auditors should use this leverage in discussions with clients about fraud and illegal acts.

To prevent litigation, the auditor should carefully assess the risk of errors and irregularities including fraud by reviewing internal controls and whether they help to prevent or detect material misstatements in the financial statements. Auditors should exercise extreme care in audits of clients that have a high degree of business risk. Professional skepticism is essential to ferret out instances of fraud.

At the end of the day, it is the ethical standards, professionalism, and practices embedded in the culture of individual auditor's and audit firms that will protect them when difficult situations arise, conflicts exist with management over an accounting or financial reporting issue, or management just wants to test the waters and see how far they can push the envelope. The public interest requires that auditors act with integrity and in accordance with the profession's ethical standards. When auditors fall short in this regard, lawsuits that are filed by clients and third parties alleging fraud are more likely to be successful against those auditors and legal liabilities can include steep financial penalties, suspension from practice, and even jail time for the offenses.

**Discussion Questions**

1. Distinguish between common-law liability and statutory liability for auditors. What is the basis for the difference in liability?

2. Explain the difference between the ethical responsibilities of auditors and auditor legal obligations.

3. Is there a conceptual difference between an error and negligence from a reasonable care perspective? Give examples of each in your response.

4. Distinguish between the legal concepts of actually foreseen third-party users and reasonably foreseeable third-party users. How does each concept establish a basis for an auditor's legal liability to third parties?

5. Describe what the law requires with respect to the legal rulings in *Credit Alliance v. Arthur Andersen & Co.* and *Security Pacific Business Credit.* Do you think the ruling establishes a fair basis for an auditor's legal liability to third parties?

6. Explain the legal basis for a cause of action against an auditor. What are the defenses available to the auditor to rebut such charges? How does adherence to the ethical standards of the accounting profession relate to these defenses?

7. A subsequent event is one that occurs after the date of the financial statements (i.e., December 31, 2013) but prior to the auditor having dated (or possibly issued) the audit report (i.e., March 15, 2014). One type of subsequent event is where additional evidence becomes available before the statements have been issued that sheds light on certain estimates previously made in the statements. A good example is additional evidence about the collectibility of a receivable that relates to its valuation in the December 31, 2013, financial statements but is not uncovered until January 31, 2014. Why is it important from an auditing perspective that an auditor be required to adjust the financial statement amounts for some material subsequent events? If an auditor fails to live up to this standard, what is the potential liability exposure for the auditor?

8. What are the legal requirements for a third party to sue an auditor under Section 10 and Rule 10b-5 of the Securities Exchange Act of 1934? How do these requirements relate to the *Hochfelder* decision?

9. Valley View Manufacturing Inc., sought a $500,000 loan from First National Bank. National insisted that audited financial statements be submitted before it would extend credit. Valley View agreed to this and also agreed to pay the audit fee. An audit was performed by an independent CPA who submitted her report to Valley View to be used solely for the purpose of negotiating a loan from National. National, upon reviewing the audited financial statements decided in good faith not to extend the credit desired. Certain ratios which as a matter of policy were used by National in reaching its decision, were deemed too low. Valley View used copies of the audited financial statements to obtain credit elsewhere. It was subsequently learned that the CPA, despite the exercise of reasonable care, had failed to discover a sophisticated embezzlement scheme by Valley View's chief accountant. Under these circumstances, what liability might the CPA have?

10. Nixon and Co., CPAs, issued an unmodified opinion on the 2013 financial statements of Madison Corp. These financial statements were included in Madison's annual report and Form 10-K filed with the SEC. Nixon did not detect material misstatements in the financial statements as a result of negligence in the performance of the audit. Based upon the financial statements, Harry purchased stock in Madison. Shortly thereafter, Madison became insolvent, causing the price of the stock to decline drastically. Harry has commenced legal action against Nixon for damages based upon Section 10(b) and Rule 10b-5 of the Securities Exchange Act of 1934. What would be Nixon's best defense to such an action? Explain.

11. Distinguish between legal and illegal insider trading. Evaluate the ethics of the practice.

12. The legal concept of *in pari delicto* holds that in a "case of equal or mutual fault [in a financial fraud] the position of the defending party [auditor] is the stronger one." The predicate for this defense is imputation: holding the corporation responsible for the acts of its officers. The leading case authority is *Cenco Inc. v Seidman & Seidman,* a 1982 case where the court permitted an audi-

tor to invoke the *in pari delicto* doctrine to defeat a claim against it for failing to detect fraud by the management of an audit client. From an ethical perspective, do you think auditors should be able to escape legal liability for failing to uncover fraud under the doctrine?[106]

13. According to a 2012 study by *Fortune* magazine, 86.5 percent of *Fortune* 100 companies have adopted clawback provisions that allow them to recover cash bonuses or stock from errant executives.[107] Apparently, such provisions now have become a widely accepted corporate governance practice. What practice(s) typically trigger clawback actions by the SEC? Do you think trying to enforce contested clawbacks are in shareholders' best interests? Why or why not?

14. Some auditors claim that increased exposure under Section 404 of SOX creates a litigation environment that is unfairly risky for auditors. Do you think that the inability of auditors to detect a financial statement misstatement due to internal control fraud in a timely manner should expose auditors to litigation? Why or why not?

15. Under Dodd-Frank, whistleblowers can obtain a monetary award if a violation of securities laws involves potential wrongdoing by an accountant's auditing firm, including—but not limited to—failing to comply with the requirements of Section 10A of the Exchange Act of 1934. As a future member of the accounting profession, do you believe you would bring forth such an allegation and, if so, under what circumstances. If you do not believe you would do so, explain why not.

16. The following quotation was in the court ruling in the case of the *Public*[108] *Employees' Retirement Association of Colorado v. Deloitte & Touche, LLP*:

   > It is not an accountant's fault if its client actively conspires with others in order to deprive the accountant of accurate information about the client's finances. It would be wrong and counter to the purposes of the Private Securities Litigation Reform Act to find an accountant liable in such an instance.

   a. Evaluate this statement from the perspective of the scienter requirements discussed in the text.

   b. Explain the implications of the PSLRA for audit responsibilities and auditor legal liability.

17. On December 31, 2009, the SEC sued Alameda, California–based telecommunications company UTStarcom, Inc., with violations of the FCPA for authorizing millions of dollars in unlawful payments by its wholly owned Chinese subsidiary to foreign government officials in Asia. UTStarcom agreed to settle the SEC's charges and pay a $1.5 million fine to the SEC and another $1.5 million to the Department of Justice. One of the items cited as violating the FCPA was a payment of nearly $7 million between 2002 and 2007 for hundreds of overseas trips by employees of Chinese government-controlled telecommunications companies that were customers of UTStarcom, purportedly to provide customer training. In reality, the trips were entirely for sightseeing.[109]

   a. Why would such payments by UTStarcom violate the FCPA?

   b. The FCPA permits a company to assert an affirmative defense against allegations of violating the FCPA if the payments were lawful under the written laws of the foreign country. Do you believe it is ethically appropriate to allow such a defense when illegal payments are made? Why or why not?

18. Given the discussion of the FSGFO in this chapter, comment on the statement that workplaces based on the FSGFO are better places to work.

19. In her article about possible changes to the legal liability of auditors due to the modification of GAAS and the audit report as a result of "The Clarity Project," Nancy Reimer points out that although the goal of the "clarified standards" is to make GAAS easier to read, understand, and apply, the new modified standards establish a higher "standard of care." A failure to meet these modified standards could increase a practitioner's exposure to legal liability.[110] Explain how the auditor's legal liability might increase as a result of changes to the audit report discussed in Chapter 5.

20. Has the accounting profession created a situation in which the auditors' ethical behavior is impaired by their professional obligations? How does the profession's view of such obligations relate to how courts tend to view the legal liability of auditors?

**Endnotes**

1. Available at www.securities.stanford.edu/1039/BSC_01/2009716_r01x_08md1963.pdf.

2. In Re Longtop Financial Technologies Limited Securities Litigation, Civ. 3658, Available at http://newsandinsight.thomsonreuters.com/uploadedFiles/Reuters_Content/2013/04_-_April/longtopclassaction–deloiteopinion.pdf.

3. Herbert W. Snyder, "Client Confidentiality and Fraud: Should Auditors Be Able to Exercise More Ethical Judgment?" *Fraud Magazine,* January/February 2011, pp. 28–30.

4. *Couch v. United States,* 409 U.S. 322, 335 n.1 (1973).

5. Snyder.

6. *SAS 54, Illegal Acts by Clients,* AU Section 317; *SAS 59,* This should be: *The Auditor's Consideration of an Entity's Ability to Continue as a Going Concern SAS 99, Consideration of Fraud in a Financial Statement Audit. (end note) SAS 316. SAS 316 is a section reference in professional standards for SAS 99 so please change delete it*

7. *United States v. Arthur Young,* 465 U.S. 805, www.caselaw.lp.findlaw.com.

8. Snyder.

9. American Institute of CPAs, *Professional Standards Volume II, as of June 1, 2012,* Statement on Auditing Standards No. 99, *Consideration of Fraud in Financial Statements,* (New York: AICPA, 2012), AU Section 316.

10. Dodd-Frank Wall Street Reform and Consumer Protection Act (HR 4173), www.sec.gov/about/laws/wallstreetreform-cpa.pdf.

11. Eileen Z. Taylor and Jordan A. Thomas, "Enhanced Protections for Whistleblowers Under the Dodd-Frank Act," *The CPA Journal,* January 2013, pp. 66–71.

12. E. Norman Veasay, *State-Federal Tension in Corporate Governance and the Professional Responsibilities of Advisors,* 28 J. Corp. L. 441, 447 (2003).

13. Leo L. Strine, Jr., *Derivative Impact? Some Early Reflections on the Corporation Law Implications of the Enron Debacle,* 57 Bus. Law. 1371, 1373 (2002).

14. Strine.

15. *Brehm v. Eisner,* 746 A.2d 244, 254 (Del. 2000).

16. *Caremark International Derivative Legislation, 1996 De. Ch LEXIS 125 (Del. 1996).*

17. Available at www.delawarelitigation.com>ChanceryCourtUpdates.

18. Dodd-Frank Wall Street Reform and Consumer Protection Act (HR 4173),

19. *SEC v. Michael A. Baker and Michael T. Gluk,* Case No. A-12-CA-285-SS, Available at www.newsandinsight.thomsonreuters.com/uploadedFiles/Reuters_Content/2012/11_-_November/secvbaker--mtdopinion.pdf.

20. Sarbanes-Oxley Act of 2002, Pub. L. No. 107-204, §302(a)(5), 116 Stat. 745, 777 (codified at 15 U.S.C. §7241(a)(5) (Supp.II2002)).

21. *See* Kevin Iurato, Comment, *Warning! A Position on the Audit Committee Could Mean Greater Exposure to Liability: The Problems with Applying a Heightened Standard of Care to the Corporate Audit Committee,* 30 Stetson L. Rev.977,987–97(2001) (collecting cases).

22. Del. Code Ann.tit.8,§220 (Supp.2004).

23. No. CIV.A.20262, 2003 WL 21517869, at *1-2 (Del. Ch. July I, 2003), *aff'd,* 829 A.2d 935 (Del. 2003).

24. *See* No. CIV.A.18553, 2002 WL 31657622, at *11-12, *15 (Del. Ch. Oct. 25, 2002). *But see* McKesson HBOC, Inc. v. Superior Court, 9 Cal. Rptr. 3d 812, 815, 821 (Cal. Ct. App. 2004) (compelling disclosure of documents given to the SEC under a confidentiality agreement).

25. Timothy J. Louwers, Robert J. Ramsay, David H. Sinason, Jerry R. Strawser, and Jay C. Thibodeau, *Auditng and Assurance Services* (New York: McGraw-Hill Irwin, 2013).

26. Zoe-Vonna Palmrose, *Empirical Research in Auditor Litigation: Considerations and Data, Studies in Accounting Research No. 33* (Sarasota, FL: American Accounting Association, 1999).

27. William F. Messier Jr., Steven M. Glover, and Douglas F. Prawitt, *Auditing and Assurance Services: A Systematic Approach* (New York: McGraw-Hill Irwin, 2012).

28. Louwers et al., p. 637.

29. Louwers et al., p. 637.

30. Louwers et al., pp. 637–638.

31. *Ultramares v. Touche,* 174 N.E. 441 (N.Y. 1931).

32. *Credit Alliance v. Arthur Andersen & Co.,* 483 N.E. 2d 100 (N.Y. 1985).

33. *Security Pacific Business Credit v. Peat Marwick Main & Co.,* 165 AD2d 622, 626), July 1, 1992, www.law.cornell.edu/nyctap/I92_0135.htm.

34. Messier et al., pp. 692–693.

35. *Rusch Factors, Inc. v. Levin,* 284. F.Supp. 85, 91.

36. *Restatement (Second) Law of Torts,* Section 652-A-E (1997), www.tomwbell.com/NetLaw/Ch05/R2ndTorts.html.

37. *Blue Bell, Inc. v. Peat, Marwick, Mitchell & Co.,* 715 S.W. 2d 408 (Dallas 1986).

38. *Rosenblum, Inc. v. Adler,* 93 N.J. 324 (1983).

39. *Citizens State Bank v. Timm, Schmidt & Company* (1983), www.wisbar.org/res/capp/2007/2006ap002290.htm.

40. Dan M. Goldwasser and Thomas Arnold, *Accountants' Liability* (New York: Practising Law Institute, 2009).

41. *Bily v. Arthur Young,* 834 P. 2d 745 (Cal. 1992).

42. *Murphy v. BDO Seidman, LLP* (2003), www.precydent.com/citation/CA1App1(2nd)/B154584M.

43. *1136 Tenants Corp. v. Max Rothenberg & Co.,* 27 App. Div. 2d 830, 277 NYS 2d 996 (1967).

44. Messier et al., p. 705.

45. *State Street Trust Co. v. Ernst,* Court of Appeals, N.Y. (1938), 278 N.Y. 104. 15 N.E.2d 416.

46. Messier et al., p. 705.

47. *Phar-Mor v. Coopers & Lybrand,* www.cases.justia.com/us-court-of-appeals/F3/22/1228/579478/.

48. *Houbigant v. Deloitte & Touche LLP,* Supreme Court, Appellate Division, First Department, New York, Available at www.caselaw.findlaw.com/ny-supreme-court-appellate-division/1304421.html.

49. *Reisman v. KPMG Peat Marwick LLP,* Appeals Court of Massachusetts, Suffolk. Available at www.caselaw.findlaw.com/ma-court-of-appeals/1287058.html.

50. *Houbigant v. Deloitte & Touche LLP.*

51. Louwers et al., pp. 641–642.

52. Louwers et al., pp. 642–643.

53. *Grant Thornton LLP v. Prospect High Income Fund, et al.,* July 2, 2010, Available at www.supreme.courts.state.tx.us/historical/2010/jul/060975.htm.

54. *U.S. v. Philip Peltz, 433 F. 2d 48, September 17, 1970,* https://bulk.resource.org/courts.gov/c/F2/433/433.F2d.48.141.34578_1.html.

55. *U.S. v. Robert Schwartz, 464 F. 2d 499, July 17, 1972,* https://bulk.resource.org/courts.gov/c/F2/464/464.F2d.499.71-1871.456.html.

56. Securities Exchange Act of 1934, Title 15 of the U.S. Code.

57. O. Lee Reed, Marisa Anne Pagnattaro, Daniel R. Cahoy, Peter J. Shedd, and Jere W. Morehead, *The Legal and Regulatory Environment of Business* (New York: McGraw-Hill Irwin, 2013).

58. Reed et al.

59. *Escott v. BarChris Construction Corp.,* U.S. District Court for the Southern District of New York, 1968, 283 F.Supp. 643.

60. *Securities and Exchange Commission v. Eddie Antar, Sam E. Antar, Mitchell Antar, Isaac Kairey, David Panoff, Eddie Gindi, and Kathleen Morin,* Civil Action No. 89-3773 (JCL), Litigation Release 15251, February 10, 1997, www.sec.gov/litigation/litreleases/lr15251.txt.

61. Securities Exchange Act of 1934, Title 15 of the U.S. Code.

62. Louwers et al., p. 648.

63. Messier et al., p. 709.

64. Messier et al., p. 709.

65. Securities Exchange Act of 1934.

66. *Andrew J. Maxwell v. KPMG LLP,* U.S. Court of Appeals 7th Circuit, March 21, 2008. Available at www.caselaw.findlaw.com/us-7th-circuit/1239253.html.

67. *Ernst & Ernst v. Hochfelder,* 425 U.S. 185 (1976).

68. *United States of America Before the Securities and Exchange Commission in the Matter of McKesson and Robbins, Inc. (Accountancy in Transition)* (New York: Garland Publishing, 1982).

69. *United States v. McKesson & Robbins, Inc.* - 351 U.S. 305 (1956)

70. *In re Equity Funding Corporation of America Securities Litigation,* 603 F. 2d 1353 (1979).

71. *In re Equity Funding Corporation of America Securities Litigation,* 603 F. 2d 1353 (1979).

72. David R. Hancox, "Equity Funding: Could It Happen Again?" Available at www.davehancox.com/hancox---sulem---public-speaking/publications/equity-funding.

73. Steven M. Davidoff, "In Insider and Enron Cases, Balancing Lies and Thievery," Available at www.dealbook.nytimes.com/2012/06/19/in-insider-and-enron-cases-balancing-lies-and-thievery/.

74. *Skilling v. United States,* Certiorari to the United States Court of Appeals for the Fifth Circuit, No. 08-1394 (2010).

75. 15 United States Code (U.S.C.) Section 78.

76. O. Lee Reed et al., pp. 562–563.

77. Available at www.sec.gov/spotlight/insidertrading/cases.shtml.

78. Available at http://www.sec.gov/news/press/2012/2012-195.htm.

79. U.S. District Court Southern District of New York, *United States v. Martha Stewart and Peter Bacanovi*c Superseding Indictment, http://news.findlaw.com/hdocs/.../mstewart/-usmspb 10504sind.html.

80. Available at www.businessinsider.com/martha-stewart-back-finally-on-the-board-after-five-year-sec-ban-2011-9.

81. *SEC v. James P. Gansman, Donna B. Murdoch, and Gerald L. Brodsky,* U.S. District Court So District of NY, May 29, 2008, Available at www.sec.gov/litigation/complaints/2008/comp20603 .pdf.

82. 15 U.S.C. Section 78u-4(g).

83. 15 United States Code (U.S.C.) Section 78.

84. *Securities and Exchange Commission v. KPMG LLP, Joseph T. Boyle, Michael A. Conway, Anthony P. Dolanski, and Ronald A. Safaran,* Civil Action No. 03-CV-0671 (DLC), Available at www.sec.gov/litigation/complaints/comp17954.htm.

85. J. M. Cooke, E.M. Freedman, R. J. Groves, Jon C. Madonna, S. F. O'Malley, and L. A. Weinbach, "The Liability Crisis in the United States: Impact on the Accounting Profession," *Journal of Accountancy,* November, pp. 19–23 (1992).

86. HR 3763: Sarbanes-Oxley Act in full Available at www.sec.gov/about/laws/soa2002.pdf.

87. *Higginbotham v. Baxter Int'l.,* 2005 WL 1272271 (N.D. Ill. May 25, 2005).

88. *In re Lattice Semiconductor Corp. Secs. Litig.,* 2006 U.S. Dist. LEXIS 262 (Jan. 3, 2006 Dist. Ore.).

89. *In re WatchGuard Secs. Litig.,* 2006 U.S. Dist. LEXIS 272717 (W.D.Wash., April 21, 2006).

90. *In re WatchGuard Secs. Litig.*

91. *Minding Your 302s: Assessing Potential Civil, Administrative, and Criminal Liability for False Financial Statement Certifications.* Available at www.pli.edu/emktg/compliance_coun/ Minding_302s_CC_34.pdf.

92. *United States v. Richard Scrushy,* Available at www.justice.gov/archive/dag/cftf/chargingdocs/ scrushyindictment.pdf.

93. *SEC Litig. Release No. 19719* (June 7, 2006).

94. *Minding Your 302s: Assessing Potential Civil, Administrative and Criminal Liability for False Financial Statement Certifications.*

95. *Sarbanes Oxley: A Decade Later,* Financial Executives Institute, Available at www.financi alexecutives.org/KenticoCMS/Financial-Executive-Magazine/2012_07/Sarbanes-Oxley-A-Decade-Later.aspx#axzz2JxEZXfNl.

96. FCPA Available at http://library.findlaw.com.

97. Richard D. Ramsey and A. F. Alkhafaji, "The 1977 Foreign Corrupt Practices Act and the 1988 Omnibus Trade Bill," *Management Decision* 29, no. 6., pp. 22–39

98. SEC Charges Pfizer with FCPA Violations, Available at www.sec.gov/news/press/2012/2012-152.htm.

99. Available at www.protiviti.com/en-US/Documents/White-Papers/Risk-Solutions/Strategies-to-Combat-Corruption-Risk-Protiviti.pdf.

100. *SEC v. Tyco International Ltd.*, 06 CV 2942 (S.D.N.Y. filed April 17, 2006) Available at www .sec.gov/litigation/litreleases/2006/lr19657.htm.

101. *SEC v. Tyco International Ltd.*, 1:12-CV-01583 (D.D.C. filed Sept. 24, 2012), Available at www .sec.gov/litigation/litreleases/2012/lr22491.htm.

102. Available at www.ethics.org/fsgo.

103. Shearman & Sterling LLP, FCPA Digest: "Cases and Review Releases Relating to Bribes to Foreign Officials under the Foreign Corrupt Practices Act of 1977," http://www.shearman.com/files/Publication/287c1af0-f9cb-4c11-805d-91c409975b41/Presentation/Publication Attachment/83d9dc0b-b80c-4ca4-877b-9efbba0952e7/FCPA-Digest-Jan2013_010213.pdf.

104. Available at www.ethisphere.com/ethisphere-institute-unveils-2012-worlds-most-ethical-companies/.

105. Available at www.management.fortune.cnn.com/2012/08/16/executive-pay-clawbacks/.

106. Available at http://apps.americanbar.org/buslaw/blt/content/2011/01/0002b.pdf.

107. Nancy M. Reimer, "Accountants Should Prepare Now for New Auditing Standards," October 22, 2012, Available at www.corporatecomplianceinsights.com/accountants-should-prepare-now-for-new-auditing-standards/.

108. *Public Employees Retirement Association of Colorado v. Deloitte & Touche, LLP,* U.S. District Court in Maryland, January 5, 2009, Available at http://www.ca4.uscourts.gov/Opinions/Published/071704.P.pdf.

109. *SEC v. UTStarcom,* CV 90 6094m December 31, 2009, Available at http://www.sec.gov/litigation/complaints/2009/comp21357.pdf.

110. Available at http://www.leclairryan.com/news/xprNewsDetail.aspx?xpST=NewsDetail&news=874.

# Chapter 6 Cases

## Case 6-1

# *SEC v. Halliburton Company and KBR, Inc.*

On February 11, 2009, the SEC announced settlements with KBR, Inc., and Halliburton Company to resolve SEC charges that KBR subsidiary Kellogg Brown & Root LLC bribed Nigerian government officials over a 10-year period, in violation of the FCPA, in order to obtain construction contracts. The SEC also charged that KBR and Halliburton engaged in books and records violations and internal controls violations related to the bribery.[1]

The SEC had alleged that beginning as early as 1994, members of the joint venture determined that it was necessary to pay bribes to officials within the Nigerian government in order to obtain the construction contracts. The former CEO of the predecessor entities, Albert "Jack" Stanley, and others involved in the joint venture met with high-ranking Nigerian government officials and their representatives on at least four occasions to arrange the bribe payments. To conceal the illicit payments, the joint venture entered into sham contracts with two agents, one based in the United Kingdom (U.K.) and one based in Japan, to funnel money to Nigerian officials.

The SEC complaint describes a "cultural committee" to decide how to carry out the bribery scheme. The committee decided to use the U.K. agent to make payments to high-ranking Nigerian officials and to use the Japanese agent to make payments to lower-ranking Nigerian officials. The joint venture took payments on a construction project, and in turn made payments to the Japanese agent and to the Swiss and Monaco bank accounts of the U.K. agent. The total payments to the two agents exceeded $180 million. After receiving the money, the U.K. agent made substantial payments to accounts controlled by Nigerian government officials and, beginning in 2002, paid $5 million in cash to a Nigerian political party.

The SEC's complaint also alleged that the internal controls of Halliburton, the parent company of the KBR predecessor entities from 1998 to 2006, failed to detect or prevent the bribery, and that Halliburton records were falsified as a result of the bribery scheme. In September 2008, Stanley pleaded guilty to bribery and related charges and entered into a settlement with the SEC. Stanley's high profile and punishment—he faces a potential seven-year sentence, the longest in the history of the federal statute outlawing the bribing of foreign officials—also signal the federal government's willingness to seek long prison terms rather than fines and court injunctions.

Without admitting or denying the SEC's allegations, KBR and Halliburton consented to be permanently enjoined from violating the antibribery, records, and internal control provisions in SEC laws. The SEC also imposed an independent consultant for Halliburton to review its policies and procedures as they relate to compliance with the FCPA.

As a result of the indemnity and the KBR subsidiary's criminal plea, Halliburton has agreed to pay $559 million (including $177 million in disgorgement) of $579 million in criminal fines payable by KBR, with KBR consenting to pay the remaining $20 million.

## Questions

1. The mission of a global group called Transparency International is to stop corruption and promote transparency, accountability, and integrity at all levels and across all sectors of society. The organization's "Core Values" are transparency, accountability, integrity, solidarity, courage, justice, and democracy. Each year, the organization evaluates business corruption in each country and produces a *Corruptions Perception Index (CPI)*. The 2012 CPI ranks Nigeria 139 of 174 nations. Exhibit 1 provides a complete set of rankings.

    Writing for Transparency International, Chinyere Nwafor states that "One of the reasons why there are so many foreign bribery cases going on related to Nigeria is basically that corruption in Nigeria is deeply entrenched in almost every area of the public sector."[2] In Nigeria, facilitating payments called "dash" are a way of life and necessity to get things done.

    Given the apparent corrupt culture in Nigeria, why shouldn't U.S. businesses just consider payoffs to Nigerian officials as a cost of doing business in that country and not a payment in violation of the FCPA?

2. Comment on the following statement from a values perspective: "Ethics must be global, not local."

3. Use ethical reasoning to respond to the following statement by a U.S. executive:

    > Bribery is bad for business. Bribery is inefficient; it's wasteful. It often doesn't accomplish what its original purpose was. You may be competing with another company that may ultimately out-bribe you. And then at the end of the day, of course, there is a huge risk that the bribery is uncovered, that you are the subject of a protracted investigation. And the costs can be quite, quite high at the end of the day.

---

[1] Securities and Exchange Commission, Accounting and Auditing Enforcement Release No. 2935A, February 11, 2009, *SEC v. Halliburton Company and KBR, Inc.*, www.sec.gov/litigation/litreleases/2009/lr20897a.htm.

[2] Chinyere Nwafor, "Bribery in Nigeria tackled globally, but not at home," September 10, 2012, http://blog.transparency.org/2012/09/10/bribery-in-nigeria-tackled-globally-but-not-at-home/.

**EXHIBIT 1**
**CPI 2012[3]**

| Rank | Country | CPI | Rank | Country | CPI |
|---|---|---|---|---|---|
| 1 | Denmark | 90 | 39 | Cape Verde | 60 |
| 1 | Finland | 90 | 39 | Israel | 60 |
| 1 | New Zealand | 90 | 41 | Dominica | 58 |
| 4 | Sweden | 88 | 41 | Poland | 58 |
| 5 | Singapore | 87 | 43 | Malta | 57 |
| 6 | Switzerland | 86 | 43 | Mauritius | 57 |
| 7 | Australia | 85 | 45 | Korea (South) | 56 |
| 7 | Norway | 85 | 46 | Brunei | 55 |
| 9 | Canada | 84 | 46 | Hungary | 55 |
| 9 | Netherlands | 84 | 48 | Costa Rica | 54 |
| 11 | Iceland | 82 | 48 | Lithuania | 54 |
| 12 | Luxembourg | 80 | 50 | Rwanda | 53 |
| 13 | Germany | 79 | 51 | Georgia | 52 |
| 14 | Hong Kong | 77 | 51 | Seychelles | 52 |
| 15 | Barbados | 76 | 53 | Bahrain | 51 |
| 16 | Belgium | 75 | 54 | Czech Republic | 49 |
| 17 | Japan | 74 | 54 | Latvia | 49 |
| 17 | United Kingdom | 74 | 54 | Malaysia | 49 |
| 19 | United States | 73 | 54 | Turkey | 49 |
| 20 | Chile | 72 | 58 | Cuba | 48 |
| 20 | Uruguay | 72 | 58 | Jordan | 48 |
| 22 | Bahamas | 71 | 58 | Namibia | 48 |
| 22 | France | 71 | 61 | Oman | 47 |
| 22 | Saint Lucia | 71 | 62 | Croatia | 46 |
| 25 | Austria | 69 | 62 | Slovakia | 46 |
| 25 | Ireland | 69 | 64 | Ghana | 45 |
| 27 | Qatar | 68 | 64 | Lesotho | 45 |
| 27 | United Arab Emirates | 68 | 66 | Kuwait | 44 |
| 29 | Cyprus | 66 | 66 | Romania | 44 |
| 30 | Botswana | 65 | 66 | Saudi Arabia | 44 |
| 30 | Spain | 65 | 69 | Brazil | 43 |
| 32 | Estonia | 64 | 69 | Macedonia | 43 |
| 33 | Bhutan | 63 | 69 | South Africa | 43 |
| 33 | Portugal | 63 | 72 | Bosnia and Herzegovina | 42 |
| 33 | Puerto Rico | 63 | 72 | Italy | 42 |
| 36 | Saint Vincent and the Grenadines | 62 | 72 | Sao Tome and Principe | 42 |
| 37 | Slovenia | 61 | 75 | Bulgaria | 41 |
| 37 | Taiwan | 61 | 75 | Liberia | 41 |

[3]Transparency International, *Corruptions Perception Index 2012*, Available at www.cpi.transparency.org/cpi2012/results/.

## EXHIBIT 1 (*continued*)

| Rank | Country | CPI | Rank | Country | CPI |
|------|---------|-----|------|---------|-----|
| 75 | Montenegro | 41 | 113 | Timor-Leste | 33 |
| 75 | Tunisia | 41 | 118 | Dominican Republic | 32 |
| 79 | Sri Lanka | 40 | 118 | Ecuador | 32 |
| 80 | China | 39 | 118 | Egypt | 32 |
| 80 | Serbia | 39 | 118 | Indonesia | 32 |
| 80 | Trinidad and Tobago | 39 | 118 | Madagascar | 32 |
| 83 | Burkina Faso | 38 | 123 | Belarus | 31 |
| 83 | El Salvador | 38 | 123 | Mauritania | 31 |
| 83 | Jamaica | 38 | 123 | Mozambique | 31 |
| 83 | Panama | 38 | 123 | Sierra Leone | 31 |
| 83 | Peru | 38 | 123 | Vietnam | 31 |
| 88 | Malawi | 37 | 128 | Lebanon | 30 |
| 88 | Morocco | 37 | 128 | Togo | 30 |
| 88 | Suriname | 37 | 130 | Côte d'Ivoire | 29 |
| 88 | Swaziland | 37 | 130 | Nicaragua | 29 |
| 88 | Thailand | 37 | 130 | Uganda | 29 |
| 88 | Zambia | 37 | 133 | Comoros | 28 |
| 94 | Benin | 36 | 133 | Guyana | 28 |
| 94 | Colombia | 36 | 133 | Honduras | 28 |
| 94 | Djibouti | 36 | 133 | Iran | 28 |
| 94 | Greece | 36 | 133 | Kazakhstan | 28 |
| 94 | India | 36 | 133 | Russia | 28 |
| 94 | Moldova | 36 | 139 | Azerbaijan | 27 |
| 94 | Mongolia | 36 | 139 | Kenya | 27 |
| 94 | Senegal | 36 | 139 | Nepal | 27 |
| 102 | Argentina | 35 | 139 | Nigeria | 27 |
| 102 | Gabon | 35 | 139 | Pakistan | 27 |
| 102 | Tanzania | 35 | 144 | Bangladesh | 26 |
| 105 | Algeria | 34 | 144 | Cameroon | 26 |
| 105 | Armenia | 34 | 144 | Central African Republic | 26 |
| 105 | Bolivia | 34 | 144 | Congo Republic | 26 |
| 105 | Gambia | 34 | 144 | Syria | 26 |
| 105 | Kosovo | 34 | 144 | Ukraine | 26 |
| 105 | Mali | 34 | 150 | Eritrea | 25 |
| 105 | Mexico | 34 | 150 | Guinea-Bissau | 25 |
| 105 | Philippines | 34 | 150 | Papua New Guinea | 25 |
| 113 | Albania | 33 | 150 | Paraguay | 25 |
| 113 | Ethiopia | 33 | 154 | Guinea | 24 |
| 113 | Guatemala | 33 | 154 | Kyrgyzstan | 24 |
| 113 | Niger | 33 | 156 | Yemen | 23 |

**EXHIBIT 1 (*continued*)**

| Rank | Country | CPI | Rank | Country | CPI |
|------|---------|-----|------|---------|-----|
| 157 | Angola | 22 | 165 | Haiti | 19 |
| 157 | Cambodia | 22 | 165 | Venezuela | 19 |
| 157 | Tajikistan | 22 | 169 | Iraq | 18 |
| 160 | Democratic Republic of the Congo | 21 | 170 | Turkmenistan | 17 |
| 160 | Laos | 21 | 170 | Uzbekistan | 17 |
| 160 | Libya | 21 | 172 | Myanmar | 15 |
| 163 | Equatorial Guinea | 20 | 173 | Sudan | 13 |
| 163 | Zimbabwe | 20 | 174 | Afghanistan | 8 |
| 165 | Burundi | 19 | 174 | Korea (North) | 8 |
| 165 | Chad | 19 | 174 | Somalia | 8 |

## Case 6-2

# Con-way Inc.

## Summary of Findings

Con-way is a Delaware corporation headquartered in San Mateo, California. It is an international freight transportation and logistics services company that conducts operations in a number of foreign jurisdictions. During the relevant period, the company was named CNF, Inc.; it changed its name to Con-way in April 2006. Con-way's common stock is registered with the SEC pursuant to Section 12(b) of the Exchange Act and is listed on the NYSE.[1]

Menlo Worldwide Forwarding, Inc. (Menlo Forwarding), was a wholly owned U.S-based subsidiary of Con-way that Con-way purchased in 1989. During the relevant period, Menlo Forwarding was headquartered in Redwood City, California, and had a 55 percent voting interest in Emery Transnational (Emery). Con-way sold Menlo Forwarding to United Parcel Service of America, Inc. (UPS), in December 2004.

California-based Con-way Inc., a global freight forwarder, was charged by the SEC with making payments that violated the FCPA. The company paid a $300,000 penalty and accepted a cease-and-desist order to settle the FCPA enforcement action. Con-way's FCPA violations were caused by a Philippines-based subsidiary, Emery Transnational. It made about $244,000 in improper payments between 2000 and 2003 to officials at the Philippines Bureau of Customs and the Philippine Economic Zone Area, and $173,000 in improper payments to officials at 14 state-owned airlines. In connection with the improper payments, Con-way failed to record these payments accurately on the company's books and records and knowingly failed to implement or maintain a system of effective internal accounting controls.

## Lack of Oversight over Emery Transnational

During the relevant period, Con-way and Menlo Forwarding engaged in little supervision or oversight over Emery. Neither Con-way nor Menlo Forwarding took steps to devise or maintain internal accounting controls concerning Emery, to ensure that it acted in accordance with Con-way's FCPA policies, or to make certain that its books and records were detailed or accurate.

During the relevant period, Con-way and Menlo Forwarding required only that Emery periodically report back to Menlo its net profits, from which Emery then paid Menlo a yearly 55 percent dividend. Menlo incorporated the yearly 55 percent

[1] Securities and Exchange Commission, *In the Matter of Con-way Inc.,* Accounting and Auditing Enforcement Release No. 2867, August 27, 2008, www.sec.gov/litigation/admin/2008/34-58433.pdf.

dividend into its financial results, which were then consolidated in Con-way's financial statements. Neither Con-way nor Menlo asked for or received any other financial information from Emery. Accordingly, neither Con-way nor Menlo maintained or reviewed any of the books and records of Emery—including the records of operating expenses, which should have reflected the illicit payments made to foreign officials.

## Payments to Philippine Customs Officials

Emery made hundreds of small payments to foreign officials at the Philippines Bureau of Customs and the Philippine Economic Zone Area between 2000 and 2003 in order to obtain or retain business. These payments were made to influence the acts and decisions of these foreign officials and to secure a business advantage or economic benefit. By these payments, foreign officials were induced to (1) violate customs regulations by allowing Emery to store shipments longer than otherwise permitted, thus saving the company transportation costs related to its inbound shipments; (2) improperly settle Emery's disputes with the Philippines Bureau of Customs, or (3) reduce or not enforce otherwise legitimate fines for administrative violations.

To generate funding for these payments, Emery employees submitted a *Shipment Processing and Clearance Expense Report* to Emery's finance department. These reports requested cash advances to complete customs processing. The cash advances were then issued via checks made payable to Emery employees, who cashed the checks and paid the money to designated foreign officials. Unlike legitimate customs payments, the payments at issue were not supported by receipts from the Philippines Bureau of Customs and the Philippine Economic Zone Area. Emery did not identify the true nature of these payments in its books and records. From 2000 to 2003, these payments totaled at least $244,000.

## Payments to Officials of Majority State-Owned Airlines

To obtain or retain business, Emery also made numerous payments to foreign officials at 14 state-owned airlines that did business in the Philippines between 2000 and 2003. These payments were made with the intent of improperly influencing the acts and decisions of these foreign officials and to secure a business advantage or economic benefit. Emery Transnational made two types of payments. The first type was known as "weight-shipped" payments, which were made to induce airline officials to reserve space for Emery on the airplanes improperly. These payments were valued based on the volume of the shipments the airlines carried for Emery. The second type were known as "gain shares" payments, which were paid to induce airline officials to falsely underweigh shipments and to consolidate multiple shipments into a single shipment, resulting in lower shipping charges. Emery paid the foreign officials 90 percent of the reduced shipping costs.

Both types of payments to foreign airline officials were paid in cash by members of Emery's management team. Checks reflecting the amount of the weight-shipped and gain shares payments were issued to these managers, who cashed the checks and personally distributed the cash payments to the foreign airline officials. Emery Transnational did not characterize these payments in its books and records as bribes. During the 2000–2003 period, these payments totaled at least $173,000. Neither Con-way nor Menlo requested or received any records of these payments or any of Emery's expenses during this period.

## Discovery of Improper Payments and Internal Investigation

Con-way discovered potential FCPA issues in early 2003. Starting in January 2003, Menlo initiated steps to increase Emery's internal reporting requirements, including requiring Emery to begin reporting its income and expenses, in addition to its net profits. As a result, in reviewing Emery's records, Menlo employees noticed unusually high customs and airline-related expenditures.

Menlo conducted an internal investigation of the suspicious payments at Emery and determined that Emery employees had been making regular cash payments to customs officials and employees of majority state-owned airlines. Based on Menlo's investigation, Con-way conducted a broader review of all of Menlo foreign businesses and voluntarily disclosed the existence of possible FCPA violations to the staff. After completing its internal investigation, Con-way imposed heightened financial reporting and compliance requirements on Emery. Menlo terminated a number of the Emery employees involved in the misconduct, and Con-way provided additional FCPA training and education to its employees and strengthened its regulatory compliance program. In December 2004, Con-way sold Emery to UPS.

## Legal Analysis

The FCPA, enacted in 1977, added Exchange Act Section 13(b)(2)(A) to require public companies to make and keep books, records, and accounts that, in reasonable detail, accurately and fairly reflect the transactions and dispositions of the assets of the issuer, and added Exchange Act Section 13(b)(2)(B) to require such companies to devise and maintain a system of internal accounting controls sufficient to provide reasonable assurances that (1) transactions are executed in accordance with management's general or specific authorization; and (2) transactions are recorded as necessary to permit preparation of financial statements in conformity with generally accepted accounting principles or any other criteria applicable to such statements, and to maintain accountability for assets.

As already detailed, Con-way's books, records, and accounts did not properly reflect the illicit payments made by Emery to Philippine customs officials and to officials of majority state-owned airlines. As a result, Con-way violated SEC Exchange Act Section 13(b)(2)(A). Con-way also failed to devise or maintain sufficient internal controls to ensure that Emery Transnational complied with the FCPA and to ensure that the payments it made to foreign officials were accurately reflected on its books and records. As a result, Con-way violated Section 13(b)(2)(B) of the Act.

Securities Exchange Act Section 13(b)(5) prohibits any person or company from knowingly circumventing or knowingly failing to implement a system of internal accounting controls as described in Section 13(b)(2)(B), or knowingly falsifying any book, record, or account as described in Section 13(b)(2)(A). By knowingly failing to implement a system of internal accounting controls concerning Emery Transnational, Con-way also violated Exchange Act Section 13(b)(5).

According to the SEC's complaint, none of Emery's improper payments were reflected accurately in Con-way's books and records. Also, Con-way knowingly failed to implement a system of internal accounting controls concerning Emery that would both ensure that Emery complied with the FCPA and require that the payments that it made to foreign officials were reflected accurately on its books and records.

## Questions

1. The FCPA distinguishes between so-called facilitating payments and more serious activities. Do you think such a distinction and the related penalties for violations under the Act make sense from an ethical perspective? Use the utilitarian analysis of harms and benefits of facilitating payments to support your position.

2. Securities Exchange Act Section 13(b)(5), 15 U.S.C. §78m(b)(5) prohibits any person or company from knowingly circumventing or knowingly failing to implement a system of internal accounting controls or knowingly falsifying any book, record, or account. What is the purpose of the accounting provisions in the SEC laws and FCPA? Assume the auditors of Con-way knew about the accounting for FCPA payments in the books and records of the company. Do you think the auditors would be guilty of: (1) ordinary negligence; (2) gross negligence; or (3) fraud? Explain.

3. Given that the FCPA permits facilitating payments, do you believe it is ethically appropriate for companies to deduct such payments from their income taxes? Why or why not? What about outright bribery payments? What does the law require in each instance with respect to tax deductibility?

## Case 6-3

# Insider Trading and Accounting Professionals

The following two cases deal with insider trading by accounting professionals.

a. Vincent Klein is a CPA and an employee benefits specialist on client audits with Foster & Lewis, a large public accounting firm in Denver, Colorado. One day while working on a client engagement, Klein learned about material, nonpublic information concerning the client's first earnings release after the company went public. Klein purchased securities of the client and tipped off two friends about some of the information, and both traded on Klein's communications. Klein felt obligated to do so because his stockbroker friends had informed him a year ago about the client's potential acquisition of a competitor company.

   1. Evaluate the ethics of trading on client securities by Klein, given that he was an employee benefits specialist on the audit.
   2. Did Klein's actions violate any rules of conduct in the AICPA Code? Why or why not?
   3. Do you think Klein would have any legal liability for his actions? Explain.

b. Marissa Lowe is an audit partner of a CPA firm and owns stock in one of the firm's clients. She does not participate in any attest engagements for this client, is not in a position to influence the client's attest engagements or the professional staff performing those engagements, and works in an office of the firm that performs none of the attest work for the client. At a recent meeting, Marissa learns about certain nonpublic activities of the client that are not material in and of themselves. Marissa combines that information with other publicly available information about the client and the industry and concludes that the client's stock price will decline.

   1. Was it ethical for Marissa to own stock in the client, given she had no involvement with the audit engagement?
   2. Assume that Marissa calls her best friend, who also owns stock in the audit client and works in the tax department of the firm. Marissa tells her friend about the expected stock price decline. Has Marissa violated any laws by contacting her friend about the matter? Has she violated her ethical obligations?
   3. Assume that you also work for the firm and know about Marissa's stock ownership. You approach Marissa and tell her she should sell her shares in the client. Marissa declines to do so and tells you it is none of your business. What would you do at this point and why?

## Case 6-4

# *Anjoorian et al.:* Third-Party Liability

In the case of *Paul V. Anjoorian v. Arnold Kilberg & Co., Arnold Kilberg, and Pascarella & Trench,* the Superior Court of the State of Rhode Island used prior SEC rulings to guide its decision on what is the auditor's liability to third parties. The court denied the defendant's motion for summary judgment.[1] The facts of the case are described in Exhibit 1.

## Duties Owed by Accountants in the Preparation of Financial Statements

The defendants argued that they are entitled to summary judgment on the plaintiff's negligence claim because P&T owed no duty to him as a shareholder of FCC. The Supreme Court has acknowledged that the duty of accounting professionals to third parties is an open question in Rhode Island, but it did identify at least three competing views: the foreseeability test, the near-privity test, and the *Restatement* test.[2]

There are two competing policy concerns underlying each of the tests. The first is compensation, because a person who relies on an accountant's work product should not have to bear the loss arising from that accountant's malpractice.[3] However, a second policy favors limiting liability for accountants to certain individuals or groups of individuals in order to make the risk of loss manageable. In the financial world, there is a significant potential for the widespread dissemination of the information from financial statements beyond the uses for which it was prepared.[4]

An auditor can balance the risks and rewards involved with the uses of financial information only if she knows

the uses to which the information will be put.[5] "By receiving notice of the third parties to whom potential liability may be incurred, the auditor can decide whether to accept the engagement, adjust the audit plan to meet the needs of third parties, and/or negotiate audit fees that are commensurate with the scope of liability." Therefore, many courts have placed limits on the scope of an auditor's potential liability so that they might successfully manage the risks inherent in their profession.[6]

## Case Analysis

The court found that the addressing of the reports to the shareholders, while not conclusive, is a strong indication that P&T intended the shareholders to rely upon them. Therefore, the court concluded that genuine issues of fact exist as to whether P&T intended for Anjoorian to rely on these financial statements. Perhaps the court would have reached a different conclusion for a widely held public corporation with a potentially unlimited number of shareholders whose identities change regularly. Here, however, FCC was a close corporation with only four shareholders, giving greater significance to the fact that the financial statements were addressed "to the shareholders."

The defendants also argued that, in order to find a duty to third parties, an accountant must have contemplated a specific transaction for which the financial statement would be used and that no such transaction was contemplated here.[7] The court found this argument unconvincing, stating that the case is unusual in that the alleged malpractice did not arise from a specific financial transaction. The typical case involves a person whose reliance on a defective financial statement induces the person to advance credit or invest new equity into the corporation.[8] When the investment is lost, or the loan unpaid, the person sues the accountant. In this case, however, Anjoorian had already invested his capital in the corporation when P&T was hired, and he alleged that he used the financial statements as a tool to evaluate the value of that investment. The alleged malpractice did not result in his advancing new value to the corporation and then losing his investment, but instead resulted in Anjoorian failing to withdraw his capital from the corporation while its value was higher.

[1]Superior Court, State of Rhode Island, *Paul V. Anjoorian v. Arnold Kilberg & Co., Arnold Kilberg, and Pascarella & Trench,* November 27, 2006.

[2]*Bowen Court Assocs. v. Ernst & Young,* 818 A.2d 721, 728 n.2 (R.I. 2003); see Carl Pacini, Mary Jill Martin, and Lynda Hamilton, "At the Interface of Law and Accounting: An Examination of a Trend Toward a Reduction in the Scope of Auditor Liability to Third Parties in the Common Law Countries," *American Business Law Journal* 37 (Winter 2000), pp. 171, 175. (The authors noted that the standards lie on a continuum, and each may produce different results for the same set of facts.)

[3]U.S. Court of Appeals, *Rusch Factors Inc. v. Levin,* 284 F.Supp. 85, 90–91 (D.R.I. 1968).

[4]See *Restatement (Second) of Torts,* § 522, com. a (1977); see also *Ultramares Corp. v. Touche Niven & Co.,* 255 N.Y. 170, 179–180 (N.Y. 1931) (J. Cardozo noted that "if liability for negligence exists, a thoughtless slip or blunder, the failure to detect a theft or forgery beneath the cover of deceptive entries, may expose accountants to a liability in an indeterminate amount for an indeterminate time to an indeterminate class. The hazards of a business conducted on these terms are so extreme as to enkindle doubt whether a flaw may not exist in the implication of a duty that exposes to these consequences.")

[5]*Restatement (Second) of Torts,* § 522, com. a (1977).
[6]See Pacini et al., pp. 175–179.
[7]See *Restatement (Second) of Torts,* § 552(2)(b) (concluding in illustration 10 that an accountant would not have a duty to a bank where he conducted an audit "of the customary scope for the corporation" and a bank subsequently relied upon it to advance credit to the corporation).
[8]See, e.g., *Rusch Factors, Inc.,* 284 F.Supp. at 86–87; *Credit Alliance,* 483 N.E.2d at 111.

## Exhibit 1
### *Anjoorian et al.:* Third-Party Liability

### Facts of the Case

The defendants Pascarella and Trench, general partners of the accounting firm Pascarella & Trench (P&T), asked the court for summary judgment in their favor with respect to plaintiff Anjoorian's claim that P&T committed malpractice in the preparation of financial statements, and that the plaintiff (Anjoorian) suffered pecuniary harm as a result.

Anjoorian formerly owned 50 percent of the issued shares of Fairway Capital Corporation (FCC), a Rhode Island corporation. The other 50 percent of the shares were held by the three children of Arnold Kilberg. Arnold Kilberg himself owned no stock in the corporation, but he served as the day-to-day manager of the company. FCC was in the business of making and servicing equity loans to small businesses under the regulation of the U.S. Small Business Administration (SBA), and was capitalized by loans from the SBA and a $1.26 million investment by Anjoorian.

Beginning in 1990, P&T provided accounting services to FCC. The firm audited FCC's annual financial statements following the close of each calendar year between 1990 and 1994. In its representation letter (similar to current Section 302 requirement under SOX), P&T stated that FCC was "responsible for the fair presentation in the financial statements of financial position." P&T's responsibility was to perform an audit in accordance with GAAS and to "express an opinion on the financial statements" based on the firm's audit. The first page of each financial statement contained the auditor's opinion that "the financial statements referred to above present fairly, in all material respects, the financial position of FCC in conformity with generally accepted accounting principles." Each report is addressed to "The Board of Directors and Shareholders." The 1990–1994 statements indicate that "it is management's opinion that all accounts presented on the balance sheet are collectible." In addition, the 1991–1994 statements indicate that "all loans are fully collateralized" according to the board of directors.

On March 2, 1994, Anjoorian filed a complaint and motion for a temporary restraining order seeking the dissolution of FCC on various grounds. P&T was not a party to that suit. As a result of that action, the three Kilberg children exercised their right to purchase the plaintiff's shares of the corporation. The court appointed an appraiser to determine the value of Anjoorian's shares, which the other shareholders would have to pay. The bulk of FCC's assets comprised its right to receive payment for the loans that it had made. The appraiser determined that the value of the corporation was $2,395,000, plus a payroll adjustment of $102,000, and minus a "loss reserve" adjustment to account for the fact that 10 of FCC's 30 outstanding loans were delinquent. The loss reserve adjustment reduced the total appraised value of the corporation by $878,234. Consequently, Anjoorian's 50 percent interest in the corporation was reduced accordingly by $439,117. He ultimately received a judgment for $809,382.85 against the other shareholders in exchange for the buyout of his shares.

In 1997, Anjoorian brought the lawsuit against Kilberg, Kilberg's company, and P&T. He claimed that P&T was negligent in preparing the annual financial statements for FCC because it did not include an accurate loan loss reserve in the statements. Anjoorian argued that he relied on the financial statements prepared by the defendants, and that if the statements had included a loan loss reserve, he would have sought dissolution of the corporation much earlier than 1994, when his shares would have been more valuable. Anjoorian submitted an appraisal suggesting that the appropriate loan loss reserve figure would have been much less—and, therefore, his share value much higher—in the years 1990 and 1991. He alleged that he lost over $300,000 in share value between 1990 and March 2, 1994. Nine years later, the defendants moved for summary judgment on the grounds that P&T owed no duty to Anjoorian as a shareholder, and that his claims are barred by the statute of limitations.

### Statute of Limitations

A claim for accounting malpractice must be commenced within three years from the time of the occurrence of the incident that gave rise to the action. The acts of malpractice alleged by Anjoorian are the failure of P&T to include an accurate loan loss reserve in each of four financial statements for the years 1990 through 1993. Anjoorian filed his complaint on February 27, 1997, which meant that acts of malpractice that occurred prior to February 27, 1994, were barred unless the discovery rule applied. The *discovery rule* provides that for injuries or damages "which could not in the exercise of reasonable diligence be discoverable at the time of the occurrence of the incident which gave rise to the action, the lawsuit shall be commenced within three years of the time that the act or acts of the malpractice should, *in the exercise of reasonable diligence,* have been discovered." Because the defendants did not present evidence that foreclosed this possibility, the court found that there existed a genuine issue as to when the pertinent facts were discovered, and therefore, the court could not conclude that Anjoorian's claims should be barred for purposes of this summary judgment motion.

The court opined that it would have no difficulty finding a duty in this case, in the absence of a specific financial transaction, if it can be shown that P&T intended the shareholders to rely on the financial statements for the purpose of evaluating the financial health of the company and, therefore, their investment in the company. In this case, the "particular transaction" contemplated by the *Restatement* relates to the purpose for which the financial statements would be used—the shareholders' decision whether to withdraw capital or not. While it remains to be proved that P&T actually did foresee that its financial statements would be used by the shareholders in this manner, the absence of a particular financial transaction does not preclude the finding of a duty in this case. Because the value of the shareholders' investment was limited to the amounts reflected in the company balance sheets, any loss from malpractice was an insurable risk for which accounting professionals can plan.[9] Further, the accountants may have further curtailed their exposure by placing an appropriate disclaimer on the financial statements to warn shareholders that they rely on the financial statements at their peril.[10] Therefore, the policy that would justify limits on accountant liability would not apply if the requisite intent were found.

The defendants argued that the plaintiff's theory of damages is speculative and against public policy. Anjoorian based his damage claims on the assertion that he relied on four annual audited financial statements to evaluate the status of his $1.26 million investment in FCC. Because the statements failed to include a loan loss reserve figure, he argued that the statements overstated the value of the corporation at the end of each year from 1990 to 1993. When Anjoorian sought dissolution in 1994, the value he obtained for his shares was significantly less than his expectation. He contended that if he had accurate financial information, he would have liquidated his investment earlier when his shares were more valuable. At issue was the existence and amount of the loan loss reserve. An appraiser of the value of the corporation in the dissolution action determined that the inclusion of a loan loss reserve in the financial statements was proper, and that created a genuine issue as to whether a breach of the duty of care occurred. The defendant had questioned the computation of the loan loss reserve but the court disagreed. (A detailed analysis of the amount of loan loss reserve has been omitted.)

## Questions

1. The auditors (P&T) claimed to have no duty to Anjoorian as a shareholder of FCC. The Rhode Island Supreme Court acknowledged that the duty of accounting professionals to third parties is an open question in the state, but it did identify at least three competing views: the foreseeability test, the near-privity test, and the *Restatement* test. Briefly describe the legal reasoning with respect to each of the three liability standards and how they pertain to the facts of the case.

2. The court decision refers to the importance of the auditors' knowing about third-party usage of the audited financial statements. What role does such knowledge play in enabling auditors to meet their professional and ethical responsibilities?

[9] See *Rusch Factors, Inc.,* 284 F.Supp. at 91.
[10] See, e.g., *First Nat'l Bank v. Sparkmon,* 442 S.E.2d 804, 806 (Ga. Ct. App. 1994) (finding disclaimers effective "to preclude any justifiable reliance by a third party upon the . . . reports they prefaced").

## Case 6-5

# *Vertical Pharmaceuticals Inc. et al. v. Deloitte & Touche LLP*[1]

On December 13, 2012, Vertical Pharmaceuticals Inc. and an affiliated company sued Deloitte & Touche LLP in New Jersey state court for alleged accountant malpractice, claiming the firm's false accusations of fraudulent conduct scrapped a public company's plans to acquire Vertical for more than $50 million.

Vertical is a privately owned company that sells niche prescription drugs geared toward women's health and pain management. Trigen Laboratories (TLI) sells and markets generic drugs. Deloitte was auditing the 2011 financial statements of Vertical and TLI, which are owned by the same three partners, when it abruptly suspended that review because of supposedly troubling items that two whistleblowers brought to the firm's attention, according to the complaint, which was filed November 21 in Morris County Superior Court.

Deloitte insisted that Vertical hire independent counsel and conduct an internal investigation with a forensic audit, the complaint said. Vertical agreed to those steps, but Deloitte eventually notified Vertical that it was resigning rather than finishing its work, according to the complaint.

"As a forensic audit later discovered—no money was being pilfered from the company. No partner was stealing money from another. No improper conduct was taking place," the complaint said.

The revelation that Deloitte resigned from the 2011 audit and the allegations of potential criminal conduct and financial improprieties that the auditor passed on to the audit committee left the acquisition for dead, the complaint said. The public company found another pharmaceutical company to acquire.

The deal would have helped rapidly grow Vertical's business and established a revenue stream for the company of more than $500 million, the complaint contends. "Deloitte knew the deal would be final once the 2011 audit was completed. Without Deloitte's interference in concocting a series of false, negligent statements regarding Vertical's financials, the 2011 audit would have been issued and the deal completed."

Vertical has asked for $200 million or more in damages on multiple counts, including accounting malpractice and breach of fiduciary duty. Deloitte also demanded and received $120,000 for all of its invoiced services before resigning, according to the complaint, which seeks back those funds as well.

Deloitte's allegedly slanted statements involved accusations that Vertical was pilfering company funds through two LLCs, inappropriately paying company employees through car allowances, committing fraud by having an owner's father as tax auditor, and paying an owner's wife off the books, according to the complaint.

The firm also falsely claimed Vertical's books were in terrible shape and that its management was unreliable, the complaint said. "A subsequent forensic audit initially to assuage Deloitte was ultimately completed . . . which found: None of these items had merit nor did they consider any resolution items justified to engender Deloitte's resignation; that Deloitte was well aware of the nature prior to its supposed whistleblower disclosures of the items; and that many of these items were in the process of being resolved based on advice provided by Deloitte as early as May 2011," the complaint said.

## Questions

1. Do you believe Deloitte & Touche breached its fiduciary duty to Vertical Pharmaceuticals in this case? Why or why not?

2. Do you believe Deloitte was guilty of malpractice as alleged by Vertical? Use the discussion in this chapter to answer the question.

3. Do you think it was ethical for Deloitte to resign from the engagement without waiting for the results of the investigation and forensic audit that was conducted at Deloitte's insistence?

[1]The case is *Vertical Pharmaceuticals Inc. et al v. Deloitte & Touche LLP,* case number L-2852-12, case filed on December 13, 2012, in the Superior Court of New Jersey, Morris County.

## Case 6-6

# *SEC v. DHB Industries, Inc., n/k/a Point Blank Solutions, Inc.*

## Background

In the past few years, the SEC has stepped up its enforcement actions against independent directors of publicly traded companies. While the commission historically has not pursued public company directors, it does so when it deems the directors to have knowingly permitted or facilitated violations of securities laws. Historically, the SEC pursues cases against independent directors only when it believes that they personally have engaged in improper conduct or have repeatedly ignored significant red flags. The action discussed below illustrates how the commission may choose to use some of its new enforcement powers under Dodd-Frank.

On February 28, 2011, the SEC charged DHB, a major supplier of body armor to the U.S. military and law enforcement agencies, with engaging in a massive accounting fraud. The agency separately charged three of the company's former outside directors and audit committee members for their complicity in the scheme. Exhibit 1 summarizes the accounting issues included in the SEC's filing against the company for violations of Section 10(b) and Rule 10b(5) of the Securities Exchange Act of 1934. The filing alleges the following:

> From at least 2003 through 2005, DHB, in connection with the purchase or sale of securities as described herein, by the use of means or instrumentalities of interstate commerce or of the mails, directly or indirectly, knowingly, willfully, or recklessly: (a) employed devices, schemes, or artifices to defraud; (b) made untrue statements of material facts or omitted to state material facts necessary in order to make the statements made, in the light of the circumstances under which they were made, not misleading; or (c) engaged in acts, practices, or courses of business which operated as a fraud or deceit upon other persons.[1]

## Action Against Independent Directors and Audit Committee Members

The commission filed a complaint in federal court against three former "independent" directors of DHB Industries, Inc. ("DHB"), now known as Point Blank Solutions, Inc., who had served as members of the audit committee. The complaint alleged that the three former board members—Jerome Krantz, Cary Chasin, and Gary Nadelman—facilitated DHB's securities violations through their "willful blindness to red flags signaling fraud" between 2003 and 2006. Their actions allegedly allowed senior management to file materially

false and misleading filings with the commission and use corporate funds to pay for personal expenses.

The complaint also alleged that the directors' actions allowed DHB's then-CEO David Brooks and CFO Dawn Schlegel to divert corporate funds to a personally controlled entity. The complaint further alleged that the three directors lacked independence because of their business relationships and decades-long social relationships with the CEO. The complaint alleged that the directors omitted from the official board minutes discussions of company expenditures that had no legitimate business purpose (e.g., paying for prostitution services), made little or no effort to understand their audit committee responsibilities, and "turned a blind eye to numerous, significant, and compounding red flags". The red flags included, among other warning signs, the following:

- The August 2003 issuance of a material weakness letter to the audit committee concerning DHB's internal controls over financial reporting by DHB's then-auditor Grant Thornton LLP and its subsequent resignation

- Numerous concerns reported to the audit committee by DHB's new auditors Weiser LLP ("Weiser") in March 2004

- Concerns raised with Weiser by the company's controller and the controller's intention to resign over inventory overvaluation

- Weiser's recommendation to the audit committee to investigate the inventory overvaluation issue

- Weiser's objection to the filing of DHB's 2004 annual report and a March 2005 material weakness letter issued by Weiser, followed by its resignation

- The January 2004 resignation of Gibson, Dunn & Crutcher LLP ("Gibson Dunn"), which had been hired as outside counsel to investigate potential related-party transactions between the CEO and an entity allegedly controlled by the CEO

- The CEO's insistence that he oversee any future investigation of related-party transactions by the law firm Pepper Hamilton LLP and the consulting firm FTI Consulting, Inc. ("FTI"), hired after the resignation of Gibson Dunn, and the subsequent firing of FTI by the CEO after FTI began to question the CEO's corporate expenses

- An April 2006 statement to the audit committee by DHB's new auditors, Rachlin, Cohen & Holtz LLP, detailing DHB's inventory manipulations in the first three quarters of 2005

The complaint alleged that the three audit committee members systematically and repeatedly failed to investigate these and other red flags, failed to address specific concerns, and allowed fraudulent activity by the CEO and other members of the senior management to continue unabated.

[1] *SEC v DHB Industries, Inc., n/k/a Point Blank Solutions, Inc.,* U.S. District Court Southern District of Florida, February 28, 2011, Available at www.sec.gov/litigation/complaints/2011/comp21867-directors.pdf.

## Exhibit 1
## Accounting Fraud Issues at DHB

On April 3, 2006 and August 18, 2006, DHB filed a Form 8-K stating that its interim reports for 2005 and financials for 2003–2004 could not be relied upon. On October 1, 2007, DHB filed a comprehensive Form 10-K, which included restated financial statements for 2003, 2004, and 2005. The restated Form 10-K disclosed that DHB's gross profit margins and net income for 2003 and 2004 were materially lower than the company had previously reported. These restated financials eliminated all of DHB's 2003 and 2004 profits.

### Overstated Inventories

Between 2003 and 2005, DHB overstated its inventory quantities and created bogus, unsubstantiated bills of material to price its "work in process" and "finished goods" inventory. These fraudulent bills of material overstated labor costs, the amount of raw materials, overhead costs, and the unit prices of DHB's four primary vest components. Throughout this period, DHB falsely adjusted its inventory schedules to increase the inventory value. Schlegel and Brooks were aware the inventory was overvalued, but did nothing to correct the company's financial statements.

   These manipulations caused DHB's annual reports to overvalue inventories materially by $24 million in 2003 and $30 million in 2004, and caused the company to overvalue its inventories materially by $33 million in its quarterly report as of September 2005. By overvaluing its inventories, DHB also materially overstated its reported gross profit and net income during these periods.

### Excess and Obsolete Inventory

Between 2003 and 2005, DHB further manipulated its inventory valuation by failing to account properly for excess and obsolete inventory as GAAP required (i.e., valuing inventory at the lower of cost or market value and accounting for impairments in value). DHB's failure to report its inventory values properly inflated its gross profit and net income falsely in its public filings and earnings releases.

   In 2004, approximately $12.5 million of hard armor plates, a key component of DHB's vests, became obsolete when the U.S. Army changed specifications for the plates. Because the U.S. military was DHB's main customer, this meant that the company could not use those armor plates in marketable vests.

   An additional $4.5 million of inventory became obsolete due to other specification changes, including the discontinuation of certain vest colors and fabrics. The changed specifications left DHB with a large inventory of plates and fabrics that it could not sell.

   DHB and others should have disclosed the known material risk and uncertainty concerning the marketability of these plates and established an inventory valuation reserve by recognizing an obsolescence charge for the plates in its 2004 Form 10-K. However, the company failed to do so, thereby falsely misrepresenting and overstating its inventory, gross profit, and pretax income for 2004 by at least $17 million.

   DHB and others additionally failed to recognize charges for impaired inventory totaling $1 million in 2003 and $6 million as of September 2005. This caused DHB to materially understate its cost of goods sold and materially overstate its gross profit and pretax income stated in its annual reports.

### Internal Controls

DHB failed to devise and maintain internal controls sufficient to provide reasonable assurance that DHB accounted for its inventory, cost of goods sold, gross profit, gross margin, selling, general, and administrative expenses, pretax income, net income, and other key figures in conformity with GAAP. DHB's lack of internal controls resulted in the filing of materially false and misleading earnings releases and public filings with the SEC.

   DHB lacked internal accounting controls over the use of corporate checks and credit cards, enabling Brooks to use DHB as his personal piggy bank. Between 1997 and 2005, Brooks used DHB checks, and corporate credit cards to divert approximately $4.7 million in company funds to his private entities and to pay for millions of dollars in personal expenses.

   These expenses, which benefited Brooks and others, included such items as luxury cars, jewelry, art, real estate, extravagant vacations, use of personal aircraft, prostitutes, horse training, and clothing and accessories from high-fashion designers such as Hermes and Louis Vuitton, and more than $120,000 for iPods included in gift bags for guests at a multimillion-dollar party for his daughter.

   DHB paid for $975,000 of Brooks's personal expenses in 2003, $788,000 in 2004, and $1.3 million in 2005. In addition, between 1997 and 2002, DHB paid for at least $1.7 million of Brooks's personal purchases on corporate credit cards. Brooks did not repay DHB these amounts.

### Fraudulent Expense Reclassification Entries

Between 2003 and 2005, DHB and others also manipulated the company's reported gross profit margin by reclassifying amounts from cost of goods sold to "research and development," an expense category on DHB's income statement.

These reclassification entries had the effect of materially understating DHB's cost of goods sold and overstating its expenses, resulting in an overstatement of DHB's gross profit (with no effect on net income and related per-share data).

CFO Dawn Schlegel (with Brooks's knowledge) routinely directed members of the accounting staff to record journal entries that reclassified these expenses without any supporting documentation. DHB recorded these bogus amounts as research and development expenses, purportedly relating to sample vests provided to sales personnel and customers. However, these amounts were baseless because, among other things, they represented tens of thousands more sample vests than DHB normally used. Furthermore, the corresponding overstated expenses were several times greater than DHB's actual cost of samples.

DHB's fraudulently reclassified entries totaling $8.8 million in 2003, $7.1 million in 2004, and $8.2 million as of September 2005, resulting in a material increase to DHB's gross profits reported in its earnings releases and public filings.

### Related-Party Transactions

From at least 2003 through 2006, Brooks funneled approximately $10 million out of DHB to a related party and did not disclose the nature of the business arrangement.

Although Brooks's wife was listed as running the related-party entity, Brooks actually authorized and reviewed all of the entity's checks prior to disbursement, personally signed the checks, directed Schlegel to sign his wife's name to the checks, authorized the payment of bonuses to employees (including horse trainers) out of DHB's accounts, controlled the price that the entity charged DHB for plates, and made decisions regarding its capital expenditures and personnel. The entity spent the majority of proceeds that it received from the sale of the plates to DHB on Brooks's horse racing empire, or Brooks transferred the money to another entity that he controlled.

The same day that the SEC filed its complaint against the three directors of DHB, the commission filed a separate complaint against the company (which is now under new management and led by new board members) for securities fraud. DHB has settled the charges and agreed to a permanent injunction from future violations.

## Questions

1. Identify the stakeholders in this case and the ethical obligations of independent members of the board of directors and audit committee to these parties.

2. What are the legal liabilities of board members and members of the audit committee? Analyze the facts of the case and comment whether they violated their legal and ethical obligations.

3. Are there any parallels in the case with the Tyco case discussed in Chapter 5? What are they? Evaluate the role that internal controls played in each case.

## Case 6-7

# Livingston & Haynes, P. C.

This case concerns alleged violations of Section 10A of the Securities Exchange Act by Livingston & Haynes, P. C. ("L&H"), Kevin Howley, and William W. Wood in connection with L&H's 2005 and 2006 year-end audits and quarterly interim reviews of the financial statements of LocatePlus Holdings Corporation ("LocatePlus"). The SEC filed charges against L&H, Howley, and Wood on June 6, 2011.[1]

L&H is an accounting and auditing firm registered with the PCAOB. The firm provides tax preparation services, as well as services to public companies registered with the commission and to private equity clients. L&H served as the auditors on LocatePlus's audits and interim reviews for the fiscal years 2005 and 2006, from which L&H received approximately $227,800 in fees.

## Violations of Securities Exchange Act of 1934

Howley served as the engagement partner and Wood served as the concurring partner on the engagements. On October 14, 2010, the commission filed a complaint against LocatePlus alleging, in part, that LocatePlus's former CEO and CFO fraudulently inflated the company's publicly reported revenue in its periodic filings with the commission for at least FY2005 and FY2006. The complaint alleges that, as part of LocatePlus's fraud, its CEO and CFO were involved in the following action related to a fictitious customer called Omni Data Services, Inc. ("Omni Data"):

- LocatePlus improperly recognized revenue from Omni Data. The improper Omni Data revenue was included in LocatePlus's financial statements that were part of quarterly and annual reports for FY2005 and FY2006 and were included in filings with the commission.
- In total, LocatePlus falsely reported more than $6 million from Omni Data for FY2005 and FY2006, representing over 25 percent of LocatePlus's total revenue for those two years.

The SEC also charged L&H with the following in connection with its audits of LocatePlus for the years 2005 and 2006:

- L&H, Howley, and Wood failed to include procedures designed to provide reasonable assurance of detecting illegal acts that would have a direct and material effect on the determination of financial statement amounts, and thus each of them violated Section 10A(a)(1) of the Exchange Act.
- L&H, Howley, and Wood became aware of multiple allegations of illegal acts at LocatePlus, including allegations

[1]SEC, Accounting and Enforcement Release No. 3288, Administrative Proceeding File No. 3-14440, *In the Matter of Livingston & Haynes, P. C., Kevin Howley, CPA and William W. Wood, CPA.* Available at www.sec.gov/litigation/admin/2011/34-64607.pdf.

that the Omni Data revenue was fictitious, yet they failed to determine whether it was likely that an illegal act had occurred. Based on this conduct, each of them violated Section 10A(b)(1) of the Exchange Act.

- During the course of L&H's 2005 and 2006 year-end audits of LocatePlus, L&H and Howley individually became aware of red flags indicating that the Omni Data revenue was fictitious, yet the company failed to ensure that the very risky area was audited properly.
- L&H and Howley failed to plan the audits properly, test the Omni Data revenue adequately, obtain sufficient competent evidential matter to serve as a basis for L&H's audit reports, exercise due professional care, apply skepticism, and properly assess the risks of material misstatement due to fraud.

## Facts of the Case

LocatePlus is a provider of public information made available via either a CD ROM-based product or via a proprietary, Internet-accessible database. The LocatePlus product contains searchable information on individuals throughout the United States, including, for example, social security numbers, prior residences, and real estate holdings. In addition to direct purchasers, LocatePlus sells its product through "channel partner" arrangements, by which third parties access their databases in consideration for a royalty.

In 2005 and 2006, LocatePlus claimed to have secured a significant "channel partner" arrangement with Omni Data, a company that purportedly conducted its business over the Internet. Under the terms of the alleged agreement, Omni Data had unlimited access to LocatePlus's data via the Internet in exchange for a royalty fee of $300,000 per month. The agreement also stated that LocatePlus would build and maintain a website for Omni Data in exchange for $500,000.

In fact, Omni Data was a sham customer of LocatePlus created by the CFO and CEO to record false revenue. Through this fraudulent scheme, Omni Data would "buy" services from LocatePlus and make purported "payments" to LocatePlus. The CFO and CEO then caused LocatePlus to record these fictitious payments as revenue in its financial results, which were included in periodic filings with the SEC.

To fund these purported payments to LocatePlus, the CFO and CEO funneled approximately $2 million in cash to Omni Data through a series of transactions which included a "round-trip" transaction in which LocatePlus made a $650,000 payment to an entity controlled by the CFO, who then transferred $600,000 to Omni Data, which then paid the $600,000 back to LocatePlus as purported payment for services.

LocatePlus made numerous false and misleading statements regarding, among other things, its revenue in a number of periodic filings with the commission. For FY2005 and FY2006, LocatePlus improperly recognized $3.6 million and $2.7 million, respectively, in fictitious revenue from Omni Data. This caused LocatePlus to overstate its 2005 annual results by 46 percent and its 2005 quarterly results by 53 percent for the first quarter, 44 percent for the second quarter and 43 percent for the third quarter. LocatePlus overstated its 2006 annual results by 28 percent and its 2006 quarterly results by 41 percent for the first quarter, 34 percent for the second quarter and 36 percent for the third quarter.

L&H performed LocatePlus's 2005 and 2006 year-end audits and quarterly reviews. The audit reports issued for both years included an explanatory *paragraph* (i.e., emphasis of matter) stating that LocatePlus's substantial net losses raise substantial doubt about the company's ability to continue as a going concern.

## Auditor Resignation

On December 10, 2004, LocatePlus's former auditor, resigned. In a resignation letter addressed to LocatePlus's audit committee chairman, LocatePlus's former auditor cited "concerns about the timeliness of information we received and about the reliability of certain representations of your company's management."

In January 2005, Howley was contacted to inquire about L&H becoming LocatePlus's new auditors. On February 16, 2005, Howley and Wood visited the former auditor's offices and met with the partner formerly responsible for the LocatePlus engagement. The former auditor's audit partner detailed multiple reasons for its resignation, including (1) difficulty getting information from management, (2) management providing contradictory explanations to its questions, (3) management providing unsigned contracts as audit evidence, and (4) difficulty getting management to accept its proposed audit adjustments.

After L&H's meeting with LocatePlus's former auditor, Howley, Wood, and L&H's president met and determined to accept LocatePlus as a client. Because of the concerns expressed by LocatePlus's former auditor, however, L&H determined to "use extensive care" and treat LocatePlus as a high-risk audit client.

## Audit Difficulties

During the 2004 audit, L&H had difficulties getting information from LocatePlus's management about significant transactions, to the extent that, on April 11, 2005, L&H pulled out of the field because they were unable to remain productive with the amount of information they had to work with.

## Red Flags Discovered

During the course of its 2005 interim reviews of quarterly filings, L&H became aware of multiple red flags concerning the revenue recognized from Omni Data and the resulting receivable on LocatePlus's balance sheet. In a June 1, 2005, e-mail from Howley to Fields, Howley noted that (1) L&H was unable to find records for Omni Data on the Connecticut secretary of state's website (i.e., the state where Omni Data was purportedly located); (2) that the alleged president of Omni Data was not listed for any of the Omni Data entities that they did find; and (3) that L&H could not locate a website for Omni Data, despite the fact that Omni Data was purportedly a business doing data sales over the Internet.

Howley accepted management's explanations for the inconsistencies. For example, in response to an L&H inquiry about the scarcity of information available on Omni Data, LocatePlus's in-house accountant told Howley in a June 7, 2005 e-mail that "we don't make it common practice to research companies extensively with which we do business." In addition, in a June 9, 2005 e-mail, Fields claimed that "[Omni Data] does not have a corporate web site because they are trying to keep a low profile" and that Omni Data's web site was, in fact, under the name "findyourpeeps.com."

As of June 30, 2005, the Omni Data receivable was approximately $1.8 million reflecting revenue of the same amount recognized in 2005. No collections had been received as of June 30, 2005, from Omni Data for revenues earned in 2005.

## Allegations of Illegal Acts

On or about August 26, 2005, Howley received a message that a former LocatePlus board member ("the informant") wanted to speak with him. During a telephone conversation with Howley shortly thereafter, the informant made a number of allegations of wrongdoing by LocatePlus and members of management. Among other things, the informant questioned the validity of the Omni Data transactions and indicated that the alleged president of Omni Data was a former girlfriend of the former CEO and chair of the board of directors. Shortly after the telephone conversation, Howley relayed the substance of the informant's allegations to Wood.

Between at least December 2005 and March 2006, the informant contacted Howley via telephone and e-mail on numerous occasions regarding his concerns about fraud at LocatePlus. During the course of multiple e-mail exchanges with Howley, the informant provided the following information:

- Omni Data revenue was phony and there was no evidence that Omni Data existed.

- Omni Data contract was signed five months before Delaware incorporation records showed that the company was incorporated.

- The alleged president of Omni Data was a "stooge set up by the CEO" to mask phony sales and was, in fact, a ballet teacher and the CEO's former girlfriend.

- The CEO told the informant that Omni Data was a start-up that "might not be around."

- LocatePlus's audit committee chairman had a conflict of interest because he had pledged assets to secure a loan to the CEO.

- The CEO had been buying off LocatePlus's audit committee chairman through extending him high-interest loans made to the company (at 30 percent to 40 percent).

Wood read the informant's e-mails and discussed them with Howley prior to and during the course of the 2005 year-end audit. Wood also discussed the allegations with L&H's president. Howley forwarded the e-mails from the informant to LocatePlus's audit committee chairman. In e-mail correspondence, Howley recommended to LocatePlus's audit committee chairman that the audit committee chairman should plan a meeting with the informant, the audit committee's legal counsel, and Howley to address the informant's allegations. The meeting never occurred.

A major issue in this case is the failure of L&H to test the Omni Data revenue and receivable adequately. The issue involves both inappropriate accounting and the failure of the audit to identify material misstatements in the financial statements.

## 2005 Audit

L&H identified numerous risk factors indicating that LocatePlus had a high risk for fraud during the 2005 year-end audit. In a fraud "brainstorming" memo included in L&H's 2005 audit work papers, L&H specifically identified overstated and/or fictitious revenues/accounts receivable relative to Omni Data. The memo went on to state that "L&H will approach the audit with much skepticism."

Despite having identified the Omni Data transactions as a high-risk area and being aware of the allegations that Omni Data was fictitious, L&H, under Howley's direction, failed to obtain sufficient competent evidential matter that LocatePlus had delivered its product to Omni Data.

Although L&H tested delivery of products and services for other LocatePlus's customers, it did not test delivery to Omni Data even though it accounted for approximately one-third of LocatePlus's revenue. For other customers, L&H compared the amounts billed and recognized as revenue to LocatePlus's data usage logs to ensure that the customer had agreed to purchase the product and had actually used it.

However, L&H never looked at the usage logs for Omni Data. Had L&H reviewed Omni Data's usage logs, they would have discovered that there was no activity or usage in 2005. Instead, L&H relied upon the executed agreement between LocatePlus and Omni Data and confirmation received from Omni Data regarding the monies earned and owed.

## 2006 Audit

Questions persisted at L&H throughout the 2006 year-end audit of LocatePlus about the existence and collectibility of the growing Omni Data receivable balance. As of December 31, 2006, the Omni Data receivable balance was $5.1 million representing approximately 88 percent of LocatePlus's total receivables. In a work paper included in L&H's 2006 year-end audit work papers, L&H noted that "there is questionability regarding the Omni Data receivable and the existence of Omni Data (whether it is a viable entity)."

The purported Omni Data agreement had been amended, as of October 1, 2006, to extend Omni Data's payment terms to $45,000 per month for the approximately $4.2 million outstanding balance. Under the original contract terms, payments were due 30 days from the invoice date. As a result of the amendment, LocatePlus reclassified $3.8 million of the Omni Data receivable from current accounts receivable to long-term accounts receivable. It also recorded a discount and an allowance on the receivable, which was approximately $1.9 million as of December 31, 2006.

Despite these developments and the open question as to whether Omni Data was a viable entity, L&H failed to obtain sufficient competent evidential matter that the Omni Data transaction was properly stated in the financial statements.

## Failure to Adequately Plan the 2005 and 2006 Year-End Audits

L&H, under Howley's direction, failed to plan the 2005 and 2006 year-end audits of LocatePlus adequately by designing procedures that would account for the heightened risk of fraud and, specifically, for the possibility that the Omni Data revenue was fictitious, as had been alleged.

L&H's testing procedures for the Omni Data revenue included relying on the confirmation process and the existence of an executed contract and checking cash receipts. Omni Data, however, was not paying within its contract terms and, as Wood acknowledged during October 6, 2010, testimony before the Commission, if LocatePlus "set up a dummy company," as had been alleged, then the confirmation process "would not be adequate evidence."

## Failure to Evaluate Evidence Obtained by the Confirmation Process

In general, it is presumed that audit evidence is more reliable when it is obtained from knowledgeable independent sources outside the entity. During the 2005 year-end audit, L&H failed to evaluate adequately the reliability of the audit evidence obtained by the confirmation process. Exhibit 1 elaborates on the inadequacies.

## Failure to Assess the Risk of Material Misstatement Due to the Omni Data Transaction

Although L&H became aware of the informant's allegations prior to and during the course of the 2005 year-end audit, it took few steps to investigate the informant's allegations during the audit. Moreover, to the extent to which L&H developed any evidence regarding the informant's allegations, the evidence corroborated many of the informant's claims.

For example, L&H searched Connecticut and Massachusetts corporate records, but found no evidence that Omni Data was incorporated. Howley attempted to contact the alleged president of Omni Data, but was initially unable to reach her as the first confirmation sent to Omni Data was returned as undeliverable.

---

**Exhibit 1**
**Evaluation of Audit Evidence**

First, L&H initially sent its confirmation to the president of Omni Data—a person alleged by the informant to be a "stooge" of the CEO—at the address that LocatePlus had provided. Moreover, the confirmation was initially returned to L&H by the U.S. Postal Service as "undeliverable." Ultimately, a confirmation was received, signed by a person purporting to be president of Omni Data.

During the 2006 year-end audit, the confirmation sent to the Omni Data address that LocatePlus had provided was again returned as "undeliverable." When Howley questioned LocatePlus about the confirmation, he was told that Omni Data had a new president, and that it was doing business under a completely different name: Economics Data Solutions. Howley researched the new president but was unable to confirm that he was related to Omni Data. In fact, the only research contained in L&H's 2006 work papers regarding the alleged new president was a December 8, 2005, newspaper article describing an individual by the same name as an attendee at tryouts for the reality television show *Ultimate Fighting*. L&H ultimately received a confirmation signed by a person purporting to be the new president of Omni Data.

---

L&H discovered additional red flags regarding the Omni Data transaction during the 2005 interim reviews and year-end audit. For example, L&H discovered that:

- The Omni Data receivable comprised approximately 76 percent of the overall accounts receivable, but LocatePlus had collected only $250,000 in payments in 2005 from Omni Data out of approximately $3.6 million in revenue recognized.
- Payments totaling approximately $10,000 from LocatePlus to the alleged president of Omni Data.
- Payments totaling approximately $325,000 to the CEO.

Although L&H's work papers document the informant's allegations, they do not document the procedures specifically designed to assess these risks. In fact, L&H's "Fraud Risk Assessment Form," for the 2005 year-end audit, which lays out procedures intended to facilitate compliance with auditing standards is blank.

Moreover, an item on L&H's audit program (completed at the conclusion of the audit) specifically instructs that "[i]f you believe that fraud or an illegal act may have occurred, document the circumstances identified and apply the procedures for potential fraud or illegal acts in additional procedures section of this audit program."

The work paper states "none noted" next to the proposed procedure indicating that L&H never applied the additional procedures in its own audit program. Howley testified that he reviewed this work paper.

L&H's 2005 year-end work papers do not document that L&H came to *any* conclusion about the merits of the informant's allegations. L&H's 2006 year-end work papers document that the very existence of Omni Data was still an open question through the 2006 year-end audit and that L&H did not come to a final conclusion about the informant's allegations until, at the earliest, April 2007.

Despite the numerous red flags and lingering questions about the existence of the Omni Data receivable, L&H's

2006 year-end work papers also do not document an assessment of the risks of material misstatement due to fraud.

Despite being aware of the informant's allegations of fraud (and thus the risks of material misstatement), Howley did not undertake adequate audit procedures during the 2005 or 2006 year-end audit to assess these risks.

L&H's 2005 year-end audit work papers document that L&H accepted management's explanations for the red flags. For example, with regard to the Omni Data receivable, Howley accepted LocatePlus's management's representation that it was collectible despite L&H's difficulties verifying its existence and Omni Data's failure to make payments under the terms of the purported contact.

With regard to the CEO payments, Howley accepted the explanation that the payments were "bonuses" approved by the board even though the bonuses did not go through LocatePlus's payroll system. In addition, L&H did not obtain LocatePlus's board minutes to attempt to verify the explanation. Finally, with regard to the payments to the alleged president of Omni Data, Howley accepted LocatePlus's explanation that they were "referral fees" despite allegations that the alleged president was a figurehead installed by the CEO.

## Alleged Professional Violations

The SEC charged that L&H, Howley, and Wood engaged in improper professional conduct that violated Section 4C(a)(2) of the Exchange Act and Rule 102(e)(1)(ii) of the Commission's Rules of Practice. Under Rule 4C(b)(2) and Rule 102(e)(1)(iv)(B), the term "improper professional conduct" means, in part, "a single instance of highly unreasonable conduct that results in a violation of applicable professional standards in circumstances in which an accountant knows, or should know, that heightened scrutiny is warranted."

In light of the specific allegations that the Omni Data transaction was fictitious, L&H's and Howley's failure to design testing procedures adequately to address that very risk, and Wood's concurrence in the approval of the issuance of L&H's 2005 and 2006 audit reports when he knew that significant matters were unresolved, constituted highly unreasonable conduct that resulted in a violation of applicable professional standards in circumstances in which each knew, or should have known, that heightened scrutiny was warranted.

The failure of L&H and Howley to plan the audits properly, test the Omni Data revenue adequately, obtain sufficient competent evidence to serve as a basis for L&H's audit reports, and assess properly the risks of material misstatement due to fraud, and the failure of Wood to address these deficiencies also constituted highly unreasonable conduct that resulted in a violation of applicable professional standards in circumstances in which each knew, or should have known, that heightened scrutiny was warranted.

As a result of the conduct alleged in the SEC filing, L&H, Howley, and Wood violated Section 10A(a)(1) of the Exchange Act, which requires each audit to include procedures designed to provide reasonable assurance of detecting illegal acts that would have a direct and material effect on the determination of financial statement amounts.

## Questions

1. Do you think L&H's actions with respect to LocatePlus and its alleged relationship with Omni Data illustrates a case of *moral blindness?* Explain with respect to the ethics of actions by LocatePlus and its effect on audit decisions by L&H.

2. A critical element of the due care requirement is to approach an audit with professional skepticism. Evaluate the audit procedures and decisions made by L&H with respect to this ethical standard.

3. Evaluate the legal liability of L&H, Howley, and Wood using the legal concepts discussed in this chapter. Support your analysis with reasoning as to whether the auditors failed to exercise ordinary care, were grossly negligent, or committed fraud.

## Case 6-8

# Kay & Lee LLP

Kay and Lee LLP has just been retained as the auditor for Holligan Industries to audit the financial statements required by a bank, Second National Bank & Trust, as a prerequisite to extending a loan to the client. The auditor knows the bank is the client's principal lender and is aware of the bank's reliance on the financial statements, particularly the valuation of inventory and accounts receivable. Additionally, the bank and auditor have direct oral and written communication during the lending period and even meet to discuss the client's financial statements.[1]

After the audit report is issued, the bank discovers that the client's inventory and accounts receivable were overstated. The client subsequently goes bankrupt and defaults on the loan. The bank alleges that the auditor failed to communicate about the inadequacy of the client's internal recordkeeping and inventory control.

## Questions

1. What would the bank have to prove to successfully bring a lawsuit against Kay & Lee for ordinary negligence? Use legal principles to support your answer.

2. Changing the facts of the case, assume the client hired Kay & Lee to audit the financial statements, explaining that the purpose of the audit is to negotiate a loan. The name of the bank is unknown to the auditors. Under which legal principle could the auditors be held legally liable for the ordinary negligence? Which case(s) in the book support your opinion?

3. From an ethical perspective why is it important for an auditor to properly audit inventory and accounts receivable when it knows a bank may rely on the audited financial statements?

[1] The facts of this case are drawn from the following online article in the *Journal of Accountancy:* Stanley Sterna, ESQ, "Defending third-party audit claims," http://www.journalofaccountancy.com/Issues/2013/May/20137570.htm.

## Case 6-9

# *Reznor v. J. Artist Management (JAM), Inc.*[1]

Michael Trent Reznor met John Malm Jr., a part-time promoter of local rock bands who also is a licensed CPA, in Cleveland, Ohio, in 1985. Malm became Reznor's manager and formed J. Artist Management (JAM), Inc. Reznor became the lead singer in the band Nine Inch Nails, which performed its first show in 1988. Reznor and Malm signed a management agreement, under which JAM was to receive 20 percent of Reznor's gross compensation.

In 1966, Malm hired a CPA, Richard Szekelyi, and his firm, Navigent Group, to provide tax consulting services to Reznor personally; his duties also included examining Reznor's financial records. Szekelyi discovered flawed accounting between the two parties to the detriment of Reznor by about $4 million. The primary cause was that Malm received tax benefits that should have gone to Reznor.[2] Reznor filed a separate lawsuit against codefendants Szekelyi and Navigent Group, charging them with negligence, breach of fiduciary duty, and aiding and abetting fraud. The codefendants sought summary judgment to dismiss Reznor's claims, stating that they did not breach any standard of care in preparing or presenting reports of Reznor's financial status, nor did Szekelyi fail to counsel Reznor adequately concerning other transactions. The court granted the summary judgment dismissing the charges against Szekelyi and Navigent.[3] Reznor had also filed a lawsuit in 2004 in New York, claiming that former manager Malm mismanaged the band's finances and actually stole money from them. Apparently, Malm tricked Reznor into signing a contract that assigned the manager 20 percent of gross earnings. The problem is that the assignment should have been of net income, not gross earnings. This means that Malm would have received 20 percent of all earnings, before taxes and before more important distributions like his band member payments.[4]

On June 1, 2005, a verdict was rendered in favor of Reznor. Malm was ordered to pay up to $2.9 million for allegedly cheating Reznor out of millions. The verdict also awarded trademarks back to Reznor.

## Questions

1. Describe the nature of the relationship between Szekelyi and Reznor. Did a privity relationship exist between the two? Why or why not?

2. What were Szekelyi's ethical obligations to Reznor, given the nature of the services provided? Which of the ethics standards in the AICPA Code should have been of particular concern to Szekelyi in performing professional services for Reznor?

3. During the course of working as the manager for Nine Inch Nails, John Malm mismanaged the band's finances and was found guilty of those charges. Malm, who is a CPA, was not hired to perform any accounting services for Reznor or the band. Does that mean his actions are not enforceable under the AICPA Code of Professional Conduct? Would a state board of accountancy have any recourse with respect to Malm's transgressions?

---

[1] The facts in this case are the original facts. However, some material has been expanded to better develop legal liability issues.
[2] Roger LeRoy Miller and Gaylord A. Jentz, *Business Law Today,* 7th ed. (Mason, OH: Thomson West, 2007), pp. 1087–1088.
[3] *Reznor v. J. Artist Mgmt,* 365 F.Supp.2d 565 (S.D.N.Y. 2005).

[4] Available at www.cmt.com/news/country-music/1503212/nine-inch-nails-trent-reznor-wins-case-against-his-former-partner.jhtml.

## Case 6-10

# *SEC v. Zurich Financial Services*

## Background

On December 11, 2008, the SEC reached agreement with Zurich Financial Services (Zurich) to settle the commission's charges against Zurich for aiding and abetting a fraud by Converium Holding AG involving the use of finite reinsurance transactions to inflate improperly Converium's financial performance. The commission's complaint alleges that Zurich aided and abetted Converium's violation of Section 10(b) of the Securities Exchange Act of 1934 and Rule 10b-5 thereunder. Under the settlement, Zurich consented to the entry of a final judgment directing it to pay a $25 million penalty plus $1 in disgorgement and, in a related administrative proceeding, consented to the entry of a cease-and-desist order against it.[1] The accounting issue in question deals with the complex topic of reinsurance. The facts of the accounting fraud have been simplified as much as possible to focus mainly on the legal liabilities of the company.

Zurich is a corporation organized under the laws of Switzerland with its principal place of business in Zurich, Switzerland. Historically, Zurich operated its reinsurance business under the brand name Zurich Re, which operated as a separate division within Zurich Insurance Company (ZIC), a wholly owned subsidiary of Zurich, and through its North American subsidiary, Zurich Reinsurance (North America) Inc. (Zurich Re North America). Prior to Converium's IPO, Zurich restructured its reinsurance operations and transferred substantially all of the reinsurance business operated under Zurich Re to Converium. In December 2001 and January 2002, pursuant to the Registration Statement and Prospectus, Zurich sold 40 million shares of Converium in the form of shares and American Depository Shares[2] (ADSs), representing its entire stake in Converium, for proceeds of approximately $1.9 billion.

## Accounting Issues

The commission's complaint alleges that beginning in 1999, the management of Zurich Re developed three reinsurance transactions for the purpose of obtaining the financial benefits of reinsurance accounting. However, in order for a company to obtain the benefits of reinsurance accounting, the reinsurance transaction must transfer risk. Here, the management of Zurich redesigned the transactions to make them appear to transfer risk to third-party reinsurers when, in fact, no risk was transferred outside of Zurich-owned entities. For two of the transactions at issue, Zurich Re ceded risk to third-party reinsurers but took it back through reinsurance agreements—known as *retrocessions*—with another Zurich entity. For the third transaction, Zurich Re ceded the risk to a third-party reinsurer but simultaneously entered into an undisclosed side agreement with the reinsurer, pursuant to which Zurich Re agreed to hold the reinsurer harmless for any losses realized under the reinsurance contracts. Because the ultimate risk under the reinsurance contracts remained with Zurich-owned entities, these transactions should not have been accounted for as reinsurance.

The complaint also alleges that, in March 2001, Zurich announced its intent to spin off its reinsurance group into an IPO. Zurich then created and capitalized Converium, which assumed the rights and obligations of Zurich's assumed reinsurance business. On December 11, 2001, Zurich spun off Converium into an IPO. At the conclusion of the IPO, the members of Zurich Re management responsible for the three reinsurance transactions ceased to be affiliated with Zurich. As a result of the improper accounting treatment of reinsurance transactions, the historical financial statements in Converium's IPO documents, including the Form F-1[3] it filed with the SEC, were materially misleading. Among other things, Converium understated its reported loss before taxes by approximately $100 million (67 percent) in 2000 and by approximately $3 million (1 percent) in 2001. In addition, for certain periods, the transactions had the effect of artificially decreasing Converium's reported loss ratios for certain reporting segments—the ratio between losses paid by an insurer and premiums earned that is frequently cited by analysts as a key performance metric for insurance companies.

The complaint further alleges that Converium's misstatements were material to investors who purchased shares in the IPO. Through the IPO, which was the largest reinsurance IPO in history, Zurich raised significantly more than it would have raised had Zurich and Converium not improperly inflated Converium's financial performance.

---

[1] Securities and Exchange Commission, *SEC v. Zurich Financial Services*, 08 Civ. 10760 (WHP) (S.D.N.Y.), Litigation Release No. 20825, December 11, 2008, Accounting and Auditing Enforcement Release No. 2910, December 11, 2008.

[2] An American Depository Share (ADS) is a U.S. dollar-denominated equity share of a foreign-based company available for purchase on an American stock exchange. ADSs are issued by depository banks in the U.S. under agreement with the issuing foreign company; the entire issuance is called an American Depository Receipt (ADR) and the individual shares are referred to as ADSs.

[3] SEC Form F-1 is required to register securities issued by foreign issuers for which no other specialized form exists or is authorized.

## Reinsurance Accounting Principles

Reinsurance is a complicated area in accounting. Exhibit 1 describes some of the main features of the accounting rules.

From 1999 through 2001, management of Zurich Re designed three reinsurance transactions that created the appearance of risk transfer in order to benefit from reinsurance accounting. These three transactions affected the financial statements included in Converium's IPO prospectus. In two of the three transactions, Zurich Re purchased reinsurance from Inter-Ocean, which, in turn, ceded these liabilities to a Zurich entity (the Inter-Ocean transactions), in one transaction directly and in the other transaction indirectly through a third reinsurer (Company A). Zurich Re's use of Inter-Ocean as an intermediary in the transaction helped obscure the transactions' circular structure and the fact that Zurich Re had merely moved the risk from one Zurich Re entity to another. In the third transaction, Zurich Re entered into a reinsurance transaction for which the risk transfer was negated by an undisclosed and purportedly unrelated side agreement that protected the reinsurer against losses suffered under the reinsurance contract. Zurich Re improperly accounted for these transactions using reinsurance accounting.

Although Zurich Re accounted for the transactions with Inter-Ocean and Company A as reinsurance, in reality, Zurich Re had recirculated the risk from one Zurich entity to another, while interposing intermediaries (Inter-Ocean and Company A) that obscured the transactions' circular structure. Because this transaction was circular, there was no risk transfer, and Zurich Re (and later Converium) should not have accounted for the contract as reinsurance. As a result, and as reported in Converium's December 2001 Form F-1, Converium understated its pretax losses for the year ended December 31, 2000, by $1.36 million.

## The Converium IPO

On March 22, 2001, in connection with its announcement of disappointing financial results for 2000, Zurich reported that it intended to exit the assumed reinsurance business. In a September 6, 2001, press release, Zurich announced that its reinsurance business would be spun off into an IPO, and that as of October 1, 2001, the business would operate under the name "Converium."

The Registration Statement and Prospectus filed by Converium in connection with the IPO, which became effective on December 11, 2001, was derived from data from the Zurich subsidiaries combined to form Converium and failed to disclose the impact of the circular Inter-Ocean and the Z-1 facility transactions on Converium's business operations, financial results, and shareholders' equity at the time of the IPO.

Accordingly, the statements in the prospectus regarding Converium's financial results for 2000 and the first half of 2001 were materially false and misleading. As a consequence of the circular Inter-Ocean transactions and the Z-1 facility transactions, rather than reporting a loss before taxes of $48.8 million for 2000, Converium should have reported a loss of at least $148.4 million. Converium also overstated its $1.09 billion in reported shareholders' equity as of December 31, 2000, by at least $72.3 million (approximately 6.6 percent of the total reported shareholders' equity), an amount including the effect of $100 million attributable to the Inter-Ocean and Z-1 facility transactions and partially offset by $27.7 million attributable to other reinsurance transactions not addressed within the complaint.

Finally, because Converium's loss ratio for its non-life reinsurance business was directly affected by the improperly recorded reinsurance obtained through the circular Inter-Ocean

---

**Exhibit 1**
**Accounting Rules for Reinsurance**

In basic terms, reinsurance is insurance for insurers. Reinsurance is the transfer of insurance risk by the primary insurer to a second insurance carrier, called the reinsurer, in exchange for a payment or premium. Whether a contract is accounted for as reinsurance depends on whether the contract indemnifies the ceding company—here Zurich and Converium—from loss or liability. Such indemnification is known as *risk transfer*. Risk is transferred when (1) the reinsurer assumes significant insurance risk and (2) it is reasonably possible that the reinsurer will realize a significant loss in the transaction. A risk transfer analysis for a contract emphasizes substance over form and GAAP requires "an evaluation of all contractual features that . . . limit the amount of insurance risk to which the reinsurer is subject." Accordingly, under GAAP, "if agreements with the reinsurer . . . in the aggregate, do not transfer risk, the individual contracts that make up those agreements also would not be considered to transfer risk, regardless of how they are structured."

Where there is insufficient risk transfer, a transaction may not be treated as reinsurance under GAAP, and must be accounted for using the deposit method, which lacks the potential accounting benefits of reinsurance accounting. Under reinsurance accounting, when losses on the ceded business are incurred, the ceding insurer records an offset to the increase in its gross loss reserves in an amount equal to the reinsurance it expects to recover from the reinsurer, thus increasing its net income by that amount. Deposit accounting has no comparable income statement benefit.

and the Z-1 facility transactions, Converium materially under-stated its reported loss ratios.

## SEC Charges

Based on the foregoing, the SEC charged Converium with violating Section 10(b) of the Exchange Act and Rule 10b-5 in that it knowingly or recklessly made false and mislead-ing statements, or omitted to state material facts necessary in order to make the statements, in the light of the circumstances under which they were made, not misleading to purchasers of Converium securities in connection with the 2001 IPO.

Zurich substantially assisted Converium's violation of Section 10(b) of the Exchange Act and Rule 10b-5 by, among other things, entering into the finite reinsurance transactions previously described for the purpose of improperly inflating its financial performance and improperly using reinsurance

accounting rules to account for the transactions with the knowledge that such accounting was improper.

## Questions

1. Why do you think it is important for a reinsurance trans-action to transfer risk in order for a company to obtain the benefits of reinsurance accounting? Discuss the account-ing and legal issues behind such a requirement.

2. Assume that the external auditors of Zurich Re and Converium knew about the Inter-Ocean and the Z-1 facility transactions. What legal issues could have been raised by the purchasers of stock in Converium's IPO to successfully bring an action against the auditors?

3. Evaluate the ethics of Zurich Re's actions with respect to its reinsurance transactions and the transfer of economic risk.

# Earnings Management and the Quality of Financial Reporting

## Ethics Reflection

In Chapter 5, we looked at the fraud triangle that identifies red flags that provide warning signs that financial fraud may exist. In Chapter 6, we learned about legal liability issues that can arise when auditors fail to identify material misstatements in the financial statements. In Chapter 7, we examine earnings management issues and techniques used to "hype" the numbers. These chapters fit together as a cohesive unit because the failure to identify red flags may lead to lawsuits against auditors if such failings result from steps taken by a client to instigate or cover-up fraud and the auditors fail to detect the material misstatements in the financial statements. Examples of the kinds of transactions used to commit fraud are discussed in Chapter 7 under the umbrella of "financial shenanigans, a term first used by Howard Schilit a forensic investigator at the Center for Financial Research and Analysis"

The Association of Certified Fraud Examiners (ACFE) defines fraud as "deception or misrepresentation that an individual or entity makes knowing that the misrepresentation could result in some unauthorized benefit to the individual or to the entity or some other party." Greed and work pressure are the most common factors pushing management to deceive investors and creditors. They provide incentives for fraud to occur and earnings management techniques may exceed the bounds of reasonability to make it happen.

Financial statement fraud occurs (or presumably occurs) with management's knowledge and blessing. The opportunity to commit fraud exists because of management's position within the organization. As we have previously

discussed, mid-level accountants can caught up in the fraud, often because they want to be loyal and a team player, such as Betty Vinson at WorldCom, when they are convinced it is a one-time event. It rarely works that way because the methods used to commit fraud typically result in moving revenue to an earlier period or delaying expense recognition to a later period. In both cases, the company is borrowing from the future to make the current period look better and the result is a snowball effect that begins the slide down the ethical slippery slope for those caught up in the fraud. The first step tends to undermine future actions. Once a person's ethics are compromised, such as Betty Vinson, it becomes more difficult to do the right thing in the future as the employer might resort to reminding the employee of her past failure. The Jose Gomez audit of ESM Government Securities that was discussed in Chapter 4 is a case in point where Gomez missed fraud at the company and magnified the ethical lapse by borrowing money from the client that now had two levers to use against Gomez if he decided to do the right thing.

Recall that the ACFE Global Fraud Study that was discussed in Chapter 3 indicates that organizations lose 5 percent of revenues to fraud each year and while only 8 percent of the cases were from financial statement fraud schemes, they did cause the greatest median loss at $1 million. There are five basic types of financial statement fraud: fictitious sales, improper expense recognition, incorrect asset valuation, hidden liabilities, and inadequate disclosures. These techniques are discussed in the "financial shenanigans" section later in this chapter.

The vast majority of public companies engage in some form of questionable earnings management, at least at the margin, according to Ronald A. Kiima, former assistant chief accountant in the Corporation Finance Division of the U.S. Securities and Exchange Commission (SEC), who now heads a consulting firm that specializes in SEC accounting and disclosure issues and corporate governance and risk management.[1]

Financial statement restatements are indicators that previous years' financial statements contained material misstatements.

Historically, the most common reason for companies to restate their financial statements or be subject to SEC enforcement actions due to fraud has been the way in which they have recognized revenue. The higher the number in the income statement (i.e., sales revenue), the greater the effect on other profit numbers in the statement (i.e., gross profit and operating income) all the way down to net income. And within revenue recognition, the most prevalent form is premature recognition, or booking sales before prices have been fixed, contracts have been finalized, or goods or services have been delivered to customers.

In a famous 1998 speech titled "The Numbers Game," former SEC chairman Arthur Levitt used an epicurean analogy to describe the practice of improperly booking revenues. "Think about a bottle of wine," he said. "You wouldn't pop the cork on that bottle before it was ready. But some companies are doing this with their revenue—recognizing it before a sale is complete, before the product is delivered to a customer, or at a time when the customer still has options to terminate, void or delay the sale."

Financial reporting refers to the way companies show their financial performance to investors, creditors, and other interested parties by preparing and presenting financial statements. The quality is of utmost importance because it is an assessment criterion for how reliable a firm's earnings are. A company that has a high quality of reporting can more readily raise funds in the marketplace because investors feel safer with a company that has quality built into the financial reports.

As you read this chapter, reflect on the numerous ways in which financial statements can be manipulated, thereby sacrificing quality, and how accountants and auditors might do a better job looking for the red flags that signal fraud may be up ahead. Also, consider whether auditors are adequately meeting their ethical obligations and protecting the public interest with regard to fraud detection.

> Increasingly, I have become concerned that the motivation to meet Wall Street earnings expectations may be overriding common sense business practices. Too many corporate managers, auditors, and analysts are participants in a game of nods and winks. In the zeal to satisfy consensus earnings estimates and project a smooth earnings path, wishful thinking may be winning the day over faithful representation.
>
> *Arthur Levitt*

This quote by former SEC chair Arthur Levitt is from a speech to the New York University Center for Law and Business on September 28, 1998, titled "The Numbers Game." Levitt links the practice of "earnings management" to an excessive zeal to project smoother earnings from year to year that casts a pall over the quality of the underlying numbers. Levitt identifies the cause as a "culture of gamesmanship" in business rooted in the emphasis on achieving short-term results such as meeting or exceeding financial analysts' earnings expectations.[2]

Warren Buffett once said that: "Earnings can be as pliable as putty when a charlatan heads the company reporting them." The quote emphasizes the importance of having an ethical person at the head of a company because a chief executive officer (CEO) who practices fraud can twist earnings to make them look better than they really are, thereby deceiving the users of the financial statements.

The accounting scandals at companies such as Enron, WorldCom, and Tyco involved the use of inside information by top management to sell shares owned at a relatively favorable current price compared to future prices. Presumably, the executives knew the earnings had been manipulated and either the manipulation could no longer be sustained or the bubble was about to burst. While the executives sold their shares and typically enhanced their wealth, thousands of employees lost millions of dollars of accumulated wealth in stock ownership and 401(k) plans. If the company failed, they lost their jobs as well. The trigger for the sale was inside information about the future viability of the company. Clearly, these managers acted illegally in violation of securities laws motivated by their own self-interest and without due regard for their fiduciary obligations to the shareholders. It was a classic example of egoistic behavior motivated purely by self-interest.

Recall that the public relies on the integrity and strong ethical values of accountants and auditors to ensure that the financial statements are accurate and reliable and that the statements include all the information investors and creditors need (have a right) to know to make informed decisions. The Rights Theory calls for actions that are universally acceptable given, an accepted standard of behavior, and not actions motivated by an ends justifying means approach to decision making. Taken together, the statements by Levitt and Buffett point to the need for those directly involved in the financial reporting process to establish and support an ethical culture in an organization.

Companies manage earnings when they ask, "How can we best report desired results?" rather than "How can we best report economic reality (the actual results)?" Levitt attributes the practice of earnings management to the pressure on Wall Street to "make the numbers." He identifies a pattern created by earnings management whereby "companies try to meet or beat Wall Street earnings projections in order to grow market capitalization and increase the value of stock options." He notes that on the one hand, auditors are under pressure to retain clients by the firm, and on the other, they are under pressure by management "not to stand in the way."

An important quality of useful information is *representational faithfulness*. To represent the transactions and events faithfully in the financial statements, the effects of transactions and events should be reported on the basis of economic substance of the transactions instead of legal form of the transaction. For example, if a company sells an asset but is still responsible for maintaining it or other risks then if this transaction is reported as sale instead of secured loan it will not faithfully represent the transaction and thus would distort the effect of the transaction and may have the potential to influence users decisions.

# Motivation for Earnings Management

## Earnings Guidance

During the 1990s and early 2000s, meeting or beating analysts' earnings expectations emerged as an important earnings benchmark. Bartov et al. found that the stock market has been found to award firms that meet or beat analysts' forecasts and punish firms that miss earnings targets.[3] Meeting or beating earnings through earnings and expectations management has drawn concerns over the integrity of managers. For instance, an analysis of Nortel Networks Corporation by Fogarty et al. (separate from Case 7-1 later in this chapter) reveals that earnings expectations management is tied to many other missteps of managers that collectively contributed to the downfall of the giant telecommunications firm.[4] Consistent with Fuller and Jensen, this suggests that earnings expectations management sets in motion a variety of organizational behaviors that often end up damaging the firm.[5] Erhard et al. suggest that meeting or beating earnings by manipulating earnings and analysts' earnings expectations is indicative of low integrity in relations with the capital markets, resulting in calls for boards of directors to take accountability for integrity of the entire corporate system[6]. Graham et al. also advocate changes in the culture of boards of directors by focusing on long-term strategic goals and shielding managers from the short-term pressure from the capital markets.[7] Liu et al. point out that taken collectively, the arguments suggest that while managing earnings expectations may help the firm avoid missing earnings targets and market penalties, it can be detrimental to the long-term value of the firm and the capital markets.[8] We note that the behaviors described above link to Burchard's Ethical Dissonance Model described in chapter 3 with low organizational ethics in the person-organization fit and if accompanied by low individual ethics, the ethical culture of the organization is more likely to lead to unethical choices than any other fit.

In addition to maximizing bonuses, the value of stock options, and meeting investors' earnings expectations, another objective of earnings management is to avoid the consequences of violation of debt covenants. Covenants in a long-term lending contract, such as required debt-to-equity ratio or minimum working capital requirements, exist to protect the lender from the potentially adverse actions of managers. Earnings management can serve as motivation to steer managers away from violating the terms of a debt contract, because such a violation would be highly costly to the manager and could affect her ability to operate the firm freely. Earnings management gives a manager the flexibility to choose those accounting policies that avoid a close proximity to covenant violation.

While some earnings management techniques may be perfectly acceptable under generally accepted accounting principles (GAAP), others are not. It is important to understand that firms and managers engaged in accounting manipulations, when discovered, bear substantial legal penalties. The legal costs not only include substantial monetary penalties, but also violations of securities laws.

An example of a company that provided false earnings guidance and was investigated by the SEC is Waste Management. The SEC's enforcement release against Waste Management Inc. describes its earnings guidance strategy as follows:[9]

> WMI violated the antifraud provisions in June 1999 when its management publicly projected results for the company's second quarter. The June forecast was a reiteration of second quarter projections made earlier in the year. Although the earlier projections may have had a reasonable basis when first disseminated, by at least the time when the reiteration occurred, WMI was aware of significant adverse trends in its business which made its continued public support of its previously announced forecasts unreasonable.

Exhibit 7.1 provides a summary of the SEC's actions taken against Waste Management and its top officers.

**EXHIBIT 7.1**
**SEC Actions Against Waste Management**

> The Commission's Complaint against Proto and DeFrates (Proto was WMI's President, Chief Operating Officer, and a member of the WMI Board of Directors; DeFrates was WMI's Chief Financial Officer) further alleges that they made additional materially false or misleading statements in June and July 1999, about WMI's ability to meet its previously announced second quarter 1999 earnings guidance of $0.78 to $0.82 per share. The Complaint alleges that between June 7 and July 2, 1999, on at least six separate occasions, Proto and/or DeFrates confirmed the company's second quarter 1999 EPS guidance in conversations with Wall Street analysts, investment bankers, and members of the public, even though they knew, or were reckless in not knowing, that WMI would fall well short of this previously stated earnings guidance.
>
> Proto has consented to pay a total of $3,721,177. This amount represents: (1) $1,503,670 in disgorgement of his illegal insider trading losses avoided, plus prejudgment interest of $513,837; (2) a civil penalty equal to his illegal insider trading losses avoided of $1,503,670; and (3) a $200,000 civil penalty for making materially false or misleading statements regarding WMI's first quarter 1999 earnings and WMI's ability to meet its previously announced second quarter 1999 earnings guidance. DeFrates has consented to pay a total of $482,779. This amount represents: (1) $121,217 in disgorgement of his illegal insider trading losses avoided, plus prejudgment interest of $40,345; (2) a civil penalty equal to his losses avoided of $121,217; and (3) a $200,000 civil penalty for making materially false or misleading statements regarding WMI's first quarter 1999 earnings and WMI's ability to meet its previously announced second-quarter 1999 earnings guidance. (AAER No. 1904).[10]

## Income Smoothing

Levitt talks about another motivation to manage earnings: to smooth net income over time. The ideal pattern of earnings for a manager is a steady increase each year over a period of time. The results make it appear that the company is growing and doing better than it really is, and the manager should be given credit for the positive results. The market reacts by bidding up the price of the stock, and the manager is rewarded for the results by a performance bonus and stock options with a prospective value that increases over time because of income smoothing that triggers stock price increases.

Income smoothing occurs through the use of accounting techniques to level out net income fluctuations from one period to the next. Companies indulge in this practice because investors are generally willing to pay a premium for stocks with steady and predictable earnings streams, compared with stocks whose earnings are subject to wild fluctuations.

Levitt concludes that "these practices lead to erosion in the quality of earnings and therefore, the quality of financial reporting." As previously mentioned, the notion that accounting information should represent what it purports to represent, or representational faithfulness,[11] would be distorted in these cases by the use of devices such as accelerating the recognition of revenue (i.e., channel stuffing), delaying the recognition of an expense, and creating "cookie-jar reserves" to smooth net income.

Cookie-jar reserves are an overly aggressive accrual of operating expenses and the creation of liability accounts done in an effort to reduce future year operating expenses. It is an accounting practice in which a company uses generous reserves from good years against losses that might be incurred in bad years. Cookie-jar accounting is a sign of misleading accounting practices. During the 1990s, these reserve practices were given the moniker of "cookie-jar reserves" because a company set aside some reserves to be taken out of the jar and used when needed to prop up earnings.

A classic case of the use of cookie-jar reserves to manipulate income was at HealthSouth. The SEC investigated the practice and deemed it to be fraudulent. According to the SEC, the company fraudulently reduced contractual adjustments to increase revenue by more than $2.2 billion.[12] The contractual allowances represented the amount of the health care billing not expected to be reimbursed. The use of the contractual allowance as a cookie-jar reserve is explained below.

During the second quarter of 1996, HealthSouth began what was to become a systematic practice of reducing contractual adjustments—i.e., narrowing the gap between standard health care charges and anticipated reimbursements—even though the applicable contractual adjustments had not actually changed and there was otherwise no support for the reductions. This practice continued without interruption in every reporting period through mid-2002. At the same time, the company improperly reclassified a number of operating expenses to make it appear as if the expenses never occurred.

The contractual allowance account was a perfect tool to manipulate earnings from year to year to present a smoothing or increasing trend in earnings. (It serves a similar purpose as a reserve for loan losses and an allowance for uncollectibles.) HealthSouth's disclosure about the practice in its financial statements seems to muddy the waters with respect to what they were doing and, more important, why. Exhibit 7.2 presents the disclosure.

One industry that routinely uses allowances to smooth net income over time is banking. Rivard et al. studied income smoothing techniques by banks and found them to be more aggressive in using loan-loss reserves as a tool of income smoothing. The provision for loan losses is a non-cash accounting expense for banks. In theory, this expense represents expected future losses, which will eventually occur on loans extended during the previous period. These expenses accumulate on the bank's balance sheet in the loan-loss reserve account. When a loan is charged off, this reserve account is debited. Because banks have

**EXHIBIT 7.2**

**Cookie-Jar Reserve Disclosure at HealthSouth**

HealthSouth sets "standard" charges for each patient service it provides. The company's revenue, however, is determined by the amount it actually receives for those services and, like virtually all health care providers, HealthSouth rarely collects its standard charge for any particular service. Instead, both its contractual arrangements with private payors and the reimbursement rates established by government programs such as Medicare typically provide for payment at less than standard rates.

The company historically has accounted for the provision of health care services by recording both its standard charge for the service and a contractual adjustment. The first entry essentially is a constant, unaffected by the amount actually to be paid by or on behalf of a patient. The second is a variable, representing the company's estimate of a discount from the standard charge which it does not expect to collect. The amount of the variable—*the contractual adjustment*—is based on the source of payment, since different payors may reimburse different amounts for the same service. The difference between the standard charge and the contractual adjustment, frequently a significant amount, represents the company's net operating revenue.

considerable flexibility in determining the size of the annual provision for loan losses, and because this is a non-cash expense, it is an excellent tool for income smoothing. During periods of lower-than-normal earnings, the bank may understate its expected future loan loss and thus increase earnings. When profits are abnormally high, the opposite occurs. Over an extended period of time, the loan-loss reserve balance is maintained at the desired level and average earnings are unaffected. However, the variability of the earnings stream over that period is less than it would otherwise be. As the authors point out, income smoothing reduces not only earnings, but also tax liabilities in high-income years, and increases them in low-income years.[13]

# Analysis of Earnings Management from a Financial Reporting Perspective

## Definition of Earnings Management

Earnings management occurs when companies artificially inflate (or deflate) their revenues or profits, or earnings per share (EPS) figures. This is accomplished in two broad ways: (1) by using aggressive accounting techniques such as capitalizing costs that should have been expensed (e.g., WorldCom accounted for its line costs as capital expenditures rather than expensing them against revenue); and (2) by establishing/altering the elements of an estimate to achieve a desired goal (e.g., Waste Management's lengthening of the useful lives on trash hauling equipment to slow down depreciation each year).

Another perspective on earnings management is to divide the techniques into two categories: operating earnings management and accounting earnings management. Operating earnings management deals with altering operating decisions to affect cash flows and net income for a period such as easing credit terms to increase sales. Accounting earnings management deals with using the flexibility in accounting standards to alter earnings numbers (Merchant, 1989).[14]

There is no generally accepted definition of earnings management in accounting. General agreement does exist that the end result of earnings management is to distort the application of GAAP, thereby bringing into question the quality of earnings. The question to be answered is whether the distortion is the result of appropriate decision making given that choices exist in the application of GAAP, or if it is motivated by a conscious effort to manipulate earnings for one's advantage, which is fraud.

While some authors distinguish between earnings manipulation and earnings management, we believe earnings manipulation is a form of earnings management. For example, Hopwood et al. believe that earnings management is management's routine use of nonfraudulent accounting and economic discretion while earnings manipulation can refer either to the legitimate or aggressive use, or fraudulent abuse, of discretion. By their reckoning, earnings management is legitimate, while earnings manipulation can be legitimate, marginally ethical, unethical, or illegal, depending on its extent.[15] The problem with this distinction is ethics relates to one's intent to act in accordance with established principles of behavior such as honesty and integrity. If one intends to manipulate earnings through smoothing or other techniques, it is unethical because it is designed to deceive another party; if not, why engage in the practice?

There are a variety of definitions of earnings management. Schipper defines it as a "purposeful intervention in the external reporting process, with the intent of obtaining some private gain (as opposed to say, merely facilitating the neutral operation of the process)."[16] Healy and Wahlen define it as "when managers use judgment in financial reporting and in structuring transactions to alter financial reports to either mislead some stakeholders about the underlying economic performance of the company, or to influence contractual outcomes that depend on reported accounting numbers."[17]

Dechow and Skinner note the difficulty of operationalizing earnings management based on the reported accounting numbers because they center on managerial intent, which is unobservable. Dechow and Skinner offer their own view that a distinction should be made between making choices in determining earnings that may comprise aggressive, but acceptable, accounting estimates and judgments, as compared to fraudulent accounting practices that are clearly intended to deceive others.[18] These authors provide a link between earnings management and Rest's Model of how ethical decisions take place that was discussed in Chapter 2. Rest identifies ethical intent as an essential ingredient in making moral decisions. It is the first step that can lead to executing ethical decisions. Absent ethical intent, a decision-maker may be motivated to skew earnings in her favor or that of the company.

Schipper views earnings management as a purposeful act by management as might be the case when earnings are manipulated to get the stock price up in advance of cashing in stock options. Healy and Wahlen focus on management's intent to deceive the stakeholders by using accounting devices to influence reported earnings positively. The underlying motivation for such actions according to the authors is the pursuit of self-interest rather than the interests of shareholders and other stakeholders.

Thomas E. McKee wrote a book on earnings management from the executive perspective. He defines *earnings management* as "reasonable and legal management decision making and reporting intended to achieve stable and predictable financial results." McKee believes earnings management reflects a conscious choice by management to smooth earnings over time and it does not include devices designed to "cook the books." He criticizes Schipper, Healy and Wahlen, and Dechow and Skinner for taking "unnecessarily negative view[s] of earnings management." McKee contends that a more positive definition is needed that portrays managers' motives in a positive light rather than the negative view adopted by others.[19]

## Ethics of Earnings Management

The authors of this book believe that the acceptability of earnings management techniques should be judged using the ethics framework established earlier in the book. Virtue ethics examines the reasons for actions taken by the decision maker as well as the action itself. McKee's definition is self-serving from a management perspective and does not reflect virtues such as honesty (full disclosure) and dependability (reliable numbers). The definition also ignores the rights of shareholders and other stakeholders to receive fair and accurate financial information. McKee's explanation that earnings management is good because it creates a more stable and predictable earnings stream by smoothing net income cannot overcome the fact that a smooth net income by choice does not reflect what investors and creditors need or want to know because it masks true performance. Further, McKee's explanation for the "goodness" of earnings management is nothing more than a rationalization for an unethical act. Hopwood et al. provide cover for their view of the ethics of earnings management by stating that "the ethics issue might possibly be mitigated by clearly disclosing aggressive accounting assumptions in the financial statement disclosures."[20] We disagree with this characterization because disclosure should not be used to mask the ills of improper accounting that tests the limits of what does and does not present fairly financial position, results of operations, and cash flows. A disclosure may be nothing more than a rationalization for an unethical action with respect to earnings management thereby closing the fraud triangle.

One might be able to rationalize the ethics of earnings management from an act-utilitarian perspective. Under this view, a decision about how to account for and report a financial transaction could be made by weighing the benefits to management and the company of using a particular technique (to smooth net income) versus the costs of providing potentially misleading information to the shareholders. Under a rule-utilitarian perspective, however, financial statements should never be manipulated for personal gain regardless of any utilitarian benefits.

Needles points out that the difference between an ethical and an unethical accounting choice is often merely the degree to which the choice is carried out. Needles believes the problem with many accounting judgments is that there is no clear limit beyond which a choice is obviously unethical. Thus, a perfectly routine accounting decision, such as expense estimation, may be illegal if the estimated amount is extreme, but it is perfectly ethical if it is reasonable. He provides an interesting example of how a manager might use the concept of an earnings continuum to decide whether to record the expense amount at the conservative end or aggressive end.[21]

Needles's example is based on a rather modest difference in estimate from $6,000 to $30,000 (1.0 percent to 5.0 percent of net sales). Exhibit 7.3 shows a difference of $0.24 per share ($1.70–$1.94) or approximately 12–14 percent of EPS (assuming 100,000 shares outstanding). We recognize that judgment is an essential part of deciding when a difference is and is not material. Needles's continuum illustrates a possible basis for such judgments and how an auditor might go about deciding whether or not to accept management's position on the issue.

**EXHIBIT 7.3**
**Where Do You Draw the Line? The Earnings Management Continuum of Ethical Financial Reporting**

Source: Copyright © 2011. Reprinted with permission of the author, Belverd E. Needles, Jr.

| Questionable Conservative | Conservative | Neutral | Aggressive | Fraudulent |
|---|---|---|---|---|
| 2a: The Earnings Management Continuum of Ethical Financial Reporting. | | | | |
| $1.70 | $1.76 | $1.82 | $1.88 | $1.94 |
| ← | | | | → |
| Violates GAAP | | Within GAAP | | Violates GAAP |

| 2b: Overly Aggressive Earnings on the Continuum | | | | |
|---|---|---|---|---|
| Highly Conservative | Overly Conservative | Neutral | Overly Aggressive | Fraudulent |
| $1.70 | $1.76 | $1.82 | $1.88 | $1.94 |
| ← | | | | → |
| Violates GAAP | | Within GAAP | | Violates GAAP |

## How Managers and Accountants Perceive Earnings Management

Elias conducted a study of corporate ethical values and earnings management ethics. He defined corporate ethical values as a composite of the individual values of managers and both the formal and informal policies on the ethics of the organization. The tone at the top signals whether ethics policies are taken seriously by management and is, therefore, very important to create an ethical corporate environment. The study clearly shows that accountants in organizations with high ethical values perceived earnings management actions as more unethical. Certified public accountants (CPAs) in industry occupations were significantly less likely than those in public accounting to perceive high ethical values in their organizations.[22] This may be attributable to the greater pressure internally to meet financial analysts' earnings projections and provide bonuses and stock options for top management.

In a case study by Phillips et al., it was determined that managers deceive shareholders by manipulating their companies' receivables, inventories, loss contingencies, and capital asset depreciation. In the past, audit committees have often failed to protect shareholders by inadequately monitoring and controlling the accounting judgments made by management.[23]

Anna and Jacob Rose investigated whether financial knowledge and trust influences audit committee members' judgment concerning client explanation for their accounting judgments. They found that audit committee members with less financial knowledge are more likely to accept insufficient client explanations for accounting judgment and are also more likely to reject sufficient client explanations for accounting judgments than more knowledgeable audit committee members. These results imply that the requirement by the Sarbanes-Oxley Act (SOX) to have three independent members of the board, one with financial expertise, on the audit committee should help to alleviate the disconnect between auditor obligations and trust.[24]

An early first survey of about how managers view the ethics of earnings management was conducted in 1990 by Bruns and Merchant. They found that managers disagreed considerably on whether earnings management is ethically acceptable. They also found that in general, the respondents thought manipulating earnings via operating decisions (e.g., purposefully delaying making needed repairs to a subsequent year) was more ethically acceptable than manipulation by accounting methods. The authors were disturbed by these findings. They were concerned that these practices could be misleading to users of the information and, over time, reduce the credibility of accounting numbers, thereby damaging the reputation of the accounting profession.[25]

Rosenzweig and Fischer followed up on the Bruns and Merchant survey in 1995 by asking accounting professionals about factors causing earnings management. Two of these factors involve accounting manipulation, and two involve operating decisions designed to influence reported earnings. The accounting factors include actions that influence earnings by changing accounting methods. Examples include recording an expense in the wrong year or changing an inventory valuation in order to influence earnings. Examples of operating decision manipulations are deferring necessary expenditures to a subsequent year or offering unusually attractive terms to customers at year-end to include next year's sales into the current year.[26]

In a 2006 survey, Akers, Giacomino, and Bellovary surveyed accounting students and practitioners about their views of earnings management. With respect to accounting practitioners, the results show that accounting manipulation is much less acceptable ethically than operating decision manipulation. This finding parallels the attitude that Bruns and Merchant found among managers.[27] Generally, the practitioners had few ethical qualms about operating decision manipulation, with scores indicating an average rating between (fully) ethical and questionable. The practitioners, however, generally felt that operating decisions that influenced expenses were somewhat more suspect than those that influenced revenues.

The results of the survey by Akers et al. indicates that none of the 20 practices asked about were rated as "Totally Unacceptable." Additional findings include that (1) only 5 of the 20 practices were rated as a "Serious Infraction," (2) 10 practices were rated as a "Minor Infraction," (3) 4 practices were rated as a "Questionable Practice," and (4) 1 action was rated as an "Ethical Practice"—painting a capital asset ahead of schedule.

The five most serious infractions were (1) bury "scrap costs" in other expenses—no (operating) income effect; (2) request deferred billing from the supplier; (3) raise the return forecast (on purchases) from 22 to 35 percent, with actuals of 22 percent; (4) accelerate delivery to customers by 42 days; and (5) defer supply expenses by delaying recording the invoice. It is interesting to note that the most serious infraction did not even affect net income.[28] Instead, the action to bury scrap costs in other expenses shifts an operating expense into a nonoperating category, thereby increasing operating income, an amount on the income statement often considered to be a more important gauge of earnings than "bottom-line" net income. Other actions are clearly designed to manage earnings by either accelerating the recording of earnings or delaying the recording of operating expenses.

As to the 10 practices rated as minor infractions, the ethical significance of each is as follows: (1) reduce reserve for obsolescence to meet budget target; (2) increase reserve for obsolescence and reduce income; (3) accelerate delivery to the customer by 28 days; (4) defer expenses to meet the annual budget; (5) raise the return forecast from 22 to 35 percent; (6) request deferred billing from the supplier; (7) accelerate delivery to the customer by 16 days; (8) reduce reserve for obsolescence to continue work; (9) defer expenses to meet the quarterly budget; and (10) prepay expenses to reduce income by $60,000.[29]

One unexpected result is that the second most unacceptable minor infraction leads to a *decrease* in income. Students may wonder why a manager might choose to reduce reported income by increasing a reserve account with an offset that increases expenses (i.e., debit: estimated loss due to obsolescence of inventory; credit: reserve for obsolescence). A good example is the case of Sunbeam Corporation, where the newly hired CEO, Al Dunlap, directed the accountants to create a reserve account during his first few months as CEO based on the belief that increasing the expenses and showing an even larger net loss would work to his advantage in the long run because in future periods, the company could restore the reserves to increase income making it appear that Dunlap had worked his magic in turning the company around. In other words, the increase in expenses in the current period when earnings were way below expectations (and there may even be a loss), creates a cookie-jar effect, while portraying the company as looking worse than it really is. Dunlap's use of cookie jar reserves to further increase losses in a down year after he was hired and reversing it into income in subsequent years became known as "big bath accounting." Dunlap figured he could blame the poor performance on the previous CEO, and it would make him look much better in future years.

## Accruals and Earnings Management

Accruals are needed on the balance sheet because when cash flows are examined within a limited time frame, they suffer from matching and timing problems and therefore often give the wrong picture of the period's performance. By measuring performance with earnings, the matching and timing problems inherent in cash flows are decreased through the use of the revenue recognition and matching principles.[30] The revenue recognition principle states that revenues should be recognized when the firm has delivered a product or has produced a substantial portion of it, and the cash receipt is reasonably certain. Over the lifetime of the firm, cash flows and earnings are the same, but when accounting principles are applied over finite time periods, cash flows have to be adjusted to produce the earnings number as is done in the operating section of a cash flow statement. These adjustments are made with accruals on the balance sheet, and thus, earnings are the sum of a period's change in accruals and its cash flows.

Accruals provide an opportunity for management to manage earnings through aggressive estimations or more conservative ones. The fraud at Waste Management is instructive in illustrating how estimates can be used to manipulate earnings. During the investigation of the fraud by the audit committee, it was determined that certain material items were incorrectly reported. Most restatements in the financial statements were related to aggressive calculations of vehicle, equipment, and container depreciation expense and capitalized interest. By increasing depreciation and salvage value assumptions for vehicle and container assets, Waste Management was postponing and avoiding depreciation expenses effectively raising current income.

The matters reflected in prior-period restatements include earlier recognition of asset value impairments (primarily related to land, landfill, and recycling investments) and environmental liabilities (primarily landfill closure and postclosure expense accruals). It was also determined that capitalized interest relating to landfill construction projects had been miscalculated. When a company begins a construction project, so long as the project is not earning revenues, it is able to accrue the interest expense related to the project and record it as part of the cost of construction (asset account, not an expense). Basically the interest expense on construction becomes part of the constructed assets and can be depreciated over the useful life of the project. This is a common practice, but if interest expenses for construction projects are overstated, then expenses are being understated and capitalized interest is overstated.

A fertile area for earnings management is through the use of discretionary accruals. *Discretionary accruals* are items that management has full control over and is able to delay or eliminate. *Nondiscretionary accruals* are items that are estimated based on changes in the fundamental economic performance of the firm, and management has no control over them. Dividing commitments into optional and non-optional confirms that total commitments are applied to offering better information for financial statements.

Unlike nondiscretionary accruals, which arise from transactions that can be considered "normal" for a firm (i.e., recording an accrual for unbilled services that have been provided), a discretionary accrual is a non-mandatory expense that is recorded within the accounting system but has yet to be realized. An example of this would be an anticipated management bonus. Discretionary accruals are those that arise from managerial discretion and are generally interpreted as indicative of managed earnings. By recognizing accruals at a "convenient" time, companies can smooth earnings and better meet or exceed analysts' earnings projections.

## Acceptability of Earnings Management from a Materiality Perspective

### Defining Materiality

We have already discussed materiality from an auditing perspective. Recall that the Financial Accounting Standards Board (FASB) defined *materiality* in *Statement of Financial Accounting Concepts (SFAS) Statement 2, Qualitative Characteristics of Accounting Information,* as "the magnitude of an omission or misstatement of accounting information that, in the light of surrounding circumstances, makes it probable that the judgment of a reasonable person relying on the information would have been changed or influenced by the omission or misstatement." Common law precedents have established that information is material for securities fraud purposes if a reasonable investor would have viewed it as having meaningfully altered the total mix of information.

The principle of materiality underscores the concept that some financial transactions are so insignificant that they are not worth measuring and reporting with exact precision. For example, some companies may define an item as material only if it affects earnings by more than 5 percent to 10 percent. This principle allows for some judgment and flexibility in financial reporting. It can be linked to Needles's idea of a continuum of ethical and unethical financial reporting through earnings management. However, the materiality principle can be misused by companies that seek to do so. For instance, a company could manipulate revenues or expenses deliberately, and yet do so within an established maximum percentage of acceptability and claim that the misstatement is not material.

In 1999, W.R. Grace & Company settled an earnings manipulation case with the SEC. The SEC alleged that Grace & Company violated GAAP by establishing an all-purpose reserve fund to "smooth" earnings from 1991 to 1995 by hiding profits in good years and using them to disguise slower earnings in later years. Internal company and audit-firm documents revealed that Grace's auditor, Andersen, discovered the buildup of earnings in the early 1990s and repeatedly warned company executives that what they were doing was improper. However, even after Grace began shifting money into earnings in 1993 and 1994, the outside auditors continued to give the company a favorable audit opinion on their financial statements. The accounting firm based their decision on the grounds that it did not view the improprieties as "material" (Davis, 1999).

The argument that the impact of distortions leading to a smoothing of earnings is too small to matter brings into question the reason why a company would work so hard to bring this about. In today's markets, missing an earnings projection by a few cents can lead to the loss of millions of dollars in the market value of a company's securities. The SEC clearly viewed the distortions by Grace & Company as material and therefore as a violation of GAAP, as well as a violation of securities laws.

*Staff Accounting Bulletin (SAB) 99,* issued by the SEC, and that was discussed in Chapter 5, clarifies that the exclusive use of a percentage materiality criteria to assess material misstatements in the financial statements has no basis in law and is unacceptable. The commission did state that the use of a percentage as a numerical threshold, such as 5 percent, may provide the basis for a preliminary assumption that, without considering all relevant circumstances, a deviation of less than the specified percentage with respect to a particular item on the registrant's financial statements is unlikely to be material. However, the SEC ruled that both qualitative and quantitative factors must be considered when assessing materiality.[31] Materiality judgments in lawsuits against accountants rely on the "reasonable person" standard, that "a substantial likelihood that the . . . fact would have been viewed by the reasonable investor as having significantly altered the 'total mix' of information made available." If an item is material, it should be disclosed in the body of the financial statements or footnotes.

Materiality is judged both by the relative amount and by the nature of the item. For example, even a small theft by the president of a company is material because it brings into question the trustworthiness of the president, may indicate that other misappropriations have occurred, and brings into question the tone set from the top.

In *SAB 99,* the SEC lists some of the qualitative factors that may cause quantitatively small misstatements to become material, including:

- It arises from an item capable of precise measurement.
- It arises from an estimate and, if so, the degree of imprecision inherent in the estimate.
- It masks a change in earnings or other trends.
- It hides a failure to meet analysts' consensus expectations for the enterprise.
- It changes a loss into income or vice versa.
- It concerns a segment or other portion of the registrant's business that has been identified as playing a significant role in the registrant's operations or profitability.
- It affects the registrant's compliance with regulatory requirements.
- It affects the registrant's compliance with loan covenants or other contractual requirements.

- It has the effect of increasing management's compensation—for example, by satisfying the requirements for the award of bonuses or other forms of incentive compensation.
- It involves concealment of an unlawful transaction.

Auditors should be on the alert for these red flags, which signal that qualitatively material items may not have been recorded and disclosed in accordance with GAAP.

### Materiality and Legal Decisions

The concept of "materiality" is important in securities law. Whether in a registration statement, or in a filing under the 1934 Act, or in providing information to the trading markets, a company will be liable for any material misstatement, or any material omission of facts necessary to make other statements "not misleading."

This standard is most often encountered in fraud litigation brought under Section 10(b) and Rule 10b-5 under the 1934 Act, but also constitutes the linchpin standard for liabilities arising under Section 11 (false registration statements), Section 12 (false prospectuses), Section 15 (liability of controlling persons) and Section 17 (criminal fraud in securities sales) under the Securities Act of 1933. The fundamental disclosure requirements contained in the two statutes are premised upon a prohibition of material misstatement or omission.

Tests of the materiality standard occur periodically in court proceedings. One such case, *Matrixx Initiatives, Inc., v. Siracusano,*[32] occurred in 2011. The petitioners had suggested that there should be a bright-line test for materiality in a securities fraud suit. The Supreme Court adopted the position of the SEC— the "total mix" of information as viewed by a reasonable investor standard of materiality articulated earlier in *TSC Industries, Inc. v. Northway, Inc.,* 426 U.S. 438 (1976).[33]

In the *Matrixx* case, the shareholder complaint claimed that the company made false statements about its key product, Zicam, a cold remedy nasal spray. In 2003, the company made statements touting the success of Zicam. At one point, Matrixx increased its earnings guidance based on Zicam sales.

The company, however, had received information that Zicam could cause a loss of smelling ability. The data came from several medical researchers, as well as individuals. The product liability suits were filed. Nevertheless, Matrixx continued to maintain that Zicam was safe and that none of the clinical trials supported a claim that the nasal spray caused a loss of smelling ability. Reports to the contrary were simply denied. A negative report of an investigation by the U.S. Food and Drug Administration (FDA) was followed by a drop in Matrixx's share price.

The district court dismissed the complaint, concluding that the adverse product reports were not material. It held that a pharmaceutical company need not disclose such reports unless they are statistically significant. The Ninth Circuit Court reversed. It rejected the statistically significant test, concluding that it was contrary to a ruling in *Basic Inc. v. Levinson,* 485 U.S. 224 (1989).[34] The Supreme Court affirmed. The Court held that "the materiality of adverse event reports cannot be reduced to a bright-line rule.

Although in many cases reasonable investors would not consider reports of adverse events to be material information, respondents have alleged facts plausibly suggesting that reasonable investors would have viewed these particular reports as material."[35]

The *Matrixx* decision illustrates how difficult materiality determinations can be and why auditors struggle with it when assessing what is a material misstatement in the financial statements. Additional information about the *Matrixx* case appears in Exhibit 7.4.

### Materiality Considerations in Evaluating Internal Control Deficiencies Under SOX

SOX increased demands on management to prevent and detect material control weaknesses. To develop the controls, SOX requires that CPAs need to be able to identify key

**EXHIBIT 7.4**

*Matrixx Initiatives, Inc., v. Siracusano*

In U.S. District Court, Matrixx moved to dismiss the class action for failure to plead properly that any misstatement or omission was "material" and failure to plead requisite scienter (intent to deceive). The court threw out the suit, but the Ninth Circuit reversed, applying the *Basic* standard for materiality.

The Supreme Court accepted certiorari in the case, presumably because of a conflict between the Ninth Circuit opinion and case law from the Second Circuit.

The court applied *Basic's* "total mix" standard and refused to develop a bright-line rule requiring that "statistically significant data" must be shown to establish materiality. Such a rigid rule would exclude from evidence information that "would otherwise be considered significant to the trading decision of a reasonable investor."

The court stated that medical experts and the FDA often consider a variety of factors in assessing causation and don't require that these factors rise to a level of "statistical significance." The key test is whether the evidence is suggestive, not categorical, proof.

The court noted that in 2009, the FDA issued a warning to Matrixx concerning possible health risks of its drug; it cited various reports of anosmia and suggestive scientific literature, none of which rose to a level of "statistical significance."

If medical experts and the FDA infer possible causation from such data, a reasonable investor might well reach the same conclusion. In addition, medical researchers reach conclusions in cases in which statistically significant data is not always available.

The SEC filed an amicus brief supportive of the Ninth Circuit. The court also relied upon an amicus brief filed by a group of law professors, stating that the law concerning materiality as articulated in *Basic* had proven to be an effective standard in litigation since 1988.

The holding in *Matrixx* does not mean that reports of adverse events necessarily mandate disclosure. Companies have to consider the context, content, and source of the reports. But a plaintiff does not have to produce "statistically significant evidence" to prove the necessary 10b-5 element of scienter; pleaded facts may give a strong inference of an intent to deceive, defraud, or manipulate, even without specific showing of statistical significance.

control exceptions and apply a materiality concept to determine the financial impact of such exceptions. In this regard, Vorhies identifies four perspectives to help CPAs meet their responsibilities under SOX, including (1) the actual financial statement misstatement or error, (2) an internal control deficiency caused by the failure in design or operation of a control, (3) a large variance in an accounting estimate compared with the actual determined amount, and (4) financial fraud by management or other employees to enhance a company's reported financial position and operating results.[36]

Under Section 302 of SOX, companies are required to (1) review their disclosure controls and procedures quarterly, (2) identify all key control exceptions and determine which are internal control deficiencies, (3) assess each deficiency's impact on the fair presentation of their financial statements, and (4) identify and report significant control deficiencies or material weaknesses to the audit committee of the board of directors and to the company's independent auditor.

Examples of misstatements or errors include incorrectly recorded financial statement amounts and financial statement amounts that should have been recorded but were not. Any internal control failure could be a control deficiency. Such deficiencies usually are the result of a failure in control design or operation. A design failure occurs when management fails to establish a sufficient level of internal control or control activities to achieve a control objective; an operating failure is when an adequately designed control does not operate properly. Because estimation processes are evaluated based on their adequacy, an accounting estimation generally would not result in a control deficiency or an uncorrected/unrecorded misstatement if it was reasonable given the available technology and the process was "normal" for the industry, and if the company's independent auditor reviewed and approved it. Estimating financial events and balances is a necessary evil given the accrual accounting system and need to report on the income and the state of assets at artificial points in time. So long as the estimation process is reasonable, CPAs cannot conclude that a control deficiency exists when the actual amount is compared with the estimate regardless of the size of the variance. If the estimation process is flawed, broken, or unreasonable, a control deficiency exists. An uncorrected/unrecorded misstatement also may exist—the difference between the estimate calculated and recorded in error versus what the correct estimate should have been.

## Current Auditing Standards and Presumptions

### Audit Risk and Materiality

The three components of audit risk are as follows:

1. Inherent risk, which is the possibility that a material misstatement will occur within the reporting company's accounting information system
2. Control risk, which is the possibility that a material misstatement that has occurred will not be detected on a timely basis by the company's control system
3. Detection risk, which is the possibility that a material misstatement that has occurred will not be caught by the independent auditor's testing

Inherent risk and control risk are known collectively as the *risk of material misstatement. Materiality in Planning and Performing an Audit* (AU 320) includes the following guidance with respect to materiality in the context of an audit:

> The auditor's consideration of materiality is a matter of professional judgment and is influenced by the auditor's perception of the needs of users of financial statements as a group; the auditor does not consider the possible effect of misstatements on specific individual users, whose needs may vary widely. Materiality judgments are made in light of surrounding circumstances and necessarily involve both quantitative and qualitative considerations.

*AU 320* points out that the evaluation of whether a misstatement could influence economic decisions of users (and therefore be material) involves consideration of the characteristics of those users who are assumed to do the following:

- Have an appropriate knowledge of business and economic activities and accounting and a willingness to study the information in the financial statements with an appropriate diligence
- Understand that financial statements are prepared and audited to levels of materiality
- Recognize the uncertainties inherent in the measurement of amounts based on the use of estimates, judgment, and the consideration of future events
- Make appropriate economic decisions on the basis of the information in the financial statements

The determination of materiality, therefore, takes into account how users with such characteristics could reasonably be expected to be influenced in making economic decisions. *AU 320* offers the following guidance with respect to using benchmarks to evaluate materiality: "Examples of benchmarks that might be appropriate, depending on the nature and circumstances of the entity, include total revenues, gross profit, and other categories of reported income, such as profit before tax from continuing operations. For asset-based entities (for example, an investment fund) an appropriate benchmark might be net assets. Other entities (for example, banks and insurance companies) might use other benchmarks."

Financial statement disclosures of items deemed to be material should be based on professional judgment and can include the following:

- Significance of the financial statement item to the balances of earnings, financial position, and cash flows

- Quantitative significance of the item to the balances of earnings, financial position, and cash flows
- Qualitative aspects of the item and related disclosure(s) when evaluated with respect the fair presentation of financial information
- "Reasonable reader" needs (i.e., would decisions about the entity change or be influenced if the disclosure were present?)
- Whether an item in question is not applicable versus not material (when preparing disclosure checklists)

### Gemstar–TV Guide International, Inc.

The danger of relying on only a quantitative analysis to make materiality judgments can be seen in the audit by KPMG of Gemstar–TV Guide International, Inc. *Accounting and Auditing Enforcement Release (AAER) 2125,* issued by the SEC, concludes that $364 million of revenue was reported improperly and that certain disclosure policies were inconsistent with Gemstar's accounting for revenue, did not comply with GAAP disclosure requirements, or both. *AAER 2125* found that the KPMG auditors concurred in Gemstar's accounting for overstated revenue from licensing and advertising transactions in March 2000, December 2000, December 2001, and March 2002. Also, KPMG did not object to Gemstar's disclosure and issued audit reports stating that KPMG had conducted its audits in conformity with generally accepted accounting standards (GAAS) and that the financial statements fairly presented its results in conformity with GAAP. In reaching these conclusions, the KPMG auditors unreasonably relied on representations by Gemstar management, unreasonably determined that the revenues were immaterial to Gemstar's financial statements, or both. The KPMG auditors' materiality determinations were unreasonable in that they considered only quantitative materiality factors (i.e., that the amount of revenue was not a large percentage of Gemstar's consolidated financial results) and failed to also consider qualitative materiality (i.e., that the revenue related to business lines that were closely watched by securities analysts and had a material effect on the valuation of Gemstar stock).

The SEC complaint reads like a "what's what" in earnings management; it provides insight into the techniques that some companies use to manage earnings. The complaint alleges that Gemstar materially overstated its revenues by nearly $250 million through the following means[37]:

- Recording revenue under expired, disputed, or nonexistent agreements, and improperly reporting this as licensing and advertising revenue
- Recording revenue from a long-term agreement on an accelerated basis in violation of GAAP and Gemstar's own policies, which required recording and reporting such revenue ratably over the terms of the agreement (consistent with the matching theory)
- Inflating advertising revenue by improperly recording and reporting revenue amounts from multiple-element transactions
- Engaging in "round-trip" transactions, whereby Gemstar paid money to a third party to advertise its services and capitalized that cost while the third party used the funds received from Gemstar to buy advertising that Gemstar recorded 100 percent as revenue in the period of the transaction
- Failing to disclose that it had structured certain settlements for the purpose of creating cookie-jar reserves of advertising revenue to smooth net income
- Improperly recording advertising revenue from nonmonetary and barter transactions even though Gemstar could not establish the advertising's fair value properly

# Financial Statement Restatements

A *financial statement restatement* occurs when a company, either voluntarily or under prompting by its auditors or regulators, revises its public financial information that was previously reported. The number and variety of restatements of financial statements by publicly owned companies increased significantly during the 2000–2006 period, as many companies restated after disclosing accounting frauds. Since 2006, the number of restatements has gone down, in part due to stricter internal control requirements under SOX Section 404 and new auditing standards established by the PCAOB. These requirements were addressed in Chapter 5.

## The Nature of Restatements

In Chapter 5, we discussed the nature and extent of financial restatements. In 2008, these were the top 10 accounting issues implicated in restatements: debt; quasi-debt; warrants and equity security issues; expense recording issues (payroll, selling, general and administrative expenses, other); cash-flow statement (*SFAS 95*); deferred, stock-based, or executive compensation issues; acquisitions, mergers, disposals, or reorganization accounting issues; revenue recognition issues; tax expense, benefit, deferral, and other (*SFAS 109*) issues; and liabilities, payables, reserves, and accrual estimate failures.

One major cause for concern continues to be the number of "stealth restatements." The SEC requires companies to disclose within four business days a determination that past financial statements should no longer be relied on. This disclosure must appear in an 8-K report. The SEC defines a stealth restatement as one that is disclosed only in periodic reports and not in the 8-K or amended periodic report such as a 10-K/A or 10-Q/A.

The number of financial restatements remained steady in 2011, hovering at 787 compared to 790 the year before, according to the latest data from Audit Analytics.[38] Companies listed on the New York Stock Exchange (NYSE), however, saw a slight increase in restatements. During 2009, 65 NYSE companies disclosed restatements, followed by 90 in 2010 and 108 in 2011. The percentage of total restatements from stealth restatements has increased to more than 50 percent. This is a troublesome development for the SEC, as the 8-K form is designed to be an early warning system so that the public knows immediately about the financial statement restatements and does not have to wait until the statements are filed with the SEC.

The SEC issued its *Final Report of the Advisory Committee on Improvements to Financial Reporting* on August 1, 2008.[39] In that report, the commission recommended that the determination of whether an accounting error is material should be separated from the decision on how to correct the error. The SEC supports a stricter rule than the current practice on accounting errors: a company should promptly correct and prominently disclose any accounting error unless clearly insignificant. In addition, the instructions to the SEC's Form 8-K should make clear that it must be filed for all determinations of nonreliance on prior financial statements to limit the possibility of stealth restatements. On the other hand, the correction and disclosure of any accounting error should not result automatically in a financial restatement. The financial statements should be amended only if the error would be material to investors making current investment decisions.

The preparation and audit of financial statements have always required the exercise of judgment. The recent trend in accounting entails a move away from prescriptive guidance toward greater use of judgment—for example, the more frequent use of fair value involves estimates of value that may be less objectively determined than historical cost measures. Similarly, the standard applicable to audits of internal control over financial reporting, issued by the PCAOB, emphasizes the need for professional judgment in taking a risk-based approach to performing internal control audits. Moreover, international accounting standards generally contain less prescriptive guidance and more reliance on general principles than U.S. GAAP.

It is important to note the trend that the SEC wants accountants and auditors to follow; the application of professional judgment in making materiality decisions. We agree with the SEC on this matter and point out that the application of professional judgment entails an ethical approach to decision making. The qualities of an ethical auditor previously discussed include honesty, objectivity, and integrity, and professional skepticism. The shift to more professional judgments should be accompanied by better training for auditors in the area of ethical decision making. We would like to see the SEC and PCAOB address this issue.

## Restatements Due to Errors in Accounting and Reporting

An analysis of causes of restatement due to errors in accounting and reporting was made by Turner and Weirich. Results from their study with respect to the kinds of accounting errors that trigger restatements are particularly relevant to the discussion in the next section of earnings management techniques. Exhibit 7.5 presents these results.

Restatements due to errors also occur when a company switches from non-GAAP to GAAP. This is an error correction that requires restated financial statements and disclosure to the SEC. A good example of this occurred at Cubic Corporation, which announced on August 1, 2012, that the audit committee of the company's board of directors, after consultation with Ernst & Young LLP, the company's independent registered public accounting firm, determined that Cubic's financial statements for the fiscal years ending September 30, 2011, 2010, and 2009, the quarters ended March 31, 2012, and December 31, 2011, and each of the prior quarters of 2011 and 2010 can no longer be relied upon as complying with GAAP. Accordingly, Cubic informed the SEC that it will restate the financial statements.[40]

Exhibit 7.6 provides additional information on how the restatements were identified and reported.

**EXHIBIT 7.5**
**Accounting Errors that Trigger Financial Statement Restatements**

| Category | Cause of Restatements |
| --- | --- |
| Revenue recognition | Improper revenue recognition, including questionable items and misreported revenue |
| Expense recognition | Improper expense recognition, including period of recognition, incorrect amounts; includes improper lease accounting |
| Misclassification | Improper classification on income statement, balance sheet, or cash flow statement; includes nonoperating revenue in the operating category; cash outflow from operating activities in investment activities |
| Equity | Improper accounting for EPS; stock-based compensation plans, options, warrants, and convertibles |
| Other comprehensive income (OCI) | Improper accounting for OCI transactions, including unrealized gains and losses on investments in debt and equity securities, derivatives, and pension-liability adjustments |
| Capital assets | Improper accounting for asset impairments; asset placed in service dates and depreciation |
| Inventory | Improper accounting for valuation of inventory, including market adjustments and obsolescence |
| Reserves/allowances | Improper accounting for bad debt reserves on accounts receivable, reserves for inventory, and provision for loan losses |
| Liabilities/contingencies | Improper estimation of liability claims, loss contingencies, litigation matters, commitments, and certain accruals |

**EXHIBIT 7.6**
**Cubic Corporation Restatement of Financial Statements (8/1/12)**[41]

The Audit Committee's decision to restate these financial statements follows a recommendation by management that revenues in these previously issued financial statements should be adjusted due to errors in calculating revenues on certain long-term fixed-price development type contracts ("development contracts") and on certain long-term service contracts with non-U.S. Government customers ("service contracts").

Preliminary indications from the company's evaluation are that the changes described below will result in an increase in revenues and net income cumulatively over the period of the restatement and an increase in retained earnings as of March 31, 2012. Cubic Corporation is continuing to evaluate the total amount of the adjustments and the specific impact on each period covered by the restatement, which may result in an increase or decrease in previously reported amounts for individual periods.

Cubic has historically recognized sales and profits for development contracts using the cost-to-cost percentage-of-completion method of accounting, modified by a formulary adjustment. Under the cost-to-cost percentage-of-completion method of accounting, sales and profits are based on the ratio of costs incurred to estimated total costs at completion. Cubic has consistently applied a formulary adjustment to the percentage completion calculation for development contracts that had the effect of deferring a portion of the indicated revenue and profits on such contracts until later in the contrac performance period.

Cubic believed that this methodology was an acceptable variation of the cost-to-cost percentage-of-completion method as described in Accounting Standards Codification ("ASC") 605-35. The company now believes that generally accepted accounting principles do not support the practice of using a formulary calculation to defer a portion of the indicated revenue and profits on such contracts. Instead, Cubic believes that sales and profits should have been recognized based on the ratio of costs incurred to estimated total costs at completion, without using a formulary adjustment. The company is in the process of evaluating the differences resulting from this change but has not yet completed this evaluation.

While evaluating its revenue recognition for development contracts, Cubic also evaluated its long-standing practice of using the cost-to-cost percentage-of-completion method to recognize revenues for many of its se vice contracts. Under the accounting literature the cost-to-cost percentage of completion method is acceptable for U.S. Government contracts but not for contracts with other governmental customers, whether domestic or foreign.

## Earnings Management Techniques

In his remarks entitled "The Numbers Game," referred to in the beginning of the chapter, former SEC chairman Arthur Levitt described five techniques of "accounting hocus-pocus" that summarized the most glaring abuses of the flexibility inherent to accrual accounting: big bath charges, creative acquisition accounting, cookie-jar reserves, materiality, and revenue recognition:[42]

- **Big bath charges:** One example is when a company resorts to taking a one-time large restructuring charge/write-down, as opposed to appropriately recording the losses over several fiscal years. This is to avoid a succession of years of earnings decline that would have otherwise made the company financial health look bad in the eyes of stakeholders. To make it more difficult for companies to abuse "big bath charges," in 1998, the FASB adopted *SFAS 144* on impairment losses and *SFAS 146* on the timing of the recognition of restructuring obligations. Another example occurred at Sunbeam Corporation that was discussed earlier in this chapter. Sunbeam had huge losses in the late 1990s. The company fired its CEO and brought in Al Dunlap. Dunlap wanted to look like a turnaround artist so he established and purposefully overstated cookie-jar-reserves to make it look as though the losses in the year he took over were higher than reported. Dunlap then could reverse the overstated expenses and increase income in future years to make him look better. The Sunbeam fraud is discussed in Case 7-7.

- **Creative acquisition accounting:** This is when following a business acquisition, the acquirer allocates the bulk of the total purchase price to the acquiree's in-process research and development (R&D), as opposed to its long-lived assets as mandated by

GAAP, thus recording a huge expense during the year of acquisition so that earnings in future years wouldn't be significantly affected by the acquisition costs. Since 1998, however, *SFAS Nos. 141* and *142* have been adopted to provide clearer guidelines on how the purchase price in a business acquisition should be allocated.

- **Cookie-jar reserves:** The objective of using cookie-jar-reserves is to smooth net income over time. This can take place in two ways. In the first scenario, a company with record revenues overstates its bad debt expense in quarter/year 1 so as to record little bad debt expense in subsequent quarters/years when it expects to achieve below-average revenues. The Lucent case that is discussed later shows the reverse treatment where the company reduced previously recorded allowances to inflate earnings in a low earnings year. In the second scenario, a company understates revenues by inflating unearned revenues in quarter/year 1 to pad revenue figures in subsequent quarters/years should they fall below market expectations. Since 1998, the SEC has released *SAB 101,* which outlines with more clarity when deferring revenue is permissible.

- **Materiality:** The concept of materiality is a gray area of accounting; consequently, it is subject to different interpretations, as previously discussed. Sometimes publicly traded companies resort to questionable accounting practices with seemingly immaterial monetary effects, but that practice allows the company to meet or beat analysts' earnings expectations thereby creating a qualitatively material effect. In this type of situation, Levitt recommends that the misstatement be considered material because it is very likely that the company's stock price would have declined if the misstatement had been corrected. In 1999, the SEC released *SAB 99,* which provides a better understanding of the definition of materiality.

- **Revenue recognition:** Some companies accelerate the recording of revenues to help meet analysts' earnings projections, increase year-end bonuses, improve the share price of stock and stock options owned by top executives, or all of them. The HealthSouth case discussed earlier in this chapter illustrates how contractual allowances can be manipulated to show higher revenues, earnings, and EPS, all of which led to higher share prices.

## Financial Shenanigans

The term *Financial Shenanigans* refers to actions or omissions intended to hide or distort the real financial performance or financial condition of an entity. They range from minor deceptions to more serious misapplications of accounting principles.

There are two basic strategies underlying accounting shenanigans:

- *Inflating current reported income*—A company can inflate its current income by inflating current revenues and gains or deflating current expenses.

- *Deflating current reported income*—A company can deflate current revenues by deflating current revenues or gains or inflating current expenses.

Howard Schilit identifies seven common financial shenanigans. We use Schilit's framework to discuss earnings manipulations at two companies charged by the SEC with accounting fraud—Xerox and Lucent.

We explain the basic financial shenanigan techniques,[43] with the number of examples in each category limited to the three most common techniques.

## 1. Recording Revenue Too Soon or of Questionable Quality

This may be the most common technique because many opportunities arise to accomplish it, including recording revenue before the earnings process has been completed or before an unconditional exchange has occurred. Examples of this shenanigan include:

- Recording revenue when future services remain to be provided
- Recording revenue before shipment or before the customer's unconditional acceptance
- Recording revenue even though the customer is not obligated to pay

The Xerox case discussed later in this chapter illustrates how a company can move earnings into an earlier period by allocating more of the revenue in a multiyear contract to earlier years than justified given continuing servicing under the contract.

## 2. Recording Bogus Revenue

Typically, bogus revenue transactions lead to fictitious revenue. Examples include:

- Recording sales that lack economic substance
- Recording as revenue supplier rebates that are tied to future required purchases
- Releasing revenue that was held back improperly before a merger

The ZZZZ Best case discussed in Chapter 5 illustrates how a master of deception like Barry Minkow can create nonexistent revenue.

## 3. Boosting Income with One-Time Gains

The gains (and losses) from the sale of operating and investment assets that should be recorded in another (e.g., miscellaneous) income account can be classified in other ways if the intent is to boost operating income. These include:

- Boosting profits by selling undervalued assets
- Including investment income or gains as part of operating revenue
- Including investment income or gains as a reduction in operating expenses

IBM used the net proceeds from the sale of an operating unit ($300 million) to lower its operating costs, rather than accounting for it as a nonrecurring, one-time gain. We consider it fraud because it is a deliberate attempt to mislead users of the financial statements into thinking that operating income is larger than it really is. Financial analysts tend to put more emphasis on operating income than net income because of the miscellaneous, non-operating items recorded below the line of operating income to get net income.

## 4. Shifting Current Expenses to a Later or Earlier Period

A common approach to shift expenses to a later period is by capitalizing a cost in the current period and expensing it over a period of time, rather than expensing the item completely in the current period. This was the technique used by WorldCom to inflate earnings by between $11 billion and $13 billion.

Additional examples include:

- Changing accounting policies and shifting current expenses to an earlier period
- Failing to write down or write off impaired assets
- Reducing asset reserves

## 5. Failing to Record or Improperly Reducing Liabilities

The liability account is often used to manipulate earnings because when liabilities that should be recorded are not, the expenses also are understated. When liabilities are reduced improperly, the same effect on expenses occurs. The result is to overstate earnings. Some examples include:

- Failing to record expenses and related liabilities when future obligations remain
- Releasing questionable reserves (cookie-jar reserves) into income
- Recording revenue when cash is received, even though future obligations remain

The recording of discretionary accruals that was previously discussed is one application of the technique. The Lucent Technologies example discussed later in this chapter illustrates a variety of these techniques.

## 6. Shifting Current Revenue to a Later Period

Some companies act to delay the recording of revenue when the amount is relatively high in a given year. In a sense, this action sets up a "rainy day" reserve that can be used to restore earnings in low-earnings years. One way to accomplish this is to create a cookie-jar reserve with the excess revenues and release it back into the income stream at a later date, when it can do more good for the bottom line. Another method is through the use of deferred revenue. Examples include:

- Deliberately overstating the allowance for uncollectible accounts thereby understating current revenue and adjusting the allowance downward in future years to increase revenue
- Deferring revenue recognition on a year-end service transaction that was completed by December 31 and then transferring it to earned revenue in subsequent years
- Deliberately overstating the estimated sales returns account and adjusting it downward in future years

Microsoft put a large amount into deferred revenue in 1997 and 1998 and released it in the middle of 1999 to create a very substantial amount of reserve. The company shifted revenue to a later period because management sensed that business would get tougher down the road and the deferred revenue could be transferred into earned revenue when needed. Once again, we consider this fraud because the company deliberately delayed the recording of earned revenue until needed later to mislead users into thinking that the company's net income portrayed a smoothing trend.

## 7. Shifting Future Expenses to the Current Period as a Special Charge

A company might choose to accelerate discretionary expenses, such as repairs and maintenance, into the current period if the current year's revenue is relatively high in relation to expected future revenue or future expenses are expected to be relatively high. The motivation to shift future expenses to the current period might be to smooth net income over time.

The delay in recording repairs and maintenance is a technique that McKee would probably categorize as appropriate, given the goal of providing smooth and predictable earnings. Recall that in the reported studies on earnings management, the idea of managing earnings through operating decisions was not perceived to be as big a problem as altering revenue amounts. However, the decision to delay needed repairs raises several ethical issues with respect to the company's operating decisions because it creates a risk that assets such as machinery and equipment may break down prematurely. These are (1) the quality of product may suffer, leading to extra quality control and rework costs; (2) production slows and fails to meet deadlines, thereby risking customer goodwill; and (3) the costs to repair the machines can be greater than they would have been had maintenance been completed on a timely basis. Imagine, for example, that you fail to change the oil in your car on a regular basis. The result may be serious, costly repairs to the engine later on.

## Descriptions of Financial Shenanigans

In this section, we describe the financial shenanigans that occurred at Xerox, Lucent, and Enron. We chose these companies because the techniques used to manage earnings vary from the relatively simple (recording revenue too soon) to the more exotic (using special-purpose entities to hide debt and inflate earnings).

# The Case of Xerox

## Motivation for Fraudulent Scheme of Top Management

On June 3, 2003, the SEC filed a civil fraud injunctive action in the U.S. District Court for the Southern District of New York charging six former senior executives of Xerox Corporation, including its former CEOs Paul Allaire and G. Richard Thoman, and its former chief financial officer (CFO) Barry D. Romeril, with securities fraud and aiding and abetting Xerox's violations of the reporting, books and records, and internal control provisions of the federal securities laws. The complaint charged the former executives with engaging in a fraudulent scheme that lasted from 1997 to 2000 and misled investors about Xerox's earnings to "polish its reputation on Wall Street and to boost the company's stock price."[44]

The quality of the financial reports came into question as Xerox failed to disclose GAAP violations that led to acceleration in the recognition of approximately $3 billion in equipment revenues and an increase in pretax earnings by approximately $1.4 billion in Xerox's 1997–2000 financial results. The executives agreed to pay over $22 million in penalties, disgorgement, and interest without admitting or denying the SEC's allegations.

The tone at the top was one that viewed business success with meeting short-term earnings targets. Romeril directed or allowed lower-ranking defendants in Xerox's financial department to make accounting adjustments to results reported from operating divisions to accelerate revenues and increase earnings. These individuals used accounting methods to meet earnings goals and predictions of outside securities analysts. Allaire and Thoman then announced these results to the public through meetings with analysts and in communications to shareholders, celebrating that Xerox was enjoying substantially greater earnings growth than the true operating results warranted.

A description of two selected fraudulent accounting devices follows.

## Fraudulent Lease Accounting

Xerox sold copiers and other office equipment to its customers for cash, but it more frequently entered into long-term lease agreements in which customers paid a single negotiated monthly fee in return for the equipment, service, supplies, and financing. Xerox referred to these arrangements as "bundled leases."

The leases met the criteria under *SFAS 13* to be accounted for as "sales-type" leases, whereby the fair value of the equipment leased would be recognized as income in the period the lease is delivered, less any residual value the equipment is expected to retain once the lease expires. GAAP permits the financing revenue portion of the lease to be recognized only as it is earned over the life of the lease. *SFAS 13* also specifies that the portion of the lease payments that represents the fee for repair services and copier supplies be prorated over the term of the lease, matching it against the financing income.

Until the mid-1990s, Xerox followed satisfactory procedures for revenue recognition. However, the company encountered growing copier sales competition around the world and perceived a need to continue reporting record earnings. The management told KPMG that it was no longer able to reasonably assign a fair value to the equipment as it had in the past. The company abandoned the value determinations made at the lease inception, for public financial reporting purposes, but not for internal operating purposes, and substituted a formula that management could manipulate at will. Xerox did not test the value determinations to assess the reliability of the original method or if the new method did a better job of accurately reflecting the fair value of copier equipment.[45]

Xerox's "topside" lease accounting devices consistently increased the amount of lease revenues that Xerox recognized at the inception of the lease and reduced the amount it recognized over the life of the lease. One method was called *return on equity (ROE)*, which pulled forward a portion of finance income and recognized it immediately as equipment revenue. The second, called *margin normalization*, pulled forward a portion of service income and recognized it immediately as equipment revenue. These income acceleration methods did not comply with GAAP because there was no matching of revenue with the period during which (1) financing was provided, (2) copier supplies were provided, and (3) repairs were made to the leased equipment.

### "Cushion" Reserves

From 1997 through 2000, Xerox violated GAAP through the use of approximately $496 million of reserves to close the gap between actual results and earnings targets. Xerox had created reserves through charges to income prior to 1997. These cookie-jar reserves were released into income to make the numbers look better than they really were. The result was a smoothing of net income over time. This practice violated *SFAS 5, Accounting for Contingencies,* which allows a company to establish reserves only for identifiable, probable, and estimable risks and precludes the use of reserves, including excess reserves, for general or unknown business risks because they do not meet the accrual requirements of *SFAS 5.*

### Sanctions by the SEC on KPMG

The SEC issued a cease-and-desist order against KPMG on April 19, 2005, for its role in auditing the financial statements of Xerox from 1997 through 2000. *AAER 2234* details KPMG's consent to institute a variety of quality control measures, which included providing oversight of engagement partner changes of audit personnel and related independence issues.[46]

On February 22, 2006, the SEC announced that all four remaining KPMG staff members in the commission's action in connection with the $1.2 billion fraudulent earnings manipulation scheme by Xerox from 1997 through 2000 had agreed to settle the charges against them. Three KPMG partners agreed to permanent injunctions, payment of $400,000 in penalties, and suspensions from practice before the commission. Four partners were charged with filing materially false and misleading financial statements with the SEC and aiding and abetting Xerox's filing of false financial reports. The SEC charged that the partners knew or should have known about improper "topside adjustments" that resulted in $3 billion of the restated revenues and $1.2 billion of the restated earnings.[47]

The concurring review partner on the audit engagement team was cited because the adjustments enabled Xerox to change the allocations of revenues that it received from leasing photocopiers and other types of office equipment. The partner agreed to a censure from the SEC for failing to exercise due care, professional skepticism, and adhere to GAAS.

On April 20, 2005, KPMG settled with the SEC over the financial fraud at Xerox, agreeing to pay $10 million in penalties, in addition to disgorging nearly $10 million in audit fees and paying another $2.7 million in interest.

## The Case of Lucent Technologies

On May 20, 2004, the SEC charged Lucent Technologies, Inc., with securities fraud and violations of the reporting, books and records, and internal control provisions of the federal securities laws. The commission also charged nine current and former Lucent officers, executives, and employees with securities fraud and aiding and abetting Lucent's violations of federal securities laws. The SEC complaint alleged that Lucent fraudulently and improperly recognized approximately $1.148 billion of revenue and $470 million in pretax income during the fiscal year 2000.

The Lucent case is typical of the frauds that occurred in the late 1990s and early 2000s. The company's accounting techniques violated GAAP and were motivated by its drive to realize revenue, meet internal sales targets, and obtain sales bonuses. The internal controls were either violated or circumvented by top management. The board of directors and audit committee were either not involved or turned away from their obligations.

According to *AAER 2016,* Lucent officers improperly granted and/or failed to disclose various side agreements, credits, and other incentives (extracontractual commitments) made to induce Lucent's customers to purchase the company's products. The premature recognition of revenue occurred by "selling" $135 million in software to a customer that could choose from a software pool by September 29, 2001, and Lucent recognized $135 million in revenue in its fiscal year ending September 30, 2000. The parties reached an agreement to document separately additional elements of the software pool transaction that would give the customer more value in the form of side agreements. Top management postdated three letters documenting the side agreements with fictitious dates in October 2000. The effect of the postdated letters was to create the appearance that the side agreements were reached after September 30, 2000, and were not connected to the software pool agreement.[48] The accounting for these transactions enabled Lucent to manage earnings in a way that smoothed net income over time.

Lucent's story as a separate entity began in April 1996, when AT&T spun off the company. By 1999, operating income had reached $5.4 billion, tripling in two years. Net income had grown more than tenfold during that time period. These remarkable increases over a relatively short period of time should have raised a red flag for KPMG, but it did not. Exhibits 7.7 and 7.8 present the comparative amounts during the two-year period ended September 30, 1999.[49]

**EXHIBIT 7.7**
**Lucent Technologies, Inc.: Comparative Sales and Income**

| | Sales and Income Amounts (in billions) | | |
|---|---|---|---|
| Item | September 1999 | September 1998 | September 1997 |
| Sales | $48.3 | $31.8 | $27.6 |
| Operating income | 5.4 | 2.6 | 1.6 |
| Net income | 4.8 | 1.0 | 0.4 |

**EXHIBIT 7.8**
**Lucent Technologies, Inc.: Percentage Change in Sales and Income**

| | Percentage Changes in Sales and Income Amounts | |
|---|---|---|
| | September 1998 to September 1999 | September 1997 to September 1998 |
| Sales | 52% | 15% |
| Operating income | 104 | 63 |
| Net income | 380 | 150 |

**EXHIBIT 7.9**   Lucent Technologies, Inc.: Financial Shenanigans

| Technique | Description | Shenanigan Number |
|---|---|---|
| Recorded revenue too soon | Lucent restated year 2000 earnings, removing $679 million improperly included revenue. | No. 1 |
| Boosted income with one-time gains | During fiscal 1998, Lucent recorded $558 million of pension income—over 50 percent of earnings for the year. | No. 3 |
| Failed to write down impaired assets | Lucent reduced the allowance for doubtful accounts and released the previous reserves despite an increase in receivables of 32 percent. | No. 4 |
| Shifted current expenses to a later period | Lucent reduced the allowance for inventory obsolescence although the inventory balance increased. | No. 4 |
| Reduced liabilities by changing accounting assumptions | Lucent modified its accounting approach and assumptions for pensions. | No. 5 |
| Released reserves into income | Lucent released $100 million of a previously recorded restructuring reserve, boosting operating income. | No. 5 |
| Created new reserves from 10 acquisitions | Lucent wrote off $2.4 billion (58 percent of the cumulative purchase price) as an in-process R&D. This new reserve could be released into earnings later. | No. 7 |

Schilit points out that Lucent's stock price increased from a low of about $14 per share on January 1, 1997, to a high of about $78 by September 1999. The stock price began to decline after that, to a low of about $7 per share on January 1, 2002, as the fraud unfolded.

Exhibit 7.9 takes Lucent's earnings management techniques and classifies them into Schilit's financial shenanigan categories.

## The Story of Enron

The uniqueness of the decisions and manipulations at Enron and its link to the passage of SOX warrants a detailed discussion. The story of Enron is one of structuring financial transactions to keep debt off the books and report higher earnings. The failure of its corporate governance systems is the poster child for needed changes under SOX.

### In the Beginning . . .

Enron was created in 1985 through Omaha-based InterNorth Inc.'s takeover of Houston Natural Gas Corporation. InterNorth paid a huge premium for Houston Natural Gas, creating $5 million in debt. The company's debt payments of $50 million a month quickly led to the selloff of billions of dollars' worth of assets. Its debt load was so high that it forced the company into financing projects with borrowings that were kept off the balance sheet.

Jeff Skilling suggested that Enron's problem were due to a fluid market for natural gas; the industry needed long-term supply contracts. But prices were volatile, and contracts were available only for 30-day spot deals. Producers were unwilling to commit to the long term, always believing the price could go up.

### Skilling's "Gas Bank" Idea

Enron needed to find a way to bridge the gap between what the producers and big gas users wanted. Skilling discussed ways to pool the investments in gas-supply contracts and then sell long-term deals to utilities through a "Gas Bank." The Gas Bank called for Enron to write long-term contracts that enabled it to start accounting for those contracts differently. Traditionally, accounting would book revenue from a long-term contract when it came in. But Skilling wanted Enron to book all anticipated revenue immediately, as if it was writing up a marketable security. The technique lends itself to earnings management because of the subjectivity involved in estimating future market value.

Counting all expected profits immediately meant a huge earnings kick for a company that was getting deeply in debt. But it also put Enron on a treadmill: To keep growing, it would have to book bigger and bigger deals every quarter. The result was to shift focus from developing economically sound partnerships to doing deals at all costs.

The marketplace didn't seem to like the Enron deals. The initial Gas Bank plan hadn't persuaded gas producers to sell Enron their reserves. To entice the producers, the company needed to offer them money upfront for gas that would be delivered later. The problem was where to get the cash.

### Fastow's Special-Purpose Entities

In 1991, to revitalize the Gas Bank, Enron's CFO, Andy Fastow, began creating a number of partnerships. The first series of deals was called Cactus. The Cactus ventures eventually took in money from banks and gave it to energy producers in return for a portion of their existing gas reserves. That gave the producers money upfront and Enron gas over time.

Fastow worked to structure ventures that met the conditions under GAAP to keep the partnership activities off Enron's books and on the separate books of the partnership. To do so, the equity financing of the partnership venture had to include a minimum of 3 percent outside ownership. Control was not established through traditional means, which was the ownership of a majority of voting equity and combining of the partnership entity into the sponsoring organization (Enron), as is done with parent and subsidiary entities in a consolidation. Instead, the independent third parties were required to have a controlling and substantial interest in the entity. Control was established by the third-party investors exercising management rights over the entity's operations. There were a lot of "Monday morning quarterbacks" in the accounting profession who questioned the economic logic of attributing even the possibility of control to those who owned only 3 percent of the capital.

Bethany McLean and Peter Elkind are two *Fortune* magazine reporters credited with prompting the inquiries and investigations that brought down the Enron house of cards. McLean had written a story posing the simple question: "How, exactly, does Enron make its money?" Well, in the go-go years of the 1990s, all too often no one asked these kinds of questions (or, perhaps, did not want to know the answers).

According to McLean and Elkind, a small group of investors were pulled together, known internally as the "Friends of Enron." When Enron needed the 3 percent of outside ownership, it turned to the friends. However, these business associates and friends of Fastow and others were independent only in a technical sense. Though they made money on their investment, they didn't control the entities or the assets within them. "This, of course, was precisely the point," McLean and Elkind say.[50]

The 3 percent investments triggered a "special-purpose vehicle or special-purpose entity (SPE)." The advantage of the independent partnership relationship was that the SPE borrowed money from banks and other financial institutions that were willing to loan money to it with an obligation to repay the debt. The SPE enabled Enron to keep debt off its books while benefiting from the transfer and use of the cash borrowed by the SPE. The money borrowed by the SPE was often "transferred" to Enron in a sale of an operating asset no longer needed by Enron. The sale transaction typically led to a recorded gain because the cash proceeds exceeded the book value of the asset sold. The result was increased cash flow and liquidity and inflated earnings. The uniqueness of the transactions engaged in by Enron was that they initially didn't violate GAAP. Instead, Enron took advantage of the rules to engineer transactions that enabled it to achieve its goals for enhanced liquidity and profitability.

Exhibit 7.10 depicts the typical transaction between Enron and the SPE.

**EXHIBIT 7.10**
**Enron Corporation's SPEs**

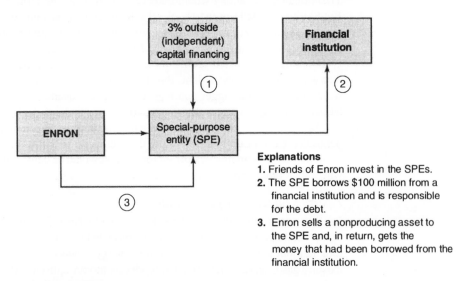

**Explanations**
1. Friends of Enron invest in the SPEs.
2. The SPE borrows $100 million from a financial institution and is responsible for the debt.
3. Enron sells a nonproducing asset to the SPE and, in return, gets the money that had been borrowed from the financial institution.

**Journal Entries**

| Enron | | | SPE | | |
|---|---|---|---|---|---|
| N/A | | | Cash | 100m | |
| | | | Due to Bank | | 100M |
| Cash | 100M | | Asset | 100m | |
| | Asset (assume) | 40M | Cash | | 100M |
| | Gain on sale | 60M | | | |

### *The Growth of SPEs*

Eventually, Enron would grow addicted to these arrangements because they hid debt. Not only did the company turn to its "friends," but increasingly, it had to borrow from banks and financial institutions that it did business with. These entities did not want to turn down a company like Enron, which was, at its peak, the seventh largest in the United States. But Enron let the risk-shifting feature of the partnerships lapse, thus negating their conformity to GAAP. Over time, the financial institutions that were involved in providing the 3 percent for the SPEs became skeptical of the ability of the SPEs to repay the interest when due. These institutions asked Enron to relieve the risk of the SPEs' failure to repay the investments. Later, partnership deals were backed by promises of Enron stock. Thus, if something went wrong, Enron would be left holding the bag. Therefore, there was no true transfer of economic risk to the SPE, and according to GAAP, the SPE should have been consolidated into Enron's financial statements.

### *The Culture at Enron*

The tension in the workplace grew with employees working later and later—first until 6 p.m. and then 11 p.m., and sometimes even into the next morning. Part of the pressure resulted from Skilling's new employee-evaluation policy. Workers called it "rank and yank." Employees were evaluated in groups, with each person rated on a scale of 1 to 5. The goal was to remove the bottom 20 percent of each group every year.

Ultimately, the system was seen as a tool for managers to reward loyalists and punish dissenters. It was seen as a cutthroat system and encouraged a "yes" culture, in which employees were reluctant to question their bosses—a fear that many would later come to regret.

### *Let the Force Be with You*

In late 1997, Enron entered a number of partnerships to improperly inflate earnings and hide debt. Enron created Chewco, named after the *Star Wars* character Chewbacca, to buy out its partner in another venture called JEDI, which was legally kept off the books. For JEDI to remain off the balance sheet, however, Chewco had to meet certain accounting requirements. But Enron skirted the already-weak rules required to keep Chewco off its books. JEDI helped overstate Enron's profits by $405 million and understate debt by $2.6 billion.

Because Enron needed to close the deal by year's end, Chewco was a rush job. Enron's executive committee presented the Chewco proposal to the board of directors on November 5. But CFO Fastow left out a few key details. He maintained that Chewco was not affiliated with Enron, but failed to mention that there was virtually no outside ownership in it. Nor did he reveal that one of his protégés, Michael Kopper, was managing the partnership. Indirectly (if not directly), Fastow would control the partnership through Kopper. Enron had a code of ethics that prohibited an officer from becoming involved with another entity that did business with Enron. Involvement by Fastow in these related-party entities was forbidden by the code. Nevertheless, the board of directors waived that requirement so Fastow could become involved with Chewco.

The board approved the deal, even though Enron's law firm, Vinson & Elkins, prepared the requisite documents so quickly that very few people actually read it before approving. Arthur Andersen, the firm that both audited Enron and did significant internal audit work for the company (pre-SOX), claimed that Enron withheld critical information. The firm billed the company only $80,000 for its review of the transaction, indicating a cursory review at best. Chewco, Fastow's involvement, the board approval, and a rapid approval process all were allowed because of a lack of internal controls. The *Star Wars* transactions were the beginning of the end for Enron. Chewco was inappropriately treated as a separate entity. Other SPE transactions eventually led to Enron's guaranteeing the debt of the SPE, using its stock as collateral. When Enron finally collapsed, its off-balance-sheet financing stood at an estimated $17 billion.

### Enron Just Keeps on Going

The greatest pressures were in Fastow's finance group. In 1999, he constructed two partnerships called LJM Cayman and LJM2 that readily passed through the board, the lawyers, and the accountants. They were followed by four more, known as the Raptors. They did it once—it worked—and then they did it again. It didn't take long to blur the lines between what's legal and what's not. When asked by a student during an interview for a position with Enron what he did at the company, one Enron employee in the finance group answered by saying, "I remove numbers from our balance sheet and inflate earnings."

As Enron pushed into new directions—wind power, water, high-speed Internet, paper, metals, data storage, advertising, etc.—it became a different company almost every quarter. Entrepreneurship was encouraged; innovation was the mantra. The quarter-by-quarter scramble to post ever-better numbers became all-consuming. Enron traders were encouraged to use "prudence reserves"—to essentially put aside some revenue until another quarter when it might be needed. Long-term energy contracts were evaluated using an adjustable curve to forecast energy prices. When a quarter looked tight, analysts were told to simply adjust the curve in Enron's favor.

### Executive Compensation

Enron's goal of setting its executive pay in the 75th percentile of its peer group—including companies like Duke Energy, Dynegy, and PG&E, which it compared itself with to assess overall corporate performance—was easily exceeded. In 2000, Enron exceeded the peer group average base salary by 51 percent. In bonus payments, it outdistanced its peers by 383 percent. The stock options granted in 2000—valued at the time at $86.5 million—exceeded the number granted by peers by 484 percent. Top management became accustomed to the large payouts, and the desire for more became of part of the culture of greed at Enron.

While Enron was the first player into the new energy market, enabling it to score huge gains, competitors caught on over time, and profit margins shrank. Skilling began looking for new pastures, and in 1996, he set his sights on electricity. Enron would do for power what it had done for natural gas. The push into electricity only added to the pressures mounting inside Enron. Earlier in 1996, Ken Lay, Enron's CEO, had predicted that the company's profits would double by 2000. This was a statement that would come back to haunt Lay in his civil trial in 2006, which alleged that he hyped Enron's stock to keep funds flowing, even though he knew the company was coming apart at the seams.

Lay pushed on as if nothing was wrong. Enron instituted a stock-option plan that promised to double employee salaries after eight years. Fresh off a $2.1 billion takeover of Portland General Corporation, an electric utility, Lay said his goal was nothing less than to make Enron the "world's greatest energy company."

Growth at all costs was the mantra at Enron. It encouraged executives to buy into this philosophy by giving out stock options that would provide cash over time and added the sweetener that if profits and the stock price went up enough, the schedule for those options would be sharply accelerated. It provided the incentive to find ways of increasing profits and improving stock price. It looked the other way when questions about ethics came up. Clearly, Enron and its officers pursued their self-interests to the detriment of all other interests and created a culture of greed. The environment at Enron reminds us of the famous quote by Gordon Gekko in the 1987 movie *Wall Street:* "Greed is good. Greed captures the essence of the evolutionary spirit."

### Congressional Investigation and Skilling's Departure

In 2000, Skilling was granted 867,880 options to buy shares, in addition to his salary and bonus that totaled $6.45 million. In that year, he exercised and sold over 1.1 million shares from options he received from prior years, and he pocketed $62.48 million. Skilling testified before Congress that he did not dump Enron shares as he told others to buy because he knew or suspected that the company was in financial trouble. Skilling's holdings of Enron shares increased because his number of options increased. Even under Enron's option plan, in which options vested fully in three years (an unusually quick rate), Skilling wound up holding many Enron shares that he couldn't legally sell.

Lay and Skilling used as their defense in the 2006 civil trial that Enron was a successful company brought down by a crisis of confidence in the market. The government contended that Enron appeared successful but actually hid its failures through dubious, even criminal accounting tricks. In fact, Enron by most measures wasn't particularly profitable—a fact obscured by its share price until late in its history. But there was one area in which it succeeded like few others: executive compensation.

As the stock market began to decline in the late 1990s, Enron's stock followed the downward trend. The never-ending number of deals, even as business slowed, gave Wall Street pause. By April 2001, concerns mounted whether the company was disclosing financial information from its off-balance-sheet financing transactions adequately.

The pressure continued both internally and externally from a slowing economy, competition from other entities that were catching on to Enron's gimmicks, and stock market declines. Differences of opinion exist why Skilling made the decision, but on August 14, 2001, Skilling, who just six months prior had been named the CEO of Enron, resigned. He gave as his public reason the ever-popular "I need to spend more time with my family."

### Sherron Watkins's Role

But Enron executive Sherron Watkins was dubious, and she sent an anonymous letter to Ken Lay, the CEO and chair of the board of directors, warning him of an impending scandal. It said in part, "Has Enron become a risky place to work? For those of us who didn't get rich over the last few years, can we afford to stay?" She described in detail problems with Enron's partnerships, problems that the letter claimed would cause huge financial upheavals at the company in as little as a year. "I am incredibly nervous that we will implode in a wave of accounting scandals," Watkins wrote. "Skilling is resigning for 'personal reasons,' but I think he wasn't having fun, looked down the road, and knew this stuff was unfixable and would rather abandon ship now than resign in shame in two years."[51]

Lay took a copy of the letter to James V. Derrick Jr., Enron's general counsel, who agreed that it needed to be investigated. They decided to assign the task to Vinson & Elkins—which had helped prepare some of the legal documents for some of the partnerships. Enron wanted answers fast, seemingly regardless of due diligence, and the company instructed the outside lawyers not to spend time examining the accounting treatment recommended by Arthur Andersen—although that was at the heart of the letter's warnings.

### Powers Committee Report

Vinson & Elkins began its investigation. Even while it investigated Fastow's role, the conflicts mounted. Kopper, who had sold his Chewco assets to Enron to deflect criticisms of Fastow's role, made a profit on the sale and then insisted that Enron cover the $2.6 million tax liability from the sale. The Powers Committee, formed by the audit committee to investigate the failure of Enron, concluded on this matter that "there is credible evidence that Fastow authorized Enron's payment to Chewco," adding that the payment—

done against the explicit instructions of Enron's general counsel—was "one of the most serious issues we identified in connection with the Chewco buyout."[52]

Three days after beginning their investigation, the Vinson & Elkins lawyers investigating Watkins's warnings reported their findings to Lay and Derrick that there was no reason for concern. Everything in Fastow's operation seemed to be on the level. They promised a written report in a matter of weeks. By then, though, it would be too late.

### The Final Days

In November 2001, Enron announced it had overstated earnings by $586 million since 1997. In December 2001, Enron made the largest bankruptcy filing ever at that time. By January 2002, the U.S. Department of Justice (DOJ) confirmed an investigation of Enron. The very next day, Andersen admitted to shredding documents related to its audit of Enron, an act of obstructing justice that would doom the firm following a DOJ lawsuit. It hardly mattered what the outcome of the lawsuit would be; Enron's clients started to abandon the firm in droves after the announcement of the lawsuit. Ultimately, the jury decided that the firm had obstructed justice, a decision that would be overturned later due to a technicality.

### The Lay-Skilling Criminal Trial

Following the unanimous jury verdict on May 26, 2006, that found both Lay and Skilling guilty of fraud and conspiracy, Lay was quoted as saying, "Certainly we're surprised," and Skilling commented, "I think it's more appropriate to say we're shocked. This is not the outcome we expected."[53]

Skilling was convicted of 19 counts of fraud, conspiracy, and insider trading. Lay was convicted on six counts in the joint trial and four charges of bank fraud and making false statements to banks in a separate nonjury trial before U.S. District Judge Sam Lake related to Lay's personal finances. The sentencing for Lay and Skilling in the case, somewhat ironically, was set for September 11, 2006. Skilling faced a maximum of 185 years in prison. For Lay, the fraud and conspiracy convictions carried a combined maximum punishment of 45 years. The bank fraud case added 120 years, 30 years for each of the four counts. Unfortunately, Ken Lay passed away just weeks after the verdict.

### Skilling's Efforts to Overturn the Verdict

On October 23, 2006, Skilling was sentenced to 24 years and 4 months in prison, and fined $45 million. As discussed in Chapter 6, Skilling has fought to overturn that sentence almost from the beginning. On June 21, 2013, it was announced by the U.S. Department of Justice that Skilling will be freed ten years early. This means he would spend a total of 14 years in jail. Skilling is eligible for parole in 2017.

### Enron: A Review of Important Accounting Issues

The fraud at Enron was caused by a variety of factors, including these:

- Improperly failing to consolidate the results of an SPE (Chewco) with Enron. Consolidation was warranted because Chewco lacked the necessary independence from Enron's management because Andy Fastow had direct or indirect control over it.
- Failing to disclose adequately the related-party relationship between Enron and the SPEs, especially those that were independent of the company under GAAP.
- Overstating earnings from using mark-to-market accounting for investments in long-term gas contracts that relied on estimates of future market value to record unrealized gains.

   The quality of financial reports was poor for the following reasons:

- Failure to disclose adequately the related-party transactions made it impossible for investors and creditors to know the full extent of these transactions, and loans were made to Enron based on vastly understated debt.

- The sale of assets to SPEs in return for the transfer of borrowed funds from the SPE, with the subsequent recording of a gain, masked Enron's true earnings and made it appear that the company was doing better than it really was.

- The use of reserves and failure to explain the basis for creation made it impossible to judge the acceptability of these transactions.

- The failure to disclose Fastow's dual role with the SPEs and as CFO of Enron made it impossible for investors and creditors to gain the information they had an ethical right to know in order to evaluate the legitimacy of off-balance-sheet transactions and their effect on the financial statements.

Enron managed earnings through the following techniques (Schilit's shenanigan numbers are indicated in parentheses):

- Used reserves to increase earnings when reported amounts were too low (#5)
- Used mark-to-market estimates to inflate earnings in violation of GAAP (#1)
- Selected which operating assets to "sell" to the SPEs, thereby affecting the amount of the gain on transfer and earnings effect (#3)

The lack of strong controls contributed to the fraud as evidenced by the following:

- Top management overrode or ignored internal controls in the approval process for Chewco, the LJM SPEs, and the Raptors.

- Oversight by the board of directors was either negligent, as was the case with the waiving of the ethics code for Fastow, or nonexistent.

- A culture was established to make the deals at any cost, thereby diluting the due diligence process that should have raised red flags on some of the transactions.

- A culture of fear was created within Enron with its "rank or yank" policy and cutthroat competition.

## FASB Rules on SPEs

While it may seem that the GAAP rules on SPEs are naïve, there are legitimate reasons for establishing the concept that an entity could isolate a business operation or some corporate assets. The idea was to control risk in a project such as investing in a new oil refinery. By following the rules to set up an SPE, an oil company could keep the large amount of debt off the books while using the funds from the SPE to construct the refinery. The off-balance-sheet effect helps control risk if the project fails. The original motivation by FASB was to establish a mechanism to encourage companies to invest in needed assets while keeping the related debt off their books.

The "creativity" of Andy Fastow was in using a less-well-known technique under GAAP to satisfy Enron's unique needs. Enron became the leader of structured transactions designed to meet specific goals rather than to present accurately its financial position and the results of its operations. These are nothing more than elaborate attempts to manage earnings.

### FASB Interpretation 46(R)

After much debate about how to fix the original SPE ownership percentage and consolidation rules, FASB issued on December 24, 2003, a revision of its proposed Interpretation: *FASB Interpretation 46(R), Consolidation of Variable Interest Entities.*[54] Basically, *Interpretation 46(R)* requires unconsolidated variable interest entities to be consolidated by their primary beneficiaries if the entities do not effectively disperse risk among parties involved. Variable-interest entities that effectively disperse risks would not be consolidated unless a single party holds an interest or combination of interests that recombines risks that were previously dispersed.

The new rules apply an economic reality test to the consolidation of a variable interest entity. No longer is there a percentage ownership test. Instead, it is the dispersion of risk that determines the consolidation status. By effectively dispersing risk, the primary beneficiary controls its own risk with respect to activities of the unconsolidated variable interest entity.

## Enron's Role in the Creation and Passage of SOX

The Enron fraud was a direct cause, along with WorldCom, of congressional passage of SOX and efforts to reform the accounting profession. The provisions of the act that were motivated by the Enron fraud include:

- Prohibiting the provision of internal audit services for audit clients. Andersen provided the major part of internal audit services for Enron. Overall, Andersen earned from Enron in its last full year as accountants $27 million from nonauditing services and $25 million from auditing services.
- Requiring that off-balance-sheet financing activities be disclosed in the notes to the financial statements. Enron's SPEs were never referred to as providing off-balance-sheet financing.
- Requiring that related-party transactions be disclosed in the notes. The activities with the SPEs qualify as related-party transactions. By some accounts, Enron had over 3,000 SPEs, yet the footnote disclosure in its last year before filing for bankruptcy was limited to one page.

Enron also suffered from the same lack of controls and inadequate corporate governance that infected so many other companies during the accounting scandals. For example, the board of directors did not act independently, and the audit committee members were not independent of management. The internal environment at Enron, especially the tone at the top, promoted a culture of making deals regardless of the risks.

The internal controls at Enron were either ignored or overridden by management (i.e., the board waived its ethics policy so that Andy Fastow could control Chewco indirectly while simultaneously serving as the CFO for Enron). This created a conflict of interest that enabled Fastow to enrich himself through control of Chewco at the expense of Enron. The result was a serious breach of fiduciary responsibilities and the failure of management to meet its obligation as an agent for the shareholders.

## Lessons to Be Learned from Enron

What is the moral of the Enron story? Certainly, we could say that weak internal controls equate with possible fraud. Also, we could point to the need for an ethical tone at the top to help prevent fraud. At Enron, once the company developed an appetite for establishing SPEs and keeping these transactions off the books, the company became more and more addicted to the cash provided through the SPEs. Even if it wanted to stop the transactions, Enron and its top management had set the company on a course that was difficult to change. Enron had started to slide down the ethical slippery slope, and there was no turning back.

The bottom-line factor that kept the Enron fraud going well past the point of no return was greed. Skilling saw Fastow getting rich, Lay saw Skilling getting rich, all the Enron employees thought they saw Lay getting rich, and then Lay hyped Enron stock to the employees for their 401(k)'s as a way for them, eventually, to get rich.

# Earnings Quality

On October 10, 2012, Dichev et al. released the results of a study of earnings quality taken from a survey of 169 CFOs of public companies and in-depth interviews of 12 CFOs and two standard setters. The results relate to the prevalence, magnitude, and detection of earnings management.[55]

Their key findings fall into three broad categories. The first includes results related to the definition, characteristics, and determinants of earnings quality. On definition, CFOs believe that earnings are high quality when they are sustainable and backed by actual cash flows. More specific quality characteristics include consistent reporting choices over time and avoidance of long-term estimates. Consistent with this view, current earnings are considered to be high quality if they serve as a good guide to the long-run profits of the firm.

The second set of results relates to how standard setting affects earnings quality. CFOs believe that reporting discretion has declined over time, and that current GAAP standards are somewhat of a constraint in reporting high-quality earnings. CFOs would like standard setters to issue fewer rules and to converge U.S. GAAP with International Financial Reporting Standards (IFRS) to improve earnings quality. Further, they believe that earnings quality would improve if reporting choices were to evolve at least partly from practice rather than being mandated from standards. As one consequence of such inflexible rules, CFOs say that the accounting standards sometimes drive operational decisions, rather than the other way around. CFOs also feel that the rules orientation of the FASB has centralized the audit function, depriving local offices of discretion in dealing with clients, and stunting the development of young auditing professionals. Overall, CFOs have come to view financial reporting largely as a compliance activity, rather than as a vehicle of innovation designed to inform stakeholders and lower the cost of capital.

The third set of results relies on observable GAAP earnings and a clear definition of earnings management, asking for within-GAAP manipulation that misrepresents performance (i.e., the researchers rule out outright fraud and performance-signaling motivations). The CFOs estimate that, in any given period, roughly 20 percent of firms manage earnings and the typical misrepresentation for such firms is about 10 percent of reported EPS. CFOs believe that 60 percent of earnings management is income-increasing, and 40 percent is income-decreasing, somewhat in contrast to the expected heavy emphasis on income-increasing results but consistent with the intertemporal setting up of accruals in settings like cookie-jar reserves and big baths. A large majority of CFOs feel that earnings misrepresentation occurs most often in an attempt to influence stock price, because of outside and inside pressure to hit earnings benchmarks, and to avoid adverse compensation and career consequences for senior executives. Finally, while CFOs caution that earnings management is difficult to unravel from the outside, they suggest a number of red flags that point to potential misrepresentation. The three most common flags are persistent deviations between earnings and the underlying cash flows, deviations from industry and other peer experience, and large and unexplained accruals and changes in accruals. There are also a number of red flags that relate to the role of the manager's character and the firm's culture, which allow and perhaps even encourage earnings management.

---

**Concluding Thoughts**

Enron, WorldCom, HealthSouth, Lucent, Waste Management, and Xerox. These are just a few of the financial statement frauds discussed in this chapter. Each fraud occurred as a result of a desire to meet financial analysts' earnings estimates or to inflate share price to make stock options worth more or to increase bonus payments to top management. The motivation for these frauds was greed, pure and simple. Techniques such as cookie-jar-reserves, accelerating revenue recognition, delaying accruals and expense recognition, and the use of SPEs to mask debt all had one thing in common—a desire to manage earnings and make the company look like it was doing better than it really was. We started discussing accounting fraud earlier in the book because it results from a lack of professional (ethical) judgment, weak corporate governance systems, and the failure of accountants and auditors to follow the profession's ethical standards in meeting their public interest obligations. In this chapter we addressed the results of such behavior that include the use of financial shenanigans to manipulate earnings and the resulting need to restate prior years' earnings once the fraud is discovered. It is interesting to note that earnings restatements had increased through 2006 and then started a downward trend. We would like to credit SOX with the reversal but feel it is too early to draw such a conclusion.

We believe that when management manipulates earnings, the quality of such information suffers. It is hard enough for most readers of financial statements to understand the underlying accounting and financial reporting techniques used to develop the statements. When such methods are manipulated, or new ones developed to put a positive spin on company results, then there is distortion effect that compromises the dependability of the statements. In the end it is the users of the statements that suffer.

At the end of the day, financial reporting needs to focus more on representational faithfulness, meaning that there should be a correspondence or agreement between the accounting measures or descriptions in financial reports and the economic events they purport to represent. Enron failed in this regard with respect to informing the public about its widespread use of SPEs to mask debt.

The accounting profession seems to recognize that the traditional term "reliability" may be misunderstood and denote an exactness that does not, and cannot exist, given a variety of choices of accounting principles and changes to them that may occur from year to year. *Statement of Financial Accounting Concepts No. 8* essentially replaces reliability as a qualitative characteristic of useful information with representational faithfulness. This is in keeping with the international accounting standards trend of doing the same as we will discuss in Chapter 8.

Faithful representation does not mean accurate in all respects. Free from error means there are no errors or omissions in the description of the event, and the process used to produce the reported information has been selected and applied with no errors in the process. In other words, a representation of an estimate can be faithful if the amount is described clearly and accurately as being an estimate, the nature and limitations of the estimating process are explained, and no errors have been made in selecting and applying an appropriate process for developing the estimate.

We are encouraged by the fact that the International Accounting Standards Board (IASB) and the FASB[56] in the U.S. have undertaken a joint project to develop an improved conceptual framework for International Financial Reporting Standards (IFRSs) and U.S. GAAP. We will explore these efforts in the next chapter.

**Discussion Questions**

1. In Arthur Levitt's speech, referred to in the opening quote, he also said: "I fear that we are witnessing an erosion in the quality of earnings, and therefore, the quality of financial reporting. Managing may be giving way to manipulation; integrity may be losing out to illusion." Explain what you think Levitt meant by this statement. What role do financial analysts' earnings expectations play in the quality of earnings?

2. Relevance and faithful representation are the qualitative characteristics of useful information under *SFAC 8*.[57] Evaluate these characteristics from an ethical perspective. That is, how does ethical reasoning enter into making determinations about the relevance and faithful representation of financial information?

3. Evaluate earnings management from a utilitarian perspective. Can earnings management be an ethical practice? Discuss why or why not.

4. Evaluate the following statements from an ethical perspective:

   "Earnings management in a narrow sense is the behavior of management to play with the discretionary accrual component to determine high or low earnings."

   "Earnings are potentially managed, because financial accounting standards still provide alternative methods."

5. Comment on the statement that materiality is in the eye of the beholder. How does this statement relate to the discussion in this chapter of how to gauge materiality in assessing financial statement restatements? Is materiality inconsistent with the notion of representational faithfulness?

6. Needles talks about the use of a continuum ranging from questionable or highly conservative to fraud to assess the amount to be recorded for an estimated expense. Discuss his concept of a continuum and the choices within a range from an ethical perspective. That is, how might a decision about the selection of one or another amount in the continuum relate to it being an ethical position to take?

7. Explain how the quality of corporate governance, risk management, and compliance systems is critical in controlling financial restatement risk within organizations.

8. In 2010, LinkedIn reported trade payable obligations totaling $10.8 million in other accrued expenses within accrued liabilities instead of accounts payable. In 2011, note 2 in the 10-K financial statements described the use of accrued liabilities instead of accounts payable as a classification. Do you believe LinkedIn's accounting qualifies as a financial shenanigan? Why or why not?

9. Comment on the statement that what a company's income statement reveals is interesting, but what it conceals is vital.

10. Maines and Wahlen[58] state in their research paper on the reliability of accounting information: "Accrual estimates require judgment and discretion, which some firms under certain incentive conditions will exploit to report non-neutral accruals estimates within GAAP. Accounting standards can enhance the information in accrual estimates by linking them to the underlying economic constructs they portray." Explain what the authors meant by this statement with respect to the possible existence of earnings management.

11. Safety-Kleen is a North American company that offers environmental products and services. The company issued a major financial restatement in 2001. In 2000, the company's board of directors initiated an investigation of possible accounting fraud within the company. The next year, Safety-Kleen restated (reduced) previously reported net income by $534 million for the period 1997–99. In the week surrounding the announcement of Safety-Kleen's investigation, the company's stock price dropped over 70% and its auditor, PricewaterhouseCoopers (PwC), withdrew its financial statement audit reports for the previous three years. PwC agreed to settle a shareholder lawsuit for failing to discover the fraud in the amount of $48 million. PwC said the audit firm admitted no wrongdoing but settled to avoid the uncertainty of a trial. Do you believe that financial restatements and withdrawing an audit report are *prima facie* indicators that a failed audit has occurred? Explain why or why not.

12. Revenue recognition for multiple-element arrangements as occurred in the Xerox case discussed in this chapter calls for determining the stand-alone selling price for each of the deliverables and using it to separate out the revenue amounts. Why do you think it is important to separate out the selling prices of each element of a bundled transaction? How might the separation affect recorded revenue in the period of sale and in future periods? How do these considerations relate to what Xerox did to manage its earnings?

13. Tinseltown Construction just received a $2 billion contract to construct a modern football stadium in the City of Industry, located in southern California, for a new National Football League (NFL) team called the Los Angeles Devils of Industry. The company estimates that it will cost $1.5 billion to construct the stadium. Explain how Tinseltown can make revenue recognition decisions each year that enable it to manage earnings over the three-year duration of the contract.

14. Explain how the use of available-for-sale securities can lead to managed earnings.

15. In the Enron case, the company eventually turned to "back-door" guaranteeing of the debt of Chewco, one of its SPEs, to satisfy equity investors. Assume that one guarantee was for a $16 million loan. The loan agreement required that Enron stock should not fall below $40 per share. If the share price did decline below that trigger amount, either the loan would be called by the bank or the bank could choose to increase the guaranteed number of Enron shares based on the new price (assume $32). If the bank decides to increase the number of shares guaranteed, what would be (1) the original number of shares in the guarantee and (2) the new number of shares? Why would it be important from an accounting and ethical perspective for Enron to disclose information about the guarantee in its financial statements?

16. On August 9, 2005, a special committee comprised of two independent directors of Krispy Kreme (the "Special Committee") presented a report of its investigation into an accounting fraud to the board of directors.

The following numbers were included in the Krispy Kreme Special Committee report with respect to reversals of accruals during the fraud period.

**Estimated Restatement Adjustments**
**Increase (decrease) in pretax earnings (in millions)**

|  | FY00 and earlier | FY ended 1/28/01 | FY ended 2/3/02 | FY ended 2/2/03 | FY ended 2/1/04 | Nine Months ended 10/31/04 | Total |
|---|---|---|---|---|---|---|---|
| **Accruals relating to employee vacation pay** | (2.0) | (0.4) | (0.5) | (0.3) | (0.5) | (0.4) | (4.1) |
| **Accruals for charitable contributions** | (0.5) | (0.5) | (0.7) | (1.7) | | | |

Devise a scenario to explain how and why the Krispy Kreme accruals were made in the amounts that they were. What might have been the motivation for such action?

17. Explain whether you believe fraudulent reporting is positively correlated with each of the following conditions: (1) more financial pressure imposed by a supervisor of a firm; (2) higher percentage of complex transactions of a firm; (3) more questionable integrity of a firm's managers; and (4) more deterioration in the relationship between a firm and its auditor.

18. Schilit recognizes that cash flow shenanigans also exist when a company takes actions to send their desirable cash inflows to the most important section (Operating) and all of the unwanted cash outflows to the other sections (Investing and Financing).[59] Given that regardless of the classification of the cash flows, the result is the same with respect to the amount of change in cash flows during the designated period, what motive might exist to shift investing and/or financing cash flows to the operating section? Is this an ethical practice? Why or why not?

19. In the study of earnings quality by Dichev et al., CFOs stated that "current earnings are considered to be high quality if they serve as a good guide to the long-run profits of the firm." Discuss how and why current earnings may *not* be a good barometer of the long-term profits of the firm.

20. Explain what is meant by the following two statements and why they may be true:

Where management does not try to manipulate earnings, there is a positive effect on earnings quality. The absence of earnings management does not, however, guarantee high earnings quality.

## Endnotes

1. David Bogoslaw, "Earnings: Watch for These Red Flags," April 09, 2009, Available at www .businessweek.com/stories/2009-04-09/earnings-watch-for-these-red-flagsbusinessweek-business-news-stock-market-and-financial-advice.

2. Arthur Levitt, "The 'Numbers Game,' Remarks by Chairman Arthur Levitt, Securities and Exchange Commission, before the NYU Center for Law and Business," September 28, 1998, www.sec.gov.

3. Eli Bartov, Dan Givoly, and Carla Hayn, "The Rewards to Meeting or Beating Earnings Expectations, *Journal of Accounting & Economics* 33, 173–204 (2002).

4. Timothy Fogarty, Michel Magnan, Garen Markarian, and Serge Bohdjalian, "Inside Agency: The Rise and Fall of Nortel," February 1, 2008, Available at http://papers.ssrn.com/sol3/papers .cfm?abstract_id=1092288.

5. Joseph Fuller and Michael C. Jensen, "Just Say No to Wall Street: Putting a Stop to the Earnings Game," *Journal of Applied Corporate Finance* 14(4), 41–46 (Winter 2002).

6. William Erhard, Michael C. Jensen, and Sam Zaffron, "Integrity: A Positive Model That Incorporates the Normative Phenomena of Morality, Ethics, and Legality—Abridged." Harvard Business School Negotiations, Organizations, and Markets (NOM) Working Paper No. 06–11; Barbados Group Working Paper No. 10-0103–06; and Simon School of Business Working Paper No. 10_07 (March 2010). Available at www://ssrn.com/Abstract_920625.

7. John R. Graham, Harvey R. Campbell, and Shiva Rajgopal, "The Economic Implications of Corporate Financial Reporting," *Journal of Accounting & Economics* 40 (1), 3–73 (December 2005).

8. M. H. Carol Liu, Samuel L. Tiras, and E. J. Ourso, "Audit Committees and Earnings Masnagement," August 2008, Available at www.aaahq.org/meetings/AUD2009/AuditCommitteesAndEarnings .pdf.

9. U.S. Securities and Exchange Commission Litigation Release No. 18422/October 22, 2003; Accounting and Auditing Enforcement Release No. 1904 (AAER No. 1904) October 22, 2003. Available at www.sec.gov/litigation/litreleases/lr18422.htm.

10. Available at www.sec.gov/divisions/enforce/friactions/friactions2003.shtml.

11. Financial Accounting Standards Board, "Recognition and Measurement in Financial Statements of Business Enterprises," *Statement of Financial Accounting Concepts (SFAC) No. 5* (Stamford, CT: FASB, May 1986).

12. Available at www.securities.stanford.edu/1008/HRC98/200482_r03c_031500.pdf.

13. Richard J. Rivard, Eugene Bland, and Gary B. Hatfield Morris, "Income Smoothing Behavior of U.S. Banks under Revised International Capital Requirements," *International Advances in Economic Research* 9(4), 288–294 (November 2003).

14. Kenneth A. Merchant, *Rewarding Results: Motivating Profit Center Managers* (Boston: Harvard Business School Press, 1989).

15. William S. Hopwood, Jay J. Leiner, and George R. Young, *Forensic Accounting and Fraud Examination* (New York: McGraw-Hill Irwin, 2012).

16. K. Schipper, "Commentary on Earnings Management," *Accounting Horizons* (December 1989), 91–102.

17. P. M. Healy and J. M. Wahlen, "A Review of Earnings Management Literature and Its Implications for Standard Setting," *Accounting Horizons* 13, 365–383 (1999).

18. P. M. Dechow and P. J. Skinner, "Earnings Management: Reconciling the Views of Accounting Academics, Practitioners, and Regulation," *Accounting Horizons* 14, 235–250 (2001).

19. Thomas E. McKee, *Earnings Management: An Executive Perspective* (Mason, OH: Thompson Corporation, 2005).

20. Hopwood et al., p. 426.

21. Belverd E. Needles, Jr., "The Role of Judgment in Ethical Financial Reporting," Beta Alpha Psi Newsletter, Vol. 2, Issue 4, Fall 2011. Available at www.bap.org/BAPNewsletter/2_4/article2.html.

22. Elias, RZ (2004). "The impact of Corporate Ethical Values on Perceptions of Earnings Management," *Managerial. Audit. Journal* 19, 84–98 (2004).

23. Frank Phillips and K. Zvinakis, "Baywatch International: A Case Linking Financial Reporting, Business, and User Decisions," *Issues in Accounting Education* 15, 605–622 (2000).

24. Anna M. Rose and Jacob Rose, "Management Attempts to Avoid Accounting Disclosure Oversight: The Effects of Trust and Knowledge on Corporate Directors' Governance Ability," *Journal of Business Ethics,* 83, 193–205 (2008).

25. William J. Bruns Jr. and Kenneth A. Merchant, "The Dangerous Morality of Managing Earnings," *Management Accounting,* August 1990, pp. 62–69.

26. K. Rosenzweig and M. Fischer, "Is Managing Earnings Ethically Acceptable?" *Management Accounting,* March 1994, pp. 44–51.

27. Michael D. Akers, Don E. Giacomino, and Jodi L. Bellovary, "Earnings Management and Its Implications: Educating the Accounting Profession," *The CPA Journal,* August 2007, pp. 33–39.

28. Akers et al.

29. Akers et al.

30. Patricia M. Dechow, "Accounting Earnings and Cash Flows as Measures of Firm Performance: The Role of Accounting Accruals," *Journal of Accounting & Economics* 18, 3–42 (1994).

31. Securities and Exchange Commission, *Staff Accounting Bulletin No. 99—Materiality,* www.sec.gov/interps/account/sab99.htm.

32. Supreme Court of the United States, *Mattrix Initiatives et al. v. Siracusano et al.* Certiorari to the U.S. Court of Appeals for the Ninth Circuit, March 22, 2011, Available at http://www.supremecourt.gov/opinions/10pdf/09-1156.pdf.

33. *TSC Industries, Inc. v. Northway, Inc.*—426 U.S. 438 (1976), Available at www.supreme.justia.com/cases/federal/us/426/438/.

34. *Basic, Inc. v. Levinson*—485 U.S. 224 (1988), Available at www.supreme.justia.com/cases/federal/us/485/224/.

35. *Mattrix Initiatives et al. v. Siracusano et al.*

36. James Brady Vorhies, "The New Importance of Materiality, *Journal of Accountancy,* May 2005, Available at http://www.journalofaccountancy.com/Issues/2005/May/TheNewImportanceOfMateriality.htm.

37. Securities and Exchange Commission, Accounting and Auditing Enforcement Release No. 2125, *In the Matter of KPMG [v. Gemstar],* www.sec.gov/litigation/admin/34-550564.html.

38. Audit Analytics, 2011 Financial Restatements: An Eleven-Year Comparison, Available at www.auditanalytics.com/0002/view-custom-reports.php?report=2cf0d91f53bc6280b23c206be796582c.

39. SEC, *Final Report of the Advisory Committee on Improvements to Financial Reporting* on August 1, 2008, Available at www.sec.gov/about/offices/oca/acifr/acifr-finalreport.pdf.

40. Available at www.markets.financialcontent.com/mi.charlotte/quote/filings/quarterly?Symbol=321%3A923159

41. Available at www.cubic.com/News/Press-Releases/ID/423/Cubic-Corporation-to-Restate-Financial-Statements

42. Levitt, "The 'Numbers Game.'"

43. Howard M. Schilit, *Financial Shenanigans: How to Detect Accounting Gimmicks and Fraud in Financial Reports,* 3d ed. (New York: McGraw-Hill, 2010).

44. Securities and Exchange Commission, Litigation Release No. 18174, *Securities and Exchange Commission v. Paul A. Allaire, G. Richard Thoman, Barry D. Romeril, Philip D. Fishbach, Daniel S. Marchibroda, and Gregory B. Tayler,* June 5, 2003, Accounting and Auditing Enforcement Release No. 1796, www.sec.gov/litigation/litreleases/lr18174.html.

45. Securities and Exchange Commission, Litigation Release No. 17645, Accounting and Enforcement Release No. 1542, *Securities and Exchange Commission v. Xerox Corporation,* Civil Action No. 02-CV-2780 (DLC) (S.D.N.Y.) (April 11, 2002).

46. Securities and Exchange Commission, Litigation Release No. 19573, Accounting and Enforcement Release No. 2379, *SEC v. KPMG LLP et al.,* Civil Action No. 03-CV 0671 (DLC) (S.D.N.Y.) (February 22, 2006).

47. Securities and Exchange Commission, Accounting and Auditing Enforcement Release No. 2234, *In the Matter of KPMG LLP,* April 19, 2005, www.sec.gov/litigation/admin/34-51574.pdf.

48. Securities and Exchange Commission, Accounting and Enforcement Release Litigation Release No. 2016, *Securities and Exchange Commission v. Lucent Technologies, Inc., Nina Aversano, Jay Carter, A. Leslie Dorn, William Plunkett, John Bratten, Deborah Harris, Charles Elliott, Vanessa Petrini, Michelle Hayes-Bullock, and David Ackerman,* Civil Action No. 04-2315 (WHW) (D.N.J.) (filed May 17, 2004, www.sec.gov/ltigation /litreleases/lr18715.htm.)

49. Securities and Exchange Commission, Accounting and Enforcement Release No. 2380, *In the Matter of Thomas J. Yoho, CPA, Respondent,* Administrative Proceeding File No. 3-12215, February 22, 2006.

50. Bethany McLean and Peter Elkind, *The Smartest Guys in the Room: The Amazing Rise and Scandalous Fall of Enron* (New York: Penguin Books, 2003).

51. Mimi Swartz and Sherron Watkins, *Power Failure: The Inside Story of the Collapse of Enron* (New York: Doubleday, 2003), pp. 275–276.

52. Report of Investigation by the Special Investigative Committee of the Board of Directors of Enron Corp., February 1, 2002, www.news.findlaw/hdocs/docs/enron/sicreport.

53. Michael Gracyzk, "Lay Says He's 'Shocked' at Enron Verdict," www.cbsnews.com/stories/2006/05/26/ap/business/mainD8HRJ2C80.shtml.

54. Financial Accounting Standards Board, *FASB Interpretation 46(R),* Consolidation of Variable Interest Entities, December 24, 2003 (Norwalk, CT: FASB, 2003).

55. Ilia Dichev, John Graham, Campbell R. Harvey, and Shiva Rajgopal, "Earnings Quality: Evidence from the Field," A research paper in progress, October 10, 2012, Available at www.faculty.fuqua.duke.edu/~charvey/Research/Working_Papers/W108_Earnings_quality_evidence.pdf.

56. Financial Accounting Standards Board, Concepts Statement No. 8, Conceptual Framework for Financial Reporting—Chapter 1, *The Objective of General Purpose Financial Reporting,* and Chapter 3, *Qualitative Characteristics of Useful Financial Information* (a replacement of FASB Concepts Statements No. 1 and No. 2) (Issue Date 9/10).

57. Financial Accounting Standards Board, Concepts Statement No. 8—Conceptual Framework for Financial Reporting—Chapter 1, *The Objective of General Purpose Financial Reporting,* and Chapter 3, *Qualitative Characteristics of Useful Financial Information* (a replacement of FASB Concepts Statements No. 1 and No. 2), Available at http://www.fasb.org/cs/BlobServer?blobkey=id&blobwhere=1175822892635&blobheader=application%2Fpdf&blobcol=urldata&blobtable=MungoBlobs.

58. Laureen A. Maines and James M. Wahlen, "The Nature of Accounting Information Reliability: Inferences from Archival and Experimental Research," Available at http://repository.binus.ac.id/content/m0034/m003421831.pdf.

59. Schilit, p. 198.

# Chapter 7 Cases

## Case 7-1

# Nortel Networks

Canada-based Nortel Networks was one of the largest tele-communications equipment companies in the world prior to its filing for bankruptcy protection on January 14, 2009, in the United States, Canada, and Europe. The company had been subjected to several financial reporting investigations by U.S. and Canadian securities agencies in 2004. The accounting irregularities centered on premature revenue recognition and hidden cash reserves used to manipulate financial statements. The goal was to present the company in a positive light so that investors would buy (hold) Nortel stock, thereby inflating the stock price. Although Nortel was an international company, the listing of its securities on U.S. stock exchanges subjected it to all SEC regulations, along with the requirement to register its financial statements with the SEC and prepare them in accordance with U.S. GAAP.

The company had gambled by investing heavily in Code Division Multiple Access (CDMA) wireless cellular technology during the 1990s in an attempt to gain access to the growing European and Asian markets. However, many wireless carriers in the aforementioned markets opted for rival Global System Mobile (GSM) wireless technology instead. Coupled with a worldwide economic slowdown in the technology sector, Nortel's losses mounted to $27.3 billion by 2001, resulting in the termination of two-thirds of its workforce.

The Nortel fraud primarily involved four members of Nortel's senior management as follows: CEO Frank Dunn, CFO Douglas Beatty, controller Michael Gollogly, and assistant controller Maryanne Pahapill. At the time of the audit, Dunn was a certified management accountant, while Beatty, Gollogly, and Pahapill were chartered accountants in Canada.

## Accounting Irregularities

On March 12, 2007, the SEC alleged the following in a complaint against Nortel:[1]

- In late 2000, Beatty and Pahapill implemented changes to Nortel's revenue recognition policies that violated U.S. GAAP, specifically to pull forward revenue to meet publicly announced revenue targets. These actions improperly boosted Nortel's fourth quarter and fiscal 2000 revenue by over $1 billion, while at the same time allowing the company to meet, but not exceed, market expectations. However, because their efforts pulled in more revenue than needed to meet those targets, Dunn, Beatty, and Pahapill

selectively reversed certain revenue entries during the 2000 year-end closing process.

- In November 2002, Dunn, Beatty, and Gollogly learned that Nortel was carrying over $300 million in excess reserves. The three did not release these excess reserves into income as required under U.S. GAAP. Instead, they concealed their existence and maintained them for later use. Further, Beatty, Dunn, and Gollogly directed the establishment of yet another $151 million in unnecessary reserves during the 2002 year-end closing process to avoid posting a profit and paying bonuses earlier than Dunn had predicted publicly. These reserve manipulations erased Nortel's *pro forma* profit for the fourth quarter of 2002 and caused it to report a loss instead.[2]

- In the first and second quarters of 2003, Dunn, Beatty, and Gollogly directed the release of at least $490 million of excess reserves specifically to boost earnings, fabricate profits, and pay bonuses. These efforts turned Nortel's first-quarter 2003 loss into a reported profit under U.S. GAAP, which allowed Dunn to claim that he had brought Nortel to profitability a quarter ahead of schedule. In the second quarter of 2003, their efforts largely erased Nortel's quarterly loss and generated a *pro forma* profit. In both quarters, Nortel posted sufficient earnings to pay tens of millions of dollars in so-called return to profitability bonuses, largely to a select group of senior managers.

- During the second half of 2003, Dunn and Beatty repeatedly misled investors as to why Nortel was conducting a purportedly "comprehensive review" of its assets and liabilities, which resulted in Nortel's restatement of approximately $948 million in liabilities in November 2003. Dunn and Beatty falsely represented to the public that the restatement was caused solely by internal control mistakes. In reality, Nortel's first restatement was necessitated by the intentional improper handling of reserves, which occurred throughout Nortel for several years, and the first restatement effort was sharply limited to avoid uncovering Dunn, Beatty, and Gollogly's earnings management activities.

---

[1] U.S. District Court for the Southern District of New York, *U.S. Securities and Exchange Commission v. Frank A. Dunn, Douglas C. Beatty, Michael J. Gollogly, and Maryanne E. Pahapill,* Civil Action No. 07-CV-2058, www.sec.gov/litigation/complaints/2007/comp20036.pdf.

[2] *Pro forma* means literally as a matter of form. Companies sometimes report income to the public and financial analysts that may not be calculated in accordance with GAAP. For example, a company might report *pro forma* earnings that exclude depreciation expense, amortization expense, and nonrecurring expenses such as restructuring costs. In general, *pro forma* earnings are reported in an effort to put a more positive spin on a company's operations. Unfortunately, there are no accounting rules on just how *pro forma* should be calculated, so comparability is difficult at best, and investors may be misled as a result.

The complaint charged Dunn, Beatty, Gollogly, and Pahapill with violating and/or aiding and abetting violations of the antifraud, reporting, and books and records requirements. In addition, they were charged with violating the Securities Exchange Act Section 13(b)(2)(B) that requires issuers to devise and maintain a system of internal accounting controls sufficient to provide reasonable assurances that, among other things, transactions are recorded as necessary to permit the preparation of financial statements in conformity with U.S. GAAP and to maintain accountability for the issuer's assets.

Dunn and Beatty were separately charged with violations of the officer certification provisions instituted by SOX under Section 302. The commission sought a permanent injunction, civil monetary penalties, officer and director bars, and disgorgement with prejudgment interest against all four defendants.

## Specifics of Earnings Management Techniques

From the third quarter of 2000 through the first quarter of 2001, when Nortel reported its financial results for year-end 2000, Dunn, Beatty, and Pahapill altered Nortel's revenue recognition policies to accelerate revenues as needed to meet Nortel's quarterly and annual revenue guidance, and to hide the worsening condition of Nortel's business. Techniques used to accomplish this goal include:

1. *Reinstituting bill and hold transactions.* The company tried to find a solution for the hundreds of millions of dollars in inventory that was sitting in Nortel's warehouses and offsite storage locations. Revenues could not be recognized for this inventory because U.S. GAAP revenue recognition rules generally require goods to be delivered to the buyer before revenue can be recognized. This inventory grew, in part, because orders were slowing and, in June 2000, Nortel had banned bill and hold transactions from its sales and accounting practices. A *bill and hold transaction* is one where the customer agrees to purchase a product but the seller (Nortel in this case) retains physical possession until the customer can accept delivery. The company reinstituted bill and hold sales when it became clear that it fell short of earnings guidance. In all, Nortel accelerated into 2000 more than $1 billion in revenues through its improper use of bill and hold transactions.
2. *Restructuring business-asset write-downs.* Beginning in February 2001, Nortel suffered serious losses when it finally lowered its earnings guidance to account for the fact that its business was suffering from the same widespread economic downturn that affected the entire telecommunications industry. As Nortel's business plummeted throughout the remainder of 2001, the company reacted by implementing a restructuring that, among other things, reduced its workforce by two-thirds and resulted in a significant write-down of assets.
3. *Creating reserves.* In relation to writing down the assets, Nortel established reserves that were used to manage earnings. Assisted by defendants Beatty and Gollogly, Dunn manipulated the company's reserves to manage Nortel's publicly reported earnings, create the false appearance that his leadership and business acumen was responsible for Nortel's profitability, and pay bonuses to these three defendants and other Nortel executives.
4. *Releasing reserves into income.* From at least July 2002 through June 2003, Dunn, Beatty, and Gollogly released excess reserves to meet Dunn's unrealistic and overly aggressive earnings targets. When Nortel internally (and unexpectedly) determined that it would return to profitability in the fourth quarter of 2002, the reserves were used to reduce earnings for the quarter, avoid reporting a profit earlier than Dunn had publicly predicted, and create a stockpile of reserves that could be (and were) released in the future as necessary to meet Dunn's prediction of profitability by the second quarter of 2003. When 2003 turned out to be rockier than expected, Dunn, Beatty, and Gollogly orchestrated the release of excess reserves to cause Nortel to report a profit in the first quarter of 2003, a quarter earlier than the public expected, and to pay defendants and others substantial bonuses that were awarded for achieving profitability on a *pro forma* basis. Because their actions drew the attention of Nortel's outside auditors, they made only a portion of the planned reserve releases. This allowed Nortel to report nearly break-even results (though not actual profit) and to show internally that the company had again reached profitability on a *pro forma* basis necessary to pay bonuses.

## Role of Auditors and Audit Committee

In the second half of 2003, Nortel's outside auditors raised concerns about Nortel's handling of reserves and, from that point forward, the defendants' scheme began to unravel. To appease the auditors, Nortel's management—led by Dunn and Beatty—conducted a purportedly comprehensive review of Nortel's assets and liabilities. This resulted in an announcement, on October 23, 2003, that Nortel would restate its financials for FY2000, FY2001, and FY2002.

Shortly after Nortel's announced restatement, the audit committee commenced an independent investigation and hired outside counsel to help it "gain a full understanding of the events that caused significant excess liabilities to be maintained on the balance sheet that needed to be restated," as well as to recommend any necessary remedial measures. The investigation uncovered evidence that Dunn, Beatty, and Gollogly and certain other financial managers were responsible for Nortel's improper use of reserves in the second half of 2002 and first half of 2003.

In March 2004, Nortel suspended Beatty and Gollogly and announced that it would "likely" need to revise and restate previously filed financial results further. Dunn, Beatty, and Gollogly were terminated for cause in April 2004.

On January 11, 2005, Nortel issued a second restatement that restated approximately $3.4 billion in misstated revenues and at least another $746 million in liabilities. All of the financial statement effects of the defendants' two accounting fraud schemes were corrected as of this date, but there remained lingering effects from the defendants' internal control and other nonfraud violations.

Nortel also disclosed the findings to date of the audit committee's independent review, which concluded, among other things, that Dunn, Beatty, and Gollogly were responsible for Nortel's improper use of reserves in the second half of 2002 and first half of 2003. The second restatement, however, did not reveal that Nortel's top executives had also engaged in revenue recognition fraud in 2000.

In May 2006, in its Form 10-K for the period ending December 31, 2005, Nortel admitted for the first time that its restated revenues in part had resulted from management fraud, stating that "in an effort to meet internal and external targets, the senior corporate finance management team . . . changed the accounting policies of the company several times during 2000," and that those changes were "driven by the need to close revenue and earnings gaps."

Throughout their scheme, the defendants lied to Nortel's independent auditor by making materially false and misleading statements and omissions in connection with the quarterly reviews and annual audits of the financial statements that were materially misstated. Among other things, each of the defendants submitted management representation letters to the auditors that concealed the fraud and made false statements, which included that the affected quarterly and annual financial statements were presented in conformity with U.S. GAAP and that they had no knowledge of any fraud that could have a material effect on the financial statements. Dunn, Beatty, and Gollogly also submitted a false management representation letter in connection with Nortel's first restatement, and Pahapill likewise made false management representations in connection with Nortel's second restatement.

The defendants' scheme resulted in Nortel issuing materially false and misleading quarterly and annual financial statements and related disclosures for at least the financial reporting periods ending December 31, 2000, through December 31, 2003, and in all subsequent filings made with the SEC that incorporated those financial statements and related disclosures by reference.

## Settlement

On October 15, 2007, Nortel, without admitting or denying the SEC's charges, agreed to settle the commission's action by consenting to be enjoined permanently from violating the antifraud, reporting, books and records, and internal control provisions of the federal securities laws and by paying a $35 million civil penalty, which the commission placed in a Fair Fund[3] for distribution to affected shareholders.[4] Nortel

also agreed to report periodically to the commission's staff on its progress in implementing remedial measures and resolving an outstanding material weakness over its revenue recognition procedures.

In settling the matter, the SEC acknowledged Nortel's substantial remedial efforts and cooperation. After Nortel announced its first restatement, the audit committee launched an independent investigation that later uncovered the improper accounting. Nortel's board took extensive remedial action that included promptly terminating employees responsible for the wrongdoing, restating its financial statements four times over four years, replacing its senior management, and instituting a comprehensive remediation program designed to ensure proper accounting and reporting practices. Nortel also shared the results of its independent investigation with the SEC. As part of the settlement, Nortel agreed to report to the commission staff every quarter until it fully implements its remediation program, and the company and its outside auditor agreed that the existing material weakness has been resolved. The commission acknowledged the assistance of the Ontario Securities Commission, which conducted its own separate, parallel investigation.

## Nortel in Canada

After a four-year investigation, on June 20, 2008, Canadian authorities arrested three high-level ex-Nortel executives on fraud charges for their alleged part in what has been described as the worst stock scandal in Canadian history. The Royal Canadian Mounted Police in Toronto arrested ex-CEO Dunn, ex-CFO Beatty, and former corporate controller Gollogly, who were each charged with seven counts of fraud. The charges include "fraud affecting public market; falsification of books and documents; and false prospectus, pertaining to allegations of criminal activity within Nortel Networks during 2002 and 2003." The three pleaded innocent and were released on bail.

On January 14, 2009, Nortel filed for protection from creditors in the United States, Canada, and the United Kingdom in order to restructure its debt and financial obligations. In June, the company announced that it no longer planned to continue operations and that it would sell off all of its business units. Nortel's CDMA wireless business and long-term evolutionary access technology (LTE) were sold to Ericsson, and Avaya purchased its Enterprise business unit.

The final indignity for Nortel came on June 25, 2009, when Nortel's stock price dropped to 18.5¢ a share, down from a high of $124.50 in 2000. Nortel's battered and bruised

---

[3]A Fair Fund is a fund established by the SEC to distribute "disgorgements" (returns of wrongful profits) and penalties (fines) to defrauded investors. Fair Funds hold money recovered from a specific SEC case. The commission chooses how to distribute the money to defrauded investors, and when completed, the fund terminates.

[4]Theresa Tedesco and Jamie Sturgeon, "Nortel: Cautionary Tale of a Former Canadian Titan," *Financial Post,* June 27, 2009, www.nationalpost.com/life/travel/sun-destinations/story .html?id=1739799#ixzz0mtBaFszD.

stock was finally delisted from the S&P/TSX composite index, a stock index for the Canadian equity market, ending a colossal collapse on an exchange on which the Canadian telecommunications giant's stock valuation once accounted for a third of its value.

## Postscript

The three former top executives of Nortel Networks Corp. were found not guilty of fraud on January 14, 2013. In the court ruling, Justice Frank Marrocco of the Ontario Superior Court found that the accounting manipulations that caused the company to restate its earnings for 2002 and 2003 did not cross the line into criminal behavior.

Accounting experts said the case is sure to be closely watched by others in the business community for the message it sends about where the line lies between fraud and the acceptable use of discretion in accounting.

The decision underlines that management still has a duty to prepare financial statements that "present fairly the financial position and results of the company" according to a forensic accountant, Charles Smedmor, who followed the case. "Nothing in the judge's decision diminished that duty."

During the trial, lawyers for the accused said that the men believed that the accounting decisions they made were appropriate at the time, and that the accounting treatment was approved by Nortel's auditors from Deloitte & Touche. Judge Marrocco accepted these arguments, noting many times in his ruling that bookkeeping decisions were reviewed and approved by auditors and were disclosed adequately to investors in press releases or notes added to the financial statements.

Nonetheless, the judge also said that he believed that the accused were attempting to "manage" Nortel's financial results in both the fourth quarter of 2002 and in 2003, but he added he was not satisfied that the changes resulted in material misrepresentations. He said that except for $80 million of reserves released in the first quarter of 2003, the rest of the use of reserves was within "the normal course of business." Judge Marrocco said the $80-million release, while clearly "unsupportable" and later reversed during a restatement of Nortel's books, was disclosed properly in Nortel's financial statements at the time and was not a material amount. He concluded that Beatty and Dunn "were prepared to go to considerable lengths" to use reserves to improve the bottom line in the second quarter of 2003, but he said the decision was reversed before the financial statements were completed because Gollogly challenged it.

In a surprising twist, Judge Marrocco also suggested the two devastating restatements of Nortel's books in 2003 and 2005 were probably unnecessary in hindsight, although he said he understood why they were done in the context of the time. He said the original statements were arguably correct within a threshold of what was material for a company of that size.

Darren Henderson, an accounting professor at the Richard Ivey School of Business at the University of Western Ontario, said that a guilty verdict would have raised the bar for management to justify their accounting judgments. But the acquittal makes it clear that "management manipulation of financial statements is very difficult to prove beyond a reasonable doubt in a court of law," he said.

It is clear that setting up reserves or provisions is still subject to management discretion, Henderson said. "The message . . . is that it is okay to use accounting judgments to achieve desired outcomes, [such as] a certain earnings target."

## Questions

1. Auditors are required to assess fraud risks as part of their ethical and professional responsibilities. What characteristics of Nortel might have caused it to be identified as a high-risk audit? Use the fraud triangle in answering this question.

2. In the Ontario Superior Court ruling, Justice Marrocco "found that the accounting manipulations that caused the company to restate its earnings for 2002 and 2003 did not cross the line into criminal behavior." Morrocco added he was "not satisfied beyond a reasonable doubt" that the trio [i.e., Dunn, Beatty, and Gollogly] had 'deliberately misrepresented' financial results.

   Review the accounting manipulations in the case and answer the following questions:
   a. What types of "financial shenanigans" were used by the trio to manipulate earnings?
   b. Do you agree with the decision of Judge Morrocco in not holding the trio legally liable? Why or why not?

3. Trust is an essential element in the relationship between the external auditor and top management. Evaluate the actions taken by the top officers with respect to their relationship with the Deloitte & Touche auditors, their fiduciary responsibilities as the head of Nortel and corporate governance in general.

## Case 7-2

# Solutions Network, Inc.

"We can't recognize revenue immediately, Paul, since we agreed to buy similar software from DSS," Sarah Young stated.

"That's ridiculous," Paul Henley replied. "Get your head out of the sand, Sarah, before it's too late."

Sarah Young is the controller for Solutions Network, Inc., a publicly owned company headquartered in Sunnyvale, California. Solutions Network has an audit committee with three members of the board of directors that are independent of management. Sarah is meeting with Paul Henley, the CFO of the company on January 7, 2014, to discuss the accounting for a software systems transaction with Data Systems Solutions (DSS) prior to the company's audit for the year ended December 31, 2013. Both Young and Henley are CPAs.

Sarah has excluded the amount in contention from revenue and net income for 2013, but Henley wants the amount to be included in the 2013 results. Henley told Sarah that the order came from the top to record the revenue on December 28, 2013, the day the transaction with DSS was finalized. Sarah pointed out that Solutions Network ordered essentially the same software from DSS to be shipped and delivered early in 2014. Therefore, according to Sarah, Solutions Network should delay revenue recognition on this "swap" transaction until that time. Henley argued against Sarah's position, stating that title had passed from the company to DSS on December 31, 2013, when the software product was shipped with FOB shipping point terms.

## Background

Solutions Network, Inc., became a publicly owned company on March 15, 2011, following a successful initial public offering (IPO). Solutions Network built up a loyal clientele in the three years prior to the IPO by establishing close working relationships with technology leaders, including IBM, Apple, and Dell Computer. The company designs and engineers systems software to function seamlessly with minimal user interface. There are several companies that provide similar products and consulting services, and DSS is one. However, DSS operates in a larger market providing IT services management products that coordinate the entire business infrastructure into a single system.

Solutions Networks grew very rapidly during the past five years. The revenue and earnings streams during those years are as follows:

| Year | Revenues (millions) | Net Income (millions) |
|---|---|---|
| 2008 | $148.0 | $11.9 |
| 2009 | 175.8 | 13.2 |
| 2010 | 202.2 | 15.0 |
| 2011 | 229.8 | 16.1 |
| 2012 | 267.5 | 17.3 |

Young prepared the following estimates for 2013:

| Year | Revenues (millions) | Net Income (millions) |
|---|---|---|
| 2013 (projected) | $287.5 | $17.9 |

## The Transaction

On December 28, 2013, Solutions Network offered to sell its Internet infrastructure software to DSS for its internal use. In return, DSS agreed to ship similar software 30 days later to Solutions Network for that company's internal use. The companies had conducted several transactions with each other during the previous five years, and while DSS initially balked at the transaction because it provided no value added to the company, it did not want to upset one of the fastest-growing software companies in the industry. Moreover, Solutions Network might be able to help identify future customers for DSS's IT service management products.

The $30 million of revenue would increase net income by $1.9 million over the projected amount for 2013. For Solutions Network, the revenue from the transaction was enough to enable the company to meet targeted goals, and the higher level of income would provide extra bonus money at year end for Young, Henley, and Ed Fralen, the CEO.

## Accounting Considerations

In her discussions with Henley, Sarah points out that the auditors will arrive on February 1, 2014; therefore, the company should be certain of the appropriateness of its accounting before that time. After all, says Sarah, "the auditors rely on us to record transactions properly as part of their audit expectations." At this point Henley reacts angrily and tells Sarah she can pack her bags and go if she doesn't support the company in its revenue recognition of the DSS transaction. To defuse the matter, Henley suggests that they meet in one week on January 14 to "put this matter to bed."

Normally, Sarah wouldn't object to Henley's proposed accounting for the transaction with DSS. However, she knows that regardless of the passage of title to DSS on December 31, 2013, the transaction is linked to Solutions Network's agreement to take the DSS product 30 days later. While she doesn't anticipate any problems in that regard, Sarah is uncomfortable with the recording of revenue on December 31 because DSS did not complete its portion of the agreement by that date. She has her doubts whether the auditors would sanction the accounting treatment.

Sarah is also concerned about the fact that another transaction occurred during the previous year that she questioned but, in the end, Sarah went along with Henley's accounting for this transaction. On December 28, 2012, Solutions Network sold a major system for $20 million to Laramie Systems but executed a side agreement with Laramie on December 29, 2012, which gave the customer the right to return the product for any reason after January 1, 2013, and for 27 additional days. Even though Solutions Network recorded the revenue on December 29,

2012, and Sarah felt uneasy about it, she did not object because Laramie did not return the product. Sarah never brought it up again. Now, she is concerned that a pattern may be developing.

## Questions

1. Describe the rules in accounting for revenue recognition in general and relate them to the two transactions mentioned in the case. Do you believe the transactions have been accounted for properly?

2. Prepare the following schedules:
   a. Percentage change in revenues from 2009 through the projected amounts in 2013
   b. Percentage of net income to revenues from 2008 through the projected amounts in 2013
   c. Redo parts (a) and (b), assuming that the DSS transaction is included in the projected results for 2013

   What questions might you raise from an ethical perspective with respect to these calculations and the motivation for Paul Henley to include the DSS transaction in 2013?

3. Assume you are Sarah Young and have decided to try to change Paul Henley's mind with respect to the accounting for the December 28, 2013 transaction. What steps might you take to counteract the position of Henley prior to the auditors' arrival on February 1, and why?

## Case 7-3

# Cubbies Cable

Ernie Binks is a big baseball fan, so it is quite natural for him, at a time like this, to recall a phrase attributed to Yogi Berra: "It was déjà vu all over again."

Binks is the partner in charge of the Cubbies Cable audit for the accounting firm of Santos & Williams LLP. Cubbies is a publicly-owned cable company headquartered in Chicago.

A situation arose with the client over the proper accounting for cable installation costs in the year-ended September 30, 2013, financial statements. The client wants to expense the costs while the audit manager has recommended capitalization. It is important to resolve the issue quickly because the client will use the September 30, 2013, audited annual statements to apply for a $10 million loan at one of two banks—Chicago First National or Bankers Trust. Binks reviewed a memorandum prepared by John Kessinger, the audit manager, that details the accounting issues. This memo is presented in Exhibit 1.

The revenue earned from the cable installation job enabled the company to complete the fourth quarter of 2013 with record earnings. Revenues at September 30, 2013, exceeded revenues at September 30, 2012, by 22 percent. Net income for the twelve months ended September 30, 2013, was 24 percent above the same amount in the prior year.

Binks is now preparing for a meeting with Rod Hondley, the advisory partner on the Cubbies Cable audit. Hondley has already made it known that he supports the client's position on the cable installation costs. Binks knows Santos & Williams operates by the simple philosophy that you have to let the client win one somewhere along the line or you may lose that client. The dilemma for Binks is he is in the uncomfortable position of going against the recommendation of the audit manager if he agrees to the client's position that Hondley supports.

Binks thinks about the fact that the situation is unique in that the client's preferred accounting treatment would actually lower earnings for the year-ended September 30, 2013, and increase it in subsequent years. He considers his options and reflects on another "Yogi-ism": "When you come to a fork in the road, take it."

---

### Exhibit 1
### Memo on Capitalization of Cable Equipment

**October 15, 2013**

We have audited the financial statements of Cubbies Cable since September 30, 2008. The audited statements are typically used by banks in granting short-term loans to Cubbies Cable.

During the 12-month period ending September 30, 2013, Cubbies constructed a major new cable system in parts of Chicago that enabled it to increase its presence in that market. The revenue from the system through September 30, 2013, exceeded projections by more than 20 percent.

A difference of opinion arose over the proper accounting for cable construction costs. The client wants to expense all of the costs during the year in the quarter ended September 30, 2013. The alternative position we recommend is to capitalize the costs and amortize them over the estimated life of the cable system.

Two different types of costs were involved:

**Cable television plant:** Costs associated with constructing the cable installation project. *SFAS 51, Financial Reporting by Cable Television Companies,* requires that cable television plant costs incurred during the prematurity (i.e., construction) periods be capitalized in full. We had protracted discussions with Cubbies Cable regarding this issue, and we were told that there was no way the company would agree to capitalize any of the costs.

**Interest cost:** The client initially expensed all interest costs related to a construction loan during the prematurity period. We convinced the client to change its accounting to capitalize the interest costs during the construction period. We used for support our reference to *SFAS 51.* This statement requires application of *SFAS 34, Capitalization of Interest Cost,* to interest costs incurred during the construction of an asset. The application of paragraphs 13 and 14 of *SFAS 34* to the client's situation requires that interest costs incurred during the prematurity period be capitalized in full by applying the interest capitalization rate to the average amount of accumulated expenditures for the asset during the period. The purpose of this procedure is to capitalize the amount of interest costs incurred during the prematurity period that theoretically could have been avoided if expenditures for construction of the cable television plant had not been made.

# Questions

1. What do you think was the motivation for Cubbies Cable in taking the position to expense all cable costs during the year ended September 20, 2013. Would you characterize the position as an attempt to manage earnings? Why or why not?

2. Who are the stakeholders in this situation? Identify the major ethical issues that should be of concern to Binks in deciding whether to just go along with the firm in its support of the client (based on Hondley's position) or support the position of the audit manager. What would you do if you were in Binks's position? Why?

3. Do you think it is ethical for CPAs to "horse trade" when negotiating with a client about the proper GAAP to apply in a particular situation? How does such negotiating relate to the accepted auditing standards of the AICPA and PCAOB discussed in Chapter 5?

## Case 7-4

# Solway, Inc.

Ben Davis is an internal accountant at Solway, Inc., a publicly owned company headquartered in Fresno, California. Ben reports to Chris Hodgins, the controller of the company; Hodgins reports to the CFO, Harry Benson; and Benson reports to George Lee, the CEO. Solway has a three-person independent audit committee that deals with financial oversight issues, including being a direct access group for matters of concern for the chief internal auditor, Sam Vines.

On January 15, 2014, Davis is approached by Hodgins and told to record an accrual for unpaid bonuses and severance payments of $50 million to be included in the December 31, 2013, financial statements. Davis asked Hodgins to explain the reason for what appeared to be an unusually high amount of money and was told the company planned to shut down a division in 2014 and the severance payments would be significant. This was the first Davis heard about a shutdown of any division, and he found it strange because the company's operating income in all divisions had set record levels in fiscal year 2013. Moreover, the bonus and severance amounts are five times the annual payroll of the division.

The numbers below show the operating income levels and accruals for 2011 through 2013:

|  | 12/31/11 | 12/31/12 | 12/31/13 |
|---|---|---|---|
| Operating Income | $100 million | $120 million | $200 million |
| Accrued bonus and severance | $10 million | $12 million | ??? |

Davis did not commit to recording the accruals because he wanted more time to think about the situation. Fortunately, Hodgins was called away on an urgent matter, bringing the meeting to an abrupt halt.

Davis decided to speak to Gloria Olson, a fellow internal accountant who graduated with Davis from college. Olson also found the amount of accruals unusually high. Davis asked Olson what the projected operating income was for December 31, 2014 based on her recent calculations. Olson told him that it was determined to be $160 million. They briefly talked about the projected decline in operating income after five straight years of increases. Davis wondered whether the reason for this could be attributable to the shutdown of the division mentioned by Hodgins.

## Questions

Assume that Davis, Hodgins, Benson, Vines, and Olson are all CPAs and hold the certificate in management accounting (CMA).

1. Review the definitions of earnings management by Schipper, Healy and Wahlen, Dechow and Skinner, and McKee that are discussed in this chapter. How would you characterize the proposed accrual for unpaid bonuses and severance payments from an earnings management perspective?

2. Place yourself in Ben Davis's shoes and consider the following in deciding whether to support Hodgins's position on the accrual:
   a. Who are the stakeholders in this case?
   b. What are the accounting issues of concern to you?
   c. What are ethical issues of concern to you with respect to your ethical and professional obligations and stakeholder interests?

3. Assume you meet with Hodgins and he instructs you in no uncertain terms to record the accrual. What would you do and why? Would whistleblowing be a consideration for you? Why or why not?

## Case 7-5

# Dell Computer

## Background

For years, Dell's seemingly magical power to squeeze efficiencies out of its supply chain and drive down costs made it a darling of the financial markets. Now we learn that the magic was at least partly the result of a huge financial illusion. On July 22, 2010, Dell agreed to pay a $100 million penalty to settle allegations by the SEC that the company had "manipulated its accounting over an extended period to project financial results that the company wished it had achieved."

According to the commission, Dell would have missed analysts' earnings expectations in every quarter between 2002 and 2006 were it not for its accounting shenanigans. This involved a deal with Intel, a big microchip maker, under which Dell agreed to use Intel's central processing unit chips exclusively in its computers in return for a series of undisclosed payments, locking out Advanced Micro Devices (AMD), a big rival. The SEC's complaint said that Dell had maintained cookie-jar reserves using Intel's money that it could dip into to cover any shortfalls in its operating results.

The SEC said that the company should have disclosed to investors that it was drawing on these reserves, but it did not. And it claimed that, at their peak, the exclusivity payments from Intel represented 76 percent of Dell's quarterly operating income, which is a shocking figure. The problem arose when Dell's quarterly earnings fell sharply in 2007 after it ended the arrangement with Intel. The SEC alleged that Dell attributed the drop to an aggressive product-pricing strategy and higher than expected component prices, when the real reason was that the payments from Intel had dried up.

The accounting fraud embarrassed the once-squeaky-clean Michael Dell, the firm's founder and CEO. He and Kevin Rollins, a former top official of the company, agreed to each pay a $4 million penalty without admitting or denying the SEC's allegations. Several senior financial executives at Dell also incurred penalties. "Accuracy and completeness are the touchstones of public company disclosure under the federal securities laws," said Robert Khuzami of the SEC's enforcement division when announcing the settlement deal. "Michael Dell and other senior Dell executives fell short of that standard repeatedly over many years."

In its statement on the SEC settlement the company played down Dell's personal involvement, saying that his $4 million penalty was not connected to the accounting fraud charges being settled by the company, but was "limited to claims in which only negligence, and not fraudulent intent, is required to establish liability, as well as secondary liability claims for other non-fraud charges."[1]

[1]Facts of the case are Available at www.economist.com/blogs/newsbook/2010/07/dells sec_settlement.

## Accounting Irregularities

The SEC charged Dell Computer with fraud for materially misstating its operating results from FY2002 to FY2005. In addition to Dell and Rollins, the SEC also charged former Dell chief accounting officer (CAO) Robert W. Davis for his role in the company's accounting fraud. The SEC's complaint against Davis alleges that he materially misrepresented Dell's financial results by using various cookie-jar reserves to cover shortfalls in operating results and engaged in other reserve manipulations from FY2002 to FY2005, including improper recording of large payments from Intel as operating expense-offsets. This fraudulent accounting made it appear that Dell was consistently meeting Wall Street earnings targets (i.e., net operating income) through the company's management and operations. The SEC's complaint further alleged that the reserve manipulations allowed Dell to misstate materially its operating expenses as a percentage of revenue—an important financial metric that Dell highlighted to investors.[2]

The company engaged in the questionable use of reserve accounts to smooth net income. Davis directed Dell assistant controller Randall D. Imhoff and his subordinates, when they identified reserved amounts that were no longer needed for bona fide liabilities, to check with him about what to do with the excess reserves instead of just releasing them to the income statement. In many cases, he ordered his team to transfer the amounts to an "other accrued liabilities" account. According to the SEC, "Davis viewed the 'Corporate Contingencies' as a way to offset future liabilities. He substantially participated in the 'earmarking' of the excess accruals for various purposes."

*FASB 5* states that a loss accrual should be recognized with a charge to income when a loss is probable and reasonably estimable. The maintenance of reserves for unspecified business risks (i.e., cookie-jar reserves) is not permitted under GAAP.

Beginning in the 1990s, Intel had a marketing campaign that paid its vendors certain marketing rebates to use their products according to a written contract. These were known as market developing funds (MDFs), which according to accounting rules, Dell could treat as reductions in operating expenses because these payments offset expenses that Dell incurred in marketing Intel's products. However, the character of these payments changed in 2001, when Intel began to

[2]Securities and Exchange Commission, *Securities and Exchange Commission v. Robert W. Davis*, Civil Action No. 1:10-cv-01464 (D.D.C.) and *Securities and Exchange Commission v. Randall D. Imhoff*, Civil Action No. 1:10-cv-01465 (D.D.C.), *Accounting and Auditing Enforcement Release No. 3177* / August 27, 2010. Available at www.sec.gov/litigation/litreleases/2010/lr21634.htm.

provide additional rebates to Dell and a few other companies that were outside the contractual agreements.

Intel made these large payments to Dell from 2001 to 2006 to refrain from using chips or processors manufactured by Intel's main rival, AMD. Rather than disclosing these material payments to investors, Dell decided that it would be better to incorporate these funds into their component costs without any recognition of their existence. The nondisclosure of these payments caused fraudulent misrepresentation, allowing Dell to report increased profitability over these years.

These payments grew significantly over the years making up a rather large part of Dell's operating income. When viewed as a percentage of operating income, these payments started at about 10 percent in FY2003 and increased to about 76 percent in the first quarter of FY2007.

When Dell began using AMD as a secondary supplier of chips in 2006, Intel cut the exclusivity payments off, which resulted in Dell having to report a decrease in profits. Rather than disclose the loss of the exclusivity payments as the reason for the decrease in profitability, Dell continued to mislead investors.

## Audit Considerations

In 2006, Dell issued a press release announcing that its audit committee had begun an independent investigation of Dell's accounting and financial reporting practices. After a year of investigation, the audit committee concluded that the financial statements for 2003, 2004, 2005, and 2006 should no longer be relied upon.

PricewaterhouseCoopers (PwC) had been Dell's independent auditor since 1986 and had signed off on every one of Dell's financial statements that were on file with the SEC. From 2003 to 2007, Dell paid PwC more than $50 million to perform auditing and other services. PwC issued clean (unmodified) audit opinions for the 2003 to 2006 financial

statements, saying that they fairly represented the financial position of Dell. However, these statements did not fairly represent Dell, as evidenced by the audit committee statement that the financial statements for these years should no longer be relied upon.

In a suit by shareholders against the firm, PwC was accused of a variety of charges, including not being truly independent and ignoring red flags. These charges were dismissed on a basis of lack of evidence to support the accusations.

## Questions

1. How would you characterize Dell's accounting for the exclusivity payments with respect to the financial shenanigans discussed in this chapter?

2. Joseph E. Abbott, the vice president and controller of West Pharmaceuticals Services, Inc., in Lionville, Pennsylvania, once said: "Investors should remember that if we do see companies start hitting estimates and not beating them, that wouldn't be such a bad thing. It could mean there is less earnings management going on." How does this statement relate to the actions of Dell in this case?

3. Identify the red flags that should have alerted PwC that Dell may have been engaging in fraud. Given that Dell issued clean opinions during the fraud years, do you think it is possible that the firm conducted its audit in accordance with GAAS? Why or why not?

## Optional Question

4. Do you agree with the statement from Dell that the actions taken were only negligent and not fraudulent? Explain your reasoning by using the discussion of legal liability in Chapter 6 for support.

## Case 7-6

# Sweat Construction Company

During the past few years, due to increasing competition, Sweat Construction Company has been more aggressive in seeking out new business opportunities. One such opportunity is the Computer Assistance Vocational Training School. It has contracted for a new 1-million-square-foot facility in San Marcos, Texas. Computer Assistance trains computer programmers for jobs in business and government. It is the largest computer training school in the southwestern United States.

Gabe Kohn is the passive owner of Sweat Construction. The company began operating in 2000, when Kohn hired Michael Woody to be the president of the company. Sweat Construction is a family-owned business that has been very successful as a mechanical contractor of heating, ventilation, and air-conditioning systems. However, increased competition has put pressure on the company to diversify its operations. Although it made a profit in 2011, the company's net income for the year was 50 percent lower than in previous years. As a result of these factors, the company decided to expand into plumbing and electrical contract work.

In March 2012, Sweat Construction successfully bid for the Computer Assistance job. The company bid low in order to secure the $3 million contract that is expected to be completed by June 30, 2013. Woody knows that the company has little margin for error on the contract. The estimated gross margin of 11.5 percent is on the low side of historical margins, which have been between 10 to 15 percent on heating,

ventilation, and air-conditioning contracts. Because it is a fixed-price contract, the company will have to absorb any cost overruns.

The Computer Assistance contract is an important one for Sweat Construction. It represents about 20 percent of the average annual revenues for the past five years. Moreover, First National Bank of Texas has been pressuring the company to speed up its interest payments on a $2 million term loan payable to the bank that is renewable on March 15, 2013. The company has been late in five of its last six monthly payments. The main reason is that some of the company's customers have been paying their bills later than usual because of tight economic conditions. However, the company expects to get back on the right track very soon after the Computer Assistance job begins.

Everything started out well on the contract. For the quarter ended June 30, 2012, Sweat Construction had an estimated cumulative gross profit of $75,000 on the contract under the percentage-of-completion method. This represents a 20 percent gross margin. Costs started to increase during the September quarter and, even though cumulative gross margin decreased to 10 percent, it was still within projected amounts. Unfortunately, the $54,000 estimated gross profit for the nine months ended December 31, 2012, represents only a 3 percent gross margin for the first year of the contract. Exhibit 1 contains cost data, billings, and collections for the year.

**EXHIBIT 1**
**SWEAT CONSTRUCTION COMPANY**
**Computer Assistance Contract**
**Year Ended December 31, 2012**

|  | Quarter Ending | | |
| --- | --- | --- | --- |
|  | **June 30** | **September 30** | **December 31** |
| Costs to date | $  300,000 | $  900,000 | $1,740,000 |
| Estimated costs to complete | 2,100,000 | 1,800,000 | 1,170,000 |
| Progress billings each quarter | 250,000 | 600,000 | 950,000 |
| Cash collections each quarter | 150,000 | 350,000 | 400,000 |

Vinny Barbieri is a CPA and the controller of Sweat Construction. Barbieri knows that cash collections on the Computer Assistance project have been slowing down—in part, because the company is behind schedule—and tension has developed between the company and Computer Assistance. He decides to contact Juan Santos, general manager for the project. Santos informs Barbieri that the tension between the company and Computer Assistance escalated recently when Santos informed top management of Computer Assistance that the electrical work may not be completed by

the June 30, 2013, deadline. If the facility does not open as scheduled for the summer months, Computer Assistance may be required to return deposits from students. Consequently, it may lose out on the revenue that is projected for the July and August summer term.

Woody calls for a meeting with Santos and Barbieri on February 6, 2013, to discuss the Computer Assistance contract. Woody knows that Sweat Construction's external auditors will begin their audit of the December 31, 2012, year-end financial statements in two weeks. Woody wants to make sure the problems with the contract have been corrected. He asks Barbieri to bring him up to date on the recent cost increases on the contract.

Barbieri informs Woody that the internal job cost data indicate that $420,000 was incurred for the month of January 2013. About 10 percent of the work was completed during that month. Barbieri emphasizes that this is consistent with recent trend data that indicate the estimated costs to complete the contract have been significantly understated. In fact, for the quarter ended December 31, 2012, the company lost approximately $40,000 on the contract, although there is a cumulative gross margin of about $60,000 for 2012. However, this cumulative margin represents only 2 percent of revenue, and the gross margin percentage is declining. Barbieri analyzed the cost data in preparation for the meeting. He estimates that total costs on the contract may be as high as $4.2 million. He recommends that the $1.17 million estimate to complete the contract should be increased by at least $1 million.

Woody is stunned by this information. He cannot understand how the company got into this predicament. The company has consistently made profits on its contracts, and there has never before been any tension with clients. The timing is particularly troublesome because First National Bank is expecting audited financial statements by March 1, 2013. Woody asks Santos whether he agrees with Barbieri's assessment about the anticipated higher level of future costs. Santos hesitates at first, but he eventually admits to the likelihood of cost overruns. He points out that the workers are not as skilled with electrical work as they are with heating, ventilation, and air-conditioning work. Consequently, some degree of learning is taking place on the job.

Woody dismisses Santos at this point and asks Barbieri what would happen if the company reports the estimated costs at December 31, 2012, without any adjustments. Woody emphasizes that the company would make the necessary adjustments in the first quarter of 2013, and gross profit on the contract with Computer Assistance ultimately will be correct. This approach would enable the company to renew its loan and give it some time to rethink its business strategy.

Barbieri immediately tells Woody that he is not comfortable with this approach because the profit on the contract for the nine months ended December 31, 2012, would be significantly overstated. He points out that the auditors are likely to question the low cost estimates. Woody becomes a bit irritated with Barbieri at this point. He tells Barbieri that the bank is not likely to renew the company's $2 million loan if the statements reflect what Barbieri suggests. He concludes by stating: "The auditors have never been a problem before. I do not expect any problems from them on this issue either, given that the firm has gone along with whatever we've asked of them in the past."

## Question

Use the integrated ethical decision-making process described in Chapter 2 to evaluate the ethical and professional issues in the case. What would you do if you were in Vinny Barbieri's position?

## Case 7-7

# Sunbeam Corporation

One of the earliest frauds during the late 1990s and early 2000s was at Sunbeam. The SEC alleged in its charges against Sunbeam that top management engaged in a scheme to fraudulently misrepresent Sunbeam's operating results in connection with a purported "turnaround" of the company. When Sunbeam's turnaround was exposed as a sham, the stock price plummeted, causing investors billions of dollars in losses. The defendants in the action included Sunbeam's former CEO and chair Albert J. Dunlap, former principal financial officer Russell A. Kersh, former controller Robert J. Gluck, former vice presidents Donald R. Uzzi and Lee B. Griffith, and Arthur Andersen LLP partner Phillip Harlow.

The SEC complaint described several questionable management decisions and fraudulent actions that led to the manipulation of financial statement amounts in the company's 1996 year-end results, quarterly and year-end 1997 results, and the first quarter of 1998. The fraud was enabled by weak or nonexistent internal controls, inadequate or nonexistent board of directors and audit committee oversight, and the failure of the Andersen auditor to follow GAAS. The following is an excerpt from the SEC's *AAER 1393*, issued on May 15, 2001:

> From the last quarter of 1996 until June 1998, Sunbeam Corporation's senior management created the illusion of a successful restructuring of Sunbeam in order to inflate its stock price and thus improve its value as an acquisition target. To this end, management employed numerous improper earnings management techniques to falsify the Company's results and conceal its deteriorating financial condition. Specifically, senior management created $35 million in improper restructuring reserves and other "cookie-jar" reserves as part of a year-end 1996 restructuring, which were reversed into income the following year. Also in 1997, Sunbeam's management engaged in guaranteed sales, improper "bill and hold" sales, and other fraudulent practices. At year-end 1997, at least $62 million of Sunbeam's reported income of $189 million came from accounting fraud. The undisclosed or inadequately disclosed acceleration of sales through "channel-stuffing" also materially distorted the Company's reported results of operations and contributed to the inaccurate picture of a successful turnaround.[1]

A brief summary of the case follows.[2]

[1] Securities and Exchange Commission, *In the Matter of Sunbeam Corporation, Respondent,* Accounting and Auditing Enforcement Release No. 1393, May 15, 2001, Available at www.sec.gov/litigation/admin/33-7976.htm.

[2] Securities and Exchange Commission, Litigation Release 17001, *Securities and Exchange Commission v. Albert J. Dunlap, Russell A. Kersh, Robert J. Gluck, Donald R. Uzzi, Lee B. Griffith, and Phillip E. Harlow,* 01-8437-CIV-Dimitrouleas (S.D. Fla., May 15, 2001), www.sec.gov/litigation/admin/33-7977.htm.

## Chainsaw Al

Al Dunlap, a turnaround specialist who had gained the nickname "Chainsaw Al" for his reputation of cutting companies to the bone, was hired by Sunbeam's board in July 1996 to restructure the financially ailing company. He promised a rapid turnaround, thereby raising expectations in the marketplace. The fraudulent actions helped raise the market price to a high of $52 in 1997. Following the disclosure of the fraud in the first quarter of 1998, the price of Sunbeam shares dropped by 25 percent, to $34.63. The price continued to decline as the board of directors investigated the fraud and fired Dunlap and the CFO. An extensive restatement of earnings from the fourth quarter of 1996 through the first quarter of 1998 eliminated half of the reported 1997 profits. On February 6, 2001, Sunbeam filed for Chapter 11 bankruptcy protection in U.S. Bankruptcy Court.

## Accounting Issues

### Cookie-Jar Reserves

The illegal conduct began in late 1996, with the creation of cookie-jar reserves that were used to inflate income in 1997. Sunbeam then engaged in fraudulent revenue transactions that inflated the company's record-setting earnings of $189 million by at least $60 million in 1997. The transactions were designed to create the impression that Sunbeam was experiencing significant revenue growth, thereby further misleading the investors and financial markets.

## Channel Stuffing

Eager to extend the selling season for its gas grills and to boost sales in 1996, CEO Dunlap's "turnaround year," the company tried to convince retailers to buy grills nearly six months before they were needed, in exchange for major discounts. Retailers agreed to purchase merchandise that they would not receive physically until six months after billing. In the meantime, the goods were shipped to a third-party warehouse and held there until the customers requested them. These bill-and-hold transactions led to recording $35 million in revenue too soon. However, the auditors (Andersen) reviewed the documents and reversed $29 million.

In 1997, the company failed to disclose that Sunbeam's 1997 revenue growth was partly achieved at the expense of future results. The company had offered discounts and other inducements to customers to sell merchandise immediately that otherwise would have been sold in later periods, a practice referred to as "channel stuffing." The resulting revenue shift threatened to suppress Sunbeam's future results of operations.

Sunbeam either didn't realize or totally ignored the fact that by stuffing the channels with product to make one year look better, the company had to continue to find outlets for their product in advance of when it was desired by customers. In other words, it created a balloon effect, in that the same amount or more accelerated amount of revenue was needed year after year. Ultimately, Sunbeam (and its customers) just couldn't keep up, and there was no way to fix the numbers.

## Sunbeam's Shenanigans

Exhibit 1 presents an analysis of Sunbeam's accounting with respect to Schilit's financial shenanigans.

## Red Flags

Schilit points to several red flags that existed at Sunbeam but either went undetected or were ignored by Andersen, including the following:[3]

1. *Excessive charges recorded shortly after Dunlap arrived.* The theory is that an incoming CEO will create cookie-jar reserves by overstating expenses, even though it reduces earnings for the first year, based on the belief that increases in future earnings through the release of the reserves or other techniques make it appear that the CEO has turned the company around, as evidenced by turning losses into profits. Some companies might take it to an extreme and pile on losses by creating reserves in a loss year, believing that it doesn't matter whether you show a $1.2 million loss for the year or a $1.8 million loss ($0.6 million reserve). This is known as the "big-bath accounting."

2. *Reserve amounts reduced after initial overstatement.* Fluctuations in the reserve amount should have raised a red flag because they evidenced earnings management as initially record reserves were restored into net income.

3. *Receivables grew much faster than sales.* A simple ratio of the increase in receivables to the increase in revenues should have provided another warning signal. Schilit provides the following for Sunbeam's operational performance in Exhibit 2 that should have created doubts in the minds of the auditors about the accuracy of reported

---

**EXHIBIT 1**
**Sunbeam Corporation's Aggressive Accounting Techniques**

| Technique | Example | Shenanigan Number |
|---|---|---|
| Recorded bogus revenue | Bill and hold sales | 2 |
| Released questionable reserves into income | Cookie jar reserves | 5 |
| Inflated special charges | Litigation reserve | 7 |

---

**EXHIBIT 2**
**Sunbeam Corporation's Operational Performance**

| | Operational Performance | | |
|---|---|---|---|
| | 9 months 9/97 ($ in millions) | 9 months 9/96 ($ in millions) | % Change |
| Revenue | $830.1 | $715.4 | 16% |
| Gross profit | 231.1 | 123.1 | 86% |
| Operating revenue | 132.6 | 4.0 | 3,215% |
| Receivables | 309.1 | 194.6 | 59% |
| Inventory | 290.9 | 330.2 | 12% |
| Cash flow from operations | (60.8) | (18.8) | N/A |

---

revenue amounts in relation to the collectibility of receivables, as indicated by the significantly larger percentage increase in receivables compared to revenues.

4. *Accrual earnings increased much faster than cash from operating activities.* While Sunbeam made $189 million in

[3]Howard M. Schilit, *Financial Shenanigans: How to Detect Accounting Gimmicks and Fraud in Financial Reports,* 2d ed. (New York: McGraw-Hill, 2002).

1997, its cash flow from operating activities was a negative $60.8 million. This is a $250 million difference that should raise a red flag, even under a cursory analytical review about the quality of recorded receivables. Accrual earnings and cash flow from operating activity amounts are not expected to be equal, but the differential in these amounts at Sunbeam seems to defy logic. Financial analysts tend to rely on the cash figure because of the inherent unreliability of the estimates and judgments that go into determining accrual earnings.

## Quality of Earnings

No one transaction more than the following illustrates questions about the quality of earnings at Sunbeam. Sunbeam owned a lot of spare parts that were used to fix its blenders and grills when they broke. Those parts were stored in the warehouse of a company called EPI Printers, which sent the parts out as needed. To inflate profits, Sunbeam approached EPI at the end of December 1997, to sell it parts for $11 million (and book an $5 million profit). EPI balked, stating that the parts were worth only $2 million, but Sunbeam found a way around that. EPI was persuaded to sign an "agreement to agree" to buy the parts for $11 million, with a clause letting EPI walk away in January 1998. In fact, the parts were never sold, but the profit was posted anyway.

Paine Webber, Inc. analyst Andrew Shore had been following Sunbeam since the day Dunlap was hired.[4] As an analyst, Shore's job was to make educated guesses about investing clients' money in stocks. Thus, he had been scrutinizing Sunbeam's financial statements every quarter and considered Sunbeam's reported levels of inventory for certain items to be unusual for the time of year. For example, he noted massive increases in the sales of electric blankets in the third quarter of 1997, although they usually sell well in the fourth quarter. He also observed that sales of grills were high in the fourth quarter, which is an unusual time of year for grills to be sold, and noted that accounts receivable were high. On April 3, 1998, just hours before Sunbeam announced a first-quarter loss of $44.6 million, Shore down-graded his assessment of the stock. By the end of the day, Sunbeam's stock prices had fallen 25 percent.

## Questions

1. Is there a difference between aggressive accounting and earnings management? Would the motivation for using the techniques described in this case influence whether they should be labeled as aggressive accounting or earnings management? Incorporate ethical considerations in your answer.

2. How did pressures for financial performance contribute to Sunbeam's culture, where quarterly sales were manipulated to influence investors? To what extent do you believe the Andersen auditors should have considered the resulting culture in planning and executing its audit?

3. Chapter 3 addresses issues related to corporate governance and ethical management. Given the facts of the case, identify the deficiencies in ethics and corporate governance failures at Sunbeam.

4. Given the variety of income adjusting techniques described in the case that were used by Sunbeam to manipulate the numbers, do you think it was proper for the Andersen auditors to dismiss $2 million of the $5 million income from the sale of the spare parts inventory? What factors do you think Andersen should have considered in addition to materiality in making the determination?

## Optional Question

5. Why is it important for auditors to use analytical comparisons such as the ratios in the Sunbeam case to evaluate possible red flags that may indicate additional auditing is required?

---

[4]"Sunbeam Corporation: 'Chainsaw Al,' Greed, and Recovery," Available at http://danielsethics.mgt.unm.edu/pdf/Sunbeam%20 Case.pdf.

## Case 7-8

# Diamond Foods

On November 14, 2012, Diamond Foods Inc. disclosed restated financial statements tied to an accounting scandal that reduced its earnings during the first three quarters of 2012 as it took significant charges related to improper accounting for payments to walnut growers. The restatements cut Diamond's earnings by 57 percent for FY2011, to $29.7 million, and by 46 percent for FY2010, to $23.2 million. By December 7, 2012, Diamond's share price had declined 54 percent for the year. A press release issued by the company explains in great detail the accounting and financial reporting issues.[1]

Diamond Foods, long-time maker of Emerald nuts and subsequent purchaser of Pop Secret popcorn (2008) and Kettle potato chips (2010), became the focus of an SEC investigation after *The Wall Street Journal* raised questions about the timing and accounting of Diamond's payments to walnut growers. The case focuses on the matching of costs and revenues. At the heart of the investigation was the question of whether Diamond senior management adjusted the accounting for the grower payments on purpose to increase profits for a given period.

The case arose in September 2011, when Douglas Barnhill, an accountant who is also a farmer of 75 acres of California walnut groves, got a mysterious check for nearly $46,000 from Diamond. Barnhill contacted Eric Heidman, the company's director of field operations, on whether the check was a final payment for his 2010 crop or prepayment for the 2011 harvest. (Diamond growers are paid in installments, with the final payment for the prior fall's crops coming late the following year.) Though it was September 2011, Barnhill was still waiting for full payment for the walnuts that he had sent Diamond in 2010. Heidman told Barnhill that the payment was for the 2010 crop, part of FY2011, but that it would be "budgeted into the next year." The problem is under accounting rules, you cannot legitimately record in a future fiscal year an amount for a prior year's crop. That amount should have been estimated during 2010 and recorded as an expense against revenue from the sale of walnuts.

An investigation by the audit committee in February 2012 found payments of $20 million to walnut growers in August 2010 and $60 million in September 2011 that were not recorded in the correct periods. The $20 million payments to growers in 2010 caught the eye of Diamond's auditors, Deloitte & Touche. However, it is uncertain whether the firm approved the accounting for the payments. It is an important determination because corporate officers can defend against securities fraud charges by arguing they did not have the requisite intent because they relied on the approval of the accountants.

The disclosure of financial restatements in November 2012 and audit committee investigation led to the resignation of former CEO Michael Mendes, who agreed to pay a $2.74 million cash clawback and return 6,665 shares to the company. Mendes's cash clawback was deducted from his retirement payout of $5.4 million. Former CFO Steven Neil was fired on November 19, 2012, and did not receive any severance.

As a result of the audit committee investigation and the subsequent analysis and procedures performed, the company identified material weaknesses in three areas: control environment, walnut grower accounting, and accounts payable timing recognition. The company announced efforts to remediate these areas of material weakness, including enhanced oversight and controls, leadership changes, a revised walnut cost estimation policy, and improved financial and operation reporting throughout the organization.

An interesting aspect of the case is the number of red flags, including unusual timing of payments to growers, a leap in profit margins, and volatile inventories and cash flows. Moreover, the company seemed to push hard on every lever to meet increasingly ambitious earnings targets and allowed top executives to pull in big bonuses, according to interviews with former Diamond employees and board members, rivals, suppliers and consultants, in addition to reviews of public and nonpublic Diamond records.

Nick Feakins, a forensic accountant, noted the relentless climb in Diamond's profit margins, including an increase in net income as a percent of sales from 1.5 percent in FY2006 to more than 5 percent in FY2011. According to Feakins, "no competitors were improving like that; even with rising Asian demand . . . it just doesn't make sense."[2] Reuters did a review of 11 companies listed as comparable organizations in Diamond's regulatory filings and found that only one, B&G Foods, which made multiple acquisitions, added earnings during the period.

Another red flag was that while net income growth is generally reflected in operating cash flow increases, at Diamond, the cash generation was sluggish in FY2010, when earnings were strong. This raises questions about the quality of earnings. Also, in September 2010, Mendes had promised EPS growth of 15 percent to 20 percent per year for the next five years. In FY2009, FY2010, and FY2011, $2.6 million of Mendes's $4.1 million in annual bonus was paid because Diamond beat its EPS goal, according to regulatory filings.

It was expected that the company would likely face a civil enforcement action by the SEC for not maintaining accurate books and records and failing to maintain adequate internal controls to report the payments properly, both of which are required for public companies. If the SEC decides to bring

[1] Available at www.investor.diamondfoods.com/phoenix.zhtml?c=189398&p=irol-newsArticle&id=1758849.

[2] Available at www.reuters.com/article/2012/03/19/us-diamond-tax-idUSBRE82I0AQ20120319.

a civil fraud case against any individuals at Diamond Foods, the Dodd-Frank Act gives it the option of filing either an administrative case or a civil injunctive action in Federal District Court. An administrative proceeding is generally considered a friendlier venue for the SEC.

## Questions

1. One of the red flags identified in the case was that operating cash flow increases did not seem to match the level of increase in net income. Explain the relationship between these two measures and why it raised questions about the quality of earnings at Diamond Foods.

2. Why were the actions of Diamond Foods with respect to its 'accounting for nuts' unethical?

3. The role of Deloitte & Touche is unclear in the case. We do not know whether the firm approved the accounting for the payments to walnut growers and periods used to record these amounts. Assume that the firm identified the improper payments and discussed the matter with management (i.e., CFO and CEO). What levers might Deloitte use to convince top management to correct the materially misstated financial statements?

## Case 7-9

# The North Face, Inc.

The North Face, Inc. (North Face) is an American outdoor product company specializing in outerwear, fleece, coats, shirts, footwear, and equipment such as backpacks, tents, and sleeping bags. North Face sells clothing and equipment lines catered towards wilderness chic, climbers, mountaineers, skiers, snowboarders, hikers, and endurance athletes. The company sponsors professional athletes from the worlds of running, climbing, skiing and snowboarding.

North Face is located in Alameda, California, along with an affiliated company, JanSport. These two companies manufacture about half of all small backpacks sold in the United States. Both companies are owned by VF Corporation, an American apparel corporation.

The North Face brand was established in 1968 in San Francisco. Following years of success built on sales to a high-end customer base, in the 1990s North Face was forced to compete with mass-market brands sold by the major discount retailers. It was at that point the company engaged in accounting shenanigans that led to it being acquired by VF Corporation.

## Barter Transactions[1]

North Face entered into two major barter transactions in 1997 and 1998. The barter company North Face dealt with typically bought excess inventory in exchange for trade credits. The trade credits could be redeemed by North Face only through the barter company, and most often the trade credits were used to purchase advertising, printing, or travel services.

North Face began negotiating a potential barter transaction in early December 1997. The basic terms were that the barter company would purchase $7.8 million of excess inventory North Face had on hand. In exchange for that inventory, North face would receive $7.8 million of trade credits that were redeemable only through the barter company.

Before North Face finalized the barter transaction, Christopher Crawford, the company's CFO, asked Deloitte & Touche, North Face's external auditors, for advice on how to account for a barter sale. The auditors provided Crawford with the accounting literature describing GAAP relating to non-monetary exchanges. That literature generally precludes companies from recognizing revenue on barter transactions when the only consideration received by the seller is trade credits.

What Crawford did next highlights one of the many ways a company can structure a transaction to manage earnings

[1]The information in this case was taken from: Securities and Exchange Commission, A Civil Complaint filed in the United States District Court Northern District of California against Christopher F. Crawford and Todd F. Katz, February 20, 2003, http://www.sec.gov/litigation/complaints/comp17978.htm.

and achieve the financial results desired rather than report what should be recorded as revenue under GAAP.

Crawford structured the transaction to recognize profit on the trade credits. First, he required the barter company to pay a portion of the purchase price in cash. Crawford agreed that North Face would guarantee that the barter company would receive at least a 60% recovery of the total purchase price when it re-sold the product. In exchange for the guarantee, the barter company agreed to pay approximately 50% of the total purchase price in cash and the rest in trade credits. This guarantee took the form of an oral side agreement that was not disclosed to the auditors.

Second, Crawford split the transaction into two parts on two days before the year-end December 31, 1997. One part of the transaction was to be recorded in the fourth quarter of 1997, the other to be recorded in the first quarter of 1998. Crawford structured the two parts of the barter sale so that all of the cash consideration and a portion of the trade credits would be received in the fourth quarter of 1997. The barter credit portion of the fourth quarter transaction was structured to allow profit recognition for the barter credits despite the objections of the auditors. The consideration for the 1998 first quarter transaction consisted solely of trade credits.

On December 29, 1997, North Face recorded a $5.15 million sale to the barter company. The barter company paid $3.51 million in cash and issued $1.64 million in trade credits. North Face recognized its full normal profit margin on the sale. Just ten days later on January 8, 1998, North Face recorded another sale to the barter company, this time for $2.65 million in trade credits, with no cash consideration. North Face received only trade credits from the barter company for this final portion of the $7.8 million total transaction. Again, North Face recognized its full normal profit margin on the sale.

## Materiality Issues

Crawford was a CPA and knew all about the materiality criteria that auditors use to judge whether they will accept a client's accounting for a disputed transaction. He realized that Deloitte & Touche would not challenge the profit recognized on the $3.51 million portion of the barter transaction recorded during the fourth quarter of fiscal 1997 because of the cash payment.

Crawford also realized that Deloitte would maintain that no profit should be recorded on the $1.64 million balance of the December 29, 1997, transaction with the barter company for which North Face would be paid exclusively in trade credits. However, Crawford was aware of the materiality thresholds that Deloitte had established for North Face's key financial statement items during the fiscal 1997 audit. He knew that the profit margin of approximately $800,000 on the $1.64 million portion of the December 1997 transaction fell slightly below

Deloitte's materiality threshold for North Face's collective gross profit. As a result, he believed that Deloitte would propose an adjustment to reverse the $1.64 million transaction but ultimately "pass" on that proposed adjustment since it had an immaterial impact on North Face's financial statements. As Crawford expected, Deloitte proposed a year-end adjusting entry to reverse the $1.64 million transaction but then passed on that adjustment during the wrap-up phase of the audit.

In early January 1998, North Face recorded the remaining $2.65 million portion of the $7.8 million barter transaction. Crawford instructed North Face's accountants to record the full amount of profit margin on this portion of the sale despite being aware that accounting treatment was not consistent with the authoritative literature. Crawford did not inform the Deloitte auditors of the $2.65 million portion of the barter transaction until after the 1997 audit was completed.

The barter company ultimately sold only a nominal amount of the $7.8 million of excess inventory that it purchased from North Face. As a result, in early 1999, North Face reacquired that inventory from the barter company.

## Audit Considerations

The auditors did not learn of the January 8, 1998 transaction until March 1998. Thus, when the auditors made the materiality judgment for the fourth quarter transaction, they were unaware that a second transaction had taken place and unaware that Crawford had recognized full margin on the second barter transaction.

In mid-1998 through 1999, the North Face sales force was actively trying to re-sell the product purchased by the barter company because the barter company was unable to sell any significant portion of the inventory. North Face finally decided, in January and February of 1999, to repurchase the remaining inventory from the barter company. Crawford negotiated the repurchase price of $690,000 for the remaining inventory.

Crawford did not disclose the repurchase to the 1998 audit engagement team, even though the audit was not complete at the time of the repurchase.

During the first week of March 1999, the auditors asked for additional information about the barter transaction to complete the 1998 audit. In response to this request, Crawford continued to mislead the auditors by failing to disclose that the product had been repurchased, that there was a guarantee, that the 1997 and 1998 transactions were linked, and that the company sales force had negotiated almost all of the orders received by the barter company.

Crawford did not disclose any of this information until he learned that the auditors were about to fax a confirmation letter to the barter company that specifically asked if any of the product had been returned or repurchased. Crawford then called the chair of North Face's audit committee, to explain that he had withheld information from the auditors. A meeting was scheduled for later that day for Crawford to make "full disclosure" to the auditors about the barter transactions.

Even at the "full disclosure" meeting with the auditors, Crawford was not completely truthful. He did finally disclose the repurchase and the link between the 1997 and 1998 transactions. He did not, however, disclose that there was a guarantee, nor did he disclose that the company's employees had negotiated most of the orders for the product.

## Deloitte & Touche

Richard Fiedelman was the Deloitte advisory partner assigned to the North Face audit engagement. Pete Vanstraten was the audit engagement partner for the 1997 North Face audit. Vanstraten was also the individual who proposed the adjusting entry near the end of the 1997 audit to reverse the $1.64 million barter transaction that North Face had recorded in the final few days of fiscal 1997. Vanstraten proposed the adjustment because he was aware that the GAAP rules generally preclude companies from recognizing revenue on barter transactions when the only consideration received by the seller is trade credits. Vanstraten was also the individual who "passed" on that adjustment after determining that it did not have a material impact on North Face's 1997 financial statements. Fiedelman reviewed and approved those decisions by Vanstraten.

Shortly after the completion of the 1997 North Face audit, Vanstraten transferred from the office that serviced North Face. In May 1998, Will Borden was appointed the new audit engagement partner for North Face. In the two months before Borden was appointed the North Face audit engagement partner, Richard Fiedelman functioned in that role.

Fiedelman supervised the review of North Face's financial statements for the first quarter of fiscal 1998, which ended on March 31, 1998. While completing that review, Fiedelman became aware of the $2.65 million portion of the $7.8 million barter transaction that Crawford had instructed his subordinates to record in early January 1998. Fiedelman did not challenge North Face's decision to record its normal profit margin on the January 1998 "sale" to the barter company. As a result, North Face's gross profit for the first quarter of 1998 was overstated by more than $1.3 million, an amount that was material to the company's first-quarter financial statements. In fact, without the profit margin on the $2.65 million transaction, North face would have reported a net loss for the first quarter of fiscal 1998 rather than the modest net income it actually reported that period.

In the fall of 1998, Borden began planning the 1998 North Face audit. An important element of that planning process was reviewing the 1997 audit workpapers. While reviewing those workpapers, Borden discovered the audit adjustment that Vanstraten had proposed during the prior year audit to reverse the $1.64 million barter transaction. When Borden brought this matter to Fiedelman's attention, Fiedelman maintained that the proposed audit adjustment should not have been included in the prior year workpapers since the 1997 audit team had *not* concluded that North Face could *not* record the $1.64 million transaction with the barter company. Fiedelman insisted that, despite the proposed audit adjustment in the 1997 audit workpapers,

Vanstraten had concluded that it was permissible for North Face to record the transaction and recognize the $800,000 of profit margin on the transaction in December 1997.

Borden accepted Fiedelman's assertion that North Face was entitled to recognize profit on a sales transaction in which the only consideration received by the company was trade credits. Borden also relied on this assertion during the 1998 audit. As a result, Borden and the other members of the 1998 audit team did not propose an adjusting entry to require North Face to reverse the $2.65 million sale recorded by the company in January 1998.

After convincing Borden that the prior year workpapers misrepresented the decision that Vanstraten had made regarding the $1.64 million barter transaction, Fiedelman began the process of documenting this revised conclusion in the 1997 working papers that related to the already issued financial statements for 1997. The SEC had concluded in its investigation that Deloitte personnel prepared a new summary memorandum and proposed adjustments schedule reflecting the revised conclusion about profit recognition, and replaced the original 1997 working papers with these newly-created working papers.

## SEC Actions against Crawford

In the SEC action against Crawford,[2] the commission charged that Crawford committed a fraud because his actions violated Section 10(b) of the Exchange Act of 1934, in that he knew or was reckless in not knowing, that (1) it was a violation of GAAP to record full margin on the trade credit portion of the sale and (2) that the auditors would consider the amount of the non-GAAP fourth quarter profit recognition immaterial and would not insist on any adjusting entry for correction.

A second charge was that Crawford aided and abetted violations of Section 13(a) of the Exchange Act that requires every issuer of a registered security to file reports with the SEC which accurately reflect the issuer's financial performance and provide other information to the public.

A third charge dealt with record-keeping and alleged violations of Section 13(b) in that the Exchange Act requires each issuer of registered securities to make and keep books, records, and accounts which, in reasonable detail, accurately and fairly reflect the business of the issuer and to devise and

[2]*In the matter of Christopher F. Crawford,* U.S. Securities and Exchange Commission Accounting and Auditing Enforcement Release No. 1751 (AAER No. 1751) April 4, 2003. Available at www.sec.gov/litigation/admin/34-47633.htm.

maintain a system of internal controls sufficient to provide reasonable assurances that, among other things, transactions are recorded as necessary to permit preparation of financial statements and to maintain the accountability of accounts.

The SEC asked the United States District Court of the Northern District of California to enter a judgment:

- permanently enjoining Crawford and the vice president of sales, Todd Katz, from violating Sections 10(b) and 13(b) (5) of the Exchange Act;

- ordering Crawford to provide a complete accounting for and to disgorge the unjust enrichment he realized, plus prejudgment interest thereon;

- ordering Crawford and Katz to pay civil monetary penalties pursuant to Section 21(d)(3) of the Exchange Act; and

- prohibiting Crawford and Katz from acting as an officer or director of a public company pursuant to Section 21(d)(2) of the Exchange Act.

Crawford agreed to the terms in a settlement with the SEC that included his suspension from appearing or practicing before the Commission as an accountant for at least five years after which time he could apply to the commission for reinstatement.

## Questions

1. A variety of definitions of earnings management are given in this chapter. Discuss the accounting techniques used by North Face by evaluating whether and why earnings management existed using the definitions provided by: Schipper, Healy & Wahlen, Dechow & Skinner, and McKee.

2. An important issue in this case is the application of materiality standards to revenue recognition on the barter transaction. Evaluate the ethics of Deloitte & Touche first proposing an audit adjustment on the $1.64 million balance of the December 29, 1997, transaction with the barter company and then passing on the adjustment based on it not having a material effect on the financial statements. Be sure to include both quantitative and qualitative materiality considerations.

3. Deloitte & Touche made audit decisions related to the barter transactions that can be criticized from an ethics perspective because of violations of the AICPA Code of Professional Conduct. Evaluate those decisions and explain the nature of the criticisms.

# Case 7-10

# Vivendi Universal

"Some of my management decisions turned wrong, but fraud? Never, never, never." This statement was made by the former CEO of Vivendi Universal, Jean-Marie Messier, as he took the stand in November 20, 2009, for a civil class action lawsuit brought against him, Vivendi Universal, and the former CFO, Guillaume Hannezo, that accused the company of hiding Vivendi's true financial condition before a $46 billion three-way merger with Seagram Company and Canal Plus. The case was brought against Vivendi, Messier, and Hannezo after it was discovered that the firm was in a liquidity crisis and would have problems repaying its outstanding debt and operating expenses (contrary to the press releases by Messier, Hannezo, and other senior executives that the firm had "excellent" and "strong" liquidity); that it participated in earnings management to achieve earnings goals; and that it had failed to disclose debt obligations regarding two of the company's subsidiaries.[1] The jury decided not to hold either Messier or Hannezo legally liable because "scienter" could not be proven. In other words, the court decided it could not be shown that the two officers acted with the intent to deceive other parties.

The stock price of the firm dropped 89 percent, from €84.70 on October 31, 2000, to €9.30 on August 16, 2002, over the period of fraudulent reporting and press releases to the media.[2]

Vivendi is a French international media giant rivaling Time Warner Inc. that spent $77 billion on acquisitions, including the world's largest music company, Universal Music Group (UMG). Messier took the firm to new heights that came with a large amount of debt through mergers and acquisitions.

The Vivendi Universal case raises a few ethical issues. For example, was it wrong for Vivendi to make improper adjustments to its earnings before interest, taxes, depreciation, and amortization (EBITDA) to meet ambitious earnings targets in 2001? Was Messier correct in stating that he made some decisions that just turned out poorly and that he was not participating in an extensive fraud scandal?

In December 2000, Vivendi acquired Canal Plus and Seagram, which included Universal Studios and its related companies, and became known as Vivendi Universal. At the time, it was one of Europe's largest companies in terms of assets and revenues, with holdings in the United States that included Universal Studios Group, UMG, and USA Networks Inc. These acquisitions cost Vivendi cash, stock, and assumed debt of over $60 billion and increased the debt associated with Vivendi's Media & Communications division

from approximately €3 billion ($4.32 billion) at the beginning of 2000 to over €21 billion ($30.25 billion) in 2002.

In July 2002, Messier and Hannezo resigned from their positions as CEO and CFO, respectively, and new management disclosed that the company was experiencing a liquidity crisis that was a very different picture than the previous management had painted of the financial condition of Vivendi Universal. This was due to senior executives using four different methods to conceal Vivendi Universal's financial problems: issuing false press releases stating that the liquidity of the company was "strong" and "excellent" after the release of the 2001 financial statements to the public, using aggressive accounting principles and adjustments to increase EBITDA and meet ambitious earnings targets, failing to disclose the existence of various commitments and contingencies, and failing to disclose part of its investment in a transaction to acquire shares of Telco, a Polish telecommunications holding company.

On March 5, 2002, Vivendi issued earnings releases for 2001, which were approved by Messier, Hannezo, and other senior executives, that their Media & Communications business had produced €5.03 billion ($7.25 billion) in EBITDA and just over €2 billion ($2.88 billion) in operating free cash flow. These earnings were materially misleading and falsely represented Vivendi's financial situation because, due to legal restrictions, Vivendi was unable unilaterally to access the earnings and cash flow of two of its most profitable subsidiaries, Cegetel and Maroc Telecom, which accounted for 30 percent of Vivendi's EBITDA and almost half of its cash flow. This contributed to Vivendi's cash flow actually being "zero or negative," making it difficult for Vivendi to meet its debt and cash obligations. Furthermore, Vivendi declared a €1 ($1.44) per share dividend because of its excellent operations for the past year, but Vivendi borrowed against credit facilities to pay the dividend, which cost more than €1.3 billion ($1.87 billion) after French corporate taxes on dividends. Throughout the following months before Messier and Hannezo's resignations, senior executives continued to lie to the public about the strength of Vivendi as a company.

In December 2000, Vivendi and Messier predicted a 35 percent EBITDA growth for 2001 and 2002, and, in order to reach that target, Vivendi used earnings management and aggressive accounting practices to overstate its EBITDA. In June 2001, Vivendi made improper adjustments to increase EBITDA by almost €59 million ($85 million), or 5 percent of the total EBITDA of €1.12 billion ($1.61 billion) that Vivendi reported. Senior executives did this mainly by restructuring Cegetel's allowance for bad debts. Cegetel, a Vivendi subsidiary whose financial statements were consolidated with Vivendi's, took a lower provision for bad debts in the period and caused the bad debts expense to be €45 million ($64.83 million) less than it would have been under historical methodology, which

---

[1] *Securities and Exchange Commission v. Vivendi Universal, S.A., Jean-Marie Messier, and Guillaume Hannezo,* www.sec.gov/litigation/complaints/comp18523.htm.
[2] As of May 15, 2013, 1 euro = $1.29, or $1 = €0.775.

in turn increased earnings by the same amount. Furthermore, after the third quarter of 2001, Vivendi adjusted earnings of UMG by at least €10.125 million ($14.77 million) or approximately 4 percent of UMG's total EBITDA of €250 million ($360.15 million) for that quarter. At that level, UMG would have been able to show EBITDA growth of approximately 6 percent versus the same period in 2000 and to outperform its rivals in the music business. They did this by prematurely recognizing revenue of €3 million ($4.32 million) and temporarily reducing the corporate overhead charges by €7 million ($10.08 million).

Vivendi failed to disclose in their financial statements commitments regarding Cegetel and Maroc Telecom that would have shown Vivendi's potential inability to meet its cash needs and obligations. They were also worried that if they disclosed this information, companies that publish independent credit opinions would have declined to maintain their credit rating of Vivendi. In August 2001, Vivendi entered into an undisclosed current account borrowing with Cegetel for €520 million ($749.11 million) and continued to grow to over €1 billion ($1.44 billion) at certain periods of time. Vivendi maintained cash pooling agreements with most of its subsidiaries, but the current account with Cegetel operated much like a loan, with a due date of the balance at December 31, 2001 (which was later pushed back to July 31, 2002), and there was a clause in the agreement that provided Cegetel with the ability to demand immediate reimbursement at any time during the loan period. If this information would have been disclosed, it would have shown that Vivendi would have trouble repaying its obligations.

Regarding Maroc Telecom, in December 2000, Vivendi purchased 35 percent of the Moroccan government–owned telecommunications operator of fixed line and mobile telephone and Internet services for €2.35 billion ($3.39 billion). In February 2001, Vivendi and the Moroccan government entered into a side agreement that required Vivendi to purchase an additional 16 percent of Maroc Telecom's shares in February 2002 for approximately €1.1 billion ($1.58 billion). Vivendi did this in order to gain control of Maroc Telecom and consolidate its financial statements with their own because Maroc carried little debt and generated substantial EBITDA. By not disclosing this information on the financial statements, Vivendi's financial information for 2001 was materially false and misleading.

The major stakeholders in the Vivendi case include (1) the investors, creditors, and shareholders of the company and its subsidiaries—by not providing reliable financial information, Vivendi misled these groups into lending credit, cash, and investing in a company that was not as strong as it seemed; (2) the subsidiaries of Vivendi and their

customers—by struggling with debt and liquidity, Vivendi borrowed cash from the numerous subsidiaries all over the globe, jeopardizing their operations; (3) the governments of these countries—because some of Vivendi's companies were government owned (such as the Moroccan company Maroc Telecom), and these governments have to regulate the fraud and crimes that Vivendi committed; and (4) Vivendi, Messier, Hannezo, and other senior management and employees—Messier was putting his future, the employees of Vivendi, and the company itself in jeopardy by making loose and risky decisions involving the sanctity of the firm.

On August 11, 2008, the SEC announced the distribution of more than $48 million to more than 12,000 investors who were victims of fraudulent financial reporting by Vivendi Universal. Investors receiving checks resided in the United States and 15 other countries. More than half bought their Vivendi stock on foreign exchanges and received their Fair Fund distribution[3] in euros.

In the Fair Funds provisions of SOX, Congress gave the commission increased authority to distribute ill-gotten gains and civil money penalties to harmed investors. These distributions reflect the continued efforts and increased capacity of the commission to repay injured investors, regardless of their physical location and their currency of choice.

## Questions

1. Why do financial analysts look at measures such as EBITDA and operating free cash flow to evaluate financial results? How do these measures differ from accrual earnings? Do you believe auditors should be held responsible for auditing such information?

2. Given the major stakeholders mentioned in the Vivendi case, evaluate the ethics of the actions taken by Messier and Hannezo as it effected stakeholder interests. Consider in your answer the fiduciary obligations of these managers.

3. Evaluate the accounting issues discussed in this case from the perspective of Schilit's financial shenanigans. Which of the various accounting decisions made by Vivendi through Messier and Hannezo can be categorized as one of the shenanigans?

---

[3]A Fair Fund is a fund established by the SEC to distribute "disgorgements" (returns of wrongful profits) and penalties (fines) to defrauded investors. Fair Funds hold money recovered from a specific SEC case. The commission chooses how to distribute the money to defrauded investors, and when completed, the fund terminates.

# Chapter 8

# International Financial Reporting: Ethics and Corporate Governance Considerations

## Ethics Reflection

In a December 6, 2012, expose of the problems inherent in auditing Chinese companies that list their stock on exchanges outside their country, such as the New York Stock Exchange (NYSE) and Toronto Stock Exchange, *New York Times* reporter Floyd Norris poses the question: "Imagine for a moment that you were auditing a company whose principal asset was trees that it would eventually cut down to sell the timber. Would you bother to verify whether the company actually owned the trees? Would you make sure that the trees the company showed to your auditors were the same trees it claimed to own?"[1]

So goes the saga of Sino-Forest Corporation, which was based in Canada but had its operations in China. The record appears to show that the Canadian affiliate of Ernst & Young (EY) failed to uncover that the assets were fake. In an e-mail to a colleague, an EY staff member involved in the audit asked "do we know that the trees" the auditors were being shown "are actually trees owned by the company? Could they show us trees anywhere and we would not know the difference?" The answer to both questions was "Yes."

The Sino-Forest bankruptcy illustrates the problems that exist for the Ontario Securities Commission and the U.S. Securities and Exchange Commission (SEC) in overseeing the financial reporting of foreign companies that sell stock in

Canada, the U.S., and numerous other countries around the world. Along with the growth in listings of foreign companies has come the challenge to auditors in the U.S. in obtaining the information necessary to conduct an audit in accordance with generally accepted auditing standards (GAAS). The problem is particularly acute for auditors of Chinese companies and can be attributed to, at least in part, different cultural values in China.

Accounting researcher Sidney Gray built on Geert Hofstede's cultural values (discussed in Chapter 1) and identifies four widely recognized accounting values that are discussed later in this chapter. One value is secrecy versus transparency. The former reflects a preference for confidentiality and the restriction of the disclosure of information about the business only to those who are closely involved with its management and financing, as in China, as opposed to the more transparent, open, publicly accountable approach that exists in the U.S. Thus, cultural values and ethical standards in a country influence the nature and extent of disclosure and resulting transparency of the financial statements.

Fraud and audit failure can occur in any country, but China is a special case because the authorities there seem to be completely uninterested in getting to the bottom of scandals whose victims have been American, Canadian, or other foreign investors. The SEC has long sought the cooperation

*(Continued)*

of the Chinese government to share audit work papers with other regulators. The Chinese insist they would provide documents only if the SEC promises not to use them in an enforcement proceeding without Chinese permission. Clearly, that defeats the purpose of getting that information.

Before we attack the Chinese for its seemingly combative approach to cooperating with regulators outside China, we need to understand that in addition to cultural differences, the Chinese government is the major stockholder in many "public" companies. China's state-owned enterprises present unique challenges for regulators in Canada, the United States, and elsewhere. So, the auditors are asking government shareholders to provide financial data on government-controlled entities. This is a challenge, to say the least.

In another case involving a Chinese company, the SEC asked a federal court to force Shanghai-based Deloitte Touche Tohmatsu CPA Ltd. to hand over its audit records on Longtop Financial Technologies, a Chinese company that allegedly committed fraud. Deloitte-Shanghai resigned as Longtop's auditor after discovering improprieties during the year ended March 31, 2011. The SEC sought information necessary to determine whether there was a fraud, who was behind it, and how it was conducted. The case had been on hold since August 2012 when the SEC sought a resolution from Chinese regulators. Chinese law bans the removal offshore of audit workpapers, and foreign regulators are not allowed to work inside China. On April 22, 2013, U.S. District Judge Gladys Kessler rejected Shanghai-based Deloitte's argument that the case should be put on hold while an administrative judge considers a separate case the regulator brought against the Chinese-based affiliates of the Big Four accounting firms. The decision may quicken the pace of litigation over the Chinese documents sought by the SEC.[2]

Chinese companies listing in the United States have fallen through a regulatory loophole, partly because U.S. audit inspectors at the Public Company Accounting Oversight Board (PCAOB) have not been allowed inside China where the audits are done. Auditors have resisted handing over records for fear of violating China's state secrets law. Dozens of Chinese companies have raised billions of dollars in the past decade listing their shares on U.S., Canadian, and other foreign exchanges. Accuracy, reliability, and transparency concerns have led to share price reductions in some of those companies amid questions about their bookkeeping and financial disclosures. From an ethical perspective, it is an issue of trust and representational faithfulness in the financial reporting. Can foreign investors trust the financial reports produced by accountants in China and audited by the Big Four CPA firms to faithfully represent what it purports to represent thereby enhancing the usefulness of such reports?

In this chapter, you will learn about the movement toward adopting one set of international accounting standards—International Financial Reporting Standards (IFRS)—international auditing and assurance standards, and corporate governance provisions. One difference in approach to standard setting is the rules-based approach in the United States as compared to a principles-based approach in many other countries. The danger of a rules-based system is that the opportunity arises to structure transactions to circumvent the rules. In principles-based systems, standards are set and decisions are made by applying professional judgment to fact situations. The danger here is the lack of guidance in making those judgments may lead to greater opportunities to manage earnings. In reality, the difference between the two systems may be more form than substance because even under a rules-based system, judgments must be made. Underlying these professional judgments are the ethical standards previously discussed. The public must trust that accountants and auditors will make such judgments with integrity, uninfluenced by pressures from employers and clients, regardless of the system used. Cultural considerations add another challenge to ethical decision-making as in the case of Chinese companies.

Global business fraud and illegal acts create challenges because of cultural variables and legal systems. In this chapter we look at global business ethics, fraud studies, and provisions of the U.K. Bribery Act as a way to better understand corporate governance outside the United States, and how it is similar to and different from corporate governance provisions under Sarbanes-Oxley (SOX) and the Dodd-Frank Financial Reform Act.

Accounting students need to be aware of international ethics and corporate governance because many will work for accounting firms and companies with operations overseas. The debate about whether it is a good idea for the U.S. to adopt IFRS to replace GAAP, or for IFRS to be converged with GAAP, misses the point that accounting professionals already need to know IFRS because those companies will likely have to use it for their overseas operations. A valid concern is whether accounting education is providing the knowledge of and commitment to ethics that is critical in today's global business and financial reporting environment. International education standards have been identified to provide the underlying foundation for professional accountants, including a framework of professional values, ethics, and attitudes to exercise professional judgment and professional skepticism. We have stressed the importance of such a foundation for ethical decision making in previous chapters and the need to place the public interest ahead of all other interests including one's employer, the client, and self-interest. We continue that theme in this chapter by examining actions and responses to questionable behavior by top management, accountants, and the auditors of multinational entities.

Sir David Tweedie, served as the chairman of the International Accounting Standards Board (IASB) for ten years ending in June 2011. The Trustees of the IFRS Foundation appointed Hans Hoogervorst to succeed Sir David Tweedie. In his speech at the spring council meeting of the American Institute of CPAs (AICPA) on May 25, 2010, Sir David Tweedie said that the move to global accounting standards is a key element of the global financial reform agenda and long-term benefits of a single set of high-quality accounting standards far outweigh the short-term difficulties of transition. "The world is moving to a single set of high-quality global accounting standards, and this is too important an area for the U.S. not to be involved. After almost a decade of work to improve IFRS and U.S. GAAP and to seek their convergence, it's time to finish the job."

---

This quote from Sir David Tweedie expresses some of the frustration in the international accounting community over the slow-paced process of adopting IFRS in the United States. The European Community first adopted IFRS in 2005. About 120 countries allow or have adopted IFRS as of June 2013. China has substantially converged its national standards with IFRS. In the United States, the migration to IFRS is being accomplished by navigating choppy waters because professional accountants are not convinced the IFRS regime produces more useful financial reports when compared to U.S. generally accepted accounting principles (GAAP).

The SEC recently announced an approach called *condorsement.* Condorsement allows the Financial Accounting Standards Board (FASB) to revise one standard at a time, moving all of U.S. GAAP toward IFRS in small increments, or vice versa. Rather than set some specific date for a single, sweeping adoption of IFRS in the United States—which would be a big deal, and require the blessing of the SEC—FASB would converge IFRS into GAAP with both systems providing acceptable alternatives.

Cynics say that condorsement neatly allows the SEC to adopt IFRS without actually adopting it; the commission simply farms out the job to FASB, which can slow-walk the U.S. financial reporting community away from U.S. GAAP and toward IFRS by 2016 or so. That spares the SEC a nasty political fight because legions of U.S. companies without much international presence have no real need to migrate to IFRS, which raises the issue whether non-public companies should be allowed to continue to use U.S. GAAP or another version that blends the two. This will be discussed later on.

## The Influence of Culture on International Financial Reporting

We addressed Hofstede's cultural values in Chapter 1, and now we return to them to close the loop on the effect of cultural values on financial reporting in the international environment. Research suggests that cultural differences cause accountants in different countries to interpret and apply accounting standards differently. This research reveals that two accounting values directly influenced by national culture are *conservatism* and *secrecy,* which affect the measurement and disclosure of financial information in financial reports and have the greatest potential to affect cross-border financial statement comparability. Hofstede's framework is the basis used to explain these findings.[3]

Three of the more important cultural values are summarized to refresh your memory:

- *Uncertainty avoidance*—how comfortable individuals in a society feel with uncertainty and ambiguity
- *Individualism*—a society's preference for a loosely knit social fabric or a more interdependent, tightly knit social fabric
- *Power distance*—how much hierarchy and unequal power distribution are accepted in a culture

Hofstede's cultural framework has been used extensively in management and other disciplines to examine the influence of national culture on organizational and individual performance. This framework can be used in an accounting context to explain the SEC's concern that "proper application encompasses not only faithful adherence to the requirements of the standards, but also understandable standards such that across the spectrum of issuers, those requirements are consistently understood and applied."[4]

Tsakumis et al. point out that the cultural values that exist in a country influence a country's accounting values (e.g., accountants' levels of conservatism and secrecy), which influence how financial reporting standards are applied. They depict the relationship as follows:

Cultural Values > Accounting Values > Application of Financial Reporting Standards[5]

Gray uses Hofstede's values to identify four widely recognized accounting values that can be used to define a country's cultural foundation with respect to financial reporting:[6]

1. Professionalism (preference for professional judgment) versus statutory control (compliance driven prescriptive legal requirements)
2. Uniformity (consistency across companies in the use of accounting practices) versus flexibility (choice of accounting practice in accordance with the perceived circumstances of individual companies)
3. Conservatism (a cautious approach to measurement to deal better with the uncertainty of future events) versus optimism (following a more hands-off, risk-taking approach)
4. Secrecy (preference for confidentiality and restrictions on disclosures) versus transparency (open and public accountability).

From an accounting perspective, high conservatism implies a tendency to defer the recognition of assets and items that increase net income while reserving for possible future declines in earnings. Within Hofstede's framework, higher levels of conservatism are most closely linked with countries that have higher *uncertainty avoidance* and lower *individualism*. High secrecy implies a tendency to restrict the disclosure of relevant information to outside parties. Higher levels of secrecy within a culture are associated with higher *uncertainty avoidance* and *power distance* and with lower *individualism*. Notwithstanding China's somewhat inexplicable low score on uncertainty avoidance, these cultural values seem to go a long way to explain the difficulty in receiving adequate disclosures in Chinese company financial reports and cooperation from China's government, as addressed earlier in this chapter.

The desire to have comparable standards has resulted in the adoption and implementation of, as well as the convergence to, IFRS. Despite the push toward convergence of these accounting standards, significant diversity remains. While discussions generally focus on the differences between specific standards and how to eliminate them, lurking in the background is the issue of why such differences exist. Cultural variables are an important part of such differences.

# Restoring the Public Trust: An International Perspective

Enron, WorldCom, Royal Dutch Shell (U.K.-Netherlands), Parmalat (Italy), and Satyam (India), all were involved in major financial statement frauds during the dark days of the first decade of the 2000s. It was a disease that infected virtually every continent in the world and brought into question whether the public trust in accountants to produce accurate and reliable financial reports had been compromised. From special-purpose entities to improper capitalization of costs to disclosing unproven reserves to recording fictitious bank accounts and management misuse of corporate resources, the dizzying array of transactions that created the frauds knew no bounds. A lack of internal controls, ineffective internal audits, and inattentive boards of directors all share blame for these frauds. In each case, an internal culture was established that made it easier for top management to perpetrate the fraud and the accountants who were on the front lines of the fraud failed to act in the public interest and report and/or stop the fraud.

The International Federation of Accountants (IFAC) is the global organization for the accountancy profession dedicated to serving the public interest. In July 2003, IFAC issued a research report, *Rebuilding Public Confidence in Financial Reporting: An International Perspective,* which examined ways of restoring the credibility of financial reporting and corporate disclosure from an international perspective. The report reflects the views of accounting professionals from six countries: Australia, Canada, France, Japan, the United Kingdom, and the United States. It identifies several key weaknesses in corporate governance from a number of corporate failures worldwide. The findings of the study include a recommendation for more effective corporate ethics codes as well as the provision of training and support for individuals within organizations to better prepare them to deal with ethical dilemmas.[7]

IFAC addresses the public interest dimension in its Policy Position Paper # 4 entitled *A Public Interest Framework for the Accountancy Profession.* The Framework is designed to enable IFAC and other professional bodies to better evaluate whether the public interest is being served through actions of the profession and its institutions. IFAC considers the "public interest" to represent the common benefits derived by stakeholders (i.e., investors and creditors) of the accounting profession through sound financial reporting. It links these benefits to responsibilities of professional accountants including the application of high standards of ethical behavior and professional judgment.[8]

The International Ethics Standards Board of Accountants (IESBA) is an independent standard-setting body that serves the public interest by setting high-quality ethical standards for professional accountants and by facilitating the convergence of international and national ethical standards, including auditor independence requirements. It has developed and published a set of ethical standards in its *Handbook of the Code of Ethics for Professional Accountants* (IFAC Code).[9] The IESBA along with the International Accounting Education Standards Board (IAESB) establish guidelines for 167 members and associates in 127 countries worldwide, representing approximately 2.5 million accountants in public practice, industry and commerce, the public sector, and education. No other accountancy body in the world and few other professional organizations have the broad-based international support that characterizes IFAC. The IAESB and IESBA standards are authoritative pronouncements that have the same force as standards promulgated by other boards operating under the auspices of IFAC, such as the International Auditing and Assurance Standards Board.

The fundamental principles of professional ethics for professional accountants identified by the IESBA include: integrity; objectivity; professional competence and due care; confidentiality; and professional behavior including compliance with laws and regulations. These principles are similar to those in the AICPA Code, state board of accountancy rules in the United States, and the codes of conduct in the United Kingdom and Australia, as well as most of the developed world.

Support exists among professional bodies for the education of future accounting professionals in professional values, ethics and attitudes in order to best serve the public interest. A survey of IFAC member bodies reported in the IAESB's information paper notes that member bodies agree that ethics education is necessary to:[10]

• Develop a sense of ethical responsibility in accountants;
• Improve the moral standards and attitudes of accountants;
• Develop the problem-solving skills that have ethical implications; and
• Develop a sense of professional responsibility or obligation.

The report considers the term 'ethics' as an over-arching term for values, ethics and attitudes. Professional values, ethics and attitudes include the ethical principles of conduct that are found in professional codes of ethics. Collectively the values, ethics and attitudes include: technical competence; core values of integrity, objectivity, independence, and confidentiality; professionalism of respect, reliability, responsibility, timeliness, due care, and courteousness; commitment to continuous improvement and life-long learning; and social responsibility.[11]

One difference between U.S. standards and those discussed above is the explicit recognition of compliance with laws and regulations as a principle of professional ethics. Recall that in the new audit report discussed in Chapter 5, a final section can be used to address compliance issues. This section, *Report on Other Legal and Regulatory Requirements,* applies only when the auditor has other reporting responsibilities. Such responsibilities result from the statutory control aspect of regulation addressed by Gray and that exist in many countries outside the United States.

# International Financial Reporting Environment

## Movement toward IFRS

For 40 years a movement has been under way to establish one set of international accounting standards for all countries around the world in order to facilitate international trade and investment. The comparability of financial statements worldwide facilitates the opening of global capital markets. Since it is no longer unusual to have foreign companies list their stock on other exchanges such as the New York Stock Exchange, London Stock Exchange, and Tokyo Stock Exchange, one common set of accounting standards should go a long way toward increasing the understandability of international financial reports.

Until recently, listing rules required that non-U.S. companies must reconcile their financial statements prepared under home country standards to U.S. GAAP. This is a tedious exercise and, unless you believe that U.S. GAAP better reflects financial position and results of operations than IFRS, the cost of reconciliation probably exceeds any benefits derived. The SEC now permits foreign companies to use IFRS without reconciliation to U.S. GAAP.

## Harmonization of Standards

The movement toward one set of international accounting standards for all countries worldwide began in 1973 when members of the International Accounting Standards Committee (IASC) used their "best efforts" to "harmonize" national standards. Notwithstanding a few cases where International standards were changed to be similar to U.S. GAAP, for all intents and purposes harmonization meant that the international standards would accommodate existing accounting practices in various countries. A major problem early that still persists today is the lack of an enforcement mechanism for the international accounting standards (IAS) set by the IASC. While IAS have morphed to IFRS over time, and the IASC has been replaced by the International Accounting Standards Board (IASB), enforcement still requires that the national securities regulator must recognize IFRS as acceptable standards. Absent an international enforcement mechanism, it is questionable whether mandatory compliance will ever occur.

One of the most contentious issues in international accounting was the use of so-called "secret reserves." Secret reserves are designed to conceal the true financial position and earnings, which are different than shown on the balance sheet and income statement thereby compromising representational faithfulness. In discussing the early differences in accounting, Zeff points out that a gulf existed between the generally accepted accounting principles in Anglo-American countries (i.e., the United States and United Kingdom) and those in countries in continental Europe and in Japan. In the latter case, it was not unusual for income tax laws to drive financial reporting and reported profit was determined by law through the use of statutory reserves.[12] The excess reserves can take the form of depreciating the fixed assets at excessively high rates or making excessive provisions for bad debts. We link this practice to our previous discussion of ethics and fraud as follows:

- Secret reserves can give the sense of financial stability to the shareholders by equalizing financial position over time.
- Secret reserves often lead to smoothing net income over time, thereby giving a false sense that earnings are stable even though that may not be the case.
- The existence of a secret reserve is generally known to management only, not to the shareholders.
- Secret reserves make the information in financial statements false and inaccurate.
- The use of secret reserves may be the cause of losing trust and confidence of the shareholders and outsiders.
- The use of secret reserves may cover up the inefficiency and fraud committed by the managers and directors.

## Comparability of Financial Statements

The effort to establish one set of accounting standards evolved into a second stage around 1990 with the *Comparability of Financial Statements Project*. The project was designed to make accounting standards worldwide more similar, and 10 revised IASs were issued and became effective in 1995. Doupnik and Perera point out that an example is the revision of *IAS 11* to require the use of the percentage of completion method when certain criteria are met, thereby removing the option to avoid the use of this method altogether.[13]

A significant event occurred when the International Organization of Securities Commissions (IOSCO) opened its membership to regulatory agencies around the world, thus giving it the potential to become a truly international organization. Today, IOSCO has members from over 100 different countries, which regulate more than 90 percent of the world's securities markets. Still, international enforcement remains problematic.

A look at the objectives of IOSCO shed light on ways in which cross-border financial statements might be regulated, even though IOSCO has no specific enforcement powers. Short of creating an "international SEC," which is unlikely to happen any time soon, "enforcement" of international financial reports falls on the regulatory agencies in each country. The objectives include the following:[14]

- Cooperate in developing, implementing, and promoting adherence to internationally recognized and consistent standards of regulation, oversight, and enforcement in order to protect investors, maintain fair, efficient, and transparent markets, and seek to address systemic risks.
- Enhance investor protection and promote investor confidence in the integrity of securities markets, through strengthened information exchange and cooperation in enforcement against misconduct and in supervision of markets and market intermediaries.

- Exchange information at both global and regional levels on their respective experiences in order to assist the development of markets, strengthen market infrastructure, and implement appropriate regulation.

In 1994, FASB and the IASC began a collaborative standard-setting effort to compare U.S. GAAP and IASC standards. The effort resulted in the FASB's publication of *The IASC-U.S. Comparison Project: A Report on the Similarities and Differences Between IASC Standards and U.S. GAAP (1996).*[15] The accomplishments of the project include:

- The IASC and IOSCO agreed on what constitutes a comprehensive set of core standards. The IASC undertook a project to complete those core standards by 1999.
- The IOSCO agreed that if it found those core standards acceptable, it would recommend endorsement of IASC standards for cross-border capital and listing purposes in all capital markets.
- As for the SEC, it issued a press release stating its intent to consider the acceptability of IASC standards as the basis for the financial reports of foreign private issuers. To be accepted by the SEC, the IASC standards would have to be (1) sufficiently comprehensive, (2) of high quality, and (3) rigorously interpreted and applied.

## Convergence of Standards

Beginning in the 1990s, efforts to harmonize accounting standards internationally evolved into a broad convergence effort. In 2001, the IASC was restructured into the IASB; and by 2009, the European Union (EU) and over 100 other countries had adopted international standards or a local variant of them.

Some countries have adopted IFRS but specifically excluded an IFRS-accepted practice. For example, in Brazil, IFRS is required but the practice of permitting the revaluation of property, plant, and equipment is not permitted by Brazilian corporate law. Other countries are still in the process of converging national standards with IFRS (i.e., U.S.) while others are considering mandatory adoption (i.e., India and Japan).[16]

The convergence project began in October 2002 as a result of the Norwalk Agreement between the FASB and the IASB, which resulted in the issuance of a *Memorandum of Understanding* formalizing the commitment of both organizations to the convergence of U.S. GAAP and IAS.[17] The project was given a big boost when the European Union announced it would require the use of IFRS for all companies doing business in the European Union, effective 2005. Following that, another memorandum was issued on February 27, 2006, reaffirming the boards' shared objective of developing high-quality, common accounting standards for use in the world's capital markets that would enhance the consistency, comparability, and efficiency of financial statements, enabling global markets to move with less friction.[18]

As a result of the Norwalk Agreement, the FASB and IASB embarked on a partnership to improve and converge U.S. GAAP and international standards. The idea is to look at specific accounting and reporting areas and decide whether the IFRS method would converge into U.S. GAAP or GAAP would converge with IFRS standards. For example, prior to its revision in 2007, IAS 23, *Borrowing Costs,* provided two methods of accounting for borrowing costs:

1. *Benchmark treatment.* Expense all borrowing costs in the period incurred.
2. *Allowed alternative treatment.* Capitalize borrowing costs to the extent that they are attributable to the acquisition, construction, or production of a qualifying asset and amortize it once the asset is placed into use; other borrowing costs are expensed in the period incurred.[19]

Adoption of the benchmark treatment would not have been acceptable under U.S. GAAP because *FASB 34* requires borrowing costs to be capitalized when related to assets that are constructed or produced for the entity's own use. As part of the convergence project, the benchmark treatment was eliminated, and the allowed alternative treatment has become the only acceptable treatment.

Convergence is a two-way street. The issue of how to account for changes in accounting principle—when an entity changes the method used to account for an item (i.e., sum-of-the-years'-digits depreciation to straight-line depreciation)—is an example of U.S. standards being converged with international standards. *IAS 8, Accounting Policies, Changes in Accounting Estimates and Error,* requires that the cumulative effect on prior periods of adopting a new accounting policy in the current period should be treated as an adjustment to the carrying amounts of the assets and liabilities affected and as an adjustment to the beginning balance in retained earnings. In the U.S., *Accounting Principles Board (APB) Opinion 20* called for the amount to be treated as a "cumulative effect" adjustment in the current income statement in the year of change rather than go through retained earnings. Here, U.S. GAAP adopted the international standard as part of the convergence project. The following statement was made when, in May 2005, the FASB issued *SFAS 154, Accounting Changes and Error Corrections,* that replaces *APB Opinion 20* and *Statement of Financial Accounting Standards (SFAS) 3:*

> "This Statement is the result of a broader effort by the FASB to improve the comparability of cross-border financial reporting by working with the International Accounting Standards Board (IASB) toward development of a single set of high-quality accounting standards. As part of that effort, the FASB and the IASB identified opportunities to improve financial reporting by eliminating certain narrow differences between their existing accounting standards. Reporting of accounting changes was identified as an area in which financial reporting in the U.S. could be improved by eliminating differences between Opinion 20 and *IAS 8,* Accounting Policies, Changes in Accounting Estimates and Errors" [now covered by *IFRS 21*].[20]

A recent European Commission study investigated the effects of mandatory IFRS adoption on accounting quality in the European Union. The study uses earnings smoothing, managing earnings toward targets, the magnitude of absolute discretionary accruals, and accruals quality as proxies for earnings management. The idea was to determine whether accounting quality was improved after mandatory IFRS adoption. The results show that accounting quality is generally improved after mandatory IFRS adoption in the European Union. That is, less earnings smoothing, more timely loss recognition, and lower magnitude of absolute discretionary accruals after mandatory IFRS adoption.[21]

With a limited number of exceptions, most stakeholders in the EU study believe that the understandability of financial statements has generally improved. While the EU Commission study found that the application of IFRS has improved the comparability and quality of financial reporting and has led to greater transparency, a more recent independent study by U.K. researchers found inconsistencies in compliance with certain impairment disclosure requirements across jurisdictions in Europe, which suggests that IFRS are not being evenly applied across jurisdictions.[22]

## Condorsement

On November 14, 2008, the SEC released for comment a proposed roadmap for the adoption of IFRS that would monitor progress until 2011, when the commission planned to consider requiring U.S. public companies to file their financial statements using IFRS. The anticipated adoption date was 2015. However, the U.S. business community was not very supportive of the SEC idea. Concerns about costs to implement and convert information systems, education and training of staff, and whether IFRS really was a better system than GAAP, all converged (so to speak) in pressuring the SEC to back off from its original plan and look for a "plan B." That is when the SEC decided to create its own language when it put forth the "condorsement" plan.

A staff paper was presented on May 26, 2011—"Work Plan for the Consideration of Incorporating International Financial Reporting Standards into the Financial Reporting System for U.S. Issuers: Exploring a Possible Method of Incorporation,"—that explains the notion of condorsement. Here is how the staff paper characterizes the condorsement approach:

> "This approach to incorporate is in essence an Endorsement Approach that would share characteristics of the incorporation approaches with other jurisdictions that have incorporated or are incorporating IFRS into their financial reporting systems. However, during the transitional period, the framework would employ aspects of the Convergence Approach to address existing differences between IFRS and U.S. The framework would retain a U.S. standard setter and would facilitate the transition process by incorporating IFRSs into U.S. GAAP over some defined period of time (e.g., five to seven years). At the end of this period, the objective would be that a U.S. issuer compliant with U.S. GAAP should also be able to represent that it is compliant with IFRS as issued by the IASB. Incorporation of IFRS through the framework would have the objective of achieving the goal of having a single set of high-quality, globally accepted accounting standards, while doing so in a practical manner that could minimize both the cost and effort needed to incorporate IFRS into the financial reporting system for U.S. issuers. It also would align the U.S. with other jurisdictions by retaining the national standard setter's authority to establish accounting standards in the U.S."[23]

Tom Selling, a well-known writer and critic of convergence in general, reviewed the staff paper and said: "The SEC has *finally* conceded that its efforts to adopt IFRS have failed. Damage control has begun in earnest, but the ship is still taking on water . . . Once upon a future time, the staff fantasized, it will be possible that financial statements prepared in accordance with U.S. GAAP will simultaneously comply with IFRS as issued by the IASB. Known informally as 'condorsement,' the paper describes the staff's wishful thinking in the form of three 'convergence' phases and a final 'endorsement' phase."[24]

Moody's Investors Service made an insightful observation with respect to the SEC staff paper and its condorsement idea. Moody's rejected it and, instead, urged the SEC to just do it: "We believe that a one-time, 'big bang' switch to IFRS, as was done in the European Union in 2005, would be more beneficial for investors."[25] The problem, according to Moody's, is that the approach being discussed by the SEC likely would become a lengthy process and push the intended goal of reaching a single set of global accounting standards further into the future. That protracted process makes financial analysis more complex for investors.

The advantages and disadvantages of U.S. GAAP and IFRS can be debated, with both sides making solid arguments in support of their respective positions. The problem now is that without the SEC making a definitive decision, companies and investors remain in accounting-rule limbo, especially midsize and smaller public companies. The reality is most large multinational entities already have gone where the SEC seems so reluctant to go. They use IFRS out of necessity—their overseas operations file financial statements using international rules.

## Auditing, Corporate Governance, and Ethics Considerations

A natural outgrowth of the movement toward IFRS has been the development of a single set of auditing standards. Auditors are charged with determining whether IFRS has been implemented properly; a common set of auditing standards adds assurance of meeting that goal. The International Auditing and Assurance Standards Board (IAASB) of the IFAC establishes international auditing and assurance standards, including International Standards on Auditing (ISAs). For the most part, these standards are similar to U.S. generally accepted auditing standards (GAAS).

The globalization of accounting and auditing standards has led to an examination of corporate governance standards around the world. Just as governance mechanisms in the U.S. help establish controls that monitor adherence to GAAP and GAAS, a similar system is needed internationally to strengthen the mechanisms needed to support conformity with IFRS and ISAs. Given that governance standards are a natural outgrowth of accounting and auditing requirements, a sound system of international corporate governance is essential to achieve quality financial reporting on a global level.

The passage of SOX in the United States and governance initiatives incorporated in the *Combined Code on Corporate Governance* issued by the Financial Reporting Council in the United Kingdom, taken together, have succeeded in getting the international business community to focus on improvements in governance. Important differences still exist, such as the two-tier versus unitary board of directors that will be discussed later in this chapter. In some countries, the most important shareholder is represented by family ownership or by a large industrial group, such as Tata Company in India. In other countries such as China, the state, through state-owned enterprises, plays a prominent role with respect to ownership requirements and management of Chinese companies. More specific corporate governance provisions in these countries will be discussed later on.

### True and Fair View versus Present Fairly

The concept of "true and fair" was created in Great Britain in 1844, when corporations were expected to fulfill the requirement of "full and fair" in the balance sheet. Traditionally, the "true and fair view" has implied a connection between the internal accounting and the external accounting. It is not possible for standards to answer all accounting questions; therefore the concept "true and fair view" is important. In a sense it is used to support other accounting rules when the standards are unclear.

The audit report in most countries that have adopted IFRS use the term "true and fair view" in lieu of the U.S. "present fairly." In the European Union, "true and fair view" is used as part of the Fourth Directive, which guides audit reporting in the community so that it applies to all members of the European Union. There are important differences between these terms because the words convey a different meaning and level of assurance to investors and creditors.

A true and fair view is the governing criterion by which financial statements are to be judged. It is therefore possible, although unusual, to override the requirements of a standard in order to give a true and fair view. This is known as the *true and fair view override.* In the United States, "present fairly" is used in conjunction with the phrase "in conformity with generally accepted accounting principles." The governing criterion in the United States is, therefore, conformity with GAAP. This distinction may be blurred as we move toward internationalization and the primacy of IFRS is achieved.[26]

# IFRS for Small and Medium-Sized Entities

On July 9, 2009, the IASB published IFRS designed for use by small and medium-sized entities (SMEs). SMEs are defined as those entities that do not have public accountability and publish general-purpose financial statements. While every entity has some public accountability, including to its owners and tax authorities, public accountability in the context of IFRS for SMEs is defined to cover entities with or seeking to have securities traded in a public market or that hold assets in a fiduciary capacity as their main business activity. The definition, therefore, is based on the nature of the entity rather than on its size.

U.S. private companies are not required to use a particular basis of accounting when preparing their financial statements, as public companies are. The factors that drive a private company's choice of which financial accounting and reporting framework to follow in preparing its financial statements depend on the company's objectives and the needs of their financial statement users. Currently, private companies in the United States can prepare their financial statements in accordance with U.S. GAAP as promulgated by the FASB, or some other comprehensive basis of accounting such as a cash or tax basis. Now, with the issuance of IFRS for SMEs, U.S. private companies have an additional option because the AICPA already has recognized the IASB as a standard setter for private-company financial reports. As previously mentioned, the status of IFRS for public companies is in the hands of the SEC.

According to the IASB, more than 95 percent of the companies in the world are eligible to use IFRS for SMEs. Unlike in the United States, the laws or government regulations of most other countries require SMEs to prepare and publish "GAAP" financial statements.

Sanders et al. point out that the primary reason that an SME would want to adopt these standards is improved access to capital. Small companies often have a difficult time getting adequate working capital, as well as capital for investment and growth. IFRS for SMEs focuses on the needs of lenders and others who prepare information about cash flows, liquidity, and solvency.[27]

The IFRS for SMEs is a self-contained standard tailored to the needs and capabilities of smaller businesses. Many of the principles in full IFRS for recognizing and measuring assets, liabilities, income, and expenses have been simplified; topics not relevant to SMEs have been omitted; and the number of required disclosures has been significantly reduced. Examples of simplifications in IFRS for SMEs appear in Exhibit 8.1.

*IFRS for SMEs* responds to the strong international demand from both developed and emerging economies for a rigorous and common set of accounting standards for small and medium-sized businesses that are much simpler than full IFRS. These standards are separate from full IFRS and can be adopted by a jurisdiction whether or not it has adopted full IFRS. Where a transaction is not addressed by the IFRS for SMEs, management is expected to use sound judgment to determine its accounting policy. If such a transaction is covered in full IFRS, management may refer to the appropriate international standard if it wishes but is not required to do so.

**EXHIBIT 8.1**
**Comparison of Accounting Rules for Full IFRS and IFRS for SMEs**

| Item | Full IFRS | IFRS for SMEs |
|---|---|---|
| Property, plant, and equipment | Cost or revaluation method | Cost method only |
| Goodwill and other intangibles | Reviewed for impairment and not amortized (indefinite lives) | Amortized (indefinite and definite lives); tested for impairment if indicated |
| Research and development costs | Research costs expensed as incurred; development costs capitalized and amortized if specific criteria met | All research and development costs expensed |
| Borrowing costs | Capitalized if certain criteria are met | Expensed |
| Pension costs | Actuarial gains or losses can be recognized immediately or amortized into profit or loss over the expected remaining working lives of participating employees | Immediate recognition and splits the expense into different components |

The overall concept of a set of IFRS for SMEs is to push down IFRS to entities that are typically not listed on a stock exchange. In general IFRS is considered too complex and onerous for non-listed entities and therefore to effectively expand its use to non-listed entities, some simplifications appear to be necessary. To some extent the proposed simplifications might be seen as the attempt for a compromise between the needs of users and preparers of IFRS financial statements. However, the frameworks of both IFRS and IFRS for SMEs highlight that the objective of financial statements is to provide information about the financial position, performance and changes in financial position of an entity that is useful to a wide range of users in making economic decisions. One of those users is potential investors in SMEs that go public. We are concerned that these users may be misled by financial statements that purport to "present fairly" or a "true and fair view" when prepared under a lesser set of IFRS.

# Principles versus Rules-Based Standards

## Ethical Considerations

The debate over whether the IFRS principles-based standards are "better" than the rules-based system in U.S. GAAP has been going on for a long time. One lesser-known provision of SOX is for a study to be conducted of the need to adopt a principles-based approach to standard setting to replace the more rules-based system in the United States. A study by the SEC notes that imperfections exist when standards are established on either a rules-based or a principles-only basis. Principles-only standards may present enforcement difficulties because they provide little guidance or structure for exercising professional judgment by preparers and auditors. Rules-based standards often provide a vehicle for circumventing the intention of the standard. As a result of its study, the SEC recommended that those involved in the standard-setting process more consistently develop standards on a principles-based or objectives-oriented basis. Such standards should have the following characteristics:[28]

- Be based on an improved and consistently applied conceptual framework.
- State clearly the accounting objective of the standard.
- Provide sufficient detail and structure so that the standard can be operationalized and applied on a consistent basis.
- Minimize exceptions from the standard.
- Avoid use of percentage tests (bright lines) that allow structuring of financial transactions to achieve technical compliance with the standard while evading the intent of the standard.

A good example of a bright line test is the 3 percent equity requirement for outside ownership of SPEs that enabled Enron to avoid consolidating SPE operations with its own operations. Instead, the "dispersion of risk" requirement of *FASB Interpretation 46(R)* that was discussed in Chapter 7 provides a more conceptual basis to determine when consolidation is appropriate.

In contrast to objectives-oriented standards, rules-based standards can provide a basis for avoidance of the accounting objectives inherent in the standards. Internal inconsistencies, exceptions, and bright-line tests reward those willing to engineer their way around the intent of standards. This can result in financial reporting that is not representationally faithful to the underlying economic substance of transactions and events. In a rules-based system, financial reporting may well come to be seen as an act of compliance rather than an act of communication. In addition, because multiple exceptions exist that could lead to internal inconsistencies, significant judgment is needed in determining where an accounting transaction falls within the myriad of possible exceptions. One example of the pitfalls under a rules-based system is accounting for leases, which we first discussed in Chapter 5. The problem here is that the rules can mask the desired objective, which is to record the lease transaction in a way that best reflects economic reality. The principle is: Does the lease transaction effectively transfer ownership to the lessee? If it does, the present value of the future lease payments is capitalized and recorded as an asset and liability on the books of the lessee.

At the other extreme, a principles-only approach typically provides insufficient guidance to make the standards reliably operational. As a consequence, principles-only standards require preparers and auditors to exercise significant judgment in applying overly broad standards to more specific transactions and events, and often do not provide a sufficient structure to frame the judgment that must be made. The result of principles-only standards can be a significant loss of comparability among reporting entities. Furthermore, under a principles-only standard-setting regime, the increased reliance on the capabilities and judgment of preparers and auditors could increase the likelihood of retrospective disagreements on accounting treatments. In turn, this could result in increased litigation with regulators for both companies and auditors.

Another example of rules-driven accounting is the use of the equity method of accounting for an investment. Under *APB 18,* an investment of 20 percent or more in the shares of stock of another entity leads to a presumption that the company (investor) can exercise significant influence over the investee and thus should account for the investment using the equity method. Under the equity method, the investor records its share of investee earnings offset by dividends received. To avoid the earnings increase, the investment can be structured to ensure that it is classified as available for sale (i.e., ensure ownership of less than 20 percent of the investment). The structured transaction would benefit the firm because the change in value of available-for-sale securities gets recognized only in earnings when the investment is sold.

In the *APB 18* example, the rules dictate the accounting treatment rather than economic substance. An economic substance criteria would provide that if the investor can, in fact, exercise significant control, then the equity method would be used rather than base that determination on an assumption of significant influence. The interesting point is the rules under IFRS are virtually the same as under U.S. GAAP. *IAS 28* establishes the same presumption for investments in "associates" as does *APB 18* for "investees." The 20 percent bright-line rule is used for both standards, and that makes us wonder whether IFRS really are more principles-based than U.S. GAAP. As previously mentioned, perhaps it is a matter more of form rather than substance.

Regardless of the approach used for standard setting, ethical considerations play an important role in the ultimate standard selected. Whether it is through the nature of professional judgment in a principles-based system or by complying with the intent of the rules in a rules-based system, professional accountants and auditors must act with honesty, objectivity, and integrity in deciding the proper application of the standard.

## Earnings Management Concerns

One concern about a principles-based system is whether an economic substance-over-form concept might lead preparers of financial statements to try and justify a specific accounting outcome with reference to commercial drivers in an attempt to manage earnings. To determine if there was a difference in the magnitude of earnings management in a principles-based versus rules-based environment, Mergenthaler examined the factors that executives consider when deciding to manage earnings. He contends that the probability of being penalized for earnings management and the penalty imposed on executives who manage are factors that influence executives' estimate of the expected cost of earnings management. Mergenthaler found a positive association between rules-based characteristics and the dollar magnitude of earnings management. He argues that this is because the expected cost of managing earnings is lower in a rules-based environment. The SEC study of principles-based standards seems to support Mergenthaler's contention. The commission expressed its concern that in a principles-based system, there may be "a greater difficulty in seeking remedies against 'bad actors' either through enforcement or litigation."[29]

French authors Thomas Jeanjean and Herve Stolowy examined the effect of IFRS conversion on earnings quality—specifically on management manipulation of earnings to avoid recognition of losses. Their work examined more than 1,100 firms in three countries to determine whether the earnings management appeared to increase or decrease after implementation of IFRS. The authors measured financial reporting quality as a reduction in earnings management. Earnings management was assessed as the frequency of small profits compared to small losses, a technique used in past studies. Australia, France, and the United Kingdom were selected for examination, as these three countries were unable to adopt IFRS before the 2005 mandatory transition date, thus eliminating any early adoption benefits. According to their research, earnings management remained consistent in Australia and the

United Kingdom after IFRS adoption. However, in France, earnings management appeared to increase, suggesting that earnings quality was not improved overall by adopting IFRS.[30]

A frequent question asked is whether principles-based accounting standards increase or decrease earnings informativeness. As outlined in the SEC study and the FASB report[31] on the principles-based approach, some argue that earnings are more informative when standards are principles based. They contend that principles-based standards do not have bright-line thresholds or exceptions that allow managers to structure transactions that technically comply with a standard while circumventing its intent. On the other hand, some argue (e.g., Herz) that principles-based standards provide more opportunities for managers to use their discretion to obfuscate earnings, thereby reducing earnings informativeness.[32] This argument suggests that rules-based standards provide guidelines that prevent management from abusing GAAP to manipulate earnings.

In a study of principles-based standards and earnings effects, Folsom et al. examined whether the reliance on principles-based standards affects the informativeness of earnings. They defined principles-based standards as standards that have fewer rules-based characteristics than rules-based standards, as evidenced by fewer bright-line thresholds, scope and legacy exceptions, large volumes of implementation guidance, and high levels of detail. The authors found that firms that rely more on principles-based standards have a stronger relation between earnings and returns. They also found that earnings map better to future cash flows and are more persistent when the firm relies on principles-based standards. Overall, these findings suggest that managers use the discretion provided by principles-based standards to convey information better to investors.[33]

## Examples of Rules-Based versus Principles-Based Standards

We provide three examples of when earnings can be managed through manipulation of the rules or in judgment-based application of principles: (1) accounting for leases, (2) valuation and recording of property, plant, and equipment, and (3) determining impairment of long-lived assets. Along with the use of the equity method previously discussed, these examples illustrate the role of judgment in interpreting accounting standards and the importance of an underlying foundation in ethical behavior, attitudes, and values.

It also highlights the importance of intent in determining whether the goal is to manage earnings. Recall that ethical intent is a critical component of making ethical decisions. These decisions should be based on the representational faithfulness of financial information and not earnings management considerations.

### Accounting for Leases

A principles-based approach to decision making is illustrated by emphasizing economic substance over legal form in lease transactions. In the United States, *SFAS 13* establishes rules that can undermine the substance-over-form concept. Recall from our discussion in Chapter 5 that if any one of four lease criteria is met, then capitalization treatment leads to recording an asset and liability on the books of the lessee using the present value of future lease payments, including any guaranteed residual value. One problem with the rules-based criteria for capitalization is they rely on implementation guidance (bright-line rules) that can be manipulated. A company might engineer a lease transaction in such a way as to achieve its desired objective of keeping the liability off its books rather than faithfully representing the underlying economic substance of the transaction. For example, to keep the liability off its books, the lessee simply does not have to guarantee to pay the residual value to the lessor. Consider the following: Present value of lease payments (excluding residual value), $107,000; fair value of leased asset, $120,000; present value of residual value, $2,000. If the residual value is unguaranteed (i.e., $107,000 is less than 90 percent of $120,000) and assuming that none of the other criteria are met, then the lease is recorded as an operating lease.

International accounting standards apply a principles-based approach to lease accounting. *IAS 17* provides that if the substance of the transaction is effectively to transfer ownership to the lessee, then it is accounted for as a purchase and sale (capitalization). The standard does establish criteria that guide capitalization, but the application relies on professional judgment. For example, the lease term must be for the *major part* of the economic life of the leased asset, and the present value of the minimum lease payments must be at least equal to *substantially all* of the fair value of the leased asset.[34] In reality, it is difficult to see how these vaguer standards produce better results, given that one company might decide that the "major part" is greater than 50 percent of the useful life of the leased asset, while another may say that it is 75 percent or more. The different applications of the standards may lead to a lack of comparability in financial reports. The problem is that even in a principles-based environment, rules might factor into the judgments made, thereby effectively negating the more conceptual principles approach. Still, if the accounting for leases does not conform to financial reporting requirements in the judgment of the auditor, then the true and fair view override (i.e., capitalizing a lease) should be exercised to ensure that economic reality is portrayed.

### Valuation and Recording of Property, Plant, and Equipment

Principles-based standards are generic and, as opposed to rules-based systems, they do not address every controversial issue but maintain considerable ambiguity about such major processes as recordkeeping and measurement. A potential drawback of the principles-based approach is a lack of precise guidelines that could create inconsistencies in the application of standards across organizations. One example is *IAS 16,* which deals with accounting for property, plant, and equipment. According to the standard, property, plant, and equipment can be accounted for under the cost method or the revaluation method. Specific rules do not exist to guide when one method should be used as opposed to the other. Moreover, the revaluations are made at fair value, with little guidance to help determine this amount except that "fair value is the amount for which an asset could be exchanged between knowledgeable, willing parties in an arm's length transaction."[35] The question is whether determinations of fair value can be made objectively over time and with sufficient precision.

Another issue is that the assets can be revalued upwards and depreciated based on the higher amount under IFRS whereas U.S. GAAP does not permit revaluation increases; only depreciation and write-downs for impairments. One has to wonder how the condorsement approach might treat such a significant difference in accounting under its "endorsement" and "convergence" philosophy.

Comparability suffers under a revaluation method because different companies may estimate the revalued amount differently. Benston contends that it is not the principles-only approach that is to blame, but the inevitable and desirable lack of comparability due to different economic environments. He states that "a company's choice of accounting measurement or presentation can convey information that is valuable to investors about the managers' operational and investment approach and decisions."[36]

### Impairment of Long-Lived Assets

The accounting for impairment of long-lived assets to be held and used depends on judgments of fair value. Generally, if the fair value of the asset is less than the carrying amount of the asset, an impairment loss is recognized. Under U.S. GAAP—*SFAS 144, Accounting for the Impairment or Disposal of Long-Lived Assets*[37], an impairment loss exists when the financial statement carrying amount exceeds its fair value and is not recoverable. A carrying amount is not recoverable if it is greater than the sum of the undiscounted cash flows expected from the asset's use and eventual disposal. FASB defines impairment loss as the amount by which the carrying value exceeds an asset's fair value. Thus, the impairment loss calculation is a two-part process. The first thing to do is to determine if impairment exists (carrying value greater than undiscounted cash flows). The second step is to determine the loss as the difference between carrying value and fair value. Under *SFAS 144,* once an impairment loss is recognized, future increases in fair value are not recognized as

**EXHIBIT 8.2**
**Impairment of**
**Long-Lived Assets**

| Determination to be Made | U.S. GAAP (*SFAS 144*) | IFRS (*IAS 36*) |
|---|---|---|
| Recognition of loss | Carrying amount > Undiscounted cash flows | Carrying amount > Recoverable amount* |
| Measurement of loss | Carrying amount minus fair value | Carrying amount minus recoverable amount |
| Reversal of impairment amount | Prohibited | Increases in recoverable recognized up to carrying amount, as adjusted for depreciation |
| Depreciation | Lower of carrying amount or fair value | Lower of carrying amount or recoverable amount, as adjusted for depreciation |

*Recoverable amount is the greater of the fair value minus cost to sell and the value in use (i.e., present value of future cash flows expected to be derived from the asset).

a recapture of the loss. Finally, asset depreciation is based on the lower fair value amount after the loss is determined. The FASB rules require judgment in estimating future cash flows and fair value, thereby providing an opportunity to "manage" the estimates and affect current and future earnings.

IFRS provides (in *IAS 36*) that an impairment loss is recognized when the carrying amount is greater than the "recoverable amount."[38] The recoverable amount is the greater of the fair value minus costs to sell and the value in use (i.e., the present value of future cash flows expected to be derived from the asset). The impairment loss is the excess of the carrying amount of the asset over its recoverable amount. Unlike U.S. standards, under IFRS, impairment losses already recognized are subject to reversal if the recoverable amount increases up to the carrying amount. Of course, the depreciation amounts also will be affected. Once again condorsement issues arise given the important difference in approaches under U.S. GAAP and IFRS. Exhibit 8.2 summarizes these rules.

Once again, looking at the rules to account for impairment losses under *IAS 36,* it is hard to see how IFRS is truly a principles-based system when the standards are based on rules that have to be interpreted and reevaluated every year. Perhaps a more principles-based standard would be to reflect the long-lived asset at its current fair value. Then, the rules could allow each entity to determine, using professional judgment, what the proper fair value for a specific asset in its particular environment is.

Exhibit 8.3 presents the authors' conceptual view of the major ingredients of a principles-based approach to making accounting judgments. Notice how, in a principles-based environment, virtue-based considerations (e.g., objectivity and integrity) form the basis to evaluate representational faithfulness and to make professional judgments about the economic substance of transactions and the assessment of a true and fair view.

## The Problem with Provisions and Reserves

The words *provisions* and *reserves* have different meanings in the United States and in many other countries around the world. In the U.S., the two terms are always synonymous, and the word *provision* means two things: (1) a liability of uncertain timing or amount (e.g., provisions for pensions); and (2) an allowance against (or impairment of) the value of an asset (e.g., bad debt provision or provision for depreciation). It is safe to say that a provision relates to a liability that does not exist at the reporting date (e.g., contingencies), whereas an allowance reflects the decline in value of an existing asset (e.g., impairments of property, plant, and equipment). Further distinctions include the following: (1) there are no legal reserves in the United States; (2) revaluation reserves relating to investments are shown as cumulative other comprehensive income if they are based on market adjustments for available-for-sale securities; (3) reserves caused by foreign currency translation are called *cumulative translation adjustments* and they, too, appear in comprehensive income; and

**EXHIBIT 8.3**
Conceptual
Framework of a
Principles-Based
Approach to Decision
Making

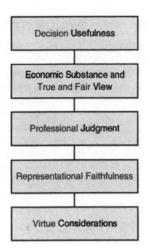

(4) profit and loss account reserves are reflected in retained earnings (e.g., appropriations of retained earnings).

The distinction between provisions and reserves is important for financial reporting because provisions are liabilities recognized by charges against profit that decrease profit and net assets (used in the U.S.). A *reserve,* on the other hand, is an element of shareholders' equity that might reflect the reduction of available profit and an increase in a corresponding equity account with no net effect on retained earnings. In either case, the provision or reserve can be manipulated to manage earnings, as might be the case by underestimating or overestimating the allowance for bad debts.

For many years, companies in the European Union used reserves to reduce reported profits because of a statutory requirement or simply to follow conservative reporting (i.e., discretionary reserves). In IFRS and U.S. GAAP, provisions for general risks should not be established simply to smooth net income. In 1998, the IASC issued *IAS 37,* which stated that a provision should be recognized when, and only when, there is a liability to a third party at the balance sheet date.[39]

Another expression that is often found, particularly under the domestic rules of prudent countries (e.g., Germany) and particularly relating to banks, is *secret* or *hidden reserves.* These would arise because a company failed to recognize an asset in its balance sheet, deliberately measured an asset at an unreasonably low value, or set up unnecessarily high provisions. Recall that in Chapter 7, we discussed cookie-jar reserves, which were used in many of the accounting scandals in the United States to smooth earnings.

Secret reserves might be recorded in the name of prudence (conservatism) or, in some countries, in order to get tax deductions. Whatever the motivation, the result is that net assets and equity will be understated. As Nobes and Parker point out, most systems of accounting contain some degree of secret reserves. For example, the IFRS, German, and U.S. systems do not recognize the internally generated asset research; and it is normal to value many assets at depreciated cost, which is often below fair value.[40]

## Global Business Ethics

Ethical practices in business depend on strong internal controls, effective corporate governance systems, and a code of ethics that guides strategic choices and decision making. We begin our discussion of global business ethics by discussing the code of ethics of the Chartered Institute of Management Accountants (CIMA), a U.K.-based professional body that is focused on accounting for business and the management accounting profession. In

**EXHIBIT 8.4**
**CIMA Code**
**of Ethics***

CIMA's code of ethics is made up of five fundamental principles: integrity, objectivity, professional competence and due care, confidentiality, and professional behavior:

- **Integrity:** Being straightforward, honest, and truthful in all professional and business relationships. You should not be associated with any information that you believe contains a materially false or misleading statement, or which is misleading by omission.
- **Objectivity:** Not allowing bias, conflict of interest, or the influence of other people to override your professional judgment.
- **Professional competence and due care:** An ongoing commitment to your level of professional knowledge and skill. Base this on current developments in practice, legislation, and techniques. Those working under your authority also must have the appropriate training and supervision.
- **Confidentiality:** You should not disclose professional information unless you have specific permission or a legal or professional duty to do so.
- **Professional behavior:** Comply with relevant laws and regulations. You also must avoid any action that could affect the reputation of the profession negatively.

**Threats**
The code identifies five categories of common threat to the five principles:

- **Self-interest threats:** Commonly called a "conflict of interest"
- **Self-review threats:** When you are required to reevaluate your own previous judgment
- **Familiarity threats:** When you become so sympathetic to the interests of others as a result of a close relationship that your professional judgment becomes compromised
- **Intimidation threats:** When you are deterred from acting objectively by actual or perceived threats
- **Advocacy threats:** Can be a problem when you are promoting a position or opinion to the point that your subsequent objectivity is compromised

**Safeguards**
The CIMA code has a "threats and safeguards" approach to resolving ethical issues. This means that if you think there is a threat, you should assess whether the threat is significant, and then take action to remove or mitigate it.

Employing institutions often have safeguards such as whistleblowing or grievance procedures that should be followed internally. External legislation that supports whistleblowing also exists such as the Sarbanes-Oxley Act and the Dodd-Frank Financial Reform Act in the U.S.

*Certified Institute of Management Accountants, *CIMA Code of Ethics* (October 2010). Available at http://www.cimaglobal.com/Documents/Professional%20ethics%20docs/code%20FINAL.pdf.

2011, the AICPA and CIMA established the Chartered Global Management Accountant (CGMA) designation to promote the professional development of management accountants across the globe. Membership in the organization obligates the professional to follow CIMA's code of ethics. Given the important role of management accountants in the corporate governance system, the CIMA Code is an important step in defining the ethical obligations of management accountants on an international basis and strengthening corporate governance systems. The CIMA code is patterned after the IFAC Code, discussed in greater detail later in this chapter, and it is similar to the AICPA Code discussed in Chapter 4. Exhibit 8.4 presents a summary of the CIMA code.

The ethics standards for members of the CIMA not only mirror those of the AICPA, but also include the threats to independence discussed in Chapter 4. One difference is the reference to compliance with relevant laws and regulations as part of professional behavior. Recall that the new audit report discussed in Chapter 5 includes an optional paragraph to address legal and regulatory issues, which in part reflects the greater weight given to such matters in Europe and other parts of the world (statutory control).

General guidance exists about handling dilemmas. There is a parallel to be drawn with the reflection step in our comprehensive ethical decision-making model, which we explained in Chapter 2. Along these lines, the CIMA guidance includes key questions to consider in resolving ethical dilemmas: (1) Would I feel comfortable about my professional peers, family, and friends knowing about the situation? and (2) How would I feel if I saw this in a newspaper?[41]

The NBES survey that was discussed in chapter 3 and CIMA survey summarized in Exhibit 8.5 both raise important concerns about corporate culture. The CIMA survey reports the troubling finding that neither senior management nor boards of directors seem to be reviewing, analyzing, and monitoring ethics information at the level recorded four years ago. In 2008, 86 percent of senior management and 68 percent of boards reviewed ethics data, according to the report. In 2012, it was 78 percent and 56 percent, respectively. This "weakened tone from the top" comes as more than a third of those surveyed (35 percent) said that they sometimes or always feel pressured to compromise their organization's standards of ethical conduct. This compares to 28 percent of respondents in 2008. Interpretation 102-4 in Exhibit 1.2 (shown in Chapter 1) describes the ethical obligations of industry CPAs to avoid subordinating professional judgment. Once again, there are parallels to be drawn with the CIMA guidance in handling dilemmas, including selecting a course of action, assessing legality/seeking legal advice, and the ultimate step

**EXHIBIT 8.5**
**NBES and CIMA**
**Surveys on Ethics***

In Chapter 3, we discussed the results of the 2011 National Business Ethics Survey (NBES) conducted by the Ethics Resource Center. The results of that study show an uptick in pressure to compromise ethical standards, a weak ethical culture, and increased reporting of misconduct, even though the percentage of respondents observing misconduct declined between 2007 and 2011.

In this chapter, we report the results of a survey, *Managing Responsible Business: A Global Survey on Business Ethics,* which was jointly completed by the AICPA and CIMA in 2012. The survey was first conducted in 2008 and focuses on four key ethical issues, including ethical culture. The following is a summary of the key findings:[42]

- There has been an increase of 10 to 15 percent in the number of organizations providing both statements of ethical values and a code of ethics, as well as related training, hotlines, and incentives such as performance-based rewards.
- A weakened "tone at the top" has potentially serious implications for the overall ethical operating culture of an organization.
- There has been an increase of almost 20 percent in organizations collecting and reporting on ethical information.
- A majority of management accountants (61 percent) believe that it is important to collect and analyze ethical information, but 20 percent of the respondents do not think that their organization will do so in the near future.
- Just over one-third agree or strongly agree that ethical standards are not fully monitored.
- Despite an increase in ethical codes and training, there is greater pressure within organizations to act unethically.
- There has been an increase in those observing ethical misconduct over the course of a year.
- Management accountants are most likely to feel pressure to compromise standards when working with colleagues in other departments. This may reflect challenges to professional objectivity when working in commercial business units.
- Bribery has risen from sixth to third in the rankings of issues of concern, reflecting the intensifying of anti-bribery and corruption legislation.

*Adapted from the CIMA Report: *Managing Responsible Business: A Global Survey on Business Ethics, 2012.*

of disassociating from the company. One reason for discussing the international ethics standards in this chapter is to emphasize the global nature of accounting practice and related ethical requirements.

The CIMA survey clearly indicates there are increased pressures within the workplace to compromise ethical standards, despite the increase of ethical codes and policies that have been put in place. We believe that the cause for the weakened culture can be found in the widening gap between the reality and rhetoric of business ethics. It seems as though lip service is being paid to ethics. It may be that a regulatory mentality fostered by laws such as SOX, Dodd-Frank, and the U.K. Bribery Act, discussed in more detail later in this chapter, has shifted the focus from ethics to compliance, thereby muddying the waters with respect to the need for top management to walk the talk of ethics.

# Global Code of Ethics

IFAC established the IESBA to develop and issue high-quality ethical standards and other pronouncements for professional accountants for use around the world. The result was the issuance of the Code of Ethics for Professional Accountants (IFAC Code), which establishes ethical requirements for professional accountants performing services in the global business arena. A member body of IFAC or a firm from its country may not apply less stringent standards than those stated in the IFAC Code. However, if a member body or firm is prohibited from complying with certain parts of this Code by national law or regulation, they should be governed by their country's requirements but comply with all other parts of the Code.

The 2012 IFAC Code contains provisions virtually identical to those embodied in the AICPA Code of Professional Conduct. The following is a brief list of similarities:[43]

1. To act in accordance with the public interest
2. To identify threats to independence (i.e., self-interest threats, advocacy threats, self-review threats, familiarity threats, and intimidation threats) and develop safeguards to mitigate such threats
3. To be independent in fact, meaning having a state of mind that permits the expression of a conclusion without being affected by influences that compromise professional judgment, allowing an individual to act with integrity, and exercising objectivity and professional skepticism
4. To maintain the appearance of independence, meaning the avoidance of facts and circumstances that are so significant that a reasonable and informed third party, having knowledge of all relevant information, including safeguards applied, would reasonably conclude that a firm's or a member of the assurance team's integrity, objectivity, or professional skepticism had been compromised
5. To adhere to standards related to integrity, objectivity, professional competence and due care, confidentiality, and professional behavior

In acting in the public interest, professional accountants must comply with their professional body's ethics code. Codes must have meaning beyond words on a piece of paper. Given the globalization of business and accounting, we believe that a principles-based code, such as the CIMA Code, IFAC Global Code, or the Principles in the AICPA Code of Professional Conduct, is better able to guide international accountants and auditors in carrying out their professional responsibilities. Rules of conduct such as those explained in Chapter 4 are important to establish when violations may occur, but they do not instill the kind of ethical values that help accountants and auditors internalize the ethics of the accounting profession as virtues.

Codes must inspire ethical behavior. Elizabeth Alexander, the former national president of the Australian Institute of Company Directors and a former national president of CPA Australia, said it best:

Codes of conduct must be transformed into powers for good, not primarily toothless forms of chastisement. The codes must become active documents which aim to encourage the professional to accept that "not everything has a price," that the professional's actions should be founded on a strong premise.[44]

# Global Fraud, Bribery, and Suspected Illegal Acts

## Global Fraud

In Chapter 3, we discussed the results of the 2012 Global Fraud Survey conducted by the Association of Certified Fraud Examiners (ACFE). The *Report to the Nations on Occupational Fraud and Abuse* studied 1,388 cases of occupational fraud—that is, asset misappropriation, corruption, and financial statement fraud schemes—reported by certified fraud examiners in 94 countries between January 2010 and December 2011. Survey participants reported 778 cases of occupational fraud in the U.S. Billing fraud continued to be the most common type of fraud scheme, followed by corruption and expense reimbursements. Although the United States experienced the greatest number of fraud cases, countries in Latin America and the Caribbean had the highest median loss.[45]

Survey participants cited an outright lack of internal controls (35.5 percent) as the most common factor contributing to global occupational fraud. Other weaknesses in fraud prevention included the override of existing internal controls (19.4 percent), lack of management review contributing to the success of the fraud (18.7 percent), and a company's poor tone at the top, which led to the fraud's occurrence (9.1 percent).

Common antifraud controls include external audits of financial statements, codes of conduct, and internal audits. This is no surprise, as a strong system of corporate governance should include these basic elements, as well as a tip line for anonymous reporting of wrongdoing and protection for whistleblowers.

In a year when many U.K. companies adopted a host of new anticorruption measures under the U.K. Bribery Act, global fraud levels also dipped, according to a new executive survey by Kroll Advisory Solutions.

The sixth annual Global Fraud Survey from Kroll, released in November 2012, polled 839 senior executives around the world. The most striking result is that there has been a notable decline in the level of fraud overall. The proportion of companies reporting that they were affected by at least one incidence of fraud dropped for the second year in a row, from 75 percent to 61 percent. The drop paid off on the bottom line too. On average, the cost of fraud to companies fell from 2.1 percent of revenues to 0.9 percent. The survey also indicates that corporations are facing a rising tide of insider threats.[46]

At the same time, the survey noted that more companies are adopting risk mitigation and compliance measures when it comes to the U.S. Foreign Corrupt Practices Act (FCPA) and the U.K. Bribery Act. "Compared with last year, far more have done a risk assessment relating to these pieces of legislation, trained senior managers appropriately, and integrated corruption issues into their due diligence activities," the report states.[47]

For example, in 2011, only 26 percent of survey respondents said they had put bribery-risk monitoring and reporting systems in place. In 2012, that figure jumped to 52 percent of respondents. Likewise, where 29 percent of companies said that they trained employees and vendors on antibribery compliance in 2011, 55 percent said that they had done so in 2012.[48]

The survey's 2012 view of insider threats looked grimmer than the previous year. About two-thirds of firms in the survey that were hit by fraud during 2012 cited an insider as a key perpetrator, rising from 60 percent in 2011 and 55 percent in 2010.[49] These results indicate the increased importance of whistleblowing actions.

Information theft also proved a stubborn and dynamic threat to corporations, according to the findings. Prevalence of this type of fraud declined only two percentage points, from 23 percent to 21 percent. Such an attack "remains the fraud to which respondents feel most vulnerable—30 percent say they are moderately or highly concerned."[50] This emerging type of fraud occurs with a class of thieves that seek customer data, as well as a company's financial and strategic data, and employees often either prove to be the innocent gateway to accessing that information or they are the culprits.

Even though occurrence has decreased, the fraud issue has been linked to employee malfeasance 35 percent of the time, more than twice the rate at which external hackers are to blame (17 percent). Moreover, employees are often unwitting accomplices to digital theft. In 51 percent of cases, the theft of an employee's technology (such as a computer or mobile phone) or an employee mistake was involved.[51]

Efforts to combat global business fraud should include the following:

- Evaluate the legal and regulatory enforcement environment.
- Motivate management to understand, commit to, and support anti-fraud and anti-corruption initiatives.
- Assess risks to the company's business, brand, and reputation.
- Maintain compliance in light of the scope and complexity of global business operations.
- Obtain legal advice when responding to compliance issues or threats.
- Work with the accountants and auditors to prevent and detect fraud.
- Educate the workforce about the risks of wrongdoing.
- Cultivate a companywide culture of compliance.

Finally, to instill an environment of compliance and ethical behavior, top management should "walk the talk" of ethics by:

- Developing an ethics training program geared toward the entity's global business operations.
- Clearly demonstrating that noncompliance will not be tolerated and that breaches will be dealt with—with no exceptions.
- Being consistent for particular offenses to avoid the appearance of selective enforcement
- Having preestablished disciplinary measures and a process for breaches, such as dismissal, prosecution for fraud or bribery, recovery of assets, etc.
- Communicating breaches and their consequences to build trust in the process.

## Global Bribery

In some countries, corruption is part of the country's culture, so fraud, bribery, and kickbacks are a way of doing business. Whether you call it "grease payments" (United States), *baksheesh* (Middle East), *mordida* (Latin America), or *ghoos* (India), these payments are designed to speed up "routine governmental action," such as processing papers, issuing permits, and other actions of an official, in order to expedite performance of duties of nondiscretionary nature (i.e., which they are already bound to perform). The payment is not intended to influence the outcome of the official's action, only its timing. These facilitation payments are one of the few exceptions to anti-bribery prohibitions of the FCPA.

In 2010, the United Kingdom passed the U.K. Bribery Act that bans facilitating payments. The act went into effect in July 2011. It defines such payments as "Small unofficial payments made to secure or expedite the performance of a routine or necessary action to which the payer has legal or other entitlement."[52] In other words, the act bans what the FCPA permits. The jury is out whether the tougher U.K. anti-bribery law will hurt U.K. multinationals as they compete with companies in countries that allow facilitating payments. It should be noted that international anti-corruption treaties also ban facilitation payments.

The act includes a new corporate criminal offense of failure to prevent bribery. The company may be guilty of a criminal offense unless they can demonstrate that they had adequate procedures in place to deal with bribery, including facilitation payments. This sounds a lot like the "good parenting" guidance provided in the U.S. Federal Sentencing Guidelines for Organizations (FSGO), discussed in Chapter 6.

The Ministry of Justice in the United Kingdom established six principles on what constitutes adequate procedures:[53]

- *Risk assessment*—Fundamental to understanding the extent to which a company has made an assessment of how and where facilitation payments take place.
- *Top-level commitment*—The extent to which senior management actually addresses the issue of facilitation payments and whether a clear policy on facilitation payments has been communicated to everyone.
- *Due diligence*—Awareness of associated persons in the organization and how they approach the tricky situation of facilitation payments when working on behalf of the company.
- *Policies and procedures*—Whether a policy exists to deal with bribery that openly addresses the issue of facilitation payments.
- *Effective implementation*—Effective policy communication, training, guidance, and project management allowing for delays caused by zero tolerance to facilitation payments.
- *Monitoring and reporting*—The company should govern and monitor the risks that they have identified, particularly in relation to third parties.

More than one year into the passage of the U.K. Bribery Act, not a single successful prosecution has been brought against a company by the United Kingdom's Serious Fraud Office (SFO), which is responsible for enforcing the law.

The SFO's approach is based on the notion that ethical business is good business. It has engaged directly with companies by communicating both its enforcement priorities and its intent to protect competition. Its position is that the Bribery Act "is not intended to penalize ethically run companies that encounter an isolated incident of bribery." As a practical matter, the SFO has effectively put the onus on companies, encouraging them to establish strong corporate governance. Companies that fail to adopt anti-corruption programs, it contends, will risk losing business to competitors.[54]

In November 2011, the SFO provided guidance as to what the agency deems to be corruption indicators, or "red flags" of corruption. While not exhaustive, the list helps to clarify those business practices that the SFO deems to be questionable:

- Abnormal cash payments.
- Pressure exerted for payments to be made urgently or ahead of schedule.
- Payments being made through a third-party country; for example, goods or services are supplied to country A but payment is made to a shell company in country B.
- Private meetings with public contractors or companies hoping to tender for contracts.
- Lavish gifts.
- Agreeing to contracts not favorable to the organization, either with terms or time period.
- Unexplained preference for certain contractors during the tendering period.

The SFO has found that to date, U.K. companies appear to be addressing the Bribery Act's requirements and reducing potential risks by ensuring that they have adequate procedures in place to prevent bribery. As part of their decision making, companies are increasingly reviewing existing policies and contracts to make sure that they comply with the law's requirements.

The U.K. Bribery Act has a potentially wide territorial reach. A non-U.K. corporation will commit an offense of offering or accepting a bribe or of bribing a foreign public official under the Bribery Act if an act that forms part of that offense takes place in the U.K. Even if the relevant act takes place outside the U.K., proceedings for the offense may still be brought in the U.K. if the person who does that act has a "close connection" with the U.K. The Bribery Act provides an exhaustive list of people who will be considered to have a "close connection" with the United Kingdom, which includes British citizens and British nationals living overseas.

For an offense to arise, the briber must be "associated" with the commercial organization, a term that applies to the organization's agents, employees, and subsidiaries. A foreign corporation which "carries on a business, or part of a business" in the U.K. may therefore be guilty of the U.K. offense even if, for example, the relevant acts were performed by the corporation's agent outside the U.K. The Bribery Act does not expand on what will constitute the carrying on of "part of a business" in the U.K., so this will be an issue for the courts to decide. However, the guidance on adequate procedures suggests that having a U.K. subsidiary or securities listed in the United Kingdom will not, of itself, be sufficient.[55]

In a recent survey of compliance, over half of all corruption incidents were identified from "tips" when a whistleblowing hotline was available, showing that having a hotline increases reporting and internal detection. Interestingly, 86 percent of respondents claim to be prepared to report potential breaches of the Bribery Act, even though 44 percent of respondents do not have, or are not aware of, clearly defined procedures for reporting Bribery Act contraventions.[56]

We believe that U.K. companies that respond to the act with rules and procedures alone are destined to have violations in the long term. Instead, companies should realize that preventing corruption is fundamentally a matter of corporate culture. Procedures, policies, rules, and systems won't work unless they are supported by a culture that is truly geared toward doing the right thing.

Culture is a very powerful force. A good perspective is to assess the way things really happen in the company. What is most rewarded? How are conflicting priorities reconciled? What happens when short-term business objectives run counter to company values? When people see something wrong, do they come forward or hold back in fear?

## Responding to a Suspected Illegal Act

In August 2012, the IESBA issued an exposure draft describing how professional accountants should respond when they discover unethical and/or illegal acts in the course of their duties. The proposal describes illegal acts of omission or commission, intentional or unintentional, committed by a client, or by those charged with governance, management, or employees of a client that are contrary to the prevailing laws or regulations.[57]

While the intended response to the illegal act is to encourage accountants to blow the whistle on unethical companies or individuals, some of the changes may conflict with other ethical responsibilities, including confidentiality requirements. Verschoor points out that research has repeatedly shown the importance of tip information to the solution of fraud and other criminal cases, but efforts to promote whistleblowing may conflict with ethics requirements contained in codes of ethics guiding professional accountants, such as the Institute of Management Accountants (IMA) Statement of Ethical Professional Practice or the AICPA Code of Professional Conduct.[58]

In its exposure draft, titled *Responding to a Suspected Illegal Act*, the IESBA seeks to modify the Code of Ethics for Professional Accountants (IFAC Code) by outlining the types of situations where a professional accountant would have an ethical responsibility to blow the whistle. Examples of behavior identified in the exposure draft include improper earnings management or balance sheet valuations.[59]

Under the proposal, a professional accountant who suspects some act or activity may be illegal would be required to take reasonable steps to confirm or resolve the suspicion and to discuss the issue with the appropriate level of management. If that doesn't put the issue to rest, the accountant would be required to take it to higher levels of management, and eventually outside authorities if necessary.[60]

The IESBA makes a distinction between an accountant and an auditor in terms of the expected response to suspected illegal acts. An auditor would be required to pursue remedies up to and including contacting legal authorities, but an accountant working either inside or outside the organization would be held to a slightly lower standard. They would be expected, but not necessarily required, to get outside authorities involved. In either case, the standard would require an accountant or an auditor to take a close look at whether her or she can remain engaged with the entity under the circumstances.[61]

The IESBA proposal seeks to strike a balance between confidentiality and the public interest. Auditors and accountants are bound to confidentiality as one of the five fundamental principles in the IFAC Code, but they may be required to set it aside when public interests are better served by disclosure of possible illegal actions. Criteria when disclosure should occur include that the suspected illegal act directly or indirectly affects the employing organizations' (or clients') financial reporting and the suspected illegal act relates to the subject matter of the professional services being provided by the professional accountant.

As previously discussed in this book, the Dodd-Frank Financial Reform Act, enacted in the United States in July 2010, contains provisions to encourage whistleblowing and protect whistleblowers when reporting suspected violations of securities laws, yet these provisions also encourage behavior from professional accountants that may conflict with their ethical responsibilities regarding confidentiality.

Recall that Dodd-Frank defines circumstances when bounties may be paid to auditing, legal, and compliance personnel, and when they can be protected from retaliatory acts if they had a reasonable belief that whistleblowing was necessary:

- To prevent substantial injury to the financial interests of the company or its shareholders, or
- That the company was about to impede an investigation of the misconduct, or
- That 120 days had passed since the whistleblower reported (or officials already knew about) the possible violations

In the United Kingdom, the Public Interest Disclosure Act of 1998 sets forth substantial legal protections against employer retaliation on workplace whistleblowers. The subject matter for disclosures is broad and includes information about crimes, miscarriages of justice, failure or likely failure to comply with any legal obligation, endangering the health or safety of any individual, damage to the environment, and information tending to show any matter falling within any one of the preceding subjects has been, is being, or is likely to be deliberately concealed.[62] Similar whistleblower protection laws exist in Australia, the Netherlands, and other countries, but the payment of cash bounties to whistleblowers is believed to be limited to the United States.

The initial response to the IESBA exposure draft has been critical. The Institute of Chartered Accountants in Australia points out that a professional obligation to breach confidentiality raises the following major concerns:[63]

- The absence of any legal protections for the accountant provided by the IFAC Code
- The risk of actionable consequences arising from such disclosure, particularly when suspicions turn out to be erroneous
- The consequent erosion of the trusted advisor relationship, which lies at the heart of the accounting profession and which in our view would affect the public interest negatively

The AICPA cautions that the guidance in the exposure draft might place a professional accountant at risk of violating her legal or contractual duties of confidentiality to a client or employer or impose a potential responsibility on a professional accountant (in the IFAC Code) to disclose suspected illegal acts to an external authority. Similar to the Institute of Chartered Accountants in Australia, which identified the absence of legal protections, the AICPA believes that a reporting obligation must include a "safe harbor" provision protecting the accountant from potential liability for allegedly unauthorized or unjustified disclosures.

The AICPA in its formal response proposed its own solution to reporting suspected illegal acts. Not surprisingly, the AICPA response is similar to its standards in Interpretation 102-4. It proposes that the IESBA might provide guidance that, *in appropriate circumstances,* a professional accountant should be expected to do the following:[64]

- Report suspected illegal acts to the appropriate levels of management of a client or employer, and possibly to those charged with governance, if management's response is not timely and appropriate.
- Consider disclosure to the external auditor, provided that such disclosure would not violate any legal or contractual confidentiality or non-disclosure requirements applicable to the engagement.
- Encourage the client or employer to disclose the matter to an appropriate authority.
- Consider his or her continuing relationship with the client or employer if the client or employer fails to address the professional accountant's concerns.

Various laws to encourage whistleblowing and protect whistleblowers exist around the world, and some countries' structures are more refined than others. But as governments work to reduce the instances of fraud, their legislative efforts create ethics challenges for accountants. The IESBA exposure draft aims to help make sense of the varied practices and deliver a set of ethical standards for professional accountants around the world.

# Comparative Corporate Governance

Corporate governance has to do with how organizations are run. Organizations with proper corporate governance have accountability and transparency. People in authority at those organizations know that their actions will be seen and judged by others. Therefore, those leaders are more likely to act in ways that benefit the organization's stakeholders. They are also less inclined to act in ways that benefit themselves personally at the expense of the organization.

## Legal and Cultural Considerations

Ethical issues exist in corporate governance systems in different countries because of legal system, business practices, and cultural considerations that directly affect the way in which companies are managed and controlled. In a series of papers, La Porta et al. show that investor protection differs significantly among countries. In common-law countries (i.e., United States and United Kingdom), the legal systems are not dependent on comprehensive compilation of legal rules and statutes but depend on court precedents (uncodified law). In these countries, there is a higher level of investor protection than civil-law countries. Civil-law countries (i.e., continental Europe, Japan) have comprehensive, continuously updated legal codes that specify all matters capable of being brought before a court, the applicable procedure, and the appropriate punishment for each offense (codified law). Lower investor protection is related to a higher ownership concentration and weaker financial markets. In such situations, the conflict between controlling and minority shareholders may be more severe than the classical agency conflict between managers and shareholders.[65]

A country's culture may be another factor that influences corporate governance. Dyck and Zingales show that the prevalence and level of private benefits of control (used as a direct proxy for investor protection) is also influenced by cultural norms within a country and not solely a result of low investor protection. In addition to legal mechanisms (i.e., accounting standards), extralegal mechanisms such as pressure coming from the public opinion curb the level of private benefits. Shareholders fear negative public opinion and reputation costs if the media uncover bad behavior. The authors conclude that apart from the legal system, cultural aspects influence the way investors are being protected.[66] Licht et al. (2005) find further empirical evidence that culture has a significant impact on corporate governance-related law.[67]

Our conclusion from this research is that the link between ownership concentration, private benefits of control, corporate governance, and the legal system is not undisputed. Factors other than the affiliation to a certain legal family also influence the firm's governance. Thus, cultural differences within legal families among and within countries potentially drive the structure of corporate governance.

## Comply or Explain Principle

In 1992, in response to a series of corporate scandals, the United Kingdom introduced what is believed to be the first code to set out best practices in corporate governance. Known as the Cadbury Code, it introduced a new regulatory concept known as "comply or explain," under which companies have the option either to follow the best practices or to explain to their shareholders why they considered that they were not appropriate in the company's particular circumstances.

The comply or explain mechanism has also been adopted more widely in other European countries, and in 2006, it was formally recognized in an EU directive that requires all companies listed on EU-regulated markets to comply with the relevant corporate governance code or explain why they have not. While the precise content of these codes varies from country to country, they all address issues such as the role, composition, and effectiveness of the board and its committees, the remuneration of executive directors, risk management and internal control, and communication with shareholders.

There are three primary reasons why the comply or explain approach is considered to be more appropriate for addressing most governance issues than more traditional forms of regulation:

- It leaves decisions about the appropriateness of a company's governance arrangements in the hands of its management and shareholders. In most cases, the primary purpose of good governance is to protect the long-term interests of the company and its owners, so it is right that they should decide collectively how to achieve that objective. In certain companies or sectors, there may also be public interest considerations, in which case the arguments for a more traditional approach to regulation may be stronger.

- While it encourages companies to follow accepted best practices, it recognizes that in certain circumstances, it may be appropriate for them to achieve good governance by other means. To be effective, good governance needs to be implemented in a way that fits the culture and organization of the individual company; these can vary enormously between companies depending on factors such as size, ownership structure, and the complexity of the business model. In general, one size does not fit all.

• By allowing a degree of flexibility, it enables codes to set more demanding standards that can be more aspirational than legislation requirements. Regulation tends to be written in terms of the minimum necessary requirements in order not to impose unjustified or disproportionate burdens on those being regulated. In contrast, a "comply or explain" code can set out market-leading practices and encourage the rest to aspire to the standards of the best.

A major theme of this text is the need for ethical corporate governance systems to ensure that decisions are made in the public interest. Cultural considerations, legal systems, and the financial markets, including shareholder interests, all influence corporate governance systems. We discussed various corporate governance mechanisms in Chapter 3, including the board of directors, audit committee, internal controls, the role of internal auditors, and the external audit. In this chapter, we look at governance provisions that differ from those in the United States, emphasizing differences in three countries: Germany, China, and India. Germany was chosen because its system mirrors that of many European countries and includes the two-tier board of director structure. China and India are two of the fastest-growing economies and have some unique aspects to their governance system. In China, a transition has been under way for quite a few years from a state-controlled to a more private enterprise system with state-representative shareholders. In India, large industrial groups (e.g., Tata) or family-owned entities are major shareholders.

## Corporate Governance in Germany

German corporate governance fundamentals and practices are generally based on the provisions of the German Stock Corporation Act, the German Codetermination Act, and the German Corporate Governance Code. German stock corporations typically have three corporate bodies in Germany—an annual general meeting of shareholders, and a dual system for its board of directors: board of management and a supervisory board.

The German Stock Corporation Act calls for a clear separation of duties between management and supervisory functions and therefore prohibits simultaneous membership on both boards. Members of the board of management and the supervisory board must exercise the standard of care of a prudent and diligent businessperson when carrying out their duties. In complying with this standard of care, members must not only take into account the interests of shareholders, as would typically be the case with a U.S. board of directors, but also the interests of other constituents, such as creditors, the company's employees, and, societal interests such as environmental concerns. The German corporation governance system has been referred to as *stakeholder capitalism*.

The board of management is responsible for managing the company and representing it in its dealings with third parties. The management board's functions are comparable to those performed in the ordinary course of business by the senior executives of a U.S. company. However, the members of the board of management of a German stock corporation are regarded as peers and share a collective responsibility for all management decisions. We believe this creates another layer of oversight that strengthens the corporate governance system in countries like Germany when compared to the U.S. where top management is responsible for the financial statements and has a vested interest in making the statements look as positive as possible. In the German system, the management board is independent of management and, potentially, better able to approach its responsibilities in a more objective manner.

The supervisory board oversees the company's board of management and appoints its members. Members of the supervisory board generally are not involved in the day-to-day management of the company. The supervisory boards of major German stock corporations are subject to employee codetermination and are comprised of representatives of the shareholders and employees. Traditionally, the shareholder representatives on the supervisory board have a good understanding of the business activities of the company. Depending on the company's total number of employees, up to half of the supervisory board members will be elected by the company's employees.

German law also has several rules applicable to supervisory board members that are designed to ensure a certain degree of independence of the board members. In addition to prohibiting members of the board of management from serving on the supervisory board, German law requires members of the supervisory board to act in the best interest of the company.

In May 2003, a German government commission promulgated a Corporate Governance Code, which has since undergone several amendments and supplementations. The Code contains additional corporate governance rules applicable to publicly quoted German stock corporations. Companies failing to comply with the Code's recommendations must disclose publicly how and why their practices differ from those recommended by the Code. This is the "comply or explain" principle that was referred to earlier.[68]

Exhibit 8.6 provides a summary of governance in German companies compared to that in the U.S.

**EXHIBIT 8.6**
**Summary of Governance in German Companies Compared to the U.S.**

1. The German corporate governance system reflects concentrated ownership and insider control, including the preponderance of family-controlled firms, in addition to management, including large shareholders, lenders, and labor. It builds on insider relationships, while the U.S. system relies on external participation.
2. In Germany, two-tier boards include the Management Board, which manages the enterprise for stakeholder groups, and the Supervisory Board, which oversees management policy carried out by the Management Board. In the U.S., a unitary approach to boards of directors is used.
3. Influential stakeholders on the German Supervisory Board include shareholders owning 25 pe cent or more of a block of stock, other blockholders (including other business enterprises, wealthy families, and large commercial banks); and there is employee representation on the board. Large institutional investors in the U.S. (e.g., CalPERS) are the only blockholders in publicly owned companies.
4. The Management Board prepares the financial statements that are examined by the outside auditors and the Supervisory Board. In the U.S., the management of the company prepares its financial statements; the audit committee oversees such statements; and the external auditors render an independent opinion on the financial statements.
5. In Germany, board and management decisions are to be made in the best interests of the company, whereas in the U.S., shareholder interests are emphasized.
6. In Germany, the "comply or explain" principle requires an explanation of noncompliance with corporate governance provisions of the Code. In the U.S., CEOs must certify compliance with corporate governance guidelines of the NYSE.
7. Germany uses a "true and fair view" concept in audit reports, rather than the "present fairly" standard in the U.S.

A major issue to be resolved for corporate governance in Germany is that ownership structures are complex and work against transparency in corporate control. Also, hybrid ownership groups and insider control create challenges for effective corporate governance. The traditional lack of protection for investors, in part due to the emphasis on bank financing, has been somewhat resolved with the expansion of stock financing in Germany.

## Corporate Governance in China

In China, the traditional state-owned enterprise (SOE) has been undergoing a process of "corporatization" since 1984, when these enterprises were encouraged to expand production and earn profits. The traditional model of state-owned and state-managed enterprises has morphed into a system in which the state uses state-owned enterprises to dominate the process of domestic wealth creation. To be sure, this is not communism; significant segments of state capitalist economies are in private hands. But the state plays the largest role in ensuring that market forces serve political ends—by ensuring that, profitable or not, businesses invest in projects that bolster social stability and protect the ruling elite's political control.

Progress has been slow in the privatization of Chinese companies because of a culture of control by the state that is part of the historical foundation of the Chinese economy. Cultural variables in China exist whereby subordinate-superior relationship tends to be polarized and there is no defense against power abuse by superiors. With a score of 80 on the power distance variable, China sits in the higher rankings of the Power Distance index (PDI)—i.e., a society that believes that inequalities among people are acceptable. Therefore, it is generally accepted that the state will yield more power and influence over Chinese businesses than private shareholders.

For all the talk in recent years about the extent to which China has embraced capitalism, huge sectors of the economy still have not fully done so: those dominated by the country's approximately 145,000 SOEs. Companies in which the state owns a majority represent 35 percent of all business activity in China. Calls for increased privatization of Chinese companies have not led to much change during the past few years, in part because the politically connected families that run many SOEs are reluctant to give up control. Unlike private companies, China's SOEs serve two masters: the Communist Party and private shareholders. And the party holds the trump card because it, not the board, appoints CEOs.

The Code of Corporate Governance for Listed Companies in China, which was issued by the Chinese Securities Regulatory Commission, a body that carries out some of the same functions as the SEC in the United States, provides a measuring stick for corporate governance practices. The company law requires corporations to form three statutory and indispensable corporate governing bodies: (1) the shareholders, acting as a body at the general meeting; (2) the board of directors; and (3) the board of supervisors. The law also introduced two new statutory corporate positions—the chair of the board of directors and the CEO.[69]

Exhibit 8.7 provides a summary of governance differences in Chinese enterprises compared to those in the U.S.

**EXHIBIT 8.7**
Summary of
Governance in
Chinese Companies
Compared to the U.S.

1. The state plays the role of an investor in China's corporatized SOEs; reporting practices are more often focused on meeting the needs of the major shareholder (i.e., the state) rather than the needs of investors, as in the case of the U.S.
2. China has a two-tier system of oversight, with overlapping responsibilities of both the supervisory board and the board of directors, and the board of directors and management compared with the unitary board in the U.S.
3. Only the chair of the audit committee need be independent in China, with a majority of independent directors on the committee. In the U.S., all members of the audit committee should be independent.
4. Directors have fiduciary duties to act in the best interests of the company and its shareholders. In the U.S., both management and the board of directors have fiduciary obligations with respect to the shareholders.
5. No required certification of financial statements by management or an internal control report, whereas in the U.S., SOX requires certification by the CEO and chief financial officer (CFO).
6. Comply or explain gaps between existing corporate governance practices and recommendations in the corporate code, although there is no penalty for failing to do so. In the U.S., CEOs must certify compliance with corporate governance guidelines of the NYSE.

The most significant issue with respect to corporate governance in China is enforcement of the many provisions that already exist in the law. Even though China has adopted many of the principles of corporate governance followed in the United States. and Germany, there is no guarantee that SOEs and public companies will implement them in the best interests of investors, given the critical role of the state shareholder and the government.

Concerns exist about potential abuses when ownership is concentrated in the hands of state investors. In recent years, there have been dozens of investigations of accounting and auditing practices of Chinese companies. Exhibit 8.8 summarizes some of the most well known allegations of fraud against Chinese companies. Notice how they run the gamut from simple falsification of bank balances to misuse of corporate resources by insiders to related-party transactions and off-balance-sheet entities.

**EXHIBIT 8.8**
**Examples of Accounting Fraud at Chinese Companies**

- In April 2012, the SEC sued SinoTech Energy and two of its executives, charging them with lying to investors about the value of the company's assets and how it used $120 million in proceeds from its initial public offering (IPO) on the National Association of Securities Dealers (NASDAQ) stock exchange in the United States. The SEC also charged that the chairman of the company secretly siphoned $40 million from the company's account at the Agricultural Bank of China.
- In May 2012, Sino-Forest was charged with false claims to have purchased Chinese standing timber in 2007 that it had already purchased through a subsidiary earlier that year. The so-called Gengma Fraud #1 resulted in an overstatement of Sino-Forest's timber holdings in the years through 2007–2009. Sino-Forest purportedly sold the timber in 2010 and then offered the same assets as collateral for a bank loan in 2011. The transaction overstated the company's revenue in the second quarter of 2010 by 52 percent, or $157.8 million, according to the SEC.
- In November 2012, the SEC charged that Longtop Financial fraudulently maintained above-market operating and gross margins by disguising expenses through a series of off-balance-sheet transfers to a wholly owned entity. In addition, the company claimed false bank balances and failed to confirm the amounts.
- In January 2013, Caterpillar's Chinese subsidiary put through a $580 million charge relating to an acquisition that Caterpillar made in China during 2012. It paid $800 million for the company, Siwei, but the target company's management team had apparently been fudging the books for quite a while before that, leading Caterpillar to overpay wildly for the acquisition. Among other things, the company inappropriately capitalized costs to inventory to overstate profits rather than expense them.
- On February 28, 2013, Keyuan Petrochemicals Inc., a China-based petrochemical company, agreed to pay $1 million to settle securities fraud charges in the United States for failing to disclose to investors related-party transactions involving its CEO and others, as well as maintaining an off-balance-sheet account to pay bonuses to senior officers and fund other expenses.

In light of the increased disclosures of accounting fraud and corruption at Chinese companies, the Chinese government began to do considerably more detailed audits of state-owned enterprises in 2013. Some critics believe that there is a growing crisis in China involving bad corporate governance that needs to be addressed immediately in order to prevent a major economic crisis in the future.[70]

Beginning in the late 2010, alleged financial frauds and serious accounting issues were revealed at a number of the smaller Chinese reverse merger companies. The problems created by such actions were explained in a speech by PCAOB board member Lewis Ferguson at California State University's (Fullerton) SEC Financial Reporting Conference in Irvine, California in September 2012:[71]

> To date, 67 of these China-based issuers have had their auditor resign, and 126 issuers have either been delisted from U.S. securities exchanges or "gone dark"—meaning that they are no longer filing current reports with the SEC. Billions of dollars of market capitalization of such companies have been lost in U.S. securities markets and it is fair to say that all of these smaller China-based companies listed on U.S. securities exchanges have suffered serious losses of both market value and investor confidence as a result of the problems of other companies.

Ferguson notes that many of the smaller Chinese companies most commonly sought access to U.S. markets by merging with existing, registered U.S. shell companies in reverse mergers, while the larger companies filed IPOs. A PCAOB study showed that in the United States alone, between January 1, 2007, and March 31, 2010, 159 Chinese companies entered the U.S. securities markets using reverse mergers and generated market capitalization of $12.8 billion.[72]

During the past several years, there have been a variety of investigations of U.S. audit firms with Chinese clients. In December 2012, it was reported that the SEC had charged the Chinese affiliates of Ernst & Young, PricewaterhouseCoopers (PwC), KPMG, Deloitte Touche Tohmatsu, and BDO China Dahua with violating U.S. securities law after the five firms failed to turn over audit work papers in connection with nine Chinese companies accused of potential accounting fraud.[73]

The issue is not so much the actions of the auditors as the deadlock between the SEC and the Chinese government, which derives essentially from a conflict in the laws of the two jurisdictions. As mentioned in the beginning of this chapter, the Chinese see SEC regulations as a challenge to its sovereignty, given that a number of companies listed in the United States are state-owned, with the Chinese government being the majority shareholder. While under U.S. securities laws, the SEC is empowered to investigate alleged fraud and require the production of audit work papers from non-U.S. accounting firms. Inspections of U.S. accounting firms in their overseas practices are required by the PCAOB. However, the audit work papers needed for such inspections constitute state secrets under Chinese laws and cannot be provided.

The PCAOB has become increasingly worried about fraud at Chinese companies. The board is seeking the ability to inspect Chinese auditing firms after accusations arose in recent years of accounting irregularities at a number of Chinese companies that trade on U.S. markets. It was announced in September 2012 that a preliminary agreement had been reached. "As a first step toward further cooperation, we are working toward and have tentatively agreed on observational visits where PCAOB inspectors would observe the Chinese authorities conducting their own audit oversight activities and the Chinese could observe the PCAOB at work," according to Lewis Ferguson. "This would not be a substitute for a PCAOB inspection but would be a trust-building exercise between regulators. Initially, such observations would focus on quality control examinations of the audit firm being examined rather than a substantive review of a specific audit. We hope such exercises will build trust and lead to further cooperation."[74]

To summarize, the main problems of corporate governance in China are:

- A high degree of state ownership of listed companies, resulting in oppression of minority shareholders.
- Separation of ownership and management control not clearly defined.
- Interference by the state in company management issues.
- Majority of directors are "inside" or executive directors; few independent directors lead to insider control.
- Lack of transparency and information disclosure.
- Lack of accountability of SOEs.
- Lax oversight by the China Securities Regulatory Commission (CSRC).

## Corporate Governance in India

Unlike China, where governance requirements exist in a corporate code, in India, various committees have studied governance and issued a variety of recommended guidelines. For example, the Kumar Mangalam Birla Committee on Corporate Governance suggests that there should be a separate section on corporate governance compliance in the annual report highlighting noncompliance with any of the mandatory recommendations and the reasons thereof.[75] This resembles the "comply or explain" provision in the codes of German companies. The auditors should also attest to the compliance of the corporate governance; recommendations and certification should be submitted to the relevant stock exchange.

There are many similarities between corporate governance systems in the U.S. and India, probably due to the historical influence of the U.K. on U.S. business structure and the longstanding influence of the U.K. in India. One major difference is that corporate conglomerates such as the Tata group in India wield great power over the economy.*

Exhibit 8.9 addresses both similarities and differences that exist in corporate governance provisions in the U.S. and India.

**EXHIBIT 8.9**

**Summary of Governance in Indian Companies Compared to the U.S.**

1. India has more diverse share ownership than in the U.S., including family and some government ownership.
2. In India, between only 33 and 50 percent of directors need to be independent, whereas a majority is required in the U.S.
3. Listed companies must have audit committees with a minimum of three directors, two-thirds of whom must be independent, whereas all three must be independent in the U.S.
4. Independence of directors can be problematic in Indian systems due to the influence of family businesses and blockholder owners. For the most part, this is not a problem in the U.S. because of SOX and the NYSE listing requirements that dictate there should be a majority of independent directors.
5. The CEO and CFO of listed companies must certify that the financial statements are fair and accept responsibility for internal controls. This is similar to U.S. requirements for audited financial statements and the assessment of management's report on internal controls.
6. Annual reports of listed companies must carry status reports about compliance with corporate governance norms. External auditors issue a certificate of assessment of compliance of corporate governance rules to be filed with the stock exchanges in India; similar requirements exist under NYSE listing requirements.
7. The Indian corporate governance system requires businesses to comply or explain any noncompliance with mandatory recommendations. Compliance explanations are also required in the U.S. under NYSE listing requirements.

An important issue in India is the lack of independent members of the board of directors in practice, notwithstanding requirements to the contrary. Many companies are traditionally owned by families whose members are part of management as well as the board of directors, making it difficult to have a level of independence that serves as a check on management behavior. According to Rajagopalan and Zhang, 45 percent of all Indian companies are family controlled.[76] The key challenge for India going forward is to strictly enforce corporate governance requirements and make recommended practices mandatory.

# CLSA Corporate Governance Watch 2012

According to the CLSA Corporate Governance Watch 2012 list, produced in collaboration with the Asian Corporate Governance Association, India's corporate governance score has improved by three percentage points between 2007 and 2012, but the ranking has remained the same. On the other hand, China's score has declined by four points and its ranking has

---

*The Tata group comprises over 100 operating companies in seven business sectors: communications and information technology, engineering, materials, services, energy, consumer products and chemicals. The group has operations in more than 80 countries across six continents, and its companies export products and services to 85 countries. The total revenue of Tata companies, taken together, was $100.09 billion in 2011–12, with 58 percent of this coming from business outside India. Tata companies employ over 450,000 people worldwide. Every Tata company or enterprise operates independently. Each of these companies has its own board of directors and shareholders, to whom it is answerable.

gone down two places. Exhibit 8.10 summarizes the rankings and Exhibit 8.11 provides the criteria used for the rankings. In each case, the reported score is based on a maximum of 100 percent. Of particular note is the low score for China in enforcement and corporate governance culture. This is consistent with the concerns that have been expressed about the number of accounting frauds in Chinese companies and lack of cooperation of Chinese regulators with the SEC as it tries to investigate such matters.

**EXHIBIT 8.10**
CLSA Asia-Pacific
Markets: Corporate
Governance Watch
2012*

| CG Watch Market Scores: 2007–2012 (percentages) | | | | |
|---|---|---|---|---|
| Market Category Scores | 2007 | 2010 | 2012 | Change 2012 vs. 2010 (% points) |
| 1. Singapore | 65 | 67 | 69 | (+2) |
| 2. Hong Kong | 67 | 65 | 66 | (+1) |
| 3. Thailand | 47 | 55 | 58 | (+3) |
| 4. Japan (tie) | 52 | 57 | 55 | (−2) |
| 4. Malaysia (tie) | 49 | 52 | 55 | (+3) |
| 6. Taiwan | 54 | 55 | 53 | (−2) |
| 7. India | 56 | 48 | 51 | (+3) |
| 8. Republic of Korea (South Korea) | 49 | 45 | 49 | (+4) |
| 9. China | 45 | 49 | 45 | (−4) |
| 10. Philippines | 41 | 37 | 41 | (+4) |
| 11. Indonesia | 37 | 40 | 37 | (−3) |

*Asian Corporate Governance Association (ACGA) "CG Watch 2012: Market Rankings," September 2012. Available at https://www.clsa.com/about-clsa/media-centre/2012-media-releases/corporate-governance-watch-2012cracks-in-asian-corporate-governance-reappear-in-recent-years.php.

**EXHIBIT 8.11**
CLSA Asia-Pacific
Markets: Corporate
Governance Watch
2012*

| Factors Used to Rate Corporate Governance (percentages) | | | | | |
|---|---|---|---|---|---|
| Market Category Scores | Total | CG Rules and Practices | Enforcement | Political and Regulatory | CG Culture |
| 1. Singapore | 69 | 68 | 64 | 73 | 54 |
| 2. Hong Kong | 66 | 62 | 68 | 71 | 53 |
| 3. Thailand | 58 | 62 | 44 | 54 | 50 |
| 4. Japan (tie) | 55 | 45 | 57 | 52 | 53 |
| 5. Malaysia (tie) | 55 | 52 | 39 | 63 | 38 |
| 6. Taiwan | 53 | 50 | 35 | 56 | 46 |
| 7. India | 51 | 49 | 42 | 56 | 43 |
| 8. Republic of Korea (South Korea) | 49 | 43 | 39 | 56 | 34 |
| 9. China | 45 | 43 | 33 | 46 | 30 |
| 10. Philippines | 41 | 35 | 25 | 44 | 29 |
| 11. Indonesia | 37 | 35 | 22 | 33 | 33 |

*Asian Corporate Governance Association (ACGA) "CG Watch 2012: Market Rankings," September 2012. Available at https://www.clsa.com/about-clsa/media-centre/2012-media-releases/corporate-governance-watch-2012cracks-in-asian-corporate-governance-reappear-in-recent-years.php.

## Concluding Thoughts

Ethical behavior takes on a new meaning in the context of international business. Multinationals must adhere to the laws of host countries, as well as their home country. While ethical standards may vary, one truth does not: Honesty, integrity, and trust are the bases for sound business relationships.

We are always on the lookout for inspiring codes of ethics or values statements of companies to pass along to our students, especially to end a course on a positive note. We found such a statement in Starbuck's Standards of Business Conduct, which addresses the company's ethical responsibilities in international business. Interestingly, the Foreign Corrupt Practices Act (FCPA) in the U.S. and the U.K. Bribery Act contains some of the same language.

Starbuck's statement speaks volumes about the integrity of the company and expectations for ethical behavior on the part of its stakeholders. Here is an excerpt:

> Starbucks is committed to the highest ethical standards in all business transactions. Partners must follow all applicable laws, rules, and regulations when conducting Starbucks business. Payments made to any foreign agent or government official must be lawful under the laws of the U.S. and the foreign country. Payments by or on behalf of Starbucks to foreign agents or government officials should always be strictly for services rendered and should be reasonable in amount given the nature of those services. Under no circumstances may a partner make payments in violation of the law or to induce government officials to do business with Starbucks. Starbucks partners at no time are permitted to influence the outcome of any business decision by exchanging bribes or kickbacks of any kind.[77]

It has been said that "good ethics is good business." We prefer to think of ethics as a limit to, a constraint on, or a correction to what business may do as business *per se*. Ethical business practices include ensuring that the highest legal and moral standards are observed in relationships with people in the organization and stakeholders that are affected by top management's actions and decisions. The laws never can cover every situation so ethical judgment is needed to make the tough calls when the laws are unclear or nonexistent.

We end our journey at the same place that we started. A strong ethics foundation is essential to act in accordance with the established standards of ethical behavior whether a company operates solely in the U.S. or in the U.S. and overseas. While standards of business practice, legal requirements, and culture may differ between countries, one thing is common to all—a high set of ethical standards are required for accountants and auditors to protect the public interest.

An ability to make ethical, reasoned judgments enables the accounting decision maker to meet professional standards and act in accordance with the public trust. We advocate the use of ethical reasoning and ethical decision-making processes to analyze ethical issues and decide on a proper course of action. However, no decision-making process can take the place of wanting to be an ethical person—doing the right thing—and be willing to carry through ethical judgment with ethical action in spite of obstacles to do otherwise. The motivation to act ethically needs to be matched by the willingness to do what it takes to make your point of view known to those in the organization who might pressure you to go along with financial wrongdoing. We leave you with this message: Don't be afraid to stand up for what you believe in your core values. Don't take short cuts and don't let others influence you to act in a way that violates ethical and professional standards. Remember that it takes a long time to build a reputation for trust in business, but that reputation can be destroyed in an instant.

## Discussion Questions

1. In this chapter, we discuss problems encountered by the PCAOB in gaining access to inspect work papers of audits by U.S. international accounting firms of Chinese companies. Explain why these problems exist, including cultural, legal, and ethical considerations.

2. What are the costs and benefits of establishing one set of accounting standards (i.e., IFRS) around the world? How do cultural factors, legal systems, and ethics influence your answer? Apply a utilitarian approach in making the analysis.

3. What are the fundamental principles of professional ethics for professional accountants identified by the IESBA and included in the IFAC Code of Ethics? How do these principles relate to the proposed standards for responding to suspected illegal acts in the IESBA exposure draft with respect to whistleblowing obligations of accountants and auditors?

4. The Institute of Chartered Accountants in England and Wales (ICAEW) has adopted a code of ethics based on the IFAC Code. In commenting on the principles-based approach used in these codes, the ICAEW states that a principles approach "focuses on the spirit of the guidance and

encourage responsibility and the exercise of professional judgment, which are key elements of professions." Explain what you believe this statement means.[78]

5. Consider the practice of making "facilitating payments" to foreign officials and others as part of doing business abroad in the context of the following statement:

> International companies are confronted with a variety of decisions that create ethical dilemmas for the decision makers. "Right-wrong," "just-unjust" derive their meaning and true value from the attitudes of a given culture. Some ethical standards are culture-specific, and we should not be surprised to find that an act that is considered quite ethical in one culture may be looked upon with disregard in another.

   Explain how culture interacts with the acceptability of making facilitating payments in a country. Use Rights Theory and Justice reasoning to analyze the ethics of allowing facilitating payments such as under the FCPA in the U.S. and prohibiting them as under the U.K. Bribery Act.

6. Do you believe that "one size fits all" with respect to corporate governance provisions in different countries around the world? Why or why not? How do legal and cultural factors influence corporate governance provisions in the U.S., Germany, China, and India?

7. Describe the different kinds of reserves that can be recorded. How do the reserves relate to the discretionary accruals discussed in Chapter 7? Can the accounting for reserves lead to a manipulation of earnings? Do you believe it would be more or less prevalent under IFRS or GAAP?

8. Critics of the IFRS argue that the more principles-based IFRS is not as precise as, and therefore is easier to manipulate than, the more rules-based GAAP. The reason for this is that IFRS requires more professional judgment from both auditors and corporate accountants with regard to the practical application of the rules. The application of professional judgment opens the door to increased opportunities for earnings management. Do you agree with these concerns expressed about principles-based IFRS? Relate your discussion to the research results discussed in this chapter.

9. What is the difference between legal and ethical compliance with corporate governance provisions? Discuss what might be the ethical compliance mechanisms from a virtue ethics perspective.

10. What is the purpose of having a two-tier system of boards of directors in countries such as Germany? How does the dual-board approach ameliorate the potential conflicts in the principal-agent relationship between investor and manager?

11. What is meant by the "true and fair view" override? When might it be applied? Do you think that the application of this principle leads to more useful financial statements from a representational faithfulness perspective? Why or why not?

12. One provision of the U.K. Bribery Act is that it applies to bribes that occur anywhere in the world by non-U.K. companies that conduct any part of their business in the United Kingdom. For example, the Bribery Act would cover a company that has a few employees working in the United Kingdom or that simply sells its goods or services in the United Kingdom. Evaluate this policy from an ethical perspective using ethical reasoning. In particular, do you think the policy is fair? Is it right?

13. Is the "comply or explain" principle an ethical approach to corporate governance? Why or why not?

14. What is the purpose of having a Global Code of Ethics? Do you think a Global Code, such as the IFAC Code, is necessary, given that codes of ethics already exist for public companies in virtually all countries?

15. IFRS for SMEs has been referred to as "IFRS lite." One of the differences between full IFRS and IFRS for SMEs is that full IFRS allows for judgment in making choices about proper accounting, whereas IFRS for SMEs is much more rigid. From a stakeholder perspective, do you think there should be a separate set of international accounting standards for small and medium-sized entities? Why or why not?

16. How do Gray's accounting values establish a basis for financial reporting in countries with different cultural systems?

17. How might earnings management practices serve to project the managerial style of firms in managing the earnings of the firms? Explain how cultural variables, such as those identified by Gray and discussed in this chapter, might impact managerial style and earnings management techniques?

18. Ernst & Young released its 2011 European Fraud survey[79] that includes a warning against the manipulation of asset impairment writedowns due to the subjective factors used and judgment

needed to draw conclusions about the proper amount of writedowns. The PCAOB found 123 audit deficiencies related to asset-valuation problems found among clients of the Big Four accounting firms in 2010, making asset valuation the most common audit problem. How do the rules for determining the impairment of long-lived assets explained in the chapter contribute to the possibility of audit deficiencies? Is this an area where GAAP should be converged with IFRS, or vice versa?

19. The 2011 Bribe Payers Index by Transparency International (TI) ranks the world's largest economies according to the likelihood of firms from these countries to bribe when doing business abroad. TI asked 3,016 senior business executives in 28 countries around the world for their perceptions of the likelihood of companies from countries they have business dealings with to engage in bribery when doing business in the executive's country. Countries are scored on a scale of 0–10, where a maximum score of 10 corresponds with the view that the companies from that country *never* bribe, and a 0 corresponds with the view that they *always* do. Here are the rankings.

| Transparency International 2011 Bribe Payer's Index* | | |
|---|---|---|
| **Rank** | **Country/Territory** | **SCORE** |
| 1 | Netherlands (tie) | 8.8 |
| 1 | Switzerland (tie) | 8.8 |
| 3 | Belgium | 8.7 |
| 4 | Germany (tie) | 8.6 |
| 4 | Japan (tie) | 8.6 |
| 6 | Australia (tie) | 8.5 |
| 6 | Canada (tie) | 8.5 |
| 8 | Singapore (tie) | 8.3 |
| 8 | United Kingdom (tie) | 8.3 |
| 10 | U.S. | 8.1 |
| 11 | France (tie) | 8.0 |
| 11 | Spain (tie) | 8.0 |
| 13 | Republic of Korea (South Korea) | 7.9 |
| 14 | Brazil | 7.7 |
| 15 | Hong Kong (tie) | 7.6 |
| 15 | Italy (tie) | 7.6 |
| 15 | Malaysia (tie) | 7.6 |
| 15 | South Africa (tie) | 7.6 |
| 19 | Taiwan (tie) | 7.5 |
| 19 | India (tie) | 7.5 |
| 19 | Turkey (tie) | 7.5 |
| 22 | Saudi Arabia | 7.4 |
| 23 | Argentina (tie) | 7.3 |
| 23 | United Arab Emirates (tie) | 7.3 |
| 25 | Indonesia | 7.1 |
| 26 | Mexico | 7.0 |
| 27 | China | 6.5 |
| 28 | Russia | 6.1 |
| **Average** | | **7.8** |

*Transparency International 2011 Bribe Payer's Index. Available at www.bpi.transparency.org/bpi2011/in_detail/.

From a cultural and a corporate governance perspective, are you surprised by the results for Germany (#4), the United States (#10), India (#19), and China (#27)? What are the ethical implications for a U.S. company doing business in each of these countries?

20. The issue of responsibility is foundational to understanding organizational ethics. Explain what this means in a global context.

## Endnotes

1. Floyd Norris, "Sorting out a Chinese Puzzle in Auditing," *New York Times,* December 6, 2012. Available at www.nytimes.com/2012/12/07/business/sorting-out-a-chinese-puzzle-in-auditing .html?pagewanted=all.

2. Tom Schoenberg, "Deloitte Loses Bid to Delay SEC Suit Over China Documents," *Bloomberg,* April 22, 2013, Available at http://www.bloomberg.com/news/2013-04-22/deloitte-loses-bid-to-delay-sec-suit-over-china-documents.html.

3. George T. Tsakumis, David R. Campbell Sr., and Timothy Doupnik, "IFRS: Beyond the Standards," *Journal of Accountancy,* February 2009. Available at www.journalofaccountancy .com/Issues/2009/Feb/IFRSBeyondtheStandards.

4. SEC Concepts Release 33-8831, August 2007, page 30. Available at www.sec.gov/rules/ concept/2007/33-8831.pdf.

5. Tsakumis et al.

6. Sidney J. Gray, "Towards a Theory of Cultural Influence on the Development of Accounting Systems Internationally," *Abacus,* March 1988, pp. 1–15.

7. International Federation of Accountants (IFAC), *Rebuilding Public Confidence in Financial Reporting: An International Perspective.* 2003. New York: IFAC.

8. International Federation of Accountants (IFAC), *A Public Interest Framework for the Accountancy Profession.* IFAC Policy Position Paper #4. (2010). New York: IFAC.

9. International Ethics Standards Board for Accountants (IESBA), *Handbook of the Code of Ethics for Professional Accountants.* 2012. New York: IFAC.

10. International Accounting Education Standards Board (IAESB), *Approaches to the Development and Maintenance of Professional Values, Ethics and Attitudes in Accounting Education Programs.* Information Paper (2006). New York: IFAC.

11. IAESB.

12. Stephen Zeff, "The Evolution of the IASC into the IASB, and the Challenges It Faces," Available at www.globalcoe-waseda-law-commerce.org/20110120Zeff_summary.pdf.

13. Timothy Doupnik and Hector Perera, *International Accounting,* 3d ed. (New York: McGraw-Hill Irwin, 2012).

14. Available at www.iosco.org/about/.

15. Available at www.fasb.org/jsp/FASB/Page/SectionPage&cid=1175801857384&pid=1218 220079468.

16. PricewaterhouseCoopers, *IFRS Adoption by Country,* April 2012, Available at http://www.pwc .com/en_US/us/issues/ifrs-reporting/publications/assets/pwc-ifrs-by-country-apr-2012.pdf.

17. International Accounting Standards Board (IASB), *Memorandum of Understanding—FASB and IASB: "The Norwalk Agreement,"* 2002. Available at www.iasb.org.

18. IASB, *A Road Map for Convergence Between IFRS and U.S. GAAP—2006–2008: Memorandum of Understanding between FASB and the IASB.* 2006. Available at www.iasb.org.

19. IASB, *IAS 23: Borrowing Costs.* Available at www.ifrs.org/Documents/IAS23.pdf.

20. FASB, Summary of Statement No. 154, "Accounting Changes and Error Corrections—A Replacement of APB Opinion No. 20 and FASB Statement No. 3." Available at www.fasb.org/ summary/stsum154.shtml.

21. *Mandatory IFRS Adoption and Accounting Quality: Evidence from the European Union.* Available at www.afaanz.org/openconf/2009/modules/request.php?module=oc_program&action=view.php& id=104.

22. Ken Tysiac, "Study by UK Researchers Shows Inconsistency in IFRS Application," *Journal of Accountancy,* January 25, 2013. Available at www.journalofaccountancy.com/news/20137251 .htm#sthash.cuR8jgIc.dpuf.

23. "Work Plan for the Consideration of Incorporating International Financial Reporting Standards into the Financial Reporting System for U.S. Issuers: Exploring a Possible Method of Incorporation," A Securities and Exchange Commission Staff Paper, May 26, 2011. Available at www.sec.gov/spotlight/globalaccountingstandards/ifrs-work-plan-paper-052611.pdf.

24. Tom Selling, "Let the 'Condorsement' Games Begin," *Accounting Onion*, August 18, 2011. Available at www.accountingonion.typepad.com/theaccountingonion/2011/08/let-the-condorsement-games-begin.html.

25. Marie Leone, "Day of the Condorsement," *CFO.com*. Available at www.cfo.com/blogs/index.cfm/detail/14580742.

26. Roger Hussey and Audry Ong, *International Financial Reporting Standards: Desk Reference* (New York: Wiley, 2006).

27. Joseph C. Sanders, Deborah L. Lindberg, and Deborah L. Seifert, "Is IFRS for SMEs a Beneficial Alternative for Private Companies?" *The CPA Journal* (February 2013), pp. 32–35.

28. SEC, *Study Pursuant to Section 108(d) of the Sarbanes-Oxley Act of 2002 on the Adoption by the U.S. Financial Reporting System of a Principles-Based Accounting System, 2003,* submitted to the Committee on Banking, Housing, and Urban Affairs of the U.S. Senate and Committee on Financial Services of the U.S. House of Representatives, www.sec.gov/news/studies/principles basedstand.htm#executive.

29. R. D. Mergenthaler, *Principles-Based versus Rules-Based Accounting Standards and Extreme Cases of Earnings Management,* a dissertation prepared for the University of Washington, 2008.

30. Thomas Jeanjean and Herve H. Stolowy, "Do Accounting Standards Matter? An Exploratory Analysis of Earnings Management before and after IFRS Adoption," *Journal of Accounting and Public Policy* 27(6) (2008), pp. 480–494.

31. Financial Accounting Standards Board, *Principles-based Approach to Standard Setting* (2002). Available at www.fasb.org/news/nr102102.shtml.

32. Herz, R. H., "A Year of Challenge and Change for the FASB," *Accounting Horizons* 17 (2003), pp. 247–255.

33. David Folsom, Paul Hribar, Rick Mergenthaler, and Kyle Peterson, "Principles-Based Standards and Earnings Attributes" (April 25, 2012). Available at SSRN: www.ssrn.com/abstract=2046190 or www.dx.doi.org/10.2139/ssrn.2046190.

34. International Accounting Standards Board, *IAS No. 17, Accounting for Leases,* 2007, www.iasb.org.

35. International Accounting Standards Board, *IAS No. 16, Accounting for Property, Plant and Equipment,* 2007, Available at www.iasb.org.

36. G. J. Benston, M. Bromwich, and A. Wagenhofer, "Principles- versus Rules-Based Accounting Standards: The FASB's Standards Setting Strategy," *Abacus* 42(2) (2006), pp. 165–188.

37. FASB, *Accounting for the Impairment or Disposal of Long-Lived Assets, Statement of Financial Accounting Standards No. 144* (August 2001). Available at www.journalofaccountancy.com/issues/2002/mar/assetimpairmentanddisposal.htm.

38. International Accounting Standards Board, *IAS No. 36, Impairment of Assets* (July 1999). Available at www.iasb.org.

39. International Accounting Standards Board, *IAS No. 37, Contingent Liabilities and Contingent Assets,* 2007. Available at www.iasb.org.

40. Christopher Nobes and Robert Parker, *Comparative International Accounting,* 10th ed. (London, England: Pearson Education Limited, 2008).

41. Certified Institute of Management Accountants, *CIMA Code of Ethics* (October 2010). Available at http://www.cimaglobal.com/Documents/Professional%20ethics%20docs/code%20FINAL.pdf.

42. CIMA, *CGMA Report: Managing Responsible Business: A Global Survey on Business Ethics,* 2012. Available at www.cgma.org/Resources/Reports/DownloadableDocuments/CGMA%20Ethics%20Report%20FINAL.pdf.

43. International Federation of Accountants, International Ethics Standards Board for Accountants, *Handbook of the Code of Ethics for Professional Accountants,* 2012 Edition. Available at www.ifac.org/sites/default/files/publications/files/2012-IESBA-Handbook.pdf.

44. www.icac.org.jm/pdf/24_3.pdf.

45. Association of Certified Fraud Examiners, *2012 Global Fraud Study: Report to the Nations on Occupational Fraud and Abuse,* www.acfe.com/uploadedFiles/ACFE_Website/Content/rttn/2012-report-to-nations.pdf.

46. *Kroll 2012 Global Fraud Report.* Available at www.krolladvisory.com/media/pdfs/KRL_FraudReport2011-12_US.pdf.

47. *Kroll 2012 Global Fraud Report.*

48. *Kroll 2012 Global Fraud Report.*

49. *Kroll 2012 Global Fraud Report.*

50. *Kroll 2012 Global Fraud Report.*

51. *Kroll 2012 Global Fraud Report.*

52. UK Ministry of Justice, UK Bribery Act 2010. Available at www.legislation.gov.uk/ukpga/2010/23/contents.

53. UK Bribery Act 2010.

54. Available at www.transparency.org.uk/our-work/bribery-act.

55. UK Bribery Act 2010.

56. Available at blogs.wsj.com/corruption-currents/2012/06/25/companies-show-little-concern-about-uk-bribery-act-enforcement/.

57. International Ethics Standards Board for Accountants (IESBA), *Responding to a Suspected Illegal Act: Exposure Draft* (August 2012). Available at www.ifac.org/sites/default/files/publications/files/IESBA-Code-of-Ethics-Illegal-Acts-Exposure-Draft.pdf.

58. Curtis C. Verschoor, "Proposed Whistleblower Standard Presents Challenges," October 4, 2102. Available at www.accountingweb.com/article/proposed-whistleblower-standard-presents-challenges/219977.

59. IESBA, *Responding to a Suspected Illegal Act.*

60. IESBA, *Responding to a Suspected Illegal Act.*

61. IESBA, *Responding to a Suspected Illegal Act.*

62. UK Public Interest Disclosure Act 1998. Available at www.legislation.gov.uk/ukpga/1998/23/contents.

63. Available at www.ifac.org/sites/default/files/publications/exposure-drafts/comments/ICAA%20Submission%20to%20IESBA%20Responding%20to%20a%20Suspected%20Illegal%20Act%20181212.pdf.

64. Available at www.aicpa.org/interestareas/professionalethics/community/commentletters/downloadabledocuments/aicpapeeccommentletteroniesbarespondingtoasuspectedillegalact.pdf.

65. Rafael La Porta, Florencio Lopez-de-Silane, Andrei Shleifer, and Robert Vishny, "Investor Protection and Corporate Governance," *Journal of Financial Economics* 58 (1–2) (July 2000), pp. 3–27.

66. A. Dyck and L. Zingales, "Private Benefits of Control: An International Comparison," *Journal of Finance* 59(2) (2004), pp. 537–600.

67. A. N. Licht, C. Goldschmidt, and S. H. Schwartz, "Culture, Law, and Corporate Governance," *International Review of Law and Economics,* 25 (2) (2005), pp. 229–255.

68. German Corporate Governance Code 2009; www.corporate-governance-code.de/eng/kodex/index.html.

69. China Securities Regulatory Commission (CSRC), State Economic and Trade Commission, Code of Corporate Governance for Listed Companies in China, January 7, 2001, www.csrc.gov.cn/en/jip.

70. Eric Jackson, "Why Corporate Governance Is So Important to China," July 6, 2011. Available at www.forbes.com/sites/ericjackson/2011/07/06/why-corporate-governance-is-so-important-to-china/.

71. Michael Cohn, "PCAOB Makes Tentative Progress on Chinese Audit Firm Inspections," September 24, 2012. Available at www.forbes.com/sites/ericjackson/2011/07/06/why-corporate-governance-is-so-important-to-china/.

72. Cohn.

73. Junheng Li, "Actions Against China Auditors: SEC Walks a Tightrope," December 13, 2012. Available at www.forbes.com/sites/junhli/2012/12/13/actions-against-china-auditors-sec-walks-a-tightrope/.

74. Cohn.

75. *Report of the Kumar Mangalam Birla Committee on Corporate Governance*, 2000, www.sebi .gov.in/commreport/corpgov.html.

76. N. Rajagopalan and Y. Zhang, "Corporate Governance Reforms in China and India: Challenges and Opportunities," *Business Horizons* 21 (2008), pp. 55–64.

77. Starbucks Standards of Business Conduct. Available at www.globalassets.starbucks.com/assets/ eecd184d6d2141d58966319744393d1f.pdf.

78. Statement Available at http://www.icaew.com/en/technical/ethics/icaew-code-of-ethics.

79. Ernst & Young, *European Fraud Survey 2011*, Available at: http://www.ey.com/GL/en/Services/ Assurance/Fraud-Investigation—Dispute-Services/European-fraud-survey-2011–recovery– regulation-and-integrity.

# Chapter 8 Cases

## Case 8-1

# *SEC v. Siemens Aktiengesellschaft*

On December 15, 2008, the SEC filed a lawsuit against Siemens Aktiengesellschaft (*Aktiengesellschaft* is German for "corporation"), charging the Munich, Germany–based manufacturer of industrial and consumer products with violations of the antibribery, books and records, and internal controls provisions of the FCPA. The SEC has the authority to bring this action because Siemens stock is listed on the NYSE. Siemens agreed to pay a total of $1.6 billion in disgorgement and fines, which is the largest amount a company has ever paid to resolve corruption-related charges. The company also agreed to pay $350 million in disgorgement to the SEC. In related actions, Siemens will pay a $450 million criminal fine to the U.S. Department of Justice (DOJ) and a fine of $569 million to the Office of the Prosecutor General in Munich, Germany. Siemens previously paid a fine of $285 million to the Munich prosecutor in October 2007. The SEC released a summary of its litigation in this matter, which is summarized in the following paragraphs.[1]

## Summary of Litigation

Between March 12, 2001, and September 30, 2007, Siemens violated the FCPA by engaging in a widespread and systematic practice of paying bribes to foreign government officials to obtain business. Siemens created elaborate payment schemes to conceal the nature of its corrupt payments, and the company's inadequate internal controls allowed the conduct to flourish. The misconduct involved employees at all levels, including former senior management, and revealed a corporate culture long at odds with the FCPA.

During this period, Siemens made thousands of payments to third parties in ways that obscured the purpose for, and the ultimate recipients of, the money. At least 4,283 of those payments, totaling approximately $1.4 billion, were used to bribe government officials in return for giving business to Siemens around the world. Among others, Siemens paid bribes on transactions to design and build metro transit lines in Venezuela; metro trains and signaling devices in China; power plants in Israel; high-voltage transmission lines in China; mobile telephone networks in Bangladesh; telecommunications projects in Nigeria; national identity cards in Argentina; medical devices in Vietnam, China, and Russia; traffic control systems in Russia; refineries in Mexico; and mobile communications networks in Vietnam. Siemens also paid kickbacks to Iraqi ministries in connection with sales of power stations and equipment to Iraq under the Oil for Food Program of the United Nations (UN). Siemens earned over

$1.1 billion in profits on these transactions. An additional 1,185 separate payments to third parties were made totaling approximately $391 million, These payments were not properly controlled and were used, at least in part, for illicit purposes, including commercial bribery and embezzlement.

From 1999 to 2003, Siemens's Management Board was ineffective in implementing controls to address constraints imposed by Germany's 1999 adoption of the Organization for Economic Co-operation and Development (OECD) anti-bribery convention that outlawed foreign bribery. The Management Board was also ineffective in meeting the U.S. regulatory and antibribery requirements that Siemens was subject to following its March 12, 2001, listing on the NYSE. Despite knowledge of bribery at two of its largest groups— Communications and Power Generation—top management was tone-deaf to the internal environment it had developed and created a corporate culture in which bribery was tolerated (and even rewarded) at the highest levels of the company. Employees obtained large amounts of cash from cash desks, which were sometimes transported in suitcases across international borders for bribery. Written authorizations for payments were removed later to eradicate any permanent record. Siemens used numerous slush funds, off-books accounts maintained at unconsolidated entities, and a system of business consultants and intermediaries to facilitate the corrupt payments.

Siemens failed to implement adequate internal controls to detect and prevent violations of the FCPA. Elaborate payment mechanisms were used to conceal the fact that bribe payments were made around the globe to obtain business. False invoices and payment documentation were created to make payments to business consultants under false business consultant agreements that identified services that were never intended to be rendered. Illicit payments were falsely recorded as expenses for management fees, consulting fees, supply contracts, room preparation fees, and commissions. Siemens inflated contracts with the United Nations (UN), signed side agreements with Iraqi ministries that were not disclosed to the UN, and recorded the after-sale-service-charge (ASSF) payments as legitimate commissions despite UN, U.S., and international sanctions against such payments.

In November 2006, Siemens's current management began to implement reforms to the company's internal controls. These reforms substantially reduced, but did not entirely eliminate, the corrupt payments. All but $27.5 million of the corrupt payments occurred before November 15, 2006. The company conducted a massive internal investigation and implemented an amnesty program to its employees to gather information.

The success of Siemens's bribery system was maintained by lax internal controls over corruption-related activities and an acceptance of such activities by members of senior

[1] *Securities and Exchange Commission v. Siemens Aktiengesellschaft,* Case 1.08-cv-02167, Litigation Release No. 20829, Accounting and Enforcement Release No. 2911, December 15, 2008, www.sec.gov/litigation/litreleases/2008/lr20829.htm.

management and the compliance, internal audit, legal, and finance departments. Siemens violated Section 30A of the Securities Exchange Act of 1934 by making illicit payments to foreign government officials in order to obtain or retain business. Siemens violated Section 13(b)(2)(B) of the Exchange Act by failing to have adequate internal controls to detect and prevent the payments. Siemens violated Section 13(b)(2)(A) of the Exchange Act by improperly recording the payments in its books.

Without admitting or denying the commission's allegations, Siemens consented to the entry of a court order permanently enjoining it from future violations of the Exchange Act; ordering it to pay $350 million in disgorgement of wrongful profits, which does not include profits factored into Munich's fine; and ordering it to comply with certain undertakings regarding its FCPA compliance program, including an independent monitor for a period of four years. On December 15, 2008, the court entered the final judgment. Since being approached by SEC staff, Siemens has cooperated fully with the ongoing investigation, and the SEC considered the remedial acts promptly undertaken by Siemens. Siemens's massive internal investigation and lower-level-employee amnesty program were essential in gathering facts regarding the full extent of Siemens's FCPA violations.

## Charges Against the Management Board

The following charges were made against Siemens's Management Board:

1. The board was ineffective in meeting the U.S. regulatory and antibribery requirements that Siemens was subject to following its listing on the NYSE on March 12, 2001.
2. The board failed to adopt meaningful compliance measures, failed to staff Siemens's compliance function adequately, and, at times failed to adopt reasonable recommendations designed to ensure compliance procedures at the company.
3. The company failed to respond to red flags, including ignoring substantial cash payments in Nigeria by senior-level employees within one of its business groups and ignoring Siemens's outside auditor KPMG's identification of approximately $5.81 million in cash that was brought to Nigeria by a Siemens employee. The FCPA compliance report prepared on the foregoing matters in November 2003 by Siemens's then-CFO did not lead to any disciplinary actions against those employees involved in the bribery, and the report was not provided to or discussed with the Management Board or the company's audit committee.

## Illicit Payment Mechanisms Used to Pay Bribes

Siemens made thousands of payments to third parties in ways that obscured the purpose for, and ultimate recipient of, the money. The principal mechanisms used to facilitate illicit payments were business consultants, payment intermediaries, slush funds, cash, and intercompany accounts.

Through its use of business consultants and payment intermediaries, Siemens funneled more than $982.7 million to third parties, including government officials. Business consultants were typically hired pursuant to business consultant agreements, contracts that on their face obligated Siemens to pay for legitimate consulting services. In reality, many business consultant agreements were shams, in that the consultants performed no services beyond funneling bribes. One business group had specific instructions on how to use a "confidential payment system" to conceal payments to business consultants. Payment intermediaries were additional entities and individuals through which Siemens funneled bribes. In many cases, Siemens would pay the intermediary an amount and simultaneously direct that the money be transferred to a third-party bank account, less a small portion as the intermediary's fee.

Siemens also funneled more than $211 million through slush funds for use as bribes. Slush funds were bank accounts held in the name of current or former senior Siemens employees, third parties, or affiliated entities. These payments were made before September 30, 2004. The most notable slush funds were maintained by a former group (i.e., consolidated entity) manager who has been convicted in Germany for his role in the payment of bribes to foreign officials, which included several slush funds held in the name of U.S. shell companies.

Siemens also used cash and cash equivalents to funnel more than $160.4 million to third parties. Its employees used "cash desks" maintained by the Siemens Real Estate Group to obtain large amounts of cash to pay bribes. Often, employees would obtain hundreds of thousands of dollars and, at times, even $1 million in various currencies from the cash desks in Germany. At times, the cash was then stored in safes maintained by Siemens employees to ensure ready access to cash to pay bribes.

As early as 2004, a Siemens corporate financial audit employee raised concerns about the use of intercompany accounts. He was phased out of his job and assigned to work on "special projects" from his home until leaving the company in 2005. Siemens thereafter began closing some of the accounts and eventually closed all of them.

Another type of internal account that employees abused was Siemens internal commission accounts. These balance-sheet accounts were intended to be used to record commissions at a business group earned on transactions with other Siemens entities. These accounts were used to make third-party payments. Many of the intercompany account payments and the internal commission account payments were done manually to bypass Siemens's automated payment system. The manual payments, executed through the system, did not require the submission of documentation in support of a payment. Siemens used a host of other schemes to make more than $25.3 million in payments to third parties. In particular, Siemens used sham supplier agreements, receivables, and other write-offs to generate payments.

In total, Siemens made bribery payments directly or indirectly to foreign government officials in connection with at least 290 projects or individual sales involving business in a variety of countries.

## Siemens Failed to Maintain Its Books, Records, and Internal Controls

Siemens failed to implement adequate internal controls to comply with the company's NYSE listing, including the detection and prevention of violations of the FCPA. As already stated, Siemens made thousands of payments to third parties in ways that obscured the purpose for, and the ultimate recipients of, the payments. Despite a policy that required two signatures on company documents to authorize transactions, a significant number of business consultant agreements were entered into and a significant number of payments were authorized in violation of the policy.

Siemens paid approximately $1.4 billion in bribes to foreign government officials. Doing so involved the falsification of Siemens's books and records by employees throughout the company. Specifically, Siemens failed to keep accurate books and records by (1) establishing and funding secret, off-books accounts; (2) establishing and using a system of payment intermediaries to obscure the source and destination of funds; (3) making payments pursuant to business consultant agreements that inaccurately described the services provided; (4) generating false invoices and other false documents to justify payments; (5) disbursing millions in cash from cash desks with inaccurate documentation authorizing or supporting the withdrawals; (6) concealing the identity of persons authorizing illicit payments; (7) recording illicit ASSF payments as legitimate commissions in Oil for Food transactions; (8) falsifying UN documents in connection with the Oil for Food program; and (9) recording bribes as payments for legitimate services.

Siemens failed to establish controls over cash disbursements, allowed manual payments without documentation, and failed to ensure the proper use of intercompany accounts. In addition, the company failed to establish an effective central compliance function. The compliance office lacked independence and was severely understaffed. Siemens's tone at the top was inadequate for a law-abiding entity, and employees engaged in bribery and other misconduct on behalf of the company were not disciplined adequately. Siemens also failed to conduct appropriate antibribery and corruption training.

## Questions

1. Evaluate the ethics of actions taken by Siemens with respect to Josephson's Six Pillars of Character and virtue-based decision making, as discussed in Chapter 1.

2. Under the German Criminal Code, much like the U.K. Bribery Act, all bribes are prohibited including facilitating payments. The Foreign Corrupt Practices Act (FCPA) in the U.S. makes a distinction between the two and permits facilitating payments made to induce a government official to carry out her designated responsibilities. From an ethical perspective, which of these two approaches are more consistent with virtue theory?

3. Comment on the following statement from an ethics perspective: Companies that make the mistake of trying to follow the bottom limits of legal behavior without championing ethics should learn from the Siemens case that once a culture of taking short cuts and ignoring values is in place, it is only a matter of time before employees cross the line into illegal conduct.

## Optional Question

4. Review the 13 cases on bribing foreign government officials described in the SEC complaint referenced below.[2] Summarize the accounting issues involved in each case and explain how the payments described violated the FCPA.

[2] *Securities and Exchange Commission v. Siemens Aktiengesellschaft,* Case 1.08-cv-02167, Litigation Release No. 20829, Accounting and Enforcement Release No. 2911, December 15, 2008, www.sec.gov/litigation/complaints/2008/comp20829.pdf.

## Case 8-2

# Parmalat: Europe's Enron

After the news broke about the frauds at Enron and WorldCom in the United States, there were those in Europe who used the occasion to beat the drum: "Our Principles-based approach to accounting standard-setting is better than your rules-based approach." Many in the U.S. started to take a closer look at the principles-based approach in the European Community, which relies less on bright-line rules to establish standards, as is the case in the U.S., but may have loopholes making it relatively easy to avoid the rules. As discussed in the chapter, a principles-based approach relies more on objective standards that guide decision making in the application of accounting standards, supported by ethical judgment to help implement the principles. The case of Parmalat illustrates why many question whether the principles-based approach leads to financial statements that more faithfully represent financial position and results of operations.

## Background

Parmalat began as a family-owned entity founded by Calisto Tanzi in 1961. During 2003, Parmalat was the eighth-largest company in Italy and had operations in 30 countries. It was a huge player in the world dairy market and was even more influential within Italian business circles. It had a network of 5,000 dairy farmers who supplied milk products and 39,000 people who were directly employed by the company. The company eventually sold shares to the public on the Milan stock exchange. The Tanzi family always held a majority, controlling stake in the company, which in 2003 was 50.02 percent. Tanzi family members also occupied the seats of CEO and chair of the board of directors.[1] The structure of Parmalat was primarily characterized by the Tanzi family and the large amount of control that it wielded over company operations. It was not unusual for family members to override whatever internal controls existed to perpetrate the accounting fraud.

The Parmalat scandal broke in late 2003, when it became known that company funds totaling almost €4 billion (approximately $5.64 billion) that were meant to be held in an account at the Bank of America did not exist. The Parmalat situation described here makes it clear that Europe is not isolated from financial fraud. It also proves that the quality of financial reporting and financial transparency are issues of global concern. At the end of the day, these issues may be more important than whether a principles-based or rules-based approach is used.

## The Italians Act

On March 19, 2004, Milan prosecutors brought charges against Parmalat founder Calisto Tanzi, other members of his family, and an inner circle of company executives for their part in the Parmalat scandal. After three months of investigation, the prosecutors charged 29 individuals, the Italian branches of the Bank of America, and the accountants Deloitte & Touche and Grant Thornton. The charges included market rigging, false auditing, and regulatory obstruction following the disclosure that €15 billion (approximately $21.15 billion) were found to be missing from the bank accounts of the multinational dairy group in December 2003. The company has since declared bankruptcy, and 16 suspects, including Carlos Tanzi, are in jail. Other suspects include Tanzi's son Stafano, his brother Giovanni, former Parmalat finance chief Fausto Tonna, and lawyer Liampaolo Zini. Former internal auditors and three former Bank of America employees also have been jailed for their roles in the fraud.[2] The judge also gave the go-ahead for Parmalat to proceed with lawsuits against the auditors. Bondi is also pursuing another lawsuit against Citigroup in New Jersey state courts. Despite all its troubles, Parmalat has recovered and today is a thriving multinational food group with operations in all five continents through either a direct presence or through license agreements.

## Parmalat Diverted Company Cash to Tanzi Family Members

In transactions that might engender pride on the part of Dennis Kozlowski, the former CEO of Tyco, Parmalat transferred approximately €350 million (approximately $494 million) to various businesses owned and operated by Tanzi family members between 1997 and 2003. These family members did not perform any equivalent services for Parmalat that would warrant such payments. Further, Parmalat failed to disclose that the transfers were to related-party interests.

## U.S. Banks Caught in the Spotlight

Italian magistrates and officials from the SEC examined the role of lenders to Parmalat, which collapsed into bankruptcy in late December 2003 following the disclosure of major holes in the financing of the company. The SEC's inquiries focused on up to approximately €1.05 billion ($1.5 billion) of notes and bonds issued in private placements with U.S. investors. The banks investigated included Bank of America, JP Morgan Chase, Merrill Lynch, and Morgan Stanley Dean Witter.

---

[1] Available at www.madhyam.org.in/admin/tender/Parmalat's %20Fall,%20Europe's%20Enron(%20ASED).pdf.

[2] Sophie Arie, "29 Named in Parmalat Case," *The Guardian*, March 19, 2004, www.guardian.co.uk/parmalat/story/0,1172990, 00.html.

Parmalat's administrator, Enrico Bondi, helped the authorities identify all the financing transactions undertaken by Parmalat from 1994 through 2003. During the investigation, it was noted that Parmalat's auditor from 1990 to 1999, Grant Thornton, did not have copies of crucial audit documents relating to the company's Cayman Islands subsidiary, Bonlat. The emergence of a €5.16 billion (approximately $7.28 billion) hole at Bonlat triggered the Parmalat collapse. The accounting firm has since handed over important audit documents to investigators.

## Accounting Fraud

One of the most notable fraudulent actions was the creation of a completely fictitious bank account in the U.S. that supposedly contained $5 billion. After media reports exposing the account surfaced, the financial institution at which the deposit existed (Bank of America) denied any such account. The company's management fooled auditors by creating a fictitious confirmation letter regarding the account. In addition to misleading the auditors about this bank account, the company's CFO, Fausto Tonna, produced fake documents and faxed them to the auditors in order to hide the fact that many of the company's dealings were completely fictitious.[3]

Parmalat's management also used "nominee" entities to transfer debt and sales in order to hide them from auditors and other interested parties. A *nominee entity* is a company created to hold and administer the assets or securities of the actual owner as a custodian.[4] These entities were clearly controlled by Parmalat and most existed only on paper.

Using nominee entities, the Parmalat management created a method to remove uncollectible or impaired accounts receivable. The bad accounts would be transferred to one of the nominee entities, thus keeping the bad debt expense or write-off for the valueless accounts off the Parmalat income statement. The transfers to nominee entities also avoided any scrutiny of the accounts by external or statutory auditors (in this case, Italian-designated auditors under the country's laws).

Creating revenues was another scheme in which the nominee or subsidiary entities were used; if a non-Italian subsidiary had a loss related to currency exchange rates, management would fabricate currency exchange contracts to convert the loss to a profit. Similar activities were undertaken to hide losses due to interest expense. Documents showing interest rate swaps were created to mislead the auditors or other parties. Interest rate swaps and currency exchange contracts are both instruments usually used to hedge on the financial markets, and sometimes to diversify the risk of certain investments. Parmalat abused these tools by creating completely fictitious contracts after the fact and claiming that they were valid and accurate. The understatement of debt was another large component of the Parmalat fraud, as was hidden debt.

On one occasion, management recorded the sale of receivables as "non-recourse," when in fact Parmalat was still responsible to ensure that the money was collectible.

There were many debt-disguising schemes in relation to the nominee entities. With one loan agreement, the money borrowed was touted as from an equity source. On another occasion, a completely fictitious debt repurchase by a nominee entity was created, resulting in the removal of a liability from the books, when the debt was still in fact outstanding. Parmalat management also incorrectly recorded many million euros' worth of bank loans as intercompany loans. This incorrect classification allowed for the loans to be eliminated in consolidation when they actually represented money owed by the company to outsiders.[5]

The fraud methods did not stop at creating fictitious accounts and documents, or even with the establishment of nonexistent foreign nominee entities and hiding liabilities. Calisto Tanzi and other management were investigated by Italian authorities for manipulating the Milan stock market. On December 20, 1999, Parmalat's management issued a press release of an appraisal of the Brazilian unit. While this release appeared to be a straightforward action, what Tanzi and others failed to disclose were the facts relating to the appraisal itself. The appraisal came from an accountant at Deloitte Touche Tohmatsu (the international name of Deloitte & Touche) and was dated July 23, 2008, nearly 19 months prior to the press release.[6] This failure to disclose information in a timely and transparent manner demonstrates yet another way that Parmalat was able to exert influence and mislead investors.

## Missing the Red Flags

The fraud that occurred at Parmalat is a case of management greed with a lack of independent oversight and fraudulent financial reporting that was taken to the extreme. As an international company, Parmalat management had many opportunities to take advantage of the system and hide the fictitious nature of financial statement items. As with many frauds, the web of lies began to untangle when the company began to run out of cash. In a discussion with a firm in New York regarding a leveraged buyout of part of the Parmalat Corporation, two members of the Tanzi family revealed that they did not actually have the cash represented in their financial statements.[7]

At the beginning of 2003, Lehman Brothers, Inc., issued a report questioning the financial status of Parmalat. Ironically, Parmalat filed a report with Italian authorities claiming that Lehman Brothers was slandering the company with the intention of hurting the Parmalat share price.[8] Financial

---

[3]Securities and Exchange Commission, *Securities and Exchange Commission v. Parmalat Finanziaria SpA*, First Amended Complaint, www.sec.gov/litigation/complaints/comp18803.pdf.

[4]Available at www.sec.gov/litigation/complaints/comp18803.pdf.

[5]*Parmalat Finanziaria SpA.*

[6]William D. Dobson, "Parmalat," http://purl.umn.edu/37555.

[7]Available at www.sec.gov/litigation/complaints/comp18803.pdf, page 14.

[8]Leonard J. Brooks and Paul Dunn, *Business and Professional Ethics for Executives, Directors, and Accountants* (Cincinnati, OH: South-Western Publishing, 2009).

institutions failed to examine the accusations thoroughly and continued to loan money to Parmalat due to the supposed strength and power wielded by the company throughout the world. (Notice the similarity with Enron, whereby U.S. banks and financial institutions bought into the fraud that was Enron and didn't want to upset what was then the seventh-largest company in the U.S.) As Luca Sala, former head of Bank of America's Italian corporate finance division, observed, "When you have a client like Parmalat, which is bringing in all that money and has industries all over the world, you don't exactly ask them to show you their bank statements."[9] This attitude and similar attitudes at Citibank led both banks, as well as many others, to write off millions of dollars of loans after the collapse. Several Bank of America employees were charged in the Parmalat fraud, mostly because of the nonexistent U.S. bank account, but also related to lending practices. Eventually, all the bank's employees were acquitted, leading the bank to state: "The crime of market manipulation with respect to BOA was found to be completely groundless."[10]

## Failure of Auditors

Parmalat accused the auditors, Grant Thornton International and Deloitte Touche Tohmatsu, of contributing to its €14 billion collapse in December 2003. Parmalat filed suit against the auditors and other third parties, seeking $10 billion in damages for alleged professional malpractice, fraud, theft of assets and civil conspiracy. Paramalat argued that the headquarters for both Grant Thornton and Deloitte had "alter ego" relationships with their Italian subsidiaries that tied them inextricably to the alleged fraud. According to the complaint, the relationships are highlighted by the firms' own claims to being "integrated worldwide accounting organizations." Judge Lewis Kaplan in U.S. District Court for the Southern District of New York granted a motion by Deloitte USA to dismiss Parmalat's first amended complaint due to Parmalat's failure to show that poor auditing of Parmalat USA was equivalent to fraud at Parmalat in Italy.

The frauds continued for many years due, in large part, to the failures of the auditors. Italian law requires both listed and unlisted companies to have a board of statutory auditors, as well as external auditors. The external auditor during the fraud, primarily Grant Thornton, SpA, failed to comply with many commonly accepted auditing practices and thus contributed to the fraud. The largest component of Parmalat's fraud that ultimately brought the company down was the nonexistent bank account with Bank of America. The auditors went through procedures to confirm this account, but they made one fatal mistake: they sent the confirmation using Parmalat's internal mail system. The confirmation request

was intercepted by Parmalat employees and subsequently forged by Tonna or an agent acting on his behalf. The forgery consisted of creating a confirmation and printing it on Bank of America letterhead and then sending it back to the auditors.

## Failure of the Board

The statutory board is intended to act as a fundamental monitor within the company and check that the board of directors is complying with laws in their actions and decisions. The Parmalat board of statutory auditors was composed of three members; the number is significant because had there been more than three seats on the statutory auditor board, minority shareholders would have had the ability to elect two of the members.[12] Parmalat's board never reported any irregularities or problems, despite receiving complaints, because of the influence of the Tanzi family. After the fraud was discovered and resolution of the issues began, it became clear that the statutory audit board did nothing to prevent or detect the fraud.

## Resolution of Outstanding Matters

Following an investigation, the founder of Parmalat, Calisto Tanzi, was sentenced in Milan to 10 years in prison in December 2008 for securities laws violations in connection with the Italian dairy company's downfall in late 2003. Tonna, the CFO, was sentenced to 30 months in jail following a trial in 2005, and other officers reached plea bargain deals.[13] Bank of America settled a civil case brought by Parmalat bondholders for $100 million.[14]

Bondholders in the U.S. and Italy had alleged the U.S. bank knew of Parmalat's financial troubles, but nevertheless sold investors Parmalat bonds that ultimately soured—allegations Bank of America denied. Both sides said the agreement cleared the way for future business between the companies. In a statement following the settlement, Bank of America stated that the record of court rulings in the case "makes it clear that no one at Bank of America knew or could have known of the true financial condition of Parmalat. We have defended ourselves vigorously in these cases and are satisfied with this outcome today."[15]

After the accounting and business problems surfaced, a court battle ensued regarding who was responsible for the audit failures. The umbrella entities of Deloitte and Grant Thornton, Deloitte Touche Tohmatsu, and Grant Thornton

---

[9]Kavaljit Singh, www.madhyam.org.in/admin/tender/Parmalat's%20Fall,%20Europe's%20Enron(%20ASED).pdf.

[10]Sara Gay Forden, "Parmalat's Tanzi Sentenced to 10 Years in Milan Trial," www.bloomberg.com/apps/news?pid520601087&sid5alrsQE4_kBPU&refer54home.

[11]Brooks and Dunn, pp. 398–399.

[12]Andrea Melis, "Corporate Governance Failures: To What Extent Is Parmalat a Particularly Italian Case?" http://papers.ssrn.com/sol3/papers.cfm?abstract_id5563223.

[13]Sara Gay Forden, "Parmalat's Tanzi Sentenced to 10 Years."

[14]Andrew Longstreth, "Bank of America Makes Peace with Parmalat for $100 million," www.law.com/jsp/article.jsp?id51202432604858.

[15]The Associated Press, "Bank of America settles Parmalat suit for $100M," July 28, 2009, Available at: http://www.utsandiego.com/news/2009/jul/28/us-bank-america-parmalat-072809/.

International, along with the U.S. branches of both firms, were included in a lawsuit by Parmalat shareholders. Questions were raised as to whether or not the umbrella entities could be held liable for the failures of a country-specific branch of their firm. The courts held that due to the level of control that the international and U.S.-based branches wielded over the other portions of the firm, they could be included in the lawsuit.[16] The extension of liability was a huge issue for accounting firms, and the external auditors were ultimately held liable. Both groups of external auditors were fined large sums to settle a class-action lawsuit by U.S. equity investors over their roles in the Italian company's 2003 collapse; Deloitte Touche Tohmatsu and its U.S. unit, Deloitte & Touche LLP, agreed to pay $8.5 million, while Grant Thornton International and its U.S. and Italian units agreed to pay $6.5 million. In addition, Deloitte agreed to pay $149 million to settle with Parmalat itself.[17]

## Legal Matters with Bank of America

On February 2, 2006, a U.S. federal judge allowed Parmalat to proceed with much of its $10 billion lawsuit against Bank of America, including claims that the bank violated U.S. racketeering laws. Enrico Bondi was appointed as the equivalent of a U.S. bankruptcy trustee to pursue claims that financial institutions, including Bank of America, abetted the company in disguising its true financial condition. Bondi accused the bank of helping to structure mostly off-balance-sheet transactions intended to "conceal Parmalat's insolvency" and of collecting fees that it did not deserve.

The lawsuit against Bank of America was dismissed.[18] Parmalat appealed the dismissal of its lawsuits, accusing Bank of America and the company's auditor, Grant Thornton LLP, of fraud in the Italian dairy company's 2003 collapse. Bondi filed notice of Parmalat's appeal to the U.S. Court of Appeals for the Second Circuit in New York. Bondi and the Parmalat Capital Finance Ltd. unit had accused Grant Thornton of helping set up fake transactions to allow insiders to steal from the company. Parmalat Capital made similar claims in a lawsuit against Bank of America. On September 18, 2009, U.S. District Judge Lewis Kaplan said Parmalat should not recover for its own fraud, noting that the transactions also generated millions of euros for the company. "The actions of its agents in so doing were in furtherance of the company's interests, even if some of the agents intended at the time they assisted in raising the money to steal some of it," Kaplan wrote.

---

[16]Thomas M. Beshere, "Questions for Accounting Firm Networks," http://mcguirewoods.com/news-resources/publications/Questions%20For%20International%20Accounting%20Firm%20Networks.pdf.
[17]Chad Bray, http://online.wsj.com/article/BT-CO-20091119-713515.html·
[18]Available at www.reuters.com/article/idUSN186214820090918, *Cached.*

## The SEC Charges

The SEC filed an amended complaint on July 28, 2004, in its lawsuit against Parmalat Finanziaria SpA in U.S. District Court in the Southern District of New York. The amended complaint alleged that Parmalat engaged in one of the largest financial frauds in history and defrauded U.S. institutional investors when it sold them more than $1 billion in debt securities in a series of private placements between 1997 and 2002. Parmalat consented to the entry of a final judgment against it in the fraud.

The complaint includes the following amended charges:

1. Parmalat consistently overstated its level of cash and marketable securities by at least $4.9 billion at December 31, 2002.
2. As of September 30, 2003, Parmalat had understated its reported debt by almost $10 billion through a variety of tactics, including:
   a. Eliminating about $6 billion of debt held by one of its nominee entities
   b. Recording approximately $1.6 billion of debt as equity through fictitious loan participation agreements
   c. Removing approximately $500 million in liabilities by falsely describing the sale of certain receivables as non-recourse, when in fact the company retained an obligation to ensure that the receivables were ultimately paid
   d. Improperly eliminating approximately $1.6 billion of debt through a variety of techniques including mischaracterization of bank debt as intercompany debt
3. Between 1997 and 2003, Parmalat transferred approximately $500 million to various businesses owned and operated by Tanzi family members.
4. Parmalat used nominee entities to fabricate nonexistent financial operations intended to offset losses of operating subsidiaries; to disguise intercompany loans from one subsidiary to another that was experiencing operating losses; to record fictitious revenue through sales by its subsidiaries to controlled nominee entities at inflated or entirely fictitious amounts; and to avoid unwanted scrutiny due to the aging of the receivables related to these sales: the related receivables were either sold or transferred to nominee entities.

In the consent agreement, without admitting or denying the allegations, Parmalat agreed to adopt changes to its corporate governance to promote future compliance with the federal securities laws, including:

- Adopting bylaws providing for governance by a shareholder-elected board of directors, the majority of whom will be independent and serve finite terms and specifically delineating in the bylaws the duties of the board of directors
- Adopting a Code of Conduct governing the duties and activities of the board of directors
- Adopting an Insider Dealing Code of Conduct
- Adopting a Code of Ethics

The bylaws also required that the positions of the chair of the board of directors and managing director be held by two separate individuals, and Parmalat must consent to having continuing jurisdiction of the U.S. District Court to enforce its provisions.

## Questions

1. In the case, Judge Kaplan dismissed Parmalat's lawsuit against Deloitte stating that Parmalat "did not show that poor auditing of Parmalat USA was equivalent to fraud." Comment on the judge's decision from the perspective of the auditor's obligation to identify fraud in the financial statements.

2. Based on the information in the case, classify the improper transactions engaged in by Parmalat into one of the seven financial shenanigans identified by Howard Schilit and discussed in Chapter 7. Explain why each transaction violated professional standards.

3. Who is to blame for the fraud at Parmalat: the company?; top management?; the auditors?; the Bank of America? How did each party violate its ethical obligations?

## Case 8-3

# Satyam: India's Enron

Satyam Computer Services, now Mahindra Satyam, is an India-based global business and information technology services company that specializes in consulting, systems integration, and outsourcing solutions. The company was the fourth-largest software exporter in India until January 2009, when the CEO and cofounder, Ramalinga Raju, confessed to inflating the company's profits and cash reserves over an eight-year period. The accounting fraud at Satyam involved dual accounting books, more than 7,000 forged invoices, and dozens of fake bank statements. The total amount of losses was Rs (rupees) 50 billion (equal to about $1.04 billion).[1] This represented about 94 percent of the company's cash and cash equivalents. The global scope of Satyam's fraud led to the labeling of it as "India's Enron." Ironically, the name "Satyam" is derived from the Sanskrit word *satya,* which translates to "truth."

Although headquartered in Hyderabad, India, Satyam's stock was listed on the NYSE since 2001. When the news of the fraud broke, Satyam's stock declined almost 90 percent in value on both the U.S. and Indian stock exchanges. Several top managers either resigned or were fired and jail terms were given to Raju, the co-founder and CEO, and Sirinivas Vadlamani, the CFO. The auditors—PricewaterhouseCoopers (PwC)—were also implicated in the fraud, and investigations against it are continuing by the Securities and Exchange Board of India (SEBI). As of June 2013, PwC was cooperating with the investigation in an attempt to fast-track a settlement ahead of protracted legal cases against the firm that are expected to take years to unravel because Satyam was India's largest-ever accounting fraud.

## Fraudulent Actions by Raju

Raju stepped down in early January 2009, admitting to falsifying financial figures of the company with respect to nonexistent cash and bank balances. Stunning his well-wishers and investors, Raju revealed the real motive behind the December 16 bid to acquire Maytas companies for $1.6 billion: to swap the fictitious cash reserves of Satyam built over years with the Maytas assets. Raju thought that the payments to Maytas could be delayed once Satyam's problem was solved. What had started as a marginal gap between actual operating profit and the one reflected in the books continued to grow over the years. It had attained unmanageable proportions as the size of the company's operations grew over the years. One lie led to another. The problem further worsened as the company had to carry additional resources and assets to justify a higher level of operations, leading to increased costs.

As things went out of hand, Raju was forced to raise Rs 1.23 billion (approximately $25.58 million) more by pledging the family-owned shares to keep the operations

[1]$1 = Rs 44 (approximately) at December 31, 2009.

going. His woes were compounded with amounts due to vendors, fleet operators, and construction companies. The offloading of the pledged shares by IL&FS Trust Company, a Mumbai-based financial institution, and others brought down the promoters' stake from 8.65 percent to a fragile 3.6 percent. By the end of the day, Raju was left facing charges from several sides. The Ministry of Corporate Affairs, the state government, and the market regulator, SEBI, decided to probe the affairs of the company and Raju's role, as well as corporate governance issues.

Going by his confessional statement to the board of Satyam in January 2009, what Raju had done over the years appears to be rather simple manipulation of revenues and earnings to show a superior performance than what was actually the case. For this, he resorted to the time-tested practice of creating fictitious billings for services that were never rendered. The offset was either an inflation of receivables or the cash in bank balance. The following is a summary of the way financial statement amounts were manipulated:

- 94 percent (Rs 5.04 billion/approximately $10.5 million) of the cash in bank account balance in the September 30, 2008, balance sheet was inflated, due largely to exaggerated profits and fictitious assets.

- An accrued interest of Rs 376 million (approximately $7.82 million) was nonexistent.

- An understated liability of Rs 1.23 billion (approximately $25.58 million) resulting from Raju's infusion of personal funds into the company was recorded as revenue.

- Inflated revenues of Rs 588 million (approximately $12.23 million) went straight to the bottom line.

## Acquisition of Maytas Properties and Maytas Infrastructure

In December 2008, Raju tried to buy two firms owned by his sons, Maytas Properties and Maytas Infrastructure (Satyam spelled backward is Maytas) for $1.6 billion. Raju tried to justify the purchase by stating that the company needed to diversify by incorporating the infrastructure market to augment its software market. However, many investors thought that the purchases of two firms were intended to line the pockets of the Raju family. Raju owned less than 10 percent of Satyam, whereas Raju's family owned 100 percent of the equity in Maytas Properties and about 40 percent of Maytas Infrastructure. Stock prices plunged dramatically after the announcement, so Raju rescinded his offer to buy the two companies.

With the prices of Satyam stock and the health of the company declining, four members of the board of directors of Satyam resigned within one month. In his confession,

Raju took full responsibility for the accounting fraud and stated that the board knew nothing about the manipulation of financial statements. He indicated a willingness to accept the legal consequences of his actions.

An important question is how independently did the "independent" directors of Satyam act in the now highly questioned and failed decision to acquire the Maytas companies? One board member, M. Rammohan Rao, dean of the prestigious Indian School of Business (ISB) with campuses in Hyderabad and Mohali, claimed that the board had taken an independent view and raised concerns about the unrelated diversification, valuation, and other issues. Two views emerged. The first was, why not stick to our core competencies and why venture into a risky proposition? The second issue was related to the valuation of the companies. Maytas Properties was valued much higher than $1.3 billion, the amount that Satyam's management came up with for the acquisition price. When asked whether the fact that the target companies—Maytas Properties and Maytas Infrastructure—were led by Raju's two sons made any difference to the board, Rao said, "We felt the valuation proposed by the Satyam management was lower and conservative, despite the family ties. We took an independent view on this."[2]

When asked if the board had taken into consideration the possible impact of the purchase of the two companies on shareholders' interests and the market reaction, the ISB dean responded, "There were concerns on these grounds as well, especially the market reaction for such an unrelated diversification." However, according to Rao, there was no way that they could gauge the market reaction at first, so they decided to take a risk. But the way the market reacted was a bit unanticipated, he added.

Questions can be raised about corporate governance with respect to the failed acquisition of the Maytas companies. A conflict of interest arose when Satyam's board agreed to invest $1.6 billion to acquire a 100 percent stake in Maytas Properties and a 51 percent stake in Maytas Infrastructure. The Raju family, which ran the Maytas companies also invited family or close friends to serve on the board of directors. These bonds created independence issues and questions about whether directors would be confrontational with top management when warranted.

## Litigation in the U.S.

Securities fraud class action lawsuits were filed on behalf of a class of persons and entities who purchased or acquired the American Depositary Shares (ADSs)[3] of Satyam on the

NYSE and/or were investors residing in the United States who purchased or acquired Satyam common stock traded on Indian exchanges between January 6, 2004, and January 6, 2009 (the class period).

The complaint alleged that Satyam, certain of its directors and officers, and the company's outside auditors (PwC) made false and misleading public statements regarding Satyam's financial condition and performance, which artificially inflated the stock price. On January 7, 2009, Satyam's chair, Ramalinga Raju, sent a letter to the company's board confessing to a massive accounting fraud. Raju admitted that the company's balance sheet and other public disclosures contained numerous false statements. For example, Raju wrote that as of September 30, 2008, the company overstated revenue by approximately 22 percent and reported cash and bank balances of Rs 53.61 billion (approximately $1.1 billion), of which Rs 50.4 billion (over $1 billion) did not exist.[4]

Reports issued since the January 7 confession indicate that Raju likely understated the scope of the fraud, and that he and members of his family engaged in widespread theft of Satyam's funds through a complex web of intermediary entities.

The complaint also asserted claims against PricewaterhouseCoopers International Ltd. and its Indian partners and affiliates including Price Waterhouse Bangalore, PricewaterhouseCoopers Private Limited, and Lovelock & Lewes (PW India firms). Satyam's outside auditors from the PW India firms were aware of the fraud but still certified the company's financial statements as accurate. A document (the charge sheet) filed in a Hyderabad court by the Indian Central Bureau of Investigation (the equivalent of the U.S. Federal Bureau of Investigation), detailing charges against numerous Satyam employees and two partners of PW India firms, alleged that the auditors received documentation from Satyam's banks that showed that the company's disclosed assets were greatly overstated. The charge sheet further alleged that these auditors received fees from Satyam that were exorbitantly higher than the fees similarly situated Indian companies paid to their outside auditors; the Central Bureau of Investigation cited these fees as evidence of a "well-knit criminal conspiracy" between Satyam and the auditors.

The complaint asserted claims against other defendants as well. In particular, the complaint alleged that members of the audit committee of the Satyam board of directors—who were responsible for overseeing the integrity of the company's financial statements, the performance and compensation of the outside auditors from PW India firms, and the adequacy and effectiveness of internal accounting and financial controls—were responsible for the publication of false and misleading public statements due to their extreme recklessness in discharging their duties and their resulting failure

---

[2]Available at www.blonnet.com/2008/12/19/stories/20081219=1600400.htm.

[3]ADSs are U.S. dollar–denominated equity shares of a foreign-based company available for purchase on a United States stock exchange. ADSs are issued by depository banks in the United States under agreement with the issuing foreign company; the entire issuance is called an American Depositary Receipt (ADR), and the individual shares are referred to as *ADSs*.

[4]*In re Satyam Computer Services, Ltd., Securities Litigation*, U.S. District Court, Southern District of New York, 09-MD-02027, January 2009.

to discover and prevent the massive accounting fraud. The complaint also alleged that Maytas Infrastructure and Maytas Properties and Raju's two sons were responsible for the false and misleading public statements. The Raju sons' false and misleading statements concerning Satyam's financial condition and performance artificially inflated the prices of the company's publicly traded securities during the class period, and caused significant damages to investors when the prices of the company's securities both in the United States. and in India experienced severe declines as a direct result of disclosures regarding Satyam's true condition.

## Actions Against PwC

PwC and its Indian affiliates initially hid behind "client confidentiality" and stated that it was "examining the contents of the statement." Realizing that this was not enough, PwC came up with a second statement claiming that "the audits were conducted in accordance with applicable auditing standards and were supported by appropriate audit evidence." This is somewhat troublesome because an audit in accordance with generally accepted auditing standards (GAAS) calls for examining the contents of the financial statements. Given that the firm did not identify the financial wrongdoing at Satyam, it would appear that the firm, at the very least, was guilty of professional negligence. At a minimum, the firm missed or failed to do the following:

- Fictitious invoices with customers were recorded as genuine.
- Raju recorded a fictional interest credit as income.
- The auditors didn't ask for a statement of confirmation of balance from banks (for cash balances) and debtors (for receivables), a basic procedure in an audit.

On January 26, 2009, Indian police arrested two partners of the Indian arm of PwC on charges of criminal conspiracy and cheating in connection with the fraud investigation at Satyam. Furious Indian investors had pressured the authorities to take such an action in light of the more than $1 billion fraud. Investors couldn't understand how a reported $1 billion in cash was really only $78 million, and how it wasn't detected by PwC. The company's financial statements were signed off by PwC on March 31, 2008.[5]

## Class Action Lawsuits in the U.S.

On January 11, 2010, India asked the authorities in the U.S. to not take any action against Satyam, as it would amount to punishing shareholders twice. Satyam can face punitive action in the United States because the company's shares are listed and traded on United States exchanges. Satyam also is contending about a dozen class action lawsuits in U.S. courts. It is also possible that the company will face charges from the SEC.

[5]Ronald Fink, "Doubt Cast on Satyam Executives' Accusations against PwC," *Financial Week*, www.financialweek.com/apps/pbcs/dll/article=/20090127/REG/901279970/10.

As many as 12 class action lawsuits were filed against the company by January 2009, and more are expected to be filed. The lawsuits were filed by investors in the ADS ever since Raju confessed to having fudged the accounts of the company for at least seven years.

The charges alleged against the defendants in the lawsuits filed to date are:

1. The defendants issued misleading financial information about the company including information contained in its annual reports, which were signed by the defendants and contained fairness opinions issued by Satyam's auditor, PwC.
2. A letter was sent by Ramalinga Raju to the board of directors of Satyam and SEBI admitting to falsification of accounts, overstatement of profits and debt owed to the company, and understatement of liabilities. The purchasers of Satyam's ADSs were injured through their purchase of stock at inflated prices because they relied on the false and misleading information provided by the defendants.
3. None of the statements made by the defendants that have been alleged to be false in the lawsuit had any qualifying cautionary statements identifying factors that could cause results to differ materially from that stated.

## Are Big-Four U.S. Accounting Firms One Global Firm or Independent Entities?

An interesting aspect of the Satyam case is whether Big-Four international CPA firms truly operate as one firm across the globe, or whether each PwC affiliated-entity is separate and apart from the U.S. firm. The issue is important because PwC in the U.S. initially claimed it should not be held legally liable for the actions of its affiliates. Although audit firms around the world use similar names and are part of global networks, the firms say they are legally independent. The international networks say they have procedures to assure that their affiliates perform high-quality audits, but those procedures appear to have broken down in this case.

Those procedures include having partners from different firms in the network review audits. While the 2008 audit was being conducted, the U.S. S.E.C. said, a partner from a different PwC firm "alerted members of the Satyam engagement team that its cash confirmation procedures appeared substantially deficient," but the Indian firm did nothing to correct the procedures.

Had the firm done as the foreign partner advised was proper, the commission said, "Satyam's fraud could have been uncovered in the summer of 2008."

## Questions

1. Madan Bahsin concludes in her research paper that examined the fraud at Satyam that "the scandal brought to light

the importance of ethics and its relevance to corporate culture." Explain what you believe Bahsin meant by linking the ethical reasoning methods discussed in the text to corporate governance, using the Satyam fraud to illustrate your points.[6]

2. Hofstede's cultural values that were discussed in Chapter 1 reflect the following scores with respect to India and the U.S.

| Cultural Dimension | India | U.S. |
|---|---|---|
| Individualism (IDV) | 48 | 91 |
| Power Distance (PDI) | 77 | 40 |
| Uncertainty Avoidance (UAI) | 40 | 46 |
| Masculinity (MAS) | 56 | 62 |
| Long-term Orientation (LTO) | 61 | 29 |

[6]Madan Bahsin, 'Corporate Accounting Frauds: A Case Study of Satyam Computers Limited," *International Journal of Contemporary Business Studies*, Available at http://akpinsight-ijcbs.webs.com/2.%20IJCBS%20Vol%203%20,No%20 10%20%20OCt%20%202012%20Madan.pdf.

Do you believe these differences in cultural values and the discussion in this chapter about corporate governance in India can be used to explain the nature and scope of the fraud at Satyam including the involvement of Raju in the acquisition of two companies owned by his sons?

3. Briefly discuss the audit failures of PwC and its affiliates with respect to the accounting issues raised in the case including fraud risk assessment. What rules of professional conduct in the AICPA Code that was discussed in Chapter 4 were violated?

## Optional Question

4. Research the current status of all legal action against Satyam, its officers, and the PwC auditors. What changes have occurred in the facts of the case since June 2013?

## Case 8-4

# Royal Dutch Shell plc[1]

From 1907 until 2005, Royal Dutch Petroleum Company, a Netherlands-based company, and the Shell Transport and Trading Company, plc., a U.K.-based company, were the two public parent companies of a group of companies known collectively as the Royal Dutch/Shell Group (the Group).[2] Operating activities were conducted through the subsidiaries of Royal Dutch and Shell Transport. In 2005, Royal Dutch Shell plc became the single parent company of Royal Dutch and Shell Transport. Today, Shell is one of the world's largest independent oil and gas companies in terms of market capitalization, operating cash flow, and oil and gas production.

## Proved Reserves

Petroleum resources represent a significant part of the group's upstream assets and are the foundation of most of its current and future activities. The group's exploration and production business depends on its effectiveness in finding and maturing petroleum resources to sustain itself and drive profitable production growth. The Group reports its proved reserves of oil and gas to the SEC as part of its 20-F filing for a foreign company selling stock on the NYSE.

Reporting internal and external volumes properly is very important to Shell. This is based on the SEC-compliant proved reserves estimation and reporting process that enables access to the funds needed for the group's capital-intensive business. The SEC requirement of "reasonable certainty" represents the high standard of evidence/confidence consistent with the meaning of the word *proved*. Proved oil and gas reserves are the estimated quantities of crude oil, natural gas, and natural gas liquids that geological and engineering data demonstrate with reasonable certainty to be recoverable in future years from known reservoirs under existing economic and operating conditions (i.e., prices and costs as of the date the estimate is made). Prices include

consideration of changes in existing prices provided by contractual arrangements, but not on escalations based upon future conditions.[3]

In 2004, Shell amended its annual report on Form 20-F/A for the calendar year 2003 financial statements following an agreement with the SEC reached on August 24, 2004, with respect to the amount of proved reserves. The SEC had charged that 4.47 billion barrels of oil equivalent (boe), or approximately 23 percent of previously reported proved reserves, did not meet the standard set by law.[4] Shell also reduced its reserves replacement ratio (RRR)—the rate at which production was replaced by new oil discoveries. According to the SEC complaint, Shell's overstatement of proved reserves, and its delay in correcting the overstatement, resulted from (1) its desire to create and maintain the appearance of a strong RRR, a key performance indicator in the oil and gas industry; (2) the failure of its internal reserves estimation and reporting guidelines to conform to applicable regulations; and (3) the lack of effective internal controls over the reserves estimation and reporting process.[5]

## Reduction of RRR

In a series of announcements between January 9 and May 24, 2004, Shell disclosed that it had recategorized 4.47 billion boe, or approximately 23 percent, of the proved reserves it reported as of year-end 2002 because they were not proved reserves as defined in Commission Rule 4-10 of Regulation S-X. This recategorization reduced the standard measure of future cash flows by approximately $6.6 billion, as reported in Shell's original 2002 Form 20-F Supplemental Information under *SFAS 69*.[6]

---

[1]The letters *plc* refer to a "public limited company." The company operates on the basis that liability of shareholders toward the public is limited to its shareholding and that they are not personally liable for debts of the company. If the company goes into bankruptcy, the personal assets of directors/shareholders are not liable for attachment.

[2]In the U.S., this would be comparable to the consolidated entity that comprises two or more separately operating subsidiaries. As in the U.S., each subsidiary would issue separate financial statements and those statements would be consolidated and combined statements would be issued in the annual report. In the Royal Dutch Shell case, all references to the financial statements are to the consolidated (Group) statements. We use a capital "G" to emphasize the business entity nature of Shell and not to confuse it with common group meanings.

[3]Petroleum Resource Volume Requirements for Resource Classification and Value Realization, www.shell.com/...and.../reserves_announcement_0906200.html.

[4]Oil equivalent refers to the conversion of gas volumes to their oil equivalent and is a measure of petroleum reserves.

[5]*Securities and Exchange Commission v. Royal Dutch Petroleum Company and the Shell Transport and Trading Company, P.L.C.,* Complaint H-04-3339, August 24, 2004, www.sec.gov/litigation/litreleases/lr18844.htm.

[6]Statement of Financial Accounting Standards (SFAS) No. 69, *Disclosures About Oil and Gas Producing Activities.* This standard requires that publicly traded enterprises that have significant oil- and gas-producing activities should disclose, among other things, "proved oil and gas reserves" as of the beginning and end of the year. Revisions of previous estimates must be disclosed separately, with appropriate explanation of significant changes.

On July 2, 2004, Shell filed an amended 2002 Form 20-F that reflected the restatement of its proved reserves and standard measure of future cash flows for the years 1999 to 2002, as follows:

| Year | Reduction in Proved Reserves | % Reduction | Reduction in Standardized Measure | % Reduction |
|---|---|---|---|---|
| 1997 | 3.13 boe | 16% | N/A | N/A |
| 1998 | 3.78 boe | 18% | N/A | N/A |
| 1999 | 4.58 boe | 23% | $7.0 billion | 11% |
| 2000 | 4.84 boe | 25% | $7.2 billion | 10% |
| 2001 | 4.53 boe | 24% | $6.5 billion | 13% |
| 2002 | 4.47 boe | 23% | $6.6 billion | 9% |

As a result of the overstatement of proved reserves, Shell also announced a reduction in its RRR for 1998 through 2002, from the previously reported 100 percent to approximately 80 percent. Had Shell reported proved reserves properly, its annual and three-year RRR over this span would have been as follows:

| Year | 1-Year RRR | | 3-Year RRR | |
|---|---|---|---|---|
| | Original | Restated | Original | Restated |
| 1998 | 182% | 134% | N/A | N/A |
| 1999 | 56% | −5% | N/A | N/A |
| 2000 | 69% | 50% | 102% | 60% |
| 2001 | 74% | 97% | 66% | 48% |
| 2002 | 117% | 121% | 87% | 90% |
| 2003 | N/A | 63% | N/A | 94% |

According to the SEC complaint, these failures led Shell to record and maintain proved reserves that it knew, or was reckless in not knowing, did not satisfy applicable regulations and to report for certain years a stronger RRR than it actually had achieved in supplemental information filed along with its 10-K report. The SEC had warned about the proved reserves, but Shell either rejected the warnings as immaterial or unduly pessimistic, or attempted to manage the potential exposure by, for example, delaying the debooking of improperly recorded proved reserves until new, offsetting proved reserves bookings materialized.

## Failure to Maintain Adequate Internal Controls

The charges against Shell include the failure to implement and maintain internal controls sufficient to provide reasonable assurance that it was estimating and reporting proved reserves accurately and in compliance with applicable requirements. These failures arose from inadequate training and supervision of the operating unit personnel responsible for estimating and reporting proved reserves and deficiencies in the internal reserves audit function. Shell's decentralized system required an effective internal reserves audit function.

To perform this function, Shell historically had engaged as Group reserves auditor a retired Shell petroleum engineer who worked only part-time and was provided limited resources and no staff to audit its vast worldwide operations. Although the Group reserves auditor was an experienced reservoir engineer, he received little, if any, training on such critical matters as how to conduct his work and the rules and standards on which his opinions should be based. He also lacked the authority to require operating unit compliance with either commission rules or group reserves guidelines. Moreover, he reported to the management of Shell's exploration and production division, which were the same people he audited.

The Group reserves auditor visited each operating unit only once every four or more years. Subsequent to his visits, he issued reports rating the operating unit's systems, compliance with Group guidelines, and audit response as "good?," "satisfactory," or "unsatisfactory," opining whether the operating unit's reported reserves met Group guidelines. From the start of his tenure in January 1999 until September 2003, the Group reserves auditor did not issue a single "unsatisfactory" rating. The Group reserves auditor also issued an annual report on the reasonableness of Shell's year-end total reserves summary. Until his February 2004 report on Shell's 2003 proved reserves, the Group reserves auditor focused as much on whether group proved reserves complied with group guidelines as he did on whether they complied with SEC requirements.

Further, the group reserves auditor failed to act independently in several respects. At times, he allowed proved reserves associated with a project to remain booked because he was more "bullish" on its prospects than the local management responsible for the project. At other times, solely to support booking proved reserves for otherwise uneconomic projects, he advised local management to submit development plans that were unlikely ever to be executed. This lack of independence facilitated the booking of questionable reserves well after they should have been debooked.

Finally, the nonexecutive directors of Royal Dutch and Shell Transport, including the members of the Group audit committee, were not provided with the information necessary for the boards of the two companies to ensure that timely and appropriate action was taken with respect to the proved reserves estimation and reporting practices.

## Group Reserves Auditor's Report

In January 2002, the Group reserves auditor's report on Shell's 2001 proved reserves stated that "recent clarifications of FASB reserves guidelines by the SEC have shown that current Group reserves practice regarding the first time booking of Proved reserves in new fields is in some cases too lenient." The auditor stated that the "g[G]roup guidelines should be reviewed [and] first-time bookings should be aligned closer with SEC guidance and industry practice and they should be allowed only for firm projects with technical maturity and full economic viability."

On February 11, 2002, an internal note addressed the divergence between Shell's guidelines and the commission's rules and estimated the possible impact of this divergence on Shell's reported proved reserves. The note explicitly stated that "recently the SEC issued clarifications that make it apparent that the Group guidelines for booking Proved Reserves are no longer fully aligned with the SEC rules." Potential exposures identified in the note included approximately 1 billion boe of proved reserves relating to projects. The note failed to recommend debookings, and Shell did not take action to debook any of these proved reserves at that time.

By September 2002, the CEO of the Exploration and Production (EP) Division internally spoke in blunt terms of his perception of the operational and performance problems facing EP, noting to his colleagues that "we are struggling on all key criteria" and that "RRR remains below 100% mainly due to aggressive booking in 1997–2000." He further observed that "we have tried to adhere to a bunch of criteria that can only be managed successfully for so long" and admonished that "given the external visibility of our issues . . . , the market can only be 'fooled' if: (1) credibility of the company is high; (2) medium and long-term portfolio refreshment is real; and/or (3) positive trends can be shown on key indicators."

A month later, the group chair e-mailed the EP CEO that he was "not contemplating a change in the external promise." The next day, the EP CEO responded, "I must admit that I become sick and tired about arguing about the hard facts and

also can not perform miracles given where we are today. If I was interpreting the disclosure requirements literally under the Sarbanes-Oxley Act and legal requirements we would have a real problem."

None of these events prompted Shell to debook significant volumes. To the contrary, Shell continued to make large, questionable proved reserves bookings during this period. By the summer of 2003, Shell's analysis of reserves exposures had progressed, but still no debookings were recommended, even though internal information indicated that "some 1040 million boe (5%) is considered to be potentially at risk." The note concluded, however, that "at this stage, no action in relation to entries in the [proved reserves exposure] Catalogue is recommended. . . . It should be noted that the total potential exposure is broadly offset by the potential to include gas fuel and flare volumes in external reserves disclosures." The note apprised the committee of steps taken to address possible noncompliance with the SEC's regulations. However, management was advised that "much, if not all, of the potential exposure is offset by Shell's practice of not disclosing reserves in relation to gas production that is consumed on site as fuel or (incidental) flaring and venting."

According to the SEC complaint, Shell had undertaken substantial remedial efforts in connection with the reserves recategorization and had cooperated with the commission in its investigation.

## Specific SEC Charges

The SEC complaint alleged the following:[7]

1. As a result of Shell's knowing or reckless overstatement of its oil and gas reserves in its financial statements, the group's commission filings, specified previously, as well as other public statements, contained materially false and misleading statements and disclosures. These filings contained untrue statements of material fact concerning the company's reported proved reserves and omitted to state facts necessary to make the statements made, in light of the circumstances under which they were made, not misleading. These statements constituted a violation of Rule 10b-5 of the Securities Exchange Act.

2. Section 13(a) of the Exchange Act requires issuers to file such annual and quarterly reports as the commission may prescribe and in conformity with such rules as the commission may promulgate. Rule 13a-1 requires the filing of accurate annual reports that comply with the SEC's Regulation S-X. Rule 12b-20 requires an issuer to include material information as may be necessary to make the required statements, in light of the circumstances under which they were made, not misleading. The following periodic reports that Royal Dutch and Shell Transport

---

[7] *Securities and Exchange Commission v. Royal Dutch Petroleum Company and the "Shell" Transport and Trading Company, P.L.C.*, Complaint H-04-3359, August 24, 2004, www.sec.gov/litigation/litreleases/lr18844.htm.

filed with the commission were not prepared in accordance with rules promulgated by the commission: Form 20-F for fiscal years 1997–2002.

3. Shell violated Section 12 of the Exchange Act, in that it failed to (1) make and keep books, records, and accounts which, in reasonable detail, accurately and fairly reflected the transactions and dispositions of its assets; (2) devise and maintain a system of internal accounting controls sufficient to provide reasonable assurances that (a) transactions were executed in accordance with management's general or specific authorization; (b) transactions were recorded as necessary to permit preparation of financial statements in conformity with GAAP or any other criteria applicable to such statements, and to maintain accountability for assets; (c) access to assets was permitted only in accordance with management's general or specific authorization; and (d) the recorded accountability for assets was compared with the existing assets at reasonable intervals and appropriate action was taken with respect to any differences.

Royal Dutch and Shell Transport agreed to settle the charges by consenting to a cease-and-desist order finding violations of the antifraud, internal controls, recordkeeping, and reporting provisions of the federal securities laws, and by paying $1 disgorgement and a $120 million penalty in a related action. Shell also committed an additional $5 million to develop and implement a comprehensive internal compliance program under the direction and oversight of the group's legal director. The companies settled without admitting or denying the commission's substantive findings.[8]

## Questions

1. Use ethical reasoning to evaluate the actions of Shell management in this case with respect to accounting for and disclosing information about proved reserves.

2. In Chapter 7 we discussed aggressive accounting and earnings management techniques. Apply your knowledge from that chapter to the facts of the Shell case with respect to its proved reserves. Be sure to address specific actions taken that illustrate aggressive accounting and earnings management.

3. Given the facts of the case, describe the failures in corporate governance including internal controls and the relationship between the Group auditor and management and explain how they contributed to the reporting problems with proved reserves at Shell.

## Optional Question

4. The following note to the financial statements of Shell for the fiscal year end December 31, 2008, appeared in its 20-F filing with SEC.

[8]U.S. Securities and Exchange Commission, Litigation Release No. 18844, August 24, 2004, www.sec.gov/litigation/litreleases/lr18844.htm.

---

### IMPAIRMENT

Other than properties with no proved reserves (where the basis for carrying costs in the Consolidated Balance Sheet is explained under "Exploration Costs"), the carrying amounts of major property, plant and equipment are reviewed for possible impairment annually, while all assets are reviewed whenever events or changes in circumstances indicate that the carrying amounts for those assets may not be recoverable. If assets are determined to be impaired, the carrying amounts of those assets are written down to their recoverable amount, which is the higher of fair value less costs to sell and value in use, the latter being determined as the amount of estimated risk-adjusted discounted future cash flows. For this purpose, assets are grouped into cash-generating units based on separately identifiable and largely independent cash inflows. Assets classified as held for sale are recognized at the lower of the carrying amount and fair value less cost to sell. No further provision for depreciation is charged on such assets.

Estimates of future cash flows used in the evaluation for impairment of assets related to hydrocarbon production are made using risk assessments on field and reservoir performance and include expectations about proved reserves and unproved volumes, which are then risk-weighted utilizing the results from projections of geological, production, recovery and economic factors.

Impairments, except those related to goodwill, are reversed as applicable to the extent that the events or circumstances that triggered the original impairment have changed. Impairment charges and reversals are reported within depreciation, depletion and amortization.

---

Compare the standards followed by Shell with respect to asset impairments that are consistent with IFRS with those generally accepted in the U.S. Explain any differences and how such differences might impact the financial statements.

## Case 8-5

# Autonomy

## Background

On November 20, 2012, Hewlett-Packard (HP) disclosed that it discovered an accounting fraud and has written down $8.8 billion of the value of Autonomy, the British software company that it bought in 2011 for $11.1 billion, after discovering that Autonomy misrepresented its finances. In May 2012, HP had fired former Autonomy CEO, Dr. Michael Lynch, citing poor performance by his unit.

According to HP, its internal probe and forensic review had uncovered that the majority of the impairment charge, over $5 billion, is linked to serious accounting improprieties, disclosure failures, and outright misrepresentations discovered by HP's internal investigation into Autonomy's practices prior to and in connection with the acquisition.

The investigation began after an unnamed "senior member" of Autonomy's leadership alleged there had been a "series of questionable accounting and business practices" prior to the acquisition. HP said that the whistleblower gave "numerous details" that HP previously had no "knowledge or visibility" of. HP said it has discovered "extensive evidence" that an unspecified number of former employees of Autonomy had cooked the books prior to HP's $11.1 billion acquisition of the software company.

The probe determined that Autonomy was "substantially overvalued at the time of its acquisition" due to misstatements of financial performance, including revenue, core growth rate, and gross margins.

HP added that it was co-operating with the U.S. DOJ, the U.S. SEC, and the United Kingdom's Serious Fraud Office.

The Autonomy disclosures are the latest efforts by CEO Meg Whitman to clean up the mess that she inherited from former CEO Leo Apotheker, who HP reminded shareholders presided over the disastrous Autonomy deal.

In a statement, Apotheker said he is both "stunned and disappointed to learn" of the alleged accounting improprieties, and the developments "are a shock to the many who believed in the company, myself included."

Apotheker said the due diligence process was "meticulous and thorough" and "it's apparent that Autonomy's alleged accounting misrepresentations misled a number of people over time—not just HP's leadership team, auditors, and directors."

## Autonomy's Position

A spokeswoman for fired CEO Lynch told Reuters that the HP allegations are "false" and Autonomy's management was "shocked to see" the fraud charges. Lynch said that HP's due diligence was intensive and the larger company's senior management was "closely involved with running Autonomy for the past year."

Lynch further commented that[1]

- HP is using this as a ruse to distract investors from its bigger problems: "People certainly realize I'm not going to be used as Hewlett-Packard's scapegoat when it's got itself in a mess."
- HP's numbers don't add up. It's questioning about $100 million in revenues, yet blaming $5 billion of the write-off on fishy accounting.
- He wants HP to explain in detail how it came up with the $5 billion in write-offs from alleged fraud.
- He not only denies all wrongdoing, but he says he has backup because Autonomy was audited quarterly and every invoice over €100,000 euros ($129,000) was approved by auditors.

Lynch also said that some of the accusations are misleading because Autonomy was following IFRS, as British companies do, not the GAAP standard used by HP, which means it recognizes revenue differently in certain situations from U.S. practices.

Exhibit 1 contains statements made by HP and Lynch in the Autonomy matter.

## Accounting and Auditing Issues

Interviews in California and England with former Autonomy employees, business partners and attorneys close to the case paint a picture of a hard-driving sales culture shaped by Lynch's desire for rapid growth. They describe him as a domineering figure, who on at least a few occasions berated employees he believed weren't measuring up.

Along the way, these people say, Autonomy used aggressive accounting practices to make sure revenue from software licensing kept growing—thereby boosting the British company's valuation. The firm recognized revenue upfront that under U.S. accounting rules would have been deferred, and struck "round-trip transactions"—deals where Autonomy agreed to buy a client's products or services while at the same time the client purchased Autonomy software, according to these people.

"The rules aren't that complicated," said Dan Mahoney of the accounting research business organization—Center for Financial Research and Analysis (CFRA),[2] who covered

---

[1]Reuters, "HP alleges Autonomy wrongdoing, takes $8.8 billion charge," November 20, 2012. Available at www.reuters.com/article/2012/11/20/us-hp-results-idUSBRE8AJ0OB20121120.
[2]Association of Certified Financial Crime Specialists, "HP-Autonomy debacle shines light on auditors, lawyers in financial crime cases," December 4, 2012, Available at http://www.acfcs.org/hp-autonomy-debacle-shines-light-on-auditors-lawyers-in-financial-crime-cases/.

## Exhibit 1
## Statements by HP and Dr. Michael Lynch at Autonomy

### HP's official statement

HP has initiated an intense internal investigation into a series of accounting improprieties, disclosure failures and outright misrepresentations that occurred prior to HP's acquisition of Autonomy. We believe we have uncovered extensive evidence of a willful effort on behalf of certain former Autonomy employees to inflate the underlying financial metrics of the company in order to mislead investors and potential buyers.

The matter is in the hands of the authorities, including the UK Serious Fraud Office (SFC), the U.S. Securities and Exchange Commission's Enforcement Division and the U.S. Department of Justice, and we will defer to them as to how they wish to engage with Dr. Lynch. In addition, HP will take legal action against the parties involved at the appropriate time.

While Dr. Lynch is eager for a debate, we believe the legal process is the correct method in which to bring out the facts and take action on behalf of our shareholders. In that setting, we look forward to hearing Dr. Lynch and other former Autonomy employees answer questions under penalty of perjury.

### For his part, Lynch offered a decidedly different narrative in a letter to HP's board that he released publicly on November 27, 2012.

To: The Board of Directors of Hewlett-Packard Company
I utterly reject all allegations of impropriety.

Autonomy's finances, during its years as a public company and including the time period in question, were handled in accordance with applicable regulations and accounting practices. Autonomy's accounts were overseen by independent auditors Deloitte LLC, who have confirmed the application of all appropriate procedures including those dictated by the International Financial Reporting Standards used in the UK.

Having no details beyond the limited public information provided last week, and still with no further contact from you, I am writing today to ask you, the board of HP, for immediate and specific explanations for the allegations HP is making. HP should provide me with the interim report and any other documents which you say you have provided to the SEC and the SFO so that I can answer whatever is alleged, instead of the selective disclosure of non-material information via background discussions with the media.

I believe it is in the interest of all stakeholders, and the public record, for HP to respond to a number of questions that I have about the allegations.

- Many observers are stunned by HP's claim that these allegations account for a $5 billion write down and fail to understand how HP reaches that number. Please publish the calculations used to determine the $5 billion impairment charge. Please provide a breakdown of the relative contribution for revenue, cash flow, profit and write down in relation to:
  a. The alleged "mischaracterization" of hardware that HP did not realize Autonomy sold, as I understand this would have no effect on annual top or bottom lines and a minor effect on gross margin within normal fluctuations and no impact on growth, assuming a steady state over the period;
  b. The alleged "inappropriate acceleration of revenue recognition with value-added resellers" and the "[creation of] revenue where no end-user customer existed at the time of sale," given their normal treatment under IFRS; and
  c. The allegations of incorrect revenue recognition of long-term arrangements of hosted deals, again given the normal treatment under IFRS.
- In order to justify a $5 billion accounting write down, a significant amount of revenue must be involved. Please explain how such issues could possibly have gone undetected during the extensive acquisition due diligence process and HP's financial oversight of Autonomy for a year from acquisition until October 2012 (a period during which all of the Autonomy finance reported to HP's CFO Cathie Lesjak).
- Can HP really state that no part of the $5 billion write down was, or should be, attributed to HP's operational and financial mismanagement of Autonomy since the acquisition?
- How many people employed by Autonomy in September 2011 have left or resigned under the management of HP?
- HP raised issues about the inclusion of hardware in Autonomy's IDOL Product revenue, notwithstanding this being in accordance with proper IFRS accounting practice. Please confirm that Ms Whitman and other HP senior management were aware of Autonomy's hardware sales before 2012. Did Autonomy, as part of HP, continue to sell third-party hardware of materially similar value after acquisition? Was this accounted for by HP and was this reported in the Autonomy segment of their accounts?
- Were Ms Whitman and Ms Lesjak aware that Paul Curtis (HP's Worldwide Director of Software Revenue Recognition), KPMG and Ernst & Young undertook in December 2011 detailed studies of Autonomy's software revenue recognition with a view to optimizing for U.S. GAAP?
- Why did HP senior management apparently wait six months to inform its shareholders of the possibility of a material event related to Autonomy?

---

**Exhibit 1 (*continued*)**

Hewlett Packard is an iconic technology company, which was historically admired and respected all over the world. Autonomy joined forces with HP with real hopes for the future and in the belief that together there was an opportunity to make HP great again. I have been truly saddened by the events of the past months, and am shocked and appalled by the events of the past week.

I am placing this letter in the public domain in the interests of complete transparency.

Yours faithfully,
Dr. Mike Lynch

---

Autonomy until it was acquired. He said that Autonomy had the hallmarks of a company that recognized revenue too aggressively. He said neither U.S. nor international accounting rules would allow companies to recognize not-yet collected revenue from customers that might be at risk.

In a statement issued on November 30, 2012, HP said its ongoing investigation into the activities of certain former Autonomy employees had uncovered numerous transactions clearly designed to inflate the underlying financial metrics of the company before its acquisition. The company said it is confident the deals are improper even under the international accounting standards Lynch cites.

In an interview with the British publication, *The Guardian,* on April 10, 2013,[3] Meg Whitman said that the board, which approved the Autonomy transaction, relied on audited information from Deloitte & Touche and additional auditing from KPMG, though she said that she's not blaming the accountants.

"Neither of them saw what we now see after someone came forward to point us in the right direction," Whitman said.

Deloitte, which served as Autonomy's auditor in the U.K., and KPMG, which performed the acquisition work for HP, are under fire for allegedly failing to detect the accounting issues.

Deloitte, said in a statement that it cannot comment further on this matter due to client confidentiality and that it will cooperate with the relevant authorities with any investigations into the allegations."[4]

[3]Juliette Garside, "HP's Meg Whitman: 'we had to be straight' on Autonomy," *The Guardian,* April 10, 2013, Available at http://www.guardian.co.uk/business/2013/apr/10/hp-autonomy-deal-meg-whitman.
[4]Francine McKenna, "Hewlett-Pckard's Allegations: A Material Writedown and all Four Audit Firms on the Spot," November 20, 2012. Available at www.forbes.com/sites/francinemckenna/2012/11/20/hewlett-packards-autonomy-allegations-a-material-writedown-puts-all-four-audit-firms-on-the-spot/.
[5]HP-Autonomy debacle shines light on auditors, lawyers in financial crime cases, Available at http://www.acfcs.org/hp-autonomy-debacle-shines-light-on-auditors-lawyers-in-financial-crime-cases/#sthash.gffH55lz.dpuf.

## Questions

1. What is meant by "earnings management" and how does it relate to the accounting techniques followed by Autonomy?

2. In an analysis by the Association of Certified Financial Crime Specialists (ACFCS) about the Autonomy merger with HP, the following statement is made: "The scandal is prompting questions about who is to blame for the soured merger. As details emerge, the case is spotlighting the difficulties that accountants and lawyers face in complex mergers and acquisitions and business deals. The case also raises the issue of what responsibility these professionals have for detecting potentially fraudulent business records where the line between accounting discrepancies and financial crime is blurred."[5] Given the facts of the case, evaluate the ethical and professional responsibilities of the external auditors with respect to the AICPA Code of Professional Conduct.

3. Meg Whitman is quoted in the case as saying that the board, which approved the Autonomy transaction, relied on audited information from Deloitte & Touche and additional auditing from KPMG. Given that auditing standards and legal requirements dictate that auditors are responsible for detecting material fraud in the financial statements of audit clients, would you blame the auditors for failing to uncover the improper accounting for revenue at Autonomy? Which audit standards are critical in making that determination?

## Optional Question

4. Revenue recognition transactions such as those described in question 2 are referred to as "linked transactions" under IFRS. Research the revenue recognition rules for linked transactions and compare them to what Autonomy did. Does it seem that Lynch's position is valid as stated in the case that the accusations against him and Autonomy for improper revenue recognition practices was not fair because Autonomy was following IFRS and they are different than the GAAP standard used by HP, which means it recognizes revenue differently in certain situations from U.S. practices?

## Case 8-6

# Olympus

### Summary of the Case

On September 25, 2012, Japanese camera and medical equipment maker Olympus Corporation and three of its former executives pleaded guilty to charges related to a $1.7 billion accounting cover-up in one of Japan's biggest corporate scandals. Olympus admitted that it tried to conceal investment losses by using improper accounting under a scheme that began in the 1990s.

The scandal was exposed in 2011 by Olympus's then-CEO, Michael C. Woodford, who was fired by the company's board after asking about deals that were later found to have been used to conceal the losses.

"The full responsibility lies with me and I feel deeply sorry for causing trouble to our business partners, shareholders and the wider public," the former chairman, Tsuyoshi Kikukawa, told the Tokyo district court. "I take full responsibility for what happened."[1]

Prosecutors charged Kikukawa; a former executive vice president, Hisashi Mori; and a former internal auditor, Hideo Yamada, with inflating the company's net worth in financial statements for five fiscal years to March 2011 due to accounting for risky investments made in the late-1980s bubble economy. The three former executives had been identified by an investigative panel, commissioned by Olympus, as the main suspects in the fraud.

An Olympus spokesman said the company would cooperate fully with the investigative authorities. It is under investigation by law enforcement agencies in Japan, Britain, and the United States.

In December 2011, Olympus filed five years' worth of corrected financial statements plus overdue first-half results, revealing a $1.1 billion hole in its balance sheet. This development led to speculation that it would need to merge or forge a business tie-up to raise capital.

### Olympus Spent Huge Sums on Inflated Acquisitions, Advisory Fees to Conceal Investment Losses

Olympus's cover-up of massive losses has shed light on several murky methods that some companies employed to clean up the mess left after Japan's economic bubble burst. Many companies turned to speculative investments as they suffered sluggish sales and stagnant operating profits. The company used "loss-deferring practices" to make losses look smaller on the books by selling bad assets to related companies.

[1]Reuters, "Olympus and Ex-Executives Plead Guilty in Accounting Fraud," September 25, 2012. Available at http://www.reuters.com/article/2012/09/25/us-olympus-trial-idUSBRE88O01920120925.

To take investment losses off its books, Olympus spent large sums of money to purchase British medical equipment maker Gyrus Group PLC and three Japanese companies and paid huge consulting fees. According to their records, Olympus paid about ¥66 billion (yen) (about $660 million), mainly in advisory fees, for their purchase of Gyrus, an apparent manipulation to conceal losses.

Olympus is suspected of having deliberately acquired Gyrus at an inflated price, and in the year following the purchases, it booked impairment losses as a result of decreases in the companies' value.

To avert a rapid deterioration of its financial standing, Olympus continued corporate acquisitions and other measures for many years, booking impairment losses to improve its balance sheet. Losses on the purchases of the three Japanese companies amounted to ¥55.7 billion. With money paid on the Gyrus deal included, Olympus may have used more than ¥100 billion in funds for past acquisitions to conceal losses on securities investments.

### Olympus Reported Only ¥17 Billion of ¥100 Billion in Losses

Olympus reported only about ¥17 billion in losses in its annual securities report for the year ending March 2000, despite the fact that its losses totaled nearly ¥100 billion at that time. Japanese accounting standards were revised in 2000 to require latent losses of financial products to be specified in annual securities reports. Olympus should have reported the actual latent losses in its report for the year ending March 2001.

The previous method that recorded stocks and other financial products by book value—the price when they were purchased—was abolished. The new method listed them by market value (mark-to-market accounting). Under this change, Olympus had to report all the losses in its March 2001 report. However, Olympus anticipated this change a year in advance and posted only about ¥17 billion of the nearly 100 billion yen as an extraordinary loss for the March 2000 settlement term. The company did not post the remainder as a deficit; rather, it deferred it using questionable measures.

### Olympus's *Tobashi* Scheme

At the heart of Olympus's action, was a once-common technique to hide losses called *tobashi,* which Japanese financial regulators tolerated before clamping down on the practice in the late 1990s. *Tobashi,* translated loosely as "to blow away," enables companies to hide losses on bad assets by selling those assets to other companies, only to buy them back later through payments, often disguised as advisory fees or other transactions, when market conditions or earnings improve.

*Tobashi* allows a company with the bad assets to mask losses temporarily, a practice banned in the early 2000s. The idea is that you pay off the losses later, when company finances are better.

Olympus appears to have pushed to settle its *tobashi* amounts from 2006 to 2008, when the local economy was picking up and corporate profits rebounding, in an effort to "clean up its act." Business was finally strong enough to be able to withstand a write-down. It was during those years that the company engineered the payouts that came under scrutiny: $687 million in fees to an obscure financial adviser over Olympus's acquisition of Gyrus in 2008, a fee that was roughly a third of the $2 billion acquisition price, more than 30 times the norm. Olympus also acquired three small Japanese companies from 2006 to 2008 with little in common with its core business for a total of $773 million, only to write down most of their value within the same fiscal year.

## Olympus Scandal Raises Questions about the "Japan Way" of Doing Business

The scandal rocked corporate Japan, not least because of the company's succession of firings, denials, admissions, and whistleblowing. It also exposed weaknesses in Japan's financial regulatory system and corporate governance.

"This is a case where Japan's outmoded practice of corporate governance remained and reared its ugly head," according to Shuhei Abe, president of Tokyo-based Sparx Group Company. "With Olympus's case, it will no longer be justifiable for Japan Inc. to continue practicing under the excuse of the 'Japan way of doing things.'" "The Japanese market is already looking unattractive to foreign investors," said Hideaki Tsukuda, managing partner at Egon Zehnder International's Tokyo office. "Japanese companies really have to get their acts together, taking this opportunity to strengthen their corporate-governance practices."[2]

On the surface, Olympus seemed to have checks on its management. For example, it hired directors and auditors from outside the company, as well as a British president who was not tied to corporate insiders. In reality, however, the company's management was ruled by former chairman Tsuyoshi Kikukawa and a few other executives who came from its financial sections.

The company's management is believed to have been effectively controlled by several executives who had a background in financial affairs, including Kikukawa and former vice president Hisashi Mori, both of whom were involved in the cover-up of past losses. Olympus's board of auditors, which is supposed to supervise the board of directors, includes full-time auditor Hideo Yamada, who also had financial expertise.

[2]"Olympus Scandal: $1.5 billion in Losses Hidden in Dodgy Acquisitions," Available at http://factsanddetails.com/japan.php?itemid=2305&catid=24&subcatid=157.

In some ways, the Olympus episode harks back to an older—and more freewheeling—era of Japanese deal-making, before the bursting of the country's economic bubble in the 1990s and subsequent regulatory reform efforts. Back then, small Japanese shareholders would threaten to cause problems at corporate annual meetings unless they were paid to be silent. In other cases, companies would pay politicians to secure government business. Culturally, you trust intermediaries and relationships so due diligence often is shortchanged.

## How Woodford Rocked the Boat at Olympus

Olympus initially said that it fired Woodford, one of a handful of foreign executives at top Japanese companies, over what it called his aggressive Western management style. Woodford disclosed internal documents to show he was dismissed after he raised questions about irregular payouts related to mergers and acquisitions. Woodford later made a bid to return to the company with a fresh slate of directors, but he abandoned that effort after Japanese institutional investors continued to back Olympus's current management.

Woodford had officially raised his concerns in a series of letters to the Olympus vice chairman, Hisashi Mori, beginning in mid-September 2011. The letters painted a picture of an increasingly frustrated Woodward as he demanded more disclosure over the acquisitions. In his fifth letter, dated September 27, he set the first of his ultimatums: Mori must, he insisted, produce documents before his return to Tokyo from London the next day and agree to a three-way summit with chairman Kikukawa.

But Kikukawa and Mori then made what seemed at the time as a puzzling move: they offered Woodford the position of CEO, to add to his post as president. The promotion was announced in a news release filled with glowing praise for Woodford, championing his cost-cutting drive and presenting him as the new global face of Olympus.

If the promotion was meant to give Woodford a greater stake in the company's future, and a greater sense of loyalty to the board, Woodford interpreted it as giving him even more ability to investigate the deals. Without the board's knowledge, he commissioned a report by PricewaterhouseCoopers (PwC) into the Gyrus deal, including the unusually high advisory fee and apparent lack of due diligence. On October 11, 2011, he circulated the report to the board and called on Kikukawa and Mori to resign. Three days later, the board fired him.

## Losses for Financial Year 2011–2012

Olympus said it posted a bigger-than-expected Group (consolidated) net loss for the fiscal year to March 2012. The consolidated net loss stood at ¥48.985 billion, compared with its projected loss of ¥32 billion and the ¥3.866 billion profit that it logged the previous year. The weaker result stemmed from additional special losses that the optical equipment maker booked to liquidate three companies that it used to conceal massive investment losses from the bubble economy.

In December 2011, Olympus filed five years' worth of corrected earnings statements to restate its accounts. It said that as of the end of September, net assets were ¥46 billion, down from a restated ¥225 billion in March 2007. It also withdrew its forecast for a ¥18 billion net profit in the current business year.

## Accounting Explanations

*Olympus hid a $1.7 billion loss through an intricate array of transactions.*

A one paragraph summary of what it did appears in the investigation report:

> The lost disposition scheme is featured in that Olympus sold the assets that incurred loss to the funds set up by Olympus itself, and later provided the finance needed to settle the loss under the cover of the company acquisitions. More specifically, Olympus circulated money either by flowing money into the funds by acquiring the entrepreneurial ventures owned by the funds at the substantially higher price than the real values, or by paying a substantially high fees to the third party who acted as the intermediate in the acquisition, resulting in recognition of large amount of goodwill, and subsequently amortized goodwill recognized impairment loss, which created substantial loss.[3]

Here is a more understandable version of the event:

> Olympus indirectly loaned money to an off-the-books subsidiary and then sold the investments that had the huge losses to the subsidiary at historical cost, eventually paying a huge premium to buy some other small companies and writing off the underwater investments as if they were goodwill impairments.

A more detailed bookkeeping analysis of the complicated transactions appears in Exhibit 1.

## Auditor Responsibilities

Arthur Andersen was the external auditor through March 31, 2002, after which Andersen was forced out of business by a U.S. DOJ investigation due to its role at Enron. Then KPMG AZSA LLC was the auditor through March 31, 2009. The 2010 and 2011 fiscal years were audited by Ernst & Young ShinNihon LLC.

The investigative report noted that the fraud was hidden quite well. Three banks were involved in hiding information from the auditors. The summary report said that all three of them agreed not to tell auditors the information that would normally be provided on an audit confirmation.

KPMG did come across one of the *tobashi* schemes carried out through one of the three different routes that had been set up. According to the investigative report:

Not everything was going smoothly. The report said that in 1999, Olympus's then-auditor, KPMG AZSA LLC, came across information that indicated the company was engaged in *tobashi*, which recently had become illegal in Japan. Mori and Yamada initially denied KPMG's assertion, but the auditor pushed them that same year to admit to the presence of one fund and unwind it, booking a loss of ¥16.8 billion. The executives assured KPMG that that was the only such deal, the report said.[4]

Questions about the auditor's role include: How do you perform an audit for a global investor audience in a local economy where intentionally hiding losses is legal? How do you function in a business environment where that is acceptable and normative?

On the other hand, notice how one audit team, from KPMG in 1999, did find one part of the scheme. Management lied by denying that it even existed. After agreeing to write it off, Olympus senior management lied again, saying that it was the only one. But the scheme expanded, without detection, for another six years or so and was in place, without detection, until the last component was unwound at the end of fiscal year 2010.

## Olympus Finally Had Enough of the Deception

The last part of the bad investments was finally written off in March 2010. That was the last month of the fiscal year, when Ernst & Young took over the audit from KPMG. Mori and Yamada had finally decided to unwind and write off the underwater financial assets and repay the loans that it had made through its unconsolidated subsidiary. Of course, by then, the financial press had gotten wind of what was going on at Olympus.

## Questions

1. In the Olympus case, Michael Woodford was abruptly fired on October 14, 2011, by the company's executive board because of what the board cited as a "management culture clash." Explain what you think this statement means in the context of the facts of the case and our discussion about the role of culture in business operations.

2. Do you think the practice of "tobashi" is a form of earnings management? Why or why not?

3. Explain the ethical issues and corporate governance failings that contributed to the fraud at Olympus, including the role of the auditors.

## Optional Question

4. What are the similarities between the actions taken in the Olympus case and those of Enron with respect to its special-purpose-entities (SPEs)?

[3]Reuters, "Olympus and Ex-Executives Plead Guilty in Accounting Fraud," September 25, 2012. Available at http://www.reuters.com/article/2012/09/25/us-olympus-trial-idUSBRE88O01920120925.

[4]"Olympus Scandal: $1.5 billion in Losses Hidden in Dodgy Acquisitions," Available at http://factsanddetails.com/japan.php?itemid=2305&catid=24&subcatid=157.

**Exhibit 1**
**Detailed Bookkeeping Analysis of Olympus's Accounting Fraud***

*Phase 1*
*Transaction 1:*
This is a summary of a complex move—it involved making a CD deposit at several banks that were asked to loan the money back to an unrelated entity, with the CD as collateral, so the subsidiary can buy investments from Olympus.

  Note: According to the investigative committee's report, three banks were involved through the course of the whole project: Commerzbank, LGT, and Société Générale. The committee's report indicates that all three banks agreed to Olympus's request not to tell the auditors about the CDs being collateral for a loan.

**(Olympus books)**
DR Certificate of deposit
CR Cash
  (CD purchase at banks; banks loan it to unconsolidated subsidiary)
**(Unconsolidated subsidiary books)**
DR Cash
CR Note payable to banks
  (Cash from banks; collateralized by Olympus)

*Transaction 2:*
**(Olympus books)**
DR Cash
CR Financial assets (Investments)
  (Proceeds from selling underwater investments to unconsolidated subsidiary; may have triggered gain on sale)
**(Unconsolidated subsidiary books)**
DR Financial assets (Investments)
CR Cash
  (To buy underwater investments from Olympus)

*Phase 2*
Eventually the CDs would have to be rolled over and brought back. In addition, the unrealized losses would have to be written down eventually, so the second phase was launched.

*Transaction 3:*
Olympus bought some tiny (startup) companies. They paid significantly more than they were worth and paid large amounts for consultants for their service as finders and intermediaries.

**(Olympus books)**
DR Investments (startup subsidiary)
DR Goodwill—(cash paid less fair market value of subsidiary net assets)
CR Cash
  (Investments in new subsidiaries)
*Note:* The investment in the consolidated subsidiary shows a large amount of goodwill, which could then be written down.

**(Entries by the newly formed consolidated subsidiary)**
DR Cash
CR Common stock
  (Cash investment from Olympus)

*Transaction 4:*
The effect of these transactions was to transfer money into the newest consolidated subsidiary, which used the money to buy the bad investments from the older, unconsolidated subsidiary. The unconsolidated subsidiary then repaid the note payable to the bank and Olympus liquidated its CD.

**(Entries by the newly formed consolidated subsidiary)**
DR Financial assets (Investments)
CR Cash
  (Buy underwater investments from unconsolidated subsidiary at book value)

**(Unconsolidated subsidiary books)**
DR Cash (from consolidated sub)
CR Financial assets (Investments)
   (Proceeds received from consolidated subsidiary from sale of underwater investments)
DR Note payable to banks
CR Cash
   (Repay loan to banks)
**Entries by Olympus**
DR Cash
CR Certificate of deposit
   (CD liquidated)

---

*Olympus Scandal: $1.5 billion in Losses Hidden in Dodgy Acquisitions," Available at http://factsanddetails.com/japan.php?itemid=2305&catid=24&subcatid=157.

# Major Cases

The following major cases are more detailed than most of the cases in the book and may require students to do research in responding to case questions. We use these cases for course summary assignments, written projects, and class discussion (i.e., group) presentations.

Major Case 1: Adelphia Communications Corporation
Major Case 2: Royal Ahold N.V. (Ahold)
Major Case 3: MicroStrategy, Inc.
Major Case 4: Cendant Corporation
Major Case 5: Navistar International
Major Case 6: Waste Management

## Major Case 1

# Adelphia Communications Corporation

On July 24, 2009, the U.S. Court of Appeals for the District of Columbia upheld the finding of the Securities and Exchange Commission (SEC) that Gregory M. Dearlove, a certified public accountant (CPA) and formerly a partner with the accounting firm Deloitte & Touche LLP (Deloitte), engaged in improper professional conduct within the meaning of Rule of Practice 102(e). Dearlove served as the engagement partner on Deloitte's audit of the financial statements of Adelphia Communications corporation. (Adelphia), a public company, for the fiscal year ended December 31, 2000. The SEC confirmed its original ruling that Adelphia's financial statements were not in accordance with generally accepted accounting principles (GAAP), and that Dearlove violated generally accepted auditing standards (GAAS). The administrative law judge (ALJ) also found that Dearlove was a cause of Adelphia's violations of the reporting and recordkeeping provisions of the Exchange Act. The ALJ permanently denied Dearlove the privilege of appearing or practicing in any capacity before the commission.

The opinion for the court was filed by Judge Douglas H. Ginsburg of the U.S. Court of Appeals for the D.C. Circuit Court. The opinion states that the SEC concluded that Dearlove engaged repeatedly in unreasonable conduct resulting in violations of applicable accounting principles and standards while serving as Deloitte's engagement partner in charge of the 2000 audit of Adelphia. Dearlove had argued that the SEC committed an error of law, misapplied the applicable accounting principles and standards, and denied him due process. Because the SEC made no error of law, and substantial evidence supports its findings of fact, the court denied the petition.

## Background Issues

John Rigas had founded Adelphia, Greek for brothers, in 1952, and Rigas and his children were the controlling shareholders in 2000. By the year 2000, Adelphia was one of the largest cable television companies in the United States. It had doubled the number of cable subscribers that it served by acquiring several other cable companies in late 1999. Although its assets were growing, Adelphia's debt grew substantially as well. The SEC found that prior to 2000, Adelphia, its subsidiaries, and some Rigas-affiliated entities entered as co-borrowers into a series of credit agreements. By 1999, Adelphia and the entities had obtained $1.05 billion in credit; in 2000, they tripled their available credit and drew down essentially all the funds available under the agreements.

Deloitte audited Adelphia's financial statements from 1980 through 2002, with Dearlove as the engagement partner. Dearlove and the Deloitte team described the 2000 audit, like many prior audits of Adelphia, as posing "much greater than normal risk" because Adelphia engaged in numerous transactions with subsidiaries and affiliated entities, many of which were owned by members of the Rigas family.

Deloitte issued its year 2000 independent auditor's report of Adelphia—signed by Dearlove—on March 29, 2001. In January 2002, in the wake of the Enron scandal, the SEC released a statement regarding the disclosure of related-party transactions. In March, Adelphia disclosed its obligations as co-debtor with the Rigas entities. Its share price declined from $30 in January 2002 to $0.30 in June, when it was delisted by the National Association of Securities Dealers (NASDAQ). In September 2002, the Department of Justice brought criminal fraud charges against Adelphia officials, including members of the Rigas family, and Adelphia agreed to pay $715 million into a victims' restitution fund as part of a settlement with the government. In April 2005 the SEC brought and settled civil actions against Adelphia, members of the Rigas family, and Deloitte.

## SEC Charges

In September 2005, the SEC charged Dearlove with improper conduct resulting in a violation of applicable professional standards, including his approval of Adelphia's method of accounting for transactions between itself and one or more Rigas entities (i.e., related-party transactions). The matter was referred to the ALJ, who presided at an administrative trial-type hearing to resolve the dispute between the SEC and Adelphia. The ALJ determined Dearlove had engaged in one instance of "highly unreasonable" conduct and repeated instances of "unreasonable" conduct, and permanently denied Dearlove the right to practice before the SEC, Adelphia, and Dearlove. Upon review of the ALJ's decision, the SEC held Dearlove had engaged in repeated instances of unreasonable conduct as defined under Rule 102 and denied him the right to practice before the SEC, but provided him the opportunity to apply for reinstatement after four years. Dearlove petitioned for review of that decision, which was denied by the U.S. Court of Appeals.[1]

SEC Rule 102(e) provides the SEC may "deny, temporarily or permanently, the privilege of appearing or practicing before [the SEC] in any way to any person who is found by the Commission . . . to have engaged in unethical or improper professional conduct." The rule defines three classes of "improper professional conduct" for accountants: (1) "Intentional or knowing conduct, including reckless conduct, that results in a violation of applicable professional standards," (2) "a single instance of highly unreasonable conduct that results in a violation of applicable professional standards," and (3) "repeated

---

[1] Securities and Exchange Commission, Accounting and Auditing Enforcement Release No. 2779, January 31, 2008, *In the Matter of Gregory M. Dearlove, CPA;* www.sec.gov/litigation/opinion/2008/34-57244.pdf.

instances of unreasonable conduct, each resulting in a violation of applicable professional standards, that indicate a lack of competence to practice before the Commission." The court supported the SEC's determination that Dearlove repeatedly engaged in unreasonable conduct.

While most of the alleged fraud at Adelphia took its form in hidden debt, the trial was also notable for examples of the eye-popping personal luxury that has marked other white-collar trials such as at Tyco.

In the court case, prosecutor Christopher Clark led off his closing argument by saying John Rigas had ordered two Christmas trees flown to New York, at a cost of $6,000, for his daughter. Rigas also ordered up 17 company cars and the company purchase of 3,600 acres of timberland at a cost of $26 million to preserve the pristine view outside his Coudersport home in Buffalo, New York. Timothy Rigas, the CFO, had become so concerned that he limited his father to withdrawals of $1 million per month.

## Deloitte's Audit

Deloitte served as the independent auditor for Adelphia, one of its largest audit clients, from 1980 through 2002. The audits were complex. Several of Adelphia's subsidiaries filed their own Forms 10-K annual reports with the SEC. For several years, Deloitte had concluded that the Adelphia engagement posed a "much greater than normal" risk of fraud, misstatement, or error; this was the highest risk category that Deloitte recognized. Risk factors that Deloitte specifically identified in reaching this assessment for the 2000 audit included the following:[2]

- Adelphia operated in a volatile industry, expanded rapidly, and had a large number of decentralized operating entities with a complex reporting structure.

- Adelphia carried substantial debt and was near the limit of its financial resources, making it critical that the company comply with debt covenants.

- Management of Adelphia was concentrated in a small group without compensating controls.

- Adelphia management lacked technical accounting expertise but nevertheless appeared willing to accept unusually high levels of risk, tended to interpret accounting standards aggressively, and was reluctant to record adjustments proposed by auditors.

- Adelphia engaged in significant related-party transactions with affiliated entities that Deloitte would not be auditing.

To help manage the audit risk, Deloitte planned, among other things, to increase Deloitte's management involvement at all stages of the audit "to ensure that the appropriate work is planned and its performance is properly supervised."

It also proposed to heighten professional skepticism "to ensure that accounting estimates, related-party transactions and transactions in the normal course of business appear reasonable and are appropriately identified and disclosed."

On March 29, 2001, Deloitte issued its independent auditor's report, signed by Dearlove, which stated that it had conducted its audit in accordance with GAAS and that such audit provided a reasonable basis for its opinion that Adelphia's 2000 financial statements fairly presented Adelphia's financial position in conformity with GAAP.

## Charges against Rigas Family and Deloitte

In the wake of Adelphia's decline, the U.S. Department of Justice (DOJ) brought criminal fraud charges against several members of the Rigas family and other Adelphia officials. The DOJ declined to file criminal charges against Adelphia as part of a settlement in which Adelphia agreed to pay $715 million in stock and cash to a victims' restitution fund once the company emerged from bankruptcy.

The SEC brought several actions related to the decline of Adelphia. On April 25, 2005, Adelphia, John Rigas, and Rigas's three sons settled a civil injunctive action in which the respondents, without admitting or denying the allegations against them, were enjoined from committing or causing further violations of the antifraud, reporting, recordkeeping, and internal controls provisions of the federal securities laws.[3] The next day, the commission instituted and settled administrative proceedings against Deloitte under Rule 102(e). Without admitting or denying the commission's allegations, Deloitte consented to the entry of findings that it engaged in repeated instances of unreasonable conduct with respect to the audit of Adelphia's 2000 financial statements. Deloitte also consented to a finding that it caused Adelphia's violations of those provisions of the Securities and Exchange Act that require issuers to file annual reports, make and keep accurate books and records, and devise and maintain a system of sufficient internal controls. Deloitte agreed to pay a $25 million penalty and to implement various prophylactic policies and procedures. The commission also settled a civil action, based on the same conduct, in which Deloitte agreed to pay another $25 million penalty. Senior manager William Caswell consented to commission findings that he committed repeated instances of unreasonable conduct and agreed to a bar from appearing or practicing as an accountant before the commission with a right to apply for reinstatement after two years.[4]

---

[2] *Securities and Exchange Commission v. Adelphia Communications Corp., et al.,* Civil Action File No. 02-CV-5776 (PKC) (S.D.N.Y. October 30, 2008), Litigation Release No. 20795, October 30, 2008; www.sec.gov/litigation/litreleases/2008/lr20795.htm.

[3] *Securities and Exchange Commission v. Adelphia Communications Corporation, John J. Rigas, Timothy J. Rigas, Michael J. Rigas, James P. Rigas, James R. Brown, and Michael C. Mulcahy,* 02 Civ. 5776 (S.D.N.Y.) (KMW), Litigation Release No. 17837, November 14, 2002; www.sec.gov/litigation/litreleases/lr17837.htm.
[4] Accounting & Auditing Enforcement Release No. 2237, *In the Matter of Deloitte & Touche LLP,* April 26, 2005; www.sec.gov/litigation/admin/34-51606.pdf.

## Violation of GAAS: General, Fieldwork, and Reporting Standards

In determining whether to discipline an accountant under Rule 102(e)(1)(iv), the commission has consistently measured auditors' conduct by their adherence to or deviation from GAAS. Certain audit conditions require auditors to increase their professional care and skepticism, as when the audit presents a risk of material misstatement or fraud. When an audit includes review of related-party transactions, auditors must tailor their examinations to obtain satisfaction concerning the purpose, nature, and extent of those transactions on the financial statements. Unless and until an auditor obtains an understanding of the business purpose of material related-party transactions, the audit is not complete. These standards can overlap somewhat, and one GAAS failure may contribute to another.

Dearlove asked the court to compare the reasonableness of his conduct to a standard used by New York state courts in professional negligence cases, that the standard for determining negligence by an accountant should be based on whether the respondent "use[d] the same degree of skill and care that other [accountants] in the community would reasonably use in the same situation." Dearlove believed that his actions should be judged in the context of the large, complex Adelphia audit and to determine whether he exercised the degree of skill and care, including professional skepticism, that a reasonable engagement partner would have used in similar circumstances. Dearlove contended that this analysis "necessarily includes . . . conclusions previously reached by other professionals," a reference to the Adelphia audits that Deloitte conducted from 1994 through 1999. Dearlove asserted that he could place some reliance on audit precedent. Moreover, in his view, the fact that prior auditors reached the same conclusions is "compelling evidence" that Dearlove acted reasonably. The court rejected any suggestion that the conduct of prior auditors should be a substitute for the standards established by GAAS, ruling that "these standards apply to audits of all sizes and all levels of complexity and describe the conduct that the accounting profession itself has established as reasonable, provid[ing] a measure of audit quality and the objectives to be achieved in an audit." The court, therefore, declined to create a separate standard of professional conduct for auditors that depends in each case on the behavior of a particular auditor's predecessors.

The SEC found that prior Deloitte audits offered little support for the conclusions reached in the 2000 audit. The record did not describe how the audits of prior financial statements were performed or what evidential matter supported those audit conclusions. Moreover, Dearlove's expert, while arguing that partner rotation does not require the new auditor to perform a "de novo audit of the client," nevertheless explained that an engagement partner "would perform . . . new audit procedures or GAAP research and consultation . . . to address changed conditions or professional standards."

In 2000, Dearlove was presented with markedly different circumstances from those presented to prior teams: since 1999, Adelphia had tripled its coborrowed debt, doubled its revenues and operating expenses, and acquired more cable subscribers. The changes implicated areas of the Adelphia audit that Deloitte had specifically identified as posing high risk—namely, its rapid expansion, substantial debt load, and significant related-party transactions. Therefore, the court rejected Dearlove's argument that the similarity of prior audit conclusions lends reasonableness to his own audit and found no reason to reject GAAS as the standard by which we judge all audits.

## Violation of Accounting and Reporting Standards

Having determined that Dearlove's conduct was unreasonable, the SEC turned to the applicable professional accounting and reporting standards. The GAAS required that when an audit posed greater than normal risk—as Dearlove had determined the Adelphia audit did—there must be "more extensive supervision by the auditor with final responsibility for the engagement during both the planning and conduct of the engagement." The SEC found no evidence in the audit workpapers or elsewhere else in the record that Dearlove gave any consideration to the propriety of at least three separate transactions: (1) offsetting receivables and payables, (2) reporting of coborrowed debt, and (3) direct placement of stock transactions.

### *Offsetting Receivables and Payables*

Accounting Principles Board Opinion No. 10 states that "it is a general principle of accounting that the offsetting of assets and liabilities in the balance sheet is improper except where a right of setoff exists." Rule 5-02 of the commission's Regulation S-X requires that issuers "state separately" amounts payable and receivable. Interpretation 39, Offsetting of Amounts Related to Certain Contracts, defines a right of setoff as "a debtor's legal right, by contract or otherwise, to discharge all or a portion of the debt of another party by applying against the debt an amount that the other party owes to the debtor. The Interpretation is consistent with Rule 5-02.

The court had concluded that Adelphia's presentation of a net figure for its related-party payables and receivables violated GAAP. Because Adelphia netted the accounts payable and receivable of its various subsidiaries against the accounts payable and receivable of various Rigas entities on a global basis, it did not comport with Interpretation 39's basic requirement that netting is appropriate only when two unrelated parties are involved.

The SEC held Adelphia violated GAAP because its netting involved more than two parties: "Adelphia netted the accounts payable and receivable of its various subsidiaries against the accounts payable and receivable of various Rigas Entities on a global basis . . . [and] netting is appropriate only when two parties are involved."

The SEC analyzed the record and determined that Dearlove's conduct was unreasonable in the circumstances and that it resulted in a violation of professional standards—both GAAS and GAAP. Because GAAS focuses upon an auditor's performance and requires him to exercise due professional care, the commission rejected Dearlove's attempt to fault the SEC for marshaling the same evidence to show that his conduct was unreasonable and that he failed to exercise due professional care in performing the audit.

### Co-borrowed Debt

Between 1996 and 2000, several Adelphia subsidiaries and some of the Rigas entities had entered as co-borrowers into a series of three credit agreements with a consortium of banks. Although the agreements differed in the amount of credit available, their terms were substantially the same: each borrower provided collateral for the loan; each could draw funds under the loan agreement; and each was jointly and severally liable for the entire amount of funds drawn down under the agreement, regardless of which entity drew down the amount. By year-end 2000, the total amount of coborrowed funds drawn under the credit agreements was $3.751 billion, more than triple the $1.025 billion borrowed at year-end 1999. Of this amount, Adelphia subsidiaries had drawn approximately $2.1 billion, and Rigas entities had drawn $1.6 billion.

Generally, an issuer must accrue on its balance sheet a debt for which it is the primary obligor. However, when an issuer deems itself to be merely contingently liable for a debt, *Statement of Financial Accounting Standards (SFAS) 5* provides the appropriate accounting and reporting treatment for that liability. *SFAS 5* establishes a three-tiered system for determining the appropriate accounting treatment of a contingent liability, based on the likelihood that the issuer will suffer a loss—that is, be required to pay the debt for which it is contingently liable. If a loss is *probable* (i.e., likely) and its amount can be reasonably estimated, the liability should be accrued on the issuer's financial statements as if the issuer were the primary obligor for the debt. If the likelihood of loss is only *reasonably possible* (defined as more than remote but less than likely), or if the loss is probable but not estimable, the issuer need not accrue the loss but should disclose the nature of the contingency and give an estimate of the possible loss or range of loss or state that such an estimate cannot be made. The issuer still must disclose the "nature and amount" of the liability, even if the likelihood of loss is only *remote* (slight).[5] From 1997 through 1999, Adelphia had included in the liabilities recorded on its balance sheet the amount that its own subsidiaries had borrowed, but it did not consider itself the primary obligor for the amount that the Rigas entities had borrowed and therefore did not include that amount on its balance sheet. Instead, Adelphia accounted for the amounts

borrowed by the Rigas entities by making the following disclosure in the footnotes to its financial statements:

> Certain subsidiaries of Adelphia are co-borrowers with Managed Partnerships (i.e., Rigas entities) under credit facilities for borrowings of up to [the total amount of all co-borrowed debt available to Adelphia and the Rigas entities that year]. Each of the co-borrowers is liable for all borrowings under this credit agreement, although the lenders have no recourse against Adelphia other than against Adelphia's interest in such subsidiaries.

Deloitte had approved this treatment in the audits it conducted from 1997 to 1999.

Dearlove knew that Adelphia considered the Rigas entities debt to be a contingent liability for which its chances of suffering a loss were merely remote, making accrual on the balance sheet unnecessary pursuant to *SFAS 5*. Deloitte created no workpapers documenting its examination of Adelphia's decision. However, from the record, it appears that Deloitte considered the matter and focused its review on the likelihood, as defined by *SFAS 5*, that Adelphia would have to pay Rigas entities's share of co-borrowed debt.

Dearlove also believed that, although the Rigas family was not legally obligated to contribute funds in the event of a default by the co-borrowers, the family would be economically compelled to protect their Adelphia holdings by stepping in to prevent a default by the entities. Dearlove did not, however, conduct any inquiry into whether the family would, in fact, use their personal assets to prevent a default by Adelphia. Dearlove estimated the value of the Rigas family's holdings of Adelphia stock by multiplying the number of shares the Rigases owned by the price per Class A share, resulting in a figure of approximately $2.3 billion, which he concluded was by itself ample to cover the debt and conclude his *SFAS 5* analysis. However, Dearlove did not determine if these Rigas family assets were already encumbered by other debt; he saw no financial statements or other proof of the family's financial condition other than local media reports that the Rigases "were billionaires." Dearlove testified that he "never asked them: Are you worth $2 billion, $3 billion, or $10 billion?" Dearlove also did not consider whether disposing of some or all of the family's stock in Adelphia might result in a downward spiral in the stock's value or in a change in their control of the company, in the event of a default by the entities under the co-borrowing agreements.

Dearlove testified that, at the end of the 2000 audit, he spoke to senior manager Caswell for about 15 minutes regarding the requirements of *SFAS 5*. During this meeting, they concluded that "the assets of the cable systems and the Adelphia common stock that the Rigases owned exceeded the amount of debt that was on the co-borrowed entities, and the overhang . . . exceeded the co-borrowing by hundreds of millions if not billions of dollars." Dearlove testified that, although other assets could have been included in an *SFAS 5* analysis, these two assets alone were sufficient to allow the auditors to conclude that Adelphia's contingent liability

---

[5] *Statement of Financial Accounting Standards (SFAS) No 5,* Accounting for Contingencies; www.fasb.org.

was remote. Deloitte therefore approved Adelphia's decision to exclude Rigas entities's $1.6 billion in co-borrowed debt from its balance sheet and to instead disclose the debt in a footnote to the financial statements.

When it reviewed the adequacy of the note disclosure that Adelphia planned to use (which was identical to the language it had used in previous years), the audit team initially believed the disclosure should be revised. During the 2000 quarterly reviews, audit manager Ivan Hofmann and others had repeatedly encouraged Adelphia management to disclose the specific dollar amount of Rigas entities's co-borrowings, but Adelphia continually ignored Deloitte's suggestions. Although Deloitte was unaware of it at the time, Adelphia management was working purposefully to obfuscate the disclosure of Rigas entities's co-borrowed debt.

In November 2000, at a third-quarter wrap-up meeting attended by Dearlove, Caswell, and Hofmann, Adelphia management (including Adelphia's vice president of finance, James Brown) agreed to make disclosures regarding the amounts borrowed by the Rigas entities under the co-borrowing agreements. Caswell and Hofmann subsequently suggested improvements to the note disclosure in written comments on at least six drafts of the 10-K; they proposed adding language that would distinguish the amount of borrowings by Adelphia subsidiaries and Rigas entities, such as the following: "A total of $____ related to such credit agreements is included in the company's consolidated balance sheet at December 31, 2000. The [Rigas] entities have outstanding borrowings of $____ as of December 31, 2000 under such facilities."

At the end of March 2001, as Deloitte was concluding its audit of the 2000 financials, Brown—despite his agreement in November 2000 to disclose the amount of Rigas entities borrowing—informed the audit team that he did not think that the additional disclosure was necessary. Instead, Brown proposed adding a phrase explaining that each of the co-borrowers "may borrow up to the entire amount available under the credit facility." Brown argued that his proposed language was more accurate than Deloitte's proposal because the lines of credit could fluctuate and, as a result, it would be better to disclose Adelphia's maximum possible exposure. Caswell agreed to take Brown's language back to the engagement team, but he told Brown that he did not agree with Brown and did not think that Deloitte would accept his proposed language.

Notwithstanding Caswell's reaction, Brown soon afterward presented his proposed language to the audit team, including Dearlove, Caswell, and Hofmann, during the audit exit meeting on March 30, 2001. Brown claimed that his proposed disclosure language had been discussed with, and approved by, Adelphia's outside counsel. Although Dearlove characterized the disclosure issue as "really one of the more minor points that [the audit team was] trying to reconcile at that point," the ALJ did not accept this testimony. Dearlove testified that he was "concerned" about "making it clear to the reader how much Adelphia could be guaranteeing," and that Brown's language was "more conservative" but "wasn't necessarily what we were attempting to help clarify." Dearlove

also testified that he told Brown, "I don't understand how that [proposed change] enhances the note" but that, after "an exchange back and forth relative to that," Dearlove "couldn't persuade him as to what he wanted." Nevertheless, Dearlove told Brown that he agreed with the proposal and approved the change. Caswell and Hofmann also indicated their agreement.

Adelphia's note disclosure of the co-borrowed debt, as it appeared in its 2000 Form 10-K with Brown's added language, read as follows:

> Certain subsidiaries of Adelphia are co-borrowers with Managed Entities under credit facilities for borrowings of up to $3,751,250,000. Each of the co-borrowers is liable for all borrowings under the credit agreements, and may borrow up to the entire amount of the available credit under the facility. The lenders have no recourse against Adelphia other than against Adelphia's interest in such subsidiaries.

## Adequacy of the Note Disclosure of Adelphia's Contingent Liability

The SEC also considered whether Adelphia's footnote disclosure of Rigas entities's co-borrowings was appropriate under GAAP. Adelphia disclosed the total amount of credit available to the co-borrowers ("up to" $3.75 billion) without indicating whether any portion of that available credit had actually been drawn down, much less that all of it had. This disclosure was inadequate to inform the investing public that Adelphia was already primarily liable for $2.1 billion and a guarantor for the remaining $1.6 billion that had been borrowed by Rigas entities. Therefore, it did not comply with the requirement in *SFAS 5* to disclose the amount of the contingent liability.

The SEC concluded that Dearlove acted unreasonably in his audit of Adelphia's note disclosure, resulting in several violations of GAAS. In high-risk audit environments such as that presented by the Adelphia engagement, GAAS specifically recommend "increased recognition of the need to corroborate management explanations or representations concerning material matters—such as further analytical procedures, examination of documentation, or discussion with others within or outside the entity" when audit risk increases. The accounting for Adelphia's co-borrowed debt implicated the extensive related-party transactions and high debt load that were part of the basis for Deloitte's high-risk assessment for the Adelphia audit. Management's insistence on its own accounting interpretation was precisely the behavior identified by the audit plan as presenting a much higher than normal risk of misstatement in the audit.

Moreover, Dearlove knew that the audit team believed that the footnote disclosure in previous years was inadequate and had urged additional disclosure that would have made clear the extent of Rigas entities's actual borrowings and Adelphia's resulting potential liability. Dearlove did not think that Brown's language helped achieve Deloitte's goal of clarifying the extent of Rigas entities's debt and Adelphia's obligation as guarantor. Yet Dearlove accepted

Brown's language without probing his reasons for the change, without understanding Adelphia's reasons for rejecting Deloitte's language and without discussing the issue with the concurring or risk review partners assigned to the audit. This unquestioning acceptance of Brown's proposed disclosure language was a clear—and at least unreasonable—departure from the requirements of GAAS to apply greater than normal skepticism and additional audit procedures in order to corroborate management representations in a high-risk environment. Dearlove's conduct resulted in violations of applicable professional standards.

Dearlove asserted that disclosure of the amount that Rigas Entities could theoretically borrow (up to $3.75 billion) was more conservative than disclosure of the $1.6 billion that it had actually borrowed. The SEC concluded that the footnote disclosure was materially misleading to investors: "Materiality depends on the significance the reasonable investor would place on the withheld or misrepresented information." If "there is a substantial likelihood that a reasonable investor would consider the information important in making an investment decision," the information is material. A reasonable investor would think it significant that the footnote disclosure spoke only in terms of potential debt when, in fact, the entire line of credit had been borrowed and $1.6 billion of it was excluded from Adelphia's balance sheet but potentially payable by Adelphia. It was especially important for this information to appear in Adelphia's financial statements because investors had no access to the financial statements of the privately held Rigas entities. The SEC rejected Dearlove's argument that Adelphia's note complied with *SFAS 5*'s requirement to disclose the amount of debt that Adelphia guaranteed.

## Debt Reclassification

After the end of the second, third, and fourth quarters of 2000, Adelphia's accounting department transferred the reporting of approximately $296 million of debt from the books of Adelphia's subsidiaries to the books of various Rigas entities. In exchange, Adelphia eliminated from its books receivables owed to it by the respective Rigas entities in the amount of debt transferred. The three transfers were in the amounts of $36 million, approximately $222 million, and more than $38 million, respectively. In each instance, the transaction took place after the end of the quarter, and each transfer involved a postclosing journal entry that was retroactive to the last day of the quarter.

A checklist prepared by Deloitte in anticipation of the 2000 audit showed that Deloitte was aware of a significant number of related-party transactions that had arisen outside the normal course of business and that past audits had indicated a significant number of misstatements or correcting entries made by Adelphia, particularly at or near year-end. An audit overview memorandum recognized as a risk area that "Adelphia records numerous post-closing adjusting journal entries" and provided as an audit response, "[Deloitte] engagement team to review post-closing journal entries recorded and review with appropriate personnel. Conclude

as to reasonableness of entries posted." An audit planning memorandum provided that "professional skepticism will be heightened to ensure that . . . related party transactions . . . are appropriately identified and disclosed" and that auditors should "increase professional skepticism in [areas] where significant related party transactions could occur."

Dearlove testified that Deloitte had identified the Rigas family's control of both Adelphia and Rigas entities as posing a special risk. Dearlove also testified that he believed that it was important to know whose debt was whose, concerning Adelphia and Rigas entities. He testified that he was "generally aware the debt was audited," but that he did not review the debt workpapers directly. He also testified: "I don't recall [debt] being [a] particularly sensitive area, . . . I don't recall issues raised to me of difficulties we had. I don't recall any particular conversation I had with the team" concerning the audit of the debt. The record does not show that Dearlove knew of the three journal entries involving debt reclassification at the time of the audit.

*Statement of Financial Accounting Standards (SFAS) 125, Accounting for Transfers and Servicing of Financial Assets and Extinguishment of Liabilities,* permits a debtor to derecognize a liability "if and only if it has been extinguished." *SFAS 125* provides that a liability is extinguished if either (1) the debtor pays the creditor and is relieved of its obligation for the liability, or (2) the debtor is legally released from being the primary obligor under the liability, either judicially or by the creditor.[6]

When the Adelphia subsidiaries posted the debt in question to their books, they acknowledged their primary liability for the amounts posted. They could not remove the debt properly from their books without first satisfying the requirements of *SFAS 125* that either the Adelphia subsidiaries repaid the debt to the creditor during the relevant reporting periods or a creditor had released the subsidiaries from their liability for repayment. The evidence does not show, and Dearlove did not contend, that either of these events occurred. Adelphia's attempt to extinguish the debt unilaterally merely by shifting the reporting to Rigas entities violated GAAP and rendered its financial statements materially misleading by making Adelphia's debt appear less than it was.

Dearlove did not dispute that "certain debt which had been posted to Adelphia was later posted to a Rigas entity." However, focusing on the statement in the initial decision that "once Adelphia's subsidiaries had posted this debt to their books they became primary obligors for the amounts posted," Dearlove argued that *SFAS 125* does not define the circumstances under which an entity recognizes debt that may be derecognized only under the *SFAS 125* criteria. He claimed that the initial decision of the commission improperly "assumed without analysis" that the posting of debt in a

---

[6] *Statement of Financial Accounting Standards No. 125,* Accounting for Transfers and Servicing of Financial Assets and Extinguishment of Liabilities; www.fasb.org.

ledger is such a circumstance. Dearlove argued that the application of *SFAS 125* is complex where entities are jointly and severally liable for an obligation, and it did not apply where an entity is secondarily or contingently rather than primarily liable. He asserted that Adelphia was arguably not required to recognize debt in cases where coborrowed funds were intended to be used by other coborrowers. He stopped short, however, of saying that the funds at issue were so intended, and our review of the record yields nothing to support such a contention. The record did not establish that all the reclassified debt was coborrowed debt, and the ALJ correctly concluded that the impropriety of Adelphia's debt reclassification was unaffected by the question whether the debt was coborrowed. In addition, Dearlove cited no authority to support his contention that *SFAS 125* is applicable only where primary obligors were required to recognize a liability, and we are aware of none.

The crucial question for the *SFAS 125* analysis is whether the debt was extinguished in one of the enumerated ways. If the debt was not extinguished as provided in *SFAS 125*, the debtor may not derecognize it. The SEC found that the debts were recognized when booked and that, because there was no evidence that the debts were extinguished under *SFAS 125*, the accounting treatment violated GAAP.

The commission also found that Dearlove's conduct in his audit of Adelphia's accounting for debt was at least unreasonable, resulting in several GAAS violations. As explained, Dearlove knew that Adelphia had a large number of decentralized operating entities with a complex reporting structure, carried substantial debt, and engaged in significant related-party transactions with affiliated entities that Deloitte would not be auditing. He also knew that Adelphia management tended to interpret accounting standards aggressively. Moreover, the audit plan specifically required that postclosing journal entries be examined in particular detail and that the audit team draw conclusions as to their reasonableness. Dearlove knew that these factors, together with others, led Deloitte to identify the Adelphia audit as posing a "much greater than normal" risk of fraud, misstatement, or error. In addition, Dearlove knew that Adelphia management netted its affiliate accounts payable and receivable and sought to reduce the amount of related-party receivables that it reported.

In this context, GAAS required Dearlove to consider the "much greater than normal" risk of the audit in determining the extent of procedures, assigning staff, and requiring appropriate levels of supervision. In addition, he was required to "direct the efforts of assistants who [were] involved in accomplishing the objectives of the audit and [to] determin[e] whether those objectives were accomplished." He was required to exercise "an attitude that includes a questioning mind and a critical assessment of audit evidence," "to obtain sufficient competent evidential matter to provide . . . a reasonable basis for forming a conclusion," and, after identifying related-party transactions, to "apply the procedures he consider[ed] necessary to obtain satisfaction concerning

the purpose, nature, and extent of these transactions and their effect on the financial statements."

The reclassified debt involved postclosing journal entries of a magnitude significant enough to require the auditors to confront management and request an explanation, as required by Deloitte's audit planning documents. After discussing the entries with appropriate Adelphia personnel, Deloitte should have documented management's explanation and Deloitte's conclusions as to whether the accounting treatment was reasonable in the audit workpapers. The record did not show that any of these steps was taken. The failure to take them was, at the very least, unreasonable.

The SEC concluded that Dearlove had acted at least unreasonably in signing an unqualified audit opinion (i.e., unmodified) stating that Deloitte had conducted its audit in accordance with GAAS and that such audit provided a reasonable basis for its opinion that Adelphia's 2000 financial statements fairly presented Adelphia's financial position in conformity with GAAP.

## Postscript

On April 21, 2005, it was announced that Time Warner and Comcast were buying bankrupt cable company Adelphia Communications in a $17.6 billion cash-and-stock deal. As a result of a settlement of actions against Adelphia and members of the Rigas Family for securities fraud and other violations, and a related criminal forfeiture action, the U.S. Department of Justice and the U.S. Securities and Exchange Commission obtained a recovery consisting of cash of approximately $729 million. The funds were distributed to eligible claimants who suffered a financial loss as a direct result of the circumstances surrounding the Adelphia fraud.

Deloitte did not fare well in the investor lawsuits. On April 5, 2010, Deloitte & Touche LLP agreed to pay up to $210 million as part of a larger $455 million amount. Also, a number of banks, including Bank of America, Citigroup, JPMorgan Chase, Wachovia, and 35 others, agreed to pay to settle an investor lawsuit. Earlier, in 2005, Deloitte had paid the SEC $50 million to settle claims that it had incorrectly audited Adelphia's 2000 financials. Not surprisingly, the defendants, Deloitte and the banks, admitted no wrongdoing, but Deloitte spokesperson, Deborah Harrington, said, "Deloitte & Touche believes it has no liability for the fraud by Adelphia and its former management. Deloitte & Touche also believes, however, that it was in the best interests of the firm and its clients to settle this action rather than to continue to face the expense and uncertainty of protracted litigation."[7]

As usual, the lawyers made out well in this case, landing a 21 percent share of the settlement (or about $94 million).

[7]"Deloitte Pays $210 million to Settle Adelphia Case: 45% of Total Sum." Available at http://www.big4.com/deloitte/deloitte-pays-210-million-to-settle-adelphia-case-45-of-total-sum-249/.

## Questions

1. Dearlove and Deloitte had identified the audit as posing much greater risk than normal. Describe the risk factors in the case that most likely would have led to this conclusion.

2. Classify each of the accounting issues in the case into the financial shenanigans identified by Schilit in Chapter 7. Are there any accounting procedures that do not fit into one of the shenanigans? If not, make up a category to describe such procedures in a general way as did Schilit. Comment on the earnings management effects as well.

3. Describe each of the auditing standards and procedures the auditors failed to adhere to given the facts of the case.

How did the failure of the auditors to follow them violate Deloitte's ethical standards as evidenced by the deficiencies in the work of Dearlove and other members of the audit engagement team?

## Optional Question:

4. Do you believe that Deloitte violated its ethical and professional responsibilities in the audit of Adelphia by being liable for negligence, gross negligence, or fraud? Explain the reasons for your answer using the discussion in Chapter 6 for support.

## Major Case 2

# Royal Ahold N.V. (Ahold)

*Note:* Case 5-9 in Chapter 5 covers many of the accounting and auditing facts of the case. We review these issues and go on to analyze the accountants' ethical and professional responsibilities in this case.

## Summary of Court Ruling

The U.S. Court of Appeals for the Fourth Circuit affirmed the lower court ruling in the case *Public Employees Retirement Association of Colorado; Generic Trading of Philadelphia, LLC v. Deloitte & Touche, LLP* that Deloitte defendants lacked the necessary scienter to conclude that they knowingly or recklessly perpetrated a fraud on Ahold's investors.

This class action securities fraud lawsuit arose out of improper accounting by Royal Ahold N.V., a Dutch corporation, and U.S. Foodservice, Inc. (USF), a Maryland-based Ahold subsidiary. The misconduct of Ahold and USF was not disputed in this appeal. The main issue is the liability of Ahold's accountants, Deloitte & Touche LLP (Deloitte U.S.) and Deloitte & Touche Accountants (Deloitte Netherlands), for their alleged role in the fraud perpetrated by Ahold and USF. Under the Private Securities Litigation Reform Act of 1995 (PSLRA), plaintiffs must plead facts alleging a "strong inference" that the defendants acted with the required scienter. As explained by the Supreme Court in *Tellabs, Inc. v. Makor Issues & Rights, Ltd.,* a strong inference "must be more than merely plausible or reasonable—it must be cogent and at least as compelling as any opposing inference of non-fraudulent intent."

The Appeals Court found that Deloitte, like the plaintiffs, were victims of Ahold's fraud rather than its enablers. In its decision, the court relied on the PSLRA and the decision in *Tellabs.* Circuit Judge Wilkinson wrote the conclusion for the court.[1] The court ruling will be explained later on.

## ERISA Class Action Settlement

Class action lawsuits are common in cases such as Ahold where dozens of separate private class action securities are combined. In this case the Employee Retirement Income Security Act (ERISA) of 1974 actions were filed against Ahold, Deloitte, and other defendants. On June 18, 2003, the Judicial Panel on Multidistrict Litigation transferred these actions to the U.S. District Court for the District of Maryland, *In re Royal Ahold N.V. Securities & "ERISA" Litigation.* Following the certification of the class action law-

suit, the U.S. District Court in Maryland ruled in favor of the ERISA plaintiffs on November 2, 2006, and awarded them $1.1 billion in the securities fraud case against Royal Ahold.[2]

## Summary of Accounting Fraud

Beginning in the 1990s, and continuing until 2003, Ahold and USF perpetrated frauds that led it to overstate its earnings on financial reports significantly: The frauds included:

- Ahold improperly "consolidated" the revenue from a number of joint ventures (JVs) with supermarket operators in Europe and Latin America. That is, for accounting purposes, Ahold treated these JVs as if it fully controlled them—and thus treated all revenue from the ventures as revenue to Ahold—when in fact, Ahold did not have a controlling stake. Under Dutch and U.S. GAAP,[3] Ahold should have consolidated only the revenue proportionally to Ahold's stake in the ventures.

- USF falsely reported its income from promotional allowances (PAs). Also known as *vendor rebates,* PAs are payments or discounts that manufacturers and vendors provide to retailers like USF to encourage the retailers to promote the manufacturers' products. To increase its stated income, USF prematurely recognized income from PAs and inflated its reported PA income beyond amounts actually received.

- On February 24, 2003, Ahold announced that its earnings for fiscal years 2001 and 2002 had been overstated by at least $500 million as a result of the fraudulent accounting for promotional allowances at USF, and that Ahold would be restating revenues because it would cease treating the joint ventures as fully consolidated. After this announcement, Ahold common stock trading on the Euronext stock exchange[4] and Ahold American

---

[1]U.S. Court of Appeals for the Fourth Circuit, *Public Employees Retirement Association of Colorado; Generic Trading of Philadelphia, LLC v. Deloitte & Touche, LLP,* January 5, 2009; www.pacer.ca4.uscourts.gov/opinion.pdf/071704.P.pdf.

[2]*In Re Royal Ahold N.V. Securities & ERISA Litigation.,* 461 F.Supp.2d 383 (2006), Available at http://www.leagle.com/xmlResult.aspx?xmldoc=2006844461FSupp2d383_1796.xml.
[3]Starting in 2005, members of the European Union (EU), including the Netherlands, adopted International Financial Reporting Standards (IFRS) as the only acceptable standards for EU companies when filing statements with securities regulators in the EU.
[4]NYSE Euronext is the result of a merger on April 4, 2007, between the NYSE and stock exchanges in Paris, Amsterdam, Brussels, and Lisbon, as well as the NYSE Liffe derivatives markets in London, Paris, Amsterdam, Brussels, and Lisbon. NYSE Euronext is a U.S. holding company that operates through its subsidiaries, and it is a listed company. NYSE Euronext common stock is dually listed on the NYSE and Euronext Paris under the symbol "NYX."

Depositary Receipts[5] trading on the NYSE lost more than 60 percent of their value. Subsequent to the February 2003 announcement, Ahold made further restatements to its earnings totaling $24.8 billion in revenues and approximately $1.1 billion in net income.

# Ahold Fraud—Joint Ventures

With respect to the JV fraud, both Deloittes advised Ahold on the consolidation of the joint ventures. Five joint ventures were at issue in this litigation: JMR, formed in August 1992; Bompreço, formed in November 1996; DAIH, formed in January 1998; Paiz-Ahold, formed in December 1999; and ICA, formed in February 2000. Ahold had a 49 percent stake in JMR and a 50 percent share of each of the other ventures at their respective times of formation. Prior to Ahold's entering into the first joint venture, Deloitte Netherlands and Deloitte U.S. gave Ahold advice about revenue consolidation under Dutch and U.S. GAAP. A memo explained that control of a joint venture is required for consolidation of the venture's revenue and discussed what situations are sufficient to demonstrate control. The memo indicated that control could be shown by a majority voting interest, a large minority voting interest under certain circumstances, or a contractual arrangement.

Ahold began consolidating the joint ventures as they were formed. The various JV agreements did not indicate that Ahold controlled the ventures. For example, the JMR joint venture agreement specified that decisions would be made by a board of directors, "deciding unanimously," and that the board would consist of three members appointed by Ahold and four members appointed by JMH, Ahold's partner in the venture. However, Ahold represented to Deloitte Netherlands that it nonetheless possessed the control requisite for consolidation. Deloitte Netherlands initially accepted these representations for the consolidation of JMR and Bompreço. But as consolidation continued, Deloitte became concerned that Ahold lacked the control necessary to consolidate these first two joint ventures.

On August 24, 1998, Deloitte Netherlands partner John van den Dries sent a letter to Michiel Meurs, Ahold's chief financial officer (CFO), advising him that Ahold's representations of control would no longer suffice—that Ahold would need to produce more evidence of control in order to justify continuing consolidation of joint venture revenue under U.S. GAAP, and that without such evidence, a financial restatement would be required. In response to Deloitte

[5]An American Depositary Receipt (ADR) represents ownership in the shares of a non-U.S. company and trades in U.S. financial markets. The stock of many non-U.S. companies trade on U.S. stock exchanges through the use of ADRs. ADRs enable U.S. investors to buy shares in foreign companies without the hazards or inconveniences of cross-border and cross-currency transactions. ADRs carry prices in U.S. dollars, pay dividends in U.S. dollars, and can be traded like the shares of U.S.-based companies.

Netherlands's requests, Ahold drafted a "control letter" addressed to BompreçoPar S.A., its partner in the Bompreço joint venture. The letter stated that the parties agreed that if they were unable to reach a consensus on a particular issue, "Ahold's proposal to solve that issue will in the end be decisive." After reviewing the draft letter, Deloitte Netherlands advised Ahold that if countersigned by the JV partner, the letter would be sufficient evidence to consolidate the venture. The letter was signed by Ahold and BompreçoPar in May 1999. By late 2000, Ahold had obtained similar countersigned control letters for the ICA, DAIH, and Paiz-Ahold joint ventures. Based on these letters and other evidence, Deloitte Netherlands concluded that consolidation was appropriate. However, in October 2002, Deloitte learned of a "side letter" sent to Ahold in May 2000 by one of Ahold's ICA joint venture partners, Canica. The letter stated that Canica did not agree with the interpretation of the shareholder agreement stated in the ICA control letter.

At this point, Deloitte Netherlands and Deloitte U.S. began trying to get Ahold to obtain an amendment to the shareholder agreement in order to justify ongoing consolidation. At a February 14, 2003, meeting, Deloitte Netherlands and Deloitte U.S. told Ahold that Ahold lacked the necessary control for consolidation. On February 22, 2003, Ahold revealed to Deloitte Netherlands side letters contradicting the Bompreço, DAIH, and Paiz-Ahold control letters. Two days later, Ahold announced that it had consolidated its joint ventures improperly and would be restating its revenues.

# USF Fraud—Promotional Allowances

Ahold acquired USF in early 2000. Prior to the acquisition, Deloitte U.S. participated in Ahold's due diligence on USF. In a February 2000 memo, Deloitte U.S. noted that USF's internal system for recording promotional allowances received was weak because it heavily relied on vendors' figures, and that the system could "easily result in losses and in frauds." Deloitte U.S. also noted in the memo that USF's use of value added service providers, special-purpose entities that bought products from vendors and then resold them to USF for a higher price, needed to be evaluated for their "tax and legal implications and associated business risks."

After Ahold's acquisition of USF was finalized, Deloitte U.S. became USF's external auditor. When performing an opening balance sheet audit of USF, Deloitte U.S. discovered that a USF division in Buffalo, New York, had been fraudulently accounting for PA income. This fraud required a restatement of $11 million of PA income. USF also downwardly adjusted its income by $90 million as a result of Deloitte U.S.'s advice that it be less aggressive in its method for recognizing PA income. USF used at interim periods a method known as the "PA recognition rate" to estimate promotional allowance income, in which PAs were estimated as a percentage of USF's total sales. The rate used by USF was

4.58 percent at the time of Ahold's acquisition of USF, but it rose as high as 8.51 percent in 2002. When USF booked final numbers, Deloitte U.S. in its audits tested USF's recognition of PAs by requesting written confirmation of PA amounts from vendors and by performing cash receipt tests. Using this confirmation process, Deloitte U.S. was able to test between 65 and 73 percent of PA receivables in its audits for 2000 and 2001.

## Auditing Issues

Because USF lacked an internal auditing department, in April 2000, Ahold hired Deloitte U.S. to perform internal auditing services at USF. The internal auditors did not report to the Deloitte U.S. external auditors.[6] Instead, they reported initially to Ahold USA's internal audit director and, later, to USF's internal audit director after he was hired. The audit was managed by Jennifer van Cleave under the supervision of Patricia Grubel, a Deloitte U.S. partner. One of the internal audit's objectives was to determine whether USF's tracking of PAs was adequate. In van Cleave's attempt to verify USF's PA numbers, she requested a number of documents from USF management, including vendor contracts. Management refused to produce a number of the requested documents. Several members of management also refused to meet with van Cleave when she asked to conduct exit meetings. Van Cleave was thus unable to complete all the audit's objectives.

In a February 5, 2001, draft report, van Cleave described how management's failure to produce requested documents resulted in her inability to complete some of the goals of the audit. Grubel instructed van Cleave to soften the report's language, and the version submitted to Michael Resnick, director of USF's Internal Audit Department, simply stated that Deloitte U.S. "was unable to obtain supporting documentation for some of the promotional allowance sample items," without more specifically detailing management's failures and lack of cooperation.

In its February 2003 external audit for 2002, Deloitte U.S. discovered through the PA confirmation process that USF had been inflating its recorded PA income. An investigation ensued. Ultimately, USF's former chief marketing officer (CMO), Mark Kaiser, was convicted on all counts of a federal indictment that alleged that he had induced USF's vendors to report PA income amounts and receivable balances falsely to Deloitte U.S., and that he had concealed the existence of written contracts with USF vendors from Deloitte U.S. Two other USF executives pled guilty to federal securities fraud charges; in their plea statements, they admitted that USF lied to and deceived Deloitte U.S., and that they induced vendors to sign false audit confirmation letters that falsely overstated

[6]Under the professional standards then in effect, an auditing firm could provide both internal and external auditing services to the same client. The Sarbanes-Oxley Act of 2002 (SOX) subsequently prohibited internal audit services for external audit clients because of independence concerns.

PA payments. In addition, 17 individuals associated with USF vendors pled guilty to various charges and admitted that they signed false audit confirmation letters in order to conceal the PA fraud from Deloitte U.S.

## PSLRA: Fraud and Scienter

In passing the PSLRA in 1995, Congress imposed heightened pleading requirements for private securities fraud actions. As a general matter, heightened pleading is not the norm in federal civil procedure. Frequently stated reasons include protecting defendants' reputations from baseless accusations, eliminating unmeritorious suits that are brought only for their nuisance value, discouraging fishing expeditions brought in the slight hope of discovering a fraud, and providing defendants with detailed information in order to enable them to defend effectively against a claim. When "alleging fraud or mistake," plaintiffs "must state with particularity the circumstances constituting fraud or mistake."

The PSLRA imposed a number of requirements designed to discourage private securities actions lacking merit. Among them is the requirement that in a private securities action "in which the plaintiff may recover money damages only on proof that the defendant acted with a particular state of mind, the complaint shall, with respect to each act or omission . . . , state with particularity facts giving rise to a strong inference that the defendant acted with the required state of mind." Complaints that do not plead scienter adequately are to be dismissed.

Because the PSLRA did not define "a strong inference," the courts of appeals disagreed on how much factual specificity plaintiffs must plead in private securities actions. The Supreme Court resolved that issue in *Tellabs,* in which the Court prescribed the following analysis for Rule 12(b)(6) motions to dismiss Section 10(b) actions:

- First, courts must, as with any motion to dismiss for failure to plead a claim on which relief can be granted, accept all factual allegations in the complaint as true.

- Second, courts must consider the complaint in its entirety, as well as other sources that courts ordinarily examine, when ruling on Rule 12(b) motions to dismiss. The inquiry, as several Courts of Appeals have recognized, is whether *all* the facts alleged, taken collectively, give rise to a strong inference of scienter, not whether any individual allegation, scrutinized in isolation, meets that standard.

- Third, in determining whether the pleaded facts give rise to a "strong" inference of scienter, the court must take into account plausible opposing inferences. The strength of an inference cannot be decided in a vacuum. The inquiry is inherently comparative. The inference of scienter must be more than merely "reasonable" or "permissible"—it must be cogent and compelling, thus strong in light of other explanations.

# Legal Reasoning

The "strong inference" requirement and the comparative analysis of inferences still leave unanswered the question of exactly what state of mind satisfies the scienter requirement of a 10b-5 action. In *Ernst & Ernst v. Hochfelder*,[7] the Supreme Court held that a plaintiff must show that the defendant possessed the "intent to deceive, manipulate, or defraud" in an action brought under Rule 10b-5 of the Securities and Exchange Act of 1934. However, the Court never made clear what mental state suffices to meet this requirement. ("We need not address here the question whether, in some circumstances, reckless behavior is sufficient for civil liability under Rule 10b-5."). The U.S. Court of Appeals held in *Ottman v. Hanger Orthopedic Group, Inc.* that "a securities fraud plaintiff may allege scienter by pleading not only intentional misconduct, but also recklessness."[8] The court defined a reckless act as one "so highly unreasonable and such an extreme departure from the standard of ordinary care as to present a danger of misleading the plaintiff to the extent that the danger was either known to the defendant or so obvious that the defendant must have been aware of it" (quoting *Phillips v. LCI Int'l, Inc.*).[9] A showing of mere negligence, however, will not suffice to support a 10(b) claim.[10]

Thus, the court ruled, the question is whether the allegations in the complaint, viewed in their totality and in light of all the evidence in the record, allow us to draw a strong inference, at least as compelling as any opposing inference, that the Deloitte defendants either knowingly or recklessly defrauded investors by issuing false audit opinions in violation of Rule 10b-5(b) or 10b-5(a) and (c). On the other hand, if it found the inference that defendants acted innocently, or even negligently, more compelling than the inference that they acted with the requisite scienter, it must affirm the lower court's ruling. Plaintiffs must show that defendants actually made a misrepresentation or omission in their audit opinions on which investors relied.

In light of the foregoing standards, the court considered first the JV fraud. The plaintiffs alleged that Deloitte U.S. and Deloitte Netherlands allowed Ahold to consolidate the joint ventures despite knowing, or being reckless with regard to the risk, that Ahold lacked the control required for consolidation. The thrust of their argument was that the control letters and Ahold's oral representations were insufficient evidence of control under Dutch and U.S. GAAP. Thus, they argued, the defendants were complicit in the fraud. According to the plaintiffs, the secret side letters, in which the JV partners contradicted Ahold's interpretations of the JV agreements in the control letters, were irrelevant because the control letters themselves did not amend the JV agreements. The plaintiffs' arguments did not

provide a basis for a strong inference that either Deloitte U.S. or Deloitte Netherlands acted knowingly or recklessly in relation to the JV fraud. The most plausible inference that one can draw from the fact that Ahold concealed the side letters from its accountants is that the accountants were uninvolved in the fraud. Ahold produced letters attesting to Ahold's control countersigned by Ahold's partners for the ICA, Bompreço, DAIH, and Paiz-Ahold joint ventures at the Deloitte defendants' request, all the while concealing the side letters from those same defendants. These facts led to a strong inference that the Deloitte defendants were attempting to ensure that Ahold had sufficient control over the joint ventures for consolidation and that Ahold was determined to prevent them from discovering otherwise. With perfect hindsight, one might posit that the defendants should have required stronger evidence of control from Ahold. Indeed, as the district court noted, it may have been negligent for the defendants to accept as the only evidence of control Ahold's repeated representations that it controlled JMR, the one joint venture for which Ahold never produced a control letter.[11] Nonetheless, the evidence as a whole leads to the strong inference that defendants were deceived by their clients into approving the consolidation. Ahold would not have needed to go out of its way to produce false evidence of control had Deloitte been complicit in the fraud, or had they been so reckless in their duties that their audit "amounted to no audit at all," as the Southern District of New York has described the standard in *SEC v. Price Waterhouse*.[12]

To establish a strong inference of scienter, plaintiffs must do more than merely demonstrate that defendants should or could have done more. They must demonstrate that Deloitte was either knowingly complicit in the fraud, or so reckless in its duties as to be oblivious to malfeasance that was readily apparent. The inference that we find most compelling based on the evidence in the record is not that the defendants were knowingly complicit or reckless, but that they were deceived by their client's repeated lies and artifices. Perhaps their failure to demand more evidence of consolidation was improper under accounting guidelines, but that is not the standard, which "requires more than a misapplication of accounting principles."[13]

The court then examined the PA fraud. The plaintiffs argued that Deloitte U.S. was knowingly complicit in the fraud when it ignored several red flags, including USF's lack of internal controls to track PA income and USF management's obstruction of the internal audit and the facts and the circumstances of USF CFO Ernie Smith's resignation. With respect to USF's problems with tracking income with PAs, it is not the case that Deloitte U.S. simply ignored the weak internal controls, as the plaintiffs alleged. Rather, Deloitte U.S. raised this issue numerous times with Ahold and USF management.

Deloitte U.S. designed a confirmation process to verify USF's reported PA income in which it contacted third-party vendors and received letters from them confirming PA amounts.

[7]U.S. Supreme Court, *Ernst & Ernst v. Hochfelder*, 425 U.S. 185 (1976).
[8]U.S. Court of Appeals, *Ottman v. Hanger Orthopedic Group, Inc.*, 353 F.3d 338, 344 (4th Cir. 2003).
[9]U.S. Court of Appeals, *Phillips v. LCI Int'l, Inc.*, 190 F.3d 609, 621 (4th Cir. 1999).
[10]*Ernst & Ernst v. Hochfelder.*

[11]U.S. Court of Appeals, *In re Royal Ahold*, 351 F.Supp. 2d.
[12]*SEC v. Price Waterhouse*, 797 F.Supp. 1217, 1240 (S.D.N.Y. 1992) [citing *McLean v. Alexander*, 599 F.2d 1190, 1198 (3d Cir. 1979)].
[13]*SEC v. Price Waterhouse.*

The plaintiffs described the confirmation process as one that "confirmed nothing." Yet instead of merely relying on USF representations, as the plaintiffs asserted, Deloitte U.S. obtained corroboration from vendors for the figures provided by USF. Deloitte U.S. would not have attempted to verify USF's figures with third parties if it were complicit in the scheme, nor can it be said that it was anything but proper to attempt to check the accuracy of representations made by USF management.

The plaintiffs attempted to suggest that the confirmation process was unsound because, for example, Deloitte U.S. accepted confirmation letters via fax and the letters were sent to brokers or sale executives instead of financial officers. But even if the confirmation process was somewhat flawed—which the defendants contested—the larger fact remains that the PA fraud went undetected initially only because USF and its vendors conspired to lie to Deloitte U.S. and to conceal important documents. Indeed, it was Deloitte U.S.'s confirmation process itself that ultimately revealed the fraud. In the course of the 2002 audit, Deloitte U.S. learned in early 2003 from a vendor from which it had requested PA confirmations that employees had signed inaccurate confirmation letters.

Shortly thereafter, Ahold authorized an internal investigation that revealed the extent of the fraud. No doubt it would have been better had the fraud been discovered earlier, but the strongest inference that one can draw from the evidence is that the fraud initially went undetected because of USF's collusion with the vendors, not because of wrongdoing by Deloitte U.S. As to the internal audit, the internal auditors reported not to the Deloitte U.S. external auditors but to USF, as was consistent with professional standards.[14]

The rest of the supposed red flags pointed to by the plaintiffs also failed to create a strong inference of scienter. With respect to the plaintiffs' allegations that Smith told Deloitte U.S. about the vendor rebate fraud, the district court twice concluded that this claim had no support in the record, and we see no reason to disagree with its conclusion. The plaintiffs alleged that facts like the high CFO turnover at USF and USF's rapid growth should have alerted Deloitte U.S. that there was fraud afoot, but they failed to explain why this was the only conclusion that Deloitte could make.

## Conclusion

"Seeing the forest as well as the trees is essential." With respect to both frauds, the plaintiffs pointed to ways that the defendants could have been more careful and perhaps discovered the frauds earlier. But the plaintiffs could not escape the fact that Ahold and USF went to considerable lengths to conceal the frauds from the accountants and that it was the defendants that ultimately uncovered the frauds. The strong inference to be drawn from this fact is that Deloitte U.S. and Deloitte Netherlands lacked the requisite scienter and instead were deceived by Ahold and USF. That inference is significantly more plausible than the competing inference that defendants somehow knew that Ahold and USF were defrauding their investors.

[14]Institute of Internal Auditors, Standards for the Professional Practice of Internal Auditing, *Statement on Internal Auditing Standards 1–18.*

The court reiterated that it is not an accountant's fault if its client actively conspires with others in order to deprive the accountant of accurate information about the client's finances. It would be wrong and counter to the purposes of the PSLRA to find an accountant liable in such an instance. The court concluded that it had found no version of the facts that would create a strong inference that the Deloitte defendants had the scienter required for a cause of action under Section 10(b); the district court rightly denied the plaintiffs' motion for leave to amend their complaint.

## Questions

1. In most of the cases in this book, the auditors have been taken to task by the courts for failing to follow generally accepted auditing standards (GAAS) and violating their ethical and professional responsibilities. The Royal Ahold case is different because the court essentially found that Deloitte should not be held liable for the efforts of the client to deprive the auditors of accurate information needed for the audit and masking the true nature of other evidence. Still, the facts of the case do raise questions about whether Deloitte compromised its ethical and professional responsibilities in accepting evidence and explanations provided by the client for the joint venture and promotional allowance transactions. Identify those instances and explain why you believe ethical and professional standards *may have been* violated.

2. Evaluate the decisions made by Deloitte from an ethical reasoning perspective. Be sure to consider the effects of its decisions on the stakeholders.

3. A shareholder may file a securities fraud claim in federal court to recover damages sustained as a result of a financial fraud. Before the PSLRA, plaintiffs could file a lawsuit simply because a stock price changed significantly and hope that the discovery process would reveal potential fraud. After the PSLRA, plaintiffs were required to bring forth particular fraudulent statements made by the defendant, to allege that the fraudulent statements were reckless or intentional and to prove that they suffered a financial loss as a result of the alleged fraud. The Ahold case is an example of how the courts have, sometimes, ruled more liberally with respect to auditors' legal obligations since the passage of the PSLRA. In the wake of Enron, WorldCom, Adelphia, and other high profile securities frauds, critics suggest that the law made it too easy to escape liability for securities fraud and thus created a climate in which frauds are more likely to occur. Comment on that statement with respect to the fraud at Royal Ahold.

## Optional Question

4. Explain the legal liability of auditors under SEC regulations and the *Telltabs* ruling relied on by the Court. Include in your discussion how scienter is determined. Do you agree with the commission's conclusion that the Deloitte auditors did not violate their *legal obligations* to shareholders? Why or why not?

## Major Case 3

# MicroStrategy, Inc.

## Background

MicroStrategy, Inc., incorporated in Wilmington, Delaware, in November 1989, has offices all over the United States and around the world. Its headquarters are in McLean, Virginia. In its early years, the company provided software consulting services to assist customers in building custom software systems to access, analyze, and use information contained in large-scale, transaction-level databases. MicroStrategy began concentrating its efforts on the development and sale of data mining and decision support software and related products during 1994 and 1995.[1]

A larger part of the company's revenues in 1996 resulted from software license sales. The company licensed its software through its direct sales force and through value-added resellers and original equipment manufacturers (OEMs). The total sales through the latter two avenues comprised more than 25 percent of the company's total revenues. Since 1996, the company revenues have been derived primarily from three sources:

- Product licenses
- Fees for maintenance, technical support, and training
- Consulting and development services

The company went public through an initial public offering (IPO) in June 1998. From the third quarter of 1998, the company began to take on a series of increasingly bigger and more complicated transactions, including the sale of software, extensive software application development, and software consulting services.

In 1998 the company began to develop an information network supported by the organization's software platform. Initially known as Telepath but later renamed Strategy.com., the network delivers personalized finance, news, weather, traffic, travel, and entertainment information to individuals through cell phones, e-mail, and fax machines. For a fee, an entity could become a Strategy.com affiliate that could offer service on a co-branded basis directly to its customers. The affiliate shared with MicroStrategy the subscription revenues from users. By the end of 2004, MicroStrategy was the leading worldwide provider of business intelligence software.

The story of MicroStrategy reflects the larger problems of the go-go years of the 1990s. The dream of many young entrepreneurs was to create a new software product or design a new Internet-based network and capitalize on the explosion in telecommunications network capacity and computer usage. Greed may have been the sustaining factor enabling the manipulation of stock value, as many chief executive officers (CEOs) and CFOs cashed in before the stock price tumbled. However, pressure to achieve financial analysts' estimates of earnings seems to have been the driving force behind the decision to "cook the books."

## Restatement of Financial Statements

On March 20, 2000, MicroStrategy announced that it planned to restate its financial results for the fiscal years 1998 and 1999. MicroStrategy stock, which had achieved a high of $333 per share, dropped over 60 percent of its value in one day, going from $260 per share to $86 per share on March 20. The stock price continued to decline in the following weeks. Soon after, MicroStrategy announced that it would also restate its fiscal 1997 financial results, and by April 13, 2000, the company's stock closed at $33 per share. The share price was quoted at its lowest price during the unraveling of the fraud $3.15 per share as of January 16, 2002.

The restatements (summarized in Table 1) reduced the company's revenues over the three-year period by about $65 million of the $312 million reported, or 21 percent. About 83 percent of these restated revenues were in 1999.

The company's main reporting failures were derived from its early recognition of revenue arising from the misapplication of AICPA *Statement of Position (SOP) 97–2*.[2] The SEC states in the Accounting and Enforcement Release: "This misapplication was in connection with multiple-element deals in which significant services or future products to be provided by the company were not separable from the up-front sale of a license to the company's existing software products." The company also restated revenues from arrangements in which it had not properly executed contracts in the same fiscal period in which revenue was recorded from the deals.

The company 10-K annual report filed with the SEC for the fiscal year ended December 31, 1998, states the following in item number 7 of Management Discussion and Analysis (MD&A):

> Our revenues are derived from two principal sources
> (i) product licenses and (ii) fees for maintenance, technical
> support, education and consulting services (collectively,
> "product support"). Prior to January 1, 1998, we recognized
> revenue in accordance with Statement of Position 91-1,
> "Software Revenue Recognition." Subsequent to December 31,
> 1997, we began recognizing revenue in accordance with
> Statement of Position 97-2, "Software Revenue Recognition."
> SOP 97-2 was amended on March 31, 1998 by SOP 98-4
> "Deferral of the Effective Date of a Provision of SOP 97-2."
> In December 1998, the AICPA issued SOP 98-9 "Modification

---

[1]Information about the case can be found at Securities and Exchange Commission, Accounting and Auditing Enforcement Release No. 1351, December 14, 2000, *In the Matter of MicroStrategy, Inc.,* December 18, 2000; www.sec.gov/litigation/admin/34-43724.htm.

[2]Available at www.aicpa.org.

### Table 1
### Impact of Restatement on Revenue and Net Income

| Reporting Period | Revenue ($ in thousands) | | Net Income ($ in thousands) | |
|---|---|---|---|---|
| | Original | Restated | Original | Restated |
| **Year ended:** | | | | |
| December 31, 1997 | $ 53,557 | $ 52,551 | $ 121 | $ (885) |
| **Quarter ended:** | | | | |
| March 31, 1998 | 19,895 | 19,160 | 542 | (193) |
| June 30, 1998 | 23,790 | 21,138 | 942 | (1,133) |
| September 30, 1998 | 27,014 | 25,960 | 1,928 | 2,055 |
| December 31, 1998 | 35,731 | 29,231 | 2,766 | (2,984) |
| **Year ended:** | | | | |
| December 31, 1998 | 106,430 | 95,489 | 6,178 | (2,255) |
| **Quarter ended:** | | | | |
| March 31, 1999 | 35,784 | 29,322 | 1,859 | (3,804) |
| June 30, 1999 | 45,638 | 40,465 | 3,211 | (3) |
| September 30, 1999 | 54,555 | 35,309 | 3,794 | (12,774) |
| December 31, 1999 | 69,352 | 46,162 | 3,756 | (17,162) |
| **Year ended:** | | | | |
| December 31, 1999 | 205,329 | 151,258 | 12,620 | (33,743) |

of SOP 97-2, Software Revenue Recognition," which amends SOP 98-4, and is effective after December 31, 1998. Management has assessed these new statements and believes that their adoption will not have a material effect on the timing of our revenue recognition or cause changes to our revenue recognition policies. Product license revenues are generally recognized upon the execution of a contract and shipment of the related software product, provided that no significant company obligations remain outstanding and the resulting receivable is deemed collectible by management. Maintenance revenues are derived from customer support agreements generally entered into in connection with initial product license sales and subsequent renewals. Fees for our maintenance and support plans are recorded as deferred revenue when billed to the customer and recognized ratably over the term of the maintenance and support agreement, which is typically one year. Fees for our education and consulting services are recognized at the time the services are performed.

The majority of MicroStrategy's sales closed in the final days of the fiscal period, which is common in the software industry and was as stated by the company in its 10-K. The following is an excerpt from the company's 10-K for the fiscal year December 31, 1998:

The sales cycle for our products may span nine months or more. Historically, we have recognized a substantial portion of our revenues in the last month of a quarter, with these revenues frequently concentrated in the last two weeks of a quarter. Even minor delays in booking orders may have a significant adverse impact on revenues for a particular quarter.

To the extent that delays are incurred in connection with orders of significant size, the impact will be correspondingly greater. Moreover, we currently operate with virtually no order backlog because our software products typically are shipped shortly after orders are received. Product license revenues in any quarter are substantially dependent on orders booked and shipped in that quarter. As a result of these and other factors, our quarterly results have varied significantly in the past and are likely to fluctuate significantly in the future. Accordingly, we believe that quarter-to-quarter comparisons of our results of operations are not necessarily indicative of the results to be expected for any future period.

## SEC Investigation and Proceedings

According to the SEC investigation, the problems for MicroStrategy began at the time of its IPO in June 1998 and continued through the announced restatement in March 2000. The software company materially overstated its revenues and earnings contrary to GAAP. The company's internal revenue recognition policy in effect during the relevant time period stated that the company recognized revenue in accordance with *SOP 97-2*. The company, however, had not complied with *SOP 97-2*, instead recognizing revenue earlier than allowed under GAAP.

The closing of a majority of the company's sales in the final days of the fiscal period resulted in the contracts department receiving numerous contracts signed by customers that needed (according to company policy) to be signed by MicroStrategy as well. To realize the desired quarterly financial results, the company held open, until after the close of the quarter, contracts that had been signed by customers but had not yet been signed by the company. After the company determined the desired financial results, the unsigned contracts were signed and given an "effective date" in the last month of the prior quarter. In some instances, the contracts were signed without affixing a date, allowing the company to assign a date at a later time. GAAP and MicroStrategy's own accounting policies required the signature of both the company and the customer prior to recognizing revenue.

SEC regulations that were violated by MicroStrategy included reporting provisions, recordkeeping requirements, and the internal control provisions. The company was required to cease and desist from committing any further violations of the relevant rules, as well as take steps to comply with the rules already violated.

## Role of the Auditor

The auditor of MicroStrategy in 1996 was Coopers & Lybrand, and Warren Martin was the engagement partner. After Coopers merged with Price Waterhouse and became known as PricewaterhouseCoopers (PwC), Martin continued as the engagement partner until April 2000. The SEC filed administrative proceedings against him on August 8, 2003, and suspended him from practicing before the commission for two years.[3]

Martin was in charge of the audit of MicroStrategy during the period of restatement and was directly responsible for the unqualified (i.e., unmodified) opinions issued on the company's inaccurate financial statements. The SEC charged him with a variety of violations of professional standards of practice, including lacking an attitude of professional skepticism, failing to obtain sufficient evidence to support revenue recognition, and demonstrating a lack of due care in carrying out professional responsibilities.

## Role of Officers of the Company

The following officers came under investigation by the SEC: Michael Saylor, cofounder and CEO; Mark Lynch, the CFO; and Sanjeev Bansal, cofounder and chief operating officer (COO). The SEC filed administrative proceedings against Saylor, Lynch, and Bansal on December 14, 2000, charging that MicroStrategy "materially overstated its revenues and earnings from the sales of software and information services contrary to GAAP." Two other officials were cited for their role in drafting the revenue recognition policies that violated GAAP—Antoinette Parsons, the corporate controller and director of finance and accounting and vice president of finance; and Stacy Hamm, an accounting manager who reported to Parsons.[4] The SEC considered that all these

officers should have been aware of the revenue recognition policies of the company. Lynch, as the CFO, had the responsibility to ensure the truthfulness of MicroStrategy's financial reports, and he signed the company's periodic reports to the SEC. Saylor also signed the periodic reports.

The CEO, CFO, and COO paid approximately $10 million in disgorgement used to repay investors who were affected by this fraud, another $1 million in penalties, and they agreed to a cease-and-desist order regarding violations of reporting, bookkeeping, and internal controls. The controller and the accounting manager agreed to a cease-and-desist order that prohibited them from violating Rules 13a and 13b of the Securities and Exchange Act. In a separate action, Lynch was denied the right to practice before the commission for three years.

On June 8, 2005, the SEC reinstated Lynch's right to appear before the commission as an accountant. Lynch agreed to have his work reviewed by the independent audit committee of any company for which he works.

## Post-Restatement Through 2004

MicroStrategy discontinued its Strategy.com business in 2001. It now has a single platform for business intelligence as its core business. Total revenues consist of revenues derived from the sale of product licenses and product support and other services, including technical support, education, and consulting services. The company's international market is rapidly developing, and it has positive earnings from operations since 2002.

For the year ended December 31, 2004, the MD&A identified its revenue recognition policy as described in Exhibit 1.

In its early years, MicroStrategy stated its revenue recognition policy in a single paragraph, saying that it followed the relevant accounting policies. Now the company provides a detailed analysis in its MD&A, as well as the notes to financial statements. The company has implemented all the requirements of the SEC. PwC continues as the auditors for MicroStrategy, and the firm has given an unqualified (i.e., unmodified) opinion on both the company's financial statements and its internal control report under SOX.

Investors sued MicroStrategy and PwC in 2000, after the software maker retracted two years of audited financial results and its stock price plunged by 62 percent in a single day, wiping out billions of dollars in shareholder wealth.

A report filed in court by the plaintiffs said the audit firm "consistently violated its responsibility" to maintain an appearance of independence. It cites e-mail evidence of a PwC auditor seeking a job at MicroStrategy while he was the senior manager on the team that reviewed the company's accounting. PwC also received money for reselling MicroStrategy software and recommending it to other clients. The accounting firm was working on setting up a business venture with its audit client, according to the plaintiff's report.

Steven G. Silber, a PwC spokesman, said the company denies "all of their allegations about our independence and the work we performed." He added: "While we believe our defense against the class-action claim was strong and compelling, we ultimately made a business decision to settle in order to avoid the further costs and uncertainties of litigation."

---

[3]Securities and Exchange Commission, Accounting and Enforcement Release No. 1835, *In the Matter of Warren Martin, CPA*, August 8, 2003; www.sec.gov/litigation/admin/34-48311.htm.

[4]U.S. Securities and Exchange Commission, "SEC Brings Civil Charges Against MicroStrategy, Three Executive Officers for Accounting Violations"; www.sec.gov/news/headlines/microstr.htm.

---

**Exhibit 1**
**Revenue Recognition**

MicroStrategy's software revenue recognition policies are in accordance with the American Institute of Certified Public Accountants' Statement of Position ("SOP") 97-2, "Software Revenue Recognition," as amended. In the case of software arrangements that require significant production, modification or customization of software, we follow the guidance in SOP 81-1, "Accounting for Performance of Construction-Type and Certain Production-Type Contracts." We also follow the guidance provided by SEC Staff Accounting Bulletin ("SAB") No. 101, "Revenue Recognition in Financial Statements," and SAB No. 104, "Revenue Recognition," which provide guidance on the recognition, presentation and disclosure of revenue in the financial statements filed with the SEC.

We recognize revenue from sales of software licenses to end users or resellers upon persuasive evidence of an arrangement, as provided by agreements or contracts executed by both parties, delivery of the software and determination that collection of a fixed or determinable fee is reasonably assured. When the fees for software upgrades and enhancements, technical support, consulting and education are bundled with the license fee, they are unbundled using our objective evidence of the fair value of the elements represented by our customary pricing for each element in separate transactions. If such evidence of fair value exists for all undelivered elements and there is no such evidence of fair value established for delivered elements, revenue is first allocated to the elements where evidence of fair value has been established and the residual amount is allocated to the delivered elements. If evidence of fair value for any undelivered element of an arrangement does not exist, all revenue from the arrangement is deferred until such time that evidence of fair value exists for undelivered elements or until all elements of the arrangement are delivered, subject to certain limited exceptions set forth in SOP 97-2.

When a software license arrangement requires us to provide significant production, customization or modification of the software, or when the customer considers these services essential to the functionality of the software product, both the product license revenue and consulting services revenue are recognized using the percentage of completion method. Under percentage of completion accounting, both product license and consulting services revenue are recognized as work progresses based upon labor hours incurred. Any expected losses on contracts in progress are expensed in the period in which the losses become probable and reasonably estimable. Contracts accounted for under the percentage of completion method were immaterial for the years ended December 31, 2004, 2003, and 2002.

If an arrangement includes acceptance criteria, revenue is not recognized until we can objectively demonstrate that the software or service can meet the acceptance criteria, or the acceptance period lapses, whichever occurs earlier. If a software license arrangement obligates us to deliver specified future products or upgrades, the revenue is recognized when the specified future product or upgrades are delivered, or when the obligation to deliver specified future products expires, whichever occurs earlier. If a software license arrangement obligates us to deliver unspecified future products, then revenue is recognized on the subscription basis, ratably over the term of the contract.

License revenue derived from sales to resellers or OEM's who purchase our products for future resale is recognized upon sufficient evidence that the products have been sold to the ultimate end users provided all other revenue recognition criteria have been met.

Technical support revenue, included in product support and other services revenue, is derived from providing technical support and software updates and upgrades to customers. Technical support revenue is recognized ratably over the term of the contract, which in most cases is one year. Revenue from consulting and education services is recognized as the services are performed.

Amounts collected prior to satisfying the above revenue recognition criteria are included in deferred revenue and advance payments in the accompanying consolidated balance sheets.[5]

---

[5]Securities and Exchange Commission, MicroStrategy 2004 10-K Report, Available at www.sec/gov/cgi-bn/browser-edgar.

---

MicroStrategy's chief of staff, Paul N. Zolfaghari, said in a statement that PwC auditors "have consistently assured us that they have been in full compliance with all applicable auditor independence requirements."

On May 8, 2011, PwC agreed to pay $55 million to settle a class action lawsuit alleging that it defrauded investors in MicroStrategy Inc. by approving financial reports that inflated the earnings and revenue of the company.[6]

[6]"Accounting Firm to Settle Suit over Audits of MicroStrategy." Available at http://mailman.lbo-talk.org/2001/2001-May/008924 .html.

## Online Resources

Your instructor may ask you to delve deeply into the accounting standards and SEC actions in answering questions in the case. The following Web sites provide extensive information that may help in that regard.

- AICPA (*SAS 55* and *SOP 97-2*): www.aicpa.org/members /div/auditstd/index.htm
- Committee of Sponsoring Organizations (COSO):
  - *Internal Control—Integrated Framework* (Executive Summary): www.coso.org/publications/executive_ summary_integrated_framework.htm

- • *Report of the National Commission on Fraudulent Financial Reporting* (Treadway Commission Report): www.coso.org/publications/NCFFR.htm
- • FASB:
  - • CON 5: www.fasb.org/pdf/con5.pdf
  - • Emerging Issues Task Force Pronouncement EITF 08-1, Revenue Arrangements with Multiple Deliverables: www.fasb.org
  - • Emerging Issues Task Force Pronouncement 09-3, Applicability of AICPA Statement of Position 97-2 to Certain Arrangements That Include Software Elements: www.fasb.org
- • Securities and Exchange Commission—Litigation Releases and Administrative Proceedings:
  - • AAER 1350: December 14, 2000: www.sec.gov/litigation/admin/34-43724.htm
  - • AAER 1351: December 14, 2000: www.sec.gov/litigation/admin/34-43725.htm
  - • AAER 1352: December 14, 2000: www.sec.gov/litigation/litreleases/lr16829.htm
  - • AAER 1359: January 17, 2001: www.sec.gov/litigation/admin/34-43850.htm
  - • AAER 1835: August 8, 2003: www.sec.gov/litigation/admin/34-48311.htm
  - • AAER 2255: June 8, 2005: www.sec.gov/litigation/admin/34-51802.pdf

## Questions

1. Evaluate the accounting decisions made by MicroStrategy from an earnings management perspective. What was the company trying to accomplish through the use of these accounting techniques? How did its decisions lead the company down the proverbial "ethical slippery slope?"

2. What motivated MicroStrategy and its management to engage in this fraud? Use the pressure and incentive side of the fraud triangle to help in answering the question. How would you characterize the company's actions in this regard with respect to ethical behavior, including a consideration of Kohlberg's stages of moral development?

3. Why is independence considered to be the bedrock of auditor responsibilities? Do you believe PwC and its professionals violated independence requirements in Rule 101 of the AICPA Code of Professional Conduct? Why or why not? Include in your discussion any threats to independence that existed .

## Major Case 4

# Cendant Corporation[1]

## The Merger of HFS and CUC

HFS Incorporated (HFS) was principally a controller of franchise brand names in the hotel, real estate brokerage, and car rental businesses, including Avis, Ramada Inn, Days Inn, and Century 21. Comp-U-Card (CUC) was principally engaged in membership-based consumer services such as auto, dining, shopping, and travel "clubs." Both securities were traded on the NYSE. Cendant Corporation was created through the December 17, 1997, merger of HFS and CUC. Cendant provided certain membership-based and Internet-related consumer services and controls franchise brand names in the hotel, residential real estate brokerage, car rental, and tax preparation businesses.

## Overview of the Scheme

The Cendant fraud was the largest of its kind until the late 1990s and early 2000s. Beginning in at least 1985, certain members of CUC's senior management implemented a scheme designed to ensure that CUC always met the financial results anticipated by Wall Street analysts. The CUC senior managers used a variety of means to achieve their goals, including:

- Manipulating recognition of the company's membership sales revenue to accelerate the recording of revenue
- Improperly using two liability accounts related to membership sales that resulted from commission payments
- Consistently maintaining inadequate balances in the liability accounts, and on occasion reversing the accounts directly into operating income

With respect to the last item, to hide the inadequate balances, senior management periodically kept certain membership sales transactions off the books. In what was the most significant category quantitatively, the CUC senior managers intentionally overstated merger and purchase reserves and subsequently reversed those reserves directly into operating expenses and revenues. CUC senior management improperly wrote off assets—including assets that were unimpaired—and improperly charged the write-offs against the company's merger reserves. By manipulating the timing of the write-offs and by improperly determining the nature of the charges incurred, the CUC senior managers used the write-offs to

inflate operating income at CUC. As the scheme progressed over the course of several years, larger and larger year-end adjustments were required to show smooth net income over time. The scheme added more than $500 million to pretax operating income during the fiscal years ended January 31, 1996; January 31, 1997; and December 31, 1997.

## SEC Filings against CUC and Its Officers

SEC complaints filed on June 14, 2000, alleged violations of the federal securities laws by four former accounting officials, including Cosmo Corigliano, CFO of CUC; Anne M. Pember, CUC controller; Casper Sabatino, vice president of accounting and financial reporting; and Kevin Kearney, director of financial reporting. The allegations against Corigliano included his role as one of the CUC senior officers who helped engineer the fraud, and he maintained a schedule that management used to track the progress of their fraud. Corigliano regularly directed CUC financial reporting managers to make unsupported alterations to the company's quarterly and annual financial results. The commission alleged that Corigliano profited from his own wrongdoing by selling CUC securities and a large number of Cendant securities at inflated prices while the fraud he helped engineer was under way and undisclosed.

The commission alleged that Pember was the CUC officer most responsible for implementing directives received from Corigliano in furtherance of the fraud, including implementing directives that inflated Cendant's annual income by more than $100 million, primarily through improper use of the company's reserves. According to the SEC, Pember profited from her own wrongdoing by selling CUC and Cendant stock at inflated prices while the fraud she helped implement was under way and undisclosed.

Sabatino and Kearney, without admitting or denying the commission's allegations, consented to the entry of final judgments settling the commission's action against them. The commission's complaint alleged that Sabatino was the CUC officer most responsible for directing lower-level CUC financial reporting managers to make alterations to the company's quarterly financial results.

In the first of the three separate administrative orders, the commission found that Steven Speaks, the former controller of CUC's largest division, made or instructed others to make journal entries that effectuated much of the January 1998 income inflation directed by Pember. In a second separate administrative order, the commission found that Mary Sattler Polverari, a former CUC supervisor of financial reporting, at the direction of Sabatino and Kearney, regularly and knowingly made unsupported alterations to CUC's quarterly financial results.

---

[1]The information for this case comes from a variety of litigation releases on the SEC Web site, including www.sec.gov/litigation/admin/34-42935.htm (June 14, 2000); www.sec.gov/litigation/admin/34-42934.htm (June 14, 2000); www.sec.gov/litigation/admin/34-42933.htm (January 24, 2001); www.sec.gov/litigation/litreleases/lr16587.htm (April 30, 2003); and www.sec.gov/litigation/complaints/comp18102.htm (April 30, 2003).

In a third administrative order, the commission found that Paul Hiznay, a former accounting manager at CUC's largest division, aided and abetted violations of the periodic reporting provisions of the federal securities laws by making unsupported journal entries that Pember had directed. Hiznay consented to the issuance of the commission's order to cease and desist from future violations of the provisions.

In a fourth and separate administrative order the commission found that Cendant violated the periodic reporting, corporate recordkeeping, and internal controls provisions of the federal securities laws, in connection with the CUC fraud. Among other things, the company's books, records, and accounts had been falsely altered, and materially false periodic reports had been filed with the commission, as a result of the long-running fraud at CUC. Simultaneous with the institution of the administrative proceeding, and without admitting or denying the findings contained therein, Cendant consented to the issuance of the commission order, which ordered Cendant to cease and desist from future violations of the provisions.

On February 28, 2001, the SEC filed a civil enforcement action in the U.S. District Court for the District of New Jersey against Walter A. Forbes, the former chair of the board of directors at CUC, and E. Kirk Shelton, the former vice chair, alleging that they directed a massive financial fraud while selling millions of dollars' worth of the company's common stock. For the period 1995–1997 alone, pretax operating income reported to the public by CUC was inflated by an aggregate amount of over $500 million. Specific allegations included:

- Forbes, CUC's chair and CEO, directed the fraud from its beginnings in 1985. From at least 1991 on, Shelton, CUC's president and COO, joined Forbes in directing the scheme.
- Forbes and Shelton reviewed and managed schedules listing fraudulent adjustments to be made to CUC's quarterly and annual financial statements. CUC senior management used the adjustments to pump up income and earnings artificially, defrauding investors by creating the illusion of a company that had ever-increasing earnings and making millions for themselves along the way.
- Forbes and Shelton undertook a program of mergers and acquisitions on behalf of CUC in order to generate inflated merger and purchase reserves at CUC to be used in connection with the fraud. Forbes and Shelton sought out HFS as a merger partner because they believed that the reserves that would be created would be big enough to bury the fraud. To entice HFS management into the merger, Forbes and Shelton inflated CUC's earnings and earnings projections.
- Forbes and Shelton profited from their own wrongdoing by selling CUC and Cendant securities at inflated prices while the fraud they had directed was under way and undisclosed. The sales brought Forbes and Shelton millions of dollars in ill-gotten gains.
- After the Cendant merger, Forbes served as Cendant's board chair until his resignation in July 1998. At the time of the merger, Shelton became a Cendant director and vice chair. Shelton resigned from Cendant in April 1998.

# Specific Accounting Techniques Used to Manage Earnings

## Making Unsupported Postclosing Entries

In early 1997, at the direction of senior management, Hiznay approved a series of entries reversing the commissions payable liability account into revenue at CUC. The company paid commissions to certain institutions on sales of CUC membership products sold through those institutions. Accordingly, at the time that it recorded revenue from those sales, CUC created a liability to cover the payable obligation of its commissions. CUC senior management used false schedules and other devices to support their understating of the payable liability of the commissions and to avoid the impact that would have resulted if the liability had been properly calculated. Furthermore, in connection with the January 31, 1997, fiscal year-end, senior management used this liability account by directing post-closing entries that moved amounts from the liability directly into revenue.[2]

In February 1997, Hiznay received a schedule from the CUC controller setting forth the amounts, effective back dates, and accounts for a series of postclosing entries that reduced the commissions payable account by $9.12 million and offsetting that reduction by increases to CUC revenue accounts. Hiznay approved the unsupported entries and had his staff enter them. They all carried effective dates spread retroactively over prior months. The entries reversed the liability account directly into revenues, a treatment that, under the circumstances, was not in accordance with GAAP.

## Keeping Rejects and Cancellations Off-Books: Establishing Reserves

During his time at CUC, Hiznay inherited, but then supervised, a longstanding practice of keeping membership sales cancellations and rejects off CUC's books during part of each fiscal year. Certain CUC membership products were processed through various financial institutions that billed their members' credit cards for new sales and charges related to the various membership products. When CUC recorded membership sales revenue from such a sale, it would allocate a percentage of the recorded revenue to cover estimated cancellations of the specific membership product being sold, as well as allocating a percentage to cover estimated rejects and chargebacks.[3] CUC used these percentage allocations to establish a membership cancellation reserve.

---

[2]*Post-closing journal entries* means entries that are made after a reporting period has ended, but before the financial statements for the period have been filed, and that have effective dates spread retroactively over prior weeks or months.

[3]Rejects resulted when the credit card to be charged was over its limit, closed, or reported as lost or stolen. Chargebacks resulted when a credit card holder disputed specific charges related to a particular membership program.

Over the years, CUC senior management had developed a policy of keeping rejects and cancellations off the general ledger during the last three months of each fiscal year. Instead, during that quarter, the rejects and cancellations appeared only on cash account bank reconciliations compiled by the company's accounting personnel. The senior managers then directed the booking of those rejects and cancellations against the membership cancellation reserve in the first three months of the next fiscal year. Because rejects and cancellations were not recorded against the membership cancellation reserve during the final three months of the fiscal year, the policy allowed CUC to hide the fact that the reserve was understated dramatically at each fiscal year-end. At its January 31, 1997, fiscal year-end, the balance in the CUC membership cancellation reserve was $29 million; CUC accounting personnel were holding $100 million in rejects and $22 million in cancellations off the books. Failing to book cancellations and rejects at each fiscal year-end also had the effect of overstating the company's cash position on its year-end balance sheet.

## Accounting and Auditing Issues

Kenneth Wilchfort and Marc Rabinowitz were partners at Ernst & Young (EY), which was responsible for audit and accounting advisory services provided to CUC and Cendant. During the relevant periods, CUC and Cendant made materially false statements to the defendants and EY about the company's true financial results and its accounting policies. CUC and Cendant made these false statements to mislead the defendants and EY into believing that the company's financial statements conformed to GAAP. For example, as late as March 1998, senior Cendant management had discussed plans to use over $100 million of the Cendant reserve fraudulently to create fictitious 1998 income, which was also concealed from the defendants and EY. CUC and Cendant made materially false statements to the defendants and EY that were included in the management representation letters and signed by senior members of CUC's and Cendant's management. The statements concerned, among other things, the creation and utilization of merger-related reserves, the adequacy of the reserve established for membership cancellations, the collectability of rejected credit card billings, and income attributable to the month of January 1997.[4]

The written representations for the calendar year 1997 falsely stated that the company's financial statements were fairly presented in conformity with GAAP and that the company had made available all relevant financial records and related data to EY. Those written representations were materially false because the financial statements did not conform to GAAP and, as discussed further, the company's management concealed material information from the defendants and EY.

In addition to providing the defendants and EY with false written representations, CUC and Cendant also adopted

procedures to hide its income-inflation scheme from the defendants and EY. Some of the procedures that CUC and Cendant employed to conceal its fraudulent scheme included (1) backdating accounting entries; (2) making accounting entries in small amounts and/or in accounts or subsidiaries the company believed would receive less attention from EY; (3) in some instances ensuring that fraudulent accounting entries did not affect schedules already provided to EY; (4) withholding financial information and schedules to ensure that EY would not detect the company's accounting fraud; (5) ensuring that the company's financial results did not show unusual trends that might draw attention to its fraud; and (6) using senior management to instruct middle- and lower-level personnel to make fraudulent entries. Notwithstanding CUC and Cendant's repeated deception, defendants improperly failed to detect the fraud. They were aware of numerous practices by CUC and Cendant indicating that the financial statements did not conform to GAAP and, as a consequence, they had a duty to withhold their unqualified opinion and take appropriate additional steps.

## Improper Establishment and Use of Merger Reserves

The company completed a series of significant mergers and acquisitions and accounted for the majority of them using the pooling-of-interests method of accounting.[5] In connection with this merger and acquisition activity, Company management purportedly planned to restructure its operations. GAAP permits that certain anticipated costs may be recorded as liabilities (or reserves) prior to their incurrence under certain conditions. However, here CUC and Cendant routinely overstated the restructuring charges and the resultant reserves and would then use the reserves to offset normal operating costs—an improper earnings management scheme. The company's improper reversal of merger and acquisition–related restructuring reserves resulted in an overstatement of operating income by $217 million.

The EY auditors provided accounting advice and auditing services to CUC and Cendant in connection with the establishment and use of restructuring reserves. The auditors excessively relied on management representations concerning the appropriateness of the reserves and performed little substantive testing, despite evidence that the reserves were established and utilized improperly.

One example of auditor failures with reserve accounting is the Cendant reserve. Cendant recorded over $500 million in merger, integration, asset impairment, and restructuring charges for the CUC-side costs purportedly associated with the merger of HFS and CUC. The company recorded a significant portion of this amount for the purpose of manipulating its earnings for December 31, 1997, and subsequent periods

---

[4]Available at www.sec.gov/litigation/complaints/comp18102 .htm.

[5]*Statement of Financial Accounting Standards (SFAS) 141, Business Combinations,* which eliminated the pooling methods for business combinations. The purchase method now must be used for all acquisitions.

and, in fact, Cendant had plans, which it did not disclose to defendants and EY, to use a material amount of the reserve to inflate income artificially in subsequent periods.

In the course of providing accounting and auditing services, the auditors failed to recognize evidence that the company's establishment and use of the Cendant reserve did not conform to GAAP. For example, CUC and Cendant provided EY with contradictory drafts of schedules when EY requested support for the establishment of the Cendant reserve. The company prepared and revised these various schedules, at least in part as a result of questions raised and information provided by the defendants. The schedules were inconsistent with regard to the nature and amount of the individual components of the reserve (i.e., component categories were added, deleted, and changed as the process progressed). While the component categories changed over time, the total amount of the reserve never changed materially. Despite this evidence, the auditors did not obtain adequate analyses, documentation, or support for changes that they observed in the various revisions of the schedules submitted to support the establishment of the reserves. Instead, they relied excessively on frequently changing management representations.

The company planned to use much of the excess Cendant reserve to increase operating results in future periods improperly. During the year ended December 31, 1997, the company wrote off $104 million of assets that it characterized as impaired as a result of the merger. Despite the size and timing of the write-off, the defendants never obtained adequate evidence that the assets were impaired as a result of the merger and, therefore, properly included in the Cendant reserve. In fact, most of the assets were not impaired as a result of the merger.

## Cash Balance from the Membership Cancellation Reserve

CUC and Cendant also inflated income by manipulating their membership cancellation reserve and reported cash balance. Customers usually paid for membership products by charging them on credit cards. The company recorded an increase in revenue and cash when it charged the members' credit card. Each month, issuers of members' credit cards rejected a significant amount of such charges. The issuers would deduct the amounts of the rejects from their payments to CUC and Cendant. CUC and Cendant falsely claimed to EY auditors that when it resubmitted the rejects to the banks for payment, it ultimately collected almost all of them within three months. CUC and Cendant further falsely claimed that for the few rejects that were not collected after three months, it then recorded them as a reduction in cash and a decrease to the cancellation reserve. The cancellation reserve accounted for members who canceled during their membership period and were entitled to a refund of at least a portion of the membership fee, as well as members who joined and were billed, but never paid for their memberships.

At the end of each fiscal year, the company failed to record three months of rejects (i.e., it did not reduce its cash and decrease its cancellation reserve for these rejects). CUC and Cendant falsely claimed to the defendants and EY that it did not record rejects for the final three months of the year because it purportedly would collect most of the rejects within three months of initial rejection. According to CUC and Cendant, the three months of withheld rejects created a temporary difference at year-end between the cash balances reflected in the company's general ledger and its bank statements. The rejects were clearly specified on reconciliations of the company's numerous bank accounts, at least some of which were provided to EY and retained in its workpapers. CUC and Cendant falsely claimed to the defendants and EY that the difference between the general ledger balance and bank statement balance did not reflect an overstatement of cash and understatement in the cancellation reserve since it collected most rejects. In fact, the majority of rejects were not collected. By not recording rejects and cancellations against the membership cancellation reserve during the final three months of each fiscal year, CUC and Cendant dramatically understated the reserve at each fiscal year-end and overstated its cash position. CUC and Cendant thus avoided the expense charges needed to bring the cancellation reserve balance up to its proper amount and the entries necessary to record CUC and Cendant's actual cash balances.

The rejects, cancellation reserve balance, and overstatement of income amounts for the period 1996 to 1997 are as follows:

| | ($ in millions) | | |
|---|---|---|---|
| Date | Rejects | Cancellation Reserve Balance | Understated Reserve/ Overstated Income |
| 1/31/96 | $ 72 | $37 | $35 |
| 1/31/97 | $100 | $29 | $28 |
| 12/31/97 | $137 | $37 | $37 |

The EY defendants did not adequately test the collectibility of these rejects and the adequacy of the cancellation reserve and instead relied primarily on management representations concerning the company's successful collection history and inconsistent statements concerning the purported impossibility of substantively testing these representations.

## Membership Cancellation Rates

The company also overstated its operating results by manipulating its cancellation reserve. The cancellation reserve accounted for members who canceled during their membership period. A large determinant of the liability associated with cancellations was CUC and Cendant's estimates of the cancellation rates. During the audits, CUC and Cendant intentionally provided EY with false estimates that were lower than the actual estimated cancellation rates. This resulted in a significant understatement of the cancellation reserve liability and an overstatement of income. To justify its understated cancellation reserve, CUC and Cendant provided to EY small, nonrepresentative samples of cancellations that understated the actual cancellation rates. The defendants allowed the company to choose the samples. EY did not test whether the samples provided were representative of the actual cancellations for the entire membership population.

## Audit Opinion

EY issued audit reports containing unqualified (i.e., unmodified) audit opinions on, and conducted quarterly reviews of, the company's financial statements that, as already stated, did not conform to GAAP. The Securities Exchange Act requires every issuer of a registered security to file reports with the commission that accurately reflect the issuer's financial performance and provide other information to the public. For the foregoing reason, the firm aided and abetted violations of the securities laws.

## Legal Issues

### SEC Settlements

Between Hiznay's arrival at CUC in July 1995 and the discovery of the fraudulent scheme by Cendant management in April 1998, CUC and Cendant filed false and misleading annual reports with the commission that misrepresented their financial results, overstating operating income and earnings and failing to disclose that the financial results were falsely represented.

The commission's complaint alleged that Sabatino, by his actions in furtherance of the fraud, violated, or aided and abetted violations of, the antifraud, periodic reporting, corporate recordkeeping, internal controls, and lying to auditors provisions of the federal securities laws. Sabatino consented to entry of a final judgment that enjoined him from future violations of those provisions and permanently bar him from acting as an officer or director of a public company.

Kearney consented to entry of a final judgment that enjoined him from future violations of those provisions, ordered him to pay disgorgement of $32,443 in ill-gotten gains (plus prejudgment interest of $8,234), and ordered him to pay a civil money penalty of $35,000. Kearney has also agreed to the issuance of a commission administrative order that barred him from practicing before the commission as an accountant, with the right to reapply after five years.

Corigliano, Pember, and Sabatino each pleaded guilty to charges pursuant to plea agreements between those three individuals and the SEC. Pursuant to his agreement, Corigliano pleaded guilty to a charge of wire fraud, conspiracy to commit mail fraud, and causing false statements to be made in documents filed with the commission, including signing

CUC's periodic reports filed with the commission and making materially false statements to CUC's auditors. Pember pleaded guilty to a charge of conspiracy to commit mail fraud and wire fraud. Sabatino, pursuant to his agreement, pleaded guilty to a charge of aiding and abetting wire fraud.

In another administrative order, the commission found that Paul Hiznay aided and abetted violations of the periodic reporting provisions of the federal securities laws, in connection with actions that he took at the direction of his superiors at CUC. Among other things, the commission alleged that Hiznay made unsupported journal entries that Pember had directed. Additional orders were entered against lower-level employees.

The commission found that Cendant violated the periodic reporting, corporate recordkeeping, and internal controls provisions of the federal securities laws, in connection with the CUC fraud in that the company's books, records, and accounts had been falsely altered, and materially false periodic reports had been filed with the SEC.

On December 29, 2009, the SEC announced a final judgment against Forbes, the former chair of Cendant, arising out of his conduct in the Cendant fraud.[6] The commission alleged that Forbes orchestrated an earnings management scheme at CUC to inflate the company's quarterly and annual financial results improperly during the period 1995 to 1997. CUC's operating income was inflated improperly by an aggregate amount exceeding $500 million.

The final judgment against Forbes, to which he consented without admitting or denying the commission's allegations, enjoined him from violating relevant sections of the securities laws and bars him from serving as an officer or director of a public company.

### Class Action Lawsuits

A class action suit by stockholders against Cendant and its auditors, led by the largest pension funds, alleged that stockholders paid more for Cendant stock than they would have had they known the truth about CUC's income. The lawsuit ended in a record $3.2 billion settlement. Details of the settlement follow.

By December 1999, a landmark $2.85 billion settlement with Cendant, was announced which far surpassed the recoveries in any other securities law class action case in history. Until the settlements reached in the WorldCom case in 2005, this stood as the largest recovery in a securities class action case, by far, and clearly set the standard in the field. In addition to the cash payment by Cendant, which was backed by a letter of credit that the company secured to protect the class, the Cendant settlement included two other very important features. First, the settlement provided that if Cendant or the former HFS officers and directors were successful in obtaining a net recovery in their continuing litigation against EY, the class would receive half of any such net recovery. As it turned out, that litigation lasted another seven years—until the end

---

[6] *Securities and Exchange Commission v. Walter A. Forbes et al.,* District Court N.J. filed February 28, 2001.

of 2007—when Cendant and EY settled their claims against each other in exchange for a payment by EY to Cendant of nearly $300 million. Based on the provision in the Cendant settlement agreement and certain further litigation and a court order, in December 2008, the class received another $132 million. This brought the total recovered from the Cendant settlement to $2.982 billion.

Second, Cendant was required to institute significant corporate governance changes that were far-reaching and unprecedented in securities class action litigation. Indeed, these changes included many of the corporate governance structural changes that would later be included within the Sarbanes-Oxley Act of 2002 (SOX). They included the following:

* The board's audit, nominating, and compensation committees would be comprised entirely of independent directors (according to stringent definitions, endorsed by the institutional investment community, of what constituted an independent director).

* The majority of the board would be independent within two years following final approval of the settlement.

* Cendant would take the steps necessary to provide that, subject to amendment of the certificate of incorporation declassifying the board of directors by vote of the required supermajority of shareholders, all directors would be elected annually.

* No employee stock option could be "repriced" following its grant without an affirmative vote of shareholders, except when such repricings were necessary to take into account corporate transactions such as stock dividends, stock splits, recapitalization, a merger, or distributions.

## The Settlement with EY

On December 17, 1999, it was announced that EY had agreed to settle the claims of the class for $335 million. This recovery was and remains today as the largest amount ever paid by an accounting firm in a securities class action case. The recovery from EY was significant because it held an outside auditing firm responsible in cases of corporate accounting fraud. The claims against EY were based on EY's "clean" (i.e., unmodified) audit and review opinions for three sets of annual financial statements, and seven quarterly financial statements, between 1995 and 1997.

The district court approved the settlements and plan of allocation in August 2000, paving the way for Cendant and EY to fund the settlements. Approximately one year later, in August 2001, the settlements and plan of allocation were affirmed on appeal by the U.S. Third Circuit Court of Appeals. And in March 2002, the U.S. Supreme Court determined that it would not hear any further appeals in the case.

## Questions

1. A statement is made in the case that Cendant manipulated the timing of write-offs and improperly determined charges in an attempt to smooth net income. Is income smoothing an ethical practice? Are there circumstances where it might be considered ethical and others where it would not? What motivated Cendant to engage in income smoothing practices in the case?

2. Representational faithfulness is a critical component of having a high quality of financial reporting. Evaluate the accounting techniques used by Cendant from the perspective of representational faithfulness and the usefulness of the financial information to the users of its financial statements.

3. Describe the failings of EY with respect to conducting an audit in accordance with GAAS. Include in your discussion any ethical violations of the AICPA Code of Professional Conduct?

4. Trust is a basic element in the relationship between auditor and client. Explain why and how trust broke down in the Cendant case including shortcomings in corporate governance.

## Major Case 5

# Navistar International

In April 2011, Navistar International Corporation sued Deloitte & Touche for $500 million, alleging "fraud, fraudulent concealment, breach of contract, and malpractice" on audits from 2002 to 2005.[1] One unusual aspect of this case is the claim by Navistar that Deloitte lied about its competency to provide audit services.

"Deloitte lied to Navistar and, on information and belief, to Deloitte's other audit clients, as to the competency of its audit and accounting services," Navistar alleged in its complaint.

Deloitte spokesman Jonathan Gandal expressed the firm's position as follows:

> A preliminary review shows it to be an utterly false and reckless attempt to try to shift responsibility for the wrongdoing of Navistar's own management. Several members of Navistar's past or present management team were sanctioned by the SEC for the very matters alleged in the complaint.

Early in the fraud, Navistar denied wrongdoing and said the problem was with "complicated" rules under SOX. Cynics reacted by saying it is hard to see how the law can be blamed for Navistar's accounting shortcomings, including management having secret side agreements with its suppliers who received "rebates"; improperly booking income from tooling buyback agreements, while not booking expenses related to the tooling; not booking adequate warranty reserves; or failing to record certain project costs. Exhibit 1 contains a detailed description of the SEC charges against Navistar and management.

In defense of Deloitte, we have to look at the bigger picture. Navistar employees committed fraud and actively took steps to avoid discovery by the auditors. The auditors did not discover the fraud, according to Navistar, and in retrospect, the company wants to hold the auditors responsible for that failure. Deloitte maintains that in each case, the fraudulent accounting scheme was nearly impossible to detect because the company failed to book items or provide information about them to the auditors.

In this case, there is little dispute that management engaged in wrongdoing. In 2010, Navistar company employees Mark Schwetschenau (controller and vice president of finance), James McIntosh (vice president of finance for the Engine Division), Thomas Akers (director of purchasing for the Engine Division), James Stanaway (director of finance for the Engine Division), Ernest Stinsa (replaced Stanaway as the director of finance for the Engine Division), and Michael Schultz (the plant controller at Navistar's foundry in Waukesha, Wisconsin), agreed to a sanction by the SEC for their role in the fraud and cover-up

Navistar and its employees did not admit to any wrongdoing in their settlement with the SEC (nothing surprising here), but the company did restate its financial statements and agree that each employee would pay a fine of $25,000 to $150,000. In addition, Navistar's CEO Daniel Ustain and CFO Robert Lannert agreed to clawbacks of $1.3 million and $1 million in bonuses that they got during the periods that Navistar's income was fraudulently inflated.

It took Navistar five years to sue Deloitte. That seems like an unusually long period of time and raises suspicions whether the company waited until its own problems were resolved with the SEC. Perhaps Navistar thought if it had sued Deloitte while the SEC investigated, it might be misconstrued by the SEC as an admission of guilt.

Deloitte may have been guilty of failing to consider adequately the risks involved in the Navistar audit. After the SOX was passed in mid-2002, all the large audit firms did some major cleanup of their audit clients and reassessed risk, an assessment that should have been done more carefully at the time of accepting the client. Big Four auditors in particular wanted to shed risky clients to protect themselves from new liability. Interestingly, to accomplish that goal with Navistar, Deloitte brought in a former Arthur Andersen partner to replace the engagement partner who might have become too close to Navistar and its management, thereby adjusting to the client's culture and *modus operandi*.

Whether because of his experience with Andersen's failure, fear of personal liability, a "not on my watch" attitude, or possibly a heads-up on interest by the SEC in some of Navistar's accounting, this new partner cleaned house. Many prior agreements between auditor and client and many assumptions about what could or could not be gotten away with were thrown out.

One problem for Navistar was that it was too dependent on Deloitte to hold its hand in all accounting matters, even after the SOX prohibited that reliance.

According to Navistar's complaint, "Deloitte provided Navistar with much more than audit services. Deloitte also acted as Navistar's business consultant and accountant. For example, Navistar retained Deloitte to advise it on how to structure its business transactions to obtain specific accounting treatment under Generally Accepted Accounting Principles (GAAP) . . . Deloitte advised and directed Navistar in the accounting treatments Navistar employed for numerous complex accounting issues apart from its audits of Navistar's financial statements, functioning as a *de facto* adjunct to Navistar's accounting department. . . . Deloitte even had a role in selecting Navistar's most senior accounting personnel by directly interviewing applicants."

---

[1]The case and subsequent facts are taken from *Navistar International Corp. v. Deloitte & Touche LLP,* 2011L004269, Cook County, Illinois, Circuit Court, Law Division (Chicago).

**Exhibit 1**
**SEC Action against Navistar[2]**

## Overview of the Case

1. At times from 2001 through 2005, Navistar overstated its pretax income by a total of approximately $137 million as the result of various instances of misconduct. Fraud at a Wisconsin foundry and in connection with certain vendor rebates and vendor tooling transactions accounted for approximately $58 million of that total. The remaining approximately $79 million resulted from improper accounting for certain warranty reserves and deferred expenses.
2. These findings do not reflect a coordinated scheme by senior management to manipulate the company's reported results or conduct committed with the intent of personal gain. Instead, these findings reflect misconduct that resulted in large part from a deficient system of internal controls, evidenced in part by insufficient numbers of employees with accounting training, a lack of written accounting policies and procedures, and flaws in the company's organizational structure.
3. The internal control deficiencies, in turn, resulted from senior management's failure to dedicate sufficient resources and attention to the adequacy of Navistar's accounting and reporting functions. The deficient internal controls failed to provide adequate checks on certain employees' efforts to meet the company's financial targets.

## Navistar's Restatement

1. In December 2007, the company filed a delayed Form 10-K for fiscal 2005 that included a restatement of its financial statements for fiscal years 2002–2004 and the first three quarters of fiscal year 2005 ("Restatement Period"). For the year ended October 31, 2004, Navistar restated its previously-reported pre-tax profit of $311 million to a pretax loss of $35 million. For the year ended October 31, 2003, the previously reported pretax loss of $49 million was restated to a pre-tax loss of $316 million. The previously reported accumulated deficit as of November 1, 2002 of $731 million was restated to an accumulated deficit of $2.4 billion. In all, Navistar restated or reclassified 16 different items. The restatement was comprised of widely varying accounting errors, related to different individuals working at different company locations, and occurred during years of profit and years of loss.
2. The restatement was required because Navistar's previously reported financial statements as filed in its annual reports in Forms 10-K and its quarterly reports in Forms 10-Q for the Restatement Period materially failed to comply with Generally Accepted Accounting Principles ("GAAP") and the financial reporting requirements under the securities laws.
3. During the 12-month period following Navistar's filing of its Form 10-K for fiscal year 2004 (later restated), and based on the company's originally reported financial results for that fiscal year, Dan Ustian, former chairman, CEO, and president, and former CFO Robert Lannert, received performance-based bonuses totaling $2 million and $1,049,503 (an original grant of $828,555, later corrected by an additional payment of $220,948) respectively. Ustian and Lannert have not reimbursed Navistar for any portion of the bonuses they received. Ustian has the dubious honor of being one of the few CEOs to have his bonus clawed back per Section 304 of the Sarbanes-Oxley Act.

## Internal Control Deficiencies

1. Navistar had numerous deficiencies throughout its system of internal controls during the relevant period, including 15 material weaknesses that were attributable, in part, to the company's failure to dedicate sufficient resources to those controls. For example, requests by managers to hire additional employees with accounting backgrounds and to assign additional employees to the company's accounting policies and procedures function were denied because of budgetary concerns; during 2000–2001 there was only one full-time employee dedicated to the policies and procedures function. The company's failure to address the internal control deficiencies contributed to at least some of the misconduct.
2. In 2002, the company's Internal Audit department warned senior management that Navistar's accounting policies and procedures needed to be updated. Although Lannert oversaw a plan to address internal audit's concerns, the policies and procedures were not updated at that time because of other perceived priorities. Additionally, James McIntosh, former vice president of finance for the Engine Division, failed to increase the number of Engine Division employees competently trained in GAAP despite being told that additional employees with such capabilities were needed. Deficient accounting policies and procedures and an inadequate number of employees trained in accounting were among the material weaknesses disclosed by the company in its Form 10-K for fiscal year 2005.

## Improper Accounting Practices at Navistar

### Vendor Rebates

1. During the 2001 to 2004 time period, Navistar ramped up its engine production beyond initial expectations and correspondingly increased its purchases of engine parts from suppliers. Navistar sought to share in those suppliers' unanticipated profits by asking them to pay a portion back to the company in the form of rebates. Under GAAP, a company could recognize rebates only when they were actually earned, i.e., when the entity had substantially accomplished what

## Exhibit 1  (continued)

was necessary to be entitled to such rebates. Accordingly, Navistar could record the full rebate as income in the then-current period *only* if no contingencies existed on its right to receive the rebate. Conversely, the company was prohibited from booking rebates as income in the then-current period if they were based on future business.

2. During this period, Navistar booked 35 rebates and related receivables from its suppliers. Of those rebates and receivables, as many as 30 were improperly booked. While these rebates and receivables took different forms—including volume-based rebates and so-called "signing bonuses" for Navistar's award of new business—all were improperly booked as income in their entirety upfront, even though, in whole or in part, they were earned in future periods. The company's eventual restatement of these rebates and receivables totaled $9.7 million of pre-tax income in 2004 and $8.5 million in 2003, which represented 27.7 percent and 2.7 percent, respectively, of the restated loss before income taxes for those years.

### Vendor Tooling

1. Prior to 2003, Navistar periodically entered into amortization agreements concerning the cost of tooling with vendors. Under these arrangements, the vendors purchased the tooling they used to make parts sold to Navistar, and the company repaid the suppliers for those tooling costs through amortization payments incorporated in the piece-price rates of the parts ultimately sold to Navistar. In 2003, the company determined that in some instances, instead of continuing these amortization payments, the company would benefit (in part through beneficial accounting treatment) by purchasing the tooling outright from the suppliers and depreciating the tooling costs going forward over a longer period. Consequently, in 2003, the company initiated a program pursuant to which Navistar arranged to terminate certain of these amortization agreements and acquired the tooling via lump sum payments to the suppliers. However, instead of paying suppliers the remaining unamortized tooling cost as of the 2003 purchase date, the company paid the suppliers a dollar amount equivalent to the unamortized tooling cost as of the beginning of the 2003 fiscal year. Since Navistar had already been paying amortization to the suppliers since the start of that fiscal year (i.e., November 1, 2002), the company arranged to receive back from those suppliers a "rebate" equivalent to those year-to-date amortization payments. The company then improperly booked these rebates into income. In addition, the company improperly deferred depreciation costs related to the tooling buybacks.

2. In 2003, two Navistar employees approached the company's outside auditor regarding the accounting for certain contemplated tooling buyback transactions. After learning of the planned accounting for the program, e-mails indicate that the auditor informed the employees that the recapture and booking of previously-paid amortization into income was improper. While certain transactions were booked in fiscal year 2003 because they were believed to be of immaterial dollar amounts, e-mails indicate that the auditor informed the company that no such transactions would be permitted in fiscal year 2004. Despite being informed of these developments, McIntosh used a "60-day rule" and authorized Engine Division employees in 2004 to record 60 days of amortization recaptured as income based on the company's payment terms. In so doing, McIntosh disregarded employees' warnings that continuing to record the recapture of amortization as income would be inconsistent with the auditor's guidance on the accounting.

### Warranty Reserve

1. Beginning in fiscal year 1999, the Engine Division Reliability & Quality ("R&Q") group, assumed responsibility for accounting for its warranty reserve, which reflected the company's estimated future warranty costs on engines installed in the majority of Navistar manufactured trucks. The warranty accrual process began with an estimated warranty cost per unit, or CPU, for each engine sold. This calculation incorporated certain "above-the-line" items, including well-established or known steps (e.g., implemented engineering fixes) that were viewed, based on historical trends or data, to have effectively reduced warranty costs. The CPU was the primary basis for the warranty reserve amount; the higher the CPU, the higher the reserve.

2. When R&Q's CPU calculation was presented to [James] Stanaway, director of finance for the Engine Division, and then ultimately to McIntosh, both typically stated that the initial estimated reserve number was too high for the Engine Division's business plan and they directed R&Q to add certain "below-the-line" items to the warranty reserve calculation process because they thought these items would reflect potential reductions that the company hoped to achieve in future warranty costs. These "below-the-line" items included anticipated vendor reimbursements and engineering fixes that lacked historical trend or other data evidencing their likely effectiveness.

3. The below-the-line items inappropriately included in the reserve calculation caused the warranty expense to be understated by $17 million in fiscal year 2002 and by $18.5 million in fiscal year 2003. The $18.5 million total represented 5.9 percent of the restated loss before income tax for that year.

### Reporting Failures Regarding Certain Deferred Start-up Costs

1. In 2000, the company entered into a long-term supply contract with an automobile manufacturer to develop and manufacture V-6 diesel engines commencing with model year 2002 and extending through 2012. From the fourth

---

**Exhibit 1 (continued)**

quarter of 2001 through the fourth quarter of 2002, the company incurred substantial start-up costs relating to the Agreement, including expenses developing the engine, constructing a plant in Huntsville, Alabama, and leasing engine assembly assets. The company began deferring some of these start-up costs in the fourth quarter of fiscal 2001 and as of the fourth quarter of 2002 had accumulated $57 million of deferred pre-production costs. Production of these engines was continually delayed until October 2002, when Navistar cancelled the Agreement and discontinued its V-6 engine program with Navistar.

2. Relevant accounting rules provided that such start-up costs could be deferred only if there exists an objectively verified and measured contractual guarantee of reimbursement. [FASB Emerging Issues Task Force Issue No. 99-5, *Accounting for Pre-Production Costs Related to Long-Term Supply Arrangements* ("EITF 99-5")].

3. Navistar deferred these start-up costs from the fourth quarter of 2001 through the fourth quarter of 2002. Specifically, the company deferred $4.3 million in the fourth quarter of fiscal year 2001, $12.8 million in the first quarter of fiscal year 2002, and $13.3 million in each of the second and third quarters of fiscal year 2002. These deferred start-up costs were not in compliance with GAAP. While oral assurances were received from Navistar senior managers that the automaker had in fact committed to reimburse the company for these start-up costs and Navistar's outside auditor was aware of and accepted the continuing deferral, the company should not have allowed the deferral because it had not received the aforementioned written guarantee of reimbursement.

---

[2] *SEC v Navistar International Corporation et al., Accounting and Auditing Enforcement Release No. 3165,* **August 5, 2010.** Available at http://www.sec.gov/litigation/admin/2010/33-9132.pdf.

---

The audit committee's role is detailed in the 2005 10-K filed in December 2007:

> The audit committee's extensive investigation identified various accounting errors, instances of intentional misconduct, and certain weaknesses in our internal controls. The audit committee's investigation found that we did not have the organizational accounting expertise during 2003 through 2005 to effectively determine whether our financial statements were accurate. The investigation found that we did not have such expertise because we did not adequately support and invest in accounting functions, did not sufficiently develop our own expertise in technical accounting, and as a result, we relied more heavily than appropriate on our then outside auditor. The investigation also found that during the financial restatement period, this environment of weak financial controls and under-supported accounting functions allowed accounting errors to occur, some of which arose from certain instances of intentional misconduct to improve the financial results of specific business segments.[3]

The 2005 10-K also addresses the issue in its first material weakness on accounting personnel. We did not have a sufficient number of accounting personnel with an appropriate level of accounting knowledge, experience and training in the application of GAAP as it relates to accounting for receivable securitization transactions. This resulted in inadequate segregation of duties and insufficient review of the information pertaining to securitization accounting. Additionally, because of the lack of internal accounting personnel, we relied heavily on our

prior independent registered public accounting firm to help us develop conclusions related to application of GAAP.

The complaint against Deloitte also references audit discrepancies cited in Public Company Accounting Oversight Board (PCAOB) inspections[4] of Deloitte. Navistar believed the discrepencies related to Deloitte's audit of the company. However, the names of companies in PCAOB inspections are not made publicly available due to confidentiality and proprietary information concerns. SOX also expressly restricts it from identifying the names of companies in the public portions of its inspection reports.

A closer look at the statute shows that the "Confidentiality" section of the act covers the handling of information that the board obtains through an inspection. It says that the board cannot be compelled to provide such information in court proceedings, including civil discovery. It also says the material is exempt from disclosure under the Freedom of Information Act.

Another section of SOX says the public portions of the board's inspection reports "shall be made available in appropriate detail," subject to "the protection of such confidential

---

[3] Available at http://files.shareholder.com/downloads/NAV/208119719x0x213905/97C07844-AC05-4F6A-A58C-FE982490BC77/Navistar%202007%20Annual%20Report.pdf=.

[4] The SOX authorizes the PCAOB to inspect registered firms for the purpose of assessing compliance with certain laws, rules, and professional standards in connection with a firm's audit work for clients that are "issuers." As of July 27, 2012, 2,398 public accounting firms, including U.S. firms and non-U.S. firms, are registered with the PCAOB. Until 2009, inspections of the Big Four CPA firms—Deloitte & Touche, PwC, KPMG, and EY—did not disclose the proportion of audits reviewed that were deemed to be defective. Among the Big Four, the board found something wrong in nearly one in six audits that it reviewed that year. A year later, the proportion had doubled to one in three.

and proprietary information as the board may determine to be appropriate." The bottom line is that the PCAOB is not legally barred from disclosing the information, but it is true that any such disclosure of client names could be overruled by the SEC.

The PCAOB's position has been made somewhat clearer by chairman James R. Doty in testimony before the U.S. House of Representatives Committee on Financial Services, Subcommittee on Capital Markets and Government Sponsored Enterprises, on March 28, 2012:

> In the early years of a relationship the auditor might be trying to build a long-term relationship by pleasing the client. In later years, however, the incentive is to avoid being the engagement partner that lost the client. It is worth exploring how we can mitigate these incentives, and the answer may not be the same for both. The PCAOB's efforts to address these problems through inspections and enforcement are ongoing. But considering the disturbing lack of skepticism we continue to see, and because of the fundamental importance of independence to the performance of quality audit work, the Board is prepared to consider all possible methods of addressing the problem of audit quality including whether mandatory audit firm rotation would help address the inherent conflict created because the auditor is paid by the client.[5]

Doty also addressed the issue of auditors keeping inspection results from audit committees or dismissing the importance of the results. In some cases, it seems, the PCAOB believe auditors have done both:

> I recognize that firms may approach such audit committee discussions with one eye on taking care not to waive any privilege the firm might have, in a different context, against compelled disclosure of inspection information. That caution, however, does not explain other more troubling assertions by firms such as that a particular audit deficiency cited by our inspectors is based on nothing more than incomplete documentation; or that it reflects merely a difference of professional judgment within a range of reasonable judgments . . .
>
> An audit committee armed with a proper understanding of our process would recognize that those kinds of assertions are seriously suspect. Those assertions are, without exception, directly at odds with the considered collective

conclusion of a group of very experienced auditors on the inspection staff. Such a conclusion means that, in a concrete, identifiable respect that is not reducible to a mere difference in professional judgment, the inspections staff has determined that the firm failed to perform an audit that provides what the audit committee contracted for and what investors deserve—reasonable assurance about whether the financial statements are free of material misstatement.

## Questions

1. Would you characterize the Deloitte audit of Navistar a failed audit? Why or why not?

2. Discuss the weaknesses in internal controls and the corporate governance system at Navistar. How should these deficiencies have affected the Deloitte audit assuming the firm was aware of these deficiencies.

3. The PCAOB audit firm inspection program was discussed in Chapters 4 and 5. What is the purpose of that program with respect to ensuring that auditors meet their ethical and professional responsibilities and obligation to place the public interest above all else? As mentioned in the case, the name of a company (client) mentioned in specific inspection report is not made publicly available. Do you believe that PCAOB inspection reports on registered CPA firms should permit the disclosure of specific details about named clients? Why or why not?

4. What is the purpose of Section 304's clawback provision in SOX? Do you think the provision is an ethical one? Use ethical reasoning to support your answer.

## Optional Question

5. Answer the following questions as directed by your instructor:

a. *Vendor rebates:* Do you believe Navistar was motivated by earnings management in its accounting for the vendor's rebates?

b. *Vendor tooling:* Evaluate Deloitte's role with respect to ethics and professionalism in providing guidance to Navistar employees on accounting for the vendor tooling costs.

c. *Warranty reserve:* Did the company's accounting for the warranty reserve comply with GAAP?

d. *Deferred start-up costs:* Evaluate the accounting for the deferred start-up costs from a matching perspective. What was the nature of the accounting that should have taken place after the automaker cancelled the agreement with Navistar in October 2002?

---

[5]James R. Doty, chairman PCAOB, "Testimony Concerning Accounting and Auditing Oversight: Pending Proposals and Emerging Issues Confronting Regulators, Standard Setters and the Economy," U.S. House of Representatives Committee on Financial Services, Subcommittee on Capital Markets and Government Sponsored Enterprises, March 28, 2012. Available at http://pcaobus.org/News/Speech/Pages/03282012_DotyTestimony.aspx.

# Major Case 6

# Waste Management

## Case Overview

This case focuses on improper accounting and management decision making at Waste Management, Inc., during the period of its accounting fraud from 1992 to 1997, and the role and responsibilities of Arthur Andersen LLP (Andersen), the Waste Management auditors, with respect to its audit of the company's financial statements. The case illustrates the kinds of financial statement frauds that were common during the late 1990s and early 2000s.

The key accounting issue was the existence of a series of Proposed Adjusting Journal Entries (PAJEs) recommended by Andersen to correct errors that understated expenses and overstated earnings in the company's financial statements. These were not recorded even though the company had promised to do so. Andersen developed a "Summary of Action Steps" that were designed to change accounting in the future in order to comply with GAAP but did not require retroactive adjustments to correct past errors. In essence, it was an agreement to do something in the future that should have been done already, with no controls or insistence by Andersen that the proposed changes would in fact, occur According to SEC Litigation Release 17435:

> Management consistently refused to make the adjustments called for by the PAJEs. Instead, defendants secretly entered into an agreement with Andersen fraudulently to write off the accumulated errors over periods of up to ten years and to change the underlying accounting practices, but to do so only in future periods.

The action steps were not followed by Waste Management. The company promised to look at its cost deferral, capitalization, and reserve policies and make needed adjustments. It never followed through, however, and the audit committee was either inattentive to the financial reporting implications or chose to look the other way. According to Litigation Release 17345, writing off the errors and changing the underlying accounting practices as prescribed in the agreement would have prevented the company from meeting earnings targets and defendants from enriching themselves. Defendants got performance-based bonuses based on the company's inflated earnings, retained their high-paying jobs, and received stock options. Some also received enhanced retirement benefits based on the improper bonuses, and some received lucrative employment contracts. Dean Buntrock, the chief executive officer (CEO) and chair of the board, Philip Rooney, director, president, and chief operating officer (COO), and James Koening, executive vice president and chief financial officer (CFO), also avoided losses by cashing in their Waste Management stock while the fraud was ongoing. Just prior to the public disclosure of the accounting

irregularities, Buntrock enriched himself by obtaining a tax benefit by donating inflated company stock to his college alma mater to fund a building in his name.

Waste Management today is a leading international provider of waste management services, with 45,000 employees serving over 20 million residential, industrial, municipal, and commercial customers; and it earned about $15 billion of revenues in 2012. It was ranked number 203 in the 2012 *Fortune* 500 listing of the largest companies in the United States. Here is a brief description of how and why the company committed fraud.

Dean Buntrock founded Waste Management in 1968 and took the company public in 1971. During the 1970s and 1980s, Buntrock built a vast waste disposal empire by acquiring and consolidating local waste hauling companies and landfill operators. At one point, the company was performing close to 200 acquisitions a year. It experienced tremendous growth in its first 20 years. From the IPO in 1971 until the end of 1991, Waste Management enjoyed 36 percent average annual growth in revenue and 36 percent annual growth in net income. The company grew from $16 million in revenue in 1971 to become the largest waste removal business in the world, with revenue of more than $7.5 billion in 1991.

Despite being a leader in the industry, Waste Management was under increasing pressure from competitors and from changes in the environmental industry. Its 1996 financial statements showed that even though its consolidated revenue for the period from December 1994 to 1996 increased 8.3 percent, its net income declined during that period by 75.5 percent. The truth was that the income numbers had been manipulated to minimize the declines over time.

The term *ill-gotten gains* refer to amounts received either dishonestly or illegally. Litigation Release 17345 identifies the following "ill-gotten gains" at Waste Management:

| Name | Positions | Amount |
|------|-----------|--------|
| Buntrock | CEO and chair of the board | $16,917,761 |
| Rooney | Director, president, and COO | $ 9,286,124 |
| Koenig | Executive vice president and CFO | $ 951,005 |
| Thomas Hau | Vice president, controller, and CAO | $ 640,100 |
| Herbert Getz | Senior vice president, general counsel, and secretary | $ 472,500 |
| Bruce Tobecksen | Vice president of finance | $ 640,100 |

These ill-gotten gains were included in a lawsuit filed by the SEC on March 26, 2002, against the six former top officers of Waste Management Inc., charging them with perpetrating a massive financial fraud lasting more than five years. The complaint, filed in U.S. District Court in Chicago, charged that defendants engaged in a systematic scheme to falsify and misrepresent Waste Management's financial results between 1992 and 1997.

According to the complaint, the defendants violated, and aided and abetted violations of, antifraud, reporting, and recordkeeping provisions of the federal securities laws. The SEC successfully sought injunctions prohibiting future violations, disgorgement of defendants' ill-gotten gains, civil money penalties, and officer and director bars against all defendants.

The complaint first identified the roles played by top management. Buntrock set earnings targets, fostered a culture of fraudulent accounting, personally directed certain of the accounting changes to make the targeted earnings, and was the spokesperson who announced the company's phony numbers. Rooney ensured that required write-offs were not recorded and, in some instances, overruled accounting decisions that would have a negative impact on operations. He reaped more than $9.2 million in ill-gotten gains from, among other things, performance-based bonuses, retirement benefits, and selling company stock while the fraud was ongoing. Koenig was primarily responsible for executing the scheme. He also ordered the destruction of damaging evidence, misled the company's audit committee and internal accountants, and withheld information from the outside auditors. He profited by more than $900,000 from his fraudulent acts. Hau was the principal technician for the fraudulent accounting. Among other things, he devised many *one-off* accounting manipulations to deliver the targeted earnings and carefully crafted the deceptive disclosures. The explanation of these manipulations is that to reduce expenses and inflate earnings artificially, management primarily used adjusting entries to conform the company's actual results to the predetermined earnings targets. The inflated earnings of prior periods then became the floor for future manipulations. The consequences created what Hau referred to as the one-off problem. To sustain the scheme, earnings fraudulently achieved in one period had to be replaced in the next. Hau profited by more than $600,000 from his fraudulent acts. Tobecksen was enlisted in 1994 to handle Hau's overflow. He profited by more than $400,000 from his fraudulent acts. Getz was the company's general counsel. He blessed the company's fraudulent disclosures and profited by more than $450,000 from his fraudulent acts.

The defendants fraudulently manipulated the company's revenues, because they were not growing enough to meet predetermined earnings targets, by manipulating current and future asset values failing to write off asset impairments, using reserve accounting to mask operating expenses, implementing improper capitalization policies, and failing to establish reserves (liabilities) to pay for income taxes and other expenses.

# Overview of Accounting and Financial Reporting Fraud

## *Improper Accounting Practices*

The accounting fraud involved a variety of practices, including improperly eliminating or deferring current period expenses in order to inflate earnings. For example, the company avoided depreciation expenses by extending the estimated useful lives of its garbage trucks while at the same time making unsupported increases to the trucks' salvage values. In other words, the more the trucks were used and the older they became, the more the defendants said they were worth. Other improper accounting practices include:

- Making unsupported changes in depreciation estimates
- Failing to record expenses for decreases in the value of landfills as they were filled with waste
- Failing to record expenses necessary to write off the costs of impaired and abandoned landfill development projects
- Improper capitalization of interest on landfill development
- Establishing inflated environmental reserves (liabilities) in connection with acquisitions so that the excess reserves could be used to avoid recording unrelated environmental and other expenses
- Netting one-time gains against operating expenses
- Manipulating reserve account balances to inflate earnings

In February 1998, Waste Management announced that it was restating its financial statements for the five-year period 1992–1996 and the first three quarters of 1997.[1] The company admitted that through 1996, it had materially overstated its reported pretax earnings by $1.43 billion and that it had understated certain elements of its tax expense by $178 million, as reported in *Accounting and Auditing Enforcement Release (AAER) 1405*:

| | |
|---|---:|
| Vehicle, equipment, and container depreciation expense | $ 509 |
| Capitalized interest | 192 |
| Environmental and closure/post-closure liabilities | 173 |
| Purchase accounting related to remediation reserves | 128 |
| Asset impairment losses | 214 |
| Software impairment reversal | (85) |
| Other | 301 |
| Pretax total | $1,432 |
| Income tax expense restatement | $ 178 |

[1]The amount for the first three-quarters of 1997 is $180,900.

Andersen audited and issued an unqualified (i.e., unmodified) report on each of Waste Management's original financial statements and on the financial statements in the restatement. In so doing, Andersen acknowledged that the company's original financial statements for the periods 1992 through 1996 were materially misstated and that its prior unqualified reports on those financial statements should not be relied upon. In the restatement, the company admitted that it had overstated its net after-tax income as follows:

**Net Income**

| Year | Reported (thousands) | Restated (thousands) | Percent Overstated |
|------|----------------------|----------------------|--------------------|
| 1992 | $850,036 | $739,686 | 15 |
| 1993 | $452,776 | $288,707 | 57 |
| 1994 | $784,381 | $627,508 | 25 |
| 1995 | $603,899 | $340,097 | 78 |
| 1996 | $192,085 | $(39,307) | 100+ |

### Netting

Top management concealed their scheme in a variety of ways, including making false and misleading statements about the company's accounting practices, financial condition, and future prospects in filings with the SEC, reports to shareholders, and press releases, and using an accounting manipulation known as *netting* to make reported results appear better than they actually were. The netting eliminated approximately $490 million in current period operating expenses and accumulated prior period accounting misstatements by offsetting them against unrelated, one-time gains on the sale or exchange of assets.

Andersen repeatedly issued unqualified audit reports on the company's materially false and misleading annual financial statements. At the outset of the fraud, management capped Andersen's audit fees and advised the Andersen engagement partner that the firm could earn additional fees through "special work." Andersen nevertheless identified the company's improper accounting practices and quantified much of the impact of those practices on the company's financial statements. Andersen annually presented company management with PAJEs to correct errors that understated expenses and overstated earnings in the company's financial statements.

### PAJEs

Management consistently refused to make the adjustments called for by the PAJEs, and Andersen accepted management's decision even though the firm knew (or should have known) that it was not in accordance with GAAP. To placate management and ease its conscience, Andersen entered into an agreement with top management to write off the accumulated errors fraudulently over periods of up to 10 years and to

change the underlying accounting practices, but to do so only in future periods. The four-page agreement or "treaty," called a Summary of Action Steps, identified improper accounting practices and prescribed 32 "must-do" steps for the company to follow to change those practices. The action steps constituted an agreement between the company and Andersen to cover up past frauds by committing additional frauds in the future. It was the smoking gun proving that Andersen knowingly participated in a fraudulent act in violation of securities laws.

Over time, the fraudulent scheme unraveled. An internal review in mid-July 1997 identified improper accounting and led to the restatement of the company's financial statements for 1992 through the third quarter of 1997. In its restated financial statements in February 1998, the company acknowledged that it had misstated its pretax earnings by approximately $1.7 billion. At the time, the restatement was the largest in corporate history.

As news of the company's overstatement of earnings became public, Waste Management's shareholders (other than the top management, who sold company stock and thus avoided losses) lost more than $6 billion of the market value of their investments when the stock declined following the public disclosure of fraud.

## SEC Sanctions against Andersen and Waste Management Officers

As for the Andersen auditors, the SEC found that the firm and four of its auditors violated the anti-fraud provisions of Rule 10b-5 of the Securities Exchange Act of 1934. These provisions make it unlawful for a CPA to (1) employ any device, scheme, or artifice to defraud; (2) make an untrue statement of material fact or omit a material fact; and (3) engage in any act, practice, or course of business to commit fraud or deceit in connection with the purchase or sale of the security.

Litigation Release No. 17039 details the charges against four partners:

| Partner | Position |
|---------|----------|
| Robert E. Allgyer | Partner in charge of Waste Management audit |
| Edward G. Maier | Risk management partner and engagement concurring partner |
| Walter Cercavschi | Partner on the Waste Management engagement |
| Robert G. Kutsenda | Central Region audit practice director |

The SEC charged that Kutsenda knew or should have known that the netting violated GAAP, that prior misstatements that he knew about would not be disclosed to investors, that the impact of the netting on the company's 1995 financial statements was material, and that an unqualified audit report was not warranted (http://www.sec.gov/litigation/admin/34-44448.htm).

On August 29, 2005 the SEC issued Litigation Release 19351, announcing that the U.S. District Court for the Northern District of Illinois entered final judgments as to defendants Dean L. Buntrock, Phillip B. Rooney, Thomas C. Hau, and Herbert A. Getz, all of whom consented to the judgments without admitting or denying the allegations. The judgments permanently barred Buntrock, Rooney, Hau, and Getz from acting as an officer or director of a public company, enjoined them from future violations of the antifraud and other provisions of the federal securities laws, and required payment of $30,869,054 in disgorgement, prejudgment interest, and civil penalties. The specific provisions of the securities acts that were violated include rules 10b-5, 12b-20, 13a-1, and 13a-13 of Sections 10(b) of the Securities Exchange Act of 1934 and Section 17(a) of the Securities Act of 1933 (http://www.sec.gov/litigation/litreleases/lr19351.htm).

The distribution of the penalty was as follows:

- Buntrock—$19,447,670 total, comprised of $10,708,032 in disgorgement, $6,439,638 of prejudgment interest, and a $2,300,000 civil penalty
- Rooney—$8,692,738 total, comprised of $4,593,764 in disgorgement, $2,998,974 of prejudgment interest, and a $1,100,000 civil penalty
- Hau—$1,578,890 total, comprised of $641,866 in disgorgement, $507,024 of prejudgment interest, and a $430,000 civil penalty
- Getz—$1,149,756 total, comprised of $472,500 in disgorgement, $477,256 of prejudgment interest, and a $200,000 civil penalty

On November 7, 2001, Connecticut attorney general Richard Blumenthal and treasurer Denise L. Nappier announced a $457 million settlement with Waste Management in a class action securities fraud case that provided monetary benefits for shareholders; it was the third-largest securities class action settlement in U.S. history at the time. Waste Management agreed to institute important changes in its corporate governance structure, including greater independence for the company's audit committee and enhanced accountability for shareholders with respect to corporate management. Members of the audit committee were required to be five years removed from employment with the company, rather than the current three years. The company also agreed to recommend to shareholders that their entire board of directors be elected annually, replacing the current system of staggered terms, with one-third of the board being elected each year (http://www.ct.gov/AG/cwp/view.asp?a=1776&q=283444). The corporate governance changes are consistent with requirements of the SOX that calls for greater independence for the audit committee and meaningful involvement in financial reporting oversight.

On June 19, 2001, the SEC announced a settlement with Arthur Andersen and the four partners in connection with the firm's audits of the annual financial statements of Waste Management for the years 1992 through 1996. The commission had alleged that Andersen and its partners failed to stand up to company management and betrayed their ultimate allegiance to Waste Management's shareholders and the investing public by sanctioning false and misleading audit reports. Thus, the firm violated its public interest obligation. As for top management at Waste Management, it failed in its fiduciary responsibilities to safeguard company assets and knowingly condoned fraudulent financial reporting.

# Details of Andersen's Involvement in the Fraud

As previously mentioned, in order to conceal the understatement of expenses, top officials resorted to an undisclosed practice known as netting. They used one-time gains realized on the sale or exchange of assets to eliminate unrelated current period operating expenses and accounting misstatements that had accumulated from prior periods. These one-time gains were offset against items that should have been reported as operating expenses in current or prior periods, and thus concealed the impact of their fraudulent accounting and the deteriorating condition of the company's core operations. Although Andersen advised company management that the use of " 'other gains' to bury charges for balance sheet cleanups . . . and the lack of disclosure . . . [was] an area of SEC exposure," the practice persisted. In fact, Andersen prepared a PRJE (post-reclassification journal entry) to reduce pretax income from continuing operations, but the company refused to record it. Over the course of the fraud, Waste Management used netting secretly to erase approximately $490 million in current period expenses and prior-period misstatements. The netting procedure effectively acknowledged that the company's accounting practices were wrong and that the netted prior period items were, in fact, misstatements (http://www.sec.gov/litigation/litreleases/lr18913.htm).

## Andersen's Relationship with Waste Management

The SEC was very critical of Andersen's relationship with Waste Management. Litigation Release 17039 notes that the firm had audited Waste Management since before it became a public company in 1971 and considered the client its "crown jewel." Until 1997, every CFO and chief accounting officer (CAO) in Waste Management's history as a public company had previously worked as an auditor at Andersen. During the 1990s, approximately 14 former Andersen employees worked for Waste Management, most often in key financial and accounting positions. Andersen selected Allgyer to be the managing partner of the Waste Management audit because he had demonstrated a "devotion to client service" and had a personal style that "fit well with Waste Management officers." During the time of the audit, Allgyer held the title of "Partner in Charge of Client Service" for Andersen's Chicago office and served as "marketing director." He coordinated marketing efforts of the office including, among other things, cross-selling non-attest services to audit clients. Shortly after Allgyer's appointment as engagement partner, Waste Management capped Andersen's corporate audit fees at the prior year's level but allowed the firm to earn additional fees for "special work." Andersen reported to the audit committee that it had billed Waste Management approximately $7.5 million in audit fees. Over the seven-year period, while Andersen's corporate audit fees remained capped, Andersen also billed the company $11.8 million in other fees. A related entity, Andersen Consulting, also billed Waste Management approximately $6 million in additional non-audit fees, $3.7 million of which were related to a strategic review that analyzed the company's overall business structure. The firm ultimately made a recommendation on implementing a new operating model designed to "increase shareholder value." Allgyer was a member of the steering committee that oversaw the strategic review, and Andersen Consulting billed his time for these services to the company. In setting Allgyer's compensation, Andersen took into account, among other things, the firm's billings to Waste Management for audit and non-audit services (http://www.sec.gov/litigation/litreleases/lr17435.htm).

## SEC Charges and Sanctions against Andersen and Partners

Allgyer was charged in connection with Andersen's audit of Waste Management's 1992 financial statements. The SEC alleged that he knew or was reckless in not knowing that the firm's audit report on the company's 1992 financial statements was materially false and misleading because in addition to quantified misstatements totaling $93.5 million, which, if corrected, would have reduced the company's net income before accounting changes by 7.4 percent, there were additional known and likely misstatements that had not been quantified and estimated. Allgyer further knew that the company had netted, without disclosure, $111 million of current-period expenses and prior-period misstatements against a portion of a one-time gain from an unrelated IPO of securities, which had the effect of understating Waste Management's 1992 operating expenses and overstating the company's income from operations. The SEC further alleged that Allgyer engaged in similar conduct in connection with the 1993 through 1996 audits. That is, he knew or was reckless in not knowing that Andersen's unqualified audit report for each of the years 1993 through 1996 was materially false and misleading [*In the Matter of Robert E. Allgyer, CPA* (Release Nos. 33-7986, 34-44445) June 19, 2001].

Allgyer, the partner responsible for the Waste Management engagement, consented (1) to the entry of a permanent injunction enjoining him from violating section 10(b) of the

Exchange Act and rule 10b-5 thereunder and section 17(a) of the Securities Act of 1933; (2) to pay a civil money penalty of $50,000; and (3) in related administrative proceedings pursuant to rule 102(e), to the entry of an order denying him the privilege of appearing or practicing before the SEC as an accountant, with the right to request his reinstatement after five years.

The SEC charged that Kutsenda, the central region audit practice director responsible for Andersen's Chicago, Kansas City, Indianapolis, and Omaha offices, engaged in improper professional conduct within the meaning of rule 102(e)(1)(ii) of the commission's rules of practice with respect to the 1995 audit. During that audit, he was informed of the non-GAAP netting of a $160 million one-time gain against unrelated expenses and prior-period misstatements and that the amount represented 10 percent of Waste Management's 1995 pretax earnings. Although not part of the engagement team, Kutsenda was consulted by two of the engagement partners and, therefore, he was required under GAAS to exercise due professional care so that an unqualified audit report was not issued on financial statements that were materially misstated [*In the Matter of Robert G. Kutsenda, CPA* (Release No. 34-44448), June 19, 2001]. Kutsenda consented in administrative proceedings pursuant to rule 102(e) to the entry of an order, based on the commission's finding that he engaged in improper professional conduct, that denied him the privilege of appearing or practicing before the SEC as an accountant, with the right to request reinstatement after one year.

*AAER 1410* was issued on June 19, 2001 and details the sanctions against Andersen and its partners. The following discussion describes the sanctions imposed on the firm (http://www.sec.gov/litigation/litreleases/lr17039.htm).

The SEC complaint against Andersen charged that the firm knew of Waste Management's exaggerated profits during its audits of the financial statements from 1992 through 1996 and repeatedly pleaded with the company to make changes. Each year, Andersen gave in and issued unqualified opinions on the company's financial statements even though they did not conform to GAAP. A summary of the findings against Andersen follows (http://www.sec.gov/litigation/litreleases/lr17435.htm):

- Knowingly or recklessly issuing false and misleading unqualified audit reports on Waste Management's annual financial statements for the years 1993 through 1996.

- Failing to quantify and estimate all known and likely misstatements due to non-GAAP accounting practices.

- In 1995, the company did not implement the action steps and continued to utilize accounting practices that did not conform with GAAP; Andersen knew but did nothing about it.

- Determining the materiality of misstatements improperly; failing to record or disclose information about such transactions; issuing an unqualified audit report.

- Written recognition in a memorandum prepared by Andersen of the company's improper netting practices and identification of SEC exposure; monitored continuing practice but failed to adequately disclose the effect on current earnings.

Andersen consented to a (1) permanent injunction enjoining it from violating section 10(b) of the Securities Exchange Act of 1934 and rule 10b-5 thereunder; (2) to pay a civil penalty of $7 million; and (3) in related administrative proceedings, to the entry of an order pursuant to rule 102(e) censuring it based upon the SEC's finding that it engaged in improper professional conduct and the issuance of the permanent injunction. The ink on the agreement barely had time to dry when, on December 2, 2001, Enron, Andersen's most infamous client, filed for Chapter 11 protection in the United States after getting embroiled in its own financial scandal.

# Corporate Governance at Waste Management

The fraud at Waste Management was perpetrated by top management. The board of directors either did not know about it or chose to look the other way. Members of top management had signed agreements with Andersen that included action steps to correct for past improper accounting by adjusting future income and adopting proper accounting procedures. Top management failed to live up to any of its agreements.

As the Waste Management fraud progressed over the years, the inflated earnings of prior periods became the floor for future manipulations—one-time adjustments made to achieve a number in one period had to be replaced in the next—and created the one-off accounting problem. In early 1997, Hau explained to the audit committee that "we've had one-off accounting every year that has to be replaced the next year. We've been doing this long enough that the problem has mounted." . . . (http://www.sec.gov/litigation/complaints/complr17435.htm). Essentially, the company created a fiction of inflated earnings and had to duplicate the fiction in subsequent years. Perhaps not surprisingly, greed ruled the day, and the company wasn't simply satisfied with meeting fictitious earnings levels in subsequent years. Instead, there needed to be a higher earnings level to keep the stock price growing and enhance stock option values for top company officials each year. In essence, the company took the first step down the ethical slippery slope in 1992 and couldn't (or wouldn't) find its way back up to the high road. It hit rock bottom in 1997, when the fraud eventually unraveled. In mid-1997, the company's board of directors brought in a new CEO, who ordered a review of the accounting and then resigned after barely four months because, reportedly, he thought that the accounting was "spooky." At that time, the proverbially red flag was raised for the public to see, and Andersen's negligence came to the forefront.

In February 1998, Waste Management acknowledged "past mistakes" and announced that it would restate its financial statements for the period 1992–1996 and the first three quarters of 1997. It concluded that, for this period, the company had overstated its reported pretax earnings by approximately $1.7 billion and understated certain elements of its income tax expense by approximately $190 million. In restating its financial statements, the company revised every accounting practice identified in the action steps—practices that defendants had agreed, but had failed, to change four years earlier.

As news of the company's overstatement of earnings became public, Waste Management's shareholders lost over $6 billion in the market value of their investments when the stock price plummeted from $35 to $22 per share. Although shareholders lost billions of dollars, top company officials profited handsomely from their fraud.

## Questions

1. The SEC charged Andersen with failing to quantify and estimate all known and likely misstatements due to non-GAAP practices. What is the purpose of doing this from an auditing perspective?

2. Classify each of the accounting techniques described in the case that contributed to the fraud into one of Schilit's accounting shenanigans. Include a brief discussion of how each technique violated GAAP.

3. Review the facts of the case with respect to Andersen's role in the fraud and describe the provisions of the AICPA Code of Professional Conduct that you believe were violated by the firm. Comment on Andersen's risk assessment as part of its audit procedures.

# References

American Institute of CPAs (AICPA). 2012a. *AICPA Professional Standards: Volume 1.* As of June 1, 2012. New York: AICPA.

AICPA. 2012b. *AICPA Professional Standards: Volume 2.* As of June 1, 2012. New York: AICPA.

American Law Institute. 2008. *Principles of Law—Principles of Corporate Governance.* Philadelphia: The American Law Institute.

*Brown v. Kendall,* 60 Mass. 292 (1850).

*In the Matter of Arthur Andersen, LLP, AAER 1405* [Release No. 34-44444] (June 19, 2001).

*In the Matter of Robert G. Kutsenda, CPA* [Release No. 34-44448] (June 19, 2001); *AAER 1409;* June 19, 2001: http://www.sec.gov/litigation/admin/34-44448.htm.

*In the Matter of Waste Management, Inc.* Securities Exchange Act of 1934 [Release No. 42968] *AAER 1277,* June 21, 2000; http://www.sec.gov/litigation/admin/34-42968.htm.

New York Stock Exchange. 2003. Final New York Stock Exchange Corporate Governance Rules: Section 303A. Available at www.nyse.com/pfds/finalcorpogovrules.pdf.

Rezaee, Z. 2009. *Corporate Governance and Ethics.* New York: John Wiley & Sons, Inc.

*SEC v. Arthur Andersen LLP, et al.,* No. 1:01CV01348 (JR) (D.D.C.) [Release No. LR-17039] *AAER 1410* (June 19, 2001); http://www.sec.gov/litigation/litreleases/lr17039.htm.

*SEC v. Buntrock, et al.,* Civil Action No. 02-C-2180 (N.D. Ill. March 26, 2002) (Andersen, J.); *AAER 132* [Release No. LR-17435] (March 26, 2002). http://www.sec.gov/litigation/litreleases/lr17435.htm.

*SEC v. Buntrock, et al.,* Civil Action No. 02-C-2180 (N.D. Ill.) (Andersen, J.) [Release No. LR-18913] *AAER* 2116: (September 30, 2004); http://www.sec.gov/litigation/litreleases/lr18913.htm.

*SEC v. Buntrock, et al.,* Civil Action No. 02-C-2180 (Andersen, J.) [Release No. LR-19351] (Aug. 29, 2005); http://www.sec.gov/litigation/litreleases/lr19351.htm.

SEC. Complaint: *SEC v. Dean L. Buntrock, Phillip B. Rooney, James E. Koenig, Thomas C. Hau, Herbert A. Getz, and Bruce D. Tobecksen:* Litigation Release 17435. *AAER 132.* March 26, 2002; http://www.sec.gov/litigation/litreleases/lr17345.htm.

SEC. Settlement with Koenig, CFO of Waste Management: January 3, 2008; http://www.sec.gov/news/press/2008/2008-2.htm.

SEC. SEC Staff Accounting Bulletin No. 99—Materiality http://www.sec.gov/interps/account/sab99.htm.

Shleifer, A. and R. Vishny. 1997. A survey of corporate governance. *Journal of Finance.* 52(2): 737–775.

Solomon, J. 2007. *Corporate Governance and Accountability.* West Sussex, U.K.: John Wiley & Sons, Ltd.

Tuttle, B., M. Coller, and R. D. Plumlee. 2002. The effect of misstatements of varying magnitude on the decisions of financial statement users: An experimental investigation of materiality thresholds. *Auditing: A Journal of Practice & Theory,* 21(1): 383–419.

U.S. Supreme Court. *TSC Industries, Inc. v. Northway, Inc.,* 426 U.S. 438 (1976).

# Name Index

Page numbers followed by n indicate notes.

# Subject Index

Page numbers followed by n indicate notes.